Cases and Materials on the Law of the Sea, Second Edition

Cases and Materials on the Law of the Sea

Second Edition

Louis B. Sohn†

John E. Noyes, *California Western School of Law*

Erik Franckx, *Vrije Universiteit Brussel*

Kristen G. Juras, *University of Montana School of Law*

BRILL
NIJHOFF

LEIDEN | BOSTON

Library of Congress Cataloging-in-Publication Data

Cases and materials on the law of the sea / Edited by Louis B. Sohn, John E. Noyes, California Western School of Law, Erik Franckx, Vrije Universiteit Brussel, Kristen Gustafson, University of Montana School of Law.—Second edition.
pages cm
Includes index.
ISBN 978-90-04-16990-6 (hardback : alk. paper)—ISBN 978-90-04-20356-3 (e-book) 1. Law of the sea—Cases. I. Sohn, Louis B., editor. II. Franckx, Erik, 1957– editor. III. Juras, Kristen Gustafson, editor.

KZA1145.S66 2014
341.4'5—dc23

2014000259

This publication has been typeset in the multilingual 'Brill' typeface. With over 5,100 characters covering Latin, IPA, Greek, and Cyrillic, this typeface is especially suitable for use in the humanities.
For more information, please see brill.com/brill-typeface.

ISBN 978 90 04 16990 6 (hardback)
ISBN 978 90 04 20356 3 (e-book)

This book is printed on acid-free paper.

Contents

Preface

Much has changed since the publication of the first edition of this text—Louis B. Sohn & John E. Noyes, Cases and Materials on the Law of the Sea—in 2004. The oceans have faced continuing environmental stresses, increased interest in the resources of the continental shelf and the deep seabed, new security threats, tensions over contested maritime boundaries, and significant developments in shipping. These challenges have prompted changes in international law, and international law in turn has helped to shape how the world reacts to these challenges. Reactions have come not just from states, but from international organizations and international judicial and arbitral bodies. The pages of this second edition reflect many of these significant developments.

Readers familiar with the first edition will note a change in emphasis in this second edition. The first edition sought both to present a sensibly organized set of teaching materials and to survey the full range of law of the sea issues, in order to at least introduce topics and point readers to relevant commentary. In this second edition we focus primarily on teaching materials, opting for depth rather than breadth of coverage. To provide an overview of the broad field of the law of the sea, we recommend that these Cases and Materials be used in conjunction with Louis B. Sohn, Kristen Gustafson Juras, John E. Noyes & Erik Franckx, Law of the Sea in a Nutshell (West, 2d ed. 2010).

The organization of this second edition of Cases and Materials on the Law of the Sea tracks that of the Nutshell. Chapter 1 introduces the law of the sea and questions about international law and international legal process. Chapters 2, 3, and 4 examine the basic concepts of high seas freedoms, vessel nationality, and flag state jurisdiction. The next two chapters concern matters that are fundamental in determining the location of various coastal zones: baselines (Chapter 5), and principles and processes applicable to maritime boundary delimitations (Chapter 6). Although many substantive issues, e.g., fisheries, cut across different zones of coastal state sovereignty or jurisdiction, such zones have been of central importance in the law of the sea, and we explore them in Chapters 7 (internal waters), 8 (the territorial sea, contiguous zone, straits, and archipelagic waters), 9 (the exclusive economic zone), and 10 (the continental shelf). Chapter 11 then examines the regime governing mineral resources in the Area, i.e., the seabed beyond the limits of national jurisdiction, and the controversy over access to genetic material in the Area. In Chapters 12, 13, 14, and 15, we explore matters where new norms and institutions have transformed traditional practice. Chapter 12 concerns marine pollution and principles of international environmental law. Chapter 13 examines high seas fisheries and the roles of regional and global organizations in conserving and managing fish stocks that range across various zones of the oceans. In Chapter 14 the focus is on maritime security. Finally, Chapter 15 analyzes the dispute settlement system created by the 1982 United Nations Convention on the Law of the Sea. The Appendix includes the 1982 Convention on the Law of the Sea and the 1994 Part XI Implementation Agreement, so that students can have ready access to essential treaty material in one volume; other treaties are excerpted throughout the text.

Different instructors may of course emphasize different themes, and—particularly if there is not time to cover the entire text—they may wish to pick and choose among different materials. In courses emphasizing security issues, Chapter 2, Chapter 4, Sections D–F, and Chapters 7, 8, and 14 deserve particular emphasis. A focus on environmental issues would certainly include Chapter 2, Sections D and G, Chapter 4, Sections A and B, Chapter 7, Section C, Chapter 11, Section D, and Chapters 12 and 13. An instructor concentrating on international litigation may want to select international court and arbitral tribunal decisions from throughout the book, and should particularly emphasize Chapters 12, 13, and 15 (and indeed may wish to assign Chapter 15 early in the course). In a course concerning the allocation of offshore resources, Chapters 5, 6, 8, 9, 10, 11, and 13 deserve significant attention.

Although this text includes much modern material, it also seeks to place the law of the sea in historical context. Current legal formulations draw on previous ones, and past solutions may still hold valuable lessons for lawyers and policy makers seeking ways to address current problems. Throughout the book, we have given attention both to traditional law of the sea topics and to topics—such as port security, the depletion of fish stocks, and the operation of new international institutions—that have gained much attention in recent years.

This set of law of the sea materials is also, we believe, useful in examining core issues of international law and international legal process. These issues have relevance to a wide variety of subject areas. For example, what are generally understood to be sources of international law, and what is the priority of each source vis-à-vis other sources? Why are some rules (e.g., those governing maritime delimitation) open-textured, while others are much more determinate? The great significance of treaties in international law requires consideration of how treaty law is made and how complex multilateral treaties change. What are the advantages and disadvantages of different mechanisms for change? What are the roles of "soft law" in the development of international law? How are problems of collective action addressed with respect to common spaces and common resources? What is the legal status of non-state actors, such as international organizations, and what functions should they carry out? Some questions about the rights of individuals under international law are explored in this volume. What are the functions of international dispute settlement mechanisms? Why do parties choose one forum over another? Various tribunals—the International Court of Justice, the International Tribunal for the Law of the Sea, arbitral tribunals, claims commissions, regional international courts such as the European Court of Justice, and municipal courts—are examined throughout the book. What challenges are posed by the proliferation of international tribunals? How should overlaps in jurisdictional competencies of international courts and tribunals be addressed? Finally, how should conflicts be resolved between the municipal laws of different states? Principles of private international law (conflict of laws) may be applied to conflicts between the laws of flag states and coastal states concerning events on board vessels, particularly when vessels are located in internal waters or the territorial sea. We hope this volume will prompt students to think about such issues, as well as about law of the sea topics.

Readers seeking more information about particular topics in the law of the sea quickly discover what may seem an overwhelming number of books and articles. Law of the Sea in a Nutshell and Notes in this Cases and Materials volume introduce some valuable reference materials. Additional citations to and overviews of law of the sea topics may be found in such excellent recent treatises as R.R. Churchill & A.V. Lowe, The Law of the Sea (3d ed. 1999), Donald R. Rothwell & Tim Stephens, The International Law of the Sea (2010), and Yoshifumi Tanaka, The International Law of the Sea (2012).

A few technical notes: Omissions in the edited readings in this book are indicated either by ellipses or by brackets. However, some citations and footnotes have been omitted with no such indications. We have updated the status of treaties as of September 2013. Internet citations were also accurate as of September 2013.

The name of our colleague and mentor, Louis B. Sohn, remains on this edition of Cases and Materials on the Law of the Sea, the first since his death in 2006. Louis Sohn greatly influenced modern international law. He participated in the 1945 San Francisco drafting conference that established the United Nations and, during 1969-1971, worked as the first Counselor on International Law at the U.S. Department of State. His vision, dedication, vast knowledge, and skill made him instrumental in the development of the modern law of the sea. In his capacity as a U.S. delegate to the Third United Nations Conference on the Law of the Sea from 1974 to 1982, he was one of the primary architects of the dispute settlement provisions of the 1982 Law of the Sea Convention.

Louis Sohn also contributed significantly to many other areas of international law, including human rights, international environmental law, international organizations, arms control and disarmament, and dispute settlement. Those active in the International Law Section of the American Bar Association, the American Society of International Law, and the American Branch of the International Law Association know about his dedication to and leadership of those organizations. Louis Sohn also served as a reporter for the American Law Institute's Restatement (Third) of the Foreign Relations Law of the United States (1986). In his distinguished career as a scholar and teacher at Harvard Law School, the University of Georgia School of Law (where he taught Kristen Gustafson Juras and Erik Franckx), and The George Washington University Law School, he encouraged many of his students to pursue careers in international law. Reflections about Professor Sohn and the law of the sea appear in John E. Noyes, Louis B. Sohn and the Law of the Sea, 16 Willamette J. Intl. L. & Dispute Resolution 238 (2008).

In preparing the two editions of this book, we have benefited from the insights, comments, and support of many colleagues—a few now sadly departed—including William Aceves, Craig Allen, Caitlyn Antrim, David Bederman, William Burke, David Caron, Jonathan Charney, James Cooper, Barry Hart Dubner, Richard Finkmoore, Paul Irwin, Mark W. Janis, James Kraska, Dino Kritsiotis, Barbara Kwiatkowska, Coalter Lathrop, William Lynch, Phyllis Marion, Stephen McCaffrey, Richard McLaughlin, Samuel P. Menefee, John Norton Moore, John Murphy, James Nafziger, Dolliver Nelson, Myron Nordquist, Alex Oude Elferink, Bernard Oxman, Michael Reed, Ashley Roach, Shabtai Rosenne, Harry Scheiber, George Taft, Jon Van Dyke, Jorge Vargas, and George Walker. David Swanson of David Swanson Cartography expertly prepared the maps and diagrams used in this edition. Rachel Smith provided essential research support for the first edition, and much of her work has found its way into this second edition. Students at California Western School of Law, the University of Georgia School of Law, Harvard Law School, and the University of San Diego's Oxford summer program also offered valuable comments about drafts of these materials. The help of student research assistants—Joey Bentzley, Elizabeth Bonner, Carmen Casado, Pamela Combo, Cavan Cox, Stacey Meinen, Omar Nassar, Jill Klein, Karine Peropyolkina, Elizabeth Pietanza, Lara Prodanovich, Scott Robinson, Justin Tipp, Jessica Walker-Keleher, Liam Vavasour, and Ashkan Yekrangi—is gratefully acknowledged, as is the work of California Western School of Law's Faculty Support Services (especially Joyce Stallworth, Heddy Fujikawa, Jackie Sewell, and Ana Contreras). We also thank the library staffs at California Western School of Law (especially William Bookheim, Linda Weathers, and Bobbi Weaver), the University of Virginia School of Law (especially Xinh Luu), and the University of Montana School of Law (especially Cynthia Condit, Phil Cousineau, and Stacey Gordon).

John E. Noyes
San Diego

Erik Franckx
Brussels

Kristen Gustafson Juras
Missoula

Table of Acknowledgements

Excerpts from the following sources appear with the kind permission of the copyright holders and/or publishers.

Articles, Books, and Treatises

Allen, Craig H., Protecting the Oceanic Gardens of Eden: International Law Issues in Deep-Sea Vent Resource Conservation and Management, 13 Georgetown Intl. Envtl. L. Rev. 563, © 2001 Georgetown International Environmental Law Review

Charney, Jonathan I., International Agreements and the Development of Customary International Law, 61 Wash. L. Rev. 971, © 1986 Washington Law Review

Churchill, R.R. and Lowe, A.V., The Law of the Sea 228 (3d ed.), © 1999 Juris Publishing, Inc.

Franckx, Erik, Fisheries in the South China Sea: A Centrifugal or Centripetal Force?, 11 Chinese J. Intl. L. 727, © 2012 Oxford University Press

Janis, Mark W. and Noyes, John E., International Law Cases and Commentary (4th ed.), © 2011 West

Kim, Doo-Young, Advisory Proceedings before the International Tribunal for the Law of the Sea as an Alternative Procedure to Supplement the Dispute-Settlement Mechanism under Part XV of the United Nations Convention on the Law of the Sea, Issues in Legal Scholarship, Vol. 7, Issue 1: Frontier Issues in Ocean Law: Marine Resources, Maritime Boundaries, and the Law of the Sea, Article No. 6, © 2008 Law of the Sea Institute, University of California, Berkeley

Kimball, Lee A., Introductory Note on Memorandum of Understanding on Port State Control in the Caribbean Region, 36 Intl. Leg. Materials 231, © 1997 American Society of International Law

Nandan, Satya, Administering the Mineral Resources of the Deep Seabed, in The Law of the Sea: Progress and Prospects (David Freestone, Richard Barnes & David M. Ong eds.), © 2006 Oxford University Press

Organization for Economic Cooperation and Development, Maritime Transport Committee, Security in Maritime Transport: The Risk Factors and Economic Impact, © 2003 Organization for Economic Cooperation and Development

Oxman, Bernard H., The 1994 Agreement and the Convention, 88 Am. J. Intl. L. 687, © 1994 American Society of International Law

Oxman, Bernard H., The Third United Nations Conference on the Law of the Sea: The Ninth Session (1980), 75 Am. J. Intl. L. 211, © 1981 American Society of International Law

Sohn, Louis B., Juras, Kristen Gustafson, Noyes, John E., and Franckx, Erik, Law of the Sea in a Nutshell (2d ed.), © 2010 West

Sohn, Louis B., Peaceful Settlement of Disputes in Ocean Conflicts: Does UNCLOS III Point the Way?, 46 Law & Contemp. Probs. No. 2 at 195, © 1983 Duke University School of Law

Sohn, Louis B., The Law of the Sea: Customary International Law Developments, 34 Am. U.L. Rev. 271, © 1985 American University Law Review

International Maritime Organization

http://www.imo.org; http://docs.imo.org

The International Maritime Organization (IMO) owns the copyrights to the following excerpted materials, and has granted permission to reproduce them. Readers should be aware that the excerpted material may not be the complete and accurate version of the original IMO document and that the original may have subsequently been amended. In cases of doubt the authentic text should be consulted and will prevail in the event of conflict.

Adoption, Designation and Substitution of Archipelagic Sea Lanes, IMO Doc. SN/Circ.200/Add.1 (2003)

IMO Code for the Implementation of Mandatory IMO Instruments, IMO Res. A.1054(27) (2011)

IMO Website Explanation, International Convention for the Prevention of Pollution from Ships (MARPOL) (as of Sept. 1, 2013)

IMO Website Explanation, International Convention for the Safety of Life at Sea (SOLAS), 1974 (as of Sept. 1, 2013)

IMO Website Explanation, International Convention on Standards of Training, Certification and Watchkeeping for Seafarers (STCW) (as of Sept. 1, 2013)

Review of Safety Measures and Procedures for the Treatment of Persons Rescued at Sea, IMO Res. A.920(22) (2002)

International Tribunal for the Law of the Sea

http://www/itlos.org

The International Tribunal for the Law of the Sea owns the copyrights to the following excerpted materials, and has granted permission to reproduce them.

Bangladesh/Myanmar Dispute Concerning Delimitation of the Maritime Boundary in the Bay of Bengal (2012)

Grand Prince Case (Belize v. France) (Prompt Release) (2001)

M/V Saiga (No. 2) Case (St. Vincent and the Grenadines v. Guinea) (Admissibility and Merits) (1999)

MOX Plant Case (Ireland v. United Kingdom) (Provisional Measures) (2001)

Responsibilities and Obligations of States Sponsoring Persons and Entities with respect to Activities in the Area (Advisory Opinion) (2011)

Tomimaru Case (Japan v. Russian Federation) (Prompt Release) (2007)
Volga Case (Russian Federation v. Australia) (Prompt Release) (2002)

International Seabed Authority
http://www.isa.org

Statement by Satya N. Nandan, Secretary-General of the International Seabed Authority to the 62nd Session of the General Assembly of the United Nations (2007)

International Tribunal Decisions

See United Nations for International Court of Justice decisions.

Canada/France Delimitation of Maritime Areas (St. Pierre and Miquelon), 31 Intl. Leg. Materials 1145, © 1992 American Society of International Law
Compañia de Navegación Nacional (Panama) v. United States, 6 Rep. Intl. Arb. Awards 382, © 2006 United Nations
Ebony Maritime SA and Loten Navigation Co. Ltd. v. Prefetto Della Provincia di Brindisi and Others, © 1997 European Union
France/United Kingdom Continental Shelf Case, 18 Intl. Leg. Materials 397, © 1979 American Society of International Law
Kate A. Hoff (United States) v. Mexico, 4 Rep. Intl. Arb. Awards 444, © 2006 United Nations
MOX Plant Case: Commission of the European Communities v. Ireland, © 2006 European Union
MOX Plant Case: Dispute Concerning Access to Information under Article 9 of the OSPAR Convention (Ireland v. United Kingdom) (OSPAR Arbit. 2003), 23 Rep. Intl. Arb. Awards 59, © 2006 United Nations
MOX Plant Case: Dispute Concerning International Movements of Radioactive Materials, and the Protection of the Marine Environment of the Irish Sea (Ireland v. United Kingdom) (Annex VII Arbit.), © 2003, 2008 Permanent Court of Arbitration
Muscat Dhows Case (France/United Kingdom), © 1905 Permanent Court of Arbitration
Saudi Arabia v. Arabian American Oil Co. (Aramco) (1958), 27 Intl. L. Rep. 117, © 1963 Oxford University Press
Southern Bluefin Tuna Case (Australia and New Zealand v. Japan), 39 Intl. Leg. Materials 1359, © 2000 American Society of International Law
The S.S. Lotus (France v. Turkey), © 1927 League of Nations, reprinted with permission of the United Nations

United Nations
http://www/un.org

The United Nations (or its respective agencies) own the copyrights to the following excerpted materials, and has granted permission to reproduce them.

Food and Agriculture Organization	The State of World Fisheries and Aquaculture 2010, Part 1: World Review of Fisheries and Aquaculture (2010)
General Assembly	Declaration of a Zone of Peace and Co-operation of the South Atlantic, UN Doc. A/RES/41/11 (1986)
	Declaration of Principles Governing the Sea-Bed and the Ocean Floor, and the Subsoil Thereof, beyond the Limits of National Jurisdiction, UN Doc. A/RES/25/ 2749 (1970)
	Explanatory Statements Concerning Votes on the Moratorium Resolution, UN Doc. A/PV.1833 (1969)
	Letter Dated 16 March 2010 from the Co-chairpersons of the Ad Hoc Open-ended Informal Working Group [on Conservation and Sustainable Use of Marine Biological Diversity beyond the Limits of National Jurisdiction] to the President of the General Assembly, UN Doc. A/65/68 (2010)
	Measures to Prevent International Terrorism, UN Doc. A/ RES/40/61 (1985)
International Court of Justice	Anglo-Norwegian Fisheries Case (United Kingdom v. Norway) (1951)
	Barcelona Traction, Light & Power Co., Second Phase (Belgium v. Spain) (1970)
	Constitution of the Maritime Safety Committee of the Intergovernmental Maritime Consultative Organization (Advisory Opinion) (1960)
	Corfu Channel Case (United Kingdom v. Albania) (1949)
	Fisheries Jurisdiction Case (Spain v. Canada) (1998)
	Fisheries Jurisdiction Case (Spain v. Canada) (Application Instituting Proceedings) (1995)
	Gulf of Maine Delimitation (Canada/United States) (1984)
	Libya/Malta Continental Shelf Case (1985)
	North Sea Continental Shelf Cases (Federal Republic of Germany v. Denmark; Federal Republic of Germany v. Netherlands) (1969)
	Nuclear Tests Case (Australia v. France) (1974)
	Oil Platforms Case (Iran v. United States) (2003)

	Qatar/Bahrain Maritime Delimitation and Territorial Questions Case (2001)
	Romania v. Ukraine Maritime Delimitation in the Black Sea (2009)
	Tunisia/Libya Continental Shelf Case (1982)
International Law Commission	Draft Articles on Diplomatic Protection, UN Doc. A/61/10 (2006)
	Report of the International Law Commission, 1956, UN Doc. A/3159 (1956)
Security Council	Final Report of the Security Council Committee Established Pursuant to Resolution 724, UN Doc. S/1996/946 (1996)
	Security Council Resolution 552, UN Doc. S/RES/552 (1984)
	Security Council Resolution 787, UN Doc. S/RES/787 (1992)
	Security Council Resolution 820, UN Doc. S/RES/820 (1993)
Miscellaneous	Agreement between the Kingdom of Belgium and the French Republic Concerning the Delimitation of the Territorial Sea, Law of the Sea Bull. 27 (1991)
	Agreement between the Kingdom of Belgium and the French Republic Concerning the Delimitation of the Continental Shelf, Law of the Sea Bull. 29 (1991)
	Convention on Future Cooperation in the Northwest Atlantic Fisheries, 1135 U.N.T.S. 369 (1978)
	Declaration of People's Republic of China upon Ratification of the Law of the Sea Convention (1996)
	Statute on the International Régime of Maritime Ports, 58 L.N.T.S. 285, © 1923 League of Nations, reprinted with permission of the United Nations
	Summary of Recommendations of the Commission on the Limits of the Continental Shelf in regard to the Submission made by the United Kingdom of Great Britain and Northern Ireland in respect of Ascension Island on 9 May 2008 (2010)
	The Law of the Sea: Navigation on the High Seas (UN Sales No. E.89.V.2) (1989)
	UNCLOS III Discussion of Straits Used for International Navigation, 2 UNCLOS III Official Records 124 (1974)
	United Nations High Commissioner for Refugees, Refugees at Sea (1984)

Table of Figures

Table of Abbreviations

Abbreviations of national and international case law reporters, statutory compilations, law reviews, and journals are not included in this Table. We have primarily followed the ALWD Citation Manual (Aspen 4th ed.) as our citation format for these types of publications. See also the Table of Treaties and Other International Instruments for abbreviations relating to those documents.

Abbreviation	
ADIZ	Air Defense Identification Zone
ASIL	American Society of International Law
ASLP	Archipelagic sea lanes passage
BCN	Biological, chemical, and nuclear [weapons]
CBP	[U.S.] Customs Border and Protection
CDEM	Construction, design, equipment, and manning
CLCS	Commission on the Limits of the Continental Shelf
CSI	Container Security Initiative
C-TPAT	Customs-Trade Partnership against Terrorism
DISERO	Disembarkation resettlement offers
DOALOS	See UNDOALOS
EC	European Community
ECFI	European Court of First Instance
ECJ	European Court of Justice
ECOSOC	United Nations Economic and Social Council
EEC	European Economic Community
EEZ	Exclusive Economic Zone
EU, E.U.	European Union
FAO	United Nations Food and Agriculture Organization
FOS	Foot of the slope
GMDSS	Global maritime distress and safety system
IAEA	International Atomic Energy Agency
ICAO	International Civil Aviation Organization
ICE	[U.S.] Immigration and Customs Enforcement
ICJ	International Court of Justice
ILA	International Law Association
ILC	International Law Commission
ILO	International Labor Organization

IMCO	Inter-Governmental Maritime Consultative Organization (now IMO)
IMDG Code	International Maritime Dangerous Goods Code
IMO	International Maritime Organization
ISA	International Seabed Authority
ITLOS	International Tribunal for the Law of the Sea
IUU	Illegal, unreported, and unregulated [fishing]
LL/GDS	Land-locked/geographically disadvantaged states
MAR	Mid-Atlantic Ridge
MOR	Mid-ocean ridge
MOU	Memorandum of Understanding
MSC	Maritime Safety Committee
NAFO	Northwest Atlantic Fisheries Organization
NATO	North Atlantic Treaty Organization
NGO	Non-governmental organization
NIEO	New International Economic Order
OECD	Organization for Economic Cooperation and Development
PCA	Permanent Court of Arbitration
PCIJ	Permanent Court of International Justice
PREPCOM	Preparatory Commission for the International Seabed Authority and for the International Tribunal for the Law of the Sea
PSI	Proliferation Security Initiative
RFMO	Regional fishery management organization
SBC	Seabed Disputes Chamber of the International Tribunal for the Law of the Sea
SFRY	Socialist Federal Republic of Yugoslavia
SOFIA	State of World Fisheries and Aquaculture
TAC	Total allowable catch
UN, U.N.	United Nations
UNCED	United Nations Conference on Environment and Development
UNCLOS I	First United Nations Conference on the Law of the Sea
UNCLOS II	Second United Nations Conference on the Law of the Sea
UNCLOS III	Third United Nations Conference on the Law of the Sea
UNDOALOS	United Nations Division for Ocean Affairs and the Law of the Sea
UNEP	United Nations Environment Programme
UNESCO	United Nations Educational, Scientific and Cultural Organization

UNHCR	United Nations High Commissioner for Refugees
VMS	Vehicle monitoring system
WEU	Western European Union
WHO	United Nations World Health Organization
WMD	Weapons of mass destruction
WTO	World Trade Organization

Table of Cases

Cases appearing as principal readings are in bold. Full citations are contained within the text.

Table (*cont.*)

Decisions of International Courts and Tribunals

Table (*cont.*)

Table (*cont.*)

Decisions of International Courts and Tribunals	
Name of Case	**Page**
Qatar/Bahrain Maritime Delimitation and Territorial Questions Case (ICJ 2001)	**251**, 253, 260, 292
Rainbow Warrior (Greenpeace v. France) (Arbit. 1987)	77
Rainbow Warrior (New Zealand v. France) (Arbit. 1986)	77
Rainbow Warrior (New Zealand v. France) (Arbit. 1990)	77
Red Crusader, The (Denmark v. United Kingdom) (Arbit. 1962)	220
Request for an Advisory Opinion Submitted by the Sub-Regional Fisheries Commission (SRFC) (ITLOS submitted 2013)	756
Request for an Examination of the Situation in Accordance with Paragraph 63 of the Court's Judgment of 20 December 1974 in the Nuclear Tests Case (New Zealand v. France) (ICJ 1995)	77
Responsibilities and Obligations of States Sponsoring Persons and Entities with Respect to Activities in the Area (ITLOS 2011)	**598**, 606, 607, 691
Romania v. Ukraine Maritime Delimitation in the Black Sea (ICJ 2009)	325, **326**, 330
Saudi Arabia v. Arabian American Oil Co. (Aramco) (Arbit. 1958)	**350**
Southern Bluefin Tuna Cases (Australia v. Japan; New Zealand v. Japan) (Provisional Measures) (ITLOS 1999)	623, 691, 770, 774
Southern Bluefin Tuna Case (Australia and New Zealand v. Japan) (Annex VII Arbit. 2000)	**770**, 781
Tomimaru Case (Japan v. Russian Federation) (Prompt Release) (ITLOS 2007)	**143**, **763**, 768, 769, 770
Tunisia/Libya Application for Revision and Interpretation of the Judgment of 24 February 1982 (ICJ 1985)	304
Tunisia/Libya Continental Shelf Case (ICJ 1982)	36, 38, 285, **294**, 301, 303, 306, 316, 317, 319, 343, **489**, 492, 493, 494
Volga Case (Russian Federation v. Australia) (Prompt Release) (ITLOS 2002)	**756** , 767, 768, 769, 770

Decisions of National Courts

Table (*cont.*)

Decisions of National Courts

Table (*cont.*)

Decisions of National Courts	
Name of Case	**Page**
United States v. Bustos-Useche (U.S. 2001)	200
United States v. Caicedo (U.S. 1995)	207
United States v. California (U.S. 1947)	222
United States v. California (U.S. 1965)	**222**
United States v. Conroy (U.S. 1979)	219
United States v. Dire (U.S. 2012)	**178**, 186, 189
United States v. Flores (U.S. 1933)	383
United States v. Havenschap Delfzijl/Eemshaven (Neth. 1999)	365
United States v. La Jeune Eugenie (U.S. 1822)	195
United States v. Louisiana (U.S. 1950)	222, 537
United States v. Louisiana (U.S. 1969)	**243**
United States v. Pinto-Mejia (U.S. 1984)	**202**
United States v. Ray (U.S. 1970)	**532**
United States v. Reagan (U.S. 1971)	383
United States v. Royal Caribbean Cruises Ltd. (U.S. 1998)	**387**, 394, 395, 396, 398, 401
United States v. Shi (U.S. 2008)	710
United States v. Shibin (U.S. 2012)	**712**, 716
United States v. Taiyo Maru (U.S. 1975)	218
Victory Transport, Inc. v. Comisaria General (U.S. 1964)	90
Warshauer v. Lloyd Sabaudo, S.A. (U.S. 1934)	**102**
Whitney v. Robertson (U.S. 1888)	541
Wildenhus's Case (U.S. 1887)	**366**, 372, 373, 374, 375, 377, 394

Table of Treaties and Other International Instruments

Treaties and other instruments appearing as principal readings are in bold. The Table does not indicate the current status of a treaty or whether the treaty has entered into force.

Table (*cont.*)

Date and Short Title	Full Title and Citation	Page
1919 Paris Convention on the Regulation of Aerial Navigation	Paris Convention relating to the Regulation of Aerial Navigation, Oct. 13, 1919, 11 L.N.T.S. 173	50, 51
1919 Treaty of Versailles	Treaty of Peace between the Allied and Associated Powers and Germany, June 29, 1919, 225 Consol. T.S. 189, 13 Am. J. Intl. L. Supp. 151 (1919)	349
1923	**Statute on the International Régime of Maritime Ports,** Dec. 9, 1923, 58 L.N.T.S. 285, 22 Am. J. Intl. L. Supp. 69 (1928)	**347**, 351, 355, 356, 357
1923 Convention of Lausanne	Treaty of Peace, July 24, 1923, 28 L.N.T.S. 11	167, 168, 176, 177
1924 United States-United Kingdom Anti-Smuggling Convention	Convention for the Prevention of Smuggling of Intoxicating Liquors, United States-United Kingdom, Jan. 23, 1924, 43 Stat. 1761, T.S. No. 685	373
1926	Convention to Suppress the Slave Trade and Slavery, Sept. 25, 1926, 46 Stat. 2183, 60 L.N.T.S. 253	195
1941 United States-Mexican Claims Commission Convention	Final Settlement of Certain Claims, United States-Mexico, Nov. 19, 1941, 56 Stat. 1347, T.S. No. 980	386
1942 United Kingdom-Venezuela Gulf of Paria Treaty	Treaty between Great Britain and Northern Island and Venezuela relating to the Submarine Areas of the Gulf of Paria, Feb. 26, 1942, 205 L.NT.S. 1211	513
1944 Chicago Convention	Convention on International Civil Aviation, Dec. 7, 1944, 61 Stat. 1180, 15 U.N.T.S. 295	50, 51, 101, 451

Table (*cont.*)

Date and Short Title	Full Title and Citation	Page
1945 ICJ Statute	**Statute of the International Court of Justice**, June 26, 1945, 59 Stat. 1031, 1055, T.S. No. 993	**16**, 26, 30, 31, 32, 68, 69, 77, 118, 164, 223, 227, 284, 297, 303, 304, 305, 325, 334, 336, 489, 678, 755, 780
1945 U.N. Charter	**United Nations Charter**, June 26, 1945, 59 Stat. 1031, T.S. No. 993, 1 U.N.T.S. XVI	31, 32, 80, 83, 91, 93, 96, 97, 100, 101, 131, 207, **208**, 209, 210, 211, 215, 277, 284, 355, 478, 484, 729, 738, 753, 755
1947 General Agreement on Tariffs and Trade (GATT)	General Agreement on Tariffs and Trade, Oct. 30, 1947, 61 Stat. A 11, 55 U.N.T.S. 188	349
1947 Rio Treaty	Inter-American Treaty of Reciprocal Assistance, Sept. 2, 1947, 62 Stat. 1681, 21 U.N.T.S. 77	80, 81, 82, 83
1948 IMO Convention	Convention on the Intergovernmental Maritime Consultative Organization, Mar. 6, 1948, 9 U.S.T. 621, 289 U.N.T.S. 48	117, 118, 119, 120
1949	North Atlantic Treaty, Apr. 4, 1949, T.I.A.S. No. 1964, 34 U.N.T.S. 243	215, 486
1951 European Coal and Steel Community Treaty	Treaty Establishing the European Coal and Steel Community, Apr. 18, 1951, 261 U.N.T.S. 140	648
1952 Convention on Civil Jurisdiction in Matters of Collision	International Convention on Certain Rules Concerning Civil Jurisdiction in Matters of Collision, May 10, 1952, 439 U.N.T.S. 217	176
1952 Convention on Penal Jurisdiction in Matters of Collision	International Convention for the Unification of Certain Rules Relating to Penal Jurisdiction in Matters of Collision or Other Incidents of Navigation, May 10, 1952, 439 U.N.T.S. 233	176, 417

Table (*cont.*)

Date and Short Title	Full Title and Citation	Page
1955	Treaty of Amity, Economic Relations and Consular Rights, United States-Iran, Aug. 15, 1955, 8 U.S.T. 899, 284 U.N.T.S. 93	93, 94, 95, 96, 99, 100
1956 Supplementary Convention on the Abolition of Slavery	Supplementary Convention on the Abolition of Slavery, the Slave Trade and Institutions and Practices Similar to Slavery, Sept. 7, 1956, 18 U.S.T. 3201, 266 U.N.T.S. 3	195, 196
1956	**Treaty of Friendship, Commerce and Navigation, United States-Netherlands,** Mar. 27, 1956, 8 U.S.T. 2043, 285 U.N.T.S. 231	**346**, 349
1957	Treaty Establishing the European Atomic Energy Community, Mar. 25, 1957, 298 U.N.T.S. 167	615, 620, 648, 651, 652, 653, 654
1957	Treaty Establishing the European Economic Community, Mar. 25, 1957, 298 U.N.T.S. 11	211, 620, 633, 643, 648, 649, 650, 651, 652, 653, 677
1958 Continental Shelf Convention	Convention on the Continental Shelf, Apr. 29, 1958, 15 U.S.T. 471, 499 U.N.T.S. 311	3, 17, 18, 19, 20, 21, 22, 23, 24, 25, 30, 35, 223, 271, 273, 283, 284, 285, 286, 287, 288, 329, 344, 513, 521, 530, 532, 534, 535, 536, 538, 540, 541, 545
1958 Fishing on the High Seas Convention	Convention on Fishing and Conservation of the Living Resources of the High Seas, Apr. 29, 1958, 17 U.S.T. 138, 559 U.N.T.S. 285	487
1958 High Seas Convention	Convention on the High Seas, Apr. 29, 1958, 13 U.S.T. 2312, 450 U.N.T.S. 82	47, 50, 60, 61, 62, 74, 83, 84, 85, 87, 111, 119, 121, 126, 127, 145, 166, 176, 182, 183, 187, 194, 203, 204, 218, 475, 476, 481, 488

Table (*cont.*)

Date and Short Title	Full Title and Citation	Page
1958 Territorial Sea Convention	Convention on the Territorial Sea and the Contiguous Zone, Apr. 29, 1958, 15 U.S.T. 1606, 516 U.N.T.S. 205	45, 219, 222, 224, 227, 240, 241, 242, 243, 244, 248, 253, 258, 266, 269, 284, 354, 409, 417, 420, 421, 422, 427, 435, 469
1958 Optional Protocol on Compulsory Dispute Settlement	Optional Protocol of Signature Concerning the Compulsory Settlement of Disputes [Arising out of the 1958 Law of the Sea Conventions], Apr. 29, 1958, 450 U.N.T.S. 169	3, 532, 744, 779
1959	Antarctic Treaty, Dec. 1, 1959, 12 U.S.T. 794, 402 U.N.T.S. 71	15
1959	North-East Atlantic Fisheries Convention, Jan. 24, 1959, T.I.A.S. No. 7078, 486 U.N.T.S. 169	483
1961	Agreement Concerning the Fishery Zone around Iceland, Iceland-Germany, July 19, 1961, 409 U.N.T.S. 47	482
1961	Single Convention on Narcotic Drugs, Mar. 30, 1961, 18 U.S.T. 1407, 520 U.N.T.S. 204	200
1961 Exchange of Notes (Iceland-United Kingdom)	Agreement Settling the Fisheries Dispute between the Government of Iceland and the Government of the United Kingdom of Great Britain and Northern Ireland, Mar. 11, 1916, 397 U.N.T.S. 275	473, 474, 476, 477, 479, 480, 481, 482, 483, 485
1963 Limited Test Ban Treaty	Treaty Banning Nuclear Weapon Tests in the Atmosphere, Ban Treaty in Outer Space and Under Water, Aug. 5, 1963, 14 U.S.T. 1313, 480 U.N.T.S. 43	68

Table (*cont.*)

Date and Short Title	Full Title and Citation	Page
1965	International Maritime Dangerous Goods (IMDG) Code, available at http://www.imo.org/Publications/IMDGCode/Pages/Default.aspx	157
1965 Maritime Traffic Convention	Convention on Facilitation of International Maritime Traffic, Apr. 9, 1965, 18 U.S.T. 411, 591 U.N.T.S. 265	357
1966 Load Lines Convention	International Convention on Load Lines, Apr. 5, 1966, 18 U.S.T. 1857, 640 U.N.T.S. 133	162, 357
1967 Treaty of Tlateloco	Treaty for the Prohibition of Nuclear Weapons in Latin America, Feb. 14, 1967, 22 U.S.T. 762, 634 U.N.T.S. 281	92
1968	Treaty on the Non-Proliferation of Nuclear Weapons, July 1, 1968, 21 U.S.T. 483, 729 U.N.T.S. 161	719, 720, 734
1969	Vienna Convention on the Law of Treaties, May 23, 1969, 1155 U.N.T.S. 331	30, 31, 131, 160, 337, 421, 509, 541, 590, 603, 627, 628, 629, 771
1969 Convention on Tonnage Measurement of Ships	International Convention on Tonnage Measurement of Ships, June 23, 1969, 34 U.S.T. 2363, 1291 U.N.T.S. 3	162
1969 Moratorium Resolution	GA Res. 2574-D, UNGAOR, 24th Sess., Supp. No. 30 at 11, UN Doc. A/7630 (1969)	4, 561, 562, 564, 567
1970 Principles Resolution	**Declaration of Principles Governing the Sea-Bed and the Subsoil Thereof Beyond the Limits of National Jurisdiction**, GA Res. 2749, Dec. 17, 1970, UNGAOR, 25th Sess., Supp. No. 28 at 24, UN Doc. A/8028 (1971)	4, **564**, 567, 572

Table (*cont.*)

Date and Short Title	Full Title and Citation	Page
1970 Hague Convention for the Suppression of Unlawful Seizure of Aircraft	Convention for the Suppression of Unlawful Seizure of Aircraft, Dec. 16, 1970, 860 U.N.T.S. 105	709
1971 Montreal Convention for the Suppression of Unlawful Acts Against the Safety of Civil Aviation	Convention for the Suppression of Unlawful Acts against the Safety of Civil Aviation, Sept. 23, 1971, 24 U.S.T. 564, 974 U.N.T.S. 177	709
1971	Convention on Psychotropic Substances, Feb. 21, 1971, 32 U.S.T. 543, 1019 U.N.T.S. 175	200
1971	Protocol between Denmark, the Federal Republic of Germany and the Netherlands, Jan. 28, 1971, 10 Intl. Leg. Materials 600 (1971)	284
1971 Federal Republic of Germany-Denmark North Sea Continental Shelf Delimitation Treaty	Treaty between the Federal Republic of Germany and the Kingdom of Denmark relating to the Delimitation of the Continental Shelf under the North Sea, Jan. 28, 1971, 10 Intl. Leg. Materials 603 (1971)	284
1971 Federal Republic of Germany-Netherlands North Sea Continental Shelf Treaty	Treaty between the Kingdom of the Netherlands and the Federal Republic of Germany on the Delimitation of the Continental Shelf under the North Sea, Jan. 28, 1971, 10 Intl. Leg. Materials 607 (1971)	284
1972 Biological and Toxin Weapons Convention	Convention on the Prohibition of the Development, Production and Stockpiling of Bacteriological (Biological) and Toxin Weapons and on Their Destruction, Apr. 10, 1972, 26 U.S.T. 583, 1015 U.N.T.S. 163	734

Table (*cont.*)

Date and Short Title	Full Title and Citation	Page
1972 London Convention on the Dumping of Wastes at Sea	Convention on the Prevention of Marine Pollution by Dumping of Wastes and Other Matter, Dec. 29, 1972, 26 U.S.T. 2403, 1046 U.N.T.S. 120	75
1972 Oslo Convention for the Prevention of Marine Pollution	Convention for the Prevention of Marine Pollution by Dumping from Ships and Aircraft, Feb. 15, 1972, 932 U.N.T.S. 3	75
1972 Santo Domingo Declaration	Declaration of Specialized Conference of Caribbean Countries Concerning the Problems of the Sea: Declaration of Santo Domingo, June 7, 1972, UNGAOR, 27th Sess., Supp. No. 21, UN Doc. A/8721 at 70 (1972), 11 Intl. Leg. Materials 892 (1972)	4, 75
1972 Stockholm Declaration	Declaration of the United Nations Conference on the Human Environment, June 16 1972, UN Doc. A/CONF/48/14/Rev.1 (1972)	75
1972 Yaoundé Conclusions	Conclusions in the General Report of the African States Regional Seminar on the Law of the Sea (Yaoundé), June 20–30, 1972, UN Doc. ST/LEG/SER.B/16 at 601 (1972)	5
1973 Convention for the Prevention of Pollution from Ships, as modified by the 1978 Protocol (MARPOL)	**International Convention for the Prevention of Pollution by Ships**, Nov. 2, 1973, 1340 U.N.T.S. 184, amended by Protocol of 1978 Relating to the International Convention for the Prevention of Pollution from Ships, 1973, Feb. 17, 1978, 1340 U.N.T.S. 61	125, **154**, 156, 162, 387, 388, 389, 390, 393, 394, 396, 400, 661
1974 Safety of Life at Sea (SOLAS) Convention	**International Convention for the Safety of Life at Sea**, Convention Nov. 1, 1974, 32 U.S.T. 47, 1184 U.N.T.S. 2	105, 125, **153**, 155, 156, 157, 160, 162, 355, 357, 378, 400, 727, 728

Table (*cont.*)

Date and Short Title	Full Title and Citation	Page
1976	Agreement Concerning British Fishing in Icelandic Waters, Iceland-United Kingdom, June 1, 1976, 15 Intl. Leg. Materials 878 (1976)	486
1977 Torremolinos Convention	International Convention for the Safety of Fishing Vessels, Apr. 2, 1977, Cmnd. 7252	156
1978 Northwest Atlantic Fisheries Convention	**Convention on Future Multilateral Cooperation in the Northwest Atlantic Fisheries**, October 24, 1978, 1135 U.N.T.S. 369	164, 165, 667, 668, 669, 678, **694**
1978 Seafarer Training, Certification and Watchkeeping (STCW) Convention	**International Convention on Standards of Training, Certification and Watchkeeping for Seafarers**, July 7, 1978, U.S. Sen. Exec. Doc. No. EE (1979), 1361 U.N.T.S. 190	**154**, 156, **158**, 160, 162, 400
1979 Maritime Search and Rescue Convention	International Convention on Maritime Search and Rescue, Apr. 27, 1979, T.I.A.S. No. 11093, 1405 U.N.T.S. 97	105, 110
1981	Agreement relating to Establishment of a Cooperative Program of Interdiction and Selective Return of Certain Haitian Migrants and Vessels, Sept. 23, 1981, United States-Haiti, 33 U.S.T. 3359, 1537 U.N.T.S. 175	109
1981	**United States-United Kingdom Agreement to Facilitate the Interdiction of Vessels Suspected of Trafficking in Drugs,** Nov. 13, 1981, 33 U.S.T. 4224, 1285 U.N.T.S. 197	**198**
1982 LOS Convention	United Nations Convention on the Law of the Sea, Dec. 10, 1982, U.S. Sen. Treaty Doc. No. 103–39 (1994), 1833 U.N.T.S. 3	See LOS Convention Table and Appendix

Table (*cont.*)

Date and Short Title	Full Title and Citation	Page
1982 Paris MOU	Memorandum of Understanding on Port State Control in Implementing Agreements on Maritime Safety and Protection of the Marine Environment, Jan. 26, 1982, 21 Intl. Leg. Materials 1 (1982)	399, 400, 401, 402
1985	South Pacific Nuclear Free Zone Treaty, Aug. 6, 1985, 24 Intl. Leg. Materials 1440 (1985)	91
1986	**Declaration of a Zone of Peace and Co-operation of the South Atlantic**, GA Res. 41/11, Oct. 27, 1986, UNGAOR, 41st Sess., UN Doc. A/RES/41/11 (1986)	**90**
1988 Convention for the Suppression of Unlawful Acts Against the Safety of Civil Aviation	Protocol for the Suppression of Unlawful Acts of Violence at Airports Serving International Civil Aviation, Supplementary to the Convention for the Suppression of Unlawful Acts Against the Safety of Civil Aviation, Feb. 24, 1988, 1589 U.N.T.S. 474	101
1988 Protocol for the Suppression of Unlawful Acts against the Safety of Fixed Platforms	Protocol for the Suppression of Unlawful Acts against the Safety of Fixed Platforms Located on the Continental Shelf, Mar. 10, 1988, 1678 U.N.T.S. 304	709
1988 SUA Convention	**Convention for the Suppression of Unlawful Acts against the Safety of Maritime Navigation**, Mar. 10, 1988, 1678 U.N.T.S. 222	**706**, 709, 710, 711, 712, 713, 714, 715, 716, 719
1988	**United Nations Convention against Illicit Traffic in Narcotic Drugs and Psychotropic Substances,** Dec. 20, 1988, U.S. Sen. Treaty Doc. No. 101-4 (1989)	**197**

Table (*cont.*)

Date and Short Title	Full Title and Citation	Page
1989	**Uniform Interpretation of Rules of International Law Governing Innocent Passage, U.S.-U.S.S.R.,** Sept. 23, 1989, Dept. State Bull. No. 2152 at 26 (Nov. 1989), 28 Intl. Leg. Materials 1445 (1989)	418, 419, 421, 422
1989 Salvage Convention	International Convention on Salvage, Apr. 28, 1989, U.S. Sen. Treaty Doc. No. 102-12 (1991), 1953 U.N.T.S. 165	360
1990 Belgium-France Continental Shelf Agreement	**Agreement between the Kingdom of Belgium and the French Republic Concerning the Delimitation of the Continental Shelf**, Oct. 8, 1990, 19 Law of the Sea Bull. 29 (1991)	269, 270, 271, 286
1990 Belgium-France Territorial Sea Agreement	**Agreement between the Kingdom of Belgium and the French Republic Concerning the Delimitation of the Territorial Sea,** Oct. 8, 1990, 19 Law of the Sea Bull. 27 (1991)	265, 268, 269, 271, 286
1992 Agenda 21	Agenda 21 of the United Nations Conference on Environment and Development, 1 Report of the United Nations Conference on Environment and Development, UN Doc. A/CONF.15/26/Rev.1 at 9	681, 688
1992 Convention on Biological Diversity	Convention on Biological Diversity, June 5, 1992, U.S. Sen. Treaty Doc. No. 103-20 (1993), 31 Intl. Leg. Materials 818 (1992)	609, 611, 612
1992	Memorandum of Understanding, United Kingdom-Albania, 63 Brit. Y.B. Intl. L. 1992 at 615, 781 (1993)	435
1992 OSPAR Convention	Convention for the Protection of the Marine Environment of the North-East Atlantic, Sept. 22, 1992, 32 Intl. Leg. Materials 1069 (1993)	619, 624, 625, 626, 627, 629, 630, 631, 633, 634, 635, 636, 637, 638, 640, 642, 648, 658, 781

Table (*cont.*)

Date and Short Title	Full Title and Citation	Page
1993 Chemical Weapons Convention	Convention on the Prohibition of the Development, Production, Stockpiling and Use of Chemical Weapons and on Their Destruction, Jan. 13, 1993, 1975 U.N.T.S. 3	734
1993 Convention for the Conservation of Southern Bluefin Tuna (CCSBT)	Convention for the Conservation of Southern Bluefin Tuna, May 10, 1993, 1819 U.N.T.S. 360	770, 772, 776, 777, 780, 781
1993 FAO Flag State Compliance Agreement	Agreement to Promote Compliance with International Conservation and Management Measures by Fishing Vessels on the High Seas, Nov. 24, 1993, U.S. Sen. Treaty Doc. No. 103-24 (1993), 2221 U.N.T.S. 91	127, 156, 688
1993 Torremolinos Protocol	Protocol of 1993 relating to the Torremolinos International Convention for the Safety of Fishing Vessels, Apr. 12, 1993, in 1993 Torremolinos Protocol and Torremolinos International Convention for the Safety of Fishing Vessels, Consolidated Edition 1995, at 9, Sales No. IMO-793E (1995)	156
1994 Implementation Agreement	**Agreement relating to the Implementation of Part XI of the Agreement of the United Nations Convention on the Law of the Sea of 10 December 1982**, July 28, 1994, GA Res. 48/263 (1994), U.S. Sen. Treaty Doc. No. 103–39 (1994), 1836 U.N.T.S. 3	11, 12, 13, 62, 572, **580**, 582, 583, 584, 585, 586, 587, 588, 589, 590, 591, 592, 597, 604, 606, 607, 611, 612, 689 and Appendix
1995 Treaty of Pelindaba	African Nuclear-Weapon-Free Zone Treaty, June 21–23, 1995, 35 Intl. Leg. Materials 698 (1996)	92

Table (*cont.*)

Date and Short Title	Full Title and Citation	Page
1995 Fish Stocks Agreement	**Agreement for the Implementation of the Provisions of the United Nations Convention on the Law of the Sea of 10 December 1982 Relating to the Conservation and Management of Straddling Fish Stocks and Highly Migratory Fish Stocks**, Dec. 4, 1995, U.S. Sen. Treaty Doc. No. 104-24 (1996), 2167 U.N.T.S. 88	12, 127, 156, **397**, 398, 667, **681**, 688, 689, 690, 691, 692, 693, 699, 702, 747
1995	Global Program of Action for the Protection of the Marine Environment from Land-based Activities, UN Doc. UNEP(OCA)/LBA/IG.2/7 (1995)	614
1995	Treaty on the Southeast Asia Nuclear-Weapon-Free Zone, Dec. 15, 1995, 1981 U.N.T.S. 129	92
1996	**Declaration of People's Republic of China upon Ratification of the Law of the Sea Convention (1996)**, available at http://www.un.org/Depts/los/convention_agreements/convention_declarations.htm#China%20Upon%20ratification	**418**
2000	Protocol to Prevent, Suppress and Punish Trafficking in Persons, Especially Women and Children, supplementing the United Nations Convention Against Transnational Organized Crime, Nov. 2, 2000, GA Res. 55/25, Annex II, UN Doc. A/RES/55/25 (2000), 40 Intl. Leg. Materials 377 (2001)	196

Table (*cont.*)

Date and Short Title	Full Title and Citation	Page
2001	International Law Commission, Draft Articles on Responsibility of States for Internationally Wrongful Acts, GA Res. 56/83, Annex, UN Doc. A/RES/56/83 (2001)	78, 131, 357, 500
2001 UNESCO Underwater Cultural Heritage Convention	Convention on the Protection of the Underwater Cultural Heritage, Nov. 6, 2001, 41 Intl. Leg. Materials 40 (2002)	12, 542, 543, 544
2002 International Ship and Port Facility Security (ISPS) Code	IMO Doc. SOLAS/CONF.5/34, Annex 1 (2002)	355, 727, 728
2003 Revised Seafarers' Identity Documents Convention (No. 185)	ILO Convention (No. 185) Revising the 1958 Seafarers' Identity Documents Convention, June 19, 2003, 2304 U.N.T.S. 121	729
2004	Regional Cooperation Agreement on Combating Piracy and Armed Robbery against Ships in Asia, Nov. 11, 2004, 2398 U.N.T.S. 199	189
2004 European Community-United States Container Security Cooperation Agreement	Agreement on Intensifying and Broadening the Agreement on Customs Cooperation and Mutual Assistance in Customs Matters to Include Cooperation on Container Security and Related Matters, European Community-United States, Apr. 22, 2004, T.I.A.S. No. 04-422, 2004 O.J. L. 304/34	736
2005	Agreement on Cooperation to Suppress the Proliferation of Weapons of Mass Destruction, Their Delivery Systems, and Related Materials by Sea, United States-Belize, Aug. 4, 2005, T.I.A.S. No. 05-1019	734

Table (*cont.*)

Date and Short Title	Full Title and Citation	Page
2005	Code of Safety for Fishermen and Fishing Vessels, Feb. 2. 2005, IMO Doc. MSC 79/23/Add.3, Annex 38 (2005)	157
2005	**Protocol of 2005 to the Convention for the Suppression of Unlawful Acts against the Safety of Maritime Navigation**, Nov. 1, 2005, IMO Doc. LEG/CONF.15/21 (2005)	717
2006	Maritime Labor Convention, Feb. 23, 2006, available at http://www.mlc2006.com	157, 398
2008	**Amendment to the Convention on Future Multilateral Cooperation in the Northwest Atlantic Fisheries,** Sept. 28, 2008, GC Doc. 07/4	695
2009	Code of Practice for the Investigation of Crimes of Piracy and Armed Robbery Against Ships, Dec. 2, 2009, IMO Doc. A 22/Res. 922, Annex	188, 189
2009 Djibouti Code of Conduct	Djibouti Code of Conduct Concerning the Repression of Piracy and Armed Robbery against Ships in the Western Indian Ocean and the Gulf of Aden, Jan. 29, 2009, IMO Doc. C 102/14, Annex (2009)	189
2009	FAO Agreement on Port State Measures to Prevent, Deter and Eliminate Illegal, Unreported and Unregulated Fishing, Nov. 22, 2009, FAO Doc. C 2009/LIM/11 Rev. 1	398, 689

Table (*cont.*)

Date and Short Title	Full Title and Citation	Page
2009 Convention on South Pacific High Seas Fishery Resources	Convention on the Conservation and Management of High Seas Fishery Resources in the South Pacific Ocean, Nov. 14, 2009, U.S. Sen. Treaty Doc. No. 113-1 (2013)	701
2011	**International Maritime Organization (IMO) Code for the Implementation of Mandatory IMO Instruments**, IMO Res. A.1054(27) (2011)	**161**
2012 Cape Town Agreement	Cape Town Agreement on the Implementation of the Provisions of the 1993 Torremolinos Protocol Relating to the 1977 International Convention for the Safety of Fishing Vessels, Oct. 11, 2012, available at http://www.imo.org	156

Table of 1982 LOS Convention Articles

The United Nations Convention on the Law of the Sea, Dec. 10, 1982, U.S. Sen. Treaty Doc. 103–39 (1994), 1833 U.N.T.S. 3. See Appendix.

Table (*cont.*)

Article	Page
37	453, 794
38	453, 469, 795
39	51, 453, 461, 462, 463, 795
40	453, 462, 796
41	453, 454, 796
42	453, 462, 463, 797
43	453, 797
44	453, 798
46	258, 259, 467, 796
47	241, 254, 255, 258, 262, 467, 798
48	258, 467, 799
49	258, 467, 799
50	258, 800
51	55, 258, 800
52	52, 258, 421, 466, 467, 800
53	258, 454, 459, 461, 462, 464, 466, 467, 469, 800
54	258, 461, 462, 463, 802
55	505, 802
56	488, 497, 498, 500, 501, 503, 506, 507, 508, 510, 546, 802
57	488, 803
58	47, 52, 55, 187, 427, 497, 498, 499, 500, 501, 502, 503, 504, 505, 506, 508, 509, 510, 512, 803
59	495, 508, 510, 511, 512, 803
60	499, 538, 803
61	512, 684, 804
62	504, 512, 805
63	688, 692, 806
64	688, 692, 770, 771, 807
73	758, 759, 761, 762, 763, 764, 765, 767, 768, 769, 812
74	323, 329, 344, 812
76	285, 305, 306, 315, 319, 332, 333, 335, 337, 338, 339, 340, 341, 343, 545, 546, 547, 548, 549, 550, 551, 552, 553, 554, 556, 557, 558, 813
77	316, 335, 545, 814
78	545, 546, 815
79	55, 545, 546, 815
80	538, 545, 815

Table (*cont.*)

Table (*cont.*)

Table (*cont.*)

Article	Page
191	607, 740, 745, 755, 864
192	613, 616, 619, 621, 864
193	616, 619, 621, 864
194	152, 616, 619, 621, 864
196	613, 865
197	616, 619, 621, 660, 866
199	660, 866
200	660, 866
201	660, 866
206	617, 619, 621, 868
207	616, 619, 621, 868
209	612, 869
211	358, 395, 463, 616, 619, 621, 870
212	619, 621, 872
213	616, 619, 621, 872
217	152, 873
218	388, 393, 394, 395, 396, 401, 874
219	398, 401, 875
220	396, 761, 768, 875
223	395, 877
224	395, 878
225	395, 878
226	395, 660, 761, 768, 878
227	395, 879
228	388, 390, 392, 393, 395, 879
229	395, 880
230	395, 880
231	395, 880
232	395, 880
233	395, 453, 880
235	660, 881
246	546, 884
256	611, 889
279	738, 745, 775, 777, 896
280	745, 775, 778, 896
281	642, 646, 745, 770, 771, 772, 775, 777, 778, 779, 780, 896

Table (*cont.*)

Article	Page
282	619, 620, 642, 643, 646, 649, 650, 658, 896
283	642, 745, 778, 896
284	745, 777, 778, 897
285	745, 897
286	745, 771, 772, 775, 778, 897
287	333, 344, 615, 618, 619, 641, 644, 650, 654, 656, 745, 754, 757, 770, 897
288	619, 642, 745, 747, 770, 777, 898
289	745, 898
290	123, 615, 616, 618, 620, 623, 749, 754, 767, 769, 770, 773, 774, 779, 780, 781, 899
291	745, 900
292	123, 130, 137, 140, 141, 395, 745, 749, 754, 757, 758, 759, 760, 761, 762, 763, 764, 765, 766, 767, 768, 769, 900
293	51, 142, 642, 651, 652, 745, 900
294	745, 900
295	745, 901
296	325, 646, 650, 745, 901
297	345, 692, 693, 740, 742, 745, 748, 773, 778, 901
298	740, 741, 747, 773, 903
299	745, 904
301	62, 80, 84, 905
303	428, 544, 905
308	580, 907
309	580, 907
311	51, 55, 421, 544, 771, 908
312	13, 589, 908
313	13, 589, 909
314	13, 589, 909
318	573, 911
Annex II	345, 548, 914
Annex II, Art. 1	556, 914
Annex II, Art. 3	337, 549, 914
Annex II, Art. 5	549, 915
Annex II, Art. 9	338, 916
Annex III	573, 595, 598, 917
Annex III, Art. 1	548, 592, 917

Table (*cont.*)

CHAPTER 1

Introduction

This chapter introduces the international law of the sea and some of the international law sources, processes, and institutions important to its development. Section A provides an overview of the history of the law of the sea and of the major treaty in the field, the 1982 United Nations Convention on the Law of the Sea (LOS Convention). Section B then examines the sources of law international lawyers consult, as well as introducing one forum in which the law of the sea has been interpreted and applied.

A Overview*

1 *Developments to 1972*

Diligent historians of international law can easily trace the beginnings of the law of the sea to ancient Greece and Rome, and with a little more effort to Phoenicia and Carthage, as well as to ancient China and India. Such medieval authors as Bartolus da Sassoferrato and Baldus de Ubaldis helped to develop the law of the sea, as did the practice of Great Britain, France, Venice, Genoa, Asian countries, the Scandinavian states, and the Hanseatic cities.

An important dispute between those who favored closed seas (mare clausum) and those who advocated the freedom of the seas (mare liberum) arose in the eastern Mediterranean and the Adriatic in the 16th and early 17th centuries. The Spanish and Portuguese governments had attempted to close vast areas of the oceans, especially in the East and West Indies, to international trade. This attempt exacerbated the mare clausum-mare liberum dispute and ran counter to an Asian tradition of freedom of the seas. A Dutch author, Hugo Grotius (de Groot), and a British author, John Selden, waged an important "battle of the books" in the early 1600s, with Grotius promoting the freedom of the seas and Selden arguing for the right of states to extend their jurisdiction over the seas. Grotius defended the interests of the Dutch government in general, and those of the Great United Company of the East Indies in particular, while Selden argued the position of the British government, which then sought,

---

* Section A is an expanded and edited version of Louis B. Sohn, Kristen Gustafson Juras, John E. Noyes & Erik Franckx, Law of the Sea in a Nutshell 1–11 (2d ed. 2010).

 | DOI 10.1163/9789004203563_002

inter alia, to protect the rich fishing grounds around the British isles from depletion by foreign fishermen. See Edward Gordon, Grotius and the Freedom of the Seas in the Seventeenth Century, 16 Willamette J. Intl. L. & Dis. Res. 252 (2008).

The practice of major maritime powers influenced the acceptance of the principle of freedom of the seas. As Great Britain gained strength as a maritime power, the British government abandoned its efforts to license foreigners to fish in "British seas" and to impose tolls on the passage of foreign vessels. The supremacy of British sea power during the 19th century solidified a customary international law regime based on the principle of the freedom of the seas, a principle that still carries weight today.

The principle of freedom of the seas encompasses specific freedoms that any state may exercise on the high seas. These include the freedoms of navigation, overflight, fishing, and laying of submarine cables and pipelines, along with the freedoms to engage in scientific research and to construct artificial islands and platforms. States have a duty to exercise these freedoms with reasonable regard for the right of other states to exercise their freedoms. A ship on the high seas is normally subject only to the jurisdiction of the state whose flag it flies. Limited exceptions to this rule apply, for example in cases of so-called "hot pursuit" from zones of coastal jurisdiction for wrongs committed in those zones. A vessel committing piratical acts on the high seas is subject to the jurisdiction of any state.

It has traditionally been recognized that the coastal state can claim control for various purposes over certain coastal waters, such as bays and a belt known as the territorial sea. In the 19th century many states agreed that this belt should not exceed three nautical miles, although several states claimed four, six, or twelve nautical miles. (A nautical mile, in illustrations and tables abbreviated as "M," is 1852 meters (6076.115 feet), while the geographical or statute mile is 1609.344 meters (5280 feet).) The topic of "territorial waters" was on the agenda of a 1930 Hague Conference for the Codification of International Law, arranged by the Assembly of the League of Nations. Although the Second Committee of the Conference agreed on a number of important rules with respect to the regime of the territorial sea, it was not able to reach a decision on whether existing international law recognized any fixed breadth of the belt of territorial sea.

Beginning in the mid-20th century, national concerns with guaranteeing access to offshore natural resources, coupled with improvements in technology, prompted states to extend their jurisdiction from their coasts. In 1945, the United States, through two proclamations by President Truman, made certain limited claims to jurisdiction over continental shelf resources and over coastal fisheries. This unilateral act was followed by similar or more extensive claims on the part of other states and by resolutions of various international bodies.

These developments prompted and shaped efforts at codification at the United Nations. In 1949 the International Law Commission, an expert body operating within the U.N. system, began to draw up articles on the regime of the high seas and related subjects. Drafts prepared by the Commission served as the basis for negotiations at the First United Nations Conference on the Law of the Sea, held at Geneva in 1958. The Conference adopted four conventions relating to: (1) the territorial sea and the contiguous zone; (2) the high seas; (3) fishing and conservation of the living resources of the high seas; and (4) the continental shelf. It adopted also an optional protocol concerning the compulsory settlement of disputes arising out of the interpretation and application of these conventions. But again no agreement could be reached on the breadth of the territorial sea.

The Second United Nations Conference on the Law of the Sea in 1960 tackled again the problem of the breadth of the territorial sea. By a vote of 54 in favor to 28 against (one vote short of the required two-thirds majority) the Conference failed to adopt a joint Canadian-U.S. compromise proposal for a six-nautical-mile territorial sea and an additional six-nautical-mile fishing zone.

One result of this fiasco was the abandonment of the three-nautical-mile limit, as many countries unilaterally extended their territorial seas or at least their fishing limits to twelve nautical miles. Major maritime powers became concerned that this change in international practice might affect the freedom of navigation through many international straits. The United States and the Soviet Union, independently and separately, started exploring the possibility of an agreement on a package relating to the territorial sea, straits, and fishing rights. The possibility of a conference on this subject was raised in 1967.

In the meantime, one "success" of the 1958 Conference started running into new difficulties. That Conference had been able to agree that the coastal state is entitled to exercise "sovereign rights" over the continental shelf "for the purpose of exploring it and exploiting its natural resources." The agreed-upon text included an open-ended definition of the continental shelf as the seabed and subsoil of the submarine area adjacent to the coast "to a depth of 200 metres or, beyond that limit, to where the depth of the superjacent waters admits of the exploitation of the natural resources of the said areas." 1958 Continental Shelf Convention, Articles 1–2. Nobody then thought that any important resources were located below the depth of 200 meters, and in any case there were not then any practical means for exploiting such depths.

By 1967, however, it became generally believed that important resources lay at the bottom of the deep oceans—more than a trillion tons of polymetallic nodules containing manganese, nickel, copper, and cobalt. Several methods for recovering deep seabed mineral resources were being considered in the United States, Europe, and Japan.

At the 1967 General Assembly of the United Nations, Ambassador Arvid Pardo of Malta proposed that the seabed and ocean floor underlying the high seas beyond the limits of national jurisdiction be declared "a common heritage of mankind," that its resources be used for the benefit of humankind as a whole, and that the United Nations study the implications of establishing an international regime and an international agency to administer it. The General Assembly established an ad hoc committee for the purpose, which in 1968 was transformed into a permanent committee. This so-called Sea-Bed Committee grew from 42 to, eventually, 91 states. In 1969, over the opposition of 27 states, the General Assembly passed a "moratorium" resolution, declaring that, pending the establishment of an international regime, states and persons "are bound to refrain from all activities of exploitation of the resources of the area of the sea-bed and ocean floor, and the subsoil thereof, beyond the limits of national jurisdiction." GA Res. 2574D, UNGAOR, 24th Sess., Supp. No. 30 at 11 (1969). See also the 1970 Declaration of Principles, GA Res. 2749, UNGAOR, 25th Sess., Supp. No. 28 at 24 (1970). The Assembly decided to convene a Third Conference on the Law of the Sea in 1973 to deal not only with the question of "an equitable international régime—including an international machinery—for the area and the resources of the sea-bed and ocean floor, and the subsoil thereof, beyond the limits of national jurisdiction," but also with "a broad range of related issues" (i.e., high seas, continental shelf, territorial sea, international straits, contiguous zone, fishing and conservation of the living resources of the high seas, preservation of the marine environment, and scientific research). GA Res. 2750C, UNGAOR, 25th Sess., Supp. No. 28 at 26 (1970).

Besides the seabed question, another issue loomed large by the time the Conference met. Certain Latin American states had claimed 200-nautical-mile zones off their coasts. While these claims were originally intended to protect fishing interests, some of them were broader in scope and pretended to extend the territorial sea to 200 nautical miles. While many other states protested against this extension of national jurisdiction, the three original claimants—Chile, Peru, and Ecuador—slowly gathered support not only in Latin America but also in Africa and Asia. In the 1970s two new concepts emerged. The first was that of a "patrimonial sea" of 200 nautical miles, espoused by a group of Caribbean states led by Colombia, Mexico, and Venezuela and embodied in the 1972 Santo Domingo Declaration. In the patrimonial sea, coastal states would have sovereignty over both living and nonliving resources, as well as the right to regulate scientific research and to adopt measures for the protection of the environment, and other states would retain the freedoms of navigation and overflight. The second new concept was that of an "economic zone," elaborated by African states in the 1972 Yaoundé Conclusions. This economic zone concept would provide coastal states with rights similar to those in a patrimonial sea, but those rights would be "without prejudice to" any of the four high seas freedoms of navigation, overflight, fishing, and laying cables.

2 *The Third United Nations Conference on the Law of the Sea and the 1982 LOS Convention*

The first, procedural, session of the Third United Nations Conference on the Law of the Sea (UNCLOS III) convened in New York, December 3–15, 1973. Rules of procedure, including provisions for reaching decisions by consensus and for elaborate voting arrangements if no consensus could be reached, were adopted at the second session in Caracas, which met June 20–August 29, 1974. In preparing draft treaty articles for the Conference, the Sea-Bed Committee had established three subcommittees. These subcommittees dealt, respectively, with: (a) the seabed, and (b) the main issues of the law of the sea, other than (c) the preservation of the marine environment and scientific research. UNCLOS III divided the subjects similarly among its three committees. The Conference—which met over a period of ten years, involved virtually every state in the world, and eventually concluded the LOS Convention—provides rich materials for studying the process of international lawmaking. UNCLOS III had to manage a flood of proposals from states, allow for the work of experts and informal working groups, and recognize the interests of various groups of states holding divergent positions in various issue areas. Texts prepared by the chairs of the Conference's three committees or the President of the Conference served as focal points for negotiation.[**]

By its seventh session in 1978, the Conference was focusing much attention on seven specific "hard-core" issues that were proving difficult to resolve. Three

** Studies of the negotiating process at UNCLOS III include Robert L. Friedheim, Negotiating the New Ocean Regime (1993), Edward L. Miles, Global Ocean Politics: The Decision Process at the Third United Nations Conference on the Law of the Sea 1973–1982 (1998), and Tommy T.B. Koh & Shanmugam Jayakumar, The Negotiating Process of the Third United Nations Conference on the Law of the Sea, in 1 The United Nations Convention on the Law of the Sea: A Commentary 29 (Myron Nordquist ed., 1985). Records of the Conference are found in the 17-volume Official Records of the Third United Nations Conference on the Law of the Sea and in a 18-volume compilation entitled Third United Nations Conference on the Law of the Sea: Documents, edited by Renate Platzöder. The draft texts prepared by the chairs of the Conference's committees or the of these issues related to seabed matters, and the others related, respectively, to the rights of land-locked and so-called geographically disadvantaged states (LL/GDS), the settlement of disputes relating to the exercise of the sovereign rights of coastal states in the exclusive economic zone, the outer limits of the continental shelf, and the delimitation of maritime boundaries between states. The negotiating groups addressing these issues had made progress by the tenth session in 1981, but the Conference was unable to complete its work then because the newly elected U.S. administration objected to the provisions relating to deep seabed mining.

On April 30, 1982, at the conclusion of its 11th session, held in New York, UNCLOS III adopted the LOS Convention, subject to adjustment of the various language versions by the Drafting Committee. The vote, which was held at the request of the United States, was 130 votes to four (Israel, Turkey, the United States, and Venezuela), with seventeen abstentions (eight Eastern

President of the Conference, which served as negotiating focal points, included: the Informal Single Negotiating Texts (ISNT) authorized at the third Geneva session of the Conference in 1975 (4 UNCLOS III Official Records 137); the Revised Single Negotiating Texts (RSNT prepared at the fourth session in New York in 1976 (5 id. 111 and 6 id. 144); and the Informal Composite Negotiation Text (ICNT) authorized at the sixth session in New York in 1977 (UN Docs. A/CONF.62/WP.10 and Add.1 (1977), 8 UNCLOS III Official Records 1). Subsequent texts included: revisions of the icnt in 1979 and 1980 (UN Doc. A/CONF.62/WP.10/Rev.1 (1979), 18 Intl. Leg. Materials 686 (1979), and UN Doc. A/CONF.62/WP.10/ Rev.2 (1980)); the Draft Convention on the Law of the Sea (Informal Text) in 1980 (UN Doc. A/CONF.62/WP.10/Rev.3* (1980)); and the Draft Convention on the Law of the Sea in 1981 (UN Doc. A/CONF.62/L.78 (1981), 15 UNCLOS III Official Records 172). Volumes 2–7 of United Nations Convention on the Law of the Sea 1982: A Commentary (Myron H. Nordquist ed.-in-chief, 1989–2011) provide an article-by-article history of the Convention.

Developments at the negotiating sessions of the Conference were reported in a series of articles published in the American Journal of International Law, the first two written by John R. Stevenson and Bernard H. Oxman and the last six by Oxman alone: The Third United Nations Conference on the Law of the Sea: The 1974 Caracas Session, 69 Am. J. Intl. L. 1 (1975); The Third United Nations Conference on the Law of the Sea: The 1975 Geneva Session, 69 id. 763 (1975); The Third United Nations Conference on the Law of the Sea: The 1976 New York Sessions, 71 id. 247 (1977); The Third United Nations Conference on the Law of the Sea: The 1977 New York Session, 72 id. 57 (1978); The United Nations Conference on the Law of the Sea: The Seventh Session (1978), 73 id. 1 (1979); The Third United Nations Conference on the Law of the Sea: The Eighth Session (1979), 74 id. 1 (1980); The Third United Nations Conference on the Law of the Sea: The Ninth Session (1980), 75 id. 211 (1981); and The Third United Nations Conference on the Law of the Sea: The Tenth Session (1981), 76 id. 1 (1982). Other sources include 1-2 A Handbook on the New Law of the Sea (René-Jean Dupuy & Daniel Vignes eds., 1991).

European states, seven Western European states, Mongolia, and Thailand). The Conference adopted at the same time various resolutions, including a resolution establishing a Preparatory Commission for the International Seabed Authority and the International Tribunal for the Law of the Sea, and a resolution governing preparatory investment in pioneer seabed mining activities. The final text, as amended by the Drafting Committee, was approved by the Conference at the resumed 11th session held in New York, September 22–24, 1982. This text consists of 320 articles and nine annexes. At the final part of the 11th session, in Montego Bay, Jamaica, December 6–10, 1982, 119 states and entities signed both the LOS Convention and the Final Act of the Conference, which contains a history of UNCLOS III and the final texts of the various UNCLOS III resolutions.

The LOS Convention codifies some existing rules of law, but it also contains many new treaty rules and provides for new institutions. The Convention, along with numerous other treaties, customary international law developments, and contributions of judicial bodies and international organizations, will occupy us throughout this book. In broad outline, the Convention and current international law recognize several zones of the oceans in which coastal states and other states have rights and responsibilities:

Zones of Coastal State Sovereignty:

- internal waters, such as ports. Internal waters are located inside a coastal state's baseline, which often conforms to the low-water mark of its coastline but in some instances may be a straight line that diverges from the coastline. We study baselines in Chapter 5 and internal waters in Chapter 7.
- the territorial sea, which extends up to twelve nautical miles from the baseline. A coastal state has sovereignty over its territorial sea, although other states have the right to sail their vessels in innocent passage through the territorial sea. The right of innocent passage had long been recognized, but the LOS Convention incorporates a specific list of activities that would render passage non-innocent. We consider the territorial sea and innocent passage in Chapter 8.

Zones of Coastal State Limited Functional Jurisdiction:

- the contiguous zone (also discussed in Chapter 8), which is located outside the territorial sea. The contiguous zone extends up to 24 nautical miles from the baseline. In this zone a coastal state may prevent violations of its fiscal, customs, immigration, and sanitary laws.

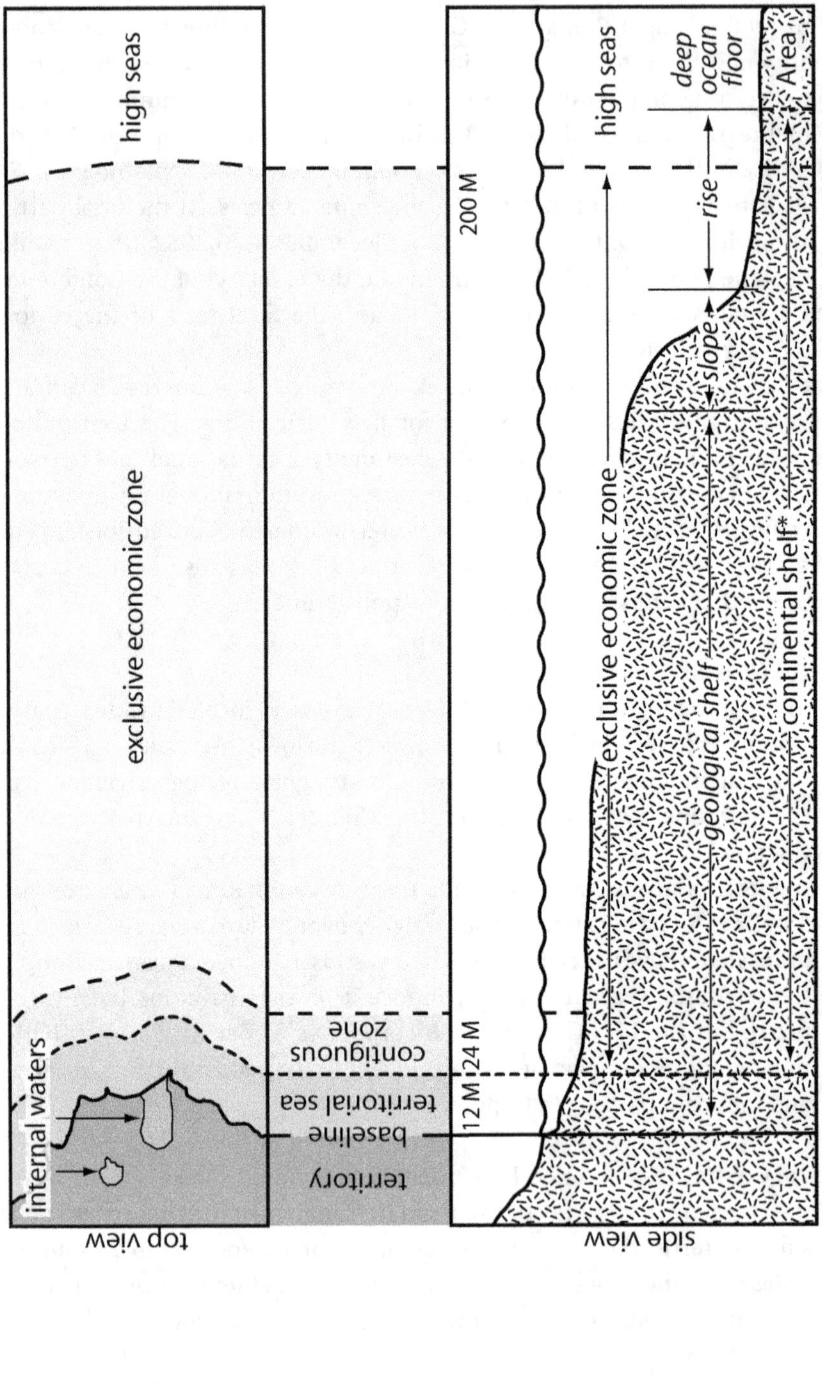

* The legal continental shelf extends at least to 200 M. In certain circumstances it may extend beyond 200 M.

FIGURE I.A *Zones of National Jurisdiction*

- the exclusive economic zone (EEZ), located outside the territorial sea and extending up to 200 nautical miles from the baseline. The EEZ was a concept newly recognized in the UNCLOS III negotiations. The coastal state has sovereign rights or jurisdiction over natural resources and certain economic uses in the EEZ. Other states may exercise specified high seas freedoms in the EEZ. See Chapter 9.
- the continental shelf, also located beyond the territorial sea and in general extending as far as the EEZ and in some cases beyond it. The continental shelf comprises the seabed and subsoil of a coastal state's land territory. The coastal state enjoys exclusive sovereign rights to exploit the natural resources of the continental shelf. The LOS Convention created a technical body, the Commission on the Limits of the Continental Shelf (CLCS), to make recommendations to the coastal state concerning the location of the outer limits of the continental shelf beyond 200 nautical miles from the baseline. We study the continental shelf and the CLCS in Chapter 10.

Regions Beyond the Limits of Coastal State Jurisdiction:

- waters beyond coastal state jurisdiction, often referred to as the high seas, where states enjoy high seas freedoms and are subject to various obligations (Chapter 2).
- the seabed and subsoil beyond the limits of national jurisdiction, known as the Area, where a special regime applies to the exploration and exploitation of mineral resources (Chapter 11).

The LOS Convention does not merely set out the various coastal zones noted above and prescribe the rights and responsibilities of states in those zones. It also deals with a wide range of other legal issues important to the rights and duties of coastal states, flag states, and the international community generally. Some Convention provisions reflect long-established international law, while other provisions were new. Issues addressed in the LOS Convention have also been the subject of many other treaties and international legal developments. Among these issues are:

- the nationality of vessels, flag state jurisdiction over vessels, and exceptions to flag state jurisdiction (Chapters 3 and 4);
- maritime boundaries between adjacent and opposite states (Chapter 6);
- transit passage through straits, an issue of great importance to maritime powers seeking to insure their ability to navigate through strategic straits (Chapter 8);

- archipelagic states and archipelagic sea lanes passage (Chapter 8);
- marine scientific research;
- protection of the marine environment from pollution (Chapter 12);
- the conservation and management of marine mammals, high seas fish stocks, and stocks that swim between the EEZ and the seas beyond (Chapter 13);
- terrorism and maritime security, an area of law consistent with, but developed largely outside, the LOS Convention (Chapter 14); and
- the system of international third-party dispute settlement established in the LOS Convention, involving in part the International Tribunal for the Law of the Sea, a new court created by the LOS Convention (Chapter 15).

3 *Developments Since 1982*

Concerns about some of the LOS Convention's deep seabed mining provisions, which were eventually modified, initially prevented widespread acceptance of the Convention. The United States, along with Belgium, Italy, Luxembourg, the United Kingdom, and West Germany, refused to sign, much less ratify, the LOS Convention when UNCLOS III concluded in 1982. Their opposition focused only on certain aspects of Part XI, which contains detailed rules and procedures concerning seabed mining beyond the limits of national jurisdiction. (Indeed, President Reagan found that the "navigation and overflight" and most other provisions of the Convention to be "consistent with U.S. interests" and to "serve well the interests of all nations." Ronald Reagan, Statement on United States Actions Concerning the Conference on the Law of the Sea (July 9, 1982), Dept. State Bull., Aug. 1982 at 71.) The Reagan administration, however, considered Part XI's provisions setting limits on seabed mineral production, requiring payments from miners, and mandating the transfer of technology to the Enterprise (the mining arm of the new International Seabed Authority) to be incompatible with market principles. The United States also sought a greater decision-making role for itself in the Authority and objected to procedures for amending Part XI. Concern grew during the 1980s that the Convention might gain the 60 ratifications necessary for its entry into force without any major developed states being parties to it.

In 1983, the Preparatory Commission for the International Seabed Authority and for the International Tribunal for the Law of the Sea (PREPCOM), which was established pursuant to Resolution I attached to the Final Act of UNCLOS III, began meeting in Jamaica. PREPCOM's mandate included registering "pioneer investors" to conduct deep seabed exploration activities under the Part XI regime. One concern, however, was that developed states would authorize their own nationals to engage in deep seabed mining activities through unilateral legislation. Various developed states with "interim" unilateral legislation, e.g., the U.S. Deep Seabed Hard Minerals Resource Act of 1980, 30 U.S.C. §§ 1401–1473 (1994), entered so-called reciprocating states treaties. These treaties respected licenses issued under national laws and sought to avoid overlaps in claims to mining areas.

A compromise agreement to meet the objections of developed states emerged through a series of meetings, beginning in July 1990, held at the initiative of the U.N. Secretary-General. The 1994 Agreement Relating to the Implementation of Part XI of the United Nations Convention on the Law of the Sea modified or set aside the technical and organizational features of Part XI that developed states had found objectionable. The Agreement is to be interpreted and applied together with the LOS Convention as a single instrument. Although labeled an "implementing agreement," the 1994 Agreement fundamentally altered many aspects of the original 1982 Convention's provisions on deep seabed mining.

The 1994 Implementation Agreement cleared the way for the Convention's widespread acceptance by developed as well as developing states, and the Convention entered into force on November 16, 1994, one year after the deposit of the 60th instrument of ratification. As of September 1, 2013, the LOS Convention had 166 parties. Among those accepting the Convention after the conclusion of the 1994 Agreement were Argentina, Australia, Austria, Belgium, Canada, Chile, China, the European Community, France, Germany, Greece, India, Italy, Japan, the Netherlands, Russia, South Korea, Spain, and the United Kingdom. Although the United States has not yet accepted the LOS Convention, U.S. policy is "to act in a manner consistent with" the Convention's "provisions relating to traditional uses of the oceans and to encourage other countries to do likewise." Presidential Letter of Transmittal of the Law of the Sea Convention, 6 October 1994, Sen. Treaty Doc. No. 103-39 at iii (1994). Since 1994 both Democratic and Republican U.S. administrations, the U.S. Navy, the U.S. Coast Guard, environmental organizations, and U.S. oil, seabed mining, shipping, and telecommunciations industries have urged U.S. acceptance of the Convention as modified by the 1994 Implementation Agreement.

Institutions created by the LOS Convention are now fully operational. These are the International Seabed Authority (see http://www.isa.org.jm), the International Tribunal for the Law of the Sea (see http://www.itlos.org), and the Commission on the Limits of the Continental Shelf (see http://www.un.org/Depts/los/clcs_new/clcs_home.htm). The Convention has also served as a framework for more detailed treaties, especially treaties related to the marine environment and resource conservation and management issues. Particularly notable is the 1995 Fish Stocks Agreement, as of September 1, 2013 accepted by 79 states and the European Union, which implements the general provisions of the LOS Convention concerning straddling and highly migratory fish stocks.

Numerous specialized and regional oceans organizations, many of which were active even before UNCLOS III, continue their treaty-making, regulatory, advice-giving, and study activities. The LOS Convention serves a so-called umbrella function: It provides general rules and helps to allocate regulatory authority, but leaves most technicalities to national legislation or to other treaties already existing or still to be elaborated. Many organizations operating consistently with the LOS Convention have devoted attention to the serious challenges facing the marine environment. The International Maritime Organization (see http://www.imo.org), which has prepared several conventions on navigational safety and maritime terrorism, has also devoted much attention to marine pollution. Independent regional organizations or bodies established within the U.N. Food and Agriculture Organization (FAO) regulate fishing activities. See http://www.fao.org/fishery/en. Groups of states have begun to cooperate to improve the marine environment in certain areas of intensive industrial activity; agreements have been concluded relating to the Baltic and Mediterranean Seas, the Persian Gulf area, the Caribbean, and many other regional seas. The United Nations Environment Programme (see http://www.unep.org) also exercises functions relating to the ocean environment. Non-governmental organizations study marine environmental issues, participate in international conferences, and contribute to the work of international organizations.

Other organizations have made important contributions with respect to other oceans issues. The United Nations Educational, Scientific and Cultural Organization (UNESCO) (see http://www.unesco.org) has developed a treaty on the protection of underwater cultural heritage. UNESCO's Intergovernmental Oceanographic Commission (see http://ioc-unesco.org) deals with marine scientific research. The United Nations Conference on Trade and Development (see http://unctad.org) has considered the transfer of marine technology and such shipping questions as the treatment of vessels in ports.

The United Nations Division of Ocean Affairs and the Law of the Sea (UNDOALOS) provides a range of legal and technical services to states and international organizations. See http://untreaty.un.org/ola/div_doalos.aspx. UNDOALOS conducts research, prepares studies, and provides advice relating to the LOS Convention, the 1994 Implementation Agreement, and the 1995 Fish Stocks Agreement. The Division seeks to advance understanding of these treaties and to promote their acceptance, consistent application, and effective implementation. Overall, however, the work of international organizations involved with law of the sea issues is decentralized; there is no hierarchical structure among the organizations. One challenge is to improve cooperation and optimize efficiency in the work of global and regional international organizations involved with the law of the sea. The activities of various international organizations are considered throughout this book.

The international law of the sea intersects with other areas of international law. For example, the World Trade Organization (see http://wto.org) and international trade lawyers have had to grapple with the relationship between free trade rules and measures that restrict trade in an effort to protect endangered species of ocean life. The 1992 United Nations Conference on Environment and Development, the 2002 World Summit on Sustainable Development, and the 2012 Rio+20 Conference linked issues of marine pollution and the conservation of living resources to broad themes of international development and international environmental law.

The LOS Convention continues to serve as a foundational document for a wide range of oceans issues. Unlike many international environmental conventions, however, the LOS Convention does not provide a quasi-legislative role for a Conference of the Parties authorized to supplement or modify treaty provisions. There is an annual Meeting of States Parties to the LOS Convention, at which major oceans issues are discussed, but the Meeting of States Parties lacks any formal authority to change the Convention. In November 1999, the U.N. General Assembly, in Resolution 54/33 (UN Doc. A/RES/54/33 (2000)), decided to establish an open-ended consultative process to facilitate an annual review of developments in ocean affairs, to suggest issues that the U.N. Secretary-General should consider in his annual report, and to identify areas where intergovernmental and inter-agency cooperation can be improved. This process also cannot authorize changes to the text of the Convention.

It is debatable whether the LOS Convention will be formally amended. The Convention provides elaborate mechanisms for amendments (see LOS Convention, Articles 155, 312–314; 1994 Implementation Agreement, Annex, § 4), but commentators have questioned whether these procedures will ever be invoked. See Stability and Change in the Law of the Sea: The Role of the LOS Convention (Alex G. Oude Elferink ed., 2005). In theory, another global treaty-making conference could be convened to develop new law to respond to new challenges facing the oceans. At present, however, there appears to be no political will for convening a Fourth United Nations Convention on the Law of the Sea. At least over the near term, it seems more likely that the LOS Convention's often-general provisions may be supplemented by bilateral or regional treaties or by global "implementing agreements," such as the 1995 Fish

Stocks Agreement. State practice and the practice of international organizations will also continue to influence the law of the sea.

The modern law of the sea encompasses a complex and varied array of issues, treaties, non-treaty norms, and institutional arrangements. The U.N. Secretary-General's annual reports on oceans and the law of the sea (available at http://www.un.org/Depts/los/general_assembly/general_assembly_reports.htm) present a picture of current issues and initiatives.

Complex political, economic, technological, environmental, and institutional developments affect the oceans. These changes generate legal challenges, concerning both the evolution of new legal norms and the implementation of existing ones. Some recent trends include:

- warming and increased acidification of the world's oceans, leading to melting Arctic sea ice, effects on marine habitats, and migration of fish species;
- spreading dead zones, the result of land-based pollution, and other environmental threats, both from tanker spills and deepwater oil blowouts, such as the 2010 Deep Water Horizon disaster in the Gulf of Mexico;
- increasingly intense fishing activities, including illegal fishing, with the FAO deeming 75 percent of the world's fisheries fully exploited, overexploited, recovering, or depleted;
- intensified maritime transport activities—seaborne trade (measured in ton-miles) more than quadrupled from 1968 to 2008; the average size of container vessels increased from 155 tons in 1987 to over 2,700 tons in 2010; the largest passenger cruise ships grew from approximately 46,000 tons in 1985 to 225,000 tons in 2013; and the number of passengers on North American cruises increased from approximately seven million in 2000 to seventeen million in 2012—leading to increased concerns over vessel safety, vessel pollution, and port capacity;
- an increase in invasive alien marine species, transported by ships and discharged in ballast water;
- the destruction of marine habitats due to intensified uses of coastal areas for agriculture and aquaculture and due to bottom trawling;
- intensifying disputes over ownership of islands and maritime zones in the South China Sea and other regions;
- a significant increase in piracy, especially off Africa, and other new threats to maritime security;
- human rights concerns related to the scourge of human trafficking and to the plight of refugees at sea;

- the deployment of unmanned seagoing devices with capacity for marine scientific research or military uses;
- the impact of technology on maritime search and rescue of vessels in distress, including in the Arctic Ocean;
- the development of technology permitting offshore production of energy through wind or waves, and the production, transport, and processing of liquified natural gas;
- the invention and laying of transoceanic fiber-optic cables;
- discoveries of underwater wrecks and heightened concern about underwater cultural heritage;
- increased activity in Antarctica, raising questions about how the 1959 Antarctic Treaty System's treatment of national claims, fisheries management and conservation, and environmental issues intersects with the international law of the sea; and
- bioprospecting and biological/pharmaceutical uses of marine resources, including diverse genetic resources found at deep-sea thermal vents, leading to legal questions about access to and use of those resources.

For introductions to these challenges, see Davor Vidas & Peter Johan Schei, The World Ocean in Globalisation, Challenges and Responses for the Anthropocene Epoch, in The World Ocean in Globalisation 3 (Davor Vidas & Peter Johan Schei eds., 2011), and Harry N. Schieber, Economic Uses of the Oceans and the Impacts on Marine Environments: Past Trends and Challenges Ahead, in id. at 65. National oceans commissions have assessed needed steps relating to the oceans, including the integration of national policies with regional and global measures. See, e.g., Pew Oceans Commn., America's Living Oceans: Charting a Course for Sea Change (2003); U.S. Commn. on Ocean Policy, An Ocean Blueprint for the 21st Century: Final Report (2004); and the work of the Joint Ocean Commission Initiative, available at http://www.jointoceancommission.org. How well the law of the sea can respond to various new challenges remains an open question. New developments show no signs of slowing down and do not allow much time for consolidation and reflection.

B International Law and International Legal Process

As Section A of this chapter suggests, the 20th century saw a significant move toward codification of the international law of the sea, and codification efforts have continued in the 21st century. Although treaties are a major source of rules of international law, customary international law and nonconsensual sources are also cited and used as sources of law. A wide variety of national and international forums construe and apply treaties and other sources of international law. This section introduces sources of international law and provides one example of a forum that uses them.

STATUTE OF THE INTERNATIONAL COURT OF JUSTICE
June 26, 1945, 59 Stat. 1031

Article 38

1. The Court, whose function is to decide in accordance with international law such disputes as are submitted to it, shall apply:

   (a) international conventions, whether general or particular, establishing rules expressly recognized by the contesting States;

   (b) international custom, as evidence of a general practice accepted as law;

   (c) the general principles of law recognized by civilized nations;

   (d) subject to the provisions of Article 59, judicial decisions and the teachings of the most highly qualified publicists of the various nations, as subsidiary means for the determination of rules of law.

2. This provision shall not prejudice the power of the Court to decide a case *ex aequo et bono*, if the parties agree thereto.

Notes

1. *Sources of International Law*. The Statute of the International Court of Justice (ICJ) provides a list of sources commonly used by international lawyers, even outside the Court. The term "sources" refers both to places where lawyers find rules of international law and to shared conceptions of just what constitutes international law. The list of sources in Article 38 is not exclusive. Judges and international lawyers may also refer, for example, to equity, jus cogens (fundamental norms permitting no derogation), and the resolutions of international organizations. The ICJ refers to equity and jus cogens in the North Sea Continental Shelf cases, excerpted below.

2. *Ex Aequo et Bono*. According to Article 38(2) of the ICJ's Statute, the Court may decide a case by "what is right and good," if the parties to a dispute explicitly so agree. Under such an ex aequo et bono authorization, the Court would not need to refer to formal sources of international law. The Court has never been authorized to decide a case ex aequo et bono.

NORTH SEA CONTINENTAL SHELF CASES

Federal Republic of Germany v. Denmark and Federal Republic of Germany v. Netherlands, 1969 I.C.J. 3

[By two Special Agreements, the parties submitted to the ICJ certain differences regarding the delimitation between them of the continental shelf in the North Sea. The parties asked the Court to decide the applicable principles and rules of international law that should apply in the delimitation. The parties had already agreed to the boundaries in the immediate vicinity of the coast, shown as dotted lines in Figure I.B following this case excerpt. Denmark and the Netherlands argued that the equidistance method should be applied in the zone beyond the agreed boundaries. The Federal Republic of Germany argued that the correct rule to be applied would grant each party a "just and equitable share" of the available continental shelf, in proportion to the length of its coastline. The Court, in paragraph 20 of its judgment, rejects the "just and equitable" share principle, and then considers whether an equidistance rule exists in international law.]

25. The Court now turns to the legal position regarding the equidistance method. The first question to be considered is whether the 1958 Geneva Convention on the Continental Shelf is binding for all the Parties in this case—that is to say whether, as contended by Denmark and the Netherlands, the use of this method is rendered obligatory for the present delimitations by virtue of the delimitations provision (Article 6) of that instrument, according to the conditions laid down in it. Clearly, if this is so, then the provisions of the Convention will prevail in the relations between the Parties, and would take precedence of any rules having a more general character, or derived from another source. On that basis the Court's . . . sole remaining task would be to interpret those provisions, in so far as their meaning was disputed or appeared to be uncertain, and to apply them to the particular circumstances involved.

26. The relevant provisions of Article 6 of the Geneva Convention, paragraph 2 of which Denmark and the Netherlands contend not only to be applicable as a conventional rule, but also to represent the accepted rule of general international law on the subject of continental shelf delimitation, as it exists independently of the Convention, read as follows:

> . . . 2. Where the same continental shelf is adjacent to the territories of two adjacent States, the boundary of the continental shelf shall be determined by agreement between them. In the absence of agreement, and

> unless another boundary line is justified by special circumstances, the boundary shall be determined by application of the principle of equidistance from the nearest points of the baselines from which the breadth of the territorial sea of each State is measured.

The Convention received 46 signatures and, up-to-date, there have been 39 ratifications or accessions. It came into force on 10 June 1964, having received the 22 ratifications or accessions required for that purpose (Article 11), and was therefore in force at the time when the various delimitations of continental shelf boundaries described earlier . . . took place between the Parties. But, under the formal provisions of the Convention, it is in force for any individual State only in so far as, having signed it within the time-limit provided for that purpose, that State has also subsequently ratified it; or, not having signed within that time-limit, has subsequently acceded to the Convention. Denmark and the Netherlands have both signed and ratified the Convention, and are parties to it, the former since 10 June 1964, the latter since 20 March 1966. The Federal Republic was one of the signatories of the Convention, but has never ratified it, and is consequently not a party.

27. It is admitted on behalf of Denmark and the Netherlands that in these circumstances the Convention cannot, as such, be binding on the Federal Republic, in the sense of the Republic being contractually bound by it. But it is contended that the Convention, or the régime of the Convention, and in particular of Article 6, has become binding on the Federal Republic in another way,—namely because, by conduct, by public statements and proclamations, and in other ways, the Republic has unilaterally assumed the obligations of the Convention; or has manifested its acceptance of the conventional régime; or has recognized it as being generally applicable to the delimitation of continental shelf areas. . . .

28. As regards these contentions, it is clear that only a very definite, very consistent course of conduct on the part of a State in the situation of the Federal Republic could justify the Court in upholding them; and, if this had existed—that is to say if there had been a real intention to manifest acceptance or recognition of the applicability of the conventional regime—then it must be asked why it was that the Federal Republic did not take the obvious step of giving expression to this readiness by simply ratifying the Convention. In principle, when a number of States, including the one whose conduct is invoked, and those invoking it, have drawn up a convention specifically providing for a particular method by which the intention to become bound by the régime of the convention is to be manifested—namely by the carrying out of certain prescribed formalities (ratification, accession), it is not lightly to be presumed that a State which has not carried out these formalities, though at

all times fully able and entitled to do so, has nevertheless somehow become bound in another way. Indeed if it were a question not of obligation but of rights,—if, that is to say, a State which, though entitled to do so, had not ratified or acceded, attempted to claim rights under the convention, on the basis of a declared willingness to be bound by it, or of conduct evincing acceptance of the conventional régime, it would simply be told that, not having become a party to the convention it could not claim any rights under it until the professed willingness and acceptance had been manifested in the prescribed form....

30. Having regard to these considerations of principle, it appears to the Court that only the existence of a situation of estoppel could suffice to lend substance to this contention,—that is to say if the Federal Republic were now precluded from denying the applicability of the conventional régime, by reason of past conduct, declarations, etc., which not only clearly and consistently evinced acceptance of that régime, but also had caused Denmark or the Netherlands, in reliance on such conduct, detrimentally to change position or suffer some prejudice. Of this there is no evidence whatever in the present case....

37. It is maintained by Denmark and the Netherlands that the Federal Republic, whatever its position may be in relation to the Geneva Convention, considered as such, is in any event bound to accept delimitation on an equidistance-special circumstances basis, because the use of this method is not in the nature of a merely conventional obligation, but is, or must now be regarded as involving, a rule that is part of the *corpus* of general international law;—and, like other rules of general or customary international law, is binding on the Federal Republic automatically and independently of any specific assent, direct or indirect, given by the latter. This contention has both a positive law and a more fundamentalist aspect. As a matter of positive law, it is based on the work done in this field by international legal bodies, on State practice and on the influence attributed to the Geneva Convention itself,—the claim being that these various factors have cumulatively evidenced or been creative of the *opinio juris sive necessitatis*, requisite for the formation of new rules of customary international law. In its fundamentalist aspect, the view put forward derives from what might be called the natural law of the continental shelf, in the sense that the equidistance principle is seen as a necessary expression in the field of delimitation of the accepted doctrine of the exclusive appurtenance of the continental shelf to the nearby coastal State, and therefore as having an *a priori* character of so to speak juristic inevitability.

39. The *a priori* argument starts from the position... according to which the right of the coastal State to its continental shelf areas is based on its sovereignty over the land domain, of which the shelf area is the natural prolongation into and under the sea.... Denmark and the Netherlands, for their part,

claim that the test of appurtenance must be "proximity," or more accurately "closer proximity": all those parts of the shelf being considered as appurtenant to a particular coastal State which are (but only if they are) closer to it than they are to any point on the coast of another State. Hence delimitation must be effected by a method which will leave to each one of the States concerned all those areas that are nearest to its own coast. Only a line drawn on equidistance principles will do this. Therefore, it is contended, only such a line can be valid (unless the Parties, for reasons of their own, agree on another), because only such a line can be thus consistent with basic continental shelf doctrine. . . .

44. [E]quidistance . . . cannot be identified with the notion of natural prolongation or extension, since . . . the use of the equidistance method would frequently cause areas which are the natural prolongation or extension of the territory of one State to be attributed to another, when the configuration of the latter's coast makes the equidistance line swing out laterally across the former's coastal front, cutting it off from areas situated directly before that front. . . .

46. [T]he notion of equidistance as being logically necessary, in the sense of being an inescapable *a priori* accompaniment of basic continental shelf doctrine, is incorrect. . . .

60. The conclusions so far reached leave open, and still to be considered, the question whether on some basis other than that of an *a priori* logical necessity, i.e., through positive law processes, the equidistance principle has come to be regarded as a rule of customary international law, so that it would be obligatory for the Federal Republic in that way, even though Article 6 of the Geneva Convention is not, as such, opposable to it. For this purpose it is necessary to examine the status of the principle as it stood when the Convention was drawn up, as it resulted from the effect of the Convention, and in the light of State practice subsequent to the Convention. . . .

61. . . . Denmark and the Netherlands themselves . . . stated that they had not in fact contended that the delimitation article (Article 6) of the Convention "embodied already received rules of customary law in the sense that the Convention was merely declaratory of existing rules." Their contention was, rather, that although prior to the Conference, continental shelf law was only in the formative stage, and State practice lacked uniformity, yet "the process of the definition and consolidation of the emerging customary law took place through the work of the International Law Commission, the reaction of governments to that work and the proceeding of the Geneva Conference"; and this emerging customary law became "crystallized in the adoption of the Continental Shelf Convention by the Conference."

62. [T]he Court cannot accept [this contention] as regards the delimitation provision (Article 6), the relevant parts of which were adopted almost

unchanged from the draft of the International Law Commission that formed the basis of discussion at the Conference. The status of the rule in the Convention therefore depends mainly on the processes that led the Commission to propose it. [T]he principle of equidistance, as it now figures in Article 6 of the Convention, was proposed by the Commission with considerable hesitation, somewhat on an experimental basis, at most *de lege ferenda*, and not at all *de lege lata* or as an emerging rule of customary international law. This is clearly not the sort of foundation on which Article 6 of the Convention could be said to have reflected or crystallized such a rule.

63. The foregoing conclusion receives significant confirmation from the fact that Article 6 is one of those in respect of which, under the reservations article of the Convention (Article 12) reservations may be made by any State on signing, ratifying or acceding,—for, speaking generally, it is a characteristic of purely conventional rules and obligations that, in regard to them, some faculty of making unilateral reservations may, within certain limits, be admitted;—whereas this cannot be so in the case of general or customary law rules and obligations which, by their very nature, must have equal force for all members of the international community, and cannot therefore be the subject of any right of unilateral exclusion exercisable at will by any one of them in its own favour. Consequently, it is to be expected that when for whatever reason, rules or obligations of this order are embodied, or are intended to be reflected in certain provisions of a convention, such provisions will figure amongst those in respect of which a right of unilateral reservation is not conferred, or is excluded. This expectation is, in principle, fulfilled by Article 12 of the Geneva Continental Shelf Convention, which permits reservations to be made to all the articles of the Convention "other than to Articles 1 to 3 inclusive"—these three Articles being the ones which, it is clear, were then regarded as reflecting, or as crystallizing, received or at least emergent rules of customary international law relative to the continental shelf, amongst them the question of the seaward extent of the shelf; the juridical character of the coastal State's entitlement; the nature of the rights exercisable; the kind of natural resources to which these relate; and the preservation intact of the legal status as high seas of the waters over the shelf, and the legal status of the superjacent air-space.

64. The normal inference would therefore be that any articles that do not figure among those excluded from the faculty of reservation under Article 12, were not regarded as declaratory of previously existing or emergent rules of law; and this is the inference the Court in fact draws in respect of Article 6 (delimitation)....

69. [T]he Geneva Convention did not embody or crystallize any pre-existing or emergent rule of customary law, according to which the delimitation of

continental shelf areas between adjacent States must, unless the Parties otherwise agree, be carried out on an equidistance-special circumstances basis. A rule was of course embodied in Article 6 of the Convention, but as a purely conventional rule. Whether it has since acquired a broader basis remains to be seen: *qua* conventional rule however, as has already been concluded, it is not opposable to the Federal Republic.

70. The Court must now proceed to the last stage in the argument put forward on behalf of Denmark and the Netherlands. This is to the effect that even if there was at the date of the Geneva Convention no rule of customary international law in favour of the equidistance principle, and no such rule was crystallized in Article 6 of the Convention, nevertheless such a rule has come into being since the Convention, partly because of its own impact, partly on the basis of subsequent State practice,—and that this rule, being now a rule of customary international law binding on all States, including therefore the Federal Republic, should be declared applicable to the delimitation of the boundaries between the Parties' respective continental shelf areas in the North Sea.

71. In so far as this contention is based on the view that Article 6 of the Convention has had the influence, and has produced the effect, described, it clearly involves treating that Article as a norm-creating provision which has constituted the foundation of, or has generated a rule which, while only conventional or contractual in its origin, has since passed into the general *corpus* of international law, and is now accepted as such by the *opinio juris*, so as to have become binding even for countries which have never, and do not, become parties to the Convention. There is no doubt that this process is a perfectly possible one and does from time to time occur: it constitutes indeed one of the recognized methods by which new rules of customary international law may be formed. At the same time this result is not lightly to be regarded as having been attained.

72. It would in the first place be necessary that the provision concerned should, at all events potentially, be of a fundamentally norm-creating character such as could be regarded as forming the basis of a general rule of law. Considered *in abstracto* the equidistance principle might be said to fulfil this requirement. Yet in the particular form in which it is embodied in Article 6 of the Geneva Convention, and having regard to the relationship of that Article to other provisions of the Convention, this must be open to some doubt. In the first place, Article 6 is so framed as to put second the obligation to make use of the equidistance method, causing it to come after a primary obligation to effect delimitation by agreement. Such a primary obligation constitutes an unusual preface to what is claimed to be a potential general rule of law. Without attempting to enter into, still less pronounce upon any question of *jus cogens*, it is well understood that, in practice, rules of international law can,

by agreement, be derogated from in particular cases, or as between particular parties,—but this is not normally the subject of any express provision, as it is in Article 6 of the Geneva Convention. Secondly the part played by the notion of special circumstances relative to the principle of equidistance as embodied in Article 6, and the very considerable, still unresolved controversies as to the exact meaning and scope of this notion, must raise further doubts as to the potentially norm-creating character of the rule. Finally, the faculty of making reservations to Article 6, while it might not of itself prevent the equidistance principle being eventually received as general law, does add considerably to the difficulty of regarding this result as having been brought about (or being potentially possible) on the basis of the Convention: for so long as this faculty continues to exist... it is the Convention itself which would, for the reasons already indicated, seem to deny to the provisions of Article 6 the same norm-creating character as, for instance, Articles 1 and 2 possess.

73. With respect to the other elements usually regarded as necessary before a conventional rule can be considered to have become a general rule of international law, it might be that, even without the passage of any considerable period of time, a very widespread and representative participation in the convention might suffice of itself, provided it included that of States whose interests were specially affected. In the present case however, the Court notes that, even if allowance is made for the existence of a number of States to whom participation in the Geneva Convention is not open, or which, by reason for instance of being land-locked States, would have no interest in becoming parties to it, the number of ratifications and accessions so far secured is, though respectable, hardly sufficient. That nonratification may sometimes be due to factors other than active disapproval of the convention concerned can hardly constitute a basis on which positive acceptance of its principles can be impled: the reasons are speculative, but the facts remain.

74. As regards the time element, the Court notes that it is over ten years since the Convention was signed, but that it is even now less than five since it came into force in June 1964, and that when the present proceedings were brought it was less than three years, while less than one had elapsed at the time when the respective negotiations between the Federal Republic and other two parties for a complete delimitation broke down on the question of the application of the equidistance principle. Although the passage of only a short period of time is not necessarily, or of itself, a bar to the formation of a new rule of customary international law on the basis of what was originally a purely conventional rule, an indispensable requirement would be that within the period in question, short though it might be, State practice, including that of States whose interests are specially affected, should have been both extensive and virtually uniform in the sense of the provision invoked;—and should moreover

have occurred in such a way as to show a general recognition that a rule of law or legal obligation is involved.

75. The Court must now consider whether State practice in the matter of continental shelf delimitation has, subsequent to the Geneva Convention, been of such a kind as to satisfy this requirement. [S]ome fifteen cases have been cited in the course of the present proceedings, occurring mostly since the signature of the 1958 Geneva Convention, in which continental shelf boundaries have been delimited according to the equidistance principle—in the majority of the cases by agreement, in a few others unilaterally—or else the delimitation was foreshadowed but has not yet been carried out. Amongst these fifteen are ... four North Sea delimitations.... But even if these various cases constituted more than a very small proportion of those potentially calling for delimitation in the world as a whole, the Court would not think it necessary to enumerate or evaluate them separately, since there are, *a priori*, several grounds which deprive them of weight as precedents in the present context.

76. To begin with, over half the States concerned, whether acting unilaterally or conjointly, were or shortly became parties to the Geneva Convention, and were therefore presumably, so far as they were concerned, acting actually or potentially in the application of the Convention. From their action no inference could legitimately be drawn as to the existence of a rule of customary international law in favour of the equidistance principle. As regards those States, on the other hand, which were not, and have not become parties to the Convention, the basis of their action can only be problematical and must remain entirely speculative. Clearly, they were not applying the Convention. But from that no inference could justifiably be drawn that they believed themselves to be applying a mandatory rule of customary international law. There is not a shred of evidence that they did and ... there is no lack of other reasons for using the equidistance method, so that acting, or agreeing to act in a certain way, does not of itself demonstrate anything of a juridical nature.

77. [E]ven if these instances of action by non-parties to the Convention were much more numerous than they in fact are, they would not, even in the aggregate, suffice in themselves to constitute the *opinio juris*;—for, in order to achieve this result, two conditions must be fulfilled. Not only must the acts concerned amount to a settled practice, but they must also be such, or be carried out in such a way, as to be evidence of a belief that this practice is rendered obligatory by the existence of a rule of law requiring it. The need for such a belief, i.e., the existence of a subjective element, is implicit in the very notion of the *opinio juris sive necessitatis*. The States concerned must therefore feel that they are conforming to what amounts to a legal obligation. The frequency, or even habitual character of the acts is not in itself enough. There are many

international acts, e.g., in the field of ceremonial and protocol, which are performed almost invariably, but which are motivated only by considerations of courtesy, convenience or tradition, and not by any sense of legal duty.

78. In this respect the Court follows the view adopted by the Permanent Court of International Justice in the *Lotus* Case, as stated in the following passage, the principle of which is, by analogy, applicable almost word for word, *mutatis mutandis*, to the present case (*P.C.I.J., Series A, No.* 10, 1927, at p. 28): "Even if the rarity of the judicial decisions to be found . . . were sufficient to prove . . . the circumstance alleged . . ., it would merely show that States had often, in practice, abstained from instituting criminal proceedings, and not that they recognized themselves as being obliged to do so; for only if such abstention were based on their being conscious of having a duty to abstain would it be possible to speak of an international custom. The alleged fact does not allow one to infer that States have been conscious of having such a duty; on the other hand, . . . there are other circumstances calculated to show that the contrary is true." Applying this dictum to the present case, the position is simply that in certain cases—not a great number—the States concerned agreed to draw or did draw the boundaries concerned according to the principle of equidistance. There is no evidence that they so acted because they felt legally compelled to draw them in this way by reason of a rule of customary law obliging them to do so—especially considering that they might have been motivated by other obvious factors. . . .

81. The Court accordingly concludes that if the Geneva Convention was not in its origins or inception declaratory of a mandatory rule of customary international law enjoining the use of the equidistance principle for the delimitation of continental shelf areas between adjacent States, neither has its subsequent effect been constitutive of such a rule; and that State practice up-to-date has equally been insufficient for the purpose. . . .

83. The legal situation therefore is that the Parties are under no obligation to apply either the 1958 Convention, which is not opposable to the Federal Republic, or the equidistance method as a mandatory rule of customary law, which it is not. But as between States faced with an issue concerning the lateral delimitation of adjacent continental shelves, there are still rules and principles of law to be applied; and in the present case it is not the fact either that rules are lacking, or that the situation is one for the unfettered appreciation of the Parties. . . .

85. [I]f [the equidistance method] were to be compulsorily applied in all situations, this would not be consonant with certain basic legal notions which . . . have from the beginning reflected the *opinio juris* in the matter of delimitation; those principles being that delimitation must be the object of agreement between the States concerned, and that such agreement must be

arrived at in accordance with equitable principles. On a foundation of very general precepts of justice and good faith, actual rules of law are here involved which govern the delimitation of adjacent continental shelves—that is to say, rules binding upon States for all delimitations;—in short, it is not a question of applying equity simply as a matter of abstract justice, but of applying a rule of law which itself requires the application of equitable principles, in accordance with the ideas which have always underlain the development of the legal régime of the continental shelf in this field, namely:

(*a*) the parties are under an obligation to enter into negotiations with a view to arriving at an agreement, and not merely to go through a formal process of negotiation as a sort of prior condition for automatic application of a certain method of delimitation in the absence of agreement; they are under an obligation so to conduct themselves that the negotiations are meaningful, which will not be the case when either of them insists upon its own position without contemplating any modification of it;

(*b*) the parties are under an obligation to act in such a way that, in the particular case, and taking all the circumstances into account, equitable principles are applied,—for this purpose the equidistance method can be used, but other methods exist and may be employed, alone or in combination, according to the area involved;

(*c*) ... the continental shelf of any State must be the natural prolongation of its land territory and must not encroach upon what is the natural prolongation of the territory of another State....

88. The Court comes next to the rule of equity. The legal basis of that rule in the particular case of the delimitation of the continental shelf as between adjoining States has already been stated. It must however be noted that the rule rests also on a broader basis. Whatever the legal reasoning of a court of justice, its decisions must by definition be just, and therefore in that sense equitable. Nevertheless, when mention is made of a court dispensing justice or declaring the law, what is meant is that the decision finds its objective justification in considerations lying not outside but within the rules, and in this field it is precisely a rule of law that calls for the application of equitable principles. There is consequently no question in this case of any decision *ex aequo et bono*, such as would only be possible under the conditions prescribed by Article 38, paragraph 2, of the Court's Statute....

89. It must next be observed that, in certain geographical circumstances which are quite frequently met with, the equidistance method, despite its known advantages, leads unquestionably to inequity, in the following sense:

(*a*) The slightest irregularity in a coastline is automatically magnified by the equidistance line as regards the consequences for the delimitation of the continental shelf. Thus it has been seen in the case of concave or convex coastlines that if the equidistance method is employed, then the greater the irregularity and the further from the coastline the area to be delimited, the more unreasonable are the results produced. So great an exaggeration of the consequences of a natural geographical feature must be remedied or compensated for as far as possible, being of itself creative of inequity.

(*b*) In the case of the North Sea in particular, where there is no outer boundary to the continental shelf, it happens that the claims of several States converge, meet and intercross in localities where, despite their distance from the coast, the bed of the sea still unquestionably consists of continental shelf. A study of these convergences, as revealed by the maps, shows how inequitable would be the apparent simplification brought about by a delimitation which, ignoring such geographical circumstances, was based solely on the equidistance method. . . .

91. Equity does not necessarily imply equality. There can never be any question of completely refashioning nature, and equity does not require that a State without access to the sea should be allotted an area of continental shelf, any more than there could be a question of rendering the situation of a State with an extensive coastline similar to that of a State with a restricted coastline. Equality is to be reckoned within the same plane, and it is not such natural inequalities as these that equity could remedy. But in the present case there are three States whose North Sea coastlines are in fact comparable in length and which, therefore, have been given broadly equal treatment by nature except that the configuration of one of the coastlines would, if the equidistance method is used, deny to one of these States treatment equal or comparable to that given the other two. Here indeed is a case where, in a theoretical situation of equality within the same order, an inequity is created. What is unacceptable in this instance is that a State should enjoy continental shelf rights considerably different from those of its neighbours merely because in the one case the coastline is roughly convex in form and in the other it is markedly concave, although those coastlines are comparable in length. It is therefore not a question of totally refashioning geography whatever the facts of the situation but, given a geographical situation of quasi-equality as between a number of States, of abating the effects of an incidental special feature from which an unjustifiable difference of treatment could result. . . .

101. For these reasons,

THE COURT, by eleven votes to six, finds that, in each case,

(A) the use of the equidistance method of delimitation not being obligatory as between the Parties; and

(B) there being no other single method of delimitation the use of which is in all circumstances obligatory;

(C) the principles and rules of international law applicable to the delimitation as between the Parties of the areas of the continental shelf in the North Sea which appertain to each of them beyond the partial boundary determined by the agreements of 1 December 1964 and 9 June 1965, respectively, are as follows:

> (1) delimitation is to be effected by agreement in accordance with equitable principles, and taking account of all the relevant circumstances, in such a way as to leave as much as possible to each Party all those parts of the continental shelf that constitute a natural prolongation of its land territory into and under the sea, without encroachment on the natural prolongation of the land territory of the other;
>
> (2) if, in the application of the preceding sub-paragraph, the delimitation leaves to the Parties areas that overlap, these are to be divided between them in agreed proportions or, failing agreement, equally, unless they decide on a régime of joint jurisdiction, user, or exploitation for the zones of overlap or any part of them;

(D) in the course of the negotiations, the factors to be taken into account are to include:

> (1) the general configuration of the coasts of the Parties, as well as the presence of any special or unusual features;
>
> (2) so far as known or readily ascertainable, the physical and geological structure, and natural resources, of the continental shelf areas involved;
>
> (3) the element of a reasonable degree of proportionality, which a delimitation carried out in accordance with equitable principles ought to bring about between the extent of the continental shelf areas appertaining to the coastal State and the length of its coast measured in the general direction of the coastline, account being taken for this purpose of the effects, actual or prospective, of any other continental shelf delimitations between adjacent States in the same region.

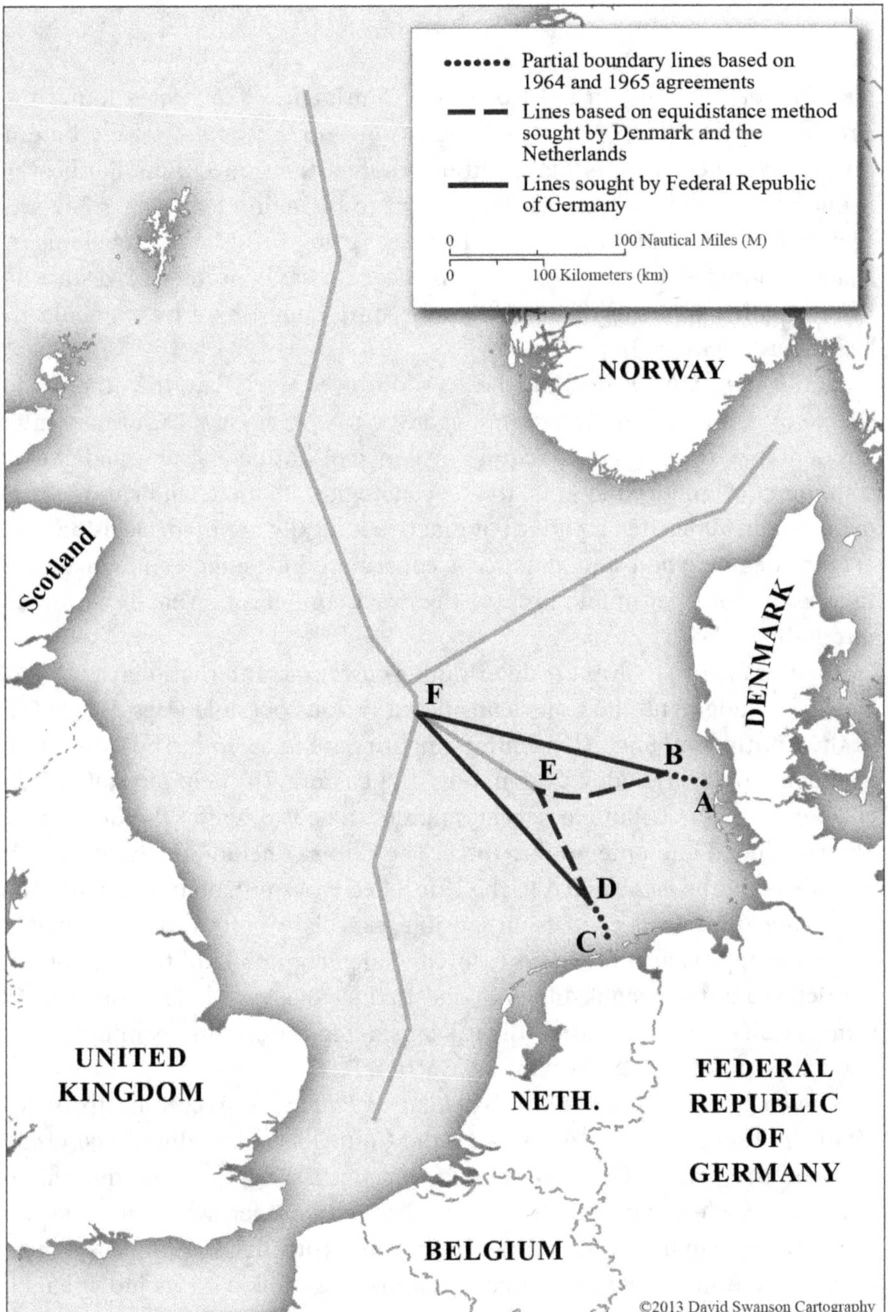

FIGURE I.B *Actual and Proposed North Sea Maritime Boundaries*

Notes

1. *Treaties*. The ICJ in the North Sea Continental Shelf cases found that Article 6 of the 1958 Continental Shelf Convention was not legally binding on Germany because Germany had not ratified the Convention. Ratification is one way a state may express its consent to be bound by a treaty. See 1969 Vienna Convention on the Law of Treaties, Articles 11–16. What explains the legally binding effect of a treaty to which a state has consented? If a state has not formally expressed its consent to become bound by a treaty, could the treaty ever become binding on it?

2. *Customary International Law*. In addition to treaty law, the other major source of contemporary international law is customary law. Customary international law is often said to require evidence of both consistent and general state practice and opinio juris, the "psychological element" indicating states' beliefs or attitudes that a pattern of practice is legally required. Decision makers may debate when state practice is consistent and general enough, or how to ascertain or infer opinio juris, or the exact content of a rule of customary international law.

Treaties may be relevant in determining customary international law. In the North Sea judgment, the Court considered various possible ways Article 6(2) of the Continental Shelf Convention might relate to custom. The Convention in theory could (a) codify or "embody" the custom, (b) help "crystallize" the custom, or (c) contribute to development of the custom after the Convention was concluded and entered into force. The Court concluded that no customary rule could be established in the North Sea cases pursuant to any of these three categories. Is its conclusion sensible, especially with respect to category (c)? Is the approach of the Lotus case, cited in paragraph 78 of the opinion, too restrictive a test for establishing custom? In the 1980s, even before the 1982 LOS Convention entered into force, the ICJ considered the customary international law status of the EEZ. See Chapter 9, Section B.

3. *Judicial Decisions and the Teaching of Publicists*. According to Article 59 of the ICJ's Statute, "a decision of the Court has no binding force except between the parties and in respect of that particular case." The doctrine of judicial precedent, familiar in common law national legal systems, does not formally apply in international law. In later maritime delimitation cases, however, the International Court cited and apparently relied on its judgments in the North Sea cases and in other cases. See, e.g., Libya/Malta Continental Shelf Case, 1985 I.C.J. 13. Is such reliance appropriate? See Article 38(1)(d) of the Court's Statute. With respect to a matter such as maritime boundary delimita-

tion, where treaties provide few concrete rules, are judicial opinions confined to the "subsidiary" role suggested in Article 38(1)(d)?

4. *Other Sources of International Law.* The ICJ in the North Sea cases also referred to other sources, including jus cogens and equity. Jus cogens is the notion that some norms are of such great importance that they cannot be derogated from by treaty or by normal customary international law. See 1969 Vienna Convention on the Law of Treaties, Article 53; Alfred von Verdross, Forbidden Treaties in International Law, 31 Am. J. Intl. L. 571 (1937). The Court did not rely on jus cogens in the North Sea cases, referring to the concept only in passing in paragraph 72, but it did invoke principles of equity. The Court did not, however, claim the authority to decide ex aequo et bono, pursuant to Article 38(2) of its Statute. What then is the authority or explanation for the use of principles of equity in the North Sea cases? Is the Court's justification for its use of equity persuasive?

5. *Hierarchy of Sources.* International lawyers debate the hierarchy of sources of international law. Does the order in which the International Court addressed sources in the North Sea cases, and the order in which sources are listed in Article 38(1) of the Court's Statute—first treaties, then customary international law, then other sources—necessarily mean that treaties "trump" customary international law and custom "trumps" other sources? Are judicial opinions always a "subsidiary" source?

6. *The ICJ and the Variety of International Forums.* Only states may be parties in contentious cases before the ICJ, which is the principal judicial organ of the United Nations. See U.N. Charter, Article 92; ICJ Statute, Article 34(1). The Court may hear interstate cases only if the states involved mutually consent. In the North Sea cases, the parties conferred jurisdiction on the Court via a special agreement, a type of treaty. How else may states provide the necessary mutual consent to the Court's jurisdiction? See Article 36 of the Court's Statute.

The ICJ is only one of many forums available to hear international legal disputes. As the materials in this book illustrate, international law of the sea disputes are heard, and international law is used, in a wide variety of formal and informal forums. These forums include diplomatic exchanges and interstate negotiations, national courts and agencies, international arbitral tribunals, conciliation commissions, international claims commissions, regional international courts, and specialized tribunals such as the International Tribunal for the Law of the Sea. Some of these forums are open to non-state entities.

7. *The Roles of the ICJ.* In the North Sea cases the ICJ set out principles to guide the parties' future negotiations concerning their continental shelf

boundaries. The states involved, relying on the Court's judgment, did in fact successfully reach agreement on the delimitation of their continental shelves in early 1971. See Figure VI.B in Chapter 6. In other maritime delimitation cases, the ICJ has, at the parties' request, delimited precise boundaries. What other roles and functions could the Court fulfill in law of the sea disputes? One such function could be providing advice, via advisory opinions, to the U.N. General Assembly, Security Council, or (when so authorized by the General Assembly) other U.N. organs and specialized agencies. U.N. Charter, Article 96; ICJ Statute, Article 65.

8. *Maritime Boundary Delimitations*. There have been numerous international arbitral and judicial decisions regarding maritime boundary delimitations. We examine this area of law in Chapter 6.

LOUIS B. SOHN, THE LAW OF THE SEA: CUSTOMARY INTERNATIONAL LAW DEVELOPMENTS
34 Am. U. L. Rev. 271 (1985)

Two recent events have revived the debate about the role of international agreements in the development of customary international law. The adoption of the United Nations Law of the Sea Convention (the Convention) by an almost unanimous vote, followed by the signature of the Convention by 159 countries, has led to the contention that a large part of the Convention, and maybe even all of it, somehow had been incorporated in customary international law, applicable to both signatories and nonsignatories alike, regardless of the fact that only a few States have ratified this document.

Traditionally, a treaty entered into force only when the requisite number of ratifications or accessions had been deposited and was binding only on the States that had ratified it or had acceded to it. The Convention, however, is a treaty that is still far from collecting the necessary sixty ratifications, but nevertheless is treated as if it were in force. Some States are already claiming rights under the Convention, and others are accusing some States of having violated this instrument, though some of the accusers have themselves not signed the Convention and most of them are not yet ready to ratify it....

The second event that complicated the situation was the shifting of gears by the main opponent of the Convention. This opponent not only accepted an important part of the Convention and made it part of domestic law, but also issued a broad statement of ocean policy praising most parts of the Convention as confirming existing maritime law and practice and fairly balancing the interests of all States. Some have greeted this event as an acceptance of the inevitable, and others have regarded it as an attempt to break up the package that made the consensus on the Convention's several hundred provisions possible. While one group claims the right to pick and choose, the other group insists on the all or nothing proposition.

Is all this unprecedented or is it simply a result of a recent evolution in the way international law is made? It is quite clear that the second proposition is the correct one and that there has been such a revolutionary change in the rules relating to sources of international law and in the ways of finding evidence that the practice of States has reached the point at which a new rule of customary international law has been generally accepted as such.

We are far from the early nineteenth century view that the best evidence of a rule of international law can be found in the writings of eminent international lawyers who have made a diligent analysis of State practice and have concluded that a rule of international law exists. Since those days, the practice of States in each field of international law has increased in manifold ways and few writers can encompass even a small part of it. Diplomatic correspondence has reached such proportions that even the major powers are unable to publish in a timely fashion more than a minor part of it. Policy statements on issues of international law are made in many fora, not only in parliaments or international conferences, but also before press conferences, on radio, and on television. No longer can a newspaper boast that it publishes all the news that is fit to print—there is not enough paper for it. Some think that computers might solve the problem of locating new evidence of international practice, but for a long time this will remain a costly and unsatisfactory process....

The result of all these developments is general frustration about traditional approaches to both the sources of international law and the evaluation of evidence of the creation or development of customary international law. Instead of focusing on what the various foreign ministries have been doing, singly or through bilateral diplomatic correspondence, the modern tendency is to pay more attention to what the governments are doing together at gatherings in which most States are represented. International lawyers no longer rely on a crisis producing an outpouring of statements from which a principle of international law might be deduced. They no longer wait for one of those great cases like the *North Atlantic Coast Fisheries Case* in 1910, where twelve volumes of hitherto hidden documents were presented to a tribunal of the Permanent Court of Arbitration, on the basis of which the tribunal was able to announce some important decisions concerning the existence of several rules of customary international law. We can no longer rely on a scholar disappearing in the archives of a particular State and after many years of research producing a set of volumes on the international law practice of that State. We are all grateful to John Bassett Moore, Green Hackworth, and Marjorie Whiteman for what they have given us in their Digests of International Law, and there are now similar collections in several other countries. Even if there still are scholars willing to do that, it is quite clear that one's lifetime is not long enough to even scratch the surface of the treasure troves hidden in the multiplying archives of many nations. While I am one of those who loves to embark on a search through history to try to trace the origin and evolution of a particular principle of international law, I have long ago lost the illusion that a definitive history of any such principle can be written. Many times I have put on paper the result of perhaps more thorough research of a particular principle than anyone had done before, with the full realization that there were still hundreds of tantalizing references that came to my attention but which I did not have time to locate and read. The Romans realized it long ago that *ars longa, vita brevis*—life is too short to study all that humanity has produced, even if we limit ourselves to a small segment.

It is clear that we have to find a better way to deal with this important subject. I believe that by trial and error we have found it. The first step was the resort to multilateral treaties in place of hundreds of bilateral ones. What a great event it was when in 1874 the Universal Postal Union was established, its treaty replacing a host of bilateral arrangements that were both inefficient and costly. Encouraged by such multilateral agreements, the two great associations of international lawyers, the Institute of International Law and the International Law Association, started preparing codes of international law on various subjects, hoping that an international conference would finally be called to adopt them. The Hague Conferences of 1899 and 1907 proved that this method can work, as is testified by the wide acceptance of both the various conventions relating to the laws of war on land and at sea and the pioneering conventions on the peaceful settlement of international disputes.

This new method of establishing rules of international law blossomed after the First World War. [T]his movement to cover one field after another with multipartite instruments increased geometrically after the Second World War.... Although every one of these multipartite agreements adds a brick to the edifice of international law, some of them are more law-making than others. In recent years, international lawyers have learned to pay special attention to treaties carefully prepared by various international organizations either directly or through such special bodies as the International Law Commission of the United Nations and similar commissions and committees functioning under other international auspices. Among them are such codificatory instruments as the Vienna conventions on diplomatic and consular relations and on the law of treaties, the Geneva conventions on humanitarian law, and the many conventions on the law of the sea and the protection of the marine environment.

The various conventions mentioned above have combined the codification of existing law with the development of the new law, and even an expert finds it difficult to determine which provisions of a particular treaty belong to one category or the other. Frequently, these conventions are applied by governments and international tribunals from the moment of their approval, without waiting for their ratification. This is true in particular of the Convention on the Law of Treaties, which was widely applied long before its coming into force in 1980. Although the United States has not ratified that Convention, both the Department of State and the courts of the United States have applied the Convention as "declaratory of customary international law." We see that process developing with respect to the 1982 Law of the Sea Convention. In fact, it began before the conclusion of the conference that prepared that treaty as some States started putting into force some parts of the Convention as soon as they were generally agreed on, especially certain provisions relating to the rights of coastal States. On the other hand, major maritime States stopped protesting against the exercise of these new rights as soon as they obtained general assurance that freedom of navigation in important coastal areas would be effectively protected.

It is not surprising, therefore, that the next step was to consider the consensus reached on the new Convention on the Law of the Sea as evidence of its general acceptance as emerging customary law. . . .

When the Law of the Sea Conventions were adopted at the First United Nations Law of the Sea Conference in 1958, the Convention on the High Seas stated in its preamble that its provisions were "generally declaratory of established principles of international law," and no States nonparties to that Convention have disputed that statement. Although other 1958 Conventions did not state expressly that their texts have become a part of customary international law, most of their provisions have also been considered as reflecting the existing or emerging customary international law. For instance, the International Court of Justice in the North Sea Continental Shelf Cases pointed out that certain articles of the 1958 Convention on the Continental Shelf, "it is clear, were then regarded as reflecting, or as crystallizing, received or at least emergent rules of customary international law." In the same case, the Court also noted that a rule that is conventional in origin can pass into the general *corpus* of international law and be accepted as such by the *opinio juris* and thus "become binding even for countries which had never, and do not, become parties to the Convention"; and added that this "constitutes indeed one of the recognized methods by which new rules of customary international law may be formed."

It is this process that came to fruition at the Third Conference on the Law of the Sea. In a case decided at the beginning of the Conference, the International

Court of Justice stated that it was premature to examine the proposals submitted to the Third United Nations Conference on the Law of the Sea, as they "must be regarded as manifestations of the views and opinions of individual States and as vehicles of their aspirations, rather than expressing principles of existing law"; the Court added that it cannot "anticipate the law before the legislator has laid it down."[1] In a later case, however, decided when the drafting of the new Convention was far advanced, but the Convention was not yet signed, the Court stated that even if the parties had not asked it, in the special agreement submitting the case to the Court, to base its decision on "the new accepted trends in the Third Conference on the Law of the Sea" it would have taken *proprio motu* account of the progress made by the Conference. The Court explained that "it could not ignore any provision of the draft convention if it came to the conclusion that the content of such provision is binding upon all members of the international community because it embodies or crystallizes a preexisting or emergent rule of customary law."[2]

The Court is thus willing to pay attention not only to a text that has codified preexisting principles of customary international law, but also to one that has crystallized an "emergent rule of customary law." It seems, therefore, that once a consensus is reached at an international conference, a rule of customary international law can emerge without having to wait for the signature of the convention. Once a convention is signed by a vast majority of the international community, its stature as customary international law is thereby strengthened, as such signatures are a clear evidence of an *opinio juris* that the convention contains generally acceptable principles.

International law does not impose any formal restrictions on the means by which States may express their common will. If in the last decades of the twentieth century they should decide that consensus at a conference plus a signature by a vast majority of the participants creates a general norm of international law, this new method of creating new principles and rules of international law would thereby become a legitimate method of law creation. There is no rule of international law preventing all States assembled in conference to agree that a particular set of rules represents a satisfactory product of "mutual accommodation, reasonableness and co-operation."[3] In addition, States may be willing to accept these rules as binding on them from the very

1 Fisheries Jurisdiction Case (U.K. v. Ice.), 1974 I.C.J. 3, 23–24.

2 Case Concerning the Continental Shelf (Tunisia v. Libyan Arab Jamahiriya), 1982 I.C.J. 18, 38.

3 Fisheries Jurisdiction Case (U.K. v. Ice.), 1974 I.C.J. 3, 23.

moment of their adoption. Whether States are willing actually to accept the last proposition depends on the circumstances of the case, and very often the agreement on the immediate acceptance of the rule as customary law is more implicit than explicit. If a sufficient number of States having a special interest in the application of a new rule start acting in accordance with it, and no States object to it, there is a clear presumption that the rule agreed on at the conference, although the agreement has not yet been ratified, has become an accepted rule of customary international law.

In its statement on the U.S. Ocean Policy, issued in March 1983, the United States has gone quite far in the direction of accepting all the provisions of the Law of the Sea Convention, except those relating to deep seabed mining. President Reagan pointed out that the Convention "contains provisions with respect to traditional uses of the oceans which generally confirm existing maritime law and practice and fairly balance the interests of all states." President Reagan also announced that the United States "is prepared to accept and act in accordance with the balance of interests" thus achieved, and that it "will recognize the rights of other states in the waters off their coasts, as reflected in the Convention, so long as the rights and freedoms of the United States and others under international law are recognized by such coastal states."

Thus, there is an agreement between the signatories to the Convention and the United States that most of the provisions of the Convention have become customary international law. The United States' refusal to accept the deep seabed mining part of the Convention does not prevent even that part from becoming customary international law, in full or in part (e.g., distinguishing between certain general principles and various institutional and administrative provisions). The only effect of the United States' refusal to join consensus on this part of the Convention is that the rules contained in this part, and in this part only, cannot bind the United States. As the International Court of Justice has noted in several cases, if a State has consistently opposed from the beginning an emerging rule of customary law, that rule, although generally applicable, does not apply to the protesting State. This is a small price to pay for this tremendous step forward in the process of the formation of new international law that has been pioneered by the Law of the Sea Conference. Some have already said that this Conference is as important as the Conference at San Francisco that created the United Nations. While I would not go so far, I agree that this Conference is likely to go down in history as the most important event in the process of development of a viable international law.

JONATHAN I. CHARNEY, INTERNATIONAL AGREEMENTS AND THE DEVELOPMENT OF CUSTOMARY INTERNATIONAL LAW

61 Wash. L. Rev. 971 (1986)

For years many states have asserted that resolutions of the United Nations General Assembly can make instant international law. Others have argued that resolutions cannot provide the necessary state practice and *opinio juris* to establish new norms. Still other observers maintain that certain resolutions can contribute important evidence to support new norms but that resolutions alone may not make new law. This dispute remains unresolved.

A similar conflict has now arisen with regard to the role that the negotiation, adoption, and conclusion of international agreements may play in developing new norms of customary international law. It has long been recognized that international agreements have an important role in the development of such norms. Recently, however, writers, international courts, and statesmen have given support to the view that international agreements, with little more, could give rise to new customary international law that is binding on all states regardless of whether or not they participated in the negotiations or became parties to the agreement. There is even some support for the view that international agreements that are not yet in force could give rise to instant international law. Such developments in the rules for establishing customary international law would have profound implications for the international legal system.

Traditionally, the International Court of Justice identified three relatively uncontroversial circumstances in which international agreements may be relevant to finding customary international law: they can codify the existing law, they can cause the law to crystallize, and they can initiate the progressive development of new law. In each of these circumstances states' negotiation and adoption of certain international agreements can add to the evidence of customary international law. But with the exception of some recent judgments, the Court had been clear that state practice dehors the agreements, that *opinio juris* were the principal considerations, and that international agreements played limited roles.[4] . . .

---

4 . . . Some contrary indications may be found in the recent judgments in ocean boundary cases before the Court. The negotiations at the Third United Nations Conference on the Law of the Sea and the resulting Convention on the Law of the Sea appear to have been given considerable importance. *See* Continental Shelf (Malta v. Libyan Arab Jamahiriya), 1985 I.C.J. 13, 29–30; Maritime Boundary in the Gulf of Maine Area (Can. v. U.S.), 1984 I.C.J. 246, 294; Continental Shelf (Tunisia v. Libyan Arab Jamahiriya), 1982 I.C.J. 3, 38, 48–49.

I Background

[T]he law does permit some individual rules found in international agreements to merge into customary law apart from the overall agreement. Certain factors are appropriately considered when determining whether a rule found within an international agreement may give rise to new customary international law. These factors include:

1. *The nature of the subject matter.* An agreement which addresses generalized interests and aspirations of the international community may be more likely to produce new law than an agreement which focuses on specific state interests.

2. *The nature of the negotiations.* A particular rule that was the product of compromises across the range of provisions in the agreement may be less appropriate for merger into customary law than a rule that resulted from a more atomized negotiation.

3. *The nature of the obligation.* A rule that is interlinked with other provisions in the agreement would be less able to be considered as a customary rule separated from the fabric of the agreement than a rule that is independent of other obligations.

4. *The nature of the rule.* A rule that requires highly technical methods of implementation would require the specificity of an international agreement, as contrasted with more generalized obligations that are possible to implement as custom. Furthermore, if international institutions are required to be used or established, customary law is inappropriate.

. . . An examination of the treatment of the law of the sea may shed more light on the role that international agreements may play in the making of customary law. . . .

. . . In its introduction to the law of the sea chapter, the Restatement [(Third) of Foreign Relations Law of the United States (1986)] reports that although the LOS Convention is not in force and the United States is not a signatory, it is an important basis for the customary law of the sea now in effect. This conclusion is consonant with the view recently expressed by the Chamber of the International Court of Justice that determined the Gulf of Maine boundary dispute between the United States and Canada.

The Restatement points out that much of the Convention merely restates the law found in the previous 1958 Law of the Sea Conventions which in part codified customary law existing at that time. More importantly, the Restatement reports that the LOS Convention has given rise to new rules of customary international law: "Other provisions in the Convention set forth rules that, whether or not they were law in 1958, became law since that time, as they were accepted at the Conference by consensus and have influenced, and by now reflect, the practice of states."

... On its face, this statement suggests that the Convention and the negotiations standing alone would not be sufficient to establish customary law.

The Restatement cautiously declares that the entire Convention has not merged into customary law. Thus, it points out that a few parts of the Convention, such as the deep seabed regime, have not merged into customary law due to the lack of supporting evidence dehors the Convention. The Restatement is therefore admittedly selective in its use of rules found in the LOS Convention.

Caution is particularly appropriate in this case. Some of the reasons that justify such caution are:

1. *The nature of the subject matter.* Much of the law of the sea under negotiation concerned real state interests, not noble aspirations of a general humanitarian kind.

2. *The nature of the negotiations.* It is beyond dispute that the negotiations at the Law of the Sea Conference were conducted on the basis of a package deal. Trade-offs between subjects were common.

3. *The nature of the obligation.* All portions of the Convention were thereby linked together as a political matter.

4. *The nature of the rule.* The Convention establishes international organizations and sets out detailed obligations, sometimes with numerical specifications. Such institutions and requirements are not susceptible to implementation by customary international law.

In addition to these considerations a few other facts suggest care should be taken before concluding that the LOS Convention has given rise to customary international law. First, many of the provisions of the Convention embody new concepts created at the negotiations, and states have not implemented them in practice. Second, the views of authorities about the effect of the Convention on customary law differ. Some have declared it to be evidence of existing law while others refuse to accept it as law except in regard to states which become parties to the agreement. Third, the Convention was adopted only three years ago by the Law of Sea Conference on a split vote; it has not come into force for any state....

In its treatment of the law of the sea the Restatement assigns international treaty negotiations a greater role in the formation of customary law than in any other substantive area of international law. First, the Restatement permits the selective use of portions of an international agreement that are the result of a compromise of real and direct state interests. Second, highly technical solutions to state relations that, in other substantive areas, had limited the impact of treaty relations on customary law, presented no obstacle to finding new customary law of the sea. Third, the complex behavior at the Law of the Sea Conference, and the controversial adoption of the Convention, provided virtually the sole basis for finding new rules of customary law. It is thus presumed that a conference and a multilateral convention that is not yet in force can, without additional evidence, provide the necessary state practice and *opinio juris* for the establishment of new rules of customary law....

II Analysis

The question ... is what role should international law give to the negotiation and conclusion of international agreements when a search is to be made for the operative rules of customary international law. Conferences held to negotiate international agreement provide a vehicle by which states communicate their views for the purpose of producing rules of law. Agreements reached at such fora do change nations' perceptions of their rights and duties. If this process were irrelevant to customary law development, some law may become frozen in time and fail to reflect movement realized at international negotiations. The gap that could develop between custom and treaty law might complicate interstate relations....

... The conclusion that more than the agreement itself must be shown before customary law is found presents problems for one seeking to find evidence of state practice and *opinio juris*. In cases where the required widespread adherence to the agreement exists, substantial evidence of state actions taken in circumstances where the agreement is not directly applicable may be hard to obtain. As a consequence, support for new rules of customary law will have to be found in the agreement and in secondary evidence derived from writers, and perhaps in self-serving official state policy statements. It is this dilemma that may force some to use tenuous evidence in support of new norms of customary international law.

If, however, an isolated rule contained within an agreement can form the basis upon which customary law is established, then one must assume that the negotiation and acceptance of the agreement as a whole can be relied upon to provide the elements of customary law. This would be difficult. For example, it is not clear how such proof can support the conclusion that there has been acceptance or *opinio juris* with respect to a rule that is isolated from the context of the agreement as a whole. In the unique circumstance of the restrictions on the use of force found within the United Nations Charter, the centrality of that rule might permit such a conclusion. In cases where the rule is not preeminent, such a conclusion would be highly questionable in the absence of independent evidence dehors the agreement. Furthermore, this approach might lead in the direction of establishing ad hoc multilateral negotiations as de facto international legislatures.

Professor Louis Sohn has taken the view that the negotiation of international agreements can readily develop new norms of international law. He has suggested that this development arises out of the difficulty faced by authorities seeking to distill patterns of state practice and *opinio juris* from the overwhelming quantity of public and secret information generated by states. In seeking a more manageable method for finding and defining customary international law, he has suggested that the international community may be expanding the role which conferences called to negotiate international agreements may play in developing new customary international law. He maintains that when a rule is the subject of agreement at a conference, that rule is presumed to give rise to custom once a number of interested states behave in conformity with the rule and no state objects. He also suggests that the international community might decide that "consensus at a conference plus a signature by a vast majority of the participants creates a general norm of international law . . . binding on [states] from the very moment of [the] adoption [of the international agreement]." . . .

As a method to facilitate the establishment of new rules of international law, this approach has much appeal. Unfortunately, it also presents certain difficulties. Some of these difficulties have been identified above. How, for example, would one determine whether a rule developed in a negotiation can be separated from the fabric of the agreement? How could one distinguish between actions and statements of officials that support the negotiated agreement as an agreement, and statements intended to support the rule as customary law? The answer to both of these questions might be that one looks to the official statements of state representatives at the negotiations for *opinio juris* supporting the rule as a norm of international law.

The record of the negotiations may be clear on the question, but that is unlikely. It certainly was not clear in the case of the Law of the Sea Conference that was the focus of Sohn's article. Even if the record were clear, such strong reliance on the intent of the negotiators to create international law may weaken the foundations of customary international law.

[I]nternational law, being a rudimentary system of law, is fragile. To the extent that customary law is effective as law, it must reflect the real interests of the members of the international community. To a certain extent, it must also reflect the normative aspirations of the community. At the same time, it must not be so divergent from actual state practice and true state interests that it becomes an unrealistic dream. As a consequence, the traditional rules for determining whether there is a rule of customary international law seek to make the most accurate appraisal of states' positions. This is why it is important to consider the actual behavior of states in real situations.

Statements of officials faced with real situations have been very significant. Information on states' views derived from abstract situations has provided less authoritative information on their true positions. While resolutions of international organizations, such as those of the United Nations General Assembly, have become accepted evidence to support rules of international law, there is much debate over their utility. The debate arises because resolutions are likely to represent highly politicized positions of state representatives divorced from the reality of international life. Even when a resolution is utilized as evidence of international law, care should be taken to determine the specific nature of the resolution and the facts surrounding its adoption.

The negotiation of international agreements at international conferences falls somewhere between actions of states faced with specific real situations and votes to adopt resolutions at meetings of international organizations. Some negotiations are closer to real and pressing international disputes than others, and positions taken at the former are more likely to represent real decisions of the participating states. Adherence to an international agreement by a state represents an even stronger decision. But negotiations and agreements do differ. Those like the United States-Iran agreements that led to the freeing of the hostages, are based strictly on specific live disputes. Others, like the human rights conventions, are not focused on any specific incident. While the former may closely reflect what states are willing to do in real situations, it is the latter that are more likely to be considered as forming the basis for new rules of international law. The latter, however, are least likely to reflect the reality of state policy. But it is the reality of state policy that should be given the greatest attention when searching for customary international law, not the more abstract activities of state representatives at multilateral fora.

It is this paradox that the legal community must face if greater reliance is to be placed on international agreements in defining customary international law. The negotiation and conclusion of international agreements might allow one to posit new rules of international law. Unfortunately, those rules may not reflect the true normative standards that guide states in reality.

It is, perhaps, for these reasons that the importance of state practice as a critical element in establishing customary international law, even when the norm is found in multilateral conventions, has received renewed emphasis in the words of the most recent judgments of the International Court of Justice. In its 1985 Judgment on the ocean boundary between Libya and Malta, the Court wrote: "It is of course axiomatic that the material of customary international laws is to be looked for primarily in the actual practice and *opinio juris* of States, even though multilateral conventions may have an important role to play in recording and defining rules deriving from custom, or indeed in developing them." . . .

Of course, law should not reflect merely what the subjects of the law would do in the absence of law. The function of law is to promote positive behavior by setting a normative standard toward which the subjects of the law will strive. Rules derived from international negotiations may reflect ideals that are unsullied by the realities of normal international discourse. The risk, however, is that these ideals may be so removed from the reality of international behavior that they would not serve effectively as legal norms.

This conclusion does not require the rejection of international conference negotiations and international agreements as evidence of international law. Rather, before it is concluded that such negotiations provide useful evidence of new rules of international law, they should be carefully viewed in the context of state practice and *opinio juris*. The subsidiary rules suggested above may help to discriminate between those international agreements that could be invoked to support new rules of international law and those that ought not to be so utilized.

Such a cautious approach may result in findings that customary law is substantially different from obligations states assume under international agreements. If that difference becomes unacceptable, states can certainly take the necessary actions and make new customary law. The rules found in international agreements support the development of new law. But in the absence of significant additional actions, it is unwise to presume that new customary law arises out of international agreements even with some state practice. It would risk defining customary law rules that do not reflect reality and do not effectively influence the actions of states.

Notes

1. *Searching for State Practice and Rules of Customary International Law.* Part of Professor Sohn's rationale for suggesting that the outcomes of multilateral treaty-making conferences could establish rules of customary international law was the difficulty of finding evidence of state practice. Does current internet technology cure this difficulty? Where exactly should one look for evidence of state practice? To the communications of diplomats? The pronouncements and actions of executive branches? Enactments by national legislatures? Decisions of national courts? Is reliance on state practice biased toward the positions of major powers, because their practice tends to be more

readily ascertainable? How is one to find evidence of opinio juris, the other traditional element of customary international law, outside a treaty-making conference? Professor Charney, in his later scholarship, emphasized that "[s]tates are increasingly aware that the work of multilateral forums contributes to the development of general international law," citing as examples "the rapid acceptance of both the 200-nautical-mile exclusive economic zone and the twelve-nautical-mile territorial sea after consensus was reached at" UNCLOS III. Jonathan I. Charney, Universal International Law, 87 Am. J. Intl. L. 529, 548 (1993).

Should international lawyers be seeking to ascertain the shared expectations of a broad "international community" comprising a range of actors, rather than merely seeking evidence of the customary practice of states? To what extent are the actions and values of private actors relevant in determining rules of international law?

Is it surprising that the existence or specific content of rules of customary international law is sometimes highly debatable? How are such debates resolved? What happens if they are not resolved? Is it surprising that some rules of customary international law *are* widely regarded as clearly established? Can you, at this stage, identify any clearly established customary international law of the sea rules?

2. *Customary International Law and Non-parties to the LOS Convention.* Professors Sohn and Charney wrote the articles excerpted above shortly after the conclusion of UNCLOS III. At that time, many states had not ratified the LOS Convention, and it had not entered into force as treaty law. Thus, it was important for many states to consider the customary international law status of LOS Convention provisions.

As of September 1, 2013, the LOS Convention is in force for 166 parties, including all the major powers except the United States. For the United States and the few other non-parties (many of which are land-locked states), do all the provisions of the LOS Convention now represent customary international law? Or only some provisions? May the United States legally consider as customary international law those Convention provisions it finds advantageous—such as those concerning the right of transit passage through straits or the right to an extended continental shelf—while rejecting any provisions it does not like? Does the United States remain legally bound by the most recent treaties that it has accepted, e.g., the 1958 Territorial Sea Convention? If a new rule of customary international law emerges, does it take precedence over a prior treaty obligation? Revisit these questions as you read about specific law of the sea issues throughout this text.

CHAPTER 2

Freedom of the High Seas

As noted in Chapter 1, the principle of the freedom of the high seas (mare liberum) prevailed over the attempts of some states to assert sovereignty over vast areas of the seas to the exclusion of other states (mare clausum). However, even under the principle of the freedom of the high seas, the right of a state to exercise control over a belt of "territorial waters" close to its coast was recognized. In the latter half of the 20th century, there was an extension of coastal state jurisdiction farther into the sea. Today, the high seas include the largest part of the 71 percent of the earth's surface that is covered by oceans. In the high seas, the ships of all nations, including even those of land-locked states, have the right to navigate and engage in certain other activities without hindrance by other states. In these activities, a ship is governed by international law and the law of its flag state. Chapters 3 and 4 consider the problems relating to the nationality of ships and the exercise of jurisdiction by a state over the ships flying its flag. Later chapters deal with the other side of the coin: the gradual extension of the jurisdiction of coastal states into the oceans.

Section A of this chapter introduces the principle of the freedom of the high seas as codified in the 1982 United Nations Convention on the Law of the Sea (LOS Convention). Sections B through F address particular high seas freedoms: the freedom of navigation, the freedom of overflight, the freedom of fishing, the freedom to lay submarine cables and pipelines, and other freedoms. We then explore important constraints on the exercise of high seas freedoms: the requirement that states exercise high seas freedoms with reasonable regard to the interests of other states (Section G), and the requirement that the high seas be used for peaceful purposes (Section H). Finally, Section I addresses the duty to render assistance to those in distress on the high seas.

A Introduction

Section 1 of Part VII (High Seas) of the LOS Convention contains general provisions governing the freedom of the high seas. In addition to important general limitations that a state must observe in exercising these freedoms, several of the enumerated freedoms are specifically made subject to other provisions of the LOS Convention, including measures regarding the conservation and

 | DOI 10.1163/9789004203563_003

management of the living resources of the high seas found in Section 2 of Part VII. Many provisions of Part XII of the Convention (Protection and Preservation of the Marine Environment) also apply to activities in the high seas. The exercise by individual states of their high seas freedoms involves a consideration of global community interests.

LAW OF THE SEA CONVENTION

Articles 86–87 and 89

See Appendix

Notes

1. *Limitations on the Exercise of High Seas Freedoms*. Article 87 notes several general limitations that must be observed by states in exercising their high sea freedoms, including "conditions laid down by this Convention" and "other rules of international law." What would be an example of another "rule of international law" that might limit a state's ability to exercise one or more of its freedoms?

Article 87(2) obligates states to exercise their freedoms "with due regard for the interests of other states." Article 88 of the LOS Convention provides that the "high seas shall be reserved for peaceful purposes." The "due regard" and "peaceful purposes" limitations are discussed in Sections G and H.

In addition to these general limitations, the freedoms of laying submarine cables, constructing artificial installations, fishing, and marine research are specifically made "subject to" other LOS Convention provisions. What are some of the specific limitations imposed on these four freedoms by other LOS Convention provisions?

2. *Defining the "High Seas."* "High seas" is defined in Article 1 of the 1958 High Seas Convention as "all parts of the sea that are not included in the territorial sea or in the internal waters of a State." In drafting the LOS Convention, the United States and other major maritime states took the position that the exclusive economic zone (EEZ) is a part of the high seas, subject to special rights of the coastal states. Other states advanced the view that the EEZ is not a part of the high seas, but instead constitutes a special zone of coastal state jurisdiction, subject to the freedoms of navigation and overflight. As finally adopted, does the LOS Convention define the "high seas"? Read Article 58(1) of the LOS Convention in the Appendix, as well as considering Article 86. We revisit this issue in Chapter 9.

B Freedom of Navigation

The concept of common ownership of the oceans and the associated freedom of navigation formed a part of the laws and traditions of many areas of the world, including the Roman Empire and Asia. In the late 15th century, after Columbus's discovery of America, Portugal and Spain asserted exclusive rights to explore and acquire ownership, respectively, of undiscovered lands in the eastern and western halves of the world, including the sole right to navigate and trade in those areas. In objection to these claims, Grotius wrote *De Mare Liberum* to support Dutch access to the East Indian trade.

HUGO GROTIUS, THE FREEDOM OF THE SEAS (1633)
7–8, 27–28, 37–38 (Ralph van Deman Magoffin trans. & James Brown Scott ed., 1916; reprinted 2001)

My intention is to demonstrate briefly and clearly that the Dutch—that is to say, the subjects of the United Netherlands—have the right to sail to the East Indies, as they are now doing, and to engage in trade with the people there. I shall base my argument on the following most specific and unimpeachable axiom of the Law of Nations, called a primary rule or first principle, the spirit of which is self-evident and immutable, to wit; every nation is free to travel to every other nation, and to trade with it.

... For do not the ocean[s], navigable in every direction with which God has encompassed all the earth, and the regular and the occasional winds which blow now from one quarter and now from another, offer sufficient proof that Nature has given to all peoples a right of access to all other peoples? ...

Two conclusions may be drawn from what has thus far been said. The first is, that which cannot be occupied, or which never has been occupied, cannot be the property of any one, because all property has arisen from occupation. The second is, that all that which has been so constituted by nature that although serving some one person it still suffices for the common use of all other persons, is today and ought in perpetuity to remain in the same condition as when it was first created by nature....

The air ... is not susceptible of occupation; and ... its common use is destined for all men. For the same reasons the sea is common to all, because it is so limitless that it cannot become a possession of any one, and because it is adapted for the use of all....

... The Portuguese claim as their own the whole expanse of the sea which separates two parts of the world so far distant the one from the other, that in all the preceding centuries neither one has so much as heard of the other. Indeed, if we take into account the share of the Spaniards, whose claim is the same as that of the Portuguese, only a little less than the whole ocean is found to be subject to two nations, while all the rest of the peoples in the world are restricted to the narrow bounds of the northern seas [. If in] a thing so vast as the sea a man were to reserve to himself from general use nothing more than mere sovereignty, still he would be considered a seeker after unreasonable power. If a man were to enjoin other people from fishing, he would not escape the reproach of monstrous greed. But the man who even prevents navigation, a thing which means no loss to himself, what are we to say of him?...

...For it is most outrageous for you to appropriate a thing, which both by ordinance of nature and by common consent is as much mine as yours, so exclusively that you will not grant me a right of use in it which leaves it no less yours than it was before.

Notes

1. *Underpinnings of the Freedom of Navigation.* Grotius relied on natural law, derived from God and reason, and cited Roman law and classical poets, philosophers, and jurists to support his positions. How do natural law and Grotius's proofs differ from the sources and evidence of modern international law? Are there any similarities?

As noted in Chapter 1, British sea power in the 19th century helped to solidify the prominence of the principle of freedom of the high seas, and in particular the freedom of navigation. Today, international law, as reflected in Article 90 of the LOS Convention, provides that "[e]very State, whether coastal or land-locked, has the right to sail ships flying its flag on the high seas." Article 87 provides for freedom of navigation. What legal and policy considerations today support unrestricted navigation rights across the high seas? Are these considerations the same as in Grotius's day or as in the 19th century?

2. *Limitations on the Freedom of Navigation.* The freedom to navigate applies not only to warships and other state-owned vessels, but to ships that are authorized by a particular state (the "flag state") to fly its flag. Chapter 4 discusses the rights and duties of the flag state with respect to its vessels. Why should Article 87 of the LOS Convention condition the freedom of navigation on compliance with legal rules, such as those found in Article 94?

The freedom of navigation does not extend to vessels that are engaged in certain prohibited activities, including piracy, the slave trade, or unauthorized broadcasting. See Chapter 4, Section D.

C Freedom of Overflight

With the development of air navigation at the beginning of the 20th century, two opposing ideas were advanced: one, that there should be an absolute freedom of air navigation, and the other, that air navigation should be subject to the sovereignty of the subjacent state. The latter theory was incorporated into the 1919 Paris Convention on the Regulation of Aerial Navigation, which in Article 1 recognized the complete and exclusive sovereignty of every state over the air space above its territory and territorial waters. As a corollary to this principle, all states enjoy the freedom of overflight above the high seas, where there are no subjacent states. Article 2(4) of the 1958 High Seas Convention and Article 87(1)(b) of the LOS Convention codify this freedom.

UNITED STATES PROTEST TO ECUADOR
2 Marian Nash-Leich, Cumulative Digest of United States Practice in International Law 1755 (1981–1988)

In 1986, the Department of State instructed the American Embassy at Quito to protest Ecuadoran interference with the flight of a U.S. Air Force plane flying over the high seas more than 175 miles from the Ecuadoran coast, as follows:

> 1. Airway Upper Lima 308 comes no closer than 175 nautical miles (NM) to the Ecuadoran coast, and customary law as reflected in the 1982 Law of the Sea Convention (which neither the U.S. nor Ecuador has signed,* but for different reasons) permits a territorial sea claim over the sea and adjacent airspace (*i.e.*, sovereignty) of no more than 12 nm from the coast. Ecuador claims a 200 nm territorial sea, which the U.S. does not recognize and which we protested in 1967. Except as might be required under the Convention on International Civil Aviation (Chicago Convention), the U.S. would oppose any attempt by Ecuador to require aircraft to give prior notice or seek prior permission in order to overfly areas beyond 12 nm from the coast.
>
> 2. Under Annex 2 to the Chicago Convention civil aircraft which expect to transit a Flight Information Region (FIR) must file a flight plan, either at least 30 minutes prior to take off or at least 10 minutes prior to entering a particular FIR, so to that extent civil aircraft are subject to a prior notification requirement. Civil aircraft must also abide by local flight regulations and instructions while in that FIR. While Annex 2 envisions variations from the 30/10 minute filing rule, the U.S. is generally

* Ecuador became a party to the LOS Convention in September 2012. [Eds.]

opposed to efforts by any country to impose more burdensome requirements in the absence of compelling circumstances.

3. The Embassy can approach appropriate [Government of Ecuador] officials to reiterate our concern that such an incident not happen again, that the U.S. does not recognize Ecuadoran territorial sea/airspace claims beyond 12 nautical miles from the coast, and our hope that any new Ecuadoran regulations will be in full conformity with international aviation standards.

Notes

1. *Diplomatic Protests*. One way states assert their rights under international law is through diplomatic communications and protests. Protests relating to alleged violations of the international law of the sea have been a significant part of U.S. practice. Other instances are compiled in Digests of United States Practice in International Law, in the U.S. Department of State Bulletin, in issues of the American Journal of International Law, and in J. Ashley Roach & Robert W. Smith, United States Responses to Excessive Maritime Claims (3d ed. 2012).

2. *The Chicago Convention and Rules Concerning Air Safety*. Lawyers concerned with the law of the sea recognize that not all matters affecting the oceans are codified in the LOS Convention or in other "law of the sea" treaties. The 1919 Paris Convention was superseded by the more comprehensive 1944 Chicago Convention on International Civil Aviation. Pursuant to Article 12 of the Chicago Convention, civil aircraft flying over the high seas must observe the Rules of the Air enacted by the International Civil Aviation Organization (ICAO). State aircraft must operate at all times with due regard for the safety of navigation. State aircraft are normally required to comply with safety measures enacted by ICAO, although appropriate exceptions may apply. How does the LOS Convention take account of other rules of international law? See, e.g., LOS Convention, Articles 39(3) (which relates to transit passage but embodies a general principle), 87, 293, 311.

3. *Overflight in the Exclusive Economic Zone*. According to the Secretariat of the ICAO, the freedom of overflight over the high seas also applies fully in airspace over a coastal state's exclusive economic zone: "For the purposes of the Chicago Convention, its Annexes and other air law instruments, the EEZ should be deemed to have the same legal status as the high seas and any reference in these instruments to the high seas should be deemed to encompass the EEZ." United Nations Convention on the Law of the Sea—Implications, if any, for the application of the Chicago Convention, its Annexes and other international air law instruments, ICAO Doc. C.WP/7777 (1984), quoted in

3 United Nations Convention on the Law of the Sea 1982: A Commentary ¶ 87.9(d) at 82 (Satya N. Nandan & Shabtai Rosenne eds., 1995).

What if a military plane flying over another state's EEZ is engaged in espionage? On April 1, 2001, a U.S. Navy surveillance aircraft collided with a Chinese jet fighter approximately 75 miles southeast of Hainan Island, China, over the South China Sea. The damaged U.S. plane landed in China; China searched the plane and detained its crew for ten days. One issue was whether the United States was legally exercising the freedom of overflight at the time of the collision. China asserted that the use of a military plane for surveillance activities failed to give "due regard" to the sovereign rights of China within its EEZ. Do you agree with China's position? What arguments might be raised on the part of the United States?

Several states have established "air defense identification zones" (ADIZs) and require foreign and domestic aircraft intending to enter the ADIZ to file flight plans and provide periodic position reports. As a matter of international law, does a coastal state strengthen its position that it may limit overflights of its EEZ if it has proclaimed an ADIZ that extends seaward of its territorial sea? China's 2013 declaration of an East China Sea ADIZ has proved controversial. For background on international legal ramifications of ADIZs, see Peter A. Dutton, *Caelum Liberam*: Air Defense Identification Zones Outside Sovereign Airspace, 103 Am. J. Intl. L. 691 (2009).

More generally, which high seas freedoms set out in Article 87 of the LOS Convention may be exercised within the EEZ of another state? Which may not be? See LOS Convention, Articles 58, 86. For further discussion, see Chapter 9.

D Freedom of Fishing

When Grotius propounded the principle of open seas, he was convinced that restrictions on fishing were intolerable and that fish were an inexhaustible resource. According to Grotius, as quoted in the excerpt from his work in Section B, "[i]f a man were to enjoin other people from fishing, he would not escape the reproach of monstrous greed." Today, fishery resources are no longer viewed as an inexhaustible resource. As discussed in Chapter 9, concern over fishery resources resulted in the creation of the exclusive economic zone (EEZ), in which a coastal state may limit access to fisheries by domestic and foreign fishing vessels in order to manage and conserve the living resources within its EEZ.

Article 87(1)(e) of the LOS Convention codifies the freedom of all states to fish on the high seas. However, this freedom is expressly made subject to general obligations concerning the conservation and management of living resources in the high seas found in Articles 116 through 120 of the Convention, which are discussed in Chapter 13.

UNITED NATIONS FOOD AND AGRICULTURE ORGANIZATION, THE STATE OF WORLD FISHERIES AND AQUACULTURE: 2010

Available at http://www.fao.org

PART 1: WORLD REVIEW OF FISHERIES AND AQUACULTURE

Global production of marine capture fisheries reached a peak of 86.3 million tonnes in 1996 and then declined slightly to 79.5 million tonnes in 2008, with great interyear fluctuations. . . .

The proportion of stocks estimated to be underexploited or moderately exploited declined from 40 percent in the mid-1970s to 15 percent in 2008. . . . In contrast, the proportion of overexploited, depleted or recovering stocks increased from 10 percent in 1974 to 32 percent in 2008. The proportion of fully exploited stocks has remained relatively stable at about 50 percent since the 1970s, with scattered, slightly lower levels between 1985 and 1997. In 2008, 15 percent of the stock groups monitored by FAO were estimated to be underexploited (3 percent) or moderately exploited (12 percent) and, therefore, able to produce more than their current catches. This is the lowest percentage recorded since the mid-1970s. Slightly more than half of the stocks (53 percent) were estimated to be fully exploited and, therefore, their current catches are at or close to their maximum sustainable productions, with no room for further expansion. The remaining 32 percent were estimated to be either overexploited (28 percent), depleted (3 percent) or recovering from depletion (1 percent) and, thus, yielding less than their maximum potential production owing to excess fishing pressure in the past, with a need for rebuilding plans. This combined percentage is the highest in the time series. While the degree of uncertainty about these estimates may be great . . ., the apparently increasing trend in the percentage of overexploited, depleted and recovering stocks and the decreasing trend in underexploited and moderately exploited stocks do give cause for concern.

Most of the stocks of the top ten species, which account in total for about 30 percent of the world marine capture fisheries production in terms of quantity . . ., are fully exploited and, therefore, have no potential for increased production, while some stocks are overexploited and increases in their production could only be possible with effective rebuilding plans in place. . . . Of the 23 tuna stocks, most are more or less fully exploited (possibly up to 60 percent), some are overexploited or depleted (possibly up to 35 percent) and only a few appear to be underexploited (mainly skipjack).

Notes

1. *The Tragedy of the Commons.* In 1968, Garrett Hardin published an influential article describing how a common resource will likely be depleted as a result of each user's choice to maximize his own short-term self-interest. The Tragedy of the Commons, 162 Science 1243 (1968). The potential for overexploitation of a common fishery resource provides a classic example of this principle, and was a major impetus behind the development of the EEZ.

2. *International Legal Responses to the Tragedy of the Commons.* How has and should international law respond to the challenges facing fisheries? In general, one response to the tragedy of the commons has been to allocate property rights in a resource. Compare the LOS Convention's treatment of rights and obligations concerning living resources in the EEZ (Chapter 9) and on the high seas (Chapter 13).

How effectively can technology respond to the stresses on world fisheries noted in the FAO reading? The expansion of marine and freshwater aquaculture production has alleviated some pressures on wild fisheries. In 1950, marine capture was the source of 86 percent of total world fish production. In 2009, 49 percent of the world's fish production came from marine capture compared to 21 percent from marine aquaculture, 23 percent from freshwater aquaculture, and six percent from inland capture. FAO, Review of the State of World Marine Fisheries Resources, Part A: Global Overview (2011), available at http://www.fao.org.

E Freedom to Lay Submarine Cables and Pipelines

After years of trial and error, the first successful transoceanic telegraph cable was laid in 1866. Today, the world depends upon an extensive and sophisticated transoceanic submarine cable network for the transmission of fax, phone, video, internet, and other data. This important network, which consists primarily of fiber optic cables, connects all continents except Antarctica. Submarine cables are also used for other purposes, such as the delivery of electricity generated by offshore wind farms.

The freedom to lay submarine pipelines assures access to offshore natural resources, which account for approximately 30 percent and 50 percent of worldwide oil and natural gas production, respectively. Once extracted offshore, these oil and gas resources are transported through thousands of miles of submarine pipelines, most of which are located on the continental shelf.

The LOS Convention also contains provisions on submarine cables and pipelines in Part VII on the High Seas (Articles 87(1)(c) and 112–115), as well as in parts of the Convention governing various coastal zones. See LOS Convention, Articles 21(1)(c), 51(2), 58(1), and 79. Treaties other than the LOS Convention are also relevant to problems relating to cables and pipelines and may be applied consistently with Article 311(2) of the LOS Convention. One treaty that remains in force is the 1884 Convention for the Protection of Submarine Cables. As of September 1, 2013 over 40 states, including the United States and Russia, were parties to it. The 1884 Convention provided the basis for the following claim asserted by the United States against the Soviet Union.

ALLEGED DAMAGE TO UNITED STATES SUBMARINE CABLES BY SOVIET VESSELS

40 Dept. State Bull. 555 (1959)

1. *United States Aide Memoire to the Soviet Union Ministry of Foreign Affairs, February 28, 1959...*

Between February 21–25, 1959, four telegraphic and one voice transatlantic cables were damaged and put out of service. Aerial investigation disclosed that the Soviet trawler *Novorossiisk* No. RT-99 was in the area of these cable difficulties.

In accordance with the "Convention for Protection of Submarine Cables" of 1884, to which the Soviet Union and the United States are parties, a U.S. naval vessel put a visiting party on board the *Novorossiisk* on February 26 to investigate whether the trawler had violated the Convention.

After discussion with the trawler Captain and examination of the log, the boarding officer from the U.S.S. *R.O. Hale* made an appropriate entry in the journal of the trawler as required by Article X of the Convention and the visiting party left the vessel. The trawler's log indicated that the ship had been in the area of cable damage at the time of the last service interruption. It is understood that the trawler proceeded on its way without delay. A cable repair ship is en route to the area of cable damage for final investigation and repair.

2. *Note from the Soviet Ministry of Foreign Affairs to the United States Embassy in Moscow, March 4, 1959...*

According to information available to competent Soviet organs the Soviet trawler *Novorossiisk* was engaged in fishing in the open sea in the Northern Atlantic ocean and caused no damage of any kind to the underwater telegraph or telephone Trans-Atlantic cables. Reports concerning this question appearing in the American press are figments of the imagination.

Consequently, the American naval vessel *R.O. Hale* had no reason for detaining and inspecting the aforementioned Soviet trawler. Attention must be called to the fact that these actions of the American authorities were undertaken specifically with respect to a Soviet vessel at a time in the region of Newfoundland when there were hundreds of vessels from other countries engaged in fishing and, as reported, many of which have more than once damaged Trans-Atlantic cables.

The Soviet Government cannot ignore the fact that in connection with the above-indicated actions of the United States authorities numerous reports have appeared in the American press containing various anti-Soviet fabrications concerning the purpose of the presence of a Soviet fishing vessel in this region. These articles in the American press are of such a kind that the impression is unavoidable that all this venture with the detention of the Soviet trawler was undertaken with provocative purposes. Not the least among these purposes is an attempt to strain Soviet-American relations. It is impossible in this connection not to draw attention to the responsibility which the American Government takes upon itself by taking such steps.

The Soviet Government protests against the detention and inspection of the Soviet fishing trawler *Novorossiisk* by the American naval vessel and anticipates that the Government of the United States will take all necessary measures to prevent further such completely unjustified actions with respect to Soviet fishing vessels engaged in the fishing trade in waters of the open sea.

3. *Note from the United States Embassy to the Soviet Ministry of Foreign Affairs, March 23, 1959 . . .*

For the reasons set out hereinafter, the United States Government considers there is no basis for a protest in this case and the Soviet protest is therefore rejected. Furthermore, the United States Government is surprised that the Soviet Government should make a charge that the detention of the Soviet trawler was for "provocative purposes" with no other basis than apparent irritation at articles in American newspapers speculating on the purposes of Soviet trawlers in certain waters. As the Soviet Government well knows, the American press is free within legal limits to publish its opinions and these do not engage the responsibility of the Government. Charges based on such flimsy support are not themselves calculated to further friendly relations.

The facts of the matter are as follows.

During the period of February 21 through February 25, 1959, communications were disrupted by damage to five transatlantic cables in the Newfoundland area located within a rectangle bounded by [specified] coordinates. . . .

The first break occurred on February 21, 1959, at 10:43 a.m., eastern standard time, in the transatlantic cable owned and operated in part jointly with a Canadian company by the American Telephone and Telegraph Company, a United States corporation having its head office at New York, New York. The cable has its west terminus in Newfoundland and the east terminus in Scotland, and is ultimately connected with the United States of America by submarine cable and radio relay.

The second break occurred on February 24, 1959, at 2:20 p.m., eastern standard time, in the transatlantic cable 1-VA, connecting Newfoundland and Ireland. The third break occurred on February 25, 1959, at 2:50 a.m., eastern standard time, in the transatlantic cable 3-PZ connecting Newfoundland and England. The fourth cable break occurred on February 25, 1959, at 11:20 a.m., eastern standard time, in the transatlantic cable 2-VA connecting Newfoundland with Ireland. The fifth break occurred on February 25, 1959, at 4:20 p.m., eastern standard time, in the transatlantic cable 4-PZ connecting Newfoundland and England. These four submarine cables connect ultimately with the United States, and are owned and operated by The Western Union Telegraph Company, a United States corporation with its head office at New York, New York.

Subsequent examination showed that there were a total of twelve breaks in the five cables. Nine of these were tension breaks and three were manmade cuts severing the cables.

Aerial observation conducted by the American Telephone and Telegraph Company sighted the Soviet trawler *Novorossiisk* RT-99 on the morning of February 25, 1959, in the approximate position latitude 49° 34' N. and longitude 50° 0' W., steaming on a southerly course at a speed of about three knots. No other vessels were visible at the time in the immediate vicinity. The aircraft succeeded in dropping a note on the deck of the trawler *Novorossiisk* advising it that it had cut four cables and requesting that it cease trawling in the area.

The Government of the United States, acting under the provisions of Article X of the Convention for the Protection of Submarine Cables, of 1884, to which both the United States and the Union of Soviet Socialist Republics adhere, and also in conformity with United States law (47 United States Code, Section 26), implementing the convention, on February 25, 1959, dispatched the United States radar picket escort U.S.S. *Roy O. Hale* to the area to investigate the reported breaks in the submarine cables. On February 26, 1959, about 11:55 a.m., eastern standard time, the Commander of the U.S.S. *Roy O. Hale* sent a party consisting of one officer and four enlisted men, without arms, aboard the Soviet trawler *Novorossiisk*. At the time of the visit the trawler was in position latitude 48° 26' N., longitude 49° 10' W. There were no other ships in the immediate vicinity.

The last four cable breaks referred to above were all located within 14 miles of each other and were each within a 12-mile radius of the observed position of the trawler *Novorossiisk* on February 25, 1959, with the nearest two breaks no more than five miles distant. The five reported cable breaks all occurred within a radius of 52 miles of one another. (All references are to nautical miles.) A line joining the last four reported positions of the breaks is a straight line with the breaks occurring in succession in the direction of approximately 160° T. A vessel in that vicinity trawling in a general southerly direction during the period in question would have been in the locations necessary to cause the breaks.

The boarding officer, communicating by means of French through an interpreter, duly informed and explained to the master of the trawler *Novorossiisk* the purpose of his visit and his authority to do so under the provisions of the convention of 1884. He examined, with the consent and acquiescence of the master, the papers of the trawler which appeared to be in order.

The boarding officer found that the latitude and longitude which the trawler *Novorossiisk* recorded in her journal for the previous days' positions also showed her to have been in the immediate vicinity of all five cable breaks. Upon request, the master produced the message dropped on the deck of the trawler on the previous day from the aircraft of the American Telephone and Telegraph Company. On the basis of the foregoing evidence, the boarding officer concluded that an examination of the fishing gear and equipment was justified to determine whether the trawler was capable of causing the cable breaks.

The unarmed boarding officer, with the consent of the master of the trawler, observed without deep examination, on the upper main deck of the trawler only, the trawling equipment and fishing gear. The boarding officer noted that the trawling equipment was of the type for deep sea fishing, and was in general fairly new, with the exception of the otter boards and net discs which were well worn and in poor condition. The trawling cable was estimated to be about 300 fathoms in length, sufficiently long enough to drag the gear on the bottom at the depth in the area—about 180 fathoms. Two broken sections of trawling cable each about 60 feet in length were observed wrapped around the hatch on deck. The four ends of these cables were shredded and frayed and appeared to have parted as a result of a sudden strain such as could have been caused by snagging the gear. These sections are identical in type, age, and condition with the trawling cable. Some of the fish observed lying frozen on the deck were of the bottom type.

The visit on board the trawler lasted about 70 minutes, and was completed at 1:05 p.m., eastern standard time. At the time of his departure the boarding officer made [entries in the trawler's journal in accordance with Article X of the 1884 Convention].

A preliminary report emanating from the cable repair ship *Lord Kelvin* which has since repaired the first broken cable states that the eastern portion of the damaged cable had been badly scraped and scuffed for about a mile east of the break. The cable had been severed by cutting. The technical opinion is that such evidence indicates that a trawler had picked up the cable with its drag, then having pulled it on deck, had cut it to release the nets.

The protection of submarine telecommunications cables on the high seas constitutes an international obligation. The locations and presence of the transatlantic submarine cables that have been cut are widely known among world fishing and maritime circles. They are shown and marked on United States admiralty and navigation maps which are available to the general public.

The above-stated record of events shows that, contrary to the assertions and charges made in the above-mentioned note of the Union of Soviet Socialist Republics, the visit to the Soviet trawler *Novorossiisk* under the circumstances shown was entirely justified and was in every respect in accordance with international law and applicable treaty provisions.

The Government of the United States is satisfied that the evidence in its possession raises a strong presumption that the master and crew of the Soviet trawler *Novorossiisk* have violated Article II of the Convention of 1884 above-mentioned which provides that "the breaking or injury of a submarine cable, done willfully or through culpable negligence, and resulting in the total or partial interruption" of telegraphic communication shall be a punishable offense.

Article VIII *et seq*. of the Convention place the responsibility for the repression of these violations of the Convention and trial and punishment of the violators on the Soviet Union. Therefore, the Government of the United States calls upon the Government of the Union of Soviet Socialist Republics to discharge its international obligations as summarily as its laws and regulations will permit, by promptly making such investigations and taking such measures as are necessary to punish those who may be found to be guilty.

The Government of the United States reserves the right to make such claims for damages as may be found to be warranted.

The Government of the United States further expects that the Government of the Union of Soviet Socialist Republics will take effective measures to prevent Soviet fishing trawlers on the high seas from damaging or cutting submarine cables in the future.

The Government of the United States further states that it will continue to fulfill its international obligations with regard to the protection of submarine cables.

Notes

1. *Injury to Submarine Cables.* An estimated 100 to 150 submarine cable injuries occur each year that result in disrupted transmissions. Most breaks are caused by trawling and anchoring, and occur on the continental shelf in depths of 100 meters or less. Other causes include natural disasters and extraction activities. Many cable owners have entered into agreements to re-route transmission traffic in the event of a cable break and to provide for cooperative maintenance measures. See Douglas Burnett, Recovery of Cable Repair Ship Cost Damages from Third Parties That Injure Submarine Cables, 35 Tulane Mar. L.J. 103 (2010). The International Cable Protection Committee, an industry organization, promotes the safety of submarine cables. See http://www.iscpc.org. Some states, including China and India, require that a cable owner seek a permit before making repairs to cables located on their continental shelves. Does a coastal state have the authority under the LOS Convention to limit or regulate repairs to submarine cables located outside of its territorial sea?

2. *Penal Sanctions for Injury to Submarine Cables.* Article 113 of the LOS Convention requires states to adopt penal sanctions for certain acts of injury to a submarine cable. The language of Article 113 is similar to Article II of the 1884 Convention for the Protection of Submarine Cables, which provides that "[t]he breaking or injury of a submarine cable, done willfully or through culpable negligence, and resulting in the total or partial interruption or embarrassment of telegraphic communication, shall be a punishable offense[.]" Certain doubts arose as to the meaning of the word "willfully" in Article II of that Convention; an explanatory memorandum was agreed on in 1886, embodying the understanding "that the imposition of penal responsibility, mentioned in the said article, does not apply to cases of breaking or of injuries occasioned accidentally or necessarily in repairing a cable, when all precautions have been taken to avoid such breakings or damages." Charles I. Bevans, 1 U.S. Department of State, Treaties and Other International Agreements of the United States of America (1776–1949) 112. For U.S. law implementing the 1884 Convention, see 47 U.S.C. §§ 21–39. Are these U.S. laws, enacted in 1888 in the telegraph era, adequate to address injuries to today's sophisticated submarine fiber optic network? At the level of international law, are Articles 112–115 of the LOS Convention (which are substantially similar to Articles 26–29 of the 1958 High Seas Convention) and the 1884 Convention still adequate?

3. *Civil Remedies Relating to Injury to Submarine Cables.* According to Article II of the 1884 Convention for the Protection of Submarine Cables, criminal punishment for injury to submarine cables shall not bar civil actions for damages. Several national courts in fact have awarded civil damages to

the owners of cables injured by third parties. See, for example, Netherlands (PTT) & Post Office (London) v. Nedlloyd (Neth. Dist. Ct. of Rotterdam, 1977), 74 Intl. L. Rep. 212; AT&T Corp. v. Tyco Telcoms (U.S.) Inc., 255 F. Supp. 2d 294 (SDNY 2003). Article 114 of the LOS Convention also requires states to adopt laws and regulations providing that owners of a submarine cable or pipeline who break or injure another cable or pipeline shall bear the cost of repairs. Read LOS Convention, Article 115. Who is to be held responsible for injuries sustained by ship owners that lose gear in order to avoid injury to a cable or pipeline?

4. *Due Regard, the Freedom of Fishing, and the Freedom to Lay Submarine Cables*. We consider in Section G the important principle that particular freedoms on the high seas must be conducted with "due regard" for other freedoms. Does that principle apply with respect to submarine cables or pipelines in other zones of the oceans? As the excerpt above shows, fishing may interfere with submarine cables. Could the reverse be true as well? What steps should the submarine cable industry follow to take into account the interests of the fishing industry? What are the possibilities for cooperative planning to reconcile competing uses? See the website of the Oregon Fishermen's Cable Committee (http://www.ofcc.com/news.htm) for a discussion of various cooperative agreements negotiated by that Committee with fiber optic cable companies to protect fishing grounds and submarine cables. Note the significance of maps in assisting with planning. A map of the pipelines on the U.S. continental shelf in the Gulf of Mexico is available at the website of the U.S. Bureau of Ocean Energy Management, http://www.boem.gov.

F Other Freedoms

The 1958 High Seas Convention explicitly recognizes the freedoms of navigation, overflight, and fishing, and the freedom to lay submarine cables and pipelines. Article 2 of the 1958 Convention also refers to "other [freedoms] which are recognized by the general principles of international law." That phrase is not repeated in Article 87 of the LOS Convention. Article 87, however, adds the "freedom of scientific research" and the "freedom to construct artificial islands and other installations permitted under international law."

Are there yet other freedoms of the high seas? The words "inter alia" in Article 87(1), which also appear in the International Law Commission's draft and in Article 2 of the 1958 High Seas Convention, suggest there may be. See ILC, Summary Record of the 7th session, 320th meeting, ¶ 30, 1955–2 Y.B. Intl. L. Commn. 220, 222. The content of such additional freedoms has been debated. A 1956 suggestion of the International Law Commission that the freedom of the high seas included the freedom to explore or exploit the subsoil of the high seas was echoed by the United States. Report of the International Law Commission covering the work of its eighth session (UN Doc. A/3159), Article 27; 1956–2 Y.B. Intl. L. Commn. 253, 278. However, the deep seabed mining regime of Part XI of the LOS Convention, as modified by the 1994 Agreement concerning Part XI's implementation, has gained widespread acceptance. Under that regime, unilateral actions to explore for or recover seabed minerals beyond the limits of national jurisdiction would be regarded as illegal. See Chapter 11.

The launching of satellites from the high seas may be an "inter alia" freedom under Article 87(1). In March 1999 Sea Launch Co. launched a rocket from a floating platform stationed on the high seas 1,400 miles south of Hawaii. The company has since launched more than 30 satellites from this platform.

Several states have also conducted military exercises and weapons tests in areas of the high seas. Such exercises and tests must be conducted in accordance with applicable treaties and customary international law. The "due regard for the interests of other States in the exercise of the freedom of the high seas" clause of Article 87 of the LOS Convention, and the "peaceful uses" requirements of Articles 88 and 301, are among the limits on military activities on the high seas. These limits are considered in the next two sections of this chapter.

G Due Regard to Interests of Other States

As use of the high seas has become heavier, the potential for conflicts among uses has increased. Article 87 provides that all states must act with "due regard" for other states' interests in exercising the freedoms of the high seas. Similarly, Article 2 of the 1958 High Seas Convention requires that high seas freedoms "be exercised by all States with reasonable regard to the interests of other States in their exercise of the freedom of the high seas." Note also that Article 87 requires states to exercise "due regard for the rights under [the LOS] Convention with respect to activities in the Area," i.e., with respect to seabed mining beyond the limits of national jurisdiction. See Chapter 11.

The readings in this section primarily explore conflicts between weapons testing on the high seas, on the one hand, and rights concerning navigation, fishing, and the environment, on the other.

WARNING AREAS
The Commander's Handbook on the Law of Naval Operations ¶ 2.6.3 (NWP1–14M, July 2007)

All ships and aircraft, including warships and military aircraft, enjoy complete freedom of movement and operation on and over the high seas. For warships, this includes task force maneuvering, flight operations, military exercises, surveillance, intelligence gathering activities, and ordinance testing and firing. . . . All of these activities must be conducted with due regard for the rights of other nations and the safe conduct and operation of other ships and aircraft.

Any nation may declare a temporary warning area in international waters and airspace to advise other nations of the conduct of activities that, although lawful, are hazardous to navigation and/or overflight. The United States and other nations routinely declare such areas for missile testing, gunnery exercises, space vehicle recovery operations, and other purposes entailing some danger to other lawful uses of the high seas by others. Notice of the establishment of such areas must be promulgated in advance, in the form of a special warning to mariners, notice to mariners (NOTMAR), notice to airmen (NOTAM), Hydro Atlantic/Hydro Pacific (HYDROLANT/HRDROPAC) messages, and the Global Maritime Distress and Safety System.

Ships and aircraft of other nations are *not* required to remain outside a declared warning area, but are obliged to refrain from interfering with activities therein. Consequently, ships and aircraft of one nation may operate in a warning area within international waters and airspace declared by another nation, collect intelligence and observe the activities involved, subject to the requirement of due regard for the rights of the declaring nation to use international waters and airspace for such lawful purposes. The declaring nation may take reasonable measures including the use of proportionate force to protect the activities against interference.

Note

1. *Warning Areas and the Due Regard Principle.* Does the establishment of temporary warning zones for military exercises unreasonably interfere with the right of other states to navigate through or fish in those zones? Identify three or four factors that should be considered in determining whether interference is unreasonable.

LEGALITY OF USING THE HIGH SEAS IN CONNECTION WITH NUCLEAR WEAPONS TESTS IN THE PACIFIC OCEAN

Paper prepared by U.S. Delegation to UNCLOS I, Feb. 20, 1958, in Marjorie M. Whiteman, 4 Digest of International Law 546 (1965).

[The U.S. delegation to the First United Nations Conference on the Law of the Sea acknowledged that U.S. nuclear testing in and around the Marshall Islands in the Pacific Ocean required "a considerable amount of space to absorb their temporarily harmful effects." It also noted that concerns with long-range fallout "raises a question of the right to conduct such tests anywhere," but argued that the question should not be determined by a specialized law of the sea conference. In the course of its paper, the U.S. delegation addressed the issue of accommodation among uses of the oceans.]

The United States maintains that its actions . . . are not contrary to the principle of the freedom of the seas. Nor is there any specific rule of international law forbidding the acts in question.

In the first place it should be borne in mind that the principle of the freedom of the seas has been one of the major equalizing influences within the community of nations. This principle has given the smaller and less wealthy state[s] the opportunity to offset the otherwise natural advantages of the countries with extensive land areas.

A second cardinal point on this matter of the freedom of the seas is that this principle has never been ascribed any fixed content. This was most recently recognized by the ILC itself when it observed that the four specific freedoms enumerated in its Article 27 on the Freedom of the High Seas is not a "restrictive" list since the Commission was "aware that there are other freedoms." Commentary to Article 27, para. 2, Report of ILC 8th Sess., A/3159, p. 24 (1956). And since the conduct of military naval and air exercises, including weapons testing, has been one of the traditional uses of the high seas it is not surprising to find that the Commission did not denounce the use of the high seas for nuclear weapons tests despite considerable pressure to do so. . . .

. . . Every use by the nationals of one state interferes with, or adversely affects, to some extent the potential use of the seas or its resources by the nationals of other states. . . . While freedom of the seas was initially advanced in the interests of fishing and surface navigation, the principle has been sufficiently flexible to encompass the newer uses made possible by technological progress. For example, air and subsurface navigation are now uses of stature rivaling that of the traditional ones. Now electrically-guided missiles race through the air above the sea, oil wells are sunk into the continental shelf; and radar towers loom out of the waters far out at sea. Each use creates a new risk and an additional inconvenience for those who fish and navigate ocean waters.

Some uses with largely undesirable effects are unquestionably valid. Belligerent activity is tolerated even though it may very materially interfere with peaceful uses of the sea. Other examples, dumping unwanted ammunition, waste oil and excess ballast into the high seas, are less severe. And although the resulting water pollution is of growing concern, however, abolition is not envisaged—merely regulation so as to minimize interference with other rights.

Hence a prospective use would not seem to be invalid merely because some undesirable effects from the standpoint of other users of the sea will ensue from its exercise. The tolerable amount, i.e., the reasonable amount, would have to be determined case by case. In the case of military operations, nations have become accustomed to accepting more and more interference therefrom.

During the last 25 years the high seas have probably been used for military maneuvers and target practice more than at any time since the crystallization of the principle of the freedom of the seas.

Apparently there has been no essential change in attitude in recent years even though rather substantial portions of international space are being utilized as military aircraft target and maneuver ranges for relatively long periods of time. There are today numerous United States military aircraft practice zones over international waters in the Atlantic, Gulf and Pacific areas. And there are at present dozens of United States Navy, Army and Air Force training areas covering portions of the high seas just off Japan itself.

The British have similar military aircraft practice zones over portions of international waters near the British Isles. These are in such regular use that commercial aircraft must regularly detour them on flights to and from the continent.

In addition, there are extensive submarine exercise areas in portions of the high seas. And there is shore to sea artillery and anti-aircraft battery practice.

Nations have acquiesced in such use for many years. Its validity is so accepted that the standard texts rarely deal with the point. When they do, such as did the Harvard Research in 1929, the validity of these activities at some point on the high seas is at least implicitly recognized since the matter is discussed from the standpoint of the coastal state's right to insist that these activities should not be conducted near its shores. In this situation large land masses—Japan, the Philippines and New Guinea—are over a thousand miles from the outer edge of the testing area.

International acquiescence from ten years of testing at the Pacific Proving Grounds suggests its validity despite the comparatively large area necessary. This is reinforced by international acquiescence in (1) a comparably sized area for the British tests last year (roughly 900 miles square) and (2) an extensive area for British-Australian tests off the Northwestern coast of Australia, running 600 miles out to sea, the outer limits of which zone were within 67 miles of one Indonesian island and within 102 miles of Java.

Even the Soviet Union has had to make use of extensive portions of the high seas for military weapons purposes. Just last September the USSR conducted surface and air maneuvers and weapons exercises in the Barents and Kara Seas which necessitated a danger area approximately 1,900 × 400 miles, apparently the largest danger area of record....

The Delegation should bear in mind, however, it does not necessarily follow as seemingly suggested by McDougal and Schlei [The Hydrogen Bomb Tests in Perspective, 64 Yale L.J. 648 (1955)], that a nation may unilaterally appropriate for its exclusive use a portion of the high seas for this purpose. In particular, the United States has been careful not to claim the right to establish a prohibited or restricted area which is tantamount to closing off a portion of the seas as a matter of enforceable right, action customarily taken only within the limits of territorial waters.

In contrast Danger or Warning areas on the high seas are predicated on the principle of voluntary compliance. As a matter of comity these areas are generally observed.... International Law Situation and Documents (1956) of the U.S. Naval War College ... states in a Note at p. 627:

> The nuclear testing areas in question have been established as danger areas, warning all vessels and aircraft to stay clear, but not prohibiting them from entering the hazard area.

Observance on that basis presupposes, of course, the reasonableness of the area or zone from the standpoint of size, duration and location. On the basis of those objective standards the Danger Areas for the United States tests would seem internationally acceptable since the area is situated in a relatively remote portion of the ocean off the track of normal surface or air routes [an American airline is the only one which is required to detour from its usual route] and in an area that is not historically a fertile fishing ground.

Furthermore, the tests are now conducted in what is considered the less fruitful fishing months. And while the Japanese have claimed their observance of the Danger Area for the tests imposes a diversionary or detour burden on their fishermen, thus far there has been no demonstration [that] the tests have brought about a reduction in the normal level of earnings.

Most important, however, is the fact that there has been no protest [up to this time] of the United States conduct of its tests in the Pacific. In short the international community has recognized the international validity of the United States position.

It would appear, therefore, that the proper yardstick for resolving conflicts between uses of the high seas is more accurately reflected by the standards suggested by the ILC in Article 71 that one use "must not result in any unjustifiable interference with" the other freedoms of the seas.

Notes

1. *U.S. Nuclear Tests and Payments for Resulting Harm.* Beginning in 1946, the United States conducted nuclear weapons tests on atolls in the Pacific Ocean. The U.S. Atomic Energy Commission was authorized to establish danger zones, which U.S. citizens and other persons under U.S. jurisdiction were prohibited from entering. Other vessels were warned to stay clear of the areas, which covered extensive portions of the high seas. Why did the United States make this distinction?

On March 1, 1954, when the Japanese vessel *Fukuryu Maru* was sailing fourteen miles outside the nuclear testing area surrounding the island of Eniwetok in the Marshall Islands, radioactive fallout from a nuclear test injured 23 members of its crew; one of them died six months later. By an agreement effected by an exchange of notes on January 4, 1955, the United States tendered, ex gratia, "as an additional expression of its concern and regret over the injuries sustained" by the Japanese fishermen, the sum of US$ 2 million. A portion of this sum was to be distributed by the Japanese government to each of them in an equitable manner, taking into account not only their personal injuries but also the damage to the Japanese fishing industry resulting from the destruction of fish contaminated by radioactivity. A portion also went to repay the Japanese government for its medical and hospitalization expenses. 6 U.S.T. 1, 237 U.N.T.S. 197. See also Marjorie M. Whiteman, 4 Digest of International Law 565–67, 570–71 (1965). This same nuclear test also injured 82 people on the neighboring Rangelap Atoll, after an unexpected windshift. These people received medical care and other assistance, and the sum of US$ 950,000 was distributed in equal amounts to them. Id. at 567, 570.

2. *Proposals at UNCLOS I Concerning Nuclear Tests on the High Seas.* The use of the high seas for nuclear tests caused great controversy. At the First United Nations Law of the Sea Conference in 1958, Czechoslovakia, Poland, the Soviet Union, and Yugoslavia proposed including in the High Seas Convention an article stating "[s]tates are bound to refrain from testing nuclear weapons on the high seas." UN Doc. A/CONF.13/C.2/L.30 (1958), 4 UNCLOS I Official Records 124. India then stated "that there is a serious and genuine apprehension on the part of many States that nuclear explosions on the high seas constitute an infringement of the freedom of the seas," and proposed referring

the matter to the U.N. General Assembly for appropriate action. UN Doc. A/CONF.13/C.2/L.71 (1958), 4 id. 134. The Indian proposal was overwhelmingly adopted, and the four-power proposal was not put to a vote.

3. *Treaty Prohibition on Nuclear Tests*. The 1963 Limited Test Ban Treaty addresses nuclear weapons testing on the high seas. Article I(a) of the Treaty prohibits nuclear tests or explosions "under water, including territorial waters or high seas." Does this language cover tests under inland waters? Under the surface of the water, or only on or under the beds of oceans or other bodies of water? See Marjorie M. Whiteman, 11 Digest of International Law 790 (1968).

The 1963 Limited Test Ban Treaty entered into force for the United States on October 10, 1963. The Treaty has been widely accepted; as of September 1, 2013, 126 states were parties. France is one of the few major powers that has not accepted the Treaty. French nuclear testing has given rise to legal challenges relating to interference with the freedom of the high seas, as suggested in the following excerpt from the oral arguments in the 1974 Nuclear Tests case. As you read the excerpt, consider the advantages and disadvantages of responding to nuclear tests, or other activities posing significant threats to the ocean environment, through international litigation rather than through multilateral treaties such as the Limited Test Ban Treaty.

NUCLEAR TESTS CASE

Australia v. France, 1 International Court of Justice, Pleadings, Oral Arguments, Documents: Nuclear Tests Cases 514 (1974)

[From 1966 to 1974 the French government undertook a series of atmospheric tests of nuclear weapons in the South Pacific. A French-owned atoll, Mururoa, was used for these tests. During the testing periods each year "Prohibited Zones" for aircraft were declared around the atoll and "Dangerous Zones" were declared for both aircraft and ships. The zones extended into the high seas around the atoll. Mururoa is something less than 4,000 miles east of Australia. The Australian government claimed that the French tests caused radioactive fallout on Australian territory. Without effect, it protested the French activity through diplomatic channels.

On May 9, 1973, Australia brought the matter before the International Court of Justice by an Application founding jurisdiction on Article 17 of the 1928 General Act for the Pacific Settlement of International Disputes, read together with Articles 36(1) and 37 of the ICJ Statute. Alternatively, the Application relied on Article 36(2) of the Statute. By a letter dated May 16, 1973, France indicated that it believed the Court to be incompetent to entertain the case, and that it did not accept jurisdiction. The Court declined to remove the case from the Court's list.

By order of June 22, 1973, the Court specified interim measures in response to an Australian request under Article 41 of the ICJ Statute and Article 33 of the 1928 General Act. The Court ordered France to avoid nuclear tests causing fallout in Australia. 1973 I.C.J. 99. The Order called for memorials and oral argument on the questions of jurisdiction and the admissibility of the Australian Application.

The Australian government filed its memorial, but the French government failed to respond. When the case was argued in July of 1974, France did not appear. The French government continued its atmospheric tests in the late summer of 1973 and the summer of 1974.

In its Application, Australia claimed, inter alia, that "the interference with ships and aircraft on the high seas and in the superjacent airspace, and the pollution of the high seas by radioactive fall-out, constitute infringements of the freedom of the high seas." The following excerpt is from the oral argument by Australia's Solicitor General on the question of the admissibility of Australia's claim.]

MR. BYERS: Mr. President, I turn now to Australia's legal interest to require that France respect Australia's right to its freedom of the seas. There are two aspects of this question, namely, Australia's right to freedom of navigation and Australia's right to fish in uncontaminated waters.

Every legal right has its necessary correlative; necessary, because without it the right ceases to be such. Just as the right to territorial integrity has its correlative in the duty of each State to respect the integrity of each other State, so Australia's right to freedom of navigation has, as a correlative, the duty of other States neither to prevent nor impair its proper exercise. So too with Australia's right to fish. The correlative in this case also is the obligation neither to prevent Australia's proper exercise of its right nor to impair that exercise. The right is impaired, for example, either by denying the fishing fleets access to the fishing grounds or by contaminating the waters in which the fish are caught or those from which they migrate, whether by deliberately caused oil slicks or deliberately caused radioactive nuclear pollution.

Abstract considerations alone yield such a result. But the matter does not stop there, for on 17 December 1970, as the Court will remember, the General Assembly adopted resolution 2749 (XXV) part of which reads: "The sea-bed and ocean floor, and the subsoil thereof, beyond the limits of national jurisdiction . . . as well as [its] resources . . . are the common heritage of mankind."

It is no doubt true to say that the legal regime of freedom of the high seas differs from that which governs the international sea-bed viewed as part of the common heritage of mankind. But there is a common factor. In both cases one State may not appropriate those areas to the exclusion or limitation of the rights of others. The existence of this common factor and the necessarily related subject matters make reference to the common heritage of mankind legitimate, indeed necessary, in a consideration of those two aspects of the freedom of the high seas which I have mentioned.

The course I propose to follow is to deal with the closure by France of the high seas. Thereafter I shall discuss the effect of pollution of those seas by radio-active nuclear fallout. I shall in each case do so only to the extent necessary to establish Australia's legal interest to propound its claim that France's action in each regard is a breach of Australia's legal rights....

Let me now examine what the French Government has done. The French practice of declaring prohibited zones for aircraft and dangerous zones for shipping has been described in [our] Application. On 4 July 1973, in addition, it formally suspended navigation by all vessels in a proclaimed security zone surrounding Mururoa Atoll. [T]he American yacht Fri and the Canadian yacht Greenpeace III were forcibly boarded and seized and removed from the danger area. In 1974 the same powers have been reactivated in connection with the current tests.

Of the illegality of such closures of the high seas one of the foremost authorities on the law of the sea, Gilbert Gidel, had no doubt. He said, and this is my translation:

> It is not possible, therefore, in our opinion, to avoid the conclusion that the conduct of nuclear tests affecting areas of the high seas is contrary to actual rules of law applicable to those areas and covered by the term "freedom of the sea." [G. Gidel, "Explosions nucléaires experimentales et liberté de la haute mer," *Fundamental Problems of International Law, Festschrift für Jean Spiropoulos*, p. 198.]

The security zone created around Mururoa Atoll means that Australian vessels have been forbidden to sail there, and Australian aircraft have been forbidden to fly there during the periods of prohibition. The fact that they may or may not then wish to do so is immaterial. The point is that there is a legal question as between Australia and France concerning their right to do so. That question requires decision, and legal argument needs to be addressed to the Court for that decision to be made. In every meaning of the expression, it follows that a case which raises this question must be admissible. The additional *zones dangereuses* mean that the Australian vessels and aircraft may not exercise their rights of passage without the possibility of being subject to gross hazards....

Involved in this question is the determination of the state of customary international law. It is sufficient to demonstrate the extent to which State practice would need to be evaluated for this purpose if I recall that, in marked contrast with the current French practice to which I have referred, the current United States practice... is to prohibit entry into a warning area of 50 nautical miles radius around Amchitka Islands only to United States citizens and to persons subject to the jurisdiction of the United States. A decision on the question of law would need to take into account the fact that the United States delegation to the Law of the Sea Conference at Geneva in 1958 was explicitly instructed as follows:

> that action against foreign ships in the warning areas in the high seas around the Bikini and Eniewetok test sites was predicated on the principle of voluntary compliance and that there was no intention to drive away ships which did not comply. The only vessel in fact interfered with was an American yacht, owned by an American, and arrested for violation of a United States law applicable to United States citizens in the high seas. All this is set out in Whiteman's *Digest of International Law*, Volume 4, at page 595.

It appears, then, to come down to this: The Court must determine whether there is a special rule of international customary law derogating from the freedom of the seas so as to enable enclosure of areas of the high seas for the purpose of nuclear testing. If enclosure is legitimate, this could only be by virtue of a claim that nuclear testing is itself an exercise of the freedom of the seas, to which other exercises have to accommodate themselves even to the point of being entirely excluded or substantially subordinated.

The question, which will need to be examined at the merits stage, is whether the freedom of navigation can be reduced because the seas are used for what is alleged to be defence purposes.

In their well-known essay on nuclear testing in the *Yale Law Journal*, 1955 (64 *Yale Law Journal*, p. 648), Professor McDougal and Mr. Schlei propagated the notion that battlefleets on maneuvers had traditionally occupied areas of the ocean to the exclusion of other shipping. [In reply, Australia notes] that universal practice, as embodied in the clear range procedures of the navies of such countries as Great Britain and the United States, and of Australia and France as well, requires that the firing ship ensure that the range is clear before shell splash or missile splash is authorized, even in zones which are proclaimed as dangerous. Whiteman's *Digest* again, furnishes details of Soviet protests and American replies amply verifying this. (Whiteman's *Digest of International Law*, Vol. 4, pp. 552–553.)

While no-one would claim that the right of navigation was so absolute that gunnery practice would be illegal; neither would one wish to say that a right to gunnery practice is so absolute as to cancel the right of navigation. I have already submitted that it is now established as a proposition of law that the testing of nuclear weapons in the atmosphere is illegal and this would deprive the prohibition of navigation of any justification. But even if it were legal, it still would not follow that the assertion of the legality of the prohibition of navigation would be plausible, because the situation would fundamentally be no different from any other naval exercise on the high seas.

[T]here exists a drastic difference between gunnery practice and the atmospheric explosion of nuclear devices, not only in their respective natures but also in their respective extents.

True it was that an American and a Canadian vessel respectively were interfered with by the French navy, not an Australian vessel. True it is that this is a remote part of the ocean, outside regular shipping routes. France might perhaps say that Australia has suffered no injury since no ship of Australian nationality has been interfered with, and the likelihood of any such ship diverting because of the prohibition is slight.

Let us for a moment consider the consequences of such an approach being upheld. It would mean that no State which asserts its authority in the high seas contrary to the rule now enshrined in Article 1 of the Geneva Convention on the High Seas could be challenged in that assertion unless and until it interfered with the ships of another.

Now we all know that for jurisdictional reasons international legal procedures for remedying such interference are not always available. So, the existence of the remedy would then depend upon the fortuitous coincidence of interference with a flag ship of a State which has a jurisdictional basis for the remedy. The coincidence may or may not be likely, but one thing is certain, and that is that neighboring States with the most immediate interest in resisting illicit encroachments in the high seas might have no remedy except resistance by force.

It is precisely to avoid conflict at sea that international law necessarily invests each State with an interest in the maintenance of the freedom of the seas. Were it otherwise, force would be the only defense to wrongful action. We all know the powerful role played by effectiveness in the creation of derogations from legal principles in international relations. How could the consolidation into customary international law of originally illicit claims be prevented if one had to await the coincidence of circumstances to which I have referred before arresting their effects?

This, Mr. President, may be one reason why States have the right to protest against excessive maritime claims. The right to assert freedom of the seas is not limited to those States whose ships are immediately or directly affected by the unlawful action. In other words, all States have a legal interest in the freedom of the seas and each State is free to seek the recognition of that freedom by all available means of legal redress.

Some examples of protests which have been made are given in . . . the Australian Memorial. Two additional examples may be mentioned. On 18 September 1973 the Permanent Representatives of Egypt and the Syrian Arab Republic wrote to the President of the Security Council bringing to the attention of the Council the fact that a Cuban merchant ship had been attacked in the high seas by the Chilean Navy and Air Force and had suffered serious damage. The way in which these two countries expressed their interest is significant. They said that the attack was wholly incompatible "with the international rules of navigation recognized by States" (S/11001).

The Soviet Union made the same point when it protested on 11 May 1972 to the United States about the mining of Haiphong. Recalling Article 1 of the Convention on the High Seas, the Soviet Union protested at the alleged "violation of the universally recognized principle of freedom of navigation in direct threat to many States' vessels" (S/10643).

The fact, Mr. President, that States have a common interest in the freedom of the seas does not mean that they have no individual interest. . . .

Just how this general interest is also an individual one was made clear by this Court in the *Anglo-Norwegian Fisheries case* (*I.C.J. Reports* 1951, p. 116). The Judgment in that case confirms what may, at first, appear to be a slightly unusual proposition, namely that any maritime State, were it so minded, could have brought an action against Norway in respect of its claims. The Court spoke of:

> "The general toleration of foreign States with regard to the Norwegian practice is an unchallenged fact." (*Ibid.*, p. 138.) Later it spoke of the United Kingdom as "a maritime Power traditionally concerned with the law of the sea and concerned particularly to defend the freedom of the seas" (*ibid.*, p. 139).

Perhaps most importantly it said that:

> The notoriety of facts, the general toleration of the international community, Great Britain's position in the North Sea, her own interest in the question, and her prolonged abstention would in any case warrant [Norway's] enforcement of her system against the United Kingdom. (*Ibid.*)

The first passage of interest in this question is the reference to "Great Britain's position in the North Sea." This consideration obviously played a major role in the development of the Court's reasoning. Naturally, the Court felt confident in asserting that a country in the position of Great Britain would have taken action, indeed may even have instituted proceedings before the Court much earlier, had it really considered Norway's claim to be opposable. That factor alone, quite separate from her own interest in the question, would have conferred a legal interest on Great Britain.

This is not the stage of the proceedings at which it would be appropriate to lead substantial evidence concerning Australia's maritime and marine interests in the Pacific Ocean. But I am sure that the Court will be well aware that those interests are extensive and are of importance in the area. Like Great Britain in the North Sea, Australia has an established position in the South Pacific and has her own interest in the question of freedom of navigation in that area. Thus, this factor, the position of the country bringing the proceedings, is a relevant consideration at this stage and of itself is sufficient to confer a legal interest upon Australia to have this matter determined by this tribunal.

But, in addition to this, I recall the Court's reference to the United Kingdom as "a maritime power traditionally concerned with the law of the seas and concerned particularly to defend the freedom of the seas." It indicates that this fact alone would have given Great Britain standing to protest. Australia does not pretend to rival Great Britain as a general maritime power, but in the South Pacific she falls in the same category.

It is this interest in the protection of the freedom of the high seas that, apart from considerations as to her position in the Pacific, constitutes in large part the Australian interest in the present case, and which gives Australia standing to allege a breach of the fundamental freedoms of the sea by the French nuclear activities in the South Pacific area....

The consideration which this Court gave to the legal interest of States in the matter of fisheries leads me now to the question of Australia's interest in preventing the pollution of the sea by reason of nuclear fall-out. The fact that the tests are conducted at a remote place is not to the point. Fallout occurs in varying levels around the globe. Fisheries can be contaminated in various places. We hear much talk, at Caracas and elsewhere, of legal interests in respect of different types of anadromous and other migratory fish, which swim over vast distances and can ingest food which is contaminated by radioactive fall-out far from their home rivers or the places where they are caught....

...Progressively, from Article 25 of the Geneva Convention of the High Seas of 1958, the community of nations has seen to it that the grip of international law upon the preservation of the natural resources of the marine environment including the high seas from environmental hazards has become ever more tenacious. [O]ne thing is now absolutely clear, and that is the duty of States not to subject the natural resources of the high seas to any unwarranted environmental hazard.

[Mr. Byers cites statements from the 1970 Declaration of Principles Governing the Sea-Bed and the Subsoil Thereof Beyond the Limits of National Jurisdiction, the 1972 Declaration of Santo Domingo, the 1971 Draft Articles on Ocean Dumping adopted by the Intergovernmental Working Group on Marine Pollution, the 1972 London Convention on the Dumping of Wastes at Sea, the 1972 Oslo Convention for the Prevention of Marine Pollution, and Recommendation 92 of the 1972 U.N. Conference on the Human Environment at Stockholm. He continues:]

Principle 7 adopted by the 1972 Stockholm Conference sums up the position in the clearest of terms:

> States shall take all possible steps to prevent pollution of the seas by substances that are liable to create hazards to human health, to harm living resources and marine life, to damage amenities or to interfere with other legitimate uses of the sea....

Australia [submits] that all of this signifies the emergence of a rule of customary law to outlaw acts whereby pollution can occur, not merely to establish the liability of the polluter for the damage that actually results. For, if we are to await the damage, and the processes of proof, what chance then would we have of conserving the common heritage of mankind? There has never been any doubt about State responsibility for actual harm, as witness the payment of damages by the United States when a cargo of radioactive contaminated fish was landed in Japan following the United States Pacific tests. The current effort is to enhance the tenacity of the law so that actual harm does not result....

People naturally fear to eat fish from waters in which fallout has occurred. The consequence economically, upon the fishing and export industries, might not be inconsiderable. Indeed recently the Australian Department of Primary Industry was asked by an importer of fish to Italy for a certificate that the fish was free from radioactivity. It would seem that he was required by the Italian customs authorities to produce such a certificate before the fish could be landed. The requirement in question was an administrative one only, not backed, so far as Australia has been able to ascertain, by any law or regulation. The requirement does not seem to have been further enforced.

Nevertheless, this request strongly supports the existence of apprehension of danger to health from radioactive marine pollution. It further indicates the possibility of the existence of special burdens placed on Australia as a result of French testing....

... Australia is deeply involved in the South Pacific area. It is there that her maritime activities are carried on and her economic interests are centered.

Countries in the region of the Southern Pacific are necessarily affected because of the direct effect of the nuclear pollution on the economic and marine activities, and the environment of the region as a whole. [M]arine pollution can have international implications if it harms living resources that are part of the patrimony of all States, creates hazards to human health and hinders marine activities including fishing.

As the Australian Memorial notes, it is the protection of the freedom of the sea which constitutes in part the Australian interest in the present case and gives Australia a sufficient legal interest to allege a fundamental breach of that freedom by the French nuclear tests in the Pacific. The need of such an interest in all States was from Australia's point of view lent an additional emphasis by yesterday's nuclear explosion in the South Pacific.

Notes

1. *The Outcome of the Nuclear Tests Case and French Nuclear Testing in the Pacific*. Following the oral argument, while the case was under advisement, French officials made statements that the ICJ found constituted binding promises not to undertake further atmospheric testing beyond the 1974 series. On the basis of these statements, the Court found in its judgment of November 30, 1974, that Australia had obtained substantially everything sought in its Application. The Court, by nine votes to six, decided that it was "therefore not called upon to give a decision" on the Australian claim. 1974 I.C.J. 253, 272. The Court reached the same result in a related case brought by New Zealand. Nuclear Tests Case (New Zealand v. France), 1974 I.C.J. 457, 478.

Beginning in 1975, France conducted underground nuclear tests on atolls in the Pacific. A round of French tests in the mid-1990s led states in and bordering the Pacific Ocean to protest. New Zealand complained to the ICJ, arguing that it was entitled to "request an examination of the situation" related to France's 1974 commitment concerning its future conduct, in accordance with paragraph 63 of the Court's 1974 decision. New Zealand cited evidence concerning the leakage of radioactivity into the marine environment following testing on atolls, and the resultant risk of serious harm to the marine environment. Request for an Examination of the Situation, 21 August 1995, available at http://www.icj-cij.org/docket/files/97/7187.pdf. New Zealand argued that resumption of underground nuclear testing would breach international law by violating the right to freedom of the high seas, as well as other rights claimed in its 1973 Application. Id., ¶¶ 13, 72. The Court, however, dismissed New Zealand's Request, noting that the 1974 challenge concerned atmospheric testing, and that the more recent French testing was non-atmospheric. Request for an Examination of the Situation in Accordance with Paragraph 63 of the Court's Judgment of 20 December 1974 in the Nuclear Tests Case (New Zealand v. France), 1995 I.C.J. 288. Furthermore, the Court lacked jurisdiction over an entirely new challenge to France's testing, because France had withdrawn its acceptance of the Court's jurisdiction under Article 36(2) of the ICJ Statute following the Court's 1974 decisions. Judge Weeramantry, Judge Koroma, and Judge ad hoc Palmer filed dissenting opinions, noting the risk of contamination of the marine environment and arguing that New Zealand had made a sufficiently compelling case to allow the court to reexamine the situation.

Non-governmental organizations such as Greenpeace have been involved in efforts to publicize and protest French nuclear testing in the Pacific. In 1985, French secret service agents affixed mines to a Greenpeace vessel, the *Rainbow Warrior*, in a harbor in New Zealand. The mines detonated as the vessel was leaving to participate in further protests. The incident led to numerous national and international legal proceedings, including criminal proceedings brought by New Zealand against the French secret agents who affixed the mines that sank the *Rainbow Warrior*; claims brought by individual family members of a photographer killed aboard the *Rainbow Warrior* that resulted in a negotiated settlement; two arbitrations between New Zealand and France, 74 Intl. L. Rep. 241 (1986) and 82 Intl. L. Rep. 500 (1990); and a 1987 arbitration between Greenpeace, as the owner of the vessel, and France, in which the arbitral tribunal ordered France to pay Greenpeace US$ 8.1 million. See Christopher Harding, Vingt Ans Après: *Rainbow Warrior*, Legal Ordering and Legal Complexity, 10 Singapore Y.B. Intl. L. 99 (2006); Philip Shabecoff, France Must Pay Greenpeace $8 Million in Sinking of Ship, N.Y. Times, Oct. 3, 1987 at A2.

2. *Standing before the International Court and Obligations Erga Omnes.* In addition to establishing the jurisdiction of the ICJ to hear the 1974 Nuclear Tests case between itself and France, Australia had to demonstrate that the case was admissible. One admissibility issue was essentially whether Australia had "standing" to bring the matter to the Court. Should Australia have standing when, as Mr. Byers conceded, the French navy interfered with U.S. and Canadian vessels, rather than an Australian vessel? Alternatively, should every state, even if not a maritime power, have standing to complain about France's nuclear tests on the high seas? On what grounds?

In dictum in the Case Concerning the Barcelona Traction, Light & Power Co., Second Phase (Belgium v. Spain), 1970 I.C.J. 3, the ICJ recognized the concept of obligations erga omnes:

> [A]n essential distinction should be drawn between the obligations of a State towards the international community as a whole, and those

> arising vis-à-vis another State in the field of diplomatic protection. By their very nature the former are the concern of all States. In view of the importance of the rights involved, all States can be held to have a legal interest in their protection; they are obligations *erga omnes*.
>
> Such obligations derive, for example, in contemporary international law, from the outlawing of acts of aggression, and of genocide, as also from the principles and rules concerning the basic rights of the human person, including protection from slavery and racial discrimination.

Id. at 32.

Should serious threats to the marine environment qualify as erga omnes violations? Should any state be able to pursue a claim with respect to such violations? If so, to what remedies should that state be entitled? In 1976, the International Law Commission endorsed the concept of erga omnes obligations. The Commission accepted the list of obligations the ICJ noted in the Barcelona Traction case, and also suggested that obligations essential to preservation of the human environment—such as those prohibiting massive pollution of the seas or the atmosphere—qualified as erga omnes obligations. UNGAOR, 31st Sess., Supp. No. 10 at 170, UN Doc. A/31/10 (1976), Article 19(3), reprinted in 1976–2 Y.B. Intl. L. Commn. 73. Article 48 of the ILC's 2001 Draft Articles on Responsibility of States for Internationally Wrongful Acts provides: "Any State other than an injured State is entitled to invoke the responsibility of another state . . . if [t]he obligation breached is owed to a group of States including that State, and is established for the protection of a collective interest of the group." GA Res. 56/83, Annex (2001). See also Edith Brown Weiss, Invoking State Responsibility in the Twenty-first Century, 96 Am. J. Intl. L. 798 (2002), and the discussion of erga omnes in the Responsibilities and Obligations of States Sponsoring Persons and Entities with Respect to Activities in the Area case, excerpted in Chapter 11, Section D. For discussion of some of the dramatic changes in the field of international environmental law as applied to the oceans, see Chapters 12 and 13 below.

3. *The Common Heritage Principle*. Mr. Byers drew an analogy between the freedom of the high seas and the common heritage principle, highlighting the point that "one State may not appropriate" the high seas "to the exclusion or limitation of the rights of others." Features often associated with the common heritage principle include:

- a prohibition of acquisition of, or exercise of sovereignty over, the area or resources in question;
- the vesting of rights to the resources in question in humankind as a whole;

- reservation of the area in question for peaceful purposes;
- protection of the natural environment;
- an equitable sharing of benefits associated with the exploitation of the resources in question, paying particular attention to the interests and needs of developing states; and
- governance via a common management regime.

John E. Noyes, The Common Heritage of Mankind: Past, Present, and Future, 40 Den. J. Intl. L. & Poly. 447, 450–51 (2012). The common heritage principle has been linked to the regime for mining the seabed beyond the limits of national jurisdiction, a topic we explore in Chapter 11.

4. *Nuclear Activities on the High Seas*. Nuclear testing is only one of many threats to the oceans posed by nuclear activities. Other challenges include: the shipment of depleted and reprocessed nuclear fuel; accidents or runoff involving nuclear plants and waste storage facilities in coastal zones; nuclear-powered warships carrying nuclear weapons (with both warships and weapons having occasionally been lost at sea); the transport of weapons of mass destruction by terrorists or terrorist attacks on nuclear vessels; and the dumping of radioactive waste from ships. How international law will address the legacy of nuclear activities and ongoing risks presents extraordinarily difficult challenges. See The Oceans in the Nuclear Age: Legacies and Risks (David D. Caron & Harry N. Scheiber eds., 2010), reviewed in John E. Noyes, Book Review, 106 Am. J. Intl. L. 191 (2012).

5. *Evaluating the Due Regard Principle*. Do the materials in this section suggest that the due regard principle is so indeterminate that its application by different decision makers will necessarily be unpredictable? What factors and values should lead a decision maker to conclude that a particular use of the high seas is undertaken either with or without due regard for other uses? What concerns do the materials in this section suggest about the feasibility of relying on broad international law principles, such as the due regard principle, to regulate the unique dangers of nuclear activities or other intensive uses of the oceans? In light of increased knowledge about the dangers of radiation, should the declaration of an exclusion zone for purposes of nuclear testing ever be considered a reasonable use of the high seas?

H Reservation of the High Seas for Peaceful Purposes

Article 88 of the LOS Convention provides that "[t]he high seas shall be reserved for peaceful purposes." Article 301 of the LOS Convention further requires that states, in exercising their rights and duties under the Convention, "shall refrain from any threat or use of force against the territorial integrity or political independence of any State, or in any other manner inconsistent with the principles of international law embodied in the Charter of the United Nations." The LOS Convention does not define "peaceful purposes."

Despite some debate at UNCLOS III, these provisions do not preclude the use of the high seas for lawful military activities. For centuries, the navies of numerous states have engaged in various activities on the oceans, including military exercises, surveillance, and law enforcement. As long as such military uses comply with the U.N. Charter and other applicable rules of international law, they are permitted on the high seas. In contrast, no state may undertake on the high seas an act that constitutes an unlawful threat or use of force, as proscribed under Article 2(4) of the U.N. Charter.

This section discusses three instances in which military actions on the high seas interfered with navigation and, in some cases, overflight. As you read about these events, evaluate the role of international law in these highly politicized situations, consider what forums are available to evaluate the legality of the military actions, and assess the efficacy of those forums.

1 *The 1962 Cuban Missile Crisis*

In 1962, the United States obtained information that the Soviet Union was secretly constructing nuclear missile sites in Cuba. The United States responded by announcing its intent to establish a "strict quarantine" around Cuba to prevent military equipment from entering Cuba. The United States also sought the collective assistance of the Organization of American States under the 1947 Inter-American Treaty of Reciprocal Assistance (the Rio Treaty).

THE SOVIET THREAT TO THE AMERICAS
Address by President John F. Kennedy (Oct. 22, 1962), 47 Dept. State Bull. 715 (1962)

Neither the United States of America nor the world community of nations can tolerate deliberate deception and offensive threats on the part of any nation, large or small. . . .

For many years both the Soviet Union and the United States, recognizing this fact, have deployed strategic nuclear weapons with great care, never upsetting the precarious status quo which insured that these weapons would not be used in the absence of some vital challenge. Our own strategic missiles have never been transferred to the territory of any other nation under a cloak of secrecy and deception; and our history, unlike that of the Soviets since the end of World War II, demonstrates that we have no desire to dominate or conquer any other nation or impose our system upon its people. Nevertheless, American citizens have become adjusted to living daily on the bull's eye of Soviet missiles located inside the USSR or in [its] submarines. . . .

Acting, therefore, in the defense of our own security and of the entire Western Hemisphere, and under the authority entrusted to me by the Constitution as endorsed by the resolution of the Congress, I have directed that the following initial steps be taken immediately:

> First: To halt this offensive buildup, a strict quarantine on all offensive military equipment under shipment to Cuba is being initiated. All ships of any kind bound for Cuba from whatever nation or port will, if found to contain cargoes of offensive weapons, be turned back. This quarantine will be extended, if needed, to other types of cargo and carriers. . . .
>
> Fifth: We are calling tonight for an immediate meeting of the Organ of Consultation, under the Organization of American States, to consider this threat to hemisphere security and to invoke articles 6 and 8 of the Rio Treaty in support of all necessary action. . . .
>
> Sixth: Under the Charter of the United Nations, we are asking tonight that an emergency meeting of the Security Council be convoked without delay to take action against this latest Soviet threat to world peace. Our resolution will call for the prompt dismantling and withdrawal of all offensive weapons in Cuba, under the supervision of U.N. observers, before the quarantine can be lifted.
>
> Seventh and finally: I call upon Chairman Khrushchev to halt and eliminate this clandestine, reckless, and provocative threat to world peace and to stable relations between our two nations. . . .

This nation is prepared to present its case against the Soviet threat to peace, and our own proposals for a peaceful world, at any time and in any forum—in the OAS, in the United Nations, or in any other meeting that could be useful—without limiting our freedom of action.

RESOLUTION OF COUNCIL OF THE ORGANIZATION OF AMERICAN STATES

Meeting as the Provisional Organ of Consultation of Oct. 23, 1962, 47 Dept. State Bull. 722 (1962)

Whereas,

The Inter-American Treaty of Reciprocal Assistance of 1947 (Rio Treaty) recognizes the obligation of the American Republics to "provide for effective reciprocal assistance to meet armed attacks against any American state and in order to deal with threats of aggression against any of them." . . .

The Council of the Organization of American States, Meeting as the Provisional Organ of Consultation, Resolves:

> 1. To call for the immediate dismantling and withdrawal from Cuba of all missiles and other weapons with any offensive capability;
>
> 2. To recommend that the member states, in accordance with Articles 6 and 8 of the Inter-American Treaty of Reciprocal Assistance, take all measures, individually and collectively, including the use of armed force, which they may deem necessary to ensure that the Government of Cuba cannot continue to receive from the Sino-Soviet powers military material and related supplies which may threaten the peace and security of the Continent and to prevent the missiles in Cuba with offensive capability from ever becoming an active threat to the peace and security of the Continent.

Notes

1. *Proclamation Authorizing Interception of Vessels.* On the basis of the Resolution of the OAS Council, President Kennedy issued a proclamation effective October 24, 1962 authorizing: the interception of any vessel proceeding toward Cuba for the purpose of identifying it and its cargo; a visit and search of any such vessel; directing it, if carrying prohibited material, to proceed to another destination; and taking it into custody if it failed or refused to obey such direction. 47 Dept. State Bull. 717 (1962). In a letter delivered on October 24, 1962 to President Kennedy, Soviet Chairman Khrushchev characterized this action as a "naval blockade" in violation of international law:

> The Soviet Government considers that the violation of the freedom to use international waters and international air space is an act of aggression which pushes mankind toward the abyss of a world nuclear-missile war. Therefore, the Soviet Government cannot instruct the captains of Soviet vessels bound for Cuba to observe the orders of American naval forces blockading that Island. Our instructions to Soviet mariners are to observe strictly the universally accepted norms of navigation in international waters and not to retreat one step from them. And if the American side violates these rules, it must realize what responsibility will rest upon it in that case. Naturally we will not simply be bystanders with regard to piratical acts by American ships on the high seas. We will then be forced

> on our part to take the measures we consider necessary and adequate in order to protect our rights. We have everything necessary to do so.

U.S. Department of State, Foreign Relations of the United States, 1961–1963, Vol. XI, Doc. 61. After an exchange of messages between the U.S. and Soviet governments, the Soviet Union agreed to remove the missiles and bombers from Cuba, and the United States terminated the interdiction of deliveries to Cuba. 47 Dept. State Bull. 740–46, 762, 874–75, 918 (1962).

2. *Collective Defense under the Rio Treaty.* Article 6 of the 1947 Inter-American Treaty of Reciprocal Assistance (the Rio Treaty) provides that the Organ of Consultation shall meet to agree upon "appropriate measures" to be taken for the common defense of any American country whose territory, sovereignty, or political independence is threatened by an act of aggression that is not an armed attack. Article 8 authorizes several possible measures that the Organ of Consultation may take, including "partial or complete interruption of economic relations or of rail, sea, air, postal, telegraphic, telephonic, and radiotelephonic or radiotelegraphic communications." Both the United States and Cuba were parties to the Rio Treaty at the time of the Cuban missile crisis.

3. *Use of Force under the U.N. Charter.* Article 2(4) of the U.N. Charter prohibits the "threat or use of force against the territorial integrity or political independence of any state." There are, however, several important exceptions. Article 51 recognizes "the inherent right of individual or collective self-defence" against "armed attacks." Article 52 states that "[n]othing in the present Charter precludes the existence of regional arrangements or agencies for dealing with such matters relating to the maintenance of international peace and security as are appropriate for regional action provided that such arrangements or agencies and their activities are consistent with the Purposes and Principles of the United Nations." However, Article 53 provides that "no enforcement action shall be taken under regional arrangements or by regional agencies without the authorization of the Security Council." Did the naval quarantine and interception of vessels violate the U.N. Charter? Was the OAS Council's Resolution a lawful exercise of the right of collective self-defense under U.N. Charter Articles 51–53? Would the Security Council have been an effective forum for resolving the Cuban missile crisis? Both the United States and the Soviet Union (now Russia) are permanent members of the U.N. Security Council, with the right to veto any proposal brought before the Council.

4. *The 1958 High Seas Convention and the LOS Convention.* At the time of the Cuban missile crisis, the United States was a party to the 1958 High Seas Convention, which had just entered into force on September 30, 1962. The 1958 High Seas Convention does not contain provisions comparable to

Articles 88 and 301 of the 1982 LOS Convention. In light of other applicable law, such as the U.N. Charter, what, if anything, do Articles 88 and 301 add that is legally relevant?

5. *Blockades and Quarantines.* The United States characterized its action as a "quarantine"; the Soviet Union characterized it as a blockade. What is the difference? According to one U.S. authority:

> Although it has been compared to and used synonymously with blockade, quarantine is a peacetime military action that bears little resemblance to a true blockade.... Quarantine is distinguished from blockade, in that:
>
> 1. Quarantine is a measured response to a threat to national security or an international crisis; blockade is an act of war against an identified belligerent.
> 2. The goal of quarantine is de-escalation and return to the *status quo ante* or other stabilizing arrangement; the goal of a blockade is denial and degradation of an enemy's capability with the ultimate end-state being capitulation in armed conflict.
> 3. Quarantine is selective in proportional response to the perceived threat; blockade requires impartial application to all nations—discrimination by a blockading belligerent renders the blockade legally invalid.
>
> Maritime quarantine is an action designed to address crisis-level confrontations during peacetime that present extreme threats to U.S. forces or security interests, with the ultimate goal of returning conditions to a stable *status quo*.

The Commander's Handbook on the Law of Naval Operations, ¶ 4.4.8 (NWP1–14M, July 2007).

2 *The 1982 Falkland/Malvinas War*

Both Argentina and the United Kingdom have claimed the Falkland Islands (Malvinas) in the South Atlantic, although the British government has controlled them. When Argentina, on April 2, 1982, occupied the Islands, the U.N. Security Council immediately called for the withdrawal of Argentine forces from the Islands and for an immediate cessation of hostilities. UN Doc. S/RES/502 (1982). The U.N. Secretary-General tried to promote a cease-fire and a negotiated end to the Falkland/Malvinas conflict.

Maritime exclusion zones played a significant role in the Falkland/Malvinas war. The United Kingdom responded to Argentina's occupation of the Islands by establishing a maritime exclusion zone around the Islands within a 200-

nautical-mile radius, seeking to stop the flow of Argentine reinforcements to the Islands. The United Kingdom threatened to sink any Argentine ship entering the zone, and sent a fleet to the South Atlantic to recover the Islands "in the exercise of the inherent right of self-defense." At the end of April 1982, the United Kingdom proclaimed a total exclusion zone, banning the ships of all nations from the 200-nautical-mile zone around the Islands. The Soviet Union protested this extension of the scope of the zone, considering it a violation of the 1958 High Seas Convention. Argentina responded with the creation of its own 200-nautical-mile zone, extending from Argentina and all the contested islands in the South Atlantic. In Argentina's zone, all British ships and aircraft, whether military or civil, including even fishing vessels, were to be considered as "hostile and treated accordingly." The United Kingdom responded on May 7, 1982, by announcing that it would treat as hostile any Argentine warship or plane found beyond twelve nautical miles of the Argentine mainland. Several Argentine and British vessels were sunk during the Falkland/Malvinas war. The hostilities ended with the British reoccupation of the Islands and the surrender of Argentine forces.

AMERADA HESS SHIPPING CORP. v. ARGENTINE REPUBLIC

830 F.2d 421 (2d Cir. 1987)

FEINBERG, Chief Justice:

This case presents the important question whether a federal district court has jurisdiction over a claim that a foreign sovereign, in violation of international law, attacked on the high seas a neutral ship engaged in the United States domestic trade. Amerada Hess Shipping Corporation (Amerada) and United Carriers, Inc. (United) appeal from a decision of the United States District Court for the Southern District of New York... dismissing their complaint for lack of jurisdiction. Appellants argue that both the Alien Tort Statute, 28 U.S.C. § 1350, and the Foreign Sovereign Immunities Act (FSIA), 28 U.S.C. §§ 1330, 1602–1611, provide jurisdiction over their claims that the Republic of Argentina destroyed an oil tanker on the high seas in violation of international law. We conclude that the Alien Tort Statute[1] does provide jurisdiction and that the FSIA does not bar it. Accordingly, we reverse and remand to the district court.

---

1 The Alien Tort Statute, 28 U.S.C. § 1350, provides: "The district courts shall have original jurisdiction of any civil action by an alien for a tort only, committed in violation of the law of nations or a treaty of the United States." [Eds.]

I Background

Because the district court dismissed United's complaint for lack of jurisdiction, we must accept appellants' allegations as true. In 1977, Amerada entered a long-term time-charter agreement with United for use of the oil tanker HERCULES. Amerada used HERCULES to carry oil from Alaska, around the southern tip of South America, to its refinery in the United States Virgin Islands. This route took HERCULES near the area in the South Atlantic where, in April 1982, an armed conflict began between Argentina and the United Kingdom that became known in this country as the Falklands War.

On May 25, 1982, HERCULES embarked from the Virgin Islands, without cargo but fully fueled, headed for Alaska. On June 3, in an effort to protect United States interest ships, the United States Maritime Administration telexed to both the United Kingdom and Argentina a list of United States flag vessels and United States interest Liberian tankers (like HERCULES) that would be traversing the South Atlantic, to ensure that these neutral vessels would not be attacked. The list included HERCULES. By June 8, HERCULES was about 600 nautical miles off the Argentine coast and nearly 500 miles from the Falkland Islands, in international waters, well outside the "exclusion zones" declared by the warring parties. That afternoon, HERCULES was attacked without warning in three different strikes by Argentine aircraft using bombs and air-to-surface rockets.

Following these attacks, HERCULES, damaged but not destroyed, headed for safe refuge in the port of Rio de Janeiro, Brazil. Although HERCULES arrived safely in Brazil, her deck and hull had both suffered extensive damage, and a bomb that had penetrated her side remained undetonated in one of her tanks. Following an investigation by the Brazilian navy, United determined that it would be unreasonably hazardous to attempt removal of the undetonated bomb. Accordingly, on July 20, 1982, approximately 250 miles off the Brazilian coast, HERCULES was scuttled. United's loss on the sunken ship is claimed at [US$] 10,000,000 and Amerada's loss on the fuel that went down with the ship is claimed at [US$] 1,901,259.07.

Following a series of unsuccessful attempts to receive a hearing of their claims by the Argentine government or to retain Argentine attorneys to prosecute their claims in the courts of that country, appellants filed their suits in the district court. The district court found that a "foreign state is subject to jurisdiction in the courts of this nation if, and only if, an FSIA exception empowers the court to hear the case." 638 F. Supp. at 75. Concluding that no FSIA exception covered these facts, the district court dismissed the suits for lack of jurisdiction. This consolidated appeal followed.

II Violation of International Law

The facts alleged by appellants, if proven, would constitute a clear violation of international law. "The law of nations 'may be ascertained by consulting the works of jurists, writing professedly on public law; or by the general usage and practice of nations; or by judicial decisions recognizing and enforcing that law.'" *Filartiga v. Pena-Irala*, 630 F.2d 876, 880 (2d Cir. 1980) (quoting *United States v. Smith*, 18 U.S. (5 Wheat.) 153, 160–61 (1820)).... In this case, treaties, case law and treatises establish that Argentina's conduct, as alleged by appellants, violates settled principles of international law.

International treaties and conventions dating at least as far back as the last century recognize the right of a neutral ship to free passage on the high seas. Broad international recognition of the rights of neutrals can be found in paragraph 3 of the Declaration of Paris of 1856: "Neutral goods, with the exception of contraband of war, are not liable to capture under enemy's flag."

A more contemporary statement of the international concern and accord on this issue may be found in the Geneva Convention on the High Seas of 1958 (Convention on the High Seas), to which both Argentina and the United States were signatories. The Convention on the High Seas maps the general usage and practice of nations with regard to the rights of neutral ships in time of war. Article 22 of that treaty states that a warship encountering a foreign merchant vessel on the high seas may not board her without grounds for suspecting her of engaging in piracy, or the slave trade, or traveling under false colors. Even when there are grounds for such suspicion, the proper course is to investigate by sending an officer to inspect the ship's documents or even to board her, not to commence an attack. If such inspection fails to support the suspicions, the merchant vessel shall "be compensated for any loss or damage that may have been sustained." Article 23 of the Convention on the High Seas makes similar provisions for aircraft that have grounds to suspect a neutral vessel. Clearly, Argentina's alleged conduct in this case, bombing HERCULES and refusing compensation, violates the Convention on the High Seas. More recently, the Law of the Sea Convention of 1982 explicitly incorporated these provisions into its text. Argentina is a signatory to the Law of the Sea Convention and the United States has endorsed the relevant sections of it.

Other international accords adopted by the United States supporting a similar view of the rights of neutral ships include the [Declaration adopted by the] London Naval Conference of 1909, the International Convention Concerning the Rights and Duties of Neutral Powers in Naval War (Hague Convention, 1907) and the Pan-American Convention Relating to Maritime Neutrality of 1928, to which Argentina was a signatory. No agreement has been called to our attention that would cast doubt on this line of authority.

As to "judicial decisions recognizing and enforcing" the rights of neutral ships on the high seas, federal courts have long recognized in a variety of contexts that attacking a merchant ship without warning or seizing a neutral's goods on the high seas requires restitution. See, e.g., *Talbot v. Jansen*, 3 U.S. (3 Dall.) 133, 161 (1795); *The Lusitania*, 251 F. 715, 732–36 (S.D.N.Y. 1918) (dictum); cf. The I'm Alone (Canada v. United States), 3 U.N. Rep. Int. Arb. Awards 1609 (1933). Similarly, the academic literature on the rights of neutrals is of one voice with regard to a neutral's right of passage. See, e.g., Rappaport, "Freedom of the Seas," 2 Encyclopedia of Amer. For. Policy 387 (1978); Restatement of Foreign Relations Law of the United States (Revised) § 521 reporters' note 1, § 522 (Tent. Draft No. 6 1985).

In short, it is beyond controversy that attacking a neutral ship in international waters, without proper cause for suspicion or investigation, violates international law. Indeed, the relative paucity of cases litigating this customary rule of international law underscores the long-standing nature of this aspect of freedom of the high seas. Where the attacker has refused to compensate the neutral, such action is analogous to piracy, one of the earliest recognized violations of international law. See 4 W. Blackstone, Commentaries 68, 72. Argentina has cited no contrary authority. Accordingly, we turn to the jurisdictional ramifications of our holding that appellants have stated a claim of a violation of international law.

[The Second Circuit concludes that the Alien Tort Statute provided jurisdiction over Argentina, and that the Foreign Sovereign Immunities Act did not preempt the jurisdictional grant of the Alien Tort Statute.]

Notes

1. *Law of Naval Warfare.* Was the Falklands/Malvinas conflict governed by the law of the sea? The exercise of the high seas freedoms is subject to "other rules of international law." LOS Convention, Article 87(1). In times of armed conflict, a special body of international law (lex specialis) referred to as the "law of war" may displace otherwise applicable rules of international law. The law of war encompasses international humanitarian law. The 1949 Geneva Conventions, as amended by the 1977 Protocols, apply primarily to land warfare. In 1986, the 25th International Conference of the Red Cross adopted Resolution VII, noting that "some areas of international humanitarian law relating to sea warfare are in need of reaffirmation and clarification on the basis of existing fundamental principles of international humanitarian law" and calling on "governments to co-ordinate their efforts in appropriate fora in order to review the necessity and the possibility of updating the relevant texts of international humanitarian

law relating to sea warfare." In response, the San Remo International Institute of International Law convened a series of annual meetings, in cooperation with a number of other institutions, including the International Committee of the Red Cross. After seven years of collaboration, the Institute adopted the non-binding San Remo Manual on International Law Applicable to Armed Conflicts at Sea (Louise Doswald-Beck ed., 1995), available at http://www.icrc.org. See also The Commander's Handbook on the Law of Naval Operations (NWP1–14M, July 2007) published by the U.S. Department of Navy, available at http://www.lawofwar.org.

2. *Exclusion Zones*. How do the exclusion zones established by the United Kingdom and Argentina differ from the temporary warning areas that states may declare for gunnery exercises or to recover space vehicles, as discussed in Section G? During times of armed conflict, should belligerent nations have the right to establish exclusion zones that interfere with the freedom of navigation of enemy vessels? Of vessels flying the flag of states that are not a party to the conflict? What are the practical reasons for establishing exclusion zones around areas of active conflict? Were the 200-nautical-mile zones established by Argentina and the United Kingdom an appropriate size? Would the attack on the *Hercules* have been legal had the vessel been inside a declared exclusion zone?

3. *Neutral Merchant Vessels*. Under the law of neutrality, vessels flying the flags of neutral states are immune from attack and capture during a war unless they are engaged in certain specific activities, such as trading contraband with a belligerent, transporting enemy armed forces, operating under enemy control, or attempting to breach a blockade. Furthermore, merchant vessels sailing in a convoy accompanied by warships, and flying the same flag as the accompanying warships, are exempt from visit and search by a belligerent warship seeking to ensure that the merchant vessels are not carrying contraband. What international law evidence did the Second Circuit rely on to support its conclusion "that attacking a neutral ship in international waters, without proper cause for suspicion or investigation, violates international law"? If a state attacks a neutral merchant vessel on the high seas in violation of international law, what recourse is available to the owner of the merchant vessel or its cargo? The Amerada Hess case was an attempt to use a national court to challenge the legality of the Argentinian attack.

4. *The U.S. Foreign Sovereign Immunities Act*. On appeal of the Amerada Hess case, the U.S. Supreme Court overturned the decision of the Second Circuit on the ground that the Foreign Sovereign Immunities Act (FSIA) provides the sole basis for U.S. courts to exercise subject matter jurisdiction over foreign governments. A violation of international law is not, in and of itself, a basis for jurisdiction in U.S. courts, unless the violation falls within an

enumerated FSIA exception to immunity. Because the plaintiff could not prove that Argentina's acts fell within an enumerated FSIA exception to immunity, jurisdiction was lacking. Argentine Republic v. Amerada Hess Shipping Corp., 488 U.S. 428 (1989). One effect of the 1976 FSIA was to reverse the presumption with respect to immunity: prior to the FSIA, Argentina would have had to prove that it was entitled to immunity; the plaintiff would not have had to demonstrate that there was an exception to immunity. See Victory Transport, Inc. v. Comisaria General, 336 F.2d 354 (2d Cir. 1964), cert. denied, 381 U.S. 934 (1965).

5. *Violations of International Law and Sovereign Immunity*. Because of the Supreme Court's ruling concerning sovereign immunity, the Court did not reach the Second Circuit's conclusion that Argentina's alleged bombing of the *Hercules* violated international law. Should a state that has violated international law be immune from jurisdiction in U.S. court? Should the U.S. Congress amend the FSIA to provide that a foreign government's violation of international law will constitute an exception to immunity? What other redress may be available to a person injured by a state's violation of international law?

DECLARATION OF A ZONE OF PEACE AND CO-OPERATION OF THE SOUTH ATLANTIC

UN Doc. A/RES/41/11 (1986)

The General Assembly . . .

Recalling the principles and norms of international law applicable to ocean space, in particular the principle of the peaceful uses of the oceans,

Convinced that the establishment of a zone of peace and cooperation in the South Atlantic would contribute significantly to the strengthening of international peace and security and to promoting the principles and purposes of the United Nations,

1. *Solemnly declares* the Atlantic Ocean, in the region situated between Africa and South America, a "Zone of peace and co-operation of the South Atlantic";

2. *Calls upon* all States of the zone of the South Atlantic to promote further regional cooperation, *inter alia*, for social and economic development, the protection of the environment, the conservation of living resources and the peace and security of the whole region;

3. *Calls upon* all States of all other regions, in particular the militarily significant States, scrupulously to respect the region of the South Atlantic as a zone of peace and cooperation, especially through the reduction and eventual

elimination of their military presence there, the non-introduction of nuclear weapons or other weapons of mass destruction and the non-extension into the region of rivalries and conflicts that are foreign to it;

4. *Calls upon* all States of the region and of all other regions to co-operate in the elimination of all sources of tension in the zone, to respect the national unity, sovereignty, political independence and territorial integrity of every State therein, to refrain from the threat or use of force, and to observe strictly the principle that the territory of a State shall not be the object of military occupation resulting from the use of force in violation of the Charter of the United Nations, as well as the principle that the acquisition of territories by force is inadmissible.

Notes

1. *The Vote on Resolution 41/11.* The recorded vote on General Assembly Resolution 41/11 was 124 states in favor (including Argentina and the United Kingdom), one against (the United States), and eight abstaining (Belgium, France, the Federal Republic of Germany, Italy, Japan, Luxembourg, the Netherlands, and Portugal). Eight absent states also later informed the U.N. Secretariat that they had intended to vote in favor of the Resolution.

2. *The Legal Effect of General Assembly Resolutions.* Although the U.N. General Assembly has the authority to adopt some resolutions that are binding on its members, such as those relating to the budget of the United Nations, most of its resolutions are recommendations only. U.N. Charter, Chapter IV. Could General Assembly resolutions be relevant evidence of customary international law? Or could they serve as authoritative interpretations of the U.N. Charter? What factors could contribute to one General Assembly resolution having more legal significance than another? Can you identify a General Assembly resolution that reflects customary international law?

3. *The Content of Resolution 41/11.* Exactly what conduct does Resolution 41/11 purport to affect? For example, does the Resolution address the movement of military vessels on the high seas in the South Atlantic?

4. *Nuclear Weapons Treaties.* What is the distinction between "zones of peace" declared by the U.N. General Assembly and "nuclear weapons free zones" that have been established by treaties, such as the 1985 South Pacific Nuclear Free Zone Treaty? See Scott Parrish, Nuclear-Weapons-Free Zones and Maritime Transit of Nuclear Weapons in The Oceans in the Nuclear Age: Legacies and Risks 337 (David D. Caron & Harry N. Scheiber eds., 2010). See also the 1967 Treaty for the Prohibition of Nuclear Weapons in Latin America

(the Treaty of Tlatcloco), the 1995 African Nuclear-Weapon-Free Zone Treaty (the Treaty of Pelindaba), and the 1995 Treaty on the Southeast Asia Nuclear-Weapon-Free Zone.

3 *The 1980–1988 Iran-Iraq War*

The Persian Gulf is one of the most strategic waterways in the world due to its importance in world oil transportation. The war between Iran and Iraq, which started in 1980, increasingly impacted shipping in the Persian Gulf as each side tried to disrupt its opponent's trade and destabilize its economy. Beginning in April 1984, many oil tankers were bombed, destroyed, or crippled, affecting not only the two belligerents but other oil-producing Gulf states as well as oil-consuming states. In response to a letter from the representatives of several Gulf states "complaining against Iranian attacks on commercial ships en route to and from the ports of Kuwait and Saudi Arabia," the U.N. Security Council adopted the following resolution in June 1984.

UNITED NATIONS SECURITY COUNCIL RESOLUTION 552
UN Doc. S/RES/552 (1984)

The Security Council . . .

Deeply concerned over the recent attacks on commercial ships en route to and from the ports of Kuwait and Saudi Arabia,

Convinced that these attacks constitute a threat to the safety and stability of the area and have serious implications for international peace and security,

1. *Calls upon* all states to respect, in accordance with international law, the right of free navigation;

2. *Reaffirms* the right of free navigation in international waters and sea lanes for shipping en route to and from all ports and installations of the littoral States that are not parties to the hostilities; . . .

4. *Condemns* the recent attacks on commercial ships en route to and from the ports of Kuwait and Saudi Arabia;

5. *Demands* that such attacks should cease forthwith and that there should be no interference with ships en route to and from States that are not parties to the hostilities;

6. *Decides*, in the event of noncompliance with the present resolution, to meet again to consider effective measures that are commensurate with the gravity of the situation in order to ensure the freedom of navigation in the area; . . .

8. *Decides* to remain seized of the matter.

Notes

1. *Enforcement Measures*. The U.N. Security Council is authorized to make legally binding decisions. See U.N. Charter, Article 25. However, Resolution 552 contained no enforcement measures. During the Cold War, the possibility of a veto by one or another of the permanent members of the Security Council (China, France, the Soviet Union, the United Kingdom, and the United States) usually precluded the Security Council from adopting forceful resolutions. When the Soviet Union dissolved in 1991 and Russia succeeded to the Soviet seat, the permanent members of the Security Council were more often able to agree on measures to counteract threats to international peace and security. Several recent U.N. Security Council resolutions have authorized naval interdictions to help enforce Security Council sanctions against states that were found to pose threats to international peace and security. The legal effects and details of these Council resolutions are explored in Chapter 4, Section E.

2. *State-initiated Protective Measures*. The Arab states on the western shore of the Gulf, which were members of the Gulf Cooperation Council, established in 1984 the Persian Gulf Protected Shipping Zone, and the Council agreed to arrange for protective patrols by vessels and planes of Saudi Arabia and other member states. Kuwait took the unusual step of asking several neutral countries, including the United States, to re-flag Kuwaiti vessels to ensure their protection. The United States subsequently placed eleven Kuwaiti vessels under U.S. registry, and in 1987 began to provide naval escorts to all U.S.-flagged vessels operating in the Gulf. Several other states also sent warships to the region to protect international shipping. Does the use of warships to escort neutral merchant vessels constitute a "peaceful purpose" under LOS Convention Article 88? In what circumstances would the warships be allowed to fire on other vessels or installations? The International Court of Justice had the opportunity to consider the latter issue in the following case.

OIL PLATFORMS CASE

Iran v. United States, 2003 I.C.J. 161

[In 1992, Iran instituted proceedings against the United States before the International Court of Justice, challenging the legality of attacks conducted in 1987 and 1988 by U.S. warships against several offshore oil production complexes owned and operated by the National Iranian Oil Company. Iran contended that the United States had breached various provisions of the 1955 Treaty of Amity, Economic Relations and Consular Rights between the

United States and Iran, as well as other international law. After the ICJ ruled, by virtue of a clause in the 1995 Treaty, that it had jurisdiction over Iran's claims alleging certain violations of that Treaty, the United States filed a counterclaim asserting that Iran had breached the 1955 Treaty by laying mines in the Persian Gulf and by attacking U.S.-flag or U.S.-owned vessels.]

22. [B]oth Iran's claim and the counter-claim of the United States can be upheld only so far as a breach or breaches of Article X, paragraph 1, of the 1955 Treaty may be shown[.] Article X, paragraph 1, of the 1955 Treaty reads as follows: "Between the territories of the two High Contracting Parties there shall be freedom of commerce and navigation."

23. ... The actions giving rise to both the claim and the counter-claim occurred in the context of the general events that took place in the Persian Gulf between 1980 and 1988, in particular the armed conflict that opposed Iran and Iraq. That conflict began on 22 September 1980, when Iraqi forces advanced into the western areas of Iranian territory, and continued until the belligerent parties accepted a ceasefire in the summer of 1988, pursuant to United Nations Security Council resolution 598 (1987) of 20 July 1987. During the war, combat occurred in the territories of both States, but the conflict also spread to the Persian Gulf—which is an international commercial route and line of communication of major importance—and affected commerce and navigation in the region. From the very beginning of the conflict, on 22 September 1980, Iran established a defence exclusion zone around its coasts; shortly after, in early October 1980, Iraq declared a "prohibited war zone" and later established a "naval total exclusive zone" in the northern area of the Persian Gulf. In 1984, Iraq commenced attacks against ships in the Persian Gulf, notably tankers carrying Iranian oil. These were the first incidents of what later became known as the "Tanker War": in the period between 1984 and 1988, a number of commercial vessels and warships of various nationalities, including neutral vessels, were attacked by aircraft, helicopters, missiles or warships, or struck mines in the waters of the Persian Gulf. Naval forces of both belligerent parties were operating in the region, but Iran has denied responsibility for any actions other than incidents involving vessels refusing a proper request for stop and search. The United States attributes responsibility for certain incidents to Iran, whereas Iran suggests that Iraq was responsible for them.

24. A number of States took measures at the time aimed at ensuring the security of their vessels navigating in the Persian Gulf. In late 1986 and early 1987, the Government of Kuwait expressed its preoccupation at Iran's alleged targeting of its merchant vessels navigating in the Persian Gulf. It therefore requested the United States, the United Kingdom and the Soviet Union to "reflag" some of these vessels to ensure their protection. Following this request,

the Kuwaiti Oil Tanker Company was able to charter a number of Soviet vessels, and to flag four ships under United Kingdom registry and 11 ships under United States registry. In addition, the Government of the United States agreed to provide all United States-flagged vessels with a naval escort when transiting the Persian Gulf, in order to deter further attacks; these escort missions were initiated in July 1987, under the designation "Operation Earnest Will." Other foreign Powers, including Belgium, France, Italy, the Netherlands and the United Kingdom, took parallel action, sending warships to the region to protect international shipping. Despite these efforts, a number of ships, including reflagged Kuwaiti vessels, merchant tankers carrying Kuwaiti oil and warships participating in "Operation Earnest Will," suffered attacks or struck mines in the Persian Gulf between 1987 and the end of the conflict.

25. Two specific attacks on shipping are of particular relevance in this case. On 16 October 1987, the Kuwaiti tanker *Sea Isle City*, reflagged to the United States, was hit by a missile near Kuwait harbour. The United States attributed this attack to Iran, and three days later, on 19 October 1987, it attacked Iranian offshore oil production installations, claiming to be acting in self-defence.... On 14 April 1988, the warship USS *Samuel B. Roberts* struck a mine in international waters near Bahrain while returning from an escort mission; four days later the United States, again asserting the right of self-defence, employed its naval forces to attack and destroy simultaneously the Nasr ["Sirri"] and Salman ["Sassan"] complexes.

26. These attacks by United States forces on the Iranian oil platforms are claimed by Iran to constitute breaches of the 1955 Treaty; and the attacks on the *Sea Isle City* and the USS *Samuel B. Roberts* were invoked in support of the United States' claim to act in self-defence....

31. ... The task of the Court is thus to ascertain whether there has been a breach by the United States of the provisions of Article X, paragraph 1; other provisions of the Treaty are only relevant in so far as they may affect the interpretation or application of that text....

32. In that respect, the Court notes that the United States has relied on Article XX, paragraph 1(*d*), of the Treaty as determinative of the question of the existence of a breach of its obligations under Article X. That paragraph provides that

> The present Treaty shall not preclude the application of measures:...
>
> (*d*) necessary to fulfil the obligations of a High Contracting Party for the maintenance or restoration of international peace and security, or necessary to protect its essential security interests.

It is the contention of the United States that the actions complained of by Iran were measures necessary to protect the essential security interests of the United States, and that accordingly, if those actions would otherwise have been breaches of Article X, paragraph 1, of the Treaty, which the United States denies, the effect of Article XX, paragraph 1(*d*), is that they are justified under the terms of the Treaty itself, and thus do not constitute breaches of it....

34. If in the present case the Court is satisfied by the argument of the United States that the actions against the oil platforms were, in the circumstances of the case, "measures ... necessary to protect [the] essential security interests" of the United States, within the meaning of Article XX, paragraph 1(*d*), of the 1955 Treaty, it must hold that no breach of Article X, paragraph 1, of the Treaty has been established....

37. ... The contention of the United States at the time was that its attacks on the oil platforms were justified as acts of self-defence, in response to what it regarded as armed attacks by Iran, and on that basis it gave notice of its action to the Security Council under Article 51 of the United Nations Charter. Before the Court, it has continued to maintain that it was justified in acting as it did in exercise of the right of self-defence; it contends that, even if the Court were to find that its actions do not fall within the scope of Article XX, paragraph 1(*d*), those actions were not wrongful since they were necessary and appropriate actions in self-defence....

43. The Court will thus examine first the application of Article XX, paragraph 1(*d*), of the 1955 Treaty, which in the circumstances of this case, as explained above, involves the principle of the prohibition in international law of the use of force, and the qualification to it constituted by the right of self-defence. On the basis of that provision, a party to the Treaty may be justified in taking certain measures which it considers to be "necessary" for the protection of its essential security interests. As the Court emphasized, in relation to the comparable provision of the 1956 USA/Nicaragua Treaty in the case concerning *Military and Paramilitary Activities in and against Nicaragua*, "the measures taken must not merely be such as tend to protect the essential security interests of the party taking them, but must be 'necessary' for that purpose"; and whether a given measure is "necessary" is "not purely a question for the subjective judgment of the party" (*I.C.J. Reports* 1986, p. 141, para. 282), and may thus be assessed by the Court. In the present case, the question whether the measures taken were "necessary" overlaps with the question of their validity as acts of self-defence. As the Court observed in its decision of 1986 the criteria of necessity and proportionality must be observed if a measure is to be qualified as self-defence (see *I.C.J. Reports* 1986, p. 103, para. 194)....

51. Despite having thus referred to attacks on vessels and aircraft of other nationalities, the United States has not claimed to have been exercising collective self-defence on behalf of the neutral States engaged in shipping in the Persian Gulf; this would have required the existence of a request made to the United States "by the State which regards itself as the victim of an armed attack" (*I.C.J. Reports* 1986, p. 105, para. 199). Therefore, in order to establish that it was legally justified in attacking the Iranian platforms in exercise of the right of individual self-defence, the United States has to show that attacks had been made upon it for which Iran was responsible; and that those attacks were of such a nature as to be qualified as "armed attacks" within the meaning of that expression in Article 51 of the United Nations Charter, and as understood in customary law on the use of force. As the Court observed in the case concerning *Military and Paramilitary Activities in and against Nicaragua*, it is necessary to distinguish "the most grave forms of the use of force (those constituting an armed attack) from other less grave forms" (*I.C.J. Reports* 1986, p. 101, para. 191), since "In the case of individual self-defence, the exercise of this right is subject to the State concerned having been the victim of an armed attack" (*ibid.*, p. 103, para. 195). The United States must also show that its actions were necessary and proportional to the armed attack made on it, and that the platforms were a legitimate military target open to attack in the exercise of self-defence.

52. Since it was the missile attack on the *Sea Isle City* that figured most prominently in the United States contentions, the Court will first examine in detail the evidence relating to that incident. The *Sea Isle City* was a Kuwaiti tanker reflagged to the United States[.] [O]n 16 October 1987 it had just ended a voyage under "Operation Earnest Will" (see paragraph 24 above), when it was hit by a missile near Kuwait's Al-Ahmadi Sea Island (or Mina al-Ahmadi) terminal. This incident, which caused damage to the ship and injury to six crew members, was claimed by the United States to be the seventh involving Iranian anti-ship cruise missiles in the area in the course of 1987....

64. [T]he question is whether that attack, either in itself or in combination with the rest of the "series of... attacks" cited by the United States can be categorized as an "armed attack" on the United States justifying self-defence. The Court notes first that the *Sea Isle City* was in Kuwaiti waters at the time of the attack on it, and that a Silkworm missile fired from (it is alleged) more than 100 km away could not have been aimed at the specific vessel, but simply programmed to hit some target in Kuwaiti waters. [T]hese incidents do not seem to the Court to constitute an armed attack on the United States, of the kind that the Court, in the case concerning *Military and Paramilitary Activities*

in and against Nicaragua, qualified as a "most grave" form of the use of force (see paragraph 51 above)....

71. As in the case of the attack on the *Sea Isle City*, the first question is whether the United States has discharged the burden of proof that the USS *Samuel B. Roberts* was the victim of a mine laid by Iran. The Court notes that mines were being laid at the time by both belligerents in the Iran-Iraq war, so that evidence of other minelaying operations by Iran is not conclusive as to responsibility of Iran for this particular mine. In its communication to the Security Council in connection with the attack of 18 April 1988, the United States alleged that "The mines were laid in shipping lanes known by Iran to be used by US vessels, and intended by them to damage or sink such vessels." Iran has claimed that it laid mines only for defensive purposes in the Khor Abdullah Channel, but the United States has submitted evidence suggesting that Iran's mining operations were more extensive. The main evidence that the mine struck by the USS *Samuel B. Roberts* was laid by Iran was the discovery of moored mines in the same area, bearing serial numbers matching other Iranian mines, in particular those found aboard the vessel Iran Ajr. This evidence is highly suggestive, but not conclusive.

72. The Court notes further that, as on the occasion of the earlier attack on oil platforms, the United States in its communication to the Security Council claimed to have been exercising the right of self-defence in response to the "attack" on the USS *Samuel B. Roberts*, linking it also with "a series of offensive attacks and provocations Iranian naval forces have taken against neutral shipping in the international waters of the Persian Gulf." Before the Court, it has contended, as in the case of the missile attack on the *Sea Isle City*, that the mining was itself an armed attack giving rise to the right of self-defence and that the alleged pattern of Iranian use of force "added to the gravity of the specific attacks, reinforced the necessity of action in self-defense, and helped to shape the appropriate response." No attacks on United States-flagged vessels (as distinct from United States-owned vessels), additional to those cited as justification for the earlier attacks on the Reshadat platforms, have been brought to the Court's attention, other than the mining of the USS *Samuel B. Roberts* itself. The question is therefore whether that incident sufficed in itself to justify action in self defence, as amounting to an "armed attack." The Court does not exclude the possibility that the mining of a single military vessel might be sufficient to bring into play the "inherent right of self-defence"; but in view of all the circumstances, including the inconclusiveness of the evidence of Iran's responsibility for the mining of the USS *Samuel B. Roberts*, the Court is unable to hold that the attacks on the Salman and Nasr platforms have been shown to have been justifiably made in response to an "armed attack" on the United States by Iran, in the form of the mining of the USS *Samuel B. Roberts*....

73. As noted above (paragraph 43), in the present case a question of whether certain action is "necessary" arises both as an element of international law relating to self-defence and on the basis of the actual terms of Article XX, paragraph 1(*d*), of the 1955 Treaty, already quoted, whereby the Treaty does "not preclude . . . measures . . . necessary to protect [the] essential security interests" of either party. In this latter respect, the United States claims that it considered in good faith that the attacks on the platforms were necessary to protect its essential security interests, and suggests that "A measure of discretion should be afforded to a party's good faith application of measures to protect its essential security interests." Iran was prepared to recognize some of the interests referred to by the United States—the safety of United States vessels and crew, and the uninterrupted flow of maritime commerce in the Persian Gulf—as being reasonable security interests of the United States, but denied that the United States actions against the platforms could be regarded as "necessary" to protect those interests. The Court does not however have to decide whether the United States interpretation of Article XX, paragraph 1(*d*), on this point is correct, since the requirement of international law that measures taken avowedly in self-defence must have been necessary for that purpose is strict and objective, leaving no room for any "measure of discretion." The Court will therefore turn to the criteria of necessity and proportionality in the context of international law on self-defence. . . .

76. The Court is not sufficiently convinced that the evidence available supports the contentions of the United States as to the significance of the military presence and activity on the Reshadat oil platforms; and it notes that no such evidence is offered in respect of the Salman and Nasr complexes. However, even accepting those contentions, for the purposes of discussion, the Court is unable to hold that the attacks made on the platforms could have been justified as acts of self-defence. . . . In the case both of the attack on the *Sea Isle City* and the mining of the USS *Samuel B. Roberts*, the Court is not satisfied that the attacks on the platforms were necessary to respond to these incidents. . . .

77. As to the requirement of proportionality, the attack of 19 October 1987 might, had the Court found that it was necessary in response to the *Sea Isle City* incident as an armed attack committed by Iran, have been considered proportionate. In the case of the attacks of 18 April 1988, however, they were conceived and executed as part of a more extensive operation entitled "Operation Praying Mantis[.]" [T]he Court cannot assess in isolation the proportionality of that action to the attack to which it was said to be a response; it cannot close its eyes to the scale of the whole operation, which involved, *inter alia,* the destruction of two Iranian frigates and a number of other naval vessels and aircraft. As a response to the mining, by an unidentified agency, of a single United States warship, which was severely damaged but not sunk, and

without loss of life, neither "Operation Praying Mantis" as a whole, nor even that part of it that destroyed the Salman and Nasr platforms, can be regarded, in the circumstances of this case, as a proportionate use of force in self-defence.

78. The Court thus concludes from the foregoing that the actions carried out by United States forces against Iranian oil installations on 19 October 1987 and 18 April 1988 cannot be justified, under Article XX, paragraph 1(*d*), of the 1955 Treaty, as being measures necessary to protect the essential security interests of the United States, since those actions constituted recourse to armed force not qualifying, under international law on the question, as acts of self-defence, and thus did not fall within the category of measures contemplated, upon its correct interpretation, by that provision of the Treaty. . . .

Notes

1. *Final Ruling.* Although the ICJ found, by a vote of fourteen to two, that the U.S. attacks could not be justified as self-defense and constituted an illegal use of force, the Court nevertheless concluded that the U.S. attacks did not violate the 1955 U.S.-Iran Treaty of Amity, Economic Relations and Consular Rights because they did not affect commerce "between the territories" of the United States and Iran, as Article X(1) of the Treaty requires. The Court, by a vote of fifteen to one, also rejected the U.S. counterclaim, because the alleged Iranian actions did not damage vessels engaged in navigation or commerce "between the territories" of the two states. For more background on the Iran-Iraq War and the U.S. role in it, see George K. Walker, The Tanker War, 1980–88: Law and Policy (Vol. 74, International Law Studies, 2000).

2. *Evaluating the Oil Platforms Decision.* In the Oil Platforms case, the ICJ applied international law relating to recourse to force and self-defense. How does this body of law differ from the "law of naval warfare" we discussed in connection with the Falkland/Malvinas War? Was it necessary or appropriate for the ICJ to consider U.N. Charter law on self-defense, given that the issues in the case arose under a bilateral U.S.-Iran treaty? In construing the law of self-defense, did the ICJ impose too high a burden of proof on the United States, e.g., regarding Iran's alleged laying of mines that threatened U.S. vessels? How could the United States satisfy the burden of proof required to defend its vessels? Do you agree with the ICJ's assertion, in paragraph 73, that "the requirement of international law that measures taken avowedly in self-defence must have been necessary for that purpose is strict and objective, leaving no room for any 'measure of discretion'"? In paragraph 72, the ICJ found that one

incident directed at the USS *Samuel B. Roberts* was insufficiently serious to amount to an "armed attack" that would trigger the right to self-defense under Article 51 of the U.N. Charter. Do you agree that there should be a "gravity" threshold that must be satisfied before the use of force in self-defense is legally authorized? If such a threshold is warranted, what may a vessel that is the subject of a "minor" attack do in response? How would you characterize the differences between the ICJ's approach to the law governing recourse to force and self-defense and the approach of the United States? See John E. Noyes, Unit Self-Defense at Sea: Views from the United States and the International Court of Justice, in The Exercise of Jurisdiction over Vessels: New Developments in the Fields of Pollution, Fisheries, Crimes at Sea and Trafficking of Weapons of Mass Destruction—Transatlantic Perspectives 185 (Erik Franckx & Philippe Gautier eds., 2010); W.H. Taft IV, Self-defense and the Oil Platforms Decision, 29 Yale J. Intl. L. 295 (2004).

3. *The Iranian Airbus Controversy.* Other U.S.-Iran controversies during the Iran-Iraq War were also brought to the International Court of Justice and other international forums. In July 1988, while patrolling in the Persian Gulf, the USS *Vincennes* shot down an Iranian civil aircraft, which crashed into the Gulf, killing the 290 people on board. On July 20, 1988, the U.N. Security Council unanimously adopted Resolution 616, which welcomed a fact-finding investigation by the International Civil Aviation Organization. The November 1988 Report of ICAO Fact-Finding Investigation, which was adopted by the ICAO's Council in March 1989, is reproduced at 28 Intl. Leg. Materials 900 (1989). The United States indicated its willingness to make ex gratia compensation to the families of victims, in general at the rate of US$ 250,000 for each full-time wage earner and US$ 100,000 for each other passenger. The United States pursued settlement on this basis with five states whose nationals were killed in the crash. 28 Intl. Leg. Materials 897 (1989).

In May 1989 Iran filed an application with the ICJ against the United States. Iran asked the Court to determine whether, by shooting down the Iranian commercial airliner, the United States had violated the 1944 Chicago Convention on International Civil Aviation and the 1988 Convention for the Suppression of Unlawful Acts Against the Safety of Civil Aviation, and, if so, to determine the amount of compensation due. The ICJ case was discontinued and the matter was settled in 1996, when the United States paid Iran approximately US$ 100 million, US$ 61.8 million of which was to go to relatives of the Iranian victims and the balance of which was for the downing of the aircraft. Case Concerning the Aerial Incident of 3 July 1988 (Iran v. United States), 1996 I.C.J. 9 (Order).

4. *Evaluating Forums.* Note the variety of forums involved with "peaceful uses of the high seas" in this section. Which do you think the most effective? Which are the most appropriate to use?

I Duty to Render Assistance

The first international instrument to impose a duty to render assistance at sea was the 1910 International Salvage Treaty. Subsequent multilateral treaties have continued to embody the duty to render assistance at sea, including Article 98 of the LOS Convention.

WARSHAUER v. LLOYD SABAUDO, S.A.
71 F.2d 146 (2d Cir.), cert. denied, 293 U.S. 610 (1934)

SWAN, Circuit Judge.

This is an action at law by the plaintiff Warshauer, a citizen of the United States and a resident of New York City, against an Italian corporation which owned and operated the steamship Conte Biancamano. In substance the complaint alleges that on the afternoon of October 31, 1931, the plaintiff and a companion were adrift on the high seas in a disabled motorboat, without gasoline and without food, when the defendant's steamer passed within hailing distance; that he exhibited a recognized signal of distress and requested the steamer to come to his assistance, and the defendant's servants on said steamer, particularly its operating personnel, clearly observed his signals of distress, but refused to heed them or to stop and take the plaintiff aboard, although they could have done so without peril to themselves or their vessel; that two days later the plaintiff was rescued by a Coastguard cutter. In the meantime and in consequence of the exposure and deprivations to which he was subjected by the failure of the defendant's steamship to render the requested aid, the plaintiff suffered permanent physical injuries for which, together with the attendant pain and subsequently incurred medical expenses, he demands damages. On motion to dismiss, ... the District Court held the complaint insufficient, and the correctness of this ruling is the issue presented by this appeal.

Argument of counsel has taken a wider range than the precise issue presented by the pleadings requires. The question chiefly debated was whether the common law or the law of the sea recognizes the existence of a legal duty coextensive with the universally admitted moral duty to rescue a stranger from peril, when this can be done without risk to the one called upon for help.

This interesting problem we pass by as unnecessary to the decision, as did the District Court.

The precise issue is whether a shipowner is liable for damages to a stranger in peril on the high seas to whom the ship's master has failed to give aid. This situation, it may be noted, involves no personal dereliction of a moral duty by the person sought to be held to respond in damages. Such dereliction was that of the master, and only by applying the doctrine of respondeat superior can it be imputed to the ship's owner; moral obliquity is not imputed to one personally innocent. It is conceded that no authority can be found which has imposed legal liability on the owner in such circumstances. The absence of specific precedent, however, is no insuperable barrier, for the law of the sea can grow by judicial decision no less than the common law. But a court should be slow to establish a new legal principle not in harmony with the generally accepted views of the great maritime nations.

Their views on this subject are disclosed in the International Salvage Treaty, which was drafted by representatives of more than twenty nations, meeting at Brussels in 1910, and to which both Italy and the United States are parties. Articles 11 and 12 of the treaty relate to the matter under consideration and read as follows:

> *Article 11*
>
> Every master is bound, so far as he can do so without serious danger to his vessel, her crew and passengers, to render assistance to everybody, even though an enemy, found at sea in danger of being lost.
>
> The owner of the vessel incurs no liability by reason of contravention of the foregoing provision.
>
> *Article 12*
>
> The High Contracting Parties whose legislation does not forbid infringements of the preceding article bind themselves to take or to propose to their respective legislatures the measures necessary for the prevention of such infringements....

The treaty was ratified by the United States in 1912, to become effective on March 1, 1913. In the meantime Congress passed legislation in fulfillment of the obligation imposed by article 12 of the treaty. Section 2 of the Act of Aug. 1, 1912, provides as follows (37 Stat. 242, 40 USCA § 728):

> Sec. 2. That the master or person in charge of a vessel shall, so far as he can do so without serious danger to his own vessel, crew, or passengers,

> render assistance to every person who is found at sea in danger of being lost; and if he fails to do so, he shall, upon conviction, be liable to a penalty of not exceeding $1,000 or imprisonment for a term not exceeding two years, or both.

The appellant contends that the declaration in article 11 that the shipowner "incurs no liability by reason of contravention" of the master's obligation to render assistance refers only to criminal liability of the owner. Such an interpretation would seem a most unlikely meaning. Unless it was intended to cover civil liability, no reason is apparent for mentioning the shipowner's exemption from liability. It is almost inconceivable that criminal responsibility should be imputed to an owner who had not directed the dereliction of his agent. In the United States, at least, imputed crime is substantially unknown. A penal statute is construed to apply only to the class of persons to whom it specifically refers. The same principle should be equally applicable to the construction of a treaty. Hence if the first sentence of article 11 refers only to the master's public duty, breach of which is to be enforced by the criminal law, there was no need to express the owner's exemption from responsibility. If, however, the master's liability may be civil as well as criminal, then the provision referring to the owner serves a purpose and clearly relieves him from civil liability.

It is further urged that the treaty is not self-executing, that article 11 is no more than an expression of policy and by the very terms of article 12 requires legislation to carry it into effect (cf. Foster v. Neilson, 2 Pet. 253, 314, 7 L.Ed. 415), and that Congress in enacting such legislation dealt only with the criminal liability of the master, leaving untouched the civil liability of both master and owner, so that no implication can be drawn, either from the treaty or the statute, that civil liability does not exist. On the contrary, the argument proceeds, the enactment of a criminal statute for the protection of a class creates a right of civil action in a member of the class who is caused harm by an infraction of the statute. Granting all this, the appellant advances no further than to establish a cause of action against the violator of the criminal statute; that is, the master. He must still prove that the master's breach of duty is imputable to his employer. It is at this point that the absence of precedent and the declaration of the treaty against liability on the part of the owner stands in his way. As a declaration of the views of the great maritime nations, the treaty needs no "implementation" by legislation. We are not at liberty to make new law in the face of that declaration. See article 15 of the Treaty (37 Stat. 1672).

Judgment affirmed.

Notes

1. *The Duty to Render Assistance.* Under the common law, there traditionally is no liability for failing to come to the aid of someone in need, at least absent a special relationship between the rescuer and the party in distress. Although the admiralty law of salvage rewards a person for rescuing property, "a court of admiralty has no authority to allow a reward merely for the saving of life. That, as is observed by Lord Stowell, 'must be left to the bounty of individuals.'" The Emblem, 8 F. Cas. 611, 612 (D. Maine 1840). Several countries, including England and Canada, have enacted legislation allowing a salvage reward for the "mere" saving of life, but those statutes do not impose a duty to come to the aid of a person in peril on the high seas. Why should a legal duty to render assistance have arisen in international law with respect to those in distress at sea? In what instances is the duty to render assistance excused? See LOS Convention, Article 98.

2. *The Use of Treaties in U.S. Judicial Opinions.* A treaty whose terms are sufficiently definite and which is deemed to create judicially cognizable rights may apply directly in U.S. courts, without the need for any implementing legislation. Such a treaty is said to be "self-executing." See Foster & Elam v. Neilson, 27 U.S. (2 Pet.) 253 (1829). Treaties are part of the "supreme Law of the Land, and the Judges in every State shall be bound thereby," according to Article VI of the U.S. Constitution, the Supremacy Clause. What other roles does the Warshauer opinion suggest that treaties may play in the U.S. legal system, even when they are not self-executing?

3. *Implementing the Duty to Render Assistance.* How can the duty to render assistance best be furthered? Under the 1979 Maritime Search and Rescue Convention, the International Maritime Organization divided the world's oceans into thirteen search and rescue areas; parties to the Convention are assigned responsibilities within each region. International communications networks are also important in implementing rescue operations. To improve communication of maritime safety information and distress signals, the worldwide Global Maritime Distress and Safety System (GMDSS) was implemented pursuant to an amendment of the 1974 SOLAS Convention. Since 1999, all passenger ships and all cargo ships of 300 gross tons or more on international voyages must carry search and rescue transponders and satellite emergency position-indicating radio beacons to increase the probability of locating ships and rescuing passengers after an accident.

4. *The Costs of Rendering Assistance: Disembarcation.* Once a rescue at sea has occurred, who is responsible for the well-being of the rescued persons? Must the rescuing ship provide medical care and provisions? Where, when,

and how should the rescued persons be disembarked? Who is responsible for any costs incurred as a result of the rescue? Several of these issues are discussed in the following article.

UNITED NATIONS HIGH COMMISSIONER FOR REFUGEES, RESCUE AT SEA
2 Refugees 21 (Feb. 1984)

Whichever way the figures are examined the message is clear. Fewer ships from fewer nations are rescuing fewer Vietnamese boat people in distress at sea. This is true in absolute numbers but, more significantly, as a proportion of total boat people arrivals in the region. In 1980, 20 percent of all Vietnamese asylum seekers arriving in South-East Asian refugee camps had been picked up by passing vessels in the South China Sea. By 1982, the figures had dropped to 15 percent. In 1983 to 12 percent. In December, the 14 passengers of a single small craft were the only ones fortunate enough to thus find safety before reaching shore.

The number of boats leaving Vietnam has significantly decreased and the economic recession experienced around the world in recent years has reduced the volume of commercial shipping. But this cannot entirely account for the fact that from 33 in 1981, the number of countries whose vessels rescued refugees fell to 15 in 1983.

Statistical trends tell only part of the story. The contractual terms of "time charter" agreements now routinely burden shipowners with expenditure incurred as a result of the rescue of refugees. This represents a deviation from past practice and may serve as a deterrent to shipmasters who represent the owners on board, when considering rescue. Whether or not this fear is justified, the new wording is a reflection of the defensive attitudes prevailing today. The saga of the boat people no longer commands the almost universally compassionate response of a few years ago.

In the spring and summer of 1979—which witnessed the largest tide of Vietnamese refugee arrivals in the region—ships from the French, Italian and US navies rescued thousands of asylum seekers. Subsequently, several private associations—from France, the Federal Republic of Germany, the United States, Switzerland and elsewhere—mounted special rescue operations in the area with a varying but generally notable degree of success. The principal difficulty faced by the promoters of such operations was the obligation to secure resettlement guarantees for the persons they rescued. As long as the countries under whose flags the rescue vessel was sailing formally undertook to provide the resettlement places required, these operations could continue. Today, US navy vessels constitute the only non-commercial rescuers in the region.

The duty to rescue persons in distress at sea has been universally recognized from time immemorial. It is an age-old practice based on moral considerations which predate laws and which no one ever saw fit to challenge. There are no records anywhere of shipmasters prosecuted for failing to rescue.

The efforts undertaken since the beginning of this century to codify the law of the sea have not only concentrated on such matters as freedom of the high seas, the exploitation of the continental shelf or the maximum width of territorial waters. The duty to rescue has been repeatedly underlined. But what the lawmakers systematically had in mind were classic shipwrecks and sailors surrounding whom no attendant legal problem was suspected. Nationals of any given state, they could expect to be repatriated from the rescue ships' first port of call. In the case of asylum-seekers, however, repatriation must be ruled out. Whose responsibility they should become is something on which international law is practically silent.

Asylum-seekers by definition cannot benefit from the protection and services of their own country of origin. What would normally be a consular issue becomes one of international protection at the forefront of which lies the question of disembarkation.

Faced with a continuing influx of boat people arriving directly on their shores, the states bordering the South China Sea consider that they are under no obligation to give haven in addition to those rescued on the high seas. As a result, none can be disembarked in the absence of formal, time-limited guarantees of resettlement abroad. These are usually given by the ship's flag state or, where the country concerned is unable to offer resettlement opportunities, drawn from a special pool [Disembarkation Resettlement Offers] (DISERO) set up to that effect. The grace period is normally limited to 90 days.

The principle of flag-state responsibility . . . evolved from practice in the absence of an alternative. The fact that it has functioned well and benefitted over 17,000 asylum-seekers rescued at sea is evidence of considerable international solidarity. But the link between the ability to disembark those rescued and the obligation to resettle them also gives rise to concern. The many captains who have chosen to bypass small craft in distress in the South China Sea in recent times may well have considered that rescuing boat people would cost more time and money than they could afford.

To address this problem UNHCR [United Nations High Commissioner for Refugees] has embarked on a vast information campaign aimed ultimately at the masters of every oceangoing vessel afloat, explaining the procedures whereby refugees can be promptly disembarked. These procedures are simple and efficient. Every captain on every ship encountering refugees should be convinced that the price of saving lives is very small indeed. . . .

Briefly, the [UNHCR's *Guidelines for Disembarkation of Refugees*] tell ships' masters how to get the refugees they rescue safely and quickly disembarked. Country to country, procedures may vary, but the *Guidelines* point out that delay and expense can be minimized or avoided by early advice to the authorities of the next scheduled port of call, and by calling on the assistance of the local UNHCR office. Some expenses too can be recovered, including costs of care and disembarkation.

Over the past years, more than 17,000 Vietnamese refugees have been picked up in the South China Sea. Half or more have disembarked in Singapore, with the remainder turning up in Hong Kong, Japan, Korea, the Philippines and Thailand. All countries in the region, however, allow only temporary entry for rescued refugees who generally must be on their way to resettlement countries within 90 days. Frequently it will be the flag state of the rescuing ship which gives the necessary "resettlement guarantee," but many rescues are made by ships flying so-called flags of convenience, or registered in countries which cannot be expected to offer resettlement.

For such cases the *Guidelines* point out that UNHCR will contact countries which have contributed to a special pool of resettlement places known as DISERO . . ., to obtain the necessary guarantee. Many disembarked under this special procedure will finally go to other countries where they have relatives or special links. Faced with an alarming decrease in places available under DISERO, UNHCR has appealed urgently to governments to come into the scheme or to expand their contribution.

Notes

1. *Vietnamese "Boat People."* In July 1979, President Jimmy Carter ordered ships of the U.S. Seventh Fleet to rescue Vietnamese "boat people" in distress and in danger of drowning in the South China Sea. The Ministry of Foreign Affairs of the Socialist Republic of Vietnam "strongly denounced" the U.S. dispatch of ships and planes to the South China Sea area to pick up refugees, and demanded that the United States cease such activities. The U.S. Department of State issued the following statement in response:

> Tradition provides that ship captains shall rescue individuals in distress at sea and bring them to the closest port for disembarkation. Thousands of Indochinese refugees have been rescued on the high seas, but in some cases vessels have reportedly ignored distress signals.
>
> In December 1978, the U.N. High Commissioner for Refugees and the Inter-Governmental Maritime Consultative Organization issued a joint appeal to governments, shipowners, and ship masters to continue the

> rescue of refugees on the high seas. Three times since mid-1978 the U.S. Government has reminded American line operators and their captains of their obligations in this regard and has also provided a guarantee of resettlement for refugees rescued by U.S.-owned or U.S.-registered vessels if those refugees are not accepted by another country.
>
> Major maritime nations, for the most part, have stated that they have instructed their carriers to rescue refugees at sea. The major problem appears to lie with carriers operating under flags of convenience. Ship masters are coming under additional pressure as a result of stiffening resistance among the ports of the region to the landing of refugees without guarantees of resettlement.

79 Dept. State Bull. No. 2031 at 2, 3 (Oct. 1979), reprinted in 1979 Digest of United States Practice in International Law 1115.

2. *U.S. Practice in the Caribbean Sea.* Beginning in 1981, the United States interdicted numerous boat people fleeing from Haiti. Most were returned to Haiti, although those found to have a credible fear of persecution if returned to Haiti could pursue an asylum claim in the United States. U.S. interdiction of Haitian vessels suspected of transporting illegal immigrants was authorized by a 1981 bilateral Agreement relating to Establishment of a Cooperative Program of Interdiction and Selective Return of Certain Haitian Migrants and Vessels. According to a 1992 U.S. executive order, the U.S. Coast Guard was authorized not only to interdict on the high seas boats carrying people seeking to escape from Haiti, but also to return the passengers to Haiti without inquiring whether they would be persecuted when they were returned. Executive Order No. 12,807, 57 Fed. Reg. 23,133 (1992). In 1994, the United States confirmed that boat people from other Caribbean states also would not be allowed into the United States. Instead, the United States, "acting with other regional nations and the UN High Commissioner for Refugees," would place those interdicted at sea in "safe haven" camps elsewhere. To this end, the United States in 1994 issued a joint communiqué with Cuba and entered into agreements with Jamaica, the United Kingdom and the Turks and Caicos Islands, Dominica, St. Lucia, Suriname, and Panama. Marion Nash (Leich), Contemporary Practice of the United States Relating to International Law, 89 Am. J. Intl. L. 96, 98–102 (1995).

3. *The* Tampa *Incident and International Initiatives.* In August 2001, the Norwegian-flag cargo vessel *Tampa* rescued 440 people from an Indonesian ferry that was sinking about 75 nautical miles northwest of Christmas Island, Australia. Those rescued were mostly individuals who were fleeing the Taliban regime in Afghanistan. When the *Tampa* sought to offload its passengers in

Australia, that country, concerned with an influx of immigrants, refused to accept them. Following lengthy negotiations, New Zealand and Nauru eventually accepted the refugees, many of whose claims were processed by the U.N. High Commissioner for Refugees.

The *Tampa* incident led to renewed efforts to improve international legal mechanisms to address issues related to refugees in distress at sea. The International Maritime Organization (IMO) called for a review of treaties and IMO instruments, and for appropriate action in conjunction with the UNHCR and other international institutions, to help insure that:

> – survivors of distress incidents are given assistance regardless of nationality or status or of the circumstances in which they are found;
> – ships which have retrieved persons in distress at sea are able to deliver the survivors to a place of safety; and
> – survivors, regardless of nationality or status, including undocumented migrants, asylum seekers, refugees and stowaways, are treated while on board in the manner prescribed in the relevant IMO instruments and in accordance with relevant international agreements and long-standing humanitarian maritime traditions[.]

IMO Res. A.920(22) (2001). Subsequently, amendments to the 1974 SOLAS Convention and the 1979 Maritime Search and Rescue Convention were adopted and entered into force in 2006. Among other matters, these amendments obligate contracting states to assist ship masters in delivering persons rescued at sea to a place of safety, with minimum further deviation from the ship's planned voyage. In 2004, the IMO Maritime Safety Committee adopted Guidelines on the Treatment of Persons Rescued at Sea, providing further guidance to states in fulfilling their obligations under international law to provide a place of safety to persons rescued at sea. MSC Res. 167(78) app. P 1 MSC Doc. 78/26/Add.2 Annex 34 (2004).

4. *Recent Migration Challenges.* European states—especially Greece, Italy, Malta, and Spain—have recently faced significant migration by sea from Africa, Asia, and the Middle East. The Office of the UNHCR reported that in 2011, a record 58,000 migrants, asylum-seekers, and refugees reached Europe in boats; at least 1,500 died in transit. In the Middle East, a record 103,000 refugees, asylum-seekers and migrants crossed the high seas in 2011 to reach Yemen, most of whom were leaving from Somalia and other Horn of Africa countries. Annual statistics regarding migration at sea are available at the UNHCR website, http://www.unhcr.org.

CHAPTER 3

Nationality of Vessels

This chapter examines the concept of nationality of vessels. The nationality of vessels has been, in theory, central to the system of control of activities on the high seas, and to a significant extent in other zones of the oceans as well. Vessel nationality is important in part because of the desirability of applying consistent legal standards to vessels. The flag state—the state of the ship's nationality—has jurisdiction over its ships on the high seas and is obligated to enforce rules regarding navigation, safety, and administrative, technical, and social matters. We explore flag state obligations in Chapter 4.

Section A of this chapter introduces the concept of vessel nationality, exploring when states may confer nationality on vessels and the requirement that there be a "genuine link" between a vessel and its flag state. Registration of vessels, which is the primary method by which states indicate grants of nationality, and ships' documents are the subjects of Section B. The chapter concludes with Section C, concerning just what is a ship or a vessel.

A The Concept of Vessel Nationality

This section considers what the concept of "nationality" means in the context of ships and explores the limits that do or should exist on a state's right to confer its nationality on a vessel. We first examine two classic incidents—one a diplomatic exchange between the United States and Spain concerning the arrest of the *Virginius* and the second the Muscat Dhows arbitration between France and Great Britain—that concern the right of states to make vessels their nationals.

The 1958 High Seas Convention incorporated in Article 5(1) the requirement of a "genuine link" between the flag state and the ship. This requirement also appears in Article 91(1) of the United Nations Convention on the Law of the Sea (LOS Convention). The next two excerpts—the arguments of states before the International Court of Justice (ICJ) in the IMCO case and the decision of the International Tribunal for the Law of the Sea (ITLOS) in the M/V Saiga (No. 2) case—discuss the meaning, importance, and application of this genuine link requirement.

This section concludes with an excerpt from the International Law Commission's Draft Articles on Diplomatic Protection, which examines the

 | DOI 10.1163/9789004203563_004

right of a flag state to pursue claims on behalf of its vessels. The right to pursue claims helps us to understand the concept of vessel nationality.

THE VIRGINIUS INCIDENT

John Bassett Moore, 2 A Digest of International Law § 309 at 898–99 (1906)

[On October 31, 1873, the *Virginius*, a vessel flying a U.S. flag, was pursued and captured on the high seas by a Spanish warship. Spain alleged that the seizure did not violate international law because the owners of the ship were in fact Cuban and had fraudulently obtained U.S. registration of the ship. Spanish authorities, which had been hunting the *Virginius* for two years prior to her capture, claimed that the vessel was carrying arms to Cuban insurrectionists who were challenging Spain's control of Cuba. Following the capture, Spain executed several of the *Virginius*'s crew members, among them U.S. citizens. A diplomatic crisis ensued. Spain and the United States eventually reached a negotiated settlement concerning matters related to the *Virginius*, the terms of which were embodied in an 1873 protocol. The U.S. Attorney General, referring to this protocol between the United States and Spain, issued the following opinion.]

Assuming the question to be what appears to conform to the intent of the protocol, whether or not the *Virginius*, at the time of her capture, had a right, as against the United States, to carry the American flag, I am of the opinion that she had no such right because she had not been registered according to law; but I am also of the opinion that she was as much exempt from interference on the high seas by another power, on that ground, as though she had been lawfully registered. Spain no doubt has a right to capture a vessel with an American register and carrying the American flag, found in her own waters, assisting, or endeavoring to assist the insurrection in Cuba, but she has no right to capture such a vessel on the high seas upon an apprehension that, in violation of the neutrality or navigation laws of the United States, she was on her way to assist said rebellion. Spain may defend her territory and people from the hostile attack of what is, or appears to be, an American vessel, but she has no jurisdiction whatever over the question as to whether or not such vessel is on the high seas in violation of any law of the United States. Spain cannot rightfully raise that question as to the *Virginius*, but the United States may, and, as I understand the protocol, they have agreed to do it; and, governed by that agreement, and without admitting that Spain would otherwise have any interest in the question, I decide that the *Virginius* at the time of her capture was without right and improperly carrying the American flag.

Notes

1. *The Nationality of Unregistered Vessels.* If the *Virginius* was in fact not legally registered in the United States, why should Spain have "no jurisdiction whatsoever" over the *Virginius* on the high seas? Today, does Article 91(1) of the LOS Convention answer the question? For more about the *Virginius* incident, see Richard H. Bradford, The Virginius Affair (1980).

A ship that is not authorized to fly the flag of a state, and therefore has no nationality, is, in modern parlance, deemed "stateless." Should a stateless vessel be subject to seizure by any state for any reason? May those on board be arrested for any (or no) reason? See LOS Convention, Article 110(1)(d). We explore these questions further in Chapter 4, Section D.4.

2. *Self-defense.* The U.S. Attorney General noted that "Spain may defend her territory and people from... hostile attack." When will the modern law of self-defense justify interference with foreign flag vessels on the high seas? See Chapter 2, Section H.

CASE OF THE MUSCAT DHOWS

France/Great Britain (1905), The Hague Arbitration Cases 64 (George G. Wilson ed., 1915), available at http://www.pca-cpa.org

[Muscat (today Oman) medically quarantined five Muscat subjects, who escaped. At the Sultan of Muscat's request, the British recaptured them. These Muscat subjects held French papers, however, and France, claiming jurisdiction over them, demanded their release. Britain, which was contending with France for influence in the Persian Gulf, agreed to advise the Sultan to release the men on the condition that France arbitrate several matters. One of the matters that was arbitrated, which we consider in the excerpt below, concerned the rights of ships flying the French flag. Our immediate topic is the nationality of vessels, but note how the case relates to efforts to suppress the slave trade, a matter that we study formally in Chapter 4, Section D.2.]

The Tribunal of Arbitration constituted in virtue of the Compromis concluded at London on October 13, 1904 between Great Britain and France;

Whereas the Government of His Britannic Majesty and that of the French Republic have thought it right by the Declaration of March 10, 1862 "to engage reciprocally to respect the independence" of His Highness the Sultan of Muscat,

Whereas difficulties as to the scope of that Declaration have arisen in relation to the issue, by the French Republic, to certain subjects of His Highness the Sultan of Muscat of papers authorizing them to fly the French flag, and also as to the nature of the privileges and immunities claimed by subjects of His Highness who are owners or masters of dhows and in possession of such papers or are members of the crew of such dhows and their families, especially as to the manner in which such privileges and immunities affect the jurisdiction of His Highness the Sultan over his said subjects,

Whereas the two Governments have agreed by Compromis of October 13, 1904 that these questions shall be determined by reference to arbitration[;]

As to the First Question:

Whereas generally speaking it belongs to every Sovereign to decide to whom he will accord the right to fly his flag and to prescribe the rules governing such grants, and whereas therefore the granting of the French flag to subjects of His Highness the Sultan of Muscat in itself constitutes no attack on the independence of the Sultan,

Whereas nevertheless a Sovereign may be limited by treaties in the exercise of this right, and ... whereas therefore the question arises, under what conditions Powers which have acceded to the General Act of the Brussels Conference of July 2, 1890 relative to the African Slave Trade, especially to article 32 of this Act, are entitled to authorize native vessels to fly their flags,

Whereas by article 32 of this Act the faculty of the Signatory Powers to grant their flag to native vessels has been limited for the purpose of suppressing slave trading and in the general interests of humanity, irrespective of whether the applicant for the flag may belong to a state signatory of this Act or not, and whereas at any rate France is in relation to Great Britain bound to grant her flag only under the conditions prescribed by this Act,

Whereas in order to attain the above mentioned purpose, the Signatory Powers of the Brussels Act have agreed in its article 32 that the authority to fly the flag of one of the Signatory Powers shall in future only be granted to such native vessels, which shall satisfy all the three following conditions:

1. Their fitters-out or owners must be either subjects of or persons protected by [protégés of] the Power whose flag they claim to fly,

2. They must furnish proof that they possess real estate situated in the district of the authority to whom their application is addressed, or supply a solvent security as a guarantee for any fines to which they may eventually become liable,

3. Such fitters-out or owners, as well as the captain of the vessel, must furnish proof that they enjoy a good reputation, and especially that they have never been condemned for acts of slave trade,

Whereas in default of a definition of the term "protégé" in the General Act of the Brussels Conference this term must be understood in the sense which corresponds best as well to the elevated aims of the Conference and its Final Act, as to the principles of the laws of nations, as they have been expressed in treaties existing at that time, in internationally recognized legislation and in international practice,

Whereas the aim of the said article 32 is to admit to navigation in the seas infested by slave trade only those native vessels which are under the strictest surveillance of the Signatory Powers, a condition which can only be secured if the owners, fitters-out and crews of such vessels are exclusively subjected to the sovereignty and jurisdiction of the State, under whose flag they are sailing,

[The tribunal examines the meaning of the term "protégé."]

Whereas the fact of having granted before the ratification of the Brussels Act on January 2, 1892 authorizations to fly the French flag to native vessels not satisfying the conditions prescribed by article 32 of this Act was not in contradiction with any international obligation of France,

For These Reasons, decides and pronounces as follows:

1. *before the 2nd of January 1892 France was entitled to authorize vessels belonging to subjects of His Highness the Sultan of Muscat to fly the French flag, only bound by her own legislation and administrative rules;*

2. *owners of dhows, who before 1892 have been authorized by France to fly the French flag, retain this authorization as long as France renews it to the grantee;*

3. *after January 2, 1892 France was not entitled to authorize vessels belonging to subjects of His Highness the Sultan of Muscat to fly the French flag, except on condition that their owners or fitters-out had established or should establish that they had been considered and treated by France as her "protégés" before the year 1863.*

As to the 2nd Question:

Whereas the legal situation of vessels flying foreign flags and of the owners of such vessels in the territorial waters of an Oriental State is determined by the general principles of jurisdiction, by . . . treaties and by the practice resulting therefrom,

Whereas the terms of the Treaty of Friendship and Commerce between France and the Iman of Muscat of November 17, 1844, [preclude visits by the authorities of the Sultan to French vessels without the consent of such vessels],

Whereas, although it cannot be denied that by admitting the right of France to grant under certain circumstances her flag to native vessels and to have these vessels exempted from visitation by the authorities of the Sultan or in his name, slave trade is facilitated, because slave traders may easily abuse the French flag, for the purpose of escaping from search, the possibility of this abuse, which can be entirely suppressed by the accession of all Powers to article 42 of the Brussels Convention, cannot affect the decision of this case, which must only rest on juridical grounds, . . .

For These Reasons, decides and pronounces as follows:

1. *dhows of Muscat authorized as aforesaid to fly the French flag are entitled in the territorial waters of Muscat to the inviolability provided by the French-Muscat Treaty of November 17, 1844*[.]

Done at The Hague, in the Permanent Court of Arbitration, August 8, 1905.

Notes

1. *The Muscat Dhows Arbitration*. The Muscat Dhows case was litigated in the Permanent Court of Arbitration, an arbitral institution founded by the 1899 Hague Peace Conference and headquartered at The Hague in the Netherlands. Muscat (Oman) was not a party; the Sultan was willing to have Britain serve as Muscat's agent, but France rejected that proposal, and the result was a British-French arbitration. Following the tribunal's decision, France and Britain took more than three years to decide which particular French dhows and protégés were subject to French nationality. See Briton Cooper Busch, Britain and the Persian Gulf, 1894–1914 at 154–86 (1967), and Dolliver Nelson, The Muscat Dhows, in 7 Max Planck Encyclopedia of Public International Law 426 (Rüdiger Wolfrum ed., 2012).

2. *The Nationality of Ships*. Would treating the dhows as French interfere with the independence of the Sultan of Muscat? Great Britain argued that "Frenchifying" the vessels would mean that dhows owned by Muscat nationals could not be visited and searched by Muscat warships, thus withdrawing those dhows "from their natural jurisdiction." The Times (London), July 25, 1905 at 5. Despite Britain's argument, the arbitral tribunal affirmed what is now a general rule: a state may authorize any vessel to fly its flag, which serves as a symbol of its nationality. For current views about vessel nationality, see Articles 91–92 of the LOS Convention.

Is it misleading to use the term "nationality" in reference to ships? Does the term, as applied to vessels, obscure other important connections, e.g., between various states and a vessel's owner, master, crew, and cargo? Is a ship better conceptualized as the national of a state, as a floating bit of state territory, or as having some sui generis connection to a state?

3. *Treaty-based Limits on Vessel Nationality.* States generally have been reluctant to accept treaty-based limitations on their right to grant nationality to vessels. In the Muscat Dhows case, the tribunal noted that states accepting the 1890 General Act of the Brussels Conference had accepted certain limits in an effort to combat the African slave trade. In particular, according to Article 32 of the General Act, "native vessels" could only gain the nationality of a state party to the General Act if their owners were either subjects of, or certain "protected persons" of, the state; if those persons owned real estate or furnished security as a guarantee for any possible fines; and if they furnished "proof that they enjoy a good reputation, and especially that they have never been condemned for acts of slave trade." Would any treaty-based limits on the nationality of vessels be appropriate responses to modern challenges facing the oceans?

4. *Flag State and Coastal State Jurisdiction.* As we will explore in Chapter 4, a flag state traditionally has had exclusive jurisdiction over ships flying its flag on the high seas. See LOS Convention, Article 94. The second question discussed in the Muscat Dhows case suggests that a coastal state may visit foreign flag vessels while they are in the territorial sea, a zone of coastal state sovereignty that today may extend up to twelve nautical miles from a coastal state's baselines. The coastal state may by treaty limit its rights in this regard, as Muscat had done in that case. We further consider coastal state jurisdiction in the territorial sea, as well as the right of foreign vessels to engage in "innocent passage" through the territorial sea, in Chapter 8. Chapter 7 examines the allocation of jurisdictional competence between flag states and port states in internal waters.

CONSTITUTION OF THE MARITIME SAFETY COMMITTEE OF THE INTER-GOVERNMENTAL MARITIME CONSULTATIVE ORGANIZATION
International Court of Justice, Pleadings, Oral Arguments, Documents: Constitution of the Maritime Safety Committee of the Inter-Governmental Maritime Consultative Organization 250–52, 259, 297–98, 318, 364–65 (1960)

[The Inter-Governmental Maritime Consultative Organization (IMCO) was established pursuant to the Convention signed at Geneva, March 6, 1948, which forms the constitution of the Organization. The Convention entered into force in 1958. The Organization (since renamed the International Maritime Organization) is responsible for international cooperation in maritime matters including navigation and pollution. One of its principal working bodies is the Maritime Safety Committee (sometimes abbreviated "M.S.C."). Article 29 of the Convention charges this Committee with consideration of such matters as: aids to navigation; the construction, equipment, and manning of vessels; and maritime safety procedures. Article 28(a) of the Convention provides in part that:

> The Maritime Safety Committee shall consist of fourteen members elected by the Assembly from the Members, governments of those nations having an important interest in maritime safety, of which not less than eight shall be the largest ship-owning nations.

On January 15, 1959, the IMCO Assembly elected the members of the Maritime Safety Committee. Panama and Liberia, although IMCO members, were not elected. Liberia and Panama were, respectively, third and eighth in gross registered tonnage among IMCO members, according to Lloyd's Register of Shipping for 1958. (This Register, although produced by a private organization, is widely regarded as an authoritative source of statistical information on shipping.) This information had been before the Assembly when the elections were being held.

A question arose in the Assembly as to whether the eight members with the greatest registered tonnage were not automatically the "largest ship-owning nations." Panama, Liberia, and the United States contended that this was the correct reading of Article 28(a). Other states, including the United Kingdom, the Netherlands, and Norway, contended that the Assembly had discretion to consider other factors in determining which states were the largest ship owners.

On January 19, 1959, the Assembly decided to seek from the International Court of Justice—in accordance with Article 56 of the IMCO Convention and Article 6(2) of the ICJ Statute—an advisory opinion on the following question:

> Is the Maritime Safety Committee of the Inter-Governmental Maritime Consultative Organization, which was elected on 15 January 1959, constituted in accordance with the Convention for the Establishment of the Organization?

On June 8, 1960, the Court rendered its opinion, holding that the largest ship-owning nations were those with the greatest registered tonnage. 1960 I.C.J. 150. The Court found, therefore, that the January 15th election had not been in accordance with Article 28(a) of the IMCO Constitution. Most of the Court's opinion concerned questions not directly related to the nationality of ships, such as the function of the Maritime Safety Committee, the meaning of the word "elect," and the drafting history of Article 28. However, several countries, in their oral and written statements to the Court, discussed the relation between a vessel and its state of registry. Portions of these statements are set out below. Note that the 1958 High Seas Convention, Article 5(1) of which contains the genuine link requirement, was not in force at the time of this case, although the Convention had been negotiated and signed.]

1. *Written Statement of the Netherlands Government, Dec. 4, 1959*

[I]n the course of the debates with reference to the election of the present M.S.C. on January 15, 1959, it was contended that registration is the *only* criterion for determining whether a State is eligible under the title of "largest ship-owning nation." [T]his interpretation seems to be based on the erroneous assumption that each State is completely free to determine which ships are entitled to fly its flag and that, for the purpose of the composition of the M.S.C.—an international body—the size of a State's commercial fleet should be measured according to such sovereign determination by that State. As to the latter assumption it would seem to need no elaborate comment that a clause such as Article 28 of the IMCO Convention, which envisages a representation of States in an intergovernmental body in accordance with the relative weight of their interests, cannot be held to make the determination of such weight simply dependent upon the national legislation of the State concerned.

Furthermore, and quite apart from the application of Article 28 of the IMCO Convention, States are *not* completely free in fixing the conditions for the right to fly their flag. In this respect it is significant that Article 5 of the Convention on the High Seas, signed at Geneva 29th April, 1958, expressly states: "There must exist a genuine link between the State and the ship; in particular, the State must effectively exercise its jurisdiction and control in administrative, technical and social matters over ships flying its flag." This provision, which forms part of a Convention adopted as a codification of the rules of international law . . . clearly imposes limitations to the freedom of a State to determine which ships "belong" to that State. . . .

A brief comparison of the conditions, imposed by the national legislation of the member States of IMCO for the grant to ships of the right to fly its flag, shows that all the States at present members of the M.S.C. under the title of "largest ship-owning nations" require ownership by nationals as a condition for registration, whereas under the legislation of Panama and Liberia registration is open to all applicants irrespective of their nationality. In case of partnerships, associations and unincorporated companies, all members, or—in some countries—at least the majority of the members should possess the nationality of the State of registration according to the legislation of the first-mentioned group of States; no such condition is required under the legislation of Panama and Liberia.

As to ships owned by corporations, there is more variety in the legislation of the group of States elected as members of the M.S.C. under the title of "largest ship-owning nations" with regard to the link between the corporation and the State concerned, imposed as a condition for registration of a ship owned by that corporation. Incorporation under the laws of the State concerned is not always expressly required. However, if there is no such condition—and, in some countries, even if there is—other conditions ensuring the national character of the corporation is established, such as the nationality of the members of the board of directors or the seat of the real centre of business. Contrariwise, the legislations of Panama and Liberia do not contain either the requirement of incorporation under the laws of the State concerned or any condition as to the nationality of the management.

In view of the above, it is submitted that the Assembly in proceeding on 15th January, 1959, to the election of the M.S.C. as presently constituted, acted in accordance with the IMCO Convention and the general rules of international law by *not* giving decisive weight—for the election of "the largest ship-owning nations"—to the amount of tonnage registered under the flags of Panama and Liberia. The legislations of the States presently elected under the title of "largest ship-owning nations" all require certain connecting factors between ships flying their flags and the State, which connecting factors are *not* required under the legislations of Panama and Liberia.

2. *Written Statement of the Government of India*

[T]he economic success of ship-owning and ship operating business depends upon a reasonably reliable forecast of the laws and regulations which will apply to the ship. The law as to the nationality of the ship must be definitely known in advance. It cannot be left to the general decision of a judge or a tax officer or a crew welfare administrator while the voyage is going on or after the voyage is concluded. The proposition that authorities may look behind the law of the flag to try to discover facts about national control of sums of money invested in the ships leads to the splitting of the nationality of the ship, which is destructive of the economic, social and legal conduct of the shipping business. It will result in international legal anarchy and in the disruption of the legal order which has already been established and followed.

3. *Oral Statement of Mr. Weeks (Liberia), Apr. 27, 1960*

[T]he "genuine link" concept as included in the High Seas Convention . . . probably does not refer at all to the conditions which should exist prior to registration. The particulars given of the concept, namely, the effective exercise by the flag State of jurisdiction and control in administrative, technical and social matters, indicate that the concept was in its final form intended to relate not to events before registration, but to events after registration. It became, in effect, an exhortation to States to do something vis-à-vis ships under their flag.

[A] difficulty affect[s] the application of the concept of the "genuine link." At what moment is it to be applied to any particular vessel? If the genuine link exists at the time of registration, but ceases thereafter, does the registration become invalid? Or if there was no genuine link at the time of registration, but one came into existence afterwards, is the registration retrospectively validated? Questions such as these exemplify the uncertainty which is introduced into an area where the need for certainty is essential. Not only must ships not have two nationalities. It is essential that the one nationality which they have should be readily, rapidly and confidently ascertainable. . . .

4. *Oral Statement of Dr. Fábrega (Panama), Apr. 27, 1960 . . .*

A ship has one flag and only one flag, and so, if that flag is not respected, if it is not properly regarded, you are creating a situation of lack of proper order and law at sea. [A]n individual, whatever his nationality, [who] goes to a foreign country, usually and normally . . . has the protection of the laws of that country which protects nationals and foreigners; he has police protection, sanitary protection, all the normal protections that a State grants to nationals and foreigners. But when a ship is at sea, that ship only has the protection of the State of its flag. So it is . . . a very dangerous proposition to start experimenting and introducing vague and complex notions of "beneficial ownership" or "genuine link," or some other, against the well-known rule and principle of the law of the flag.

5. *Oral Statement of Mr. Seyersted (Norway), Apr. 29, 1960 . . .*

It is *not* in accordance with sound principles of law to let the right of a country depend exclusively upon facts which it is within the exclusive power of the Government concerned to create. Should one consider such a criterion to provide a single test for establishing certain international rights of the State, one must at least ascertain that the State has exercised its power within certain limits laid down in international law. Otherwise one would arrive at complete arbitrariness.

Notes

1. *Open Registry.* A system of flag state control poses particular difficulties if a flag state cannot or will not control its ships. Recall that the tribunal in the Muscat Dhows case cautioned that "slavetraders may easily abuse the French flag, for the purpose of escaping from search." Modern concerns relating to a lack of flag state supervision relate to poor labor conditions on board ships, unsafe vessels, and risks of pollution. These concerns are often linked to open registry or "flag of convenience" vessels. A 1970 British committee headed by Lord Rochdale identified six features common to open registry:

> (i) The country of registry allows ownership and/or control of its merchant vessels by non-citizens;
> (ii) Access to the registry is easy. A ship may usually be registered at a consul's office abroad. Equally important, transfer from the registry at the owner's option is not restricted;
> (iii) Taxes on the income from the ships are not levied locally or are low. A registry fee and an annual fee, based on tonnage, are normally the only charges made. A guarantee or acceptable understanding regarding future freedom from taxation may also be given;
> (iv) The country of registry is a small power with no national requirement under any foreseeable circumstances for all the shipping registered, but receipts from very small charges on a large tonnage may produce a substantial effect on its national income and balance of payments;
> (v) Manning of ships by non-nationals is freely permitted; and
> (vi) The country of registry has neither the power nor the administrative machinery effectively to impose any government or international regulations; nor has the country the wish or the power to control the companies themselves.

Commn. of Inquiry into Shipping, Report 51, Cmnd. 4337 (1970).

The practice of open registry grew rapidly after World War II. What are the advantages of open registry for ship owners and flag of convenience states? What are the disadvantages of flags of convenience for various interests? Why do not all vessel owners seek flag of convenience nationality? How in fact have open registry states implemented and enforced labor, environmental, and safety standards on ships flying their flags? See Elizabeth R. De Sombre,

Flagging Standards: Globalization and Environmental, Safety, and Labor Regulations (2006).

2. *Evaluating the Genuine Link Requirement.* Was development of a genuine link requirement sensible with respect to vessels? The genuine link requirement originated outside the context of the law of the sea, in cases involving dual nationals, and the ICJ controversially extended the concept to find that one country was not obliged to recognize the nationality of the citizen of another country with whom that country had no "genuine link." Nottebohm Case (Liechtenstein v. Guatemala), 1955 I.C.J. 4. Is a genuine link a condition of nationality? What other functions could the requirement serve? See Vincent P. Cogliati-Bantz, Disentangling the "Genuine Link": Enquiries in Sea, Air and Space Law, 79 Nordic J. Intl. L. 383 (2010); John E. Noyes, Interpreting the 1982 Law of the Sea Convention and Defining Its Terms, in Definitions for the Law of the Sea: Terms Not Defined by the 1982 Convention 45, 69–78 (George K. Walker ed., 2011).

THE M/V SAIGA (NO. 2) CASE

St. Vincent and the Grenadines v. Guinea (Admissibility and Merits), ITLOS Case No. 2 (1999), 3 ITLOS Rep. 10, 120 Intl. L. Rep. 143, 38 Intl. Leg. Materials 1323 (1999), available at http://www.itlos.org

[The *Saiga*, a tanker flying the flag of Saint Vincent and the Grenadines, was engaged in supplying fuel oil to fishing vessels in the exclusive economic zone (EEZ) of Guinea. On October 28, 1997, a Guinean patrol boat attacked the *Saiga* after, according to the tanker's logbook, it had moved into the EEZ of Sierra Leone. The vessel was then arrested and, along with its crew, brought to port in Conkary, Guinea, where the master was detained and the cargo of fuel oil was discharged. Guinea claimed the *Saiga*'s supplying of fuel to fishing vessels violated Guinean customs laws and filed criminal charges against the master, who ultimately received a suspended sentence of six months' imprisonment and a fine.

The incident gave rise to various proceedings before the International Tribunal for the Law of the Sea, in accordance with the compulsory dispute settlement provisions of Part XV of the LOS Convention, to which both Saint Vincent and the Grenadines and Guinea are parties. On November 13, 1997, Saint Vincent and the Grenadines submitted an application for the prompt release of the *Saiga* and its crew, pursuant to Article 292 of the LOS Convention. The ITLOS, on December 4, 1997, ordered the prompt release of the vessel and crew on the posting of a US$ 400,000 bond. 1 ITLOS Rep. 16, 110 Intl. L. Rep. 736,

37 Intl. Leg. Materials 360 (1998). The vessel was released on February 28, 1998, and remaining crew members also left Conkary then.

On January 13, 1998, pursuant to Article 290 of the LOS Convention, Saint Vincent and the Grenadines filed a request for provisional measures with the ITLOS, concerning the arrest and detention of the *Saiga* and its crew. On March 11, 1998, the Tribunal prescribed provisional measures, ordering Guinea to refrain from taking enforcement measures against the vessel. 117 Intl. L. Rep. 111, 37 Intl. Leg. Materials 1202 (1998). The ITLOS then heard and decided the merits of the case pursuant to an agreement between Saint Vincent and the Grenadines and Guinea dated February 20, 1998. In the proceedings on the merits, Saint Vincent and the Grenadines claimed, inter alia, that Guinea interfered with the rights of a Vincentian vessel to navigate in Guinea's EEZ, violated the Convention's provisions on the right of hot pursuit, and used excessive force in stopping and arresting the vessel. There are additional excerpts from the M/V Saiga (No. 2) case in Chapter 4, Section F (hot pursuit) and Chapter 9 (EEZ). The Tribunal, in its judgment of July 1, 1999, ruled in favor of Saint Vincent and the Grenadines on several issues, awarding US$ 2,123,357 as compensation.

The ITLOS also addressed arguments by Guinea urging that, as a threshold matter, the claims of Saint Vincent and the Grenadines were inadmissible. One admissibility argument, concerning the issue of genuine link, appears in the excerpt below; we see another such argument, concerning the alleged lack of proper registration of the *Saiga*, in Section B.]

75. The next objection to admissibility raised by Guinea is that there was no genuine link between the *Saiga* and Saint Vincent and the Grenadines. Guinea contends that "without a genuine link between Saint Vincent and the Grenadines and the M/V '*Saiga*,' Saint Vincent and the Grenadines' claim concerning a violation of its right of navigation and the status of the ship is not admissible before the Tribunal *vis-à-vis* Guinea, because Guinea is not bound to recognize the Vincentian nationality of the M/V '*Saiga*,' which forms a prerequisite for the mentioned claim in international law."

76. Guinea further argues that a State cannot fulfill its obligations as a flag State under the Convention with regard to a ship unless it exercises prescriptive and enforcement jurisdiction over the owner or, as the case may be, the operator of the ship. Guinea contends that, in the absence of such jurisdiction, there is no genuine link between the ship and Saint Vincent and the Grenadines and that, accordingly, it is not obliged to recognize the claims of Saint Vincent and the Grenadines in relation to the ship.

77. Saint Vincent and the Grenadines maintains that there is nothing in the Convention to support the contention that the existence of a genuine link

between a ship and a State is a necessary precondition for the grant of nationality to the ship, or that the absence of such a genuine link deprives a flag State of the right to bring an international claim against another State in respect of illegal measures taken against the ship.

78. Saint Vincent and the Grenadines also challenges the assertion of Guinea that there was no genuine link between the *Saiga* and Saint Vincent and the Grenadines. It claims that the requisite genuine link existed between it and the ship. Saint Vincent and the Grenadines calls attention to various facts which, according to it, provide evidence of this link. These include the fact that the owner of the *Saiga* is represented in Saint Vincent and the Grenadines by a company formed and established in that State and the fact that the *Saiga* is subject to the supervision of the Vincentian authorities to secure compliance with the International Convention for the Safety of Life at Sea (SOLAS), 1960 and 1974, the International Convention for the Prevention of Pollution from Ships, 1973, as modified by the Protocol of 1978 relating thereto (MARPOL 73/78), and other conventions of the International Maritime Organization to which Saint Vincent and the Grenadines is a party. In addition, Saint Vincent and the Grenadines maintains that arrangements have been made to secure regular supervision of the vessel's seaworthiness through surveys, on at least an annual basis, conducted by reputable classification societies authorized for that purpose by Saint Vincent and the Grenadines. Saint Vincent and the Grenadines also points out that, under its laws, preference is given to Vincentian nationals in the manning of ships flying its flag. It further draws attention to the vigorous efforts made by its authorities to secure the protection of the *Saiga* on the international plane before and throughout the present dispute.

79. Article 91, paragraph 1, of the [LOS] Convention provides: "There must exist a genuine link between the State and the ship." Two questions need to be addressed in this connection. The first is whether the absence of a genuine link between a flag State and a ship entitles another State to refuse to recognize the nationality of the ship. The second question is whether or not a genuine link existed between the *Saiga* and Saint Vincent and the Grenadines at the time of the incident.

80. With regard to the first question, the Tribunal notes that the provision in article 91, paragraph 1, of the Convention, requiring a genuine link between the State and the ship, does not provide the answer. Nor do articles 92 and 94 of the Convention, which together with article 91 constitute the context of the provision, provide the answer. The Tribunal, however, recalls that the International Law Commission, in article 29 of the Draft Articles on the Law of the Sea adopted by it in 1956, proposed the concept of a "genuine link" as a criterion not only for the attribution of nationality to a ship but also for the recognition by other States of such nationality. After providing that "ships

have the nationality of the State whose flag they are entitled to fly," the draft article continued: "Nevertheless, for purposes of recognition of the national character of the ship by other States, there must exist a genuine link between the State and the ship." This sentence was not included in article 5, paragraph 1, of the Convention on the High Seas of 29 April 1958 (hereinafter "the 1958 Convention"), which reads, in part, as follows:

> There must exist a genuine link between the State and the ship; in particular, the State must effectively exercise its jurisdiction and control in administrative, technical and social matters over ships flying its flag.

Thus, while the obligation regarding a genuine link was maintained in the 1958 Convention, the proposal that the existence of a genuine link should be a basis for the recognition of nationality was not adopted.

81. The Convention follows the approach of the 1958 Convention. Article 91 retains the part of the third sentence of article 5, paragraph 1, of the 1958 Convention which provides that there must be a genuine link between the State and the ship. The other part of that sentence, stating that the flag State shall effectively exercise its jurisdiction and control in administrative, technical and social matters over ships flying its flag, is reflected in article 94 of the Convention, dealing with the duties of the flag State.

82. Paragraphs 2 to 5 of article 94 of the Convention outline the measures that a flag State is required to take to exercise effective jurisdiction as envisaged in paragraph 1. Paragraph 6 sets out the procedure to be followed where another State has "clear grounds to believe that proper jurisdiction and control with respect to a ship have not been exercised." That State is entitled to report the facts to the flag State which is then obliged to "investigate the matter and, if appropriate, take any action necessary to remedy the situation." There is nothing in article 94 to permit a State which discovers evidence indicating the absence of proper jurisdiction and control by a flag State over a ship to refuse to recognize the right of the ship to fly the flag of the flag State.

83. The conclusion of the Tribunal is that the purpose of the provisions of the Convention on the need for a genuine link between a ship and its flag State is to secure more effective implementation of the duties of the flag State, and not to establish criteria by reference to which the validity of the registration of ships in a flag State may be challenged by other States.

84. This conclusion is not put into question by the United Nations Convention on Conditions for Registration of Ships of 7 February 1986 invoked by Guinea. This Convention (which is not in force) sets out as one of its principal objectives the strengthening of "the genuine link between a State and ships

flying its flag." In any case, the Tribunal observes that Guinea has not cited any provision in that Convention which lends support to its contention that "a basic condition for the registration of a ship is that also the owner or operator of the ship is under the jurisdiction of the flag State."

85. The conclusion is further strengthened by the Agreement for the Implementation of the Provisions of the United Nations Convention on the Law of the Sea of 10 December 1982 Relating to the Conservation and Management of Straddling Fish Stocks and Highly Migratory Fish Stocks opened for signature on 4 December 1995 and the Agreement to Promote Compliance with International Conservation and Management Measures by Fishing Vessels on the High Seas of 24 November 1993. These Agreements, neither of which is in force, set out, *inter alia*, detailed obligations to be discharged by the flag States of fishing vessels but do not deal with the conditions to be satisfied for the registration of fishing vessels.

86. In the light of the above considerations, the Tribunal concludes that there is no legal basis for the claim of Guinea that it can refuse to recognize the right of the *Saiga* to fly the flag of Saint Vincent and the Grenadines on the ground that there was no genuine link between the ship and Saint Vincent and the Grenadines.

87. With regard to the second question, the Tribunal finds [by eighteen votes to two] that, in any case, the evidence adduced by Guinea is not sufficient to justify its contention that there was no genuine link between the ship and Saint Vincent and the Grenadines at the material time.

Notes

1. *The International Tribunal for the Law of the Sea.* The International Tribunal for the Law of the Sea, which decided the M/V Saiga (No. 2) case, was created by the LOS Convention and began operating after the Convention entered into force in November 1994. Located in Hamburg, Germany, the ITLOS is a component of the Convention's compulsory third-party dispute settlement system, which we explore in Chapter 15.

2. *The Genuine Link Requirement in the LOS Convention.* Article 5 of the 1958 High Seas Convention provides in part: "There must exist a genuine link between the State and the ship; in particular, the State must effectively exercise its control in administrative, technical and social matters over ships flying its flag." Article 91 of the LOS Convention only retains the language before the semicolon. The language after the semicolon is found at the start of Article 94, which then addresses in more detail flag state obligations to control administrative, technical, and social matters. We consider Article 94 and the

responsibilities of flag states in Chapter 4. Does dividing the quoted sentence from Article 5 of the High Seas Convention between Articles 91 and 94 of the LOS Convention have legal significance? Does it weaken the argument that a flag state's failure to perform its duties under Article 94 would provide evidence of the lack of a genuine link between it and the ship at issue?

3. *Lack of Genuine Link and Nonrecognition of Vessel Nationality*. If a flag state lacks a genuine link with a ship flying its flag, should another state be entitled to refuse to recognize the ship as a national of the flag state? If nonrecognition is precluded, how else may violations of the genuine link requirement be "enforced" or deterred?

4. *The Indeterminacy of the Genuine Link Requirement.* Does the indeterminacy or "softness" of the genuine link requirement mean it is of no importance? What are the prospects for an international agreement that would add more specific content to the genuine link requirement? How else do international law and process respond to the concerns about flag of convenience vessels that prompted adoption of the requirement?

INTERNATIONAL LAW COMMISSION, DRAFT ARTICLES ON DIPLOMATIC PROTECTION

Report of the International Law Commission on the Work of its Fifty-eighth Session, UNGAOR, 61st Sess., Supp. No. 10, Draft Article 18, UN Doc. A/61/10 (2006)

Article 18

Protection of ships' crews

The right of the State of nationality of the members of the crew of a ship to exercise diplomatic protection is not affected by the right of the State of nationality of a ship to seek redress on behalf of such crew members, irrespective of their nationality, when they have been injured in connection with an injury to the vessel resulting from an internationally wrongful act.

Commentary

(1) The purpose of draft article 18 is to affirm the right of the State or States of nationality of a ship's crew to exercise diplomatic protection on their behalf, while at the same time acknowledging that the State of nationality of the ship also has a right to seek redress on their behalf, irrespective of their nationality, when they have been injured in the course of an injury to a vessel resulting from an internationally wrongful act. It has become necessary to affirm the right of the State of nationality to exercise diplomatic protection on behalf of the members of a ship's crew in order to preclude any suggestion that this right

has been replaced by that of the State of nationality of the ship. At the same time it is necessary to recognize the right of the State of nationality of the ship to seek redress in respect of the members of the ship's crew. Although this cannot be characterized as diplomatic protection in the absence of the bond of nationality between the flag State of a ship and the members of a ship's crew, there is nevertheless a close resemblance between this type of protection and diplomatic protection.

(2) There is support in the practice of States, in judicial decisions and in the writings of publicists, for the position that the State of nationality of a ship (the flag State) may seek redress for members of the crew of the ship who do not have its nationality. There are also policy considerations in favour of such an approach.

(3) The early practice of the United States, in particular, lends support to such a custom. Under American law foreign seamen were traditionally entitled to the protection of the United States while serving on American vessels. The American view was that once a seaman enlisted on a ship, the only relevant nationality was that of the flag State. This unique status of foreigners serving on American vessels was traditionally reaffirmed in diplomatic communications and consular regulations of the United States. Doubts have, however, been raised, including by the United States, as to whether this practice provides evidence of a customary rule.

(4) International arbitral awards are inconclusive on the right of a State to extend protection to non-national seamen, but tend to lean in favour of such right rather than against it. In *McCready (US) v. Mexico* the umpire, Sir Edward Thornton, held that "seamen serving in the naval or mercantile marine under a flag not their own are entitled, for the duration of that service, to the protection of the flag under which they serve." In the *"I'm Alone"* case, which arose from the sinking of a Canadian vessel by a United States coast guard ship, the Canadian Government successfully claimed compensation on behalf of three non-national crew members, asserting that where a claim was on behalf of a vessel, members of the crew were to be deemed, for the purposes of the claim, to be of the same nationality as the vessel. In the *Reparation for Injuries* advisory opinion two judges, in their separate opinions, accepted the right of a State to exercise protection on behalf of alien crew members.

(5) In 1999, the International Tribunal for the Law of the Sea handed down its decision in *The M/V "Saiga" (No. 2)* case (*Saint Vincent and the Grenadines v. Guinea*) which provides support for the right of the flag State to seek redress for non-national crew members. The dispute in this case arose out of the arrest and detention of the *Saiga* by Guinea, while it was supplying oil to fishing vessels off the coast of Guinea. The *Saiga* was registered in St. Vincent and the

Grenadines ("St. Vincent") and its master and crew were Ukrainian nationals. There were also three Senegalese workers on board at the time of the arrest. Following the arrest, Guinea detained the ship and crew. In proceedings before the International Tribunal for the Law of the Sea, Guinea objected to the admissibility of St. Vincent's claim, *inter alia*, on the ground that the injured crew members were not nationals of St. Vincent. The Tribunal dismissed these challenges to the admissibility of the claim and held that Guinea had violated the rights of St. Vincent by arresting and detaining the ship and its crew. It ordered Guinea to pay compensation to St. Vincent for damages to the *Saiga* and for injury to the crew.

(6) Although the Tribunal treated the dispute mainly as one of direct injury to St. Vincent, the Tribunal's reasoning suggests that it also saw the matter as a case involving the protection of the crew something akin to, but different from, diplomatic protection. Guinea clearly objected to the admissibility of the claim in respect of the crew on the ground that it constituted a claim for diplomatic protection in respect of non-nationals of St. Vincent. St. Vincent, equally clearly, insisted that it had the right to protect the crew of a ship flying its flag "irrespective of their nationality." In dismissing Guinea's objection the Tribunal stated that the United Nations Convention on the Law of the Sea in a number of relevant provisions, including article 292, drew no distinction between nationals and non-nationals of the flag State. It stressed that "the ship, every thing on it, and every person involved or interested in its operations are treated as an entity linked to the flag State. The nationalities of these persons are not relevant."

(7) There are cogent policy reasons for allowing the flag State to seek redress for the ship's crew. This was recognized by the Law of the Sea Tribunal in *Saiga* when it called attention to "the transient and multinational composition of ships' crews" and stated that large ships "could have a crew comprising persons of several nationalities. If each person sustaining damage were obliged to look for protection from the State of which such a person is a national, undue hardship would ensue." Practical considerations relating to the bringing of claims should not be overlooked. It is much easier and more efficient for one State to seek redress on behalf of all crew members than to require the States of nationality of all crew members to bring separate claims on behalf of their nationals.

(8) Support for the right of the flag State to seek redress for the ship's crew is substantial and justified. It cannot, however, be categorized as diplomatic protection. Nor should it be seen as having replaced diplomatic protection. Both diplomatic protection by the State of nationality and the right of the flag State to seek redress for the crew should be recognized, without priority being

accorded to either. Ships' crews are often exposed to hardships emanating from the flag State, in the form of poor working conditions, or from third States, in the event of the ship being arrested. In these circumstances they should receive the maximum protection that international law can offer.

(9) The right of the flag State to seek redress for the ship's crew is not limited to redress for injuries sustained during or in the course of an injury to the vessel but extends also to injuries sustained in connection with an injury to the vessel resulting from an internationally wrongful act, that is as a consequence of the injury to the vessel. Thus such a right would arise where members of the ship's crew are illegally arrested and detained [e.g., after a wrongful attack].

Notes

1. *The International Law Commission.* The International Law Commission (ILC), one outgrowth of 19th- and early 20th-century international law codification efforts, was established by the U.N. General Assembly in 1947. GA Res. 147(II) (1947). The ILC furthers the goal of Article 13(1) of the U.N. Charter, which calls on the General Assembly to "initiate studies and make recommendations for the purpose of... encouraging the progressive development of international law and its codification." The General Assembly elects international law experts from various countries to serve as members of the ILC. Article 15 of the Commission's Statute distinguishes two roles: progressive development, i.e., "the preparation of draft conventions on subjects which have not yet been regulated by international law or in regard to which the law has not yet been sufficiently developed in the practice of States," and codification, i.e., "the more precise formulation and systematization of rules of international law in fields where there already has been extensive State practice, precedent and doctrine." Since its inception, the ILC has prepared highly influential draft treaties. Of particular interest in this book is the ILC's work on draft treaties used in negotiating the four 1958 law of the sea conventions; we have noted that ILC effort in Chapters 1 and 2. ILC draft treaties also helped pave the way for the 1969 Vienna Convention on the Law of Treaties and the Rome Statute on the International Criminal Court. In addition, the ILC has prepared important documents that have not become treaties, including the 2001 Draft Articles on State Responsibility. One of the ILC's current projects is the Draft Articles on Diplomatic Protection, excerpted above. For more information about the ILC, see http://www.un.org/law/ilc.

2. *Nationality of Vessels and Espousal of Claims.* The concept of nationality of vessels serves several functions. These include clarifying what legal authority governs a vessel on the high seas and providing a basis for a

country's military protection of merchant vessels—recall the reflagging of Kuwaiti ships as U.S. vessels during the Iran-Iraq war in the 1980s, an issue discussed in Chapter 2, Section H.3. Another function of vessel nationality, at issue in the ILC excerpt above, is allowing the flag state to espouse claims concerning infringements of the rights of its vessels and crew members. In paragraph 8 of its Commentary to Draft Article 18 on Diplomatic Protection, the ILC concluded that "[b]oth diplomatic protection by the State of nationality and the right of the flag State to seek redress for the crew should be recognized, without priority being accorded to either." But if the state of nationality of a crew member, cargo interest, or vessel owner espouses a claim for injuries to its nationals along with the flag state, is not some priority among claims required? To whom should a state that has interfered with the rights of a foreign crew member of a flag state's vessel pay any damages? To the flag state or to the state of nationality of the crew member?

If a flag state pursues a claim, does the ship-as-unit doctrine apply to crew members of the same nationality as the respondent state? The issue arose when Russia seized a Greenpeace vessel, and the Netherlands, as flag state, sought the release of the vessel and her crew, some of whom were Russian nationals. See the Arctic Sunrise Case (Netherlands v. Russia) (Provisional Measures), ITLOS Case No. 22 (2013), ¶¶ 95, 105(1), available at http://www.itlos.org; Separate Opinion of Judge Jesus, id. ¶¶ 19-20; and Dissenting Opinion of Judge Golitsyn, id. ¶ 46.

Why even require vessel owners or crew members to persuade some state to espouse their claims? Could individuals pursue claims on their own? Should an international tribunal provide a forum for crew members to pursue claims directly against states for violating the crew members' rights under international law?

B Registration and Documentation

States normally grant nationality to vessels by registering them in accordance with national legislation. The excerpts below from the M/V Saiga (No. 2) and Grand Prince cases analyze the relationship between nationality and registration. States issue documents to ships as evidence of their registration, and the documents can be used as proof of nationality. The last reading in this section outlines the traditional significance of a ship's documents.

THE M/V SAIGA (NO. 2) CASE
St. Vincent and the Grenadines v. Guinea (Admissibility and Merits), ITLOS Case No. 2 (1999), 3 ITLOS Rep. 10, 120 Intl. L. Rep. 143, 38 Intl. Leg. Materials 1323 (1999), available at http://www.itlos.org

[For a summary of this case, see Section A. One of Guinea's objections to the admissibility of the claims of Saint Vincent and the Grenadines was that the latter state lacked standing. Guinea argued that when the *Saiga* was arrested, it was "not validly registered under the flag of Saint Vincent and the Grenadines." ¶ 55. Consequently, according to Guinea, Saint Vincent and the Grenadines could not pursue claims related to the ship or those on board. Guinea emphasized that the *Saiga*'s provisional Vincentian registration certificate stated that it expired on September 12, 1997, and that a permanent registration certificate was not issued until November 28, 1997. Thus, Guinea maintained, the *Saiga* was "*a ship without nationality* at the time of its attack on October 28, 1997." ¶ 57 (emphasis in original). The ITLOS rejected this objection to the admissibility of the Vincentian claims, noting that "the consistent conduct of Saint Vincent and the Grenadines provides sufficient support for the conclusion that the *Saiga* retained" that state's registration and nationality "at all times material to the dispute." ¶ 73(b). The excerpt below, from the Separate Opinion of ITLOS Vice-President Wolfrum, discusses legal principles related to vessel registration.]

Separate Opinion of Vice-President Wolfrum

17. Registration of ships has to be seen in close connection with jurisdictional powers flag States have over ships flying their flag and their obligation concerning the implementation of rules of international law in respect to these ships.... Th[e] subjection of the high seas to the rule of international law is organized and implemented by means of a permanent legal relation between ships flying a particular flag and the State whose flag they fly. This link enables and, in fact, obliges States to implement and enforce international as well as their national law governing the utilization of the high seas. The Convention upholds this principle. It further establishes a legal regime balancing the jurisdictional powers of the flag State and the powers and competencies of coastal States or port States concerning foreign ships whenever they enter maritime areas under the jurisdiction of the latter or enter respective ports. Since the juridical order of the maritime spaces is based upon the institution of the nationality of ships, it is necessary that this nationality be easily identifiable, that, in case of disputing claims or situations requiring the identification of

the ship, its nationality may be established on the basis of verifiable objective data. These essential principles are not reflected adequately in the Judgment when it considers some signs of Vincentian nationality, e.g. some documents, including the ship's seal, produced by the charterer or owner, on board of the ship and, in particular, the subsequent conduct of Saint Vincent and the Grenadines as sufficient to prove it to have had the nationality of Saint Vincent and the Grenadines at the time of the arrest.

18. Traditionally the nationality of ships has been established and implemented by linking national rules on the nationality of ships with international ones and in particular by obliging States to mutually respect the national rules on the nationality of ships. It is the traditional rule of international law, frequently confirmed in international and national adjudication, that the national law of each particular country determines which ship should be eligible for receiving the nationality of the particular State. It has been equally recognized that each State may decide upon the criteria of eligibility which must be recognized by other States. Article 91, paragraph 1, first sentence, of the Convention has codified this rule of international customary law.

19. This rule constitutes as much a right as an obligation of States. The provision embraces the prescriptive jurisdiction of every State to establish the respective conditions ships have to meet for being granted the right to fly the flag of that particular State. The wording of the provision further clearly indicates that States are under an obligation to enact respective national regulations.

20. Article 91, paragraph 1, of the Convention refers to nationality as well as registration without clarifying the relationship between the two concepts. This again is an area where States have considerable discretion. Different systems are applied in municipal law; however it is common to all of them that the attribution of nationality for merchant ships requires a constitutive act from the side of the responsible authorities of the given State. It is the prevailing practice that—except for warships and sometimes smaller vessels—such constitutive act rests in the registration e.g. that nationality is granted through registration.

21. The obligation to enter ships into a register of ships has developed in national law[.]

22. To attribute effectively the right to fly its flag to a ship and to be certain that this will be respected a State must take further steps with the view to make other States cognizant of this fact. The mode most traditionally upheld to prove the registration and/or nationality of a particular ship is in making such formal attribution through appropriate documentation. This has been confirmed in

hundreds of treaties of friendship, commerce, and navigation. Although different clauses are used they all confirm that the nationality of vessels shall be reciprocally recognized on the basis of documents and certificates on board of the vessel issued by the proper authorities of either of the contracting Parties.

23. The Convention follows this approach in its article 91, paragraph 2. The wording of this provision indicates that certificates of registration or equivalent documents issued by the respective national authorities constitute the proof for a particular ship to have the right to fly the flag of that State. The authorities of other States or international authorities, as the case may be, are under an obligation to respect these documents as being accurate and valid[;] in particular, they must not—except under special circumstances—challenge the validity or accuracy of such documents on the ground that they do not correspond to the national law of the State having issued the documents. Only such understanding of the objective of the documents referred to in article 91, paragraph 2, of the Convention corresponds to the content of the general rule enshrined in article 91, paragraph 1, first sentence, of the Convention. To consider documents as referred to in article 91, paragraph 2, of the Convention as being the authoritative statement of the responsible State on the status of a given ship thus is the necessary mechanism to protect the right of every State to establish its own regime on registration and nationality of ships and to apply it according to its national law....

25. When establishing whether the *Saiga* was registered under the flag of Saint Vincent and the Grenadines the Tribunal... disregards the content of the Provisional Certificate of Registration and the Register of Ships. Instead, as already indicated, the Judgment relies as evidence on the "overt signs of Vincentian nationality on the ship or carried on board," the conduct of Saint Vincent and the Grenadines after the arrest of the *Saiga* and on the failure of Guinea to challenge the registration or nationality of the *Saiga*. The disregard of the wording of the Provisional Certificate of the *Saiga* and of the entry in the Register of Ships, as printed out 15 April 1997, is at the roots of my disagreement with the reasoning of the Judgment on the issue of registration/nationality of the *Saiga*.

26. The Judgment should have proceeded from the documents Saint Vincent and the Grenadines had to issue, according to article 91, paragraph 2, of the Convention, to the *Saiga*, namely the Provisional Certificate of Registration relevant at the time of the arrest of the ship. This Certificate of Registration was marked to be a provisional one and clearly stated that it expired on 12 September 1997. An examination of the Register of Ships... submitted by Saint Vincent and the Grenadines confirms that the registration

of the *Saiga* (ex *Sunflower*) was entered on 12 March 1997 and was valid until 12 September 1997.... Since the permanent registration of the *Saiga* was entered in the Register of Ships of Saint Vincent and the Grenadines only on 28 November 1997 the Judgment should have come to the conclusion that the *Saiga* was, according to the documents referred to in article 91, paragraph 2, of the Convention, not registered at the time of its arrest. The further and only possible conclusion to be drawn is that, according to the Merchant Shipping Act of Saint Vincent and the Grenadines the *Saiga* at the time of its arrest did not have the nationality of Saint Vincent and the Grenadines.

27. [T]he nationality of a ship is a fact to be determined, like other facts in dispute before the Tribunal, on the basis of evidence adduced by the parties.... In international litigation a State does not have the exclusive power to interpret its national law to the detriment of the other party.

[Vice-President Wolfrum concludes that the Merchant Shipping Act of Saint Vincent and the Grenadines did not support the contention that the *Saiga* remained registered after the expiry date of its provisional registration.]

33. It is well established in international law that the primary requisite for the making of an international claim is the existence of an interest recognized by law at the time the alleged violation of that interest occurred. This condition is not fulfilled since the *Saiga* did not have the nationality at the time of the arrest and later conduct of Saint Vincent and the Grenadines cannot cure this deficit. Apart from that the Convention on the Law of the Sea rules out that a State becomes the flag State of a ship retroactively and by mere conduct. [A]rticle 91, paragraph 1, of the Convention... does not allow a State to claim the flag State position in international proceedings although there is no valid registration when the very State considers this to be in its interest and to reject it if its interests so require.

[Vice-President Wolfrum nevertheless concurs with the ITLOS's decision that the claims of Saint Vincent and the Grenadines are admissible. He finds that Guinea was estopped from challenging the nationality of the Saiga because Guinea failed to challenge, in earlier stages of the proceedings, the flag state status of Saint Vincent and the Grenadines, and because Guinea negotiated and accepted a bank guarantee from Saint Vincent for release of the vessel. ¶ 41. Judge Wolfrum also finds that Guinea had acquiesced in Saint Vincent being the flag state of the Saiga by failing to raise the lack of the vessel's registration at the outset of the proceedings. ¶ 43.]

THE GRAND PRINCE CASE

Belize v. France (Prompt Release), ITLOS Case No. 8 (2001), 125 Intl. L. Rep. 273, available at http://www.itlos.org

[The *Grand Prince*, a fishing vessel with a Spanish master and a crew of Spanish and Chilean nationals, was arrested on December 26, 2000, off the French Kerguelen Islands, in the exclusive economic zone of the French Southern and Antarctic Territories. French authorities claimed that the master of the *Grand Prince* was fishing without authorization in the French EEZ, and that he had, in violation of French law, failed to announce his entry into the EEZ and to declare the fish carried on board. A French frigate escorted the *Grand Prince* to a port in Réunion, where it arrived on January 9, 2001, and was detained during French legal proceedings there. On March 6, 2001, Belize authorized an application to be brought on its behalf to the ITLOS under Article 292 of the LOS Convention, seeking an order for the prompt release of the *Grand Prince* on the posting of a reasonable bond. The evidence revealed that the *Grand Prince* was flying the flag of Belize at the time of its arrest, but, according to Belize, "at the time of its detention, it was going to be reflagged and registered in Brazil." ¶ 33. The Tribunal considered whether Belize was indeed the flag state of the *Grand Prince*, in order to determine whether the Tribunal could exercise jurisdiction over the prompt release application.]

66. It is necessary here to examine the question of which entity has the *locus standi* to seek the release of a vessel from detention. In the scheme of article 292 of the Convention, it is the flag State of the vessel that is given the *locus standi* to take up the question of release in an appropriate court or tribunal. Any other entity may make an application only on behalf of the flag State of the vessel. As provided in article 292, paragraph 2, the application for release may be made "only by or on behalf of the flag State of the vessel."

67. The initial burden of establishing that Belize was the flag State when the Application was made is on the Applicant. In seeking to discharge this burden, the Applicant submitted the following documents:

(a) Letter dated 15 March 2001 from the Attorney General of Belize;

(b) Provisional patent of navigation issued by IMMARBE [the International Merchant Marine Registry of Belize];

(c) Certification dated 30 March 2001 issued by IMMARBE and headed "TO WHOM IT MAY CONCERN."

68. The Attorney General's letter, authorizing Mr. Alberto Penelas Alvarez to make an application on behalf of Belize under article 292 of the Convention, stated that the vessel was "of Belize flag, which holds registration number 07972047 and call letters V3UJ7."

69. The date of issuance of the provisional patent of navigation was given as 16 October 2000 and the date of its expiration was given as 29 December 2000.

70. The IMMARBE certification of 30 March 2001 stated:

> TO WHOM IT MAY CONCERN
>
> The undersigned, Director and Senior Deputy Registrar of the International Merchant Marine Registry of Belize, duly empowered by the Merchant Ships Act, 1989/1996, hereby certifies that the vessel GRAND PRINCE is registered under the flag of Belize, holding registration Number 07972047 and call letters V3UJ7.

It is also certified that there are documents relating to the status of the vessel that are pending to be processed,—including the cancellation of status which execution was suspended—based on particular circumstances involving the situation of the vessel and relating to the detention instructed by the French authorities.

It is further certified that, despite the expiration of the Patent of navigation and Ship station license, the vessel is still considered as registered in Belize until final decision of this Administration pending to the result of the court proceeding in which the vessel is engaged at the present time.

71. The Respondent drew the attention of the Tribunal to the following documents:

(a) Note verbale dated 4 January 2001 sent by the Ministry of Foreign Affairs, Belize, to the Embassy of France in El Salvador;

(b) Letter dated 26 March 2001 sent by IMMARBE to the Honorary Consul of France in Belize City.

72. In the note verbale of 4 January 2001, the Ministry of Foreign Affairs of Belize stated:

> The Ministry of Foreign Affairs of Belize presents its compliments to the Embassy of France in El Salvador and has the honour to refer to the Note of 3 January 2001 with reference to the detention of Belize-flagged vessel "Grand Prince."
>
> The Ministry of Foreign Affairs wishes to inform that Belize's shipping registry has confirmed that the vessel was registered with the Belize Registry. However, as this is the second reported violation committed by

> the vessel, the punitive measures being imposed by the Belizean authority is [sic] its de-registration effective today 4 January 2001....

74. In the letter dated 26 March 2001, IMMARBE stated:

> This is in reply to your request for an update on the latest developments relating to the vessel GRAND PRINCE, which was detained by the French Authorities due to alleged infringement of the fishing regulation in the exclusive economic zone of Kerguelen.
>
> We would like to inform you that while we were in the process of canceling ex-officio the vessel's status, the owners requested an opportunity to defend themselves of the accusations by submitting an appeal to the Tribunal for the Law of the Sea.
>
> Under this context and being Belize a member of the Convention on the Law of the Sea we considered fair to allow the affected party to file its petition for which purposes we requested our competent authorities to grant the authorization for them to represent themselves at the mentioned Tribunal.
>
> Depending on the result of this court proceeding we will decide whether or not to enforce our decision to delete the vessel from our records....

76. The question arises as to whether the registration of the vessel in Belize continued following the expiry of the provisional patent of navigation or, as the case may be, was revived following the de-registration of the vessel with effect from 4 January 2001. The Tribunal considers that the documents placed before it by the parties disclose on their face contradictions and inconsistencies in matters relating to expiration of the provisional patent of navigation, de-registration of the vessel and suspension of de-registration, all of which give rise to reasonable doubt as to the status of the vessel when the Application was made. This doubt has a bearing on the question of jurisdiction of the Tribunal.

77. According to the settled jurisprudence in international adjudication, a tribunal must at all times be satisfied that it has jurisdiction to entertain the case submitted to it. For this purpose, it has the power to examine *proprio motu* the basis of its jurisdiction....

81. As observed by the Tribunal in the M/V "SAIGA" (No. 2) Case, the Tribunal considers that "the nationality of a ship is a question of fact to be determined, like other facts in dispute before it, on the basis of evidence adduced by the parties."...

83. In Belize, under the Registration of Merchant Ships Act, 1989, the right of a fishing vessel to fly the Belizean flag flows from the act of registration.

Accordingly, unless a fishing vessel like the *Grand Prince* is registered in Belize, Belize would not be the flag State of that vessel. It is necessary that there is sufficient evidence to establish that a vessel is registered and, therefore, has the right to fly the flag of Belize at the relevant time.

84. Of the documents before the Tribunal in the present case, the only document issued to the *Grand Prince* by Belize under the Registration of Merchant Ships Act, 1989, was the provisional patent of navigation. This document expressly stated that its date of expiration was 29 December 2000. The Applicant has not claimed that the shipowners sought extension of the period of the provisional patent of navigation, or that the provisional patent of navigation was extended or replaced by another statutory certificate. What were placed before the Tribunal were a letter and a certification from IMMARBE dated 26 March 2001 and 30 March 2001, respectively (IMMARBE communications), documents which on their face were intended to serve the purpose of authorizing the shipowners to make an "appeal" to the Tribunal. This is shown in particular by the statements contained in the IMMARBE communication of 26 March 2001 that the shipowners wanted an opportunity "to defend themselves of the accusations by submitting an appeal to the Tribunal for the Law of the Sea" and that IMMARBE "considered fair to allow the affected party to file its petition for which purposes we [IMMARBE] requested our competent authorities to grant the authorization for them to represent themselves at the mentioned Tribunal."

85. The Tribunal notes that the assertion made in the IMMARBE communication dated 30 March 2001 that "despite the expiration of the Patent of navigation and the Ship station license, the vessel is *still considered* as registered in Belize" (emphasis supplied) remained unsubstantiated and has to be understood in the light of what is stated in paragraph 84. In the view of the Tribunal, the assertion that the vessel is "still considered as registered in Belize" contains an element of fiction and does not provide sufficient basis for holding that Belize was the flag State of the vessel for the purposes of making an application under article 292 of the Convention. The IMMARBE communications cannot be treated as "documents" within the meaning of article 91, paragraph 2, of the Convention.

86. The Tribunal considers that the IMMARBE communications are in the nature of administrative letters, unsupported by references to any entries in the merchant marine register of Belize or any other action required by law. It is also noted that these communications were issued after the Application was made in this case.

87. The IMMARBE communications must be read together with the provisional patent of navigation and the note verbale of the Ministry of Foreign Affairs of Belize of 4 January 2001. On its face, the provisional patent of navi-

gation became spent on 29 December 2000. The note verbale was an official communication from Belize to France, setting out the legal position of the Government of Belize with respect to the registration of the vessel. Having first noted that the vessel was registered in Belize, this note verbale declared that "as this is the second reported violation committed by the vessel, the punitive measures being imposed by the Belizean authority is its de-registration effective today 4 January 2001." [T]he act of de-registration must be taken to have commenced with effect from 4 January 2001.

88. The Attorney General's letter of 15 March 2001 does not offer any more clarity on the question of registration and nationality than the IMMARBE communications.

89. In the M/V "SAIGA" (No. 2) Case, the Tribunal considered that the conduct of a flag State, "at all times material to the dispute," was an important consideration in determining the nationality or registration of a ship. The Tribunal finds that the Applicant did not act "at all times material to the dispute" on the basis that the *Grand Prince* was a vessel of its nationality. To the contrary, on 4 January 2001, Belize communicated to France, by means of a note verbale from the Ministry of Foreign Affairs, its decision to de-register the *Grand Prince* with effect from 4 January 2001.

90. In this connection, the Tribunal wishes to note that the Registration of Merchant Ships Act, 1989, was amended in 1996 with a view to strengthening the powers of the Registrar to de-register vessels. Section 25 of the Act, in its amended form, provides:

> Where a vessel registered in IMMARBE infringes, violates or engages in an activity in breach of this Act, or any regulations, resolutions or circular notes or letters made or issued thereunder, or any international convention to which Belize is a party, or any United Nations sanctions, the Registrar may revoke the registration of such vessel from IMMARBE or impose a fine not exceeding fifty thousand dollars.

91. The provisional patent of navigation issued in favour of the *Grand Prince* also carried an endorsement in line with section 25. In this connection, the Tribunal notes the efforts of Belize towards fulfilling its international responsibilities with respect to combating illegal fishing....

93. In the light of the expiration of the provisional patent of navigation or, as the case may be, in the light of the de-registration of the *Grand Prince*, referred to in the note verbale of 4 January 2001, and on the basis of an overall assessment of the material placed before it, the Tribunal concludes that the documentary evidence submitted by the Applicant fails to establish that Belize was the flag State of the vessel when the Application was made. Accordingly,

the Tribunal finds [by 12 votes to 9] that it has no jurisdiction [under article 292 of the LOS Convention] to hear the Application.

Notes

1. *The Interplay of National and International Law*. The ITLOS must apply the LOS Convention "and other rules of international law not incompatible with this Convention." LOS Convention, Article 293(1); Annex VI, Article 23. But when international law leaves it to each state to fix the conditions for granting nationality to ships and for registering ships, the Tribunal must also take account of national law. What challenges are presented by this state of affairs? For a review of national laws on registration of vessels, see Sompong Sucharitkul, Liability and Responsibility of the State of Registration or the Flag State in Respect of Sea-Going Vessels, Aircraft and Spacecraft Registered by National Registration Authorities, 54 Am. J. Comp. L. 409, 421–29 (2006) (surveying laws of twelve countries).

In the Grand Prince case the ITLOS had to determine whether, under Belize's laws, the *Grand Prince* could be considered to have Belizean nationality. Vice President Nelson, in his Separate Opinion, cited Judge Anzilotti's opinion in Legal Status of Eastern Greenland, a case of the Permanent Court of International Justice, P.C.I.J. Ser. A/B, No. 53 at 91 (1933), to suggest that the note verbale from Belize's Ministry of Foreign Affairs (indicating deregistration of the *Grand Prince* on January 4, 2001) was "binding" on Belize "or at least must be of high persuasive value." The dissenting judges, to the contrary, believed that the evidence supported the view that Belize had suspended deregistration procedures, and that the statements by IMMARBE officials satisfied Belize's initial burden of establishing that the *Grand Prince* had Belizean nationality. Joint Dissenting Opinion of Judges Caminos, Marotta Rangel, Yankov, Yamamoto, Akl, Vukas, Marsit, Eiriksson, and Jesus, ¶¶ 5, 10, 14. Some judges noted that the lawyer whom Belize authorized to pursue the case on its behalf—a lawyer in private practice in Spain—was not in the best position to help the Tribunal reconcile apparently contradictory information concerning Belize's position as to the nationality of the vessel. See Declaration of Judge ad hoc Cot, ¶ 14; Separate Opinion of Judge Anderson.

2. *Continuity of Nationality*. The ITLOS would have had jurisdiction to entertain the application only if it had found the *Grand Prince* to have Belizean nationality. But at what time must that nationality be established? When the vessel was first arrested? At the start of the detention of the vessel in French port? When the application was filed with the ITLOS on behalf of Belize? Should admissibility require continuous nationality between, on the one hand,

the time of arrest or detention and, on the other hand, the time the application was filed?

3. *Loss of Nationality*. Should deregistration necessarily mean that the vessel's nationality is lost? Should deregistration preclude a flag state from exercising diplomatic protection in the prompt release context, if that state still claims the vessel as its own? Did the ITLOS overlook the possibility that nationality remained continuous in the Grand Prince case even if the *Grand Prince* was deregistered? See Vaughan Lowe & Robin Churchill, The International Tribunal for the Law of the Sea: Survey for 2001, 17 Intl. J. Marine & Coastal L. 463, 474–75 (2002).

Suppose that a coastal state seizes and then, pursuant to its laws, confiscates a foreign flag vessel for violating the state's coastal fishing regulations. Does the confiscated vessel retain its original nationality? The issue arose in the Tomimaru Case (Japan v. Russia), ITLOS Case No. 15 (2007), a prompt release application. According to the ITLOS, "the confiscation of a vessel does not result *per se* in an automatic change of the flag or in its loss. Confiscation changes the ownership of a vessel but ownership of a vessel and the nationality of a vessel are different issues." ¶ 70. Why should confiscation not change a vessel's nationality?

4. *Temporary and Provisional Registrations*. A state may temporarily authorize a ship to fly its flag in a variety of situations, e.g., to permit ships purchased abroad to be delivered to the buyer's country. See, for example, 46 U.S.C. § 12115. What are the consequences if flag of convenience states maintain loose control over their systems of provisional registration, as arguably was the case with the operation of the system of provisional registration maintained by Saint Vincent and the Grenadines, at issue in the M/V Saiga (No. 2) case? Consider the views of ITLOS President Mensah in his Separate Opinion in that case:

> 22. . . . I find it necessary to express my concerns regarding certain unusual features of the legislation of Saint Vincent and the Grenadines and the administrative practices of its Maritime Authorities concerning the issue of documents to ships. [T]he Merchant Shipping Act permits provisional registration to last for as long as twelve months. This long period of provisional registration provides scope for abuse by unscrupulous shipowners who may wish to operate sub-standard ships, for it makes possible for them to switch such ships between flags on consecutive "provisional registrations" for one year at a time. . . . It is also a cause for concern that the Maritime Administration appears to allow and condone the practice by which ships operate under provisional registration without valid certificates of any kind. In this regard, I refer to the statement

> by the Deputy Commissioner for Maritime Affairs that "it is common practice for owners to allow the provisional certificate to lapse for a short time before obtaining either a further Provisional Certificate or a Permanent Certificate." The lack of diligence on the part of shipowners in renewing or replacing certificates at the appropriate time, and the toleration of such lapses by Saint Vincent and the Grenadines, can have undesirable implications for the effective implementation of the provisions of the Convention on nationality of ships and the duties of flag States. The practice could also encourage abuses and create difficulties in international maritime transport. Specifically, it could encourage or condone neglect on the part of owners and managers of ships and thus lead to situations where, as in the present case, a ship is able to operate for more than six weeks without having on board a currently valid document testifying that it was in fact registered with the State whose flag it was flying. [A] certificate of registration is the most important evidence of the nationality of a ship for third States and other parties who may have an interest in the identity of the flag State or in the discharge of flag State responsibilities under the Convention and other international agreements dealing with safety at sea and the prevention and control of pollution of the marine environment from ships. It is . . . imperative that every ship operating internationally should have a valid certificate of registration at all times.

St. Vincent and the Grenadines v. Guinea (Admissibility and Merits), ITLOS Case No. 2 (1999), Pres. Mensah, Sep. Op., ¶ 22, available at http://www.itlos.org.

Should there be uniform international standards concerning provisional vessel registration and deregistration? All vessel registration and deregistration?

CALVO, LE DROIT INTERNATIONAL THÉORIQUE ET PRATIQUE
(5th ed. 1896), translated in John Bassett Moore, 2 A Digest of International Law § 321 at 1002 (1906)

§ 426. . . . In all cases the vessel should be furnished with proof of its nationality by means of authentic documents, or of certain distinctive signs which enable one to tell at first sight to what nation it belongs.

§ 427. The flag is the visible sign of the national character of a ship. Each state has its own colors, under which its nationals sail and which cannot be used without its permission. . . .

§ 428. The flag alone does not suffice to prove the nationality of the ship; it offers too great facilities for abuse and usurpations. In order to have a more certain means of control, maritime nations have agreed that every merchant ship must be provided with papers or sea letters, which the captain is bound to produce whenever it is legitimately required. The ship's papers most usually consist of an act indicating the signal of the ship, its dimensions, its name, the details of its construction; the act authorizing the vessel to bear the national flag; a crew list mentioning the names and nationality of the sailors; and a bill of sale of property and a passport or patent of navigation.

Notes

1. *Documents*. Calvo described the traditional effects and content of ship documents. The flag symbolizes the nationality of a ship, but in the event of a discrepancy between a ship's flag and its documents, the documents control the question of nationality. ITLOS Vice-President Wolfrum, in paragraphs 22–23 of his Separate Opinion in the M/V Saiga (No. 2) case excerpted above, also discussed the significance of documentation and the links between registration and documentation. What other purposes may documents serve, in addition to establishing a vessel's nationality for international purposes?

When a state grants a ship the right to fly its flag, it must issue "documents to that effect." LOS Convention, Article 91(2); 1958 High Seas Convention, Article 5(2). In paragraph 84 of the Grand Prince case, the ITLOS emphasized that not all of the "documents" in the case relating to the nationality of the *Grand Prince* could be "treated as 'documents' within the meaning of Article 91, paragraph 2, of the Convention." Why not?

2. *Reviewing Concepts.* How does registration link to nationality? How does documentation link to registration and to nationality? Compare and contrast: vessel nationality; registration; documentation; flag; genuine link.

C What Is a Ship or Vessel?

STEWART v. DUTRA CONSTRUCTION CO.
543 U.S. 481 (2005)

JUSTICE THOMAS delivered the opinion of the Court.

The question in this case is whether a dredge is a "vessel" under § 2(3)(G) of the Longshore and Harbor Workers' Compensation Act (LHWCA), 33 U.S.C. § 902(3)(G). We hold that it is.

I

As part of Boston's Central Artery/Tunnel Project, or "Big Dig," the Commonwealth of Massachusetts undertook to extend the Massachusetts Turnpike through a tunnel running beneath South Boston and Boston Harbor to Logan Airport. The Commonwealth employed respondent Dutra Construction Company to assist in that undertaking. At the time, Dutra owned the world's largest dredge, the *Super Scoop*, which was capable of digging the 50-foot-deep, 100-foot-wide, three-quarter-mile-long trench beneath Boston Harbor that is now the Ted Williams Tunnel.

The *Super Scoop* is a massive floating platform from which a clamshell bucket is suspended beneath the water. The bucket removes silt from the ocean floor and dumps the sediment onto one of two scows that float alongside the dredge. The *Super Scoop* has certain characteristics common to seagoing vessels, such as a captain and crew, navigational lights, ballast tanks, and a crew dining area. But it lacks others. Most conspicuously, the *Super Scoop* has only limited means of self-propulsion. It is moved long distances by tugboat. (To work on the Big Dig, it was towed from its home base in California through the Panama Canal and up the eastern seaboard to Boston Harbor.) It navigates short distances by manipulating its anchors and cables. When dredging the Boston Harbor trench, it typically moved in this way once every couple of hours, covering a distance of 30-to-50 feet each time.

Dutra hired petitioner Willard Stewart, a marine engineer, to maintain the mechanical systems on the *Super Scoop* during its dredging of the harbor. At the time of Stewart's accident, the *Super Scoop* lay idle because one of its scows, Scow No. 4, had suffered an engine malfunction and the other was at sea. Stewart was on board Scow No. 4, feeding wires through an open hatch located about 10 feet above the engine area. While Stewart was perched beside the hatch, the *Super Scoop* used its bucket to move the scow. In the process, the scow collided with the *Super Scoop*, causing a jolt that plunged Stewart head-first through the hatch to the deck below. He was seriously injured.

Stewart sued Dutra in the United States District Court for the District of Massachusetts under the Jones Act, 46 U.S.C. App. § 688(a), alleging that he was a seaman injured by Dutra's negligence. He also filed an alternative claim under § 5(b) of the LHWCA, 33 U.S.C. § 905(b), which authorizes covered employees to sue a "vessel" owner as a third party for an injury caused by the owner's negligence.

[The Court traces the complex procedural history of the case, which resulted in summary judgments in favor of Dutra on the two claims, with both rulings affirmed by the First Circuit. Of primary concern is petitioner's Jones Act claim, providing a cause of action for injured "seamen." Since that term has been construed in terms of the LHWCA's reference to "a master or member of a crew of any vessel," 33 U.S.C. § 902(3)(G), the Court concludes that "it is the LHWCA's use of the term 'vessel' that matters." 543 U.S. at 488 n.1.]

We granted certiorari to resolve confusion over how to determine whether a watercraft is a "vessel" for purposes of the LHWCA.

II...

A

Just as Congress did not define the term "seaman" in the Jones Act, it did not define the term "vessel" in the LHWCA itself. However, Congress provided a definition elsewhere. At the time of the LHWCA's enactment, §§ 1 and 3 of the Revised Statutes of 1873 specified:

> In determining the meaning of the revised statutes, or of any act or resolution of Congress passed subsequent to February twenty-fifth, eighteen hundred and seventy-one, ... [t]he word "vessel" includes every description of water-craft or other artificial contrivance used, or capable of being used, as a means of transportation on water. 18 Stat., pt. 1, p. 1.

Sections 1 and 3 show that, because the LHWCA is an Act of Congress passed after February 25, 1871, the LHWCA's use of the term "vessel" "includes every description of water-craft or other artificial contrivance used, or capable of being used, as a means of transportation on water."

Section 3's definition, repealed and recodified in 1947 as part of the Rules of Construction Act, 1 U.S.C. § 3, has remained virtually unchanged from 1873 to the present. Even now, § 3 continues to supply the default definition of "vessel" throughout the U.S. Code, "unless the context indicates otherwise." 1 U.S.C. § 1. The context surrounding the LHWCA's enactment indicates that § 3 defines the term "vessel" for purposes of the LHWCA.

Section 3 merely codified the meaning that the term "vessel" had acquired in general maritime law. In the decades following its enactment, § 3 was regularly used to define the term "vessel" in maritime jurisprudence. Taking only the issue presented here—whether a dredge is a vessel—prior to passage of the Jones Act and the LHWCA, courts often used § 3's definition to conclude that dredges were vessels....

[E]arly cases show that at the time Congress enacted the Jones Act and the LHWCA in the 1920's, it was settled that § 3 defined the term "vessel" for purposes of those statutes. It was also settled that a structure's status as a vessel under § 3 depended on whether the structure was a means of maritime transportation. For then, as now, dredges served a waterborne transportation function, since in performing their work they carried machinery, equipment, and crew over water.

This Court's cases have continued to treat § 3 as defining the term "vessel" in the LHWCA, and they have continued to construe § 3's definition in light of the term's established meaning in general maritime law.... Since [*Norton* v. *Warner Co.*, 321 U.S. 565 (1944),] this Court has often said that dredges and comparable watercraft qualify as vessels under the Jones Act and the LHWCA.

B

Despite this Court's reliance on § 3 in cases like... *Norton*, Dutra argues that the Court has implicitly narrowed § 3's definition. Section 3 says that a "vessel" must be "used, or capable of being used, as a means of transportation on water." 18 Stat, pt 1, p 1. In a pair of cases, the Court held that a drydock, *Cope* v. *Vallette Dry Dock Co.*, 119 U.S. 625, 630 (1887), and a wharfboat attached to the mainland, *Evansville & Bowling Green Packet Co.* v. *Chero Cola Bottling Co.*, 271 U.S. 19, 22 (1926), were not vessels under § 3, because they were not practically capable of being used to transport people, freight, or cargo from place to place. According to Dutra, *Cope* and *Evansville* adopted a definition of "vessel" narrower than § 3's text....

Cope and *Evansville* did no more than construe § 3 in light of the distinction drawn by the general maritime law between watercraft temporarily stationed in a particular location and those permanently affixed to shore or resting on the ocean floor. Simply put, a watercraft is not "capable of being used" for maritime transport in any meaningful sense if it has been permanently moored or otherwise rendered practically incapable of transportation or movement.

This distinction is sensible: A ship and its crew do not move in and out of Jones Act coverage depending on whether the ship is at anchor, docked for loading or unloading, or berthed for minor repairs, in the same way that ships taken permanently out of the water as a practical matter do not remain vessels merely because of the remote possibility that they may one day sail again. See *Pavone* v. *Mississippi Riverboat Amusement Corp.*, 52 F.3d 560, 570 (CA5 1995) (floating casino was no longer a vessel where it "was moored to the shore in a semi-permanent or indefinite manner"); *Kathriner* v. *Unisea, Inc.*, 975 F.2d 657, 660 (CA9 1992) (floating processing plant was no longer a vessel where a "large opening [had been] cut into her hull," rendering her incapable of moving over the water). Even if the general maritime law had not informed the meaning of § 3, its definition would not sweep within its reach an array of fixed structures not commonly thought of as capable of being used for water transport....

C

The Court of Appeals, relying on its previous en banc decision in *DiGiovanni* v. *Traylor Brothers, Inc.*, 959 F.2d 1119 (CA1 1992), held that the *Super Scoop* is not a "vessel" because its primary purpose is not navigation or commerce and because it was not in actual transit at the time of Stewart's injury. Neither prong of the Court of Appeals' test is consistent with the text of § 3 or the established meaning of the term "vessel" in general maritime law.

Section 3 requires only that a watercraft be "used, or capable of being used, as a means of transportation on water" to qualify as a vessel. It does not require that a watercraft be used primarily for that purpose. As the Court of Appeals recognized, the *Super Scoop*'s "function was to move through Boston Harbor, ... digging the ocean bottom as it moved." 343 F.3d, at 12. In other words, the *Super Scoop* was not only "capable of being used" to transport equipment and workers over water—it *was* used to transport those things. Indeed, it could not have dug the Ted Williams Tunnel had it been unable to traverse the Boston Harbor, carrying with it workers like Stewart.

Also, a watercraft need not be in motion to qualify as a vessel under § 3.... Just as a worker does not "oscillate back and forth between Jones Act coverage and other remedies depending on the activity in which the worker was engaged while injured," *Chandris*, [*Inc.* v. *Latsis*,] 515 U.S. [347,] 363 [(1995)], neither does a watercraft pass in and out of Jones Act coverage depending on whether it was moving at the time of the accident.

Granted, the Court has sometimes spoken of the requirement that a vessel be "in navigation," *id.*, at 373–374, but never to indicate that a structure's locomotion at any given moment mattered. Rather, the point was that structures may lose their character as vessels if they have been withdrawn from the water for extended periods of time. The Court did not mean that the "in navigation" requirement stood apart from § 3, such that a "vessel" for purposes of § 3 might nevertheless not be a "vessel in navigation" for purposes of the Jones Act or the LHWCA.

Instead, the "in navigation" requirement is an element of the vessel status of a watercraft. It is relevant to whether the craft is "used, or capable of being used" for maritime transportation. A ship long lodged in a drydock or shipyard can again be put to sea, no less than one permanently moored to shore or the ocean floor can be cut loose and made to sail. The question remains in all cases whether the watercraft's use "as a means of transportation on water" is a practical possibility or merely a theoretical one. In some cases that inquiry may involve factual issues for the jury, but here no relevant facts were in dispute. Dutra conceded that the *Super Scoop* was only temporarily stationary while Stewart and others were repairing the scow; the *Super Scoop* had not been taken out of service, permanently anchored, or otherwise rendered practically incapable of maritime transport.

... The LHWCA does not meaningfully define the term "vessel" as it appears in either § 902(3)(G) or § 905(b), and 1 U.S.C. § 3 defines the term "vessel" throughout the LHWCA....

The judgment of the Court of Appeals is reversed, and the case is remanded for further proceedings consistent with this opinion.

Notes

1. *Defining Ship or Vessel.* The issue of what is a ship or vessel arises in applying legislation and treaties. The definition may be much debated. Do you agree that the Supreme Court reached the proper conclusion in Stewart v. Dutra Construction Co.? Or should the Court instead have looked to the dredge's primary function, i.e., construction, and considered that the dredge's stationary status at the time of Stewart's accident meant that it was not involved in transportation? Should the intent of the owner of a putative vessel have any bearing on how it is categorized?

In U.S. law, the definition in 1 U.S.C. § 3 is a default definition that other statutes may qualify or vary. See, e.g., 33 U.S.C. § 453 (certain navigation regulations apply to "vessels under control and running under their own power"); 33 U.S.C. § 1601(1) (statute implementing International Regulations for Preventing Collisions at Sea defines "vessel" as "every description of watercraft, including nondisplacement craft and seaplanes, used or capable of being used as a means of transportation on water"). Is it appropriate for the same word to mean different things in different treaties or different contexts? Does the answer depend on the context in which the definition is to apply?

The LOS Convention uses the terms "vessel" and "ship" interchangeably, but it does not define the terms. (The Convention does define "warship" in Article 29.) Should "ship" and "vessel" be defined for purposes of the LOS Convention? If so, what should be the definition? Might any definition lead to confusion or inconsistencies when the LOS Convention is applied alongside other treaties that specifically define "ship" or "vessel"? See John E. Noyes, Interpreting the 1982 Law of the Sea Convention and Defining Its Terms, in Definitions for the Law of the Sea: Terms Not Defined by the 1982 Convention 45, 55–61 (George K. Walker ed., 2011).

How should floats or gliders used to conduct marine scientific research be categorized? What about so-called "unmanned marine vehicles," used by military services, which vary considerably in their size, appearance, missions, and degree of autonomous operation? Which, if any, of these devices are "vessels"? See Craig H. Allen, The Seabots are Coming Here: Should They be Treated as "Vessels"?, 65 J. Navigation 749 (2012); Katharina Bork et al., The Legal Regulation of Floats and Gliders—In Quest of a New Regime?, 39 Ocean Dev. & Intl. L. 298 (2008).

2. *Defining Navigation.* Will there also be debate over the meaning of "navigation" or "transportation"? See Lozman v. City of Riviera Beach, 133 S. Ct. 735 (2013). A study prepared by the U.N. Office for Ocean Affairs and the Law of the Sea pointed out:

> There is no definition of "navigation" given in any of the Conventions on the law of the sea, nor in any other treaty which might be referred to by way of analogy. One might therefore refer to the ordinary dictionary usage of the term "navigate"—"to go from one place to another in a ship or ships, to sail," or of the term "navigation"—"the action or practice of passing on water in ships or other vessels." [2 The Shorter Oxford English Dictionary (3d ed. 1973).] Thus it can be taken to connote the calculated movement of ships or the capacity to move them (from the Latin *navis* (ship) and *agere* (to drive)). In other words, by the term "navigation" we refer to marine transportation and the use of ships and vessels.

The Law of the Sea: Navigation on the High Seas 5 (UN Sales No. E.89.V.2, 1989).

CHAPTER 4

Jurisdiction of the Flag State

The 1982 Law of the Sea Convention (LOS Convention) and numerous other international treaties specify obligations of the flag state with respect to administrative, technical, social, and safety matters for ships flying its flag. Section A of this chapter highlights these obligations. We review the generally recognized rule of a flag state's exclusive jurisdiction over its vessels and the events that occur on them in Section B. Sections C through F then explore specific exceptions to this rule. Port states and coastal states may also exercise jurisdiction over a flag state's vessels in some situations, particularly with respect to vessels in a state's ports, internal waters, or territorial sea, as discussed in Chapters 7 (Internal Waters) and 8 (Territorial Sea).

A Flag State Obligations

Article 94(1) of the LOS Convention requires every state to "effectively exercise its jurisdiction and control in administrative, technical and social matters over ships flying its flag." Under LOS Convention Articles 94(3) and (4), each state must adopt measures to ensure the safety at sea of vessels flying its flag. Article 94 is not the only provision in the LOS Convention that specifies flag state obligations: Articles 194(3)(b) and 217 concern flag state obligations with respect to pollution of the marine environment.

In enacting safety measures, the flag state must "conform to generally accepted international regulations, procedures and practices." LOS Convention, Article 94(5). Similarly, with regard to pollution control measures, the flag state must ensure that its vessels comply with "applicable international rules and standards, established through the competent international organization or general diplomatic conference." Id., Article 217(1). The LOS Convention provides a broad legal framework establishing a flag state's obligations; these obligations are to be implemented through a flag state's participation in or observance of additional international agreements providing uniform and comprehensive regulations governing the safety, administrative, technical, and social aspects of a ship's operation.

 | DOI 10.1163/9789004203563_005

1 *International Maritime Organization Conventions and "Generally Accepted" International Regulations*

The International Maritime Organization (IMO), a U.N. specialized agency, was formed to facilitate the adoption of uniform standards in matters concerning maritime safety, navigation, and prevention and control of marine pollution from ships. As of September 1, 2013, it was comprised of 170 member states. The IMO has adopted numerous international agreements affecting the obligations of flag states, three of the most important of which are described below.

INTERNATIONAL CONVENTION FOR THE SAFETY OF LIFE AT SEA (SOLAS), 1974
http://www.imo.org (as of Sept. 1, 2013)

The SOLAS Convention in its successive forms is generally regarded as the most important of all international treaties concerning the safety of merchant ships. The first version was adopted in 1914, in response to the Titanic disaster, the second in 1929, the third in 1948, and the fourth in 1960. The 1974 version [which entered into force May 25, 1980] includes the tacit acceptance procedure—which provides that an amendment shall enter into force on a specified date unless, before that date, objections to the amendment are received from an agreed number of Parties. As a result the 1974 Convention has been updated and amended on numerous occasions....

The main objective of the SOLAS Convention is to specify minimum standards for the construction, equipment and operation of ships, compatible with their safety. Flag States are responsible for ensuring that ships under their flag comply with its requirements, and a number of certificates are prescribed in the Convention as proof that this has been done. Control provisions also allow Contracting Governments to inspect ships of other Contracting States if there are clear grounds for believing that the ship and its equipment do not substantially comply with the requirements of the Convention—this procedure is known as port State control. The current SOLAS Convention includes Articles setting out general obligations, amendment procedure and so on, followed by an Annex divided into 12 Chapters. [The Annex chapters address in detail ship construction, fire protection, life saving arrangements, radio communications, navigation safety services, cargo carriage, carriage of dangerous goods, nuclear-powered ships, safety management, special high-speed craft safety measures, maritime security, and special requirements for bulk carriers.]

INTERNATIONAL CONVENTION FOR THE PREVENTION OF POLLUTION FROM SHIPS (MARPOL)

http://www.imo.org (as of Sept. 1, 2013)

The International Convention for the Prevention of Pollution from Ships (MARPOL) is the main international convention covering prevention of pollution of the marine environment by ships from operational or accidental causes. The MARPOL Convention was adopted on 2 November 1973 at IMO. The Protocol of 1978 was adopted in response to a spate of tanker accidents in 1976–1977. As the 1973 MARPOL Convention had not yet entered into force, the 1978 MARPOL Protocol absorbed the parent Convention. . . .

The Convention includes regulations aimed at preventing and minimizing pollution from ships—both accidental pollution and that from routine operations—and currently includes six technical Annexes. [Annexes I (oil) and II (noxious liquid substances carried in bulk) entered into force Oct. 2, 1983; Annex III (harmful substances carried in packaged form) entered into force July 1, 1992; Annex IV (sewage from ships) entered into force Sept. 27, 2003; Annex V (garbage from ships) entered into force Dec. 31, 1998; and Annex VI (air pollution from ships) entered into force May 19, 2005.]

INTERNATIONAL CONVENTION ON STANDARDS OF TRAINING, CERTIFICATION AND WATCHKEEPING FOR SEAFARERS (STCW)

http://www.imo.org (as of Sept. 1, 2013)

The 1978 STCW Convention [which entered into force Apr. 28, 1984] was the first to establish basic requirements on training, certification and watchkeeping for seafarers on an international level. Previously the standards of training, certification and watchkeeping of officers and ratings were established by individual governments, usually without reference to practices in other countries. As a result standards and procedures varied widely, even though shipping is the most international of all industries. . . .

The 1995 amendments [which entered into force Feb. 1, 1997], adopted by a Conference, represented a major revision of the Convention, in response to a recognized need to bring the Convention up to date and to respond to critics who pointed out the many vague phrases, such as "to the satisfaction of the Administration," which resulted in different interpretations being made. . . . One of the major features of the revision was the division of the technical annex into regulations, divided into Chapters as before, and a new STCW Code, to which many technical regulations were transferred. Part A of the Code is mandatory while Part B is recommended. . . .

Another major change was the requirement for Parties to the Convention to provide detailed information to IMO concerning administrative measures taken to ensure compliance with the Convention. This represented the first time that IMO had been called upon to act in relation to compliance and implementation—generally, implementation is [the responsibility of] the flag States, while port State control also acts to ensure compliance. Under Chapter I, regulation I/7 of the revised Convention, Parties are required to provide detailed information to IMO concerning administrative measures taken to ensure compliance with the Convention, education and training courses, certification procedures and other factors relevant to implementation. The information is reviewed by panels of competent persons, nominated by Parties to the STCW Convention, who report on their findings to the IMO Secretary-General, who, in turn, reports to the [IMO's] Maritime Safety Committee (MSC) on the Parties which fully comply. The [MSC] then produces a list of "confirmed Parties" in compliance with the STCW Convention. . . .

The Manila amendments to the STCW Convention and Code were adopted on 25 June 2010, marking a major revision of the STCW Convention and Code. The 2010 amendments entered into force on 1 January 2012 under the tacit acceptance procedure and are aimed at bringing the Convention and Code up to date with developments since they were initially adopted and to enable them to address issues that are anticipated to emerge in the foreseeable future.

Notes

1. *Flag State Conformity to "Generally Accepted" International Regulations.* Read Article 94 of the LOS Convention. The reference in Article 94(5) to "generally accepted regulations, procedures and practices" suggests that a flag state may be bound by an IMO standard that the flag state has not specifically adopted, so long as the standard is "generally accepted." What determines whether a standard has been "generally accepted"? Is the inquiry identical to whether the standard has been accepted as customary international law? Is the practice of ship owners or other private entities relevant in determining "general acceptance"? For discussion of the phrase "generally accepted," see Comm. on Coastal State Jurisdiction Relating to Marine Pollution, Final Report, in Intl. L. Assoc., Report of the Sixty-Ninth Conference (London) 443, 473–81 (2000), reprinted in Vessel-source Pollution and Coastal State Jurisdiction 75, 105–13 (Erik Franckx ed., 2001).

2. *Acceptance of IMO Conventions.* Many of the major IMO conventions have been widely accepted. For example, as of September 30, 2013: the 1974 SOLAS Convention had 162 contracting states as parties, representing 98.77

percent of the world's shipping tonnage; MARPOL 73/78 (Annex I/II) had 152 parties, representing 99.20 percent of the world's shipping tonnage; and the 1978 STCW Convention had 157 parties, representing 99.23 percent of the world's shipping tonnage. What explains the widespread acceptance of these IMO conventions?

3. *Flag State Duties and Fishing Vessels.* Does the obligation of states to adopt measures to ensure the safety of its vessels apply to fishing vessels? Fishing vessels are exempt from most of the requirements of the 1974 SOLAS Convention because of the significant differences in design and operation between fishing vessels and other types of ships. In 1977, the IMO adopted the Torremolinos International Convention for the Safety of Fishing Vessels, which contained safety requirements for the construction and equipment of new fishing vessels of 24 meters (78.5 feet) in length or more, including vessels processing their catch. The Convention, which the major fishing nations considered too stringent, did not gain sufficient ratifications to enter into force. In 1993, the IMO adopted the 1993 Torremolinos Protocol, which updated the 1977 Torremolinos Convention to incorporate technological advances and limited many of its mandatory regulations to fishing and processing vessels of 45 meters (147.5 feet) in length or more. The 1993 Torremolinos Protocol has also failed to gain sufficient ratifications to enter into force.

In 2012, an IMO conference adopted the Cape Town Agreement on the Implementation of the 1993 Torremolinos Protocol, which is intended to replace and supersede the 1993 Protocol. To encourage and facilitate adoption of the 2012 Cape Town Agreement, state parties may adopt a plan to phase in the implementation of certain requirements over a five-year period (ten years for radiocommunication measures). The Agreement also allows a flag state to exempt any fishing vessels flying its flag from compliance if the application of the Agreement would be unreasonable or impracticable, provided that the vessel complies with adequate safety measures appropriate for its type and use. An exempt vessel may only undertake fishing activities within the territorial sea and exclusive economic zone of the flag state, except to the extent that the flag state has entered into an agreement with another state regarding the operation of an exempt vessel within the territorial sea or exclusive economic zone of that state, or a common fishing ground.

What are some of the major impediments to enacting uniform standards governing the safety of fishing vessels? Numerous fisheries treaties, including the 1995 Fish Stocks Agreement, the 1993 FAO Flag State Compliance Agreement, and various regional fisheries agreements, provide for flag state obligations toward fishing vessels. We consider these treaties in Chapter 13. Are they better vehicles for regulating the safety of fishing vessels? Why or why not? Can regional agreements represent "generally accepted international regulations, procedures and practices"?

4. *International Labor Organization Conventions and the Safety and Working Conditions of Seafarers.* According to the International Labor Organization (ILO), there are more than 1.2 million seafarers worldwide. The ILO—like the IMO, a U.N. specialized agency—has adopted numerous conventions relating to working and living conditions of seafarers and to their safety, health, welfare, repatriation, and social security. The 2006 Maritime Labor Convention, which entered into force on August 20, 2013, consolidated and updated 37 existing ILO maritime conventions and related recommendations. For a discussion of the 2006 Maritime Labor Convention and other instruments adopted by the ILO, see http://www.ilo.org.

5. *IMO Recommendations and Codes.* The IMO's Assembly, composed of all member states, adopts numerous resolutions containing recommendations to member states. These recommendations, which are usually prepared by various IMO committees, are not legally binding. They are, in common international law parlance, a type of "soft law." Several of the IMO Assembly's recommendations are detailed codes or guidelines that address matters such as signals, construction, equipment, and safe practices for a wide range of situations. See, for example, the 2005 Code of Safety for Fishermen and Fishing Vessels. Despite the non-binding character of recommendations and many codes, states often incorporate them into their national laws and regulations. Are non-mandatory instruments among the types of "generally accepted international regulations, procedures and practices" that a flag state is obliged to follow under Article 94 of the LOS Convention?

Some codes are also eventually incorporated into treaties, at which point they become legally binding for states that are parties to those treaties. One of the most important of these is the International Maritime Dangerous Goods (IMDG) Code. First adopted by the IMO Assembly in 1965 to provide guidance to mariners, shippers, packers, and others involved in the carriage of dangerous goods by sea, the IMDG Code was incorporated by amendment into the 1974 SOLAS Convention, and now binds contracting states.

2 *Updating IMO Conventions*

Technology regarding navigation, pollution control measures, and other matters subject to flag state regulation changes very rapidly, resulting in the need to constantly review and update IMO conventions that address these subjects. The traditional IMO treaty amendment procedure, requiring approval of a specified percentage of contracting states (typically two thirds), made it difficult to timely implement technological advances. To address this problem, the IMO developed and began to incorporate into treaties an expedited amendment procedure known as "tacit acceptance."

INTERNATIONAL CONVENTION ON STANDARDS OF TRAINING, CERTIFICATION AND WATCHKEEPING OF SEAFARERS
July 7, 1978, U.S. Sen. Exec. Doc. No. EE (1979), 1361 U.N.T.S. 2

Article XII. Amendments

(1) The Convention may be amended by either of the following procedures:

(a) Amendments after consideration within the [International Maritime] Organization:

(i) Any amendment proposed by a Party shall be submitted to the Secretary-General, who shall then circulate it to all Members of the Organization, all Parties and the Director-General of the International Labour Office at least six months prior to its consideration;

(ii) Any amendment so proposed and circulated shall be referred to the Maritime Safety Committee of the Organization for consideration;

(iii) Parties, whether or not Members of the Organization, shall be entitled to participate in the proceedings of the Maritime Safety Committee for consideration and adoption of amendments;

(iv) Amendments shall be adopted by a two-thirds majority of the Parties present and voting in the Maritime Safety Committee expanded as provided for in sub-paragraph (*a*)(iii) (hereinafter referred to as the "expanded Maritime Safety Committee") on condition that at least one third of the Parties shall be present at the time of voting;

(v) Amendments so adopted shall be communicated by the Secretary-General to all Parties for acceptance;

(vi) An amendment to an Article shall be deemed to have been accepted on the date on which it is accepted by two thirds of the Parties;

(vii) An amendment to the Annex shall be deemed to have been accepted:

1. At the end of two years from the date on which it is communicated to Parties for acceptance; or
2. At the end of a different period, which shall be not less than one year, if so determined at the time of its adoption by a two-thirds majority of the Parties present and voting in the expanded Maritime Safety Committee;

however, the amendments shall be deemed not to have been accepted if within the specified period either more than one third of Parties, or Parties the combined merchant fleets of which constitute not less than fifty per cent of the gross tonnage of the world's merchant shipping of ships of 100 gross register tons or more, notify the Secretary-General that they object to the amendment;

(viii) An amendment to an Article shall enter into force with respect to those Parties which have accepted it, six months after the date on which it is deemed to have been accepted, and with respect to each Party which accepts it after that date, six months after the date of that Party's acceptance;

(ix) An amendment to the Annex shall enter into force with respect to all Parties, except those which have objected to the amendment under sub-paragraph (*a*)(vii) and which have not withdrawn such objections, six months after the date on which it is deemed to have been accepted. Before the date determined for entry into force, any Party may give notice to the Secretary-General that it exempts itself from giving effect to that amendment for a period not longer than one year from the date of its entry into force, or for such longer period as may be determined by a two-thirds majority of the Parties present and voting in the expanded Maritime Safety Committee at the time of the adoption of the amendment; or

(b) Amendment by a conference:

(i) Upon the request of a Party concurred in by at least one third of the Parties, the Organization shall convene, in association or consultation with the Director-General of the International Labour Office, a conference of Parties to consider amendments to the Convention;

(ii) Every amendment adopted by such a conference by a two-thirds majority of the Parties present and voting shall be communicated by the Secretary-General to all Parties for acceptance;

(iii) Unless the conference decides otherwise, the amendment shall be deemed to have been accepted and shall enter into force in accordance with the procedures specified in sub-paragraphs (*a*)(vi) and (*a*)(viii) or sub-paragraphs (*a*)(vii) and (*a*)(ix) respectively, provided that references in these sub-paragraphs to the expanded Maritime Safety Committee shall be taken to mean references to the conference.

Notes

1. *Amendment by Tacit Acceptance.* Under the law of treaties, amendments bind only those states that expressly accept them, unless the treaty being amended provides otherwise. See 1969 Vienna Convention on the Law of Treaties, Articles 39–40. The 1978 STCW Convention is one of several IMO conventions that allows amendment other than by express acceptance. An amendment to the STCW Convention may be adopted either by the Maritime Safety Committee (expanded to include all STCW contracting parties, even if a contracting party is not a member of the IMO) or by a conference of state parties. Once an amendment has been "adopted," how does a state become bound by it? Amendments to an Annex of the STCW Convention are subject to the "tacit acceptance procedure"; annexes typically contain technical provisions. Why should amendments to the more general articles of the Convention be excluded from the "tacit acceptance" procedure? Once an amendment to an Annex has been adopted, how may a state party prevent its "deemed acceptance" of the amendment? How many state parties must object in order to prevent an amendment to an Annex from entering into force under the tacit acceptance procedure? If the requisite number of state parties does not timely object, when does the amendment enter into force? Is the amendment effective as to any party that does timely object?

2. *Effectiveness of Tacit Acceptance Procedure.* The tacit acceptance procedure has proven effective in allowing regular and rapid amendments to those IMO conventions that have incorporated the procedure. For example, the 1974 SOLAS Convention has been amended more than 40 times since 1981; most amendments have addressed technical matters and were implemented by use of the tacit acceptance procedure.

3 *Implementing Flag State Obligations*

A flag state's acceptance of an IMO convention is not sufficient in and of itself to fulfill its obligation to effectively exercise jurisdiction and control over vessels flying its flag. The flag state must also ensure, through adoption and enforcement of national legislation and regulations, that the ships flying its flag actually comply with the requirements established in those conventions. In 2003, the IMO adopted the Voluntary IMO Member State Audit Scheme in an effort to objectively assess whether flag states were effectively administering and implementing their treaty obligations. Although initially participation was voluntary, the IMO Assembly has approved the implementation of a mandatory audit scheme for several important IMO conventions.

INTERNATIONAL MARITIME ORGANIZATION (IMO) CODE FOR THE IMPLEMENTATION OF MANDATORY IMO INSTRUMENTS

IMO Res. A.1054(27) (2011)

THE ASSEMBLY, . . .

REAFFIRMING that States, in their capacity as flag States, have the primary responsibility to have in place an adequate and effective system to exercise control over ships entitled to fly their flag and to ensure that they comply with relevant international rules and regulations in respect of maritime safety, security and protection of the marine environment,

REAFFIRMING ALSO that States, in their capacity as port and coastal States, have other obligations and responsibilities under applicable international law in respect of maritime safety, security and protection of the marine environment,

NOTING that, while States may realize certain benefits by becoming party to instruments aiming at promoting maritime safety, security and protection of the marine environment, these benefits can only be fully realized when all parties carry out their obligations as required by the instruments concerned,

NOTING ALSO that the ultimate effectiveness of any instrument depends, *inter alia*, on all States:

(a) becoming party to all instruments related to maritime safety, security and protection of the marine environment;

(b) implementing and enforcing such instruments fully and effectively;

(c) reporting to the Organization, as required,

NOTING FURTHER that, in the context of the Voluntary IMO Member State Audit Scheme, the enactment of appropriate legislation and its implementation and enforcement are the three key issues on which a Member State's performance can be measured,

BEARING IN MIND that the Voluntary IMO Member State Audit Scheme contains references to the Code for the Implementation of Mandatory IMO Instruments, as appropriate; and that the Code, in addition to providing guidance for the implementation and enforcement of IMO instruments, forms the basis of the Audit Scheme, in particular concerning the identification of the auditable areas,

HAVING CONSIDERED the recommendations made by the Maritime Safety Committee, at its eighty-ninth [May 2011] session, and the Marine Environment Protection Committee, at its sixty-second [July 2011] session,

1. ADOPTS the Code for the Implementation of Mandatory IMO Instruments, 2011, set out in the annex to the present resolution;

2. URGES Governments of all States in their capacity as flag, port and coastal States to implement the Code on a national basis[.]

Notes

1. *Flag State Compliance.* The issue of how to promote flag state implementation and enforcement of the full range of flag state obligations has gained increasing attention in recent years. See 2003 Oceans and the Law of the Sea: Report of the Secretary-General ¶¶ 85–91, UN Doc. A/58/65 (2003) (discussing various initiatives). The International Chamber of Shipping publishes annually a report compiling data regarding the performance of various flag states in implementing and enforcing international regulations, available at http://www.ics-shipping.org.

In addition to the audit scheme excerpted above, several other measures promote compliance with IMO conventions. Some conventions require certificates to be carried on board to show that the ship has been inspected and has met the required standards. Port state inspections, which are discussed in Chapter 7 of this book, also promote adherence by flag states and vessel owners to IMO standards. As another effort to assure flag state compliance, the IMO Technical Cooperation Division provides training and other assistance to governments of developing states to assist in implementing technical standards in the conventions and codes.

2. *IMO Audit Scheme.* By the end of 2012, approximately 70 IMO member states had volunteered to participate in the audit scheme. A specially trained IMO audit team conducts audits pursuant to IMO-established procedures, which include a review of national legislation as well as national implementation and enforcement measures. The scope of the audit is established by agreement between the participating state and the IMO Secretary-General. The IMO audit scheme will become mandatory through amendments (scheduled to occur in 2013, for entry into force in 2015) to several widely adopted IMO conventions, including the 1966 Convention on Load Lines, 1969 Convention on Tonnage Measurement of Ships, 1972 Convention on the Prevention of Collisions at Sea, 1973 Convention for the Prevention of Pollution from Ships (MARPOL 73/78), 1974 Safety of Life at Sea (SOLAS) Convention, and 1978 Convention on Standards of Training, Certification and Watchkeeping for Seafarers (STCW).

3. *The Scope of Article 94.* Can you identify some of the important issues regarding the governance of ships or its crews or passengers that fall outside of the scope of Article 94 of the LOS Convention? What laws govern those issues?

B Overview of Flag State Jurisdiction

According to Article 92 of the LOS Convention, ships sailing on the high seas are subject to the exclusive jurisdiction of the flag state, "save in exceptional cases provided for in international treaties or in this Convention." "Jurisdiction," meaning "competence" or "authority," may be exercised by a state's legislature (jurisdiction to prescribe or legislative jurisdiction), enforcement agencies or officials (executive or enforcement jurisdiction), or courts (judicial jurisdiction).

NOTE VERBALE NO. 10 FROM THE MINISTRY OF FOREIGN AFFAIRS OF SPAIN TO THE EMBASSY OF CANADA

Application Instituting Proceedings, Annex 3, Fisheries Jurisdiction Case (Spain v. Canada), available at http://www.icj-cij.org

[In an effort to conserve important fisheries in the northwest Atlantic that straddled the Canadian exclusive economic zone (EEZ) and the high seas beyond it, Canada enacted legislation authorizing the application and enforcement of Canadian conservation measures against foreign fishing vessels on the high seas in certain circumstances. Pursuant to this legislation, a Canadian warship boarded and seized a Spanish fishing vessel on the high seas near the Canadian EEZ and arrested its commanding officer. Spain responded initially with a diplomatic protest.]

The Ministry of Foreign Affairs of Spain presents its compliments to the Embassy of Canada in Madrid and, in connection with the boarding of the fishing boat *Estai*, flying the Spanish flag, by the Canadian authorities on 9 March 1995 in international waters, makes the following statement:

In carrying out the said boarding operation, the Canadian authorities breached the universally accepted norm of customary international law codified in Article 92 and articles to the same effect of the 1982 Convention on the Law of the Sea, according to which ships on the high seas shall be subject to the exclusive jurisdiction of the flag State. In the light of this serious incident, which has caused substantial damage to Spanish nationals, Spain lodges the most vigorous protest and at the same time demands the immediate release of the crew and the vessel and reserves the right to claim appropriate compensation.

The Spanish Government considers that the wrongful act committed by ships of the Canadian navy can in no way be justified by presumed concern to conserve fisheries in the area, since it violates the established provisions of the NAFO [Northwest Atlantic Fisheries Organization] Convention to which Canada is a party.

The boarding of the vessel constitutes a serious offence against international law, not in keeping with the usual conduct of a responsible State, carried out under cover of unilateral legislation not opposable to other States. Consequently, the Spanish Government demands the repeal of the legislation in question.

The Spanish Government finds itself constrained, in the light of these events, to reconsider its relations with Canada, and reserves the right to take whatever measures it considers appropriate.

The Ministry of Foreign Affairs takes this opportunity to reiterate to the Embassy of Canada in Spain the assurances of its highest consideration.

Madrid, 10 March 1995.

Notes

1. *The* Estai *Dispute*. In responding to Spain's Note Verbale, Canada asserted that "the *Estai* resisted the efforts to board her made by Canadian inspectors in accordance with international practice" and that "the arrest of the *Estai* was necessary in order to put a stop to the overfishing of Greenland halibut by Spanish fishermen." Fisheries Jurisdiction Case (Spain v. Canada), 1998 I.C.J. 432, ¶ 20. Read Articles 92 and 110 of the LOS Convention. Which, if any, exceptions to the exclusive jurisdiction of the flag state might Canada invoke in support of its position that its arrest of the *Estai* was lawful under international law? Is the list of exceptions inclusive or exclusive?

Shortly after the *Estai* incident, Spain initiated proceedings against Canada in the International Court of Justice (ICJ), seeking, among other measures, a declaration "that the legislation of Canada, in so far as it claims to exercise a jurisdiction over ships flying a foreign flag on the high seas, outside the exclusive economic zone of Canada, is not opposable to the Kingdom of Spain." Fisheries Jurisdiction Case (Spain v. Canada), 1998 I.C.J. 432, ¶ 10. The ICJ concluded that it lacked jurisdiction over the case because the requisite mutual consent of the parties was missing. Canada had filed a reservation, under Article 36(2) of the ICJ Statute, that excluded "disputes arising out of or concerning conservation and management measures taken by Canada with respect to vessels fishing in the NAFO Regulatory Area... and the enforcement of such measures" from its acceptance of the ICJ's jurisdiction. 1998 I.C.J. 432, ¶ 87. See Louise De La Fayette, The Fisheries Jurisdiction Case (*Spain* v. *Canada*), Judgment on Jurisdiction of 4 December 1998, 48 Intl. & Comp. L.Q. 664 (1999). If both countries had been parties to the LOS Convention at the time—Spain had accepted the Convention in 1997, but Canada did not join until 2003—would Spain have been able to bring the *Estai* dispute to a third-party tribunal under the dispute settlement provisions of the LOS Convention? See Chapter 15.

The incident was eventually settled by negotiation and by changes to the 1978 Northwest Atlantic Fisheries Convention, including reallocation of quotas available to NAFO members and institution of an observer program on all vessels fishing in the NAFO regulatory area. NAFO, 1995 Annual Report. In Chapter 13 we consider legal efforts to promote the conservation and management of straddling fish stocks that range between one country's EEZ and the high seas.

2. *Treaty-based Exceptions to the Flag State's Exclusive Jurisdiction.* Both Articles 92 and 110 of the LOS Convention recognize that a flag state may by treaty authorize another state to exercise jurisdiction over its vessels. At the time of the *Estai* incident, Canada and the European Economic Community (of which Spain was a member) were parties to the 1978 Northwest Atlantic Fisheries Convention. Article XVIII of that Convention provides:

> The Contracting Parties agree to maintain in force and to implement within the Regulatory Area a scheme of joint international enforcement.... This scheme shall include provision for reciprocal rights of boarding and inspection by the Contracting Parties and for flag State prosecution and sanctions on the basis of evidence resulting from such boardings and inspections.

Under this treaty provision, did Canada have the right to board and inspect the *Estai*? To seize and detain the vessel? To prosecute the vessel's master? If Canada had referred any alleged violations of fishery conservation measures to Spain as the flag state, what recourse would be available to Canada if Spain declined to prosecute the vessel or its officers?

In addition to fisheries treaties, several treaties concerning the interdiction of immigrants on ships provide for exceptions to the flag state's exclusive jurisdiction. See Chapter 2, Section I. Treaties intended to eliminate maritime drug traffic also frequently contain such exceptions. See Section D.3 below. In addition, under bilateral treaties between the United States and other countries, foreign flag vessels calling at deepwater port facilities outside U.S. territorial waters are subject to U.S. jurisdiction. See Marian Nash (Leich), 2 Cumulative Digest of United States Practice in International Law 1981–1988, 2078–79 (1994) (listing such bilateral treaties).

3. *Immunity of Warships*. Warships and government vessels used for non-commercial service on the high seas have complete immunity from interference by states other than the flag state. LOS Convention, Articles 95–96; 1958 High Seas Convention, Articles 8(1), 9. Why should warships and government vessels enjoy immunity from boarding and seizure? Read the definition of "warship" found at LOS Convention, Article 29. What criteria must be satisfied in order to be classified as a warship? Would an unmanned submersible vessel used for surveillance or other purposes by the U.S. Navy enjoy warship immunity?

For discussion of the jurisdiction a coastal state may exercise over a foreign warship or non-commercial government vessel within its internal waters, ports, and territorial sea, see Chapters 7 and 8.

4. *Procedures against Vessels during Armed Conflict*. The materials in this chapter focus on when a state may legally visit, board, search, or seize a foreign flag vessel on the high seas during peacetime. For discussion of available procedures against foreign merchant vessels of a belligerent or neutral state during armed conflict, see Chapter 2, Sections G and H.

C Jurisdiction in Matters of Collision

It is not uncommon for vessels to collide. The Lotus case, decided by the Permanent Court of International Justice in 1927, addressed the issue of jurisdictional competence when a flag state's vessel wrongfully collides with another state's vessel on the high seas. The Lotus case also raised broader issues concerning the concept of "jurisdiction" and the jurisprudential basis for determining the legality of a state's actions under international law.

THE S.S. LOTUS
France v. Turkey, 1927 P.C.I.J. (ser. A) No. 9

[A French steamer, the *Lotus*, collided with a Turkish collier, the *Boz-Kourt*, on the high seas; the Turkish vessel sank with a loss of eight lives. When the French vessel arrived in Constantinople, Turkey with the Turkish survivors of the collision, the watch officer, Lieutenant Demons, a French national, was arrested and tried for manslaughter. A Turkish court found Demons guilty, fined him, and sentenced him to 80 days' imprisonment. By a special agreement between France and Turkey, the following question was submitted to the Permanent Court of International Justice: "Has Turkey, contrary to Article 15 of the Convention of Lausanne of July 24th, 1923, respecting conditions of residence and business and jurisdiction, acted in conflict with the principles of international law—and if so, what principles—by instituting … criminal proceedings in pursuance of Turkish law against M. Demons …?"

The French government made several arguments against Turkey's action. First, "according to international law as established by the practice of civilized nations, in their relations with each other, a State is not entitled, apart from express or implicit special agreements, to extend the criminal jurisdiction of its courts to include a crime or offence committed by a foreigner abroad solely in consequence of the fact that one of its nationals has been a victim of the crime or offense." Second, "acts performed on the high seas on board a merchant ship are, in principle and from the point of view of criminal proceedings, amenable only to the jurisdiction of the courts of the State whose flag the vessel flies." Third, in collision cases "the culpable character of the act causing the collision must be considered in the light of purely national regulations which apply to the ship and the carrying out of which must be controlled by the national authorities." Finally, France argued that a collision cannot "be localized in the vessel sunk, such a contention being contrary to the facts."

The Turkish government, on the other hand, argued that "[v]essels on the high seas form part of the territory of the nation whose flag they fly, and in the case under consideration, the place where the offense was committed being the S.S. *Boz-Kourt* flying the Turkish flag, Turkey's jurisdiction in the proceedings taken is as clear as if the case had occurred in her territory—as is borne out by analogous cases." Turkey also took the position that "as no principle of international criminal law exists which would debar Turkey from exercising the jurisdiction which she clearly possesses to entertain an action for damages, that country has jurisdiction to institute criminal proceedings."]

The Law

I

1. – The collision which occurred on August 2nd, 1926, between the S.S. *Lotus*, flying the French flag, and the S.S. *Boz-Kourt*, flying the Turkish flag, took place on the high seas: the territorial jurisdiction of any State other than France and Turkey therefore does not enter into account.

2. – The violation, if any, of the principles of international law would have consisted in the taking of criminal proceedings against Lieutenant Demons. It is not therefore a question relating to any particular step in these

proceedings—such as his being put to trial, his arrest, his detention pending trial or the judgment given by the Criminal Court of Stamboul—but of the very fact of the Turkish Courts exercising criminal jurisdiction. . . .

The prosecution was instituted because the loss of the *Boz-Kourt* involved the death of eight Turkish sailors and passengers. It is clear, in the first place, that this result of the collision constitutes a factor essential for the institution of the criminal proceedings in question; secondly, it follows from the statements of the two Parties that no criminal intention has been imputed to either of the officers responsible for navigating the two vessels; it is therefore a case of prosecution for involuntary manslaughter. The French Government maintains that breaches of navigation regulations fall exclusively within the jurisdiction of the State under whose flag the vessel sails; but it does not argue that a collision between two vessels cannot also bring into operation the sanctions which apply to criminal law in cases of manslaughter.

[Q]uestions of criminal law relating to the justification of the prosecution and consequently to the existence of a *nexus causalis* between the actions of Lieutenant Demons and the loss of eight Turkish nationals are not relevant to the issue so far as the Court is concerned. Moreover, . . . there is no doubt that [the eight deaths] may be regarded as the direct outcome of the collision, and the French Government has not contended that this relation of cause and effect cannot exist. . . .

II

[T]he Court must now ascertain which were the principles of international law that the prosecution of Lieutenant Demons could conceivably be said to contravene.

It is Article 15 of the Convention of Lausanne of July 24th, 1923, respecting the conditions of residence and business and jurisdiction, which refers the contracting Parties to the principles of international law as regards the delimitation of their respective jurisdiction.

This clause is as follows:

> Subject to the provisions of Article 16, all questions of jurisdiction shall, as between Turkey and the other contracting Powers, be decided in accordance with the principles of international law.

The French Government maintains that the meaning of the expression "principles of international law" in this article should be sought in the light of the evolution of the Convention. Thus it states that during the preparatory work, the Turkish Government, by means of an amendment to the relevant article of a draft for the Convention, sought to extend its jurisdiction to crimes committed in the territory of a third State, provided that, under Turkish law, such crimes were within the jurisdiction of Turkish Courts. This amendment, in regard to which the representatives of France and Italy made reservations, was definitely rejected by the British representative; and the question having been subsequently referred to the Drafting Committee, the latter confined itself in its version of the draft to a declaration to the effect that questions of jurisdiction should be decided in accordance with the principles of international law. The French Government deduces from these facts that the prosecution of Demons is contrary to the intention which guided the preparation of the Convention of Lausanne.

The Court must recall in this connection what it has said in some of its preceding judgments and opinions, namely, that there is no occasion to have regard to preparatory work if the text of a convention is sufficiently clear in itself. Now the Court considers that the words "principles of international law," as ordinarily used, can only mean international law as it is applied between all nations belonging to the community of States. . . .

III

The Court, having to consider whether there are any rules of international law which may have been violated by the prosecution in pursuance of Turkish law of Lieutenant Demons, is confronted in the first place by a question of principle which, in the written and oral arguments of the two Parties, has proved to be a fundamental one. The French Government contends that the Turkish Courts, in order to have jurisdiction, should be able to point to some title to jurisdiction recognized by international law in favor of Turkey. On the other hand, the Turkish Government takes the view that Article 15 allows Turkey jurisdiction whenever such jurisdiction does not come into conflict with a principle of international law.

The latter view seems to be in conformity with the special agreement itself, . . . which asks the Court to say whether Turkey has acted contrary to the principles of international law and, if so, what principles. According to the special agreement, therefore, it is not a question of stating principles which would permit Turkey to take criminal proceedings, but of formulating the principles, if any, which might have been violated by such proceedings. This way of stating the question is also dictated by the very nature and existing conditions of international law.

International law governs relations between independent States. The rules of law binding upon states therefore emanate from their own free will as expressed in conventions or by usages generally accepted as expressing principles of law and established in order to regulate the relations between those coexisting independent communities or with a view to the achievement of common aims. Restrictions upon the independence of States cannot therefore be presumed.

Now the first and foremost restriction imposed by international law upon a State is that—failing the existence of a permissive rule to the contrary—it may not exercise its power in any form in the territory of another State. In this sense jurisdiction is certainly territorial; it cannot be exercised by a State outside its territory except by virtue of a permissive rule derived from international custom or from a convention.

It does not, however, follow that international law prohibits a State from exercising jurisdiction in its own territory, in respect of any case which relates to acts which have taken place abroad, and in which it cannot rely on some permissive rule of international law. Such a view would only be tenable if international law contained a general prohibition to States to extend the application of their laws and the jurisdiction of their courts to persons, property and acts outside their territory, and if, as an exception to this general prohibition, it allowed States to do so in certain specific cases. But this is certainly not the case under international law as it stands at present. Far from laying down a general prohibition to the effect that States may not extend the application of their laws and the jurisdiction of their courts to persons, property and acts outside their territory, it leaves them in this respect a wide measure of discretion which is only limited in certain cases by prohibitive rules; as regards other cases, every State remains free to adopt the principles which it regards as best and most suitable....

Though it is true that in all systems of law the principle of the territorial character of criminal law is fundamental, it is equally true that all or nearly all these systems of law extend their action to offences committed outside the territory of the State which adopts them, and they do so in ways which vary from State to State. The territoriality of criminal law, therefore, is not an absolute principle of international law and by no means coincides with territorial sovereignty....

IV

The Court will now proceed to ascertain whether general international law... contains a rule prohibiting Turkey from prosecuting Lieutenant Demons....

The arguments advanced by the French Government, other than those considered above, are, in substance, the three following:

(1) International law does not allow a State to take proceedings with regard to offences committed by foreigners abroad, simply by reason of the nationality of the victim; and such is the situation in the present case because the offence must be regarded as having been committed on board the French vessel.

(2) International law recognizes the exclusive jurisdiction of the State whose flag is flown as regards everything which occurs on board a ship on the high seas.

(3) Lastly, this principle is especially applicable in a collision case.

As regards the first argument, the Court feels obliged in the first place to recall that its examination is strictly confined to the specific situation in the present case, for it is only in regard to this situation that its decision is asked for.

[T]he characteristic features of the situation of fact are as follows: there has been a collision on the high seas between two vessels flying different flags, on one of which was one of the persons alleged to be guilty of the offence, whilst the victims were on board the other.

This being so, the Court does not think it necessary to consider the contention that a State cannot punish offences committed abroad by a foreigner simply by reason of the nationality of the victim. For this contention only relates to the case where the nationality of the victim is the only criterion on which the criminal jurisdiction of the State is based. Even if that argument were correct, generally speaking—and in regard to this the Court reserves its opinion—it could only be used in the present case if international law forbade Turkey to take into consideration the fact that the offence produced its effects on the Turkish vessel and consequently in a place assimilated to Turkish territory in which the application of Turkish criminal law cannot be challenged, even in regard to offences committed there by foreigners. But no such rule of international law exists. No argument has come to the knowledge of the Court from which it could be deduced that States recognize themselves to be under an obligation towards each other only to have regard to the place where the author of the offence happens to be at the time of the offence. On the contrary, it is certain that the courts of many countries, even of countries which have given their criminal legislation a strictly territorial character, interpret criminal law in the sense that offences, the authors of which at the moment of commission are in the territory of another State, are nevertheless to be regarded as having been committed in the national territory, if one of the constituent elements of the offence, and more especially its effects, have taken place there.... Consequently, once it is admitted that the effects of the offence were produced on the Turkish vessel, it becomes impossible to hold that there is a rule of international law which prohibits Turkey from prosecuting Lieutenant Demons because of the fact that the author of the offence was on board the French ship....

The second argument put forward by the French Government is the principle that the State whose flag is flown has exclusive jurisdiction over everything which occurs on board a merchant ship on the high seas.

It is certainly true that—apart from certain special cases which are defined by international law—vessels on the high seas are subject to no authority except that of the State whose flag they fly. In virtue of the principle of the freedom of the seas, that is to say, the absence of any territorial sovereignty upon the high seas, no State may exercise any kind of jurisdiction over foreign vessels upon them. Thus, if a war vessel, happening to be at a spot where a collision occurs between a vessel flying its flag and a foreign vessel, were to send on board the latter an officer to make investigations or to take evidence, such an act would undoubtedly be contrary to international law.

But it by no means follows that a State can never in its own territory exercise jurisdiction over acts which have occurred on board a foreign ship on the high seas. A corollary of the principle of the freedom of the seas is that a ship on the high seas is assimilated to the territory of the State the flag of which it flies, for, just as in its own territory, that State exercises its authority upon it, and no other State may do so. All that can be said is that by virtue of the principle of the freedom of the seas, a ship is placed in the same position as national territory; but there is nothing to support the claim according to which the rights of the State under whose flag the vessel sails may go farther than the rights which it exercises within its territory properly so called. It follows that what occurs on board a vessel on the high seas must be regarded as if it occurred on the territory of the State whose flag the ships flies. If, therefore, a guilty act committed on the high seas produces its effects on a vessel flying another flag or in foreign territory, the same principles must be applied as if the territories of two different States were concerned, and the conclusion must therefore be drawn that there is no rule of international law prohibiting the State to which the ship on which the effects of the offence have taken place belongs, from regarding the offence as having been committed in its territory and prosecuting, accordingly, the delinquent.

This conclusion could only be overcome if it were shown that there was a rule of customary international law which, going further than the principle stated above, established the exclusive jurisdiction of the State whose flag was flown. The French Government has endeavored to prove the existence of such a rule, having recourse for this purpose to the teachings of publicists, to decisions of municipal and international tribunals, and especially to conventions which, whilst creating exceptions to the principle of the freedom of the seas by permitting the war and police vessels of a State to exercise a more or less extensive control over the merchant vessels of another State, reserve jurisdiction to the courts of the country whose flag is flown by the vessel proceeded against.

In the Court's opinion, the existence of such a rule has not been conclusively proved.

In the first place, as regards teachings of publicists, and apart from the question as to what their value may be from the point of view of establishing the existence of a rule of customary law, it is no doubt true that all or nearly all writers teach that ships on the high seas are subject exclusively to the jurisdiction of the State whose flag they fly. But the important point is the significance attached by them to this principle; now it does not appear that in general, writers bestow upon this principle a scope differing from or wider than that explained above and which is equivalent to saying that the jurisdiction of a State over vessels on the high seas is the same in extent as its jurisdiction in its own territory. On the other hand, there is no lack of writers who, upon a close study of the special question whether a state can prosecute for offences committed on board a foreign ship on the high seas, definitely come to the conclusion that such offences must be regarded as if they have been committed in the territory of the state whose flag the ship flies, and that consequently the general rules of each legal system in regard to offences committed abroad are applicable.

[T]here is no lack of cases in which a State has claimed a right to prosecute for an offence, committed on board a foreign ship, which it regarded as punishable under its legislation. Thus Great Britain refused the request of the United States for the extradition of John Anderson, a British seaman who had committed homicide on board an American vessel, stating that she did not dispute the jurisdiction of the United States but that she was entitled to exercise hers concurrently. This case, to which others might be added, is relevant in spite of Anderson's British nationality, in order to show that the principle of the exclusive jurisdiction of the country whose flag the vessel flies is not universally accepted.

The cases in which the exclusive jurisdiction of the State whose flag was flown has been recognized would seem rather to have been cases in which the foreign State was interested only by reason of the nationality of the victim, and in which, according to the legislation of that State itself or the practice of its courts, that ground was not regarded as sufficient to authorize prosecution for an offence committed abroad by a foreigner.

Finally, as regards conventions expressly reserving jurisdiction exclusively to the State whose flag is flown, it is not absolutely certain that this stipulation is to be regarded as expressing a general principle of law rather than as corresponding to the extraordinary jurisdiction which these conventions confer on the state-owned ships of a particular country in respect of ships of another country on the high seas. Apart from that, it should be observed that these conventions relate to matters of a particular kind, closely connected with the policing of the seas, such as the slave trade, damage to submarine cables, fisheries, etc., and not to common-law offences. Above all it should be pointed out that the offences contemplated by the conventions in question only concern a single ship; it is impossible therefore to make any deduction from them in regard to matters which concern two ships and consequently the jurisdiction of two different States.

The Court therefore has arrived at the conclusion that the second argument put forward by the French Government does not, any more than the first, establish the existence of a rule of international law prohibiting Turkey from prosecuting Lieutenant Demons.

It only remains to examine the third argument advanced by the French Government and to ascertain whether a rule specially applying to collision cases has grown up, according to which criminal proceedings regarding such cases come exclusively within the jurisdiction of the State whose flag is flown.

In this connection, the Agent for the French Government has drawn the Court's attention to the fact that questions of jurisdiction in collision cases, which frequently arise before civil courts, are but rarely encountered in the practice of criminal courts. He deduces from this that, in practice, prosecutions only occur before the courts of the State whose flag is flown and that that circumstance is proof of a tacit consent on the part of States and, consequently, shows what positive international law is in collision cases.

In the Court's opinion, this conclusion is not warranted. Even if the rarity of the judicial decisions to be found among the reported cases were sufficient to prove in point of fact the circumstance alleged by the Agent for the French Government, it would merely show that States had often, in practice, abstained from instituting criminal proceedings, and not that they recognized themselves as being obliged to do so; for only if such abstention were based on their being conscious of having a duty to abstain would it be possible to speak of an international custom....

So far as the Court is aware there are no decisions of international tribunals in this matter; but some decisions of municipal courts have been cited. Without pausing to consider the value to be attributed to the judgments of municipal courts in connection with the establishment of the existence of a rule of international law, it will suffice to observe that the decisions quoted sometimes support one view and sometimes the other.

[As] municipal jurisprudence is thus divided, it is hardly possible to see in it an indication of the existence of the restrictive rule of international law which alone could serve as a basis for the contention of the French Government.

On the other hand, the Court feels called upon to lay stress upon the fact that it does not appear that the States concerned have objected to criminal proceedings in respect of collision cases before the courts of a country other than the flag of which was flown, or that they have made protests: their conduct does not appear to have differed appreciably from that observed by them in all cases of concurrent jurisdiction. This fact is directly opposed to the existence of a tacit consent on the part of States to the exclusive jurisdiction of the State whose flag is flown, such as the Agent for the French Government has thought it possible to deduce from the infrequency of questions of jurisdiction before criminal courts....

In support of the theory in accordance with which criminal jurisdiction in collision cases would exclusively belong to the State of the flag flown by the ship, it has been contended that it is a question of the observance of the national regulations of each merchant marine and that effective punishment does not consist so much in the infliction of some months' imprisonment upon the captain as in the cancellation of his certificate as master, that is to say, in depriving him of the command of his ship.

In regard to this, the Court must observe that in the present case a prosecution was instituted for an offence at criminal law and not for a breach of discipline. Neither the necessity of taking administrative regulations into account (even ignoring the circumstance that it is a question of uniform regulations adopted by States as a result of an international conference) nor the impossibility of applying certain disciplinary penalties can prevent the application of criminal law and of penal measures of repression.

The conclusion at which the Court has therefore arrived is that there is no rule of international law in regard to collision cases to the effect that criminal proceedings are exclusively within the jurisdiction of the State whose flag is flown.

This conclusion moreover is easily explained if the manner in which the collision brings the jurisdiction of two different countries into play be considered.

The offence for which Lieutenant Demons appears to have been prosecuted was an act—of negligence or imprudence—having its origin on board the *Lotus*, while its effects made themselves felt on board the *Boz-Kourt*. These two elements are, legally, entirely inseparable, so much so that their separation renders the offence non-existent. Neither the exclusive jurisdiction of either State, nor the limitations of the jurisdiction of each to the occurrences which took place on the respective ships would appear calculated to satisfy the requirements of justice and effectively to protect the interests of the two States. It is only natural that each should be able to exercise jurisdiction and to do so in respect of the incident as a whole. It is therefore a case of concurrent jurisdiction....

FOR THESE REASONS,

The Court . . . gives, by the President's casting vote—the votes being equally divided—, judgment to the effect

(1) that, following the collision which occurred on August 2nd, 1926, on the high seas between the French steamship *Lotus* and the Turkish steamship *Boz-Kourt*, and upon the arrival of the French ship at Stamboul, and in consequence of the loss of the *Boz-Kourt* having involved the death of eight Turkish nationals, Turkey, by instituting criminal proceedings in pursuance of Turkish law against Lieutenant Demons, officer of the watch on board the *Lotus* at the time of the collision, has not acted in conflict with the principles of international law, contrary to Article 15 of the Convention of Lausanne of July 24th, 1923, respecting conditions of residence and business and jurisdiction[.]

Notes

1. *The Lotus Court.* The Lotus case was decided by the Permanent Court of International Justice (PCIJ), established after World War I as part of the League of Nations. When the League was dissolved and the United Nations created after World War II, the PCIJ was succeeded by the International Court of Justice, which continued the essential features of the PCIJ.

2. *Treaty Modification of the Lotus Rule.* Read Article 97 of the LOS Convention, which relates to penal jurisdiction in matters of collision or any other incident of navigation. How does this provision modify the rule enunciated in the Lotus case? What advantages might be achieved under the Convention's approach? The 1952 Convention on Penal Jurisdiction in Matters of Collision, the 1952 Convention on Civil Jurisdiction in Matters of Collision, and Article 11 of the 1958 High Seas Convention have also modified the Lotus rule.

3. *Legislative and Enforcement Jurisdiction.* The Lotus court ruled that Turkey's laws could apply with respect to the collision with the Turkish vessel on the high seas—that is, Turkey had "legislative jurisdiction." But what did the Court state regarding enforcement jurisdiction? Could Turkey have boarded the French vessel, the *Lotus*, on the high seas and brought the vessel to port? This question did not arise in the case, because the *Lotus* sailed into a Turkish port after the collision, where Turkish authorities arrested Lt. Demons. Suppose the collision involved the *Lotus* and the vessel of a third state (rather than a Turkish vessel), and suppose Turkey arrested and tried Lt. Demons after the *Lotus* entered Turkish port. Under the Court's analysis, would that exercise

of both enforcement and legislative jurisdiction by Turkey have been permissible under international law? Would it matter whether the vessel of the third state carried Turkish passengers who were injured?

4. *The Lotus Case and Positivism.* The Lotus case is a significant example of a state-centric positivist view of international law. The Court's statements that "rules of law binding upon States ... emanate from their own free will as expressed in conventions or by usages generally accepted as expressing principles of law" and that "[r]estrictions upon the independence of States ... cannot be presumed" are strong expressions of the positivist position. Did the positivist orientation of the PCIJ remove all judicial discretion, leaving applicable rules of international law to be determined by expressions of state consent? Consider, for example, why—given the issue submitted to the Court, i.e., the meaning of Article 15 of the 1923 Convention of Lausanne—the PCIJ examined customary international law. Was the decision to look to customary international law an act of judicial discretion?

The Court's strong positivist orientation led it to place the burden of proof on France rather than Turkey. In order for France to prevail, it had to prove the existence of a rule of customary international law restricting Turkey's authority to exercise jurisdiction. Note the evenly split vote of the Court. Would there likely have been a different result if the Court had placed the burden on Turkey to show that its prosecution of Lieutenant Demons was justified under international law?

Was the Court's positivist approach appropriate in the Lotus case? Is it appropriate today with respect to all law of the sea issues?

D Illegal Acts and Stateless Vessels

Paragraphs (1)(a), (b), and (c) of Article 110 of the LOS Convention list three circumstances that justify the boarding of a foreign ship: reasonable grounds to suspect that the ship is engaged in piracy, the slave trade, or unauthorized broadcasting. Under Article 110(d), a warship may board a stateless vessel. This section takes a closer look at the piracy and slave trade exceptions to the exclusive jurisdiction of a flag state, and also explores whether international law allows a state to interfere, on the high seas, with a foreign flag vessel that is involved in drug trafficking—an act not specifically listed in Article 110.

1 *Piracy*

UNITED STATES v. DIRE
680 F.3d 446 (4th Cir. 2012), cert. denied, 133 S. Ct. 982 (2013)

[During the spring of 2010, in two unrelated events, boats off the coast of Somalia approached U.S. naval vessels and opened fire. The crews of the boats involved in these events were arrested and brought to trial, in two separate cases, in U.S. federal district court on charges of committing the crime of "piracy [under] the law of nations." In both cases, the defendants moved to dismiss the piracy count, alleging that the facts pleaded by the United States failed to satisfy the elements of piracy as defined under international law. Despite the similarities between the cases, the judges presiding over the two cases reached opposite conclusions as to whether the alleged actions of the defendants constituted piracy. Both cases were appealed to the U.S. Court of Appeals for the Fourth Circuit.]

Opinion by JUDGE KING:

In the early morning hours of April 1, 2010, on the high seas between Somalia and the Seychelles (in the Indian Ocean off the east coast of Africa), the defendants ... imprudently launched an attack on the USS Nicholas, having confused that mighty Navy frigate for a vulnerable merchant ship. The defendants, all Somalis, were swiftly apprehended and then transported to the Eastern District of Virginia, where they were convicted of the crime of piracy, as proscribed by 18 U.S.C. § 1651, plus myriad other criminal offenses. In this appeal, the defendants challenge their convictions and life plus-eighty-year sentences on several grounds, including that their fleeting and fruitless strike on the Nicholas did not, as a matter of law, amount to a § 1651 piracy offense. As explained below, we reject their contentions and affirm.

According to the trial evidence, the USS Nicholas was on a counter-piracy mission in the Indian Ocean when, lit to disguise itself as a merchant vessel, it encountered the defendants shortly after midnight on April 1, 2010. The Nicholas was approached by an attack skiff operated by defendant Hasan and also carrying defendants Dire and Ali, while defendants Umar and Gurewardher remained with a larger mother-ship some distance away. From their posts on the Nicholas, crew members could see by way of night-vision devices that Hasan was armed with a loaded rocket-propelled grenade launcher (commonly referred to as an "RPG"), and that Dire and Ali carried AK-47 assault rifles.

... When the defendants' attack skiff was within sixty feet of the Nicholas's fantail (its lowest and thus most accessible point), Dire and Ali discharged the first shots—bursts of rapid, automatic fire from their AK-47s aimed at the Nicholas and meant to attain its surrender. The Nicholas's crew responded in kind, resulting in an exchange of fire that lasted less than thirty seconds. Bullets from Dire and Ali's AK-47s struck the Nicholas near two of its crew members, but the defendants' brief attack was (thankfully) casualty-free. Dire, Ali, and Hasan then turned their skiff and fled, with the Nicholas in pursuit.

... Dire, Ali, and Hasan threw various items from the skiff overboard into the Indian Ocean, discarding the RPG, the AK-47s, and a ladder that would have enabled them to board the Nicholas. About thirty minutes into the pursuit, the Nicholas captured the three defendants in the skiff. Thereafter, the Nicholas chased and captured the two defendants in the mothership....

The defendants' strike on the USS Nicholas was consistent with an accustomed pattern of Somali pirate attacks, designed to seize a merchant ship and then return with the vessel and its crew to Somalia, where a ransom would be negotiated and secured. Indeed, on April 4, 2010, during questioning aboard the Nicholas, the defendants separately confessed to participating willingly in a scheme to hijack a merchant vessel, and they provided details about their operation....

In these consolidated appeals, the defendants first contend that their ill-fated attack on the USS Nicholas did not constitute piracy under 18 U.S.C. § 1651, which provides in full:

> Whoever, on the high seas, commits the crime of piracy as defined by the law of nations, and is afterwards brought into or found in the United States, shall be imprisoned for life.

According to the defendants, the crime of piracy has been narrowly defined for purposes of § 1651 as robbery at sea, i.e., seizing or otherwise robbing a vessel. Because they boarded the Nicholas only as captives and indisputably took no property, the defendants contest their convictions on Count One [Piracy], as well as the affixed life sentences.

[The district court, in United States v. Hasan, 747 F.Supp. 2d 599, 602 (E.D. Va. 2010), referred to here as *Hasan I*, denied the defendants' motion to dismiss the piracy count, based upon its conclusion that piracy "under the law of nations" encompassed acts of violence committed on the high seas for private ends.]

The *Hasan I* opinion was issued on the heels of the August 17, 2010 published opinion in United States v. Said, 757 F.Supp.2d 554 (E.D.Va. 2010), wherein a different judge of the Eastern District of Virginia essentially took these defendants' view of the piracy offense by recognizing a robbery element. Like these defendants, the *Said* defendants have been charged with piracy under 18 U.S.C. § 1651 for attacking—but not seizing or otherwise robbing—a United States Navy ship.... The *Said* court granted the defendants' pretrial motion ... to dismiss the piracy count from the indictment because no taking of property was alleged.

As the *Said* court recognized, article I of the Constitution accords Congress the power "[t]o define and punish Piracies and Felonies committed on the high Seas, and Offences against the Law of Nations." ... In its present form, the language of 18 U.S.C. § 1651 can be traced to an 1819 act of Congress, which similarly provided, in pertinent part:

> That if any person or persons whatsoever, shall, on the high seas, commit the crime of piracy, as defined by the law of nations, and such offender or offenders, shall afterwards be brought into or found in the United States, every such offender or offenders shall, upon conviction thereof, ... be punished....

Examining the Act of 1819 in its United States v. Smith decision of 1820, the Supreme Court recognized:

> There is scarcely a writer on the law of nations, who does not allude to piracy, as a crime of a settled and determinate nature; and whatever may be the diversity of definitions, in other respects, all writers concur, in holding, that robbery, or forcible depredations upon the sea, animo furandi [i.e., with intent to steal] is piracy.

18 U.S. (5 Wheat.) 153, 161 (1820). Accordingly, the *Smith* Court, through Justice Story, articulated "no hesitation in declaring, that piracy, by the law of nations, is robbery upon the sea."

Invoking the principle that a court "must interpret a statute by its ordinary meaning at the time of its enactment," the *Said* court deemed *Smith* to be the definitive authority on the meaning of piracy under 18 U.S.C. § 1651.... The *Said* court noted ... "the only substantive change to § 1651 since its enactment has been the removal of the death penalty for the offense as opposed to the current penalty of life imprisonment."

[A]lthough the *Said* court acknowledged contemporary international law sources defining piracy to encompass the *Said* defendants' violent conduct, the court deemed such sources to be too "unsettled" to be authoritative. The court further determined that relying on those international law sources would violate due process, explaining that, if "the definition of piracy [were adopted] from the [ ] debatable international sources whose promulgations evolve over time, defendants in United States courts would be required to constantly guess whether their conduct is proscribed by § 1651[,] render[ing] the statute unconstitutionally vague." Thereby undeterred from employing the "clear and authoritative" definition in *Smith* "of piracy as sea robbery," the court dismissed the piracy count from the *Said* indictment.

[In *Hasan I*] the district court took a different tack, ... denying these defendants' pretrial motion to dismiss the Count One piracy charge from their Indictment. That is, the court focused on piracy's unusual status as a crime defined by the law of nations and subject to universal jurisdiction.

The district court began by recognizing that, "[f]or centuries, pirates have been universally condemned as hostis humani generis—enemies of all mankind—because they attack vessels on the high seas, and thus outside of any nation's territorial jurisdiction, ... with devastating effect to global commerce and navigation."

[According to the district court in *Hasan I*,] "piracy on the high seas was a unique offense because it permitted nations to invoke universal jurisdiction, such that any country could arrest and prosecute pirates in its domestic courts, irrespective of the existence of a jurisdictional nexus." (citing 4 William Blackstone, Commentaries 71).... "Indeed, by the Eighteenth Century ... the international crime of piracy was well established as the *only* universal jurisdiction crime." [S]ee The Chapman, 5 F. Cas. 471, 474 (N.D.Cal.1864) (No. 2602)....

With that history in mind, the district court recognized that the Define and Punish Clause "accords to Congress the special power of criminalizing piracy in a manner consistent with the exercise of universal jurisdiction." The court further recognized, however, that Congress encountered early difficulties in criminalizing "general piracy" (that is, piracy in contravention of the law of nations), rather than solely "municipal piracy" (i.e., piracy in violation of United States law). On the one hand, "[w]hile municipal piracy is flexible enough to cover virtually any overt act Congress chooses to dub piracy, it is necessarily restricted to those acts that have a jurisdictional nexus with the United States." (citing Dole v. New Eng. Mut. Marine Ins. Co., 7 F. Cas. 837, 847 (C.C.D.Mass.1864) (No. 3966).... On the other hand, "general piracy can be prosecuted by any nation, irrespective of the presence of a jurisdictional nexus." (citing Sosa v. Alvarez–Machain, 542 U.S. 692, 762 (2004) (Breyer, J., concurring in part and concurring in the judgment) ("[I]n the 18th century, nations reached consensus not only on the substantive principle that acts of piracy were universally wrong but also on the jurisdictional principle that any nation that found a pirate could prosecute him.")). Importantly, though, "because it is created by international consensus, general piracy is restricted in substance to those offenses that the international community agrees constitute piracy."

[A]s the district court recounted, "Congress passed the Act of 1819 to make clear that it wished to proscribe not only piratical acts that had a nexus to the

United States, but also piracy as an international offense subject to universal jurisdiction." . . .

Having noted that "[n]o other Supreme Court decision since *Smith* has directly addressed the definition of general piracy," and recognizing the necessity of looking to foreign sources to determine the law of nations, the district court then focused on case law from other countries. . . . The court deemed the Privy Council of England's 1934 decision in In re Piracy Jure Gentium [general piracy], [1934] A.C. 586 (P.C.), to be "[t]he most significant foreign case dealing with the question of how piracy is defined under international law." There, the defendants were "a number of armed Chinese nationals" who, while "cruising in two Chinese junks" on the high seas, had chased a Chinese cargo vessel "for over half an hour, during which shots were fired by the attacking party." Similar to the present case, however, those defendants were captured before accomplishing any robbery. The defendants were transported to Hong Kong for trial and found guilty of piracy, but only subject to the question of the hour: "Whether an accused person may be convicted of piracy in circumstances where no robbery has occurred." Premised on the Full Court of Hong Kong's subsequent determination that a robbery was required, the defendants were ultimately acquitted.

Though with no intent to disturb that judgment, the Privy Council revisited the issue upon referral from "His Majesty in Council." . . . The precise question before the Privy Council was "whether actual robbery is an essential element of the crime of piracy jure gentium, or whether a frustrated attempt to commit a piratical robbery is not equally piracy jure gentium." Significantly, the Privy Council answered: "Actual robbery is not an essential element in the crime of piracy jure gentium. A frustrated attempt to commit a piratical robbery is equally piracy jure gentium." . . .

In addition to the Privy Council's In re Piracy Jure Gentium decision, the district court in *Hasan I* examined Kenya's 2006 Republic v. Ahmed prosecution of "ten Somali suspects captured by the United States Navy on the high seas"—"[t]he most recent case on [general piracy] outside the United States of which [the district court was] aware." The High Court of Kenya affirmed the *Ahmed* defendants' convictions for piracy jure gentium, culling from international treaties a modern definition of piracy that encompasses acts of violence and detention. . . .

As detailed in *Hasan I*, "there are two prominent international agreements that have directly addressed, and defined, the crime of general piracy." The first of those treaties is the [1958 High Seas Convention], which was adopted in 1958 and ratified by the United States in 1961, rendering the United States one of today's sixty-three parties to that agreement. . . .

The second pertinent treaty is the United Nations Convention on the Law of the Sea (the "UNCLOS"), which has amassed 162 parties since 1982—albeit not the United States, which has not ratified the UNCLOS "but has recognized that its baseline provisions reflect customary international law." . . . Relevant here, the UNCLOS [Article 101] provides that

> [p]iracy consists of any of the following acts:
> (a) any illegal acts of violence or detention, or any act of depredation, committed for private ends by the crew or the passengers of a private ship or a private aircraft, and directed:
> (i) on the high seas, against another ship or aircraft, or against persons or property on board such ship or aircraft;
> (ii) against a ship, aircraft, persons or property in a place outside the jurisdiction of any State;
> (b) any act of voluntary participation in the operation of a ship or of an aircraft with knowledge of facts making it a pirate-ship or aircraft;
> (c) any act of inciting or of intentionally facilitating an act described in subparagraph (a) or (b).

. . . Upon comparing the High Seas Convention with the UNCLOS, the district court in *Hasan I* recognized that the latter treaty "defines piracy in exactly the same terms as the [1958 High Seas Convention], with only negligible stylistic changes." . . . The [district] court also observed that the UNCLOS "represents the most recent international statement regarding the definition . . . of piracy." . . .

"Having concluded that Congress's proscription of 'piracy as defined by the law of nations' in 18 U.S.C. § 1651 necessarily incorporates modern developments in international law," the district court next endeavored to "discern the definition of piracy under the law of nations at the time of the alleged offense in April 2010." In so doing, the court observed that the law of nations is ascertained today via the same path followed in 1820 by the Supreme Court in *Smith*: consultation of "the works of jurists, writing professedly on public law[s]"; consideration of "the general usage and practice of nations"; and contemplation of "judicial decisions recognising and enforcing that law." (quoting *Smith*). Engaging in that analysis, the court concluded:

> As of April 1, 2010, the law of nations, also known as customary international law, defined piracy to *include* acts of violence committed on the high seas for private ends without an actual taking. More specifically, . . . the definition of general piracy under modern customary inter-

> national law is, at the very least, reflected in Article 15 of the 1958 High Seas Convention and Article 101 of the 1982 UNCLOS.

[The *Hasan I* court also concluded that] "[t]oday, 'the law of nations has become synonymous with the term "customary international law," which describes the body of rules that nations in the international community universally abide by, or accede to, out of a sense of legal obligation and mutual concern.'" Narrowing customary international law to one of those two treaties, the court chose the UNCLOS, which—in addition to "contain[ing] a definition of general piracy that is, for all practical purposes, identical to that of the High Seas Convention"—"has many more states parties than the High Seas Convention" and "has been much more widely accepted by the international community than the High Seas Convention."

In the course of its discussion of the High Seas Convention and the UNCLOS, the district court recognized that "[t]reaties are proper evidence of customary international law because, and insofar as, they create legal obligations akin to contractual obligations on the States parties to them." (quoting Kiobel v. Royal Dutch Petroleum Co., 621 F.3d 111, 137 (2d Cir. 2010)). According to the court, "[w]hile all treaties shed some light on the customs and practices of a state, 'a treaty will only constitute sufficient proof of a norm of customary international law if an overwhelming majority of States have ratified the treaty, and those States uniformly and consistently act in accordance with its principles.'" (quoting *Kiobel*).... With those principles in mind, the [district] court recognized [that] "UNCLOS's definition of piracy has a norm-creating character and reflects an existing norm of customary international law that is binding on even those nations that are not a party to the Convention, including the United States."

The district court further observed "that UNCLOS does not represent the first time that acts of violence have been included in the definition of general piracy." Rather, even accepting that "actual robbery on the high seas" was once an essential element of general piracy, "the view that general piracy does not require an actual robbery on the sea has certainly gained traction since the Nineteenth Century, as evidenced by [intervening case law], the Harvard Draft Convention on Piracy, the High Seas Convention, and UNCLOS."...

Additionally, the court recognized that "[c]ontemporary scholarly sources... appear to agree that the definition of piracy in UNCLOS represents customary international law.... While writers on the issue do present disagreements regarding the definition of general piracy," the court acknowledged, "such disagreements do not implicate the core definition provided in UNCLOS."

(explaining that "writers [instead] disagree about the outer boundaries of the definition of general piracy, such as whether UNCLOS's requirement of 'private ends' prohibits its application to terrorist activities, or whether piracy can arise in situations involving just one ship rather than two")....

The *Hasan I* opinion further rejected the *Said*-approved theory "that applying the contemporary customary international law definition of general piracy violates fundamental due process protections." ... According to *Hasan I*, "§ 1651's express incorporation of the definition of piracy provided by 'the law of nations,' which is today synonymous with customary international law, provides fair warning of what conduct is proscribed by the statute." In support of that conclusion, the district court in *Hasan I* recapped the Supreme Court's 1820 holding in *Smith* "that, by incorporating the definition of piracy under the law of nations, Congress had proscribed general piracy as clearly as if it had enumerated the elements of the offense in the legislation itself." ...

The district court then reaffirmed that, as of the alleged offense date of April 2010, the definition of piracy under the law of nations was found in the substantively identical High Seas Convention and UNCLOS, the latter having "been accepted by the overwhelming majority of the world as reflecting customary international law."

[The district court concluded that the facts supported an allegation of piracy against all defendants. At a subsequent trial, all defendants were convicted of piracy, which resulted in this appeal to the Fourth Circuit Court of Appeals.]

We ... agree with the [*Hasan I*] district court that the definition of piracy under the law of nations, at the time of the defendants' attack on the USS Nicholas and continuing today, had for decades encompassed their violent conduct. That definition, spelled out in the UNCLOS, as well as the High Seas Convention before it, has only been reaffirmed in recent years as nations around the world have banded together to combat the escalating scourge of piracy. For example, in November 2011, the United Nations Security Council adopted Resolution 2020, recalling a series of prior resolutions approved between 2008 and 2011 "concerning the situation in Somalia"; expressing "grave[ ] concern[ ] [about] the ongoing threat that piracy and armed robbery at sea against vessels pose"; and emphasizing "the need for a comprehensive response by the international community to repress piracy and armed robbery at sea and tackle its underlying causes." Of the utmost significance, Resolution 2020 reaffirmed "that international law, as reflected in the [UNCLOS], sets out the legal framework applicable to combating piracy and armed robbery at sea." Because the district court correctly applied the UNCLOS definition of piracy as customary international law, we reject the defendants' challenge to their Count One piracy convictions, as well as their mandatory life sentences....

Notes

1. *The Evils of Piracy.* Why has piracy been so universally condemned? What precepts of the law of the sea do pirates threaten? In light of the values threatened by piracy and developments since the 1820 United States v. Smith decision, did the Dire court use the correct definition of piracy? The Dire court echoed the British Privy Council in In re Piracy Jure Gentium, [1934] A.C. 586, 592: "International law was not crystallized in the 17th century, but is a living and expanding code."

2. *The Requirement of "Private Ends."* Read Articles 100–102 of the LOS Convention. Note the requirement that the acts must be "committed for private ends." What were the "private ends" of the defendants convicted in the Dire case? If the vessel of a non-governmental organization (NGO), such as Greenpeace or the Sea Shepherds, were to attack vessels engaged in activities that the NGO opposes (such as whaling), has the "private ends" requirement been satisfied? See Castle John v. NV Mabeco (Cours de Cass. Belgium), reprinted at 77 Intl. L. Rep. 537 (1987); Institute of Cetacean Research v. Sea Shepherd, 708 F.3d 1099 (9th Cir. 2013).

3. *Privateers.* In the 19th century and earlier, states would commission, or authorize, private vessels (referred to as "privateers") to attack merchant vessels flying the flags of enemies. A municipal prize court would adjudicate the status of any alleged enemy vessel seized by a privateer. If condemned, the vessel and its cargo would be sold, and the captain and crew of the vessel that captured the "prize" would be awarded a portion of the sales price. Does the practice of privateering help explain the "private ends" requirement?

The 1856 Paris Declaration Respecting Maritime Law proclaimed that "[p]rivateering is, and remains, abolished." Why is privateering no longer tolerated? See Dino Kritsiotis, The Contingencies of Piracy, 41 Cal. W. Intl. L.J. 305 (2011); Nicholas Parrillo, The De-Privatization of American Warfare: How the U.S. Government Used, Regulated, and Ultimately Abandoned Privateering in the Nineteenth Century, 19 Yale J.L. & Human. 1 (2007).

4. *Distinguishing Insurgents from Pirates.* If a government warship were attacked by insurgents of the same nationality in an attempt to overthrow the existing government, has the "private ends" element of piracy been satisfied? If it is determined that insurgents are acting for political purposes rather than private ends, are they entitled to prisoner of war status or other rights under international humanitarian law? Does international humanitarian law apply to pirates? In the Ambrose Light Case, 25 F. 408 (S.D.N.Y. 1885), the court ruled that because the insurgent owner and crew members of a vessel that engaged in hostile activities on the high seas were not recognized as belligerents by

their own country (Colombia) or by any other states, their acts were for "private" rather than political ends. According to James Brown Scott:

> Notwithstanding the opinion in the [Ambrose Light], it is today recognized in practice as well as in theory, that a vessel belonging to insurgents who have not yet been recognized, will not be treated as a pirate engaged in a piratical enterprise, if it limits its actions to the parent state.

Cases on International Law 548 n.6 (1922).

5. *The Private Ship Limitation.* Both Article 15 of the 1958 High Seas Convention and Article 101 of the LOS Convention limit piratical acts to those committed by the crew or passengers of private ships (or by those voluntarily participating in operating pirate ships, or by those "inciting or intentionally facilitating" piratical acts). In May 1975, a Cambodian government patrol boat seized the U.S. merchant ship *Mayaguez*. The seizure took place approximately 52 nautical miles from the Cambodian coast in waters that, in the view of the United States, were high seas. President Ford condemned the act as "piracy." 1975 Digest of United States Practice in International Law 423, 424. Was this a valid legal characterization? If piracy is not applicable, what other claims might the United States bring against Cambodia as a result of this incident?

6. *Place of Occurrence.* What geographical limitations are set forth in Article 101 of the LOS Convention? To what "place" is Article 101(a)(ii) addressed? According to the International Law Commission's commentary on its draft Article 39, which corresponds to Article 15(1)(b) of the 1958 High Seas Convention (and in turn to Article 101(a)(ii) of the LOS Convention): "In considering as 'piracy' acts committed in a place outside the jurisdiction of any State, the Commission had chiefly in mind acts committed by a ship or aircraft on an island constituting terra nullius or on the shores of an unoccupied territory." 1956-2 Y.B. Intl. L. Commn. 253, 282. Does that explanation cover all reasonable interpretations of the clause as used in the LOS Convention? Are acts of violence committed for private ends against another vessel in the exclusive economic zone properly characterized as piracy? See LOS Convention, Article 58.

More generally, why is piracy limited to the high seas and other locations outside the jurisdiction of states? Does the crime of piracy reflect a sensitivity to traditional jurisdictional and law enforcement prerogatives of states?

If an act that otherwise meets the requirements of piracy occurs within the territorial sea of a coastal state, may the warship of another state intervene without the coastal state's consent? At the request of Somalia, the U.N. Security Council has adopted a series of resolutions authorizing certain foreign warships to enter the territorial waters of Somalia to repress acts of piracy. See, for example, UN Doc. S/RES/1816 (2008); UN Doc. S/RES/2020 (2011). These resolutions specifically note that they are not to be considered as establishing, under customary international law, a right to enter territorial waters to suppress piracy.

7. *The Requirement of Two Ships.* According to Article 101(a) of the LOS Convention, piracy involves the act of one ship or aircraft against another ship or aircraft. If a group of armed individuals board a vessel at port, and then overtake the vessel on the high seas, killing passengers and committing other depradations, has piracy occurred? This type of incident occurred in 1961, when armed men boarded a Portuguese passenger vessel, the *Santa Maria*, at various ports, and then overtook the vessel on the high seas. See Marjorie M. Whiteman, 4 Digest of International Law 665–66 (1965). Similarly, the passenger ship *Achille Lauro* was boarded by terrorists at port in 1985; the terrorists then overtook the vessel on the high seas. A special convention prepared by the IMO on the subject, the 1988 Convention for the Suppression of Unlawful Acts against the Safety of Maritime Navigation, is considered in Chapter 14.

8. *Distinguishing Armed Robbery from Piracy.* The International Maritime Organization has recognized that "armed robbery against ships" is distinct from piracy:

> Armed robbery against ships means any of the following acts:
>
> 1. any illegal act of violence or detention or any act of depredation, or threat thereof, other than an act of "piracy," committed for private ends and directed against a ship or against persons or property on board such ship, within a State's internal waters, archipelagic waters and territorial sea;
>
> 2. any act of inciting or of intentionally facilitating an act described above.

Code of Practice for the Investigation of Crimes of Piracy and Armed Robbery Against Ships, IMO Res. A.1025(26), Annex, ¶ 2.2. How exactly does "armed robbery against ships" differ from piracy?

9. *Criminal Prosecution.* Under LOS Convention Article 100, did the United States have an obligation to prosecute the individuals involved in the attack on the USS *Nicholas*, or was the decision to prosecute discretionary? What considerations might have supported the decision to prosecute the Somali crew members in the United States, rather than releasing them into the custody of Somalia? Was there a jurisdictional nexus between the Somali crew

members and the United States? According to the Dire court, piracy is a crime of "universal jurisdiction," i.e., a crime that any state can prosecute even though it has no connection to the conduct or participants. Do you agree that any state could have prosecuted the crew members involved in the attack against the USS *Nicholas*? Would you expect that most piracy prosecutions involve cases in which there is some nexus with the prosecuting state? See Eugene Kontorovich & Steven Art, Empirical Examination of Universal Jurisdiction for Piracy, 104 Am. J. Intl. L. 436 (2010).

In Resolution 1918, adopted on April 27, 2010, the Security Council called on member states to criminalize piracy under their domestic laws and to favorably consider the prosecution and imprisonment of suspected pirates. UN Doc. S/RES/1918 (2010). The U.N. Secretary-General has prepared several reports identifying options regarding the prosecution of suspected pirates. See, e.g., UN Doc. S/2012/50 (2012).

10. *"Municipal" Piracy.* May a state adopt national legislation that defines piracy more broadly than it is defined under the LOS Convention? For example, could a state eliminate the requirement of "private ends" or the requirement that two ships be involved? If a state chooses to prosecute a person for piracy as defined under municipal law (rather than "the law of nations"), must a jurisdictional nexus exist? What factors might satisfy such a jurisdictional nexus?

11. *Modern Incidents of Piracy and Armed Robbery at Sea.* Acts of piracy and armed robbery committed against ships have greatly increased in recent decades. To help address the problem of modern-day piracy, the IMO has adopted a Code of Practice for the Investigation of the Crimes of Piracy and Armed Robbery against Ships, IMO Res. A.922(22) (2001). Regional cooperation among States plays an important role in suppressing piracy. See, for example, the 2009 Djibouti Code of Conduct concerning the Repression of Piracy and Armed Robbery against Ships in the Western Indian Ocean and the Gulf of Aden, MSC Doc. 102/14 (2009), and the 2004 Regional Cooperation Agreement on Combating Piracy and Armed Robbery against Ships in Asia, available at http://www.recaap.org. The IMO prepares monthly and annual piracy reports, available at http://imo.org, and the non-governmental International Maritime Bureau Piracy Reporting Centre of the International Chamber of Commerce also compiles detailed records, available at http://www.icc-ccs.org/piracy-reporting-centre. The IMO reported 544 incidents of piracy and armed robbery in 2011 and 341 such incidents in 2012. MSC.4/Circ.180 (2012), MSC.4/Circ.193 (2013).

2 *Slavery*

LE LOUIS

2 Dods. 210, 165 Eng. Rep. 1464 (High Court of Admiralty, 1817)

[*Le Louis*, a brig flying the French flag, sailed from the West Indies in January of 1816, bound for Africa. On March 11, 1816, she was seized by a British colonial armed cutter, the *Queen Charlotte*. In the course of resisting the seizure the crew of the brig killed twelve crew members of the *Charlotte*.

Following the seizure, *Le Louis* was taken to the British colony of Sierra Leone. The Crown proceeded against her for condemnation in the Vice-Admiralty Court. The British authorities alleged that the French brig was engaged in the slave trade, which had been made illegal both by a French municipal law and by an Additional Article to the Treaty of Vienna of 1815 between Britain and France. The British authorities further claimed that the British vessel had a right in those circumstances to visit, search, and seize the French vessel on the high seas. They claimed that resistance to such a search was piratical. The Vice-Admiralty Court condemned *Le Louis* for participating in the slave trade in violation of the law of nations.

On appeal, the High Court of Admiralty reversed, finding no act of piracy, on the ground that there was no right of visit and search in time of peace and that the slave trade was not prohibited by French law. The following discussion appears in Sir William Scott's opinion for the High Court.]

[N]o information is distinctly conveyed to the Court what preliminaries led to this unfortunate conflict; in which no fewer than twelve lives were lost on the British side, and three on the other, and in which several persons on both sides were wounded. The Court is left to infer, from the general course of the transaction, that it originated in a demand to visit and search the vessel, on a suspicion of her being a slave trader, and in a resistance to that demand; the demand and the resistance being maintained to the length of producing the calamitous event which I have described....

At the outset of the proceedings the seizor describes himself as commissioned to make *captures* and seizures. It certainly appeared to be a singular commission that authorized him to make captures in time of peace.... It may, however, be sufficient to state that this commission professes to be issued by the governor of Sierra Leone, on the 25th of January 1816; to be founded on the Slave Trade Act, 51 G. 3, and to authorise the commander to seize and detain (for I do not find that the word *capture* occurs) all ships and vessels offending against that Act, or any other Act abolishing the slave trade; and ... to observe, that neither this British Act of Parliament, nor any commission founded on it, can affect any right or interest of foreigners, unless they are founded upon principles and impose regulations that are consistent with the law of nations. That is the only law which Great Britain can apply to them; and the generality of any terms employed in an Act of Parliament must be narrowed in construction by a religious adherence thereto....

Assuming the fact... that there was a demand, and a resistance producing the deplorable results here described, I think that the natural order of things compels me to enquire first, whether the party who demanded had a right to search; for if not, then not only was the resistance to it lawful, but likewise the very fact on which the other ground of condemnation rests is totally removed. For if no right to visit and search, then no ulterior right of seizing and bringing in, and proceeding to adjudication; and it is in the course of those proceedings alone, that the facts are produced, that she is a French ship trading in slaves; and if these facts are made known to the seizor by his own unwarranted acts, he cannot avail himself of discoveries thus unlawfully produced, nor take advantage of the consequences of his own wrong. Supposing, however, that it should appear that he had a right to visit and search, and therefore to avail himself of all the information he so acquired, the question would then be, whether that information has established all the necessary facts? The first is, that it was a French ship intentionally employed in the slave trade, which... appears to be sufficiently shewn. The second is, that such a trading is a contravention of the French law; for it has been repeatedly admitted that the Court, in order to support this sentence of condemnation, must have the foundation of the trade being prohibited by the law of the country to which the party belongs.

Upon the first question, whether the right of search exists in time of peace, I have to observe, that two principles of public law are generally recognized as fundamental. One is the perfect equality and entire independence of all distinct states. Relative magnitude creates no distinction of right; relative imbecility, whether permanent or casual, gives no additional right to the more powerful neighbour; and any advantage seized upon that ground is mere usurpation. This is the great foundation of public law, which it mainly concerns the peace of mankind, both in their politic and private capacities, to preserve inviolate. The second is, that all nations being equal, all have an equal right to the uninterrupted use of the unappropriated parts of the ocean for their navigation. In places where no local authority exists, where the subjects of all states meet upon a footing of entire equality and independence, no one state, or any of its subjects, has a right to assume or exercise authority over the subjects of another. I can find no authority that gives the right of interruption to the navigation of states in amity upon the high seas, excepting that which the rights of war give to both belligerents against neutrals....

The right of visitation being in this present case exercised in time of peace, the question rises, how is it to be legalised? And looking to what I have described as the known existing law of nations evidenced by all authority and all practice, it must be upon the ground that the captured vessel is to be taken *legally* as a pirate, or else some new ground is to be assumed on which this right, which has been distinctly admitted not to exist generally in time of peace, can be supported. Wherever it has existed, it has existed upon the ground of repelling injury, and as a measure of self-defence. No practice that exists in the world carries it further. It is perfectly clear, that this vessel cannot be deemed a pirate from any want of a national character legally obtained. She is the property not of sea rovers, but of French acknowledged domiciled subjects. She has a French pass, French register, and all proper documents, and is an acknowledged portion of the mercantile marine of that country. If, therefore, the character of a pirate can be impressed upon her, it must be only on the ground of her occupation as a slave trader; no other act of piracy being imputed. The question then comes to this:—Can the occupation of this French vessel be legally deemed a piracy, inferring, as it must do, if it be so, all the pains and penalties of piracy? . . . I think it requires no labour of proof to shew that such an occupation cannot be deemed a legal piracy. The very statute lately passed which makes it a transportable offence in any British subject to be concerned in this trade, affords a decisive proof that it was not liable to be considered as a piracy, and a capital offence, as it would be in foreigners as well as British subjects, if it was a piracy at all. In truth it [lacks] some of the distinguishing features of that offence. It is not the act of freebooters, enemies of the human race, renouncing every country, and ravaging every country in its coasts and vessels indiscriminately, and thereby creating an universal terror and alarm; but of persons confining their transactions (reprehensible as they may be) to particular countries, without exciting the slightest apprehension in others. It is not the act of persons insulting and assaulting coasts and vessels against the will of the Governments and the course of their laws, but of persons resorting thither to carry on *a traffic* (as it is there most unfortunately deemed), not only recognised but invited by the institutions and administrations of those barbarous communities. . . . Be the malignity of the practice what it may, it is not that of piracy, in legal consideration.

Piracy being excluded, the Court has to look for some new and peculiar ground: but in the first place a new and very extensive ground is offered to it by the suggestion, which has been strongly pressed, that this trade, if not the crime of piracy, is nevertheless *crime*, and that every nation, and indeed every individual has not only a right, but a duty, to prevent in every place the commission of crime. It is a sphere of duty sufficiently large that is thus opened out to communities and to their members. But to establish the consequence required, it is first necessary to establish that the right to interpose by force to prevent the commission of crime, commences, not upon the commencement of the overt act, nor upon the evident approach towards it, but on the bare surmise grounded on the mere possibility; for unless it goes that length it will not support the right of forcible enquiry and search. What are the proximate circumstances which confer on you the right of intruding yourself into a foreign ship, over which you have no authority whatever, or of demanding the submission of its crew to your inquiry whether they mean to deal in the traffic of slaves, not in your country, but in one in which you have no connection? Where is the law that has defined those circumstances and created that right under their existence? Secondly, it must be shewn that the act imputed to the parties is unquestionably and legally criminal by the universal law of nations; for the right of search claimed makes no distinctions, and in truth can make none; for till the ship is searched it cannot be known whether she is a slave trader or not, and whether she belongs to a nation which admits the act to be criminal, or to one which maintains it to be simply commercial, and I say *legally* criminal, because neither this Court nor any other can carry its private apprehensions, independent of law, into its public judgments on the quality of actions.... It must look to the legal standard of morality; and upon a question of this nature, that standard must be found in the law of nations as fixed and evidenced by general and ancient and admitted practice, by treaties and by the general tenour of the laws and ordinances and the formal transactions of civilised states; and looking to those authorities, I find a difficulty in maintaining that the traffic is legally criminal....

Within these few years, a considerable change of opinion has taken place, particularly in this country. Formal declarations have been made, and laws enacted, in reprobation of this practice; and pains, ably and zealously conducted, have been taken to induce other countries to follow the example; but at present with insufficient effect: for there *are* nations which adhere to the practice, under all the encouragement which their own laws can give it. What is the doctrine of our Courts of the Law of Nations relatively to them? Why, that their practice is to be respected; that their slaves if taken are to be restored to them; and if not taken under innocent mistake, to be restored with costs and damages. All this, surely, upon the ground that such conduct on the part of any state is no departure from the law of nations; because, if it were, no such respect could be allowed to it, upon an exemption of its own making; for no nation can privilege itself to commit a crime against the law of nations by a mere municipal regulation of its own. And if our understanding and administration of the law of nations be, that every nation, independently of treaties, retains a legal right to carry on this traffic, and that the trade carried on under that authority is to be respected by all tribunals, foreign as well as domestic, it is not easy to find any consistent grounds on which to maintain that the traffic, according to our views of that law, is criminal.

[If visit and search are] not permitted in time of peace it will be extremely difficult to suppress the traffic. [T]he suppression, however desirable, and however sought, is attended with enormous difficulties; difficulties which have baffled the most zealous endeavors for many years.... But the difficulty of the attainment will not legalise measures that are otherwise illegal. To press forward to a great principle by breaking through every other great principle that stands in the way of its establishment; to force the way to the liberation of Africa by trampling on the independence of other states in Europe; in short, to procure an eminent good by means that are unlawful; is as little consonant to private morality as to public justice. Obtain the concurrence of other nations, if you can, by application, by remonstrance, by example, by every peaceable instrument which man can employ to attract the consent of man. But a nation is not justified in assuming rights that do not belong to her merely because she means to apply them to a laudable purpose; nor in setting out upon a moral crusade of converting other nations by acts of unlawful force. Nor is it to be argued, that because other nations approve the ultimate purpose, they must therefore submit to every measure which any one state or its subjects may inconsiderately adopt for its attainment. In this very case nothing can be clearer than that the only French law produced is in direct contradiction to such a notion; because approving as it does (though to a very limited extent) the abolition, it nevertheless reserves to its own authorities the cognisance of each cause and the appropriation of the penalties.

[Scott continues with an analysis of French law, concluding that at the time of the seizure slave trading was still permissible under that law.]

Notes

1. *The Evolution of International Norms.* Today, many consider the prohibition against slavery and the slave trade to reflect fundamental precepts of international human rights law. Under Article 13 of the 1958 High Seas Convention and Article 99 of the LOS Convention, every state must take effective measures to prevent and punish the transport of slaves in ships authorized to fly its flag. How did the prohibition against slavery evolve? In the 19th century, several states enacted legislation prohibiting trading in slaves and/or ownership of slaves. According to Sir William Scott, can national legislation alone establish customary international law? What roles do national legislation play in the

development of international law? In United States v. La Jeune Eugenie, 26 F. Cas. 832 (Cir. Ct., D. Mass. 1822) (15,551), Justice Story relied on bilateral treaties outlawing the slave trade as evidence of international law prohibiting the slave trade, as well as on natural law concepts. How might natural law support a prohibition against slavery?

Between 1815 and 1957, approximately 300 bilateral and multilateral agreements were implemented to suppress slavery. Office of the U.N. High Commissioner for Human Rights, Abolishing Slavery and Its Contemporary Forms, HR/Pub/02/4 ¶ 2 (2002). Recall the treaty provisions combating the slave trade that were at issue in the Muscat Dhows Case in Chapter 3. Some 19th-century treaties also provided for international procedural mechanisms to combat the slave trade. See Leslie Bethell, The Mixed Commissions for the Suppression of the Transatlantic Slave Trade in the Nineteenth Century, 7 J. African History 79 (1966). Two important 20th-century multilateral conventions are the 1926 Convention to Suppress the Slave Trade and Slavery and the 1956 Supplementary Convention on the Abolition of Slavery. As of September 1, 2013, 123 states were parties to the latter treaty.

2. *The Right to Board Ships Suspected of Engaging in the Slave Trade.* Review Article 110 of the LOS Convention. If a warship suspects that a foreign merchant ship on the high seas is transporting slaves, what exactly is the warship authorized to do? Compare LOS Convention, Article 105. What enforcement actions may a warship take against a ship engaged in piracy? What reasons support the different enforcement actions that a foreign warship may take toward a ship engaged in piracy and a ship engaged in transporting slaves? Would it be more appropriate to treat instances of slave trading like piracy? Or should the slave trade be treated like other instances of illegal immigration, addressed through treaties authorizing visits or searches of flag vessels by foreign warships? See Chapter 2, Section I.

3. *Modern Instances of Slave Trading and Trafficking in Persons.* Although the African slave trade had largely ended by the start of the 20th century, today the transport of illegal immigrants and their subsequent use as forced labor, and sex trafficking in women and children, pose significant problems. See Economic and Social Council, Commn. on Human Rights, Sub-Commn. on Prevention of Discrimination and Protection of Minorities, Contemporary Forms of Slavery: Report of the Working Group on Contemporary Forms of Slavery on its Twenty-Third Session, UN Doc. E/CN.4/Sub.2/1998/14 (1998); U.S. Dept. State, Trafficking in Persons Report (June 2013), available at http://www.state.gov. Is the transportation of persons intended to be used in forced labor or prostitution encompassed within the prohibition against the transport of slaves as enunciated in Article 99 of the LOS Convention? What problems

might arise if the term "slave" as used in Article 99 of the LOS Convention were broadly construed?

Consider Article 7(c) of the 1956 Supplementary Convention on the Abolition of Slavery, which defines "slave trade" as including:

> all acts involved in the capture, acquisition or disposal of a person with intent to reduce him to slavery; all acts involved in the acquisition of a slave with a view to selling or exchanging him; all acts of disposal by sale or exchange of a person acquired with a view to being sold or exchanged; and, in general, every act of trade or transport in slaves by whatever means of conveyance.

For background, see Jean Allain, The Slavery Conventions (2008). Compare this definition of "slave trade" to the definition of "trafficking in persons" in Article 3(a) of the 2000 Protocol to Prevent, Suppress and Punish Trafficking in Persons, Especially Women and Children, supplementing the United Nations Convention Against Transnational Organized Crime:

> the recruitment, transportation, transfer, harbouring or receipt of persons, by means of the threat or use of force or other forms of coercion, of abduction, of fraud, of deception, of the abuse of power or of a position of vulnerability or of the giving or receiving of payments or benefits to achieve the consent of a person having control over another person, for the purpose of exploitation. Exploitation shall include, at a minimum, the exploitation of the prostitution of others or other forms of sexual exploitation, forced labour or services, slavery or practices similar to slavery, servitude or the removal of organs[.]

As of September 1, 2013, there were 157 parties to the Trafficking Protocol. This Protocol requires state parties to enact legislation criminalizing human trafficking activities, and to implement or consider implementing various measures to protect and assist the victims of human trafficking. There is no provision in the Protocol allowing a party's warships to board the vessels of other parties that are suspected of engaging in human trafficking.

3 *Illicit Drug Traffic*

Unlike piracy, the slave trade, and unauthorized broadcasting, illicit drug traffic is not specifically listed in Article 110 of the LOS Convention as one of the circumstances that could justify interference with a flag state's exclusive jurisdiction. In accordance with Articles 92 and 110 of the LOS Convention, however, such interference may be authorized pursuant to treaty. Following are examples from both a multilateral and bilateral treaty granting enforcement authority to a contracting state over the vessels of other state parties in certain circumstances. As you read, note the differences in the enforcement authority granted under each treaty over the vessels of other contracting states.

UNITED NATIONS CONVENTION AGAINST ILLICIT TRAFFIC IN NARCOTIC DRUGS AND PSYCHOTROPIC SUBSTANCES

Dec. 20, 1988, U.S. Sen. Treaty Doc. No. 101–4 (1989), 1678 U.N.T.S. 201, 28 Intl. Leg. Materials 497 (1989)

Article 17

1. The Parties shall co-operate to the fullest extent possible to suppress illicit traffic by sea, in conformity with the international law of the sea.

2. A Party which has reasonable grounds to suspect that a vessel flying its flag or not displaying a flag or marks of registry is engaged in illicit traffic may request the assistance of other Parties in suppressing its use for that purpose. The Parties so requested shall render such assistance within the means available to them.

3. A Party which has reasonable grounds to suspect that a vessel exercising freedom of navigation in accordance with international law and flying the flag or displaying marks of registry of another Party is engaged in illicit traffic may so notify the flag State, request confirmation of registry and, if confirmed, request authorization from the flag State to take appropriate measures in regard to that vessel.

4. In accordance with paragraph 3 or in accordance with treaties in force between them or in accordance with any agreement or arrangement otherwise reached between those Parties, the flag State may authorize the requesting State to, *inter alia*:

(a) Board the vessel;

(b) Search the vessel;

(c) If evidence of involvement in illicit traffic is found, take appropriate action with respect to the vessel, persons and cargo on board.

5. Where action is taken pursuant to this article, the Parties concerned shall take due account of the need not to endanger the safety of life at sea, the security of the vessel and the cargo or to prejudice the commercial and legal interests of the flag State or any other interested State.

6. The flag State may, consistent with its obligations in paragraph 1 of this article, subject its authorization to conditions to be mutually agreed between it and the requesting Party, including conditions relating to responsibility.

7. For the purposes of paragraphs 3 and 4 of this article, a Party shall respond expeditiously to a request from another Party to determine whether a vessel that is flying its flag is entitled to do so, and to requests for authorization made pursuant to paragraph 3. At the time of becoming a Party to this Convention, each Party shall designate an authority or, when necessary, authorities to receive and respond to such requests. Such designation shall be notified through the Secretary-General to all other Parties within one month of the designation.

8. A Party which has taken any action in accordance with this article shall promptly inform the flag State concerned of the results of that action.

9. The Parties shall consider entering into bilateral or regional agreements or arrangements to carry out, or to enhance the effectiveness of, the provisions of this article.

10. Action pursuant to paragraph 4 of this article shall be carried out only by warships or military aircraft, or other ships or aircraft clearly marked and identifiable as being on government service and authorized to that effect.

11. Any action taken in accordance with this article shall take due account of the need not to interfere with or affect the rights and obligations and the exercise of jurisdiction of coastal States in accordance with the international law of the sea.

UNITED STATES-UNITED KINGDOM AGREEMENT TO FACILITATE THE INTERDICTION OF VESSELS SUSPECTED OF TRAFFICKING IN DRUGS

Nov. 13, 1981, 33 U.S.T. 4224, 1285 U.N.T.S. 197

1. The Government of the United Kingdom of Great Britain and Northern Ireland agree that they will not object to the boarding by the authorities of the United States, outside the limits of the territorial sea and contiguous zone of the United States and within the areas described in paragraph 9 below, of private vessels under the British flag in any case in which those authorities reasonably believe that the vessel has on board a cargo of drugs for importation into the United States in violation of the laws of the United States.

2. On boarding the vessel the authorities of the United States may address enquiries to those on board, examine the ship's papers and take such other measures as are necessary to establish the place of registration of the vessel. When these measures suggest that an offence against the laws of the United States relative to the importation of narcotic drugs is being committed, the

Government of the United Kingdom agree that they will not object to the authorities of the United States instituting a search of the vessel.

3. If the authorities of the United States then believe that an offence against the laws referred to in paragraph 2 above is being committed, the Government of the United Kingdom agree that they will not object to the vessel being seized and taken into a United States port.

4. The Government of the United Kingdom may, within 14 days of the vessel's entry into port, object to the continued exercise of United States jurisdiction over the vessel for purposes of the laws referred to in paragraph 2 above, and the Government of the United States shall thereupon release the vessel without charge. The Government of the United States shall not institute forfeiture proceedings before the end of the period allowed for objection.

5. The Government of the United Kingdom may, within 30 days of the vessel's entry into port, object to the prosecution of any United Kingdom national found on board the vessel, and the Government of the United States shall thereupon release such person. The Government of the United Kingdom agree that they will not otherwise object to the prosecution of any person found on board the vessel.

6. Any action by the authorities of the United States shall be taken in accordance with this Agreement and United States law.

7. In any case where a vessel under the British flag is boarded the authorities of the United States shall promptly inform the authorities of the United Kingdom of the action taken and shall keep them fully informed of any subsequent developments.

8. If any loss or injury is suffered as a result of any action taken by the United States in contravention of these arrangements or any improper or unreasonable action taken by the United States pursuant thereto, representatives of the two Governments shall meet at the request of either to decide any question relating to compensation. Representatives of the two Governments shall in any case meet from time to time to review the working of these Arrangements.

9. The areas referred to in paragraph 1 above comprise the Gulf of Mexico, the Caribbean Sea, that portion of the Atlantic Ocean West of longitude 55° West and South of latitude 30° North and all other areas within 150 miles of the Atlantic coast of the United States.

Notes

1. *Multilateral Conventions Addressing Drug Trafficking*. Two other important multilateral conventions, the 1961 Single Convention on Narcotic Drugs,

Article 35 and the 1971 Convention on Psychotropic Substances, Article 21, impose duties on parties to cooperate among themselves and with international organizations in efforts to suppress traffic in illicit drugs. However, neither of these conventions provides a right to board vessels of other parties suspected of engaging in illicit drug traffic. The 1988 U.N. Convention excerpted above was drafted in response to a U.N. General Assembly resolution requesting the Commission on Narcotic Drugs to initiate "the preparation of a draft convention against illicit traffic in narcotic drugs" that would consider especially aspects of the problem "not envisaged in existing international instruments." UN Doc. A/RES/39/141 (1984). The 1988 Convention entered into force in 1990; as of September 1, 2013, 187 states and the European Union were parties. As of September 1, 2013, there were 153 parties to the 1961 Convention and 183 parties to the 1971 Convention.

2. *Enforcement Measures.* Read Articles 108 and 110 of the LOS Convention and contrast the enforcement actions that a warship of a party may take against a foreign vessel suspected of engaging in illicit drug traffic under that article, the multilateral 1988 Convention, and the bilateral U.S.-U.K. agreement. Which framework grants the greatest enforcement authority to a warship of a state party that encounters a vessel of another state party suspected of engaging in drug trafficking? Why is it often more difficult to negotiate greater enforcement rights in a multilateral, rather than a bilateral, treaty?

3. *Flag State Consent.* Under the U.S. Maritime Drug Law Enforcement Act, which is discussed in more detail below, consent to board a foreign vessel suspected of engaging in drug trafficking may be obtained from the flag state "by radio, telephone, or similar oral or electronic means." 46 U.S.C. § 70502(c)(2) (2013). Is such informal consent valid under international law? The U.S. statute provides that such consent "is proved conclusively by certification of the [U.S.] Secretary of State [or his designee.]" U.S. courts have ruled that only the flag state (and not the individual defendant) has standing to challenge the validity of the consent under international law. See, e.g., United States v. Bustos-Useche, 273 F.3d 622 (5th Cir. 2001).

Recall Articles 92 and 110 of the LOS Convention, which provide that acts of interference with a flag state's jurisdiction must be authorized by treaty, if not otherwise specifically approved in the Convention. What reasons support this treaty requirement? Could a flag state by treaty provide for informal ways to grant its consent? As of March 2013, the United States has entered 45 maritime counterdrug bilateral agreements or operational procedures with other states. U.S. Dept. State, Bureau for Intl. Narcotics and Law Enforcement Affairs, International Narcotics Control Strategy Report, Vol. 1 at 42 (2013).

4 *Stateless Vessels*

Article 110 of the LOS Convention authorizes the officers of a warship to board, on the high seas, a vessel that is reasonably suspected of being "without nationality." As a part of its effort to combat illicit drug traffic, the United States has enacted the following legislation, which extends U.S. criminal jurisdiction to any person aboard a stateless vessel who possesses, with the intent to manufacture or distribute, a controlled substance.

UNITED STATES MARITIME DRUG LAW ENFORCEMENT ACT
46 U.S.C. § 70503 (2013)

(a) Prohibitions. An individual may not knowingly or intentionally manufacture or distribute, or possess with intent to manufacture or distribute, a controlled substance on board—

(1) a vessel of the United States or a vessel subject to the jurisdiction of the United States; or

(2) any vessel if the individual is a citizen of the United States or a resident alien of the United States.

(b) Extension beyond territorial jurisdiction. Subsection (a) applies even though the act is committed outside the territorial jurisdiction of the United States.

[Several of the terms used in the preceding section are specifically defined in the Act:]

46 U.S.C. § 70502 (2013)

(c) Vessel subject to the jurisdiction of the United States.

(1) [T]he term "vessel subject to the jurisdiction of the United State" includes—

(A) a vessel without nationality;

(B) a vessel assimilated to a vessel without nationality under paragraph (2) of article 6 of the 1958 Convention on the High Seas;

(C) a vessel registered in a foreign nation if that nation has consented or waived objection to the enforcement of United States law by the United States;

(D) a vessel in the customs waters of the United States;

(E) a vessel in the territorial waters of a foreign nation if the nation consents to the enforcement of United States law by the United States; and

(F) a vessel in the [24-mile] contiguous zone of the United States that . . .

(i) is entering the United States,

(ii) has departed the United States, or

(iii) is a hovering vessel as defined in section 401 of the Tariff Act of 1930 (19 U.S.C. 1401).

(2) Consent or waiver of objection. Consent or waiver of objection by a foreign nation to the enforcement of United States law by the United States under paragraph (1)(C) or (E)—

(A) may be obtained by radio, telephone, or similar oral or electronic means; and

(B) is proved conclusively by certification of the Secretary of State or the Secretary's designee.

(d) Vessel without nationality.

(1) [T]he term "vessel without nationality" includes—

(A) a vessel aboard which the master or individual in charge makes a claim of registry that is denied by the nation whose registry is claimed;

(B) a vessel aboard which the master or individual in charge fails, on request of an officer of the United States authorized to enforce applicable provisions of United States law, to make a claim of nationality or registry for that vessel; and

(C) a vessel aboard which the master or individual in charge makes a claim of registry and for which the claimed nation of registry does not affirmatively and unequivocally assert that the vessel is of its nationality. . . .

(e) Claim of nationality or registry. A claim of nationality or registry under this section includes only—

(1) possession on board the vessel and production of documents evidencing the vessel's nationality as provided in article 5 of the 1958 Convention on the High Seas;

(2) flying its nation's ensign or flag; or

(3) a verbal claim of nationality or registry by the master or individual in charge of the vessel.

UNITED STATES v. PINTO-MEJIA

720 F.2d 248 (2d Cir. 1983), modified, 728 F.2d 142 (2d Cir. 1984)

[The U.S. Coast Guard spotted a vessel 100 miles off the coast of Maine headed southwesterly. The vessel, the *Ricardo*, was not flying a flag. The Coast

Guard suspected that the vessel was engaged in drug smuggling. The Coast Guard boarded the vessel, opened the main hold, and discovered twenty tons of marijuana. The crew members, all Colombian nationals, were arrested for violation of the Marijuana on the High Seas Act, the predecessor of the Maritime Drug Law Enforcement Act. The Coast Guard confirmed with Venezuelan authorities that, although the vessel had once been registered in Venezuela, its registration had lapsed, thereby rendering the vessel stateless. The court held that under Article 6 of the 1958 High Seas Convention, the boarding of the stateless vessel did not violate international law. The defendants argued that even if the search and seizure were not unlawful, there was an insufficient nexus between the vessel and the United States to establish jurisdiction.]

Defendants contend that even a proper finding that the RICARDO was stateless would not establish that the vessel was subject to the jurisdiction of the United States since international law prohibits a state's exercise of penal jurisdiction over a stateless vessel on the high seas unless there is some nexus between the state and the vessel. We disagree with defendant's interpretation of international law.

First, we note that in enacting statutes, Congress is not bound by international law. If it chooses to do so, it may legislate with respect to conduct outside the United States, in excess of the limits posed by international law. As long as Congress has expressly indicated its intent to reach such conduct, "a United States court would be bound to follow the Congressional direction unless this would violate the due process clause of the Fifth Amendment," Leasco Data Processing Equipment Corp. v. Maxwell, 468 F.2d 1326, 1334 (2d Cir. 1972). Our review of the language and history of §§ 955a et seq. persuades us that, assuming that the RICARDO was stateless, Congress intended these sections to reach the conduct of the defendants in this case. In § 955a(h) [the predecessor to 46 U.S.C. § 70503], Congress expressly stated its intention to reach acts committed "outside the territorial jurisdiction of the United States." In addition, in the legislative history of § 955a, there is evidence that Congress had as a primary goal the ability to reach stateless possessors of narcotics who could not be proved to have intent to distribute the narcotics in the United States.... Experts who testified at the hearing on H.R. 2538 noted that many drug traffickers responsible for transporting drugs that ended up in the United States were able to travel with impunity over the high seas because of the then-existing requirement that the traffickers intend to distribute the drugs in the United States before being subject to prosecution there. The difficulty of proving intent allowed many such traffickers to go free, although their wares were in fact intended to be distributed in the United States. Section 955a was enacted to close this loophole. Thus, the House of Representatives Report accompanying H.R. 2538 observed that United States jurisdiction was to be extended to "vessels without nationality on the high seas," and that "[a]ny person on board such a vessel, of either U.S. or foreign citizenship, is prohibited from ... possessing with the intent to ... distribute any controlled substance." H.R.Rep. No. 323, 96th Cong., 1st Sess. 9 (1979). The Report noted that "[t]he intent to distribute need not be within the United States. Moreover, the intent element may be inferred by proof of a presence of a large quantity of the narcotic or dangerous drug, giving rise to the inference of trafficking," *id.* at 10, and that "it would not be necessary to prove that the vessel or the controlled substance was bound for the United States," *id.* at 12. Congress's explicit intention, therefore, was to extend the reach of § 955a to foreigners on stateless vessels on the high seas who possess large quantities of narcotics that they may or may not intend for distribution in the United States.

Defendants point out that despite this explicit intention, Congress also expressed its intention that § 955a be consistent with the strictures of international law, see, e.g., H.R. Rep. at 11 ("section [955a] is designed to prohibit all acts of illicit trafficking in controlled substances on the high seas which the United States can reach under international law"), and they argue that international law permits the extension of the jurisdiction envisioned by Congress only if there is some nexus between the vessel and the state seeking to assert jurisdiction. Defendant's argument fails, however, since it apparently was Congress's understanding—and correctly so—that international law does not provide such protection to vessels that are stateless.

One of the basic principles of international law is that "all nations have an equal and untrammeled right to navigate on the high seas." United States v. Marino-Garcia, 679 F.2d 1373, 1380 (11th Cir. 1982), cert. denied, 459 U.S. 1114 (1983); see [1958] Convention on the High Seas Art. 2. With this right, of course, comes responsibility. To preserve all nations' freedom to travel on the high seas and to avoid conflict among nations, Article 2 of the Convention provides that each state must exercise its right "with reasonable regard to the interests of other States in their exercise of the freedom of the high seas."

To enforce compliance with these principles among individual ships traveling on the high seas, Articles 5 and 6 of the Convention provide that a ship has the nationality of the state whose flag it flies and that the ship is subject to that state's jurisdiction. Each state has the responsibility of fixing the conditions "for the grant of its nationality to ships, for the registration of ships in its territory, and for the right to fly its flag. [I]n particular, the State must effectively exercise its jurisdiction and control in administrative, technical and social matters over ships flying its flag." *Id.* Art. 5. To eliminate any confusion over which state has jurisdiction over a ship, Article 6 provides that a ship may sail under the flag of only one state and that while doing so, it is generally subject to that state's exclusive jurisdiction. A ship may not change flags during a voyage except when a real transfer of ownership or registry occurs, and a ship that flies under the flags of more than one state, claiming the nationality of whichever it deems convenient, is considered to be a ship without nationality that may not claim the protection of any of the nationalities in question.

The suggestion underlying these principles is that a stateless vessel, which does not sail under the flag of one state to whose jurisdiction it has submitted, may not claim the protection of international law and does not have the right to travel the high seas with impunity. There is ample evidence that Congress properly understood that these principles were consistent with its desire that § 955a reach stateless vessels on the high seas whether or not the narcotics carried were intended for distribution in the United States. During the hearings on H.R. 2538, Congress was repeatedly presented with statements by experts, reflecting what was apparently a common understanding among those interested in the bill, that the United States could, consistent with international law, assert jurisdiction over stateless vessels on the high seas.

In light of these principles and Congress's manifest intentions, courts have agreed uniformly that stateless vessels on the high seas are, by virtue of their statelessness, subject to the jurisdiction of the United States. As the court in *Marino-Garcia* put it,

> [v]essels without nationality are international pariahs. They have no internationally recognized right to navigate freely on the high seas.... Moreover, flagless vessels are frequently not subject to the laws of a flag-state. As such, they represent "floating sanctuaries from authority" and constitute a potential threat to the order and stability of navigation on the high seas....
>
> The absence of any right to navigate freely on the high seas coupled with the potential threat to order on international waterways has led various courts to conclude that international law places no restrictions upon a nation's right to subject stateless vessels to its jurisdiction. Thus, the assertion of jurisdiction over stateless vessels on the high seas in no way transgresses recognized principles of international law. 679 F.2d at 1382 (citations omitted).

We find inapposite the authorities invoked by defendants in their effort to show that a nexus must exist before the United States may exercise jurisdiction over a stateless vessel on the high seas. The nexus requirement has been applied only to a vessel that is registered with, and is flying the flag of, one state to whose jurisdiction it has submitted. In such cases, international law requires the state seeking to assert jurisdiction to show a nexus between it and the foreign vessel that is sufficient to justify supplanting the flag state's normally "exclusive jurisdiction" granted by Article 6 of the Convention on the High Seas. Only a limited number of such nexuses have been found to be sufficient to warrant permitting a state to assert jurisdiction over another state's vessel. Restatement (Second) of Foreign Relations Law of the United States §§ 18 (vessel engaged in illegal activity intended to have an effect in the state), 33 (vessel engaged in an activity that threatens the state's security or governmental functions), 34 (vessel engaged in a universally prohibited activity, such as piracy) (1965). But we find no authority in international law for requiring any nexus where the ship otherwise would be subject to the jurisdiction of no state.

We conclude, therefore, that international law provides no bar to an assertion of jurisdiction over a stateless vessel by the United States pursuant to § 955a(a), even absent proof that the vessel's operators intended to distribute their cargo in the United States. Consequently, we conclude that a properly supported finding by the district court that the RICARDO was stateless would, in itself, be sufficient to establish the court's jurisdiction over the defendants.

Notes

1. *Stateless Vessels and Jurisdictional Nexus*. What authority may a state assert over a stateless vessel after boarding, if it determines that the stateless vessel is engaged in an unlawful activity? The LOS Convention does not specifically authorize the seizure of a stateless vessel found on the high seas or the arrest of its crew members, unless there are reasonable grounds to believe that the vessel is engaged in piracy (Article 105) or unauthorized broadcasting (Article 109), or if another treaty authorizes the seizure or arrest (Articles 92, 110). The Pinto-Mejia court concluded that "international law provides no bar" to the U.S.'s assertion of jurisdiction over stateless vessels and their crew members under its drug enforcement statute. Do you agree?

Drug trafficking has not been recognized as an offense, such as piracy or genocide, that any state may punish under the international law principle of "universal jurisdiction." See Restatement (Third) Foreign Relations Law of the United States § 404 (1986). Where universal jurisdiction does not apply, international law requires a connection between a state, on the one hand, and the state's territory, citizens, vessels, government operations, or security on the other hand, in order for the state validly to exercise jurisdiction. Recall the decision in the Lotus case; what was the nexus between the French officer and Turkey upon which jurisdiction was based? Under the reasoning of the Pinto-Mejia court, would the United States have jurisdiction over a stateless vessel and its foreign crew arrested 2,000 miles from U.S. territory, if no evidence established that drugs found on board were destined for the United States? For U.S. courts, should "nexus" be determined in accordance with international law conceptions of permissible jurisdiction? See United States v. Caicedo, 47 F.3d 370 (9th Cir. 1995).

2. *Jurisdiction over Crew Members.* The Pinto-Mejia court concluded that the fact that the vessel "was stateless would, in itself, be sufficient to establish the court's jurisdiction over the defendants." Is it sensible to draw a distinction between jurisdiction with respect to the vessel and jurisdiction over those on board? That is, even assuming that a U.S. exercise of authority over a stateless vessel is legal, does it follow that the United States has legislative and enforcement jurisdiction over the vessel's foreign crew members? Would such crew members, or their state of nationality, have a legitimate complaint under international law if they were tried under U.S. law without a showing of jurisdictional nexus to the United States?

E United Nations Security Council Decisions, Threats to International Peace and Security, and the Interdiction of Vessels

The U.N. Security Council has the primary responsibility, under Chapter VII of the U.N. Charter, to take action with respect to threats to the peace, breaches of the peace, and acts of aggression. Security Council decisions made under Chapter VII, which must be adopted by nine of its fifteen members and not vetoed by one of its permanent members (China, France, Russia, the United Kingdom, and the United States), are legally binding. Some Security Council decisions have imposed economic sanctions on states found to threaten international peace and security, and have authorized the interdiction of shipping to or from the sanctioned states.

This section examines U.N. Security Council actions related to the interdiction of vessels. The first excerpt includes U.N. Charter articles relating to the Security Council's authority; Articles 39–42 and 48 are part of the Charter's Chapter VII. Following are excerpts from two Security Council resolutions concerning measures relating to jurisdiction over vessels. These resolutions were adopted in response to activities of the Federal Republic of Yugoslavia in the state of Bosnia and Herzegovina during the early 1990s. Two additional readings—a European Court of Justice decision and an excerpt from a U.N. report—concern the enforcement of these resolutions.

UNITED NATIONS CHARTER

June 26, 1945, 59 Stat. 1031, T.S. No. 993

Article 25

The Members of the United Nations agree to accept and carry out the decisions of the Security Council in accordance with the present Charter.

Article 39

The Security Council shall determine the existence of any threat to the peace, breach of the peace, or act of aggression and shall make recommendations, or decide what measures shall be taken in accordance with Articles 41 and 42, to maintain or restore international peace and security.

Article 40

In order to prevent an aggravation of the situation, the Security Council may, before making the recommendations or deciding upon the measures provided for in Article 39, call upon the parties concerned to comply with such provisional measures as it deems necessary or desirable. . . .

Article 41

The Security Council may decide what measures not involving the use of armed force are to be employed to give effect to its decisions, and it may call upon the Members of the United Nations to apply such measures. These may include complete or partial interruption of economic relations and of rail, sea, air, postal, telegraphic, radio, and other means of communication, and the severance of diplomatic relations.

Article 42

Should the Security Council consider that measures provided for in Article 41 would be inadequate or have proved to be inadequate, it may take such action by air, sea, or land forces as may be necessary to maintain or restore international peace and security. Such action may include demonstrations, blockade, and other operations by air, sea, or land forces of Members of the United Nations.

Article 48

1. The action required to carry out the decisions of the Security Council for the maintenance of international peace and security shall be taken by all the Members of the United Nations or by some of them, as the Security Council may determine.

2. Such decisions shall be carried out by the Members of the United Nations directly and through their action in the appropriate international agencies of which they are members.

Article 103

In the event of a conflict between the obligations of the Members of the United Nations under the present Charter and their obligations under any other international agreement, their obligations under the present Charter shall prevail.

Note

1. *Security Council Resolutions and the Interdiction of Vessels Bound for Bosnia-Herzegovina.* Bosnia-Herzegovina, a region within the Socialist Federal Republic of Yugoslavia (SFRY), became an independent state when the SFRY broke apart in the early 1990s. Other states recognized Bosnia and Herzegovina, and it was admitted to the United Nations as a Member State on May 2, 1992.

The Federal Republic of Yugoslavia (Serbia and Montenegro, now succeeded by Serbia) provided military and other assistance to Bosnian Serbs, who gained control over much of Bosnia and Herzegovina. In response, the Security Council passed resolutions mandating, inter alia, various economic sanctions against the Federal Republic. In Resolution 713, which was adopted on September 12, 1991, the Council invoked Chapter VII of the U.N. Charter (Articles 39–51) and decided "that all States shall . . . immediately implement a general and complete embargo on all deliveries of weapons and military equipment to Yugoslavia." In Resolution 757 (May 30, 1992), the Council decided, inter alia, that "all States shall prevent" imports into their territories from the Federal Republic, as well as most exports to Yugoslavia "by their nationals or from their territories or using their flag vessels or aircraft."

The excerpts from Resolutions 787 (Nov. 16, 1992) and 820 (Apr. 17, 1993), which follow, concern the interdiction of shipping bound to and from Yugoslavia.

UNITED NATIONS SECURITY COUNCIL RESOLUTION 787
UN Doc. S/RES/787 (1992)

The Security Council, . . .

12. Acting under Chapters VII and VIII of the Charter of the United Nations, *calls upon* States, acting nationally or through regional agencies or arrangements, to use such measures commensurate with the specific circumstances as may be necessary under the authority of the Security Council to halt all inward and outward maritime shipping in order to inspect and verify their cargoes and destinations and to ensure strict implementation of the provisions of resolutions 713 (1991) and 757 (1992); . . .

15. *Requests* all States to provide in accordance with the Charter of the United Nations such assistance as may be required by those States acting nationally or through regional agencies and arrangements in pursuance of paragraphs 12 and 13 of the present resolution[.]

UNITED NATIONS SECURITY COUNCIL RESOLUTION 820
UN Doc. S/RES/820 (1993)

The Security Council, . . .

Determined to strengthen the implementation of measures imposed by its earlier relevant resolutions,

Acting under Chapter VII of the Charter of the United Nations, . . .

19. *Reminds* States of the importance of strict enforcement of measures imposed under Chapter VII of the Charter, and *calls upon* them to bring proceedings against persons and entities violating the measures imposed by resolutions 713 (1991), 757 (1992), 787 (1992) and the present resolution and to impose appropriate penalties; . . .

25. *Decides* that all States shall detain pending investigation all vessels, freight vehicles, rolling stock, aircraft and cargoes found in their territories and suspected of having violated or being in violation of resolutions 713 (1991), 757 (1992), 787 (1992) or the present resolution, and that, upon a determination that they have been in violation, such vessels, freight vehicles, rolling stock and aircraft shall be impounded and, where appropriate, they and their cargoes may be forfeit to the detaining State; . . .

28. *Decides* to prohibit all commercial maritime traffic from entering the territorial sea of the Federal Republic of Yugoslavia (Serbia and Montenegro) except when authorized on a case-by-case basis by the Committee established by resolution 724 (1991) or in case of *force majeure*;

29. *Reaffirms* the authority of States acting under paragraph 12 of resolution 787 (1992) to use such measures commensurate with the specific circumstances as may be necessary under the authority of the Security Council to enforce the present resolution and its other relevant resolutions, including in the territorial sea of the Federal Republic of Yugoslavia (Serbia and Montenegro)[.]

EBONY MARITIME SA AND LOTEN NAVIGATION CO. LTD v. PREFETTO DELLA PROVINCIA DI BRINDISI AND OTHERS
Case C-177/95, 1997 E.C.R. I-1111 (ECJ 1997)

By order of 11 April 1995, received at the Court on 6 June 1995, the Consiglio di Stato (Council of State [of Italy]) referred for a preliminary ruling under Article 177 of the EC Treaty three questions on the interpretation of Article 1(1)(c) and (d) and Article 10 of Council Regulation (EEC) No 990/93 of 26 April 1993 concerning trade between the European Economic Community and the Federal Republic of Yugoslavia (Serbia and Montenegro)....

The questions have been raised in proceedings brought by Ebony Maritime, a company established under the law of Liberia, and Loten Navigation, a company established under Maltese law, for annulment of a decision taken by the Prefetto (Prefect) of the Province of Brindisi on 22 July 1994 ordering the vessel *Lido II* to be seized pursuant to [1993 Italian laws] imposing an embargo on the States of the former Yugoslavia.

According to the recitals in its preamble, the Regulation seeks to implement within the Community certain aspects of the sanctions decided on against the Federal Republic of Yugoslavia by the United Nations Security Council, which, on the basis of Chapter VII of the United Nations Charter, adopted Resolutions 713 (1991), 757 (1992) and 787 (1992) and reinforced those sanctions by Resolution 820 (1993)....

The scope of the Regulation ...

Article 9 of the Regulation, read in conjunction with Article 1(1)(c) thereof, requires the competent authorities of the Member States to detain, pending investigations, all vessels and cargoes suspected of having breached the prohibition of entry into the territorial sea of the Federal Republic of Yugoslavia for purposes of trade. Under Article 10, the Member State concerned may confiscate vessels and cargoes once it has been established that they have infringed the prohibition.

It follows from the wording of those provisions that the detention and confiscation measures apply to all vessels, with no distinction being drawn on the basis of the vessel's flag or owner. Further, the application of those measures is not subject to the condition that the breach of the prohibitions set out in the Regulation should take place within Community territory. In any case, the prohibition on entry into the territorial sea of the Federal Republic of Yugoslavia, set out in Article 1(1)(c) of the Regulation, can be breached only outside Community territory.

The competent authorities of the Member State concerned must therefore, under Article 9 of the Regulation, detain all vessels suspected of having breached the sanctions imposed against the Federal Republic of Yugoslavia, even if they are flying the flag of a non-member country, belong to non-Community nationals or companies, or if the alleged breach of sanctions occurred outside Community territory. Likewise, national authorities may, under... Article 10 of the Regulation, confiscate those vessels and their cargoes once the infringement has been established.

Since ... the Regulation applies within the whole territory of the Community, Articles 9 and 10 are applicable once those vessels are within the territory of a Member State and thus under the territorial jurisdiction of that State, even if the alleged infringement occurred outside its territory....

The first and second questions

By its first and second questions, the national court is in substance seeking to ascertain whether Article l(l)(c) and (d) of the Regulation prohibits only actual entry of commercial traffic into the territorial sea of the Federal Republic of Yugoslavia or whether it also prohibits conduct occurring in international waters which gives good reason to believe that the vessel concerned is on course for that territorial sea for the purposes of commercial traffic.

It must be noted in this regard that Article 1(1)(c) of the Regulation prohibits the entry of all commercial traffic into Yugoslav territorial waters.

That provision is intended to prevent any entry whatever of commercial traffic into those waters. It was introduced pursuant to Resolution 820 (1993), which was designed to reinforce the sanctions imposed against the Federal Republic of Yugoslavia by previous resolutions of the United Nations Security Council. In order to guarantee that those sanctions would be effective, it was deemed vital to prevent all commercial traffic in Yugoslav territorial waters.

Effective prevention of all commercial traffic in Yugoslav territorial waters implies that the prohibition set out in Article 1(1)(c) of the Regulation should apply not only to actual entries, but also to attempted entries into those territorial waters by vessels in international waters. Any other interpretation would risk rendering the prohibition ineffective.

Furthermore, Article 1(1)(d) of the Regulation, which prohibits any activity the object or effect of which is, directly or indirectly, to promote the entry of any commercial traffic into the territorial sea of the Federal Republic of Yugoslavia, confirms that a breach of the sanctions laid down by the Regulation may result from conduct occurring in international waters.

The answer to the first and second questions must therefore be that Article 1(1)(c) and (d) of the Regulation prohibits not only the actual entry of commercial traffic into the territorial sea of the Federal Republic of Yugoslavia but also conduct occurring in international waters which gives good reason to believe that the vessel concerned is on course for that territorial sea for the purpose of commercial traffic.

FINAL REPORT OF THE SECURITY COUNCIL COMMITTEE ESTABLISHED PURSUANT TO RESOLUTION 724
UN Doc. S/1996/946 at 32 (1996)

During the first half of 1993, NATO [the North Atlantic Treaty Organization] and WEU [the Western European Union] continued their patrolling missions in the Adriatic Sea, which the two organizations had begun in July 1992 in order to ensure compliance by maritime traffic in the area with Security Council resolutions. Since June 1993, following the coming into force of resolution 820 (1993), NATO and WEU joined their efforts in a combined naval enforcement operation named "Sharp Guard." The mission was twofold: first, to check all vessels entering or leaving the Adriatic Sea (on average, 50 vessels a day), if necessary diverting them to Italian harbours for inspection of their cargo and documents, in order to prevent the supply of weapons and military equipment by sea to the countries of the former Yugoslavia; and second, preventing all commercial maritime traffic from entering the territorial sea of the Federal Republic of Yugoslavia. The use of force against vessels attempting to evade was authorized, in accordance with paragraph 28 of resolution 820 (1993), but the Committee is not aware of any instance when fire power was needed, although, from 16 July 1992 to 18 June 1996, NATO/WEU forces challenged 74,332 merchant vessels, inspected 5,975 at sea and diverted 1,416 to ports. Fourteen nations provided maritime and airborne assets to the joint operation, deploying almost 4,500 military personnel and 20 ships. Italy provided Coast Guard resources, port and inspection facilities, logistical and other support to the efforts to enforce mandatory measures. The Committee benefited from weekly situation reports by Italy on the operation, on behalf of the

Presidency of WEU, as well as from regular reports by the Executive Office of the General Secretary of NATO[.]

Notes

1. *The Efficacy of U.N. Security Council Sanctions*. What factors influence the efficacy of U.N. Security Council decisions? Although Security Council sanctions have sometimes been violated, the above excerpts indicate some of the ways in which they may be made effective. What steps could be taken, in addition to Security Council-authorized enforcement actions at sea, and regional and national legislative and judicial measures against foreign flag ships violating the sanctions? Flag states also penalize violations involving their own vessels. For example, Greece prosecuted the ship owners and captains of Greek ships that violated the U.N. sanctions against the Federal Republic, and Honduras cancelled the registration and licenses of violators. See Final Report of the Security Council Committee Established Pursuant to Resolution 724, UN Doc. S/1996/946 at 13 (1996).

The Security Council lifted various sanctions against the Federal Republic of Yugoslavia in Resolution 1022 (1995), UN Doc. S/RES/1022 (1995). That Resolution endorsed the results of the 1995 General Framework Agreement for Peace in Bosnia and Herzegovina with Annexes (the Dayton Accords).

2. *Other Security Council Sanctions Regimes*. The Security Council has also established other sanctions regimes involving, inter alia, maritime interdiction. For example, Iraq's invasion of Kuwait in August 1990 led to several strong Security Council resolutions, among them Resolutions 661 and 665. Resolution 661 of August 6, 1990, UN Doc. S/RES/661 (1990), imposed several sanctions, including the requirement that all states ban imports to Iraq and Kuwait, as well as exports from those states. On August 16, 1990, the United States announced that its forces would intercept and search ships in zones in the Persian Gulf, the Gulf of Oman, and the Red Sea, as part of a multinational effort to enforce Resolution 661. The intercept operation is described in U.S. Dept. Navy, Special Warning No. 80, Aug. 17, 1990, reprinted in Kuwait Crisis: Basic Documents 245 (E. Lauterpacht et al. eds., 1991). The Security Council passed Resolution 665 on August 25, 1990. UN Doc. S/RES/665 (1990). Resolution 665 called on states cooperating with Kuwait that had maritime forces in the Gulf to use necessary measures "to halt all inward and outward maritime shipping in order to inspect and verify their cargoes and destinations and to ensure strict implementation" of Resolution 661's mandatory sanctions. States understood Resolution 665 as an authorization to use naval force to stop the shipping to and from Iraq and Kuwait. Oscar Schachter, United Nations Law in the Gulf Conflict, 85 Am. J. Intl. L. 451, 454 (1991).

3. *Regional Organizations and Sanctions.* As indicated in the Security Council resolutions and the Final Report excerpted above, regional organizations often help enforce sanctions established by the U.N. Security Council. Chapter VIII of the U.N. Charter specifically envisions roles for "regional arrangements or agencies" in contributing to the maintenance of international peace and security, in cooperation with the United Nations. See also Position Paper of the Secretary-General on the Occasion of the Fiftieth Anniversary of the United Nations, A/50/60-S/1995/1, 3 January 1995, in An Agenda for Peace 1995 at 5 (UN Sales No. E.95.I.15, 2d ed. 1995). When may the North Atlantic Treaty Organization (NATO), which was established as a regional self-defense organization in the 1949 North Atlantic Treaty, legally interfere with maritime commerce? In 1999 NATO proposed, in response to the bombing of Kosovo by the Federal Republic of Yugoslavia, to interdict ships—including ships not flying the flags of NATO member states—that were suspected of carrying oil to the Federal Republic. The proposal was criticized as illegal because of a lack of Security Council authorization as required under Article 53 of the U.N. Charter.

F Hot Pursuit

THE M/V SAIGA (NO. 2) CASE

St. Vincent and the Grenadines v. Guinea (Admissibility and Merits), ITLOS Case No. 2 (1999), 3 ITLOS Rep. 10, 120 Intl. L. Rep. 143, 38 Intl. Leg. Materials 1323 (1999), available at http://www.itlos.org

[A summary of this case appears in Chapter 3, Section A. A Vincentian flag vessel, the *Saiga*, was stopped, seized, and detained by Guinea for offloading gas oil to fishing vessels in a Guinean "customs radius" in violation of Guinea's customs laws. Saint Vincent and the Grenadines claimed that Guinea's application of its rules in its full "customs radius" violated international law because those waters constituted part of Guinea's exclusive economic zone (EEZ), extending well beyond its contiguous zone, and application of customs rules in the EEZ was impermissible. The International Tribunal for the Law of the Sea agreed that application by Guinea of its customs rules in its EEZ beyond its contiguous zone was impermissible. (See Chapter 9 for consideration of the scope of permissible coastal state jurisdiction in the EEZ.) Saint Vincent and the Grenadines also argued that Guinea's pursuit of the *Saiga* violated Article 111 of the LOS Convention, which governs hot pursuit. The International Tribunal for the Law of the Sea (ITLOS)'s consideration of the hot pursuit issue follows.]

139. Saint Vincent and the Grenadines contends that, in arresting the *Saiga*, Guinea did not lawfully exercise the right of hot pursuit under article 111 of the Convention. It argues that since the *Saiga* did not violate the laws and regulations of Guinea applicable in accordance with the Convention, there was no legal basis for the arrest. Consequently, the authorities of Guinea did not have "good reason" to believe that the *Saiga* had committed an offence that justified hot pursuit in accordance with the Convention.

140. Saint Vincent and the Grenadines asserts that, even if the *Saiga* violated the laws and regulations of Guinea as claimed, its arrest on 28 October 1997 did not satisfy the other conditions for hot pursuit under article 111 of the Convention. It notes that the alleged pursuit was commenced while the ship was well outside the contiguous zone of Guinea. The *Saiga* was first detected (by radar) in the morning of 28 October 1997 when the ship was either outside the exclusive economic zone of Guinea or about to leave that zone. The arrest took place after the ship had crossed the southern border of the exclusive economic zone of Guinea.

141. Saint Vincent and the Grenadines further asserts that, wherever and whenever the pursuit was commenced, it was interrupted. It also contends that no visual and auditory signals were given to the ship prior to the commencement of the pursuit, as required by article 111 of the Convention.

142. Guinea denies that the pursuit was vitiated by any irregularity and maintains that the officers engaged in the pursuit complied with all the requirements set out in article 111 of the Convention. In some of its assertions, Guinea contends that the pursuit was commenced on 27 October 1997 soon after the authorities of Guinea had information that the *Saiga* had committed or was about to commit violations of the customs and contraband laws of Guinea and that the pursuit was continued throughout the period until the ship was spotted and arrested in the morning of 28 October 1997. In other assertions, Guinea contends that the pursuit commenced in the early morning of 28 October 1997 when the *Saiga* was still in the exclusive economic zone of Guinea. In its assertions, Guinea relies on article 111, paragraph 2, of the Convention.

143. Guinea states that at about 0400 hours on 28 October 1997 the large patrol boat P328 sent out radio messages to the *Saiga* ordering it to stop and that they were ignored. It also claims that the small patrol boat P35 gave auditory and visual signals to the *Saiga* when it came within sight and hearing of the ship. The Guinean officers who arrested the ship testified that the patrol boat sounded its siren and switched on its blue revolving light signals.

144. Guinea admits that the arrest took place outside the exclusive economic zone of Guinea. However, it points out that since the place of arrest was not in the territorial sea either of the ship's flag State or of another State, there was no breach of article 111 of the Convention....

146. The Tribunal notes that the conditions for the exercise of the right of hot pursuit under article 111 of the Convention are cumulative; each of them has to be satisfied for the pursuit to be legitimate under the Convention. In this case, the Tribunal finds that several of these conditions were not fulfilled.

147. With regard to the pursuit alleged to have commenced on 27 October 1997, the evidence before the Tribunal indicates that, at the time the Order for the Joint Mission of the Customs and Navy of Guinea was issued, the authorities of Guinea, on the basis of information available to them, could have had no more than a suspicion that a tanker had violated the laws of Guinea in the exclusive economic zone. The Tribunal also notes that, in the circumstances, no visual or auditory signals to stop could have been given to the *Saiga*. Furthermore, the alleged pursuit was interrupted. According to the evidence given by Guinea, the small patrol boat P35 that was sent out on 26 October 1997 on a northward course to search for the *Saiga* was recalled when information was received that the *Saiga* had changed course. This recall constituted a clear interruption of any pursuit, whatever legal basis might have existed for its commencement in the first place.

148. As far as the pursuit alleged to have commenced on 28 October 1998 is concerned, the evidence adduced by Guinea does not support its claim that the necessary auditory or visual signals to stop were given to the *Saiga* prior to the commencement of the alleged pursuit, as required by article 111, paragraph 4, of the Convention. Although Guinea claims that the small patrol boat (P35) sounded its siren and turned on its blue revolving light signals when it came within visual and hearing range of the *Saiga*, both the Master who was on the bridge at the time and Mr. Niasse who was on the deck, categorically denied that any such signals were given. In any case, any signals given at the time claimed by Guinea cannot be said to have been given at the commencement of the alleged pursuit.

149. The Tribunal has already concluded that no laws or regulations of Guinea applicable in accordance with the Convention were violated by the *Saiga*. It follows that there was no legal basis for the exercise of the right of hot pursuit by Guinea in this case.

150. For these reasons, the Tribunal finds that Guinea stopped and arrested the *Saiga* on 28 October 1997 in circumstances which did not justify the exercise of the right of hot pursuit in accordance with the Convention.

151. The Tribunal notes that Guinea, in its pleadings and submissions, suggests that the actions against the *Saiga* could, at least in part, be justified on the ground that the *Saiga* supplied gas oil to the fishing vessels in the contiguous zone of the Guinean island of Alcatraz. However, in the course of the oral proceedings, Guinea stated:

> [T]he bunkering operation of the ship in the Guinean contiguous zone is also of no relevance in this context, although it may be relevant to the application of the criminal law. The relevant area here is the customs radius. This is a functional zone established by Guinean customs law within the realm of the contiguous zone and a part of the Guinean exclusive economic zone. One can describe it as a limited customs protection zone based on the principles of customary international law which are included in the exclusive economic zone but which are not a part of the territory of Guinea.

152. The Tribunal has not based its consideration of the question of the legality of the pursuit of the *Saiga* on the suggestion of Guinea that a violation of its customs laws occurred in the contiguous zone. The Tribunal would, however, note that its conclusion on this question would have been the same if Guinea had based its action against the *Saiga* solely on the ground of an infringement of its customs laws in the contiguous zone. For, even in that case, the conditions for the exercise of the right of hot pursuit, as required under article 111 of the Convention, would not have been satisfied for the reasons given in paragraphs 147 and 148.

Notes

1. *Violations Permitting a Right of Hot Pursuit.* For what sorts of violations may a coastal state pursue a foreign flag vessel? See LOS Convention, Article 111(1)–(2). Was the reason for which Guinea pursued the *Saiga* legal, according to Article 111(1)–(2)?

Compare United States v. Taiyo Maru, 395 F. Supp. 413 (S.D. Maine 1975), involving the U.S. Coast Guard's hot pursuit and seizure on the high seas of a Japanese fishing vessel for violating U.S. fisheries laws applicable in a nine-mile U.S. fishery management zone that extended beyond the three-mile U.S. territorial sea. The Japanese vessel was located within this nine-mile zone when pursuit began. The U.S. district court upheld the legality of the pursuit, dismissing arguments that the vessel was unlawfully seized on the high seas. Assuming that the United States followed all the procedural requirements associated with the right of hot pursuit, did the Taiyo Maru court's decision comply with U.S. international law obligations? Article 23 of the 1958 High Seas Convention, to which the United States is a party, provides:

> The hot pursuit of a foreign ship may be undertaken when the competent authorities of the coastal State have good reason to believe that the ship has violated the laws and regulations of that State. Such pursuit

> must be commenced when the foreign ship or one of its boats is within the internal waters or the territorial sea or the contiguous zone of the pursuing State.... If the foreign ship is within a contiguous zone, as defined in article 24 of the Convention on the Territorial Sea and the Contiguous Zone, the pursuit may only be undertaken if there has been a violation of the rights for the protection of which the zone was established.

At the time the United States had a twelve-nautical-mile contiguous zone. However, Article 24 of the 1958 Territorial Sea Convention authorizes coastal state control in its contiguous zone only to "prevent infringement" of the coastal state's "customs, fiscal, immigration or sanitary regulations within its territory or territorial sea," or to "punish infringement" of those regulations "committed with its territory or territorial sea." Fishing, which a coastal state may regulate in its territorial sea, is not mentioned in Article 24 as a subject of coastal state authority in the contiguous zone. In Chapter 9 we discuss the evolution of coastal state fisheries zones and the EEZ.

2. *Territorial Limits on Hot Pursuit.* Read Article 111(3) of the LOS Convention. The right of hot pursuit ceases as soon as the ship being pursued enters the territorial sea of its own state or of a third state. However, the pursuing vessel may continue its pursuit if authorized by the state whose territorial waters have been entered. United States v. Conroy, 589 F.2d 1258 (5th Cir.), cert. denied, 444 U.S. 831 (1979). What policy reasons support this territorial limit on hot pursuit?

3. *The Signal to Stop.* Article 111(4) of the LOS Convention requires that "pursuit may only be commenced after a visual or auditory signal to stop has been given at a distance which enables it to be seen or heard by the foreign ship." Should this language be construed strictly, because pursuit derogates from the general rules favoring freedom of navigation and flag state control? Or should account be taken of changes in technology? Which approach did the ITLOS follow in the Saiga (No. 2) Case? In Regina v. The Mills, discussed in William C. Gilmore, Hot Pursuit: The Case of *R. v. Mills and Others*, 44 Intl. & Comp. L.Q. 949 (1995), the judge found that communication by UHF radio to the vessel being pursued satisfied the signal requirement for hot pursuit. The judge also considered relevant the fact that government helicopters were hovering close to the vessel when the radio signals were transmitted.

4. *Constructive Presence.* Many hot pursuit cases involve the pursuit of a vessel that itself never entered a relevant coastal zone. Pursuit is valid, according to Article 111(4) of the LOS Convention, if the pursuing state has satisfied itself "that the ship pursued or one of its boats or other craft working as a team and using the ship pursued as a mother ship" is within the relevant zone. How should the terms "working as a team" and "mother ship" be construed? In

Regina v. The Mills, noted in Note 3, the court found that the critical element was transhipment of contraband by prearrangement, even though the unloading vessel and the receiving vessel were engaged in a one-shot transfer rather than a continuing relationship. The transfer occurred far outside the British contiguous zone, and the trawler to which the contraband was unloaded (but not the unloading vessel) proceeded into the British territorial sea. The trawler, which had departed from Ireland rather than from Britain, was not a boat of the unloading vessel. The British court nonetheless upheld the hot pursuit of the unloading vessel.

5. *The Use of Force in Hot Pursuit.* What procedures should be used to stop a vessel that is being pursued? When should the use of force be allowed? In The I'm Alone (Canada v. United States) (1933), 3 Rep. Intl. Arb. Awards 1613, 1615 (2006), the commissioners approved, if there is a right of hot pursuit, a state's use of "necessary and reasonable force for the purpose of effecting the objects of boarding, searching, seizing and bringing into port the suspected vessel; and if sinking should occur incidentally, as a result of the exercise of necessary and reasonable force for such purpose, the pursuing vessel might be entirely blameless." In the M/V Saiga (No. 2) case, the ITLOS made the following statements:

> 155.... Although the Convention does not contain express provisions on the use of force in the arrest of ships, international law... requires that the use of force must be avoided as far as possible and, where force is unavoidable, it must not go beyond what is reasonable and necessary in the circumstances. Considerations of humanity must apply in the law of the sea, as they do in other areas of international law.
>
> 156. These principles have been followed over the years in law enforcement operations at sea. The normal practice used to stop a ship at sea is first to give an auditory or visual signal to stop, using internationally recognized signals. Where this does not succeed, a variety of actions may be taken, including the firing of shots across the bows of the ship. It is only after the appropriate actions fail that the pursuing vessel may, as a last resort, use force. Even then, appropriate warning must be issued to the ship and all efforts should be made to ensure that life is not endangered.

38 Intl. Leg. Materials at 1355. See also The Red Crusader, Denmark-United Kingdom, 35 Intl. L. Rep. 485 (1962).

CHAPTER 5

Baselines

The baseline is an essential notion in the law of the sea. As we noted in Chapter 1 and will examine more closely in the next several chapters, the law of the sea is divided into different maritime zones. See Figure I.A in Chapter 1. With respect to all of them the baseline serves as the point of departure in order to measure, at least partly or indirectly, the spatial extent of the zone in question. The breadth of the territorial sea, contiguous zone, and exclusive economic zone, as discussed in Chapters 8 and 9, is measured from the baseline. As far as the continental shelf (Chapter 10) is concerned, we must distinguish between cases where the continental margin, which comprises the submerged prolongation of the land mass and consists of the seabed and the subsoil of the shelf, the slope, and the rise, does not extend beyond 200 nautical miles and cases where it does. In the first situation, the baseline serves as the basis for determining the outer limits of the continental shelf. If, however, the continental margin does extend beyond 200 nautical miles, other factors—e.g., the foot of the slope or the 2,500 meter isobath—help determine the outer limits of the continental shelf, although the location of the baseline remains relevant. See Figures X.B, X.C, and X.D in Chapter 10. Finally, the baseline determines the location of the Area, albeit indirectly. The Area, discussed in Chapter 11, is defined as "the seabed and ocean floor and the subsoil thereof, beyond the limits of national jurisdiction." LOS Convention, Article 1(1)(1).

Section A of this chapter concerns the normal baseline. The general principle is that the low-water line along the coast marks the normal baseline, but this apparently simple concept gives rise to a number of rather intricate problems when applied in practice. Section B explores straight baselines in the international law of the sea. Once the International Court of Justice (ICJ) ruled in 1951 that straight baselines were not contrary to international law, this notion quickly found its reflection in treaty law as well as state practice. Some countries have interpreted the treaty provisions rather loosely, and the United States, occasionally joined by other countries, has protested such aggressive straight baseline claims. The ICJ revisited this issue in 2001. Finally, Section C examines the issue of archipelagic baselines, a new concept codified by the LOS Convention.

 | DOI 10.1163/9789004203563_006

A Normal Baseline

The following case concerns Article 3 of the 1958 Territorial Sea Convention, which was carried over to become Article 5 of the 1982 Law of the Sea Convention (LOS Convention). Article 3 of the 1958 Convention, to which the United States is a party, reads: "Except where otherwise provided in these articles, the normal baseline for measuring the breadth of the territorial sea is the low-water line along the coast as marked on large-scale charts officially recognized by the coastal State."

UNITED STATES v. CALIFORNIA
381 U.S. 139 (1965)

[In 1945 the United States sued California to determine ownership and mineral rights in the seabed under the three-mile territorial sea off the coast of California. In that case the Supreme Court held that all seabed rights seaward of the ordinary low-water mark and outside of inland waters belonged to the federal government, not to California. United States v. California, 332 U.S. 19 (1947). See also United States v. Louisiana, 339 U.S. 699 (1950); United States v. Texas, 339 U.S. 707 (1950).

Pursuant to the California decision a Special Master was appointed to determine in detail the application of the terms "ordinary low-water mark" and "inland waters" in certain areas of the coast. He filed his report, largely favoring the United States, in 1952. 344 U.S. 872 (1952). However, on May 23, 1953, the U.S. Congress passed the Submerged Lands Act, 43 U.S.C. §§ 1301–1315, which reversed the California decision and awarded submerged lands three nautical miles seaward of the "limit of inland waters" to the coastal state. The Act did not define "inland waters."

The Submerged Lands Act rendered the Special Master's Report moot because the steep slope of the California coastal seabed made drilling more than a mile or two offshore impossible with the technology of the time. By 1963, however, new techniques had made drilling in deeper waters possible. Exceptions to the Special Master's Report were renewed, and the case came again to the Supreme Court, essentially to determine the principles according to which inland waters should be delimited.

In the 1965 decision excerpted here, the Court finds that Congress had intentionally left the definition of inland waters to the Court, and further found that the 1958 Territorial Sea Convention, which entered into force for the United States on September 10, 1964, was controlling. In the course of approving the Special Master's Report with minor modifications, the Court made various observations about how the principles of the 1958 Convention applied. One of the Court's observations is reproduced here.]

Along the California coast there are two low tides each day, one of which is generally lower than the other. The assertion of the United States, with which the Special Master agreed, is that the line of ordinary low water is obtained by taking the average of all the low tides. California would average only the lower low tides. We hold that California's position represents the better view of the matter. The Submerged Lands Act defines coastline in terms of the "line of ordinary low water." The [Territorial Sea] Convention (Art. 3) uses "the low-water line along the coast as marked on large-scale charts officially recognized by the coastal State" (i.e., the United States). We interpret the two lines thus indicated to conform, and on the official United States coastal charts of the Pacific Coast prepared by the United States Coast and Geodetic Survey, it is the lower low water line which is marked.

Notes

1. *Sources of International Law.* Why is it useful to mention a decision of the highest judicial organ of a particular country in a book on international law of the sea? Are decisions of national judicial organs subsumed under Article 38(1)(d) of the ICJ Statute (reproduced in Chapter 1), which is generally relied on as a list of the different sources of international law? May national court decisions be taken into consideration under any other subsection of Article 38(1)? Did the U.S. Supreme Court both rely on international law and help to develop international law in United States v. California? Note that Article 59 of the ICJ Statute provides that a "decision of the Court has no binding force except between the parties and in respect of that particular case."

2. *The Roles of Baselines.* As noted in the introductory paragraph to this chapter, baselines mark the starting point of various international zones extending seaward. Why else are baselines legally significant? Why was the location of baselines important in the 1965 United States v. California decision?

3. *The Low-water Line.* The preference for the low-water line over the high-water line as the baseline in the international law of the sea was apparently an easy choice to make because, as succinctly stated by the ICJ, "[t]his criterion is the most favorable to the coastal State and clearly shows the character of territorial waters as appurtenant to the land territory." Fisheries Case (United Kingdom v. Norway), 1951 I.C.J. 116, 128. Why might a country nevertheless prefer the high-water line? See for instance the reservation made by Iran when it signed the 1958 Continental Shelf Convention, to which it is still not a party. The reservation reads in part: "With respect to the phrase 'and unless another

boundary line is justified by special circumstances' included in paragraphs 1 and 2 of this article, the Iranian Government accepts this phrase on the understanding that one method of determining the boundary line in special circumstances would be that of measurement from the high water mark." Available at http://treaties.un.org/pages/ViewDetails.aspx?src=TREATY&mtdsg_no=XXI-4&chapter=21&lang=en. Consider the bathymetry of the Persian Gulf in this respect.

When proposing the low-water line as the normal baseline in its draft articles on the territorial sea, the International Law Commission (ILC) admitted that this notion "may have different meanings." Report of the International Law Commission, UNGAOR, 11th Sess., Supp. No. 9, UN Doc. A/3159 (1956), reprinted in 1956-2 Y.B. Intl. L. Commn. 253, 267. The ILC found support for this assertion in the work of the 1930 Hague Codification Conference, where the responses of coastal states to a questionnaire about the exact method employed to determine the low-water line indicated that different meanings could be given to the concept. Bases of Discussion Drawn up for the Conference by the Preparatory Committee, II Territorial Waters, League of Nations Doc. C.74.M.39.1929.V. (1929), reprinted in Official Documents: Conference for the Codification of International Law, 24 Am. J. Intl. L. Supp. 30 (1930). O'Connell, for instance, distinguished four different methods: the lowest astronomical tide, the mean low-water springs (the lowest level to which spring tides retreat on average over a period of time), the mean lower low-water, and the mean higher low-water. D.P. O'Connell, 1 The International Law of the Sea 173–74 (1982). In view of this divergence in state practice, the Hague Codification Conference agreed that, instead of trying to impose a single vertical datum, it was preferable to allow states to continue to use the methods already relied on in their charts. The ILC confirmed this approach by considering "that it is permissible to adopt as the base line the low-water mark as indicated on large-scale charts officially recognized by the coastal State," thus leaving some discretion to the coastal states. Report of the International Law Commission, supra. This reference to "large-scale charts officially recognized by the coastal State" was retained in the 1958 Territorial Sea Convention (Article 3) as well as in the LOS Convention (Article 5). Did the U.S. Supreme Court in 1965 agree that the official U.S. chart determined the kind of low-water line relied on by the United States? Which of the different methods distinguished by O'Connell applied in this case? In Europe we see a trend toward a common standard, namely the lowest astronomical tide.

4. *The Low-water Line as Marked on Large-scale Charts Officially Recognized by the Coastal State.* As seen in Note 3, the chart determines the kind of low-water line on which the coastal state relies. But today, when instruments that

accurately measure tidal data are no longer solely in the hands of the coastal state, another issue arises in applying Article 5 of the LOS Convention. What happens if a discrepancy occurs between the low-water line drawn on the chart and the one actually "on the ground," even if the low-water line is measured using the same standard as the one indicated on the chart? A Dutch court faced this issue in a case involving fishermen who were accused of violating fishing regulations applicable in the Dutch territorial sea. After they heard that a low-tide elevation would no longer be shown on an upcoming revision of the official chart, the fishermen calculated their position without taking into account that particular feature. They argued that on December 15, 2004 they were fishing outside the twelve-nautical-mile limit because the low-tide elevation in question was now completely submerged and could no longer be used as a territorial sea base point. The court held, however, that until December 22, 2004—the day on which the new chart became available—the defendants had to rely on the official chart in existence at that time, i.e., a chart dated January 3, 2002, because "in law only the officially recognized chart is determinative." Rechtbank Amsterdam, Parketnummers 13/501817-05 and 13/500730-05 (A) (June 29, 2007), available at http://www.rechtspraak.nl/Pages/default.aspx (translation by one of the authors).

Would it make any difference if the dispute were not between a state and a natural person subjected to its laws, but rather between one state disputing the low-water mark indicated on the charts of another state in a maritime delimitation case? The issue arose in a recent delimitation case in which Guyana contested parts of the baseline indicated on an official chart of Suriname, revised in 2005 after the proceedings in this arbitration had commenced. The tribunal rejected Guyana's claim, but only after considering the evidence advanced by the parties to the dispute. In re Guyana/Suriname (Annex VII Arb., 2007), 47 Intl. Leg. Materials 166, 222 (2008).

To which of these two types of cases does United States v. California best compare? For additional background on the normal baseline, see Comm. on Baselines under the International Law of the Sea, Report, in Intl. L. Assn., Report of the Seventy-Fifth Conference (Sofia) 385 (2012).

B Straight Baselines

International law permits variation from normal baselines in specific situations. This section investigates the system of straight baselines, which the ICJ recognized in the 1951 Anglo-Norwegian Fisheries case and which is now codified in Article 7 of the LOS Convention. In this section we excerpt not only the

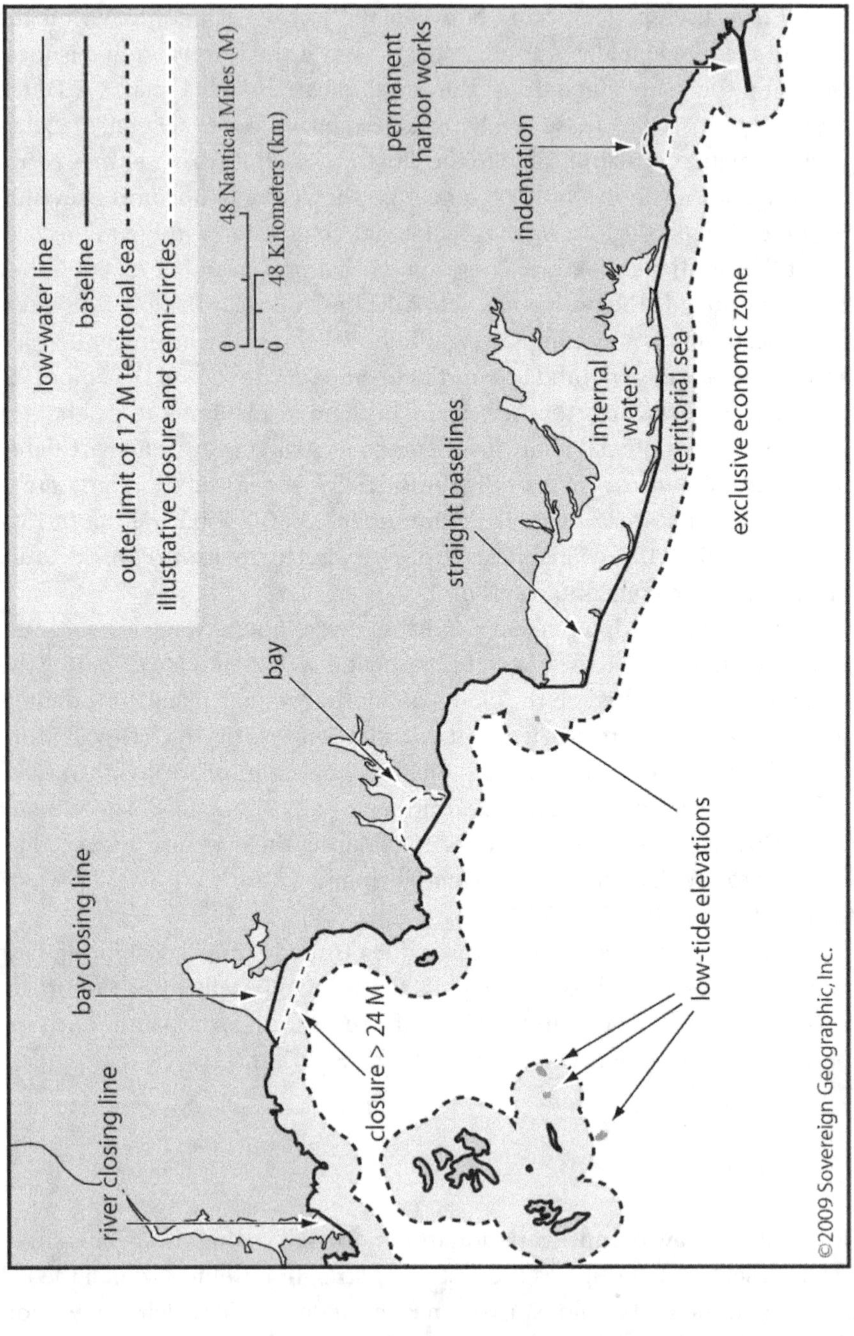

FIGURE V.A *Baselines*

Anglo-Norwegian Fisheries case, but a U.S. Supreme Court case, a diplomatic protest of a straight baseline claim, and a 2001 ICJ case considering the possible use of straight baselines in a maritime delimitation dispute.

Article 7 does not capture every situation in which straight baselines may be used. For example, they may also be used to close off the mouths of bays (LOS Convention, Article 10; 1958 Territorial Sea Convention, Article 7) or rivers (LOS Convention, Article 9; 1958 Territorial Sea Convention, Article 13). For a visualization of such closures by straight lines see Figure V.A, which also highlights other features influencing the baseline, such as low-tide elevations (LOS Convention, Article 13; 1958 Territorial Sea Convention, Article 11) and permanent harbor works (LOS Convention, Article 11; 1958 Territorial Sea Convention, Article 8). Another occurrence of straight baselines concerns the case of archipelagic states, which we specifically consider in Section C.

ANGLO-NORWEGIAN FISHERIES CASE
United Kingdom v. Norway, 1951 I.C.J. 116

[On September 28, 1949, the United Kingdom filed an application instituting proceedings against Norway before the ICJ. The subject of the proceedings was the validity under international law of the lines of delimitation of the Norwegian fisheries zone laid down by a Norwegian decree in 1935. These lines are shown in Figure V.B below. The application referred to the declarations by which the United Kingdom and Norway had accepted the compulsory jurisdiction of the ICJ in accordance with Article 36(2) of the Statute. Norway did not contest the jurisdiction of the ICJ.]

The historical facts laid before the Court establish that as the result of complaints from the King of Denmark and of Norway, at the beginning of the seventeenth century, British fishermen refrained from fishing in Norwegian coastal waters for a long period, from 1616–1618 until 1906.

In 1906 a few British fishing vessels appeared off the coasts of Eastern Finnmark. From 1908 onwards they returned in greater numbers. These were trawlers equipped with improved and powerful gear. The local population became perturbed, and measures were taken by the Norwegian Government with a view to specifying the limits within which fishing was prohibited to foreigners.

The first incident occurred in 1911 when a British trawler was seized and condemned for having violated these measures. Negotiations ensued between the two Governments. These were interrupted by the war in 1914. From 1922 onwards incidents recurred. Further conversations were initiated in 1924. In 1932, British trawlers, extending the range of their activities, appeared in the sectors off the Norwegian coast west of the North Cape, and the number of warnings and arrests increased. On July 27th, 1933, the United Kingdom Government sent a memorandum to the Norwegian Government complaining that in delimiting the territorial sea the Norwegian authorities had made use of unjustifiable base-lines. On July 12th, 1935, a Norwegian Royal Decree was enacted delimiting the Norwegian fisheries zone north of 66° 28.8' North latitude.

The United Kingdom made urgent representations in Oslo in the course of which the question of referring the dispute to the Permanent Court of International Justice was raised. Pending the result of the negotiations, the Norwegian Government made it known that Norwegian fishery patrol vessels would deal leniently with foreign vessels fishing a certain distance within the fishing limits. In 1948, since no agreement had been reached, the Norwegian Government abandoned its lenient enforcement of the 1935 Decree; incidents then became more and more frequent. A considerable number of British trawlers were arrested and condemned. It was then that the United Kingdom Government instituted the present proceedings.

The Norwegian Royal Decree of July 12th, 1935, concerning the delimitation of the Norwegian fisheries zone sets out in the preamble the considerations on which its provisions are based. In this connection it refers to "well-established national titles of right," "the geographical conditions prevailing on the Norwegian coasts," "the safeguard of the vital interests of the inhabitants of the northern-most parts of the country"; it further relies on the Royal Decrees of February 22nd, 1812, October 16th, 1869, January 5th, 1881, and September 9th, 1889.

The Decree provides that "lines of delimitation towards the high sea of the Norwegian fisheries zone as regards that part of Norway which is situated northward of 66° 28.8' North latitude… shall run parallel with straight base-lines drawn between fixed points on the mainland, on islands or rocks, starting from the final point of the boundary line of the Realm in the easternmost part of the Varangerfjord and going as far as Traena in the County of Nordland." An appended schedule indicates the fixed points between which the base-lines are drawn.

The subject of the dispute is clearly indicated under point 8 of the Application instituting proceedings: "The subject of th dispute is the validity or otherwise under international law of the lines of delimitation of the Norwegian fisheries zone laid down by the Royal Decree of 1935 for that part of Norway which is situated northward of 66° 28.8' North latitude." And further on: "… the question at issue between the two Governments is whether the lines prescribed by the Royal Decree of 1935 as the base-lines for the delimitation of the fisheries zone have or have not been drawn in accordance with the applicable rules of international law."

Although the Decree of July 12th, 1935, refers to the Norwegian fisheries zone and does not specifically mention the territorial sea, there can be no doubt that the zone delimited by this Decree is none other than the sea area which Norway considers to be her territorial sea. That is how the Parties argued the question and that is the way in which they submitted it to the Court for decision....

The coastal zone concerned in the dispute is of considerable length. It lies north of latitude 66° 28.8' N., that is to say, north of the Arctic Circle, and it includes the coast of the mainland of Norway and all the islands, islets, rocks and reefs, known by the name of the "skjærgaard" (literally, rock rampart), together with all Norwegian internal and territorial waters. The coast of the mainland, which, without taking any account of fjords, bays and minor indentations, is over 1,500 kilometres in length, is of a very distinctive configuration. Very broken along its whole length, it constantly opens out into indentations often penetrating for great distances inland: the Porsangerfjord, for instance, penetrates 75 sea miles inland. To the west, the land configuration stretches out into the sea: the large and small islands, mountainous in character, the islets, rocks and reefs, some always above water, others emerging only at low tide, are in truth but an extension of the Norwegian mainland. The number of insular formations, large and small, which make up the "skjærgaard," is estimated by the Norwegian Government to be one hundred and twenty thousand. From the southern extremity of the disputed area to the North Cape, the "skjærgaard" lies along the whole of the coast of the mainland; east of the North Cape, the "skjærgaard" ends, but the coast line continues to be broken by large and deeply indented fjords.

Within the "skjærgaard," almost every island has its large and its small bays; countless arms of the sea, straits, channels and mere waterways serve as a means of communication for the local population which inhabits the islands as it does the mainland. The coast of the mainland does not constitute, as it does in practically all other countries, a clear dividing line between land and sea. What matters, what really constitutes the Norwegian coast line, is the outer line of the "skjærgaard."

The whole of this region is mountainous. The North Cape, a sheer rock little more than 300 metres high, can be seen from a considerable distance; there are other summits rising to over a thousand metres, so that the Norwegian coast, mainland and "skjærgaard," is visible from far off.

Along the coast are situated comparatively shallow banks, veritable underwater terraces which constitute fishing grounds where fish are particularly abundant; these grounds were known to Norwegian fishermen and exploited by them from time immemorial. Since these banks lay within the range of vision, the most desirable fishing grounds were always located and identified by means of the method of alignments ("*meds*"), at points where two lines drawn between points selected on the coast or on islands intersected.

In these barren regions the inhabitants of the coastal zone derive their livelihood essentially from fishing.

Such are the realities which must be borne in mind in appraising the validity of the United Kingdom contention that the limits of the Norwegian fisheries zone laid down in the 1935 Decree are contrary to international law.

The Parties being in agreement on the figure of 4 miles for the breadth of the territorial sea, the problem which arises is from what base-line this breadth is to be reckoned. The Conclusions of the United Kingdom are explicit on this point: the base-line must be [the] low-water mark on permanently dry land which is a part of Norwegian territory, or the proper closing line of Norwegian internal waters.

The Court has no difficulty in finding that, for the purpose of measuring the breadth of the territorial sea, it is the low-water mark as opposed to the high-water mark, or the mean between the two tides, which has generally been adopted in the practice of States. This criterion is the most favourable to the coastal State and clearly shows the character of territorial waters as appurtenant to the land territory. The Court notes that the Parties agree as to this criterion, but that they differ as to its application....

The Court finds itself obliged to decide whether the relevant low-water mark is that of the mainland or of the "skjærgaard." Since the mainland is bordered in its western sector by the "skjærgaard," which constitutes a whole with the mainland, it is the outer line of the "skjærgaard" which must be taken into account in delimiting the belt of Norwegian territorial waters. This solution is dictated by geographic realities.

Three methods have been contemplated to effect the application of the low-water mark rule. The simplest would appear to be the method of the *tracé parallèle*, which consists of drawing the outer limit of the belt of territorial waters by following the coast in all its sinuosities. This method may be applied without difficulty to an ordinary coast, which is not too broken. Where a coast is deeply indented and cut into, as is that of Eastern Finnmark, or where it is bordered by an archipelago such as the "skjærgaard" along the western sector of the coast here in question, the base-line becomes independent of the low-water mark, and can only be determined by means of a geometrical construction. In such circumstances the line of the low-water mark can no longer be put forward as a rule requiring the coastline to be followed in all its sinuosities.

Nor can one characterize as exceptions to the rule the very many derogations which would be necessitated by such a rugged coast; the rule would disappear under the exceptions. Such a coast, viewed as a whole, calls for the application of a different method; that is, the method of base-lines which, within reasonable limits, may depart from the physical line of the coast.

It is true that the experts of the Second Sub-Committee of the Second Committee of the 1930 Conference for the codification of international law formulated the low-water mark rule somewhat strictly ("following all the sinuosities of the coast"). But they were at the same time obliged to admit many exceptions relating to bays, islands near the coast, groups of islands. In the present case this method of the *tracé parallèle,* which was invoked against Norway in the Memorial, was abandoned in the written Reply, and later in the oral argument of the Agent of the United Kingdom Government. Consequently, it is no longer relevant to the case. "On the other hand," it is said in the Reply, ["]the *courbe tangente*—or, in English, 'envelopes of arcs of circles'—method is the method which the United Kingdom considers to be the correct one."

The arcs of circles method, which is constantly used for determining the position of a point or object at sea, is a new technique in so far as it is a method for delimiting the territorial sea. This technique was proposed by the United States delegation at the 1930 Conference for the codification of international law. Its purpose is to secure the application of the principle that the belt of territorial waters must follow the line of the coast. It is not obligatory by law, as was admitted by Counsel for the United Kingdom Government in his oral reply....

The principle that the belt of territorial waters must follow the general direction of the coast makes it possible to fix certain criteria valid for any delimitation of the territorial sea; these criteria will be elucidated later. The Court will confine itself at this stage to noting that, in order to apply this principle, several States have deemed it necessary to follow the straight base-lines method and that they have not encountered objections of principle by other States. This method consists of selecting appropriate points on the low-water mark and drawing straight lines between them. This has been done, not only in the case of well-defined bays, but also in cases of minor curvatures of the coast line where it was solely a question of giving a simpler form to the belt of territorial waters.

It has been contended, on behalf of the United Kingdom, that Norway may draw straight lines only across bays. The Court is unable to share this view. If the belt of territorial waters must follow the outer line of the "skjærgaard," and if the method of straight baselines must be admitted in certain cases, there is no valid reason to draw them only across bays, as in Eastern Finnmark, and not also to draw them between islands, islets and rocks, across the sea areas separating them, even when such areas do not fall within the conception of a bay. It is sufficient that they should be situated between the island formations of the "skjærgaard," *inter fauces terrarum*. . . .

In the opinion of the United Kingdom Government, Norway is entitled, on historic grounds, to claim as internal waters all fjords and sunds which have the character of a bay. She is also entitled on historic grounds to claim as Norwegian territorial waters all the waters of the fjords and sunds which have the character of legal straits . . ., and, either as internal or as territorial waters, the areas of water lying between the island fringe and the mainland. . . .

By "historic waters" are usually meant waters which are treated as internal waters but which would not have that character were it not for the existence of an historic title. The United Kingdom Government refers to the notion of historic titles both in respect of territorial waters and internal waters, considering such titles, in both cases, as derogations from general international law. In its opinion Norway can justify the claim that these waters are territorial or internal on the ground that she has exercised the necessary jurisdiction over them for a long period without opposition from other States, a kind of *possessio longi temporis*, with the result that her jurisdiction over these waters must now be recognized although it constitutes a derogation from the rules in force. Norwegian sovereignty over these waters would constitute an exception, historic titles justifying situations which would otherwise be in conflict with international law.

[T]he United Kingdom Government concedes that Norway is entitled to claim as internal waters all the waters of fjords and sunds which fall within the conception of a bay as defined in international law whether the closing line of the indentation is more or less than ten sea miles long. But the United Kingdom Government concedes this only on the basis of historic title; it must therefore be taken that that Government has not abandoned its contention that the ten-mile rule is to be regarded as a rule of international law.

In these circumstances the Court deems it necessary to point out that although the ten-mile rule has been adopted by certain States both in their national law and in their treaties and conventions, and although certain arbitral decisions have applied it as between these States, other States have adopted a different limit. Consequently, the ten-mile rule has not acquired the authority of a general rule of international law.

In any event the ten-mile rule would appear to be inapplicable as against Norway inasmuch as she has always opposed any attempt to apply it to the Norwegian coast.

The Court now comes to the question of the length of the base-lines drawn across the waters lying between the various formations of the "skjærgaard." Basing itself on the analogy with the alleged general rule of ten miles relating to bays, the United Kingdom Government still maintains on this point that the length of straight lines must not exceed ten miles.

In this connection, the practice of States does not justify the formulation of any general rule of law. The attempts that have been made to subject groups of islands or coastal archipelagoes to conditions analogous to the limitations concerning bays (distance between the islands not exceeding twice the breadth of the territorial waters, or ten or twelve sea miles), have not got beyond the stage of proposals.

Furthermore, apart from any question of limiting the lines to ten miles, it may be that several lines can be envisaged. In such cases the coastal State would seem to be in the best position to appraise the local conditions dictating the selection.

Consequently, the Court is unable to share the view of the United Kingdom Government, that "Norway, in the matter of baselines, now claims recognition of an exceptional system." As will be shown later, all that the Court can see therein is the application of general international law to a specific case.

[The Court considers and rejects the British argument that waters shoreward of the skjærgaard that are used as a navigational route are territorial waters rather than internal waters. The British argument that only waters "falling within the conception of a bay" can be considered internal waters is also rejected.]

It does not at all follow that, in the absence of rules having the technically precise character alleged by the United Kingdom Government, the delimitation undertaken by the Norwegian Government in 1935 is not subject to certain principles which make it possible to judge as to its validity under international law. The delimitation of sea areas has always an international aspect; it cannot be dependent merely upon the will of the coastal State as expressed in its municipal law. Although it is true that the act of delimitation is necessarily a unilateral act, because only the coastal State is competent to undertake it, the validity of the delimitation with regard to other States depends upon international law.

In this connection, certain basic considerations inherent in the nature of the territorial sea, bring to light certain criteria which, though not entirely precise, can provide courts with an adequate basis for their decisions, which can be adapted to the diverse facts in question.

Among these considerations, some reference must be made to the close dependence of the territorial sea upon the land domain. It is the land which confers upon the coastal State a right to the waters off its coasts. It follows that while such a State must be allowed the latitude necessary in order to be able to adapt its delimitation to practical needs and local requirements, the drawing of base-lines must not depart to any appreciable extent from the general direction of the coast.

Another fundamental consideration, of particular importance in this case, is the more or less close relationship existing between certain sea areas and the land formations which divide or surround them. The real question raised in the choice of base-lines is in effect whether certain sea areas lying within these lines are sufficiently closely linked to the land domain to be subject to the regime of internal waters. This idea, which is at the basis of the determination of the rules relating to bays, should be liberally applied in the case of a coast, the geographical configuration of which is as unusual as that of Norway.

Finally, there is one consideration not to be overlooked, the scope of which extends beyond purely geographical factors: that of certain economic interest peculiar to a region, the reality and importance of which are clearly evidenced by a long usage.

Norway puts forward the 1935 Decree as the application of a traditional system of delimitation, a system which she claims to be in complete conformity with international law. The Norwegian Government has referred in this connection to an historic title, the meaning of which was made clear by Counsel for Norway at the sitting on October 12th, 1951: "The Norwegian Government does not rely upon history to justify exceptional rights, to claim areas of sea which the general law would deny; it invokes history, together with other factors, to justify the way in which it applies the general law." This conception of an historic title is in consonance with the Norwegian Government's understanding of the general rules of international law. In its view, these rules of international law take into account the diversity of facts and, therefore, concede that the drawing of base-lines must be adapted to the special conditions obtaining in different regions. In its view, the system of delimitation applied in 1935, a system characterized by the use of straight lines, does not therefore infringe the general law; it is an adaptation rendered necessary by local conditions.

The Court must ascertain precisely what this alleged system of delimitation consists of, what is its effect in law as against the United Kingdom, and whether it was applied by the 1935 Decree in a manner which conformed to international law.

It is common ground between the Parties that on the question of the existence of a Norwegian system, the Royal Decree of February 22nd, 1812, is of cardinal importance. This Decree is in the following terms: "We wish to lay down as a rule that, in all cases when there is a question of determining the limit of our territorial sovereignty at sea, that limit shall be reckoned at the distance of one ordinary sea league from the island or islet farthest from the mainland, not covered by the sea; of which all proper authorities shall be informed by rescript."

This text does not clearly indicate how the base-lines between the islands or islets farthest from the mainland were to be drawn. In particular, it does not say in express terms that the lines must take the form of straight lines drawn between these points. But it may be noted that it was in this way that the 1812 Decree was invariably construed in Norway in the course of the 19th and 20th centuries.

[The Court reviews how Norway construed the 1812 Decree in government decrees, decisions, and reports dated 1869, 1889, 1912, 1929, and 1934.]

It should, however, be pointed out that whereas the 1812 Decree designated as base-points "the island or islet farthest from the mainland not covered by the sea," Norwegian governmental practice subsequently interpreted this provision as meaning that the limit was to be reckoned from the outermost island and islets "not continuously covered by the sea."

The 1812 Decree, although quite general in its terms, had as its immediate object the fixing of the limit applicable for the purposes of maritime neutrality. However, as soon as the Norwegian Government found itself impelled by circumstances to delimit its fisheries zone, it regarded that Decree as laying down principles to be applied for purposes other than neutrality....

The 1869 Statement of Reasons brings out all the elements which go to make up what the Norwegian Government describes as its traditional system of delimitation: base-points provided by the islands or islets farthest from the mainland, the use of straight lines joining up these points, the lack of any maximum length for such lines. The [1934] judgment of the Norwegian Supreme Court in the *St. Just* case upheld this interpretation and added that the 1812 Decree had never been understood or applied "in such a way as to make the boundary follow the sinuosities of the coast or to cause its position to be determined by means of circles drawn round the points of the Skjaergaard or of the mainland furthest out to sea—a method which it would be very difficult to adopt or to enforce in practice, having regard to the special configuration of this coast." Finally, it is established that, according to the Norwegian system, the baselines must follow the general direction of the coast, which is in conformity with international law.

Equally significant in this connection is the correspondence which passed between Norway and France between 1869–1870. On December 21st, 1869, only two months after the promulgation of the Decree of October 16th relating to the delimitation of Sunnmöre, the French Government asked the Norwegian

Government for an explanation of this enactment. It did so basing itself upon "the principles of international law." In a second Note dated December 30th of the same year, it pointed out that the distance between the base-points was greater than 10 sea miles, and that the line joining up these points should have been a broken line following the configuration of the coast. In a Note of February 8th, 1870, the Ministry for Foreign Affairs, also dealing with the question from the point of view of international law, replied as follows:

> By the same Note of December 30th, Your Excellency drew my attention to the fixing to the fishery limit in the Sunnmöre Archipelago by a straight line instead of a broken line. According to the view held by our Government, as the distance between the islets of Svinöy and Storholmen is more than 10 sea miles, the fishery limit between these two points should have been a broken line following the configuration of the coast line and nearer to it than the present limit. In spite of the adoption in some treaties of the quite arbitrary distance of 10 sea miles, this distance would not appear to me to have acquired the force of an international law. Still less would it appear to have any foundation in reality: one bay, by reason of the varying formations of the coast and sea-bed, may have an entirely different character from that of another bay of the same width. It seems to me rather that local conditions and considerations of what is practicable and equitable should be decisive in specific cases. The configuration of our coasts in no way resembles that of the coasts of other European countries, and that fact alone makes the adoption of any absolute rule of universal application impossible in this case.
>
> I venture to claim that all these reasons militate in favour of the line laid down by the Decree of October 16th. A broken line, conforming closely to the indentations of the coast line between Svinöy and Storholmen, would have resulted in a boundary so involved and so indistinct that it would have been impossible to exercise any supervision over it....

Language of this kind can only be construed as the considered expression of a legal conception regarded by the Norwegian Government as compatible with international law. And indeed, the French Government did not pursue the matter. In a Note of July 27th, 1870, it is said that, while maintaining its standpoint with regard to principle, it was prepared to accept the delimitation laid down by the Decree of October 16th, 1869, as resting upon "a practical study of the configuration of the coast line and of the conditions of the inhabitants."...

In the light of these considerations, and in the absence of convincing evidence to the contrary, the Court is bound to hold that the Norwegian authorities applied their system of delimitation consistently and uninterruptedly from 1869 until the time when the dispute arose.

From the standpoint of international law, it is now necessary to consider whether the application of the Norwegian system encountered any opposition from foreign States.

Norway has been in a position to argue without any contradiction that neither the promulgation of her delimitation Decrees in 1869 and in 1889, nor their application, gave rise to any opposition on the part of foreign States. Since, moreover, these Decrees constitute, as has been shown above, the application of a well-defined and uniform system, it is indeed this system itself which would reap the benefit of general toleration, the basis of an historical consolidation which would make it enforceable as against all States.

The general toleration of foreign States with regard to the Norwegian practice is an unchallenged fact. For a period of more than sixty years the United Kingdom Government itself in no way contested it....

The United Kingdom Government has argued that the Norwegian system of delimitation was not known to it and that the system therefore lacked the notoriety essential to provide the basis of an historic title enforceable against it. The Court is unable to accept this view. As a coastal State on the North Sea, greatly interested in the fisheries in this area, as a maritime Power traditionally concerned with the law of the sea and concerned particularly to defend the freedom of the seas, the United Kingdom could not have been ignorant of the Decree of 1869 which had at once provoked a request for explanations by the French Government. Nor, knowing of it, could it have been under any misapprehension as to the significance of its terms, which clearly described it as constituting the application of a system. The same observation applies *a fortiori* to the Decree of 1889 relating to the delimitation of Romsdal and Nordmöre which must have appeared to the United Kingdom as a reiterated manifestation of the Norwegian practice.

Norway's attitude with regard to the North Sea Fisheries (Police) Convention of 1882 is a further fact which must at once have attracted the attention of Great Britain. There is scarcely any fisheries convention of greater importance to the coastal States of the North Sea or of greater interest to Great Britain. Norway's refusal to adhere to this Convention clearly raised the question of the delimitation of her maritime domain, especially with regard to bays, the question of their delimitation by means of straight lines of which Norway challenged the maximum length adopted in the Convention. Having regard to the fact that a few years before, the delimitation of Sunnmöre by the 1869 Decree had been presented as an application of the Norwegian system, one cannot avoid the conclusion that, from that time on, all the elements of the problem of Norwegian coastal waters had been clearly stated. The steps subsequently taken by Great Britain to secure Norway's adherence to the Convention clearly show that she was aware of and interested in the question.

The Court notes that in respect of a situation which could only be strengthened with the passage of time, the United Kingdom Government refrained from formulating reservations.

The notoriety of the facts, the general toleration of the international community, Great Britain's position in the North Sea, her own interest in the question, and her prolonged abstention would in any case warrant Norway's enforcement of her system against the United Kingdom.

The Court is thus led to conclude that the method of straight lines, established in the Norwegian system, was imposed by the peculiar geography of the Norwegian coast; that even before the dispute arose, this method had been consolidated by a constant and sufficiently long practice, in the face of which the attitude of governments bears witness to the fact that they did not consider it to be contrary to international law.

The question now arises whether the Decree of July 12th, 1935, which in its preamble is expressed to be an application of this method, conforms to it in its drawing of the base-lines, or whether, at certain points, it departs from this method to any considerable extent....

In the absence of convincing evidence to the contrary, the Court cannot readily find that the lines adopted in these circumstances by the 1935 Decree are not in accordance with the traditional Norwegian system....

Finally, it has been contended by the United Kingdom Government that certain, at least, of the base-lines adopted by the Decree are, irrespective of whether or not they conform to the Norwegian system, contrary to the principles stated above by the Court as governing any delimitation of the territorial sea. The Court will consider whether, from the point of view of these principles, certain of the base-lines which have been criticized in some detail really are without justification.

The Norwegian Government admits that the base-lines must be drawn in such a way as to respect the general direction of the coast and that they must be drawn in a reasonable manner. The United Kingdom Government contends that certain lines do not follow the general direction of the coast, or do not follow it sufficiently closely, or that they do not respect the natural connection existing between certain sea areas and the land formations separating or surrounding them. For these reasons, it is alleged that the line drawn is contrary to the principles which govern the delimitation of the maritime domain....

The United Kingdom Government has directed its criticism more particularly against two sectors, the delimitation of which they represented as extreme cases of deviation from the general direction of the coast: the sector of Sværholthavet (between base-points 11 and 12) and that of Lopphavet (between basepoints 20 and 21). The Court will deal with the delimitation of these two sectors from this point of view.

The base-line between points 11 and 12, which is 38.6 sea miles in length, delimits the waters of the Sværholt lying between Cape Nordkyn and the North Cape. [The Court reviews the geographical details.] The Court concludes that Sværholthavet has the character of a bay.

The delimitation of the Lopphavet basin has also been criticized by the United Kingdom.... The Lopphavet basin constitutes an ill-defined geographic whole. It cannot be regarded as having the character of a bay. It is made up of an extensive area of water dotted with large islands which are separated by inlets that terminate in the various fjords. The base-line has been challenged on the ground that it does not respect the general direction of the coast. It should be observed that, however justified the rule in question may be, it is devoid of any mathematical precision. In order properly to apply the rule, regard must be had for the relation between the deviation complained of and what, according to the terms of the rule, must be regarded as the *general* direction of the coast. Therefore, one cannot confine oneself to examining one sector of the coast alone, except in a case of manifest abuse; nor can one rely on the impression that may be gathered from a large scale chart of this sector alone. In the case in point, the divergence between the base-line and the land formations is not such that it is a distortion of the general direction of the Norwegian coast.

Even if it were considered that in the sector under review the deviation was too pronounced, it must be pointed out that the Norwegian Government has relied upon an historic title clearly referable to the waters of Lopphavet, namely, the exclusive privilege to fish and hunt whales granted at the end of the 17th century to Lt.-Commander Erich Lorch under a number of licenses....

These ancient concessions tend to confirm the Norwegian Government's contention that the fisheries zone reserved before 1812 was in fact much more extensive than the one delimited in 1935. It is suggested that it included all fishing banks from which land was visible, the range of vision being, as is recognized by the United Kingdom Government, the principle of delimitation in force at that time. The Court considers that, although it is not always clear to what specific areas they apply, the historical data produced in support of this contention by the Norwegian Government lend some weight to the idea of the survival of traditional rights reserved to the inhabitants of the Kingdom over fishing grounds included in the 1935 delimitation, particularly in the case of Lopphavet. Such rights, founded on the vital needs of the population and attested by very ancient and peaceful usage, may legitimately be taken into account in drawing a line which, moreover, appears to the Court to have been kept within the bounds of what is moderate and reasonable....

For these reasons,

THE COURT...

Finds

by ten votes to two,

that the method employed for the delimitation of the fisheries zone by the Royal Norwegian Decree of July 12th, 1935, is not contrary to international law;

and by eight votes to four,

that the base-lines fixed by the said Decree in application of this method are not contrary to international law.

Notes

1. *Straight Baselines and International Law.* When the ILC considered the issue of straight baselines in preparation for the First United Nations Conference on the Law of the Sea (UNCLOS I), the Commission concluded, by a vote of ten to two, that the ICJ had expressed the law in force. The Commission "accordingly drafted the article [on straight baselines] on the basis of this judgement." Report of the International Law Commission, UNGAOR, 11th Sess., Supp. No. 9, UN Doc. A/3159 (1956), reprinted in 1956-2 Y.B. Intl. L. Commn. 253, 267 (1957). Consider Article 4 of the 1958 Territorial Sea Convention, which reads:

FIGURE V.B *Norway's Straight Baselines Under its 1935 Decree*

1. In localities where the coast line is deeply indented and cut into, or if there is a fringe of islands along the coast in its immediate vicinity, the method of straight baselines joining appropriate points may be employed in drawing the baseline from which the breadth of the territorial sea is measured.

2. The drawing of such baselines must not depart to any appreciable extent from the general direction of the coast, and the sea areas lying within the lines must be sufficiently closely linked to the land domain to be subject to the régime of internal waters.

3. Baselines shall not be drawn to and from low-tide elevations, unless lighthouses or similar installations which are permanently above sea level have been built on them.

4. Where the method of straight baselines is applicable under the provisions of paragraph 1, account may be taken, in determining particular baselines, of economic interests peculiar to the region concerned, the reality and the importance of which are clearly evidenced by a long usage.

5. The system of straight baselines may not be applied by a State in such a manner as to cut off from the high seas the territorial sea of another State.

6. The coastal State must clearly indicate straight baselines on charts, to which due publicity must be given.

Compare this 1958 provision with Article 7 of the LOS Convention. The paragraph in Article 7 about deltas and unstable coastlines is new, as is the last part of paragraph 4. Paragraph 6 of the 1958 Territorial Sea Convention was not carried over to the LOS Convention's Article 7 on straight baselines, but has been moved to a special article on charts, lists, and geographical coordinates. LOS Convention, Article 16(1). Article 16(1) obligates the coastal state to publish most of the baselines discussed so far, namely straight baselines and closing lines in mouths of rivers and bays. Archipelagic baselines also need to be published. LOS Convention, Article 47(9). Only the normal baseline is not made the subject of an explicit LOS Convention publication requirement. Is this point relevant to the issue explored in Note 4 following United States v. California above, namely whether the line on the chart or the line "on the ground" should prevail?

2. *Length of Straight Baselines*. Did the ICJ, in the Anglo-Norwegian Fisheries case, establish a maximum length for straight baseline segments, as the United Kingdom had urged? The average segment length of the Norwegian system was 11.9 nautical miles. The longest segment, between points 20 and

21 (Lopphavet) measured 43.6 nautical miles, while the one between points 11 and 12 (Særholthavet) was 38.6 nautical miles long. May we conclude that lengths up to approximately 45 nautical miles are acceptable in international law, or did the ICJ take other considerations into account in justifying the length of those two segments? An International Law Commission draft initially included, "[a]s a general rule," a ten-nautical-mile maximum segment length. Report of the International Law Commission, UNGAOR, 11th Sess., Supp. No. 9, UN Doc. A/3159 (1956), reprinted in 1956-2 Y.B. Intl. L. Commn. 253, 267. After some governments spoke out against this provision, the Commission deleted it from its draft by a majority vote. Id., 267–68. What are the advantages and disadvantages of specifying a maximum segment length? Of not doing so? Keep this background in mind as you read about the other examples of state practice in the rest of this chapter.

3. *The Persistent Objector Rule.* According to the Court, "the ten-mile rule would appear to be inapplicable as against Norway inasmuch as she has always opposed any attempt to apply it to the Norwegian coast." This statement became the basis of the doctrine of the persistent objector, which was later applied in other cases and situations. See Ted L. Stein, The Approach of the Different Drummer: The Principle of the Persistent Objector in International Law, 26 Harv. Intl. L.J. 457 (1985). Should this doctrine be recognized in international law? For critical comments about it, see Jonathan I. Charney, The Persistent Objector Rule and the Development of Customary International Law, 56 Brit. Y.B. Intl. L. 1 (1985). For a present-day appraisal, with further references, see Olufemi Elias, Persistent Objector, in 8 Max Planck Encyclopedia of Public International Law 280 (Rüdiger Wolfrum ed., 2012).

4. *Other Issues.* In this excerpt from the Anglo-Norwegian Fisheries case, the ICJ touched on other crucial issues of the law of the sea and general international law besides the persistent objector rule mentioned in Note 3.

First, the ICJ clarified the determination of the outer limit of the territorial sea. How did the ICJ evaluate the different methods sometimes used by states? Which of them gained the ICJ's approval? How did the ICJ's remarks on this topic influence the development of treaty law? Read LOS Convention, Article 4 in the Appendix. Article 4 is identical to Article 6 of the 1958 Territorial Sea Convention.

Second, the ICJ's decision included this often-quoted statement concerning the determination of national maritime zones: "Although it is true that the act of delimitation is necessarily a unilateral act, because only the coastal State is competent to undertake it, the validity of the delimitation with regard to other States depends upon international law."

Third, the ICJ reformulated a fundamental principle that the land dominates the sea. This principle was first enunciated in 1909 by an arbitral tribunal in the Grisbådarna case between Norway and Sweden. The Grisbådarna tribunal stated that its decision conformed with "fundamental principles of the law of nations, both ancient and modern, in accordance with which the maritime territory is an essential appurtenance of land territory." 1 The Hague Court Reports 121, 127 (James Brown Scott ed., 1916; reprinted 2004). The ICJ's reformulation read: "It is the land which confers upon the coastal State a right to the waters off its coast."

Fourth, the ICJ accepted the Norwegian contention that the general toleration of the Norwegian practice with respect to straight baselines led to the consolidation of an historical title, i.e., a right which finds its source in history. It held that the Norwegian delimitation method "had been consolidated by a constant and sufficiently long practice."

Fifth, the ICJ saw in the behavior of the United Kingdom a classic example of the application of the theory of acquiescence in international law, for that country had waited more than sixty years before contesting Norway's straight baselines.

UNITED STATES v. LOUISIANA
349 U.S. 11, 72–73 (1969)

[This case concerns the discretion to draw straight baselines. If a coastal state finds itself in a situation in which it is legally entitled to draw such baselines, must it do so? Or does it retain the discretion not to employ them? Consider these questions as your read this excerpt.]

In *United States v. California*, 381 U.S. 139, 168, we held that "the choice under [the 1958 Territorial Sea Convention] to use the straight-base-line method for determining inland waters claimed against other nations is one that rests with the Federal Government, and not with the individual States." Since the United States asserts that it has not drawn and does not want to draw straight baselines along the Louisiana coast, that disclaimer would, under the *California* decision, be conclusive of the matter. Louisiana argues, however, that because the Louisiana coast is so perfectly suited to the straight baseline method, and because it is clear that the United States would employ it in the conduct of its international affairs were it not for this lawsuit, the Court should reconsider its holding in *California* and itself draw appropriate baselines. While we agree that the straight baseline method was designed for precisely such coasts as the Mississippi River Delta area, we adhere to the position that the selection of this optional method of establishing boundaries should be left to the branches of Government responsible for the formulation and implementation of foreign policy. It would be inappropriate for this Court to review or overturn the considered decision of the United States, albeit partially motivated by a domestic concern, not to extend its borders to the furthest extent consonant with international law.

Note

1. *U.S. Practice to Refrain from Drawing Straight Baselines.* Why would a country not want to use a system of straight baselines, provided for not only in treaty law and court decisions, but probably also in customary international law? See Note 1 following the Anglo-Norwegian Fisheries case. In the Supreme Court's judgment the U.S. federal government's decision not to use straight baselines was partly based on foreign policy and partly on domestic concerns. What would the foreign policy concerns have been? Domestic concerns are illustrated by United States v. Alaska, 521 U.S. 1 (1997), in which the discretion of the federal government to draw straight baselines was also at issue. In that case Alaska argued that the United States had consistently followed a policy of drawing straight baselines connecting fringe islands when the islands were no more than ten miles apart. Application of this ten-mile rule would result in treating waters in Stefansson Sound along Alaska's Arctic coast as internal ("inland") waters, in which case, pursuant to the U.S. Submerged Lands Act, 43 U.S.C. §§ 1301–1315, Alaska would own the submerged lands beneath such waters. The parties agreed that Alaska's coastline satisfied the prerequisite for straight baselines in Article 4 of the 1958 Territorial Sea Convention. 521 U.S. at 9. The Court reviewed the position of the United States toward the ten-mile rule in its foreign relations, as well as in its disputes with states of the United States concerning ownership of submerged land. According to the Court, Alaska had not established that the United States followed a "firm and continuing" ten-mile rule for connecting islands. Thus, "Alaska's entitlement to submerged lands along its Arctic Coast must be determined by applying the Convention's normal baseline principles." Id. at 21. In United States v. Louisiana and United States v. Alaska, was it appropriate for the U.S. Supreme Court to rely on international legal principles to settle national disputes between the federal and state governments?

Are the U.S. cases consistent with the staunch support of the United States for the initiative of the ILC, mentioned in Note 2 following the Anglo-Norwegian Fisheries case, to limit the maximum length of straight baseline segments to ten nautical miles? The United States reacted to the Commission's decision to delete the ten-mile rule by stating: "The removal of the ten-mile limit on the length of the base lines which may be used . . . open[s] the way for abuses of a principle which should be restricted to extraordinary cases as was made clear by the International Court of Justice in the Fisheries Case between the United Kingdom and Norway." Comments by Governments on the Provisional Articles Concerning the Regime of the High Seas and the Draft Articles on the Regime of the Territorial Sea adopted by the International Law Commission at its Seventh Session, UN Doc. A.CN.4/99 and Add.1-9 (1956), 1956-2 Y.B. Intl. L. Commn. 94.

UNITED STATES PROTEST OF OMAN'S STRAIGHT BASELINES
U.S. Dept. of State, Limits in the Seas No. 113, Straight Baseline Claims: Djibouti and Oman (1992), available at http://www.state.gov/documents/organization/58382.pdf

THE CLAIM: By Royal Decree No. 38/82 and accompanying Notice of June 1, 1982 . . . Oman has claimed straight baselines along four sections of its

OMAN'S STRAIGHT BASELINES

Group "A" (Along the Musandam Peninsula)		**Group "C" (Along Oman's east coast)**	
Segment	**Length (miles)**	**Segment**	**Length (miles)**
1–2	1.03	. . .	
2–3	10.63	31–32	16.76
3–4	1.15	. . .	
4–5	0.95	35–36	20.90
5–6	10.7	36–37	19.31
6–7	11.59		
7–8	1.06	**Group "D" (Along Oman's southeast coast)**	
. . .			
13–14	9.74		
14–15	3.86	38–39	24.88
15–16	8.36	39–40	20.54
		40–41	10.29
		41–42	16.06
[Group "B" claims omitted]		42–43	17.67

coast (identified as Groups A, B, C, and D, see map). This claim implemented the enabling legislation Oman had passed on July 2, 1972.

ANALYSIS: Oman consists of two non-contiguous regions separated by the United Arab Emirates. It occupies the northern extremity of the Ru'us (peninsula) al Jibal, comprising the Musandam Peninsula and offshore islands. The major territorial segment of Oman is situated in the south and west, below the 25th parallel of north latitude, along the shores of the Gulf of Oman and the Arabian Sea.

Generally, Oman's coastline is quite smooth. The straight baseline claim involves less than half Oman's coastline. In those areas where straight baselines are not claimed the territorial sea is measured from the normal baseline, which, according to Article 5 of the LOS Convention "is the low-water line along the coast as marked on large-scale charts officially recognized by the coastal State." . . .

As a result of conducting an analysis similar to the above, the United States delivered to the Government of Oman a diplomatic note on August 12, 1991, protesting many segments of this baseline system, [portions of which are excerpted below:]

[Complimentary opening] and refers to Oman's Declarations of 17 August 1989 accompanying the deposit of its ratification of the 1982 United Nations Convention of the Law of the Sea, confirming Oman's Notice of June 1, 1982, establishing straight baselines along portions of Oman's coast, pursuant to Article 2(C) of Royal Decree No. 15/81. . . .

The Government of the United States wishes to recall to the Government of Oman that, as recognized in customary international law and as reflected in the 1982 United Nations Convention on the Law of the Sea, unless exceptional circumstances exist, baselines are to conform to the low-water line along the coast as marked on a state's official large-scale charts. Straight baselines may only be employed in localities where the coastline is deeply indented and cut into, or where there is a fringe of islands along the immediate vicinity of the coast. Where employed, straight baselines must not depart to any appreciable extent from the general direction of the coast. The coast of Oman does not meet any of these criteria. For example, the coastline is too smooth landward of points 1–5, 14–16, and 38–43; and too few islands mask Oman's coastline at points 6–7 and 38–43. On the other hand, the line connecting points 36–37 encloses a juridical bay, and while point 6 is situated on an island, instead of the mainland, segment 5–6 essentially encloses juridical bays. . . .

The Government of the United States therefore objects to the claims described above and made by Oman in ratifying the 1982 United Nations

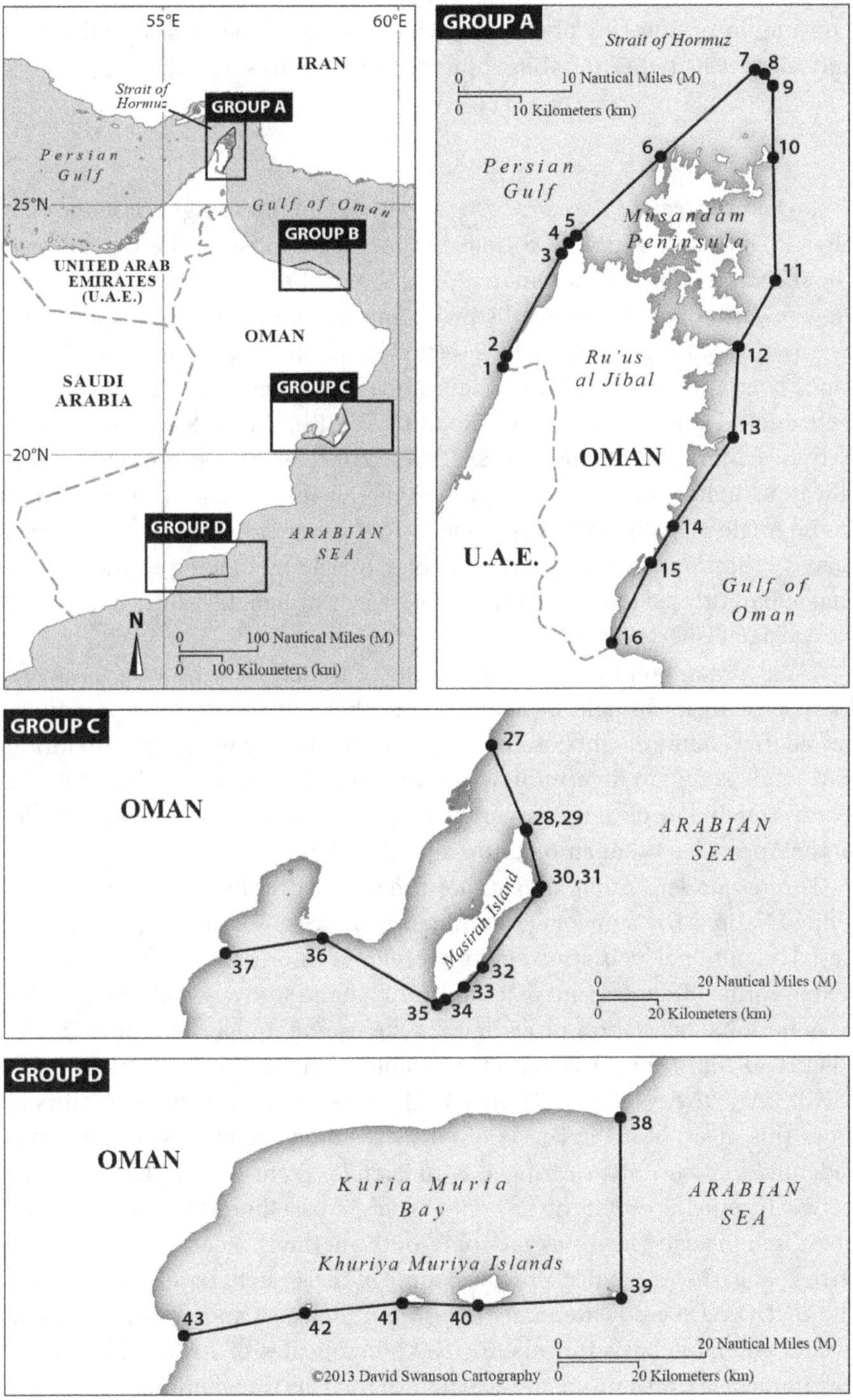

FIGURE V.C *Oman's Straight Baselines*

Convention on the Law of the Sea, which are not valid in international law, and reserves its rights and those of its nationals in this regard.

Notes

1. *Oman's Straight Baselines.* Do you think Oman's straight baselines comply with Article 7 of the LOS Convention? In response to the U.S. protest of Oman's straight baselines, Oman replied that its baselines were "drawn with a view toward maintaining the distinguishing economic interests of the region in question, interests which have established their significance and importance over a long period." American Embassy Muscat telegram 5320, Dec. 4, 1991, quoted in J. Ashley Roach & Robert W. Smith, United States Responses to Excessive Maritime Claims 85 n.83 (3d ed. 2012). Is this a persuasive legal justification, in light of Article 7(5) of the LOS Convention and the ICJ's concerns in the Anglo-Norwegian Fisheries case? To the extent that Article 7 is ambiguous, is it appropriate to supplement that Article by looking to the purposes that apparently led the ICJ to approve Norway's straight baselines in the Anglo-Norwegian Fisheries case?

Could Oman point to other provisions of the LOS Convention to justify at least some of its straight baselines? Note that the U.S. diplomatic note suggested that some straight baseline segments might be closing lines for juridical bays. How is one to determine when a coastal indentation is a juridical bay? What straight bay closing lines are permitted? See LOS Convention, Article 10 in the Appendix. What ambiguities does that Article not resolve?

2. *International Straight Baseline Practice.* According to a study by the United Nations Division for Ocean Affairs and the Law of the Sea (UNDOALOS), based on national legislation and other reliable information, as of July 15, 2011, no fewer than 87 states (out of a total of 152 in the study)—including Oman—have national legislation providing for the use of straight baselines. Table of Claims to Maritime Jurisdiction, available at http://www.un.org/Depts/los/LEGISLATIONANDTREATIES/PDFFILES/table_summary_of_claims.pdf. Does this mean that the coasts of all these states are at least in part deeply indented and cut into, or fringed with islands? States do not have to choose between applying either the normal or straight baseline system for their entire coastline; instead they may combine both methods. Read LOS Convention, Article 14 in the Appendix. However, some of the straight baselines reported in the UNDOALOS study are many miles from the coast and appear not to have even a colorable basis for meeting the prerequisites of Article 4 of the 1958 Territorial Sea Convention and Article 7 of the LOS Convention.

3. *Diplomatic Protests.* The U.S. protest to Oman is just one of numerous U.S. protests of straight baselines that the United States considers excessive, made in the form of formal protest notes, notes verbale, or aides mémoire. See Roach & Smith, supra Note 1, at 59–133. Other states also submit diplomatic protests, as illustrated by the 1933 British protest of Norway's system of maritime delimitation, discussed in the Anglo-Norwegian Fisheries case. When Vietnam set up its system of straight baselines in 1982, China, France, the Federal Republic of Germany, and Thailand all joined the United States in protesting the enactment. Id. at 99. When Canada established straight baselines around its Arctic archipelago in 1985, not only the United States, as the state most directly concerned, but also member states of the European Community addressed a letter of protest to the Canadian government. Id. at 111–12. For a critical analysis of the Canadian claim by a high-level European official, see Daniel Vignes, La conformité au droit de la mer des lignes de base droites tracées par le Canada au nord du 70ème parallèle nord, in International Law at a Time of Perplexity: Essays in Honour of Shabtai Rosenne 1005 (Yoram Dinstein & Mala Tabory eds., 1989). Why would a state take the serious step of filing a diplomatic protest with another state, despite there being friendly relations between the two states?

4. *Operational Responses to Straight Baseline Claims.* The United States may respond operationally, as well as with diplomatic protests, to what it regards as illegal straight baseline claims and other state actions that interfere with the freedom of navigation. These operational responses are made under what is known as the Freedom of Navigation Program. This policy has been expressed in the following terms:

> The United States will exercise and assert its navigation and overflight rights and freedoms on a worldwide basis in a manner that is consistent with the balance of interests reflected in the [1982 LOS] convention. The United States will not, however, acquiesce in unilateral acts of other states designed to restrict the rights and freedoms of the international community in navigation and overflight and other related high seas uses.

Statement on United States Oceans Policy, Mar. 10, 1983, 22 Intl. Leg. Materials 464 (1983). The U.S. Department of Defense prepared a manual reporting maritime claims of other states and indicating many instances of protests and operational assertions under the Freedom of Navigation Program. U.S. Dept. of Defense, Maritime Claims Reference Manual (DoD 2005.1-M, 2005), available at http://www.jag.navy.mil/organization/documents/mcrm/MCRM.pdf. What are the advantages and disadvantages of such a program? Would

Part XV of the LOS Convention on the settlement of disputes, discussed in Chapter 15, offer a better solution? Why has Part XV not yet been of any substantial help in settling divergent views on the legality of certain systems of straight baselines?

5. *Lengths of Straight Baseline Segments in State Practice.* Given the lack of clear guidance on the maximum length of baselines in the Anglo-Norwegian Fisheries case as well as treaty law, a certain evolution can be discerned in state practice. In the 1950s and 1960s states very often mirrored their practice on Norway's example, which the ICJ approved in the Anglo-Norwegian Fisheries case. For instance, when the United Kingdom established its own system of straight baselines in 1964, the average segment length was 11.25 nautical miles, and the longest segment 40.25 nautical miles. U.S. Dept. of State, Limits in the Seas No. 23, Straight Baselines: United Kingdom (1970), available at http://www.state.gov/documents/organization/61604.pdf. Compare these figures with those of the Norwegian system as accepted by the ICJ in 1951.

Little by little, however, states started to increase these numbers. The average segment length of the 1985 Canadian system, discussed in Note 3, is about 17 nautical miles, with the longest segment measuring 99.5 nautical miles. Donat Pharand, Canada's Arctic Waters in International Law 162 (1988). For the Vietnamese system established three years earlier, and also mentioned in Note 3, these figures are 84.6 and 161.8 nautical miles, with 40 percent of the segments measuring more than 100 nautical miles. U.S. Dept. of State, Limits in the Seas No. 99, Straight Baselines: Vietnam 8 (1983), available at http://www.state.gov/documents/organization/58573.pdf. Following this general trend, the Chinese system around the mainland and Hainan Island, established about a decade after the Canadian one, has an average length approaching the maximum segment in the Anglo-Norwegian Fisheries case, and a maximum segment length of 121.7 nautical miles, with six percent of its segments measuring more than 100 nautical miles. U.S. Dept. of State, Limits in the Seas No. 117, Straight Baselines: China 4 (1996), available at http://www.state.gov/documents/organization/57692.pdf. Recall that China itself saw fit to lodge a protest against the Vietnamese system in 1982! The Chinese system, it is true, is not as extreme as the Vietnamese one—all the Chinese figures are lower, namely the average and maximum segment length as well as the percentage of segments measuring more than 100 nautical miles—but it covers more than twice as much coastline as does the Vietnamese one. For more discussion of the Chinese system of straight baselines, see Note 3 following the excerpt on Fiji's archipelagic baselines in Section C.

Even some countries that had restrictively applied straight baselines have now liberalized them to some extent. Finland provides an example. Finland first legislatively established a system of straight baselines in 1966. Finland's legislation was characterized by a few rather unusual features. First, the Finnish law provided that the maximum length of the segments could not be more than twice the width of the territorial sea, which in Finland at that time was still four nautical miles. As a consequence, the average segment length was only 4.4 nautical miles. U.S. Dept. of State, Limits in the Seas No. 48, Straight Baselines: Finland 8 (1970), available at http://www.state.gov/documents/organization/61523.pdf. Second, the system was subject to a periodic review every 30 years. When Finland conducted a review in 1995, applicable to the period 1995–2014, it could extend the length of its straight baseline segments because its legislature had expanded its territorial sea limit from four to twelve nautical miles. By 1995 the legislature had also repealed the statutory provision requiring that the distance between two base points be at most twice the width of the territorial sea. See UNDOALOS, Law of the Sea Bull. No. 29 at 56 (1995), available at http://www.un.org/Depts/los/doalos_publications/LOSBulletins/bulletinpdf/bulletinE29.pdf. As of the end of 2013, the average segment length is 13.6 nautical miles.

6. *Action-reaction Pattern in the Practice of States.* Professor Scovazzi, an expert on straight baselines, concluded that two opposing tendencies meet each other with respect to straight baselines. On the one hand are the excessive claims of what he calls a minority of coastal states. On the other hand are the diplomatic protests and occasional military maneuvers—Scovazzi asks whether these maneuvers are also excessive—of one great naval power. See Tullio Scovazzi, L'établissement de systèmes de lignes de base droites de la mer territoriale: les règles et la pratique, 2 Annuaire du Droit de la Mer 160, 176 (1997). As illustrated not only by the previous Notes but also by the many U.S. sources relied on in Section B (and in Section C on archipelagic baselines as well), the United States attaches particular importance to the question of straight baselines. Why is the United States so concerned with this issue? Consider again Note 3 following the excerpt from the Anglo-Norwegian Fisheries case as well as the U.S. Freedom of Navigation Program, discussed in Note 4 above, when formulating your answer. Are there international community interests, rather than simply U.S. interests, that are served by reining in excessive straight baseline claims?

CASE CONCERNING MARITIME DELIMITATION AND TERRITORIAL QUESTIONS BETWEEN QATAR AND BAHRAIN

2001 I.C.J. 40

210. Bahrain has contended that, as a multiple-island State, its coast consists of the lines connecting its outermost islands and such low-tide elevations

as lie within their territorial waters. Without explicitly referring to Article 4 of the 1958 Convention on the Territorial Sea and the Contiguous Zone or Article 7 of the 1982 Convention on the Law of the Sea, Bahrain in its reasoning and in the maps provided to the Court applied the method of straight baselines....

211. Bahrain maintains that as a multiple-island State characterized by a cluster of islands off the coast of its main islands, it is entitled to draw a line connecting the outermost islands and low-tide elevations. According to Bahrain, in such cases the external fringe should serve as the baseline for the territorial sea.

212. The Court observes that the method of straight baselines, which is an exception to the normal rules for the determination of baselines, may only be applied if a number of conditions are met. This method must be applied restrictively. Such conditions are primarily that either the coastline is deeply indented and cut into, or that there is a fringe of islands along the coast in its immediate vicinity.

213. The fact that a State considers itself a multiple-island State or a *de facto* archipelagic State does not allow it to deviate from the normal rules for the determination of baselines unless the relevant conditions are met. The coasts of Bahrain's main islands do not form a deeply indented coast, nor does Bahrain claim this. It contends, however, that the maritime features off the coast of the main islands may be assimilated to a fringe of islands which constitute a whole with the mainland.

214. The Court does not deny that the maritime features east of Bahrain's main islands are part of the overall geographical configuration; it would be going too far, however, to qualify them as a fringe of islands along the coast. The islands concerned are relatively small in number. Moreover, in the present case it is only possible to speak of a "cluster of islands" or an "island system" if Bahrain's main islands are included in that concept. In such a situation, the method of straight baselines is applicable only if the State has declared itself to be an archipelagic State under Part IV of the 1982 Convention on the Law of the Sea, which is not true of Bahrain in this case.

215. The Court, therefore, concludes that Bahrain is not entitled to apply the method of straight baselines.... It is on this basis that the equidistance line must be drawn.

Notes

1. *Development of International Law.* With more than half of the states claiming straight baselines (see Note 2 following the excerpt on Oman's Straight Baselines), how is it still possible for the ICJ to qualify the method of straight baselines as "an exception to the normal rule"? Recall that the ICJ, in

the Anglo-Norwegian Fisheries case excerpted above, stated that if one were to apply normal baselines to the Norwegian coast, "the [normal baseline] rule would disappear under the exceptions." What do you believe will be the impact of paragraph 212 of the Qatar-Bahrain judgment on the further evolution of state straight baseline practice? Will paragraph 212 affect the already-existing national legislation reviewed in Note 5 following the excerpt on Oman's Straight Baselines? Recall that much national legislation had rather loosely interpreted the conditions imposed by the ICJ in the Anglo-Norwegian Fisheries case, as later codified in Article 4 of the 1958 Territorial Sea Convention and in Article 7 of the LOS Convention. The United States—given its opinion when the ILC retracted its ten-nautical-mile maximum limit for straight baselines (see Note 1 following the United States v. Louisiana case above)—must have been comforted by the ICJ's Qatar-Bahrain decision.

2. *Straight Baselines in Maritime Delimitation Cases.* As mentioned above, states have not contested excessive baselines directly under Part XV dispute settlement procedures. Yet straight baseline questions often arise in maritime boundary delimitations, as in the Qatar-Bahrain case. In that case, the ICJ concluded that Bahrain was not entitled to apply the method of straight baselines; Bahrain had relied on archipelagic baselines, discussed in the next section, without having declared itself to be an archipelagic state. We will see in Chapter 6 how arbiters and judges have dealt with the sensitive issue of baseline claims in many other maritime delimitation cases.

C Archipelagic Baselines

FIJI'S ARCHIPELAGIC BASELINES

U.S. Dept. of State, Limits in the Seas No. 101, Fiji's Maritime Claims (1984), available at http://www.state.gov/documents/organization/58567.pdf

Introduction

By Acts No. 18 of 1977 and No. 15 of 1978 the Government of Fiji enacted the Marine Spaces Act which, inter alia, set forth Fiji's maritime limits.... The Fiji Royal Gazette Supplement subsequently published several legal notices, cited as Marine Spaces Orders, including one that specified geographical coordinates for Fiji's archipelagic straight baselines and for the seaward limits of its exclusive economic zone (Legal Notice No. 117), and one that specified straight baseline turning points for the island of Rotuma (see map following p. 4) and adjacent islands (Legal Notice No. 118; see Annex 2 for the Legal Notices published on November 27, 1981, pertaining to the Marine Spaces Act). These orders entered into force on December 1, 1981.

Fiji, an island state situated in the southwest Pacific Ocean, comprises about 320 islands ranging in size from Viti Levu (10,390 square kilometers) to uninhabited rocks a few square meters in area.... The total land area of Fiji (not including the water area within the fringing reefs) is approximately 18,272 square kilometers. The capital city of Suva is located on the southeast coast of Viti Levu.

With the exception of some outlying islands, the so-called Fiji Archipelago generally forms a circular configuration. The distances between extreme Fijian islands are approximately 570 nautical miles (1,055 kilometers) between the northern island of Rotuma and Ceva-i-Ra in the south and about 288 nautical miles (533 kilometers) between the easternmost island in the Lau Group (on the Mbukatatanoa Reefs) and Viwa Island in the west.

For the purpose of its Marine Spaces Act, the Government of Fiji has distinguished the Fiji Archipelago from the Island of Rotuma and its dependencies and from the island of Ceva-i-Ra. Separate baseline systems are defined for each of these areas. Because of distances between Rotuma and the main island group and between Ceva-i-Ra and the main island group, it was impossible for Fiji, under the provisions of the [LOS Convention], to draw one archipelagic baseline system that would incorporate every Fijian island.

Baselines

Fiji's legislation establishes two different types of baselines. Archipelagic baselines join most of the country's islands to form the Fiji Archipelago; seaward of those baselines [are] the territorial sea and high seas, landward of them are archipelagic waters and internal waters. The other type of baseline delimits the internal waters from archipelagic waters (if situated inside archipelagic baselines) or from the territorial sea (as in the Rotuma Island area).

The archipelagic straight baseline system comprises 34 turning points and connects the outer point of the outer islands and drying reefs. Legal Notice 117 (paragraph 2) states that the geographical coordinates of the basepoints are based on the World Geodetic System 1972 (WGS72) and that the listings given in the First Schedule are correct, minus 7 seconds of latitude and 14 seconds of longitude in each case. The distance between basepoints ranges from 1.0 nautical miles (between points 19 and 20) to 119.9 nautical miles (between points 15 and 16), with a mean length of 27.7 nautical miles.... The baseline length criterion cited in Article 47(2) of the LOS Convention is met. This paragraph states:

> The length of such baselines shall not exceed 100 nautical miles, except that up to 3 percent of the total number of baselines enclosing any archipelago may exceed that length, up to a maximum length of 125 nautical miles.

These baselines, along with the depiction of the internal waters and the territorial sea limit, are officially illustrated on Fiji Marine Spaces Chart 81/2 which is based on British Admiralty Chart 2691, 1970. The attached chart (which does not show the internal waters) is based on U.S. DMAHTC chart 605 and is produced solely for the purpose of this study.

According to Article 47(1) of the LOS Convention:

> An archipelagic State may draw straight archipelagic baselines joining the outermost points of the outermost islands and drying reefs of the archipelago provided that within such baselines are included the main islands and an area in which the ratio of the area of the water to the area of the land, including atolls, is between 1 to 1 and 9 to 1.

It would appear that Fiji's archipelagic baseline system meets these requirements. As shown on Fiji's Marine Spaces Chart 81/2, 30 of the 34 baseline turning points seem to be located on drying reefs and only 4 turning points (Nos. 1, 8, 26, and 33) fall on land. The total area enclosed by the archipelagic baselines is approximately 174,300 square kilometers (50,900 sq. nautical miles). Based on Fiji's internal waters claim this area includes the following components:

> Land = 18,272 sq. kilometers
> Internal waters = 25,558 sq. kilometers
> Archipelagic waters = 130,470 sq. kilometers

For the purpose of calculating the water-to-land area ratio, Article 47(7) allows the use of "waters lying within the fringing reefs of islands and atolls. . . ." In Fiji's case these waters, claimed as internal waters, are about 1.4 times the total land area. The resulting water-area-to-land-area ratio is well within the LOS Convention range:

> 130,470 : 43,830 = 2.98 : 1.

It is with respect to fringing reefs that most of the questions regarding the internal baselines arise. Article 6 of the LOS Convention provides:

> In the case of islands situated on atolls or of islands having fringing reefs, the baseline for measuring the breadth of the territorial sea is the seaward low-water line of the reef, as shown by the appropriate symbol on charts officially recognized by the coastal State.

A fundamental omission from the LOS Convention is a provision designating appropriate reef closing lines similar to the provisions given for "rivers" and "bays" found in Articles 9 and 10, respectively. Many of the reefs surrounding Fijian islands extend from the land and are unbroken physical features. Other reefs, however, contain one or several entrances to the lagoons that they surround. Fiji arbitrarily has drawn closing lines for these reef entrances. Depending on one's interpretation of the LOS text, it may be questionable whether Fiji can legally claim much of the enclosed waters as internal. An examination of the Fijian chart shows at least four areas where Fiji's claimed internal water baseline may be somewhat far reaching.

The first area is at the Heemskercq Reefs [see Figure V.D], located near the northeast corner of the archipelago, east of Vanua Levu. Although there may be a problem of chart symbol interpretation, the baseline appears to follow along a symbol depicting a submerged feature for about 13 nautical miles. Off the west coast of Vanua Levu an internal water baseline has been drawn along the Pascoe Reefs (to the southwest of the Great Sea Reef). Across Round Island Passage, to the east of Yasawa Group, internal water baselines have been drawn along an area labeled Tivolei on the Fiji chart. In both areas the chart symbols indicate submerged features rather than drying reefs. And finally, south of Viti Levu the small island of Mbengga contains two internal water baselines that do not appear to follow along drying reefs. To conform to the LOS Convention it would appear that some adjustments to the internal water baseline should be made, adjustments that would not affect significantly the archipelagic water to land area ratio.

The baseline for Ceva-i-Ra is the low-water line of the drying reefs that surround the island. The island itself measures only about 100 meters by 325 meters, and the internal waters enclosed by the claimed baselines are approximately 2.5 sq. kilometers.

The baseline claimed by Fiji for its northern island of Rotuma may be questionable. In the Marine Spaces Act Rotuma is defined as the "Rotuma archipelago" comprising Rotuma and its dependencies, which include about six smaller islands situated between 1.5 and 4.5 nautical miles to the west of Rotuma. Currently before Fiji's Parliament is an amendment to the Marine Spaces Act which, inter alia, deletes reference to Rotuma as an archipelago. Instead, the waters within the baselines are intended to be internal waters and

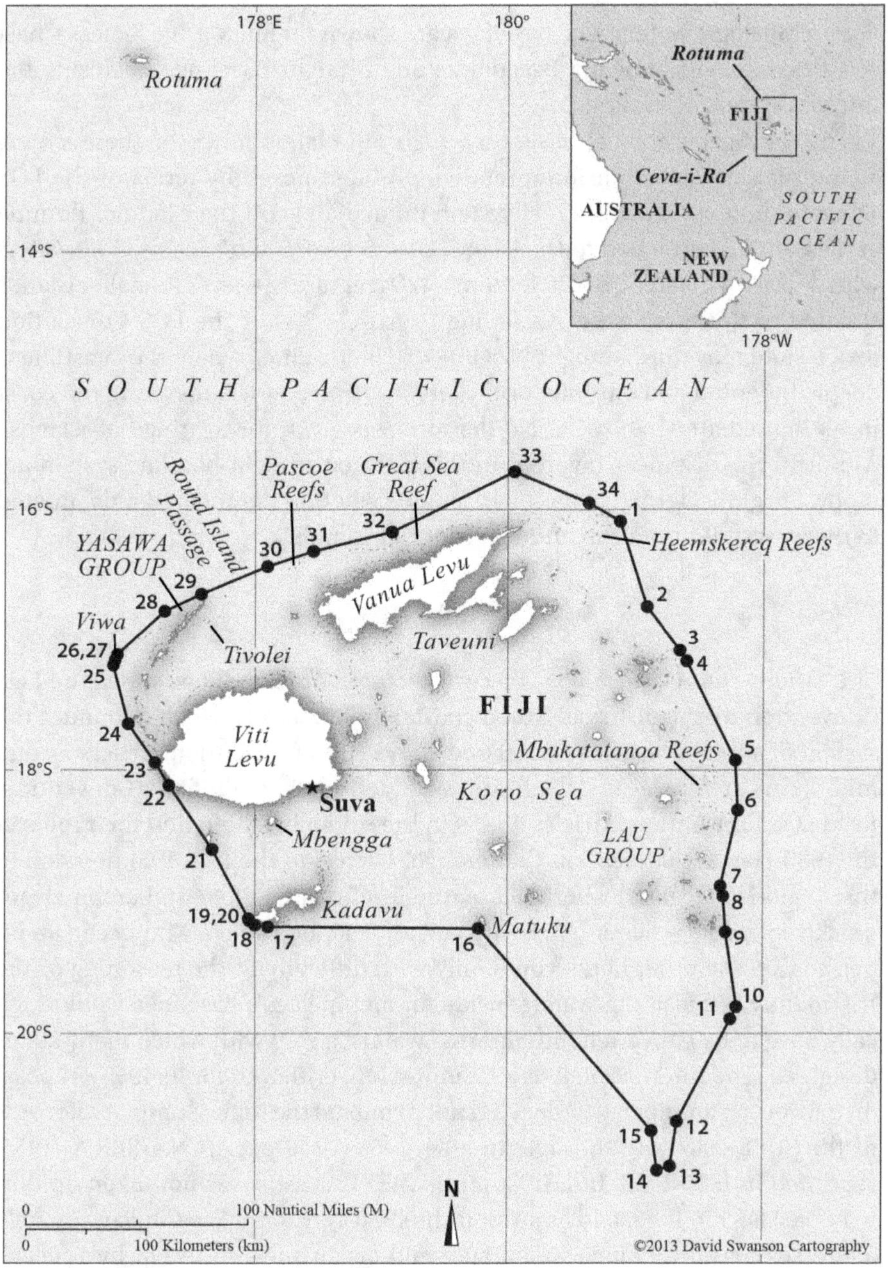

FIGURE V.D *Fiji's Straight Archipelagic Baselines*

not archipelagic waters. The baselines are shown on Fiji Marine Spaces Chart 81/1 titled, "Chart Showing Basepoints and Straight Baselines Enclosing the Internal Waters of Rotuma."....

The legal-geographical basis on which Fiji claims much of these waters as internal highlights an interpretative problem posed by terms of the LOS Convention text. There is a reef system immediately off the island of Rotuma and essentially attached to the island. Distinct from and separated by waters with depths of greater than 20 fathoms (120 feet) are the several smaller islands situated to Rotuma's west. According to Article 7(1) of the LOS Convention text, a state may draw straight baselines, "[i]n localities where the coastline is deeply indented and cut into, or if there is a fringe of islands along the coast in its immediate vicinity...." No definition is given for a "fringe of islands." Although the distances involved in this claimed straight baseline system are modest in global terms..., it is questionable whether the small islands situated to the west of Rotuma constitute a "fringe of islands."

Notes

1. *Mid-ocean Archipelagos: A New Concept in the LOS Convention.* The LOS Convention distinguishes between coastal archipelagos, which fall under the system of straight baselines discussed above (LOS Convention, Article 7), and mid-ocean archipelagos, which are regulated in Part IV of the Convention. Read LOS Convention, Articles 46–54 in the Appendix. Both find their roots in the 1930 Hague Codification Conference. Thanks to the ICJ's 1951 decision in the Anglo-Norwegian Fisheries case, the legal regime of coastal archipelagos quickly found its reflection in treaty law, as described above. Mid-ocean archipelagos, on the other hand, could only with difficulty fit the reasoning of the ICJ, mainly because the waters inside an archipelago's baselines would logically have to be converted into internal waters, a step with which many states disagreed. The International Law Commission, criticized for its 1955 proposal on mid-ocean archipelagos, decided not to pursue the topic. Summary Records of the 7th Session, 319th Mtg., June 24, 1955, UN Doc. A/CN.4/SER.A /1955, reprinted in 1955-1 Y.B. Intl. L. Commn. 218. The issue was not taken up during UNCLOS I in 1958, and as a result the 1958 Territorial Sea Convention only addresses coastal archipelagos and not mid-ocean ones. It was Fiji, by a speech of its delegate to the Seabed Committee on July 22, 1971, that placed this issue back on the international agenda. Part IV of the LOS Convention finally dealt with the legal status of mid-ocean archipelagos.

2. *Archipelagic State Status.* If a state fits the Article 46(a) and (b) definitions of "archipelagic state" and "archipelago" (a concept used in the definition of "archipelagic state"), is it ipso jure an archipelagic state under the LOS

Convention? Can such a state automatically rely on all the provisions found in Part IV of the LOS Convention, including entitlement to draw straight archipelagic baselines? Consider the Qatar-Bahrain Maritime Delimitation case when formulating your answer. What rules applied to Bahrain's baselines, according to the ICJ? Or, to approach the same issue from a different angle, what is the legal relevance of the Fijian legal enactments of the late 1970s? Besides Fiji, the following twenty states have, as of July 15, 2011 enacted enabling legislation relating to their status as archipelagic states: Antigua and Barbuda, Bahamas, Cape Verde, Comoros, Indonesia, Grenada, Jamaica, Kiribati, Maldives, the Marshall Islands, Mauritius, Papua New Guinea, the Philippines, Saint Vincent and the Grenadines, Sao Tome and Principe, Seychelles, Solomon Islands, Trinidad and Tobago, Tuvalu, and Vanuatu. See UNDOALOS, Table of Claims to Maritime Jurisdiction, available at http://www.un.org/Depts/los/LEGISLATIONANDTREATIES/PDFFILES/table_summary_of_claims.pdf. All these countries did so either during the UNCLOS III negotiations (1972–1982), like Fiji, or afterwards, and all of them are parties to the LOS Convention. In 2007 the Dominican Republic also proclaimed its archipelagic status, although at the time the country was not yet a party to the LOS Convention. (It only became a party in 2009.) Special about the Dominican Republic is that it shares its main island with Haiti. The United Kingdom and the United States jointly protested a few months after the Dominican Republic's proclamation. Joint Demarche of October 18, 2007, Undertaken by the United Kingdom of Great Britain and Northern Ireland and the United States of America in Relation to the Law of the Dominican Republic No. 66-07 of May 22, 2007, UNDOALOS, Law of the Sea Bull. No. 66 at 98 (2008). But see Sophia Kopela, 2007 Archipelagic Legislation of the Dominican Republic: An Assessment, 24 Intl. J. Marine & Coastal Law 501, 503–09 (2009) (supporting, after thorough analysis, the archipelagic state status of the Dominican Republic).

3. *Non-geographical Criteria for Archipelagic State Status.* The definitions of "archipelagic state" and "archipelago" in Article 46(a) and (b) of the LOS Convention combine pure geographical requirements with additional ones. An archipelagic state must be "wholly" constituted by archipelagos and islands. LOS Convention, Article 46(a). The islands and other features constituting an "archipelago" must be closely interrelated in order to form an intrinsic geographical, economic, and political entity or to have been historically so considered. Id., Article 46(b). What explains these requirements? Did the UNCLOS III negotiators believe that colonial powers, like France and Portugal, which possess a number of mid-ocean archipelagos, sometimes very far from their capitals, should be allowed to benefit from Part IV of the LOS Convention? Consider again the list of archipelagic states in Note 2.

Consider also the Canadian legislation of 1985, which we discussed in Section B in Note 3 following the excerpt on Oman's Straight Baselines. The preamble of this legislation begins: "Whereas Canada has long maintained and exercised sovereignty over the waters of the Canadian Arctic *archipelago.*" Available at http://laws-lois.justice.gc.ca/eng/regulations/SOR-85-872/page-1.html#fn_SOR-85-872_e_hq_4078 (emphasis added). Is Canada entitled to archipelagic state status?

In 1992 China established the baselines of its territorial sea. A first part of the Chinese legislation established straight baselines around the mainland and Hainan Island, already referred to in Note 5 following the excerpt on Oman's straight baselines. A second part, however, concerned the baselines around the Xisha (Paracel) Islands, composed of around 40 insular features and reefs, the largest of which only measures 1.62 square kilometers (.625 square miles). China totally enclosed these Islands with 27 segments of straight baselines. The United States commented on these baselines by stating:

> China (or Vietnam) would not be allowed to establish archipelagic straight baselines around the Paracel Islands, since the LOS Convention is quite clear in stating that an archipelagic State "means a State constituted wholly by one or more archipelagoes and may include other islands." And, an archipelago "means a group of islands, including parts of islands, interconnecting waters and other natural features which are so closely interrelated that such islands, waters and other natural features form an intrinsic geographic, economic and political [entity], or which historically have been regarded as such." As continental states, China and Vietnam cannot establish archipelagic straight baselines around islands belonging to them.

U.S. Dept. of State, Limits in the Seas No. 117, China: Straight Baselines Claim 8 (1996), available at http://www.state.gov/documents/organization/57692.pdf. This U.S. comment raises at least two issues. First, the Chinese legislation nowhere uses the notion of archipelagic baselines. Is China not allowed to rely on Article 7 of the LOS Convention to draw straight baselines around these islands? When answering this question, take into account what the ICJ had to say on this issue in the Qatar-Bahrain Maritime Delimitation case. Second, the U.S. comment also twice mentioned "Vietnam" when analyzing the straight baselines established by China around the Paracel Islands. What was the United States suggesting by doing so?

4. *Archipelagic Baselines: General Considerations.* Archipelagic straight baselines enclose archipelagic waters, a topic we explore in Chapter 8, Section D.

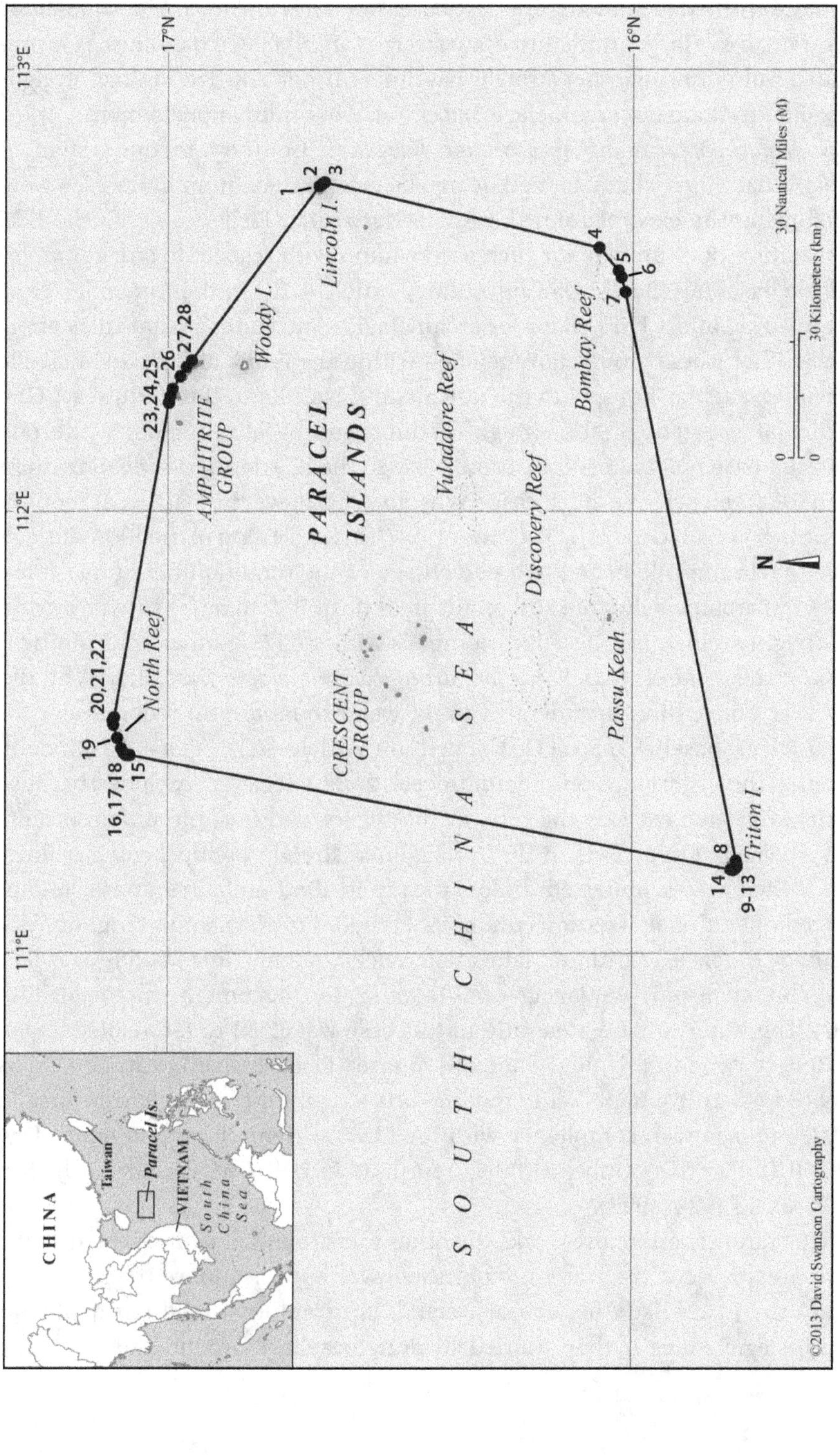

FIGURE V.E *China's Straight Baselines Claim around the Paracel Islands*

Is a state entitled to draw archipelagic baselines if it is not an archipelagic state? If a state, like Fiji, is entitled to draw straight archipelagic baselines, is it precluded from drawing other straight baselines? If it is entitled to draw straight baselines that are not archipelagic baselines, what rules apply to them?

5. *Length of Straight Archipelagic Baselines.* Contrary to the system of straight baselines, characterized by an absence of maximum limits (see Note 2 following the excerpt from the Anglo-Norwegian Fisheries case), the LOS Convention does provide for such a maximum with respect to straight archipelagic baselines. Read LOS Convention, Article 47(2) in the Appendix. How did this rule affect Fiji's claim for archipelagic state status? What rules apply to the other island groups not included within the limits of Fiji's archipelagic baselines, such as Rotuma to the north and Ceva-i-Ra to the southwest? One particular segment of the straight archipelagic baselines, namely the one between base points 15 and 16, came close to the 125-nautical-mile maximum limit tolerated in exceptional cases. Why do you believe this particular requirement was included in the LOS Convention? This exception to the 100-nautical-mile maximum rule is tied to a percentage of the total number of baselines. Does the archipelagic state still retain great flexibility to make sure its system of straight archipelagic baselines complies with the 125-nautical-mile limit?

6. *Water-to-land Area Ratio for Straight Archipelagic Baselines.* Why did the LOS Convention include a 1:1 to 9:1 water-to-land ratio requirement for archipelagic baselines? See LOS Convention, Article 47(1). Fiji has no difficulty meeting this criterion, but other mid-ocean archipelagos are excluded because their water area exceeds the ratio at the higher end (i.e., more than 9 units water). When Cape Verde in 1977 proclaimed straight archipelagic baselines, the United States protested diplomatically in 1980 and 1989 and also conducted operational assertions under its Freedom of Navigation Program. U.S. Dept. of Defense, Maritime Claims Reference Manual (DoD 2005.1-M, 2005), available at http://www.jag.navy.mil/organization/documents/mcrm/MCRM.pdf). The water-to-land area ratio in this case was 12.54 to 1. J. Ashley Roach & Robert W. Smith, United States Responses to Excessive Maritime Claims 209 (3d ed. 2012). Cape Verde modified its straight archipelagic baselines in 1992, and is now in compliance with the LOS Convention requirements. Law No. 60/IV/92 of December 21, 1992, reprinted in UNDOALAS, Law of the Sea Bull. No. 26 at 24 (1994).

This ratio criterion also works the other way around. It can well be that the land area exceeds the water area at the lower end (i.e., more than one unit land). Countries like Australia or Ireland, for example, would not qualify as archipelagic states if they wanted to draw baselines around their outlying islands, even assuming that all other criteria were met, because their landmass would not allow them to satisfy this ratio.

7. *Evaluating the LOS Convention's Archipelagic Baselines Criteria.* Consider all the criteria that a state must fulfill in order to be able to draw archipelagic baselines under the LOS Convention. Can they all be characterized as scientific in nature? Some of the archipelagic baseline criteria have been spelled out in much more detail than the Article 7 straight baseline requirements. For example, the archipelagic baseline rules include a maximum limit for segments between two turning points. As illustrated by the Fiji example, do these more determinate criteria eliminate all subjectivity when trying to apply the rules in practice? Also consider the case of the Dominican Republic, discussed in Note 2, when answering this question.

CHAPTER 6

Maritime Delimitation

The international law of the sea distinguishes the establishment of maritime zones by coastal states, on the one hand, from the delimitation of maritime zones between adjacent and opposite states, on the other. As discussed in Chapter 5, establishing maritime zones depends on the baseline and is by its nature a unilateral act that can only be undertaken by the coastal state, even though the validity of this unilateral act with respect to other states is governed by international law. However, states cannot delimit maritime zones unilaterally. The need for delimitation arises where the zones of two adjacent coastal states touch, or where the distance between opposite states is less than twice the width of the zone to be delimited. Most often, delimitation difficulties arise in the context of the continental shelf and the exclusive economic zone (EEZ), for these zones extend up to 200 nautical miles. Since the 1982 United Nations Convention on the Law of the Sea (LOS Convention) allows states in certain circumstances to extend their continental shelves beyond 200 nautical miles (see Chapter 10, Section C), the need for delimitation may extend to such expanded continental shelves as well. Delimitation may also be necessary in the territorial sea if less than 24 nautical miles separates two opposing coasts, as for instance between France and the United Kingdom in the English Channel/La Manche. States normally settle delimitation issues by bilateral agreement, but they may also elect to use other methods of peaceful dispute settlement.

This chapter provides examples of the diverse methods states use to delimit maritime boundaries, including both bilateral agreements and cases from arbitral tribunals, the International Court of Justice (ICJ), and the International Tribunal for the Law of the Sea (ITLOS). In Section A we consider the delimitation of the territorial sea. Because this zone remains limited in area, it has caused relatively little difficulty between states. We next address, in Section B, zones extending up to 200 nautical miles. Here, the use of one particular boundary line over another may affect who has jurisdiction over thousands of square nautical miles. Although numerous continental shelf and EEZ boundaries have already been settled, many others remain undefined. This situation has contributed to interstate tensions and has created uncertainties for private entities desiring to use the oceans or recover its resources. For example, unresolved boundaries in the South China Sea have contributed to tensions in the region. Finally, Section C deals with the delimitation of extended continental

 | DOI 10.1163/9789004203563_007

shelves, i.e., continental shelves beyond 200 nautical miles from baselines. Because these extended continental shelves may abut the Area, which is the common heritage of mankind, additional legal complexities arise.

States in general prefer diplomatic over juridical means when trying to settle their disputes in international law, and the settlement of maritime delimitation disputes fully confirms this general rule. Most maritime boundary disputes have been resolved through direct negotiations. Sections A and B each start out with one example of such a bilateral agreement, relating to the territorial sea and continental shelf respectively. However, the decisions of international judicial bodies have played a more significant role in developing the substantive law applicable to maritime delimitation than has state practice. Hence, despite the fact that delimitation agreements far outnumber maritime boundaries settled through third-party adjudication, most of the excerpts included in this chapter are from arbitral and judicial decisions.

A Territorial Sea

AGREEMENT BETWEEN THE KINGDOM OF BELGIUM AND THE FRENCH REPUBLIC CONCERNING THE DELIMITATION OF THE TERRITORIAL SEA

19 Law of the Sea Bull. 27 (1991)

The Government of the French Republic and the Government of the Kingdom of Belgium;

Desiring to establish the course of the line delimiting the territorial sea of the French Republic and that of the Kingdom of Belgium;

Desiring to take account of all the existing rules applicable to the delimitation of maritime spaces, with a view to arriving at an equitable solution;

Have agreed as follows:

Article 1

1. The boundary between the territorial sea of the French Republic and the territorial sea of the Kingdom of Belgium shall be a line composed of loxodromes connecting, in the sequence given, the points defined as follows by their coordinates:

	East longitude	North latitude
Point 1	02° 32' 37"	51° 05' 37"
Point 2	02° 23' 25"	51° 16' 09"

2. The coordinates of the points specified in paragraph 1 are defined on European Datum (1st Adjustment 1950).

3. The line defined in paragraph 1 has been drawn, for purposes of illustration only, on the map annexed to this Agreement.

Article 2

The points defined above have been determined by taking into account low-tide elevations at the approaches to the French and Belgian coasts. However, the application by France and Belgium of different methods for calculating the elevations has resulted in two different delineations. It has therefore been agreed that the area comprised within these two delineations shall be divided into two equal parts.

Article 3

Each Contracting Party shall notify the other of the completion of the constitutional procedures required for the entry into force of this Agreement. This Agreement shall enter into force on the date of receipt of the last notification.

IN WITNESS WHEREOF, the undersigned, duly authorized by their respective Governments, have signed this Agreement.

DONE at Brussels on 8 October 1990.

Notes

1. *Applicable Law.* What did the parties mean when in the preamble they stated that they intended to "take account of all the existing rules applicable to the delimitation of maritime spaces"? In order to answer that question, you need to know that when the 1990 Belgium-France Agreement was signed, only Belgium was a party to the 1958 Territorial Sea Convention, and neither state had accepted the LOS Convention. Article 12(1) of the 1958 Convention provides:

> Where the coasts of two States are opposite or adjacent to each other, neither of the two States is entitled, failing agreement between them to the contrary, to extend its territorial sea beyond the median line every point of which is equidistant from the nearest points on the baselines from which the breadth of the territorial seas of each of the two States is measured. The provisions of this paragraph shall not apply, however, where it is necessary by reason of historic title or other special circumstances to delimit the territorial seas of the two States in a way which is at variance with this provision.

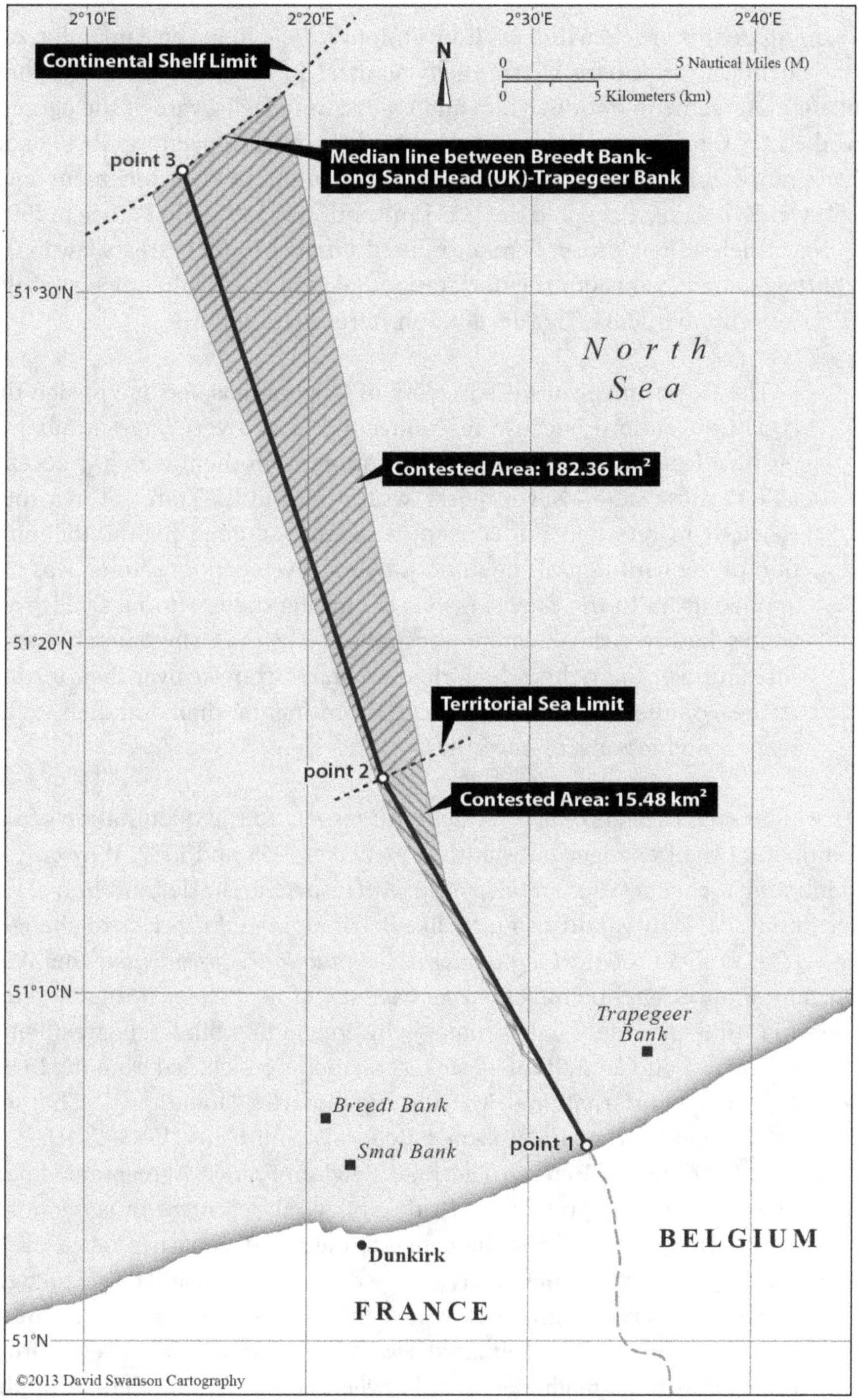

FIGURE VI.A *Belgium-France Territorial Sea and Continental Shelf Delimitation*

Compare this article with LOS Convention, Article 15 in the Appendix. Are they identical, or at least substantially similar? In 1990, when signing their bilateral Agreement, both Belgium and France were well aware of the content of the LOS Convention. Belgium had signed the LOS Convention in 1984, as had France in 1982. They both became legally bound by that document soon afterwards: Belgium accepted the LOS Convention in 1998, and France in 1996.

Nevertheless, Belgium and France refused simply to refer to treaty law in the 1990 Agreement. Consider the declaration Belgium made when it signed the LOS Convention in 1984. This declaration starts out as follows:

> The Government of the Kingdom of Belgium has decided to sign the [LOS Convention] because the Convention has a very large number of positive features and achieves a compromise on them which is acceptable to most States. Nevertheless, with regard to the status of maritime space, it regrets that the concept of equity, adopted for the delimitation of the continental shelf and the exclusive economic zone, was not applied again in the provisions for delimiting the territorial sea. It welcomes, however, the distinctions established by the Convention between the nature of the rights which riparian States exercise over their territorial sea, on the one hand, and over the continental shelf and their exclusive economic zone, on the other.

As will be seen in Section B, the rules with respect to the delimitation of the continental shelf changed substantially between 1958 and 1982. Why do you think similar changes did not take place with respect to the delimitation of the territorial sea? Why would a country like Belgium "regret" this lack of change?

2. *The Broader Context of Bilateral Delimitation Agreements*. The 1990 Belgium-France Agreement is but one example of how states normally settle their maritime boundary issues, namely by concluding bilateral agreements. For an overview and analysis of all such agreements concluded from the 1940s to date, see 1–6 International Maritime Boundaries (Jonathan I. Charney, Lewis M. Alexander, David A. Colson & Robert W. Smith eds., 1993–2011).

3. *The Delimitation Method*. The 1990 Belgium-France Agreement differs from the overwhelming majority of other bilateral delimitation agreements because it expressly mentions the concrete method the parties relied on to arrive at their maritime boundary. What are the advantages and disadvantages of indicating the exact manner in which the line was drawn? Even though the coast in the area to be delimited was rather rectilinear, it is clear from Figure VI.A that the straight segment between points 1 and 2 delimiting the territorial sea between the parties was not a line "*every point* of which is

equidistant from the nearest points on the baselines from which the breadth of the territorial seas of each of the two States is measured" (emphasis added), as provided in the 1958 Territorial Sea and LOS Conventions. The line, in other words, was not a true equidistant line, but a so-called simplified equidistant line where area compensation had been applied. May states diverge from the method provided in a treaty in force between them when settling their dispute by agreement?

4. *Importance of the Baseline for Delimitation.* This 1990 Agreement demonstrates how small differences with respect to the calculation of the low-water line can have major implications as far as maritime delimitation is concerned. In this situation, a 30-centimeter (approximately one-foot) dispute over the low-water line resulted in a disputed territorial sea area of about 15 square kilometers (5.8 square miles). The dispute derived from the fact that, according to Belgian charts, Trapegeer and Smal were the only existing low-tide elevations in the area, but according to the French charts Breedt also emerged at low tide. Read LOS Convention, Article 13 in the Appendix to fully appreciate the importance of low-tide elevations. This difference resulted from the fact that Belgium's low-water line was based on the local mean lower low-water, i.e., the mean of the lower of the two daily low waters, whereas the French relied on the lowest astronomical tide, i.e., a level, based on astronomical conditions that do not regularly recur, that is not reached every year. The French system, as a consequence, resulted in a low-water line that lies 30 centimeters below the actually measured daily low-water line relied on by Belgium. See Erik Franckx, Maritime Boundary Agreements: The Case of Belgium, 25 Belgian Rev. Intl. L. 390, 423–25 (1992).

B Exclusive Economic Zone and Continental Shelf

AGREEMENT BETWEEN THE KINGDOM OF BELGIUM AND THE FRENCH REPUBLIC CONCERNING THE DELIMITATION OF THE CONTINENTAL SHELF

19 Law of the Sea Bull. 29 (1991)

The Government of the French Republic and the Government of the Kingdom of Belgium;

Desiring to establish the course of the line delimiting the continental shelf between the French Republic and that of the Kingdom of Belgium;

Desiring to take account of all the existing rules applicable to the delimitation of maritime spaces, with a view to arriving at an equitable solution;

Have agreed as follows:

Article 1

1. The boundary between the continental shelf of the French Republic and the continental shelf of the Kingdom of Belgium shall be a line composed of loxodromes connecting[,] in the sequence given, the points defined as follows by their coordinates:

	East longitude	North latitude
Point 2	02° 23' 25"	51° 16' 09"
Point 3	02° 14' 18"	51° 33' 28"

2. The coordinates of the points specified in paragraph 1 are defined on European Datum (1st Adjustment 1950).

3. The line defined in paragraph 1 has been drawn, for purposes of illustration only, on the map annexed to this Agreement.

Article 2

The points defined above have been arrived at after an attempt to find an equitable solution on the basis mainly of a compromise between two assumptions, one taking into account the low-tide elevations at the approaches to the French and Belgian coasts, and one taking into account the low-water line of the coast.

Article 3

Each Contracting Party shall notify the other of the completion of the constitutional procedures required for the entry into force of this Agreement. This Agreement shall enter into force on the date of receipt of the last notification.

IN WITNESS WHEREOF, the undersigned, duly authorized by their respective Governments, have signed this Agreement.

DONE at Brussels on 8 October 1990.

Notes

1. *Applicable Law.* As explained in Note 1 following the 1990 Belgium-France Territorial Sea Delimitation Agreement, the treaty law relating to the delimitation of the territorial sea had remained essentially unchanged between the 1958 Territorial Sea Convention and the LOS Convention. By contrast,

as we will see in this section, the treaty rules concerning continental shelf delimitation had changed substantially between 1958 and 1990, when Belgium and France settled their continental shelf boundary. However, no treaty law applied between the parties. This time it was France that was a party to the relevant 1958 treaty—the Continental Shelf Convention—while Belgium was not. As of 1990, both countries had signed the LOS Convention, but neither was yet legally bound by it. Why did Belgium and France refer in their 1990 Continental Shelf Delimitation Agreement to "all the existing rules applicable to the delimitation of maritime spaces"? Did they have different motivations for including the same phrase in their Territorial Sea Agreement?

2. *Timing of the Bilateral Delimitation Agreements.* Belgium was the last country in the North Sea to delimit its maritime boundaries with its neighbors, namely France, the United Kingdom, and the Netherlands. The 1990 Belgium-France Continental Shelf Agreement, together with the Territorial Sea Delimitation Agreement concluded on the same day, were the first of these Belgian treaties. Why did it take so long, given the friendly relations between the parties, to arrive at a mutually acceptable solution? Why were Denmark, Norway, the Netherlands, and the United Kingdom, and even Germany with the help of the ICJ (see the North Sea Continental Shelf cases, excerpted below and in Chapter 1, Section B), able to reach agreements much earlier? Why, moreover, were maritime boundaries more completely constructed in the Baltic Sea by the early 1990s? The states concluding Baltic Sea maritime boundary delimitations included the Soviet Union, Soviet bloc states, and European states, even though the Baltic Sea region at that time was still the focal point of Cold War animosity.

3. *The Delimitation Method.* The bilateral 1990 Belgium-France Continental Shelf Agreement—like the 1990 Territorial Sea Agreement—is again special when compared to the overwhelming majority of other bilateral delimitation agreements, because it expressly mentions the concrete method the parties relied on to arrive at their maritime boundary. The reason provided in Article 2 is somewhat less specific than with respect to the territorial sea. It still mentions the different positions of the parties, but it no longer indicates precisely how the division of the disputed zone was to be effectuated. The basic position of the two parties was not the same in the two cases, for with respect to the continental shelf Belgium believed that the low-tide elevations should simply be ignored. The Continental Shelf Agreement did not divide the disputed area into two equal parts, as was the case with the territorial sea. Instead, the Continental Shelf Agreement only referred to "an attempt to find an equitable solution" without explaining why finally Belgium received four-fifths of the disputed area and France one-fifth. France insisted on relying on low-tide elevations in delimiting the continental shelf, but the compromise gave less

than full effect to these features. According to France's measurements, Breedt, located in front of the French coast, was ten centimeters above sea level, while Trapegeer, in front of the Belgian coast, was 40 centimeters above sea level. The parties therefore considered the ratio of one-to-four to be equitable in dividing the disputed continental shelf zone. See David Anderson, Belgium-France (Rpt. No. 9–16), in 2 International Maritime Boundaries 1891 (Jonathan I. Charney & Lewis M. Alexander eds., 1993); see also Erik Franckx, Maritime Boundary Agreements: The Case of Belgium, 25 Belgian Rev. Intl. L. 390, 429 (1992).

4. *Importance of the Baseline for Delimitation.* As we saw with respect to the territorial sea, a small difference in the low-water mark can markedly impact the maritime zones claimed by the parties. See Note 4 following the Belgium-France Territorial Sea Delimitation Agreement in Section A. The disputed zone generated by such a small difference at the baseline becomes dramatically larger as one moves farther out to sea. For Belgium and France, a difference of 30 centimeters with respect to the calculation of the low-water line resulted in a disputed area of about fifteen square kilometers in the territorial sea. With respect to the continental shelf the disputed area increased more than tenfold to about 182 square kilometers (approximately 70 square miles)—and this in an area where geography prohibits the parties from claiming a full 200-nautical-mile zone, much less a possible extended continental shelf, as discussed in Section C of this chapter and Chapter 10, Section C.

5. *Sequence of the Conclusion of Delimitation Agreements.* When states agree to delimit different maritime zones at the same time, an analysis of state practice reveals that they normally rely on one document. What explains this preference? Why did Belgium and France conclude two separate agreements, even though both agreements were treated as a single package, being concluded on the same day in 1990 and entering into force on the same day, namely April 7, 1993?

Of course, delimitation of different maritime zones does not always take place at the same time. The continental shelf notion predates that of the EEZ (compare Chapter 10, Section A with Chapter 9, Section A), and some states started delimiting their continental shelves before turning their attention to the EEZ. When Belgium and France concluded their 1990 Continental Shelf Agreement, neither state had proclaimed an EEZ, even though both states would soon accept the LOS Convention, which recognized the concept of the EEZ, and even though the ICJ had already stated that the EEZ had become part and parcel of customary international law (see Chapter 9, Section A). Belgium and France chose not to mention the EEZ at all, leaving those states with the potential need to delimit overlapping EEZs, should they be subsequently proclaimed. What options are available for states that do not want to return to the negotiating table at a later time?

NORTH SEA CONTINENTAL SHELF CASES

Federal Republic of Germany v. Denmark; Federal Republic of Germany v. Netherlands, 1969 I.C.J. 3

[In these two joined cases, the International Court of Justice was asked, by two Special Agreements, "[w]hat principles and rules of international law are applicable to the delimitation as between the Parties of the areas of the continental shelf in the North Sea which appertain to each of them," beyond partial boundaries that had been determined by previous agreement. Significant portions of these cases are reproduced in Chapter 1. For a map showing the previously agreed partial boundaries (lines A–B and C–D on the map) and the proposed boundaries argued by the parties, see Figure I.A. As noted in the excerpt from these cases in Chapter 1, the ICJ rejects a "just and equitable share" principle urged by the Federal Republic of Germany. The ICJ also finds that Article 6 of the 1958 Continental Shelf Convention is not binding on the parties as treaty law. Denmark and the Netherlands subsequently argue that, based on "*a priori* logical necessity" and on customary international law, an equidistance rule should be used to delimit the boundaries between Germany and Denmark, and between Germany and the Netherlands. The ICJ rejects those arguments.

The portions of the judgment reproduced below concern the principle of natural prolongation, some considerations applicable to the maritime boundary between opposite rather than adjacent states, the principle that the parties are obligated to negotiate with a view to arriving at an agreement, and the equitable principles that apply to the delimitation.]

43. More fundamental than the notion of proximity appears to be the principle—constantly relied upon by all the Parties—of the natural prolongation or continuation of the land territory or domain, or land sovereignty of the coastal State, into and under the high seas, via the bed of its territorial sea which is under the full sovereignty of that State. There are various ways of formulating this principle, but the underlying idea, namely of an extension of something already possessed, is the same, and it is this idea of extension which is, in the Court's opinion, determinant. Submarine areas do not really appertain to the coastal State because—or not only because—they are near it. They are near it of course; but this would not suffice to confer title, any more than, according to a well-established principle of law recognized by both sides in the present case, mere proximity confers *per se* title to land territory. What

confers the *ipso jure* title which international law attributes to the coastal State in respect of its continental shelf, is the fact that the submarine areas concerned may be deemed to be actually part of the territory over which the coastal State already has dominion,—in the sense that, although covered with water, they are a prolongation or continuation of that territory, an extension of it under the sea. From this it would follow that whenever a given submarine area does not constitute a natural—or the most natural—extension of the land territory of a coastal State, even though that area may be closer to it than it is to the territory of any other State, it cannot be regarded as appertaining to that State;—or at least it cannot be so regarded in the face of a competing claim by a State of whose land territory the submarine area concerned is to be regarded as a natural extension, even if it is less close to it.

44. In the present case, although both sides relied on the prolongation principle and regarded it as fundamental, they interpreted it quite differently. Both interpretations appear to the Court to be incorrect. Denmark and the Netherlands identified natural prolongation with closest proximity and therefrom argued that it called for an equidistance line: the Federal Republic seemed to think it implied the notion of the just and equitable share, although the connection is distinctly remote.... As regards equidistance, it clearly cannot be identified with the notion of natural prolongation or extension, since ... the use of the equidistance method would frequently cause areas which are the natural prolongation or extension of the territory of one State to be attributed to another, when the configuration of the latter's coast makes the equidistance line swing out laterally across the former's coastal front, cutting it off from areas situated directly before that front.

45. The fluidity of all these notions is well illustrated by the case of the Norwegian Trough.... Without attempting to pronounce on the status of that feature, the Court notes that the shelf areas in the North Sea separated from the Norwegian coast by the 80–100 kilometres of the Trough cannot in any physical sense be said to be adjacent to it, nor to be its natural prolongation. They are nevertheless considered by the States parties to the relevant delimitations ... to appertain to Norway up to the median lines.... True these median lines are themselves drawn on equidistance principles; but it was only by first ignoring the existence of the Trough that these median lines fell to be drawn at all.

46. The conclusion drawn by the Court from the foregoing analysis is that the notion of equidistance as being logically necessary, in the sense of being an inescapable *a priori* accompaniment of basic continental shelf doctrine, is incorrect.... The appurtenance of a given area, considered as an entity, in no way governs the precise delimitation of its boundaries, any more than

uncertainty as to boundaries can affect territorial rights. There is for instance no rule that the land frontiers of a State must be fully delimited and defined, and often in various places and for long periods they are not, as is shown by the case of the entry of Albania into the League of Nations (*Monastery of Saint Naoum, Advisory Opinion, 1924, P.C.I.J., Series B, No.* 9, at p. 10).

47. A review of the genesis and development of the equidistance method of delimitation can only serve to confirm the foregoing conclusion. Such a review may appropriately start with the instrument, generally known as the "Truman Proclamation," issued by the Government of the United States on 28 September 1945.... The Truman Proclamation ... soon came to be regarded as the starting point of the positive law on the subject, and the chief doctrine it enunciated, namely that of the coastal State as having an original, natural, and exclusive (in short a vested) right to the continental shelf off its shores, came to prevail over all others, being now reflected in Article 2 of the 1958 Geneva Convention on the Continental Shelf. With regard to the delimitation of lateral boundaries between the continental shelves of adjacent States, ... the Truman Proclamation stated that such boundaries "shall be determined by the United States and the State concerned in accordance with equitable principles." These two concepts, of delimitation by mutual agreement and delimitation in accordance with equitable principles, have underlain all the subsequent history of the subject....

[The ICJ surveys the work of the International Law Commission and a Committee of Experts in developing the equidistance/special circumstances principle. The ICJ concludes that an equidistance rule was not established by "*a priori* logical necessity" or any "inherent necessity of continental shelf doctrine."]

57. Before going further it will be convenient to deal briefly with two subsidiary matters. Most of the difficulties felt in the International Law Commission related, as here, to the case of the lateral boundary between adjacent States. Less difficulty was felt over that of the median line boundary between opposite States, although it too is an equidistance line. For this there seems to the Court to be good reason. The continental shelf area off, and dividing, opposite States, can be claimed by each of them to be a natural prolongation of its territory. These prolongations meet and overlap, and can therefore only be delimited by means of a median line; and, ignoring the presence of islets, rocks and minor coastal projections, the disproportionally distorting effect of which can be eliminated by other means, such a line must effect an equal division of the particular area involved.... This type of case is therefore different from that of laterally adjacent States on the same coast with no immediately opposite coast in front of it, and does not give rise to the same kind of problem....

58. [W]hereas a median line divides equally between the two opposite countries areas that can be regarded as being the natural prolongation of the territory of each of them, a lateral equidistance line often leaves to one of the States concerned areas that are a natural prolongation of the territory of the other. . . .

83. The legal situation therefore is that the Parties are under no obligation to apply either the 1958 Convention, which is not opposable to the Federal Republic, or the equidistance method as a mandatory rule of customary law, which it is not. But as between States faced with an issue concerning the lateral delimitation of adjacent continental shelves, there are still rules and principles of law to be applied. . . .

85. It emerges from the history of the development of the legal régime of the continental shelf, which has been reviewed earlier, that the essential reason why the equidistance method is not to be regarded as a rule of law is that, if it were to be compulsorily applied in all situations, this would not be consonant with certain basic legal notions which . . . have from the beginning reflected the *opinio juris* in the matter of delimitation; those principles being that delimitation must be the object of agreement between the States concerned, and that such agreement must be arrived at in accordance with equitable principles. On a foundation of very general precepts of justice and good faith, actual rules of law are here involved which govern the delimitation of adjacent continental shelves—that is to say, rules binding upon States for all delimitations;—in short, it is not a question of applying equity simply as a matter of abstract justice, but of applying a rule of law which itself requires the application of equitable principles, in accordance with the ideas which have always underlain the development of the legal régime of the continental shelf in this field, namely:

(*a*) the parties are under an obligation to enter into negotiations with a view to arriving at an agreement, and not merely to go through a formal process of negotiation as a sort of prior condition for automatic application of a certain method of delimitation in the absence of agreement; they are under an obligation so to conduct themselves that the negotiations are meaningful, which will not be the case when either of them insists upon its own position without contemplating any modification of it;

(*b*) the parties are under an obligation to act in such a way that, in the particular case, and taking all the circumstances into account, equitable principles are applied,—for this purpose the equidistance method can be used, but other methods exist and may be employed, alone or in combination, according to the areas involved;

(*c*) for the reasons given in paragraph 43 and 44, the continental shelf of any State must be the natural prolongation of its land territory and must not encroach upon what is the natural prolongation of the territory of another State.

86. It is now necessary to examine these rules more closely, as also certain problems relative to their application. So far as the first rule is concerned, the Court would recall not only that the obligation to negotiate which the Parties assumed by Article 1, paragraph 2, of the Special Agreements ... merely constitutes a special application of a principle which underlies all international relations, and which is moreover recognized in Article 33 of the Charter of the United Nations as one of the methods for the peaceful settlement of international disputes....

87. As the Permanent Court of International Justice said in its Order of 19 August 1929 in the case of the *Free Zones of Upper Savoy and the District of Gex*, the judicial settlement of international disputes "is simply an alternative to the direct and friendly settlement of such disputes between the parties" (*P.C.I.J., Series A, No. 22*, at p. 13). Defining the content of the obligation to negotiate, the Permanent Court, in its Advisory Opinion in the case of *Railway Traffic between Lithuania and Poland*, said that the obligation was "not only to enter into negotiations but also to pursue them as far as possible with a view to concluding agreements," even if an obligation to negotiate did not imply an obligation to reach agreement (*P.C.I.J., Series A/B, No. 42*, 1931, at p. 116). In the present case, it needs to be observed that whatever the details of the negotiations carried on in 1965 and 1966, they failed of their purpose because the Kingdoms of Denmark and the Netherlands, convinced that the equidistance principle alone was applicable, in consequence of a rule binding upon the Federal Republic, saw no reason to depart from that rule; and equally, given the geographical considerations ..., the Federal Republic could not accept the situation resulting from the application of that rule. So far therefore the negotiations have not satisfied the conditions indicated in paragraph 85(*a*), but fresh negotiations are to take place on the basis of the present Judgment.

88. The Court comes next to the rule of equity....

89. [I]n certain geographical circumstances which are quite frequently met with, the equidistance method, despite its known advantages, leads unquestionably to inequity, in the following sense:

(*a*) The slightest irregularity in a coastline is automatically magnified by the equidistance line as regards the consequences for the delimitation of the continental shelf. Thus it has been seen in the case of concave or convex coastlines that if the equidistance method is employed, then the greater the irregularity and the further from the coastline the area to be delimited, the more unreasonable are the results produced. So great an exaggeration of the consequences of a natural geographical feature must be remedied or compensated for as far as possible, being of itself creative of inequity.

(*b*) In the case of the North Sea in particular, where there is no outer boundary to the continental shelf, it happens that the claims of several States converge, meet and intercross in localities where, despite their distance from the coast, the bed of the sea still unquestionably consists of continental shelf. A study of these convergences, as revealed by the maps, shows how inequitable would be the apparent simplification brought about by a delimitation which, ignoring such geographical circumstances, was based solely on the equidistance method.

90. If for the above reasons equity excludes the use of the equidistance method in the present instance, as the sole method of delimitation, the question arises whether there is any necessity to employ only one method for the purposes of a given delimitation. There is no logical basis for this. [T]he international law of continental shelf delimitation does not involve any imperative rule and permits resort to various principles or methods, as may be appropriate, or a combination of them, provided that, by the application of equitable principles, a reasonable result is arrived at.

91. Equity does not necessarily imply equality. There can never be any question of completely refashioning nature, and equity does not require that a State without access to the sea should be allotted an area of continental shelf, any more than there could be a question of rendering the situation of a State with an extensive coastline similar to that of a State with a restricted coastline. Equality is to be reckoned within the same plane, and it is not such natural inequalities as these that equity could remedy. But in the present case there are three States whose North Sea coastlines are in fact comparable in length and which, therefore, have been given broadly equal treatment by nature except that the configuration of one of the coastlines would, if the equidistance method is used, deny to one of these States treatment equal or comparable to that given the other two. Here indeed is a case where, in a theoretical situation of equality within the same order, an inequity is created. What is unacceptable in this instance is that a State should enjoy continental shelf rights considerably different from those of its neighbours merely because in the one case the coastline is roughly convex in form and in the other it is markedly concave, although those coastlines are comparable in length. It is therefore not a question of totally refashioning geography whatever the facts of the situation but, given a geographical situation of quasi-equality as between a number of States,

of abating the effects of an incidental special feature from which an unjustifiable difference of treatment could result.

92. [T]he problem above all [is] one of defining the means whereby the delimitation can be carried out in such a way as to be recognized as equitable. Although the Parties have made it known that they intend to reserve for themselves the application of the principles and rules laid down by the Court, it would, even so, be insufficient simply to rely on the rule of equity without giving some degree of indication as to the possible ways in which it might be applied in the present case, it being understood that the Parties will be free to agree upon one method rather than another, or different methods if they so prefer.

93. In fact, there is no legal limit to the considerations which States may take account of for the purpose of making sure that they apply equitable procedures, and more often than not it is the balancing-up of all such considerations that will produce this result rather than reliance on one to the exclusion of all others. The problem of the relative weight to be accorded to different considerations naturally varies with the circumstances of the case.

94. In balancing the factors in question it would appear that various aspects must be taken into account. Some are related to the geological, others to the geographical aspect of the situation, others again to the idea of the unity of any deposits. These criteria, though not entirely precise, can provide adequate bases for decision adapted to the factual situation.

95. The institution of the continental shelf has arisen out of the recognition of a physical fact; and the link between this fact and the law, without which that institution would never have existed, remains an important element for the application of its legal régime. The continental shelf is, by definition, an area physically extending the territory of most coastal States into a species of platform which has attracted the attention first of geographers and hydrographers and then of jurists. The importance of the geological aspect is emphasized by the care which, at the beginning of its investigation, the International Law Commission took to acquire exact information as to its characteristics, as can be seen in particular from the definitions to be found on page 131 of Volume I of the *Yearbook of the International Law Commission* for 1956. The appurtenance of the shelf to the countries in front of whose coastlines it lies, is therefore a fact, and it can be useful to consider the geology of that shelf in order to find out whether the direction taken by certain configurational features should influence delimitation because, in certain localities, they point-up the whole notion of the appurtenance of the continental shelf to the State whose territory it does in fact prolong.

96. The doctrine of the continental shelf is a recent instance of encroachment on maritime expanses which, during the greater part of history, appertained to no-one. [T]he principle is applied that the land dominates the sea; it is consequently necessary to examine closely the geographical configuration of the coastlines of the countries whose continental shelves are to be delimited. This is one of the reasons why the Court does not consider that markedly pronounced configurations can be ignored; for, since the land is the legal source of the power which a State may exercise over territorial extensions to seaward, it must first be clearly established what features do in fact constitute such extensions. . . .

97. Another factor to be taken into consideration in the delimitation of areas of continental shelf as between adjacent States is the unity of any deposits. The natural resources of the subsoil of the sea in those parts which consist of continental shelf are the very object of the legal régime established subsequent to the Truman Proclamation. Yet it frequently occurs that the same deposit lies on both sides of the line dividing a continental shelf between two States, and since it is possible to exploit such a deposit from either side, a problem immediately arises on account of the risk of prejudicial or wasteful exploitation by one or other of the States concerned. To look no farther than the North Sea, the practice of States shows how this problem has been dealt with, and all that is needed is to refer to the undertakings entered into by the coastal States of that sea with a view to ensuring the most efficient exploitation or the apportionment of the products extracted. . . . The Court does not consider that unity of deposit constitutes anything more than a factual element which it is reasonable to take into consideration in the course of the negotiations for a delimitation. The Parties are fully aware of the existence of the problem as also of the possible ways of solving it.

98. A final factor to be taken account of is the element of a reasonable degree of proportionality which a delimitation effected according to equitable principles ought to bring about between the extent of the continental shelf appertaining to the States concerned and the lengths of their respective coastlines,—these being measured according to their general direction in order to establish the necessary balance between States with straight, and those with markedly concave or convex coasts, or to reduce very irregular coastlines to their truer proportions. The choice and application of the appropriate technical methods would be a matter for the parties. One method . . . consists in drawing a straight baseline between the extreme points at either end of the coast concerned, or in some cases a series of such lines. Where the parties wish to employ in particular the equidistance method of delimitation, the establishment

of one or more baselines of this kind can play a useful part in eliminating or diminishing the distortions that might result from the use of that method.

99. In a sea with the particular configuration of the North Sea, and in view of the particular geographical situation of the Parties' coastlines upon that sea, the methods chosen by them for the purpose of fixing the delimitation of their respective areas may happen in certain localities to lead to an overlapping of the areas appertaining to them. The Court considers that such a situation must be accepted as a given fact and resolved either by an agreed, or failing that by an equal division of the overlapping areas, or by agreements for joint exploitation, the latter solution appearing particularly appropriate when it is a question of preserving the unity of a deposit....

101. For these reasons,

THE COURT,
by eleven votes to six,
finds that, in each case,

(A) the use of the equidistance method of delimitation not being obligatory as between the Parties; and

(B) there being no other single method of delimitation the use of which is in all circumstances obligatory;

(C) the principles and rules of international law applicable to the delimitation as between the Parties of the areas of the continental shelf in the North Sea which appertain to each of them beyond the partial boundary determined by the agreements of 1 December 1964 and 9 June 1965, respectively, are as follows:

(1) delimitation is to be effected by agreement in accordance with equitable principles, and taking account of all the relevant circumstances, in such a way as to leave as much as possible to each Party all those parts of the continental shelf that constitute a natural prolongation of its land territory into and under the sea, without encroachment on the natural prolongation of the land territory of the other;

(2) if, in the application of the preceding sub-paragraph, the delimitation leaves to the Parties areas that overlap, these are to be divided between them in agreed proportions or, failing agreement, equally, unless they decide on a régime of joint jurisdiction, user, or exploitation for the zones of overlap or any part of them;

(D) in the course of the negotiations, the factors to be taken into account are to include:

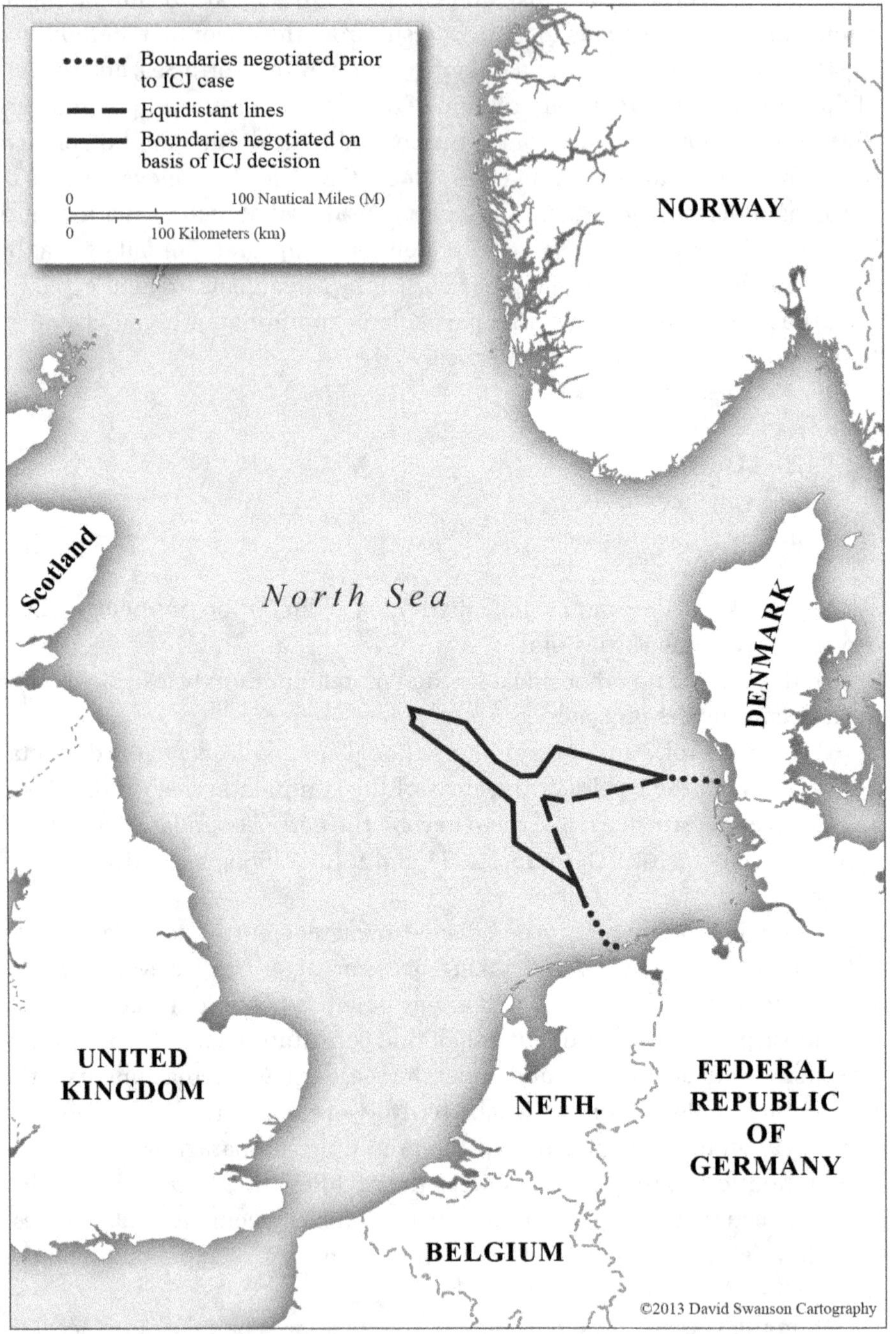

FIGURE VI.B *Negotiated Boundaries Following the ICJ's Decision in the North Sea Continental Shelf Cases*

(1) the general configuration of the coasts of the Parties, as well as the presence of any special or unusual features;

(2) so far as known or readily ascertainable, the physical and geological structure, and natural resources, of the continental shelf areas involved;

(3) the element of a reasonable degree of proportionality, which a delimitation carried out in accordance with equitable principles ought to bring about between the extent of the continental shelf areas appertaining to the coastal State and the length of its coast measured in the general direction of the coastline, account being taken for this purpose of the effects, actual or prospective, of any other continental shelf delimitations between adjacent States in the same region.

Notes

1. *Applicable Law*. As already discussed in Chapter 1, Section B, Note 2 following the North Sea Continental Shelf cases, Article 6(2) of the 1958 Continental Shelf Convention relating to the delimitation between adjacent states neither codified preexisting customary law, helped to crystallize it, or contributed to the development of the custom after the Convention was concluded and had entered into force. Article 6 reads in full:

> 1. Where the same continental shelf is adjacent to the territories of two or more States whose coasts are opposite each other, the boundary of the continental shelf appertaining to such States shall be determined by agreement between them. In the absence of agreement, and unless another boundary line is justified by special circumstances, the boundary is the median line, every point of which is equidistant from the nearest points of the baselines from which the breadth of the territorial sea of each State is measured.
>
> 2. Where the same continental shelf is adjacent to the territories of two adjacent States, the boundary of the continental shelf shall be determined by agreement between them. In the absence of agreement, and unless another boundary line is justified by special circumstances, the boundary shall be determined by application of the principle of equidistance from the nearest points of the baselines from which the breadth of the territorial sea of each State is measured.
>
> 3. In delimiting the boundaries of the continental shelf, any lines which are drawn in accordance with the principles set out in paragraphs 1 and 2 of this article should be defined with reference to charts and geographical features as they exist at a particular date, and reference should be made to fixed permanent identifiable points on the land.

How does this rule compare to the rule in the 1958 Territorial Sea Convention for delimiting the territorial sea? See Note 1 following the 1990 Belgium-France Territorial Sea Delimitation Agreement in Section A. While the territorial sea delimitation rule in the 1958 Territorial Sea Convention was carried over to the LOS Convention, Article 6 of the 1958 Continental Shelf Convention was not. Read LOS Convention, Article 83 in the Appendix. If the delimitation of the continental shelf in 1969 was governed neither by treaty law nor by customary international law, on what did the ICJ base its legal reasoning?

2. *The International Court's Advisory Function.* The North Sea Continental Shelf cases were contentious cases, in which the ICJ's jurisdiction was based on Article 36 of its Statute. The ICJ may also render advisory opinions on any legal question when the U.N. General Assembly or Security Council (or another U.N. organ or specialized agency authorized by the General Assembly to request an advisory opinion) so requests. See U.N. Charter, Article 96; ICJ Statute, Article 65. Nevertheless, the ICJ in the North Sea judgment seemed to fulfill an advisory or declaratory judgment function, in light of the parties' desire to continue negotiations concerning the precise delimitation of the continental shelf boundary.

3. *Boundary Agreements between the Parties to the Dispute following the North Sea Judgment.* The three countries reached agreement on the delimitation of their continental shelves in January 1971. 1971 Protocol between Denmark, the Federal Republic of Germany and the Netherlands; 1971 Federal Republic of Germany-Denmark North Sea Continental Shelf Delimitation Treaty; and 1971 Federal Republic of Germany-Netherlands North Sea Continental Shelf Treaty. See Figure VI.B, showing the agreed boundaries, along with the difference between them and the equidistance line boundaries. The final result was a highly irregular delimitation line. In German this line has been called the "Entenschnabel" (beak of a duck), which, with some imagination, it resembles. The irregularity in the negotiated line is explained by the decision to leave undisturbed certain Danish licensees on the Danish side of the line. Rainer Lagoni, Oil and Gas Deposits across National Frontiers, 73 Am. J. Intl. L. 215, 241–42 (1979).

4. *Boundary Agreements in the North Sea Region following the North Sea Judgment.* The North Sea Continental Shelf cases had a major impact on the development of legal conceptions about the continental shelf. See Chapter 10. The cases also influenced the regional practice of states surrounding the North Sea. If prior to this decision bilateral agreements had been guided by the strict equidistance rule, afterwards "[a]ll the agreements were based to a greater or lesser extent upon equitable principles other than equidistance." David

Anderson, Region IX: Northern and Western European Maritime Boundaries, in 1 International Maritime Boundaries 331, 335 (Jonathan I. Charney & Lewis M. Alexander eds., 1993). Do the territorial sea and continental shelf agreements concluded between Belgium and France, discussed above, confirm this trend?

5. *The Land Dominates the Sea.* The ICJ emphasized a basic premise of the international law of the sea: the land dominates the sea. In what other context had the ICJ already relied on this foundational concept?

With respect to the continental shelf, the principle that the land dominates the sea may relate either to geography or geology. In the North Sea Continental Shelf cases the ICJ explicitly relied on this principle when discussing geography. See ¶ 96. After having dismissed the application of the principle of equidistance between adjacent states, what geographical factor did the ICJ finally invoke to help guide the parties in how to resolve their maritime delimitation dispute? Explain in this context what the ICJ meant by its statement: "Equity does not necessarily imply equality." Instead of using the equidistance/special circumstances rule of Article 6 of the 1958 Continental Shelf Convention, which did not apply to the parties either as treaty law or as customary international law, the ICJ relied instead on the equity/relevant circumstances principle. Is there any substantial difference in content?

As far as the geological dimension was concerned, the ICJ relied on the premise that the land dominates the sea, without explicitly mentioning it, to justify its view that the continental shelf is the natural prolongation of the land territory. Although the 1958 Continental Shelf Convention does not even mention the notion of natural prolongation, it figures prominently in the LOS Convention's definition of the continental shelf. Read LOS Convention, Article 76(1) in the Appendix. To use the words of the ICJ itself in a later decision, it was its decision in the 1969 North Sea Continental Shelf cases that "gave currency to the expression 'natural prolongation' as part of the vocabulary of the international law of the sea." Tunisia/Libya Continental Shelf Case, 1982 I.C.J. 46, ¶ 43. As the later readings in this chapter will demonstrate, the notion of "natural prolongation" in maritime delimitation cases has had a checkered history. The major role this notion still seems to play with respect to the continental shelf is not so much related to delimitation, discussed in this chapter, but rather to appurtenance beyond 200 nautical miles (see Chapter 10, Section C).

6. *Opposite and Adjacent States.* In paragraphs 57–58 of its decision in the North Sea Continental Shelf cases, the ICJ considered briefly whether similar procedures should apply in drawing boundaries between opposite and

adjacent states. Initially, Mr. François, Special Rapporteur, proposed different regimes for adjacent and opposite coasts. Second Report to the International Law Commission, 1951–2 Y.B. Intl. L. Commn. 75, 103. For adjacent states, Mr. François recommended prolongation of the territorial sea boundary. For opposite states, he recommended a median line rule. Read the text of Article 6 of the 1958 Continental Shelf Convention set forth in Note 1 above. Is there a difference between applying a median line as called for in Article 6(1) of the 1958 Convention and applying an equidistant line under Article 6(2) of the 1958 Convention? The court of arbitration in the 1977 France/United Kingdom Arbitration pronounced, in paragraph 95, the following dictum on the matter:

> [T]he distinction drawn by the Court [in the North Sea Continental Shelf cases] between the two geographical situations is one derived not from any legal theory but from the very substance of the difference between the two situations. Whereas in the case of "opposite" States a median line will normally affect a broadly equitable delimitation, a lateral equidistance line extending outwards from the coasts of adjacent States for long distances may not infrequently result in an inequitable delimitation by reason of the distorting effect of individual geographical features. In short, it is the combined effect of the side-by-side relationship of the two States and the prolongation of the lateral boundary for great distances to seawards which may be productive of inequity and is the essence of the distinction between "adjacent" and "opposite" coasts situations.

18 Intl. Leg. Materials 397, 426 (1979). Belgium and France are examples of adjacent states where the application of a lateral equidistant line could easily have resulted in an inequitable delimitation because of the distorting effect of low-tide elevations in the vicinity of the coast. See the 1990 Belgium-France Territorial Sea Delimitation Agreement in Section A and the 1990 Belgium-France Continental Shelf Delimitation Agreement in this Section B.

7. *Joint Development Zones.* In paragraph 99 of its judgment, the ICJ noted that states may agree on joint development zones to provide for equitable access to living or nonliving resources. A joint development zone may be concluded with or without delimiting a maritime boundary that cuts through the zone. What are the advantages and disadvantages of negotiating a joint development zone without agreeing on a maritime boundary? See D.H. Anderson, Strategies for Dispute Resolution: Negotiating Joint Arrangements, in Boundaries and Energy: Problems and Prospects 473 (Gerard Blake et al. eds., 1998).

CONTINENTAL SHELF BOUNDARY ARBITRATION BETWEEN FRANCE AND THE UNITED KINGDOM

18 Intl. Leg. Materials 397 (1979)

[The elaborate decision of the tribunal in the France/United Kingdom arbitration was rendered on June 30, 1977. The following excerpts focus particularly on the legal and equitable standards that govern this delimitation of a maritime boundary between non-adjacent states and on the influence of islands on the location of the maritime boundary.

This arbitration concerns the proper delimitation between France and the United Kingdom of the continental shelf from a point in the eastern section of the English Channel/La Manche westward to the 1000-meter isobath, which is located some 175 nautical miles west of the end of the Brittany peninsula. The area in question is shown in Figure VI.C. The entire seabed area between the British and French coasts is substantially less than 200 meters (656 feet) deep. The parties agreed—except with respect to a minor geological question, which did not figure in the decision—that the seabed area between the two states constitutes a single continuous geographic unit. At the extreme eastern end of the Channel, the coasts of the two states are separated by less than twenty nautical miles of water; in its western reaches the Channel is almost 130 nautical miles across. Near the French coast are several small groups of islands, including the Channel Islands group centering on the Guernsey and Jersey Islands. The Channel Islands are British dependencies; some of their smaller islands are less than seven nautical miles from the French coast.

The two states found in 1975 that they were unable to agree on the proper boundary throughout this entire region. On July 10, 1975, they entered into a special agreement (compromis) by which the matter was submitted to a court of arbitration. The U.K. government appointed Sir Humphrey Waldock as its member, and the French government appointed Paul Reuter, who was later replaced by André Gros. Three other judges were appointed jointly: Herbert Briggs, Endre Ustov, and Erik Castren, who served as President.

The court gives detailed consideration to the question of applicable law. It finds that the effect of a French reservation to the 1958 Continental Shelf Convention, combined with the British rejection of that reservation, is to exclude the Channel Islands region from the Convention's application. In this region the boundary "must accordingly be determined by reference to the rules of customary law." ¶ 74. As to the rest of the disputed area, the court finds that Article 6 of the 1958 Continental Shelf Convention applies "in principle," stating

> 75. ... This does not, however, mean that the Court considers the rules of customary law discussed in the judgment in the *North Sea Continental Shelf* cases to be inapplicable in the present case. [T]he provisions of Article 6 [of the 1958 Convention] do not define the conditions for the application of the equidistance-special circumstances rule; moreover, the equidistance-special circumstances rule and the rules of customary law have the same object—the delimitation of the boundary in accordance with equitable principles. In the view of this Court, therefore, the rules of customary law are a relevant and even essential means both for interpreting and completing the provisions of Article 6.

In making this finding, the court considers that "it should take due account of the evolution of the law of the sea" since 1958. ¶ 48. In elaborating these applicable principles of law, the court finds in general that customary international law and the 1958 Continental Shelf Convention tend to lead to the same conclusion.]

97. [T]he appropriateness of the equidistance method or any other method for the purpose of effecting an equitable delimitation is a function or reflection of the geographical and other relevant circumstances of each particular case. The choice of the method or methods of delimitation in any given case, whether under the 1958 Convention or customary law, has therefore to be determined in the light of those circumstances and of the fundamental norm that the delimitation must be in accordance with equitable principles. Furthermore, in appreciating the appropriateness of the equidistance method as a means of achieving an equitable solution, regard must be had to the difference between a "lateral" boundary between "adjacent" States and a "median" boundary between "opposite" States.

[The court points out that the notion of "proportionality" has a place in equitable delimitation, but not with reference to any particular geographical feature such as length of coastline. Instead, proportionality is introduced to determine whether, by the application of equidistance, a distortion results that produces inequity or "disproportion" under all relevant circumstances.

The court then considers the three principal points in dispute. First, it decides to give full weight, in drawing the median line through the Channel, to the Eddystone Rocks located eight nautical miles from the the British coast. These uninhabited elevations, including one on which a 51.2-meter-high lighthouse is located, are submerged at spring high tides twice a year.]

139. The Court emphasizes that it is not concerned in these proceedings to decide the general question of the legal status of the Eddystone Rocks as

an island or of its entitlement to a territorial sea of its own. Indeed, ... the Arbitration Agreement does not invest it with competence to resolve differences between the Parties regarding the delimitation of the territorial sea of either of them. In the present proceedings the Court is concerned with the Eddystone Rocks only as an element in the delimitation of the continental shelf boundary in the English Channel. Thus, what the Court is called upon to decide is not the general question of their legal status as an island but their relevance in the delimitation of the median line in the Channel as between the United Kingdom and the French Republic. No doubt, having regard to the role normally played by the baseline of the territorial sea in the delimitation of a median line, there is a certain connexion between the two questions. But it still remains true that the Court is here concerned with the Eddystone Rocks only in the particular context of the delimitation of the continental shelf by a median line in the Channel as between the Parties now before the Court....

143. The Eddystone Rock, as is confirmed by the Court's own expert, was treated as relevant to the delimitation of the median line in the Channel in 1971. Consequently, the French Government's statement, that it has never accepted "officiellement" the coordinates communicated to it so far as concerns the use of Eddystone Rock, does not seem to the Court sufficient to counterbalance the evidence of its use in 1971 by both Parties. This evidence is, moreover, reinforced by the French Government's earlier acceptance of the relevance of the Eddystone Rock in the delimitation of the United Kingdom's fishery limits. In these circumstances, the Court need not examine the further question, indicated by the United Kingdom, of the possible relevance of the right which it claims to establish a 12-mile territorial sea that would bring Eddystone within the territorial sea of England.

144. In the light of all the foregoing considerations and without taking any position on the difference between the Parties as to the precise legal status of Eddystone Rock, the Court concludes that it should treat the Rock as a relevant base-point for delimiting the continental shelf boundary in the Channel.

[The second point concerns the effect to be given to the British Channel Islands near the French coast:]

194. The true position, in the opinion of the Court, is that the principle of natural prolongation of territory is neither to be set aside nor treated as absolute in a case where islands belonging to one State are situated on continental shelf which would otherwise constitute a natural prolongation of the territory of another State. The application of that principle in such a case, as in other cases concerning the delimitation of the continental shelf, has to be appreciated in the light of all the relevant geographical and other circumstances....

195. ... In other words, the question is whether the Channel Islands should be given the full benefit of the application of the principle of natural prolongation in the areas to their north and north-west or whether their situation close to the mainland of France requires, on equitable grounds, some modification of the application of the principle in those areas.... Any ground of equity, the Court considers, is... to be looked for in the particular circumstances of the present case and in the particular equality of the two States in their geographical relation to the continental shelf of the Channel.

196. [T]he Court... draw[s] attention to the approximate equality of the mainland coastlines of the Parties on either side of the English Channel, and to the resulting equality of their geographical relation to the continental shelf of the Channel, if the Channel Islands themselves are left out of account. The presence of these British islands close to the French coast, if they are given full effect in delimiting the continental shelf, will manifestly result in a substantial diminution of the area of continental shelf which would otherwise accrue to the French Republic. This fact by itself appears to the Court to be, *prima facie*, a circumstance creative of inequity and calling for a method of delimitation that in some measure redresses the inequity. If this conclusion is tested by applying the equidistance-special circumstances rule of Article 6, instead of the rules of customary law, it appears to the Court that the presence of the Channel Islands close to the French coast must be considered, *prima facie*, as constituting a "special circumstance" justifying a delimitation other than the median line proposed by the United Kingdom.

[As a result, the court draws the principal line equidistant between the two mainland coasts—as if the islands were not there. The islands themselves are then given twelve-mile shelf "enclaves" within the French shelf. As the court is empowered only to delimit the continental shelves between the two states, and as the area between the islands and the French coast consisted entirely of the territorial seas of the two parties, the court refrains from drawing the line between the islands and the French mainland and draws only a twelve-mile line on the seaward side of the islands.

The third principal issue is the delimitation in the Atlantic Ocean, west of the Channel. Here the question comes down to the weight to be given to the Scilly Isles, a group off the southwest tip of England. The court reaches this question after rejecting arguments for employing methods other than equidistance in this area.]

249. [I]t seems to the Court to be in accord not only with the legal rules governing the continental shelf but also with State practice to seek the solution in a method modifying or varying the equidistance method rather than to have recourse to a wholly different criterion of delimitation. The appropriate

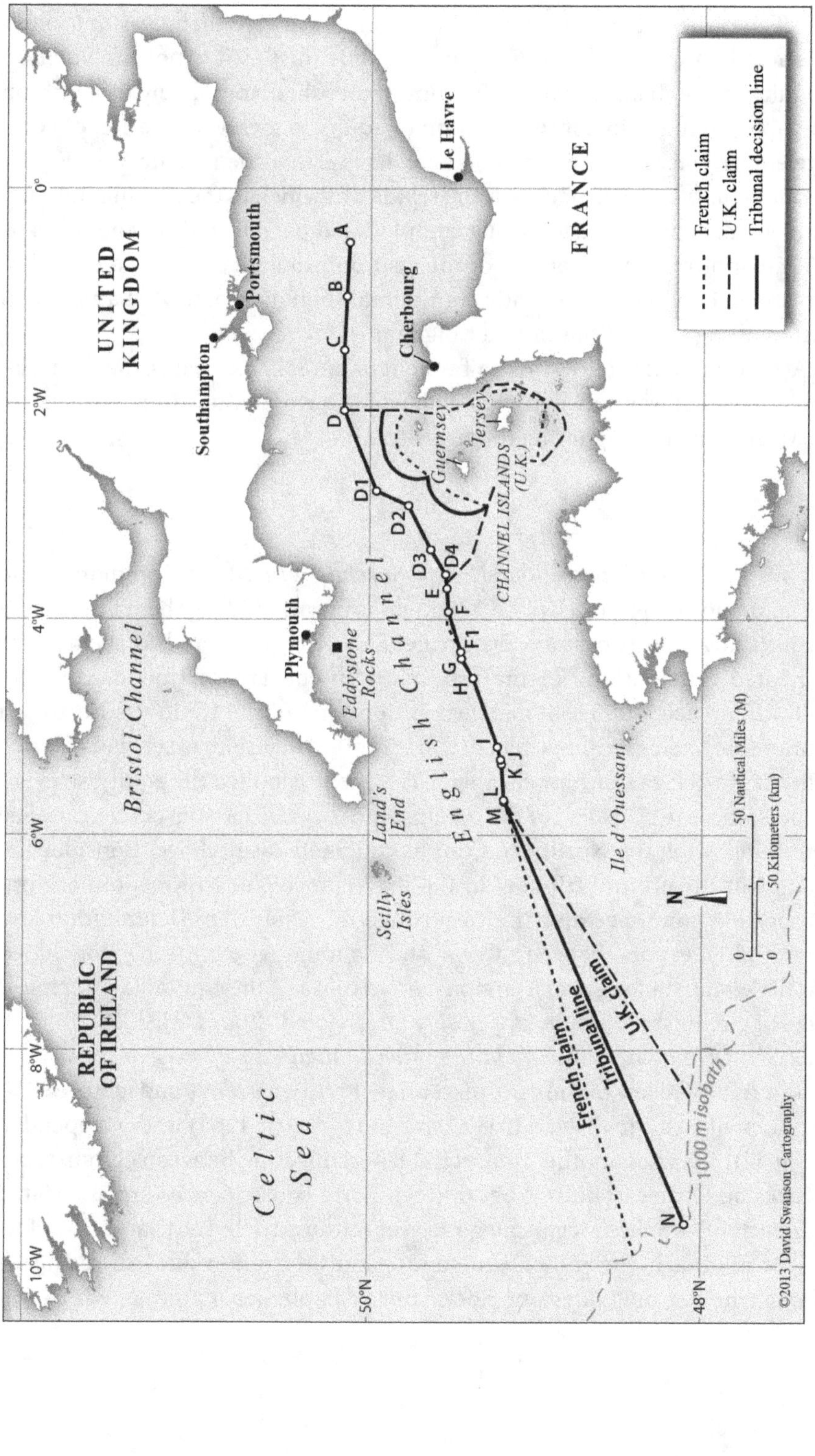

FIGURE VI.C *France/United Kingdom Continental Shelf Delimitation*

method, in the opinion of the Court, is to take account of the Scilly Isles as part of the coastline of the United Kingdom but to give them less than their full effect in applying the equidistance method. Just as it is not the function of equity in the delimitation of the continental shelf completely to refashion geography, so it is also not the function of equity to create a situation of complete equity where nature and geography have established an inequity. Equity does not, therefore, call for coasts, the relation of which to the continental shelf is not equal, to be treated as having completely equal effects. What equity calls for is an appropriate abatement of the disproportionate effects of a considerable projection on to the Atlantic continental shelf of a somewhat attenuated portion of the coast of the United Kingdom.

[Accordingly, the court gives half weight to the Scillies. That is, the delimitation is made halfway between a line that would have resulted from giving them full weight and a line ignoring them entirely.]

Notes

1. *Does the Equidistance Rule Have a Special Status?* In the opinion of the arbitrators in the France/United Kingdom arbitration, does the equidistance rule have any priority over any other rule? Should opposite and adjacent states be treated differently? Did the arbitrators in the France/United Kingdom arbitration reach a different conclusion from that of the ICJ in the North Sea Continental Shelf cases? See paragraph 75 of that decision, excerpted above.

In the North Sea Continental Shelf cases the ICJ applied the equity/relevant circumstances rule instead of the equidistance/special circumstances rule. See Note 5 following the North Sea Continental Shelf cases above. Consider the remarks of the arbitral tribunal in the 1977 France/United Kingdom arbitration on this point. See also the case concerning Maritime Delimitation and Territorial Questions between Qatar and Bahrain, where the ICJ concluded that the equidistance/special circumstances rule and the equitable principles/relevant circumstances rule "are closely interrelated." 2001 I.C.J. 40, ¶ 231.

2. *The Definition of Islands in the International Law of the Sea.* How does the international law of the sea differentiate between islands and features that do not qualify as such? Read LOS Convention, Article 121(1) in the Appendix. Article 121(3) makes another important distinction: that between certain types of rocks and other islands. What different legal consequences are associated with each of the three legal categories set out in Article 121(1) and (3)? How was the tribunal in the France/United Kingdom arbitration able to avoid determining whether the Eddystone Rocks, the exact physical nature of which was

highly contested between the parties, were able to generate their own territorial sea?

Was there a difference, according to the court, between the baselines from which the territorial sea is measured, as discussed in Chapter 5, and base points that serve as starting points for measuring a maritime delimitation line? If states can contest a baseline that has been drawn contrary to the applicable rules of international law as discussed in Chapter 5, Section B, can third states also contest a bilateral delimitation agreement based on a base point located on such a contested baseline? Does one need to distinguish between (a) a bilateral delimitation line dividing an area that would otherwise be beyond twice the permissible limits of the zone to be delimited and (b) a line that does not extend jurisdiction beyond such limit? See Louis B. Sohn, Baseline Considerations, in 1 International Maritime Boundaries 153, 156 (Jonathan I. Charney & Lewis M. Alexander eds., 1993).

3. *The Role of Islands in Maritime Delimitation.* Leaving aside the exact status of the Eddystone Rocks, the France/United Kingdom arbitration was very much centered around the effect to be given to islands in a maritime delimitation. No single rule of international law sets out the exact effect to be given to islands. Much will depend on the particular characteristics of the islands in question, including their location in the area to be delimited. States normally solve such issues by concluding bilateral delimitation agreements. Only in about ten percent of disputes involving islands do direct negotiations lead to a stalemate, with states submitting their dispute to third-party settlement. Victor Prescott & Gillian Triggs, Islands and Rocks and their Role in Maritime Delimitation, in 5 International Maritime Boundaries 3245, 3279 (David A. Colson & Robert W. Smith eds., 2005). After a meticulous analysis, Derek Bowett concluded, with respect to islands: "The situations are so diverse that generalizations are hazardous, and to attempt to postulate 'rules' would be to fall into the error which the courts have persistently, and rightly, avoided. The most that can be done is to identify certain tendencies in state practice." Derek Bowett, Islands, Rocks, Reefs, and Low-tide Elevations in Maritime Boundary Delimitations, in 1 International Maritime Boundaries 131, 150 (Jonathan I. Charney & Lewis M. Alexander eds., 1993).

In the France/United Kingdom arbitration, the tribunal came up with totally different solutions for the Scilly Isles and the Channel Islands. The Scillies are a group of 48 British islands, with about 2,500 people inhabiting six of them. They are located off the southwest tip of England between 21 and 31 nautical miles from the southwestern extremity of the English mainland, and cover a total area of about sixteen square kilometers (six square miles). The Channel

Islands are British islands located off the French coast. They measure approximately 195 square kilometers (75 square miles) and have a total population of 130,000. Why did the court consider it appropriate to treat these two islands groups differently? Did the court explain why precisely half effect, and not for instance three-fourths effect, was attributed to the Scilly Isles?

TUNISIA/LIBYA CONTINENTAL SHELF CASE
1982 I.C.J. 18

[By Special Agreement Libya and Tunisia requested the ICJ to specify the principles and rules of international law that may be applied in delimiting the continental shelf between them. The ICJ was also asked to consider "equitable principles, and the relevant circumstances which characterize the area, as well as the new accepted trends in the Third Conference on the Law of the Sea," and "to clarify the practical method for the application of these principles and rules in this specific situation." The ICJ, in paragraph 24 of its judgment, comments on this reference to "new accepted trends":

> The Court is thus authorized by the Special Agreement to take into account "new accepted trends" which can be considered, as the term "trends" suggests, as having reached an advanced stage of the process of elaboration. The Third United Nations Conference on the Law of the Sea has however not yet come to an end. The draft convention of 28 August 1981 is not yet the final text to be submitted for signature. It would no doubt have been possible for the Parties to have identified in the Special Agreement certain specific developments in the law of the sea of this kind, and to have declared that in their bilateral relations in the particular case such rules should be binding as *lex specialis*. The Parties have however not been so specific, and in the light of their replies to a question put by a Member of the Court on the point, it does not appear that it was their intention to go so far as to impose additional or supplementary rules on themselves in this way in the context of this case. According to Tunisia, the "trends," so far as they do not constitute general international law, are to be taken into account as "factors in the interpretation of the existing rules." In any event, however, any consideration and conclusion of the Court in connection with the application of the "trends" is confined exclusively to the legal relations of the Parties in the present case. Furthermore, the Court would have had *proprio motu* to take account of the progress made by the Conference even if the Parties had not alluded to it in their Special Agreement; for it could not ignore any provision of

> the draft convention if it came to the conclusion that the content of such provision is binding upon all members of the international community because it embodies or crystallizes a pre-existing or emergent rule of customary law.

Both Libya and Tunisia argue that a boundary line should be drawn in accordance with the "natural prolongation" of their land area; neither proposes an equidistant line. Libya argues that a boundary due north from Ras Ajdir (see Figure VI.D) would reflect the prolongation of its landmass. Tunisia argues that the natural prolongation of the continent in the boundary area is eastward.]

44. Both Parties to the present case have in effect based their argument upon the idea that because a delimitation should, in accordance with the Judgment in the *North Sea Continental Shelf* cases, leave to each Party "all those parts of the continental shelf that constitute a natural prolongation of its land territory into and under the sea" (*I.C.J. Reports 1969*, p. 53, para. 101(C)(1)), therefore the determination of what constitutes such natural prolongation will produce a correct delimitation. The Court in 1969 did not regard an equitable delimitation and a determination of the limits of "natural prolongation" as synonymous, since in the operative clause of its Judgment, just quoted, it referred only to the delimitation being effected in such a way as to leave "as much as possible" to each Party the shelf areas constituting its natural prolongation. The Court also clearly distinguished between a principle which affords the justification for the appurtenance of an area to a State and a rule for determining the extent and limits of such area: "the appurtenance of a given area, considered as an entity, in no way governs the precise delimitation of its boundaries" (*I.C.J. Reports 1969*, p. 32, para. 46). The Court is therefore unable to accept the contention of Libya that "once the natural prolongation of a State is determined, delimitation becomes a simple matter of complying with the dictates of nature." It would be a mistake to suppose that it will in all cases, or even in the majority of them, be possible or appropriate to establish that the natural prolongation of one State extends, in relation to the natural prolongation of another State, just so far and no farther, so that the two prolongations meet along an easily defined line. Nor can the Court approve the argument of Tunisia that the satisfying of equitable principles in a particular geographical situation is just as much a part of the process of the identification of the natural prolongation as the identification of the natural prolongation is necessary to satisfy equitable principles. The satisfaction of equitable principles is, in the delimitation process, of cardinal importance, ... and identification of natural prolongation may, where the geographical

circumstances are appropriate, have an important role to play in defining an equitable delimitation, in view of its significance as the justification of continental shelf rights in some cases; but the two considerations—the satisfying of equitable principles and the identification of the natural prolongation—are not to be placed on a plane of equality.

[After reviewing the detailed arguments of the parties relating to such historical geological features as plate tectonics and the allegedly "northward thrust" of the African continent, and to various geomorphological or bathymetric features, the Court concludes its findings in this respect:]

61. The conclusion which, in the Court's view, has ineluctably to be drawn from this analysis is that, despite the confident assertions of the geologists on both sides that a given area is "an evident prolongation" or "the real prolongation" of the one or the other State, for legal purposes it is not possible to define the areas of continental shelf appertaining to Tunisia and to Libya by reference solely or mainly to geological considerations. The function of the Court is to make use of geology only so far as required for the application of international law. It is of the view that what must be taken into account in the delimitation of shelf areas are the physical circumstances as they are today; that just as it is the geographical configuration of the present-day coasts, so also it is the present-day sea-bed, which must be considered. It is the outcome, not the evolution in the long-distant past, which is of importance.

[After rejecting the claims of the parties based on the notion of "natural prolongation," the Court returns to a discussion of "equitable principles applicable to delimitation of shelf areas." ¶ 68.]

70. Since the Court considers that it is bound to decide the case on the basis of equitable principles, it must first examine what such principles entail, divorced from the concept of natural prolongation which has been found not to be applied for purposes of delimitation in this case. The result of the application of equitable principles must be equitable.... It is... the result which is predominant; the principles are subordinate to the goal. The equitableness of a principle must be assessed in the light of its usefulness for the purpose of arriving at an equitable result. It is not every such principle which is in itself equitable; it may acquire this quality by reference to the equitableness of the solution. The principles to be indicated by the Court have to be selected according to their appropriateness for reaching an equitable result. From this consideration it follows that the term "equitable principles" cannot be interpreted in the abstract; it refers back to the principles and rules which may be appropriate in order to achieve an equitable result. This was the view of the Court when it said, in its Judgment of 1969:

> it is a truism to say that the determination must be equitable; rather is the problem above all one of defining the means whereby the delimitation can be carried out in such a way as to be recognized as equitable (*I.C.J. Reports 1969*, p. 50, para. 92).

71. Equity as a legal concept is a direct emanation of the idea of justice. The Court whose task is by definition to administer justice is bound to apply it. In the course of the history of legal systems the term "equity" has been used to define various legal concepts. It was often contrasted with the rigid rules of positive law, the severity of which had to be mitigated in order to do justice. In general, this contrast has no parallel in the development of international law; the legal concept of equity is a general principle directly applicable as law. Moreover, when applying positive international law, a court may choose among several possible interpretations of the law the one which appears, in the light of the circumstances of the case, to be closest to the requirements of justice. Application of equitable principles is to be distinguished from a decision *ex aequo et bono*. The Court can take such a decision only on condition that the Parties agree (Art. 38, para. 2, of the Statute), and the Court is then freed from the strict application of legal rules in order to bring about an appropriate settlement. The task of the Court in the present case is quite different: it is bound to apply equitable principles as part of international law, and to balance up the various considerations which it regards as relevant in order to produce an equitable result. While it is clear that no rigid rules exist as to the exact weight to be attached to each element in the case, this is very far from being an exercise of discretion or conciliation; nor is it an operation of distributive justice.

[The Court excludes economic factors because they are extraneous variables that are highly unpredictable: "A country might be poor today and become rich tomorrow." ¶ 107.]

109. Before considering the methods of delimitation discussed by the Parties in argument, the Court thinks it appropriate to make some observations on the equidistance method. The Court held in the *North Sea Continental Shelf* cases, which also concerned adjacent States, that the equidistance method of delimitation of the continental shelf is not prescribed by a mandatory rule of customary law (*I.C.J. Reports 1969*, p. 46, para. 83; p. 53, para. 101). On the other hand it emphasized the merits of this rule in cases in which its application leads to an equitable solution. The subsequent practice of States, as is apparent from treaties on continental shelf boundaries, shows that the equidistance method has been employed in a number of cases. But it also shows

that States may deviate from an equidistance line, and have made use of other criteria for the delimitation, whenever they found this a better way to arrive at an agreement. One solution may be a combination of an equidistance line in some parts of the area with a line of some other kind in other parts, as dictated by the relevant circumstances. Examples of this kind are provided by the 1977 arbitration on the Delimitation of the Continental Shelf between France and the United Kingdom, and by the Convention between France and Spain on the Delimitation of the Continental Shelves of the two States in the Bay of Biscay of 29 January 1974. Treaty practice, as well as the history of Article 83 of the draft convention on the Law of the Sea, leads to the conclusion that equidistance may be applied if it leads to an equitable solution; if not, other methods should be employed.

110. Nor does the Court consider that it is in the present case required, as a first step, to examine the effects of a delimitation by application of the equidistance method, and to reject that method in favour of some other only if it considers the results of an equidistance line to be inequitable. A finding by the Court in favour of a delimitation by an equidistance line could only be based on considerations derived from an evaluation and balancing up of all relevant circumstances, since equidistance is not, in the view of the Court, either a mandatory legal principle, or a method having some privileged status in relation to other methods.

114. [I]n the view of the Court, the proper appreciation and taking into account of the "relevant circumstances which characterize the area" call for the area close to the coasts of the Parties to be treated differently from the areas further offshore. The Court will therefore deal with the area as divided into two sectors. It must, however, be emphasized that such difference of treatment is ultimately dictated by the primordial requirement of achieving an overall equitable result.

115. The considerations which dictate this difference of treatment of the two sectors of continental shelf for the purposes of delimitation are intimately related to the varying influences of the individual circumstances characterizing the area, and will be considered below. However, it should be noted at the outset that the extent of the area to be delimited is such that the terminal point to seaward of the delimitation line ... will be at a considerable distance from the nearest point on the coasts of the two Parties and from the frontier point of Ras Ajdir. Where the delimitation to be effected is upon such a scale as this, the use of any one method of delimitation which may seem appropriate, in the light of relevant circumstances, close to the shores of the States concerned, may well suffer from the defect noted in 1969 with respect to the equidistance method, that the distorting effects of certain factors on the course of the line

> under certain conditions of coastal figuration are . . . comparatively small within the limits of territorial waters, but produce their maximum effect in the localities where the main continental shelf areas lie further out (*I.C.J. Reports 1969*, p. 37, para. 59),

and "the further from the coastline the area to be delimited, the more unreasonable are the results produced" (*ibid.*, p. 49, para. 89(*a*)). In such a situation, a possible means (though not the only one) of avoiding an inequitable result is to employ one method of delimitation up to a given distance from the coasts, and thenceforth to employ a different method. In the view of the Court, the situation in the present case calls for an approach of this kind.

[Considering the land frontier between the parties and their prior conduct in establishing a boundary for the granting of petroleum concessions, the Court determines that for the sector close to shore, the boundary line should be a line perpendicular to the coast. Taking into account the radical change in the general direction of the Tunisian coastline in the Gulf of Gabes, the Court applies a line parallel to the general direction of the coast, giving a modified effect to the Kerkennah Islands, following the lead of the France/United Kingdom arbitration. See ¶¶ 121, 129.]

132. [In concluding, the Court] recalled the historic evolution of the concept of continental shelf, from its inception in the Truman Proclamation of 28 September 1945, through the Geneva Convention of 1958, through the *North Sea Continental Shelf* cases and subsequent jurisprudence, up to the draft convention of the Third Law of the Sea Conference, and its evolution in State practice, and [pointed out that it] has endorsed and developed those general principles and rules which have thus been established. Clearly each continental shelf case in dispute should be considered and judged on its own merits, having regard to its peculiar circumstances; therefore, no attempt should be made here to overconceptualize the application of the principles and rules relating to the continental shelf.

133. For these reasons,

> THE COURT,
> by ten votes to four,
> finds that:

A. The principles and rules of international law applicable for the delimitation, to be effected by agreement in implementation of the present Judgment, of the areas of continental shelf appertaining to the Republic of Tunisia and the Socialist People's Libyan Arab Jamahiriya respectively, in the area of the

Pelagian Block in dispute between them as defined in paragraph B, subparagraph (1), below, are as follows:

(1) the delimitation is to be effected in accordance with equitable principles, and taking account of all relevant circumstances;

(2) the area relevant for the delimitation constitutes a single continental shelf as the natural prolongation of the land territory of both Parties, so that in the present case, no criterion for delimitation of shelf areas can be derived from the principle of natural prolongation as such;

(3) in the particular geographical circumstances of the present case, the physical structure of the continental shelf areas is not such as to determine an equitable line of delimitation.

B. The relevant circumstances referred to in paragraph A, subparagraph (1), above, to be taken into account in achieving an equitable delimitation include the following:

(1) the fact that the area relevant to the delimitation in the present case is bounded by the Tunisian coast from Ras Ajdir to Ras Kaboudia and the Libyan coast from Ras Ajdir to Ras Tajoura and by the parallel of latitude passing through Ras Kaboudia and the meridian passing through Ras Tajoura, the rights of third States being reserved;

(2) the general configuration of the coasts of the Parties, and in particular the marked change in direction of the Tunisian coastline between Ras Ajdir and Ras Kaboudia;

(3) the existence and position of the Kerkennah Islands;

(4) the land frontier between the Parties, and their conduct prior to 1974 in the grant of petroleum concessions, resulting in the employment of a line seawards from Ras Ajdir at an angle of approximately 26° east of the meridian, which line corresponds to the line perpendicular to the coast at the frontier point which had in the past been observed as a de *facto* maritime limit;

(5) the element of a reasonable degree of proportionality, which a delimitation carried out in accordance with equitable principles ought to bring about between the extent of the continental shelf areas appertaining to the coastal State and the length of the relevant part of its coast, measured in the general direction of the coastlines, account being taken for this purpose of the effects, actual or prospective, of any other continental shelf delimitation between States in the same region.

C. The practical method for the application of the aforesaid principles and rules of international law in the particular situation of the present case is the following:

(1) the taking into account of the relevant circumstances which characterize the area defined in paragraph B, subparagraph (1), above, including its extent, calls for it to be treated, for the purpose of its delimitation between the Parties to the present case, as made up of two sectors, each requiring the application of a specific method of delimitation in order to achieve an overall equitable solution;

(2) in the first sector, namely in the sector closer to the coast of the Parties, the starting point for the line of delimitation is the point where the outer limit of the territorial sea of the Parties is intersected by a straight line drawn from the land frontier point of Ras Ajdir through the point 33° 55' N, 12°E, which line runs at a bearing of approximately 26° east of north, corresponding to the angle followed by the north-western boundary of Libyan petroleum concessions numbers NC 76, 137, NC 41 and NC 53, which was aligned on the south-eastern boundary of Tunisian petroleum concession "Permis complémentaire offshore du Golfe de Gabès" (21 October 1966); from the intersection point so determined, the line of delimitation between the two continental shelves is to run northeast through the point 33° 55' N, 12°E, thus on the same bearing, to the point of intersection with the parallel passing through that most westerly point of the Tunisian coastline between Ras Kaboudia and Ras Ajdir, that is to say, the most westerly point on the shoreline (low-water mark) of the Gulf of Gabes;

(3) in the second sector, namely in the area which extends seawards beyond the parallel of the most westerly point of the Gulf of Gabes, the line of delimitation of the two continental shelves is to veer to the east in such a way as to take account of the Kerkennah Islands; that is to say, the delimitation line is to run parallel to a line drawn from the most westerly point of the Gulf of Gabes bisecting the angle formed by a line from that point to Ras Kaboudia and a line drawn from that same point along the seaward coast of the Kerkennah Islands, the bearing of the delimitation line parallel to such bisector being 52° to the meridian; the extension of this line northeastwards is a matter falling outside the jurisdiction of the Court in the present case, as it will depend on the delimitation to be agreed with third States.

Notes

1. *The ICJ's Use of Equity*. In paragraph 71 of its decision in the Tunisia/Libya case, the Court emphasized that the "[a]pplication of equitable principles is

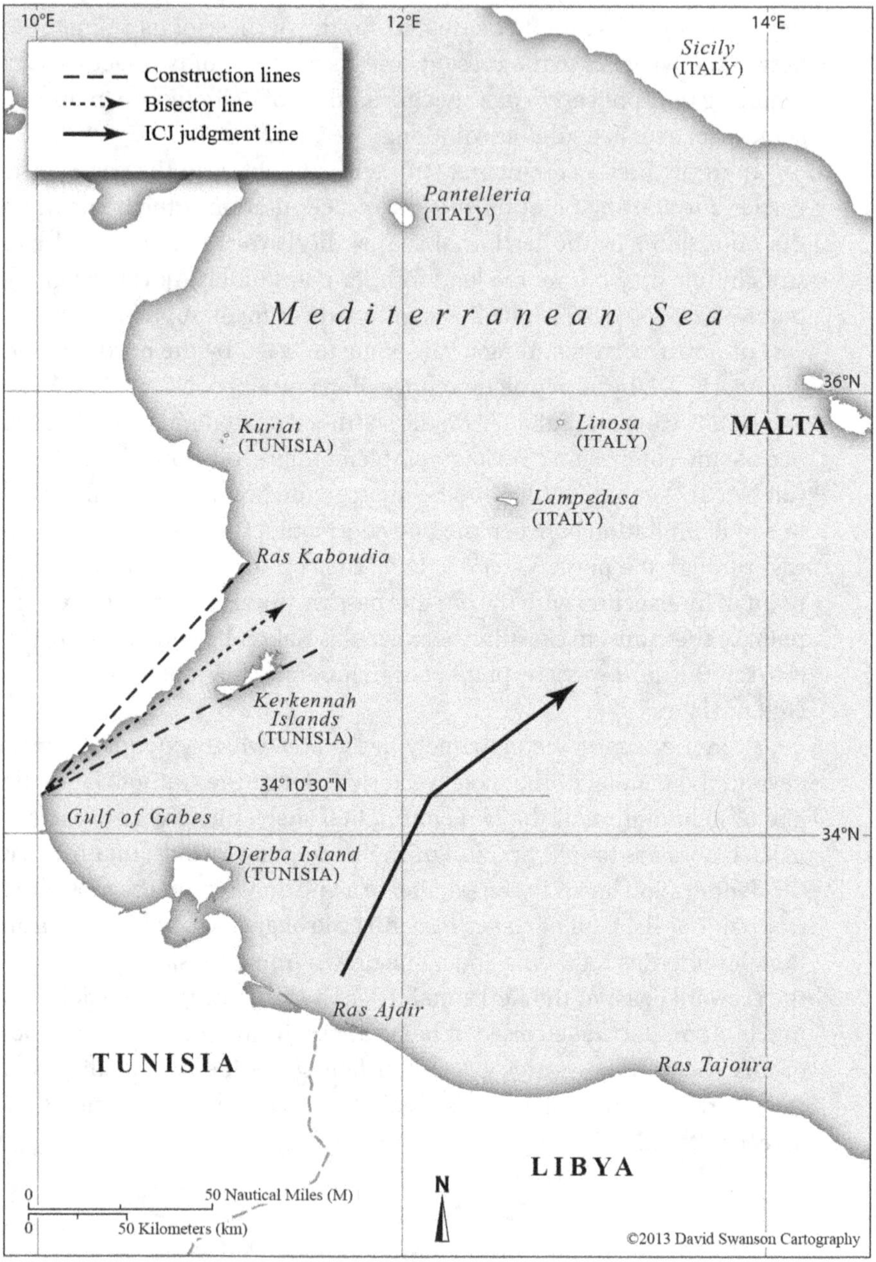

FIGURE VI.D *Tunisia/Libya Continental Shelf Delimitation*

to be distinguished from a decision *ex aequo et bono*." A decision ex aequo et bono rests purely in the discretion of the Court; it is not based on any legal rules or principles. The Court acknowledged that it was bound "to apply equitable principles as a part of international law. While it is clear that no rigid rules exist... this is very far from being an exercise of discretion or conciliation." Some dissenting judges, however, criticized the majority's opinion as "stray[ing] into subjectivism" and as "*ex aequo et bono*." 1982 I.C.J. at 156 (Gros), 157 (Oda). Did the Court's discussion of various factors—historic, economic, geologic, equidistance—narrow the discretion available to the judges in their search for an "equitable result"?

2. *The ICJ's Use of Natural Prolongation*. Following the emphasis placed by the ICJ in the North Sea Continental Shelf cases on the concept of natural prolongation with respect to the continental shelf, as mentioned in Note 5 following those cases, Libyan geologists and Tunisian geomorphologists spent considerable effort trying to persuade the judges that the natural prolongation in the area to be delimited favored their national positions. How did the ICJ dispose of the issue in the Tunisia/Libya case?

3. *The ICJ's Use of Equidistance*. In 1969, the ICJ in the North Sea Continental Shelf cases decided that, absent a specific agreement, equidistance was not an obligatory rule of international law. Is it nevertheless logical for courts and tribunals to establish an equidistant line in cases of adjacency, possibly adjusting that line in a second phase in light of relevant circumstances? Would such an approach add determinacy to the legal methodology for making maritime delimitations?

4. *The Treatment of Islands*. How did the ICJ solve the conflicting claims of the parties with respect to the effect to be given to the Kerkennah Islands, located about ten nautical miles from the mainland? These islands measure 180 square kilometers (69.5 square miles) and have a population of about 14,000. The ICJ's method seems comparable to the one applied by the France/United Kingdom arbitral tribunal with respect to the Scilly Isles, even though the Kerkennah Islands are more than ten times as big, have a population about 5.6 times larger, and are located one third of the distance closer to shore. Does the ICJ explain precisely why it attributed half effect, and not for instance three-fourths effect, to the Kerkennah Islands?

5. *Interpretation and Requested Revision of the Judgment*. In 1984 Tunisia, relying on Articles 60 and 61 of the ICJ Statute, asked the Court to revise and interpret its 1982 judgment. The Court interpreted some parts of the 1982 judgment, but Tunisia's application requesting revision was deemed inadmissible. Tunisia failed to base its application for revision on a fact that could be

a "decisive factor" and that was previously unknown to Tunisia and the Court, as required by Article 61(1) of the Court's Statute. Application for Revision and Interpretation of the Judgment of 24 February 1982 in the Case Concerning the Continental Shelf (Tunisia v. Libya), 1985 I.C.J. 192.

LIBYA/MALTA CONTINENTAL SHELF CASE
1985 I.C.J. 13

[This case was submitted to the ICJ by Special Agreement on July 26, 1982, following the exercise of good offices by the U.N. Secretary-General to persuade the two states to submit their dispute to the Court. The parties asked the Court to decide the following question:

> What principles and rules of international law are applicable to the delimitation of the area of the continental shelf which appertains to the Republic of Malta and the area of continental shelf which appertains to the Libyan Arab Republic, and how in practice such principles and rules can be applied by the two Parties in this particular case in order that they may without difficulty delimit such areas by an agreement as provided in Article III.

On March 21, 1984, the Court rejected an application by Italy for permission to intervene. The Court concluded that Italy was in fact asking the Court to adjudicate its disputes with Libya and Malta without the consent of those countries—disputes over which the Court lacked jurisdiction. In addition, the Court noted that the final judgment in the main case would be without prejudice to the rights and titles of other states. 1984 I.C.J. 3, 18–24. Consequently, in the final judgment the Court limits its decision "in geographical scope so as to leave the claims of Italy unaffected"; it points out again that "the Court has not been endowed with jurisdiction to determine what principles and rules govern delimitations with third States, or whether the claims of the Parties outside that area prevail over the claims of those third States in the region." 1985 I.C.J. at ¶ 21.]

26. The Parties are broadly in agreement as to the sources of the law applicable in this case. Malta is a party to the 1958 Geneva Convention on the Continental Shelf, while Libya is not; the Parties agree that the Convention, and in particular the provisions for delimitation in Article 6, is thus not as such applicable in the relations between them. Both Parties have signed the 1982 United Nations Convention on the Law of the Sea, but that Convention has not yet entered into force, and is therefore not operative as treaty-law; the

Special Agreement contains no provisions as to the substantive law applicable. Nor are there any other bilateral or multilateral treaties claimed to be binding on the Parties. The Parties thus agree that the dispute is to be governed by customary international law. This is not at all to say, however, that the 1982 Convention was regarded by the Parties as irrelevant: the Parties are again in accord in considering that some of its provisions constitute, to a certain extent, the expression of customary international law in the matter. The Parties do not however agree in identifying the provisions which have this status, or the extent to which they are so treated.

27. It is of course axiomatic that the material of customary international law is to be looked for primarily in the actual practice and *opinio juris* of States, even though multilateral conventions may have an important role to play in recording and defining rules deriving from custom, or indeed in developing them.... Nevertheless, it cannot be denied that the 1982 Convention is of major importance, having been adopted by an overwhelming majority of States; hence it is clearly the duty of the Court, even independently of the references made to the Convention by the Parties, to consider in what degree any of its relevant provisions are binding upon the Parties as a rule of customary international law. In this context particularly, the Parties have laid some emphasis on a distinction between the law applicable to the basis of entitlement to areas of continental shelf—the rules governing the existence, "*ipso jure* and *ab initio*," and the exercise of sovereign rights of the coastal State over areas of continental shelf situated off its coasts—and the law applicable to the delimitation of such areas of shelf between neighbouring States. The first question is dealt with in Article 76 of the 1982 Convention, and the second in Article 83 of the Convention. Paragraph 1 of that Article provides that:

> The delimitation of the continental shelf between States with opposite or adjacent coasts shall be effected by agreement on the basis of international law, as referred to in Article 38 of the Statute of the International Court of Justice, in order to achieve an equitable solution.

Paragraph 10 of Article 76 provides that "The provisions of this article are without prejudice to the question of delimitation of the continental shelf between States with opposite or adjacent coasts." That the questions of entitlement and of definition of continental shelf, on the one hand, and of delimitation of continental shelf on the other, are not only distinct but are also complementary is self-evident. The legal basis of that which is to be delimited, and of entitlement to it, cannot be other than pertinent to that delimitation.

28. [T]he Court would . . . first recall that, as it noted in its Judgment in the case concerning the *Continental Shelf* (*Tunisia/Libyan Arab Jamahiriya*),

> In the new text, any indication of a specific criterion which could give guidance to the interested States in their effort to achieve an equitable solution has been excluded. Emphasis is placed on the equitable solution which has to be achieved. The principles and rules applicable to the delimitation of continental shelf areas are those which are appropriate to bring about an equitable result . . . (*I.C.J. Reports 1982*, p. 49, para. 50.)

The Convention sets a goal to be achieved, but is silent as to the method to be followed to achieve it. It restricts itself to setting a standard, and it is left to States themselves, or to the courts, to endow this standard with specific content. Secondly, the Court in 1982 observed the disappearance, in the last draft text of what became Article 83, paragraph 1, of reference to delimitation by agreement "in accordance with equitable principles" (*I.C.J. Reports 1982*, p. 49, para. 49). It found however that it was "bound to decide the case on the basis of equitable principles" as well as that "The result of the application of equitable principles must be equitable" (*ibid.*, p. 59, para. 70). . . .

33. In the view of the Court, even though the present case relates only to the delimitation of the continental shelf and not to that of the exclusive economic zone, the principles and rules underlying the latter concept cannot be left out of consideration. As the 1982 Convention demonstrates, the two institutions—continental shelf and exclusive economic zone—are linked together in modern law. Since the rights enjoyed by a State over its continental shelf would also be possessed by it over the sea-bed and subsoil of any exclusive economic zone which it might proclaim, one of the relevant circumstances to be taken into account for the delimitation of the continental shelf of a State is the legally permissible extent of the exclusive economic zone appertaining to that same State. This does not mean that the concept of the continental shelf has been absorbed by that of the exclusive economic zone; it does however signify that greater importance must be attributed to elements, such as distance from the coast, which are common to both concepts. . . .

39. [S]ince the development of the law enables a State to claim that the continental shelf appertaining to it extends up to as far as 200 miles from its coast, whatever the geological characteristics of the corresponding sea-bed and subsoil, there is no reason to ascribe any role to geological or geophysical factors within that distance either in verifying the legal title of the States concerned or in proceeding to a delimitation as between their claims. [S]ince

the distance between the coasts of the Parties is less than 400 miles, so that no geophysical feature can lie more than 200 miles from each coast, the feature referred to as the "rift zone" cannot constitute a fundamental discontinuity terminating the southward extension of the Maltese shelf and the northward extension of the Libyan as if it were some natural boundary....

42. Neither, however, is the Court able to accept the argument of Malta—almost diametrically opposed to the Libyan rift-zone argument—that the new importance of the idea of distance from the coast has, at any rate for delimitation between opposite coasts, in turn conferred a primacy on the method of equidistance.... Malta rejects the view that natural prolongation in the physical sense is the basis of title of the coastal State, and bases its approach to continental shelf delimitation on the "distance principle": each coastal State is entitled to continental shelf rights to a certain distance from its coast, whatever may be the physical characteristics of the sea-bed and subsoil. Since there is not sufficient space between the coasts of Malta and Libya for each of them to enjoy continental shelf rights up to the full 200 miles recognized by international law, the delimitation process must, according to Malta, necessarily begin by taking into consideration an equidistance line between the two coasts. The delimitation of the continental shelf must start from the geographical facts in each particular case; Malta regards the situation as one of two coastal States facing each other in an entirely normal setting. Malta does not assert that the equidistance method is fundamental, or inherent, or has a legally obligatory character. It does argue that the legal basis of continental shelf rights—that is to say, for Malta, the "distance principle"—requires that as a starting point of the delimitation process consideration must be given to a line based on equidistance; though it is only to the extent that this primary delimitation produces an equitable result by a balancing up of the relevant circumstances that the boundary coincides with the equidistance line. As a provisional point of departure, consideration of equidistance "is required" on the basis of the legal title.

43. The Court is unable to accept that, even as a preliminary and provisional step towards the drawing of a delimitation line, the equidistance method is one which *must* be used, or that the Court is "required, as a first step, to examine the effects of a delimitation by application of the equidistance method" (*I.C.J. Reports 1982*, p. 79, para. 110).... That a coastal State may be entitled to continental shelf rights by reason of distance from the coast, and irrespective of the physical characteristics of the intervening sea-bed and subsoil, does not entail that equidistance is the only appropriate method of delimitation, even between opposite or quasi-opposite coasts, nor even the only permissible point of departure. The application of equitable principles in the particular

relevant circumstances may still require the adoption of another method, or combination of methods, of delimitation, even from the outset. . . .

45. Judicial decisions are at one—and the Parties themselves agree . . .—in holding that the delimitation of a continental shelf boundary must be effected by the application of equitable principles in all the relevant circumstances in order to achieve an equitable result. . . . It is . . . the goal—the equitable result—and not the means used to achieve it, that must be the primary element in this duality of characterization. . . . Yet . . . the justice of which equity is an emanation, is not abstract justice but justice according to the rule of law; which is to say that its application should display consistency and a degree of predictability; even though it looks with particularity to the peculiar circumstances of an instant case, it also looks beyond it to principles of more general application. This is precisely why the courts have, from the beginning, elaborated equitable principles as being, at the same time, means to an equitable result in a particular case, yet also having a more general validity and hence expressible in general terms; for, as the Court has also said, "the legal concept of equity is a general principle directly applicable as law" (*I.C.J. Reports 1982*, p. 60, para. 71).

46. The normative character of equitable principles applied as a part of general international law is important because these principles govern not only delimitation by adjudication or arbitration, but also, and indeed primarily, the duty of Parties to seek first a delimitation by agreement, which is also to seek an equitable result. That equitable principles are expressed in terms of general application, is immediately apparent from a glance at some well-known examples: the principle that there is to be no question of refashioning geography, or compensating for the inequalities of nature; the related principle of non-encroachment by one party on the natural prolongation of the other, which is no more than the negative expression of the positive rule that the coastal State enjoys sovereign rights over the continental shelf off its coasts to the full extent authorized by international law in the relevant circumstances; the principle of respect due to all such relevant circumstances; the principle that although all States are equal before the law and are entitled to equal treatment, "equity does not necessarily imply equality" (*I.C.J. Reports 1969*, p. 49, para. 91), nor does it seek to make equal what nature has made unequal; and the principle that there can be no question of distributive justice.

47. The nature of equity is nowhere more evident than in these well-established principles. In interpreting them, it must be borne in mind that the geography which is not to be refashioned means those aspects of a geographical situation most germane to the legal institution of the continental shelf; and it is "the coast of each of the Parties," which

> constitutes the starting line from which one has to set out in order to ascertain how far the submarine areas appertaining to each of them extend in a seaward direction, as well as in relation to neighbouring States situated either in an adjacent or opposite position (*I.C.J. Reports 1982*, p. 61, para. 74).

In a semi-enclosed sea like the Mediterranean, that reference to neighbouring States is particularly apposite, for, as will be shown below, it is the coastal relationships in the whole geographical context that are to be taken account of and respected.

48. The application of equitable principles thus still leaves the Court with the task of appreciation of the weight to be accorded to the relevant circumstances in any particular case of delimitation. There is a much-quoted *dictum* of the Court in its 1969 Judgment to this effect:

> In fact, there is no legal limit to the considerations which States may take account of for the purpose of making sure that they apply equitable procedures, and more often than not it is the balancing-up of all such considerations that will produce this result rather than reliance on one to the exclusion of all others. The problem of the relative weight to be accorded to different considerations naturally varies with the circumstances of the case. (*I.C.J. Reports 1969*, p. 50, para. 93.)

Yet although there may be no legal limit to the considerations which States may take account of, this can hardly be true for a court applying equitable procedures. For a court, although there is assuredly no closed list of considerations, it is evident that only those that are pertinent to the institution of the continental shelf as it has developed within the law, and to the application of equitable principles to its delimitation, will qualify for inclusion. Otherwise, the legal concept of continental shelf could itself be fundamentally changed by the introduction of considerations strange to its nature.

49. It was argued by Libya that the relevant geographical considerations include the landmass behind the coast, in the sense that that landmass provides in Libya's view the factual basis and legal justification for the State's entitlement to continental shelf rights, a State with a greater landmass having a more intense natural prolongation. The Court is unable to accept this as a relevant consideration. Landmass has never been regarded as a basis of entitlement to continental shelf rights, and such a proposition finds no support in the practice of States, in the jurisprudence, in doctrine, or indeed in the

work of the Third United Nations Conference on the Law of the Sea. It would radically change the part played by the relationship between coast and continental shelf.... What distinguishes a coastal State with continental shelf rights from a landlocked State which has none, is certainly not the landmass, which both possess, but the existence of a maritime front in one State and its absence in the other. The juridical link between the State's territorial sovereignty and its rights to certain adjacent maritime expanses is established by means of its coast. The concept of adjacency measured by distance is based entirely on that of the coastline, and not on that of the landmass.

50. It was argued by Malta, on the other hand, that the considerations that may be taken account of include economic factors and security. Malta has contended that the relevant equitable considerations, employed not to dictate a delimitation but to contribute to assessment of the equitableness of a delimitation otherwise arrived at, include the absence of energy resources on the island of Malta, its requirements as an island developing country, and the range of its established fishing activity. The Court does not however consider that a delimitation should be influenced by the relative economic position of the two States in question, in such a way that the area of continental shelf regarded as appertaining to the less rich of the two States would be somewhat increased in order to compensate for its inferiority in economic resources. Such considerations are totally unrelated to the underlying intention of the applicable rules of international law. It is clear that neither the rules determining the validity of legal entitlement to the continental shelf, nor those concerning delimitation between neighbouring countries, leave room for any considerations of economic development of the States in question. While the concept of the exclusive economic zone has, from the outset, included certain special provisions for the benefit of developing States, those provisions have not related to the extent of such areas nor to their delimitation between neighbouring States, but merely to the exploitation of their resources. The natural resources of the continental shelf under delimitation "so far as known or readily ascertainable" might well constitute relevant circumstances which it would be reasonable to take into account in a delimitation, as the Court states in the *North Sea Continental Shelf* cases (*I.C.J. Reports 1969*, p. 54, para. 101(D)(2)). Those resources are the essential objective envisaged by States when they put forward claims to sea-bed areas containing them. In the present case, however, the Court has not been furnished by the Parties with any indications on this point.

[As far as national security is concerned, the delimitation made by the Court in this decision will not be "so near the coast of either Party as to make questions of security a particular consideration in the present case." ¶ 51.]

54. Malta has also invoked the principle of sovereign equality of States as an argument in favour of the equidistance method pure and simple, and as an objection to any adjustment based on length of coasts or proportionality considerations. It has observed that since all States are equal and equally sovereign, the maritime extensions generated by the sovereignty of each State must be of equal juridical value, whether or not the coasts of one State are longer than those of the other. The first question is whether the use of the equidistance method or recourse to proportionality considerations derive from legal rules accepted by States. If, for example, States had adopted a principle of apportionment of shelf on a basis of strict proportionality of coastal lengths (which the Court does not consider to be the case), their consent to that rule would be no breach of the principle of sovereign equality between them. Secondly, it is evident that the existence of equal entitlement, *ipso jure* and *ab initio*, of coastal States, does not imply an equality of extent of shelf, whatever the circumstances of the area; thus reference to the length of coasts as a relevant circumstance cannot be excluded *a priori*. The principle of equality of States has therefore no particular role to play in the applicable law.

[Libya relies on proportionality as an important equitable principle, arguing that the delimitation "should take account of the significant difference in lengths of the respective coastlines which face the area in which delimitation is to be effected." ¶ 11. The Court points out that proportionality is not a "principle" but only one "factor" or "criterion" among several others to be taken into account. ¶ 57.]

58. [To] use the ratio of coastal lengths as of itself determinative of the seaward reach and area of continental shelf proper to each Party, is to go far beyond the use of proportionality as a test of equity, and as a corrective of the unjustifiable difference of treatment resulting from some method of drawing the boundary line. If such a use of proportionality were right, it is difficult indeed to see what room would be left for any other consideration; for it would be at once the principle of entitlement to continental shelf rights and also the method of putting that principle into operation. [T]he use of proportionality as a method in its own right is wanting of support in the practice of States, in the public expression of their views at (in particular) the Third United Nations Conference on the Law of the Sea, or in the jurisprudence. It is not possible for the Court to endorse a proposal at once so far-reaching and so novel. That does not however mean that the "significant difference in lengths of the respective coastlines" is not an element which may be taken into account at a certain stage in the delimitation process; this aspect of the matter will be returned to at the appropriate stage in the further reasoning of the Court....

60. In applying the equitable principles thus elicited, within the limits defined above, and in the light of the relevant circumstances, the Court intends to proceed by stages; thus, it will first make a provisional delimitation by using a criterion and a method both of which are clearly destined to play an important role in producing the final result; it will then examine this provisional solution in the light of the requirements derived from other criteria, which may call for a correction of this initial result.

61. [A]s the Court has found above, the law applicable to the present dispute, that is, to claims relating to continental shelves located less than 200 miles from the coasts of the States in question, is based not on geological or geomorphological criteria, but on a criterion of distance from the coast or, to use the traditional term, on the principle of adjacency as measured by distance. It therefore seems logical to the Court that the choice of the criterion and the method which it is to employ in the first place to arrive at a provisional result should be made in a manner consistent with the concepts underlying the attribution of legal title.

62. . . . The Court has itself noted that the equitable nature of the equidistance method is particularly pronounced in cases where delimitation has to be effected between States with opposite coasts. [The Court recites its statements in paragraphs 57 and 58 of the North Sea Continental Shelf cases excerpted above.] But it is in fact a delimitation exclusively between opposite coasts that the Court is, for the first time, asked to deal with. It is clear that, in these circumstances, the tracing of a median line between those coasts, by way of a provisional step in a process to be continued by other operations, is the most judicious manner of proceeding with a view to the eventual achievement of an equitable result.

63. The median line drawn in this way is thus only provisional. Were the Court to treat it as final, it would be conferring on the equidistance method the status of being the only method the use of which is compulsory in the case of opposite coasts. [U]nder existing law, it must be demonstrated that the equidistance method leads to an equitable result in the case in question. . . .

66. The Court has already examined, and dismissed, a number of contentions made before it as to relevant circumstances in the present case (paragraphs 48–54 above). [T]here remains however the very marked difference in the lengths of the relevant coasts of the Parties, and the element of the considerable distance between those coasts referred to by both Parties, and to be examined below. In connection with lengths of coasts, attention should be drawn to an important distinction . . . between the relevance of coastal lengths as a pertinent circumstance for a delimitation, and use of those lengths in

assessing ratios of proportionality ... between lengths of coasts and areas of continental shelf attributed on the basis of those coasts. It has been emphasized that this latter operation is to be employed solely as a verification of the equitableness of the result arrived at by other means.... Consideration of the comparability or otherwise of the coastal lengths is a part of the process of determining an equitable boundary on the basis of an initial median line; the test of a reasonable degree of proportionality, on the other hand, is one which can be applied to check the equitableness of any line, whatever the method used to arrive at that line.

67. In order to assess any disparity between lengths of coasts it is first necessary to determine which are the coasts which are being contemplated; but that determination need only be in broad terms.... If the disparity in question only emerges after scrupulous definition and comparison of coasts, it is *ex hypothesi* unlikely to be of such extent as to carry weight as a relevant circumstance....

68. ... If the coasts of Malta and the coast of Libya from Ras Ajdir to Ras Zarruq are compared, it is evident that there is a considerable disparity between their lengths, to a degree which, in the view of the Court, constitutes a relevant circumstance which should be reflected in the drawing of the delimitation line. The coast of Libya from Ras Ajdir to Ras Zarruq, measured following its general direction, is 192 miles long, and the coast of Malta from Ras il-Wardija to Delimara Point, following straight baselines but excluding the islet of Filfla, is 24 miles long. In the view of the Court, this difference is so great as to justify the adjustment of the median line so as to attribute a larger shelf area to Libya; the degree of such adjustment does not depend upon a mathematical operation and remains to be examined.

69. In the present case, the Court has also to look beyond the area concerned in the case, and consider the general geographical context in which the delimitation will have to be effected. The Court observes that that delimitation, although it relates only to the continental shelf appertaining to two States is also a delimitation between a portion of the southern littoral and a portion of the northern littoral of the Central Mediterranean. If account is taken of that setting, the Maltese islands appear as a minor feature of the northern seaboard of the region in question, located substantially to the south of the general direction of that seaboard, and themselves comprising a very limited coastal segment. From the viewpoint of the general geography of the region, this southward location of the coasts of the Maltese islands constitutes a geographical feature which should be taken into account as a pertinent circumstance; its influence on the delimitation line must be weighed in order to arrive at an equitable result....

71. In the light of these circumstances, the Court finds it necessary, in order to ensure the achievement of an equitable solution, that the delimitation line between the areas of continental shelf appertaining respectively to the two Parties, be adjusted so as to lie closer to the coasts of Malta. Within the area with which the Court is concerned, the coasts of the Parties are opposite to each other, and the equidistance line between them lies broadly west to east, so that its adjustment can be satisfactorily and simply achieved by transposing it in an exactly northward direction.

72. Once it is contemplated that the boundary requires to be shifted northward of the median line between Libya and Malta, it seems appropriate first to establish what might be the extreme limit of such a shift. This is easily done and indeed the calculation is, in broad terms, apparent from any map of the area as a whole, showing the wider geographical context which the Court has found to be relevant. Let it be supposed, for the sake of argument, that the Maltese islands were part of Italian territory, and that there was a question of the delimitation of the continental shelf between Libya and Italy, within the area to which this Judgment relates. Again, between opposite coasts, with a large, clear area between them, that boundary would not then be the median line, based solely upon the coasts of Libya to the south and Sicily to the north. At least some account would be taken of the islands of Malta; and even if the minimum account were taken, the continental shelf boundary between Italy and Libya would be somewhat south of the median line between the Sicilian and Libyan coasts. Since Malta is not part of Italy, but is an independent State, it cannot be the case that, as regards continental shelf rights, it will be in a worse position because of its independence. Therefore, it is reasonable to assume that an equitable boundary between Libya and Malta must be to the south of a notional median line between Libya and Sicily; for that is the line, as we have seen, which allows no effect at all to the islands of Malta.... A transposition northwards through 24' of latitude of the Malta-Libya median line would therefore be the extreme limit of such northward adjustment.

73. The position reached by the Court at this stage of its consideration of the case is therefore the following. It takes the median line (ignoring Filfla as a basepoint) as the first step of the delimitation. But relevant circumstances indicate that some northward shift of the boundary line is needed in order to produce an equitable result. These are first, the general geographical context in which the islands of Malta appear as a relatively small feature in a semi-enclosed sea; and secondly, the great disparity in the lengths of the relevant coasts of the two Parties. The next step in the delimitation is therefore to determine the extent of the required northward shift of the boundary line. Here, there are two important parameters which the Court has already

mentioned above. First, there is the outside limit of any northward shift, of some 24' (see paragraph 72 above). Second, there is the considerable distance between the coasts (some 195' difference of latitude, in round terms, between Benghisa Point and the Libyan coast due south of that point), which is an obviously important consideration when deciding whether, and by how much, a median line boundary can be shifted without ceasing to have an approximately median location, or approaching so near to one coast as to bring into play other factors such as security. In the present case there is clearly room for a significant adjustment, if it is found to be required for achieving an equitable result. Weighing up these several considerations in the present kind of situation is not a process that can infallibly be reduced to a formula expressed in actual figures. Nevertheless, such an assessment has to be made, and the Court has concluded that a boundary line that represents a shift of around three-quarters of the distance between the two outer parameters—that is to say between the median line and the line 24' north of it—achieves an equitable result in all the circumstances. It has therefore decided that the equitable boundary line is a line produced by transposing the median line northwards through 18' of latitude.... The course of the delimitation line dictated by the method adopted is shown, for the purposes of illustration only, on Map No. 3 [Figure VI.E] appended hereto....

77. The Court has...had occasion to note the development which has occurred in the customary law of the continental shelf, and which is reflected in Articles 76 and 83 of the United Nations Convention on the Law of the Sea, concerning the relationship between the concept of the continental shelf as the natural prolongation of the land territory of the coastal State and the factor of distance from the coast. As the Court has explained, in a geographical situation like that with which the present case is concerned, where a single continental shelf falls to be delimited between two opposite States, so that no question arises, as between those States, of delimitation by reference to a continental margin extending beyond 200 miles from the baselines round the coast of either State, the legal concept of natural prolongation does not attribute any relevance to geological or geophysical factors either as basis of entitlement or as criterion for delimitation. Each coastal State is entitled to exercise sovereign rights over the continental shelf off its coasts for the purpose of exploring it and exploiting its natural resources (Art. 77 of the Convention) up to a distance of 200 miles from the baselines—subject of course to delimitation with neighbouring States—whatever the geophysical or geological features of the sea-bed within the area comprised between the coast and the 200-mile limit. The introduction of this criterion of distance has not however had the effect of...conferring upon the equidistance method of delimitation the

status of a general rule or an obligatory method of delimitation, or of a priority method, to be tested in every case (cf. *Continental Shelf (Tunisia/Libyan Arab Jamahiriya), I.C.J. Reports 1982*, p. 79, para. 110). The fact that the Court has found that, in the circumstances of the present case, the drawing of a median line constitutes an appropriate first step in the delimitation process, should not be understood as implying that an equidistance line will be an appropriate beginning in all cases, or even in all cases of delimitation between opposite States.

78. Having drawn the initial median line, the Court has found that that line requires to be adjusted in view of the relevant circumstances of the area, namely the considerable disparity between the lengths of the coasts of the Parties here under consideration, the distance between those coasts, the placing of the basepoints governing any equidistance line, and the general geographical context. Taking these into consideration, and setting as an extreme limit for any northward displacement of the line the notional median line which, on the hypothesis of a delimitation between Italy and Libya on the basis of equidistance, in the area to which the Judgment relates, would deny any effect whatever to Malta, the Court has been able to indicate a method making it possible for the Parties to determine the location of a line which would ensure an equitable result between them. This line gives a result which seems to the Court to meet the requirements of the test of proportionality, and more generally to be equitable, taking into account all relevant circumstances, finds that,

79. For these reasons,

THE COURT
by fourteen votes to three

finds that, with reference to the areas of continental shelf between the coasts of the Parties within the limits defined in the present Judgment, namely the meridian 13° 50' E and the meridian 15° 10' E:

A. The principles and rules of international law applicable for the delimitation, to be effected by agreement in implementation of the present Judgment, of the areas of continental shelf appertaining to the Socialist People's Libyan Arab Jamahiriya and to the Republic of Malta respectively are as follows:

(1) the delimitation is to be effected in accordance with equitable principles and taking account of all relevant circumstances, so as to arrive at an equitable result;

(2) the area of continental shelf to be found to appertain to either Party not extending more than 200 miles from the coast of the Party concerned, no criterion for delimitation of shelf areas can be derived from the principle of natural prolongation in the physical sense.

B. The circumstances and factors to be taken into account in achieving an equitable delimitation in the present case are the following:

(1) the general configuration of the coasts of the Parties, their oppositeness and their relationship to each other within the general geographical context;

(2) the disparity in the lengths of the relevant coasts of the Parties and the distance between them;

(3) the need to avoid in the delimitation any excessive disproportion between the extent of the continental shelf areas appertaining to the coastal State and the length of the relevant part of its coast, measured in the general direction of the coastlines.

C. In consequence, an equitable result may be arrived at by drawing, as a first stage in the process, a median line every point of which is equidistant from the low-water mark of the relevant coast of Malta (excluding the islet of Filfla), and the low-water mark of the relevant coast of Libya, that initial line being then subject to adjustment in the light of the above mentioned circumstances and factors.

D. The adjustment of the median line referred to in subparagraph C above is to be effected by transposing that line northwards through 18' of latitude (so that it intersects the meridian 15° 10' E at approximately latitude 34° 30' N) such transposed line then constituting the delimitation line between the areas of continental shelf appertaining to the Socialist People's Libyan Arab Jamahiriya and to the Republic of Malta respectively.

Notes

1. *The Influence of the LOS Convention Negotiations on Continental Shelf Delimitations.* The Third United Nations Conference on the Law of the Sea (UNCLOS III) was in its final years while the Libya/Malta case was before the ICJ. It was clear that the final LOS Convention would contain a provision that the continental shelf would extend at least 200 nautical miles from a coastal state's baseline. See LOS Convention, Article 76. We consider the development of the concept of the continental shelf in detail in Chapter 10.

2. *The ICJ's Use of Natural Prolongation.* Contrary to the Tunisia/Libya case, where the parties could not convince the ICJ that distinctive geological or geomorphological features were present, the Libya/Malta case featured

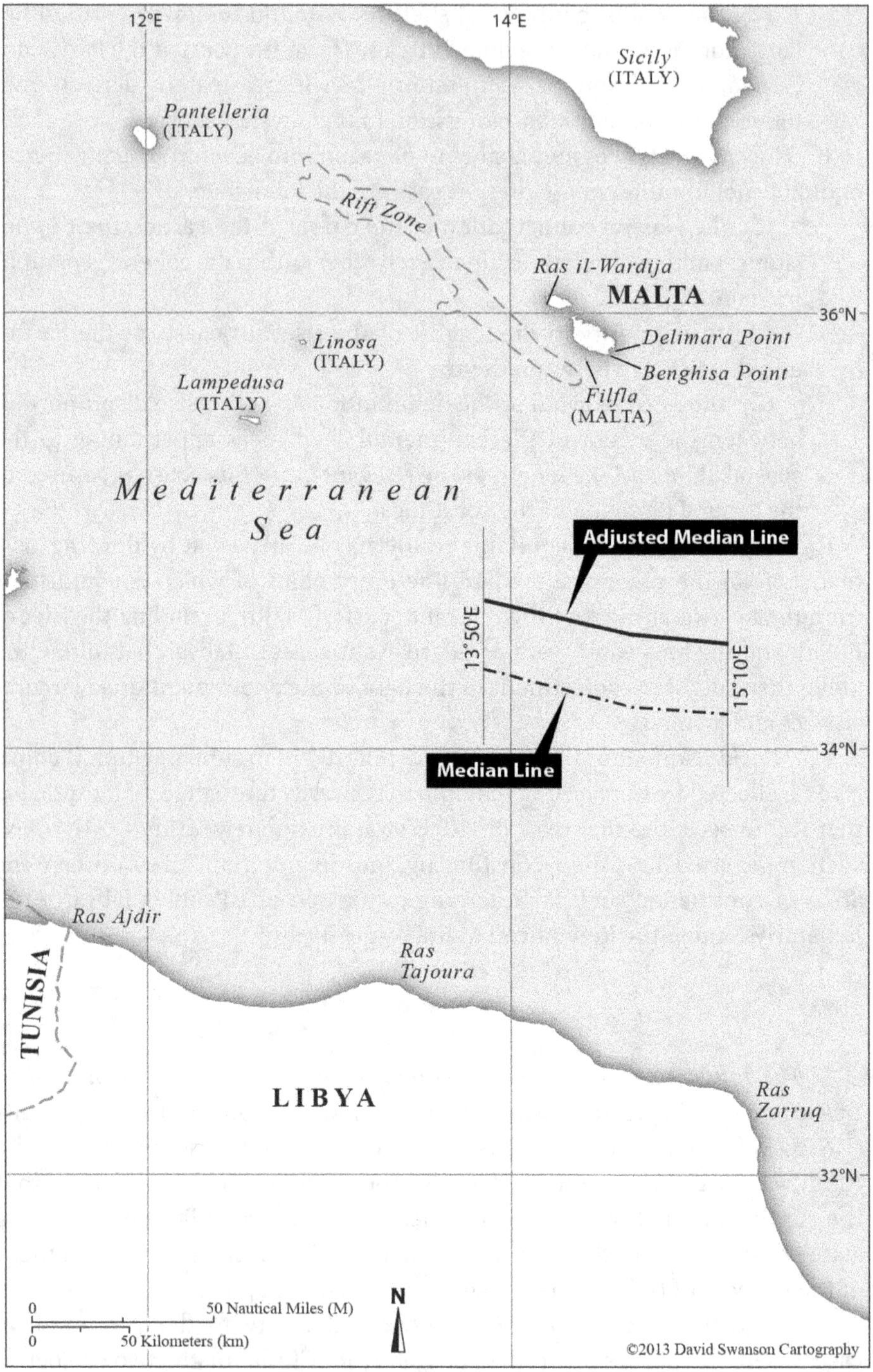

FIGURE VI.E *Libya/Malta Continental Shelf Delimitation*

a prominent rift zone. See Figure VI.E. This rift zone appeared on the international bathymetric chart of the Mediterranean as the "Malta Trough," the "Pantellera Trough," and the "Linosa Trough." ¶ 37. In paragraph 45 of the 1969 North Sea Continental Shelf cases, excerpted above, the ICJ had cited the Norwegian Trough as an example of a physical feature that could, in the Court's opinion, influence continental shelf appurtenance. The Norwegian Trough was only 200–650 meters (656–2,133 feet) deep, and Libya was convinced that the Malta Trough, located much closer to the Maltese coast than to the Libyan coast and reaching depths of over 1,000 meters (3,281 feet), would be a decisive criterion in its maritime delimitation with Malta. As in the Tunisia/Libya case, the ICJ was able to dispose of the natural prolongation argument, discussed in Note 2 following that case, but this time on other grounds. ¶ 39. What were those grounds, and is their influence likely to be more lasting? Can you think of any continental shelf delimitation situations in which features such as troughs might still be relevant? See David A. Colson, The Delimitation of the Outer Continental Shelf Between Neighboring States, 97 Am. J. Intl. L. 91 (2003).

3. *The Treatment of Islands in Maritime Delimitations.* First, in the Libya/Malta case, the ICJ decided to totally ignore Filfla Island as a base point for constructing an equidistant line. ¶ 73. This uninhabited island, which forms part of the Maltese straight baseline system, has a height of 60 meters (197 feet) and is consequently permanently above water. The ICJ confirmed its earlier opinion that baselines used by the coastal state to determine their maritime zones do not necessarily have to coincide with base points used for delimitation purposes:

> The Court does not express any opinion on whether the inclusion of Filfla in the Maltese baselines was legally justified; but in any event the baselines as determined by coastal States are not *per se* identical with the points chosen on a coast to make it possible to calculate the area of continental shelf appertaining to that State.

¶ 64. Compare the characteristics of Filfla with those of Eddystone Rocks in the France/United Kingdom arbitration, which the arbitral tribunal accepted as base points. How do you explain this difference in treatment?

Second, how did the fact that one of the states was an island influence the delimitation in the Libya/Malta case? Did the ICJ explain clearly why shifting the latitude of the median line 18' northward represented an equitable solution in this case?

4. *The ICJ's Use of Equidistance.* Is equidistance in the absence of an agreement, even though not obligatory as a rule of treaty or customary law as decided in 1969, nevertheless a logical first method to be applied by courts and tribunals in cases of opposite states, to be possibly adjusted in a second phase by relevant circumstances?

CASE CONCERNING DELIMITATION OF MARITIME AREAS (ST. PIERRE AND MIQUELON)
Canada/France, Court of Arbitration, 31 Intl. Leg. Materials 1145 (1992)

[Canada and France in 1972 delimited the overlapping territorial sea between the French islands of Saint Pierre and Miquelon, with a total area of 237 square kilometers (91.5 square miles), and the opposing Canadian coast. With respect to the remainder of the maritime boundary, however, the parties held widely divergent positions. France argued that the equidistance principle should be applied. Canada urged that these two French islands be enclaved by a territorial sea of twelve nautical miles; the France/United Kingdom arbitral tribunal, as discussed above, had used such an enclave system with respect to the English Channel Islands in front of the French coast. When Canada and France could not solve their maritime dispute through negotiations, they signed a compromis in 1989 to submit their dispute to a court of arbitration. During these proceedings both parties further develop their initial positions. The court dismisses both arguments. It first refuses to follow the France/United Kingdom arbitration.]

42. In the course of these proceedings repeated reference was made by the Parties to the treatment given to the Channel Islands in the 1977 decision in the Anglo-French Arbitration. This Court does not consider that decision to provide a precedent for the present case. The situation of the Channel Islands is substantially different from the present one, because of the proximity of the English coast. The Channel Islands were seen by the Court as an incidental feature in a delimitation between two mainland, and approximately commensurate, coasts.

[The court subsequently, perhaps with some irritation, dismisses the claims of the parties in a section of its ruling entitled "Exaggeration in the Claims of the Parties" where it states:

> This Court does not consider that either of the proposed solutions provides even a starting point for the delimitation. The Court's conclusion is similar to that drawn by the Chamber of the International Court of Justice in the Gulf of Maine case, namely "that it must undertake this final stage

of the task entrusted to it and formulate its own solution independently of the proposals made by the Parties" (ICJ Reports, 1984, para. 190).

¶ 65. It continues to give its own assessment independent of proposals made by the parties in a section that it calls "The Solution."]

66. In order to reach an equitable result, it is necessary to examine separately two different sectors of the maritime area where the delimitation is to be effected. This distinction between two separate seaward projections of the coasts of the French islands was suggested in the French Memorial, which says: "la zone dans laquelle doit intervenir la délimitation comporte deux secteurs nettement distincts, l'un à l'ouest et au sud-ouest des Iles, l'autre au sud et au sud-est de ces Iles" (¶ 307). [Eds.' translation: "the zone within which the delimitation must take place consists of two markedly distinct sectors, one toward the west and southwest of the Islands, the other toward the south and southeast of these Islands."]

67. With respect to the first sector, which may be called the western seaward projection, it is unavoidable that any seaward extension of the French coasts beyond their territorial sea would cause some degree of encroachment and cut off to the seaward projection towards the south from points located in the southern shore of Newfoundland. Both Parties, however, recognize that "some degree of cut off may be inherent in any delimitation," and such effect is "inherent in the mere presence of the islands close to the Newfoundland shore"...; it has also been stated that any solution "amputera... inéluctablement une partie de leurs droits. Tel est l'esprit de toute opération de délimitation." [Eds.' translation: "will amputate... inescapably a part of their rights. Such is the purpose of all delimitation proceedings."]

68. This Court has already concluded that the specific Canadian proposal of the enclave is not equitable because it denies the islands any maritime area beyond that already recognized as territorial sea. A limited extension of the enclave beyond the territorial sea in this western sector would meet to some degree the reasonable expectations of France of title beyond the narrow belt of territorial sea, even if causing some encroachment to certain Canadian seaward projections.

69. A reasonable and equitable solution for the western sector would be to grant to Saint Pierre and Miquelon an additional twelve nautical miles from the limit of its territorial sea, for its exclusive economic zone. That area will have the extent of the contiguous zone referred to in Article 33 of the 1982 Convention on the Law of the Sea, which grants to the coastal State jurisdiction to prevent infringement of its customs, fiscal, immigration or sanitary regulations. Beginning at point 9 of the delimitation referred to in Article 8 of the Agreement of 27 March, 1972, the line of delimitation shall be a straight

line in a southwesterly direction to the furthest point of intersection of arcs of circles of 12 nautical miles radius centred on the nearest points of the baselines described below. Thence it shall be an equidistant line between Canada and the French islands to a position 24 nautical miles from the nearest points on those baselines, from where it will follow a 24 nautical miles limit measured from the nearest points of the baseline of the French islands as far as the western limit of the second sector. In the case of Canada the baseline is to be that given in the Territorial Sea and Fishing Zones Geographical Co-ordinates Order, and in the case of the French islands the baseline is to be the low-water line of the islands, islets, above-water rocks or low-tide elevations.

70. In the second sector, towards the south and the southeast the geographical situation is completely different. The French islands have a coastal opening towards the south which is unobstructed by any opposite or laterally aligned Canadian coast. Having such a coastal opening, France is fully entitled to a frontal seaward projection towards the south until it reaches the outer limit of 200 nautical miles, as far as any other segment of the adjacent southern coast of Newfoundland. There is no foundation for claiming that Saint Pierre and Miquelon frontal projection in this area should end at the 12 mile limit of the territorial sea. On the other hand, such a seaward projection must not be allowed to encroach upon or cut off a parallel frontal projection of the adjacent segments of the Newfoundland southern coast.

71. In order to achieve this result the projection towards the south must be measured by the breadth of the coastal opening of the French islands towards the south. Thus, a balanced application of the principles and criteria invoked by the Parties leads to the solution of a second maritime area for Saint Pierre and Miquelon, in the southern sector extending to a distance of 188 nautical miles from a 12 nautical miles limit measured from the baselines already described, with its axis extending due south along the meridian half way between the two meridian described below, its eastern and western limits being formed by lines parallel to that axis and its width being determined by the distance between the meridians passing through the easternmost point of the island of St. Pierre and the westernmost point of Miquelon respectively and measured at the mean latitude of those two points, or approximately 10.5 nautical miles. From the northeastern point of the limit thus described, as far as point 1 referred to in the 1972 Agreement, the delimitation shall be a twelve nautical miles limit measured from the nearest points on the baseline of the French islands.

72. Canada has contended that in determining the seaward projection towards the South of Saint Pierre and Miquelon, account must be taken of the projection towards the east from the coasts of Cape Breton Island, 140 nautical

miles away, or from other more distant points in Nova Scotia. Both Parties considered in this connection the hypothetical situation that would arise if Nova Scotia would have been an independent country. Canada contended that it could not derive less maritime rights for the sole reason that Nova Scotia is a Canadian province.

73. The objections of Canada against the southern projection of the coast of Saint Pierre and Miquelon, based on an eastern projection from Nova Scotia and Cape Breton Island are not compelling. Geographically, the coasts of Nova Scotia have open oceanic spaces for an unobstructed seaward projection towards the south in accordance with the tendency, remarked by Canada, for coasts to project frontally, in the direction in which they face. In the hypothesis of a delimitation exclusively between Saint Pierre and Miquelon and Nova Scotia, as if the southern coast of Newfoundland did not exist, it is likely that corrected equidistance would be resorted to, the coasts being opposite. In that event it is questionable whether the area hypothetically corresponding to Nova Scotia, would reach the maritime areas towards the south appertaining to Saint Pierre and Miquelon.

74. In the light of the geographical situation, the Court finds no incompatibility or inconsistency in admitting a limited westward projection of the west coast of Saint Pierre and Miquelon, as well as a full seaward projection to 200 miles of the unobstructed south coast of the French islands.

Notes

1. *Single Maritime Boundary.* This is the first case in this chapter in which both the continental shelf and the EEZ needed to be delimited. In Article 2(1) of their compromis the parties asked the court to draw a single maritime boundary, i.e., a boundary that would delimit at the same time the continental shelf as well as the EEZ. Is this an obligation under international law? In the LOS Convention, two articles (Articles 74 and 83) deal separately with the delimitation of the continental shelf and the EEZ. Today, however, state practice indicates that, in the overwhelming majority of cases, parties seeking delimitation opt for a single maritime boundary. This trend is apparent when parties reach an agreement themselves. A similar tendency can be noted when parties opt for third-party settlement, either by mutual consent, as in the Canada/France arbitration, or when one of the parties unilaterally institutes a case. Even though state practice to the contrary does exist, states generally prefer single maritime boundaries. Why?

2. *Islands Located Close to the Shore of Another Country.* The court in the Canada/France arbitration refused to draw a parallel between Saint Pierre and

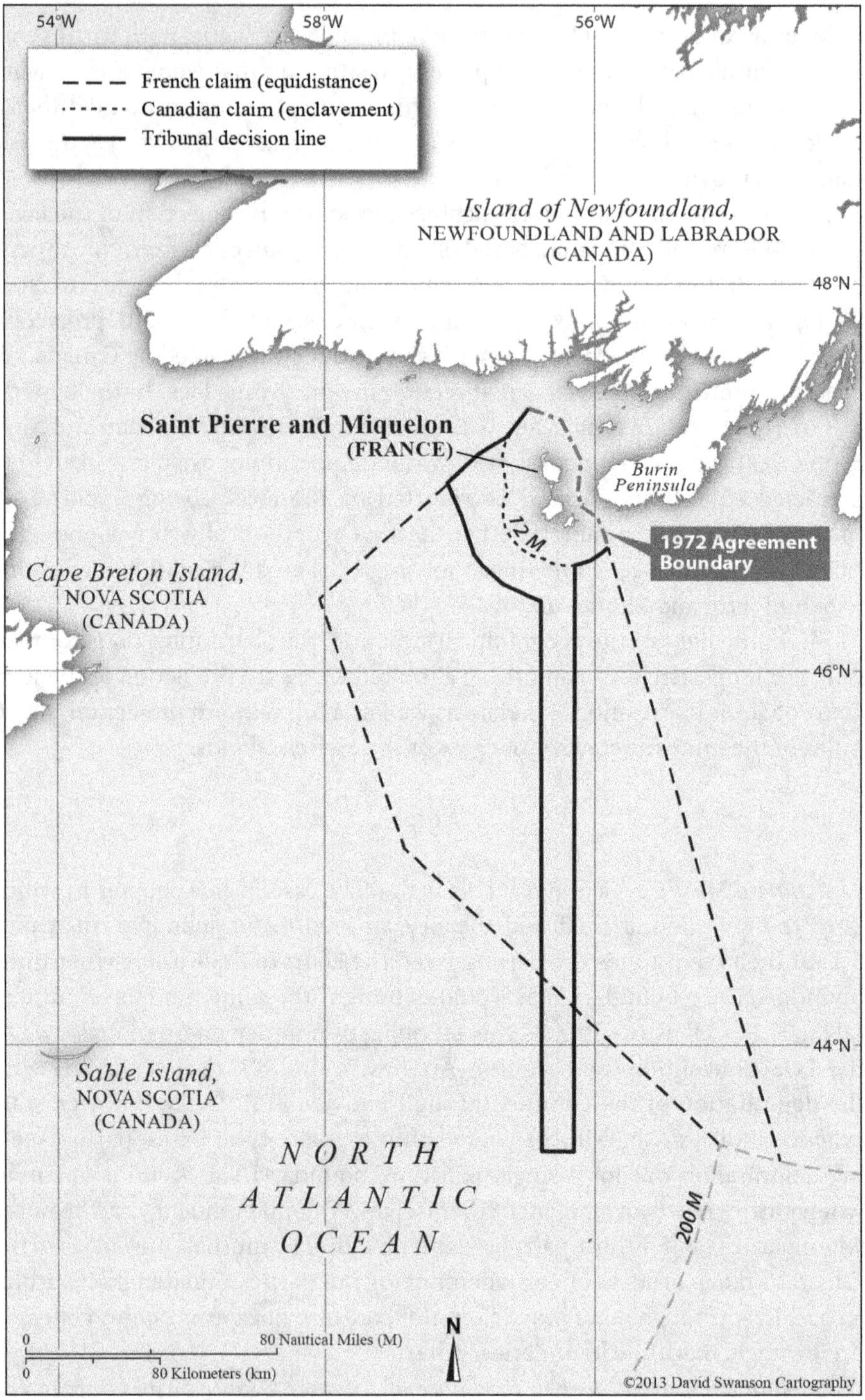

FIGURE VI.F *Maritime Delimitation in the Canada/France Arbitration*

Miquelon and the Channel Islands in the France/United Kingdom arbitration. Was this because the court fundamentally disagreed with how the arbiters solved the dispute concerning the Channel Islands in 1977, or did it rather try to distinguish the two cases? The law of maritime delimitation has sometimes been compared to a system of judge-made law in the common law tradition. Tribunals and courts often refer to one another when rendering decisions in maritime delimitation cases. See for instance paragraph 65 of the Canada/France arbitration. As will be seen, the ICJ often refers back to its own previous judgments, while the ITLOS does not distinguish between courts and tribunals and cites both ICJ and arbitral decisions. See, for example, the ICJ's Romania v. Ukraine case in Section C, ¶¶ 362 and 382–83. The normal rule is that the decision of an international judicial or arbitral body has "no binding force except between the parties and in respect of th[e] particular" case or dispute between them. ICJ Statute, Article 59; LOS Convention, Article 296(2). But do international courts and tribunals in reality follow a system of stare decisis? How can one explain this general deference of a court to its own earlier decisions, and even to decisions of other courts and tribunals?

3. *The Demise of Equidistance in Maritime Delimitation Law?* The Canada/France arbitration has been labeled "a full departure from the equidistance method." Victor Prescott & Gillian Triggs, Islands and Rocks and their Role in Maritime Delimitation, in 5 International Maritime Boundaries 3245, 3264 (David A. Colson & Robert W. Smith eds., 2005). The parties to the dispute could hardly have imagined beforehand that the court would eventually arrive at something like "The Solution"! It struck them, and many commentators, as a deus ex machina. As one of the arbiters wrote in his dissenting opinion:

> 1. I am at a loss to identify the principles and rules which could justify in law the delimitation which has been decided, and I fear that the Decision may in some respects jeopardize the development of the law of maritime delimitation....
>
> 2. My essential reason for voting against the Decision is that the delimitation in the strange form of a mushroom which is its result does not seem to me to be founded "on the basis of law."

Dissenting Opinion of Prosper Weil, ¶¶ 1–2. Did the tribunal, for instance, explain at all why on the left cap of the mushroom it granted a limited extension beyond the territorial sea, whereas on the right cap of the mushroom it did not?

We may discern a similar development in the jurisprudence of the ICJ. According to a former President of the ICJ, during the mid-1980s the

> case law and treaty law had become so unpredictable that there was extensive debate . . . on whether there still existed a law of delimitations or whether, in the name of equity, we were not ending up with arbitrary solutions. Sensitive to these criticisms, in subsequent years the Court proceeded to develop its case law in the direction of greater certainty.

Speech by His Excellency Judge Gilbert Guillaume, President of the International Court of Justice, to the Sixth Committee of the General Assembly of the United Nations, Oct. 31, 2001, available at http://www.icj-cij.org. According to President Guillaume, this new tendency started to change with the Libya/Malta case in 1985. Review the position of the ICJ with respect to the equidistance rule in that case. The Court categorically refused to recognize the obligatory nature of the equidistance rule, but did the Court's use of the principle undercut its statements about it?

The last two cases in this chapter, one before the ICJ and one before the ITLOS, suggest that the law of maritime delimitation has now attained a higher level of certainty.

MARITIME DELIMITATION IN THE BLACK SEA
Romania v. Ukraine, 2009 I.C.J. 61

[Romania and Ukraine had a longstanding dispute about the effect to be attributed to Serpents' Island, which belongs to Ukraine, on the two states' maritime boundary in the Black Sea. Serpents' Island covers an area of 0.17 square kilometers (0.065 square miles) and is located about twenty nautical miles from the delta of the Danube River, which forms the land boundary between the parties. Although Serpents' Island has housed a lighthouse since the middle of the 19th century, the parties disputed whether the island had its own fresh water resources, a point arguably relevant to the status of Serpents' Island under Article 121(3) of the LOS Convention. Romania brought this case before the ICJ on the basis of previous agreements reached by the parties stipulating that if after two years of negotiations no boundary agreement had been reached, one party could unilaterally seize the ICJ. In this decision, the Court clarifies its maritime boundary delimitation methodology.]

115. When called upon to delimit the continental shelf or exclusive economic zones, or to draw a single delimitation line, the Court proceeds in defined stages.

116. These separate stages, broadly explained in the case concerning *Continental Shelf* (*Libyan Arab Jamahiriya/Malta*) (*Judgment, I.C.J. Reports 1985*, p. 46, para. 60), have in recent decades been specified with precision.

First, the Court will establish a provisional delimitation line, using methods that are geometrically objective and also appropriate for the geography of the area in which the delimitation is to take place. So far as delimitation between adjacent coasts is concerned, an equidistance line will be drawn unless there are compelling reasons that make this unfeasible in the particular case (see *Territorial and Maritime Dispute between Nicaragua and Honduras in the Caribbean Sea (Nicaragua* v. *Honduras), Judgment, I.C.J. Reports 2007 (II)*, p. 745, para. 281). So far as opposite coasts are concerned, the provisional delimitation line will consist of a median line between the two coasts. No legal consequences flow from the use of the terms "median line" and "equidistance line" since the method of delimitation is the same for both.

117. Equidistance and median lines are to be constructed from the most appropriate points on the coasts of the two States concerned, with particular attention being paid to those protuberant coastal points situated nearest to the area to the delimited. The Court considers elsewhere ... the extent to which the Court may, when constructing a single-purpose delimitation line, deviate from the base points selected by the Parties for their territorial seas. When construction of a provisional equidistance line between adjacent States is called for, the Court will have in mind considerations relating to both Parties' coastlines when choosing its own base points for this purpose. The line thus adopted is heavily dependent on the physical geography and the most seaward points of the two coasts.

118. In keeping with its settled jurisprudence on maritime delimitation, the first stage of the Court's approach is to establish the provisional equidistance line. At this initial stage of the construction of the provisional equidistance line the Court is not yet concerned with any relevant circumstances that may obtain and the line is plotted on strictly geometrical criteria on the basis of objective data.

119. In the present case the Court will thus begin by drawing a provisional equidistance line between the adjacent coasts of Romania and Ukraine, which will then continue as a median line between their opposite coasts.

120. The course of the final line should result in an equitable solution (Articles 74 and 83 of UNCLOS). Therefore, the Court will at the next, second stage consider whether there are factors calling for the adjustment or shifting of the provisional equidistance line in order to achieve an equitable result (*Land and Maritime Boundary between Cameroon and Nigeria* (*Cameroon* v. *Nigeria: Equatorial Guinea intervening*), *Judgment, I.C.J. Reports 2002*, p. 441, para. 288). The Court has also made clear that when the line to be drawn covers several zones of coincident jurisdictions, "the so-called equitable principles/relevant circumstances method may usefully be applied, as in these maritime

FIGURE VI.G *Romania v. Ukraine Maritime Delimitation*

zones this method is also suited to achieving an equitable result" (*Territorial and Maritime Dispute between Nicaragua and Honduras in the Caribbean Sea (Nicaragua* v. *Honduras), Judgment, I.C.J. Reports 2007 (II)*, p. 741, para. 271).

121. This is the second part of the delimitation exercise to which the Court will turn, having first established the provisional equidistance line.

122. Finally, and at a third stage, the Court will verify that the line (a provisional equidistance line which may or may not have been adjusted by taking into account the relevant circumstances) does not, as it stands, lead to an inequitable result by reason of any marked disproportion between the ratio of the respective coastal lengths and the ratio between the relevant maritime area of each State by reference to the delimitation line.... A final check for an equitable outcome entails a confirmation that no great disproportionality of maritime areas is evident by comparison to the ratio of coastal lengths. This is not to suggest that these respective areas should be proportionate to coastal lengths—as the Court has said "the sharing out of the area is therefore the consequence of the delimitation, not vice versa" (*Maritime Delimitation in the Area between Greenland and Jan Mayen (Denmark* v. *Norway), Judgment, I.C.J. Reports 1993*, p. 67, para. 64).

Notes

1. *Delimitation Methodology.* The ICJ in this case provides an authoritative statement of the delimitation methodology used in modern maritime delimitation cases. What are the three steps involved? How exactly does the methodology differ from that used in earlier cases, such as the Libya/Malta case, where the Court also referred to an equidistant line? Does the fact that this decision was unanimous give more weight to this submission? Why are unanimous decisions in ICJ cases in general, and maritime delimitation cases in particular, rather exceptional?

2. *Opposite and Adjacent States.* As already discussed under Note 6 following the North Sea Continental Shelf cases, the 1958 Continental Shelf Convention makes a distinction between opposite and adjacent states as far as the applicable delimitation method is concerned. What does the ICJ in the present judgment add to this discussion?

3. *Is Serpents' Island an Island or a Rock?* In the international law of the sea an important difference exists between naturally formed islands (LOS Convention, Article 121(1)) and natural features that we may for convenience label "non-islands." See Note 2 following the France/United Kingdom arbitration. The law of the sea moreover differentiates naturally formed islands, which have a territorial sea, continental shelf, and an EEZ, from certain types

of rocks, which have a territorial sea but no EEZ or continental shelf. Review LOS Convention, Article 121(3). What characteristics does a rock need to have in order not to be downgraded to this paragraph 3 exception? How easily can these characteristics be applied in practice?

As stated before, Serpents' Island constituted a basic bone of contention between Romania and Ukraine. Central to the discussion was the question whether this feature was to be considered an island, as argued by Ukraine, or instead a rock that cannot sustain human habitation or economic life of its own, as contended by Romania. The ICJ sidestepped this issue by totally ignoring Serpents' Island in the process of delimitation. It neither served as a base point for the construction of the provisional equidistance line, since it did not form part of the general configuration of the coast, nor was it considered a relevant circumstance calling for the adjustment of that provisional equidistance line. ¶¶ 149, 189. Serpents' Island itself consequently had no effect on the delimitation. The twelve-nautical-mile arc of its territorial sea did serve as part of the delimitation line, but that arc was based on an agreement between the parties. ¶ 188. The ICJ concluded that it did "not need to consider whether Serpents' Island falls under paragraphs 2 or 3 of Article 121 of [the LOS Convention] nor their relevance to this case." ¶ 187. Why do you think courts and tribunals have so far evaded deciding the legal status of "rocks," even though the issue often arises in maritime delimitation disputes?

C Extended Continental Shelf

DISPUTE CONCERNING DELIMITATION OF THE MARITIME BOUNDARY BETWEEN BANGLADESH AND MYANMAR IN THE BAY OF BENGAL

ITLOS Case No. 16 (2012), available at http://www.itlos.org

[This is the first maritime delimitation case to be submitted to the ITLOS. In this judgment, the ITLOS first confirms the maritime dispute methodology put forward by the ICJ in the Romania v. Ukraine case. After carefully analyzing the evolution in this field the ITLOS concludes that today "jurisprudence has developed in favour of the equidistance/relevant circumstances method." ¶ 238; see also ¶¶ 225–37 and 239. Consequently, it applies that method, following the three-stage approach. Note that the delimitation aspect of the decision—concerning the territorial sea as well as the EEZ and the continental shelf—is decided by a vote of 21 to 1. This margin may suggest that delimitation methodology has become more predictable than it was in some of the earlier case law.

The ITLOS also deals with the difficult issue of Saint Martin's Island. This island belongs to Bangladesh but is near Myanmar's coast because it is located just south of the mouth of the Naaf River, which forms the land boundary between the two countries. Because of the configuration of the coasts, the island is about the same distance from the coast of each country. Both parties recognized that Saint Martin's is an island within the meaning of LOS Convention Article 121(1)–(2), but disagreed on the effect to be given to it. The ITLOS at two occasions in its judgment states what it believes to be the general rule applicable to islands, or rather the absence of any such rule: "The Tribunal notes that neither case law nor State practice indicates that there is a general rule concerning the effect to be given to islands in maritime delimitation." ¶ 147. "There is no general rule in this respect. Each case is unique and requires specific treatment, the ultimate goal being to reach a solution that is equitable." ¶ 317. The ITLOS analyzes carefully the claims of the parties and, in a short section, sets out its decision. With respect to the territorial sea delimitation, the Tribunal gives full effect to the island, while attributing no effect to it with respect to the delimitation of the EEZ and the continental shelf. ¶¶ 146–52, 316–19. The ITLOS only marginally elucidates why an island that is relevant to the delimitation of the territorial sea loses all significance with respect to other coastal zones.

The real novel contribution of this judgment to the law of maritime delimitation, however, concerns the delimitation of the continental shelf beyond the 200-nautical-mile limit. As will be explained in Chapter 10, all coastal states have a continental shelf of at least this distance, but depending on the thickness of the sediments, some of them may also claim a continental shelf extending beyond that limit. Up to this point, courts and tribunals had never decided how to delimit the continental shelf beyond 200 nautical miles, either because they refused to do so as a matter of principle in the case before them, or because the issue did not arise.]

IX. Continental shelf beyond 200 nautical miles

Jurisdiction to delimit the continental shelf in its entirety

341. While the Parties are in agreement that the Tribunal is requested to delimit the continental shelf between them in the Bay of Bengal within 200 nm, they disagree as to whether the Tribunal has jurisdiction to delimit the continental shelf beyond 200 nm and whether the Tribunal, if it determines that it has jurisdiction to do so, should exercise such jurisdiction.

342. ... Myanmar does not dispute that "as a matter of principle, the delimitation of the continental shelf, including the shelf beyond 200 [nm], could fall within the jurisdiction of the Tribunal." However, it raises the issue of the advisability in the present case of the exercise by the Tribunal of its jurisdiction with respect to the delimitation of the continental shelf beyond 200 nm.

343. Myanmar states in its Counter Memorial that the question of the jurisdiction of the Tribunal regarding the delimitation of the continental shelf beyond 200 nm in general should not arise in the present case because the delimitation line, in its view, terminates well before reaching the 200 nm limit from the baselines from which the territorial sea is measured.

344. At the same time Myanmar submits that "[e]ven if the Tribunal were to decide that there could be a single maritime boundary beyond 200 [nm] (*quod non*), the Tribunal would still not have jurisdiction to determine this line because any judicial pronouncement on these issues might prejudice the rights of third parties and also those relating to the international seabed area."

345. Myanmar further submits that "[a]s long as the outer limit of the continental shelf has not been established on the basis of the recommendations" of the Commission on the Limits of the Continental Shelf (hereinafter "the Commission"), "the Tribunal, as a court of law, cannot determine the line of delimitation on a hypothetical basis without knowing what the outer limits are." It argues in this regard that:

> A review of a State's submission and the making of recommendations by the Commission on this submission is a necessary prerequisite for any determination of the outer limits of the continental shelf of a coastal State "on the basis of these recommendations" under article 76(8) of UNCLOS and the area of continental shelf beyond 200 [nm] to which a State is potentially entitled; this, in turn, is a necessary precondition to any judicial determination of the division of areas of overlapping sovereign rights to the natural resources of the continental shelf beyond 200 [nm]. [...] To reverse the process [...], to adjudicate with respect to rights the extent of which is unknown, would not only put this Tribunal at odds with other treaty bodies, but with the entire structure of the Convention and the system of international ocean governance.

346. In support of its position, Myanmar refers to the Arbitral Award in the *Case concerning the Delimitation of Maritime Areas between Canada and France* of 10 June 1992, which states: "[i]t is not possible for a tribunal to reach a decision by assuming hypothetically the eventuality that such rights will in fact exist" (*Decision of 10 June 1992, ILM, Vol. 31* (*1992*), p. 1145, at p. 1172, para. 81).

347. Myanmar asserts that in the case concerning *Territorial and Maritime Dispute between Nicaragua and Honduras in the Caribbean Sea* (*Nicaragua* v. *Honduras*), the ICJ declined to delimit the continental shelf beyond 200 nm between Nicaragua and Honduras because the Commission had not yet made recommendations to the two countries regarding the continental shelf beyond 200 nm.

348. During the oral proceedings Myanmar clarified its position, stating, *inter alia*, that in principle it did not question the jurisdiction of the Tribunal. The Parties accepted the Tribunal's jurisdiction on the same terms, in accordance with the provisions of article 287, paragraph 1, of the Convention, "for the settlement of dispute [...] relating to the delimitation of maritime boundary between the two countries in the Bay of Bengal." According to Myanmar, the only problem that arose concerned the possibility that the Tribunal might in this matter exercise this jurisdiction and decide on the delimitation of the continental shelf beyond 200 nm.

349. Myanmar further observed that if the Tribunal "nevertheless were to consider the Application admissible on this point—*quod non*—you could not but defer judgment on this aspect of the matter until the Parties, in accordance with Article 76 of the Convention, have taken a position on the recommendations of the Commission concerning the existence of entitlements of the two Parties to the continental shelf beyond 200 [nm] and, if such entitlements exist, on their seaward extension—i.e., on the outer (not lateral, *outer*) limits of the continental shelf of the two countries."

350. Bangladesh is of the view that the Tribunal is expressly empowered by the Convention to adjudicate disputes between States arising under articles 76 and 83, in regard to the delimitation of the continental shelf. As the Convention draws no distinction in this regard between jurisdiction over the inner part of the continental shelf, i.e., that part within 200 nm, and the part beyond that distance, according to Bangladesh, delimitation of the entire continental shelf is covered by article 83, and the Tribunal plainly has jurisdiction to carry out delimitation beyond 200 nm.

351. Responding to Myanmar's argument that "in any event, the question of delimiting the shelf beyond 200 [nm] does not arise because the delimitation line terminates well before reaching the 200 [nm] limit," Bangladesh states that "Myanmar's argument that Bangladesh has no continental shelf beyond 200 [nm] is based instead on the proposition that once the area *within* 200 [nm] is delimited, the terminus of Bangladesh's shelf falls short of the 200 [nm] limit." Bangladesh contends that "[t]his can only be a valid argument if the Tribunal first accepts Myanmar's arguments in favour of an equidistance line within 200 [nm]. Such an outcome would require the

Tribunal to disregard entirely the relevant circumstances relied upon by Bangladesh."

352. With reference to Myanmar's argument regarding the rights of third parties, Bangladesh states that a potential overlapping claim of a third State cannot deprive the Tribunal of jurisdiction to delimit the maritime boundary between two States that are subject to the jurisdiction of the Tribunal, because third States are not bound by the Tribunal's judgment and their rights are unaffected by it. Bangladesh points out that so far as third States are concerned, a delimitation judgment by the Tribunal is merely *res inter alios acta* and that this assurance is provided in article 33, paragraph 2, of the Statute.

353. Bangladesh also observes that Myanmar's contention "with regard to the international seabed area disregards its own submission to the CLCS, which makes clear that the outer limits of the continental shelf *vis-à-vis* the international seabed are far removed from the maritime boundary with Bangladesh."

354. Bangladesh observes that with respect to the potential areas of overlap with India, Myanmar accepts that even if the Tribunal cannot fix a tripoint between three States, it can indicate the "general direction for the final part of the maritime boundary between Myanmar and Bangladesh," and that doing so would be "in accordance with the well-established practise" of international courts and tribunals.

355. In summarizing its position on the issue of the rights of third parties and the jurisdiction of the Tribunal, Bangladesh states that:...

> 2. The delimitation by the Tribunal of a maritime boundary in the continental shelf beyond 200 [nm] does not prejudice the rights of third parties. In the same way that international courts and tribunals have consistently exercised jurisdiction where the rights of third States are involved, ITLOS may exercise jurisdiction, even if the rights of the international community to the international seabed were involved, which in this case they are not.
>
> 3. With respect to the area of shelf where the claims of Bangladesh and Myanmar overlap with those of India, the Tribunal need only determine which of the two Parties in the present proceeding has the better claim, and effect a delimitation that is only binding on Bangladesh and Myanmar. Such a delimitation as between the two Parties to this proceeding would not be binding on India.

356. Bangladesh observes that there is no conflict between the roles of the Tribunal and the Commission in regard to the continental shelf and that,

to the contrary, the roles are complementary. Bangladesh also states that the Tribunal has jurisdiction to delimit boundaries within the outer continental shelf and that the Commission makes recommendations as to the delineation of the outer limits of the continental shelf with the Area, as defined in article 1, paragraph 1, of the Convention, provided there are no disputed claims between States with opposite or adjacent coasts.

357. Bangladesh adds that the Commission may not make any recommendations on the outer limits until any such dispute is resolved by the Tribunal or another judicial or arbitral body or by agreement between the parties, unless the parties give their consent that the Commission review their submissions. According to Bangladesh, in the present case, "the Commission is precluded from acting due to the Parties' disputed claims in the outer continental shelf and the refusal by at least one of them (Bangladesh) to consent to the Commission's actions."

358. Bangladesh points out that if Myanmar's argument were accepted, the Tribunal would have to wait for the Commission to act and the Commission would have to wait for the Tribunal to act. According to Bangladesh, the result would be that, whenever parties are in dispute in regard to the continental shelf beyond 200 nm, the compulsory procedures entailing binding decisions under Part XV, Section 2, of the Convention would have no practical application. Bangladesh adds that "[i]n effect, the very object and purpose of the UNCLOS dispute settlement procedures would be negated. Myanmar's position opens a jurisdictional black hole into which all disputes concerning maritime boundaries in the outer continental shelf would forever disappear."

359. Summarizing its position, Bangladesh states that in portraying recommendations by the Commission as a prerequisite to the exercise of jurisdiction by the Tribunal, Myanmar sets forth a "circular argument" that would make the exercise by the Tribunal of its jurisdiction with respect to the continental shelf beyond 200 nm impossible, which is inconsistent with Part XV and with article 76, paragraph 10, of the Convention.

360. The Tribunal will now consider whether it has jurisdiction to delimit the continental shelf beyond 200 nm.

361. Article 76 of the Convention embodies the concept of a single continental shelf. In accordance with article 77, paragraphs 1 and 2, of the Convention, the coastal State exercises exclusive sovereign rights over the continental shelf in its entirety without any distinction being made between the shelf within 200 nm and the shelf beyond that limit. Article 83 of the Convention, concerning the delimitation of the continental shelf between States with opposite or adjacent coasts, likewise does not make any such distinction.

362. In this regard, the Tribunal notes that in the *Arbitration between Barbados and Trinidad and Tobago*, the Arbitral Tribunal decided that "the dispute to be dealt with by the Tribunal includes the outer continental shelf, since [...] it either forms part of, or is sufficiently closely related to, the dispute [...] and [...] in any event there is in law only a single 'continental shelf' rather than an inner continental shelf and a separate extended or outer continental shelf" (*Decision of 11 April 2006, RIAA, Vol. XXVII*, p. 147, at pp. 208–209, para. 213).

363. For the foregoing reasons, the Tribunal finds that it has jurisdiction to delimit the continental shelf in its entirety. The Tribunal will now consider whether, in the circumstances of this case, it is appropriate to exercise that jurisdiction.

Exercise of jurisdiction

364. The Tribunal will first address Myanmar's argument that Bangladesh's continental shelf cannot extend beyond 200 nm because the maritime area in which Bangladesh enjoys sovereign rights with respect to natural resources of the continental shelf does not extend up to 200 nm.

365. The Tribunal notes that this argument cannot be sustained, given its decision, as set out in paragraph 339, that the delimitation line of the exclusive economic zone and the continental shelf reaches the 200 nm limit.

366. The Tribunal will now turn to the question of whether the exercise of its jurisdiction could prejudice the rights of third parties.

367. The Tribunal observes that, as provided for in article 33, paragraph 2, of the Statute, its decision "shall have no binding force except between the parties in respect of that particular dispute." Accordingly, the delimitation of the continental shelf by the Tribunal cannot prejudice the rights of third parties. Moreover, it is established practice that the direction of the seaward segment of a maritime boundary may be determined without indicating its precise terminus, for example by specifying that it continues until it reaches the area where the rights of third parties may be affected.

368. In addition, as far as the Area is concerned, the Tribunal wishes to observe that, as is evident from the Parties' submissions to the Commission, the continental shelf beyond 200 nm that is the subject of delimitation in the present case is situated far from the Area. Accordingly, the Tribunal, by drawing a line of delimitation, will not prejudice the rights of the international community.

369. The Tribunal will now examine the issue of whether it should refrain in the present case from exercising its jurisdiction to delimit the continental shelf beyond 200 nm until such time as the outer limits of the continental

shelf have been established by each Party pursuant to article 76, paragraph 8, of the Convention or at least until such time as the Commission has made recommendations to each Party on its submission and each Party has had the opportunity to consider its reaction to the recommendations.

370. The Tribunal wishes to point out that the absence of established outer limits of a maritime zone does not preclude delimitation of that zone. Lack of agreement on baselines has not been considered an impediment to the delimitation of the territorial sea or the exclusive economic zone notwithstanding the fact that disputes regarding baselines affect the precise seaward limits of these maritime areas. However, in such cases the question of the entitlement to maritime areas of the parties concerned did not arise.

371. The Tribunal must therefore consider whether it is appropriate to proceed with the delimitation of the continental shelf beyond 200 nm given the role of the Commission as provided for in article 76, paragraph 8, of the Convention and article 3, paragraph 1, of Annex II to the Convention.

372. Pursuant to article 31 of the Vienna Convention, the Convention is to be interpreted in good faith in accordance with the ordinary meaning of its terms in their context and in the light of its object and purpose. As stated in the Advisory Opinion of the Seabed Disputes Chamber, article 31 of the Vienna Convention is to be considered "as reflecting customary international law" (*Responsibilities and obligations of States sponsoring persons and entities with respect to activities in the Area (Request for Advisory Opinion submitted to the Seabed Disputes Chamber), 1 February 2011*, para. 57).

373. The Convention sets up an institutional framework with a number of bodies to implement its provisions, including the Commission, the International Seabed Authority and this Tribunal. Activities of these bodies are complementary to each other so as to ensure coherent and efficient implementation of the Convention. The same is true of other bodies referred to in the Convention.

[The ITLOS reviews the functions of the Commission, which we consider in Chapter 10, Section C.]

376. There is a clear distinction between the delimitation of the continental shelf under article 83 and the delineation of its outer limits under article 76. Under the latter article, the Commission is assigned the function of making recommendations to coastal States on matters relating to the establishment of the outer limits of the continental shelf, but it does so without prejudice to delimitation of maritime boundaries. The function of settling disputes with respect to delimitation of maritime boundaries is entrusted to dispute settlement procedures under article 83 and Part XV of the Convention, which include international courts and tribunals.

377. There is nothing in the Convention or in the Rules of Procedure of the Commission or in its practice to indicate that delimitation of the continental shelf constitutes an impediment to the performance by the Commission of its functions.

378. Article 76, paragraph 10, of the Convention states that "[t]he provisions of this article are without prejudice to the question of delimitation of the continental shelf between States with opposite or adjacent coasts." This is further confirmed by article 9 of Annex II, to the Convention, which states that the "actions of the Commission shall not prejudice matters relating to delimitation of boundaries between States with opposite or adjacent coasts."

379. Just as the functions of the Commission are without prejudice to the question of delimitation of the continental shelf between States with opposite or adjacent coasts, so the exercise by international courts and tribunals of their jurisdiction regarding the delimitation of maritime boundaries, including that of the continental shelf, is without prejudice to the exercise by the Commission of its functions on matters related to the delineation of the outer limits of the continental shelf.

380. Several submissions made to the Commission, beginning with the first submission, have included areas in respect of which there was agreement between the States concerned effecting the delimitation of their continental shelf beyond 200 nm. However, unlike in the present case, in all those situations delimitation has been effected by agreement between States, not through international courts and tribunals.

381. In this respect, the Tribunal notes the positions taken in decisions by international courts and tribunals.

382. The Arbitral Tribunal in the *Arbitration between Barbados and the Republic of Trinidad and Tobago* found that its jurisdiction included the delimitation of the maritime boundary of the continental shelf beyond 200 nm (*Decision of 11 April 2006, RIAA, Vol. XXVII*, p. 147, at p. 209, para. 217). The Arbitral Tribunal, in that case, did not exercise its jurisdiction stating that:

> As will become apparent, however, the single maritime boundary which the Tribunal has determined is such that, as between Barbados and Trinidad and Tobago, there is no single maritime boundary beyond 200 nm. (*ibid.*, at p. 242, para. 368)

383. In the case concerning *Territorial and Maritime Dispute between Nicaragua and Honduras in the Caribbean Sea* (*Nicaragua* v. *Honduras*), the ICJ declared that:

> The Court may accordingly, without specifying a precise endpoint, delimit the maritime boundary and state that it extends beyond the 82nd meridian without affecting third-States rights. It should also be noted in this regard that in no case may the line be interpreted as extending more than 200 [nm] from the baselines from which the breadth of the territorial sea is measured; any claim of continental shelf rights beyond 200 miles must be in accordance with Article 76 of UNCLOS and reviewed by the Commission on the Limits of the Continental Shelf established thereunder. (*Judgment, I.C.J. Reports 2007*, p. 659, at p. 759, para. 319).

384. The Tribunal observes that the determination of whether an international court or tribunal should exercise its jurisdiction depends on the procedural and substantive circumstances of each case.

385. Pursuant to rule 46 of the Rules of Procedure of the Commission, in the event that there is a dispute in the delimitation of the continental shelf between States with opposite or adjacent coasts, submissions to the Commission shall be considered in accordance with Annex I to those Rules. Annex I, paragraph 2, provides:

> In case there is a dispute in the delimitation of the continental shelf between opposite or adjacent States, or in other cases of unresolved land or maritime disputes, related to the submission, the Commission shall be:
>
> (a) Informed of such disputes by the coastal States making the submission; and
>
> (b) Assured by the coastal States making the submission to the extent possible that the submission will not prejudice matters relating to the delimitation of boundaries between States.

386. Paragraph 5(a) of Annex I to the same Rules further provides:

> 5. (a) In cases where a land or maritime dispute exists, the Commission shall not consider and qualify a submission made by any of the States concerned in the dispute. However, the Commission may consider one or more submissions in the areas under dispute with prior consent given by all States that are parties to such a dispute.

387. In the present case, Bangladesh informed the Commission by a note verbale dated 23 July 2009, addressed to the Secretary-General of the United Nations, that, for the purposes of rule 46 of the Rules of Procedure of the

Commission, and of Annex I thereto, there was a dispute between the Parties and, recalling paragraph 5(a) of Annex I to the Rules, observed that:

> given the presence of a dispute between Bangladesh and Myanmar concerning entitlement to the parts of the continental shelf in the Bay of Bengal claimed by Myanmar in its submission, the Commission may not "consider and qualify" the submission made by Myanmar without the "prior consent given by all States that are parties to such a dispute."

388. Taking into account Bangladesh's position, the Commission has deferred consideration of the submission made by Myanmar[.] (Statement by the Chairman of the Commission on the progress of work in the Commission, CLCS/64 of 1 October 2009, p. 10, paragraph 40)

389. The Commission also decided to defer the consideration of the submission of Bangladesh,

> in order to take into account any further developments that might occur in the intervening period, during which the States concerned might wish to take advantage of the avenues available to them, including provisional arrangements of a practical nature as outlined in annex I to the rules of procedure. (Statement by the Chairman of the Commission on the progress of work in the Commission, CLCS/72 of 16 September 2011, p. 7, paragraph 22)

390. The consequence of these decisions of the Commission is that, if the Tribunal declines to delimit the continental shelf beyond 200 nm under article 83 of the Convention, the issue concerning the establishment of the outer limits of the continental shelf of each of the Parties under article 76 of the Convention may remain unresolved. The Tribunal notes that the record in this case affords little basis for assuming that the Parties could readily agree on other avenues available to them so long as their delimitation dispute is not settled.

391. A decision by the Tribunal not to exercise its jurisdiction over the dispute relating to the continental shelf beyond 200 nm would not only fail to resolve a long-standing dispute, but also would not be conducive to the efficient operation of the Convention.

392. In the view of the Tribunal, it would be contrary to the object and purpose of the Convention not to resolve the existing impasse. Inaction in the present case, by the Commission and the Tribunal, two organs created by the Convention to ensure the effective implementation of its provisions, would

leave the Parties in a position where they may be unable to benefit fully from their rights over the continental shelf.

393. The Tribunal observes that the exercise of its jurisdiction in the present case cannot be seen as an encroachment on the functions of the Commission, inasmuch as the settlement, through negotiations, of disputes between States regarding delimitation of the continental shelf beyond 200 nm is not seen as precluding examination by the Commission of the submissions made to it or hindering it from issuing appropriate recommendations.

394. For the foregoing reasons, the Tribunal concludes that, in order to fulfil its responsibilities under Part XV, Section 2, of the Convention in the present case, it has an obligation to adjudicate the dispute and to delimit the continental shelf between the Parties beyond 200 nm. Such delimitation is without prejudice to the establishment of the outer limits of the continental shelf in accordance with article 76, paragraph 8, of the Convention.

[The ITLOS subsequently addresses entitlement to the continental shelf beyond 200 nautical miles. Because delimitation presupposes overlapping entitlements, the ITLOS has to determine whether there are entitlements and whether they overlap. In answering these questions affirmatively, the ITLOS emphasizes that it is the coastal state and not the Commission on the Limits of the Continental Shelf (discussed in Chapter 10, Section C) that establishes the limits of the continental shelf beyond 200 nautical miles. But, just as a country may be entitled to land territory where its boundaries are uncertain, entitlement to the continental shelf beyond 200 nautical miles does not require fixed outer limits. Bangladesh disputes that Myanmar has an entitlement beyond 200 nautical miles mainly because of a lack of natural prolongation, arguing that the sediments found in the area are all transported by the Ganges-Brahmaputra river system and thus are of Bangladeshi origin. The ITLOS, however, construing the text of Article 76 of the LOS Convention, finds that natural prolongation in its geological sense is not a separate legal test for entitlement. The Tribunal determines that the geomorphological requirement of paragraph 4(a)(i) of that Article is met because a "thick layer of sedimentary rocks covers practically the entire floor of the Bay of Bengal, including areas appertaining to" both Bangladesh and Myanmar. ¶ 445.

Having determined that overlapping entitlements exist beyond 200 nautical miles, the ITLOS then proceeds to delimit this area of overlap. Bangladesh maintains that the Ganges-Brahmaputra river system and its deposits give that country "the most natural prolongation" in the Bay of Bengal, and consequently argues that this element is a relevant circumstance that the ITLOS must take into account when delimiting the area beyond 200 nautical miles. ¶ 457. Continuing its reasoning that natural prolongation "is not an

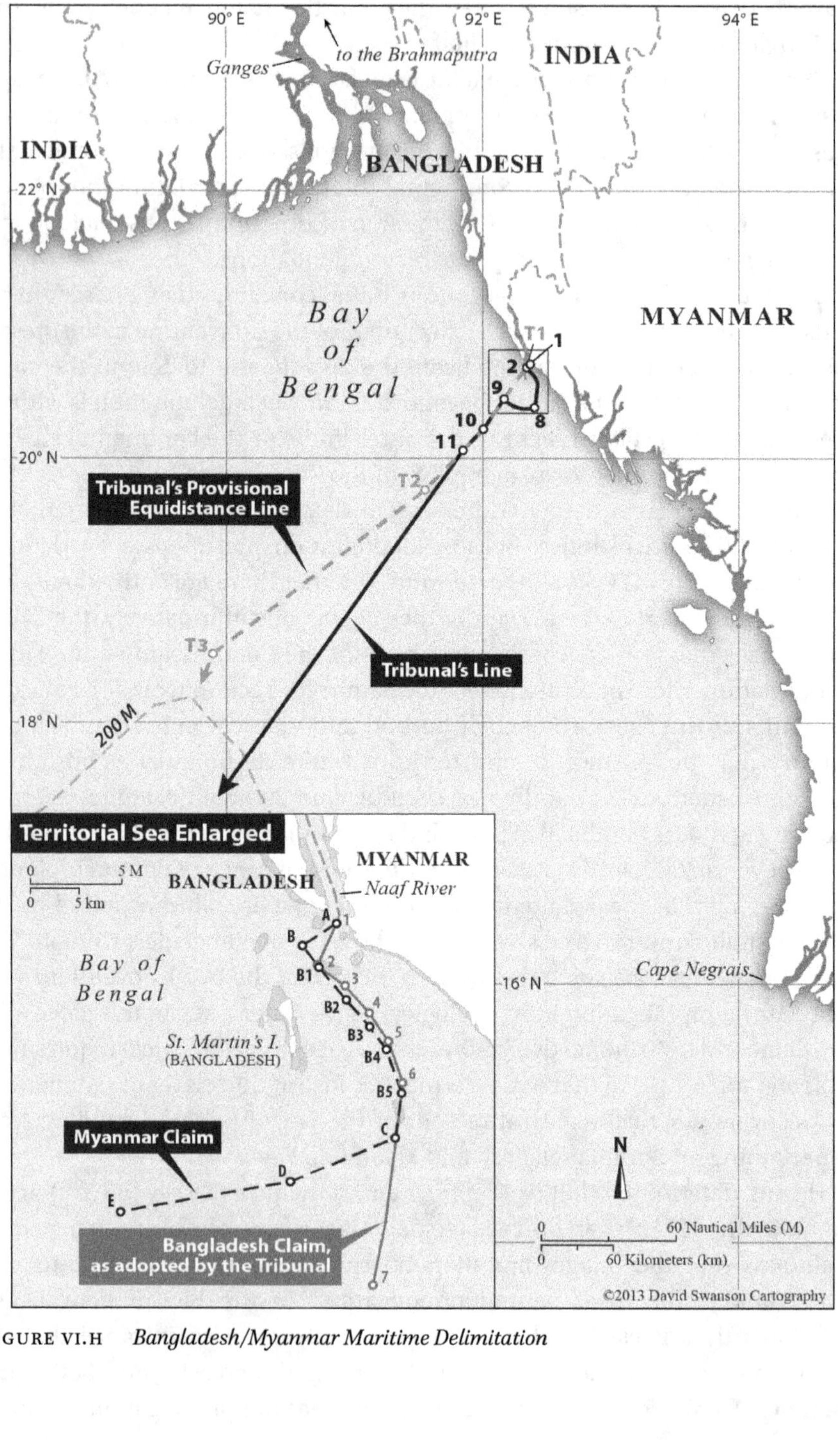

FIGURE VI.H *Bangladesh/Myanmar Maritime Delimitation*

independent basis for entitlement and should be interpreted in the context of" other provisions of Article 76 of the LOS Convention, the ITLOS simply dismisses Bangladesh's argument. ¶ 460. The Tribunal applies the same criteria it used to delimit the maritime boundary inside the 200-nautical-mile limit and continues its delimitation line in the same direction until it reaches the area where the rights of third states may be affected. ¶ 462.]

Notes

1. *The Continental Shelf beyond 200 Nautical Miles.* As stated in the introduction to this case, courts and tribunals had previously not delimited the continental shelf beyond 200 nautical miles from baselines. Does this case mean that from now on courts and tribunals will decide the issue when the parties request delimitation of a maritime zone between them that includes the continental shelf, or even propriu motu? After all, as the ITLOS noted in paragraph 361 of its opinion, Article 76 makes no distinction between the sovereign rights exercised by a coastal state over the so-called inner or outer continental shelf. What prompted the ITLOS to delimit the outer, or extended, continental shelf in the Bangladesh/Myanmar case? In the Canada/France arbitration, discussed above, the court stated, when asked to delimit the continental shelf beyond 200 nautical miles:

> Any decision by this Court recognizing or rejecting any rights of the Parties over the continental shelf beyond 200 nautical miles, would constitute a pronouncement involving a delimitation, not "between the Parties" but between each one of them and the international community, represented by organs entrusted with the administration and protection of the international sea-bed Area (the sea-bed beyond national jurisdiction) that has been declared to be the common heritage of mankind. This Court is not competent to carry out a delimitation which affects the rights of a Party which is not before it.

¶¶ 78–79. How was the ITLOS able to sidestep this cogent argument in the Bangladesh/Myanmar case? The Area will be discussed in more detail in Chapter 11.

2. *What Remains of Natural Prolongation?* The ICJ introduced the notion of natural prolongation in 1969. With respect to the legal relevance of natural prolongation, have we now come full circle to where we were prior to the North Sea cases? Later ICJ judgments downgraded and eventually dismissed this notion as far as its effect is concerned inside the 200-nautical-mile zone, as illustrated by the Tunisia/Libya and Libya/Malta cases. Yet the idea remained

that "natural prolongation" might still be relevant beyond 200 nautical miles, because in that instance one was dealing only with the delimitation of a single maritime zone, namely the continental shelf. See Note 2 following the Libya/Malta case. In the Bangladesh/Myanmar case, Bangladesh stressed just that point. Did the ITLOS definitively settle the question of the importance to be attributed to natural prolongation in maritime delimitation cases? Consider a continental shelf beyond 200 nautical miles that needs to be delimited but is characterized by a trough or a rift zone.

3. *Development of the Applicable Law.* The law governing maritime delimitation of the EEZ and the continental shelf first went through a period of uncertainty, as this section has demonstrated. Starting from the equidistance/special circumstances method contained in Article 6(2) of the 1958 Continental Shelf Convention, the method of delimitation was transformed into the equity/relevant circumstances rule. See Note 5 following the North Sea Continental Shelf cases. Articles 74 and 83 of the LOS Convention, governing the delimitation of the EEZ and the continental shelf, are themselves highly indeterminate, providing no concrete method to be applied but merely a result to be obtained. However, around the time the LOS Convention entered into force, judgments of courts and arbitral tribunals started to converge around yet another standard, now called the equidistance/relevant circumstances method. In the Bangladesh/Myanmar case, the ITLOS noted "that jurisprudence has developed in favour of the equidistance/relevant circumstances method," and the Tribunal found it the appropriate method to apply. ¶¶ 238–39. Semantically, this method comes very close to the "equidistance/special circumstances" method found in Article 6 of the 1958 Continental Shelf Convention. How, if at all, do the two methods differ?

4. *Choice of Forum.* On October 8, 2009, Bangladesh initiated an arbitral tribunal proceeding against Myanmar in accordance with Article 287 and Annex VII of the LOS Convention. As discussed in Chapter 15, this is the default procedure when parties to a dispute do not opt for the same choice of procedure. Read LOS Convention, Article 287 in the Appendix. Neither Bangladesh nor Myanmar had made any choice under Article 287. Once Myanmar was no longer in a position to avoid adjudication, it made a declaration in accordance with Article 287(1) on November 4, 2009, in which it accepted the jurisdiction of the ITLOS for this particular case. On December 12, 2009 Bangladesh issued an almost identical declaration:

> Pursuant to Article 287, paragraph 1 of the 1982 United Nations Convention on the Law of the Sea, the Government of the People's Republic of Bangladesh declares that it accepts the jurisdiction of the

> International Tribunal for the Law of the Sea for the settlement of dispute between the People's Republic of Bangladesh and the Union of Myanmar relating to the delimitation of their maritime boundary in the Bay of Bengal.

Bangladesh/Myanmar, ITLOS Case No. 16, Notification submitted by Bangladesh (Dec. 13, 2009), available at http://www.itlos.org. In effect, Bangladesh accepted the offer made by Myanmar and the procedure was changed from an Annex VII arbitration to a case before the ITLOS. Id., Order 2010/1 (Jan. 28, 2010). Did the ITLOS consider that this case was introduced unilaterally or by mutual consent? The answer to this question can have major implications for subsequent procedures, as for instance if one of the parties were to contest the jurisdiction of the ITLOS. In his Declaration appended to the Tribunal's final judgment, Judge Treves notes that similar "transfers" from Annex VII arbitration to the ITLOS had already occurred in three other of its cases. Id., Declaration of Judge Treves (Mar. 14, 2012). After the ITLOS had been properly seized, Myanmar withdrew its declaration. Id., Judgment (Mar. 14, 2012), ¶ 8. What is the legal effect of withdrawing consent once a court or tribunal has been regularly seized? This maneuvering illustrates the high level of flexibility that characterizes the dispute settlement provisions of the LOS Convention, as will be further discussed in Chapter 15.

If two states have difficulty negotiating a maritime boundary, does the indeterminancy in the law of maritime delimitation law make it more or less likely that those states will submit their maritime boundary disputes to a third-party tribunal for a binding decision? What are the relative advantages and disadvantages of arbitration, the ICJ, a chamber of the ICJ, the ITLOS, and a chamber of the ITLOS as forums to settle maritime boundary disputes? Non-binding conciliation, another dispute settlement option that has been used on occasion, is also available under the LOS Convention. See R.R. Churchill, Maritime Delimitation in the Jan Mayen Area, 9 Marine Policy 16 (1985); LOS Convention, Article 297 and Annex V.

5. *Single Maritime Boundary.* When Bangladesh and Myanmar appeared before the ITLOS, they agreed that a single delimitation line should be drawn for their continental shelf and EEZ boundaries. See ¶¶ 178–81. Why is a single maritime boundary the preferred method of settling complex maritime boundaries, i.e., those applicable to more than one maritime zone? See also Note 1 following the Canada/France arbitration.

CHAPTER 7

Internal Waters and Ports

This chapter explores international legal issues related to internal waters and ports. A state has sovereignty over its internal waters, which are bordered to the seaward by the territorial sea or by archipelagic waters of archipelagic states. Internal waters are located on the landward side of the baseline and include lakes, rivers, bays, historic waters, and many ports. A port, where cargo and passengers are loaded or unloaded, is generally an integral part of the coastline. However, ships may also anchor and load or unload cargoes at roadsteads or deepwater ports at a distance from the coast.

Section A of this chapter explores whether foreign vessels have a right of access to ports. Section B analyzes the resolution of conflicts of jurisdiction that arise when foreign flag vessels and their crews are present in internal waters. Finally, Section C considers port state jurisdiction and control over foreign flag vessels pursuant to treaties regulating environmental, safety, and labor matters; these treaties have led to an enlarged scope for port state jurisdiction.

A Access to Ports

If foreign flag vessels have a right of access to a coastal state's ports, the "sovereignty" of the coastal state over its internal waters is correspondingly qualified. This section explores whether such a right of access exists at international law, along with the conditions that a state may attach to access to its ports. The section includes excerpts from a bilateral treaty and a multilateral treaty, an international arbitral decision, and two decisions of municipal courts discussing international law.

NETHERLANDS-UNITED STATES TREATY OF FRIENDSHIP, COMMERCE AND NAVIGATION

Mar. 27, 1956, 8 U.S.T. 2043, 285 U.N.T.S. 231

Article 19(2)

Vessels of either Party shall have liberty, on equal terms with vessels of the other Party and on equal terms with vessels of any third country, to come with their cargoes to all ports, places and waters of such other Party open to foreign commerce and navigation. Such vessels and cargoes shall in all respects

 | DOI 10.1163/9789004203563_008

be accorded national treatment and most-favored nation treatment within the ports, places and waters of such other Party.

STATUTE ON THE INTERNATIONAL RÉGIME OF MARITIME PORTS
Opened for signature Dec. 9, 1923, 58 L.N.T.S. 285, 22 Am. J. Intl. L. Supp. 69 (1928)

Article 1

All ports which are normally frequented by sea-going vessels and used for foreign trade shall be deemed to be maritime ports within the meaning of the present Statute.

Article 2

Subject to the principle of reciprocity and to the reservation set out in the first paragraph of Article 8,* every Contracting State undertakes to grant the vessels of every other Contracting State equality of treatment with its own vessels, or those of any other State whatsoever, in the maritime ports situated under its sovereignty or authority, as regards freedom of access to the port, the use of the port, and the full enjoyment of the benefits as regards navigation and commercial operations which it affords to vessels, their cargoes and passengers.

The equality of treatment thus established shall cover facilities of all kinds, such as allocation of berths, loading and unloading facilities, as well as dues and charges of all kinds levied in the name or for the account of the Government, public authorities, concessionaires or undertakings of any kind.

Article 3

The provisions of the preceding Article in no way restrict the liberty of the competent port authorities to take such measures as they may deem expedient for the proper conduct of the business of the port provided that these measures comply with the principle of equality of treatment as defined in the said Article. . . .

Article 13

This Statute applies to all vessels, whether publicly or privately owned or controlled. It does not, however, apply in any way to warships or vessels

* According to Article 8(1), each Contracting State "reserves the power . . . of suspending the benefit of equality of treatment from any vessel of a State which does not effectively apply . . . this Statute to the vessels of the said Contracting State." [Eds.]

performing police or administrative functions, or, in general, exercising any kind of public authority, or any other vessels which for the time being are exclusively employed for the purposes of the Naval, Military or Air Forces of a State.

Article 14

This Statute does not in any way apply to fishing vessels or to their catches....

Article 16

Measures of a general or particular character which a Contracting State is obliged to take in case of an emergency affecting the safety of the State or the vital interests of the country may, in exceptional cases, and for as short a period as possible, involve a deviation from the provisions of Articles 2 to 7 inclusive; it being understood that the principles of the present Statute must be observed to the utmost possible extent.

Article 17

No Contracting State shall be bound by this Statute to permit the transit of passengers whose admission to its territories is forbidden, or of goods of a kind of which the importation is prohibited, either on grounds of public health or security, or as a precaution against diseases of animals or plants. As regards traffic other than traffic in transit, no Contracting State shall be bound by this Statute to permit the transport of passengers whose admission to its territories is forbidden, or of goods of which the import or export is prohibited, by its national laws.

Each Contracting State shall be entitled to take the necessary precautionary measures in respect of the transport of dangerous goods or goods of a similar character, as well as general police measures, including the control of emigrants entering or leaving its territory, it being understood that such measures must not result in any discrimination contrary to the principles of the present Statute.

Nothing in this Statute shall affect the measures which one of the Contracting States is or may feel called upon to take in pursuance of general international conventions to which it is a party, or which may be concluded hereafter, particularly conventions concluded under the auspices of the League of Nations, relating to the traffic in women and children, the transit, export or import of particular kinds of articles such as opium or other dangerous drugs, arms, or the produce of fisheries, or in pursuance of general conventions intended to prevent any infringement of industrial, literary or artistic property, or relating to false marks, false indications of origin or other methods of unfair competition.

Notes

1. *Access to Ports and Bilateral Treaties.* Numerous bilateral treaties incorporate the principle of freedom of access to ports. Article 19(2) of the 1956 United States-Netherlands Treaty of Friendship, Commerce and Navigation provides an example. Why would countries often include this principle of free access in bilateral treaties?

2. *Access to Ports and Multilateral Treaties.* Multilateral treaties do not normally reflect the bilateral practice by explicitly providing for access to ports. One exception is the Statute on the International Régime of Maritime Ports, which entered into force on July 26, 1926, and is still in force. As of September 1, 2013, ratifications, accessions, or notifications of succession had been deposited by 42 states (including Germany, Japan, and the United Kingdom, but excluding the United States), the most recent in 2001. M. Sugimura, the Rapporteur of the 1919 League of Nations Ports Committee, noted that Article 23(e) of the 1919 Covenant of the League of Nations and Article 379 of the 1919 Treaty of Versailles supported development of the Statute. According to the Rapporteur, the "fundamental idea which we have constantly borne in mind" in negotiating the Statute was "facilitating maritime transport and international trade as far as possible." Report of the Ports Committee to the Conference, in League of Nations, Second General Conference on Communications and Transit, Geneva, 15 Nov.–9 Dec. 1923, Records and Texts Relating to the Convention and Statute on the International Regime of Maritime Ports 90, League of Nations Doc. C.29.M.15.1924.VIII (1924).

Do other multilateral treaties support a right of access to ports? The 1982 United Nations Convention on the Law of the Sea (LOS Convention) does not explicitly provide for such a right. However, Articles 17 and 18(1)(b) of the LOS Convention provide a right of innocent passage through the territorial sea for the purpose of entering or leaving internal waters.

Do provisions of the widely accepted 1947 General Agreement on Tariffs and Trade, which promotes the reduction and elimination of trade barriers, support a right of access to ports? According to Article V(2) of the GATT, "[t]here shall be freedom of transit through the territory of each contracting party... for traffic in transit to or from the territory of other contracting parties. No distinction shall be made which is based on the flag of vessels... or on any circumstances relating to the ownership of... vessels." Article XI provides as a general rule that "[n]o prohibitions or restrictions other than duties, taxes or other charges... shall be instituted or maintained by any contracting party" on imports from or exports to other contracting parties. GATT Article XX, however, provides for nondiscriminatory measures that, inter alia, are "necessary to protect human, animal or plant life or health" or relate to customs enforcement. Permissible port state conditions on access are discussed later in this section. For an introduction to the effect of international trade law on port access, see Ted L. McDorman, Regional Port State Control Agreements: Some Issues of International Law, 5 Ocean & Coastal L.J. 207, 219–22 (2000).

SAUDI ARABIA v. ARABIAN AMERICAN OIL CO. (ARAMCO)
Arbitration Tribunal (1958), 27 Intl. L. Rep. 117 (1963)

[This case concerns the interpretation of two Saudi Arabian agreements. By the first, signed on May 29, 1933, and later amended, Saudi Arabia ("the Government" in the opinion) granted to Aramco (sometimes "the Company") the exclusive right to transport oil taken from Aramco's concession area in Saudi Arabia. By a 1954 agreement with A.S. Onassis and his company, Saudi Arabian Maritime Tankers Ltd. ("Satco"), Saudi Arabia gave Satco vessels a 30-year "right of priority" to carry Saudi Arabian oil. That agreement also provided that the Satco fleet would be of Saudi Arabian registry. Aramco claimed that the Onassis agreement contravened its rights under the 1933 agreement to transport Saudi Arabian oil in vessels of its own choosing, by improperly forcing Aramco to use Satco's Saudi-flagged tankers.

The arbitral tribunal, composed of Referee Badawi and Arbitrators Habachy and Sauser-Hall (succeeded by Hassan), decides in favor of Aramco by two votes to one. Among the points discussed in the extensive majority opinion is the question of the Saudi government's control over access to its ports.]

[T]he Government . . . believes . . . that it has the right, by virtue of its sovereignty, to create a national fleet, to grant it any prerogatives and privileges it deems fit, and to regulate at its own discretion the conditions of access and of departure of foreign ships to and from the State ports. The Government contends that this right is of particular importance, as regards the transportation by sea of the main commercial product of its national economy. Therefore a priority right can be granted to tankers flying the national flag. This right is far from being absolute in the Government's intention, but is limited by the implied covenant, recognized by the Government, that nothing will be done which could have the effect of preventing or impeding the export of oil by the concessionary Company. The Government invokes in this connection its rights of territorial sovereignty and its power to regulate the exercise of the concessions granted for the exploitation and development of the national resources of its subsoil.

It is indisputable that every sovereign State has the right to control its ports, for they are a part of its maritime communications. It has the international competence, by virtue of its internal independence and of its territorial supremacy, to regulate as it deems best, transportation from its territory, whether by land or by sea. With regard to the development and safeguard of its economic and financial interests particularly, a State has undeniably the right to regulate and to control importation into, and exportation from, its territory of articles of every description; this right of control embraces the right to prohibit the ingress or egress of certain goods, and to levy duties upon imports and exports. International case-law and doctrine unanimously admit that "for the purpose of furthering its commercial, fiscal and political interests, a state must be able to supervise all ships entering, leaving or anchoring in its territorial waters" (Higgins and Colombos, *The International Law of the Sea*, 3rd ed. 1954, paragraph 77, p. 66). Reference may be made to a judicial decision in this sense, that of Arbitrator Borel (dated July 18, 1932) in the case of the ships *Kronprins Gustav Adolf* and *Pacific* between Sweden and the United States of America (*U.N.R.I.A.A.*, vol. II, p. 1256).*

However, the territorial sovereignty of the State over its means of maritime communications is not unrestricted. It can only be exercised within the limits of customary international law, of the treaties the State has concluded and of the particular undertakings it has assumed.

According to a great principle of public international law, the ports of every State must be open to foreign merchant vessels and can only be closed when the vital interests of the State so require (Guggenheim, *Traité de droit international public*, vol. I, 1953, p. 419). This is clearly provided in Article 16 of the Statute on the international régime of maritime ports, of 9 December 1923, established by the Second Conference on Communications in Geneva. Freedom for foreign vessels to enter the ports of a State implies the right to load and to unload goods. It follows that the Company, by virtue of the rules of the Law of Nations, is plainly entitled to sell its oil and its products to any purchasers it chooses, under such terms and conditions as are agreed upon with them, and thus to conclude f.o.b. [free on board] sales, in which tankers are supplied by the buyers. It cannot be impeded by discrimination based on

* This case concerned the allegedly improper detention of two Swedish merchant vessels in U.S. ports during the First World War. The sole arbitrator, Borel of Switzerland, found for the United States on the narrow point that the detention did not violate 1783 and 1827 treaties between Sweden and the United States. The point about port access cited here is an observation *obiter* that, in accordance with the preamble of the 1783 treaty, the ports of either party were "subject to the territorial sovereignty of the State concerned and to the interior regulations, respecting navigation and commerce, which the State remained at liberty to make as it deemed convenient." The "Kronprins Gustaf Adolf" (1932), 2 Rep. Intl. Arb. Awards 1239, 1256 (2006). [Eds.]

nationality of the ships and resulting in the exclusion, from the loading and transport of oil for export, of customers who wish to carry away the oil on their own tankships or on tankships especially chartered for this purpose. The only right which the Government could invoke, on the basis of international law, would be the right of every State to reserve coasting navigation to vessels flying the national flag. However, Saudi Arabia recognizes Aramco's exclusive right of maritime transport in all its territorial waters included in the Concession area.

In the exercise of its sovereignty, the State of Saudi Arabia has imposed restrictions upon itself in order to grant to the concessionary Company, for a valuable consideration of the importance stipulated in the 1933 Concession Agreement, an exclusive right of transportation by land and by sea for a limited period of time. It has guaranteed to the Company that it would not exercise its sovereignty in any way contrary to the obligations it has undertaken towards Aramco and to the rights it has granted. The sovereignty of the State is not limited by some exterior cause; it is the State itself which undertakes the (negative) obligation not to impede the grantee's exercise of its rights. The principle of respect for acquired rights prevents the State from derogating from this undertaking. By the signing of the 1933 Concession Agreement, the Government has already exercised its right to supervise the ingress and egress of ships into and from its territorial waters.... "No one may derogate from his own grant" is a legal maxim which is universally accepted. It is recognized by the Hanbali school of Moslem law, as has been found by the Tribunal; it applies to all legal relationships, whether in private law or in public law.

In the oral proceedings, Government's Counsel have put forward the proposition that a State may control all activities carried on within its frontiers and its territorial waters, even those which involve communications or transport across its borders, when, in fact, they have repercussions beyond these borders, either on the high seas or within the territory of a foreign State.

The Government contends, in other words, that it has the right to fix the conditions on which petroleum may cross the national borders of Saudi Arabia, whether by pipeline or by tankships. It also contends that, while it exercises this right—which has inevitably some effects outside its territorial domain, in foreign countries or on the high seas—it does not go beyond the limits of its competence under international law. The Government concludes therefrom that, in respect of goods produced within its territory and subject to its jurisdiction, it is entitled to impose upon the concessionaire the obligation to transport these goods overseas on vessels flying its national flag and enjoying the monopoly it wishes to grant to such vessels.

The Arbitration Tribunal is unable to agree with such an argumentation, which overlooks the exclusive right of transport by sea belonging to the concessionaire of an integral oil enterprise—a right which has been clearly confirmed by a complete and objective analysis of all the governing texts.

The Government's thesis is refutable, since both Parties admit that Aramco's exclusive right to transport, pursuant to Article 2 of the 1933 Concession Agreement, covers the territorial sea of Saudi Arabia as well as its "offshore waters" in the Persian Gulf comprised in the "exclusive area." While the Government recognized this exclusive right of maritime transport with regard to the whole extent of its territorial waters, and even to its offshore waters—which implies the right to cross the frontier—it contended at the same time that the right to cross the line constituting the maritime frontier in order to enter the high seas would be excluded from that right of maritime transport. This argumentation is untenable. It is illogical to consider as a violation of the concessionary's obligations the exercise by him, on the high seas, of his exclusive right of transport which is not contested within the maritime frontiers of Saudi Arabia. A contention which is so contrary to the needs of international commerce cannot be accepted by the Arbitration Tribunal, for it involves a restriction of the principle of freedom of the high seas which finds no justification whatever in the Law of Nations. Under this law, the sovereignty of the State is, in principle, limited to its territorial domain and an extension of its power beyond those limits is only admitted under exceptional conditions which do not exist in the present dispute.

Notes

1. *A Right of Access to Ports and Customary International Law.* What was the basis for the arbitral tribunal's statement in the Aramco case that "[a]ccording to a great principle of international law, ports of every State must be open to foreign merchant vessels and can only be closed when the vital interests of a State so require"? Is this principle a necessary corollary of the high seas freedom of navigation? Is the principle established by combination of the general practice of states in opening their ports to commercial traffic, the multilateral Statute on the International Régime of Maritime Ports, and the web of bilateral treaties recognizing a right of access to ports (see Note 1 following the treaty excerpts above)? Or do the exceptions to the Statute on the International Régime of Maritime Ports and "the plethora of bilateral port access agreements in existence" instead indicate, as one scholar has put it, "the absence of a right of access to ports under customary international law"? Erik Jaap Molenaar, Port State Jurisdiction: Toward Comprehensive, Mandatory and Global Coverage, 38 Ocean Dev. & Intl. L. 225, 227 (2007). According to the International Court of Justice (ICJ), "in order to enjoy access to ports, foreign

vessels possess" a right of innocent passage through the territorial sea to and from internal waters as a matter of customary international law, and that if a "right of access to the port is hindered[,] what is infringed is the freedom of communications and of maritime commerce." Case Concerning Military and Paramilitary Activities in and against Nicaragua (Nicaragua v. United States), 1986 I.C.J. 4, 111–12. Do the ICJ's statements support a customary international law right of access to ports?

Publicists have expressed different views concerning the existence of a right of access to ports under customary international law. See, e.g., George C. Kasoulides, Port State Control and Jurisdiction 1–22 (1993); Vasilios Taskias, The Regime of Maritime Port Access: A Relook at Contemporary International and United States Law, 5 Loyola Maritime L.J. 1 (2007). Many authorities deny a right of access to ports. Why? A.V. Lowe would resolve equivocal evidence in favor of "the right of the coastal State to deny entry," because of the "sovereignty of States over their ports and the fundamental rule of international law that limitations upon sovereignty must be established by those claiming their existence." A.V. Lowe, The Right of Entry into Maritime Ports in International Law, 14 San Diego L. Rev. 597, 619 (1977). In the absence of a treaty providing a right of access to ports, should decision makers resolve conflicting evidence in accordance with the "fundamental rule" Lowe describes? What are the alternatives?

2. *Sovereignty of Coastal States over Internal Waters*. What does it mean to say, as the LOS Convention recognizes in Article 2(1), that a coastal state has "sovereignty" with respect to its internal waters? Does it mean that international law has nothing to say about a coastal state's actions affecting these waters? Does it mean that international law reserves a coastal state's actions concerning its ports and internal waters to that state's absolute discretion? Some international law limitations explicitly affect a coastal state's control over its internal waters. For example, if a state establishes a straight baseline that encloses as internal waters areas that previously had not been considered internal waters, a right of innocent passage exists in those waters. LOS Convention, Article 8(2); 1958 Territorial Sea Convention, Article 5(2). Furthermore, according to the ICJ in Land, Island and Maritime Frontier Dispute (El Salvador/Honduras; Nicaruaga intervening), 1992 I.C.J. 351, 593, "rights of innocent passage are not inconsistent with a regime of historic waters," such as historic bays, although each case of historic waters must be analyzed separately to determine whether rights of innocent passage obtain. For more on innocent passage, see Chapter 8. How else does international law affect how a coastal state must treat its internal waters?

3. *Port Access in Times of War or Threats to National Security*. As noted in the Aramco case, ports may "be closed when the vital interests of a State so require." Should the determination of "when vital interests so require" be left to the unilateral discretion of port states? States regularly do prohibit or restrict access to their ports in times of war or threats to national security. Article 18 of the 1923 Statute on the International Régime of Ports excludes its application in time of war with regard to the rights and duties of belligerents. Article 16 of the Statute also permits emergency measures deviating from Articles 2 through 7 of the Statute in exceptional cases where the safety or vital interests of the port state are concerned; such measures are to be in effect for as short a period as possible.

Other international arbitral decisions have also recognized the legality of port closures during times of conflict. The Orinoco Steamship Co. Case (United States v. Venezuela) (1904; 1910), 9 Rep. Intl. Arb. Awards 191 (2006), 11 id. 227 (2006), involved the closure of Venezuelan ports to a U.S. company's vessels in 1902, during a revolutionary period in Venezuela. The steamship company, which claimed to be the exclusive concessionaire for trade to certain ports, complained that denying access to those ports was arbitrary and discriminatory, especially since those same ports remained open to non-company vessels. Venezuela claimed that the challenged acts had been taken to prevent rebel forces from receiving support and supplies, and that the claimant was friendly to the rebels. The umpire (Barge) found that the prohibition was permissible: "[T]he right to open and close, as a sovereign on its own territory, certain harbors, ports and rivers in order to prevent the trespassing of fiscal laws is not and could not be denied to the Venezuelan Government, much less this right can be denied when used . . . in defense of the very existence of the Government." 9 Rep. Intl. Arb. Awards at 203.

The September 11, 2001, terrorist attacks in the United States prompted significant national and international security measures affecting ports and port access. In the United States, the Maritime Transportation Security Act of 2002, 46 U.S.C. §§ 70101 et seq., was one U.S. response. The International Maritime Organization (IMO) has adopted a variety of measures concerning port security and threats of maritime terrorism, including an International Ship and Port Facility Security (ISPS) Code and related amendments to the 1974 Safety of Life at Sea (SOLAS) Convention. The U.N. Security Council, acting under Chapter VII of the U.N. Charter, may also issue legally binding decisions relating to transport to address threats to international peace and security. See, e.g., UN Doc. S/RES/1540, ¶ 3 (2004). The problem of securing ports is daunting. For example, in 2000, just before the 9/11 attacks, U.S. ports handled 33 million containers. For more on maritime security, see Chapter 14.

KHEDIVIAL LINE, S.A.E. v. SEAFARERS' INTERNATIONAL UNION
278 F.2d 49 (2d Cir. 1960)

[The plaintiff, a corporation organized under the laws of the United Arab Republic and the owner and operator of a U.A.R.-flagged cargo vessel, the *S.S. Cleopatra*, sought an injunction and damages against the defendant. The complaint alleged

> that the Cleopatra having docked at Pier 16, East River, on April 13, 1960, in New York Harbor, defendant Seafarers' International Union placed a picket line in the vicinity of the vessel and induced defendant International Longshoremen's Association to picket her and to instruct said defendant's members, who would normally discharge and load her cargo, to refuse to work. The basis of the picketing was a pamphlet, signed by both unions, bearing the legend "We Protest Nasser's Blacklist of American Ships." The complaint alleged that by reason of the picket line and defendants' activities, combination and conspiracy, the Cleopatra had been unable to discharge or load cargo, to plaintiff's irreparable damage[.]

278 F.2d at 50. Among the bases on which plaintiff sought relief was the Alien Tort Claims Act, 28 U.S.C. § 1350, which gives U.S. federal district courts "original jurisdiction of any civil action by an alien for a tort only, committed in violation of the law of nations or a treaty of the United States." The court denied relief, and on the Alien Tort Claim Act count reasoned that the plaintiff had "presented no precedents or arguments to show either that the law of nations accords an unrestricted right of access to harbors by vessels of all nations or that, if it does, this is a right of the foreign national rather than solely of the nation." 278 F.2d at 52. The court found that a right of port access was treaty-based:]

International law recognizes a right of innocent passage through the territorial sea. However, the access of foreign vessels to ports is usually provided for in a treaty of friendship, commerce and navigation, see, e.g., the treaty of February 2, 1948 between the United States and Italy, 63 Stat. 2256, 2284. A Convention and Statute respecting the International Regime of Maritime Ports, signed at Geneva on December 9, 1923, provides that on a basis of reciprocity the vessels of the contracting parties shall enjoy equality of treatment in, and freedom of access to, their maritime ports; but the United States is not a party to this Convention.

Notes

1. *Port Closures Due to Private Actions*. The Khedivial Line case involved a suit directly against the union allegedly responsible for the port closure. If a right to port access did exist pursuant to treaty (or customary international law), could the port state itself be responsible for port closures due to the conduct of non-state actors? Could a state be responsible at international law for failing to act with due diligence to prevent a port closure by private actors? For discussion of state responsibility, see the International Law Commission's Draft Articles on Responsibility of States for Internationally Wrongful Acts, GA Res. 56/83, Annex (2001).

2. *Government Conditions on Port Access*. If a government, rather than purely private actors, were to close its ports to vessels of the U.A.R. because of concern over some of that country's policies, would the port closure be legal at international law? Must authority for a port closure be found in the 1923 Statute on the International Régime of Maritime Ports or some other treaty? What if no treaty specifies conditions on port access?

Certainly, as suggested in Note 3 in the previous set of Notes, restricting access to ports in time of war or for reasons of national security is permissible. Other, more mundane conditions on access to ports—relating, for example, to how port business is to be conducted or to the safety of vessels entering ports—are also uncontroversial. Article 3 of the 1923 Statute on the International Régime of Maritime Ports permits a state to condition a foreign ship's access to a port on compliance with laws and regulations governing "the conduct of the business of the port." Various international conventions, such as the 1965 Maritime Traffic Convention and the 1966 Convention on Load Lines, provide for standard vessel certificates and establish recommended practices with respect to documents that may need to be presented on entrance to a port.

Other conditions on port access are common. Port states impose conditions related to sanitary and health concerns (including passengers with contagious diseases), national customs and immigration requirements, the transport of hazardous materials, and, in some cases, nuclear-powered ships or ships with nuclear cargoes—all matters with respect to which port states may have strong concerns. Consider, for example, what conditions you think should apply to the entry of a nuclear-powered ship into port.

What about conditioning port access on a foreign flag vessel having particular equipment on board? International conventions, such as the 1974 Safety of Life at Sea (SOLAS) Convention, require detailed measures relating to ship construction, design, equipment, and manning (CDEM), which may be difficult to modify as a ship moves from port to port. According to Article 21(2) of the LOS Convention, coastal state laws and regulations applicable to foreign flag vessels in innocent passage (see Chapter 8) "shall not apply to the design, construction, manning or equipment of foreign ships unless they are giving effect to generally accepted international rules or standards." But may a port state impose more stringent national CDEM standards as a condition for access to its ports? May a port state consider a foreign flag vessel's entry into port illegal if, outside the port state's territorial sea, the vessel has not used certain equipment? See Lindy S. Johnson, Coastal State Regulation of International Shipping 40–43, 52–54 (2004), and the discussion in Sections B and C of this chapter.

What limitations, if any, exist on the conditions a port state may apply to ships entering its ports, if the port state has not agreed to specific limitations by treaty? Read Article 25 of the LOS Convention, which appears in Part II of the Convention (entitled "Territorial Sea and Contiguous Zone"), and Article 211(3), found in Part XII (on "Protection and Preservation of the Marine Environment"), which refer to conditions on access to ports. Do these articles suggest that a port state has residual jurisdiction to impose whatever conditions it likes on access to its ports? For example, may a port state selectively impose conditions, discriminating against particular flag states? Must a port state publicize conditions before applying them?

3. *Enforcing Conditions on Port Access.* What steps is a port state entitled to take if a foreign flag vessel does not comply with the port state's legitimate conditions on access? Certainly, the port state may deny access to its ports altogether. What other steps may legally be taken? Some enforcement measures, such as confiscating a ship or its cargo, are likely to be more draconian than, say, simply prohibiting the landing of certain cargo that does not conform to a port state's municipal regulations.

GUANGZHOU OCEAN SHIPPING CO. v. MINISTER OF TRANSPORT, PUBLIC WORKS AND WATER MANAGEMENT

Council of State, Administrative Justice Division (1995), 27 Neth. Y.B. Intl. L. 354 (1996)

The Facts: On 4 March 1992 a seagoing ship—the '*Long Lin*'—belonging to the China State shipping line Guangzhou Ocean Shipping Company, was seriously damaged by a collision on the North Sea and lost part of its cargo (barrels of resin) overboard; its tanks were also hit and emptied into the sea. After contracting Smit Tak, the salvage company, and the Scheldepoort ship repair yard, the Dutch agent of the shipping line, Cosco Guangzhou, requested the permission of the Dutch authorities for the vessel to enter territorial waters. The respondent immediately made a thorough inspection of the condition of the ship and imposed a number of technical requirements regarding the transport, which were then fulfilled. The respondent also demanded an unconditional payment commitment, first for a sum of 20 million guilders and later for a sum of 10 million guilders, for all costs incurred and yet to be incurred by the State in respect of the present incident and its handling, including the escorting of the vessel to the port of Vlissingen, sinking [of the damaged vessel if necessary], measures to combat oil pollution, etc. The insurers of the shipping line stated that they would be prepared to provide the requested guarantee, provided that it was added to the guarantee that the shipping line or, as the case may be, the insurers reserved the right to limit liability (this was in fact the full extent of the insurer's liability to the shipping line under the conditions of the [insurance] policy). The respondent did not accept the reservation and prohibited the *Long Lin* from entering Dutch territorial waters as long as its conditions were not met.

The appellant then appealed against this decision on 1 April 1992 to [the Administrative Justice Division]....

As regards the merits of the case: What is in dispute is the question whether the respondent was entitled to refuse the appellant entry into Dutch territorial waters on the ground that the appellant did not meet the conditions set by the respondent for entry.

The appellant takes the view that the respondent acted in breach of both international and national law by refusing the ship access to Dutch territorial waters. In the first place, the appellant disputes (by reference to various treaties) the power of the respondent to make the order at issue in the action. It then disputes the lawfulness of the conditions set by the respondent. The Division holds as follows in this respect.

The appellant is not entitled to invoke the "right of innocent passage" within the meaning of Article 14 of the Convention on the Territorial Sea and the Contiguous Zone of 29 April 1958. This is because the term "passage" as referred to in Article 14 means continuous and expeditious passage through the territorial waters for the purposes of ordinary navigation. In the present case, the vessel entered Dutch territorial and coastal waters in a damaged condition....

Although the State has indeed signed the International Convention on Salvage 1989 and has therefore indicated its intention of subscribing to the provisions of this Convention, the appellant's reliance on the preamble and in particular Article 11* cannot succeed if only because at the time of the contested decision the Convention had not yet come into force.

In principle, the State of the Netherlands and hence the respondent derive the power to impose a prohibition from the sovereignty of the State. On the other hand, under international law the respondent may not go so far as to prevent a ship which is in distress and requires repairs from entering territorial and coastal waters and seeking safety in a port or elsewhere along the coast. In such a case, the seriousness of the situation in which the ship finds itself should be weighed against the threat which the ship poses to the coastal State. The Division also considers that the State may obtain security in such a case for recovery of the potential costs to the State resulting from the entry of the ship. Such a condition is after all intended to cover any disadvantages which entry into Dutch territorial waters may entail. Since these costs, if they occur, must be borne primarily by the State despite its right of recovery against the shipping line, it was logical to request a guarantee in favour of the State of the Netherlands.

As regards the payment condition imposed in the present case, the Division holds as follows.

The amount for which the guarantee must be issued should not exceed the amount which would be payable by the State in the event of an unfavourable end to the passage through territorial waters to the proposed terminus (a ship repair yard in Vlissingen). No reasoning whatever is given in this respect in the contested order. . . .

In view of the above, the Division is of the opinion that the contested order is in breach of the generally recognized principle of proper administration, i.e., that a decision should be supported by the grounds on which it is stated to be based and which are known to the person concerned.

The order should therefore be quashed[.] When reviewing the order, the respondent should take into account all possible mishaps which occur during the journey to the repair yard, but not cases which it was certain or virtually certain at the time of the contested order would not occur.

Notes

1. *The Right of Entry into Port in Distress.* Does a vessel in distress have a right to enter a foreign port? When vessels have entered foreign ports in

---

* Article 11 of the 1989 Salvage Convention provides:

A State Party shall, whenever regulating or deciding upon matters relating to salvage operations such as admittance to ports of vessels in distress or the provision of facilities to salvors, take into account the need for co-operation between salvors, other interested parties and public authorities in order to ensure the efficient and successful performance of salvage operations for the purpose of saving life or property in danger as well as preventing damage to the environment in general.

[Eds.]

distress, their entry traditionally has been regarded as permissible under international law. On this point, "all writers agree." Louise de La Fayette, Access to Ports in International Law, 11 Intl. J. Marine & Coastal L. 1, 11 (1996). See the Kate A. Hoff case in Section B. What determines whether a vessel is in distress? Traditional formulations stress the imminent loss of a ship, its cargo, and its crew, due either to conditions on board, such as structural failure, or external factors, such as a storm. See John E. Noyes, Ships in Distress, in 9 Max Planck Encyclopedia of Public International Law 173, ¶ 1 (Rüdiger Wolfrum ed., 2012). Must the lives of those on board necessarily be at risk for a vessel to be in distress? Is the right of entry into a port in distress prompted primarily by humanitarian concerns for those on board? Will those concerns be less common today than in the past, since technology facilitates air rescues of people on board a floundering vessel?

Does it make a difference whether the entry into port of a ship in distress is regarded as pursuant to a right under international law, or whether the entry is technically wrongful but "excused" by the distress? Professor Lowe has posed the example of a ship that is in distress because of defective steering equipment, enters a foreign port, and, because of the defective equipment, damages a wharf. Should the wharf owner be entitled to compensation? On what grounds? See Vaughan Lowe, Precluding Wrongfulness or Responsibility: A Plea for Excuses, 10 European J. Intl. L. 405, 410–11 (1999).

2. *Places of Refuge and Conditions on Port Entry of Ships in Need of Assistance.* The IMO has addressed the problem of a "ship in need of assistance," defined as a "ship in a situation, apart from one requiring rescue of persons on board, that could give rise to loss of the vessel or an environmental or navigational hazard," by adopting non-binding Guidelines on Places of Refuge for Ships in Need of Assistance. IMO Doc. A/23/RES/949 (2004). If a ship in need of assistance threatens harm to a coastal state's territorial or internal waters, may that state deny port entry? Even if refusing entry poses greater dangers for other states or the marine environment? Was it appropriate for the Dutch court to impose conditions on entry in the Guangzhou Ocean Shipping Co. case? Are other solutions preferable with respect to providing "places of refuge"? How should such solutions be implemented? See John E. Noyes, Places of Refuge for Ships, 36 Denver J. Intl. L. & Policy 135 (2008).

B Port State Jurisdiction over Foreign Vessels While in Port

When a foreign flag vessel enters a port or internal waters of a coastal state, conflicts of jurisdiction may arise, with the flag state and port state each seeking to have its laws and enforcement mechanisms apply to events on board or related to the vessel. The cases in this section explore port state jurisdiction in a variety of settings: jurisdiction over government vessels; jurisdiction over criminal activities of crew members on board a private vessel; application of port state labor and tort law with respect to foreign flag vessels; and application of port state law to vessels that have entered port in distress. Consider what legal standards should be used to resolve conflicts of jurisdiction.

THE SCHOONER EXCHANGE v. MCFADDON
11 U.S. (7 Cranch) 116 (1812)

[McFaddon and another, both U.S. citizens, claimed that they owned the schooner *Exchange*, which left Baltimore, Maryland, bound for Spain on October 27, 1809. They alleged that while at sea, on December 30, 1810, the *Exchange* was seized by persons acting under orders of the Emperor of France. On August 24, 1811, appellees libeled a French flag vessel in the port of Philadelphia, on a claim for attachment and restoration as the schooner *Exchange*. The U.S. Attorney filed a suggestion that, since France and the United States were at peace, French public vessels may enter and leave U.S. ports freely and without detention or molestation. The suggestion also claimed that the libeled vessel had entered the port in distress and out of necessity, and asked that process of attachment be quashed. The U.S. Attorney produced the French consul's verification of the vessel captain's commission, which stated that the vessel had been armed in France.

The U.S. District Court for the District of Pennsylvania dismissed the libel on the ground that under the circumstances as suggested by the U.S. Attorney the vessel was not subject to the process of U.S. courts. The Circuit Court reversed, and the U.S. Attorney appealed to the Supreme Court.]

MARSHALL, Ch. J., delivered the opinion of the Court as follows:

This case involves the very delicate and important inquiry, whether an American citizen can assert, in an American court, a title to an armed national vessel, found within the waters of the United States.... The jurisdiction of the nation within its own territory is necessarily exclusive and absolute. It is susceptible of no limitation not imposed by itself. [F]ull and absolute territorial jurisdiction being alike the attribute of every sovereign, and being incapable of conferring extra-territorial power, would not seem to contemplate foreign sovereigns nor their sovereign rights as its objects. One sovereign being in no respect amenable to another; and being bound by obligations of the highest character not to degrade the dignity of his nation, by placing himself or its sovereign rights within the jurisdiction of another, can be supposed to enter a foreign territory only under an express license, or in the confidence that the immunities belonging to his independent sovereign station, though not expressly stipulated, are reserved by implication, and will be extended to him.

This perfect equality and absolute independence of sovereigns, and this common interest impelling them to mutual intercourse, and an interchange of good offices with each other, have given rise to a class of cases in which every sovereign is understood to waive the exercise of a part of that complete exclusive territorial jurisdiction, which has been stated to be the attribute of every nation.

1st. One of these is admitted to be the exemption of the person of the sovereign from arrest or detention within a foreign territory.

If he enters that territory with the knowledge and license of its sovereign, that license, although containing no stipulation exempting his person from arrest, is universally understood to imply such stipulation....

3d. A third case in which a sovereign is understood to cede a portion of his territorial jurisdiction is, where he allows the troops of a foreign prince to pass through his dominions.

[T]he general license to foreigners to enter the dominions of a friendly power, is never understood to extend to a military force; and an army marching into the dominions of another sovereign, may justly be considered as committing an act of hostility; and, if not opposed by force, acquiesces no privilege by its irregular and improper conduct....

But the rule which is applicable to armies, does not appear to be equally applicable to ships of war entering the ports of a friendly power. The injury inseparable from the march of an army through an inhabited country and the dangers often, indeed generally, attending it, do not ensue from admitting a ship of war, without special license, into a friendly port. A different rule, therefore, with respect to this species of military force has been generally adopted. If, for reasons of state, the ports of a nation generally, or any particular ports be closed against vessels of war generally, or the vessels of any particular nation, notice is usually given of such determination. If there be no prohibition, the ports of a friendly nation are considered as open to the public ship of all powers with whom it is at peace, and they are supposed to enter such ports and to remain in them while allowed to remain, under the protection of the government of the place....

To the Court, it appears, that where, without treaty, the ports of a nation are open to the private and public ships of a friendly power, whose subjects have also liberty without special license, to enter the country for business or amusement, a clear distinction is to be drawn between the rights accorded to private individuals or private trading vessels, and those accorded to public armed ships which constitute a part of the military force of the nation....

When private individuals of one nation spread themselves through another as business or caprice may direct, mingling indiscriminately with the inhabitants of that other, or when merchant vessels enter for the purposes of trade, it would be obviously inconvenient and dangerous to society, and would subject the laws to continual infraction, and the government to degradation, if such individuals or merchants did not owe temporary and local allegiance, and were not amenable to the jurisdiction of the country. Nor can the foreign sovereign have any motive for wishing such exemption [from territorial jurisdiction]. His subjects thus passing into foreign countries, are not employed by him, nor are they engaged in national pursuits. Consequently there are powerful motives for not exempting persons of this description from the jurisdiction of the country in which they are found, and no one motive for requiring it. The implied license, therefore, under which they enter can never be construed to grant such exemption.

But in all respects different is the situation of a public armed ship. She constitutes a part of the military force of her nation; acts under the immediate and direct command of the sovereign; is employed by him in national objects. He has many and powerful motives for preventing those objects from being defeated by the interference of a foreign state. Such interference cannot take place without affecting his power and his dignity. The implied license, therefore, under which such vessel enters a friendly port, may reasonably be construed, and, it seems to the Court, ought to be construed, as containing an exemption from the jurisdiction of the sovereign, within whose territory she claims the rites of hospitality.... It seems then to the Court, to be a principle of public law, that national ships of war, entering the port of a friendly power open for their reception, are to be considered as exempted by the consent of that power from its jurisdiction.

Without doubt, the sovereign of the place is capable of destroying this implication. He may claim and exercise jurisdiction, either by employing force, or by subjecting such vessels to the ordinary tribunals. But until such power be exerted in a manner not to be misunderstood, the sovereign cannot be considered as having imparted to the ordinary tribunals a jurisdiction, which it would be a breach of faith to exercise. Those general statutory provisions therefore which are descriptive of the ordinary jurisdiction of the judicial tribunals, which give an individual whose property has been wrested from him, a right to claim that property in the courts of the country in which it is found, ought not, in the opinion of this Court, to be so construed as to give them jurisdiction in a case, in which the sovereign power has impliedly consented to waive its jurisdiction....

If the preceding reasoning be correct, the *Exchange*, being a public armed ship, in the service of a foreign sovereign, with whom the government of the United States is at peace, and having entered an American port open for her reception, on the terms on which ships of war are generally permitted to enter the ports of a friendly power, must be considered as having come into the American territory, under an implied promise, that while necessarily within it, and demeaning herself in a friendly manner, she should be exempt from the jurisdiction of the country.

If this opinion be correct, there seems to be a necessity for admitting that the fact might be disclosed to the Court by the suggestion of the Attorney for the United States. [T]he sentence of the Circuit Court, reversing the sentence of the District Court, in the case of the *Exchange* [is] reversed, and that of the District Court, dismissing the libel, [is] affirmed.

Notes

1. *The Schooner Exchange and Types of Jurisdiction.* Was the Supreme Court in The Schooner Exchange concerned with legislative jurisdiction (i.e., the question of which state's law should apply)? Or was it concerned with judicial jurisdiction? Or with both types of jurisdiction? Review the Lotus case in Chapter 4, concerning types of jurisdiction.

2. *Sovereign Immunity and Territorial Sovereignty.* What was the rationale for the Supreme Court's decision to accord immunity to the French warship in The Schooner Exchange? Is the case consistent with the proposition that a state has full territorial sovereignty over its land and internal waters? Today, a port state will refuse to exercise jurisdiction over offenses committed on board foreign warships or government ships used for noncommercial purposes. Such ships are also immune from arrest, attachment, or execution. The Netherlands Supreme Court, citing numerous treaties, state practice, and the comments of publicists, ruled that a U.S. warship or military supply ship, which had caused damage in a Dutch harbor, was immune from jurisdiction under international law. United States v. Havenschap Delfzijl/Eemshaven (1999), noted in 32 Neth. Y.B. Intl. L. 240 (2001). See also Restatement (Third) of Foreign Relations Law of the United States § 512, reporters' note 6 (1986).

3. *Access of Warships to Ports.* The Schooner Exchange case concerns jurisdiction over a warship once it is in port. Do or should warships have a right of access to port in the first place? Treaties concerning access to ports typically

apply only to commercial vessels. See Article 13 of the Statute on the International Régime of Maritime Ports, which is reproduced in Section A, and Access to, or Anchorage in, the Port of Danzig, Advisory Opinion, 1931 P.C.I.J. Ser. A/B No. 43, 128–29. Should warships in distress have a right of access to ports?

4. *Sovereign Immunity and Government Vessels Used for Commercial Purposes.* Some countries have used government vessels for commercial purposes. Should such a vessel be entitled to sovereign immunity? In Berizzi Brothers Co. v. The S.S. Pesaro, 271 U.S. 562, 574 (1926), the U.S. Supreme Court held that government commercial ships "must be held to have the same immunity as warships." In Mexico v. Hoffman, 324 U.S. 30 (1945), however, the Supreme Court denied sovereign immunity to a commercial ship owned by but not in possession of the Mexican government. In 1976, Congress enacted the Foreign Sovereign Immunities Act (FSIA), primarily codified at 28 U.S.C. §§ 1602–1611. The Act provides that a foreign state shall not be immune from U.S. judicial jurisdiction in any case "in which the action is based upon a commercial activity" linked to the United States and "carried on... by the foreign state." The commercial activity must be carried on in whole or in part in the United States, or must have a direct effect in the United States. Id., § 1605(a)(2).

The FSIA also addresses enforcement jurisdiction. The Act provides that a foreign state is not immune from jurisdiction in any admiralty case brought to enforce a maritime lien against a vessel of the foreign state, when the "maritime lien is based upon a commercial activity of the foreign state," provided that certain notice requirements are met. Id., § 1605(b). Furthermore, the court may not award a money judgment against the foreign state in an amount greater than the value of the vessel or its cargo in such an action. Id., § 1605(c).

WILDENHUS'S CASE
120 U.S. 1 (1887)

This appeal brought up an application made to the Circuit Court of the United States for the District of New Jersey, by Charles Mali, the "Consul of His Majesty the King of the Belgians, for the States of New York and New Jersey, in the United States," for himself as such consul, "and in behalf of one Joseph Wildenhus, one Gionviennie Gobnbosich, and one John J. Ostenmeyer," for the release, upon a writ of *habeas corpus*, of Wildenhus, Gobnbosich, and Ostenmeyer from the custody of the keeper of the common jail of Hudson County, New Jersey, and their delivery to the consul, "to be dealt with according to the law of Belgium." The facts on which the application rested were thus stated in the petition for the writ: ...

Second. That on or about the sixth day of October, 1886, on board the Belgian steamship Noordland, there occurred an affray between the said Joseph Wildenhus and one Fijens, wherein and whereby it is charged that the said Wildenhus stabbed with a knife and inflicted upon the said Fijens a mortal wound, of which he afterwards died.

Third. That the said Wildenhus is a subject of the Kingdom of Belgium and has his domicile therein, and is one of the crew of the said steamship Noordland, and was such when the said affray occurred.

Fourth. That the said Fijens was also a subject of Belgium and had his domicile and residence therein, and at the time of the said affray, as well as at the time of his subsequent death, was one of the crew of the said steamship.

Fifth. That at the time said affray occurred the said steamship Noordland was lying moored at the dock of the port of Jersey City, in said state of New Jersey.

Sixth. That the said affray occurred and ended wholly below the deck of the said steamship, and that the tranquillity of the said port of Jersey City was in nowise disturbed or endangered thereby.

Seventh. That said affray occurred in the presence of several witnesses all of whom were and still are of the crew of the said vessel, and that no other person or persons except those of the crew of said vessel were present or near by.

Article XI of a Convention between the United States and Belgium "concerning the rights, privileges, and immunities of consular officers," concluded March 9, 1880, and proclaimed by the President of the United States, March 1, 1881, is as follows:

The respective consuls-general, consuls, vice-consuls, and consular agents shall have exclusive charge of the internal order of the merchant vessels of their nation, and shall alone take cognizance of all differences which may arise, either at sea or in port, between the captains, officers, and crews, without exception, particularly with reference to the adjustment of wages and the execution of contracts. The local authorities shall not interfere, except when the disorder that has arisen is of such a nature as to disturb tranquility and public order on shore, or in the port, or when a person of the country or not belonging to the crew, shall be concerned therein.

In all other cases, the aforesaid authorities shall confine themselves to lending aid to the consuls and vice-consuls or consular agents, if they are

> requested by them to do so, in causing the arrest and imprisonment of any person whose name is inscribed on the crew list, whenever, for any cause, the said officers shall think proper.

MR. CHIEF JUSTICE WAITE, after stating the case as above reported, delivered the opinion of the court....

It is part of the law of civilized nations that when a merchant vessel of one country enters the ports of another for the purposes of trade, it subjects itself to the law of the place to which it goes, unless by treaty or otherwise the two countries have come to some different understanding or agreement; for, as was said by Chief Justice Marshall in *The Exchange*, 7 Cranch, 116, 144, "it would be obviously inconvenient and dangerous to society, and would subject the laws to continual infraction, and the government to degradation, if such ... merchants did not owe temporary and local allegiance, and were not amenable to the jurisdiction of the country." And the English judges have uniformly recognized the rights of the courts of the country of which the port is part to punish crimes committed by one foreigner on another in a foreign merchant ship. As the owner has voluntarily taken his vessel for his own private purposes to a place within the dominion of a government other than his own, and from which he seeks protection during his stay, he owes that government such allegiance for the time being as is due for the protection to which he becomes entitled.

From experience, however, it was found long ago that it would be beneficial to commerce if the local government would abstain from interfering with the internal discipline of the ship, and the general regulation of the rights and duties of the officers and crew towards the vessel or among themselves. And so by comity it came to be generally understood among civilized nations that all matters of discipline and all things done on board which affected only the vessel or those belonging to her, and did not involve the peace or dignity of the country, or the tranquility of the port, should be left by the local government to be dealt with by the authorities of the nation to which the vessel belonged as the laws of that nation or the interests of its commerce should require. But if crimes are committed on board of a character to disturb the peace and tranquility of the country to which the vessel has been brought, the offenders have never by comity or usage been entitled to any exemption from the operation of the local laws for their punishment, if the local tribunals see fit to assert their authority.

Such being the general public law on this subject, treaties and conventions have been entered into by nations having commercial intercourse, the purpose of which was to settle and define the rights and duties of the contracting parties with respect to each other in these particulars, and thus prevent the inconvenience that might arise from attempts to exercise conflicting jurisdictions....

The form of the provision found in the present convention with Belgium first appeared in a convention with Austria concluded in 1870, Art. XI, 17 Stat. 827, and it is found now in substantially the same language in all the treaties and conventions which have since been entered into by the United States on the same subject.

It thus appears that at first provision was made only for giving consuls police authority over the interior of the ship and jurisdiction in civil matters arising out of disputes or differences on board, that is to say, between those belonging to the vessel. Under this police authority the duties of the consuls were evidently confined to the maintenance of order and discipline on board. This gave them no power to punish for crimes against the peace of the country. In fact, they were expressly prohibited from interfering with the local police in matters of that kind. The [1806 French Conseil d'Etat] cases of *The Sally* and *The Newton* are illustrative of this position. That of *The Sally* related to the discipline of the ship, and that of *The Newton* to the maintenance of order on board. In neither case was the disturbance of a character to affect the peace or the dignity of the country.

In the next conventions consuls were simply made judges and arbitrators to settle and adjust differences between those on board. This clearly related to such differences between those belonging to the vessel as are capable of adjustment and settlement by judicial decision or by arbitration, for it simply made the consuls judges or arbitrators in such matters. That would of itself exclude all idea of punishment for crimes against the State which affected the peace and tranquility of the port; but, to prevent all doubt on this subject, it was expressly provided that it should not apply to differences of that character.

Next came a form of convention which in terms gave the consuls authority to cause proper order to be maintained on board and to decide disputes between the officers and crew, but allowed the local authorities to interfere if the disorders taking place on board were of such a nature as to disturb the public tranquility, and that is substantially all there is in the convention with Belgium which we have now to consider. This treaty is the law which now governs the conduct of the United States and Belgium towards each other in this particular. Each nation has granted to the other such local jurisdiction within its own dominion as may be necessary to maintain order on board a merchant vessel, but has reserved to itself the right to interfere if the disorder on board is of a nature to disturb the public tranquility.

The treaty is part of the supreme law of the United States, and has the same force and effect in New Jersey that it is entitled to elsewhere. If it gives the consul of Belgium exclusive jurisdiction over the offence which it is alleged has been committed within the territory of New Jersey, we see no reason why he may not enforce his rights under the treaty by writ of *habeas corpus* in any proper court of the United States. This being the case, the only important question left for our determination is whether the thing which has been done—the disorder that has arisen—on board this vessel is of a nature to disturb the public peace, or, as some writers term it, the "public repose" of the people who look to the state of New Jersey for their protection. If the thing done—"the disorder," as it is called in the treaty—is of a character to affect those on shore or in the port when it becomes known, the fact that only those on the ship saw it when it was done is a matter of no moment. Those who are not on the vessel pay no special attention to the mere disputes or quarrels of the seamen while on board, whether they occur under deck or above. Neither do they as a rule care for anything done on board which relates only to the discipline of the ship, or to the preservation of order and authority. Not so, however, with crimes which from their gravity awaken a public interest as soon as they become known, and especially those of a character which every civilized nation considers itself bound to provide a severe punishment for when committed within its own jurisdiction. In such cases inquiry is certain to be instituted at once to ascertain how or why the thing was done, and the popular excitement rises or falls as the news spreads and the facts become known. It is not alone the publicity of the act, or the noise and clamor which attends it, that fixes the nature of the crime, but the act itself. If that is of a character to awaken public interest when it becomes known, it is a "disorder" the nature of which is to affect the community at large, and consequently to invoke the power of the local government whose people have been disturbed by what was done. The very nature of such an act is to disturb the quiet of a peaceful community, and to create, in the language of the treaty, a "disorder" which will "disturb tranquility and public order on shore or in the port." The principle which governs the whole matter is this: Disorders which disturb only the peace of the ship or those on board are to be dealt with exclusively by the sovereignty of the home of the ship, but those which disturb the public peace may be suppressed, and, if need be, the offenders punished by the proper authorities of the local jurisdiction. It may not be easy at all times to determine to which of the two jurisdictions a particular act of disorder belongs. Much will undoubtedly depend on the attending circumstances of the particular case, but all must concede that felonious homicide is a subject for the local jurisdiction, and that if the proper authorities are proceeding with the case in a regular way, the consul has no right to interfere to prevent it....

This is fully in accord with the practice in France, where the government has been quite as liberal towards foreign nations in this particular as any other, and where, as we have seen in the cases of *The Sally* and *The Newton*, by a decree of the Council of State, representing the political department of the government, the French courts were prevented from exercising jurisdiction. But afterwards, in 1859, in the case of *Sally*, the mate of an American merchantman, who had killed one of the crew and severely wounded another on board the ship in the port of Havre, the Court of Cassation, the highest judicial tribunal of France, upon full consideration held, while the Convention of 1853 [10 Stat. 996] was in force, that the French courts had rightful jurisdiction, for reasons which sufficiently appear in the following extract from its judgment:

> Considering that it is a principle of the law of nations that every state has sovereign jurisdiction throughout its territory;
>
> Considering that by the terms of Article 3 of the Code Napoleon the laws of police and safety bind all those who inhabit French territory, and that consequently foreigners, even *transeuntes*, find themselves subject to those laws;
>
> Considering that merchant vessels entering the port of a nation other than that to which they belong cannot be withdrawn from the territorial jurisdiction, in any case in which the interest of the state of which that port forms part finds itself concerned, without danger to good order and to the dignity of the government;
>
> Considering that every state is interested in the repression of crimes and offences that may be committed in the ports of its territory, not only by the men of the ship's company of a foreign merchant vessel towards men not forming part of that company, but even by men of the ship's company among themselves, whenever the act is of a nature to compromise the tranquillity of the port, or the intervention of the local authority is invoked, or the act constitutes a crime by common law, [*droit commun*, the law common to all civilized nations,] the gravity of which does not permit any nation to leave it unpunished, without impugning its rights of jurisdictional and territorial sovereignty, because that crime is in itself the most manifest as well as the most flagrant violation of the laws which it is the duty of every nation to cause to be respected in all parts of its territory.

[The Supreme Court affirms the Circuit Court's decision refusing to deliver the prisoners to the Belgian consul.]

Notes

1. *Territorial Jurisdiction and Resolving Conflicts of Jurisdiction.* According to Wildenhus's Case and The Schooner Exchange, what should be the primary basis for jurisdiction governing foreign flag vessels in U.S. port? Why in each case did the U.S. Supreme Court not insist on extending U.S. jurisdiction to foreign vessels in port?

Some other U.S. cases also have emphasized a territorial basis of jurisdiction over foreign vessels in port or in the territorial sea. In Cunard S.S. Co. v. Mellon, 262 U.S. 100 (1923), for example, several steamship companies sought an injunction against the enforcement of the 18th Amendment to the U.S. Constitution and the National Prohibition Act with regard to foreign vessels in U.S. ports. The 18th Amendment, in effect between 1920 and 1933, prohibited "the manufacture, sale, or transportation of intoxicating liquors within, the importation thereof into, or the exportation thereof from the United States and all territory subject to the jurisdiction thereof for beverage purposes." According to the Supreme Court:

> The merchant ship of one country voluntarily entering the territorial limits of another subjects herself to the jurisdiction of the latter. The jurisdiction attaches in virtue of her presence, just as with other objects within those limits. During her stay she is entitled to the protection of the laws of that place and correlatively is bound to yield obedience to them. Of course, the local sovereign may out of considerations of public policy choose to forego the exertion of its jurisdiction or to exert the same in only a limited way, but this is a matter resting solely in its discretion. . . .
>
> In principle, therefore, it is settled that the Amendment could be made to cover both domestic and foreign merchant ships when within the territorial waters of the United States. And we think it has been made to cover both when within those limits. It contains no exception of ships of either class and the terms in which it is couched indicate that none is intended. Such an exception would tend to embarrass its enforcement and to defeat the attainment of its obvious purpose, and therefore cannot reasonably be regarded as implied.

Id. at 124–26.

2. *The Effect of Treaties on the Exercise of Port State Jurisdiction.* As indicated in Wildenhus's Case, treaties often provide for flag state jurisdiction over some matters related to a vessel while in a foreign port. The controversy over the Prohibition Act in the Cunard case, discussed in Note 1, was defused when,

in 1924, the United States relented and concluded a convention with Great Britain. Article 3 of the 1924 United States-United Kingdom Anti-Smuggling Convention permitted British vessels to carry alcoholic liquors when "voyaging to or from ports of the United States, ... provided that such liquors shall be kept under seal continuously" while in U.S. territorial waters and "that no part of such liquors shall at any time or place be unladen within the United States." At the same time, Great Britain agreed that private vessels under British flag suspected of trying to import alcoholic beverages into the United States could be boarded by U.S. authorities outside U.S. territorial waters up to a distance of one-hour sailing time. May treaties affect the interpretation of a provision of the U.S. Constitution—in this situation, the 18th Amendment?

3. *The Peace of the Port Doctrine in Treaty Law and Customary International Law.* Chief Justice Waite began his opinion in Wildenhus's Case with a strong statement of territorial jurisdiction: "When a merchant vessel of one country enters the ports of another for the purposes of trade, it subjects itself to the law of the place to which it goes." The rule may be modified if "by treaty or otherwise the two countries have come to some different understanding or agreement." In Wildenhus's Case, Belgium and the United States had come to such a "different understanding" in their 1880 treaty. Note that, according to Article VI of the U.S. Constitution, a treaty is part of the "supreme law of the land," which the Belgian consul could invoke in a habeas petition in U.S. court without the need for U.S. legislation implementing the treaty.

Is the peace of the port doctrine also a rule of customary international law, or is any deference to flag state jurisdiction instead a matter of coastal state discretion in the absence of a treaty? On this point, views are split. The United Kingdom takes the position that, although the port state authorities will not usually intervene unless the peace of the port is affected, "derogation from the exercise of local criminal jurisdiction is a matter of comity and discretion." Ian Brownlie, Principles of Public International Law 319 (7th ed. 2008). In an Italian case, however, in which a Greek sailor on a Cypriot vessel in an Italian harbor was arrested by Italian authorities for drug possession, the Italian court found that only Cyprus, not Italy, would have criminal jurisdiction: "Modern writers on international law and international state practice ... recognise the existence of an international custom whereby a foreign ship retains its separate identity as long as it does not interfere in local life by acts which cause or are likely to cause a breach of the peace on shore." Only when there is such an interference would the port state "be entitled to intervene because of its interest in the peaceful course of life in its own community on shore." State v. Jannopulos (Court of Naples, 1974), 1 Italian Y.B. Intl. L. 268, 269 (1975). Does the existence of numerous bilateral treaties such as the one at issue in

Wildenhus's Case reinforce arguments that the peace of the port doctrine is a rule of customary international law? Why might it matter in practice whether the peace of the port doctrine is a rule of customary international law or a matter of discretion?

4. *Actions Affecting the Peace of the Port.* In determining whether the peace of the port is affected, what factors need a court or public official take into account?

5. *Port State Jurisdiction over Non-crew Members on Foreign Flag Vessels.* In determining whether a port state should exercise jurisdiction, should it matter whether a person accused of violating port state law is not of the same nationality as the foreign flag vessel? Should it matter if the accused is not a crew member? In Complaint of Mikkelsen, 1953-1 Sirey, Cour de Cassation (Crim.) 79, noted at 48 Am. J. Intl. L. 164 (1954), the French Court of Cassation distinguished the cases of the *Sally* and the *Newton*, which Chief Justice Waite discussed in Wildenhus's Case. The court held that port state jurisdiction was not excluded when the person aboard ship who was the object of that jurisdiction was not part of the ship's company, even though he was a foreign national.

BENZ v. COMPANIA NAVIERA HIDALGO
353 U.S. 138 (1957)

[The S.S. *Riviera* was a Liberian flag cargo ship owned by Compania Naviera Hidalgo, S.A., a Panamanian corporation. It was crewed entirely by nationals of countries other than the United States, working under British articles of agreement. The voyage began in Germany and was to continue for two years or until the vessel returned to a European port.

While the *Riviera* was docked in Portland, Oregon, during this voyage, the crew went on strike. After picketing the vessel for seventeen days the crew was ordered off the vessel by the U.S. district court pursuant to a possessory libel filed by the ship's owner. In the course of this picketing the crew had appointed a U.S. union as its collective bargaining agent, despite the fact that no crew member was a member of it or any other U.S. union. The union and other unions picketed the *Riviera* following the crew's dismissal. Each was enjoined from picketing pursuant to actions brought by the ship's owner. After the vessel sailed, the owner continued the actions against the unions' representatives, and the district court awarded damages, finding that the unions had violated Oregon common law. The district court found that federal law did not preempt the field since the Labor Management Act of 1947, 61 Stat. 136, 29 U.S.C. § 141 (sometimes "the Act" in the opinion), did not apply to what was essentially a foreign dispute. On this point the court of appeals agreed, and the case went to the Supreme Court on a writ of certiorari.

In the course of reviewing and affirming this conclusion, the Supreme Court (Clark, J.) surveys the applicability of U.S. labor law to foreign vessels.]

It is beyond question that a ship voluntarily entering the territorial limits of another country subjects itself to the laws and jurisdiction of that country. *Wildenhus's Case*, 120 U.S. 1 (1887). The exercise of that jurisdiction is not mandatory but discretionary. Often, because of public policy or for other reasons, the local sovereign may exert only limited jurisdiction and sometimes none at all. It follows that if Congress had so chosen, it could have made the Act applicable to wage disputes arising on foreign vessels between nationals of other countries when the vessel comes within our territorial waters. The question here therefore narrows to one of intent of the Congress as to the coverage of the Act.

The parties point to nothing in the Act itself or its legislative history that indicates in any way that the Congress intended to bring such disputes within the coverage of the Act. Indeed the District Court found to the contrary, specifically stating that the Act does not "cover a dispute between a foreign ship and its foreign crew." The Court of Appeals, though not passing on the question, noted that "It may well be that American laws should not be construed to apply, without some more explicit Congressional indication than we are able to find in the National Labor Relations Act, as amended, to situations with as many points of foreign contact as the situation at bar." 233 F.2d, at 65.

Our study of the Act leaves us convinced that Congress did not fashion it to resolve labor disputes between nationals of other countries operating ships under foreign laws. The whole background of the Act is concerned with industrial strife between American employers and employees. In fact, no discussion in either House of Congress has been called to our attention from the thousands of pages of legislative history that indicates in the least that Congress intended the coverage of the Act to extend to circumstances such as those posed here. It appears not to have even occurred to those sponsoring the bill. The Report made to the House by its Committee on Education and Labor and presented by the coauthor of the bill, Chairman Hartley, stated that "the bill herewith reported has been formulated as a bill of rights both for *American* workingmen and for their employers." The report declares further that because of the inadequacies of legislation "the *American* workingman has been deprived of his dignity as an individual," and that it is the purpose of the bill to correct these inadequacies. (Emphasis added.) What was said inescapably describes the boundaries of the Act as including only the workingmen of our own country and its possessions.

The problem presented is not a new one to the Congress. In the Seamen's Act of March 4, 1915, 38 Stat. 1164, the Congress declared it unlawful to pay a seaman wages in advance and specifically declared the prohibition applicable to foreign vessels "while in waters of the United States." *Id.*, at 1169. In *Sandberg* v. *McDonald*, 248 U.S. 185 (1918), this Court construed the Act as not covering advancements "when the contract and payment were made in a foreign country where the law sanctioned such contract and payment.... Had Congress intended to make void such contracts and payments a few words would have stated that intention, not leaving such an important regulation to be gathered from implication." *Id.*, at 195.... In 1920 Congress amended § 4 of the Seamen's Act of 1915, and granted to every seaman on a vessel of the United States the right to demand one-half of his then earned wages at every port the vessel entered during a voyage. The section was made applicable to "seamen on foreign vessels while in harbors of the United States, and the courts of the United States shall be open to such seamen for its enforcement." This Court in *Strathearn Steamship Co.* v. *Dillon*, 252 U.S. 348 (1920), upheld the applicability of the section to a British seaman on a British vessel under British articles. The Court pointed out:

> [the act] manifests the purpose of Congress to place American and foreign seamen on an equality of right in so far as the privileges of this section are concerned, with equal opportunity to resort to the courts of the United States for the enforcement of the act. Before the amendment... the right to recover one-half the wages could not be enforced in face of a contractual obligation to the contrary. Congress, for reasons which it deemed sufficient, amended the act so as to permit the recovery upon the conditions named in the statute. *Id.*, at 355.

In 1928, *Jackson* v. *S.S. Archimedes*, 275 U.S. 463, was decided by this Court. It involved advance payments made by a British vessel to foreign seamen before leaving Manchester on her voyage to New York and return. It was contended that the advances made in Manchester were illegal and void. That there was "no intention to extend the provisions of the statute," the Court said, "to advance payments made by foreign vessels while in foreign ports, is plain. This Court had pointed out in the *Sandberg* case [*supra*], that such a sweeping provision was not specifically made in the statute...." *Id.*, at 470. Soon thereafter several proposals were made in Congress designed to extend the coverage of the Seamen's Act so as to prohibit advancements made by foreign vessels in foreign ports. A storm of diplomatic protest resulted. Great Britain, Italy, Sweden,

Norway, Denmark, the Netherlands, Germany, and Canada all joined in vigorously denouncing the proposals. In each instance the bills died in Congress.

And so here such a "sweeping provision" as to foreign applicability was not specified in the Act. The seamen agreed in Germany to work on the foreign ship under British articles. We cannot read into the Labor Management Relations Act an intent to change the contractual provisions made by these parties. For us to run interference in such a delicate field of international relations there must be present the affirmative intention of the Congress clearly expressed. It alone has the facilities necessary to make fairly such an important policy decision where the possibilities of international discord are so evident and retaliative action so certain. We, therefore, conclude that any such appeal should be directed to the Congress rather than the courts.

Notes

1. *Congressional Intent and the Application of U.S. Labor Law to Foreign Flag Vessels in U.S. Ports.* Did the Benz Court's approach to determining the applicable law differ from the U.S. Supreme Court's approach in The Schooner Exchange and Wildenhus's Case? The Benz Court, in determining that the U.S. Labor Management Act did not apply to the foreign crew of a foreign flag vessel in U.S. port, claimed to consider the "intent of the Congress as to the coverage of the Act." Will congressional intent always be informative? Should "vessels not [merely] temporarily in United States waters but operating in a regular course of trade between foreign ports and those of the United States," McCulloch v. Sociedad Nacional de Marineros de Honduras, 372 U.S. 10, 18–19 (1963), be subject to the application of U.S. labor law? In McCulloch the Court refused to distinguish Benz on this ground alone, referring to "the well-established rule of international law that the law of the flag state ordinarily governs the internal affairs of a ship." *Id.* at 21. The Court in International Longshoremen's Assn. v. Ariadne Shipping Co., 397 U.S. 195 (1970), distinguished Benz and McCulloch and found that the U.S. National Labor Relations Board had exclusive jurisdiction in a labor dispute; but in that case the dispute was between a foreign flag vessel in a U.S. port and U.S. workers hired to be longshoremen for the vessel while there. Were these decisions based on what Congress in fact intended concerning the scope of application of the U.S. Labor Management Act? If specific evidence of congressional intent is missing, what considerations determine whether U.S. law applies?

2. *The Internal Affairs Rule.* U.S. courts have sometimes addressed the exercise of port state control over foreign flag vessels in terms of Congress's

"implied consent" to leave jurisdiction over a ship's internal affairs to the flag state. In McCulloch (Note 1) the U.S. Supreme Court quoted the internal affairs rule approvingly. The Benz Court indicated that the United States could extend its jurisdiction to the internal affairs of foreign ships within its ports if U.S. legislative intent were sufficiently clear. See the Court's discussion of Sandberg v. McDonald, 248 U.S. 185 (1918).

The U.S. Supreme Court again considered the internal affairs rule in Spector v. Norwegian Cruise Lines Ltd., 545 U.S. 119 (2005). The U.S. Court of Appeals for the Fifth Circuit had invoked the Benz "clear statement" rule in dismissing claims that the Americans with Disabilities Act (ADA), 42 U.S.C. §§ 12181 et seq., applied to a foreign cruise ship. The Supreme Court, influenced by the fact that the foreign flag ship's base of operations was in the United States and that many passengers were U.S. citizens, reversed with respect to some ADA provisions, concluding that the cruise ship fell within the ADA's coverage as a "public accommodation" and "public transportation." However, the defendant was exempted from ADA-specified modifications that were not "readily achievable," such as those requiring the removal of barriers to allow wheelchair access. What factors affect whether a modification is readily achievable? Should a court conclude that if the 1974 Safety of Life at Sea (SOLAS) Convention mandates certain construction, then modifications to that construction are not readily achievable? Spector's plurality opinion and several concurring and dissenting opinions discussed the internal affairs rule.

Do a ship's internal affairs depend on how a vessel operates or functions, or instead on the vessel's contacts with the port state? Should a court conclude that a matter does not concern a ship's internal affairs if the port state has an interest in applying its laws, e.g., because its citizens are on board? If a court is balancing interests, is the internal affairs rule needed? Should the internal affairs rule be confined to practices that a vessel has a treaty obligation to carry out? If so, which treaties should matter: those of the port state or those of the flag state? Is the internal affairs rule as applied by U.S. courts merely a specific example of the "Charming Betsy rule"? According to this rule, "an act of congress ought never to be construed to violate the law of nations if any other possible construction remains." Murray v. Schooner Charming Betsy, 6 U.S. (2 Cranch) 64, 118 (1804). Or is the goal of the internal affairs rule more broadly to avoid potential conflicts with the national law of the flag state? What are the implications of always applying port state law, or of narrowly construing the scope of a foreign ship's internal affairs, if a ship visits ports in many different countries?

HELLENIC LINES LTD. v. RHODITIS

389 U.S. 306 (1970)

MR. JUSTICE DOUGLAS delivered the opinion of the Court.

This is a suit under the Jones Act[1] by a seaman who was injured aboard the ship *Hellenic Hero* in the Port of New Orleans. The District Court, sitting without a jury, rendered judgment for the seaman. The Court of Appeals affirmed. . . .

Petitioner Hellenic Lines Ltd. is a Greek corporation that has its largest office in New York and another office in New Orleans. More than 95% of its stock is owned by a United States domiciliary who is a Greek citizen—Pericles G. Callimanopoulos (whom we call Pericles). He lives in Connecticut and manages the corporation out of New York. He has lived in this country since 1945. The ship *Hellenic Hero* is engaged in regularly scheduled runs between various ports of the United States and the Middle East, Pakistan, and India. The District Court found that its entire income is from cargo either originating or terminating in the United States.

Respondent, the seaman, signed on in Greece, and he is a Greek citizen. His contract of employment provides that Greek law and a Greek collective-bargaining agreement apply between the employer and the seaman and that all claims arising out of the employment contract are to be adjudicated by a Greek court. And it seems to be conceded that respondent could obtain relief through Greek courts, if he desired.

The Jones Act speaks only of "the defendant employer" without any qualifications. In *Lauritzen v. Larsen*, 345 U.S. 571, however, we listed seven factors to be considered in determining whether a particular shipowner should be held to be an "employer" for Jones Act purposes:

---

1 The Act provided:

> Any seaman who shall suffer personal injury in the course of his employment may, at his election, maintain an action for damages at law, with the right of trial by jury, and in such action all statutes of the United States modifying or extending the common-law right or remedy in cases of personal injury to railway employees shall apply; and in case of the death of any seaman as a result of any such personal injury the personal representative of such seaman may maintain an action for damages at law with the right of trial by jury, and in such action all statutes of the United States conferring or regulating the right of action for death in the case of railway employees shall be applicable. Jurisdiction in such actions shall be under the court of the district in which the defendant employer resides or in which his principal office is located.

41 Stat. 1007, 46 U.S.C. § 688 [as of September 1, 2013, codified as amended at 46 U.S.C. § 30104].

> (1) the place of the wrongful act; (2) the law of the flag; (3) the allegiance or domicile of the injured seaman; (4) allegiance of the defendant shipowner; (5) the place where the contract of employment was made; (6) the inaccessibility of a foreign forum; and (7) the law of the forum.

Of these seven factors it is urged that four are in favor of the shipowner and against jurisdiction: the ship's flag is Greek; the injured seaman is Greek; the employment contract is Greek; and there is a foreign forum available to the injured seaman.

The *Lauritzen* test, however, is not a mechanical one. We indicated that the flag that a ship flies may, at times, alone be sufficient. The significance of one or more factors must be considered in light of the national interest served by the assertion of Jones Act jurisdiction. Moreover, the list of seven factors in *Lauritzen* was not intended as exhaustive. [T]he owner's *base of operations* is another factor of importance in determining whether the Jones Act is applicable; and there well may be others.

In *Lauritzen* the injured seaman had been hired in and was returned to the United States, and the shipowner was served there. Those were the only contacts of that shipping operation with this country.

The present case is quite different.

Pericles became a lawful permanent resident alien in 1952. We extend to such an alien the same constitutional protections of due process that we accord citizens. The injury occurred here. The forum is a United States court. Pericles' base of operations is New York. The *Hellenic Hero* was not a casual visitor; rather, it and many of its sister ships were earning income from cargo originating or terminating here. We see no reason whatsoever to give the Jones Act a strained construction so that this alien owner, engaged in an extensive business operation in this country, may have an advantage over citizens engaged in the same business by allowing him to escape the obligations and responsibility of a Jones Act "employer." The flag, the nationality of the seaman, the fact that his employment contract was Greek, and that he might be compensated there are in the totality of the circumstances of this case minor weights in the scales compared with the substantial and continuing contacts that this alien owner has with this country. If... the liberal purposes of the Jones Act are to be effectuated, the facade of the operation must be considered as minor, compared with the real nature of the operation and a cold objective look at the actual operational contacts that this ship and this owner have with the United States. By that test the Court of Appeals was clearly right in holding that petitioner Hellenic Lines was an "employer" under the Jones Act.

Affirmed.

Notes

1. *A Balancing Test to Resolve Port State-Flag State Conflicts of Jurisdiction.* According to the Jones Act, any seaman who is injured or dies in the course of his employment may maintain an action for damages in U.S. court. Should the Jones Act apply to foreign crew members injured while on board a foreign flag vessel in a U.S. port? In the absence of a treaty specifying some international rule or choice-of-law solution, consider which of the following three approaches to this question of conflict of laws is preferable, or whether yet another approach would be better. First, a port state could apply its laws on the grounds that the conduct occurred in its territory. Should port state law apply in all instances involving a foreign flag vessel in internal waters? If not, what exceptions to a principle of territorial jurisdiction should apply?

Second, a port state could focus on legislative intent, like the Benz Court did. If the flag state's legislature and the port state's legislature each intended that its own law should apply, should the forum (port) state's law invariably be applied? What should be done if it is not clear whether the port state's legislature intended for its law to apply to foreign flag vessels or their crews?

Third, a port state's court could use a multifactor balancing approach, such as the one outlined in Rhoditis, to determine whether the port state's law applies to foreign flag vessels in U.S. ports. The Rhoditis Court cited Lauritzen v. Larsen, 541 U.S. 571, 577 (1954), which set out the balancing approach and linked that approach to international law: "By usage as old as the Nation, [U.S. shipping] statutes have been construed to apply only to areas and transactions in which American law would be considered operative under prevalent doctrines of international law." Should the Benz Court have applied a multi-factor balancing test? Has the Supreme Court outlined the appropriate factors to use in a multifactor balancing approach? Why is each factor important? Are some factors more significant than others? How does a multifactor balancing approach work in practice? Did the Supreme Court, in concluding that the Jones Act applied in Rhoditis, strike the correct balance in applying the various factors? Consider the opinion of Justice Harlan, who, joined by Justice Stewart and Chief Justice Burger, dissented in Rhoditis:

> Today's decision suggests that courts have become mesmerized by contacts, and notwithstanding the purported eschewal of a mechanical application of the *Lauritzen* test, they have lost sight of the primary purpose of *Lauritzen* which, as I conceive it, was to reconcile the all-embracing language of the Jones Act with those principles of comity embodied in international and maritime law that are designed to "foster amicable and workable commercial relations." 345 U.S., at 582. *Lauritzen*, properly

> understood, should, I submit, be taken to focus the juridical inquiry on the purpose of Congress and the presence or absence of an adequate basis for the assertion of American jurisdiction, when that purpose may be furthered by application of the statute in the circumstances presented.
>
> Where, as in the case before us, the injured plaintiff has no American ties, the inquiry should be directed toward determining what jurisdiction is primarily concerned with plaintiff 's welfare and whether that jurisdiction's rule may, consistent with those notions of due process that determine the presence of legislative jurisdiction, govern recovery. In the case before us, there is no reason to disregard either the law of the flag or plaintiff's contractual undertaking to accept Greek law as controlling, thereby in effect assuming that he signed articles under conditions that would justify disregarding the contractual choice of law. Rhoditis is a Greek national who resides in Greece. Under those circumstances Greek law provides the appropriate rule. I would reverse the judgment of the Court of Appeals, and hold that the Jones Act affords no redress to this seaman.

398 U.S. at 318. Was it reasonable to apply U.S. (port state) law in Rhoditis? What disadvantages attended the refusal to apply the law of the flag state in that case? What disadvantages would have attended the application of U.S. law in Benz?

2. *Flag State Assertions of Jurisdiction*. Each of the principal cases in this section was decided by the court of a port state, with the court considering whether the port state should exercise judicial or legislative jurisdiction over a foreign vessel located there, or over individuals on board it. How should the analysis differ if the flag state is considering whether to exercise judicial jurisdiction or apply its laws with respect to an incident occurring in another country's internal waters? Is it persuasive to argue that a vessel is a "floating part of territory" of the flag state, and thus subject to jurisdiction on a territorial basis? In a criminal case, is it plausible for the flag state to assert jurisdiction over someone on board who is accused of a crime on the grounds that the accused is a national of the flag state? What if the accused is a non-national of the flag state? Should the flag state in either case defer to the jurisdiction of the state in whose port the vessel is located? Should the answer turn on how far port state proceedings have advanced? In the case of In re Bianchi, 24 Intl. L. Rep. 173 (Cámara Nacional Especial, 1957), an Argentine court held that Bianchi, a member of the crew of a ship of Argentine registry who committed a theft on board that ship while in the Brazilian port of Rio de Janeiro,

could be tried in an Argentine court, as Brazil did "not choose to exercise its right to institute proceedings because it considers that the act has not affected the community at large or the peace of the port." In such a case the flag state may assert full authority over the ship "for the purpose of restoring order and discipline on board or protecting the rights of passengers." Id., at 174. What if a port state has preliminarily detained a crew member on a foreign flag vessel? Or indicted him? Or tried him? See United States v. Flores, 289 U.S. 137, 158–59 (1933) (upholding U.S. flag state jurisdiction over crimes involving U.S. citizens committed on board a U.S. vessel in Belgian internal waters, where Belgium asserted no jurisdiction); United States v. Reagan, 453 F.2d 165 (6th Cir. 1971), cert. denied, 406 U.S. 946 (1972) (upholding U.S. flag state jurisdiction over crime involving U.S. citizens committed on board U.S. vessel in German internal waters, where German authorities had, in a "preliminary proceeding," taken defendant into custody, committed him to a mental institution, and then released him).

What principles should a flag state use to analyze whether its noncriminal laws apply to its vessels in foreign ports? Is a balancing test—such as the one used in Rhoditis—appropriate? Is some other approach preferable? In National Labor Relations Board v. Dredge Operators, Inc., 19 F.3d 206 (5th Cir. 1994), the NLRB sought to enforce its order that the defendant, which operated a U.S. flag vessel, bargain with a U.S. union. The vessel, the *Stuyvestant*, was operating in Hong Kong indefinitely, conducting dredging work for the Hong Kong international airport under contract with the government of Hong Kong. The union was elected to represent the crew members, slightly over half of whom were U.S. nationals. The court stated that "a United States flag vessel is considered American territory," id. at 212, and held that the application of U.S. law was warranted. What if Hong Kong insisted on the operation of its own labor laws? Dredge Operators (DOI) in fact claimed "that Hong Kong labor laws requiring the hiring of a certain percentage of Hong Kong employees conflicted with United States labor laws mandating that a United States flag vessel employ only Americans." Id. at 208. The court concluded, however, that no conflict affected the defendant's ability to negotiate with the U.S. union. Neither Hong Kong nor the United States had insisted on full compliance with its own hiring rules, although Hong Kong had issued work permits to DOI specifying that a significant number of Hong Kong crew members be employed. Hong Kong also had not required DOI to accept a different union. See id. at 213.

KATE A. HOFF (UNITED STATES) v. MEXICO
Mixed Claims Commission under the Convention of 1923 (1929), 4 Rep. Intl. Arb. Awards 444 (2006)

[The *Rebecca*, a U.S. schooner, sailed from the United States in January 1884, with cargo consigned for a Texas port and also for Tampico, Mexico. While offshore the Texas port a strong adverse wind drove the vessel to sea until it found itself off Tampico in a damaged and leaking condition. The vessel accordingly entered the latter port and lodged a "protest of distress" with the U.S. consul in Tampico. Mexican customs officials seized the cargo destined for Texas, without giving any receipt for it, and arrested the master on a charge of attempt to smuggle. He was tried, acquitted, and released, but was rearrested and held under bond for over two months. The *Rebecca* and its cargo were sold by court order, part of the proceeds being paid over to the Federal Treasury and the rest being distributed among certain customs employees.]

It is of course well established that, when a merchant vessel belonging to one nation enters the territorial waters of another nation, it becomes amenable to the jurisdiction of the latter and is subject to its laws, except in so far as treaty stipulations may relieve the vessel from the operation of local laws. On the other hand, there appears to be general recognition among the nations of the world of what may doubtless be considered to be an exception....

Recognition has been given ... to the immunity of a ship whose presence in territorial waters is due to a superior force. The principles with respect to the status of a vessel in "distress" find recognition both in domestic laws and in international law....

Domestic courts have frequently considered pleas of distress in connection with charges of infringement of customs laws. Interesting cases in which pleas of distress were raised came before American courts in the cases of vessels charged with violation of the interesting American so-called "non-intercourse" acts forbidding trade with French and British possessions. In these cases it was endeavored in behalf of the vessels to seek immunity from prosecution under these laws by alleging that the vessels had entered forbidden ports as a result of *vis major*. A Mexican law of 1880 which was cited in the instant case appears to recognize in very comprehensive terms the principles of immunity from local jurisdiction which have so frequently been invoked.

The enlightened principle of comity which exempts a merchant vessel, at least to a certain extent, from the operation of local laws has been generally stated to apply to vessels forced into port by storm, or compelled to seek refuge for vital repairs or for provisioning, or carried into port by mutineers.

It has also been asserted in defense of a charge of attempted breech [sic] of blockade. It was asserted by as early a writer as Vattel, *The Law of Nations*, p. 128. In the instant case we are concerned simply with distress said to have been occasioned by violent weather.

While recognizing the general principle of immunity of vessels in distress, domestic courts and international courts have frequently given consideration to the question as to the degree of necessity prompting vessels to seek refuge. It has been said that the necessity must be urgent. It seems possible to formulate certain reasonably concrete criteria applicable and controlling in the instant case. Assuredly a ship floundering in distress, resulting either from the weather or from other causes affecting management of the vessel, need not be in such a condition that it is dashed helplessly on the shore or against rocks before a claim of distress can properly be invoked in its behalf. The fact that it may be able to come into port under its own power can obviously not be cited as conclusive evidence that the plea is unjustifiable. If a captain delayed seeking refuge until his ship was wrecked, obviously he would not be using his best judgment with a view to the preservation of the ship, the cargo and the lives of people on board. Clearly an important consideration may be the determination of the question whether there is any evidence in a given case of a fraudulent attempt to circumvent local laws. And even in the absence of any such attempt, it can probably be correctly said that a mere matter of convenience in making repairs or in avoiding a measure of difficulty in navigation cannot justify a disregard of local laws.

The *Rebecca* did sail into Tampico, as observed by the judge who condemned the vessel, under its own power. However, it did not enter the port until after it had for three days, in a crippled condition, been contending with a storm in an attempt to enter the port at Brazos Santiago, Texas. [A] well grounded apprehension of the loss of the vessel and cargo and persons on board prompted the captain to turn south towards Tampico. [T]he captain had no intent to perpetrate a fraud on Mexican customs laws. [T]he captain [also] had no intent merely as a matter of convenience to flout Mexican laws. This very small vessel had been driven before a strong north wind; its cabin had been damaged; its pumps had been broken and repaired; the cooking stove on the vessel had been rendered useless; there were one and a half to two feet of water in the vessel; and it had been leaking.

[I]t is unnecessary to discuss [whether Mexico misapplied its own laws in condemning the ship and cargo] in view of the conclusions reached by the Commission with respect to the conditions under which the vessel entered Tampico. The ship entered the port of Tampico in distress, and the seizure of both the vessel and cargo was wrongful.

Notes

1. *U.S.-Mexican Claims Commission.* The United States and Mexico entered several agreements establishing commissions to consider claims involving citizens of the two states. A three-person General Claims Commission heard the Kate A. Hoff case. The Commission operated during 1924–1931, deciding almost 200 claims that had arisen since July 4, 1868. In the 1941 United States-Mexican Claims Convention the United States accepted US$ 40,000,000 in settlement of claims of U.S. citizens, and agreed to pay more than US$ 500,000 with respect to Commission awards in favor of Mexican nationals against the United States. American Mexican Claims Commissions, Report to the Secretary of State 71–72 (1948). The United States then enacted the Settlement of Mexican Claims Act of 1942, 56 Stat. 1058, creating a national body to administer the distribution of claims received under the 1941 Claims Convention. For discussion of the role of international claims commissions in dispute settlement, see David Bederman, The Glorious Past and Uncertain Future of International Claims Commissions, in International Courts for the Twenty-First Century 161 (Mark W. Janis ed., 1992).

2. *Port State Jurisdiction over Vessels in Distress.* Should port state jurisdiction be precluded in all instances over foreign flag vessels that enter port in distress? What if an action on board disrupts the peace of the port? What if, in the Kate A. Hoff case, Mexico had not seized the vessel and cargo, but had taken some less intrusive action, such as demanding an inventory of goods on board? See John E. Noyes, Ships in Distress, in 9 Max Planck Encyclopedia of Public International Law 173, ¶¶ 21–24 (Rüdiger Wolfrum ed., 2012).

C Enlarged Port State Jurisdiction

In Sections A and B, we considered the application of port state laws to foreign flag vessels and examined how conflicts of jurisdiction between flag states and port states are resolved. States traditionally conditioned access to their ports, or applied their laws to foreign flag vessels in port, with respect to such matters as immigration, health and sanitation, customs, and security. Today, port state jurisdiction is "enlarged" to encompass the failure of foreign flag states to effectively exercise jurisdiction over their vessels with respect to a range of international obligations. The LOS Convention and instruments developed by the International Maritime Organization, the International Labor Organization, and the Food and Agriculture Organization authorize port states, subject to limitations, to inspect or otherwise exercise jurisdiction over foreign flag vessels to help promote compliance with international pollution, vessel safety, labor, and fisheries management standards. In some situations, port states may institute proceedings against foreign flag vessels for violating these standards even if the violations occurred outside the territorial jurisdiction of the port state. The port state, in short, may be enlisted to help insure the efficacy of international regulatory standards. The materials below—one U.S. case, one treaty provision, and one reading about a regional initiative—introduce such enlarged port state jurisdiction.

UNITED STATES v. ROYAL CARIBBEAN CRUISES LTD.
11 F. Supp. 2d 1358 (S.D. Fla. 1998)

The Defendant, Royal Caribbean Cruises, Ltd. (RCCL), is accused in this case with the knowing use or presentation of a false writing, specifically an Oil Record Book for the cruise ship the *Nordic Empress*, during a United States Coast Guard inspection on February 1, 1993. This conduct is alleged to be in violation of Title 18 of the United States Code, section 1001, also known as the "False Statements Act." For the purposes of the Motion to Dismiss, we consider the facts as alleged in the Indictment.

On February 1, 1993, at approximately 3:00 a.m., a Coast Guard aircraft on patrol observed, via Forward Looking Infra-red Radar, the *Nordic Empress* discharging oil from the vessel. This discharge occurred in Bahamian waters, en route to the United States and the destination port of Miami, Florida. Upon its arrival into Miami, the Coast Guard conducted a document and safety inspection. During its review of the Oil Record Book, the Coast Guard observed that there was no entry indicating an overboard discharge of oil on February 1, 1993. Based upon the suspicion that an alleged discharge violation had occurred, the United States referred this matter to a representative of the government of Liberia via the Department of State. The referral letter addressed an "alleged discharge violation" but referred the Coast Guard Report in its entirety, including the reference to potential violations of the Oil Record Book, to Liberia. On February 10, 1994, Liberia filed its Determination that there was reasonable doubt that the *Nordic Empress* was in contravention of MARPOL and that it was "difficult" to respond to the allegations of "improperly recorded" Oil Record Book entries under the facts as presented, and recommended expunging the allegation. There was no appeal for reconsideration or review made to the International Maritime Organization pursuant to the protocol set forth in MARPOL.

The indictment in this case was returned on February 19, 1998. The Indictment charges a violation of 18 U.S.C. § 1001. In pertinent part, it charges that:

> On or about February 1, 1993, in the port of Miami, within the Southern District of Florida, the defendant Royal Caribbean Cruises Ltd knowingly and willfully used a false writing, in a matter within the jurisdiction of the United States Coast Guard, knowing the same to contain materially false, fictitious and fraudulent entries, to wit, an Oil Record Book for the Nordic Empress, that falsely represented that all overboard discharges of oil contaminated bilge waste occurred only after treatment of the bilge waste through 15 parts per million equipment, that is, the Oil Water Separator, and which failed to record the overboard discharge of oil contaminated bilge waste without the use of the Oil Water Separator.

The instant Motion to Dismiss by RCCL was filed on March 25, 1998, based on both domestic and international law principles....

RCCL's Motion to Dismiss based upon international law is based upon the contention that prosecution is precluded by binding provisions of international law under both MARPOL (the Protocol of 1978 Relating to the International Convention for the Prevention of Pollution from Ships, 1973) and UNCLOS (the Law of the Sea Convention of 1982). Defendant first argues that the relevant provisions of MARPOL require dismissal of this case, as domestic prosecution of the alleged fabrication of the Oil Record Book is properly addressed via an international regime mandating referral to the flag state, Liberia. Second, Defendant argues that this action violates UNCLOS. Defendant contends that... at least three provisions of UNCLOS are implicated by this prosecution: the international equivalent of a prohibition on double jeopardy contained within Article 228.1; the Article 228.2 three-year statute of limitations on proceedings to impose penalties on foreign vessels; and Article 218.2, which prohibits institution of proceedings with respect to a "discharge violation" unless requested by the flag state or a state damaged or threatened by the discharge.... We will address each of these arguments in turn.

[The court reviews RCCL's contentions that prosecution was barred under U.S. law, but refuses to dismiss the case on those grounds.]

II. International Law & Applicability of 18 U.S.C. § 1001: MARPOL

The next set of arguments which RCCL invokes in favor of dismissal is that the charging theory of this case is inconsistent with international law. RCCL contends that prosecution is precluded by binding provisions of international law under both MARPOL and UNCLOS. [T]he expert testimony presented by both sides regarding this issue was most informative and helpful. The former Ambassador-at-Large and Special Representative of the President of the United States to the Third United Nations Conference on the Law of the Sea,

Elliot L. Richardson, testified as to the international law issues presented in this matter. Professor Bernard Oxman, a senior member of the U.S. Delegation to the Third U.N. Conference on the Law of the Sea, also testified regarding the implications to the law of the sea in this case. On behalf of the government, Rear Admiral Paul Blaney, Chief Counsel of the United States Coast Guard, Captain Thomas Gilmour, Director of Field Activities for Marine Safety and Environmental Protection, United States Coast Guard, and Robert K. Harris, Assistant Legal Adviser for Oceans International Environment and Scientific Affairs at the Department of State testified by Affidavit regarding the position of the United States in this matter.

The MARPOL Protocol, more formally known as the Protocol of 1978 Relating to the International Convention for the Prevention of Pollution from Ships, 1973, is a treaty to which the United States is a party; its provisions are codified as U.S. law as APPS, the Act to Prevent Pollution from Ships, at 33 U.S.C. § 1901 *et seq*. MARPOL establishes a framework for addressing discharges of pollutants on the high seas. Among the requirements, under MARPOL is that ships must maintain an Oil Record Book in which entries of activities relating to oil discharges are to be entered. As a result, the *Nordic Empress* was under an obligation by MARPOL to maintain an Oil Record Book; make proper entries in that book of all oil discharge activities; and keep the Oil Record Book available for inspection. For jurisdictional purposes, the requirements concerning the Oil Record Book apply to a ship that operates under the authority of a country other than the United States, such as the *Nordic Empress*, while the ship is "in the navigable waters of the United States, or while at port or terminal under the jurisdiction of the United States." 33 C.F.R. § 151.09(a)(5). While MARPOL authorizes, *inter alia*, a port state to inspect a ship to verify a discharge in violation of MARPOL, it requires a port state finding a discharge violation contravening the Convention to forward the report to the Secretary [of the department in which the Coast Guard is operating] for further action from the flag state. 33 U.S.C. § 1907(c)(2); MARPOL, Art. 6(2). RCCL contends that the authority of port states is strictly limited to providing assistance to the flag state by enforcing the recordkeeping requirement through inspections, and that the United States does not have jurisdiction to enforce Oil Record Book violations occurring outside the navigable waters of the United States under MARPOL. Any violations of MARPOL, including a violation of Oil Book requirements, must be responded to by way of the referral system outlined above....

MARPOL constitutes valid United States law because of the enactment of APPS, not because it is self-executing or directly enforceable without enacting legislation. We have held in the context of domestic law issues that MARPOL/APPS does not preclude this § 1001 prosecution ... and we are not convinced that the result should be any different under applicable international law....

We agree with RCCL that the careful international regulatory balance created by MARPOL must be respected. Equally compelling, however, is the right of the United States to enforce its laws within its borders. If the policy goal of a comprehensive regime of anti-pollution measures is to be achieved, it is necessary that domestic and international law work together to the extent possible to maximize enforcement. The discharge of oil in an improper manner is one crime; the failure to keep an Oil Record Book as required under MARPOL/APPS is another; and the deliberate presentation of a false material writing to the U.S. Coast Guard is another. [T]o the extent possible, international and domestic law should cooperate in regulation and enforcement. We refer to the testimony of Captain Thomas Gilmour, United States Coast Guard, who opines that "[a]ny holding that would undermine the ability of port states to ensure accuracy and truthfulness in these certificates and records would adversely affect the goal of the IMO, the Congress, and the Coast Guard to eliminate substandard ships and operations. This same principle applies to many other domestic laws and regulations that are based on international standards." Referral to the flag state may be proper in one instance; prosecution under United States law appropriate in another. We necessarily do not entertain the question of the proper policy choices regarding the wisdom of the decision to prosecute this matter as opposed to referral; such arguments are reserved for consideration by the Executive Branch. Assuming without deciding the standing of RCCL to assert MARPOL in its defense, we do not believe that under the facts as presented, MARPOL/APPS would preclude this prosecution.

III. International Law & Applicability of 18 U.S.C. § 1001: UNCLOS

RCCL also invokes UNCLOS, the United Nations Convention on the Law of the Sea, contending that several provisions thereunder preclude this action. RCCL argues that although UNCLOS has not yet been ratified by the U.S. Senate, it should nonetheless be given the weight of law such that it bars this prosecution....

RCCL argues that various provisions of UNCLOS are violated by this prosecution. Article 228 of UNCLOS effectively sets out the international equivalent of a double jeopardy prohibition, and Liberia has already instituted and concluded its own proceedings. As a result, proceeding with this case would violate the provisions of Article 228.1, which applies to "proceedings to impose penalties in respect of any violation of... international rules and standards relating to the prevention, reduction, and control of pollution from vessels committed by a foreign vessel beyond the territorial sea of the State instituting proceedings...." RCCL contends that as the matter referred to Liberia was the entire

Coast Guard report, including the alleged discharge and the Oil Book violation, this double jeopardy provision prevents this prosecution. The second UNCLOS provision cited by RCCL is Article 228.2, which establishes that "proceedings to impose penalties on foreign vessels shall not be instituted after the expiry of three years from the date on which the violation was committed...." As the alleged violation occurred on or about February 1, 1993, and this case was filed on February 19, 1998, RCCL asserts that the statute of limitations provision is violated.... Finally, UNCLOS 218.2 prohibits the United States from initiating a prosecution absent a request from Liberia, the flag state, or Bahamas, the state "damaged or threatened by the discharge violation." No such request has occurred; in fact Liberia has lodged a Diplomatic Note concerning this action with the United States Department of State. RCCL claims we have no jurisdiction over the instant action and must dismiss on that basis as well.

The government first contends that RCCL lacks standing to raise the provisions of UNCLOS in its defense.... To the extent that RCCL has standing to invoke the provisions of UNCLOS, the government argues that UNCLOS is inapplicable to this case. This action addresses a crime committed in port, and UNCLOS does not explicitly or implicitly regulate what a nation may do to enforce its domestic laws in port. Finally, the government asserts that none of the provisions of UNCLOS are violated by this prosecution....

We first analyze whether or not UNCLOS should be accorded the weight of law in these proceedings. We are not convinced that UNCLOS, a treaty which all parties agree applies to protect navigational freedoms and the law of the sea, has any bearing on this domestic prosecution. The alleged crime occurred in port in Miami, Florida, and involved presentation of a materially false writing to the United States Coast Guard. The extent to which this action is so connected to the protocols set forth in UNCLOS such that the law of the sea is properly invocable is, as was acknowledged by former Ambassador Richardson, a question of degree. As an obvious hypothetical, the expert testimony of both former Ambassador Richardson and Professor Oxman concurred that assault and battery upon a Coast Guard Boarding Officer investigating an incident of possible pollution is not a violation in respect of pollution, and thus the United States would have jurisdiction to prosecute it. Ambassador Richardson agreed that false statements or obstruction of justice pursuant to legal proceedings, even pursuant to this legal proceeding, would not be cognizable under the law of the sea convention. Professor Oxman also agreed that bribery of an officer of a ship in an attempt to conceal an incident of pollution should probably not be regarded as a violation in respect of pollution violations.... These hypotheticals indicate the continuum along which infractions of domestic law related to, but not necessarily implicating, international law of the sea occur.

Presentation of a false Oil Record Book seems more appropriately characterized, as do the above examples, as an essentially domestic law violation over which the United States properly has jurisdiction.

[Assuming, however, that UNCLOS is at issue] RCCL argues ... that UNCLOS should be considered customary international law and thus be considered binding on this Court. It does appear from all of the testimony produced in this case, as well as the caselaw in this area, that UNCLOS is properly considered customary international law.... Mr. Oxman explains that the requirements of UNCLOS should be respected under international law

> ... by the established principle that U.S. statutes are not to be interpreted and applied in a manner inconsistent with international law if any other interpretation is possible, by the clear undertaking by President Reagan to respect the relevant rules of the Convention, and by the firm position of the Executive Branch that the United States will respect the rules set forth in the Convention regarding navigation and other matters, expects other nations to do the same, and reserves the right to take such measures as may be necessary to ensure that they do so.

[The court determines that RCCL lacks "standing to litigate its rights under UNCLOS."]

Even assuming UNCLOS is properly considered customary international law and RCCL possesses standing, however, we find no violation of UNCLOS occurred. The first provision invoked by RCCL is Article 228.1, which addresses "Suspension and restrictions on institution of proceedings." Article 228.1 states that:

> [p]roceedings to impose penalties in respect of any violation of applicable laws and regulations or international rules and standards relating to the prevention, reduction, and control of pollution from vessels *committed by a foreign vessel beyond the territorial seas of the State instituting proceedings* shall be suspended upon the taking of proceedings to impose penalties in respect of corresponding charges by the flag state.... (emphasis added).

By its own terms, Article 228.1 applies to violations committed at sea. As we have held, the violation alleged in this Indictment, presentation of a materially false Oil Record Book, occurred in port. To the extent that Liberia did evaluate alleged Oil Record Book improprieties, the pending Indictment refers to knowing presentation of a false statement while in port to the United States Coast Guard, which is a different matter than the allegedly referred charge of falsifying an Oil Record Book at the time of an alleged illegal discharge. We agree that even if this issue were referred under MARPOL/UNCLOS, it is unlikely that Liberia would possess venue or jurisdiction to adjudicate it properly, and thus find that the asserted "double jeopardy" provision in Article 228.1 is not violated by this prosecution.

The relevant part of the second provision raised, Article 228.2, requires that "[p]roceedings to impose penalties on foreign vessels shall not be instituted after the expiry of three years from the date on which the violation was committed. . . ." We do not believe that Defendant's interpretation, which argues that the statute of limitations in UNCLOS applies to *all* proceedings by non-flag states to penalize activities of foreign-flagged vessels, is tenable. Reading Article 228.2 that broadly would potentially change hundreds of statutes of limitations established in United States law simply because a foreign-flagged vessel were involved, upsetting the balance between domestic and international maritime law with which this action is so concerned. The more realistic interpretation is to read the provisions of Article 228.2 to limit, as they do by implication, non-flag states to three years in which to sanction foreign-flagged vessels for violations of UNCLOS. Following that reading, the three-year statute of limitations provision is inapplicable to this matter, as the violation alleged in this action is a violation of 18 U.S.C. § 1001, not UNCLOS.

The final provision raised by Defendant, Article 218.1 [and 218.2], addresses "Enforcement by port States." It mandates that no proceedings

> in respect of any discharge from that vessel outside the internal waters, territorial sea, or exclusive economic zone . . . shall be instituted in respect of a discharge violation in the internal waters, territorial sea, or exclusive economic zone of another State unless requested by that State, the flag State, or a state damaged or threatened by the discharge violation[.]

It is uncontested that there has been no request by Liberia, the flag state, or the Bahamas, the coastal state. By its own language, Article 218 limits itself to proceedings "in respect of any discharge from a vessel outside the internal waters, territorial sea, or exclusive economic zone." While the interpretation of the term "in respect of" is admittedly imprecise, Article 218.1 plainly directs its prohibitions to discharge violations and not domestic port violations. As a result, we do not find that the provisions of Article 218.1 are violated by this action.

Even assuming UNCLOS has the weight of law and Defendant RCCL possesses standing to raise UNCLOS as an individual litigant, because we do not find that any of the cited provisions of UNCLOS are violated by this proceeding, we deny the Motion to Dismiss on those grounds.

Notes

1. *International Law in U.S. Courts.* As we saw in Wildenhus's Case in Section B, "self-executing" U.S. treaties apply in U.S. courts without being implemented by legislation. MARPOL, however, was applicable in U.S. courts not because it was self-executing, but because it had been incorporated into U.S. law by statute, the Act to Prevent Pollution from Ships, 33 U.S.C. §§ 1901–1915.

On what basis could the LOS Convention apply in a U.S. court? Since the United States had not ratified the Convention, the Royal Caribbean Cruises court had to consider whether its provisions were customary international law. The court believed they were, but was not convinced that the defendant could invoke them in court. There has been much debate concerning when customary international law may supply a rule of decision in U.S. courts. In one frequently cited passage, the U.S. Supreme Court made the following statement:

> International law is part of our law, and must be ascertained and administered by the courts of justice of appropriate jurisdiction, as often as questions of right depending upon it are duly presented for their determination. For this purpose, where there is no treaty, and no controlling executive or legislative act of judicial decision, resort must be had to the customs and usages of civilized nations[.]

The Paquete Habana, 175 U.S. 677, 700 (1900). If a customary international law norm is not applied as a rule of decision in a case, how else could it be used in litigation?

2. *Port State Jurisdiction in the Royal Caribbean Cruises Case.* Does the material we considered earlier in this chapter support the U.S. exercise of port state jurisdiction in the Royal Caribbean Cruises case? Does international law allow a port state to prescribe and enforce rules and standards that are more stringent than those called for in international treaties?

3. *Port State Jurisdiction With Respect to Pollutant Discharges and the LOS Convention.* The Royal Caribbean Cruises court noted that, under Article 218 of the LOS Convention, port state authority exists even with respect to certain pollution discharges from vessels occurring outside the internal waters, territorial sea, or exclusive economic zone of the port state. The court did not directly rely on Article 218, since it did not base its holding on a discharge violation. If a court were to apply Article 218 to the facts of this case, would a prosecution for a discharge violation have been upheld? What is novel about Article 218? How does the port state jurisdiction provided for in the Article compare with traditional international law bases for the exercise of jurisdiction? Review the Lotus case in Chapter 4, and the discussion there about bases of prescriptive

jurisdiction under international law. What justifies the Article 218 "enlarged" basis for port state jurisdiction? If the effects of a vessel's discharge of pollutants beyond a port state's coastal waters are not felt in those waters, does port state jurisdiction under Article 218 depend on the notion that such jurisdiction furthers "international community concerns"? Do Articles 218 and 228 of the LOS Convention allocate too much or too little jurisdictional authority to the port state?

Article 218 appears in Part XII ("Protection and Preservation of the Marine Environment"), Section 6 ("Enforcement") of the LOS Convention. Does the Article also provide authority for a port state to apply its own laws, as well as to exercise enforcement jurisdiction? Does Article 211(3) provide sufficient authority for a port state to apply its own laws in a case falling within Article 218? See also LOS Convention, Article 25(2).

4. *Port State Obligations to Transmit Information and to Suspend Proceedings.* The Royal Caribbean Cruises court reported that the United States, the port state in the case, had transmitted the Coast Guard's records of its investigation to Liberia, the flag state. Note the obligation contained in Article 218(4) of the LOS Convention, and see also Article 228(1), which concerns the suspension of proceedings "to impose penalties in respect of" pollution prevention and control obligations. Were the U.S. proceedings in the Royal Caribbean Cruises case "in respect of " pollution? How should the United States have replied to Liberia's diplomatic note?

5. *Safeguards.* The provisions of Article 228 concerning suspension of proceedings and restrictions on the institution of proceedings are only some of the LOS Convention's "safeguards" against overzealous port state or coastal state enforcement of pollution measures. Among the other safeguards in Section 7 of Part XII of the Convention (Articles 223–233) is the requirement of non-discrimination in the treatment of foreign vessels (Article 227). Article 230 provides that only monetary penalties may be imposed when foreign vessels commit pollution violations beyond the territorial sea; the same limitation applies to violations in the territorial sea, "except in the case of a willful and serious act of pollution." Article 226 regulates the investigation of foreign vessels for pollution violations and requires the prompt release of such vessels subject to the posting of reasonable financial security. See also Article 292 and the discussion of applications for the prompt release of vessels and crews in Chapter 15.

Do any of the safeguards restrict port state measures concerning the construction, design, equipment, or manning (CDEM) of foreign flag vessels to measures that give effect to generally accepted international rules or standards? Should there be safeguards concerning CDEM matters? Compare LOS Convention, Article 21(2) concerning limits on coastal state laws and regulations relating to innocent passage in the territorial sea.

6. *Application to Vessels Voluntarily in Port.* A port state has jurisdiction under Article 218 "[w]hen a vessel is voluntarily within a port or at an off-shore terminal of a State." Article 220(1), which authorizes port state enforcement with respect to pollution violations occurring in the port state's own territorial sea or EEZ, similarly applies only to vessels voluntarily in port. What explains this limitation? What should be done with respect to polluting vessels that enter ports involuntarily?

7. *Port State Jurisdiction under MARPOL.* Article 4(2) of MARPOL requires each party to impose sanctions for violations of MARPOL standards "within the jurisdiction" of that party, i.e., in its internal waters or territorial sea. MARPOL also provides for extensive port state enforcement actions against foreign flag vessels. Articles 5 and 6 contain detailed provisions concerning denials of entry into port, port state inspections, and follow-up actions if evidence is found of vessel discharges or conditions that may pose an unreasonable threat of harm to the marine environment. MARPOL also links to the LOS Convention. For example, Article 218(1) of the LOS Convention authorizes port state investigations and proceedings "in respect of any discharge from [a] vessel outside the internal waters, territorial sea or exclusive economic zone of that State in violation of applicable international rules and standards established through the competent international organization or general diplomatic conference." The applicable international "rules include the discharge standards contained in the Annexes to MARPOL 73/78, which have achieved the level of 'generally accepted.'" Erik Jaap Molenaar, Port State Jurisdiction: Toward Comprehensive, Mandatory and Global Coverage, 38 Ocean Dev. & Intl. L. 225, 235 (2007).

8. *The Royal Caribbean Cruises Case and Expanded Bases for Port State Jurisdiction.* The Royal Caribbean Cruises court ultimately relied on a U.S. statute penalizing false reporting of oil discharges to find a violation by the Liberian-flagged *Nordic Empress*, suggesting one technique port states may use to expand the scope of their jurisdiction. In addition to penalizing the provision of false information, consider the following techniques for expanded port state jurisdiction:

- setting conditions for vessel departure, such as the mandatory disposal of all waste in port facilities, as a condition for entry into port;
- prohibiting vessels of flag states not bound to observe the regulations of regional fisheries management organizations (RFMOs) from entering port or landing catch unless they provide vessel management system (VMS) data verifying fisheries practices consistent with RFMO regulations;

- exercising port state jurisdiction over vessels that take, possess, transport, or sell fish in violation of the law of a *foreign* country (see, e.g., the U.S. Lacey Act, 16 U.S.C. §§ 3371 et seq.);
- exercising port state jurisdiction over unregistered vessels for activities that the flag state's own vessels are prohibited from conducting.

See Molenaar, supra Note 7, at 241–44. At what point will the exercise of port state jurisdiction upset the allocation of authority set out in the LOS Convention, e.g., its provisions regulating pollution discharges? For more on marine pollution, see Chapter 12.

AGREEMENT FOR THE IMPLEMENTATION OF THE PROVISIONS OF THE [LOS CONVENTION] RELATING TO THE CONSERVATION AND MANAGEMENT OF STRADDLING FISH STOCKS AND HIGHLY MIGRATORY FISH STOCKS (1995 FISH STOCKS AGREEMENT)
Dec. 4, 1995, U.S. Sen. Treaty Doc. No. 104-24 (1996), 2167 U.N.T.S. 88

Article 23
Measures taken by a port State

1. A port State has the right and the duty to take measures, in accordance with international law, to promote the effectiveness of subregional, regional and global conservation and management measures. When taking such measures a port State shall not discriminate in form or in fact against the vessels of any State.

2. A port State may, *inter alia*, inspect documents, fishing gear and catch on board fishing vessels, when such vessels are voluntarily in its ports or at its offshore terminals.

3. States may adopt regulations empowering the relevant national authorities to prohibit landings and transshipments where it has been established that the catch has been taken in a manner which undermines the effectiveness of subregional, regional or global conservation and management measures on the high seas.

4. Nothing in this article affects the exercise by States of their sovereignty over ports in their territory in accordance with international law.

Notes

1. *Port State Jurisdiction and Matters of International Community Concern.* Article 23 of the 1995 Fish Stocks Agreement concerns matters that affect

the international community, as well as port state constituencies. As of September 1, 2013, the 1995 Fish Stocks Agreement is in force for 80 states and the European Union. See also the 2009 FAO Agreement on Port State Measures to Prevent, Deter and Eliminate Illegal, Unreported and Unregulated Fishing. In addition to fisheries conservation and management, which is the subject of Article 23, and pollution control, which is addressed in the Royal Caribbean Cruises case and the Notes following it, labor conditions on board vessels may also be the subject of enlarged port state jurisdiction. See 2006 Maritime Labor Convention, Article V(4). In general, "the scope of port state jurisdiction has expanded enormously, not just due to the updating of relevant international instruments, but also due to their continuous expansion into related or entirely new subject areas." Erik Jaap Molenaar, Port State Jurisdiction: Toward Comprehensive, Mandatory and Global Coverage, 38 Ocean Dev. & Intl. L. 225, 240 (2007).

2. *Mandatory Exercise of Port State Jurisdiction?* Note that Article 23(1) of the 1995 Fish Stocks Agreement provides that port states have not only the right but the duty to take enforcement measures. Although the exercise of port state jurisdiction is often discretionary, some other treaty provisions make it mandatory. See, e.g., LOS Convention, Article 219 (concerning port state measures relating to the seaworthiness of vessels to prevent pollution). Should port state measures to promote compliance with international labor, environmental, and fisheries conservation requirements always be mandatory? What steps should be taken to avoid the problem of "ports of convenience," which refuse to inspect vessels that may be lax in complying with environmental, labor, or fisheries conservation measures?

3. *Savings Clauses.* Paragraph 4 of Article 23 of the 1995 Fish Stocks Agreement is known as a "savings clause." Does this provision confirm that a port state may extend the port state measures referred to in Article 23 to ships that fly the flag of non-parties to the Fish Stocks Agreement? Or does paragraph 4 mean that port states may take enforcement measures more onerous than those named in Article 23, with respect to all foreign flag vessels in port that have caught fish in violation of global conservation and management standards? See Molenaar, supra Note 1, at 234–35. More generally, what limits exist on port state enforcement jurisdiction? Would it be desirable to have all port states impose the same enforcement measures with respect to the conservation of straddling or highly migratory fish stocks, or high seas fish stocks, or other matters of international concern?

LEE A. KIMBALL, INTRODUCTORY NOTE ON MEMORANDUM OF UNDERSTANDING ON PORT STATE CONTROL IN THE CARIBBEAN REGION

36 Intl. Leg. Materials 231 (1997)

The Memorandum of Understanding (MOU) on Port State Control in the Caribbean Region is the fourth in a series commencing in 1982 with the Paris Memorandum (Europe). The other two cover the Latin American (1992) and Asia Pacific (1993) regions, and further regional developments are in the offing. These documents represent an innovative exercise by port states at the regional level to guard against accidents and pollution caused by vessels that do not conform with generally accepted international rules and standards. Following the practice of the Paris MOU, most also ensure conformity with international standards for seafarers to ensure acceptable living and working conditions on board ships. Each MOU identifies the relevant rules by reference to specific conventions adopted under the auspices of the International Maritime Organization (IMO) and the International Labor Organization (ILO). That is, they do not impose requirements additional to those in the identified conventions. Nevertheless, for vessels which due to their size are not covered by the international conventions, some of the MOUs permit maritime authorities to take necessary actions to ensure that these ships are not hazardous to safety, health, or the environment. . . .

The purpose of the MOUs is to reinforce flag State responsibilities to comply with international rules and standards. They seek to improve and harmonize a system of port state inspections for this purpose and avoid distorting competition among ports. Pre-empting unilateral approaches has also been a factor in their conclusion. The MOUs provide for consultation, cooperation, and information exchange among the signatory maritime authorities. In the case of the Caribbean, they call for each authority to strive to inspect, within three years of entry into force of the Memorandum, 15% of the estimated number of foreign ships which enter its ports during a representative twelve-month period. (This target varies among the four MOUs.)

The MOUs rely on a computerized databank and electronic communications to record inspection results and forward them to other states in the region so that future ports of call can be alerted to any deficiencies. Inspection results are conveyed also to flag states and deficiencies reported to the IMO. In order to avoid disruptions to navigation, ships may not be inspected more frequently than every six months unless there are clear grounds for doing so, thus effectively targeting problem vessels.

The inspections cover technical requirements and equipment and, since 1992, operational requirements. Their intensity proceeds from routine review of relevant certificates and documents on board the vessel and a cursory survey, to more detailed inspection if clear grounds exist for doing so, to detention of the vessel until serious deficiencies are rectified. If deficiencies are clearly hazardous and cannot be remedied in the port of inspection, the ship may proceed to another port, subject to any appropriate conditions determined by the maritime authority of the inspecting State to ensure that the vessel does not pose unreasonable danger to safety, health or the environment. The ship's next port of call would be informed of the situation. (The Paris MOU provides for agreement by the flag State regarding such conditions. Ships violating these terms will be denied access to ports whose maritime authorities are signatories to the MOU until satisfactory evidence of compliance with all applicable instruments is forthcoming.)

Verifying compliance with international operational requirements entails additional responsibilities for inspectors in assessing crew capabilities to handle equipment and communicate in emergency situations. A 1992 IMO-approved resolution explicitly expands the scope of port state control to operational matters "when there are clear grounds for believing that the master or crew are not familiar with essential shipboard procedures relating to the safety of ships," with "clear grounds" defined in an annex to the resolution (A.742(18)). The 19th IMO Assembly adopted an omnibus resolution on port State control which incorporates all previous resolutions on the subject (A.787(19)). It adds guidance for the detention of ships, qualification and training requirements for port state control officers, and procedural guidelines for them to follow. Recent amendments to the Safety of Life at Sea (SOLAS), Prevention of Pollution from Ships (MARPOL 73/78) and Standards of Training, Certification and Watchkeeping for Seafarers (STCW) conventions... incorporate a legal basis for port state control regarding operational requirements.

The MOUs do not themselves provide a legal basis for intervention to detain a substandard foreign ship, nor do the relevant conventions. This must be provided in national legislation. Since undue detention and delay involve the risk of compensation to the shipowner, such action is not taken lightly. When detention occurs, the responsible flag State must be notified.

Port state control arrangements are reinforced by the 1982 UN Convention on the Law of the Sea....

The right of the port State to verify compliance by foreign vessels with international shipping conventions is a long-standing one, but until the 1980s it had not been widely or systematically exercised. The Paris MOU was triggered largely by the grounding of the Amoco Cadiz in March 1978 off France, but it reflected growing doubts that international shipping in the region was complying with widely accepted maritime safety conventions and heightened concern over the risks of maritime accidents.... Entry into effect of the MOU provided a cornerstone for dealing with enforcement of international rules on ship safety and pollution control in the wake of the Amoco Cadiz.

Concern that substandard ships might be moving to other regions led to early cooperation between the Paris MOU and individual States to harmonize inspection procedures and exchange information electronically. The success of the European arrangement inspired the IMO to endorse such regional arrangements in 1991 (A.682(17)). Since then, the secretariats of both the Paris MOU and the IMO have provided advice and assistance to other regions in developing their own accords. The issue of reciprocal recognition of inspection results among the regions has been raised, but the achievements of the different regions have not yet reached an adequate degree of commonality. There are ongoing efforts to ensure compatibility among the regions and promote electronic information exchange. The IMO is working on an international ship information database to store national and regional inspection information and assist flag and port States to control substandard ships.

Initial skepticism of the Paris MOU on the part of shipowners has modified as the results have demonstrated a reduction in substandard ships, removing "free riders" from international shipping competition. Inspection results also serve as a guide to likely defects and the causes of accidents so that preventive measures may be improved. This may be undertaken through the competent international organizations and at the national level. Inquiries of the Paris MOU from national maritime authorities about their ships' inspections have led to improved vigilance and corrective action.

[The Paris MOU] regime has recently been strengthened by the European Union Council Directive on Port State Control, which entered into force on July 1, 1996 (95/21/EC, June 19, 1995).

Notes

1. *Port State Control Measures Relating to Vessel Seaworthiness*. Some commentators distinguish "port state jurisdiction" from "port state control." Port state control means that "the port State limits itself to taking an administrative measure of control, such as detaining a ship in port until various corrective measures have been taken or ordering it to proceed to the nearest shipyard for repairs." With port state control, unlike with port state jurisdiction, "the port State does not prosecute the vessel for an alleged breach of its legislation." Ho-Sam Bang, Port State Jurisdiction and Article 218 of the UN Convention on the Law of Sea, 40 J. Maritime L. & Com. 291, 292 (2009). Article 219 of the LOS Convention, which was not at issue in the Royal Caribbean Cruises case, is one provision authorizing port state control measures. Article 219 provides that when a port state has ascertained that a vessel in one of its ports "is in

violation of applicable international rules and standards relating to seaworthiness of vessels and thereby threatens damage to the marine environment," the port state "shall, as far as practicable, take administrative measures to prevent the vessel from sailing," except to a repair yard; "upon removal of the causes of the violation," the port state "shall permit the vessel to continue immediately." Which "international rules and standards" will be "applicable"?

2. *Port State Memoranda of Understanding.* The maritime authorities of twenty Caribbean states and territories negotiated the Memorandum of Understanding on Port State Control in the Caribbean Region, and nine states signed it when it opened for signature in February 1996. As of September 1, 2013, fifteen states were members of the Caribbean MOU, and France is an associate member. See http://www.caribbeanmou.org. Given that several treaties authorize port state inspections and other control measures, why are port state control MOUs needed? How do such MOUs further port state control goals?

As noted by Lee Kimball, states have gained considerable experience in implementing the 1982 Paris MOU, in which, as of September 1, 2013, 26 European maritime authorities and Canada participate. In 2012, over 18,000 inspections of 14,646 vessels registered in 113 different flag states occurred in the Paris MOU region. Fifty-seven percent of all inspected vessels had at least one deficiency; there were 669 detentions of vessels for serious deficiencies related to health, safety, or pollution; and fifteen ships were banned. In 2011, the Paris MOU instituted a new inspection system, with increased targeting of high-risk vessels and periodic regional inspections of all vessels. As a result of the new system, recorded deficiencies have decreased from 64,698 in 2010 to 49,261 in 2012. See Paris MOU, Port State Control: Annual Report 2012, 18–20, available at http://www.parismou.org.

Most of the world is now served by nine MOUs. As of September 1, 2013, these are, in addition to the Paris MOU and the Caribbean MOU: the Viña del Mar MOU (Latin America) (http://www.acuerdolatino.int.ar); the Tokyo MOU (Asia/Pacific region) (http://www.tokyo-mou.org); the Mediterranean MOU (http://www.medmou.org); the Indian Ocean MOU (http://www.iomou.org); the Riyadh MOU (Persian Gulf) (http://www.riyadhmou.org); the Black Sea MOU (http://www.bsmou.org); and the Abuja MOU (West and Central Africa) (http://www.abujamou.org). No North American MOU exists, but Canada participates in the Paris MOU (for its Atlantic coast) and the Tokyo MOU (for its Pacific coast). What are the prospects for increased interregional cooperation to promote compatible port state control efforts? Note that the Tokyo MOU, the Caribbean MOU, the Mediterranean MOU, the Black Sea MOU, the Riyadh MOU, and the U.S. Coast Guard have observer status with the Paris MOU, and eight members of the Paris MOU are also members of other MOUs. See Paris MOU, Port State Control: Annual Report 2012, 16–17.

CHAPTER 8

Territorial Sea, Contiguous Zone, Straits, and Archipelagic Waters

This chapter first examines the territorial sea, a narrow band of coastal waters over which the coastal state traditionally has exercised authority. Subsection 1 of Section A explores the breadth of the territorial sea and its juridical status in international law. In Subsection 2 we focus on the right of foreign vessels to engage in innocent passage, which constitutes one significant limit on the authority of a coastal state over its territorial sea. Subsection 2 also considers the coastal state's jurisdiction over foreign flag vessels passing through the territorial sea.

The remainder of this chapter investigates the rights of coastal and flag states in other zones near baselines. In Section B we look at the contiguous zone, which extends beyond the territorial sea, and the conceptual links between the territorial sea and the contiguous zone. Sections C and D examine two navigational regimes developed at the Third United Nations Conference on the Law of the Sea (UNCLOS III) and codified in the 1982 United Nations Convention on the Law of the Sea (LOS Convention): transit passage through straits and archipelagic sea lanes passage through archipelagic waters.

A The Territorial Sea

1 *Status of the Territorial Sea*

Does international law provide that a coastal state has plenary jurisdiction over its territorial sea for all purposes, comparable to its jurisdiction over its land territory? Or is the coastal state's authority limited, dependent on affirmative acts of the coastal state, which it may take only if necessary to protect particular interests, such as security or fisheries? And just how broad is this territorial sea, within which the coastal state has authority? The 1876 case of Regina v. Keyn concerned such questions, and subsequent treaties have addressed them as well.

 | DOI 10.1163/9789004203563_009

REGINA v. KEYN
2 Ex. D. 63 (1876)

[When a German merchant ship, the *Franconia*, accidentally struck and sunk a British vessel, the *Strathclyde*, a woman aboard the *Strathclyde* drowned. The collision occurred at a point in the English Channel less than three miles from the British coast. Ferdinand Keyn, the German captain of the *Franconia*, was tried for manslaughter in a British criminal court and convicted.

Keyn appealed his conviction, and the case came before the Court for Crown Cases Reserved on the issue of the jurisdiction of British courts over acts by foreign nationals aboard foreign vessels in British coastal waters. A thirteen-judge bench finds, by a vote of seven to six, that British courts lacked jurisdiction. Only two judges think Keyn's negligent acts were constructively taken aboard the British vessel, since their effects were felt there. The majority (Phillimore disagrees on this point) conclude Parliament could grant the courts jurisdiction over acts committed in a belt of open sea appurtenant to the coast, but find Parliament had not yet done so. The opinions of the judges, occupying over 170 pages of the court reports, discuss in detail the literature on the subject and explore thoroughly the basis, nature, and extent of coastal state jurisdiction over the marginal sea. We reproduce here only a portion of two of the opinions.]

SIR R. PHILLIMORE . . .

The question as to dominion over portions of the seas enclosed within headlands or contiguous shores . . . is not now under consideration. It is enough to say that within [the] term "territory" are certainly comprised the ports and harbours, and the space between the flux and reflux of tide, or the land up to the furthest point at which the tide recedes. But it is at this point that the difficulty presented by the case before us begins, and here the following questions present themselves for solution:

1. Is a state entitled to any extension of dominion beyond low-water mark?
2. If so, how far does this territory, or do these territorial waters, as they are usually called, extend?
3. Has a state the same dominion over these territorial waters as over the territory of her soil and in her ports, or is it of a more limited character and confined to certain purposes?

With respect to the first of these questions the answer may be given without doubt or hesitation, namely, that a state is entitled to a certain extension of territory, in a certain sense of that word, beyond low-water mark.

With respect to the second question, the distance to which the territorial waters extend, it appears on an examination of the authorities that the distance has varied (setting aside even more extravagant claims) from 100 to 3 miles, the present limit. . . .

The third question . . . remains to be substantively considered; it is one of much importance, viz., whether, admitting that the state has a dominion over three miles of adjacent water, it is the same dominion which the possessor has over her land and her ports, or is it of a more limited character—limited to the purpose of protecting the adjacent shore, for which it was granted, and not extending to a general sovereignty over all passing vessels. . . .

The consensus of civilized independent states has recognized a maritime extension of frontier to the distance of three miles from low-water mark, because such a frontier of belt of water is necessary for the defense and security of the adjacent state.

It is for the attainment of these particular objects that a dominium has been granted over this portion of the high seas.

This proposition is materially different from the proposition contended for, namely, that it is competent to a state to exercise within these waters the same rights of jurisdiction and property which appertain to it in respect to its lands and its ports. There is one obvious test by which the two sovereignties may be distinguished.

According to modern international law, it is certainly a right incident to each state to refuse a passage to foreigners over its territory by land, whether in time of peace or war. But it does not appear to have the same right with respect to preventing the passage of foreign ships over this portion of the high seas. . . .

The reason of the thing, that is, the defense and security of the state, does not require or warrant the exclusion of peaceable foreign vessels from passing over these waters; and the custom and usage of nations has not sanctioned it.

Consequences fraught with mischief and injustice might flow from the opposite doctrine, which would render applicable to a foreign vessel while in *itinere* from one foreign port to another, passing over these waters, all the criminal law of the adjacent territory. No single instance has been brought to our notice of the practical exercise by any nation of this jurisdiction.

The authorities cited in order to show that a foreign vessel is subject to the laws of the foreign port which she enters appear to me inapplicable to the present case.

A foreign merchant vessel going into the port of a foreign state subjects herself to the ordinary law of the place during the period of her commorancy there; she is as much a *subditus temporaneus* as the individual who visits the interior of the country for the purposes of pleasure or business. . . .

If, indeed, as has been contended, there be no difference between the jurisdiction by the adjacent state over vessels in ports and over passing and commorant vessels, then the whole criminal law of England was applicable to the crew and those on board the German vessel, so long as she was within a marine league of the English shore.

The consequences of such a position of law appear to me, especially in the absence of any precedent, sufficient to render it untenable.

There is yet another argument, already partially adverted to, which appears to me entitled to great weight in an English court of justice.

Upon the subject of the three-miles belt of territorial water, Parliament has frequently legislated. It might perhaps be not impertinently asked, why, if these waters are territorial in the same sense as the land, and those who traverse them are already subject to the law. But, passing by this observation, it will be found on examination of the statutes that the provisions in them are either framed exclusively for British subjects and ships, or that they relate to the protection and peace of the state....

Upon the whole, I am of opinion that the Court had no jurisdiction over this foreigner for an offence committed on board a foreign ship on the high seas, though within three miles of the coast; that he is governed by the law of the state to which his flag belongs; and that the conviction cannot be sustained....

COCKBURN, C.J.

...There can be no doubt that the suggestion of Bynkershoek, that the sea surrounding the coast to the extent of cannon-range should be treated as belonging to the state owning the coast, has, with but very few exceptions, been accepted and adopted by the publicists who have followed him during the last two centuries. But it is equally clear that, in the practical application of the rule, in respect of the particular of distance, as also in the still more essential particular of the character and degree of sovereignty and dominion to be exercised, great difference of opinion and uncertainty have prevailed, and still continue to exist....

One set of writers ... ascribe to the state territorial property and sovereignty over the three miles of sea, to the extent of the right of excluding the ships of all other nations, even for the purpose of passage—a doctrine flowing immediately from the principle of territorial property, but which is too monstrous to be admitted. Another set concede territorial property and sovereignty, but make it subject to the right of other nations to use these waters for the purpose of navigation. Others ... deny any right of territorial property, but concede "jurisdiction"; by which I understand them to mean the power of applying the law, applicable to persons on the land, to all who are within the territorial water, and the power of legislating in respect of it, so as to bind every one who comes within the jurisdiction, whether subjects or foreigners. Some . . . would confine this jurisdiction to purposes of "safety and police"—by which I should be disposed to understand measures for the protection of the territory, and for the regulation of the navigation, and the use of harbours and roadsteads, and the maintenance of order among the shipping therein, rather than the general application of the criminal law.

Other authors . . . would restrict the jurisdiction to certain specified purposes in which the local state has an immediate interest, namely, the protection of its revenue and fisheries, the exacting of harbour and light dues, and the protection of its coasts in time of war.

Some of these authors . . . make a most important distinction between a commorant and a passing ship. According to [one] author, while the commorant ship is subject to the general law of the local state, the passing ship is liable to the local jurisdiction only in matters of "military and police regulations, made for the safety of the territory and population of the coast." None of these writers, it should be noted, discuss the question, or go the length of asserting that a foreigner in a foreign ship, using the waters in question for the purpose of navigation solely, on its way to another country, is liable to the criminal law of the adjoining country for an offence committed on board.

Now, when it is remembered that it is mainly on the statements and authority of these writers, and to opinions founded upon them, that we are called upon to hold that foreigners on the so-called territorial sea are subject to the general law of this country, the discrepancy of opinion which I have been pointing out becomes very material. Looking to this, we may properly ask those who contend for the application of the existing law to the littoral sea independently of legislation, to tell us the extent to which we are to go in applying it. Are we to limit it to three miles, or to extend it to six? Are we to treat the whole body of the criminal law as applicable to it, or only so much as relates to "police and safety"? Or are we to limit it, as one of these authors proposes, to the protection of fisheries and customs, the exacting of harbour and light dues, and the protection of our coasts in time of war? Which of these writers are we to follow? What is there in these conflicting views to guide us, in the total absence of precedent or legal sanction, as to the extent to which we may subject foreigners to our law? What is there in them which authorizes us to assume not only that Parliament can of right deal with the three-mile zone as forming part of our territory, but also that, by the mere assent of other nations, the sea to this extent has become so completely a part of our territory as to be subject, without legislation, to the whole body of our existing law, civil and criminal?

But it is said that, although the writers on international law are disagreed on so many essential points, they are all agreed as to the power of a littoral state to deal with the three-mile zone as subject to its dominion, and that consequently we may treat it as subject to our law. But this reasoning strikes me as unsatisfactory; for what does this unanimity in the general avail us when we come to the practical application of the law in the particular instance, if we are left wholly in the dark as to the degree to which the law can be legitimately enforced? This unanimity of opinion that the littoral sea is, at all events for some purposes, subject to the dominion of the local state, may go far to show that, by the concurrence of other nations, such a state may deal with these waters as subject to its legislation. But it wholly fails to show that, in the absence of such legislation, the ordinary law of the local state will extend over the waters in question—which is the point which we have to determine.

Notes

1. *Parliament's Response.* Regina v. Keyn was sharply criticized when it was decided. Within two years the British Parliament passed a law that, inter alia, permitted the exercise of criminal jurisdiction over acts occurring within a marginal sea extending "to such a distance as is necessary for the defence and security of [the Queen's] dominions." Territorial Waters Jurisdiction Act, 41 and 42 Victoria, c. 73 (1878).

2. *The Breadth of the Territorial Sea.* Although many states recognized three nautical miles as the maximum breadth of the territorial sea at the time of Regina v. Keyn, state practice was not uniform. Practice continued to diverge well into the 20th century. See Donald R. Rothwell & Tim Stephens, The International Law of the Sea 59–68 (2010); John E. Noyes, Territorial Sea, in 4 The Oxford Encyclopedia of Maritime History 125 (John B. Hattendorf ed., 2007). The issue of the maximum permissible breadth of the territorial sea was not resolved until agreement at UNCLOS III on the language contained in Article 3 of the LOS Convention.

The United States extended its territorial sea from three to twelve nautical miles for international purposes in 1988, by Presidential Proclamation No. 5928, 54 Fed. Reg. 777 (1989). See Bruce E. Alexander, The Territorial Sea of the United States: Is It Twelve Miles or Not?, 20 J. Maritime L. & Commerce 449 (1989); John E. Noyes, United States of America Presidential Proclamation No. 5928: A 12-Mile U.S. Territorial Sea, 4 Intl. J. Estuarine & Coastal L. 142 (1989). Why did the United States delay so long before extending its territorial sea? Some other countries hesitated as well. The United Kingdom did not extend its territorial sea to twelve nautical miles until 1987. Territorial Sea Act 1987,

c. 49 (entered into force Oct. 1, 1987). Why might some states that were not maritime powers also have been reluctant to proclaim a broader territorial sea? For example, Belgium also delayed its twelve-nautical-mile extension until 1987. Act Establishing the Breadth of the Territorial Sea of Belgium, 6 October 1987, available at http://www.un.org/depts/los/LEGISLATIONANDTREATIES/PDFFILES/BEL_1987_Act.pdf (entered into force Nov. 1, 1987). Erik Franckx, Belgium Extends its Territorial Sea up to 12 Nautical Miles, 20 Belgian Rev. Intl. L. 41 (1987).

A few countries still do not assert a territorial sea to the maximum extent permissible. Why should this be so? Does Regina v. Keyn suggest possible reasons? What reasons prevail today?

3. *Justifications for Coastal State Authority in the Territorial Sea.* Justice Phillimore and Chief Justice Cockburn mentioned several reasons for coastal state authority over a territorial sea. Do those reasons still apply today? Are there now other reasons for the existence of such a territorial belt that were either not present or not fully appreciated in 1876?

Note the distinction in Chief Justice Cockburn's opinion between coastal state control over a passing vessel and control over a commorant (stopping) one. Why should there be such a distinction? In addition, should vessels passing through the territorial sea on the way to or from a local port be treated differently from those just passing by the coastal state's shores?

4. *"Sovereignty" over the Territorial Sea.* In the early 20th century, the position of states and writers moved toward the view that the territorial sea—along with the airspace above it and the subsoil and seabed below—was subject to the "sovereignty" of the coastal state. For example, the Territorial Waters Committee of the 1930 Hague Conference put forward a text providing that "[t]he territory of a State includes a belt of sea described in this Convention as the territorial sea. Sovereignty over this belt is exercised subject to the conditions prescribed by the present Convention and the other rules of international law." League of Nations Doc. C.351(b).M.145(b).1930.V at 212, reprinted in 4 League of Nations Conference for the Codification of International Law 1414 (Shabtai Rosenne ed., 1975). Would this formulation, or the formulation in Article 2 of the LOS Convention (which tracked Article 1 of the 1958 Territorial Sea Convention), resolve the dilemmas that troubled Chief Justice Cockburn in Regina v. Keyn?

Is Article 2(3) of the LOS Convention superfluous? In a multi-polar world, is not a state's freedom of action—its "sovereignty"—always defined by what freedom of action is allowed to states pursuant to international law? At the least, Article 2(3) emphasizes that the scope of a state's sovereignty in its territorial sea is not identical to its sovereignty within its land territory. In particular, foreign flag vessels have a right of innocent passage through the territorial sea; there is no comparable right of passage for foreigners over land territory.

2 *Innocent Passage and Jurisdiction over Passing Vessels*

The LOS Convention and other treaties have recognized and defined the right of foreign flag vessels to engage in innocent passage through the territorial sea. What is meant by "innocent passage"? When may a coastal state exercise jurisdiction over a foreign flag merchant vessel passing through the coastal state's territorial sea? Can the passage of warships through the territorial sea be "innocent," and, if so, may a coastal state require that a foreign warship give notice before it engages in innocent passage in the coastal state's territorial sea? We explore such questions in this subsection.

COMPAÑIA DE NAVEGACIÓN NACIONAL (PANAMA) v. UNITED STATES
Arbitration under the Conventions of 1926 and 1932 (1933), in U.S. Dept. State, American and Panamanian General Claims Arbitration 765 (1934), 6 Rep. Intl. Arb. Awards 382 (2006)

[In 1923 the *David*, a Panamanian flag vessel, and the *Yorba Linda*, a U.S. flag vessel, collided at sea. Two years later the General Petroleum Corporation, owner of the *Yorba Linda*, libeled the *David*, owned by the Compañia de Navegación Nacional, a Panamanian company, in the U.S. District Court for the Canal Zone. The libel alleged that the collision had occurred in U.S. territorial waters and that it had been caused by the *David*'s negligence. Pursuant to this libel the *David* was arrested in waters that the tribunal determined were part of the three-mile territorial sea of the Canal Zone. Her owners put up a US$ 30,000 bond to obtain her release from U.S. authorities. In 1927 the parties arrived at a court-approved settlement whereby the Panamanian company paid the U.S. corporation US$ 16,250. The Panamanian company then brought the present claim to the American-Panamanian Claims Commission, alleging that the damages paid, reputation lost, and costs incurred by the company as a result of the U.S. lawsuit were all due to the improper arrest of the *David*.

Both sides agreed that, if the *David* was found to have been arrested in the U.S. territorial sea, she was there only while in transit from one part of the Panamanian territorial sea to another. On these premises, the Panamanian agent argues that the arrest did not conform with existing international law on innocent passage. The following is an excerpt from his brief on this point.]

... The right of innocent transit is a real, effective *right*; it is more than that; it is a limitation imposed by international law upon the sovereignty of the littoral state in favor of the maritime navigation of other powers.

In truth, this right of *innocent transit* is so old and so firmly established that I consider it superfluous to prove it. However, here is one of its many manifestations:

> It is laid down that foreign ships have a right of innocent passage through the marginal sea. (Moore, *Digest* [*of International Law*], I, p. 700.) [See also ... Rivier, *Principes du droit des gens*, 1, 152; Hall, *International Law* (4th [ed.]) 212.]

In a series of resolutions adopted by the Institut de Droit International at Paris, in 1894, it was established (art. 5) that all vessels without distinction possess *the right of innocent passage* through the territorial waters. (Moore, *supra*, p. 701.) This principle was reiterated in article 8, which provided:

> ARTICLE 8. Ships of any nationality, by the mere fact of being in territorial waters, are subject to the jurisdiction of the riparian state, unless they are merely passing by. (Moore, *Digest*, I, p. 701.)

[E]ven over the marine belt of three miles the jurisdiction of the Sovereign of the shore is qualified by those modifications which the law of necessity has wrought into international law. Fishing boats or other vessels, traversing those rough waters, have the right, not merely of free transit of which I have spoken, but of relief, when suffering from want of necessaries, from the shore. *Extract from the communication sent by Mr. Bayard, Secretary of State of the United States, to Mr. Manning, Secretary of the Treasury, on May 28, 1886.* (Moore, *Digest*, I, p. 721.)

In the year 1929, the most noted internationalists of the United States prepared a draft convention which was to serve and did serve as the basis of the First Conference on the Codification of International Law held at The Hague in 1930....

In the chapter on Territorial Waters it was provided in article 14, as follows:

> ART. 14. A state must permit innocent passage through its marginal seas by the vessels of other states, but it may prescribe reasonable regulation for such passage.

And in article 16, it was provided:

> ART. 16. A state may not exercise civil jurisdiction over a vessel of another state while it is in course of innocent passage through the marginal sea, except in respect of an act committed by the vessel during the course of the innocent passage and not relating solely to the internal economy of the vessel.

It is not possible to find a clearer or more authorized establishment of the right of innocent passage. As may be seen, the only two limitations of this right do not include a passage like that of the *David*; said limitations consist, according to article 14, in that the littoral state may "prescribe reasonable regulations for such passage." This refers merely to measures of security, to a distinction which may be made between different classes of vessels, such as submarines, warships, merchant ships, etc. It has been so understood by the authors who drafted article 14, on commenting upon said article in *Research in International Law, Draft Conventions on Nationality. Responsibility of States, Territorial Waters*, Harvard Law School, p. 295. But it has never been suggested, and it would even be absurd to suppose it, that the right to regulate this innocent passage includes the right to destroy it.

The other limitation imposed on this right according to the aforesaid article 16, is that the littoral state may exercise civil jurisdiction over a vessel in innocent passage only "with respect to an act committed by said vessel during the course of that innocent passage and not relating solely to the internal economy of the vessel." It is obvious that this exception is not applicable in this claim.

The comment made by the aforementioned authors on the limitation imposed by Article 16 is very interesting and particularly applicable in this claim. In fact, the commentators cite as example a hypothetical case which exactly is analogous to the case of the *David*, expressing themselves as follows:

> Moreover, the exercise of civil jurisdiction should clearly be limited, as the text provides, to those acts committed by the vessel itself or by those on board during the innocent passage, and it should not extend to matters relating solely to the internal economy of the vessel. This limitation clearly excludes the state's exercise of civil jurisdiction with reference to acts committed before the vessel entered marginal seas on the particular passage concerned. If for instance, a British vessel had been in a collision on the high seas or in French territorial waters, jurisdiction should not be taken by the United States with respect to that collision when this British vessel is in innocent passage through the American marginal sea.

Thus, it is clearly established that the right of *innocent passage* through the marginal seas *is not a simple permit or act of grace, but a right* in the proper sense of the word, that is to say, a limitation imposed by international law upon the jurisdiction and sovereignty of the littoral state. This right was violated when the authorities of the Zone exercised jurisdiction over the *David* by arresting her, and consequently the United States is obliged to indemnify the claimant for the damages sustained as a result of this usurpation of jurisdiction.

[The U.S. agent counters by arguing that, even if the *David* were in "innocent passage," international law did not prohibit the coastal state authorities from exercising civil jurisdiction as the U.S. marshal had when he arrested the *David*. The following extracts are from the U.S. agent's reply brief in support of this contention.]

[U]nder treaty stipulations between the two Governments as well as under the general principles of international law, there can be no question regarding the right of the United States to exercise general jurisdiction over the waters of the Canal Zone extending 3 miles into the Pacific. The question arises, therefore, whether the jurisdictional rights of the United States *are* limited by the right of innocent passage in such a manner that the arrest of the *David*, while in transit through Canal Zone waters, constituted a violation of international law. . . .

In his [1927] work, *The Law of Territorial Waters and Maritime Jurisdiction*, Jessup states:

> As a general principle, the right of innocent passage requires no supporting argument or citation of authority; it is firmly established in international law. There is, however, a divergency of opinion on two points: first, whether war vessels may exercise the right; second, to what extent such transient vessels are subjected to the authority of the littoral state. [P. 120.]
>
> In so far as concerns the extent to which merchant vessels passing through territorial waters are subject to the authority of the local sovereign, there is little express authority. This is due to the fact that national laws and decrees rarely specify whether the vessels dealt with therein are those bound for the national ports or those merely passing through on a foreign voyage. It is interesting to note that for nearly one hundred and twenty-five years the American customs laws providing for the examination of foreign ships within twelve miles of shore (and therefore also within territorial waters) were applicable only to ships bound for American ports. Since the Tariff Act of 1922, even ships in passage are included within the letter of the law. [P. 121.]

> In conclusion it may be said that the right of innocent passage does not guarantee to the vessel exercising it a total immunity from the processes of the local law. [P. 121.]

The eminent authority Hall, who regards the right of innocent passage as "established in the most complete manner," makes the following statements concerning the matter of local jurisdiction over merchant vessels engaged in the exercise of the right:

> ... It would ... be convenient that the amount of jurisdiction to be exercised by a state in its ports and in its territorial waters in general should be made the same under a practice or understanding sufficiently wide to become authoritative. There is no reason for any distinction between the immunities of a ship in the act of using its right of innocent passage, and of a ship at rest in the harbours of the state; and if there were any reason, it would still be difficult to settle the point at which a distinction should be made. [*International Law*, p. 215.]
>
> Looking at the case of passing vessels by itself, there being at present no clear usage in the matter, a state must be held to preserve territorial jurisdiction, in so far as it may choose to exercise it, over the ships and the persons on board, as fully as over ships and persons within other parts of its territory. [*Ibid.*, p. 215.]

[T]he replies made by various governments to questions formulated by the Preparatory Committee for the Codification Conference held at The Hague in 1930, are of particular interest. The following inquiries were made concerning the matter of limitations upon the criminal and civil jurisdiction of the coastal state:

> Is the coastal State precluded from exercising jurisdiction: (*a*) in civil cases; (*b*) in criminal cases?
>
> Is jurisdiction only exercisable in respect of occurrences happening during the passage?
>
> Are there distinctions to be made according to whether the ship is passing through the territorial waters on its way to or from a port of the coastal state or is merely passing through such waters?

The replies of some of the governments are, in part, as follows, Publication of League of Nations, C.74.M.39.1929.V, p. 78:

> *Australia*: . . . A State is entitled to exercise jurisdiction in civil or criminal cases over foreign merchant vessels, and persons and property on board them, in its territorial waters; such jurisdiction is not limited to occurrences happening during the voyage or affected in law by whether the vessel is merely passing through territorial waters or *en route* to or from a port of the coastal State or whether the effect of the occurrence does or does not extend beyond the ship itself or the persons on board. . . .
>
> *Denmark*: 1. (*a*) The Danish State must be regarded as possessing the unrestricted right, from the most ancient times, to subject any foreign merchant vessel passing through its waters to its civil jurisdiction. Nevertheless, this question does not appear ever to have been decided by the Danish Courts. Denmark would, however, be prepared to adopt a rule providing that the mere fact of passage would not suffice to subject a foreign merchant vessel to the civil jurisdiction of the coastal State; provided, however, that such passage does not produce consequences extending beyond the ship itself, as, for instance, in the case of a collision or an accident at sea, etc. The Danish Government sees no reason to distinguish between the cases of vessels entering or leaving the port of a coastal State, or merely passing through its waters.

[The U.S. agent also quotes the replies of several other governments.]

The above statements of various governments concerning the matter of the littoral state's civil jurisdiction over vessels passing through marginal waters support the conclusion reached by Hall that there is "no clear usage in the matter." Consequently, as stated by Jessup, the right of innocent passage "does not guarantee to the vessel exercising it a total immunity from the processes of the local law," and, as stated by Hall, . . . with respect to "passing vessels"—

> . . . a state must be held to preserve territorial jurisdiction, in so far as it may choose to exercise it, over the ships and persons on board, as fully as over ships and persons within other parts of its territory.

It will be obvious, therefore, that while under the existing principles of international law foreign merchant vessels have a right of passage through marginal seas, no right of extra-territoriality attaches to such vessels during such passage.

[The Commission finds in favor of the United States on this point as well as on the merits of the whole case. The majority opinion (per D.W. van Heeckeren

(Netherlands), Presiding Commissioner, and Elihu Root, Jr., Commissioner) gives the following summary treatment to the innocent passage question:]

We now turn to the question raised by the assertion that the *David* should have been exempted from arrest under the rule of innocent passage.... The general rule of the extension of sovereignty over the 3-mile zone is clearly established. Exceptions to the completeness of this sovereignty should be supported by authority. There is a clear preponderance of authority to the effect that this sovereignty is qualified by what is known as the right of innocent passage, and that this qualification forbids the sovereign actually to prohibit the innocent passage of alien merchant vessels through its territorial waters.

There is no clear preponderance of authority to the effect that such vessels when passing through territorial waters are exempt from civil arrest. In the absence of such authority, the Commission cannot say that a country may not, under the rules of international law, assert the right to arrest on civil process merchant ships passing through its territorial waters.

[The Panamanian commissioner, H.F. Alfaro, dissents, disagreeing generally with the majority's holding and its finding on innocent passage. His views on the coastal state's jurisdiction follow.]

Let us pass now to the second question, the so-called right of innocent passage. The opinion of the majority admits ... the existence of that right; it admits that it constitutes a limitation of territorial sovereignty and that the sovereign cannot impede said passage, but it denies that it carries with it exemption from civil arrest by the territorial authorities.

I am not in accord with this conclusion of the majority which is contrary to the very nature of the right of innocent passage and which considerably abridges it and does not seem to be based upon creditable authorities in international law. [The right of innocent passage] has been considered as a necessary appendage to the freedom of navigation on the high seas. To subject a merchant ship sailing coastwise within the 3-mile limit to civil arrest by coastal authorities, violently interrupts such passage and notably abridges the freedom of the seas referred to. There are, on the other hand, authorities of high standing in international law, who expressly establish the lack of jurisdiction by littoral authorities in such cases. See for example the resolutions adopted in 1894 by the Institute of International Law and especially the juridical investigation carried out by the most prominent American international jurists (Research in International Law, Harvard Law School) which served as a basis for the Hague Conference on the Codification of International Law.

It is proper to point out also that the claimant does not maintain that absolute immunity exists from the jurisdiction of the littoral authorities; that it does not allege, for example, lack of jurisdiction in the case of an offense committed within territorial waters in the course of innocent passage, although some writers deny jurisdiction even in such cases; the claimant also accepts that the ship is obliged to comply with orders and maritime regulations which contribute to the safety of navigation, or that are of a sanitary or police character. The claimant maintains only that in case of a civil action growing out of a collision occurring previously beyond the jurisdiction of the littoral authorities, the latter were without jurisdiction later to interfere with the passage of the same ship by means of a civil suit not affecting in any way territorial sovereign interests.

Notes

1. *Jurisdiction over Passing Vessels.* By arresting the *David*, the United States was exercising its enforcement jurisdiction. (See the discussion of jurisdiction in Chapter 4, Section B.) Compare the result in the case of the *David* with Article 28 of the LOS Convention (which is virtually identical to Article 20 of the 1958 Territorial Sea Convention). What is the current force of the *David* decision?

What about legislative jurisdiction? Did the arbitral tribunal indicate the types of coastal state laws to which a passing vessel, such as the *David*, could be subject? The *David* apparently was engaged in innocent passage through the territorial sea of the U.S. Canal Zone. How do modern limitations on coastal state jurisdiction over vessels in innocent passage compare? Article 21 of the LOS Convention specifies coastal state laws that may apply to a vessel in innocent passage. Are there other coastal state laws to which a vessel in innocent passage may be subject today? Does Article 27, which provides for general enforcement jurisdiction of criminal laws, imply the existence of additional legislative jurisdiction? That is, will all of a coastal state's criminal laws apply to a vessel in innocent passage? How does international law limit the legislative jurisdiction of coastal states over vessels in innocent passage? See LOS Convention, Articles 21(1)–(2), 24. Note that other treaties may modify the rules set forth in the LOS Convention. See, for example, the 1952 Convention on Penal Jurisdiction in Matters of Collision. That Convention provides for the exclusive jurisdiction of the flag state in a collision case, even in the territorial sea, absent a reservation to the contrary by a coastal state with respect to offenses in its territorial sea.

What are the limits, if any, on the legislative and enforcement jurisdiction that a coastal state today may exercise with respect to a foreign ship that is engaged in non-innocent passage? Or with respect to a foreign ship in the territorial sea that is not in passage at all? See also LOS Convention, Article 25.

2. *Determining Innocence of Passage.* Why was the passage of the *David* "innocent"? Will the innocence of a passage depend solely on the activities of

the passing vessel? Could innocence turn on the mere presence of the vessel in the territorial sea? Or on the intent of the master of the passing vessel? Will any activity of a passing vessel in the territorial sea that violates a coastal state law make the vessel's passage non-innocent? Conversely, can passage be non-innocent if the passing vessel has not violated any coastal state law?

DECLARATION OF PEOPLE'S REPUBLIC OF CHINA UPON RATIFICATION OF THE LAW OF THE SEA CONVENTION

June 7, 1996, available at http://www.un.org/Depts/los/convention_agreements/convention_declarations.htm#China%20Upon%20ratification

In accordance with the decision of the Standing Committee of the Eighth National People's Congress of the People's Republic of China at its nineteenth session, the President of the People's Republic of China has hereby ratified the United Nations Convention on the Law of the Sea of 10 December 1982 and at the same time made the following statement: . . .

4. The People's Republic of China reaffirms that the provisions of the United Nations Convention on the Law of the Sea concerning innocent passage through the territorial sea shall not prejudice the right of a coastal State to request, in accordance with its laws and regulations, a foreign State to obtain advance approval from or give prior notification to the coastal State for the passage of its warships through the territorial sea of the coastal State.

UNIFORM INTERPRETATION OF RULES OF INTERNATIONAL LAW GOVERNING INNOCENT PASSAGE

U.S.S.R.-U.S., Sept. 23, 1989, Dept. State Bull. No. 2152 at 26 (Nov. 1989), 28 Intl. Leg. Materials 1445 (1989)

1. The relevant rules of international law governing innocent passage of ships in the territorial sea are stated in the 1982 United Nations Convention on the Law of the Sea (Convention of 1982), particularly in Part II, Section 3.

2. All ships, including warships, regardless of cargo, armament or means of propulsion, enjoy the right of innocent passage through the territorial sea in accordance with international law, for which neither prior notification nor authorization is required.

3. Article 19 of the Convention of 1982 sets out in paragraph 2 an exhaustive list of activities that would render passage not innocent. A ship passing through the territorial sea that does not engage in any of those activities is in innocent passage.

4. A coastal State which questions whether the particular passage of a ship through its territorial sea is innocent shall inform the ship of the reason why it questions the innocence of the passage, and provide the ship an opportunity to clarify its intentions or correct its conduct in a reasonably short period of time.

5. Ships exercising the right of innocent passage shall comply with all laws and regulations of the coastal State adopted in conformity with relevant rules of international law as reflected in Articles 21, 22, 23 and 25 of the Convention of 1982. These include the laws and regulations requiring ships exercising the right of innocent passage through its territorial sea to use such sea lanes and traffic separation schemes as it may prescribe where needed to protect safety of navigation. In areas where no such sea lanes or traffic separation schemes have been prescribed, ships nevertheless enjoy the right of innocent passage.

6. Such laws and regulations of the coastal State may not have the practical effect of denying or impairing the exercise of the right of innocent passage as set forth in Article 24 of the Convention of 1982.

7. If a warship engages in conduct which violates such laws or regulations or renders its passage not innocent and does not take corrective action upon request, the coastal State may require it to leave the territorial sea, as set forth in Article 30 of the Convention of 1982. In such case the warship shall do so immediately.

8. Without prejudice to the exercise of rights of coastal and flag States, all differences which may arise regarding a particular case of passage of ships through the territorial sea shall be settled through diplomatic channels or other agreed means.

Notes

1. *Innocent Passage of Warships and the Question of Prior Notice or Authorization.* May a coastal state require a foreign warship to obtain prior authorization for passage through the territorial sea? This question links to the issue whether warships have a right of innocent passage at all. After all, if a coastal state may insist on prior authorization, how could there be a "right" of innocent passage? China's policy, which it had maintained well before its 1996 declaration, has drawn protests from the United States and the United Kingdom. See J. Ashley Roach & Robert W. Smith, Excessive Maritime Claims § 10.3.4 at 247 n.81 (3d ed. 2012). See also Hyun-Soo Kim, The 1992 Chinese Territorial Sea Law in the Light of the UN Convention, 43 Intl. & Comp. L.Q. 894, 901–03 (1994). Paragraph 2 of the bilateral 1989 Uniform Interpretation sets out the U.S. and Russian position.

Whether warships should have a right of innocent passage has long been debated. Maritime powers have insisted on such a right without prior notice or authorization. Some coastal states have disagreed. Judge Azevedo, in his Dissenting Opinion in the Corfu Channel Case, (United Kingdom v. Albania) (Merits), 1949 I.C.J. 4, 78, reviewed early debates about this issue and highlighted why claims to a general right of innocent passage for warships have been controversial: warships threaten, and the traditional justification for freedom of navigation, i.e., to facilitate international trade, applies only to merchant vessels. Some neutral states allowed warships of belligerents to pass through their coastal waters, but this practice, according to Judge Azevedo, did not support a general rule of innocent passage. In ratifying the 1958 Territorial Sea Convention, several states entered reservations requiring previous notification or even authorization for the innocent passage of a warship through the territorial sea. See Marjorie M. Whiteman, 4 Digest of International Law 416 (1965). Despite debates at UNCLOS III, the LOS Convention does not explicitly state whether a coastal state may require prior notice or authorization for warship passage. Several states in addition to China have made declarations asserting rights to prior notification or authorization. See Yann-huei Song, Survey of Declarations or Statements Made by the Parties to the Law of the Sea Convention: 30 Years after Adoption, 28 Intl. J. Marine & Coastal L. 5, 22–25 (2013).

As a matter of international law, who has the better argument concerning a right of innocent passage for warships and whether prior notice or authorization is required? Does Article 19(2) of the LOS Convention suggest that warships have a right of innocent passage? What may be inferred from the fact that Articles 17–26 of the LOS Convention, concerning innocent passage, are located in a subsection of the Convention entitled "Rules Applicable to *All* Ships" (emphasis added)? Is not a "right" of innocent passage for warships a nullity if a coastal state may require prior authorization? Is the coastal state's obligation under Article 24(1)(a) not to "impose requirements on foreign ships which have the practical effect of denying or impairing the right of innocent passage" inconsistent with a coastal state's requiring prior authorization for passage? Prior notification? Can prior notification be justified as a necessary implication of Article 21(1)(a) of the LOS Convention? Why, in any event, should a maritime power object to a requirement of prior notification? Since the controversy over prior authorization or notification had been of concern for many years, why was it not clarified once and for all during the lengthy UNCLOS III negotiations?

How, in practice, is the situation likely to be managed if a maritime power claims that warships may engage in innocent passage without prior notice or authorization, while a coastal state insists on such notice or authorization? See R.R. Churchill & A.V. Lowe, The Law of the Sea 90 (3d ed. 1999); Roach & Smith, supra, § 10.3.4.

2. *The Uniform Interpretation of Rules of International Law Governing Innocent Passage.* The 1989 Uniform Interpretation was negotiated following bumping incidents involving U.S. and Soviet military vessels in the territorial sea of the Soviet Union in the Black Sea. The United States had sent its vessels to challenge Soviet restrictions on innocent passage. Other than Paragraph 2, concerning prior notice or authorization, does the Uniform Interpretation merely restate provisions of the LOS Convention? The Uniform Interpretation is a bilateral treaty, binding the United States and the Soviet Union (now Russia). If the United States should become a party to the LOS Convention, could the United States and Russia, which is a party, vary LOS Convention terms between themselves? See LOS Convention, Article 311(3)–(4); Vienna Convention on the Law of Treaties, Article 41. Does the Uniform Interpretation have implications for states other than the United States and Russia? For discussion of the Uniform Interpretation, see Erik Franckx, Innocent Passage of Warships: Recent Developments in US-Soviet Relations, 14 Marine Policy 484 (1990).

3. *"Subjective" vs. "Objective" Innocence of Passage.* Is innocent passage to be determined by "subjective" or "objective" criteria? Does the innocence of passage depend objectively—i.e., by reference to some externally ascertainable standard—on the actions of the vessel? Or is innocence to be determined according to the judgment, discretion, or intentions of the parties involved? For analysis of early debates about this issue, see Solomon Slonim, The Right of Innocent Passage and the 1958 Geneva Conference on the Law of the Sea, 5 Columbia J. Transnatl. L. 96 (1966). Under the LOS Convention, may a coastal state rely on subjective factors to determine whether passage is innocent? Is it any surprise that two major maritime powers, the United States and the Soviet Union, should prefer an interpretation under which the innocence of passage is to be determined by objective criteria? See Paragraph 3 of the Uniform Interpretation. Do the provisions of Article 19(2) of the LOS Convention in all respects set out objective criteria? What is the relevance of Article 19(1) of the LOS Convention, which tracks the language of Article 14(4) of the 1958 Territorial Sea Convention?

4. *Suspension of Innocent Passage.* According to Article 25(3) of the LOS Convention, referred to in Paragraph 5 of the 1989 Uniform Interpretation, a coastal state may suspend the right of innocent passage. Under what conditions? Given those conditions, why might maritime powers be concerned? As you read Part C, pay attention to how the matter of suspension of passage was

treated with respect to passage through straits, and compare Article 52(2) of the LOS Convention on the suspension of innocent passage in archipelagic waters.

5. *The Regime of Warships.* Paragraph 7 of the Uniform Interpretation refers to one of several rules in Subsection C, Section 3, Part 2 of the LOS Convention, which is entitled "Rules Applicable to Warships and Other Government Ships Operated for Non-commercial Purposes." See LOS Convention, Articles 29–32. Which of these articles apply only to the operation of warships in the territorial sea? Which require consideration of customary international law? See generally Bernard H. Oxman, The Regime of Warships Under the United Nations Convention on the Law of the Sea, 24 Va. J. Intl. L. 809 (1984).

B Contiguous Zone

Coastal states have on occasion exercised jurisdiction over foreign vessels "hovering" outside their territorial seas. This section examines the purposes for which a coastal state may apply its legislative or enforcement jurisdiction to activities in a zone contiguous to the territorial sea. We consider a classic U.S. Supreme Court case from 1804 and the influential codification of the contiguous zone in the 1958 Territorial Sea Convention.

CHURCH v. HUBBART
6 U.S. (2 Cranch) 187 (1804)

[John Church, a U.S. citizen, insured with the defendant Hubbart the cargo of the brig *Aurora*, a U.S. vessel. One of the two policies of insurance issued to cover this risk stated: "The insurers are not liable for seizure by the Portuguese for illicit trade." The other policy contained what the Court held to be the same exception in somewhat different terms.

The *Aurora* sailed from New York to South America for the purpose of selling the insured cargo at one or two Portuguese ports in Brazil. Portuguese laws dating back to 1591 prohibited foreign vessels from trading in Portuguese ports unless they had a royal license. Nevertheless, a small portion of the *Aurora*'s cargo was sold without incident in Rio de Janeiro. On the way back up the Brazilian coast, the *Aurora* anchored twelve or fifteen miles from land off the port of Para. Church, who was aboard the brig as supercargo, and two crewmembers went ashore in the longboat of a schooner that was sailing in company with the *Aurora*. Although the ostensible motive for this trip was reprovisioning, in fact Church had expressed his intention to sell what cargo he could while ashore. Before he could do so, he and the shore party were arrested. The Portuguese colonial governor found that the *Aurora* was in violation of the trade prohibition edicts, and had her and her cargo forfeited to the Portuguese Crown.

Church sued in the Massachusetts Circuit Court to recover on his insurance policies (collectively referred to in the opinion as "this contract"). The jury found against him, and he appealed. The principal grounds of his appeal were misinterpretation of the policy language and the trial court's admission into evidence of insufficiently authenticated evidence of the Portuguese edicts, sentence, and seizure. Church's counsel also made the following argument on appeal concerning the permissible extent of coastal jurisdiction:]

[T]he vessel was seized five leagues from the land, at anchor on the high seas. The seizure was not justified by [Portugal's] own laws: she was not within their territorial jurisdiction. By the law of nations, territorial jurisdiction can extend only to the distance of cannon-shot from the shore. *Vattel,* lib. 1, c. 23, § 280, 289. A vessel has a right to hover on the coast: it is no cause of condemnation. It can, at most, justify a seizure for the purpose of obtaining security that she will not violate the laws of the country. The law which is produced forbids the vessel to enter a port, but does not authorize a seizure upon the open sea. Great Britain, the greatest commercial nation in the world, has extended her revenue laws the whole length of the law of nations, to prevent smuggling. But she authorizes seizures of vessels, only within the limits of her ports, or within two leagues of the coast; and then only for the purpose of obtaining security.

The reason that the supercargo went on shore was the want of water; and the evidence proves that the want was real. For this purpose he had a right to go on shore, and although he thereby placed his person in their power, yet that did not bring the vessel into port.

[Counsel for the defendant responsed:] As to the law. The gentleman read a passage from Vattel, to show that cannon shot from the coast is by the law of nations the utmost bound of territorial jurisdiction. This passage is evidently restricted to the extent to which the rights of a neutral territory extend in time of war. The rule is apparently laid down for the sake of the inference from it, that a belligerent vessel cannot be taken under the cannon of a neutral fortress. It is a very indefinite rule, indeed, even for the purpose to which it extends, for it makes the extent of a nation's territory depend upon the weight of metal, or projectile force of her cannon. It is a right which must resolve itself into power; and comes to this, that territory extends as far as it can be made to be respected.

But this principle does not apply to the right of a nation to cause her revenue and colonial laws to be respected. Here all nations do assume at least a greater extent than cannon-shot; and other passages from Vattel show the distinctions which are acknowledged on this point. Lib. 1, § 287, 288. . . .

But the gentleman read an authority from 4 Bac. Abr. 543, upon smuggling. "The British revenue laws," says he, "go as far as the law of nations will permit, and they extend the right of boarding smugglers only to two leagues." Instead of appealing to Bacon's Abridgement, and British laws, I prefer looking into our own statute book, and take there the measure which our own government has asserted for the extent of our jurisdiction. (1 U.S. Stat. 646, § 25–27; *Ibid.* 700, § 99.) Here we see the principles are assumed of exercising this jurisdiction four leagues from the coast, and at indefinite distances within bays. All this is perfectly conformable to the law of nations. But it proves that the Aurora, when at anchor within the Bay of Para, and four or five leagues from Cape Baxos, was completely within the territorial jurisdiction of the governor of Para.

[On the issue of international law, the Court agrees with the defendant's position. Here is Chief Justice Marshall's opinion for the Court on the point.]

The risk of this illicit trade is separated from the various other perils to which vessels are exposed at sea, and excluded from the policy. Whenever the risk commences, the exception commences also, for it is apparent that the underwriters meant to take upon themselves no portion of that hazard which was occasioned by the unlawfulness of the voyage.

If it could have been presumed by the parties to this contract, that the laws of Portugal, prohibiting commercial intercourse between their colonies and foreign merchants, permitted vessels to enter their ports, or to hover off their coasts for the purposes of trade, with impunity, and only subjected them to seizure and condemnation after the very act had been committed, or if such are really their laws, then, indeed, the exception might reasonably be supposed to have been intended to be as limited in its construction, as is contended for by the plaintiff. If the danger did not commence, until the vessel was in port, or until the act of bargain and sale, without a permit from the governor, had been committed, then it would be reasonable to consider the exception as only contemplating that event.

But this presumption is too extravagant to have been made. [A]s a general principle, the nation which prohibits commercial intercourse with its colonies, must be supposed to adopt measures to make that prohibition effectual. They must, therefore, be supposed to seize vessels coming into their harbours, or hovering on their coasts, in a condition to trade, and to be afterwards governed in their proceedings with respect to those vessels, by the circumstances which shall appear in evidence. That the officers of that nation are induced occasionally to dispense with their laws, does not alter them, or legalize the trade they prohibit. As they may be executed, at the will of the governor, there is always danger that they will be executed, and that danger the insurers have not chosen to take upon themselves.

That the law of nations prohibits the exercise of any act of authority over a vessel in the situation of the Aurora, and that this seizure is, on that account, a mere marine trespass, not within the exception, cannot be admitted. To reason from the extent of protection a nation will afford to foreigners, to the extent of the means it may use for its own security, does not seem to be perfectly correct. It is opposed by principles which are universally acknowledged.

The authority of a nation, within its own territory, is absolute and exclusive. The seizure of a vessel, within the range of its cannon, by a foreign force is an invasion of that territory, and is a hostile act which it is its duty to repel. But its power to secure itself from injury may certainly be exercised beyond the limits of its territory. Upon this principle, the right of a belligerent to search a neutral vessel on the high seas, for contraband of war, is universally admitted, because the belligerent has a right to prevent the injury done to himself, by the assistance intended for his enemy: so too, a nation has a right to prohibit any commerce with its colonies. Any attempt to violate the laws made to protect this right, is an injury to itself, which it may prevent, and it has a right to use the means necessary for its prevention. These means do not appear to be limited within any certain marked boundaries, which remain the same, at all times and in all situations. If they are such as unnecessarily to vex and harass foreign lawful commerce, foreign nations will resist their exercise. If they are such as are reasonable and necessary to secure their laws from violation, they will be submitted to.

In different seas, and on different coasts, a wider or more contracted range, in which to exercise the vigilance of the government, will be assented to. Thus, in the channel, where a very great part of the commerce to and from all the north of Europe, passes through a very narrow sea, the seizure of vessels on suspicion of attempting an illicit trade, must necessarily be restricted to very narrow limits; but on the coast of South America, seldom frequented by vessels, but for the purpose of illicit trade, the vigilance of the government may be extended somewhat farther; and foreign nations submit to such regulations as are reasonable in themselves, and are really necessary to secure that monopoly of colonial commerce, which is claimed by all nations holding distant possessions.

If this right be extended too far, the exercise of it will be resisted. It has occasioned long and frequent contests, which have sometimes ended in open war. The English, it will be well recollected, complained of the right claimed by Spain to search their vessels on the high seas, which was carried so far that the *quarda costas* of that nation seized vessels not in the neighborhood of their coasts. This practice was the subject of long and fruitless negotiations, and at length, of open war. The right of the Spaniards was supposed to be exercised unreasonably and vexatiously, but it never was contended, that it could only be exercised within the range of the cannon from their batteries. Indeed, the right given to our own revenue cutters, to visit vessels four leagues from our coast, is a declaration that, in the opinion of the American government, no such principle as that contended for has a real existence. Nothing, then, is to be drawn from the laws or usages of nations, which gives to this part of the contract before the coup seizure of the Aurora, by the Portuguese governor, was an act of lawless violence.

[The Court holds, nevertheless, that the Circuit Court's judgment must be reversed as it relied on evidence that was not properly authenticated.]

Note

1. *The Concept of Hovering Zones.* In Church v. Hubbart Chief Justice Marshall suggested that the extent of coastal state control over foreign flag vessels could vary in hovering zones, in order to prevent smuggling. He noted that such control is not subject to "any certain marked boundaries, which remain the same, at all times and in all situations." There may be, "[i]n different seas, and on different coasts, a wider or more contracted range, in which to exercise the vigilance of the government." What are the advantages and disadvantages of Marshall's position?

CONVENTION ON THE TERRITORIAL SEA AND CONTIGUOUS ZONE
Apr. 29, 1958, 15 U.S.T. 1606, 516 U.N.T.S. 205

Article 24

1. In a zone of the high seas contiguous to its territorial sea, the coastal State may exercise the control necessary to:

(*a*) Prevent infringement of its customs, fiscal, immigration or sanitary regulations within its territory or territorial sea;

(*b*) Punish infringement of the above regulations committed within its territory and territorial sea.

2. The contiguous zone may not extend beyond twelve miles from the baseline from which the breadth of the territorial sea is measured.

3. Where the coasts of two States are opposite or adjacent to each other, neither of the two States is entitled, failing agreement between them to the contrary, to extend its contiguous zone beyond the median line every point of which is equidistant from the nearest points on the baselines from which the breadth of the territorial seas of the two States is measured.

Notes

1. *Coastal State Jurisdiction in the Contiguous Zone.* How does a coastal state's authority in its contiguous zone compare to its authority in its territorial sea? According to Article 24 of the 1958 Territorial Sea Convention, may a coastal state apply its laws to conduct occurring in its contiguous zone? Or may it only take enforcement measures there? Is there a difference in the treatment of incoming vessels that have not yet entered the territorial sea and outgoing vessels leaving the territorial sea? See Sir Gerald Fitzmaurice, Some Results of the Geneva Conference on the Law of the Sea: The Territorial Sea and Contiguous Zone and Related Topics, 8 Intl. & Comp. L.Q. 73, 108–21 (1959); John E. Noyes, Establishment of a 24-mile US Contiguous Zone, 15 Intl. J. Marine & Coastal L. 269 (2000); Shigeru Oda, The Concept of the Contiguous Zone, 11 Intl. & Comp. L.Q. 131 (1962); I.A. Shearer, Problems of Jurisdiction and Law Enforcement against Delinquent Vessels, 35 Intl. & Comp. L.Q. 320, 329–31 (1986).

What steps may a coastal state take to punish infringements of its customs, fiscal, immigration, or sanitary regulations? See Article 111 of the LOS Convention and the discussion of hot pursuit in Chapter 4, Section F. Does Article 24 provide a basis for stopping, boarding, or arresting outward-bound ships in the contiguous zone if such infringements have occurred, even if the strict prerequisites for hot pursuit have not been met? What steps may a state take to prevent infringements by inbound vessels? What law determines the steps that may be taken? Would a coastal state's inspection of all foreign flag vessels that are approaching its territorial sea be consistent with the right of freedom of navigation? See LOS Convention, Articles 58(1), 87.

2. *The Contiguous Zone in the 1982 LOS Convention.* Compare Article 24 of the 1958 Territorial Sea Convention with Article 33 of the 1982 LOS Convention. You will note close similarities, but also a few differences. What explains the differences?

3. *Matters Subject to Coastal State Jurisdiction in the Contiguous Zone.* Article 33 of the LOS Convention, like Article 24 of the Territorial Sea Convention, provides for coastal state jurisdiction in the contiguous zone only with respect to customs, fiscal, immigration, and sanitary matters. Article 24 grew out of Article 66 of the 1956 draft of the International Law Commission (ILC). ILC Article 66 is identical to paragraphs 1 and 2 of Article 24 of the 1958 Convention, except that Article 24 added "immigration" to the list of types of regulations comprehended within its scope. 1956–2 Y.B. Intl. L. Commn. 294. In its commentary on Article 66 the ILC noted that it had not recognized special security rights in the contiguous zone. The ILC

> considered that the extreme vagueness of the term "security" would open the way for abuses and that the granting of such rights was not necessary. The enforcement of customs and sanitary regulations will be sufficient in most cases to safeguard the security of the State. In so far as measures of self-defense against an imminent and direct threat to the security of the State are concerned, the Commission refers to the general principles of international law and the Charter of the United Nations.

Id. at 295. For discussion of self-defense, see Chapter 2, Section H. At the 1958 Geneva Conference, the First Committee approved and sent to Plenary a Polish proposal that added to Article 66 an explicit reference to the authority of the coastal state with respect to "violations of its security." 3 First United Nations Conference on the Law of the Sea, Official Records 181, UN Doc A/CONF.13/39 (UN Sales No. 58.V.4, 1958). In the Plenary, the First Committee's text, including the Polish amendment, received majority support but was short of the two-thirds approval necessary under Conference rules. 2 First United Nations Conference on the Law of the Sea, Official Records 40, UN Doc A/CONF.13/38 (UN Sales No. 58.V.4, 1958). The United States then offered a substitute text that simply eliminated explicit mention of security and contained the language now found in Article 24 of the 1958 Convention; this language was immediately and unanimously approved without discussion. Id. at 126. Would it have been preferable to include "security" within the scope of Article 24? For discussion of steps coastal states may take to help insure their security, see Chapter 14.

The LOS Convention itself authorizes coastal state control over some additional matters in the contiguous zone. What is the effect of Article 303 of the Convention? What is the effect of adoption of the concept of the exclusive economic zone (EEZ), which extends beyond the territorial sea? Based on what you read about the EEZ in Chapter 1, is the contiguous zone now superfluous? Does the contiguous zone add anything to the coastal state authority provided in the EEZ provisions of the LOS Convention? Delegates at UNCLOS III debated whether it was advisable to retain the contiguous zone, but as you can see the decision was made to include Article 33 in the Convention. More about the EEZ appears in Chapter 9.

C Straits Used for International Navigation

Many straits provide essential routes for commercial and military traffic. What standards should govern passage through international straits? The first reading in this section is an excerpt from the 1949 decision of the International

Court of Justice (ICJ) in the Corfu Channel case. Following the case are excerpts from UNCLOS III debates about straits.

CORFU CHANNEL CASE
United Kingdom v. Albania (Merits), 1949 I.C.J. 4

[On May 15, 1946, Albanian shore batteries fired on two British naval cruisers while they were cruising through Albanian territorial waters in the North Corfu Channel. Neither was hit. The United Kingdom protested to Albania, claiming that the two vessels were simply exercising a recognized right of innocent passage through a strait connecting two parts of the high seas. In particular, the North Corfu Channel is at one end of a strait running north and south between the Adriatic and Ionian seas. The Channel, which is one mile across at its narrowest, lies between the Albanian mainland and the Greek island of Kerkira (Corfu). The boundary between Greek and Albanian territorial waters runs through the Channel.

The Albanian government responded by claiming that foreign warships had no right to pass through the Channel without advance notice to and permission from Albania. In turn, the United Kingdom reasserted the right of its warships to innocent passage, and warned that if its vessels were fired upon again it would return fire. Thereafter, on October 22, 1946, four British warships—the *Mauritius, Leander, Saumarez,* and *Volage*—were cruising through the Channel. The latter two vessels struck mines that the Court found must have been placed in the channel with the actual or constructive knowledge of the Albanian government. Both ships were damaged; several crew members were killed, and others were injured. On November 12 and 13, 1946, British minesweepers covered the area and turned up 22 moored mines.

The United Kingdom submitted the matter to the U.N. Security Council, and on April 9, 1947, the Council recommended that the parties refer "the dispute" to the ICJ. On May 22nd the United Kingdom instituted proceedings before the ICJ—its first contentious case—and Albania filed a Preliminary Objection.

The Court found that by various acts Albania voluntarily accepted the Court's jurisdiction (forum prorogatum), rejected the Albanian objection, and ordered the case to proceed on the merits. Judgment of Mar. 25, 1948, 1948 I.C.J. 15. Immediately thereafter the Court was notified that the parties had reached a Special Agreement submitting the following questions for decision:

> (1) Is Albania responsible under international law for the explosions which occurred on the 22nd October 1946 in Albanian waters and for the damage and loss of human life which resulted from them and is there any duty to pay compensation?

> (2) Has the United Kingdom under international law violated the sovereignty of the Albanian People's Republic by reason of the acts of the Royal Navy in Albanian waters on the 22nd October and on the 12th and 13th November 1946 and is there any duty to give satisfaction?

By order of March 26, 1948, the Court declared that future proceedings in the case would be on the basis of this Special Agreement. 1948 I.C.J. 53.

The ICJ decided in favor of the United Kingdom on the first question by a vote of eleven to five. On the second question, the Court decided by fourteen votes to two that the October 22nd passage did not violate Albania's sovereignty. The Court unanimously decided that the minesweeping of November 12th and 13th was a violation of sovereignty.

The ICJ's discussion of the innocent passage of warships concerned the specific case of passage through a strait used for international navigation. In this context, the Court summarily rejected the innocence of the November 12th and 13th minesweeping. It considered, however, in some detail the innocence of the October 22nd passage and the characteristics of international straits.]

On May 15th, 1946, the British cruisers *Orion* and *Superb*, while passing southward through the North Corfu Channel, were fired at by an Albanian battery in the vicinity of Saranda. It appears from the report of the commanding naval officer dated May 29th, 1946, that the firing started when the ships had already passed the battery and were moving away from it; that from 12 to 20 rounds were fired; that the firing lasted 12 minutes and ceased only when the ships were out of range; but that the ships were not hit although there were a number of "shorts" and of "overs." An Albanian note of May 21st states that the Coastal Commander ordered a few shots to be fired in the direction of the ships "in accordance with a General Order founded on international law."

The United Kingdom Government at once protested to the Albanian Government, stating that innocent passage through straits is a right recognized by international law. There ensued a diplomatic correspondence in which the Albanian Government asserted that foreign warships and merchant vessels had no right to pass through Albanian territorial waters without prior notification to, and the permission of, the Albanian authorities. This view as put into effect by a communication of the Albanian Chief of Staff, dated May 17th, 1946, which purported to subject the passage of foreign warships and merchant vessels in Albanian territorial waters to previous notification to and authorization by the Albanian Government. The diplomatic correspondence continued, and culminated in a United Kingdom note of August 2nd, 1946, in which the United Kingdom Government maintained its view with regard to the right of innocent passage through straits forming routes for international maritime traffic between two parts of the high seas. The note ended with the warning that if Albanian coastal batteries in the future opened fire on any British warship passing through the Corfu Channel, the fire would be returned.

The contents of this note were, on August lst, communicated by the British Admiralty to the Commander-in-Chief, Mediterranean, with the instruction that he should refrain from using the Channel until the note had been presented to the Albanian Government. On August 10th, he received from the Admiralty the following telegram: "The Albanians have now received the note. North Corfu Strait may now be used by ships of your fleet, but only when essential and with armament in fore and aft position. If coastal guns fire at ships passing through the Strait, ships should fire back." On September 21st, the following telegram was sent by the Admiralty to the Commander-in-Chief, Mediterranean: "Establishment of diplomatic relations with Albania is again under consideration by His Majesty's Government who wish to know whether the Albanian Government have learnt to behave themselves. Information is requested whether any ships under your command have passed through the North Corfu Strait since August and, if not, whether you intend them to do so shortly." The Commander-in-Chief answered the next day that his ships had not done so yet, but that it was his intention that *Mauritius* and *Leander* and two destroyers should do so when they departed from Corfu on October 22nd.

It was in such circumstances that these two cruisers together with the destroyers *Saumarez* and *Volage* were sent through the North Corfu Strait on that date.

The Court will now consider the Albanian contention that the United Kingdom Government violated Albanian sovereignty by sending the warships through this Strait without the previous authorization of the Albanian Government.

It is . . . generally recognized and in accordance with international custom that States in time of peace have a right to send their warships through straits used for international navigation between two parts of the high seas without the previous authorization of a coastal State, provided that the passage is *innocent*. Unless otherwise prescribed in an international convention, there is no right for a coastal State to prohibit such passage through straits in time of peace.

The Albanian Government does not dispute that the North Corfu Channel is a strait in the geographical sense; but it denies that this Channel belongs to the class of international highways through which a right of passage exists, on the grounds that it is only of secondary importance and not even a necessary route between two parts of the high seas, and that it is used almost exclusively for local traffic to and from the ports of Corfu and Saranda.

It may be asked whether the test is to be found in the volume of traffic passing through the Strait or in its greater or lesser importance for international navigation. But in the opinion of the Court the decisive criterion is rather its geographical situation as connecting two parts of the high seas and the fact of its being used for international navigation. Nor can it be decisive that this Strait is not a necessary route between two parts of the high seas, but only an alternative passage between the Aegean and the Adriatic Seas. It has nevertheless been a useful route for international maritime traffic. In this respect, the Agent of the United Kingdom Government gave the Court the following information relating to the period from April lst, 1936, to December 31st, 1937: "The following is the total number of ships putting in at the Port of Corfu after passing through or just before passing through the Channel. During the period of one year nine months, the total number of ships was 2,884. The flags of the ships are Greek, Italian, Roumanian, Yugoslav, French, Albanian and British. Clearly, very small vessels are included, as the entries for Albanian vessels are high, and of course one vessel may make several journeys, but 2,884 ships for a period of one year nine months is quite a large figure. These figures relate to vessels visited by the Customs at Corfu and so do not include the large number of vessels which went through the Strait without calling at Corfu at all." There were also regular sailings through the Strait by Greek vessels three times weekly, by a British ship fortnightly, and by two Yugoslav vessels weekly and by two others fortnightly. The Court is further informed that the British Navy has regularly used this Channel for eighty years or more, and that it has also been used by the navies of other States.

One fact of particular importance is that the North Corfu Channel constitutes a frontier between Albania and Greece, that a part of it is wholly within the territorial waters of these States, and that the Strait is of special importance to Greece by reason of the traffic to and from the port of Corfu.

Having regard to these various considerations, the Court has arrived at the conclusion that the North Corfu Channel should be considered as belonging to the class of international highways through which passage cannot be prohibited by a coastal State in time of peace.

On the other hand it is a fact that the two coastal States did not maintain normal relations, that Greece had made territorial claims precisely with regard to a part of Albanian territory bordering on the Channel, that Greece had declared that she considered herself technically in a state of war with Albania, and that Albania, invoking the danger of Greek incursions, had considered it necessary to take certain measures of vigilance in this region. The Court is of opinion that Albania, in view of these exceptional circumstances, would have been justified in issuing regulations in respect of the passage of warships through the Strait, but not in prohibiting such passage or in subjecting it to the requirement of special authorization.

For these reasons the Court is unable to accept the Albanian contention that the Government of the United Kingdom has violated Albanian sovereignty by sending the warships through the Strait without having obtained the previous authorization of the Albanian Government. In these circumstances, it is unnecessary to consider the more general question, much debated by the Parties, whether States under international law have a right to send warships in time of peace through territorial waters not included in a strait.

The Albanian Government has further contended that the sovereignty of Albania was violated because the passage of the British warships on October 22nd, 1946, was not an *innocent passage*. The reasons advanced in support of this contention may be summed up as follows: The passage was not an ordinary passage, but a political mission; the ships were maneuvering and sailing in diamond combat formation with soldiers on board; the position of the guns was not consistent with innocent passage; the vessels passed with crews at action stations; the number of the ships and their armament surpassed what was necessary in order to attain their object and showed an intention to intimidate and not merely to pass; the ships had received orders to observe and report upon the coastal defenses and this order was carried out.

It is ... admitted by the United Kingdom Agent, that the object of sending the warships through the Strait was not only to carry out a passage for purposes of navigation, but also to test Albania's attitude. As mentioned above, the Albanian Government, on May 15th, 1946, tried to impose by means of gunfire its view with regard to the passage. As the exchange of diplomatic notes did not lead to any clarification, the Government of the United Kingdom wanted to ascertain by other means whether the Albanian Government would maintain its illegal attitude and again impose its view by firing at passing ships. The legality of this measure taken by the Government of the United Kingdom cannot be disputed, provided that it was carried out in a manner consistent with the requirements of international law. The "mission" was designed to affirm a right which had been unjustly denied. The Government of the United Kingdom was not bound to abstain from exercising its right of passage, which the Albanian Government had illegally denied.

It remains, therefore, to consider whether the *manner* in which the passage was carried out was consistent with the principle of innocent passage and to examine the various contentions of the Albanian Government in so far as they appear to be relevant.

[T]he British warships ... were not proceeding in combat formation, but in line, one after the other, and ... they were not maneuvering until after the first explosion. Their movements thereafter were due to the explosions and were made necessary in order to save human life and the mined ships. It is shown by the evidence of witnesses that the contentions that soldiers were on board must be due to a misunderstanding probably arising from the fact that the two cruisers carried their usual detachment of marines.

It is known from the . . . order issued by the British Admiralty on August 10th, 1946, that ships, when using the North Corfu Strait, must pass with armament in fore and aft position. That this order was carried out during the passage on October 22nd is stated by the Commander-in-Chief, Mediterranean, in a telegram of October 26th to the Admiralty. The guns were, he reported, "trained fore and aft, which is their normal position at sea in peace time, and were not loaded." It is confirmed by the commanders of *Saumarez* and *Volage* that the guns were in this position before the explosions. The navigating officer on board *Mauritius* explained that all guns on the cruiser were in their normal stowage position. The main guns were in the line of the ship, and the antiaircraft guns were pointing outwards and up into the air, which is the normal position of these guns on a cruiser both in harbour and at sea. In the light of this evidence, the Court cannot accept the Albanian contention that the position of the guns was inconsistent with the rules of innocent passage.

In the above-mentioned telegram of October 26th, the Commander-in-Chief reported that the passage "was made with ships at action stations in order that they might be able to retaliate quickly if fired upon again." In view of the firing from the Albanian battery on May 15th, this measure of precaution cannot, in itself, be regarded as unreasonable. But four warships—two cruisers and two destroyers—passed in this manner, with crews at action stations, ready to retaliate quickly if fired upon. They passed one after another through this narrow channel, close to the Albanian coast, at a time of political tension in this region. The intention must have been, not only to test Albania's attitude, but at the same time to demonstrate such force that she would abstain from firing again on passing ships. Having regard, however, to all the circumstances of the case, as described above, the Court is unable to characterize that measures taken by the United Kingdom authorities as a violation of Albania's sovereignty.

Notes

1. *The Aftermath of the Corfu Channel Case.* In its judgment of December 14, 1949, the ICJ fixed the amount of compensation due from Albania to the United Kingdom at £843,947. 1949 I.C.J. 244. In 1992, following the fall of Albania's Communist government, an agreement was reached whereby Albania would

pay the United Kingdom US$ 2,000,000 for damages from the 1946 Corfu Channel incident. As part of this agreement, Albania received £12 million in gold that had been looted by the Nazis in World War II and held since that war in the Bank of England by the Tripartite Gold Commission, an entity formed by France, the United Kingdom, and the United States. See Memorandum of Understanding, United Kingdom-Albania, May 8, 1992, reproduced in United Kingdom Materials on International Law 1992 (Geoffrey Marston ed.), 63 Brit. Y.B. Intl. L. 1992 at 615, 781 (1993); Albanian Gold Dispute Settled, Financial Times (London), Oct. 30, 1996 at 2. For an overview of the Corfu Channel case and its significance for international law, see Michael Waibel, Corfu Channel Case, in 2 Max Planck Encyclopedia of Public International Law 792 (Rüdiger Wolfrum ed., 2012).

2. *International Straits.* The ICJ concluded that the North Corfu Channel was an international strait. What criteria or test should be used to determine whether a particular strait is an international one?

3. *Innocent Passage through Straits and the Territorial Sea.* The ICJ in the Corfu Channel case seemed to indicate that innocent passage through international straits might be treated differently from innocent passage through the territorial sea, even when a strait lay within the territorial sea. The 1958 Territorial Sea Convention nevertheless addressed the issue of passage through straits under the heading of innocent passage through the territorial sea. Article 16(4) of the 1958 Convention provides: "There shall be no suspension of innocent passage of foreign ships through straits which are used for international navigation between one part of the high seas and another part of the high seas or the territorial sea of a foreign State." At UNCLOS III, a new regime evolved governing transit passage through straits.

UNCLOS III DISCUSSION OF STRAITS USED FOR INTERNATIONAL NAVIGATION

2 UNCLOS III Official Records 124–37, 139

[Beginning in the mid-1960s, the idea of a twelve-nautical-mile territorial sea gradually came to be accepted. As this acceptance grew, maritime states became concerned about the status of straits that had been traditionally used for passage from one sea or area of the sea to another. Many of the major international straits which had been high seas under the three-nautical-mile regime would become territorial sea should a twelve-nautical-mile limit come into effect. Disagreement arose as to whether passage through these newly territorial straits would be governed by a regime of, or similar to, innocent passage or instead by a high seas regime. Strictest among proposals favoring the former position was that introduced by Fiji in Sub-Committee II of the Sea-Bed Committee in 1973. 3 Report of the Sea-Bed Committee, UNGAOR, 28th Sess., Supp. No. 21 at 91–98, UN Doc. A/9021 (1973). The Fiji text treated straits as simply another part of the territorial sea, providing only for a limited and ambiguous guarantee of non-suspension of passage (in Article 4(2)). Along the same lines as this text was a draft submitted by Cyprus, Greece, Indonesia, Malaysia, Morocco, the Philippines, Spain, and Yemen (commonly called the "Eight Power" proposal). Id. at 3–10. Both drafts also introduced a new concept of ships with so-called "special characteristics." Depending on the draft, these were nuclear-powered or nuclear-armed vessels, marine scientific research vessels, or tankers or other ships carrying noxious substances. As to these, the coastal state would have still broader powers of control over passage. Both drafts would also permit severe restrictions on the passage of warships and overflight.

Taking the other position were proposals such as those submitted to the Sea-Bed Committee by the United States in 1971 and Italy in 1973. Report of the Sea-Bed Committee, UNGAOR, 26th Sess., Supp. No. 21, Annex IV, at 241, UN Doc. A/8421 (1971); 3 Report of the Sea-Bed Committee, UNGAOR, 28th Sess., Supp. No. 21, at 70–71, UN Doc. A/9021 (1973). These drafts had the effect of making territorial straits the juridical equivalent of the high seas for all purposes of navigation. The maritime powers supporting such freedom apparently considered that flag states and international organizations could adequately ensure navigational safety and environmental protection.

By the time of the 1974 Caracas session of UNCLOS III, the positions of the various parties had softened somewhat, although considerable differences still existed. Three drafts were submitted at this point in the negotiations. The first was by the United Kingdom delegation. UN Doc. A/CONF.62/C.2/L.3, 3 UNCLOS III Official Records 183, 185–86. This text favored the free or "transit passage" regime supported by maritime and naval powers. Under it, transit passage could not be suspended, and ships were allowed to operate "in the normal mode" (e.g., submarines may travel submerged through the passage). While the strait-bordering states were given considerable authority over pollution, the U.K. text provided no basis for controlling ships with special characteristics. A joint Danish-Finnish amendment to this draft, UN Doc. A/CONF.62/C.2/L.15, id. at 191, raised another issue: the amendment would have exempted from the transit passage regime only straits less than six nautical miles wide, that is, all straits that had traditionally been territorial because of the three-nautical-mile limit. The second main draft was introduced by the Soviet Union and five other Eastern European states. UN Doc. A/CONF.62/C.2/L.11, id. at 189. It also represented the freedom of navigation position and was generally similar to the U.K. text, except that it contained more extensive provisions for the prevention of security threats by ships or aircraft in transit. The third text was introduced by four straits states, Malaysia, Morocco, Oman, and Yemen. UN Doc. A/CONF.62/C.2/L.16, id. at 192, 194–95. It took up the coastal states' position formerly represented by the Fiji and Eight-Power drafts; it proposed a modified innocent passage regime, with a non-suspension provision. Under it, the coastal state would have had control over the required equipment of passing vessels and expanded powers over ships with special characteristics.

On the basis primarily of these drafts the following discussions took place in Committee II at the Caracas session of UNCLOS III in 1974. The chairman of the Committee was Andrés Aguilar of Venezuela.]

[11th Meeting, July 22, 1974]

7. [Mr. FERGO (Denmark)] A general agreement establishing a maximum limit of 12 miles for the territorial sea would result in the creation of a large number of new straits. Several delegations had pointed out that there was no justification for restricting navigation through, and overflight over, vital straits that had long been considered as high seas. In the case of "new" straits up to a breadth of 24 miles, there might be a need for a new régime of free transit passage. Such a régime should take due account of the interests of coastal States, particularly with respect to security and protection against pollution. On the other hand, his delegation failed to see the need to change the rules of innocent passage through straits less than 6 miles wide, where the right of free passage and overflight had never existed. On the contrary, it could be argued that the increased size and speed of ships as well as the increased traffic in straits justified giving increased consideration to the interest of the coastal State.

8. The problem could be solved by maintaining the existing rules of innocent passage through international straits of less than 6 miles and establishing a new régime of "transit passage" through new wide straits, which would emerge as a result of establishing a maximum limit of 12 miles for the territorial sea. . . .

9. He also stressed the fact that some straits, such as the Danish straits leading to the Baltic Sea, had never been subject to the right of free passage but had been under a special régime serving the interests of both the coastal State and the international community; such a type of arrangement should remain in effect. . . .

12. With reference to document A/CONF.62/C.2/L.11, which stated in article 1, paragraph 2(*f*) that the "coastal State shall not place in the straits any installations which could interfere with or hinder the transit of ships," he pointed

out that Denmark had geographically the character of an island country, the main island being separated from the other main parts of the country, as well as from neighbouring Sweden, by narrow international straits. It was of vital social and economic importance for Denmark and its neighbouring countries to be able to build bridges or tunnels across those straits, and the Danish Parliament had already taken a decision in principle to that effect. Existing plans took full account of the obligation not to hamper the free passage of ships in transit. His delegation took it that the reference in article 1, paragraph 2(*f*) to the placement of installations in straits did not modify the right of coastal States to build traffic links of the nature referred to, on the understanding that transit through the straits would be able to continue unhampered. . . .

14. [Mr. MANNER (Finland)] [W]ith regard to straits within or leading to enclosed sea areas, and being either completely within the territory of one coastal State, or passing through the territorial seas of States which already bordered on each other[:] If no special rules had been agreed upon, the provisions concerning innocent passage were applicable and could be applied also in the future. [T]here was no reason to require the opening of such a strait to free passage, in other words to place the strait under the régime of the high seas as far as navigation was concerned. . . .

17. Mr. DUDGEON (United Kingdom) said that his delegation regarded agenda item 4, currently under consideration, as one of the most important questions facing the Conference. Acceptance of a territorial sea of 12 miles would result in a large number of straits forming essential links for international navigation, both by sea and air, ceasing to have a strip of high seas down the middle. Hence the need to ensure that unrestricted navigation through those vital links in the world network of communications should remain available for use by the international community. His delegation had been gratified by the amount of interest shown in chapter III of its draft (A/CONF.62/C.2/L.3). He would like to reply to some very pertinent questions which had been put to it in the course of informal discussions.

18. Article 1 set out the concept of transit passage through straits connecting two parts of the high seas. The concept his delegation had tried to describe corresponded to what it believed to be the best international practice at that time. It proposed that ships and aircraft exercising the right of transit passage should not be impeded or hampered during their passage. At the same time the right was given "solely for the purpose of continuous and expeditious transit of the strait."

19 In the context of the geographical situations to which that right would apply, his delegation had first and foremost in mind the strait linking one part of the high seas with another part of the high seas. However, as particular

straits were called by other names, such as "channel" or "passage," and often did not begin at a precise line, paragraph 3 of article 1 stipulated that the article applied to "any strait or other stretch of water whatever its geographical name," as long as it was sea.

20. His delegation also had in mind the situation of the long strait which had more than one country bordering one side of the strait. Assuming a strait which had two countries on the western side, States A and B, and one country on the eastern side, State C, the United Kingdom draft proposed, first, a right of transit should the ship or aircraft be going all the way northwards or southwards through the strait; secondly, a right of transit if the ship or aircraft was proceeding down the first part of the strait between States A and C with a view to calling at a port or airport of State B. Such was the purpose of the words "or a State bordering the strait" at the end of article 1, paragraph 2.

21. Paragraph 4 of article 1 concerned two exceptional cases. The first was what might be described as a broad strait: if the strait was rather more than 24 miles wide, and had a good and wide enough high-seas route down the middle, it was unnecessary to provide a special right of transit passage since ships and aircraft could navigate on the high seas through the strait. The second case was the not infrequent one of a strait formed by an island lying less than 24 miles off the coast of a State. There again his delegation saw insufficient justification for according the right of transit passage between the island and the coast of the State, so long as an equally suitable high seas route was available on the seaward side of the island.

22. Article 2 proposed very stringent restrictions upon what ships and aircraft might do while exercising the right of transit passage. Ships and aircraft must not engage in any activities other than those which were part of their normal passage. They also had to comply with generally accepted standards for navigation and safety, thus providing safeguards for the straits States.

23. Articles 3 and 4 set out rights in relation to transit passage of States that bordered on straits used for international navigation. Article 3 recognized the value of sea-lanes and traffic separation schemes wherever it was necessary to promote the safe passage of ships, especially in the light of the volume of sea traffic passing through the waters of straits. The United Kingdom proposed that such traffic separation schemes be approved by IMCO [the Intergovernmental Maritime Consultative Organization, now the International Maritime Organization] before being brought into operation. IMCO had, in fact, already approved a scheme of that kind for the Straits of Dover, which was currently operating, and no State could unilaterally alter the regulations with which all mariners were required to comply. Furthermore, article 4 made express provision that any State bordering on a strait could prescribe laws and

regulations in order to give full effect to traffic separation schemes for navigation in straits. It also provided a basis for the straits State to take appropriate powers to control discharge of oil or other noxious substances into the strait by making laws and regulations. Foreign ships exercising the right of transit passage would have to conform with the regulations; should they fail to comply, the possibility of legal proceedings would arise in the case of merchant vessels. In the case of warships and other vessels entitled to sovereign immunity, article 4, paragraph 5, and article 7 stipulated that the flag-State was directly responsible for damage caused by noncompliance with such laws and regulations on the part of one of its ships. Namely, there would be liability on the international level or, in other words, State responsibility.

[T]he United Kingdom delegation pointed out that [Article 8] concerned three geographical cases: that of a strait used for international navigation linking a part of the high seas with the territorial sea of a State; that of a strait lying between an island and the mainland of the coastal State, where, in accordance with the provisions of article 1, paragraph 4(*b*), the right of transit passage was not involved; and lastly, that of a broad strait through which a high seas corridor ran down the middle. In those three cases, the United Kingdom delegation considered that there were no grounds to provide for the right of transit passage. Instead, it was proposed that the régime of innocent passage as described in chapter II of the draft should apply, subject to the other provisions of article 8. There were, moreover, two exceptional cases not arising from article 8, involving, in the first instance, a ship crossing from one side of a strait to the other and, in the second instance, a ship going along part of a strait bordered by a single State on passage to a port of that State. In those two cases, the United Kingdom delegation considered that the régime of innocent passage should apply and not that of transit passage. . . .

29. [Mr. DE ALWIS (Sri Lanka)] Every State bordering on a strait within its territorial sea had a legitimate right not only to safeguard the vital interests connected with its security, but also to ensure that no damage resulting from pollution or from some accident affected its marine environment; and in such an eventuality, it must be provided with adequate compensation for damage. With regard to pollution, it was gratifying to observe that that issue did not give rise to any major difficulties of substance. With reference to the effects of the passage of vessels on the security interests of the coastal State, his delegation considered that a distinction should be made between the passage of merchant vessels and that of warships. As a developing country with an export-import economy, desirous of increasing its share in an expanding world trade, Sri Lanka supported the view that it was in the interests of the

world economy that passage of merchant vessels should be unimpeded except in circumstances such as *force majeure* or navigational hazards, and that the right to transit passage should be recognized for all ships without discrimination as to flag, point of origin or destination. That involved the continuance of customary sea lanes for security reasons. The passage of merchant vessels, which should be presumed to be innocent, must nevertheless be in conformity with the coastal State's laws and regulations with regard to safeguards against damage to its marine environment and its security requirements. That legitimate right of international commercial navigation had not been opposed by coastal States bordering on straits; indeed, they had given indications that they were inclined to show flexibility on that aspect of navigation.

30. On the other hand, the question of the passage of military vessels gave rise to divergent views, although they were not necessarily irreconcilable. The extension of the territorial sea to a breadth of 12 miles was designed to accommodate the justifiable concerns of the coastal States to ensure their national security. A coastal State bordering on international straits could not be denied the safeguards granted to other coastal States, and its security interests could not be endangered merely because straits used for international navigation existed within its territorial waters. It would be unreasonable to expect the State concerned not to react to the passage along its coasts of an armada of military vessels which might have hostile intentions towards it. Sri Lanka, which was committed to a nuclear-free-zone and to zones of peace, obviously could not advocate or encourage the passage of foreign warships. Being not unmindful, however, of current realities, the delegation of Sri Lanka was inclined to adopt a flexible attitude in that respect, subject to certain safeguards in the interests of preserving coastal State security. Furthermore, the supporters of free transit through straits were not unmindful of the legitimate fears of coastal States, since they had already suggested certain acts which might be deemed prejudicial to the peace, good order or security of a coastal State. Sri Lanka, for its part, considered that it would not be unreasonable to include in the new régime provisions providing first, that warships must observe the laws and regulations of the coastal State applicable to the passage of other ships; secondly, that prior notification of the passage of any warship, specifying that such passage would take place within predetermined time-limits without necessarily indicating the actual time of passage, must be given to the coastal State, which could designate the sea lanes to be used; thirdly, that if a warship failed to comply with the laws and regulations of the coastal State, it could be required to leave the straits immediately along a route to be designated by the coastal State concerned; and, fourthly, that where more than one coastal State

was involved, those States should be required to cooperate in establishing a joint administration with a view to avoiding obstacles to transit deriving from a lack of co-ordination on the part of one of them.

[12th Meeting, July 22, 1974]

1. Mr. KOLOSOVSKY (Union of Soviet Socialist Republics), referring to the draft articles on straits used for international navigation (A/CONF.62/C.2/L.11), of which his delegation was a sponsor, underlined the importance of the principle contained in article 1, which provided that all ships in transit would enjoy equal freedom of navigation for the purpose of transit passage between straits used for international navigation between two parts of the high seas. That principle was essential for maintaining the benefits derived from the tremendous development of international trade in recent years.... The Soviet Union attached special importance to that freedom, since its only access to the Atlantic and the Far East was through straits, and its coastal shipping linking the far-flung points of its extensive territory passed through a number of straits.

2. The USSR recognized the need to protect the security of coastal States bordering on straits used for international navigation between one part of the high sea and another, but it also believed that the security and other interests of countries that used those straits, which comprised the majority, should also be taken into account. The security of the USSR depended upon communications by sea and through straits. Consequently, his delegation could not agree that matters relating to navigation through straits used for international navigation admitted unilateral solutions. Attempts to modify the traditional régime or to limit transit through those straits were against the interests of the international community....

11. Mr. TORRAS DE LA LUZ (Cuba) said that his country favoured the maintenance of freedom of navigation and overflight during the transit of ships and aircraft through and over straits used for those purposes, a position which had its origin in Cuba's particular situation and which was vindicated by historical experience. Because of the aggressive policy towards Cuba which the United States had pursued since the beginning of the Cuban Revolution, principally in the seas surrounding Cuba, it was vitally important for his country from the standpoint of both economics and defence, that there should be a guarantee that maritime communications with other continents could not be cut off[.]

12. So-called "innocent passage" gave coastal States the possibility of obstructing, on various pretexts, transit through the strait on which they bordered. The Caribbean, in view of its characteristics, could thus again come

under United States domination and that would put Cuba and other islands in a difficult position, an experience which was not confined to the Caribbean. . . .

16. Mr. MOORE (United States of America) said that the inadequacies of the traditional doctrine of innocent passage were well known. His delegation appreciated the trend in the debates as well as the various proposals in the Committee, which reflected an understanding of the importance of navigation and overflight through straits for the global flow of trade and communications and for a stable and peaceful world order and showed that there need be no conflict between the interests of States transiting and States bordering straits. The proposals reflected the three categories of concern most frequently expressed by States bordering straits: the security of the coastal State, safety of navigation and prevention of pollution. With respect to the security of States bordering straits, his delegation agreed that the chapter on passage through straits used for international navigation in the new convention might specify that the right of unimpeded transit was to be exercised solely for the purpose of continuous and expeditious transit of the strait. The convention should require that ships and aircraft in transit refrain from any threat or use of force, in violation of the Charter of the United Nations, against the territorial integrity or political independence of a State bordering the strait. With respect to safety of navigation, it was possible to achieve a balance which would fully protect the interests of States whose ships and aircraft transited a strait and the interests of States bordering the strait. The first step was necessarily to ensure that transiting vessels and aircraft complied with applicable international safety regulations. The draft articles presented by the United Kingdom (A/CONF.62/C.2/L.3), which his delegation supported, met that need. . . .

18. The third category of concern related to the prevention of pollution and in that connexion he stressed the importance of the United Kingdom proposal to require that ships in transit should comply with international regulations, procedures and practices for the prevention and control of pollution from ships. Subject to appropriate safeguards and the sovereign immunity exception, States bordering straits should be able to enforce measures against violations within the strait for deviation from approved traffic separation schemes.

19. With respect to both safety and pollution in straits, he stressed the importance of making adequate provision for compensation in case of damage; the provisions concerning liability envisaged in the United Kingdom draft articles and in the proposals submitted by a number of Eastern European States (A/CONF.62/C.2/L.11) were interesting in that connexion. Similarly, it should be remembered that some straits required special standards in addition to those universally adopted; for that reason his delegation would welcome it if States bordering a strait recommended to the appropriate international

organization for approval any special safety or pollution standards which they felt were necessary in that way. States bordering the strait would have a predominant role in the formulation of such special standards, but at the same time, the interests of the international community would be fully protected.

20. His delegation noted with satisfaction that most of the recently introduced proposals concerning transit through straits included the essential element of transit by aircraft; while there had been suggestions that the Conference should not consider questions related to overflight of aircraft, it should be recalled that such questions were inseparably linked with the law of the sea in the 1958 Geneva Conventions; moreover, since the breadth of the territorial sea would be decided by the Conference, the question of overflight could not be avoided unless some States were willing to forgo their sovereignty over the air space above their territorial sea. . . .

25. Mr. WARIOBA (United Republic of Tanzania) said that, in dealing with passage through straits used for international navigation, it was necessary to distinguish between ships performing national duties and ships performing international duties. Merchant ships performed an international duty and their passage through straits should not be hampered in any way; in that respect his delegation was ready to negotiate on a régime that would ensure them easy and safe passage; that régime should be prepared at all levels, international, regional, subregional and national, and should determine the rights and duties of all parties in respect of the passage of ships through straits; regions and States would be expected to ensure the implementation of the general norms.

26. In that connexion, the flag State, for example, would be responsible for the technical requirements of ships, such as construction standards, and the coastal State would be responsible for rules that would ensure speedy and safe passage. To that end, the coastal State would need information in order to know the amount of traffic at any time and to supervise passage accordingly. He did not therefore see any reason for objections to advance notification of a ship's passage through a particular strait and he questioned the basis for maintaining that that kind of power for the coastal State would be detrimental to international navigation.

27. With regard to warships, they were not, in his delegation's opinion, in the service of the international community; rather, they were used to further the foreign policy objectives of a few States. Warships should therefore give notification of passage and should not pass through a strait secretly because of the risks to the coastal State. In any case, why the secrecy for warships if their passage was peaceful?

[13th Meeting, July 23, 1974]

2. [Mr. BEESLEY (Canada)] All the proposals submitted so far assumed a plurality of régimes—that of the territorial sea, that of straits customarily used for international passage, the possibility of alternative routes and the problem of straits less than 24 miles wide. While care must be taken not to create systems of discrimination, the establishment of world-wide regulations did not preclude the establishment of special régimes for particular straits.

3. While the definition of a "strait used for international navigation" must take into account its geographical aspects, many straits which appeared suitable for international navigation on charts were not so used for very good reasons. In the judgment rendered by the International Court of Justice in the Corfu Channel case, the Court had adopted as a criterion of the strait's actual use for international navigation the number of ships using it and the number of flags represented. The major point was that in defining an international strait one must consider, along with the geographical element, the usage element, namely, that it must be a strait that had traditionally been used for international navigation.

4. The statement by the United States representative at the preceding meeting had drawn attention to problems of safety and pollution; he had said that some straits, because of depth or other navigational or environmental limitations, would require special standards in addition to those universally adopted. The Canadian delegation was in basic agreement with that differentiation between certain straits and their régimes. . . .

11. [Mr. ABDEL HAMID (Egypt)] welcomed the attention drawn by the United States representative to the question of the security of the coastal State, [but] he wished to ask him two questions. The first was why his country did not respect the requirement that prior authorization should be given by the coastal State for passage of warships or at least that the coastal State should be notified of such passage, and the second was how the coastal State could verify whether a submarine refrained from testing weapons of any kind during its passage through straits if it remained submerged. . . .

16. [Mr. SYMONIDES (Poland) stated that it was] unjustified in terms of international law to classify straits into those up to 6 miles wide and those from 6 to 24 miles wide, especially since an overwhelming majority of delegations recognized a 12-mile territorial sea. In both cases, the legal status was identical and the waters of such straits were territorial waters.

17. That did not, however, mean that transit through straits up to 24 miles wide could be based on the principle of innocent passage through the territorial sea. . . . It was possible to bypass a territorial sea by extending navigation

routes but it was impossible to avoid passage through certain straits. If the decision to grant or refuse passage could be taken arbitrarily on the basis of the still not well defined notion of "innocent passage," it might lead to discrimination against some States and to the limitation of the right of navigation for subjective reasons due to existing alliances, political ties and particular interests of coastal States. That was especially applicable to the passage of warships.

18. ... In the case of narrow straits, the coastal State would also have the right to trace out special corridors for transit purposes....

24. [Mr. ARIAS SCHREIBER (Peru)] The proposal submitted by the United Kingdom (A/CONF.62/C.2/L.3) and that submitted by a group of socialist countries (A/CONF.62/C.2/L.11) were based on a principle that was not in keeping with the nature of marine space or with the development of the law of the sea. Instead of referring to the passage of vessels through the territorial sea and straits used for international navigation, the proposals spoke of straits linking one part of the high seas with another part of the high seas, whereas the likelihood was that in future they would link not two parts of the high seas, but the economic zones of one or more coastal States. The definition must therefore be amended. The essential point was that the area involved was territorial sea; consequently, the provisions governing its use could not disregard the rights and jurisdiction which the coastal State exercised within that area.

25. As part of the rights and jurisdiction, it was logical that the coastal States should require notification of the passage of vessels with special status; it was even more logical to require authorization for the passage of warships. If, as the great Powers maintained, the passage was innocent, warships must prove their innocence in compliance with the convention. The same was true for the passage of submarines, whose concealment could only be for far from innocent reasons....

27. It was clear that certain maritime Powers intended to use the law of the sea as an instrument of their policy of freedom of action and to serve their plans for hegemony, and they expected other States to serve as accomplices in achieving those aims. They even went so far as to make recognition of large areas of national jurisdiction for mainly economic purposes conditional on the simultaneous acceptance of free passage through straits for mainly aggressive purposes, in the vain hope that non-straits States would accept such a deal. His country would not be a party to that maneuver.... It appeared from an initial examination that the proposals submitted by the delegation of Oman (A/CONF.62/C.2/L.16) were a step in the right direction....

41. Mr. ANDERSEN (Iceland) said that the question of a territorial sea of 12 miles, an economic zone of up to 200 miles and unimpeded passage

through straits used for international navigation were closely linked and must be resolved together. . . .

42. The right of unimpeded passage and adequate protection of the interests of the coastal State must be balanced. In that connection he supported the United Kingdom proposals (A/CONF.62/C.2/L.3), which had been supplemented by the proposals of Denmark and Finland (A/CONF.62/C.2/L.15) and similar proposals such as those put forward by six socialist countries (A/CONF.62/C.2/L.11).

43. An agreement along those lines would greatly facilitate the work of the Conference on the economic zone. He hoped that the straits issue would not become a stumbling block but rather a catalyzing factor in ensuring the successful treatment of the economic zone.

44. Mr. LING Ching (China) . . . said that the legal status of the territorial sea differed from that of the high seas. The territorial sea was undeniably an inseparable part of the territory of the coastal State, which exercised full sovereignty over it. A strait lying within the limits of the territorial sea could hardly change its status and become part of the high seas simply because it was normally used for international navigation. It stood to reason that the strait State exercised sovereignty and jurisdiction over such a strait, and had the right to make all the necessary laws and regulations governing it. . . . The Soviet proposal . . . while placing restrictions on the sovereignty and rights of the coastal State, demanded the right of equal freedom of navigation for all ships, including warships. That, in essence, was a denial of the status of such straits as territorial sea and of the coastal State's sovereignty and jurisdiction over them. Such contempt for the sovereignty of the strait State was unacceptable to his delegation. . . .

46. The passage of foreign military vessels . . . must be clearly distinguished from that of foreign merchant vessels. . . . The super-Powers had always tried to obliterate that distinction under the smoke-screen of "all ships," and had adopted pretexts of all kinds in an attempt to impose free passage through straits by warships. . . .

50. Thus, the ideas of "all ships" and "free passage" as advocated by the super-Powers were designed to enable their warships and nuclear submarines to cross the oceans of the world in implementation of their expansionist policies and their strategy of world hegemony. If that design were carried out, not only would the sovereignty of the straits States be infringed, but the peace and security of the world as a whole would be threatened. His country could not accept that approach. The draft articles submitted by Oman provided that the coastal State might require prior notification to or authorization by its

competent authorities for the passage of foreign warships through its territorial sea, in conformity with regulations in force in such a State. His delegation considered that requirement to be the undeniable right of a sovereign State and firmly supported its inclusion in the convention. . . .

64. Mr. STEVENSON (United States of America) in exercise of his right of reply, explained to the Egyptian representative, who had asked what assurance there would be that a submerged submarine in transit through a strait would respect the obligation not to threaten the security of that State, that the United States fully expected to comply with any treaty which it signed and ratified. Clearly, there was always a risk of States not complying with their legal duties, whether they related to a surface or submarine vessel; but his country's record in that respect had been a very good one. Indeed, the fact that it was seeking a right of submerged transit indicated its intention to abide by its obligations.

65. A strait was an area of confined waters in which no captain of a surface ship, much less of a submarine, would choose to take action threatening the security of a strait State. Moreover, since submarines were equipped to travel submerged, that was the safest way for them to pass through an international strait.

66. In reply to the question why the United States had not complied with the obligation of notification or authorization with respect to military vessels passing through the territorial sea, including straits overlapped by that sea, he pointed out that there was no such requirement of notification or authorization under the existing passage régime adopted in 1958 with respect to the territorial sea. In fact, the specific proposals made at the 1958 Conference to require such notification or authorization had not been adopted.

67. His delegation felt that any such requirement for warships would not be desirable, for it would tend to involve strait States much more directly in transits having nothing to do with their own interests, and might conceivably expose them to pressures to which they would not otherwise be subject.

68. The representative of Egypt and others had suggested that there might be something illegitimate about the transit of warships or military aircraft through or over straits without notice or authorization. However, it was unrealistic to entertain proposals which would discriminate against the navigation rights of warships or military aircraft. The exercise of individual and collective defence had been recognized under the United Nations Charter and in repeated actions of the United Nations. All nations, whether they bordered straits or not, recognized the importance of maintaining that right for the protection of their vital territorial and political integrity. The maintenance of transit rights for warships and military aircraft was not only consistent with the Charter but was the only policy consistent with global realities and international stability.

[14th Meeting, July 23, 1974]

1. Mr. SULEIMAN (Oman) introduced the draft articles on navigation through the territorial sea, including straits used for international navigation (A/CONF.62/C.2/L.16), and reiterated certain basic principles.

2. First, navigation through the territorial sea and through straits used for international navigation should be dealt with as an entity, since the straits in question formed part of the territorial sea.

3. Secondly, regulation of navigation through straits should establish a satisfactory balance between the particular interests of the coastal State and the interests of international maritime navigation.

4. Thirdly, the regulation should contribute both to the security of coastal States and to the safety of international maritime navigation. Those objectives could be achieved by the reasonable and adequate exercise by the coastal State of its right to regulate navigation through its territorial sea.

5. Fourthly, the regulation should take due account of the economic realities and scientific and technological developments that had taken place in recent years, and should establish appropriate rules to regulate navigation of certain ships with special characteristics.

6. Fifthly and lastly, the regulation should supply the deficiencies of the 1958 Geneva Convention on the Territorial Sea and the Contiguous Zone, especially relating to the passage of warships through the territorial sea, including straits. . . .

13. Part II of the draft articles dealt with the right of innocent passage through straits used for international navigation. Article 20 covered the straits as defined by the International Court of Justice in the Corfu Channel case and therefore did not apply to straits which historically had not been used for international navigation. Article 22, which dealt with special duties of coastal States, contained an important innovation in that it established the rule that passage of foreign merchant ships through straits should be presumed to be innocent. That presumption of innocent passage was a new idea, which was justified by the recognition that merchant ships performed an international duty to mankind and an important role in international trade, which was an instrument for development.

14. Mr. CHAO (Singapore) said that the question of international navigation through straits was important to his country first because Singapore depended to a large extent on international trade and the maintenance of the free flow of traffic through the straits was therefore vital to it, and secondly by reason of its geographical situation, since it was locked in on all sides by the territorial waters of its neighbouring States and its only access to the high seas was through the straits. . . .

15. Straits formed a vital link between different parts of the globe and the maintenance of that communication was essential for the benefit of the whole international community. Passage through territorial seas was less vital and for that reason separate régimes should be set up for the territorial sea and for straits. In any case, what was important in the last analysis was to adopt rules which would be objective. . . .

17. Mr. LACLETA Y MUÑOZ (Spain) said that the proposals submitted to the Committee reflected two different schools of thought with regard to passage through straits used in international navigation. There were three different points to be considered in connexion with those proposals: how they would affect the nature of ocean space, how they would affect the régime governing navigation in those waters, and, lastly, what attitude they indicated towards the fundamental distinction between merchant ships and warships.

18. One group of States considered that the waters of a strait were no longer, strictly speaking, part of the territorial sea. The draft submitted to the sea-bed Committee by the United States in 1971 stated in article 11, paragraph 1, that "all ships and aircraft in transit shall enjoy the same freedom of navigation and overflight, for the purposes of transit through and over such straits, as they have on the high seas." . . .

19. On the other hand, the draft submitted by Fiji to the sea-bed Committee in 1973 (A/9021 and Corr.1 and 3, vol. III, sect. 31) and the eight-Power draft (*ibid.*, sect. 6), like the draft recently submitted by Oman (A/CONF.62/C.2/L.16), rightly included the question of straits under the same heading as . . . the régime of territorial sea. . . .

21. As to the effects of the proposals on the régime governing navigation through straits, the proposals by the United Kingdom (A/CONF.62/C.2/L.3), the socialist States (A/CONF.62/C.2/L.11), and Denmark and Finland (A/CONF.62/C.2/L.15), like those by the United States in 1971, and by Italy in 1973 (A/9021 and Corr.1 and 3, vol. III, sect. 19) used the same formula: freedom of navigation for all ships and freedom of overflight for all aircraft. Their real aim was to establish the same freedom for navigation through straits as for navigation on the high seas, a freedom that had already been recognized. Certain countries were trying to get the Conference to reduce the breadth of the territorial sea to 3 miles in certain sea areas, i.e., the straits of other States.

22. The second school of thought was reflected in the 1973 eight-Power draft and the draft just submitted by Oman, which referred to the régime of navigation through straits as a "right of innocent passage." That régime achieved a balance between the interests of the coastal State and the legitimate interests of international navigation. . . .

23. [T]he navigation of merchant ships through straits must be guaranteed and facilitated as they were the carriers of trade and the means of peaceful international cooperation; but it was different with warships, whose mere passage through waters under foreign sovereignty implied a potential threat to the coastal State. The drafts in documents A/CONF.62/C.2/L.3, 11 and 15, like the draft submitted by the United States in 1971 and the one submitted by Italy in 1973, made no distinction between merchant ships and warships, and there was one very significant element in all those texts: the provision that submarines should navigate on the surface and show their flag had been dropped. It would seem then that the aim was to allow submarines to pass through the ocean space under the sovereignty of another State without that State's knowledge. Those proposals also had another characteristic in common, namely, they provided for freedom of overflight in transit for all types of aircraft, whether civil or military, over the straits. That would be tantamount to amending the Convention on International Civil Aviation, signed at Chicago in 1944, [Article 3(c) of] which required prior authorization of the State concerned for the overflight by military aircraft of its territorial sea, of which straits formed a part.

24. The régime of innocent passage applied strictly to navigation on the surface, and had nothing to do with the secret passage of submerged vessels or overflight. The 1973 eight-Power draft, like the Oman draft in document A/CONF.62/C.2/L.16, was very clear on those two points. In addition, the passage of warships was regulated by rules which, while allowing the right of passage, safeguarded the rights of the coastal State by requiring that the passage should be innocent and empowering the State concerned to require prior notification or authorization....

27. Mr. NAJAR (Israel) said that his delegation, like many others, was concerned about certain tendencies to limit freedom of navigation through straits and other maritime spaces in a period characterized by a rapid development of maritime traffic and by growing economic and technological interdependence among all States.... Israel specifically reaffirmed its support of freedom of navigation and overflight in all straits that linked two parts of the high sea or the high sea with the territorial sea of a foreign State.

28. ... His delegation could not ... accept the régime proposed in chapter III, article 8, of the United Kingdom draft articles (A/CONF.62/C.2/L.3) for straits linking the high sea with the territorial sea of a foreign State, because it considered the régime unjustified....

29. [T]he proposals of the United Kingdom and the socialist States infringed the principle of equality of treatment of all straits linking two parts

of the high sea or the high sea with the territorial sea of a foreign State, a principle of equality which had, however, been embodied in article 16, paragraph 4, of the 1958 Geneva Convention.

30. The right of freedom of navigation through straits which represented the sole means of access from the high sea to the territorial sea of a State and the reverse was a fundamental principle of international law, which prevailed over any considerations of a geographical or other nature. Such straits must be open to free navigation and overflight.

31. A new type of discrimination against partially landlocked coastal countries linked to the high sea through a strait could hardly be introduced at a time when the Conference on the Law of the Sea was attempting to give wider rights to geographically disadvantaged countries. . . .

33. [Mr. MESLOUB (Algeria)] Algeria was a geographically disadvantaged country and, what was more, its access to the oceans was exclusively through straits. As a developing country bordering on a semi-enclosed sea and practically without resources, it should logically be subject to a special régime affording access to the oceans. That right of free transit should be similar to the right whose recognition was sought for the land-locked countries, because there would be no sense in recognizing the rights of geographically disadvantaged countries to the living resources of neighbouring economic zones if those countries were simultaneously denied the means enabling them to enjoy those rights. . . .

63. Mr. AL-SAUD AL-SABAH (Kuwait), speaking . . . on behalf of Iraq, the United Arab Emirates, the Libyan Arab Republic, Saudi Arabia, Qatar and Kuwait, said that the term "straits used for international navigation" should be strictly confined to straits which connected two parts of the high seas. Because of that view, the Governments on whose behalf he was speaking had not acceded to the Convention on the Territorial Sea and the Contiguous Zone of 1958, since they opposed the interpretation of that concept in article 16, paragraph 4, of that Convention, which treated all straits alike. That provision had been politically motivated by the desire to accommodate specific interests in a particular region.

Notes

1. *Straits and the Expanded Breadth of the Territorial Sea.* When the breadth of the territorial sea expanded to twelve nautical miles, the effect was to enclose entirely within the territorial sea numerous straits used for international navigation that had previously contained a high seas corridor. Notable

among these passages were the Bering Strait, the Strait of Gibraltar, the Dover Strait, the Malacca Strait, Babel Mandeb (Red Sea), and several Caribbean straits, including the Dominica, Martinique, and St. Lucia Channels and the St. Vincent Passage. See Annotated Supplement to The Commander's Handbook on the Law of Naval Operations (1997), 73 Intl. Legal Studies 207–08, Table A2-5 (A.R. Thomas & James C. Duncan eds., 1999).

2. *Passage through Straits and the LOS Convention.* The regime of transit passage through straits is set out in Part III, Section 2 (Articles 37–44) of the LOS Convention. What different categories of straits does the LOS Convention recognize, and what legal rules regarding rights of passage apply to each? When the regime of transit passage through straits applies, how does it differ from innocent passage? From freedom of navigation on the high seas, which we explored in Chapter 2? What are the rights and duties of, respectively, straits states and maritime powers under the regime of transit passage through straits? See John Norton Moore, The Regime of Straits and the Third United Nations Conference on the Law of the Sea, 74 Am. J. Intl. L. 77 (1980); S.N. Nandan & D.H. Anderson, Straits Used for International Navigation: A Commentary on Part III of the U.N. Convention on the Law of the Sea 1982, 1989 Brit. Y.B. Intl. L. 159.

How satisfied or dissatisfied would each state that expressed views in the discussions above have been with the consensus reached concerning passage through straits in the LOS Convention? See also Article 233, which concerns coastal state enforcement measures and safeguards with respect to oil spills or other major environmental damage in straits, caused or threatened by merchant vessels and government ships on commercial service. For discussion, see Mary George, Transit Passage and Pollution Control in Straits under the 1982 Law of the Sea Convention, 33 Ocean Dev. & Intl. L. 189 (2002). To the extent that states were dissatisfied, why might they nevertheless accept the LOS Convention? Which states in the discussions above still have not accepted the Convention?

3. *Sea Lanes and the International Maritime Organization.* According to Article 41 of the LOS Convention, the "competent international organization" has a role with respect to the establishment of sea lanes or traffic separation schemes under the regime of transit passage through straits. According to the Division for Ocean Affairs and the Law of the Sea of the Office of Legal Affairs at the United Nations, the "competent international organization" under Article 41 is the International Maritime Organization. See "Competent or relevant international organizations" under the United Nations Convention on the Law of the Sea, L. Sea Bull. No. 31 at 79 (1996). Why was it necessary to involve

an international organization? How does Article 41 respond to the concerns of some delegates in the UNCLOS III discussions? Compare Article 22 of the LOS Convention, which applies to sea lanes and traffic separation schemes in the territorial sea, and Article 53, which relates to archipelagic sea lanes passage.

D Archipelagic Waters

In principle, the problem of archipelagic waters at UNCLOS III was similar, both politically and legally, to the problem of straits used for international navigation. Coastal—in this case archipelagic—states and maritime powers held opposing interests. Archipelagic states wanted a regime of innocent passage in the seas between the islands making up their land territory, or even a regime of internal waters. In contrast, maritime powers sought to freely navigate through waters that had traditionally been used for international navigation. Part IV of the LOS Convention embodied a compromise that included, inter alia, a right of "archipelagic sea lanes passage." In this section we examine one example of how the right of archipelagic sea lanes passage as agreed on in the LOS Convention has been implemented.

ADOPTION, DESIGNATION AND SUBSTITUTION OF ARCHIPELAGIC SEA LANES

IMO Doc. SN/Circ.200/Add.1 (July 3, 2003)

1. At its sixty-ninth session (11 to 20 May 1998), the Maritime Safety Committee, by resolution MSC.72(69), adopted a partial system of archipelagic sea lanes in Indonesian archipelagic waters and Indonesia undertook to inform the Organization, in accordance with paragraph 3.13 of the General Provisions for adoption, designation and substitution of archipelagic sea lanes, of the date on which the partial system would be implemented, which date would not be earlier than six months after the date of designation of the sea lanes by the Government of Indonesia.

2. On 27 June 2003, the Organization received from Indonesia a copy of Indonesian Government Regulation No. 37, 2002 dated 28 June 2002 on the Rights and Obligations of Foreign Ships and Aircraft Exercising the Right of Archipelagic Sea Lanes Passage through designated archipelagic sea lanes. Pursuant to this Regulation, the archipelagic sea lanes in the Indonesian archipelagic waters were implemented effectively on 28 December 2002 at 0000 hours local time. . . .

ANNEX: INDONESIAN GOVERNMENT REGULATION NUMBER 37, 2002 ON THE RIGHTS AND OBLIGATIONS OF FOREIGN SHIPS AND AIRCRAFT EXERCISING THE RIGHT OF ARCHIPELAGIC SEA LANE PASSAGE THROUGH DESIGNATED ARCHIPELAGIC SEA LANES . . .

Chapter II: The Rights and Obligations of Foreign Ships and Aircraft Exercising the Right of Archipelagic Sea Lane Passage

Article 2

Foreign ships and aircraft may exercise the right of Archipelagic Sea Lane Passage for the purposes of navigation and overflight from one part of the high seas or an exclusive economic zone to another part of the high seas or an exclusive economic zone through the territorial sea and archipelagic waters of Indonesia.

Article 3

1. The exercise of the right of archipelagic sea lane passage as described in article 2 is conducted through a sea lane or air route above the sea lane designated as an archipelagic sea lane for the purpose of transit in such sea lanes, as stipulated in article 11.
2. Pursuant to this regulation, to exercise the right of archipelagic sea lane passage in other parts of Indonesian waters can be conducted after such a sea lane has been designated in those waters for the purpose of this transit.

Article 4

1. Foreign ships and aircraft exercising the right of archipelagic sea lane passage must transit without delay through or above the archipelagic sea lane in normal mode solely for the purpose of continuous, expeditious and unobstructed transit.
2. Foreign ships and aircraft that exercise the right of archipelagic sea lane passage shall not deviate more than 25 nautical miles to either side of the axis lines during passage, provided that such ships and aircraft shall not navigate or fly over closer to the coast than 10 per cent of the distance between the nearest points on islands bordering the sea lane.
3. Foreign ships and aircraft exercising the right of archipelagic sea lane passage must refrain from any threat or use of force against the sovereignty, territorial integrity, or political independence of the Republic of Indonesia or in any other manner in violation of the principle of international law embodied in the Charter of the United Nations.

4. Foreign military warships and aircraft when exercising the right of archipelagic sea lane passage are not allowed to conduct war exercises or exercises using any kind of weapons with ammunition.

5. Except for a situation involving a *force majeure* or distress, aircraft exercising the right of archipelagic sea lane passage shall not land on Indonesian territory.

6. All foreign ships when exercising the right of archipelagic sea lane passage are not allowed to stop or anchor or to move back and forth while passing, except in the case of a *force majeure* or in distress or for the purpose of rendering assistance to persons or ships in distress.

7. Foreign ships and aircraft exercising the right of archipelagic sea lane passage are prohibited from carrying out unauthorized broadcasting or interfere with telecommunications systems and are prohibited from establishing direct communications with unauthorized persons or groups within the territory of Indonesia.

Article 5

Foreign ships or aircraft, including research or hydrographic vessels whilst exercising the right of archipelagic sea lane passage shall not conduct marine scientific research or hydrographic surveys either with the use of detection equipments or sample gathering equipments, unless granted permission to do so.

Article 6

1. Foreign ships, including fishing vessels exercising the right of archipelagic sea lane passage are prohibited from carrying out fishing activities.

2. Foreign fishing vessels exercising the right of archipelagic sea lane passage whilst required to fulfill the obligations stipulated in paragraph (1) must also keep their fishing gear stowed.

3. Foreign ships and aircraft exercising the right of archipelagic sea lane passage shall not embark or disembark persons, goods or currency in contravention of customs, immigration, fiscal and health laws except in the situation of a *force majeure* or distress.

Article 7

1. Foreign ships when exercising the Right of Archipelagic Sea Lane Passage shall observe the generally accepted regulations, procedures and international practices for the safety of navigation, including the regulations relating to collision prevention at sea.

2. Transiting ships in the traffic separation scheme established in the archipelagic sea lanes are obliged to observe the said scheme.

3. Foreign ships exercising the Right of Archipelagic Sea Lane Passage shall not damage or disrupt navigation facilities and submarine cables and pipelines.

4. Foreign ships exercising the right of archipelagic sea lane passage in the area where facilities for the exploitation or exploration of natural resources are located shall not sail within 500 meters of the prohibited zone around the installation.

Article 8

1. Foreign civil aircraft exercising the Right of Archipelagic Sea Lane Passage shall:

a. comply with the aviation regulations as established by the International Civil Aviation Organization concerning flight safety;

b. continuously monitor the radio frequencies as directed by the air traffic control authority or the appropriate international emergency radio frequency.

2. Foreign national aircraft exercising the Right of Archipelagic Sea Lane Passage shall:

a. respect the aviation regulations concerning flight safety as stipulated in paragraph (1)a;

b. observe the obligations as stipulated in paragraph (1)b.

Article 9

1. Foreign ships exercising the right of archipelagic sea lane passage are prohibited from discharging oil, oily waste and other dangerous materials into the marine environment, and or conducting other activities in contravention of international standards and regulations to prevent, reduce and control marine pollution originating from the ship.

2. Foreign ships exercising the right of archipelagic sea lane passage are prohibited from dumping waste into Indonesian waters.

3. Foreign nuclear-powered ships or ships carrying nuclear materials, or other inherently dangerous or noxious substances exercising the right of archipelagic sea lane passage, must bring documents and observe special precautionary measures as determined by international agreements for such vessels.

Article 10

1. Persons or legal personalities responsible for the operation of foreign cargo ships, aircraft or government-owned ships and aircraft used for commercial

purposes exercising the right of archipelagic sea lane passage shall take responsibility for any loss or damage suffered by Indonesia as a result of non-compliance with the provisions in articles 7, 8 and 9.

2. The flag state of a ship or the state of registry of an aircraft shall bear international responsibility for any loss or damage suffered by Indonesia as a result of non-compliance with the provisions in articles 7, 8 and 9, by warships or foreign aircraft when exercising the right of archipelagic sea lane passage.

Chapter III: Designation of Archipelagic Sea Lanes to be used for Exercising the Right of Archipelagic Sea Lane Passage

Article 11

[The Article specifies three north-south archipelagic sea lanes, with spurs, which are shown in Figure VIII.A.]

Article 12

1. The axis lines of the archipelagic sea lanes and connecting points of such sea lanes as stipulated in article 11 above are depicted on nautical charts for publication as required.

2. The geographical coordinates of the connecting points of the archipelagic sea lanes as stipulated in article 11 are listed in the Geographical Coordinates Table in Annex I, Annex II, Annex III, Annex III.A and Annex III.B. . . .

Chapter IV: Other Provisions

Article 13

The provisions in this government regulation shall not derogate the right of foreign ships to exercise the right of innocent passage within the archipelagic sea lanes.

Article 14

The provisions in this government regulation concerning Indonesian Archipelagic Sea Lane Passage shall not be effective for the Leti Strait and part of the Ombai Strait bordering East Timor, which due to the changing status of East Timor, such straits are no longer part of the Indonesian archipelagic waters.

Article 15

Six months after this government regulation was enforced, foreign ships and aircraft can exercise the right of archipelagic sea lane passage only through the designated Indonesian archipelagic sea lanes as stipulated in this government regulation.

Chapter V: Final Provisions

Article 16

This Government Regulation shall enter into force on the date of its promulgation [June 28, 2002].

ELUCIDATION ON GOVERNMENT REGULATION NUMBER 37, 2002 ON THE RIGHTS AND OBLIGATIONS OF FOREIGN SHIPS AND AIRCRAFT EXERCISING THE RIGHT OF ARCHIPELAGIC SEA LANE PASSAGE THROUGH DESIGNATED ARCHIPELAGIC SEA LANES

General

Law Number 6, 1996, on Indonesian Waters was enacted as the implementation of Law Number 17, 1985, on the Ratification of the United Nations Convention on Law of the Sea (UNCLOS). In accordance with this Convention, the sovereignty of the Republic of Indonesia encompasses not only the land, internal waters, territorial seas and archipelagic waters, but also the air space over those areas.

Although Indonesia has sovereignty over its territorial seas and its archipelagic waters, Law Number 6, 1996, on the Indonesian Waters pursuant to the 1982 UNCLOS includes the provisions that foreign ships and aircraft shall enjoy the right of archipelagic sea lane passage through territorial seas and archipelagic waters of Indonesia for the purpose of traversing those waters from one part of the high seas or an exclusive economic zone to another part of the high seas or other exclusive economic zone. . . .

For the implementation of such passage, and pursuant to the Convention, Indonesia may designate particular archipelagic sea lane passage by specifying sea lanes for such passage from amongst the routes normally used for international navigation.

Security risks may be an issue if the right of archipelagic sea lane passage is exercised through routes normally used for international navigation as stipulated in article 53 paragraph (12) of the Convention since transit through archipelagic sea lanes incorporates specific freedoms.

In order to reduce [those] risks, it is considered necessary to designate archipelagic sea lane passage for such transit.

The Indonesian Government designates these archipelagic sea lanes in observance of the concerns of the international community expressed through the competent organization for international navigation, namely International Maritime Organization (IMO). On 19 May 1998 the Maritime Safety Committee (MSC-69-IMO) accepted the Indonesian submission to designate 3 archipelagic sea lanes and its spurs which can be used to exercise the right of archipelagic sea lane passage through Indonesian waters. Further to the IMO's acceptance of the Indonesian proposal, the geographical coordinates of conecting [sic] lines for these 3 archipelagic sea lanes and their spurs shall be enacted into the Government Regulation.

The designation of these 3 archipelagic sea lanes and their spurs does not indicate that these 3 lanes can only be used by foreign ships for the purpose of exercising the right of archipelagic sea lane passage from one part of the high seas or an exclusive economic zone to another part of the high seas or other exclusive economic zone through the Indonesian waters. Foreign ships planning to navigate from one part of the high seas or an exclusive economic zone to one of the Indonesian ports or to another part of the high seas or other exclusive economic zone may do so with the exercise of the right of innocent passage in the Indonesian waters equally within the archipelagic sea lanes or beyond the archipelagic sea lanes.

In light of that consideration and pursuant to articles 18 and 19 of Law Number 6, 1996 on the Indonesian Waters, it is deemed necessary to enact a Government Regulation on the Rights and Obligations of Foreign Ships and Aircraft Exercising the Right of Archipelagic Sea Lane Passage through Designated Archipelagic Sea Lanes. . . .

As the implementation of Law Number 6, 1996 on Indonesian Waters, this Government Regulation constitutes the accomplishment of the ratification of the 1982 UNCLOS with Law Number 17, 1985. Accordingly, in order to ensure consistent interpretation of the provisions of this Government Regulation with that of the 1982 UNCLOS and pursuant to the elucidation of articles of Law Number 6, 1996, it is deemed necessary within the elucidation of the provisions of this Government Regulation to refer to specific articles and paragraphs of the 1982 UNCLOS, particularly where its provisions are not found in Law Number 6, 1996 on Indonesian Waters but rather in the 1982 UNCLOS.

Article by Article . . .

Article 2

The provisions on archipelagic sea lane passage may be used by foreign ships only to traverse the Indonesian waters from one part of the high seas or an exclusive economic zone to another part of the high seas or another exclusive economic zone, while the provision on innocent passage can be used by foreign ships either to traverse the Indonesian waters without entering any Indonesian seaports or anchoring in one of the Indonesian seaports.

Foreign ships sailing in the Indonesian waters wishing to enter any Indonesian seaport or the other way around must adhere to the innocent passage provisions and must accordingly whilst sailing in the archipelagic sea lanes must obey the stipulations of innocent passage and are prohibited from using the stipulations of archipelagic sea lane passage.

Article 3

Paragraph (1)

See General Explanation[,] paragraph 5.

Paragraph (2)

Sufficiently clear

Article 4

Paragraph (1)

The provision in this paragraph serves as the application of article 54 in conjunction with article 39 paragraph (1) letter a, of the [LOS] Convention.

Paragraph (2)

The provision in this paragraph serves as the application of article 53 paragraph (1), of the [LOS] Convention.

Paragraph (3)

The provision in this paragraph serves as the application of article 54 in conjunction with article 39 paragraph (1) letter b, of the [LOS] Convention.

Paragraph (4)

Whilst exercising archipelagic sea lane passage, warships and foreign military aircraft are prohibited from conducting activities as referred to in this paragraph, because it is not directly associated with the normal mode for the purpose of continuous and expeditious transit which may cause disturbance to the state's peace, order and security.

The provision in this paragraph serves as the application of article 54 in conjunction with article 39 paragraph (1) letter c of the [LOS] Convention.

[The explanations for Article 4, paragraphs 5–7 closely track that given for paragraph 4.]

Article 5

The provision in this paragraph serves as the application of article 54 in conjunction with Article 40 of the [LOS] Convention.

Article 6

Paragraph (1)

The provision in this paragraph serves as the application of the laws on fisheries and article 54 in conjunction with article 42 paragraph (1) letter c of the [LOS] Convention.

[The explanation for Article 6, paragraph 2 is identical to that given for paragraph 1.]

Paragraph (3)

The provision in this paragraph serves as the application of the laws on customs, fiscal, immigration and health along with the provision of article 54 in conjunction with article 42 paragraph (1) letter d and article 39 paragraph (1) letter c of the [LOS] Convention.

Article 7

Paragraph (1)

The provision in this paragraph serves as the application of article 54 in conjunction with article 39 paragraph (2) letter a of the [LOS] Convention.

Paragraph (2)

The provision in this paragraph serves as the application of article 53 paragraph (1) of the [LOS] Convention.

Paragraph (3)

The provision in this paragraph serves as the application of article 54 in conjunction with article 42 paragraph (1) letter a of the [LOS] Convention.

Paragraph (4)

The prohibited zone is the zone designated around the installations with a width of 500 (five hundred) meters from the outermost points of the installation, or other points constituting permanent parts of the installation whereby third party ships are prohibited from sailing.

Whilst exercising archipelagic sea lane passage, foreign ships are prohibited from performing activities as referred to in this paragraph as to protect such installations from the hazards resulting from the sailing of such foreign ships.

Article 8

Paragraph (1)

The provision in this paragraph serves as the application of article 54 in conjunction with article 39 paragraph (3) of the [LOS] Convention.

[The explanation for Article 8, paragraph 2 is identical to that given for paragraph 1.]

Article 9

Paragraph (1)

The provision in this paragraph serves as the application of article 54 in conjunction with article 42 paragraph (1) letter b and article 211 paragraph (2) of the [LOS] Convention.

Paragraph (2)

The provision in this paragraph serves as the application of article 210 paragraph (1) of the [LOS] Convention.

Paragraph (3)

The international treaties referred to in this paragraph are as follows:

1. Convention on the Physical Protection of Nuclear Materials;
2. Irradiated Nuclear Fuel (INF) Codes;
3. International Maritime Dangerous Goods (IMDG) Codes;
4. Hazardous Materials and Noxious Substances (HNS) Codes.

Article 10

Paragraph (1)

The responsibility of persons or legal bodies for the operation of cargo ships or aircraft in this paragraph have civil responsibilities such as to pay compensation for loss or damage.

Paragraph (2)

The provision in this paragraph serves as the application of article 54 in conjunction with article 42 paragraph (5) of the [LOS] Convention....

Article 12

Paragraph (1)

The addition of archipelagic sea lanes on navigational charts is meant to ensure that the navigation of foreign ships may be executed by adhering to the archipelagic sea lane passage requirements in accordance with the provision as stipulated in this Government Regulation as the implementation of the provisions of the 1982 UNCLOS.

Paragraph (2)

Geographic coordinates for the archipelagic sea lane connecting points are cited in latitude and longitude, with explanatory notes on the waters where such points are situated as well as other data as required....

Article 13

See the General Explanation[,] paragraph 7.

Article 14

The Indonesian proposal on the designation of archipelagic sea lanes has been adopted by the International Maritime Organization under Maritime Safety Committee (MSC) resolution 72 (69) during the 69th session of the MSC convened in London from May 11–20, 1998 when the Leti Strait and part of the Ombai Strait bordering East Timor were still part of the Indonesian archipelagic waters.

However due to the changing status of East Timor, the Leti Strait and part of the Ombai Strait are no longer straits constituting part of the Indonesian archipelagic waters as they have become straits situated between two countries.

Article 15

The provision in this article constitutes the specification for a change of a condition which under the provision of article 53 paragraph (12) of the [LOS] Convention, the right of passage for foreign ships and aircraft may remain using the routes normally used for international navigation to the situation whereby according to the provision laid down in this Government Regulation, such right of passage for foreign ships and aircraft can be exercised through certain sea lanes.

Six months should be sufficient time to prepare for any matter required to ensure the safety of navigation through such archipelagic sea lanes.

DIGEST OF UNITED STATES PRACTICE IN INTERNATIONAL LAW
760–62 (2003)

A telegram from the Department of State to the American embassy in Jakarta, Indonesia, dated August 8, 2003, explained that prior to the Third UN Conference on the Law of the Sea (1973–1982), international law did not permit archipelagic claims. The United States worked closely with Indonesia to reach agreement on a regime for mid-oceanic island states "to achieve international recognition of their special status as archipelagic States." The telegram continued:

> Under the regime agreed to in Part IV of the 1982 Law of the Sea Convention, an archipelagic State is entitled to draw archipelagic straight baselines around the outermost points of the outermost islands and drying reefs of the archipelago and thereby convert high seas areas within the archipelago into archipelagic waters under the sovereignty of the archipelagic State. In return, the archipelagic State recognized the right

> of ships and aircraft of all states to transit the archipelagic waters and adjacent territorial sea in the normal mode for the continuous, expeditious and unobstructed transit (i.e., the right of archipelagic sea lanes passage (ASLP)) through all routes normally used for international navigation through those waters until such time as the archipelagic State, in conjunction with the International Maritime Organization (IMO), designated archipelagic sea lanes (ASL) through the archipelago adopted by the IMO.

The United States recognized Indonesia's claim to status as an archipelagic state, conditioned on Indonesia's commitment that application of its claim was and would be in full conformity with international law reflected in Part IV of the Law of the Sea Convention. The United States had also worked with Indonesia and Australia in identifying three mutually acceptable ASLs, adopted by the IMO in 1998, at a time when East Timor was under the control of Indonesia.

The telegram requested the embassy to present a diplomatic note to the Government of Indonesia requesting clarification on four points in connection with Indonesia's June 28, 2002, Regulation No. 37 on the Rights and Obligations of Foreign Ships and Aircraft Exercising the Right of Archipelagic Sea Lanes Passage. An English copy of the regulation, which formally designated the three north-south ASLs, was made available in July 2003 through the IMO. The text of the diplomatic note, setting forth the U.S. requests for clarification, is provided below[:]

> [The United States] refers to Indonesian Regulation No. 37 of 28 June 2002 on the Rights and [O]bligations of Foreign Ships and Aircraft Exercising the Right of Archipelagic Sea Lanes Passage through designated archipelagic sea lanes, and seeks as a matter of some urgency clarification of several of its provisions.
>
> The United States recalls the Exchange of Notes accompanying the United States-Indonesia Convention for the Avoidance of Double Taxation and the Prevention of Fiscal Evasion with Respect to Taxes on Income, and Related Protocol, of July 11, 1988, by which the Government of the Republic of Indonesia agreed that it will apply the archipelagic States principles "in accordance with Part IV of the 1982 United Nations Convention on the Law of the Sea and . . . respect() the international rights and obligations pertaining to transit of the Indonesian archipelagic waters in accordance with international law and reflected in that Part."

The Government of the United States has carefully reviewed the English translation of Indonesian Regulation No. 37 of 2002 as publicized by IMO circular SN/Circ.200/Add.l of July 3, 2003.

The United States is pleased to inform the Government of the Republic of Indonesia that it considers for the most part the Regulation and its Annexes faithfully follow the provisions of Part IV of the 1982 Law of the Sea Convention and the sea lanes adopted by the IMO in 1998. In that connection, the Government of the United States wishes to inform the Government of the Republic of Indonesia of its understanding that:

—as this is a partial designation of archipelagic sea lanes through the Indonesian archipelago, the right of the ships and aircraft of all States to exercise archipelagic sea lanes passage continues on all normal routes used for international navigation through other parts of the Indonesian archipelago, as provided in Article 53(12) of the Law of the Sea Convention and paragraph 6.7 of Part H of the IMO Ships' Routeing Guide, and

—the right of innocent passage exists for the ships of all States in all of Indonesia's archipelagic waters (except for internal waters within archipelagic waters) and territorial sea, as provided in Article 52(1) of the Law of the Sea Convention and paragraph 6.5 of Part H of the IMO Ships' Routeing Guide.

The United States would appreciate a note in reply confirming that Indonesia agrees with these understandings.

In addition, the United States would appreciate being advised of the coordinates (latitude and longitude) of the southern termination of the axes of Spurs IIIA and IIIB resulting from the change in status of East Timor since the sea lanes were adopted by the IMO in 1998.

Finally, the United States would appreciate being informed of Indonesia's intentions with regard to those archipelagic straight baselines that are measured from basepoints on East Timor territory pursuant to Law No. 4 of 1960.

The United States would appreciate an early reply so that it may provide appropriate guidance to its forces prior to the implementation of the sea lanes and regulation on December 27, 2003.

The United States is prepared to engage in any necessary consultation with Indonesia officials as may be necessary to reach a mutually satisfactory clarification of these points.

Notes

1. *Archipelagic Baselines of Archipelagic States*. The determination of "archipelagic baselines" (LOS Convention, Article 47) is important to the determination of the territorial sea, contiguous zone, exclusive economic zone, and continental shelf (Article 48) of an "archipelagic state" (Article 46(1)(a)). Such baselines also enclose "archipelagic waters," over which the archipelagic state has sovereignty (Article 49), and through which other states have rights of innocent passage (Article 52) or archipelagic sea lanes passage (Article 53). Archipelagic baselines are reviewed in Chapter 5.

2. *Archipelagic Sea Lanes Passage*. Why was the International Maritime Organization involved with the issue of archipelagic sea lanes passage in waters over which Indonesia has sovereignty, and what was the IMO's role? See LOS Convention, Article 53(9); IMO Res. A.858(20) (1997); IMO Res. MSC.72(69) (1998). Was it proper for Indonesia to submit, and for the IMO to adopt, a partial system of sea lanes in Indonesian archipelagic waters in 1998, given the reference in Article 53(4) of the LOS Convention to "all" normal routes? Why did the IMO not insist that Indonesia designate all sea lanes before giving approval?

Why would Indonesia designate archipelagic sea lanes at all, in light of the permissive language in Article 53(1) of the LOS Convention? For an archipelagic state, what are the advantages and disadvantages of designating sea lanes? Following Indonesian Regulation 37 (2002) and the U.S. diplomatic reply, what mode of passage must U.S. vessels follow if they seek to traverse Indonesian archipelagic waters in an east-west direction? In a 2003 statement to the IMO's Maritime Safety Committee, Indonesia's delegates "confirm[ed] that the nature of designation of the Indonesian Sea Lanes Passage (ASLP) was a partial one." Report of the Maritime Safety Committee on its Seventy-seventh Session ¶ 25.40, MSC 77/26 (June 10, 2003). Indonesia also stated that the failure to designate sea lanes meant that "ASLP shall be conducted through all routes normally used for international navigation" and that pending full designation a "similar consequence will be applied through" such routes. MSC 77/26/Add.2, Annex 27 (June 16, 2006). Is Indonesia's international stance consistent with its 2002 Regulation No. 37? See Penny Campbell, Indonesian Archipelagic Sea Lanes, in Australian Maritime Issues 2005, Papers in Australian Maritime Affairs No. 16 (Gregory P. Gilbert & Robert J. Davit eds., 2005); Constance Johnson, A Rite of Passage: The IMO Consideration of the Indonesian Archipelagic Sea-Lanes Submission, 15 Intl. J. Marine & Coastal L. 326 (2000).

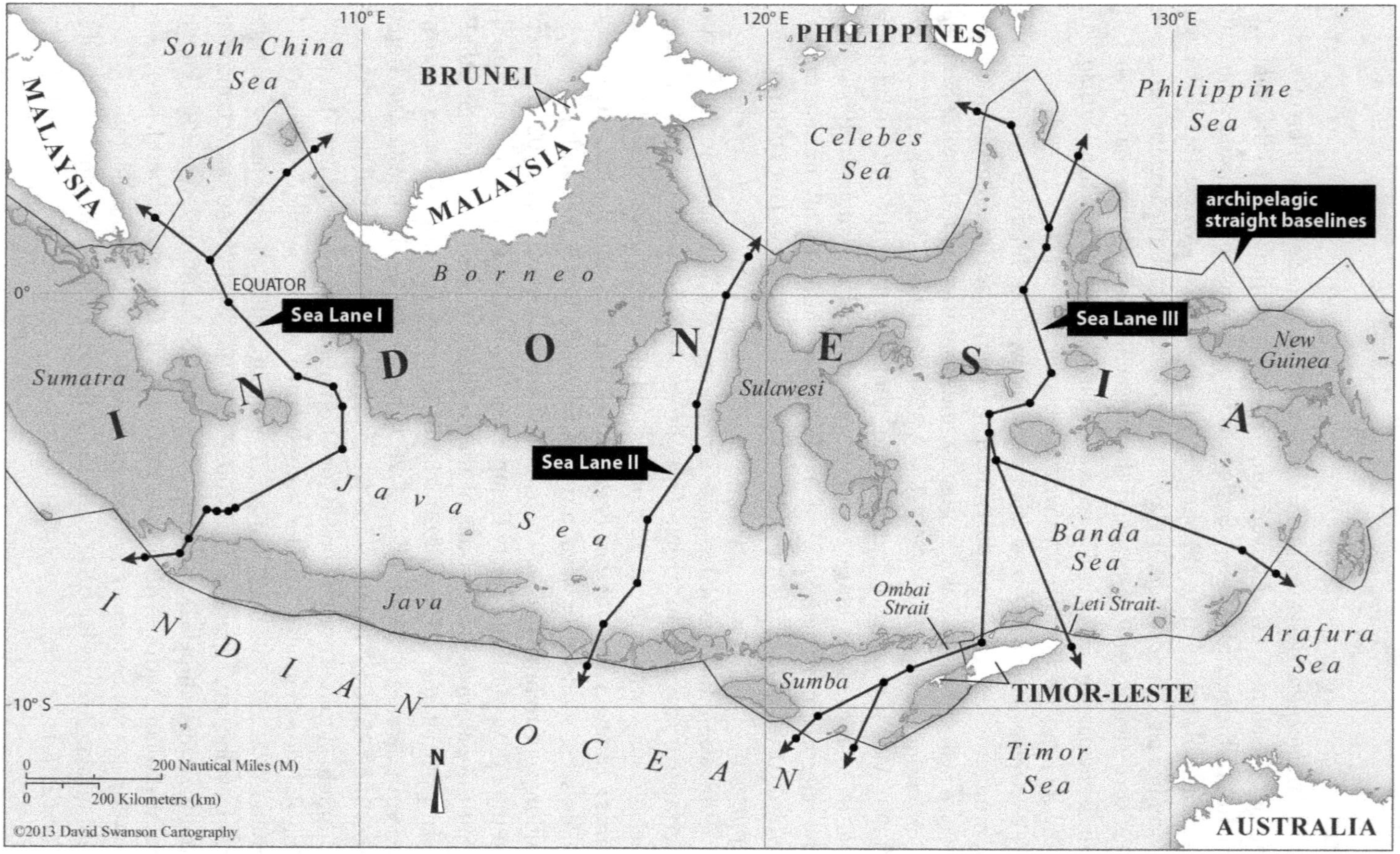

FIGURE VIII.A *Indonesia's Partial System of Archipelagic Sea Lanes*

How similar is the regime of archipelagic sea lanes passage to the regime of transit passage through straits? Compare, for example, Articles 38(2) and 53(3) of the LOS Convention. See J. Peter A. Bernhardt, The Right of Archipelagic Sea Lanes Passage: A Primer, 35 Va. J. Intl. L. 719 (1995).

3. *Rights of Non-parties to the LOS Convention.* As of September 1, 2013, the United States remained a non-party to the LOS Convention. May a non-party legally claim rights newly created in the LOS Convention—such as transit passage through straits or archipelagic sea lanes passage—without also accepting the full range of obligations set out in the Convention? Why or why not? Does the United States, a party to the 1958 Territorial Sea Convention, remain bound, at least with respect to other parties to that treaty, to comply with the limited navigational rights accorded under that treaty?

CHAPTER 9

Exclusive Economic Zone

As we will see in Chapter 10, coastal state assertions of jurisdiction over the continental shelf began in the mid-20th century, prompted in large measure by changes in oil drilling and mining technology. Changes in technology also contributed to assertions of coastal state control over fisheries zones extending beyond the territorial sea, as distant-water foreign flag trawlers and factory ships became able to capture and process huge quantities of fish near the shores of coastal states. Coastal states regarded expanded coastal zones as a way to protect, or promote the development of, their local fishing and economic interests.

In 1945 the United States made unilateral claims concerning the continental shelf and fisheries. These claims, which President Truman asserted by two proclamations issued on the same day, provide good starting points for our consideration of the law concerning the continental shelf and the exclusive economic zone (EEZ). The content of the two Truman proclamations differed significantly, as we will see, as did their impacts on the development of the law of the sea.

Iceland was the first country to proclaim a separate exclusive fishery zone beyond its territorial sea during the 1950s. Other countries that had historically fished in these waters, such as Germany and the United Kingdom, firmly objected to this unilateral behavior. Iceland increased the width of the newly proclaimed zone from four nautical miles in 1952 to twelve nautical miles in 1958 and 50 nautical miles in 1972. All sides involved their navies, and the so-called Cod Wars ensued. The dispute finally ended up before the International Court of Justice (ICJ). The Court rendered its decision in 1974, a rather awkward time because the Third United Nations Conference on the Law of the Sea (UNCLOS III), which would profoundly reshape the law of fisheries, had just started its work a year earlier. Section A covers these early developments.

The EEZ became firmly established in international law soon after UNCLOS III concluded in 1982 and states signed the United Nations Convention on the Law of the Sea (LOS Convention). The creation of this new maritime zone is a good example of how codification may sometimes precede and contribute to the formation of customary international law. Section B highlights this phenomenon.

Section C then examines some applications of the EEZ in state practice. Some activities taking place in the EEZ clearly fall under the competence of

 | DOI 10.1163/9789004203563_010

the coastal state, while others remain part of the freedoms of the high seas. However, legal competence concerning certain activities remains debatable.

A Early Developments

Early assertions of coastal state jurisdiction or control over the waters of the high seas adjacent to the territorial sea related to interests in fisheries. This section includes an example of a unilateral coastal state claim (the 1945 Truman Proclamation on fisheries) and a judicial analysis of competing claims concerning the right to fish in fisheries zones proclaimed by a coastal state (the 1974 decision of the ICJ in the United Kingdom-Iceland Fisheries Jurisdiction case).

PRESIDENTIAL PROCLAMATION NO. 2668 (TRUMAN PROCLAMATION REGARDING FISHERIES)

Sept. 28, 1945, 10 Fed. Reg. 12304 (1945), 13 Dept. State Bull. 486 (1945)

Whereas for some years the Government of the United States of America has viewed with concern the inadequacy of present arrangements for the protection and perpetuation of the fishery resources contiguous to its coasts, and in view of the potentially disturbing effect of this situation, has carefully studied the possibility of improving the jurisdictional basis for conservation measures and international cooperation in this field; and

Whereas such fishery resources have a special importance to coastal communities as a source of livelihood and to the nation as a food and industrial resource; and

Whereas the progressive development of new methods and techniques contributes to intensified fishing over wide sea areas and in certain cases seriously threatens fisheries with depletion; and

Whereas there is an urgent need to protect coastal fishery resources from destructive exploitation, having due regard to conditions peculiar to each region and situation and to the special rights and equities of the coastal State and of any other State which may have established a legitimate interest therein;

Now, therefore, I, Harry S. Truman, President of the United States of America, do hereby proclaim the following policy of the United States of America with respect to coastal fisheries in certain areas of the high seas:

In view of the pressing need for conservation and protection of fishery resources, the Government of the United States regards it as proper to establish conservation zones in those areas of the high seas contiguous to the coasts of the United States wherein fishing activities have been or in the future may be developed and maintained on a substantial scale. Where such activities have been or shall hereafter be developed and maintained by its nationals alone, the United States regards it as proper to establish explicitly bounded conservation zones in which fishing activities shall be subject to the regulation and control of the United States. Where such activities have been or shall hereafter be legitimately developed and maintained jointly by nationals of the United States and nationals of other States, explicitly bounded conservation zones may be established under agreements between the United States and such other States; and all fishing activities in such zones shall be subject to regulation and control as provided in such agreements. The right of any State to establish conservation zones off its shores in accordance with the above principles is conceded, provided that corresponding recognition is given to any fishing interests of nationals of the United States which may exist in such areas. The character as high seas of the areas in which such conservation zones are established and the right to their free and unimpeded navigation are in no way thus affected.

Notes

1. *The Truman Proclamation Regarding Fisheries and Early Efforts to Manage and Conserve Fisheries.* When the Truman Proclamation regarding fisheries was issued, all waters beyond the territorial sea and contiguous zone were viewed as the high seas over which no state had jurisdiction. See G.H. Hackworth, 2 Digest of International Law 651 (1941). Several bilateral treaties, such as the 1818 United States-Great Britain Fisheries Convention, had concerned fishery management and conservation, but by 1945 those agreements were no longer adequate, as increased fishing in waters contiguous to the coast was leading to over-exploitation of several fishery stocks. What different scenarios did the Truman Proclamation envisage? In each scenario, what U.S. actions did the Proclamation contemplate?

2. *Comparing the Truman Proclamation Regarding the Continental Shelf.* On the same day President Truman issued his proclamation regarding fisheries, he also issued a second proclamation regarding the continental shelf. Presidential Proclamation No. 2667, Sept. 28, 1945, 10 Fed. Reg. 12303 (1945), 59 Stat. 884 (1945). By that proclamation Truman considered "the natural resources of the subsoil and sea bed of the continental shelf... as appertaining to the United States, subject to its jurisdiction and control." See Chapter 10, Section A. How does this assertion compare to the content of the Truman Proclamation regarding fisheries? Does each proclamation conform to existing international law

or instead reflect a progressive development of international law? As we will see in Chapter 10, the Truman Proclamation regarding the continental shelf was a major success. In contrast, the United States never implemented fisheries conservation zones under the Truman Proclamation regarding fisheries on the basis of agreements with other countries. What explains this difference in outcomes?

3. *The Responses of Other States.* The Truman Proclamation regarding fisheries and the Truman Proclamation regarding the continental shelf contributed to the decision of several South American states to establish zones of up to 200 nautical miles. These South American states claimed complete sovereignty over the seabed, its subsoil, and superjacent waters in these zones, "in order to reserve, protect, preserve and exploit the natural resources of whatever nature found on, within and below the said seas." Chile, Presidential Declaration concerning the Continental Shelf, June 23, 1947, reproduced in Marjorie M. Whiteman, 4 Digest of International Law 794 (1965). The United States objected to this and similar decrees because the decrees asserted complete national sovereignty over the zones and failed to recognize the rights of other states. Id. at 796–97. Were these Latin American claims contrary to the letter as well as the spirit of both of the 1945 Truman proclamations?

FISHERIES JURISDICTION CASE[1]
United Kingdom v. Iceland, 1974 I.C.J. 3

[In 1948, Iceland's Parliament passed a law authorizing the Ministry of Fisheries to set "conservation zones within the limits of the continental shelf of Iceland; wherein all fisheries shall be subject to Icelandic rules and control." 1974 I.C.J., ¶ 19. In 1952, Iceland established a fisheries zone extending four nautical miles from straight baselines and prohibited foreign fishing within the zone. In 1958, Iceland proclaimed a twelve-nautical-mile fisheries zone, again prohibiting foreign fishing within the new limit. British efforts to continue fishing in the twelve-nautical-mile zone led to "incidents on the fishing grounds," id., ¶ 24, and a 1959 Icelandic parliamentary resolution emphasizing Iceland's objective to extend a fisheries zone "over the whole of the continental shelf area." Id. In a 1961 Exchange of Notes, the United Kingdom acknowledged Iceland's dependence on coastal fisheries for its livelihood and economic development and agreed not to object to the twelve-nautical-mile zone. Iceland, for

---

1 The headnote to this case and portions of the Notes following it are in part reprinted from pages 790 and 796–98 of International Law Cases and Commentary by Mark W. Janis & John E. Noyes, 4th ed. 2011, with permission of West. [Eds.]

its part, agreed to give the United Kingdom six months' notice of any further extension of Icelandic fisheries jurisdiction and agreed to refer any disputes over such an extension to the ICJ. In 1972 Iceland again extended its exclusive fisheries jurisdiction, to 50 nautical miles from its baselines, and prohibited all foreign fishing in the 50-nautical-mile zone. The United Kingdom again protested, pointing out that its vessels had historically fished in those waters.

The United Kingdom brought the matter to the ICJ, basing jurisdiction on the 1961 Exchange of Notes. Iceland refused to participate in the proceedings and to recognize the Court's jurisdiction. However, in 1973 the ICJ found that it had jurisdiction to entertain the application, and proceeded to render its final judgment in 1974.

The Federal Republic of Germany had, like Britain, protested Iceland's assertion of fisheries zones, and Germany brought a parallel application to the ICJ, based on a 1961 bilateral agreement that was similar to the 1961 Exchange of Notes between Iceland and the United Kingdom. The Court reached a similar decision with respect to jurisdiction in Germany's case, and issued a separate judgment in Germany's case in 1974. Many paragraphs in the two 1974 judgments are identical. The excerpt below is from the U.K. case, but bracketed language accompanying paragraph 70 (paragraph 62 in the decision in Germany's case) includes some additional language that appeared in the decision in Germany's case.]

11. In the course of the written proceedings, the following submissions were presented on behalf of the Government of the United Kingdom:...

The United Kingdom asks the Court to adjudge and declare:

> (*a*) that there is no foundation in international law for the claim by Iceland to be entitled to extend its fisheries jurisdiction by establishing a zone of exclusive fisheries jurisdiction extending to 50 nautical miles from the baselines...; and that its claim is therefore invalid; and
>
> (*b*) that questions concerning the conservation of fish stocks in the waters around Iceland are not susceptible in international law to regulation by the unilateral extension by Iceland of its exclusive fisheries jurisdiction to 50 nautical miles from the aforesaid baselines but are matters that may be regulated, as between Iceland and the United Kingdom, by arrangements agreed between those two countries[.]

49. The Applicant has challenged the Regulations promulgated by the Government of Iceland on 14 July 1972, and since the Court has to pronounce on this challenge, the ascertainment of the law applicable becomes necessary. As the Court stated in the *Fisheries* case:

> The delimitation of sea areas has always an international aspect; it cannot be dependent merely upon the will of the coastal State as expressed in its municipal law. Although it is true that the act of delimitation is necessarily a unilateral act, because only the coastal State is competent to undertake it, the validity of the delimitation with regard to other States depends upon international law. (*I.C.J. Reports 1951*, p. 132.)

The Court will therefore proceed to the determination of the existing rules of international law relevant to the settlement of the present dispute.

50. The Geneva Convention on the High Seas of 1958, which was adopted "as generally declaratory of established principles of international law," defines in Article 1 the term "high seas" as "all parts of the sea that are not included in the territorial sea or in the internal waters of a State." Article 2 then declares that "The high seas being open to all nations, no State may validly purport to subject any part of them to its sovereignty" and goes on to provide that the freedom of the high seas comprises, *inter alia*, both for coastal and non-coastal States, freedom of navigation and freedom of fishing. The freedoms of the high seas are however made subject to the consideration that they "shall be exercised by all States with reasonable regard to the interests of other States in their exercise of the freedom of the high seas."

51. . . . At the 1958 Conference, the main differences on the breadth of the territorial sea were limited at the time to disagreements as to what limit, not exceeding 12 miles, was the appropriate one. The question of the breadth of the territorial sea and that of the extent of the coastal State's fishery jurisdiction were left unsettled at the 1958 Conference. These questions were referred to the Second Conference on the Law of the Sea, held in 1960. Furthermore, the question of the extent of the fisheries jurisdiction of the coastal State, which had constituted a serious obstacle to the reaching of an agreement at the 1958 Conference, became gradually separated from the notion of the territorial sea. This was a development which reflected the increasing importance of fishery resources for all States.

52. The 1960 Conference failed by one vote to adopt a text governing the two questions of the breadth of the territorial sea and the extent of fishery rights. However, after that Conference the law evolved through the practice of States on the basis of the debates and near-agreements at the Conference. Two concepts have crystallized as customary law in recent years arising out of the general consensus revealed at that Conference. The first is the concept of the fishery zone, the area in which a State may claim exclusive fishery jurisdiction independently of its territorial sea; the extension of that fishery zone up to a 12-mile limit from the baselines appears now to be generally accepted.

The second is the concept of preferential rights of fishing in adjacent waters in favour of the coastal State in a situation of special dependence on its coastal fisheries, this preference operating in regard to other States concerned in the exploitation of the same fisheries, and to be implemented in the way indicated in paragraph 57 below.

53. In recent years the question of extending the coastal State's fisheries jurisdiction has come increasingly to the forefront. The Court is aware that a number of States has asserted an extension of fishery limits. The Court is also aware of present endeavours, pursued under the auspices of the United Nations, to achieve in a third Conference on the Law of the Sea the further codification and progressive development of this branch of the law, as it is of various proposals and preparatory documents produced in this framework, which must be regarded as manifestations of the views and opinions of individual States and as vehicles of their aspirations, rather than as expressing principles of existing law. The very fact of convening the third Conference on the Law of the Sea evidences a manifest desire on the part of all States to proceed to the codification of that law on a universal basis, including the question of fisheries and conservation of the living resources of the sea. Such a general desire is understandable since the rules of international maritime law have been the product of mutual accommodation, reasonableness and co-operation. So it was in the past, and so it necessarily is today. In the circumstances, the Court, as a court of law, cannot render judgment *sub specie legis ferendae*, or anticipate the law before the legislator has laid it down.

54. The concept of a 12-mile fishery zone, referred to in paragraph 52 above, as a *tertium genus* between the territorial sea and the high seas, has been accepted with regard to Iceland in the substantive provisions of the 1961 Exchange of Notes, and the United Kingdom has also applied the same fishery limit to its own coastal waters since 1964; therefore this matter is no longer in dispute between the Parties. At the same time, the concept of preferential rights, a notion that necessarily implies the existence of other legal rights in respect of which that preference operates, has been admitted by the Applicant to be relevant to the solution of the present dispute. Moreover, the Applicant has expressly recognized Iceland's preferential rights in the disputed waters and at the same time has invoked its own historic fishing rights in these same waters, on the ground that reasonable regard must be had to such traditional rights by the coastal State, in accordance with the generally recognized principles embodied in Article 2 of the High Seas Convention. If, as the Court pointed out in its dictum in the *Fisheries* case, cited in paragraph 49 above, any national delimitation of sea areas, to be opposable to other States, requires evaluation in terms of the existing rules of international law, then it becomes necessary

for the Court, in its examination of the Icelandic fisheries Regulations, to take those elements into consideration as well. Equally it has necessarily to take into account the provisions of the Exchange of Notes of 1961 which govern the relations between the Parties with respect to Iceland's fishery limits. The said Exchange of Notes, which was concluded within the framework of the existing provisions of the law of the sea, [is] a treaty which is valid and in force.

55. The concept of preferential rights for the coastal State in a situation of special dependence on coastal fisheries originated in proposals submitted by Iceland at the Geneva Conference of 1958. Its delegation drew attention to the problem which would arise when, in spite of adequate fisheries conservation measures, the yield ceased to be sufficient to satisfy the requirements of all those who were interested in fishing in a given area. Iceland contended that in such a case, when a catch-limitation becomes necessary, special consideration should be given to the coastal State whose population is overwhelmingly dependent on the fishing resources in its adjacent waters.

56. An Icelandic proposal embodying these ideas failed to obtain the majority required, but a resolution was adopted at the 1958 Conference concerning the situation of countries or territories whose people are overwhelmingly dependent upon coastal fisheries for their livelihood or economic development. This resolution, after "recognizing that such situations call for exceptional measures befitting particular needs" recommended that:

> ... where, for the purpose of conservation, it becomes necessary to limit the total catch of a stock or stocks of fish in an area of the high seas adjacent to the territorial sea of a coastal State, any other States fishing in that area should collaborate with the coastal State to secure just treatment of such situation, by establishing agreed measures which shall recognize any preferential requirements of the coastal State resulting from its dependence upon the fishery concerned while having regard to the interests of the other States.

The resolution further recommended that "appropriate conciliation and arbitral procedures shall be established for the settlement of any disagreement."

57. At the Plenary Meetings of the 1960 Conference the concept of preferential rights was embodied in a joint amendment presented by Brazil, Cuba and Uruguay which was subsequently incorporated by a substantial vote into a joint United States-Canadian proposal concerning a 6-mile territorial sea and an additional 6-mile fishing zone, thus totaling a 12-mile exclusive fishing zone, subject to a phasing-out period. This amendment provided, independently of the exclusive fishing zone, that the coastal State had:

> . . . the faculty of claiming preferential fishing rights in any area of the high seas adjacent to its exclusive fishing zone when it is scientifically established that a special situation or condition makes the exploitation of the living resources of the high seas in that area of fundamental importance to the economic development of the coastal State or the feeding of its population.

It also provided that:

> A special situation or condition may be deemed to exist when:
>
> (*a*) The fisheries and the economic development of the coastal State or the feeding of its population are so manifestly interrelated that, in consequence, that State is greatly dependent on the living resources of the high seas in the area in respect of which preferential fishing is being claimed;
>
> (*b*) It becomes necessary to limit the total catch of a stock or stocks of fish in such areas . . .

The contemporary practice of States leads to the conclusion that the preferential rights of the coastal State in a special situation are to be implemented by agreement between the States concerned, either bilateral or multilateral, and, in case of disagreement, through the means for the peaceful settlement of disputes provided for in Article 33 of the Charter of the United Nations. It was in fact an express condition of the amendment referred to above that any other State concerned would have the right to request that a claim made by a coastal State should be tested and determined by a special commission on the basis of scientific criteria and of evidence presented by the coastal State and other States concerned. The commission was to be empowered to determine, for the period of time and under the limitations that it found necessary, the preferential rights of the coastal State, "while having regard to the interests of any other State or States in the exploitation of such stock or stocks of fish."

58. State practice on the subject of fisheries reveals an increasing and widespread acceptance of the concept of preferential rights for coastal States, particularly in favour of countries or territories in a situation of special dependence on coastal fisheries. Both the 1958 Resolution and the 1960 joint amendment concerning preferential rights were approved by a large majority of the Conferences, thus showing overwhelming support for the idea that in certain special situations it was fair to recognize that the coastal State had preferential fishing rights. After these Conferences, the preferential rights of the coastal State were recognized in various bilateral and multilateral international agreements. [Two regional agreements concluded in the 1970s,] in allocating the annual shares on the basis of the past performance of the parties in the

area, assign an additional share to the coastal State on the ground of its preferential right in the fisheries in its adjacent waters. The [1973 Arrangement relating to Fisheries in Waters Surrounding the Faroe Islands] takes expressly into account in its preamble "the exceptional dependence of the Faroese economy on fisheries" and recognizes "that the Faroe Islands should enjoy preference in waters surrounding the Faroe Islands."

59. There can be no doubt of the exceptional dependence of Iceland on its fisheries. That exceptional dependence was explicitly recognized by the Applicant in the Exchange of Notes of 11 March 1961, and the Court has also taken judicial notice of such recognition, by declaring that it is "necessary to bear in mind the exceptional dependence of the Icelandic nation upon coastal fisheries for its livelihood and economic development" (*I.C.J. Reports 1972*, p. 16, para. 23).

60. The preferential rights of the coastal State come into play only at the moment when an intensification in the exploitation of fishery resources make it imperative to introduce some system of catch-limitation and sharing of those resources, to preserve the fish stocks in the interests of their rational and economic exploitation. This situation appears to have been reached in the present case....

61. The Icelandic regulations challenged before the Court have been issued and applied by the Icelandic authorities as a claim to exclusive rights thus going beyond the concept of preferential rights. Article 2 of the Icelandic Regulations of 14 July 1972 states:

> Within the fishery limits all fishing activities by foreign vessels shall be prohibited in accordance with the provisions of Law No. 33 of 19 June 1922, concerning Fishing inside the Fishery Limits.

Article 1 of the 1922 Law provides: "Only Icelandic citizens may engage in fishing in the territorial waters of Iceland, and only Icelandic boats or ships may be used for such fishing."...

62. The concept of preferential rights is not compatible with the exclusion of all fishing activities of other States. A coastal State entitled to preferential rights is not free, unilaterally and according to its own uncontrolled discretion, to determine the extent of those rights. The characterization of the coastal State's rights as preferential implies a certain priority, but cannot imply the extinction of the concurrent rights of other States, and particularly of a State which, like the Applicant, has for many years been engaged in fishing in the waters in question, such fishing activity being important to the economy of the country concerned. The coastal State has to take into account and pay regard to the position of such other States, particularly when they

have established an economic dependence on the same fishing grounds. Accordingly, the fact that Iceland is entitled to claim preferential rights does not suffice to justify its claim unilaterally to exclude the Applicant's fishing vessels from all fishing activity in the waters beyond the limits agreed to in the 1961 Exchange of Notes.

63. In this case, the Applicant has pointed out that its vessels have been fishing in Icelandic waters for centuries and that they have done so in a manner comparable with their present activities for upwards of 50 years. Published statistics indicate that from 1920 onwards, fishing of demersal [bottomfeeding] species by United Kingdom vessels in the disputed area has taken place on a continuous basis from year to year, and that, except for the period of the Second World War, the total catch of those vessels has been remarkably steady. Similar statistics indicate that the waters in question constitute the most important of the Applicant's distant-water fishing grounds for demersal species.

64. The Applicant further states that in view of the present situation of fisheries in the North Atlantic, which has demanded the establishment of agreed catch-limitations of cod and haddock in various areas, it would not be possible for the fishing effort of United Kingdom vessels displaced from the Icelandic area to be diverted at economic levels to other fishing grounds in the North Atlantic. Given the lack of alternative fishing opportunity, it is further contended, the exclusion of British fishing vessels from the Icelandic area would have very serious adverse consequences, with immediate results for the affected vessels and with damage extending over a wide range of supporting and related industries. It is pointed out in particular that wide-spread unemployment would be caused among all sections of the British fishing industry and in ancillary industries and that certain ports—Hull, Grimsby and Fleetwood—specially reliant on fishing in the Icelandic area, would be seriously affected.

65. Iceland has for its part admitted the existence of the Applicant's historic and special interests in the fishing in the disputed waters. [The Court supports this statement by quoting a 1971 statement by the Prime Minister of Iceland and drawing inferences from the 1961 Exchange of Notes.]

66. Considerations similar to those which have prompted the recognition of the preferential rights of the coastal State in a special situation apply when coastal populations in other fishing States are also dependent on certain fishing grounds. In both instances the economic dependence and the livelihood of whole communities are affected. Not only do the same considerations apply, but the same interest in conservation exists. In this respect the Applicant has recognized that the conservation and efficient exploitation of the fish stocks

in the Iceland area are of importance not only to Iceland but also to the United Kingdom.

67. The provisions of the Icelandic Regulations of 14 July 1972 and the manner of their implementation disregard the fishing rights of the Applicant. Iceland's unilateral action thus constitutes an infringement of the principle enshrined in Article 2 of the 1958 Geneva Convention on the High Seas which requires that all States, including coastal States, in exercising their freedom of fishing, pay reasonable regard to the interests of other States. It also disregards the rights of the Applicant as they result from the Exchange of Notes of 1961. The Applicant is therefore justified in asking the Court to give all necessary protection to its own rights, while at the same time agreeing to recognize Iceland's preferential position. Accordingly, the Court is bound to conclude that the Icelandic Regulations of 14 July 1972 establishing a zone of exclusive fisheries jurisdiction extending to 50 nautical miles from baselines around the coast of Iceland, are not opposable to the United Kingdom, and the latter is under no obligation to accept the unilateral termination by Iceland of United Kingdom fishery rights in the area.

68. The findings stated by the Court in the preceding paragraphs suffice to provide a basis for the decision of the present case, namely: that Iceland's extension of its exclusive fishery jurisdiction beyond 12 miles is not opposable to the United Kingdom; that Iceland may on the other hand claim preferential rights in the distribution of fishery resources in the adjacent waters; that the United Kingdom also has established rights with respect to the fishery resources in question; and that the principle of reasonable regard for the interests of other States enshrined in Article 2 of the Geneva Convention on the High Seas of 1958 requires Iceland and the United Kingdom to have due regard to each other's interests, and to the other States, in those resources.

69. It follows from the reasoning of the Court in this case that in order to reach an equitable solution of the present dispute it is necessary that the preferential fishing rights of Iceland, as a State specially dependent on coastal fisheries, be reconciled with the traditional fishing rights of the Applicant. Such a reconciliation cannot be based, however, on a phasing-out of the Applicant's fishing, as was the case in the 1961 Exchange of Notes in respect of the 12-mile fishery zone. In that zone, Iceland was to exercise exclusive fishery rights while not objecting to continued fishing by the Applicant's vessels during a phasing-out period. In adjacent waters outside that zone, however, a similar extinction of rights of other fishing States, particularly when such rights result from a situation of economic dependence and long-term reliance on certain fishing grounds, would not be compatible with the notion of preferential rights as it was recognized at the Geneva Conferences of 1958 and 1960, nor would it be

equitable. At the 1960 Conference, the concept of preferential rights of coastal States in a special situation was recognized in the joint amendment referred to in paragraph 57 above, under such limitations and to such extent as is found "necessary by reason of the dependence of the coastal State on the stock or stocks of fish, while having regard to the interests of any other State or States in the exploitation of such stock or stocks of fish." The reference to the interests of other States in the exploitation of the same stocks clearly indicates that the preferential rights of the coastal State and the established rights of other States were considered as, in principle, continuing to co-exist.

70. This is not to say that the preferential rights of a coastal State in a special situation are a static concept, in the sense that the degree of the coastal State's preference is to be considered as fixed for ever at some given moment. On the contrary, the preferential rights are a function of the exceptional dependence of such a coastal State on the fisheries in adjacent waters and may, therefore, vary as the extent of that dependence changes. Furthermore, as was expressly recognized in the 1961 Exchange of Notes, a coastal State's exceptional dependence on fisheries may relate not only to the livelihood of its people but to its economic development. In each case, it is essentially a matter of appraising the dependence of the coastal State on the fisheries in question in relation to that of the other State concerned and of reconciling them in as equitable a manner as is possible.

[Additional language appears in paragraph 62 of the Germany-Iceland Fisheries Jurisdiction case, which corresponds to the above paragraph 70 in the United Kingdom-Iceland case. Paragraph 62 addresses slight differences in wording between the 1961 Iceland-United Kingdom Exchange of Notes and the 1961 Iceland-Germany Exchange of Notes. Paragraph 62 (1974 I.C.J. at 199–200) also provides in part:

> It has been suggested by the Applicant that a situation of exceptional dependence on fisheries for purposes of economic development could only exist in respect of States which are still in a stage of development and have only a minor share in the fisheries off their coasts. Such States undoubtedly afford clear examples of special dependence; however, in the present case the recognition of the exceptional importance of coastal fisheries to the Icelandic economy was made at a time when Iceland was already a State with a comparatively developed economy and possessed a substantial share in the exploitation of the fisheries off its coasts. It is therefore not possible to accept the limited interpretation of the expression employed in the 1961 Exchange of Notes suggested by Applicant.]

71. In view of the Court's finding (paragraph 67 above) that the Icelandic Regulations of 14 July 1972 are not opposable to the United Kingdom for the reasons which have been stated, it follows that the Government of Iceland is not in law entitled unilaterally to exclude United Kingdom fishing vessels from sea areas to seaward of the limits agreed to in the 1961 Exchange of Notes or unilaterally to impose restrictions on their activities in such areas. But the matter does not end there; as the Court has indicated, Iceland is, in view of its special situation entitled to preferential rights in respect of the fish stocks of the waters adjacent to its coasts. Due recognition must be given to the rights of both Parties, namely the rights of the United Kingdom to fish in the waters in dispute, and the preferential rights of Iceland. Neither right is an absolute one; the preferential rights of a coastal State are limited according to the extent of its special dependence on the fisheries and by its obligation to take account of the rights of other States and the needs of conservation; the established rights of other fishing States are in turn limited by reason of the coastal State's special dependence on the fisheries and [their] own obligation to take account of the rights of other States, including the coastal State, and of the needs of conservation.

72. ... It is one of the advances in maritime international law, resulting from the intensification of fishing, that the former *laissez-faire* treatment of the living resources of the sea in the high seas has been replaced by a recognition of a duty to have due regard to the rights of other States and the needs of conservation for the benefit of all. Consequently, both Parties have the obligation to keep under review the fishery resources in the disputed waters and to examine together, in the light of scientific and other available information, the measures required for the conservation and development, and equitable exploitation, of those resources, taking into account any international agreement in force between them such as the North-East Atlantic Fisheries Convention of 24 January 1959, as well as such other agreements as may be reached in the matter in the course of further negotiation.

73. The most appropriate method for the solution of the dispute is clearly that of negotiation. Its objective should be the delimitation of the rights and interests of the Parties, the preferential rights of the coastal State on the one hand and the rights of the Applicant on the other, to balance and regulate equitably questions such as those of catch-limitation, share allocations and "related restrictions concerning areas closed to fishing, number and type of vessels allowed and forms of control of the agreed provisions" (*Fisheries Jurisdiction (United Kingdom v. Iceland), Interim Measures, Order of 12 July 1973, I.C.J. Reports 1973*, p. 303, para. 7). This necessitates detailed scientific knowledge

of the fishing grounds. It is obvious that the relevant information and expertise would be mainly in the possession of the Parties. The Court would, for this reason, meet with difficulties if it were itself to attempt to lay down a precise scheme for an equitable adjustment of the rights involved. . . .

74. It is implicit in the concept of preferential rights that negotiations are required in order to define or delimit the extent of those rights, as was already recognized in the 1958 Geneva Resolution on Special Situations relating to Coastal Fisheries, which constituted the starting point of the law on the subject. This Resolution provides for the establishment, through collaboration between the coastal State and any other State fishing in the area, of agreed measures to secure just treatment of the special situation.

75. The obligation to negotiate thus flows from the very nature of the respective rights of the Parties; to direct them to negotiate is therefore a proper exercise of the judicial function in this case. This also corresponds to the principles and provisions of the Charter of the United Nations concerning peaceful settlement of disputes. As the Court stated in the *North Sea Continental Shelf* cases:

> . . . this obligation merely constitutes a special application of a principle which underlies all international relations, and which is moreover recognized in Article 33 of the Charter of the United Nations as one of the methods for the peaceful settlement of international disputes (*I.C.J. Reports 1969*, p. 47, para. 86).

76. In this case negotiations were initiated by the Parties from the date when Iceland gave notice of its intention to extend its fisheries jurisdiction, but these negotiations reached an early deadlock, and could not come to any conclusion; subsequently, further negotiations were directed to the conclusion of the interim agreement of 13 November 1973. The obligation to seek a solution of the dispute by peaceful means, among which negotiations are the most appropriate to this case, has not been eliminated by the interim agreement. . . .

78. In the fresh negotiations which are to take place on the basis of the present Judgment, the Parties will have the benefit of the above appraisal of their respective rights, and of certain guidelines defining their scope. The task before them will be to conduct their negotiations on the basis that each must in good faith pay reasonable regard to the legal rights of the other in the waters around Iceland outside the 12-mile limit, thus bringing about an equitable apportionment of the fishing resources based on the facts of the particular situation, and having regard to the interests of other States which have established fishing rights in the area. It is not a matter of finding simply

an equitable solution, but an equitable solution derived from the applicable law. As the Court stated in the *North Sea Continental Shelf* cases:

> ... it is not a question of applying equity simply as a matter of abstract justice, but of applying a rule of law which itself requires the application of equitable principles (*I.C.J. Reports 1969*, p. 47, para. 85).

79. For these reasons,

THE COURT,

by ten votes to four,

(1) finds that the Regulations concerning the Fishery Limits off Iceland... promulgated by the Government of Iceland on 14 July 1972 and constituting a unilateral extension of the exclusive fishing rights of Iceland to 50 nautical miles from the baselines specified therein are not opposable to the Government of the United Kingdom;

(2) finds that, in consequence, the Government of Iceland is not entitled unilaterally to exclude United Kingdom fishing vessels from areas between the fishery limits agreed to in the Exchange of Notes of 11 March 1961 and the limits specified in the Icelandic Regulations of 14 July 1972, or unilaterally to impose restrictions on the activities of those vessels in such areas;

by ten votes to four,

(3) holds that the Government of Iceland and the Government of the United Kingdom are under mutual obligations to undertake negotiations in good faith for the equitable solution of their differences concerning their respective fishery rights in the areas specified in subparagraph 2;

(4) holds that in these negotiations the Parties are to take into account, *inter alia*:

(*a*) that in the distribution of the fishing resources in the areas specified in subparagraph 2 Iceland is entitled to a preferential share to the extent of the special dependence of its people upon the fisheries in the seas around its coasts for their livelihood and economic development;

(*b*) that by reason of its fishing activities in the areas specified in subparagraph 2, the United Kingdom also has established rights in the fishery resources of the said areas on which elements of its people depend for their livelihood and economic well-being;

(*c*) the obligation to pay due regard to the interests of other States in the conservation and equitable exploitation of these resources;

(*d*) that the above-mentioned rights of Iceland and of the United Kingdom should each be given effect to the extent compatible with the conservation and development of the fishery resources in the areas specified in subparagraph 2 and with the interests of other States in their conservation and equitable exploitation;

(*e*) their obligation to keep under review those resources and to examine together, in the light of scientific and other available information, such measures as may be required for the conservation and development, and equitable exploitation, of those resources, making use of the machinery established by the North-East Atlantic Fisheries Convention or such other means as may be agreed upon as a result of international negotiations.

Notes

1. *The Cod Wars.* During the so-called Cod Wars, Iceland boarded British vessels, arrested British fishermen, and cut the nets of British trawlers. The United Kingdom sent frigates to escort and protect British trawlers off Iceland. There were shooting and ramming incidents. Tensions were particularly high during 1958–1961, after Iceland extended its fisheries zone from four to twelve nautical miles, and during 1972–1973, after Iceland declared a 50-nautical-mile fisheries zone. Iceland's 1972 decisions to extend its fisheries zone and to denounce its 1961 agreement with the United Kingdom followed the 1971 Icelandic election, in which the Agrarian Progressive Party, which had made fisheries jurisdiction a major campaign issue, emerged as the head of a new coalition government.

Rejecting the decision in the Fisheries Jurisdiction case, Iceland extended its fishing limits from 50 to 200 nautical miles in 1975. Regulations Concerning the Fishery Limits off Iceland, July 15, 1975, 14 Intl. Leg. Materials 1282 (1975). This extension resulted in further clashes involving British and Icelandic naval units. Other states became concerned the controversy might lead Iceland to withdraw from the North Atlantic Treaty Organization and to shut down a NATO military base in Iceland that was used to monitor Soviet vessels. In June 1976, Iceland and the United Kingdom finally reached an Agreement Concerning British Fishing in Icelandic Waters, allowing British fishing within the 200-nautical-mile limit, but at a substantially reduced level. Iceland also concluded bilateral fishing agreements with Belgium, the Federal Republic of Germany, and Norway during 1975 and 1976. For perspectives on the Cod Wars, see Hannes Jónsson, Friends in Conflict: The Anglo-Icelandic Cod Wars and the Law of the Sea (1982), and Andrew Welch, The Royal Navy in the Cod Wars: Britain and Iceland in Conflict (2006).

2. *The 1958 Fishing on the High Seas Convention.* The ICJ stressed that, as a court of law, it could only rely on de lege lata, i.e., the law as it exists, as opposed to de lege ferenda, i.e., the law as it should be. At the time the ICJ was deciding the Fisheries Jurisdiction case, the 1958 Fishing on the High Seas Convention was the most significant treaty concerning fisheries beyond the territorial sea. This Convention does not create an exclusive fishing zone for the coastal state beyond its territorial sea, but rather, as suggested by its title referring explicitly to the high seas, grants special rights to these states in the conservation, management, and exploitation of fisheries in areas along their coasts contiguous to the territorial sea. Contrary to the Truman Proclamation regarding fisheries, discussed above, the 1958 Fishing on the High Seas Convention provides for a compulsory dispute settlement mechanism in case the coastal state and other states whose nationals fished in any area of the high seas adjacent to the territorial sea of the former cannot reach an agreement. According to Article 9, any dispute arising out of the application of conservation measures is to be settled by a special commission, the members of which are to be appointed by agreement between the states in dispute or, failing such agreement, by the Secretary-General of the United Nations, "in consultation with the States in dispute and the President of the International Court of Justice and the Director-General of the Food and Agriculture Organization of the United Nations." However, of the four law of the sea conventions adopted in 1958, this one has secured the fewest ratifications (as of September 1, 2013, 39 states, including the United States, are parties). The 1958 Fishing on the High Seas Convention was not binding on the parties in the Fisheries Jurisdiction case as treaty law: the United Kingdom had ratified the Convention in 1960; Iceland, although it had signed the Convention in 1958, never ratified it; Germany never signed or ratified it.

3. *The ICJ's View of Rights to Fisheries.* How satisfactorily did the ICJ, in 1974, bridge the gap between, on the one hand, existing codified and customary international law and, on the other hand, the clear indications of developments in state practice as evidenced by the negotiations taking place at UNCLOS III? Was the Court persuasive in claiming that existing international law provided preferential rights for coastal states as well as rights for states such as the United Kingdom that had historically fished off Iceland? How does the Court's invocation of equity compare with its use of equity in its maritime delimitation cases excerpted in Chapter 6? The Court concluded that Iceland and the United Kingdom should negotiate a settlement of their differences over rights to fisheries. Did this procedural recourse suggest that, at base, there

was a lack of consensus on the substantive values that would shape any norm of international law on this issue? Was the Court more interested in trying to help Britain and Iceland resolve this particular dispute than in articulating a rule of general international law?

4. *Customary International Law and Coastal State Fisheries Jurisdiction.* Judges Forster, Bengzon, Jimenez de Arechaga, Nagendra Singh, and Ruda concurred separately in the Fisheries Jurisdiction case. Although those judges agreed with the result in the majority opinion and found that a twelve-nautical-mile fisheries zone was generally accepted in international law, they did not consider that any rule of customary international law established twelve nautical miles as the obligatory maximum limit. The judges argued that 30 to 35 coastal states had extended their fisheries jurisdiction beyond twelve nautical miles, and noted the general lack of protests to such extensions and the existence of public pronouncements inconsistent with making any protest. The concurring judges also cited declarations and proposals made at the then-ongoing UNCLOS III. They questioned whether, on "a subject where practice was contradictory and lacks precision," it was "reasonable to discard entirely as irrelevant the evidence of what States are prepared to claim and to acquiesce in, as gathered from the positions taken by them in view of or in preparation for a conference for the codification and progressive development of the law on the subject." 1974 I.C.J. at 48. Finally, the judges lamented the legal uncertainty at the time regarding the maximum limit of coastal state fisheries jurisdiction, and expressed the hope that the matter would be clarified at UNCLOS III.

B The Exclusive Economic Zone and Customary International Law

Together with the Area, the EEZ is a creation of the LOS Convention that complements the maritime zones as codified in 1958 at UNCLOS I. The EEZ conception fundamentally changed the existing international law applicable to fisheries. In the past most living resources had been governed by the principle of the freedom of fishing applicable on the high seas. See 1958 High Seas Convention, Article 2. By attributing sovereign rights to the coastal state for the exploration and exploitation of the living resources in a 200-nautical-mile zone, however, Articles 56–57 of the LOS Convention subjected more than 95 per cent of all commercially exploited fish resources to the conservation and management of the coastal states. This section will assess how this new concept quickly became part of customary international law in a rather atypical manner. It will do so by analyzing the decisions of the highest judicial organ of the United Nations as well as the state practice of the only major maritime power that voted against the LOS Convention in 1982 and that continues to be a non-party today, namely the United States.

TUNISIA/LIBYA CONTINENTAL SHELF CASE
1982 I.C.J. 18, 74

[For background on this case, see Chapter 6, Section B.]

100. . . . While it may be that Tunisia's historic rights and titles are more nearly related to the concept of the exclusive economic zone, which may be regarded as part of modern international law, Tunisia has not chosen to base its claims upon that concept.

Note

1. *Judicial Decisions as a Source of International Law.* The Special Agreement concluded between Tunisia and Libya in order to bring the case before the ICJ clearly specified that the Court should only determine the principles governing the delimitation of the seabed and the subsoil, not of the superjacent waters. Its Article 1 read:

> The Court is requested to render its Judgment in the following matter: What are the principles and rules of international law which may be applied for the delimitation of the area of the continental shelf appertaining to the Republic of Tunisia and the area of the continental shelf appertaining to the Socialist People's Libyan Arab Jamahiriya and, in rendering its decision, to take account of equitable principles and the relevant circumstances which characterize the area, as well as the recent trends admitted at the Third Conference on the Law of the Sea.

1982 I.C.J. at 21.

Nevertheless, in a classical example of an obiter dictum the ICJ inserted a statement on the nature of the EEZ in a sub-phrase at the very end of a long paragraph devoted to historic rights and title. What is the legal significance of such a digression, especially in view of the fact that Article 59 of the ICJ Statute specifies that its decisions have no binding force except between the parties and in respect of the particular case before it?

Note the careful language used by the ICJ ("may be regarded"), which contrasts sharply with the following passage to be found in the separate opinion of Judge Jiménez de Aréchaga:

> The provisions of the negotiating texts and of the draft convention, and the consensus which emerged at the Conference, have had in this respect a constitutive or generating legal effect, serving as the focal point for and as the authoritative guide to a consistent and uniform practice of States. The proclamation by 86 coastal States of economic zones, fishery zones or fishery conservation zones, made in conformity with the texts of the Conference, constitutes a widespread practice of States which has hardened into a customary rule, an irreversible part of today's law of the sea.

1982 I.C.J. at 115, ¶ 54. Why did this much more assertive statement not find its way into the Court's opinion? Could the fact that the decision was rendered when the LOS Convention had not yet been signed (which happened later the same year) help to explain the ICJ's rather cautious approach?

EXCLUSIVE ECONOMIC ZONE OF THE UNITED STATES OF AMERICA
Presidential Proclamation No. 5030, Mar. 10, 1983, 48 Fed. Reg. 10605 (1983), 19 Weekly Comp. 385, 22 Intl. Leg. Materials 465 (1983)

Whereas the Government of the United States of America desires to facilitate the wise development and use of the oceans consistent with international law;

Whereas international law recognizes that, in a zone beyond its territory and adjacent to its territorial sea, known as the Exclusive Economic Zone, a coastal State may assert certain sovereign rights over natural resources and related jurisdiction; and

Whereas the establishment of an Exclusive Economic Zone by the United States will advance the development of ocean resources and promote the protection of the marine environment, while not affecting other lawful uses of the zone, including the freedoms of navigation and overflight, by other States;

Now, Therefore, I, Ronald Reagan, by the authority vested in me as President by the Constitution and laws of the United States of America, do hereby proclaim the sovereign rights and jurisdiction of the United States of America and confirm also the rights and freedoms of all States within an Exclusive Economic Zone, as described herein.

The Exclusive Economic Zone of the United States is a zone contiguous to the territorial sea, including zones contiguous to the territorial sea of the United States, the Commonwealth of Puerto Rico, the Commonwealth of the Northern Mariana Islands (to the extent consistent with the Covenant and the United Nations Trusteeship Agreement), and United States overseas territories and possessions. The Exclusive Economic Zone extends to a distance

200 nautical miles from the baseline from which the breadth of the territorial sea is measured. In cases where the maritime boundary with a neighboring State remains to be determined, the boundary of the Exclusive Economic Zone shall be determined by the United States and other State concerned in accordance with equitable principles.

Within the Exclusive Economic Zone, the United States has, to the extent permitted by international law, (a) sovereign rights for the purpose of exploring, exploiting, conserving and managing natural resources, both living and non-living, of the seabed and subsoil and the superjacent waters and with regard to other activities for the economic exploitation and exploration of the zone, such as the production of energy from the water, currents and winds; and (b) jurisdiction with regard to the establishment and use of artificial islands, and installations and structures having economic purposes, and the protection and preservation of the marine environment.

This Proclamation does not change existing United States policies concerning the continental shelf, marine mammals and fisheries, including highly migratory species of tuna which are not subject to United States jurisdiction and require international agreements for effective management.

The United States will exercise these sovereign rights and jurisdiction in accordance with the rules of international law.

Without prejudice to the sovereign rights and jurisdiction of the United States, the Exclusive Economic Zone remains an area beyond the territory and territorial sea of the United States in which all States enjoy the high seas freedoms of navigation, overflight, the laying of submarine cables and pipelines, and other internationally lawful uses of the sea.

Notes

1. *The Reagan Proclamation and the Development of Customary Law.* In a statement accompanying his EEZ Proclamation, President Reagan announced that the LOS Convention "contains provisions with respect to traditional uses of the oceans which generally confirm existing maritime law and practice and fairly balance the interests of all states." 22 Intl. Leg. Materials 461, 464 (1983). Why did the United States seem to insist that the content of this Reagan Proclamation was based on customary international law? How does the U.S. position relate to the package deal approach that had characterized UNCLOS III? What is the Reagan Proclamation's influence on the development of customary international law? See also the next excerpt in this respect.

2. *The U.S. EEZ.* The United States has an extensive coastline along its mainland and Alaska. Note also President Reagan's assertion of a U.S. EEZ

contiguous to the territorial sea of "the Commonwealth of Puerto Rico, the Commonwealth of the Northern Mariana Islands . . . and United States overseas territories and possessions." Which islands can support an EEZ, according to the LOS Convention? See Article 121. The asserted U.S. EEZ encompassed a vast area (some 2,083,400 square nautical miles, larger than the EEZ of any other country), a vast volume of water, and many metric tons of fisheries.

DELIMITATION OF THE MARITIME BOUNDARY IN THE GULF OF MAINE AREA

Canada/United States, 1984 I.C.J. 246, 294

[By Special Agreement dated March 29, 1979, Canada and the United States requested a Special Chamber of the ICJ to draw, in the Gulf of Maine area, a single line to delimit both the continental shelf and the 200-nautical-mile exclusive fishery zone. The Chamber notes that in the North Sea Continental Shelf cases and the Tunisia/Libya Continental Shelf case, the Court had been asked only to indicate the principles and rules of law applicable to those delimitations, rather than actually to draw the line, as the parties requested in this case. The Chamber also points out two other differences between this case and those previous cases: the delimitation did not relate exclusively to the continental shelf, but to both the continental shelf and the exclusive fishery zone; and the delimitation was to be by a single boundary.]

94. Turning lastly to the proceedings of the Third United Nations Conference on the Law of the Sea and the final result of that Conference, the Chamber notes in the first place that the Convention adopted at the end of the Conference has not yet come into force and that a number of States do not appear inclined to ratify it. This, however, in no way detracts from the consensus reached on large portions of the instrument and, above all, cannot invalidate the observation that certain provisions of the Convention, concerning the continental shelf and the exclusive economic zone, which may, in fact, be relevant to the present case, were adopted without any objections. The United States, in particular, in 1983, that is to say after the Special Agreement had come into force, proclaimed an economic zone on the basis of Part V of the 1982 Convention. This proclamation was accompanied by a statement by the President to the effect that in that respect the Convention generally confirmed existing rules of international law. Canada, which has not at present made a similar proclamation, has for its part also recognized the legal significance of the nature and purpose of the new 200-mile régime. This concordance of views is worthy of note, even though the present Judgment is not directed to the delimitation of the exclusive economic zone as such. In the Chamber's

opinion, these provisions, even if in some respects they bear the mark of the compromise surrounding their adoption, may nevertheless be regarded as consonant at present with general international law on the question.

Note

1. *The Relationship between State Practice and Court Decisions in the Development of Customary International Law.* Like the Continental Shelf case between Tunisia and Libya, the Gulf of Maine case did not concern delimitation of the EEZ (but rather the parties' "exclusive fishery zones"). Nevertheless the ICJ found it appropriate to make a statement about the EEZ. What evidence did the Court use to support its statement? Did the ICJ consider the state practice of the United States, described above, to be significant in the development of customary international law? What exactly did the ICJ conclude about the customary international law status of the EEZ? Note that the Court again used the word "may." Also, is it clear whether the Court was referring to the EEZ as a whole, or only to certain EEZ provisions of special interest to the ICJ, e.g., the delimitation provision? Was the authoritativeness of the Court's statement diminished because the Gulf of Maine decision was not rendered by the full ICJ, but only by a chamber?

LIBYA/MALTA CONTINENTAL SHELF CASE
1985 I.C.J. 13, 33

[For background on this case, see Chapter 6, Section B.]

34. ...It is in the Court's view incontestable that...the institution of the exclusive economic zone... is shown by the practice of States to have become a part of customary law.

Notes

1. *The Relationship between Customary Law and Codification.* Legal history indicates that customary law normally precedes written law. Also in international law, treaties often set down in writing pre-existing rules of customary law. In view of the fact that Canada had formally established an EEZ in 1997, why did the Special Agreement not mention the EEZ instead of the notion of "exclusive fishery zones"? Nevertheless, customary law can sometimes be created as a result of codification. The ICJ envisaged that possibility with respect to a convention that had already entered into force. See North Sea Continental Shelf cases, ¶ 70, excerpted in Chapter 1, Section B. By making a clear assertion about the

legal status of the EEZ in 1985, i.e., about a decade before the LOS Convention entered into force, the ICJ acknowledged that agreements not yet in force could also help generate customary international law.

In the Libya/Malta case the ICJ no longer used the term "may" to qualify its assertion about the legal status of the EEZ, and consequently it is this 1985 decision that is normally invoked to argue that the EEZ has become an integral part of customary international law. Consider, however, that in the Libya/Malta case, the ICJ based its jurisdiction on a Special Agreement, Article 1 of which closely resembled the Tunisia-Libya Special Agreement reproduced above—i.e., the ICJ was not asked to delimit the EEZ, but only the continental shelf.

2. *State Assertions of EEZs and 200-nautical-mile Fishery Zones.* Judge Jiménez de Aréchaga, in his separate opinion in the 1982 Tunisia/Libya case, reported that 86 coastal states had proclaimed economic zones or fishery zones. 1982 I.C.J. at 115, ¶ 54. By 1994, just as the LOS Convention entered into force, 93 states claimed a 200-nautical-mile EEZ (or one up to a median line with opposite states), and an additional fifteen countries claimed a 200-nautical-mile fishery zone. Law of the Sea: Report of the Secretary-General, UN Doc. A/49/631 at 11 (1994). As of July 15, 2011, the United Nations Division for Ocean Affairs and the Law of the Sea reports these figures are 131 and two respectively. See Table of Claims to Maritime Jurisdiction (as at 15 July 2011), available at http://www.un.org/Depts/los/LEGISLATIONANDTREATIES/PDFFILES/table_summary_of_claims.pdf. For maps and statistics concerning EEZs around the world, see Sea Around Us Project, Exclusive Economic Zone, http://www.seaaroundus.org/eez.

3. *Customary International Law as a Vehicle to Develop International Law.* Taking into account the 1985 ICJ pronouncement and the U.S. EEZ Proclamation reproduced above, along with the fact that a high percentage of coastal states at present do claim EEZs or fishery zones, is it safe to conclude that the whole Part V of the LOS Convention, entitled Exclusive Economic Zone and containing Articles 55–75, has become part and parcel of customary international law today?

C The Exclusive Economic Zone and its Application in Practice

Whether the EEZ is part of the high seas, although subject to special rights of coastal states, or rather part of the territorial sea subject to certain freedoms of the high seas such as navigation and overflight, was an issue that strongly divided the negotiators at UNCLOS III. Today, the EEZ is normally characterized as a tertium genus. It is part of neither the high seas nor the territorial sea, but rather forms a sui generis category. This is more than a semantic argument.

The LOS Convention does attribute rights or jurisdiction in the EEZ in certain cases, but can of course not do so for all present-day uses, much less for possible new future uses. Where attribution of rights or jurisdiction is not clear, we must ask whether residual competence resides with the coastal state, with flag states, or conceivably with some other entity. The LOS Convention tries to solve this issue by means of its Article 59, which calls for resolving conflicts concerning the attribution of rights in the EEZ "on the basis of equity and in the light of all the relevant circumstances."

THE M/V SAIGA (NO. 2) CASE

St. Vincent and the Grenadines v. Guinea (Admissibility and Merits), ITLOS Case No. 2 (1999), 3 ITLOS Rep. 10, 120 Intl. L. Rep. 143, 38 Intl. Leg. Materials 1323 (1999), available at http://www.itlos.org

[For background on this case, see Chapter 3, Section A.]

110. Saint Vincent and the Grenadines asserts that the arrest of the *Saiga* and the subsequent actions of Guinea were illegal. It contends that the arrest of the *Saiga* was unlawful because the ship did not violate any laws or regulations of Guinea that were applicable to it. It further maintains that, if the laws cited by Guinea did apply to the activities of the *Saiga*, those laws, as applied by Guinea, were incompatible with the Convention.

111. The laws invoked by Guinea as the basis for the arrest of the *Saiga* and the prosecution and conviction of its Master are the following:

(a) Law L/94/007;
(b) The Merchant Marine Code;
(c) The Customs Code;
(d) The Penal Code.

112. Articles 1, 4, 6 and 8 of Law L/94/007 read (in translation) as follows:

Article 1

> The import, transport, storage and distribution of fuel by any natural person or corporate body not legally authorized are prohibited in the Republic of Guinea.

[Articles 4, 6, and 8 of Law L/94/007 specify criminal penalties for unauthorized refueling and for the illegal importation of fuel into Guinea.]

113. Article 40 of the Merchant Marine Code reads (in translation) as follows:

> The Republic of Guinea exercises, within the exclusive economic zone which extends from the limit of the territorial sea to 188 nautical miles beyond that limit, sovereign rights concerning the exploration and exploitation, conservation and management of the natural resources, biological or non-biological, of the sea beds and their sub-soils, of the waters lying underneath, as well as the rights concerning other activities bearing on the exploration and exploitation of the zone for economic purposes.

114. Articles 1 and 34, paragraphs 1 and 2, of the Customs Code read (in translation) as follows:

> *Article 1*
>
> The customs territory includes the whole of the national territory, the islands located along the coastline and the Guinea territorial waters. However, free zones, exempt from all or some of the customs legislation and regulations, may be created within the customs territory.
>
> *Article 34*
>
> 1. The customs radius includes a marine area and a terrestrial area.
> 2. The marine area lies between the coastline and an outer limit located at sea 250 kilometres from the coast. . . .

116. The main charge against the *Saiga* was that it violated article 1 of Law L/94/007 by importing gas oil into the customs radius (*rayon des douanes*) of Guinea. Guinea justifies this action by maintaining that the prohibition in article 1 of Law L/94/007 "can be applied for the purpose of controlling and suppressing the sale of gas oil to fishing vessels in the customs radius according to article 34 of the Customs Code of Guinea." In support of this contention, Guinea declares that it is the consistent practice and the settled view of the courts of Guinea that the term "Guinea," referred to in article 1 of the Law L/94/007, includes the customs radius, and that, consequently, the prohibition of the import of gas oil into Guinea extends to the importation of such oil into any part of the customs radius. According to Guinea, the fact that the *Saiga* violated the laws of Guinea has been authoritatively established by the Court of Appeal. In its view, that decision cannot be questioned in this case because the Tribunal is not competent to consider the question whether the internal legislation of Guinea has been properly applied by the Guinean authorities or its courts. . . .

118. ... Saint Vincent and the Grenadines maintains that, on a correct interpretation of Law L/94/007 read with articles 1 and 34 of the Customs Code, the *Saiga* did not violate any laws of Guinea when it supplied gas oil to the fishing vessels in the exclusive economic zone of Guinea.

119. In the alternative, Saint Vincent and the Grenadines contends that the extension of the customs laws of Guinea to the exclusive economic zone is contrary to the Convention. It argues that article 56 of the Convention does not give the right to Guinea to extend the application of its customs laws and regulations to that zone. It therefore contends that Guinea's customs laws cannot be applied to ships flying its flag in the exclusive economic zone. Consequently, the measures taken by Guinea against the *Saiga* were unlawful.

120. In the view of the Tribunal, there is nothing to prevent it from considering the question whether or not, in applying its laws to the *Saiga* in the present case, Guinea was acting in conformity with its obligations towards Saint Vincent and the Grenadines under the Convention and general international law. In its Judgment in the *Case Concerning Certain German Interests in Polish Upper Silesia*, the Permanent Court of International Justice stated:

> From the standpoint of International Law and of the Court which is its organ, municipal laws are merely facts which express the will and constitute the activities of States, in the same manner as do legal decisions or administrative measures. The Court is certainly not called upon to interpret the Polish law as such; but there is nothing to prevent the Court's giving judgment on the question whether or not, in applying that law, Poland is acting in conformity with its obligations towards Germany under the Geneva Convention. (*Certain German Interests in Polish Upper Silesia, Merits, Judgment No. 7, 1926, P.C.I.J., Series A, No. 7*, p. 19)

121. A denial of the competence of the Tribunal to examine the applicability and scope of national law is even less acceptable in the framework of certain provisions of the Convention. One such provision, which is also relied upon by Guinea, is article 58, paragraph 3, which reads as follows:

> In exercising their rights and performing their duties under this Convention in the exclusive economic zone, States shall have due regard to the rights and duties of the coastal State and shall comply with the laws and regulations adopted by the coastal State in accordance with the provisions of this Convention and other rules of international law in so far as they are not incompatible with this Part.

Under this provision, the rights and obligations of coastal and other States under the Convention arise not just from the provisions of the Convention but also from national laws and regulations "adopted by the coastal State in accordance with the provisions of this Convention." Thus, the Tribunal is competent to determine the compatibility of such laws and regulations with the Convention.

122. The Tribunal notes that Guinea produces no evidence in support of its contention that the laws cited by it provide a basis for the action taken against the *Saiga* beyond the assertion that it reflects the consistent practice of its authorities, supported by its courts. Even if it is conceded that the laws of Guinea which the *Saiga* is alleged to have violated are applicable in the manner that is claimed by Guinea, the question remains whether these laws, as interpreted and applied by Guinea, are compatible with the Convention.

123. Saint Vincent and the Grenadines claims that, in applying its customs laws to the *Saiga* in its customs radius, which includes parts of the exclusive economic zone, Guinea acted contrary to the Convention. It contends that in the exclusive economic zone Guinea is not entitled to exercise powers which go beyond those provided for in articles 56 and 58 of the Convention. It further asserts that Guinea violated its rights to enjoy the freedom of navigation or other internationally lawful uses of the sea in the exclusive economic zone, since the supply of gas oil by the *Saiga* falls within the exercise of those rights.

124. Guinea denies that the application of its customs and contraband laws in its customs radius is contrary to the Convention or in violation of any rights of Saint Vincent and the Grenadines. It maintains that it is entitled to apply its customs and contraband laws to prevent the unauthorized sale of gas oil to fishing vessels operating in its exclusive economic zone. It further maintains that such supply is not part of the freedom of navigation under the Convention or an internationally lawful use of the sea related to the freedom of navigation but a commercial activity and that it does not, therefore, fall within the scope of article 58 of the Convention. For that reason, it asserts that the Guinean action against the *Saiga* was taken not because the ship was navigating in the exclusive economic zone of Guinea but because it was engaged in "unwarranted commercial activities."

125. Guinea further argues that the exclusive economic zone is not part of the high seas or of the territorial sea, but a zone with its own legal status (a *sui generis* zone). From this it concludes that rights or jurisdiction in the exclusive economic zone, which the Convention does not expressly attribute to the coastal States, do not automatically fall under the freedom of the high seas.

126. The Tribunal needs to determine whether the laws applied or the measures taken by Guinea against the *Saiga* are compatible with the Convention. In other words, the question is whether, under the Convention, there was justification for Guinea to apply its customs laws in the exclusive economic zone within a customs radius extending to a distance of 250 kilometres from the coast.

127. The Tribunal notes that, under the Convention, a coastal State is entitled to apply customs laws and regulations in its territorial sea (articles 2 and 21). In the contiguous zone, a coastal State may exercise the control necessary to:

> (a) prevent infringement of its customs, fiscal, immigration or sanitary laws and regulations within its territory or territorial sea;
> (b) punish infringement of the above laws and regulations committed within its territory on territorial sea. (article 33, paragraph 1)

In the exclusive economic zone, the coastal State has jurisdiction to apply customs laws and regulations in respect of artificial islands, installations and structures (article 60, paragraph 2). In the view of the Tribunal, the Convention does not empower a coastal State to apply its customs laws in respect of any other parts of the exclusive economic zone not mentioned above.

128. Guinea further argues that the legal basis of its law prohibiting the supply of gas oil to fishing vessels in the customs radius is to be found in article 58 of the Convention. It relies on the reference, contained in paragraph 3 of that article, to the "other rules of international law" to justify the application and enforcement of its customs and contraband laws to the customs radius. These "other rules of international law" are variously described by Guinea as "the inherent right to protect itself against unwarranted economic activities in its exclusive economic zone that considerably affect its public interest," or as the "doctrine of necessity," or as "the customary principle of self-protection in case of grave and imminent perils which endanger essential aspects of its public interest."

129. The Tribunal finds it necessary to distinguish between the two main concepts referred to in the submissions of Guinea. The first is a broad notion of "public interest" or "self-protection" which Guinea invokes to expand the scope of its jurisdiction in the exclusive economic zone, and the second is "state of necessity" which it relies on to justify measures that would otherwise be wrongful under the Convention.

130. The main public interest which Guinea claims to be protecting by applying its customs laws to the exclusive economic zone is said to be the

"considerable fiscal losses a developing country like Guinea is suffering from illegal off-shore bunkering in its exclusive economic zone." Guinea makes references also to fisheries and environmental interests. In effect, Guinea's contention is that the customary international law principle of "public interest" gives it the power to impede "economic activities that are undertaken [in its exclusive economic zone] under the guise of navigation but are different from communication."

131. According to article 58, paragraph 3, of the Convention, the "other rules of international law" which a coastal State is entitled to apply in the exclusive economic zone are those which are not incompatible with Part V of the Convention. In the view of the Tribunal, recourse to the principle of "public interest," as invoked by Guinea, would entitle a coastal State to prohibit any activities in the exclusive economic zone which it decides to characterize as activities which affect its economic "public interest" or entail "fiscal losses" for it. This would curtail the rights of other States in the exclusive economic zone. The Tribunal is satisfied that this would be incompatible with the provisions of articles 56 and 58 of the Convention regarding the rights of the coastal State in the exclusive economic zone.

132. It remains for the Tribunal to consider whether the otherwise wrongful application by Guinea of its customs laws to the exclusive economic zone can be justified under general international law by Guinea's appeal to "state of necessity."

133. In the *Case Concerning the Gabčíkovo-Nagymaros Project* (*Gabčíkovo-Nagymaros Project (Hungary/Slovakia), Judgment, I.C.J. Reports 1997*, pp. 40 and 41, paragraphs 51 and 52), the International Court of Justice noted with approval two conditions for the defence based on "state of necessity" which in general international law justifies an otherwise wrongful act. These conditions, as set out in article 33, paragraph 1, of the International Law Commission's Draft Articles on State Responsibility, are:

> (a) the act was the only means of safeguarding an essential interest of the State against a grave and imminent peril; and
> (b) the act did not seriously impair an essential interest of the State towards which the obligation existed.

134. In endorsing these conditions, the Court stated that they "must be cumulatively satisfied" and that they "reflect customary international law."

135. No evidence has been produced by Guinea to show that its essential interests were in grave and imminent peril. But, however essential Guinea's interest in maximizing its tax revenue from the sale of gas oil to fishing vessels,

it cannot be suggested that the only means of safeguarding that interest was to extend its customs laws to parts of the exclusive economic zone.

136. The Tribunal, therefore, finds that, by applying its customs laws to a customs radius which includes parts of the exclusive economic zone, Guinea acted in a manner contrary to the Convention. Accordingly, the arrest and detention of the *Saiga*, the prosecution and conviction of its Master, the confiscation of the cargo and the seizure of the ship were contrary to the Convention.

137. In their submissions, both parties requested the Tribunal to make declarations regarding the rights of coastal States and of other States in connection with offshore bunkering, i.e. the sale of gas oil to vessels at sea. The Tribunal notes that there is no specific provision on the subject in the Convention. Both parties appear to agree that, while the Convention attributes certain rights to coastal States and other States in the exclusive economic zone, it does not follow automatically that rights not expressly attributed to the coastal State belong to other States or, alternatively, that rights not specifically attributed to other States belong as of right to the coastal State. Saint Vincent and the Grenadines asks the Tribunal to adjudge and declare that bunkering in the exclusive economic zone by ships flying its flag constitutes the exercise of the freedom of navigation and other internationally lawful uses of the sea related to the freedom of navigation, as provided for in articles 56 and 58 of the Convention. On the other hand, Guinea maintains that "bunkering" is not an exercise of the freedom of navigation or any of the internationally lawful uses of the sea related to freedom of navigation, as provided for in the Convention, but a commercial activity. Guinea further maintains that bunkering in the exclusive economic zone may not have the same status in all cases and suggests that different considerations might apply, for example, to bunkering of ships operating in the zone, as opposed to the supply of oil to ships that are in transit.

138. The Tribunal considers that the issue that needed to be decided was whether the actions taken by Guinea were consistent with the applicable provisions of the Convention. The Tribunal has reached a decision on that issue on the basis of the law applicable to the particular circumstances of the case, without having to address the broader question of the rights of coastal States and other States with regard to bunkering in the exclusive economic zone. Consequently, it does not make any findings on that question.

Separate Opinion of Judge Zhao

I voted in favour of the Judgment in the *M/V "SAIGA" (No. 2)* case. However, I have my own opinion concerning the thorny issue of "bunkering and freedom of navigation."

1. The Applicant alleges that offshore bunkering is a global multi-million dollar industry involving all of the major oil companies and numerous independent companies. It tries to give the impression that bunkering is a lawful activity on the high seas falling within the freedom of navigation.

Indeed, some States or regions regard offshore bunkering as among their principal activities, as illustrated by the Applicant. This does not mean, however, that bunkering has become a universal practice of States. Far from it, among the 35 offshore bunkering companies illustrated by the Applicant, none is from the UK, France, Italy, Spain, Belgium or Austria in West Europe, or from East European or North American countries except one. None is from China, Russia, Japan, India, Indonesia, Brazil or Argentina, among others. Accordingly, bunkering can hardly be considered as a lawful global industry involving all the major companies.

2. This case presents the question whether bunkering fishing vessels in the contiguous zone or in the exclusive economic zone of a State is freedom of navigation or internationally lawful uses of the sea pursuant to article 58, paragraph 1, of the Convention. In other words, is bunkering an aspect of high-seas freedom of navigation?

Bunkering by its very nature is a means of evading customs duties of coastal States. The Applicant admits that it is usually preferable not to bunker in the territorial waters of a State because duties may be payable. The coastal States of West Africa were also well aware of the problem of "the control and regulation of customs and fiscal matters related to economic activities" in the exclusive economic zone, as the proposal of 18 African States at the Third United Nations Conference on the Law of the Sea and an earlier proposal by Nigeria demonstrate.

The word "navigation" means nothing but "the act of navigating" or "the making of voyages at sea." According to article 58, paragraph 1, of the Convention:

> In the exclusive economic zone, all States, whether coastal or land-locked, enjoy, subject to the relevant provisions of this Convention, the freedoms referred to in article 87 of navigation . . . and other internationally lawful uses of the sea related to these freedoms, such as those associated with the operation of ships . . .

Article 90 (right of navigation) also provides: "Every State, whether coastal or landlocked, has the right to sail ships flying its flag on the high seas." Not a single mention of bunkering or the like is made in the 1982 Convention. That is to say, there is no legitimate status for bunkering in the law of the sea.

I share the view that international law should at all times distinguish between navigation and the commercial activities of a shipping business. International lawyers and international litigation always draw a distinction between freedom of navigation and the freedom to trade, the freedom to carry goods and the freedom of movement of shipping.

3. The Applicant submits that bunkering is an aspect of the high-seas freedom of navigation or an internationally lawful use of the sea related thereto, which, under article 58, paragraph 1, of the Convention, the M/V *Saiga* enjoys in the exclusive economic zone of Guinea. It should be pointed out, however, that bunkering of fishing vessels in the exclusive economic zone is not navigation under the Convention. The exclusive economic zone, as a zone with its own legal status, is neither a part of the high seas, nor the territorial sea. Uses of the sea with regard to which the Convention has not expressly attributed rights or jurisdiction in the exclusive economic zone to the coastal State do not automatically fall under the freedom of the high seas. Therefore bunkering must not be regarded as falling within the high seas freedom of navigation or related to it. It is not navigation of the M/V *Saiga* that is involved, but its commercial activities of offshore bunkering in the exclusive economic zone of Guinea. The interpretation that freedom of navigation includes bunkering and all other activities and rights ancillary to it is incorrect. The view that bunkering is free in the exclusive economic zone because it is free on the high seas is legally not tenable.

4. In short, bunkering should not be encouraged, let alone without restraint. On the contrary, the following conditions are generally required for bunkering: (1) For States wishing to undertake bunkering activities in the exclusive economic zone to enter into agreement with the coastal State; and (2) for fishing vessels to obtain licences or approval for bunkering from those States. Unless it is conducted in accordance with these two conditions, there is no legitimate status for bunkering in the law of the sea.

Separate Opinion of Judge Anderson

. . . I have voted for the finding in operative paragraph (7) of the Judgment to the effect that the arrest, etc. of the *Saiga* in respect of its bunkering activity on 27 October 1997 violated the rights of St. Vincent. A coastal State is not empowered by the Convention to treat bunkering in its contiguous zone or EEZ as amounting *ipso facto* to the illegal import of dutiable goods into its customs territory, without further proof of matters such as the entry of the goods into its territory or territorial sea. By doing so in this instance, Guinea, in my opinion, went beyond articles 33 and 56 and failed to respect article 58 of the Convention.

I also endorse the decision recorded in paragraph 138 of the Judgment not to make any general findings on questions of bunkering in the EEZ. These questions are far from being straightforward. Today, bunkering is conducted under all manner of different circumstances and may involve distinct types of recipient vessels, including passenger vessels, warships, cargo ships and fishing vessels. For example, immediately before and after taking on bunkers, a recipient vessel may be exercising the freedom of navigation. In such a case, its bunkering could well amount to an "internationally lawful use of the sea" related to the freedom of navigation and "associated with the operation of ships" within the meaning of article 58, paragraph 1, of the Convention. To take a different example, a fishing vessel may be engaged in fishing in the EEZ with permission and subject to conditions established in the laws and regulations of the coastal State, consistent with the Convention (in particular, its article 62, paragraph 4). Here, the accent is not so much on the navigation of the fishing vessel as upon its efficient exploitation of the stocks in accordance with the terms of its licence. Yet again, a fishing vessel may also be in need of bunkers whilst navigating in transit between its home port and some distant fishing grounds. And the supply of bunkers to a ship which has run out of fuel as a result of a mishap may also have a safety or humanitarian dimension. Several other examples could be imagined. Plainly, the Tribunal could not address such varied situations in the abstract and without the necessary materials and evidence. The Tribunal was right to confine its decision to the particular question of the application of customs and fiscal legislation to bunkering in the EEZ which arose in this case and to leave aside the many other possible questions. . . .

Separate Opinion of Judge Vukas

8. According to the Memorial [of Saint Vincent and the Grenadines], freedom of navigation and related rights, guaranteed under article 58 of the Convention, include bunkering which, therefore, must not be subject to customs duties or contraband laws in Guinea's exclusive economic zone.

The last part of paragraph 101 of the Memorial reads:

> *A priori* the right to bunker gas oil within the exclusive economic zone falls squarely within freedom of navigation rights and other internationally lawful uses of the sea. This is confirmed by the text of the 1982 Convention (and its *travaux préparatoires*), by the Convention's object

> and purposes, and by state practice. It is also consistent with international judicial authority on the extent of coastal state's rights in the exclusive economic zone.

Saint Vincent and the Grenadines did not indicate precisely where in the text of the 1982 Convention it has been *confirmed* that bunkering "within the exclusive economic zone falls squarely within freedom of navigation rights and other internationally lawful uses of the sea." It also did not provide any evidence that the *travaux préparatoires* for the Convention supported the above claim, or at all referred to bunkering.

The only argument of Saint Vincent and the Grenadines concerning the freedom of navigation, which is based on the Convention, is its claim that the exclusive economic zone is a zone *sui generis* (article 55 of the Convention), in which all the "pre-existing rights of states to exercise high seas freedoms, ... including bunkering ... are unaltered, except where subject to express limits under the 1982 Convention" (Memorial, paragraph 104).

Saint Vincent and the Grenadines did not refer to any "international judicial authority" or any specific "state practice" supporting its claim concerning bunkering.

9. Guinea, on its side, claimed that bunkering was not included in the high seas freedoms applicable in the exclusive economic zone. It considered the zone a régime where rights or jurisdiction which the Convention has not expressly attributed to the coastal State do not automatically fall under the freedoms of the high seas. Concerning bunkering undertaken by the *Saiga* it stated:

> Contrary to the Applicant's opinion that "bunkering is a freedom of navigation right," Guinea contends that the M/V "Saiga's" bunkering of fishing vessels *in the Guinean exclusive economic zone* is neither comprised by the freedom of navigation referred to in article 87 of the Convention, nor does it form any other internationally lawful use of the sea related to these freedoms, such as those associated with the operation of ships. It is not navigation of the M/V "Saiga" that is at issue in this case, but its commercial activity of off-shore bunkering in the Guinean exclusive economic zone. Article 58(1) of the Convention does not apply to the mentioned bunkering activities which caused Guinea to take measures against the M/V "Saiga." ... (Counter-Memorial, paragraph 95)

In addition, Guinea made two clarifications which reduce the scope of disagreement of the parties. First, it distinguishes the situation of the buyer from that of the seller of the fuel:

> Obtaining fuel, which is necessary to sail a ship, could reasonably be considered as ancillary or related to navigation, whereas providing fuel could not. (Counter-Memorial, paragraph 97)

Thus, a ship buying fuel from a vessel engaged in bunkering in the exclusive economic zone of a third State does not violate article 58, paragraph 1, of the Convention.

Second, Guinea distinguishes between supplying bunkers to fishing vessels in the Guinean exclusive economic zone and to other vessels navigating in transit through that zone (Counter-Memorial, paragraph 101). It opposes only bunkering of fishing vessels, not of other types of ships.

10. Therefore, on the basis of the mentioned explanations provided by Guinea, it appears that both parties accept as legal the supplying of bunkers to all other types of ships in transit through an exclusive economic zone other than fishing vessels. The task of the Tribunal is thus reduced to the analysis and adjudication of the conflict of the positions of the parties respecting the bunkering only of fishing vessels.

In this respect, Saint Vincent and the Grenadines makes no distinction whatsoever. It is exactly in respect of a case of bunkering fishing vessels by the *Saiga* that it brought the case to the Tribunal. Indeed all its argumentation mentioned concerns bunkering in general.

11. On the other hand, Guinea argued against the legality of the supply of bunkers to fishing vessels in the exclusive economic zone. However, it did not want to base its opposition to the bunkering of such ships on the regard other States owe to its sovereign rights over the living resources of its exclusive economic zone. Namely, article 58, paragraph 3, in this respect reads:

> In exercising their rights and performing their duties under this Convention in the exclusive economic zone, States shall have due regard to the rights and duties of the coastal State and shall comply with the laws and regulations adopted by the coastal State in accordance with the provisions of this Convention and other rules of international law in so far as they are not incompatible with this Part.

12. Guinea decided not to base its claim on the rights it is guaranteed, as all other coastal States, in the exclusive economic zone under article 56, paragraph 1(a). It advanced two economic reasons for not permitting bunkering of

fishing vessels in its exclusive economic zone, not willing to base them on its sovereign rights granted under article 56, paragraph 1(a). Its first reason is the following.

> Through obtaining fuel at sea, a fishing vessel can spend a longer time fishing on the fishing grounds and hence can catch a greater amount of fish, before it is bound to call at a port. Accordingly the coastal State has an interest to regulate offshore bunkering in its exclusive economic zone as an aspect of its fisheries policies. (Counter-Memorial, paragraph 104)

The second reason, linked to the first, concerns fiscal interests of Guinea:

> Whereas customs revenues on oil products represent at least 33% of the total customs revenue destined for the Guinean Public Treasury, and whereas only 10% of the fishing fleet operating in the Guinean exclusive economic zone is flying the Guinean flag, customs revenues from fishing vessels flying foreign flags are an important fiscal resource for Guinea. (Counter-Memorial, paragraph 104)

13. Yet, notwithstanding the link of its arguments with fishing, Guinea insists that bunkering fishing vessels in the exclusive economic zone is not inherent to the sovereign rights of the coastal State, provided for in article 56, paragraph 1(a), of the Convention. It claims that "[a]lthough the bunkering activities are ancillary measures of a considerable importance for the fishing vessels concerned, they constitute neither fishing nor conservation or management activities with respect to the living resources themselves" (Counter-Memorial, paragraph 106).

Guinea also rejected the possibility of using the remaining part of article 56, paragraph 1(a):

> Neither does Guinea contend that the economic activities employed by the M/V "Saiga" in its exclusive economic zone are "other activities for the economic exploitation and exploration of the zone, such as the production of energy from [the] water, currents and winds" in the sense of article 56(1)(a) of the Convention. The activities envisaged in the mentioned provision are those constituting an exploitation and exploration of the zone itself and its natural resources, as the example of energy production indicates, whereas bunkering activities are of a different nature. They are business activities.... Although these activities are conducted with a view to fisheries and although they represent ancillary measures

> for the fishing vessels in the exclusive economic zone, they do not form an economic exploitation of the zone itself. In conclusion Guinea does not contend that bunkering the fishing vessels would constitute a part of its sovereign rights in its exclusive economic zone. (Counter-Memorial, paragraph 108)

14. Having rejected any link of its assertion concerning the bunkering of fishing vessels with article 56, paragraph 1(a), of the Convention, Guinea eventually points out the legal basis for its claim.

The first field in which Guinea seeks justification for its action towards foreign tankers supplying bunkers to fishing ships are rules and principles of general international law. Such rules and principles, according to Guinea, are referred to in "the last operative sentence of the preamble to the Convention" and in article 58, paragraph 3. These rules and principles of general international law serve as a source of Guinea's claim that it is justified to exercise jurisdiction in respect of such bunkering in order to protect its *public interest*:

> Guinea alleges that it has an inherent right to protect itself against unwarranted economic activities in its exclusive economic zone that considerably affect its public interest. (Counter-Memorial, paragraph 112)

Endorsing this view throughout the proceedings, Guinea submitted, as a subsidiary argument, that its actions were justified on the basis of article 59 of the Convention, which reads:

> In cases where this Convention does not attribute rights or jurisdiction to the coastal State or to other States within the exclusive economic zone, and a conflict arises between the interests of the coastal State and any other State or States, the conflict should be resolved on the basis of equity and in the light of all the relevant circumstances, taking into account the respective importance of the interests involved to the parties as well as to the international community as a whole.

However, Guinea invoked article 59 with some reluctance, as according to its Rejoinder, article 59 applies only when there is "a lacuna in the law which is not present here" (Rejoinder, paragraph 86)....

17. [T]he drafting history and the content of Part V of the Convention do not provide valid reasons for considering bunkering of any type of ships as an illegal use of the exclusive economic zone. In this respect, a note circulated at the beginning of the fifth session of UNCLOS III by the President of the

Conference should be recalled. Pleading for a consensus on the régime of the exclusive economic zone, the President wrote:

> A satisfactory solution must ensure that the sovereign rights and jurisdiction accorded to the coastal State are compatible with well-established and long recognized rights of communication and navigation which are indispensable to the maintenance of international relations, *commercial* and otherwise. (emphasis added) [footnote omitted]

Thus, the President did not see a strict separation of *ius communicationis* and *ius commercii*. It should be stressed that it was only after this President's appeal that the final formula of article 58, paragraph 1, was included in the draft of the Convention (Informal Composite Negotiating Text).

Bunkering should, although as a rather new activity at the time it was not expressly mentioned at the Conference, be considered an "internationally lawful use of the sea" in the sense of article 58, paragraph 1, of the Convention. It is related to the freedom of navigation "and associated with the operation of ships." This claim is not difficult to defend from the point of view of navigation as well as international law. Supply of bunkers is the purpose of the navigation of a tanker, and refuelling is essential for further navigation of the ship to which gas oil has been supplied. This close relationship of bunkering and navigation with the terms used in article 58, paragraph 1, forces me to recall here article 31, paragraph 1, of the 1969 Vienna Convention on the Law of Treaties, to which the parties often referred in their pleadings: "A treaty shall be interpreted in good faith in accordance with the ordinary meaning to be given to the terms of the treaty in their context and in the light of its object and purpose." …

19. Guinea itself did not provide a meaningful input into the establishment of any new customary rule concerning the rights of coastal States. In respect to the legislation it invoked in order to justifiy its actions regarding the *Saiga, grosso modo* I share the conclusions of the Tribunal (see, in particular, paragraphs 122, 127 and 136 of the Judgment).

In fact, Guinea offered interesting evidence of its awareness about the insufficiency of its existing legislation for preventing bunkering of fishing vessels in its exclusive economic zone. After the arrest of the Saiga, the Government of Guinea undertook an initiative to adopt a decree expressly regulating "the activity of refuelling fishing boats and other vessels in transit to Conakry" (draft Joint Decree No.A/98 … MEF/MCIPSP/98). In a letter of the National Director of Customs to the Minister of Economy and Finances, it is expressly stated that the proposed Decree is "*intended to close the current legal loophole* in the area of the refuelling of boats, an activity where the State currently registers large losses in customs revenue" (Counter-Memorial, paragraph 101, and Annex XVI, p. 9—emphasis added).

20. [A]n overview of the practice of States, prepared in 1994 by the Division for Ocean Affairs and the Law of the Sea of the United Nations Office of Legal Affairs, pointed out the case of an African State which is quite opposite to the tendency of Guinea. The following quotation demonstrates the attitude of Namibia, which amended its legislation in order to follow the content of the régime of the exclusive economic zone under the Convention:

> It may be noted that in 1991 Namibia adopted an amendment to section 4(3)(b) of the Territorial Sea and Exclusive Economic Zone Act of Namibia (1990), which had provided for the right to exercise powers necessary to prevent the contravention of fiscal law or any law relating to customs, immigration and health in its exclusive economic zone. The amendment deletes the reference to such right, which, under article 33 of the Convention, belongs to the contiguous zone and not to the exclusive economic zone, so that the Act may conform with the Convention.

21. However, my conclusion concerning the non-existence of additional international rules concerning the rights and duties of coastal and/or other States in the exclusive economic zone beyond those in the Convention does not mean that I rule out the possibility of the development of such rules by a constant practice of States.

Article 59 of the Convention itself is a confirmation of the awareness of States participating in UNCLOS III that the specific legal régime they have established has not attributed all possible rights and jurisdiction to the coastal States or to other States. Therefore, not only in respect of fishing vessels, but also of other types of ships or specific situations in which they can find themselves at sea, new rules may be established not only through the practice of States, but also through other sources of international law.

Separate Opinion of Judge Laing

55. If properly handled, the notion of concurrence of authority can contribute to the avoidance of potential disputes and, in the case of an actual dispute, the avoidance of a *non liquet*, given the unlikelihood that there can be easy or early negotiated reform of the Convention. These goals are also facilitated by the Convention's unique feature of a significant variety of norms and formulas to address the diverse potential disputes and matters requiring resolution. One of the formulas used in Parts V and VII has already been mentioned—language requiring States to have "due regard to the rights and duties" of other States

with which they have concurrent authority and jurisdiction. The device is used in a carefully balanced and institutionalized manner in articles 56, paragraph 2, 58, paragraph 3, and 87, paragraph 2, which evidently must interact with each other. Another formula is article 59[.]

However, neither party to this case has seriously relied on article 59. The reason might be the apparent position of the parties that the facts of this case do not call for the application of this provision. Nevertheless, without my taking a position on article 59, the "attribution" aspect of the provision might be noted. It serves as a reminder that many articles of the Convention deal with jurisdictional issues, which can be phrased in terms of attribution. The coastal State has authority and jurisdiction mainly in relation to natural resources and related matters which have been attributed to it in several provisions. Simultaneously, even in relation to the environmental protection of those resources, concurrent though non-identical, authority and jurisdiction has been attributed to port and flag States, international organizations and coastal States. It has been said that rights concerning economic interests, communication, scientific research and seabed drilling have been attributed to the coastal State by Part V. However, notwithstanding the over-complete and ambitious nature of the institutional title "exclusive economic zone," economic rights, on the whole, have not been attributed solely to that State. In view of what this Opinion reveals, the same holds true about the attribution of such other rights as those concerning communication and navigation.

56. [B]y virtue of the prevailing global economic order, all States have a right to free general and maritime economic access and non-discrimination. Against that background and my detailed examination of provisions of the Convention, a full and clear body of evidence would be required properly to address attribution and bunkering. *Prima facie*, however, the available evidence is not inconsistent with at least a measure of tolerance of the use of this maritime space by all States that are legitimate users of non-territorial waters within their respective functional or other spheres. . . .

Dissenting Opinion of Judge Warioba

91. When all the evidence is taken together it is quite clear that Guinea could properly apply customs and contraband laws against the *Saiga* when it undertook bunkering activities in the exclusive economic zone. . . .

106. [A] word of caution [is in order concerning] the danger of smuggling that may be associated with bunkering activities in the exclusive economic zones of the coastal States. For if that is not discouraged there will be no peace along the coast of Africa. It should be hoped that the silence of the Tribunal

on the issue of smuggling will not be interpreted as a licence for unwarranted bunkering activities which encourage smuggling.

Notes

1. *Coastal State Rights and Jurisdiction in the EEZ with Respect to Economic Matters.* The decision of the International Tribunal for the Law of the Sea in the M/V Saiga (No. 2) Case serves as a reminder that not every activity of economic or commercial concern to a coastal state occurring in its EEZ is a permissible subject of coastal state regulation and enforcement. The Tribunal had no difficulty in finding that Guinea's customs legislation could not be applied in the EEZ beyond the contiguous zone, even if it concerned the import, transport, storage, and distribution of fuel, which Guinean legislation regulated.

Guinea centered its whole legal argument on the application of its customs legislation up to 250 kilometers from its coast. (For more on customs jurisdiction in the contiguous zone, see Chapter 8, Section B.) Could Guinea have been more successful had it focused its argument on the fact that the import, transport, storage, and distribution of fuel in this case specifically applied to fishing vessels? Why did Guinea not pursue that line of argument? "Bunkering," i.e., supplying fuel at sea to vessels—in this case fishing vessels—allows them to remain longer at sea, and the vessels' fishing efforts are enhanced. According to the LOS Convention, the coastal state certainly does have jurisdiction over fishing activities up to 200 nautical miles from its baselines. What exactly is the scope of that jurisdiction? How does it compare with the "preferential rights" that the ICJ accorded Iceland in the 1974 Fisheries Jurisdiction case? Looking at Articles 61–62 of the LOS Convention, would Guinean regulation of bunkering of fishing vessels in its EEZ outside its contiguous zone have been permissible?

What did the Law of the Sea Tribunal have to say about the practice of bunkering? Should the Tribunal have explicitly found that a vessel engaged in bunkering was exercising the freedom of navigation, or at least was exercising some "other internationally lawful use[] of the sea related to" that freedom, under Article 58(1) of the LOS Convention? Compare the views of Judges Zhao, Anderson, Vukas, Laing, and Warioba, who all touched on this issue in their separate and dissenting opinions.

2. *Article 59 of the LOS Convention.* If an issue falls within Article 59, how should it be resolved? What is meant by "equity" in this context? Does Article 59 implicitly contemplate that international courts or arbitral tribunals will have to resolve conflicts on a case-by-case basis? What other alternatives are there for resolving conflicts over the attribution of rights or jurisdiction in the EEZ?

CHAPTER 10

Continental Shelf

Offshore oil and natural gas production is a multibillion dollar industry. Ever-improving technology has made possible the drilling of wells in extremely deep waters on the continental shelf far from shore. Other continental shelf resources include sedentary fisheries and hard minerals.

Section A of this chapter addresses the early development of the juridical concept of the continental shelf, a concept that came to be generally recognized only in the latter half of the 20th century. Section B explores the work of the International Law Commission, which led to the 1958 Continental Shelf Convention, and municipal cases applying the 1958 legal regime.

Some rules governing the continental shelf changed significantly in the 1982 United Nations Convention on the Law of the Sea (LOS Convention). In Section C we consider the 1982 rules, negotiated at the Third United Nations Conference on the Law of the Sea (UNCLOS III). Section C also examines the Commission on the Limits of the Continental Shelf, a technical body created by the LOS Convention and charged with making recommendations concerning the limits of the continental shelf beyond 200 nautical miles from a coastal state's baselines.

A Early Developments

Prior to the Second World War, individuals and states were primarily interested in the seabed and subsoil beyond the limits of the territorial sea because of sedentary fisheries. More recently, interest has focused on non-living resources. The 1942 United Kingdom-Venezuela Gulf of Paria Treaty (with respect to what was then U.K.'s colony of Trinidad and Tobago) contemplated the exploitation of the mineral resources of the seabed and subsoil of the Gulf of Paria. In 1945 concern with offshore oil reserves prompted a unilateral U.S. proclamation, which precipitated the development of the modern law of the continental shelf.

This section reproduces the 1945 U.S. continental shelf proclamation, along with explanatory statements. Also included are Chile's assertion of an extended offshore zone and the U.S. reaction to that assertion.

 | DOI 10.1163/9789004203563_011

PRESIDENTIAL PROCLAMATION NO. 2667 (TRUMAN PROCLAMATION REGARDING THE CONTINENTAL SHELF)

Sept. 28, 1945, 10 Fed. Reg. 12303 (1945), 59 Stat. 884 (1945)

Whereas the Government of the United States of America, aware of the long range world-wide need for new sources of petroleum and other minerals, holds the view that efforts to discover and make available new supplies of these resources should be encouraged; and

Whereas its competent experts are of the opinion that such resources underlie many parts of the continental shelf off the coasts of the United States of America, and that with modern technological progress their utilization is already practicable or will become so at an early date; and

Whereas recognized jurisdiction over these resources is required in the interest of their conservation and prudent utilization when and as development is undertaken; and

Whereas it is the view of the Government of the United States that the exercise of jurisdiction over the natural resources of the subsoil and sea bed of the continental shelf by the contiguous nation is reasonable and just, since the effectiveness of measures to utilize or conserve these resources would be contingent upon cooperation and protection from the shore, since the continental shelf may be regarded as an extension of the land-mass of the coastal nation and thus naturally appurtenant to it, since these resources frequently form a seaward extension of a pool or deposit lying within the territory, and since self-protection compels the coastal nation to keep close watch over activities off its shores which are of the nature necessary for utilization of these resources;

Now, therefore, I, Harry S. Truman, President of the United States of America, do hereby proclaim the following policy of the United States of America with respect to the natural resources of the subsoil and sea bed of the continental shelf.

Having concern for the urgency of conserving and prudently utilizing its natural resources, the Government of the United States regards the natural resources of the subsoil and sea bed of the continental shelf beneath the high seas but contiguous to the coasts of the United States as appertaining to the United States, subject to its jurisdiction and control. In cases where the continental shelf extends to the shores of another State, or is shared with an adjacent State, the boundary shall be determined by the United States and the State concerned in accordance with equitable principles. The character as high seas of the waters above the continental shelf and the right to their free and unimpeded navigation are in no way thus affected.

WHITE HOUSE PRESS RELEASE, SEPT. 28, 1945

13 Dept. State Bull. 484 (1945)

The policy proclaimed by the President in regard to the jurisdiction over the continental shelf does not touch upon the question of Federal versus State control. It is concerned solely with establishing the jurisdiction of the United States from an international standpoint. It will, however, make possible the orderly development of an underwater area 750,000 square miles in extent. Generally, submerged land which is contiguous to the continent and which is covered by no more than 100 fathoms (600 feet) of water is considered as the continental shelf.

Petroleum geologists believe that portions of the continental shelf beyond the three-mile limit contain valuable oil deposits. The study of sub-surface structures associated with oil deposits which have been discovered along the Gulf coast of Texas, for instance, indicates that corresponding deposits may underlie the offshore or submerged land. The trend of oil-productive salt domes extends directly into the Gulf of Mexico off the Texas coast. Oil is also being taken at present from wells within the three-mile limit off the coast of California. It is quite possible, geologists say, that the oil deposits extend beyond this traditional limit of national jurisdiction.

Valuable deposits of minerals other than oil may also be expected to be found in these submerged areas. Ore mines now extend under the sea from the coasts of England, Chile, and other countries.

While asserting jurisdiction and control of the United States over the mineral resources of the continental shelf, the proclamation in no wise abridges the right of free and unimpeded navigation of waters of the character of high seas above the shelf, nor does it extend the present limits of the territorial waters of the United States.

The advance of technology prior to the present war had already made possible the exploitation of a limited amount of minerals from submerged lands within the three-mile limit. The rapid development of technical knowledge and equipment occasioned by the war now makes possible the determination of the resources of the submerged lands outside of the three-mile limit. With the need for the discovery of additional resources of petroleum and other minerals, it became advisable for the United States to make possible orderly development of these resources. The proclamation of the President is designed to serve this purpose.

ANNUAL REPORT OF THE SECRETARY OF THE INTERIOR, FISCAL YEAR ENDED JUNE 30, 1945

Marjorie M. Whiteman, 4 Digest of International Law 760 (1965)

Approximately described, the Continental Shelf is all of the ocean floor around the United States and its Territories that is covered by no more than 600 feet of water. The whole area is almost as large as the area embraced in the Louisiana Purchase, which was 827,000 square miles, and almost twice as large as the original 13 colonies, which was 400,000 square miles. Along the Alaska coastline the shelf extends several hundred miles under the Bering Sea. On the Eastern coast of the United States the width of the shelf varies from 20 miles to 250 miles, and along the Pacific coast it is from 1 to 50 miles wide.

. . . Experts in the geology of oil lands would not be surprised if we found 22 billion barrels of oil—more than we are sure that we have on the continent—beneath one small part of the shelf that reaches into the Gulf of Mexico. Geologists also think that the shelf will yield rutile, sulphur, ilemenite, chromite, monazite and other heavy minerals.

Notes

1. *Truman's Fisheries Proclamation*. On the same day President Truman issued his continental shelf proclamation, he issued a second proclamation. By that proclamation, the United States asserted the right to regulate fishing activities in areas of the high seas contiguous to the coast of the United States where U.S. nationals alone had fished, and envisaged agreements with other states in areas of joint fishing operations. Presidential Proclamation No. 2668, Sept. 28, 1945, 10 Fed. Reg. 12304 (1945), 13 Dept. State Bull. 486 (1945). The United States never implemented fisheries conservation zones under this proclamation. For more on Truman's fisheries proclamation and the expansion of coastal fishing zones, see Chapter 9.

2. *The Continental Shelf Proclamation and the Interests of U.S. States*. Some U.S. Senators feared that the Truman Proclamation on the continental shelf might prejudice the claims of the states of the United States to submerged lands within or outside of the three-mile limit of the territorial sea. In response, a sentence was added at the last minute to Executive Order No. 9633, Sept. 28, 1945, 10 Fed. Reg. 12305 (1945), 13 Dept. State Bull. 486 (1945), which provided machinery to implement the Truman Proclamation. The sentence read: "Neither this Order nor the aforesaid proclamation shall be deemed to affect the determination by legislation or judicial decree of any issues between the United States and the several states, relating to the ownership or control of

the subsoil and sea bed of the continental shelf within or outside of the three-mile limit." The allocation of jurisdiction over the continental shelf between the U.S. federal and state governments was addressed in the 1953 Submerged Lands Act and Outer Continental Shelf Act, discussed in Section B.

3. *Development of the Truman Proclamations.* Several years of study and discussion among various U.S. executive branch departments preceded the two Truman proclamations, as did consultation with Congress. Secretary of the Interior Harold Ickes was the main architect of the proclamations. He had been advocating such steps since the late 1930s. World War II also prompted concern with ensuring a supply of natural resources. See Marjorie M. Whiteman, 4 Digest of International Law 752–56, 945–54 (1965); 1945–2 Foreign Relations of the United States 1480–1530. President Roosevelt approved the continental shelf policy in early 1945.

In the spring and summer of 1945 the U.S. State Department contacted the governments of Canada, Mexico, the United Kingdom, and the Soviet Union to obtain reactions to the proposed U.S. proclamations. Id. at 1510. The United States did not "desire to reserve the resources of the continental shelf to nationals of this country any more than it was the policy of the United States to exclude foreigners from participating in the exploitation of the mineral resources of the United States itself." Id. at 1511. The "primary [U.S.] concern was to assert the necessary control over such operations off the coasts of the United States to guard against the depletion of our mineral resources and to regulate, from point of view of security, the activity of foreigners in proximity to our coast." Id. The United Kingdom suggested concluding an agreement between the two countries, and perhaps similar agreements with Cuba, authorizing each country to exercise jurisdiction over oil exploration and exploitation in drillable areas adjacent to its own territorial waters. Id. at 1524. What would have been the advantages and disadvantages of negotiating such treaties? Was it illegal under international law for the United States unilaterally to proclaim a continental shelf? What alternatives can you envision to either bilateral agreements or unilateral claims concerning resources of the continental shelf?

4. *Other States' Claims to Offshore Zones.* The following states made some sort of claim during the late 1940s to control over the seabed areas adjacent to their coasts: Argentina (1946, following somewhat ambiguous continental shelf legislation in 1944), Chile (1947), Costa Rica (1949), Guatemala (1949), Honduras (1950), Iceland (1948), Mexico (1945), Nicaragua (1950), Panama (1946), Peru (1947), the Philippines (1949), Saudi Arabia (1949), and the United Kingdom for various colonies and areas under its protection (1945–1949). See 1 Laws and Regulations of the Regime of the High Seas 3–19, 22–38, UN

Doc. ST/LEG/SER.B/1 (UN Sales No. 1951.V.2, 1951). Chile's declaration and the U.S. response to it are reproduced below.

CHILE, PRESIDENTIAL DECLARATION CONCERNING THE CONTINENTAL SHELF, JUNE 23, 1947
El Mercurio (Santiago de Chile), June 29, 1947 at 27; translation from 2 Intl. L.Q. 135 (1948), reprinted in Marjorie M. Whiteman, 4 Digest of International Law 794 (1965)

Considering:

1. That the Governments of the United States of America, of Mexico and of the Argentine Republic, by presidential declarations made on 28 September 1945, 29 October 1945, and 11 October 1946, respectively, have categorically proclaimed the sovereignty of their respective States over the land surface or continental shelf adjacent to their coasts, and over the adjacent seas within the limits necessary to preserve for the said States the natural riches belonging to them, both known and to be discovered in the future;

2. That they have explicitly proclaimed the rights of their States to protect, preserve, control and inspect fishing enterprises, with the object of preventing illicit activities threatening to damage or destroy the considerable natural riches of this kind contained in the seas adjacent to their coasts, and which are indispensable to the welfare and progress of their respective peoples; and that the justice of such claims is indisputable;

3. That it is manifestly convenient, in the case of the Chilean Republic, to issue a similar proclamation of sovereignty, not only by the fact of possessing and having already under exploitation natural riches essential to the life of the nation and contained in the continental shelf, such as the coal-mines, which are exploited both on the mainland and under the sea, but further because, in view of its topography and the narrowness of its boundaries, the life of the country is linked to the sea and to all present and future natural riches contained within it, more so than in the case of any other country;

4. That international consensus of opinion recognizes the right of every country to consider as its national territory any adjacent extension of the epicontinental sea and the continental shelf;

5. That the State has the obligation to protect and guard the exploitation of the natural riches contained in this territory, on sea, on land, and in the air;

The President of the Republic hereby declares:

(1) The Government of Chile confirms and proclaims its national sovereignty over all the continental shelf adjacent to the continental and island

coasts of its national territory, whatever may be their depth below the sea, and claims by consequence all the natural riches which exist on the said shelf, both in and under it, known or to be discovered.

(2) The Government of Chile confirms and proclaims its national sovereignty over the seas adjacent to its coasts whatever may be their depths, and within those limits necessary in order to reserve, protect, preserve and exploit the natural resources of whatever nature found on, within and below the said seas, placing within the control of the government especially all fisheries and whaling activities with the object of preventing the exploitation of natural riches of this kind to the detriment of the inhabitants of Chile and to prevent the spoiling or destruction of the said riches to the detriment of the country and the American continent.

(3) The demarcation of the protection zones for whaling and deep sea fishery in the continental and island seas under the control of the Government of Chile will be made in virtue of this declaration of sovereignty at any moment which the Government may consider convenient, such demarcation to be ratified, amplified, or modified in any way to conform with the knowledge, discoveries, studies and interests of Chile as required in the future. Protection and control is hereby declared immediately over all the seas contained within the perimeter formed by the coast and the mathematical parallel projected into the sea at a distance of 200 nautical miles from the coasts of Chilean territory. This demarcation will be calculated to include the Chilean islands, indicating a maritime zone contiguous to the coasts of the said islands, projected parallel to these islands at a distance of 200 nautical miles around their coasts.

(4) The present declaration of sovereignty does not disregard the similar legitimate rights of other States on a basis of reciprocity, nor does it affect the rights of free navigation on the high seas.

NOTE FROM THE GOVERNMENT OF THE UNITED STATES TO THE GOVERNMENT OF CHILE, JULY 2, 1948

Marjorie M. Whiteman, 4 Digest of International Law 796 (1965)

I have the honor to refer to the Decree issued by the President of the Republic of Chile on June 25, 1947 concerning the conservation of the resources of the continental shelf and the epicontinental seas and to advise that I have been instructed by my Government to make certain reservations with respect to the rights and interests of the United States of America.

The United States Government has carefully studied this declaration of the President of the Republic of Chile. The Declaration cites the Proclamations of the United States of September 28, 1945 in the Preamble. My Government is accordingly confident that His Excellency, the President of the Republic of Chile, in issuing the Declaration, was actuated by the same long-range considerations with respect to the wise conservation and utilization of natural resources as motivated President Truman in proclaiming the policy of the United States relative to the natural resources of the subsoil and sea bed of the continental shelf and its policy relative to coastal fisheries in certain areas of the high seas. The United States Government, aware of the inadequacy of past arrangements for the effective conservation and perpetuation of such resources, views with utmost sympathy the considerations which led the Chilean Government to issue its Declaration.

At the same time, the United States Government notes that the principles underlying the Chilean Declaration differ in large measure from those of the United States Proclamations and appear to be at variance with the generally accepted principles of international law. In these respects, the United States Government notes in particular that (1) the Chilean Declaration confirms and proclaims the national sovereignty of Chile over the continental shelf and over the seas adjacent to the coast of Chile outside the generally accepted limits of territorial waters, and (2) the Declaration fails, with respect to fishing, to accord appropriate and adequate recognition to the rights and interests of the United States in the high seas off the coast of Chile. In view of these considerations, the United States Government wishes to indicate to the Chilean Government that it reserves the rights and interests of the United States so far as concerns any effects of the Declaration of June 25, 1947, or of any measures designed to carry that Declaration into execution.

The reservations thus made by the United States Government are not intended to have relation to or to prejudge any Chilean claims with reference to the Antarctic Continent or other land areas.

The Government of the United States of America is similarly reserving its rights and interests with respect to decrees issued by the Governments of Argentina and Peru which purport to extend their sovereignty beyond the generally accepted limits of territorial domain.

Notes

1. *Evaluating the Chilean Declaration and the U.S. Response.* How did the Chilean declaration differ from the Truman proclamations? After the unilateral Truman proclamations, what principled basis, if any, did the United States have for objecting to assertions by Chile and other coastal states of extensive authority over coastal zones? How and why are diplomatic protests, such as the U.S. reply to Chile, relevant to the process of developing international law?

How else could states concerned about the extension of offshore coastal zones try to influence international legal developments concerning such zones?

2. *Evolution of the Concept of the Continental Shelf in International Law.* The uncertain contours of coastal state rights over the continental shelf were reflected in a 1951 arbitral judgment. In Petroleum Dev. (Trucial States) Ltd. v. Abu Dhabi, 18 Intl. L. Rep. 144, 155 (1951), the arbitrator concluded "that there are in this field so many ragged edges and unfilled blanks, so much that is merely tentative and exploratory, that in no form can the doctrine [of the continental shelf] claim as yet to have assumed . . . the hard lineaments or the definitive status of an established rule of international law." The work of the International Law Commission (ILC) in the 1950s contributed significantly to the development of the 1958 Continental Shelf Convention and the legal regime of the continental shelf. The ILC, a body of experts of different nationalities operating within the U.N. system, works on the codification and progressive development of international law. More about the ILC appears in the last set of Notes in Chapter 3, Section A.

B Development and Implementation of the 1958 Continental Shelf Convention

This section reviews the work of the International Law Commission concerning the continental shelf. The Notes following the ILC's 1956 Report demonstrate how influential the ILC's work was in shaping the 1958 Continental Shelf Convention. This section concludes with two decisions from U.S. courts that illustrate national implementation of the 1958 Convention and explore the scope of coastal state jurisdiction on the continental shelf.

REPORT OF THE INTERNATIONAL LAW COMMISSION, 1956

UNGAOR, 11th Sess., Supp. No. 9 at 40, UN Doc. A/3159 (1956), 1956–2 Y.B. Intl. L. Commn. 253

Commentary to the Articles Concerning the Law of the Sea

[The Commission began discussing the continental shelf in 1951, and adopted the present text after several reexaminations, taking into account comments received from governments.]

(2) The Commission accepted the idea that the coastal State may exercise control and jurisdiction over the continental shelf, with the proviso that such control and jurisdiction shall be exercised solely for the purpose of exploiting its resources; and it rejected any claim to sovereignty or jurisdiction over the superjacent waters.

(3) In some circles it is thought that the exploitation of the natural resources of submarine areas should be entrusted, not to coastal States, but to agencies of the international community generally. In present circumstances, however, such internationalization would meet with insurmountable practical difficulties, and would not ensure the effective exploitation of natural resources necessary to meet the needs of mankind.

(4) The Commission is aware that exploration and exploitation of the seabed and subsoil, which involves the exercise of control and jurisdiction by the coastal State, may affect the freedom of the seas, particularly in respect of navigation. Nevertheless, this cannot be a sufficient reason for obstructing a development which, in the opinion of the Commission, can be to the benefit of all mankind. The necessary steps must be taken to ensure that this development affects the freedom of the seas no more than is absolutely unavoidable, since that freedom is of paramount importance to the international community. The Commission thought it possible to combine the needs of the exploitation of the seabed and subsoil with the requirement that the sea itself must remain open to all nations for navigation and fishing. With these considerations in mind, the Commission drafted the following articles.

Article 67

For the purposes of these articles, the term "continental shelf" is used as referring to the seabed and subsoil of the submarine areas adjacent to the coast but outside the area of the territorial sea, to a depth of 200 metres (approximately 100 fathoms), or, beyond that limit, to where the depth of the superjacent waters admits of the exploitation of the natural resources of the said areas.

Commentary

(1) In its first draft, prepared in 1951, the Commission designated the continental shelf as "the seabed and subsoil of the submarine areas contiguous to the coast, but outside the area of territorial waters, where the depth of the superjacent waters admits of the exploitation of the natural resources of the seabed and subsoil." It followed from this definition that areas in which exploitation was not technically possible by reason of the depth of the water, were excluded from the continental shelf. . . .

(3) At its fifth session, in 1953, the Commission reconsidered this decision. It abandoned the criterion of exploitability in favour of that of a depth of 200 metres. In the light of the comments submitted by certain Governments, the Commission came to the conclusion that the text previously adopted lacked

the necessary precision and might give rise to disputes and uncertainty. The Commission considered that the limit of 200 metres would be sufficient for all practical purposes at present and probably for a long time to come. It took the view that the adoption of a fixed limit would have considerable advantages, in particular with regard to the delimitation of continental shelves between adjacent States or States opposite each other. The adoption of different limits by different States might cause difficulties of the same kind as differences in the breadth of the territorial sea. The Commission was aware that future technical progress might make exploitation possible at a depth greater than 200 metres; in that case the limit would have to be revised, but meanwhile there was every advantage in having a stable limit.

(4) At its eighth session, the Commission reconsidered this provision. It noted that the Inter-American Specialized Conference on "Conservations of Natural Resources: Continental Shelf and Oceanic Waters," held at Ciudad Trujillo (Dominican Republic) in March 1956, had arrived at the conclusion that the right of the coastal State should be extended beyond the limit of 200 metres, "to where the depth of the superjacent waters admits of the exploitation of the natural resources of the seabed and subsoil." Certain members thought that the article adopted in 1953 should be modified.... While maintaining the limit of 200 metres in this article as the normal limit corresponding to present needs, they wished to recognize forthwith the right to exceed that limit if exploitation of the seabed or subsoil at a depth greater than 200 metres proved technically possible. It was therefore proposed that the following words should be added to the article, "or, beyond that limit, to where the depth of the superjacent waters admits of the exploitation of the natural resources of the said areas." In the opinion of certain members this addition would also have the advantage of not encouraging the belief that up to 200 metres depth there is a fixed zone where rights of sovereignty other than those stated in article 68 below can be exercised. Other members contested the usefulness of the addition, which in their opinion unjustifiably and dangerously impaired the stability of the limit adopted. The majority of the Commission nevertheless decided in favour of the addition.

(5) The sense in which the term "continental shelf" is used departs to some extent from the geological concept of the term. The varied use of the term by scientists is in itself an obstacle to the adoption of the geological concept as a basis for legal regulation of this problem.

(6) There was yet another reason why the Commission decided not to adhere strictly to the geological concept of the continental shelf. The mere fact that the existence of a continental shelf in the geological sense might be questioned in regard to submarine areas where the depth of the sea would

nevertheless permit of exploitation of the subsoil in the same way as if there were a continental shelf, could not justify the application of a discriminatory legal régime to these regions.

(7) While adopting, to a certain extent, the geographical test for the "continental shelf" as the basis of the juridical definition of the term, the Commission therefore in no way holds that the existence of a continental shelf, in the geographical sense as generally understood, is essential for the exercise of the rights of the coastal State as defined in these articles. Thus, if, as is the case in the Persian Gulf, the submarine areas never reach the depth of 200 metres, that fact is irrelevant for the purposes of the present article. Again, exploitation of a submarine area at a depth exceeding 200 metres is not contrary to the present rules, merely because the area is not a continental shelf in the geological sense.

(8) In the special cases in which submerged areas of a depth less than 200 metres, situated fairly close to the coast, are separated from the part of the continental shelf adjacent to the coast by a narrow channel deeper than 200 metres, such shallow areas could be considered as adjacent to that part of the shelf. It would be for the State relying on this exception to the general rule to establish its claim to an equitable modification of the rule. In case of dispute it must be a matter for arbitral determination whether a shallow submarine area falls within the rule as here formulated.

(9) ... The majority of the Commission decided to retain the term "continental shelf" because it is in current use and because the term "submarine areas" used without further explanation would not give a sufficient indication of the nature of the areas in question. The Commission considered that some departure from the geological meaning of the term "continental shelf" was justified, provided that the meaning of the term for the purpose of these articles was clearly defined. . . .

(10) The term "continental shelf" does not imply that it refers exclusively to continents in the current connotation of that word. It also covers the submarine areas contiguous to islands.

(11) Lastly the Commission ... does not intend limiting the exploitation of the subsoil of the high seas by means of tunnels, cuttings or wells dug from terra firma. Such exploitation of the subsoil of the high seas by a coastal State is not subject to any legal limitation by reference to the depth of the superjacent waters.

Article 68

The coastal State exercises over the continental shelf sovereign rights for the purpose of exploring and exploiting its natural resources.

Commentary

(1) While this article, as provisionally formulated in 1951 (article 2 of the draft), referred to the continental shelf as "subject to the exercise by the coastal State of control and jurisdiction for the purpose of exploring it and exploiting its natural resources," the article as now formulated lays down that "the coastal State exercises over the continental shelf sovereign rights for the purpose of exploring and exploiting its natural resources."

(2) The Commission desired to avoid language lending itself to interpretations alien to an object which the Commission considers to be of decisive importance, namely, the safe-guarding of the principle of the full freedom of the superjacent sea and the air space above it. Hence it was unwilling to accept the sovereignty of the coastal State over the seabed and subsoil of the continental shelf. On the other hand, the text as now adopted leaves no doubt that the rights conferred upon the coastal State cover all rights necessary for and connected with the exploration and exploitation of the natural resources of the continental shelf. Such rights include jurisdiction in connexion with the prevention and punishment of violations of the law. The rights of the coastal State are exclusive in the sense that, if it does not exploit the continental shelf, it is only with its consent that anyone else may do so.

(3) At its fifth session, the Commission decided after long discussion to retain the term "natural resources," as distinct from the more limited term "mineral resources." In its previous draft the Commission had only dealt with "mineral resources" and some members proposed adhering to that course. The Commission, however, came to the conclusion that the products of "sedentary" fisheries, in particular, to the extent that they were natural resources permanently attached to the bed of the sea should not be left outside the scope of the régime adopted, and that this aim could be achieved by using the term "natural resources." It is clearly understood that the rights in question do not cover so-called bottom-fish and other fish which, although living in the sea, occasionally have their habitat at the bottom of the sea or are bred there.

(4) At the eighth session it was proposed that the condition of permanent attachment to the seabed should be mentioned in the article itself. At the same time the opinion was expressed that the condition should be made less strict; it would be sufficient that the marine fauna and flora in question should live in constant physical and biological relationship with the seabed and the continental shelf; examination of the scientific aspects of that question should be left to the experts. The Commission however decided to leave the text of the article and of the commentary as it stood.

(5) It is clearly understood that the rights in question do not cover objects such as wrecked ships and their cargoes (including bullion) lying on the seabed or covered by the sand of the subsoil.

(6) In the view of the Commission, the coastal State, when exercising its exclusive rights, must also respect the existing rights of nationals of other States. Any interference with such rights, when unavoidably necessitated by the requirements of exploration and exploitation of natural resources, is subject to the rules of international law concerning respect for the rights of aliens. However, apart from the case of acquired rights, the sovereign rights of the coastal State over its continental shelf also cover "sedentary" fisheries in the sense indicated above. . . .

(7) The rights of the coastal State over the continental shelf do not depend on occupation, effective or notional, or on any express proclamation.

(8) The Commission does not deem it necessary to expatiate on the question of the nature and legal basis of the sovereign rights attributed to the coastal State. The considerations relevant to this matter cannot be reduced to a single factor. In particular, it is not possible to base the sovereign rights of the coastal State exclusively on recent practice, for there is no question in the present case of giving the authority of a legal rule to a unilateral practice resting solely upon the will of the States concerned. However, the practice itself is considered by the Commission to be supported by considerations of law and of fact. In particular, once the seabed and subsoil have become an object of active interest to coastal States with a view to the exploration and exploitation of their resources, they cannot be considered as res nullius, i.e., capable of being appropriated by the first occupier. It is natural that coastal States should resist any such solution. Moreover, in most cases the effective exploitation of natural resources must presuppose the existence of installations on the territory of the coastal State. Neither is it possible to disregard the geographical phenomenon whatever the term—propinquity, contiguity, geographical continuity, appurtenance or identity—used to define the relationship between the submarine areas in question and the adjacent non-submerged land. All these considerations of general utility provide a sufficient basis for the principle of the sovereign rights of the coastal State as now formulated by the Commission. As already stated, that principle, which is based on general principles corresponding to the present needs of the international community, is in no way incompatible with the principle of the freedom of the seas.

(9) Although for the reasons stated, as well as for practical considerations, the Commission was unable to endorse the idea of internationalization of the submarine areas comprised in the concept of the continental shelf, it did not discard the possibility of setting up an international body for scientific

research and assistance with a view to promoting their most efficient use in the general interest. It is possible that some such body may one day be set up within the framework of an existing international organization.

(10) The proposals made by the Commission in its report for 1953 caused some anxiety in scientific circles, where it was thought that freedom to conduct scientific research in the soil of the continental shelf and in the waters above would be endangered. In so far as such researches are conducted in the waters above a continental shelf, this anxiety seems to be unjustified since the freedom to conduct research in these waters—which still form part of the high seas—is in no way affected. The coastal State will not have the right to prohibit scientific research, in particular research on the conservation of the living resources of the sea. The consent of the State will only be required for research relating to the exploration or exploitation of the seabed or subsoil. It is to be expected that the coastal State will only refuse its consent exceptionally, and in cases in which it fears an impediment to its exclusive rights to explore and exploit the seabed and subsoil.

Article 69

The rights of the coastal State over the continental shelf do not affect the legal status of the superjacent waters as high seas, or that of the airspace above those waters.

Commentary

Article 69 is intended to ensure respect for the freedom of the seas in face of the sovereign rights of the coastal State over the continental shelf. . . . A claim to sovereign rights in the continental shelf can only extend to the seabed and subsoil and not to the superjacent waters; such a claim cannot confer any jurisdiction or exclusive right over the superjacent waters, which are and remain a part of the high seas. The articles on the continental shelf are intended as laying down the régime of the continental shelf, only as subject to and within the orbit of the paramount principle of the freedom of the seas and of the airspace above them. No modification of or exceptions to that principle are admissible unless expressly provided for in the various articles.

Article 70

Subject to its right to take reasonable measures for the exploration of the continental shelf and the exploitation of its natural resources, the coastal State may not impede the laying or maintenance of submarine cables on the continental shelf.

Commentary

(1) The coastal State is required to permit the laying of submarine cables on the seabed of its continental shelf, but in order to avoid unjustified interference with the exploitation of the natural resources of the seabed and subsoil, it may impose conditions concerning the route to be followed.

(2) The Commission considered whether this provision should not be extended to pipelines. In principle, the answer must be in the affirmative. The question is, however, complicated by the fact that it would often be necessary to install pumping stations at certain points, which might hinder the exploitation of the soil more than cables. It follows the coastal State might be less liberal in this matter than in the case of cables. As the question does not yet seem to be of practical importance, the Commission has not expressly referred to pipelines in the present article.

Article 71

1. The exploration of the continental shelf and the exploitation of its natural resources must not result in any unjustifiable interference with navigation, fishing or the conservation of the living resources of the sea.

2. Subject to the provisions of paragraphs 1 and 5 of this article, the coastal State is entitled to construct and maintain on the continental shelf installations necessary for the exploration and exploitation of its natural resources, and to establish safety zones at a reasonable distance around such installations and take in those zones measures necessary for their protection.

3. Such installations, though under the jurisdiction of the coastal State, do not possess the status of islands. They have no territorial sea of their own, and their presence does not affect the delimitation of the territorial sea of the coastal State.

4. Due notice must be given of any such installations constructed, and permanent means for giving warning of their presence must be maintained.

5. Neither the installations themselves, nor the said safety zones around them may be established in narrow channels or where interference may be caused in recognized sea lanes essential to international navigation.

Commentary

(1) While article 69 lays down in general terms the basic principle of the unaltered legal status of the superjacent sea and the air above it, article 71 applies that basic principle to the main manifestations of the freedom of the seas, namely, freedom of navigation and of fishing. Paragraph 1 of this article lays down that the exploration of the continental shelf must not result in any unjustifiable interference with navigation, fishing or the conservation of the

living resources of the sea. [H]owever, . . . what the article prohibits is not any kind of interference, but only unjustifiable interference. The manner and the significance of that qualification were the subject of prolonged discussion in the Commission. The progressive development of international law, which takes place against the background of established rules, must often result in the modification of those rules by reference to new interests or needs. The extent of that modification must be determined by the relative importance of the needs and interests involved. To lay down, therefore, that the exploration and exploitation of the continental shelf must never result in any interference whatsoever with navigation and fishing might result in many cases in rendering somewhat nominal both the sovereign rights of exploration and exploitation and the very purpose of the articles as adopted. The case is clearly one of assessment of the relative importance of the interests involved. Interference, even if substantial, with navigation and fishing might, in some cases, be justified. On the other hand interference even on an insignificant scale would be unjustified if unrelated to reasonably conceived requirements of exploration and exploitation of the continental shelf. While, in the first instance, the coastal State must be the judge of the reasonableness—or the justification—of the measures adopted, in case of dispute the matter must be settled on the basis of article 73. [Article 73 provides that any dispute regarding the interpretation or application of the articles "shall be submitted to the International Court of Justice at the request of any of the parties, unless they agree on another method of peaceful settlement."]

(2) With regard to the conservation of the living resources of the sea, everything possible should be done to prevent damage by exploitation of the subsoil, seismic exploration in connexion with oil prospecting, and leaks from pipelines.

(3) Paragraphs 2 to 5 relate to the installations necessary for the exploration and exploitation of the continental shelf, as well as to safety zones around such installations and the measures necessary to protect them. These provisions, too, are subject to the overriding prohibition of unjustified interference. Although the Commission did not consider it essential to specify the size of the safety zones, it believes that generally speaking a maximum radius of 500 metres is sufficient for the purpose. . . .

(7) While, generally, the Commission, by formulating the test of unjustifiable interference, thought it advisable to eliminate any semblance of rigidity in adapting the existing principle of the freedom of the sea to what is essentially a novel situation, it thought it desirable to rule out expressly any right of interference with navigation in certain areas of the sea. These areas are defined in paragraph 5 of this article as narrow channels or recognized sea lanes

essential to international navigation. They are understood to include straits in the ordinary sense of the word. The importance of these areas for the purpose of international navigation is such as to preclude, in conformity with the tests of equivalence and relative importance of the interests involved, the construction of installations or the maintenance of safety zones therein, even if such installations or zones are necessary for the exploration or exploitation of the continental shelf.

Notes

1. *The Work of the International Law Commission.* What were the advantages (and disadvantages, if any) of having the ILC prepare a draft treaty text, which served as the basis for states to negotiate the four 1958 Geneva conventions on the high seas, the territorial sea, fishing, and the continental shelf? Compare the process of negotiating the LOS Convention, outlined in Chapter 1.

How well did the ILC balance the rights of coastal states and other states in the portions of its draft treaty text concerning the continental shelf? What interpretive challenges or practical difficulties do the articles present?

2. *The 1958 Continental Shelf Convention.* The 1958 United Nations Conference on the Law of the Sea adopted the ILC's draft relating to the continental shelf with a few changes. As you review the changes, consider why countries wanted to make them and whether you think the changes were sensible.

First, the ILC's continental shelf articles were separated from the original all-embracing draft convention on the law of the sea, and became a separate Convention on the Continental Shelf. The United States and 57 other countries became parties to this Convention.

Second, Article 1 (corresponding to ILC Article 67) made clear that the term "continental shelf" refers also "to the seabed and subsoil of similar submarine areas adjacent to the coasts of islands." The reference to "approximately 100 fathoms" was omitted.

Third, Article 2 of the Continental Shelf Convention revised ILC Article 68. According to Article 2, "[t]he coastal State exercises over the continental shelf sovereign rights for the purpose of exploring it and exploiting its natural resources"; the word "it" did not appear in the ILC's text. In addition, Article 2 added three new paragraphs, reflecting points made in the ILC's Commentary:

> 2. The rights referred to in paragraph 1 of this article are exclusive in the sense that if the coastal State does not explore the continental shelf or exploit its natural resources, no one may undertake these activities, or make a claim to the continental shelf, without the express consent of the coastal State.

3. The rights of the coastal State over the continental shelf do not depend on occupation, effective or notional, or on any express proclamation.

4. The natural resources referred to in these articles consist of the mineral and other non-living resources of the seabed and subsoil together with living organisms belonging to sedentary species, that is to say, organisms which, at the harvestable stage, either are immobile on or under the seabed or are unable to move except in constant physical contact with the seabed or the subsoil.

Fourth, important changes were made in Article 5 (corresponding to ILC Article 71). The changes and additions are italicized:

1. The exploration of the continental shelf and the exploitation of its natural resources must not result in any unjustifiable interference with navigation, fishing or the conservation of the living resources of the sea, *nor result in any interference with fundamental oceanographic or other scientific research carried out with the intention of open publication.*

2. Subject to the provisions of paragraphs 1 and 6 of this article, the coastal State is entitled to construct and maintain *or operate* on the continental shelf installations *and other devices* necessary for *its* exploration and *the* exploitation of its natural resources, and to establish safety zones around such installations *and devices* and to take in those zones measures necessary for their protection.

3. *The safety zones referred to in paragraph 2 of this article may extend to a distance of 500 metres around the installations and other devices which have been erected, measured from each point of their outer edge. Ships of all nationalities must respect these safety zones.*

4. Such installations *and devices*, though under the jurisdiction of the coastal State, do not possess the status of islands. They have no territorial sea of their own, and their presence does not affect the delimitation of the territorial sea of the coastal State.

5. Due notice must be given *of the construction* of any such installation, and permanent means for giving warning of their presence must be maintained. *Any installations which are abandoned or disused must be entirely removed.*

6. Neither the installations *or devices*, nor the safety zones around them, may be established where interference may be caused *to the use of* recognized sea lanes essential to international navigation.

7. *The coastal State is obliged to undertake, in the safety zones, all appropriate measures for the protection of the living resources of the sea from harmful agents.*

8. *The consent of the coastal State shall be obtained in respect of any research concerning the continental shelf and undertaken there. Nevertheless, the coastal State shall not normally withhold its consent if the request is submitted by a qualified institution with a view to purely scientific research into the physical or biological characteristics of the continental shelf, subject to the proviso that the coastal State shall have the right, if it so desires, to participate or to be represented in the research, and that in any event the results shall be published.*

3. *The Continental Shelf and International Dispute Settlement.* The 1958 Continental Shelf Convention contains no counterpart to ILC Article 73 (referred to in the Commentary to ILC Article 69 above), which concerned formal third-party dispute settlement. Instead, states negotiated the 1958 Optional Protocol Concerning the Compulsory Settlement of Disputes. Why had the ILC believed it was important to provide for the jurisdiction of the International Court of Justice in matters related to the continental shelf? What are the advantages and disadvantages of making third-party dispute settlement optional? In Chapter 15 we consider the system of obligatory third-party dispute settlement established in the LOS Convention.

UNITED STATES v. RAY
423 F.2d 16 (5th Cir. 1970)

AINSWORTH, Circuit Judge:

Triumph and Long Reefs are two coral reefs which lie in international waters about four and one-half miles off the southeast coast of Florida, near Miami, and are the subject of this interesting and fantastic controversy between two rival private claimants and the United States. To the District Court (Judge Charles B. Fulton), the case was reminiscent of a fairy tale. To the defendants, the reefs were to become an island nation to be known as Grand Capri Republic; to intervenor, a new sovereign country would be established on the reefs, to be named Atlantis, Isle of Gold. Defendants would organize some semblance of a defense but have no intention of attacking the Coast Guard or Navy. Intervenor envisioned the reefs as a property worth one billion dollars, where a post office, building offices, stamp department and foreign office would be built, as well as a government palace and congress.

The fairy tale has an unhappy ending, with the granting by the District Court of the petition of the United States for a permanent injunction against the activities of defendants and intervenor on these reefs, and by the action which we take here in affirming in part and reversing in part the judgment of the trial court. The dreams of the separate groups for a new nation must perish, like the lost continent "Atlantis," beneath the waves and waters of the sea which constantly submerge the reefs.

The United States brought this action for injunctive relief against Louis M. Ray and Acme General Contractors, Inc. alleging interference with the rights of the United States on coral reefs located on its Continental Shelf on two grounds. In the first count the Government alleged that the activities of these defendants in building caissons on the reefs, dredging material from the seabed and depositing that material within the caissons was causing irreparable injury to the reefs which are subject to the control of the United States, and that these activities constituted trespass. The second count alleged that these activities were being unlawfully conducted without the required authorization of the Secretary of the Army. See 33 U.S.C. § 403; 43 U.S.C. § 1333(f). A preliminary injunction was granted against defendants. Thereafter Atlantis Development Corporation, Ltd., which was also contemplating commercial development of the reefs, was allowed by this Court to intervene in the proceedings. Intervenor filed a cross claim, alleging its superior title to the property by virtue of discovery of the reefs by its predecessor. After an extensive nonjury trial, at which numerous witnesses, lay and expert, testified and at which voluminous exhibits were introduced, the District Court adopted all of the facts stipulated by the parties and further found:

> 1. Triumph and Long Reefs are a part of the Continental Shelf extending seaward from the East Coast of Florida, and all waters overlying the reefs do not exceed one hundred fathoms in depth.
>
> 2. Triumph and Long Reefs are completely submerged at all times, except when their highest projections are fleetingly visible while awash at mean low water. Accordingly, Triumph and Long Reefs are part of the "seabed" and "subsoil" of the Outer Continental Shelf within the Outer Continental Shelf Lands Act of 1953, 43 U.S.C. § 1331, et seq.
>
> 3. These reefs, together with the organisms attached thereto, are 'natural resources' within the Outer Continental Shelf Lands Act, and the Geneva Convention on the Continental Shelf.
>
> 4. The caissons positioned by Ray and the jack platform construction or "boathouses" built on pilings proposed by Atlantis constitute "artificial

> islands and fixed structures * * * erected * * * for the purpose of * * * developing" the reefs, within the Outer Continental Shelf Lands Act.

The District Court denied all claims of defendants and intervener [and] denied the Government's claim of trespass under the first count. In so doing, the District Court recognized the sovereign rights of the United States, but concluded that those rights are limited as the claimed interest of the United States is something less than a property right, consisting of neither ownership nor possession, and consequently not supporting a common law action for trespass quare clausum fregit.

All parties have appealed. The Government's appeal is limited to the Court's denial of an injunction on count one of the amended complaint. We affirm the District Court's factual findings and its grant of injunctive relief under the Government's second count. However, we reverse the Court's denial of injunctive relief on the first count of the Government's amended complaint. . . .

It is clear that the reefs in question are within the area designated as the Continental Shelf by both national (Outer Continental Shelf Lands Act, supra) and international (Geneva Convention on the Continental Shelf, 15 U.S.T. 473, executed in 1958 and effective in 1964) law.

The Outer Continental Shelf Lands Act, 43 U.S.C. § 1331(a), in pertinent part provides:

> The term "outer Continental Shelf" means all submerged lands lying seaward and outside of the area of lands beneath navigable waters as defined in section 1301 of this title, and of which the subsoil and seabed appertain to the United States and are subject to its jurisdiction and control.

Article 1 of the international Convention on the Continental Shelf similarly reads:

> For the purpose of these articles, the term "continental shelf" is used as referring (a) to the seabed and subsoil of the submarine areas adjacent to the coast but outside the area of the territorial sea, to a depth of 200 metres or, beyond that limit, to where the depth of the superjacent waters admits of the exploitation of the natural resources of the said areas; * * * [15 U.S.T. 473.]

The evidence shows that the reefs are completely submerged at mean high water, and as the Court specifically found, "at all times, except when their highest projections are fleetingly visible while awash at mean low water." Thus the reefs are contemplated within the definition of the Outer Continental Shelf Lands Act and the Geneva Convention on the Continental Shelf, if they meet the definition of "seabed" or "subsoil" contained therein. Webster defines "seabed" as "lands underlying the sea." The evidence establishes that the term "seabed" is commonly understood to be any terrain below the high water line. The federal and common law comports with this understanding in defining the "bed" of a body of water as lands below the ordinary high water mark. The record shows that on the death of the coral, which has a natural predilection for cementing itself onto preexisting rocky structures, its skeletal remains become part of the seabed of the Continental Shelf. The District Court's finding that the reefs are part of the "seabed" of the Shelf is fully supported by substantial evidence of record.

The same national and international laws (the Outer Continental Shelf Lands Act and the Geneva Convention on the Continental Shelf) explicitly recognize the sovereign rights of the United States and the exclusiveness of those rights to explore the Shelf and exploit its natural resources.

The Outer Continental Shelf Lands Act (43 U.S.C. § 1332(a)) states:

> It is declared to be the policy of the United States that the subsoil and seabed of the outer Continental Shelf appertain to the United States and are subject to its jurisdiction, control, and power of disposition as provided in this subchapter.

To the extent that any of the terms of the Act are inconsistent with the later adopted Geneva Convention on the Continental Shelf, they should be considered superseded. See Cook v. United States, 288 U.S. 102, 118–119 (1933). But there is nothing in the pertinent language of the Geneva Convention on the Continental Shelf which detracts from or is inconsistent with the Outer Continental Shelf Lands Act. To the contrary, the Geneva Convention confirms and crystallizes the exclusiveness of those rights, particularly with reference to the natural resources of the Shelf.

Article 2 of the Geneva Convention on the Continental Shelf provides:

> 1. The coastal State exercises over the continental shelf sovereign rights for the purpose of exploring it and exploiting its natural resources.
>
> 2. The rights referred to in paragraph 1 of this article are exclusive in the sense that if the coastal State does not explore the continental shelf or exploit its natural resources, no one may undertake these activities, or make a claim to the continental shelf, without the express consent of the coastal State.

> 3. The rights of the coastal State over the continental shelf do not depend on occupation, effective or notional, or on any express proclamation.
>
> 4. The natural resources referred to in these articles consist of the mineral and other non- living resources of the seabed and subsoil together with living organisms belonging to sedentary species, that is to say, organisms which, at the harvestable stage, either are immobile on or under the seabed or are unable to move except in constant physical contact with the seabed or the subsoil.

It is unnecessary for us to decide whether the Outer Continental Shelf Lands Act, Section 1332(a), supra (which does not limit the nation's "jurisdiction, control, and power of disposition" to the natural resources of the Shelf), alone confers rights sufficient to authorize the injunctive relief sought. The right of the United States to control those resources is implicit in Article 2, paragraphs 1, 2 and 3, supra, of the Geneva Convention on the Continental Shelf, and explicitly recognized in the Submerged Lands Act, 43 U.S.C. § 1301 et seq. This Act further provides (43 U.S.C. § 1302) the definition of "natural resources" of the Continental Shelf:

> Nothing in this chapter shall be deemed to affect in any wise the rights of the United States to the natural resources of that portion of the subsoil and seabed of the Continental Shelf lying seaward and outside of the area of lands beneath navigable waters, as defined in Section 1301 of this title, all of which natural resources appertain to the United States, and the jurisdiction and control of which by the United States is confirmed.

Section 1301, referred to within the above-quoted section, defines "natural resources" as including, "without limiting the generality thereof, oil, gas and all other minerals, and fish, shrimp, oysters, clams, crabs, lobsters, sponges, kelp, and other marine animal and plant life * * *." (Emphasis supplied.) 43 U.S.C. § 1301(e).

Article 2, paragraph 4, of the Geneva Convention on the Continental Shelf includes in its definition of "natural resources" both living and non-living[10] resources, for it defines the term as consisting of "* * * mineral and other

10 Such a specific declaration renders immaterial the controversy of whether the coral composing the reefs is living or dead. Nevertheless, there is abundant evidence to corroborate the District Court's finding that the living corals attached to the reefs are sedentary.

non-living resources of the seabed and subsoil together with living organisms belonging to sedentary species. * * *."

Having thus concluded that the United States has the exclusive right for purposes of exploration and exploitation of the reefs, there remains only the question of whether injunctive relief was improperly denied to the Government on its first count which alleged trespass.

Although the complaint is inaccurately framed in terms of trespass in count one, the Government repeatedly stresses that it is not claiming ownership of the reefs. We do not question the District Court's conclusion that the Government's interest, being something less than fee simple, cannot support a common law action for trespass quare clausum fregit. But we do not understand that claim to seek such a remedy, despite the language in which the petition is couched. Damages, an inseparable element in the common law action for trespass, are not sought here, and the only relief requested is restraint from interference with rights to an area which appertains to the United States and which under national and international law is subject not only to its jurisdiction but its control as well. It is in this light that we consider the allegations of amended count one.

Neither ownership nor possession is, however, a necessary requisite for the granting of injunctive relief. This principle is implicit in the companion decisions of the Supreme Court, United States v. State of Louisiana, 339 U.S. 699 (1950); United States v. State of Texas, 339 U.S. 707 (1950), in which injunctive relief was granted to protect "paramount rights" of the United States beyond the territorial limits of Louisiana and Texas, to distances farther out in international waters than that involved here and at a time when those rights had not yet been statutorily established.[11]

... Obviously the United States has an important interest to protect in preventing the establishment of a new sovereign nation within four and one-half miles of the Florida Coast, whether it be Grand Capri Republic or Atlantis, Isle of Gold.

The rights of the United States in and to the reefs and the vital interest which the Government has in preserving the area require full and permanent injunctive relief against any interference with those rights by defendants and intervenor....

Affirmed in part, reversed in part.

---

11 Injunction from interferences with the natural resources over which the United States was claiming "sovereign rights" extended to an area 27 miles from the coast in the case against Louisiana, and to the outer edge of the Outer Continental Shelf in the case against Texas (anywhere from 75 to 150 miles of the coast).

Notes

1. *New "States" at Sea.* The Grand Capri Republic and Atlantis, Isle of Gold were only two of several putative new states built or envisioned outside the territorial sea. Other examples include: Sealand, established on an abandoned military platform six nautical miles off the east coast of Great Britain; the Republic of Minerva, planned for an artificial island approximately 300 nautical miles southwest of Tonga, to be built on coral reefs also claimed by Tonga; the short-lived Republic of Rose Island, created on a man-made platform in the Adriatic Sea seven nautical miles off the east coast of Italy; and Abalonia, planned for the Cortes Bank 110 nautical miles west of San Diego, California. See Samuel P. Menefee, "Republics of the Reefs": Nation-Building on the Continental Shelf and in the World's Oceans, 25 Cal. W. Intl. L.J. 81 (1994); Marjorie Miller & Richard Boudreaux, A Nation for Friend and Faux, L.A. Times, June 7, 2000 at A1. Some innovators pursue the possibility of "seasteading" in communities on the high seas. See http://www.seasteading.org (website of the Seasteading Institute); Cities on the Ocean, Economist, Dec. 3, 2011 at 14.

2. *Artificial Islands, Installations, and Structures on the Continental Shelf.* How would the issues posed in United States v. Ray be analyzed under the LOS Convention? Compare Article 5 of the 1958 Continental Shelf Convention with Articles 60 and 80 of the LOS Convention, which address artificial islands, installations, and structures on the continental shelf and in the exclusive economic zone. Under Articles 60 and 80, a coastal state, in its EEZ and on its continental shelf, "shall have the exclusive right to construct and to authorize and regulate the construction, operation and use of," inter alia, artificial islands. The coastal state also "shall have exclusive jurisdiction over such artificial islands, ... including jurisdiction with regard to customs, fiscal, health, safety and immigration laws and regulations."

TREASURE SALVORS, INC. v. UNIDENTIFIED WRECKED AND ABANDONED SAILING VESSEL

569 F.2d 330 (5th Cir. 1978)

[This case involves the competing claims of the federal government and private treasure salvors to a centuries-old Spanish galleon, which sank off the coast of Florida. The Notes following the case explore changes in legal standards that may apply to recovery of underwater historical material. However, the court's discussion of the law concerning the continental shelf remains noteworthy.]

GEWIN, Circuit Judge: . . .

In late summer of 1622 a fleet of Spanish galleons, heavily laden with bullion exploited from the mines of the New World, set sail for Spain. Spain, at this period in her history, was embroiled in the vicious religious conflicts of the Thirty Years' War and desperately needed American bullion to finance her costly military adventures. As the fleet entered the Straits of Florida, seeking the strongest current of the Gulf Stream, it was met by a hurricane which drove it into the reef-laced waters off the Florida Keys. A number of vessels went down, including the richest galleon in the fleet, *Nuestra Senora de Atocha*. Five hundred fifty persons perished, and cargo with a contemporary value of perhaps [US$] 250 million was lost. A later hurricane shattered the *Atocha* and buried her beneath the sands.

For well over three centuries the wreck of the *Atocha* lay undisturbed beneath the wide shoal west of the Marquesas Keys, islets named after the reef where the Marquis of Cadereita camped while supervising unsuccessful salvage operations. Then, in 1971, after an arduous search aided by survivors' accounts of the 1622 wrecks, and an expenditure of more than [US$] 2 million, plaintiffs located the *Atocha*. Plaintiffs have retrieved gold, silver, artifacts, and armament valued at [US$] 6 million. Their costs have included four lives, among them the son and daughter-in-law of Melvin Fisher, plaintiffs' president and leader of the expedition. . . .

The Antiquities Act authorizes executive designation of historic landmarks, historic and prehistoric structures, and objects of historic or scientific interest situated upon lands owned or controlled by the United States as national monuments. [T]he Antiquities Act applied by its terms only to lands owned or controlled by the Government of the United States. The wreck of the *Atocha* rests on the continental shelf, outside the territorial waters of the United States.

The government asserts that the [1953] Outer Continental Shelf Lands Act (OCSLA), 43 U.S.C. § 1331 et seq., demonstrates Congressional intent to extend the jurisdiction and control of the United States to the outer continental shelf. OCSLA was passed, along with the [1953] Submerged Lands Act, 43 U.S.C. § 1301 et seq., to clarify the respective interests of coastal states and the United States in the natural resources of the subsoil and seabed of the continental shelf.

. . . By enactment of the Submerged Lands Act, Congress recognized the coastal states' title to and ownership of the lands and natural resources beneath navigable waters within the territorial sea. In the Outer Continental Shelf Lands Act, "Congress emphatically implemented its view that the United

States has paramount rights to the seabed beyond the three-mile limit." [United States v. Maine, 420 U.S. 515, 526 (1975).]

43 U.S.C. § 1332(a) declares the policy of the United States to be "that the subsoil and seabed of the outer Continental Shelf appertain to the United States and are subject to its jurisdiction, control, and power of disposition as provided in this subchapter."

... The [OCSLA] consists almost exclusively of specific measures to facilitate exploitation of natural resources on the continental shelf. In addition, 43 U.S.C. § 1332(b) provides that the Act "shall be construed in such manner that the character as high seas of the waters above the outer Continental Shelf and the right to navigation and fishing therein shall not be affected." As the court below noted, an extension of jurisdiction for purposes of controlling the exploitation of the natural resources of the continental shelf is not necessarily an extension of sovereignty.

We believe that a limited construction of the Act comports with the primary purpose of resolving competing claims to ownership of the natural resources of the offshore seabed and subsoil. So read, the Act is consistent with Article 2 of the Convention on the Continental Shelf:

> 1. The coastal state [nation] exercises over the continental shelf sovereign rights for the purpose of exploring it and exploiting its natural resources.

The Convention on the Continental Shelf was a product of the United Nations Conference on the Law of the Sea convened at Geneva in 1958. It was the result of eight years' work by the International Law Commission. The Convention on the Continental Shelf became effective as law in the United States eleven years after passage of the Outer Continental Shelf Lands Act and superseded any incompatible terminology in the domestic statute. United States v. Ray, 423 F.2d 16, 21 (5th Cir. 1970). See Cook v. United States, 288 U.S. 102, 118–19 [(1933)].

Interpretations of the Convention and the Act by legal scholars have, with remarkable accord, reached the same conclusion regarding the nature of control of the United States over the continental shelf. The most compelling explication of the Convention regarding national control over non-resource-related material in the shelf area is contained in the comments of the International Law Commission:

> It is clearly understood that the rights in question do not cover objects such as wrecked ships and their cargoes (including bullion) lying on the seabed or covered by the sand of the subsoil.

This comment is consistent with the Commission's general perception of national jurisdiction over the continental shelf:

> [The Commission] was unwilling to accept the sovereignty of the coastal State over the seabed and subsoil of the continental shelf. [T]he text as now adopted leaves no doubt that the rights conferred upon the coastal state cover all rights necessary for and connected with the exploration and exploitation of the natural resources of the continental shelf.

We have demonstrated the limited scope of American control over the wreck site. We conclude that the remains of the *Atocha* are not situated on lands owned or controlled by the United States under the provisions of the Antiquities Act.

Notes

1. *Treaties in U.S. Judicial Opinions*. Note the uses made of the 1958 Continental Shelf Convention in United States v. Ray and Treasure Salvors. Note particularly the statements that the Convention would supersede inconsistent language in an earlier federal statute. The U.S. "last-in-time rule," applicable as between federal statutes and self-executing treaties, may be traced to Whitney v. Robertson, 124 U.S. 190 (1888). Under international law, of course, rules of substantive national law cannot justify a state's failure to apply a valid treaty. See Greco-Bulgarian Communities Case, 1930 P.C.I.J. (ser. B) No. 17 at 32; 1969 Vienna Convention on the Law of Treaties, Article 27.

2. *The Law of Salvage and the Protection of Underwater Cultural Heritage.* Recovery of wrecks has historically been governed by the general maritime law of salvage and finds. In general, the law of salvage provides compensation to salvors who assist vessel owners by rescuing property that otherwise would be lost. The law of finds allows those discovering wrecks to claim ownership if the wrecks have been long abandoned.

Should the law of salvage, traditionally applied to vessels in distress, or the law of finds be used for historic wrecks with material important to cultural heritage? In addition to salvors and vessel owners, what other groups or individuals have interests in historic wrecks? Can the traditional maritime law of salvage and finds accommodate the interests of archaeologists and the public's interest in cultural heritage? If the law of salvage is applied to an historic wreck, should the salvor have the right to exclude others from visiting, searching, surveying, or photographing the wreck? See R.M.S. Titanic, Inc. v. Haver, 171 F. 3d 943 (4th Cir.), cert. denied., 528 U.S. 825 (1999); see also R.M.S. Titanic,

Inc. v. Wrecked & Abandoned Vessel, 435 F.3d 521 (4th Cir. 2006). One international law expert has observed that, in recent years,

> [c]ourts and other national authorities have assumed greater responsibility to ensure scientifically acceptable handling of shipwrecks, their cargo, related debris, and other underwater artifacts. As a result, salvage law is adopting principles of preservation. But the . . . traditional law [of salvage] was never intended to address modern circumstances of historic wreck and other underwater heritage. Nor has it proven itself to be capable of doing so reliably.

James A.R. Nafziger, Historic Salvage Law Revisited, 31 Ocean Dev. & Intl. L. 81, 89 (2000).

Concern about underwater cultural heritage (UCH) led to negotiation, under the auspices of the United Nations Educational, Scientific and Cultural Organization (UNESCO), of the 2001 Underwater Cultural Heritage Convention. The UNESCO Convention was based on a draft prepared by the influential non-governmental International Law Association. Buenos Aires Draft Convention on the Protection of the Underwater Cultural Heritage, in Intl. L. Assn., Report of the Sixty-Sixth Conference (Buenos Aires) 432 (1994). Article 1(a) of the UNESCO Convention broadly defines UCH as "all traces of human existence having a cultural, historical or archaeological character which have been partially or totally under water, periodically or continuously, for at least 100 years." The Convention obligates parties to take appropriate measures to protect UCH and takes a position against its commercial exploitation (favoring its in situ preservation as a primary option). Article 4 concerns the application of the law of salvage and finds:

> Any activity relating to underwater cultural heritage to which this Convention applies shall not be subject to the law of salvage or law of finds, unless it:
>
> (a) is authorized by the competent authorities, and
>
> (b) is in full conformity with this Convention, and
>
> (c) ensures that any recovery of the underwater cultural heritage achieves its maximum protection.

The UNESCO Convention entered into force in January 2009; there were 45 parties as of September 1, 2013.

How should the law governing UCH take account of the rights of coastal states in various coastal zones? Consider the UNESCO Convention's treatment of the rights and obligations of coastal states parties on the continental shelf, in Article 10:

> 1. No authorization shall be granted for an activity directed at underwater cultural heritage located in the exclusive economic zone or on the continental shelf except in conformity with the provisions of this Article.
>
> 2. A State Party in whose exclusive economic zone or on whose continental shelf underwater cultural heritage is located has the right to prohibit or authorize any activity directed at such heritage to prevent interference with its sovereign rights or jurisdiction as provided for by international law including the United Nations Convention on the Law of the Sea.
>
> 3. Where there is a discovery of underwater cultural heritage or it is intended that activity shall be directed at underwater cultural heritage in a State Party's exclusive economic zone or on its continental shelf, that State Party shall:
>
> (a) consult all other States Parties which have declared an interest under Article 9, paragraph 5, on how best to protect the underwater cultural heritage;
>
> (b) coordinate such consultations as "Coordinating State," unless it expressly declares that it does not wish to do so, in which case the States Parties which have declared an interest under Article 9, paragraph 5, shall appoint a Coordinating State.
>
> 4. Without prejudice to the duty of all States Parties to protect underwater cultural heritage by way of all practicable measures taken in accordance with international law to prevent immediate danger to the underwater cultural heritage, including looting, the Coordinating State may take all practicable measures, and/or issue any necessary authorizations in conformity with this Convention and, if necessary prior to consultations, to prevent any immediate danger to the underwater cultural heritage, whether arising from human activities or any other cause, including looting. In taking such measures assistance may be requested from other States Parties.
>
> 5. The Coordinating State:
>
> (a) shall implement measures of protection which have been agreed by the consulting States, which include the Coordinating State, unless the consulting States, which include the Coordinating

State, agree that another State Party shall implement those measures;

(b) shall issue all necessary authorizations for such agreed measures in conformity with the Rules, unless the consulting States, which include the Coordinating State, agree that another State Party shall issue those authorizations;

(c) may conduct any necessary preliminary research on the underwater cultural heritage and shall issue all necessary authorizations therefore, and shall promptly inform the Director-General of the results, who in turn will make such information promptly available to other States Parties.

6. In coordinating consultations, taking measures, conducting preliminary research and/or issuing authorizations pursuant to this Article, the Coordinating State shall act on behalf of the States Parties as a whole and not in its own interest. Any such action shall not in itself constitute a basis for the assertion of any preferential or jurisdictional rights not provided for in international law, including the United Nations Convention on the Law of the Sea.

7. Subject to the provisions of paragraphs 2 and 4 of this Article, no activity directed at State vessels and aircraft shall be conducted without the agreement of the flag State and the collaboration of the Coordinating State.

Article 3 of the UNESCO Convention provides that "[n]othing in this Convention shall prejudice the rights, jurisdiction and duties of States under international law, including the United Nations Convention on the Law of the Sea." Notwithstanding Article 3 and Article 10(6), quoted above, does the UNESCO Convention in fact expand the jurisdiction of coastal states in the continental shelf? If so, why would some international actors find that to be a matter of concern? See also LOS Convention, Article 311.

The LOS Convention contains only general provisions on "archaeological and historical objects found at sea." See id., Articles 149 and 303. Does Article 303 expand the rights of coastal states with respect to such objects in at least the portion of the continental shelf comprising the contiguous zone? See id., Article 33, and Chapter 8, Section B.

3. *Oil and Natural Gas on the Continental Shelf.* The major economic use of the continental shelf has involved oil and natural gas exploitation. The U.S. Outer Continental Shelf Lands Act (OCSLA), 43 U.S.C. §§ 1331 et seq., regulations issued pursuant to that Act, and other federal statutes now govern oil, gas, and other mineral exploration, lease sales, and exploitation on the U.S. federal continental shelf. The OCSLA also provides for safety and health stan-

dards on offshore installations and in exploration or mining operations. In addition, the OCSLA mandates environmental studies and requires that the continental shelf be managed in a way that balances "economic, social, and environmental values." Id., § 1344.

C Development and Implementation of the 1982 LOS Convention Provisions on the Continental Shelf

States faced difficult questions at the Third United Nations Conference on the Law of the Sea: What accommodation should be made for coastal states with geologically narrow continental shelves? What should be the relevance, if any, of the concept of a 200-nautical-mile exclusive economic zone (see Chapter 9) to the concept of the continental shelf? Should states with shelves that geologically extend beyond 200 nautical miles from the baseline have the exclusive right to exploit the resources of those shelves? For shelves extending beyond 200 nautical miles, what should be the outer limits of the continental shelf? Should each coastal state have the authority to establish those limits unilaterally, or should there be some international oversight of outer limits lines? To the extent that the regime of the continental shelf expanded, the international Area beyond the limits of national jurisdiction (see Chapter 11) would be reduced in scope. If coastal states were to be entitled to exploit the resources of broad continental shelves beyond 200 nautical miles, should any of the resulting revenues be allocated to land-locked or developing states? Such questions complicated negotiation of Part VI of the LOS Convention.

In this section, we look first at several articles in Part VI. We close with an excerpt that illustrates the work of the Commission on the Limits of the Continental Shelf (CLCS), a technical body established by the LOS Convention.

LAW OF THE SEA CONVENTION

Articles 76–82

See Appendix

Notes

1. *The Continental Shelf in the LOS Convention.* How have legal conceptions about the continental shelf, as embodied in the 1982 LOS Convention, changed since the 1958 Continental Shelf Convention? What has remained the same? What is the continuing relevance of the work of the International Law Commission, which we considered in Section B? See Figures X.B and X.D below.

Perhaps the most significant changes in the LOS Convention concern the extent of the legal continental shelf. Does Article 76 provide a determinate limit for the continental shelf? Does it establish a core concept to guide interpretation about the extent of a coastal state's continental shelf? How does the physical continental shelf differ from the legal continental shelf?

2. *Rights of Non-coastal States.* Articles 78 and 79 of the LOS Convention concern the rights of non-coastal states, and the corresponding obligations of coastal states, on the continental shelf and in the superjacent waters. What conflicts between non-coastal and coastal states may arise with respect to the continental shelf, and what principles govern the resolution of such conflicts?

3. *Comparing the Exclusive Economic Zone to the Continental Shelf.* Article 56 of the LOS Convention, contained in Part V on the exclusive economic zone, provides that a coastal state has "sovereign rights for the purpose of," inter alia, exploring and exploiting the non-living resources of the seabed and its subsoil. Given that provision, why is there a separate Part VI for the continental shelf? How does the legal regime of the continental shelf differ from the legal regime of the EEZ?

4. *The Continental Shelf beyond 200 Nautical Miles from the Baseline.* For state parties to the LOS Convention, how do the rights and obligations of coastal states with respect to the continental shelf beyond 200 nautical miles from the baseline differ from their rights and obligations with respect to the continental shelf up to 200 nautical miles? See LOS Convention, Articles 82 and 246. Why should there be any difference?

Is a non-party to the LOS Convention entitled to any continental shelf beyond 200 nautical miles from the baseline, since, as a non-party, it has not accepted the revenue-sharing requirements of Article 82? Does Article 82 require the payment of a "royalty" or "tax" to an international body, with respect to a region "owned" by a coastal state? Or, instead, does the fee called for under Article 82 reflect part of the compromise negotiated at UNCLOS III that entitled coastal states to any continental shelf at all beyond 200 nautical miles from baselines? If parties to the LOS Convention take the view that the seabed and subsoil beyond the 200-nautical-mile limit of a non-party to the Convention is part of the Area, what are the corresponding obligations of those parties? How might those obligations affect companies seeking to exploit oil and gas from the seabed outside the 200-nautical-mile limit? See LOS Convention, Article 137(3) and Annex III, Article 1. We examine the Area and rights to its mineral resources in Chapter 11.

5. *The Commission on the Limits of the Continental Shelf.* Article 76(8) of the Convention provides that "[i]nformation on the limits of the continental shelf beyond 200 nautical miles from" baselines "shall be submitted by the coastal

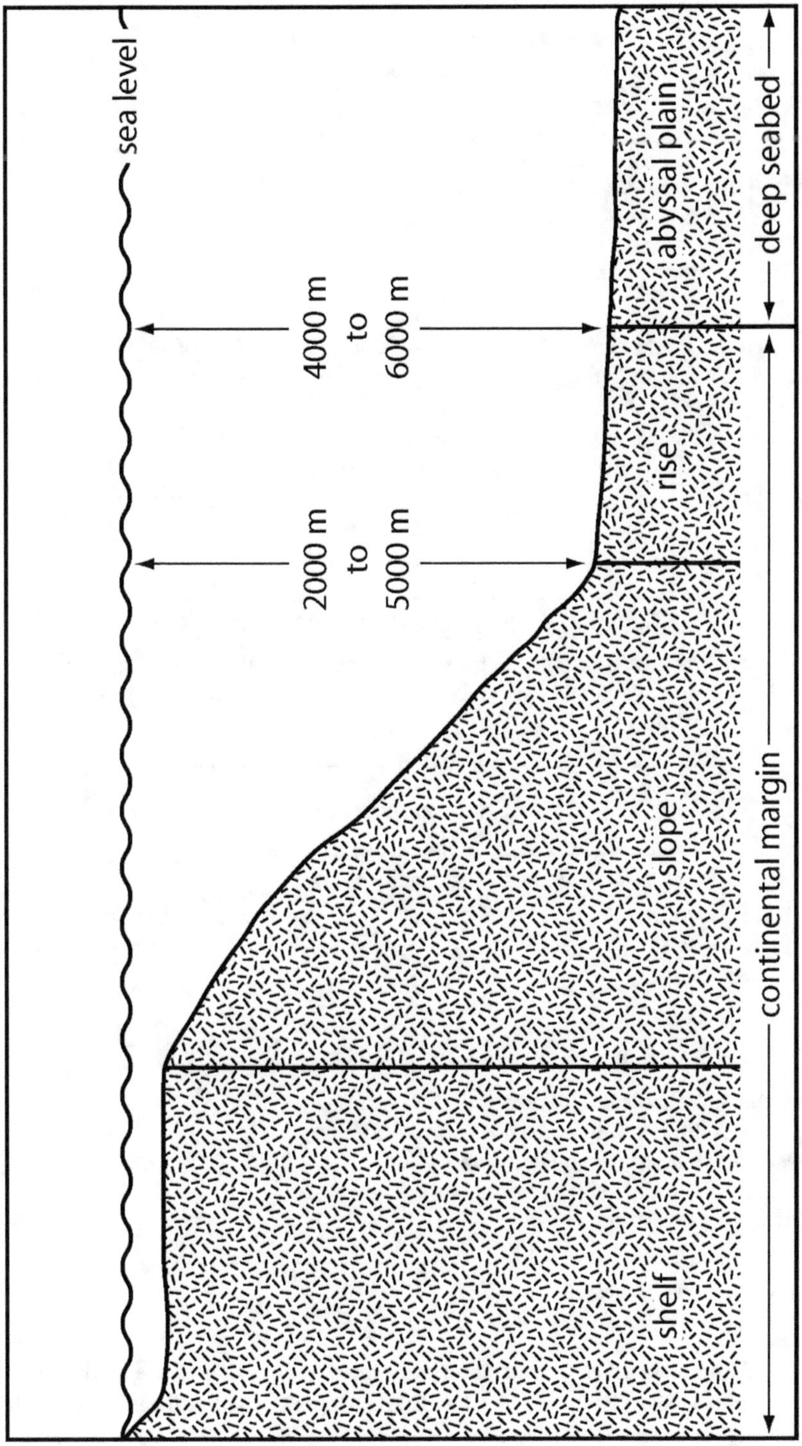

FIGURE X.A *Continental Shelf and Margin*

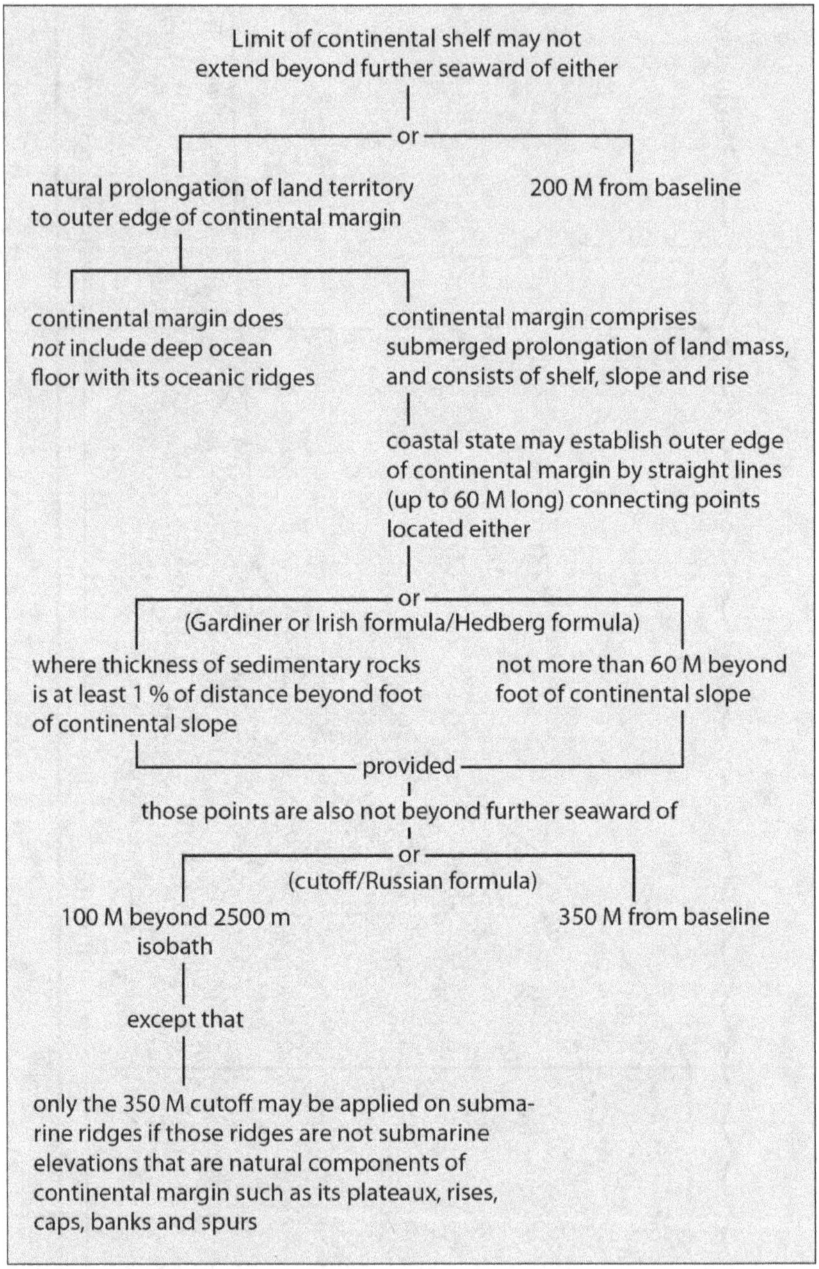

FIGURE X.B *Diagram of Article 76**

* Modified from Bernard H. Oxman, The Third United Nations Conference on the Law of the Sea: The Ninth Session (1980), 75 Am. J. Intl. L. 211, 229 (1981). Used with permission of the American Society of International Law.

State" to the CLCS, a technical body created by the LOS Convention. The CLCS "shall make recommendations to coastal States on matters related to the establishment of the outer limits of their continental shelf. The limits of the shelf established by a coastal State on the basis of these recommendations shall be final and binding." Read Annex II of the LOS Convention, which contains more details about the CLCS. Why did those negotiating the LOS Convention consider the CLCS to be necessary? What are the functions of the CLCS? What challenges does it face?

SUMMARY OF RECOMMENDATIONS OF THE COMMISSION ON THE LIMITS OF THE CONTINENTAL SHELF IN REGARD TO THE SUBMISSION MADE BY THE UNITED KINGDOM OF GREAT BRITAIN AND NORTHERN IRELAND IN RESPECT OF ASCENSION ISLAND ON 9 MAY 2008

Adopted Apr. 15, 2010, available at http://www.un.org/Depts/los/clcs_new/submissions_files/submission_gbr.htm

I. INTRODUCTION

1. On 9 May 2008, the United Kingdom of Great Britain and Northern Ireland ("the United Kingdom") submitted . . . to the Commission on the Limits of the Continental Shelf ("the Commission"), in accordance with article 76, paragraph 8, of the United Nations Convention on the Law of the Sea of 10 December 1982 ("the Convention"), information on the limits of the continental shelf beyond 200 nautical miles (M) from the baselines from which the breadth of the territorial sea is measured relating to the continental shelf of Ascension Island. The Convention entered into force for the United Kingdom on 24 August 1997. . . .

8. The Commission makes these Recommendations to the United Kingdom in fulfilment of its mandate as contained in article 76, paragraph 8, and articles 3 and 5 of Annex II to the Convention. . . .

IV. RECOMMENDATIONS

14. The Submission of the United Kingdom of 9 May 2008 relates to the area around the United Kingdom's Overseas Sovereign Territory of Ascension Island. Ascension Island is a dependency of the British Overseas Territory of Saint Helena, some 750 M to the southeast. . . .

1. *Geographical Region Description . . .*

16. Ascension Island is the sub-aerial expression of a volcanic seamount that is located in the central Atlantic Ocean about 90 km west of the median rift valley of the Mid-Atlantic Ridge (MAR). . . .

18. A series of geological, geophysical, and geochemical studies on Ascension Island and the surrounding seafloor over the last ten years have provided a consistent model for the constructional history of the Island. In this model, volcanism initiated in proximity to the spreading centre due to a weak and intermittent mantle plume or by a melting of small mantle heterogeneities and subsequently resulted in the accumulation of volcanic piles to form the present-day Ascension Island.

2. *General Considerations*

2.1. Natural prolongation of the land territory and submerged prolongation of the land mass applicable to Ascension Island

19. During the Subcommission's consideration of the data and other material submitted by the United Kingdom, differences of views arose between the Delegation and the Subcommission related to natural prolongation and submerged prolongation under article 76. . . .

21. [T]he United Kingdom outlines its views as follows:

> (i) The United Kingdom ". . . *do not regard establishment of the 'natural prolongation' of the land territory as referred to in Article 76 to require a particular 'morphology,' or set of morphological features, considered in isolation from other data. The technical arguments for natural prolongation, foot of slope position, base of slope region can all be developed and established through analyses of a range of data, including geology and geophysics, in addition to morphology.*"
>
> (ii) The United Kingdom also points out that "[*t*]*he Commission make specific reference to such landmasses* (*which include Ascension Island and several other island examples in the world's oceans*) *in paragraph 7.2.8. of the Scientific and Technical Guidelines—"Some ridges* (*including active spreading ridges*) *may have islands on them. In such cases it would be difficult to consider that those parts of the ridge belong to the deep ocean floor." Hence, such a ridge, as it extends from the island landmass and even though it passes laterally into deep ocean floor, can be included in the continental margin of the island state in question and may be regarded as a "submarine ridge" or "submarine elevation" in the sense of Article 76, and not part of the deep ocean floor.*"

(iii) The United Kingdom further states that "[*n*]*atural prolongation of the land territory is a fundamental first consideration, regardless of the composition or morphology of the landmass or the character of the surrounding seafloor, and 76(4) applied to that natural prolongation to delineate the outer edge of the continental margin—constraints permitting, of course.*"

22. The Subcommission outlined its views on natural prolongation, submerged prolongation and the delineation of the outer edge of the continental margin . . . through the following principles and considerations based on the Convention and the Guidelines:

(i) The "*natural prolongation of* [*the*] *land territory*" is based on the physical extent of the continental margin to its "*outer edge*" (article 76, paragraph 1) i.e. "*the submerged prolongation of the land mass* . . ." (article 76, paragraph 3);
(ii) The outer edge of the continental margin in the sense of article 76, paragraph 3, is established by applying the provisions of article 76, paragraph 4, through measurements from the [foot of the slope (FOS)];
(iii) The FOS determined for this purpose is always associated with an identifiable base of continental slope, pursuant to article 76, paragraph 4(b);
(iv) The principle of crustal neutrality applies: i.e. article 76 is neutral regarding the crustal nature of the land mass of a coastal State; and
(v) The regime of islands (article 121) which states that the maritime zones of an island envisaged by the Convention "*. . . are determined in accordance with the provisions of this Convention applicable to other land territory.*" This implies that for the purposes of delineating the outer limits of the continental shelf all island States have a continental margin in the sense of article 76, paragraph 3.

23. The Subcommission elaborated further on the above principles and considerations . . . as follows:

(i) Physically, and in accordance with article 76, paragraph 3, the continental margin "*consists of the seabed and subsoil of the shelf, the slope and the rise,*" and beyond that lies the "*deep ocean floor with its oceanic ridges*"; that is, a four-component subdivision of submarine morphology. These morphological components are involved in defining the continental margin of any kind of coastal State land mass, in accordance with article 76, paragraph 3, of the Convention. Therefore, it follows that the *"foot of the continental slope"* referred to in article 76, paragraph 4, is with reference to the continental slope province of the continental margin in the sense of the Convention.

(ii) The consequence of the above is that, for the purposes of the Convention, any kind of land mass (irrespective of crustal type, size etc.) of a coastal State has a continental margin that can be delineated in accordance with article 76, paragraph 4 of the Convention. The deep ocean floor occurs seaward of the continental margin and includes the oceanic features of the seafloor such as ocean basins, abyssal plains, abyssal hills, mid-ocean ridges, fracture zones, seamounts etc.

(iii) The determination of a FOS requires the existence of both continental slope and an identifiable base to that slope (see sections 5.2 and 6.2 of the Guidelines). In turn, the existence of a continental slope requires the existence of a distinct morphological feature rising from the level of the continental rise or deep ocean floor up to the continental shelf of the land mass of the coastal State.

(iv) The deep ocean floor in the sense of article 76 is the area seaward of the outer edge of the continental margin. However, the opposite also applies, i.e. that the continental margin is the area landward of the deep ocean floor. This concept is reflected in paragraph 5.4.5 of the Guidelines.

2.2. Characteristics of the Mid-Atlantic Ridge and the deep ocean floor

24. The oceanic crust of the Atlantic Ocean is produced by sea-floor spreading magmatism along the central (median) rift valley of the MAR. The MAR is part of the global mid-ocean ridge (MOR) system that has been recognised as the most striking feature of the ocean floor since the 1950s. The MAR system extends north-south from the Arctic Ocean to the Southern Ocean and is considered to be the most significant example of a slow-spreading ridge in the global MOR system. Slow-spreading processes are responsible for the rugged topography of the MAR. New crustal material (generally comprising mid-ocean ridge basalt near the surface) is accreted to the separating plates within the rift valley by extrusive and intrusive volcanism. This seafloor spreading process is the normal mechanism for the creation of new ocean floor throughout all of the world's oceans. . . .

26. The MOR, and the MAR in particular, are not typical ridge-like features in the sense of conventional morphological definitions when viewed as a whole[.] That is, they are not *"elongated narrow elevations of varying complexity having steep sides"* as defined in the International Hydrographic Organisation publication Standardization of Undersea Feature Names (Bathymetric Publication No. 6, 4th Edition, November 2008), but rather are broad swells or

undulations of the ocean floor. The main reason that the term "ridge" arose in naming the MAR is largely historic and was used to describe both the prominent central valley with its rift shoulders, as well as the broader province with its gently dipping flanks. At that time, the tectonic significance of MORs was not well understood. It is now realized that the flanks of MORs are actually normal deep ocean floor that has aged, cooled and thermally subsided as the oceanic lithosphere moved away from the active spreading centre.

27. It is generally recognised that the true oceanic features of the seafloor occur seaward of the continental margin and include both the ocean basin floor and MOR zones. This categorisation is reflected in article 76, paragraph 3, of the Convention, which states that the continental margin "*... does not include the deep ocean floor with its oceanic ridges ...*"

3. *Considerations in Respect of Ascension Island*

3.1. Submerged prolongation of the landmass of Ascension Island and entitlement to delineate the outer limits of the continental shelf beyond 200 M

28. The Commission recognises the entitlement of a coastal State to delineate the outer limits of the continental shelf beyond 200 M if the outer edge of the continental margin established from FOS points determined at its base by applying the provisions of article 76, paragraph 4, extend beyond the coastal State's 200 M limits (see section 2.2 of the Guidelines). [T]he Commission gave close consideration to the location of the base of the continental slope of Ascension Island during its examination of the entitlement of the United Kingdom to delineate the outer limits of the continental shelf beyond 200 M. . . .

33. [T]he United Kingdom stated "*... that the morphological characteristics of the seafloor elevation of which Ascension is a part, and which extends beyond 200 nautical miles to the north, south and west of the Island, does not conform to a typical form of continental margin, and does not exhibit features typical thereof, such as shelf, slope and rise. It is therefore the view of the United Kingdom that a foot of slope, in the western sector and partially in the eastern sector, should be identified by means of evidence to the contrary at appropriate positions along the elevation.*" ...

35. In the west, the United Kingdom describes its approach to defining a base of slope zone as follows: "*In the West Area there is no conventional shelf, slope and rise. Here foot of slope points were identified at locations where the westward-dipping seafloor, corresponding to the western flank of the MAR, meets the deep abyssal plain of the western South Atlantic Ocean or the eastern edge of the South American rise. We interpret this junction as being analogous to that between conventional lower slope, or rise, and deep ocean floor.*" ...

37. The United Kingdom states that Ascension Island "[...] *is a surface expression of the regional low-intensity thermal anomaly that has caused a regional elevation of the associated Mid-Atlantic Ridge and surrounding seafloor* [...]." ...

39. The United Kingdom states that ... "... *such a ridge, as it extends from the island landmass and even though it passes laterally into deep ocean floor, can be included in the continental margin of the island state in question and may be regarded as a 'submarine ridge' or 'submarine elevation' in the sense of Article 76, and not part of the deep ocean floor.*" ...

42. Based on the discussion in paragraphs 24 to 27 above, it is the view of the Commission that away from island landmasses and their associated, discrete seafloor highs, both the MAR (with its central valley, rift shoulders and flanks that dip at 0.1–0.2 degrees away from the central spreading axis) and the adjacent deep parts of the adjacent ocean basin belong to the deep ocean floor of the Atlantic Ocean.

43. ... The Commission recognises that islands surmounting discrete morphological features (including ridges) rising from this deep ocean floor are entitled to a "continental margin" and "continental shelf" (article 76, paragraphs 1 and 3). In the case of ridges surmounted by islands the question arises as to which parts of such ridges are of the deep ocean floor, and which parts represent the continental margin of the island (see paragraph 7.2.8 of the Guidelines).

44. Whether such islands are entitled to establish outer limits to their continental shelves beyond 200 M depends on the location of the base and the FOS within the submerged prolongation of those islands. Therefore, the FOS must be situated more than 140 M from the territorial sea baselines in order to establish an outer edge of continental margin beyond 200 M using the 60 M distance formula. For this to be the case for a small oceanic island like Ascension, it would have to surmount a discrete seafloor high, that itself rises above the average "ruggedness" of the deep ocean floor. In turn, such a discrete seafloor high would have to be of sufficient areal extent for the continental slope and its base to be within the necessary distance of the 200 M line or beyond. In the view of the Commission, the data submitted by the United Kingdom does not demonstrate such a situation....

47. ... The Commission is of the view that Ascension Island is distinct from the surrounding ocean floor, morphologically, geologically, geophysically and geochemically.

48. It is therefore the Commission's view that ... the base of the slope of Ascension Island [is located] at the bottom of the volcanic edifice, and not within the central valley or the fracture zones of the MAR, or where the

gently westward-dipping seafloor merges with other provinces of the deep ocean floor or the adjacent continental margins. . . .

3.2. Conclusions

51. The Commission is of the view that the rugged seafloor between the Ascension Island volcanic edifice and the axis of the MAR is part of the normal deep ocean floor (that includes the axial valley of the MAR). This volcanic edifice is a pinnacle surrounded by the deep ocean floor. Given this, any maximum change in gradient away from the base of that pinnacle (i.e. the base of the insular slope of the island surmounting the volcanic edifice) does not represent a valid FOS associated with the continental margin of the island, but is related to variations in the gradient of features of the deep ocean floor. This does not mean that islands, in general, cannot generate a continental margin that extends beyond 200 M. . . .

4. *Recommendations*

53. [T]he Commission concludes that, in the Ascension Island region, the FOS points contained in the Submission do not fulfil the requirements of article 76 and Chapters 5 and 7 of the Guidelines. The Commission recommends that these FOS points do not form the basis for the establishment of the outer edge of the continental margin in the Ascension Island region.

54. Consequently, the Commission recommends that, in the area around Ascension Island, the United Kingdom does not establish the outer limits of its continental shelf beyond 200 M on the basis of the technical and scientific documentation contained in the United Kingdom's Submission of 9 May 2008 and other data and material provided by the United Kingdom.

Notes

1. *The Commission on the Limits of the Continental Shelf and International Law.* As the excerpt above suggests, the CLCS is indeed a technical body, composed of "experts in the field of geology, geophysics or hydrography" (Annex II, Article 1) who evaluate submissions of data. As of September 1, 2013, there had been 67 submissions to the Commission, which had issued 18 recommendations; many states had also filed statements with preliminary information, indicating that additional submissions would be forthcoming. See http://www.un.org/depts/los/clcs_new/clcs_home.htm. Is the work of the CLCS, in setting standards in its Scientific and Technical Guidelines, CLCS/11 and Add. 1 (1999), and in making recommendations concerning continental shelf limits in specific cases, purely technical or scientific? Will the CLCS ever have to make

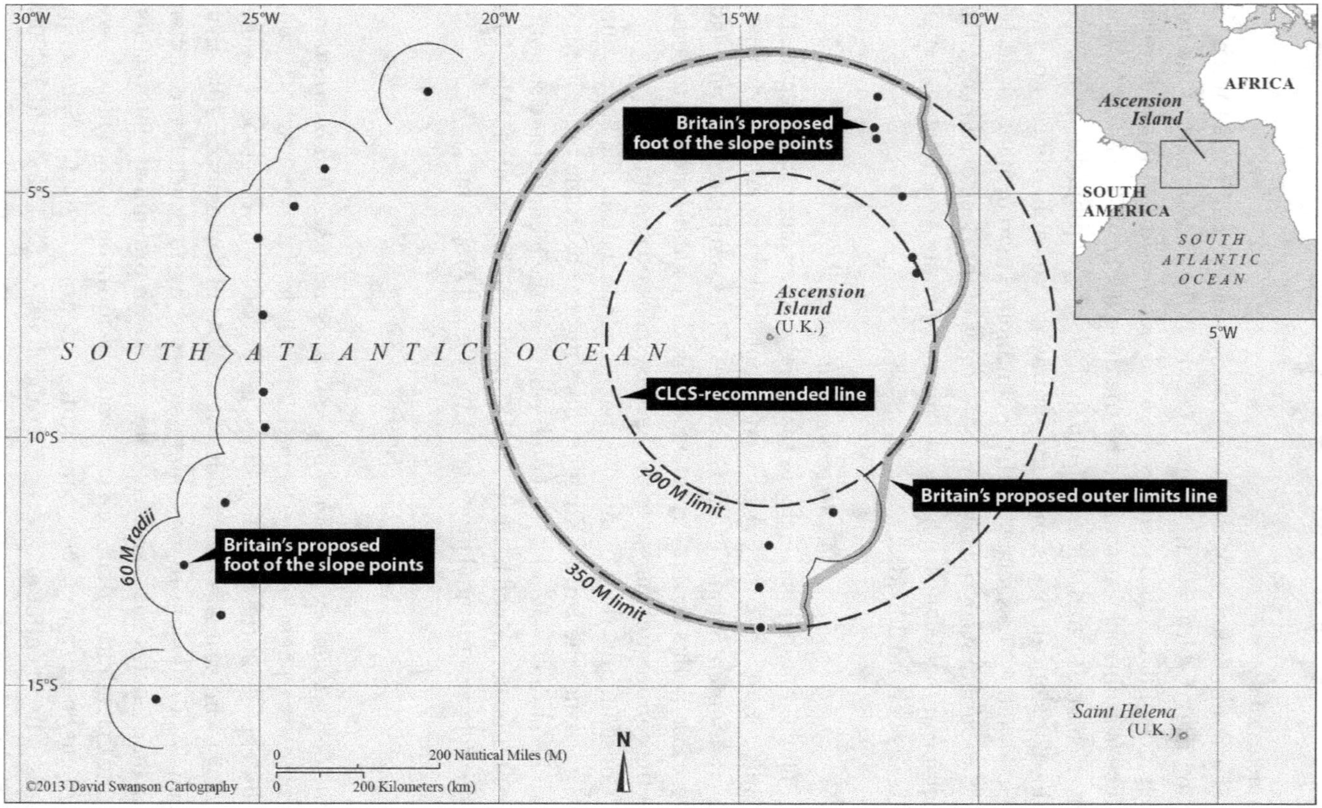

FIGURE X.C *Outer limits of the continental Shelf for Ascension Island, as proposed by the United Kingdom in 2008 and as recommended by the Commission on the Limits of the Continental Shelf in 2010*

legal determinations? Was it a mistake to leave international lawyers off the Commission?

2. *Islands and the Continental Shelf.* Why are islands entitled to any "continental" shelf at all? See LOS Convention, Articles 76, 121. In the excerpt above, the United Kingdom and the CLCS agreed that Ascension Island was entitled to a continental shelf. They disagreed, however, about whether it had a continental shelf extending beyond 200 nautical miles from the baseline. See Figure X.C. What was the British argument? Why did the United Kingdom not prevail? The CLCS confined its recommendation to Ascension Island, and in paragraph 51 of the Summary indicated that some islands perhaps could "generate a continental margin that extends beyond" 200 nautical miles from the baseline. Why should a mid-ocean island ever be able to claim a continental shelf extending beyond 200 nautical miles from its baselines? Is such an island located on an "oceanic ridge," as referred to in Article 76(3)? See Marc Benitah, Russia's Claim in the Arctic and the Vexing Issue of Ridges in UNCLOS, 11 ASIL Insights, Issue 27 (2007); Harold Brekke & Philip Symonds, Submarine Ridges and Elevations of Article 76 in Light of Published Summaries of Recommendations of the Commission on the Limits of the Continental Shelf, 42 Ocean Dev. & Intl. L. 289 (2011).

3. *CLCS Recommendations and Continental Shelf Outer Limits.* When a coastal state establishes the outer limits of a continental shelf that extends beyond 200 nautical miles from the baseline, is the coastal state legally obligated to follow exactly the CLCS's recommendations? With respect to Ascension Island, what could the United Kingdom do if it disagreed with the CLCS's recommendations? According to Article 76(8) of the LOS Convention, "limits of the shelf established by a coastal State on the basis of" CLCS recommendations "shall be final and binding." Are such limits binding only on the coastal state, or on other states?

Why, in its submission to the CLCS as shown in Figure X.C, did the United Kingdom propose outer limits that stopped at 350 nautical miles to the north, west, and south of Ascension Island, given that it had identified foot of the slope points far beyond that distance? See Article 76(5)–(6) of the LOS Convention. In its Ascension Island recommendation, did the CLCS accurately follow Article 76 of the LOS Convention? That is, was the disagreement with the United Kingdom really not about the law, but about geomorphological data, which, according to the Commission, did not support a foot of the slope outside 140 nautical miles from Ascension Island's baseline? The result of the Commission's determination was that the United Kingdom could not establish a continental shelf extending beyond 200 nautical miles from baselines. What should a coastal state do if the Commission issues a disadvantageous recommendation based on an erroneous legal interpretation of Article 76?

The United Kingdom, in a diplomatic note, stated that it was "disappointed with the final recommendations of the Commission" concerning Ascension Island, and referred to its arguments that the CLCS misinterpreted Article 76 of the LOS Convention. Note No. 08/11, United Kingdom Mission to the United Nations (Jan. 11, 2011), attaching Paper Summarising the Presentation by the United Kingdom of Great Britain and Northern Ireland to the Commission on the Limits of the Continental Shelf on Points of Legal Interpretation made on 12 April 2010, available at http://www.un.org/Depts/los/clcs_new/submissions_files/submission_gbr.htm.

In some CLCS submissions, one disputed issue has concerned how a coastal state may connect a fixed point located less than 60 nautical miles outside the 200-nautical-mile limit to that limit. May the state always connect that fixed point to the 200-nautical-mile limit by a 60-nautical-mile straight line? See Figure X.D. Do you see why the legal status of many hundreds of square miles of sea floor could be at stake? See LOS Convention, art. 76(2), (4), (7); Andrew Serdy, The Commission on the Limits of the Continental Shelf and its Disturbing Propensity to Legislate, 26 Intl. J. Marine & Coastal L. 355, 371–78 (2011).

In making its recommendations, may the CLCS consider the legality of an extensive straight baseline from which a coastal state seeks a 350-nautical-mile outer limit? May it determine whether a formation that a submitting state deems an island is really a rock that is not entitled to a continental shelf under Article 121(3) of the LOS Convention? How should the CLCS deal with such issues?

Why, in practical terms, might states be concerned if a coastal state has established outer limits in violation of international law? In what courts or tribunals, if any, may states challenge the legality of a coastal state's actions with respect to its outer limits? May the International Seabed Authority bring a challenge? The CLCS? See Erik Franckx, The International Seabed Authority and the Common Heritage of Mankind: The Need for States to Establish the Outer Limits of Their Continental Shelf, 25 Intl. J. Marine & Coastal L. 543 (2010); John E. Noyes, Judicial and Arbitral Proceedings and the Outer Limits of the Continental Shelf, 42 Vand. J. Transnatl. L. 1211 (2009). For more on dispute settlement under the LOS Convention, see Chapter 15.

4. *The Intersection of Law and Science*. Knowledge about the geology, geophysics, and geomorphology of the seabed has changed significantly since the LOS Convention was negotiated. In the excerpt above, for example, the CLCS notes new information and changing conceptions about Ascension Island and the Mid-Atlantic Ridge. Do such advances in knowledge make it difficult to interpret the Convention? Given the numerous coastal state submissions to the CLCS, it may well operate for several decades. If some new discovery casts

doubt on the scientific basis of a recommendation made years before, may the earlier recommendation be revisited? Should the CLCS, in an effort to treat submitting states even-handedly, apply the same scientific assumptions to all coastal state submissions, even if those assumptions have become outdated?

5. *Promoting Effective Access to the CLCS.* In order for coastal states to make effective submissions to the CLCS, they must be able to evaluate offshore data related to Article 76 criteria and make presentations to the CLCS. What can be done to help insure that states lacking the funds or expertise to compile all the technical data have the ability to collect and submit data? Would transparent CLCS deliberations help assure that any access to the CLCS is effective? What changes, if any, should be made to increase the transparency of CLCS deliberations?

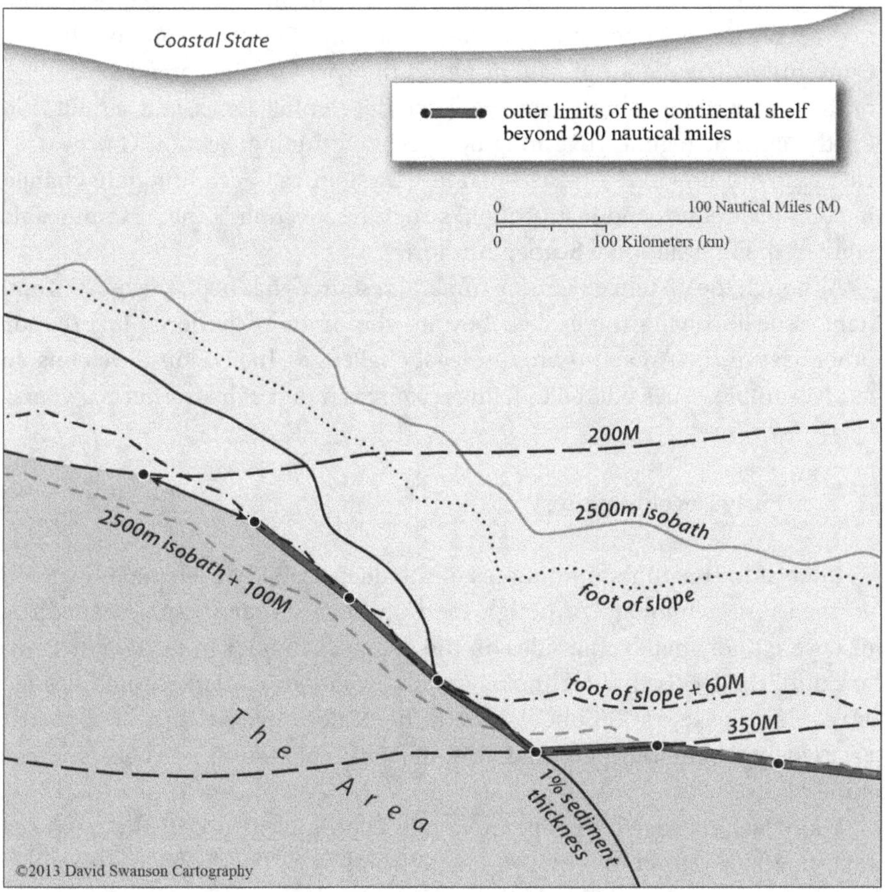

FIGURE X.D *Continental Shelf Beyond 200 Nautical Miles from Baselines*

CHAPTER 11

The Deep Seabed

This chapter primarily concerns the international legal regime for the mineral resources of the seabed and subsoil beyond the limits of national jurisdiction, a region known as the "Area." Section A traces early developments. Section B then outlines the complex provisions of Part XI of the 1982 United Nations Convention on the Law of the Sea (LOS Convention) governing deep seabed mineral resources. Those provisions involve roles for international institutions: the International Seabed Authority and the Seabed Disputes Chamber of the International Tribunal for the Law of the Sea.

As we see in Section C, a 1994 Part XI Implementation Agreement modified or set aside some controversial seabed mining provisions of the LOS Convention. This 1994 Agreement paved the way for widespread acceptance of the Convention by both developed and developing states, and set out rules for the current regime governing deep seabed mining. Section C provides a case study of how the international legal system can accommodate changes in complex treaties and institutional structures. Section D then examines the work of the International Seabed Authority.

Although the system governing mineral resources has been the most prominent issue involving the seabed beyond the limits of national jurisdiction, other uses of the Area also present legal challenges. In Section E we consider as an example issues related to living resources found at hydrothermal vents.

A Early Developments

Interest in the mineral resources of the deep seabed developed along with advances in technology. Although the *Challenger* oceanographic expedition discovered polymetallic nodules on the deep ocean floor in 1872–1876, it was not until the 1960s that technology made exploitation of these nodules feasible. John L. Mero's 1965 book, The Mineral Resources of the Seas, created excitement about the potential commercial exploitation of these strategic minerals.

Many leaders urged a cooperative approach toward use of the deep seabed. In 1966, U.S. President Lyndon Johnson said: "We must be careful to avoid a race to grab and to hold the lands under the high seas. We must ensure

 | DOI 10.1163/9789004203563_012

that the deep seas and the ocean bottoms are, and remain, the legacy of all human beings." Remarks at the Commissioning of the New Research Ship, The "Oceanographer," 2 Weekly Compilation of Presidential Documents 930, 931 (1966). In 1967 Ambassador Pardo of Malta gave an influential speech at the United Nations, noting the danger of militarization of the seabed, the risk of pollution that could permanently damage the marine environment, and the potential that technically advanced states could exclusively control the exploitation of the significant resources of the seabed beyond the limits of national jurisdiction. Ambassador Pardo thought that "escalating tensions" would be "inevitable" absent "an effective international régime over the sea-bed and the ocean floor beyond a clearly defined national jurisdiction." UNGAOR, 22d Sess., First Comm., 1516th mtg., ¶ 3, UN Doc. A/C.1/PV 1516 (1967). He proposed that a widely representative international agency, separate from the United Nations, be established to exercise regulatory powers with respect to the seabed beyond national jurisdiction and the resources found there.

In December 1967 the U.N. General Assembly voted to establish an Ad Hoc Committee to Study the Peaceful Uses of the Sea-Bed and the Ocean Floor beyond the Limits of National Jurisdiction. Following the report of the Ad Hoc Committee, the General Assembly, in December 1968, established the Committee on the Peaceful Uses of the Sea-Bed and the Ocean Floor beyond the Limits of National Jurisdiction (the Sea-Bed Committee). The work of this Committee led to important General Assembly resolutions. One was the 1969 Moratorium Resolution, in which the General Assembly, by a vote of 62 in favor and 28 against, with 28 abstentions, declared that:

> pending the establishment of the aforementioned international régime:
> (a) States and persons, physical or juridical, are bound to refrain from all activities of exploitation of the resources of the area of the sea-bed and ocean floor, and the subsoil thereof, beyond the limits of national jurisdiction;
> (b) No claim to any part of that area or its resources shall be recognized.

GA Res. 2574-D, UNGAOR, 24th Sess., Supp. No. 30 at 11, UN Doc. A/7630 (1969).

As we see in the next reading, developed and developing states held different views about the Moratorium Resolution. Also reproduced below are the General Assembly's influential 1970 Principles Resolution and a 1977 article that highlights the considerable interest in deep seabed mining during the years the LOS Convention was being negotiated.

EXPLANATORY STATEMENTS CONCERNING VOTES ON THE MORATORIUM RESOLUTION

UNGAOR, 24th Sess. at 1–3, UN Doc. A/PV.1833 (Dec. 15, 1969)

[This excerpt contains statements from the delegates of the United States and Mexico made to the U.N. General Assembly immediately prior to the recorded vote on the Moratorium Resolution. The delegates refer to the Resolution as the "draft resolution" or "draft resolution D."]

7. [Mr. *Phillips* (United States of America):] First of all, the draft resolution proceeds on a premise which is unsound and self-defeating: that the development of sea-bed exploitation, and accordingly the development of the technological capacity of such exploitation, should be retarded. What has struck us as doubly surprising about that proposition is that it is put forward in connexion with an item the very existence of which is due in substantial measure to the conviction that all mankind stands to benefit by the promotion of the exploitation of sea-bed resources. The question is, therefore, whose interests, if anybody's, would such retardation serve? This is the question to which we have as yet heard no adequate answer.

We are aware, of course, that a rather simplistic picture has sometimes been painted of developed maritime Powers monopolizing sea-bed technology and rushing greedily to exhaust sea-bed resources before the international community can establish a régime to regulate their exploitation. To knowledgeable people, however, this picture is defective in at least two respects. First, to the extent that the technology of sea-bed exploitation exists at all, it exists only in embryonic form. If its development does not move forward to the point where commercially viable exploitation of sea-bed resources is possible on a significant scale, there will be no exploitation of sea-bed resources and no benefit to anyone, developed or developing, coastal or landlocked, east or west, north or south.

8. Secondly, as far as my delegation is aware, there is simply no possibility of one country or group of countries having exclusive use of sea-bed exploitation technology, any more than one country or group of countries has exclusive use of the technology of exploiting resources on land. . . .

9. Thirdly, the tendency of this draft resolution is to encourage national action which will make the issues now entrusted to the Sea-Bed Committee for negotiation and solution progressively more difficult to solve. . . . In practical effect this draft resolution is likely to encourage some States that may feel it useful or necessary to engage in exploration or exploitation of sea-bed resources to move towards unjustifiably expansive claims of national jurisdiction

solely in order to remove those exploitation activities from the scope of the prohibition contained in the draft resolution and thus render them, in their view, legitimate. . . .

12. Finally, not the least regrettable aspect of the draft resolution before us is that its adoption would represent a breakdown, on a matter of basic importance, of those processes of cooperation and consensus which are necessary if any genuine accomplishment is to result from our joint labours on the sea-bed issues in the United Nations. . . .

14. Mr. *Garcia Robles* (Mexico): . . . Ever since this subject first came up for consideration in the General Assembly in 1967, all our work has been based upon the premise that the exploitation of the resources of the sea-bed and the ocean floor, and the subsoil thereof, beyond the limits of national jurisdiction, should be carried out in the interests of all mankind, irrespective of the geographical location of States and taking into account the special interests and needs of the developing countries.

15. To this end it is imperative for the Committee on the Sea-Bed and the Ocean Floor to come to an agreement on the establishment of an international régime that shall include appropriate international machinery to make such exploitation possible. Hence, draft resolution D, submitted by the First Committee, is limited, in the interests of all mankind, to making explicit what basically is only the necessary corollary of the principles which were clearly accepted by the General Assembly when it adopted the actual title of the agenda item and which, moreover, were expressly included by the General Assembly in previous resolutions such as resolution 2467 A (XXIII). . . .

16. [T]he basic and indeed sole objective is to ensure that while the Committee on the Sea-Bed and the Ocean Floor is deliberating on the establishment of the international régime, States and persons, physical or juridical, shall not take advantage of the inevitable delay to appropriate the resources of the region or exploit them for their own benefit. For we all remember the statement made by Mrs. Myrdal, the distinguished representative of Sweden, in the First Committee, in which she said:

> . . . while we deliberate, developments may take a course of their own. The risk that, as time passes, national property rights become acquired "by use, occupation or other means" must not be overlooked. Commercial interests are clamouring vociferously for go-ahead signals; their technical press can provide any number of quotations to that effect. Military interests seem to be no less eager. Powerful techniques are already in the hands of a few countries. . . . It thus becomes urgent for us to act immediately in order to forestall any regrettable developments.

17. The obligations of States and persons, physical or juridical, mentioned in the draft resolution are, of course, applicable only to those areas which lie outside national jurisdiction. Furthermore, the draft resolution does not undertake to decide how far the area extends or what are the limits of national jurisdiction.

Note

1. *The U.S. Position.* In May 1970, following the Moratorium Resolution but before adoption of the Principles Resolution (below), U.S. President Richard Nixon proposed that:

> all nations adopt as soon as possible a treaty under which they would renounce all national claims over the natural resources of the seabed beyond the point where the high seas reach a depth of 200 meters (218.8 yards) and would agree to regard these resources as the common heritage of mankind. The treaty should establish an international regime for the exploitation of seabed resources beyond this limit. The regime should provide for the collection of substantial mineral royalties to be used for international community purposes, particularly economic assistance to developing countries.

62 Dept. State Bull. 737 (1970). According to President Nixon, if the law of the sea "is not modernized multilaterally, unilateral action and international conflict are inevitable"; an international agreement could "save over two-thirds of the earth's surface from national conflict and rivalry, protect it from pollution and put it to use for the benefit of all." Id. Did President Nixon take the same position as that expressed by Mr. Phillips in his statement about the Moratorium Resolution? Or was the President suggesting a change in U.S. policy?

THE PRINCIPLES RESOLUTION
Declaration of Principles Governing the Sea-Bed and the Ocean Floor, and the Subsoil Thereof, beyond the Limits of National Jurisdiction, GA Res. 2749, UN Doc. A/RES/25/2749 (1970)

The General Assembly . . .
Solemnly declares that:
1. The sea-bed and ocean floor, and the subsoil thereof, beyond the limits of national jurisdiction (hereinafter referred to as the area), as well as the resources of the area, are the common heritage of mankind.

2. The area shall not be subject to appropriation by any means by States or persons, natural or juridical, and no State shall claim or exercise sovereignty or sovereign rights over any part thereof.

3. No State or person, natural or juridical, shall claim, exercise or acquire rights with respect to the area or its resources incompatible with the international régime to be established and the principles of this Declaration.

4. All activities regarding the exploration and exploitation of the resources of the area and other related activities shall be governed by the international régime to be established.

5. The area shall be open to use exclusively for peaceful purposes by all States, whether coastal or land-locked, without discrimination, in accordance with the international régime to be established.

6. States shall act in the area in accordance with the applicable principles and rules of international law, including the Charter of the United Nations and the Declaration on Principles of International Law concerning Friendly Relations and Co-operation among States in accordance with the Charter of the United Nations, adopted by the General Assembly on 24 October 1970, in the interests of maintaining international peace and security and promoting international co-operation and mutual understanding.

7. The exploration of the area and the exploitation of its resources shall be carried out for the benefit of mankind as a whole, irrespective of the geographical location of States, whether land-locked or coastal, and taking into particular consideration the interests and needs of the developing countries.

8. The area shall be reserved exclusively for peaceful purposes, without prejudice to any measures which have been or may be agreed upon in the context of international negotiations undertaken in the field of disarmament and which may be applicable to a broader area. One or more international agreements shall be concluded as soon as possible in order to implement effectively this principle and to constitute a step towards the exclusion of the sea-bed, the ocean floor and the subsoil thereof from the arms race.

9. On the basis of the principles of this Declaration, an international régime applying to the area and its resources and including appropriate international machinery to give effect to its provisions shall be established by an international treaty of a universal character, generally agreed upon. The régime shall, inter alia, provide for the orderly and safe development and rational management of the area and its resources and for expanding opportunities in the use thereof, and ensure the equitable sharing by States in the benefits derived therefrom, taking into particular consideration the interests and needs of the developing countries, whether land-locked or coastal.

10. States shall promote international co-operation in scientific research exclusively for peaceful purposes:

(*a*) By participation in international programmes and by encouraging co-operation in scientific research by personnel of different countries;

(*b*) Through effective publication of research programmes and dissemination of the results of research through international channels;

(*c*) By co-operation in measures to strengthen research capabilities of developing countries, including the participation of their nationals in research programmes.

No such activity shall form the legal basis for any claims with respect to any part of the area or its resources.

11. With respect to activities in the area and acting in conformity with the international régime to be established, States shall take appropriate measures for and shall co-operate in the adoption and implementation of international rules, standards and procedures for, *inter alia*:

(*a*) The prevention of pollution and contamination, and other hazards to the marine environment, including the coastline, and of interference with the ecological balance of the marine environment;

(*b*) The protection and conservation of the natural resources of the area and the prevention of damage to the flora and fauna of the marine environment.

12. In their activities in the area, including those relating to its resources, States shall pay due regard to the rights and legitimate interests of coastal States in the region of such activities, as well as of all other States, which may be affected by such activities. Consultations shall be maintained with the coastal States concerned with respect to activities relating to the exploration of the area and the exploitation of its resources with a view to avoiding infringement of such rights and interests.

13. Nothing herein shall affect:

(*a*) The legal status of the waters superjacent to the area or that of the air space above those waters;

(*b*) The rights of coastal States with respect to measures to prevent, mitigate or eliminate grave and imminent danger to their coastline or related interests from pollution or threat thereof or from other hazardous occurrences resulting from or caused by any activities in the area, subject to the international régime to be established.

14. Every State shall have the responsibility to ensure that activities in the area, including those relating to its resources, whether undertaken by governmental agencies, or non-governmental entities or persons under its jurisdiction, or acting on its behalf, shall be carried out in conformity with the international régime to be established. The same responsibility applies to

international organizations and their members for activities undertaken by such organizations or on their behalf. Damage caused by such activities shall entail liability.

15. The parties to any dispute relating to activities in the area and its resources shall resolve such dispute by the measures mentioned in Article 33 of the Charter of the United Nations and such procedures for settling disputes as may be agreed upon in the international régime to be established.

Notes

1. *The Vote on the Principles Resolution.* The General Assembly approved the Principles Resolution on December 17, 1970. The vote was 108 in favor, none against, and fourteen abstentions. No record of individual votes was taken. Among the states declaring their approval were France, Japan, the United Kingdom, and the United States. UNGAOR, 25th Sess., UN Docs. A/C.1/PV.1798 at 12–17, 26–37 (1970); A/C.1/PV.1799 at 6–16, 23–30 (1970). Is this U.S. position consistent with the policy that President Nixon had articulated in May 1970, quoted in the Note immediately before the Principles Resolution? Why did the United States vote in favor of the Resolution? When the Principles Resolution was adopted, the United States and several other countries in fact declared that the Resolution was not binding and did not constitute an interim deep seabed mining regime. Id. at 1, 3–4, 6. The United States also rejected the earlier Moratorium Resolution and reserved its right to begin exploring and exploiting the deep seabed on a non-exclusive basis with regard to the rights of other states, until it became a party to an international agreement establishing a new international regime. Id.

2. *The Legal Effect of General Assembly Resolutions.* What factors shape or determine the legal effect of General Assembly resolutions? What were the implications of the Principles Resolution for the shape of an international legal regime to govern the control or ownership of mineral resources of the seabed beyond national jurisdiction?

ROGER-J. BONNEL, BELGIANS AND AMERICANS ARE GETTING READY TO COLLECT OCEAN MINERALS

Le Soir [Belgian francophone edition], Aug. 19, 1977, at 1, 4, translated in U.S. Joint Publications Research Service, Translations on Law of the Sea, No. 58, Oct. 6, 1977

[Although the references to technology in this 1977 article are dated, the article conveys a sense of the excitement associated with prospects for deep seabed mining at the time the LOS Convention was being negotiated, as well as some significant background about deep seabed mineral resources.]

Several weeks from now, toward the end of September, semi-industrial exploitation tests of polymetallic oceanic nodules will begin in the Pacific, thus marking the beginning of the "sea-mining" era. What makes this news all the more interesting to us is that our country is directly involved in this great adventure of our time.

Union Minière [a Belgian corporation], through its two subsidiaries—Union Mines, with one-third of the investment and responsible for recovery of nodules, and Metallurgie Hoboken-Overpelt, with ten percent of the mining company and responsible for separation of the metals contained in the nodules—will be in partnership with the Americans. A pilot plant will be built in Belgium, showing how important the enterprise is to our country.

[Oceanic] wealth is not made up, as one might think, of oil deposits in the sea, but of nodules. . . . What is involved? Stony concretions whose dimensions vary from the size of a ping-pong ball to that of a paving stone. [T]hey are rich in multiple metals.

[P]olymetallic nodules are formed at the interface of water and sediment, far from continents, in deep, cold water at about 1 [degree centigrade] and at a pressure varying between 350 and 500 kg per square centimeter. Their concentration may vary between 0 and 50 kg to the square meter, the latter figure being the exception. The composition of the nodules varies, depending on the site where they were taken.

We had the good fortune of meeting J.-J. Saquet, president of the "Deepsea Ventures Incorporated" group, [a U.S. corporation that] specializes in collecting nodules, and president of Union Mines.

As far back as 1970 exploitation tests were conducted in the Pacific. In 1974 Union Minière became interested in "ocean mining" and decided to participate in the evaluation of nodules. Some groups which took an initial interest in this exploitation have retired from it—the Japanese, for instance. In November 1975 the only remaining shareholders were U.S. Steel, the second largest steel producer in the world, and Union Minière. In April 1977 a third partner, the American Sun group, joined with Deepsea Ventures Incorporated to carry on the planned program.

To succeed in exploiting polymetallic nodules from the ocean depths, Mr. Saquet told us, it is essential to take as a basis a two-pronged system: 1. to proceed with prospecting marine depths in order to ascertain their geologic structure. There is a ship for that purpose, "Prospector," equipped with highly technical apparatus. 2. to settle on mining methods for nodule collection.

Nodule recovery tests conducted since 1970 on the Blake Plateau, 200 nautical miles from Georgia, proved it was possible to exploit nodules. A ship was equipped with a derrick which permitted descent to a depth of 800 meters.

Although the first recoveries were accomplished with the aid of a "dredging tank," an "aspirator" system has now been perfected. This involves a pipe 4,500 meters long, suspended beneath the ship; its terminal is equipped with a dredging head which brings the nodules up to the entrance of the pipe. Compressed air is injected there, causing suction or "airlift" which enables recovery of a column of water containing nodules.

The tests were more than fruitful, since at the time of the recovery tests there was not enough room on board for storing the nodules and part of them had to be thrown overboard!

[T]he new ship, "Deepsea Ventures II" is equipped with highly perfected fittings, and continuous monitoring of what is going on in the vicinity of the dredge during mining "trawling" is possible, by means of a television camera.

In the Pacific, nodules are always found at greater depths. The most important known deposit is located North of New Guinea and Southwest of Hawaii, between 0° and 20° North and 120° and 180° West. Nodules of the highest mineral content are found in the Pacific abyssal plains, between the Clarion and Clipperton fracture zones.

"Deepsea Ventures," which converted an ore ship in order to begin semi-industrial exploitation, asked the American government for a concession for an emplacement located a thousand nautical miles South of San Francisco. The final tests are currently being completed along the coasts of the United States in order to test each equipment subsystem. The site selected covers 60,000 square km, or roughly twice the area of Belgium. Although it did not grant a concession, the Washington government responded concisely: "There is no problem. You have selected a site on the high seas which does not at present fall under national or international legal authority." . . .

The ship which will go into action at the end of September will operate at a fifth of normal commercial scale, which is one million tons per year. It will then be a matter of proceeding to extract metals. The average content of the nodules is from 25 to 30 percent manganese; 1 to 1.4 percent nickel; .8 to 1.3 percent copper; 1 per thousand to 3 per thousand cobalt; the iron average may reach 6 percent.

Such extraction poses no problem for Metallurgie Hoboken-Overpelt, the "grand master" of complex metallurgic processes. That is why the pilot plant for processing nodules in metallic form will be built in Belgium. The manganese will be converted in the United States into oxide to form a manganiferous alloy.

No one can precisely evaluate the quantity of nodules, Mr. Saquet told us, since research has been conducted in only a minimal ocean area. In addition, as he told us, the causes of nodule formation are not well known. It is known that their age varies between one and ten million years. One thing is established: they proliferate in the Pacific at a depth of 4,500 to 6,000 meters.

For a site to be exploitable, 500 million tons of nodules must be extracted. Now, it is estimated that there are between 150 and 450 sites in the world. Figuring from the lowest number, 75 billion tons of nodules could be produced, but it would be possible to find twice as much.

Twenty-five to 30 percent of nodule metals are actually recoverable. As it is estimated that it will take six to eight years to begin a real industrial exploitation, Mr. Saquet believes that in the meantime a technologic method will be discovered which will make it possible to increase the rate of metal recovery. There are enough polymetallic nodules for at least 40 years of exploitation.

Notes

1. *The Minerals in the Deep Seabed.* Attention originally focused on polymetallic nodules, which contain manganese, nickel, copper, and cobalt. Polymetallic sulphides have attracted attention in recent years. Scientists have discovered considerable deposits of polymetallic sulphides, both in shallow waters subject to national jurisdiction and near deep ocean hydrothermal vents on the seabed beyond national jurisdiction. Polymetallic sulphides contain copper, iron, and zinc sulphides and, sometimes, gold and silver. Also of interest are cobalt-rich ferromanganese crusts, which are found on seamounts and undersea ridges and plateaux. See International Seabed Authority, Polymetallic Massive Sulphides and Cobalt-Rich Ferromanganese Crusts: Status and Prospects (ISA Technical Study No. 2, 2002).

2. *Location of Nodules.* The 1977 Le Soir article mentioned the nodule-rich deep seabed area between the Clarion and Clipperton fracture zones southeast of Hawaii. Although this region of the central Pacific, between the equator and 20° N latitude and between the American continent and 155° E longitude, contains the most extensive and concentrated known deposit of commercial grade nodules, there are other areas of potential commercial interest.

3. *Nodule Recovery Technology.* Technology for recovering polymetallic nodules from the deep seabed has advanced dramatically since the system noted in the Le Soir article. For descriptions of seabed mining technologies, see Report on the International Seabed Authority's Workshop on Polymetallic Nodule Mining Technology: Current Status and Challenges Ahead, ISBA/14/C/7 (2008).

4. *Overly Optimistic Projections?* The Le Soir article struck an optimistic note about the prospects for commercially viable mining of deep seabed minerals. Many shared this optimism. In 1967, Malta's Ambassador Arvid Pardo had stirred much excitement when he discussed the potential for exploiting the "incredibly vast" non-living resources on and beneath the ocean floor beyond the limits of national jurisdiction. UNGAOR, 22d Sess., First Comm., 1515th mtg., ¶ 35, UN Doc. A/C.1/PV 1515 (1967). Pardo thought those limits would be set closer to shore than the outer limits of the continental shelf eventually authorized in the LOS Convention, and his reference to non-living resources included oil and gas resources. Nevertheless, the idea that deep seabed nodules could provide vast wealth animated many delegates at UNCLOS III.

Some economists were also enthusiastic. In 1972 one expert termed polymetallic nodules an "essentially inexhaustible source of many important industrial metals." Deep seabed mining presented an "exciting investment opportunity," which could "measurably reduc[e] pollution of the atmosphere by permitting the closing down of many pollution-prone . . . mines on land." John L. Mero, Potential Economic Value of Ocean-Floor Manganese Nodule Deposits, in Papers from a Conference on Ferromanganese Deposits on the Ocean Floor 191, 201 (David R. Horn ed., 1972). Even in the 1970s, however, most economists stressed the difficulties with accurately predicting the costs or profitability of seabed mining. See J.D. Nyhart et al., A Cost Model of Deep Ocean Mining and Associated Regulatory Issues (1978). Improved efficiencies in land-based production, the discovery of minerals in coastal zones (e.g., off Papua New Guinea), and uncertainties about the prospects for environmentally sensitive and effective deep-sea recovery methods led observers to question the economic viability of deep seabed mining.

Writing in 2006, Satya Nandan, the then Secretary-General of the International Seabed Authority, concluded:

> Given the current status of exploration and the lead time required to reach the commercial exploitation phase, it would be safe to say that unless there is a major infusion of capital, especially from the private sector, commercial exploitation of minerals from the deep seabed cannot be said to be imminent. On the other hand, it would be equally fair to say, that given the clear evidence of the presence of large-scale deposits of minerals in various forms, the growing demand for raw material, and man's ingenuity and determination, long-term prospects for successful deep seabed mining [are] very promising.

Satya Nandan, Administering the Mineral Resources of the Deep Seabed, in The Law of the Sea: Progress and Prospects 75, 91 (David Freestone, Richard

Barnes & David M. Ong eds., 2006). Changing market conditions, the high metal content of some deep seabed resources, concerns of countries with gaining secure sources of strategic metals, and improved technology have recently prompted optimistic assessments of prospects for deep seabed mining. See William J. Broad, A Gold Rush in the Abyss, N.Y. Times, July 10, 2012 at D1; Alistair Macdonald & Edward Welsch, Next Frontier: Mining the Ocean Floor, Wall St. J., June 4, 2012.

B Part XI of the 1982 LOS Convention

At the Third United Nations Conference on the Law of the Sea (UNCLOS III), negotiation of a deep seabed mining regime proved difficult. The final product, codified primarily in Part XI of the LOS Convention, set out general principles to govern seabed mining, principles that traced their origins to the early General Assembly resolutions. The Convention also contained complex articles specifying the structure and powers of a new international institution, the International Seabed Authority (ISA or Authority). In addition, the Convention provided for economic assistance for developing states, a production ceiling to safeguard land-based producers, and mechanisms allowing an international seabed institution to obtain mining technology.

This section highlights Part XI's provisions, along with critical reactions to those provisions. Many of Part XI's detailed provisions were modified or set aside in the 1994 Implementation Agreement. We examine that Agreement in Section C.

LAW OF THE SEA CONVENTION

Articles 1(1)(1), 1(1)(3), 133–50, 152–58, 170, 176, 186

See Appendix

Notes

1. *The Common Heritage Principle*. According to Article 136 of the LOS Convention, "[t]he Area and its resources are the common heritage of mankind." Paragraph 1 of the Principles Resolution, reproduced in Section A, also refers to the common heritage principle. What does "common heritage" mean in this context? That claims of sovereignty or sovereign rights over the Area or its resources are prohibited? That resources are vested in humankind as a whole (and if so, what is meant by "humankind")? That "activities in the Area,"

defined in Article 1(1)(3), must be carried out for the benefit of humankind as a whole, taking into particular consideration the interests and needs of developing states, especially landlocked and geographically disadvantaged ones? That economic benefits derived from activities in the Area must be shared equitably (and if so, what is meant by "equitably")? That other benefits must be shared (and if so, what benefits)? That the Area is to be reserved for peaceful purposes? That the marine environment must be protected from harmful effects arising from activities in the Area? That activities in the Area are to be governed under an international management regime? All of the above? Something else? See John E. Noyes, The Common Heritage of Mankind: Past, Present, and Future, 40 Denver J. Intl. L. & Policy 447 (2012); 6 United Nations Convention on the Law of the Sea, 1982: A Commentary, ¶¶ INTRO.3 to INTRO.13, 136.8(a) (Myron Nordquist et al. eds., 2003).

2. *The Original Part XI Regime.* Describe the original governance system for "activities in the Area" set out in the LOS Convention. What institutions were involved, and what were their responsibilities? What is the "parallel system"? What steps did a mining company have to take before it could explore for or exploit mineral resources in the Area? As we will see in Section C, this original system has been changed significantly.

3. *Annex III and Detailed Technical Provisions on Seabed Mining.* Many of the LOS Convention's provisions governing deep seabed mining are highly technical. Some of these provisions are contained in the Convention itself—e.g., Article 151 on production ceilings and policies—and some appear in Annexes III and IV to the Convention, which "form an integral part of" the Convention. LOS Convention, Article 318. Annex III's Article 13 concerning the financial terms of contracts provides an example of the detailed, technical nature of some of the Convention's rules on seabed mining.

Was it wise to negotiate such detailed provisions? The mining-related activities that the Convention sought to regulate were not yet economically viable, and, once undertaken, might be pursued in significantly changed circumstances. Should the drafters of the Convention instead have set down only framework principles to govern seabed mining, leaving specific details to be worked out in future protocols or through decisions of state parties to the Convention? Many environmental treaties have used such an approach.

4. *The International Political Context.* The negotiation of the seabed mining provisions of the LOS Convention proved difficult because of the different political perspectives of various groups of states. Developing and developed states held divergent views:

> The Group of 77 sought the establishment of an international seabed authority itself having the power to engage in sea-bed mining, and

> to control mining by other licensees, who would pay it royalties which, along with its own profits, would be distributed among all States as the "common heritage of mankind." The developed States, in contrast, proposed initially that the authority should be established as little more than a registry of national claims to sea-bed mining sites, having few, if any, powers to interfere with the exploitation of the Area by the mining companies.

R.R. Churchill & A.V. Lowe, The Law of the Sea 228 (3d ed. 1999). Nevertheless, not all developed states held identical positions, nor did all developing states:

> The group of landlocked and other geographically disadvantaged States . . ., for example, which included both developed and developing States, pressed hard for guarantees concerning their representation in the authority and their share in the benefits of sea-bed mining. Similarly those States, from both north and south, which have wide continental shelves, opposed the efforts of the geographically disadvantaged States, among others, to establish narrow limits to national sea-bed jurisdiction in order to maximize the area constituting the common heritage of mankind.

Id. For additional discussion of divergent economic interests regarding the deep seabed, see Bernard H. Oxman, The Third United Nations Conference on the Law of the Sea: The 1976 New York Sessions, 71 Am. J. Intl. L. 247, 251–53 (1977).

5. *The U.S. Political Context.* The United States had long favored some international regime concerning the deep seabed. See the statements of the Johnson and Nixon administrations, excerpted in Section A. Although the Nixon proposal differed from the one that evolved at UNCLOS III, the Nixon, Ford, and Carter administrations all sought consensus on the seabed mining regime at the Conference, recognizing that the complex negotiations were producing a treaty text that provided rights concerning navigation and other matters important to U.S. interests. The difficult negotiations concerning the seabed mining regime—involving some of the "hard-core" issues at UNCLOS III—were nearing a conclusion when, in 1981, a new administration took office in the United States. The Reagan administration decided to review the U.S. position toward the Convention's seabed mining provisions and, as the next excerpt reveals, ultimately decided not to sign the Convention because of objections to some of those provisions.

WHITE HOUSE OFFICE OF POLICY INFORMATION, ISSUE UPDATE NO. 10
Apr. 15, 1983

On December 10, 1982, signing ceremonies for the United Nations Convention on the Law of the Sea (LOS) were held at Montego Bay, Jamaica. While 117 countries signed the treaty, the United States and 46 other nations, together representing more than half of the world's GNP, chose not to sign the document.

President Reagan had announced on July 9, 1982, that the United States would not sign. In making this statement the President acknowledged that the treaty contained "many positive and very significant accomplishments," but noted that "the deep seabed mining part of the convention does not meet U.S. objectives" and was unacceptable.

The Administration's earlier review had identified several draft treaty provisions with regard to deep seabed mining that would be distinctly harmful to U.S. and other countries' interests. Accordingly, the President, on January 29, 1982, made explicit six major U.S. objectives in the LOS Treaty negotiations. An acceptable treaty, he said, must:

1) Not deter development of any seabed mineral resources to meet national and world demands.
2) Assure national access to these resources by current and future qualified entities to enhance U.S. security of supply, to avoid monopolization of the resources by the operating arm of the International Authority, and to promote the economic development of the resources.
3) Provide a decision-making role in the deep seabed régime that fairly reflects and effectively protects political and economic interests and the financial contributions of participating states.
4) Not allow for amendments to come into force without approval of the participating states, including the advice and consent of the U.S. Senate.
5) Not set other undesirable precedents for international organizations.
6) Be likely to receive the advice and consent of the U.S. Senate.

At the President's direction, the U.S. sought certain revisions that would have brought the document more in line with these objectives. Several U.S. allies supported that effort.

However, the Third World nations that dominated the LOS negotiations rejected the proposed revisions, preventing the LOS convention from meeting any of the U.S. objectives....

Under international law, development of . . . deep-ocean minerals is a freedom of the high seas open to exercise by any nation. The LOS treaty would eliminate this free access for all nations, and transfer control of the ocean's minerals to an international authority dominated by Third World states, which are largely hostile to free market approaches and to the interests of the industrialized nations of the free world. Granting them veto power over development of resources that are potentially valuable to western economic and security interests would thus be dangerously short-sighted. It would also be a gross perversion of this country's original goals in the LOS process.

The New International Economic Order

The United States and the other developed countries entered into the LOS negotiations primarily to achieve a balanced and mutually beneficial resolution of certain difficult issues related to the use of the world's oceans. Many of the less-developed countries, however, had another object in mind: to use the LOS process as a vehicle for the mandatory transfer of wealth and technology from "have" nations of the globe to the "have nots."

The LOS sessions were dominated from beginning to end by a coalition of these developing states, known as the "Group of 77" (which now number 120). The ultimate aim of the Group of 77 is the establishment of a New International Economic Order (NIEO), a scheme for restructuring the international economy along the socialist lines of the world's centrally-managed economies and for redistributing the world's wealth. The LOS treaty is viewed by the Group of 77 as a significant step toward this end because the seabed provisions enshrine several NIEO principles.

One of the most instrumental of the NIEOs concepts is [the] treaty's proclamation that the resources of the deep seabed are the "common heritage of mankind." This idea, first propounded in an address to the U.N. General Assembly by Ambassador Arvid Pardo of Malta in 1967, was later incorporated into a resolution by that body in 1970. The U.S. supported that resolution with the provision that it had no intrinsic legal meaning and could acquire substance only through a universally accepted treaty. Short of that, the U.S. view has consistently been that the deep seabed is the exclusive province of no one nation or group of nations, and may therefore be developed by anyone willing to expend the necessary capital and assume the inevitable risks associated with that development.

Yet the dominant Third World viewpoint is just the opposite: that the deep seabed is the collective property of all nations, that an international body—which the Third World countries would effectively control—should regulate access to the seabed, and that any fruits of development should be distributed to all countries, regardless of whoever undertakes the burden of mining.

These ideas, once established in the LOS convention, could easily be applied in other areas. In particular, the LOS treaty would set a precedent for further Third World efforts to dictate the use of resources beyond national jurisdiction, such as control of Antarctica and other unclaimed resource depositories, and, possibly, the International Monetary Fund and World Bank.

Concern over the LOS treaty therefore transcends the issue of the national or private right to mine the ocean floor, although that in itself is certainly important. In broader terms, the question is whether the United States should endorse an agreement that, by its failure to meet stated U.S. objectives, remains contrary to fundamental American political and economic principle interests.

There is a practical side to this question as well. Free-market economies have, almost without exception, generated far higher standards of living for all their peoples than have [those] rooted in socialist doctrine. Relying on the discredited centralized economic control techniques of the latter as the basis for mining the minerals of the seabed would therefore be one of the least effective means possible for promoting global prosperity.

How the "Common Heritage" Would be Divided

Nevertheless, the LOS treaty depends almost exclusively on centralized control devices. Under the provisions of the LOS convention, an International Seabed Authority (the "Authority") would have jurisdiction over deep seabed mining. Modeled loosely on the United Nations, the Authority would consist of a "supreme" policy-making Assembly in which each member nation would have one vote, and a 36-member Executive Council, corresponding respectively, but only roughly, to the U.N. General Assembly and the Security Council.

Like its U.N. counterpart, the Assembly would be dominated by the Group of 77 and be heavily influenced by the Soviet Union and its sympathizers. It would in practice be another forum to propagandize against the interests of the industrialized countries and their successful economies.

Even more troublesome, the Council of the Authority, unlike the U.N. Security Council, would have no permanent members and no Great Power veto, two devices that have repeatedly been used to protect U.S. interests in the United Nations. Most decisions would instead be made on the basis of consensus, two-thirds or three-fourths majority votes, which the Third World would have little difficulty mustering. This would permit the Group of 77 to effectively block or control, and thus dictate, the terms for seabed mining and thereby further implement the NIEO.

Mining operations would be carried out on behalf of the Authority by a commercial subsidiary called the "Enterprise," for which the United States would pay a quarter of the massive startup costs—a share that could amount to [US$] 300–350 million. The Enterprise, through an array of special privileges, could exercise a virtual monopoly over seabed mining.

At the same time, the LOS treaty would place heavy burdens on any nation or private concern that wanted to compete with the Enterprise. A company wishing to engage in deep seabed mining would have to pay the Authority a license application fee of [US$] 500,000. Yet nothing in the treaty requires the Authority to approve the company's application. It could reject the application outright, or subject it to preconditions either detrimental to ocean mining or harmful to friends of the U.S., such as a mandatory boycott of Israel as a prerequisite for mining.

If a company were actually awarded a license, it would thereafter be required to pay an annual "exploration fee" of [US$] 1 million. As if this were not enough to discourage the most intrepid entrepreneur, the LOS treaty would permit the Authority to restrict private companies' production in order to protect the market position of land-based mineral producers and the Enterprise, which is itself guaranteed a substantial level of production under the treaty.

A private competitor could also be forced to transfer its mining technology to the Enterprise or to developing countries, and would be prohibited from using any technology it did not transfer. Since the technology employed in any large mining project is typically obtained from a hundred or more third parties, companies seeking to operate under the treaty would face the virtually impossible task of either convincing all such suppliers to make their technology available to the Authority, or designing and assembling a practical mining system without the use of technology owned by these third parties, and be willing to transfer such a system, upon completion, to the Enterprise.

It is therefore unlikely that any private mining operation would be successfully assembled under the treaty. Companies, by and large, simply will not take such risks and make major investments in new technologies if they cannot expect to receive the benefits of doing so. As a result, the treaty most likely would choke off the development of the technology necessary to mine the seabed.

Other Flaws in the Treaty

There remain other serious flaws in the LOS treaty. The treaty, for example, could subsidize international terrorism. Several "national liberation groups," including the Palestine Liberation Organization (PLO) and the South-West Africa People's Organization (SWAPO), had observer status at LOS negotiations. Under the terms of the treaty, these and other similar groups could share in the distribution of seabed wealth.

Another serious objection to the treaty is that it could be amended after 20 years by a three-fourths vote and ratification by nations party to the treaty. Thus, if it ratified the treaty, the U.S. would for all practical purposes lock itself into any such changes, having little choice other than withdrawing from the treaty. Even U.S. Senate rejection of the treaty amendments would not necessarily prevent them from going into effect. The Group of 77 and its allies would comprise at least three-fourths of most conceivable sets of treaty signatories, and would effectively control the amendment process.

Effect on the Third World

The restrictions that the LOS treaty would impose on seabed mining are contrary to the interests of both industrialized and the developing countries. The latter nations in particular would have few, if any, opportunities to join in the production of seabed minerals under the treaty, and little chance of profiting from the seabed's wealth of resources.

For deep seabed mining is not yet commercially viable, and the technical difficulties and costs involved in recovering minerals from depths of up to 15,000 feet are considerable, especially since present mineral markets are weak. Unless the companies that have the capital and expertise to undertake so risky a venture have the opportunity to earn a reasonable reward for their efforts, vast quantities of mineral-rich ores could remain on the ocean bottom, and *no one* would benefit from them.

Even if deep seabed mining did come about under LOS, despite the treaty's onerous restraints, there is no reason to assume that the people in the developing countries would see any improvement in their lives. That part of the wealth from deep seabed mining taken by the Authority would first be used to fund the Authority's operation and bureaucracy, and there would be little if any left over. Moreover, by restricting the rational development of seabed mining, the LOS treaty could force up the future prices of ocean minerals to consumers in developing countries and thereby hinder these countries' economic advance. Developing countries could thus be worse off under the LOS treaty. . . .

Conclusion

The Law of the Sea Treaty's seabed mining regime is thus hopelessly flawed. It will not produce a positive consensus that would enrich international law, nor contribute to economic development that can benefit all peoples. It also violates some of the United States' fundamental principles, and would exacerbate rather than reduce global tensions.

President Reagan has said that where the mineral wealth of the Ocean floor is concerned, the aim of the United States is "to establish with other nations an order that would allow exploration and development under reasonable terms and conditions."

U.S. efforts are now directed toward developing an alternative agreement, based on customary law, that will permit seabed mining and preserve freedom of the seas for all nations. This will be a top priority of the United States in the years ahead.

Notes

1. *A Package Deal?* The United States could not accept the LOS Convention and at the same time enter reservations to the Convention's seabed mining provisions. Article 309 generally prohibits reservations. Could the United States and other maritime powers, which had negotiated provisions concerning navigation and other matters favorable to their interests, claim the benefits of those provisions as a matter of customary international law? According to some, the Convention was a "package deal," a product of numerous and complex trade-offs and compromises; a state could not claim particular rights found in the Convention (e.g., transit passage through straits) while rejecting certain obligations (e.g., those included in the seabed mining regime). Is this argument sensible? Or does it misapprehend the way in which customary international law develops? Review the material in Chapter 1 and Chapter 9, Section B on customary international law.

2. *Deep Seabed Mining and High Seas Freedoms.* Was the Reagan administration's assertion that deep seabed mining is a freedom of the high seas plausible in 1983? Read Sections C and D and then assess whether such an assertion would be plausible today.

C The 1994 Implementation Agreement

Industrialized states proved unwilling to accept the LOS Convention with Part XI in its original form. The Federal Republic of Germany and the United Kingdom joined the United States in refusing even to sign the Convention. Other industrialized states, also concerned about the Convention's deep seabed mining regime, signed the Convention but held off ratifying it.

Efforts to shape the legal regime for deep seabed mining proceeded along three tracks. One was the work of the Preparatory Commission for the International Seabed Authority and for the International Tribunal for the Law of the Sea (PREPCOM), a body established at UNCLOS III to adopt mining regulations and to plan for the entry into force of the Convention. A second was unilateral seabed mining legislation, which the United States and a few other industrialized states adopted. The third track, involving the efforts of the U.N. Secretary-General to negotiate a multilateral agreement to "implement" the LOS Convention by modifying provisions of the Convention's seabed mining regime, is the focus of this section. The U.N. Secretary-General initiated a series of informal meetings beginning in July 1990. Approximately 30 interested states, including the three major non-signatories to the Convention—Germany, the United Kingdom, and the United States—and states representing all different perspectives, initially participated. After the consultations were opened to all states in 1992, between 75 and 90 states participated. The Secretary-General's consultations resulted in the 1994 Agreement relating to the Implementation of Part XI of the United Nations Convention on the Law of the Sea. The negotiators had felt some urgency to conclude their work before November 16, 1994, when the Convention was due to enter into force. See LOS Convention, Article 308. Virtually all of the 60 ratifications required for entry into force were from developing states, and the participation of developed states was desired.

Although the 1994 Agreement is titled an "implementation agreement," it in fact significantly modified the original Part XI regime. The Agreement and the 1982 LOS Convention—which are to be applied and read together as a single instrument—have now been accepted by most developed and developing states. The International Seabed Authority (ISA or Authority) is operating under this modified 1982/1994 regime.

The first reading below highlights the substantive modifications made to the original Part XI regime. These modifications were incorporated in the 1994 Implementation Agreement's Annex, an "integral part" of the Agreement. The second reading is the Agreement itself (without its Annex), which contains several mechanisms designed to encourage establishment of a widely accepted unified seabed mining regime incorporating the provisions of the Agreement's Annex.

BERNARD H. OXMAN, THE 1994 AGREEMENT AND THE CONVENTION
88 Am. J. Intl. L. 687 (1994)

In June 1994, some twelve years after the conclusion of the Third UN Conference on the Law of the Sea, the UN Secretary-General reported to the General Assembly that informal consultations had led to agreements that appeared to have removed the obstacles to general adherence to the 1982 UN Convention on the Law of the Sea. . . .

In July 1990, UN Secretary-General Javier Perez de Cuellar initiated informal consultations to attempt to meet the objections of the industrialized states.

His successor, Boutros Boutros-Ghali, continued those consultations and saw them to conclusion. . . .

As reported by the Secretary-General, the consultations resulted in:

—a draft "Agreement relating to the Implementation of Part XI of the United Nations Convention on the Law of the Sea of 10 December 1982"; and

—a draft resolution by which the UN General Assembly would adopt the Agreement and urge states to adhere to it and to the Convention.

The resolution was adopted by the General Assembly at a resumed forty-eighth session on July 28, 1994, by a vote of 121 in favor, none against, and 7 abstentions. The Agreement was opened for signature the next day. Over fifty states have already signed the Agreement, including the United States and virtually all other industrialized states.

The Agreement, the Convention and U.S. Policy

The 1994 Agreement provides, in Article 2, that it is to be interpreted and applied together with Part XI of the Convention as a single instrument; in the event of inconsistency between them, the Agreement will prevail. It may take some time before states that have not yet ratified the Convention become party to the Convention and the 1994 Agreement. More than sixty states, however, have already ratified the Convention, which enters into force for them on November 16, 1994; it would have been unrealistic to expect that before that date all of them would become party to the new Agreement as well. The Agreement therefore contains liberal terms for its provisional application by all, and affords states several years to become party to both the Agreement and the Convention. With a large number of states, including industrial states, accepting provisional application, one may expect that Part XI will be implemented from the outset in accordance with the new Agreement and with representative participation in decision-making organs.

The purpose of the 1994 Agreement is to enhance the prospects for widespread ratification of the Convention by responding to problems with the deep seabed mining regime in Part XI, particularly those that troubled industrial states, including the United States. The Agreement is designed also to respond to developments in the decade since Part XI was completed, specifically "the growing concern for the global environment," and "political and economic changes, including in particular a growing reliance on market principles."

It may be instructive to consider how the 1994 Agreement responds to the problems identified and the concerns expressed by the United States when it sought, without success, to change Part XI in 1982.

U.S. policy regarding the 1982 Convention, as enunciated by the Reagan administration, may be summarized as follows. "While most provisions of the draft convention are acceptable and consistent with U.S. interests, some major elements of the deep seabed mining regime are not acceptable." The United States "has a strong interest in an effective and fair Law of the Sea treaty which includes a viable seabed mining régime." It was "not seeking to change the basic structure of the treaty" or "to destroy the system" but "to make it work for the benefit of all nations to enhance, not resist, seabed resource development." If negotiations could fulfill six key objectives with respect to the deep seabed mining régime, the "Administration will support ratification" of the Convention. It was the administration's "judgment that, if the President's objectives as outlined are satisfied, the Senate would approve the Law of the Sea treaty." [The article reviews the objectives identified by President Reagan, which appear in Section B of this chapter.]

How the 1994 Agreement responds to U.S. objections and U.S. requirements may be considered under several headings.

Decision Making

Like many international organizations, the International Sea-Bed Authority established by the Convention will have an Assembly in which all parties are represented, a Council of limited membership, and specialized elected organs also of limited membership.

1982 text: While all specific regulatory powers with regard to deep seabed mining are reposed exclusively or concurrently in the Council, Article 160 gives the Assembly "the power to establish general policies."

Problem: "Policymaking in the seabed authority would be carried out by a one-nation, one-vote assembly."

Response: The 1994 Agreement qualifies the general policy-making powers of the Assembly by requiring the collaboration of the Council. It also provides: "Decisions of the Assembly on any matter for which the Council also has competence or on any administrative, budgetary or financial matter shall be based on the recommendations of the Council." The Assembly may either approve the recommendations or return them.

Problem: "The executive council which would make the day-to-day decisions affecting access of U.S. miners to deep seabed minerals would not have permanent or guaranteed representation by the United States."

Response: The new Agreement guarantees a seat on the Council for "the State, on the date of entry into force of the Convention, having the largest economy in terms of gross domestic product." That state is the United States.

1982 text: Consensus on the thirty-six-member Council is required for such matters as proposing treaty amendments; adopting rules, regulations and procedures; and distributing financial benefits and economic adjustment assistance. Other substantive Council decisions require either a two-thirds or three-quarters vote.

Problem: The "United States would not have influence on the council commensurate with its economic and political interests." "The decision-making system should provide that, on issues of highest importance to a nation, that nation will have affirmative influence on the outcome. Conversely, nations with major economic interests should be secure in the knowledge that they can prevent decisions adverse to their interests."

Response: The new Agreement establishes "chambers" of states with particular interests. Two four-member chambers of the Council are likely to be effectively controlled by major industrial states, including the United States (which is guaranteed a seat in one of those chambers). The Agreement provides that "decisions on questions of substance, except where the Convention provides for decisions by consensus in the Council, shall be taken by a two-thirds majority of members present and voting, provided that such decisions are not opposed by a majority in any one of the chambers." Any three states in either four-member chamber may therefore block a substantive decision for which consensus is not required.

The Agreement further specifies: "Decisions by the Assembly or the Council having financial or budgetary implications shall be based on the recommendations of the Finance Committee." The United States and other major contributors to the administrative budget are guaranteed seats on the Finance Committee, and the committee functions by consensus.

This approach to voting enables interested states (including the United States) to block undesirable decisions. Because blocking power encourages negotiation of decisions desired by and acceptable to the states principally affected, it enhances affirmative as well as negative influence.

Production Limitation

Problem: "The United States believes that its interests . . . will best be served by developing the resources of the deep seabed as market conditions warrant. We have a consumer oriented philosophy. The draft treaty, in our judgment, reflects a protectionist bias which would deter the development of deep seabed mineral resources." Specifically, the "treaty would impose artificial limitations on seabed mineral production" and "would permit discretionary and discriminatory decisions by the Authority if there is competition for limited production allocations." The production ceiling is undesirable as a matter of principle and precedent, and the process for allocating production authorizations is a significant source of uncertainty and discriminatory treatment impeding guaranteed access to minerals by qualified miners.

Response: The new Agreement specifies that the provisions regarding the production ceiling, production limitations, participation in commodity agreements, production authorizations and selection among applicants "shall not apply." In their place, the Agreement incorporates the market-oriented GATT restrictions on subsidies. It prohibits "discrimination between minerals derived from the [deep seabed] and from other sources," and specifies that the rates of payments by miners to the Authority "shall be within the range of those prevailing in respect of land-based mining of the same or similar minerals in order to avoid giving deep seabed miners an artificial competitive advantage or imposing on them a competitive disadvantage."

Technology Transfer

Problem: "Private deep seabed miners would be subject to a mandatory requirement for the transfer of technology to the Enterprise and to developing countries." This provision was considered burdensome, prejudicial to intellectual property rights, and objectionable as a matter of principle and precedent.

Response: The new Agreement declares that the provisions on mandatory transfer of technology "shall not apply." It substitutes a general duty of cooperation by sponsoring states to facilitate the acquisition of deep seabed mining technology, "consistent with the effective protection of intellectual property rights," if the Enterprise (the operating arm of the Sea-Bed Authority) or developing countries are unable to obtain such technology on the open market or through joint-venture arrangements.

Access

Problem: "The draft treaty provides no assurance that qualified private applicants sponsored by the U.S. Government will be awarded contracts. It is our strong view that all qualified applicants should be granted contracts and that the decision whether to grant a contract should be tied exclusively to the question of whether an applicant has satisfied objective qualification standards."

Response: The new Agreement eliminates the provisions for choice among qualified applicants. Access will be on a first-come, first-served basis. The qualification standards for mining applicants are to be set forth in rules, regulations and procedures adopted by the Council by consensus and "shall relate to the financial and technical capabilities of the applicant and his performance under any previous contracts." If the applicant is qualified; if the application fee is paid; if procedural and environmental requirements are met; if the area applied for is not the subject of a prior contract or application; and if the sponsoring state would not thereby exceed maximum limits specified in the Convention, "the Authority shall approve" the application. Its failure to do so will be subject to arbitration or adjudication.

The new Agreement contains special voting rules that facilitate a decision to approve an application to explore or exploit minerals. In the Legal and Technical Commission, only a simple majority is required for recommending approval. When that recommendation reaches the Council, the application is deemed approved unless disapproved within a prescribed period (normally sixty days) by the same vote required for substantive decisions. Thus, any three industrial states in a four-member chamber may prevent disapproval.

The new Agreement accords important "grandfather" rights to the U.S. consortia that already have made investments under the U.S. Deep Seabed Hard Mineral Resources Act. They are deemed to have met the necessary financial and technical qualifications if the U.S. Government, as the sponsoring state, certifies that they have made the necessary expenditures. They are also entitled to arrangements "similar to and no less favourable than" those accorded investors of other countries that registered as pioneers with the Preparatory Commission prior to entry into force of the Convention.

Problem: U.S. objectives "would not be satisfied if minerals other than manganese nodules could be developed only after a decision was taken to promulgate rules and regulations to allow the exploitation of such minerals."

Response: The new Agreement requires the Council of the Authority to adopt necessary rules, regulations and procedures within two years of a request by a state whose national intends to apply for the right to exploit a mine site. This applies to manganese nodules or any other mineral resource. If the Council fails to complete the work on time, it must give provisional approval to an application based on the Convention and the new Agreement, notwithstanding the fact that the rules and regulations have not been adopted.

The Enterprise

Problem: "The treaty would give substantial competitive advantages to a supra-national mining company—the Enterprise." It "creates a system of privileges which discriminates against the private side of the parallel system. Rational private companies would, therefore, have little option but to enter joint ventures or other similar ventures either with the operating arm of the Authority, the Enterprise, or with developing countries. Not only would this deny the United States access to deep seabed minerals through its private companies because the private access system would be uncompetitive but, under some scenarios, the Enterprise could establish a monopoly over deep seabed mineral resources."

Response: The new Agreement provides: "The obligations applicable to contractors [private miners] shall apply to the Enterprise." It requires the Enterprise to conduct its initial operations through joint ventures "that accord with sound commercial principles," and delays the independent functioning of the Enterprise until the Council decides that those criteria have been met. The Agreement does not exclude the Enterprise either from the principle that mining "shall take place in accordance with sound commercial principles" or from its prohibitions on subsidies. It specifies that the "obligation of States Parties to fund one mine site of the Enterprise ... shall not apply and States Parties shall be under no obligation to finance any of the operations in any mine site of the Enterprise or under its joint-venture arrangements." The Agreement also eliminates mandatory transfer of technology to the Enterprise and the potentially discriminatory system for issuing production authorizations.

The Agreement makes clear that a private miner may contribute the requisite "reserved area" to the Enterprise at the time the miner receives its own exclusive exploration rights to a specific area (thus minimizing its risk and investment). That miner has "the right of first refusal to enter into a joint-venture arrangement with the Enterprise for exploration and exploitation of" the reserved area, and has priority rights to the reserved area if the Enterprise itself does not apply for exploration or exploitation rights to the reserved area within a specified period.

Finance

Problem: "The treaty would impose large financial burdens on industrialized countries whose nationals are engaged in deep seabed mining and financial terms and conditions which would significantly increase the costs of mineral production."

Response: The new Agreement halves the application fee for either exploration or exploitation to [US$] 250,000 (subject to refund to the extent the fee exceeds the actual costs of processing an application), and eliminates the detailed financial obligations of miners set forth in the 1982 text, including the million-dollar annual fee. Financial details would be supplied, when needed, by rules, regulations and procedures adopted by the Council by consensus, on the basis of general criteria that, for example, would link the rates to those prevailing for mining on land, and prohibit discrimination or rate increases for existing contracts.

With respect to state parties, in addition to eliminating any requirement that states contribute funds to finance the Enterprise or provide economic adjustment assistance to developing countries, the new Agreement provides for streamlining and phasing in the organs and functions of the Authority as needed, and for minimizing costs and meetings. Budgets and assessments for administrative expenses are subject to consensus procedures in the Finance Committee and approval by both the Council and the Assembly.

Regulatory Burdens

Problem: "The new international organization would have discretion to interfere unreasonably with the conduct of mining operations, and it could impose potentially burdensome regulations on an infant industry."

Response: The substantive changes set forth in the new Agreement, including the elimination of production limitations, production authorizations and forced transfers of technology, and the relaxation of diligence requirements, substantially narrow the area of potential abuse. The new procedural provisions, including voting arrangements in the Council and the Finance Committee, and restrictions on the Assembly, decrease the risk of unreasonable regulatory decisions. As indicated in its Preamble and in the General Assembly resolution adopting it, the new Agreement is the product of a marked shift, throughout the world, from statist and interventionist economic philosophies toward more market-oriented policies. Taken together, the new provisions and new attitudes give reason to expect the system to operate in accordance with the provisions of the Convention and the Agreement guaranteeing the miner exclusive rights to a mine site, security of tenure, stability of expectations and title to minerals extracted, and according the miner and its sponsoring state extensive judicial and arbitral remedies to protect those rights.

What cannot be supplied in advance by any blueprint for a deep seabed mining régime is the measure of confidence born of experience with a system in operation.

Distribution of Revenues

1982 text: The Convention authorizes the equitable sharing of surplus revenues from mining, "taking into particular consideration the interests and needs of the developing States and peoples who have not attained full independence or other self-governing status."

Problem: "The convention would allow funding for national liberation groups, such as the Palestine Liberation Organization and the South West Africa People's Organization."

Response: Political developments in Africa and the Middle East have mitigated this problem. Moreover, distribution to such groups would be a practical impossibility unless the Sea-Bed Authority's revenues from miners and from the Enterprise exceeded both its administrative expenses and its assistance to adversely affected land-based producers, and would be possible then only if the Council decided by consensus to include such groups in the distribution of surplus revenues. A decision on distribution of surplus funds would also be subject, under the new Agreement, to a consensus in the Finance Committee.

Review Conference

Problem: "A review conference would have the power to impose treaty amendments on the United States without its consent."

Response: The new Agreement declares that the provisions in Part XI relating to the review conference "shall not apply." Amendments to the deep seabed mining régime could not be adopted without U.S. consent.

Conclusion

The 1994 Agreement substantially accommodates the objections of the United States and other industrial states to the deep seabed mining provisions of the Law of the Sea Convention. The Agreement embraces market-oriented policies and eliminates provisions identified as posing significant problems of principle and precedent, such as those dealing with production limitations, mandatory transfer of technology, and the review conference. It increases the influence of the United States and other industrial states in the Sea-Bed Authority, and reflects their longstanding preference for emphasizing interests, not merely numbers, in the structure and voting arrangements of international organizations. Detail that is objectionable or premature is eliminated or qualified. The Sea-Bed Authority is streamlined and its regulatory discretion curtailed. The role of its operating arm—the Enterprise—is delayed and sharply confined. Deep cuts are made in the financial obligations of states and private companies.

United States accession to the Convention and ratification of the new Agreement will promote widespread adherence by states generally. This will protect not only deep seabed mining but many other important interests in the oceans. In the meantime, provisional application of the Agreement by the United States and by a substantial number of other states will help ensure that Part XI will not be implemented in unmodified form, that the full range of affected interests will be represented during the early stages of organization when important precedents and procedures are established, and that these precedents and procedures will facilitate widespread ratification of the Convention and the Agreement.

1994 AGREEMENT RELATING TO THE IMPLEMENTATION OF PART XI OF THE UNITED NATIONS CONVENTION ON THE LAW OF THE SEA

See Appendix (omit Annex to the Agreement)

Notes

1. *The 1994 Implementation Agreement.* The 1994 Implementation Agreement does not technically "amend" the LOS Convention. The Convention specifies various amendment procedures, but the 1994 Agreement did not involve any of them. See LOS Convention, Articles 155, 312–315. Instead, the 1994 Agreement is a treaty, the text of which was adopted by a resolution of the U.N. General Assembly. UN Doc. A/RES/48/263 (1994). No states voted against the resolution, although seven states abstained (Colombia, Nicaragua, Panama, Peru, the Russian Federation, Thailand, and Venezuela). In terms of the law of treaties, however, General Assembly adoption of the text of a treaty does not constitute the agreement of states to be bound by the treaty. See 1969 Vienna Convention on the Law of Treaties, Articles 9, 11. The next four Notes address how a unified LOS Convention/1994 Implementation Agreement regime could be achieved.

2. *Facilitating Acceptance of a Unified LOS Convention/1994 Implementation Agreement Regime.* The 1994 Implementation Agreement contains provisions to facilitate implementation of a unified 1982 LOS Convention/1994 Agreement regime. According to Article 2(1) of the 1994 Agreement, "[t]he provisions of this Agreement and Part XI shall be interpreted and applied together as a single instrument." Any state accepting the Convention from July 28, 1994, also consents to be bound by the Agreement, and acceptance of the Agreement requires simultaneous or previous acceptance of the Convention. 1994 Implementation Agreement, Article 4(1)–(2). In line with the law of treaties (see 1969 Vienna Convention on the Law of Treaties, Article 11), Article 4(3) of the Agreement sets forth different ways states may consent to be bound by the Agreement, including, for states that had previously accepted the Convention, mere signature of the Agreement.

What is the situation with respect to a state that had accepted the LOS Convention prior to adoption of the 1994 Implementation Agreement but that has not consented to be bound by the Agreement? As of September 1, 2013, approximately twenty states fell into this category. Does the lengthy deliberative process leading up to the 1994 Agreement—a process in which all interests were taken into account—constitute a new way to make international law, creating binding legal obligations for those twenty states?

3. *Entry into Force.* According to Article 6 of the 1994 Implementation Agreement, it enters into force 30 days after 40 states accept it. At least seven

of those 40 states must be states referred to in paragraph 1(a) of Resolution II of UNCLOS III, and at least five of those seven must be developed states. These developed states include Belgium, Canada, France, Germany, India, Italy, Japan, the Netherlands, the Soviet Union (now Russia), the United Kingdom, and the United States. The 1994 Agreement thus could not enter into force unless it received the backing of several developed states that would contribute to the ISA's expenses. The Agreement entered into force on July 28, 1996.

4. *Provisional Application.* One innovative feature of the 1994 Implementation Agreement was Article 7, authorizing provisional application of the Agreement beginning when the LOS Convention entered into force in November 1994. Article 7 insured that the ISA would operate consistently under Part XI as modified by the 1994 Agreement.

5. *Provisional Membership in the Authority.* The 1994 Implementation Agreement's Annex also provided for provisional membership in the ISA for states that had not yet accepted the Convention and Agreement. 1994 Implementation Agreement, Annex, § 1, ¶ 12. The United States and Canada obtained such provisional membership and were elected as members of the Authority's Council, but their provisional membership status lapsed in November 1998. Canada accepted the LOS Convention in 2003 and now may participate in the work of the ISA.

6. *Deep Seabed Mining Outside the LOS Convention/1994 Implementation Agreement Regime.* The United States has signed the 1994 Implementation Agreement, but as of September 1, 2013, the U.S. Senate had not given its advice and consent to U.S. acceptance of the Convention and the Agreement, which are read together as one instrument and which must be accepted together. A U.S. corporation may not use the LOS Convention/1994 Implementation Agreement regime to obtain licenses to explore for or exploit mineral resources in the Area. The Authority may approve plans of work for activities in the Area for state parties or for nationals of state parties; every member of a multinational consortium must be a national of a state party. See LOS Convention, Article 153(2) and Annex III, Articles 3–4; 1994 Implementation Agreement, Annex, § 1, ¶ 12(c)(ii).

Is the modified Part XI regime for resource-related activities in the Area an international legal obligation erga omnes? Would unilateral U.S. approval of either an exploration license or a commercial recovery permit for a U.S. mining company under the U.S. Deep Seabed Hard Mineral Resources Act (DSHMRA), 30 U.S.C. §§ 1401 et seq., now be legal under international law? Do you agree with the observation of Judge Dolliver Nelson, who, writing even before the 1994 Implementation Agreement entered into force in 1996, concluded that the position that "deep seabed mining is a freedom of the high seas" is "no longer tenable, in light of the fact that almost all the major technologically advanced countries have adopted and signed" the 1994 Agreement? L.D.M. Nelson, The New Deep Sea-Bed Mining Regime, 10 Intl. J. Marine & Coastal L. 189, 202 (1995).

Why would a U.S. company not choose to pursue the DSHMRA route? What other options are available to it? Why has Lockheed Martin, the sole U.S. company that still, as of September 1, 2013, held exploration licenses under the DSHMRA, urged U.S. accession to the LOS Convention? In a May 17, 2012, letter, Lockheed Martin gave its "strong support for speedy ratification" of the LOS Convention:

> [T]he multi-billion dollar investments needed to establish an ocean-based resource development business must be predicated upon clear legal rights established and protected under the treaty-based framework of the LOS Convention, including the International Seabed Authority. [W]ithout ratifying the LOS [Convention], the United States cannot sponsor claims with, or shape the deep seabed rules of, the ISA.

The Law of the Sea Convention (Treaty Doc. 103–39): Hearing Before the Senate Committee on Foreign Relations, 112th Cong. 74, 74–75 (2013) (Letter from Robert J. Stevens, Chairman and Chief Executive Officer, Lockheed Martin Corp., to Sen. John Kerry, Chairman, U.S. Senate Foreign Relations Committee, May 17, 2012). Could a U.S. corporation face litigation risks or other legal action if it were to exploit deep seabed minerals outside the LOS Convention/1994 Implementation Agreement regime? What are the legal obligations of state parties to the LOS Convention with respect to mining activities by non-parties in the Area? See LOS Convention, Article 137(3) and Annex III, Article 1.

D The International Seabed Authority

The International Seabed Authority (ISA or Authority) came into existence on November 16, 1994, when the LOS Convention entered into force. Headquartered in Kingston, Jamaica, the Authority is operating under the joint LOS Convention/1994 Implementation Agreement regime. Ambassador Satya Nandan of Fiji, who had played a significant role in UNCLOS III negotiations, was elected as the ISA's first Secretary-General in 1996 and served three four-year terms. His 2007 report and the 2013 report by ISA Secretary-General Nii A. Odunton of Ghana, both excerpted below, highlight recent ISA activities. The third reading in this section is an excerpt from an advisory opinion of the Seabed Disputes Chamber of the International Tribunal for the Law of the Sea

(SBC or Chamber). It sets out important principles concerning the work of the Authority and the obligations of states sponsoring seabed miners.

STATEMENT BY SATYA N. NANDAN, SECRETARY-GENERAL OF THE INTERNATIONAL SEABED AUTHORITY TO THE 62ND SESSION OF THE GENERAL ASSEMBLY OF THE UNITED NATIONS

Dec. 10, 2007, available at http://www.isa.org.jm/en/node/329

In the 1970s when we negotiated Part XI of the Convention we were led to believe that seabed mining was imminent. The initial predictions on which much of the Part XI regime was based were proved unduly optimistic in the light of changing political and economic circumstances. The result was prolonged delay as States and commercial entities adjusted their priorities to meet the demands of a changing global outlook.

The world continues to evolve. At this moment, the day when commercial mining of seabed resources becomes a reality is closer than at any time in the past 25 years.

The two main drivers of commercial activity have always been economics and technology. Human ingenuity can rapidly solve technological problems if economic conditions are such as to encourage investment in technology. Over the past few years there has been a surge in demand for most of the metals that would be derived from seabed mining, leading to a rapid and dramatic increase in the price of metals on world markets.... Much of this increase in demand and price was driven by surging economic growth in developing new economies such as China, India and Brazil....

The long delay in commercial seabed mining since 1982 has not meant that States Parties to the Convention have been idle. In fact, the delay has benefited the international community in at least three ways.

First, it has enabled States to work together to establish the International Seabed Authority on a solid footing, based on economy, efficiency and sound free market principles.

Second, it has allowed the scientists to gain an immeasurably greater understanding of the deep ocean environment through research and intensive study.

Third, it has provided sufficient time to further elaborate the legal regime for deep seabed mining through the regulations adopted by the Authority. Not only is this regime based on sound economic principles, it is also based on rigorous environmental standards, including the application of the precautionary approach.

Indeed, it is fair to say that there are few other activities in the oceans that have been studied and regulated to such a detailed extent before the activity has even taken place. Most examples of environmental regulation occur as a response to environmental degradation, often as a result of over-utilization of resources and incidental destruction of habitats. In the case of the Authority, most of the efforts over the past 10 years have been spent in encouraging the study of the deep sea environment and in working together with scientists from around the world to analyze and disseminate the results of such research for the benefit of all States. A very good example of this is the recently concluded Kaplan project, which is the first and most successful attempt to analyze the species composition and rates of gene flow of living organisms across the abyssal plains of the Clarion-Clipperton zone in the Central Pacific Ocean. . . .

One of the key outcomes of the Kaplan project is a set of recommendations as to scientific criteria for the establishment of marine protected areas, which we refer to more accurately as preservation reference zones. The purpose of these would be to safeguard biodiversity in the Clarion-Clipperton zone in anticipation of nodule mining. As far as seabed mining is concerned, the need to set aside areas to preserve their unique flora and fauna was recognized by the drafters of the Convention itself. Under article 162(2)(x) of the Convention, the Council of the Authority has the power to disapprove areas for exploitation where substantial evidence indicates the risk of serious harm to the marine environment. Similarly, under the regulations governing exploration for polymetallic nodules, contractors are required to designate so-called preservation reference zones where no mining shall occur in order to ensure representative and stable biota of the seabed. Taking into account the outcomes of the Kaplan project, the Authority intends to work with scientists, contractors and the Legal and Technical Commission to develop a comprehensive proposal to establish such reference zones in the Clarion-Clipperton zone. . . .

The increasing likelihood that commercial mining will take place in the foreseeable future makes it all the more important that the Authority completes its work on the elaboration of regulations for exploration for polymetallic sulphides and cobalt-rich crusts as soon as possible.

REPORT OF THE SECRETARY-GENERAL OF THE INTERNATIONAL SEABED AUTHORITY UNDER ARTICLE 166, PARAGRAPH 4, OF THE UNITED NATIONS CONVENTION ON THE LAW OF THE SEA
ISBA/19/A/2 (2013)

XII. Ongoing supervision of contracts for exploration and award of new contracts as necessary

56. The contractual nature of the relationship between the Authority and those wishing to conduct activities in the Area is fundamental to the legal regime

established by Part XI of the Convention and the 1994 Agreement. Annex III to the Convention, which sets out the "Basic Conditions of Prospecting, Exploration and Exploitation," also forms an integral part of this legal regime, which is to be further developed in the rules, regulations and procedures adopted by the Authority. Consequently, the administration and supervision of contracts between the Authority and qualified entities wishing to explore for or exploit deep-sea mineral resources lies at the core of the Authority's functions.

A. *Status of contracts for exploration*

57. As at April 2013, the Authority had issued 14 exploration contracts, covering approximately one million square kilometres of the seafloor. Of these, 12 cover exploration for polymetallic nodules, and 2 for polymetallic sulphides.

58. Between 2001 and 2010, the Authority concluded eight contracts for exploration for polymetallic nodules to the following qualified applicants: Yuzhmorgeologiya (Russian Federation); the Interoceanmetal Joint Organization (IOM) (Bulgaria, Cuba, Czech Republic, Poland, Russian Federation and Slovakia); the Government of the Republic of Korea; the China Ocean Mineral Resources Research and Development Association (COMRA) (China); Deep Ocean Resources Development Ltd. (DORD) (Japan); IFREMER (France); the Government of India; and the Federal Institute for Geosciences and Natural Resources of Germany (BGR) (Germany).

59. Between 2011 and 2013, the Authority entered into contracts with: Nauru Ocean Resources Inc. (Nauru), signed on 22 July 2011; COMRA (China), signed on 18 November 2011; Tonga Offshore Mining Limited (Tonga), signed on 11 January 2012; the Government of the Russian Federation, signed on 29 October 2012; G-TEC Sea Mineral Resources NV (Belgium), signed on 14 January 2013; and UK Seabed Resources Ltd. (United Kingdom), signed on 8 February 2013. Three further plans of work for exploration that were approved at the eighteenth session will be issued in the form of contracts with the Authority as soon as the necessary formalities have been concluded, during the second half of 2013. The applicants involved are IFREMER (France), Marawa Research and Exploration Ltd. (Kiribati) and the Government of the Republic of Korea. This would bring the total number of exploration contracts to 17 by the end of 2013 (not including the applications pending for consideration at the nineteenth session).

60. One of the obligations arising out of the contractual relationship between the Authority and the contractors is the timely submission of an annual activity report including progress made on exploration activities, supported by appropriate data and information. This enables the Secretary-General and the Legal and Technical Commission to be in possession of the

information necessary to the exercise of their functions, in particular those relating to the protection of the marine environment from the harmful effects of activities in the Area. . . . As of April 2013, activity reports for 2012 had been received from all contractors from which reports were due.

XIII. Progressive development of the regulatory regime for activities in the Area

67. The Authority has a fundamental role to play in ensuring that an appropriate regulatory regime is established, in accordance with the Convention and the 1994 Agreement, that provides adequate security of tenure for future exploration for and exploitation of the mineral resources of the Area, while ensuring effective protection for the marine environment. The regulatory regime would ultimately be encapsulated in a Mining Code, which would comprise the whole of the comprehensive set of rules, regulations and procedures issued by the Authority to regulate prospecting, exploration and exploitation of marine minerals in the Area.

A. *Prospecting and exploration*

68. The Mining Code currently consists of three sets of regulations covering prospecting and exploration for polymetallic nodules, polymetallic sulphides and cobalt-rich ferromanganese crusts, respectively. The Assembly approved the latter at the eighteenth session [in 2012]. In addition to specifying the process through which contracts may be applied for and granted, the regulations set out the standard terms and conditions, applicable to all entities, of contracts with the Authority. . . .

B. *Exploitation*

70. During the eighteenth session, the Council considered a report of the Secretary-General on a proposed workplan for the formulation of a regulatory framework for the exploitation of polymetallic nodules in the Area (ISBA/18/C/4). Although some members were of the opinion that the proposed timeline was somewhat optimistic and expressed their concern about whether the Authority would have the human and financial resources to complete the work involved in formulating the regulations by 2016, several delegations endorsed the workplan. . . .

72. One of the most important recommendations in the report is that the Authority develop and put in place a "staged" or "phased" provisional licensing system requiring that, prior to the expiration of an exploration licence, contractors interested in proceeding to the mining phase first apply for a provisional mining licence based upon preparation and submission of a

pre-feasibility study and workplans to undertake a detailed bankable feasibility study based upon a pilot mining operation in the contract area.

Notes

1. *Plans of Work and Exploration Contracts*. Seven of the contractors referred to in the readings above were pioneer investors registered by the Preparatory Commission, which operated between the signing of the LOS Convention in 1982 and its entry into force in 1994. In August 1997 these pioneer investors formally submitted plans of work for exploration to the ISA Council. In accordance with the 1994 Agreement, these plans of work were considered to be approved. See 1994 Implementation Agreement, Annex, § 1, ¶ 8; § 3, ¶¶ 11(a), 13. As noted in the 2013 Report of the ISA Secretary-General excerpted above, as of April 2013 the Authority had entered into fifteen-year exploration contracts with fourteen applicants, and three more contracts were pending with applicants whose plans of work had been approved in 2012.

At its July 2013 session, the ISA approved two more plans of work for exploration in the Area—both for exploration for cobalt-rich ferromanganese crusts—submitted by China Ocean Mineral Resources Research and Development Association (sponsored by China) and by Japan Oil, Gas and Metals National Corporation (Japan). By the end of 2013, the ISA had received three additional applications for plans of work from entities sponsored by Brazil, the Cook Islands, and Germany.

2. *The Mining Code*. As of September 1, 2013, the ISA has adopted: Regulations on Prospecting and Exploration for Polymetallic Nodules in the Area, ISBA/6/A/18 (2000), as amended, ISBA/19/A/9 (2013); Regulations on Prospecting and Exploration for Polymetallic Sulphides, ISBA/16/A/12 (2010); and Regulations on Prospecting and Exploration for Cobalt-rich Ferromanganese Crusts in the Area, ISBA/18/A/11 (2012). These Regulations provide different rules for prospecting (which involves a search for deposits and provides no exclusive rights) and exploration (which covers processing systems and the analysis and testing of deposits, and which does provide exclusive rights). Each set of Regulations addresses operator procedures, fees, and dispute settlement, and pays significant attention to environmental matters. The Regulations also contain standard clauses to be used in exploration contracts, and provide a broad scope for the confidentiality of information and data that seabed mining contractors are required to submit to the Authority.

3. *The ISA's Budget*. State parties to the LOS Convention fund the operations of the ISA. The Authority's budget for the 2013–2014 biennium is approximately

US$ 14.3 million. ISBA/18/A/7 (2012). A modest Voluntary Trust Fund assists with participation of members from developing states.

4. *Environmental Studies and Marine Protected Areas.* The ISA has conducted environmental workshops to study the potential impact of deep seabed mining, and has collected and disseminated information about the deep seabed environment. Does the LOS Convention give the Authority the right to establish marine protected areas in the Area? How else could marine protected areas be established for this part of the oceans? In this regard, what roles should regional fisheries organizations, the International Maritime Organization, or the U.N. General Assembly play?

RESPONSIBILITIES AND OBLIGATIONS OF STATES SPONSORING PERSONS AND ENTITIES WITH RESPECT TO ACTIVITIES IN THE AREA
Seabed Disputes Chamber of the International Tribunal for the Law of the Sea, Advisory Opinion, ITLOS Case No. 17 (2011), 50 Intl. Leg. Materials 455 (2011), available at http://www.itlos.org

1. The questions on which the advisory opinion of the Seabed Disputes Chamber of the International Tribunal for the Law of the Sea (hereinafter "the Chamber") has been requested are set forth in decision ISBA/16/C/13 adopted by the Council of the International Seabed Authority (hereinafter "the Council") on 6 May 2010 at its sixteenth session. [The Council requested an advisory opinion on three questions:]

> 1. What are the legal responsibilities and obligations of States Parties to the Convention with respect to the sponsorship of activities in the Area in accordance with the Convention, in particular Part XI, and the 1994 Agreement relating to the Implementation of Part XI of the United Nations Convention on the Law of the Sea of 10 December 1982?
>
> 2. What is the extent of liability of a State Party for any failure to comply with the provisions of the Convention, in particular Part XI, and the 1994 Agreement, by an entity whom it has sponsored under Article 153, paragraph 2(b), of the Convention?
>
> 3. What are the necessary and appropriate measures that a sponsoring State must take in order to fulfil its responsibility under the Convention, in particular Article 139 and Annex III, and the 1994 Agreement? . . .
>
> 4. . . .
>
> —On 10 April 2008, the Authority received two applications for approval of a plan of work for exploration in the areas reserved for the conduct of activities by the Authority through the Enterprise or

in association with developing States pursuant to Annex III, article 8, of the United Nations Convention on the Law of the Sea (hereinafter "the Convention"). These applications were submitted by Nauru Ocean Resources Inc. (sponsored by the Republic of Nauru) and Tonga Offshore Mining Ltd. (sponsored by the Kingdom of Tonga); . . .

—On 1 March 2010, the Republic of Nauru transmitted to the Secretary-General a proposal . . . to seek an advisory opinion from the Chamber on a number of specific questions regarding the responsibility and liability of sponsoring States;

—In support of its proposal, Nauru submitted, inter alia, the following considerations:

> In 2008 the Republic of Nauru sponsored an application by Nauru Ocean Resources Inc. for a plan of work to explore for polymetallic nodules in the Area. Nauru, like many other developing States, does not yet possess the technical and financial capacity to undertake seafloor mining in international waters. To participate effectively in activities in the Area, these States must engage entities in the global private sector (in much the same way as some developing countries require foreign direct investment). Not only do some developing States lack the financial capacity to execute a seafloor mining project in international waters, but some also cannot afford exposure to the legal risks potentially associated with such a project. Recognizing this, Nauru's sponsorship of Nauru Ocean Resources Inc. was originally premised on the assumption that Nauru could effectively mitigate (with a high degree of certainty) the potential liabilities or costs arising from its sponsorship. This was important, as these liabilities or costs could, in some circumstances, far exceed the financial capacities of Nauru (as well as those of many other developing States). Unlike terrestrial mining, in which a State generally only risks losing that which it already has (for example, its natural environment), if a developing State can be held liable for activities in the Area, the State may potentially face losing more than it actually has.
>
> Ultimately, if sponsoring States are exposed to potential significant liabilities, Nauru, as well as other developing States, may be precluded from effectively participating in activities in the Area, which is one of the purposes and principles of Part XI of the Convention[.] As a result, Nauru considers it crucial that guidance be provided on the interpretation of the relevant sections of Part XI pertaining to responsibility and liability, so that developing States can assess whether it is within

their capabilities to effectively mitigate such risks and in turn make an informed decision on whether or not to participate in activities in the Area. * * *

—The Council decided not to adopt the proposal as formulated by Nauru. In view of the wishes of many participants in the debate, it decided to request an advisory opinion on three more abstract but concise questions[.]

73. [Question I] concerns the obligations of sponsoring States. Before examining the provisions of the Convention, the 1994 Agreement as well as the Nodules Regulations [Regulations on Prospecting and Exploration for Polymetallic Nodules, ISBA/6/A/18 (2000)] and the Sulphides Regulations [Regulations on Prospecting and Exploration for Polymetallic Sulfides, ISBA/16/A/12 (2010)] (hereinafter "the Convention and related instruments"), the Chamber must determine the meaning of two of the terms used in the Question, namely: "sponsorship" and "activities in the Area." . . .

74. The notion of "sponsorship" is a key element in the system for the exploration and exploitation of the resources of the Area set out in the Convention. Article 153, paragraph 2, of the Convention describes the "parallel system" of exploration and exploitation activities indicating that such activities shall be carried out by the Enterprise, and, in association with the Authority, by States Parties or state enterprises or natural or juridical persons. It further states that, in order to be eligible to carry out such activities, natural and juridical persons must satisfy two requirements. First, they must be either nationals of a State Party or effectively controlled by it or its nationals. Second, they must be "sponsored by such States." [T]he requirement of sponsorship [applies] also to state enterprises.

75. The purpose of requiring the sponsorship of applicants for contracts for the exploration and exploitation of the resources of the Area is to achieve the result that the obligations set out in the Convention, a treaty under international law which binds only States Parties thereto, are complied with by entities that are subjects of domestic legal systems. This result is obtained through the provisions of the Authority's Regulations that apply to such entities and through the implementation by the sponsoring States of their obligations under the Convention and related instruments.

76. The role of the sponsoring State, as set out in the Convention, contributes to the realization of the common interest of all States in the proper application of the principle of the common heritage of mankind which requires faithful compliance with the obligations set out in Part XI. . . .

82. Question 1 concerns the responsibilities and obligations of sponsoring States in respect of "activities in the Area." This expression is defined in article 1, paragraph 1(3), of the Convention as "all activities of exploration for, and exploitation of, the resources of the Area." According to article 133(a) of the Convention, for the purposes of Part XI, the term "resources" means "all solid, liquid or gaseous mineral resources in situ in the Area at or beneath the seabed, including polymetallic nodules." [A]ccording to article 133(b), "resources, when recovered from the Area, are referred to as 'minerals.' "

[Transporting minerals from the waters above the part of the Area where mining occurs or processing those minerals on land do not constitute exploration or exploitation within the meaning of Article 1(1)(3). However, such activities as recovering minerals from the seabed and lifting them to the surface of the water do fall within the definition of "activities in the Area."]

99. The key provisions concerning the obligations of the sponsoring States are: article 139, paragraph 1; article 153, paragraph 4 (especially the last sentence); and Annex III, article 4, paragraph 4, of the Convention (especially the first sentence)....

110. The sponsoring State's obligation "to ensure" [that activities in the Area be carried out in conformity with Part XI] is not an obligation to achieve, in each and every case, the result that the sponsored contractor complies with the aforementioned obligations. Rather, it is an obligation to deploy adequate means, to exercise best possible efforts, to do the utmost, to obtain this result. To utilize the terminology current in international law, this obligation may be characterized as an obligation "of conduct" and not "of result," and as an obligation of "due diligence."...

117. "[D]ue diligence" is a variable concept. It may change over time as measures considered sufficiently diligent at a certain moment may become not diligent enough in light, for instance, of new scientific or technological knowledge. It may also change in relation to the risks involved in the activity. As regards activities in the Area, it seems reasonable to state that prospecting is, generally speaking, less risky than exploration activities which, in turn, entail less risk than exploitation.... The standard of due diligence has to be more severe for the riskier activities....

119. [Annex III, article 4, paragraph 4] requires the sponsoring State to adopt "laws and regulations" and to take "administrative measures which are, within the framework of its legal system, reasonably appropriate for securing compliance by persons under its jurisdiction."

120. [T]he "due diligence" obligation "to ensure" requires the sponsoring State to take measures within its legal system and that the measures must be "reasonably appropriate."...

121. The obligations of sponsoring States are not limited to the due diligence "obligation to ensure." Under the Convention and related instruments, sponsoring States also have obligations with which they have to comply independently of their obligation to ensure a certain behaviour by the sponsored contractor. These obligations may be characterized as "direct obligations."

[One direct obligation, compliance with which is also relevant in meeting the sponsoring state's due diligence "obligation to ensure," is implementation of the "precautionary approach."]

125. [R]egulation 31, paragraph 2, of the Nodules Regulations and regulation 33, paragraph 2, of the Sulphides Regulations both . . . state that sponsoring States (as well as the Authority) "shall apply a precautionary approach, as reflected in Principle 15 of the Rio Declaration" in order "to ensure effective protection for the marine environment from harmful effects which may arise from activities in the Area."

126. Principle 15 of the 1992 Rio Declaration on Environment and Development (hereinafter "the Rio Declaration") reads:

> In order to protect the environment, the precautionary approach shall be widely applied by States according to their capabilities. Where there are threats of serious or irreversible damage, lack of full scientific certainty shall not be used as a reason for postponing cost-effective measures to prevent environmental degradation.

127. The provisions of the aforementioned Regulations transform this non-binding statement of the precautionary approach in the Rio Declaration into a binding obligation. The implementation of the precautionary approach as defined in these Regulations is one of the [direct] obligations of sponsoring States. . . .

131. [T]he precautionary approach is also an integral part of the general obligation of due diligence of sponsoring States, which is applicable even outside the scope of the Regulations. The due diligence obligation of the sponsoring States requires them to take all appropriate measures to prevent damage that might result from the activities of contractors that they sponsor. This obligation applies in situations where scientific evidence concerning the scope and potential negative impact of the activity in question is insufficient but where there are plausible indications of potential risks. A sponsoring State would not meet its obligation of due diligence if it disregarded those risks. . . .

135. [T]he precautionary approach has been incorporated into a growing number of international treaties and other instruments, many of which reflect the formulation of Principle 15 of the Rio Declaration. In the view of the

Chamber, this has initiated a trend towards making this approach part of customary international law. This trend is clearly reinforced by the inclusion of the precautionary approach in the Regulations[.] So does the following statement in paragraph 164 of the ICJ Judgment in *Pulp Mills on the River Uruguay* that "a precautionary approach may be relevant in the interpretation and application of the provisions of the Statute" (i.e., the environmental bilateral treaty whose interpretation was the main bone of contention between the parties). This statement may be read in light of article 31, paragraph 3(c), of the Vienna Convention [on the Law of Treaties], according to which the interpretation of a treaty should take into account not only the context but "any relevant rules of international law applicable in the relations between the parties."

[The Chamber discusses other direct obligations of sponsoring states, e.g., obligations to apply best environmental practices, to ensure the availability of recourse for compensation for pollution damage, and to conduct environmental impact assessments. The Chamber then considers the interests and needs of developing states.]

152. [In light of language in the LOS Convention's Preamble concerning "the realization of a just and equitable international economic order which takes into account the interests and needs of mankind as a whole and, in particular, the special interests and needs of developing countries,"] it is necessary to examine whether developing sponsoring States enjoy preferential treatment as compared with that granted to developed sponsoring States under the Convention and related instruments. . . .

158. [N]one of the general provisions of the Convention concerning the responsibilities (or the liability) of the sponsoring State "specifically provides" for according preferential treatment to sponsoring States that are developing States. [T]here is no provision requiring the consideration of such interests and needs beyond what is specifically stated in Part XI. [T]he general provisions concerning the responsibilities and liability of the sponsoring State apply equally to all sponsoring States, whether developing or developed.

159. Equality of treatment between developing and developed sponsoring States is consistent with the need to prevent commercial enterprises based in developed States from setting up companies in developing States, acquiring their nationality and obtaining their sponsorship in the hope of being subjected to less burdensome regulations and controls. The spread of sponsoring States "of convenience" would jeopardize uniform application of the highest standards of protection of the marine environment, the safe development of activities in the Area and protection of the common heritage of mankind. . . .

161. [However,] Principle 15 of the Rio Declaration . . . provides that the precautionary approach shall be applied by States "according to their capabilities."

It follows that the requirements for complying with the obligation to apply the precautionary approach may be stricter for the developed than for the developing sponsoring States. . . .

162. Furthermore, the reference to "capabilities" is only a broad and imprecise reference to the differences in developed and developing States. What counts in a specific situation is the level of scientific knowledge and technical capability available to a given State in the relevant scientific and technical fields.

[The Chamber turns to Question 2, which concerns the extent of liability of a State Party should an entity it has sponsored fail to comply with requirements under Part XI of the Law of the Sea Convention and the 1994 Implementation Agreement.]

172. From the wording of article 139, paragraph 2, of the Convention, it is evident that liability arises from the failure of the sponsoring State to carry out its own responsibilities. The sponsoring State is not, however, liable for the failure of the sponsored contractor to meet its obligations. . . .

179. Neither the Convention nor the relevant Regulations . . . specifies what constitutes compensable damage, or which subjects may be entitled to claim compensation. It may be envisaged that the damage in question would include damage to the Area and its resources constituting the common heritage of mankind, and damage to the marine environment. Subjects entitled to claim compensation may include the Authority, entities engaged in deep seabed mining, other users of the sea, and coastal States.

180. No provision of the Convention can be read as explicitly entitling the Authority to make such a claim. It may, however, be argued that such entitlement is implicit in article 137, paragraph 2, of the Convention, which states that the Authority shall act "on behalf" of mankind. Each State Party may also be entitled to claim compensation in light of the *erga omnes* character of the obligations relating to preservation of the environment of the high seas and in the Area. In support of this view, reference may be made to article 48 of the [International Law Commission (ILC)] Articles on State Responsibility, which provides:

> Any State other than an injured State is entitled to invoke the responsibility of another State . . . if: (a) the obligation breached is owed to a group of States including that State, and is established for the protection of a collective interest of the group; or (b) the obligation breached is owed to the international community as a whole. . . .

184. [T]he liability of sponsoring States arises from their failure to carry out their own responsibilities and is triggered by the damage caused by sponsored contractors. There must be a causal link between the sponsoring State's failure and the damage, and such a link cannot be presumed. . . .

194. The obligation for a State to provide for a full compensation or *restituto in integrum* is currently part of customary international law. This conclusion was first reached by the Permanent Court of International Justice in the *Factory of Chorzów* case (PCIJ Series A, No. 17, p. 47). This obligation was further reiterated by the International Law Commission. According to article 31, paragraph 1, of the ILC Articles on State Responsibility: "The responsible State is under an obligation to make full reparation for the injury caused by the internationally wrongful act." . . .

200. [In accordance with Annex III, Article 22 of the Convention,] the main liability for a wrongful act committed in the conduct of the contractor's operations or in the exercise of the Authority's powers and functions rests with the contractor and the Authority, respectively, rather than with the sponsoring State. In the view of the Chamber, this reflects the distribution of responsibilities for deep seabed mining activities between the contractor, the Authority and the sponsoring State.

201. [T]he liability of the sponsoring State arises from its own failure to carry out its responsibilities, whereas the contractor's liability arises from its own non-compliance. Both forms of liability exist in parallel. There is only one point of connection, namely, that the liability of the sponsoring State depends upon the damage resulting from activities or omissions of the sponsored contractor. But, in the view of the Chamber, this is merely a trigger mechanism. Such damage is not, however, automatically attributable to the sponsoring State.

202. If the contractor has paid the actual amount of damage, as required under Annex III, article 22, of the Convention, in the view of the Chamber, there is no room for reparation by the sponsoring State.

203. [A] gap in liability may occur if, notwithstanding the fact that the sponsoring State has taken all necessary and appropriate measures, the sponsored contractor has caused damage and is unable to meet its liability in full. [A] gap in liability may also occur if the sponsoring State failed to meet its obligations but that failure is not causally linked to the damage. . . .

204. In the view of the Chamber, the liability regime established by article 139 of the Convention and in related instruments leaves no room for residual liability [of the sponsoring State, in the event of such a gap].

[We omit discussion of Question 3, concerning the "necessary and appropriate" measures a sponsoring state must take to fulfill its responsibilities under the LOS Convention and related instruments, along with the Chamber's lengthy concluding replies to all three Questions. The Chamber's replies are all unanimous.]

Notes

1. *The ISA's Regulatory Authority*. In the Responsibilities and Obligations case the SBC interpreted the phrase "activities in the Area" more restrictively than had the ISA in its Nodules Regulations and Sulphides Regulations. The Chamber noted that the LOS Convention did not encompass transportation to points on land or processing as being included among "activities in the Area," while the two sets of Regulations had included transportation and processing. See ¶¶ 87, 92, 95–96 (not reproduced in the excerpt above). Yet the Chamber also upheld the application of the precautionary approach to activities in the Area, as required in the Nodules Regulations and the Sulphides Regulations, even though the LOS Convention does not refer to that approach. See ¶¶ 125–35. How do you reconcile these holdings? What are the limits on the Authority's rulemaking or regulatory authority?

2. *The Seabed Disputes Chamber's Use of General International Law*. Was it appropriate for the SBC to rely on general international law materials in the Responsibilities and Obligations case? Does the LOS Convention invite decision makers facing an issue arising under the LOS Convention to use general international law? Or does the LOS Convention constrain such uses? See Duncan French, From the Depths: Rich Pickings of Principles of Sustainable Development and General International Law on the Ocean Floor—the Seabed Disputes Chamber's 2011 Advisory Opinion, 26 Intl. J. Marine & Coastal L. 525 (2011); Michael Wood, The International Tribunal for the Law of the Sea and General International Law, 22 Intl. J. Marine & Coastal L. 351 (2007).

3. *Obligations of Developing States*. The SBC favored "[e]quality of treatment between developing and developed sponsoring States," noting that "[t]he spread of sponsoring States 'of convenience' would jeopardize uniform application of the highest standards of protection of the marine environment, the safe development of activities in the Area and protection of the common heritage of mankind." ¶ 159. When, if ever, does it make sense for developing states to be bound by standards different from those applicable to developed states?

4. *The Common Heritage Principle and Erga Omnes Obligations*. Does the SBC's advisory opinion reinforce the view that the Area is the common heritage of humankind? Given the various changes in the 1994 Implementation Agreement favorable to developed states, which we reviewed in Section C, how

should we now characterize the features of the deep seabed "common heritage" regime? Is this regime an erga omnes one?

5. *Claims Concerning Illegal Activities*. If a contractor or a sponsoring state were to act illegally under international law, who may bring a claim? In what forum(s)? Compare the advisory jurisdiction of the SBC, which it exercised in the opinion excerpted above. See LOS Convention, Articles 186–191. For more on the dispute settlement system of the LOS Convention, see Chapter 15.

6. *Changing the Deep Seabed Mining Regime*. As noted earlier in this chapter, the 1994 Implementation Agreement significantly modified Part XI of the LOS Convention. Going forward, what avenues are most likely to be used to change the Part XI/1994 Implementation Agreement regime or how it is interpreted? The ISA's Regulations? Formal amendments to the LOS Convention? Advisory opinions from the SBC? Other judicial or arbitral decisions? To what extent may international courts or tribunals review the legality of measures adopted by the Authority? See LOS Convention, Article 189.

E Non-Mineral Resources and Uses of the Area

The International Seabed Authority (ISA or Authority) and the international legal community must also consider what roles, if any, the Authority may play with respect to new uses of the deep seabed—uses not directly related to mineral resources. In recent years, for example, attention has focused on biologically diverse bacteria and other life forms found at deep-sea hydrothermal vents. These life forms, capable of thriving in the presence of great heat, great pressure, and an extremely acidic environment, interest scientific researchers and have commercial uses. What international law rules and procedures govern the use of living resources at deep-sea hydrothermal vents? The readings and Notes in this section explore this question.

CRAIG H. ALLEN, PROTECTING THE OCEANIC GARDENS OF EDEN: INTERNATIONAL LAW ISSUES IN DEEP-SEA VENT RESOURCE CONSERVATION AND MANAGEMENT

13 Georgetown Intl. Envtl. L. Rev. 563 (2001)

. . . Under the CHM [common heritage of humankind] regime, no State has jurisdiction to establish integrated conservation and management measures or pollution prevention and control regulations for vent fields in the Area. At the same time, the ISA authority over the Area is limited to mining activities and the environmental effects of those mining activities. There is, therefore, presently no State or international organization with the needed authority to protect the vent resources against the tragedy of the commons by, for example, establishing maritime protected areas for those fields threatened by unsustainable or otherwise incompatible uses. Nor does any State or international organization have area-based jurisdiction to control marine pollution or seabed waste disposal at or near vent fields within the Area....

Although both the geographic and functional extent of the high seas freedoms was curtailed by the 1982 LOSC, particularly by Parts V and XI, the freedoms are still broad, as are the State obligations that accompany those freedoms.... It can be asserted in good faith that the collection of LMRs [living marine resources] by marine scientists from vents lying within the Area or in the surrounding waters of the high seas, or even LMR harvesting by bioprospectors in those areas, falls within the freedom to fish, to engage in marine scientific research or, perhaps, an unspecified hybrid of those two high seas freedoms. Those high seas freedoms, when exercised with due regard to the interests of other States under the Convention and in accordance with measures implementing Part XII of the Convention, embrace the freedom to capture, study, and use the living resources beyond any nation's jurisdiction. Over two decades of State practice confirms the soundness of this interpretation. Marine scientists have been collecting biological samples from the vent chimneys and the surrounding waters and seabed within the Area since at least 1979, without any apparent objection. Even after those specimens were put to commercial use in biotechnology application, there is no evidence that any State or international organization protested the activity as a violation of international law.

[S]everal factors militate against an expansive construction of the CHM concept. First, the UNCLOS III *travaux préparatoires* demonstrate that the conferees rejected a broader definition of "resources" of the Area that would have included living resources. Even Ambassador Pardo, author of the CHM concept, acknowledged that the final text of the LOSC "severely limited" the CHM regime. Second, the "exhaustibility" argument offered in support of extending the CHM to the seabed's mineral resources before the LOSC entered into force is inapposite to vent LMRs. The exhaustibility argument reasoned that because the mineral resources of the deep sea are exhaustible, if they may be legally appropriated by any entity, the technologically advanced nations will exploit them to the exclusion of developing nations. Although deep seabed vents are neither common nor easily accessible, the living resources of the vents appear to be renewable.... Third, in contrast to seabed mining claims, the rational development of which requires a regime that provides for preemptive claims to mining sites to effectively exclude all but the authorized miner, LMR collection efforts, as presently practiced, require no such exclusivity. Finally, any expansion of the CHM concept to resources other than seabed minerals is in derogation of a centuries old tradition of broad high seas freedoms, and only an express or implied intent by States to diminish the scope of those freedoms, voluntarily assumed, carries the legitimacy necessary to serve as a binding norm.

LETTER DATED 16 MARCH 2010 FROM THE CO-CHAIRPERSONS OF THE AD HOC OPEN-ENDED INFORMAL WORKING GROUP [ON CONSERVATION AND SUSTAINABLE USE OF MARINE BIOLOGICAL DIVERSITY BEYOND THE LIMITS OF NATIONAL JURISDICTION] TO THE PRESIDENT OF THE GENERAL ASSEMBLY

UN Doc. A/65/68 (2010)

70. Delegations generally recognized that the [LOS] Convention provided the framework for all activities in the oceans and seas, including in respect of marine genetic resources beyond areas of national jurisdiction. However, the view was also expressed that the Convention's scope did not encompass marine genetic resources and that only the mandate of the Convention on Biological Diversity provided the legal regime in that regard.

71. Divergent views were expressed on the relevant legal regime under the [LOS] Convention regarding marine genetic resources beyond areas of national jurisdiction. Several delegations observed that, according to General Assembly resolution 2749 (XXV) and Part XI of the Convention, which they noted was part of customary international law, the seabed and ocean floor and the subsoil thereof beyond the limits of national jurisdiction (the "Area"), as well as its resources, were the common heritage of mankind. They emphasized that the common heritage of mankind, including the fair and equitable sharing of benefits, applied to the biological resources of the Area. Several delegations noted the competence of the International Seabed Authority in that regard. Some delegations also stressed that, under the Convention, the legal regime applicable to marine resources was defined by the maritime zone in which they were found, not by their nature as mineral or biological resources.

72. Other delegations stressed that Part XI only addressed mineral resources, and expressed the view that marine genetic resources beyond areas of national jurisdiction were regulated by the high seas regime in Part VII of the Convention. They observed that the mandate of the International Seabed Authority in relation to marine biological diversity was specifically set out in

article 145 of the Convention relating to the protection of the marine environment with regard to activities in the Area.

73. A number of delegations underlined the need to address implementation gaps in this connection. Notably, delegations highlighted the following practical measures: promotion of marine scientific research; development of codes of conduct for research activities; environmental impact assessments, including the development of guidance on assessments of impacts on marine genetic resources within the general process of environmental impact assessment; establishment of mechanisms for cooperation, sharing of information and knowledge resulting from research on marine genetic resources, including by increasing participation of researchers from developing countries in relevant research projects; establishment of marine protected areas, discussion of practical options for benefit-sharing, including options for facilitating access to samples; and consideration of the intellectual property aspects of marine genetic resources beyond areas of national jurisdiction.

74. Several delegations called for the strengthening of the role of the present Working Group, including with a view to adopting specific provisions to regulate access to marine genetic resources beyond areas of national jurisdiction and exploitation. A proposal was made that the United Nations should urgently initiate a negotiating process with the aim of defining the legal aspects related to marine biodiversity beyond areas of national jurisdiction, including the establishment of an institutional structure responsible for the management and conservation of the resources. The possible adjustment of the mandate of the International Seabed Authority could be considered in that context.

75. Several delegations expressed the view that an implementing agreement on marine biodiversity beyond areas of national jurisdiction to the Convention should address marine genetic resources, and recognize the applicability of the concept of common heritage of mankind in this respect. . . . Other delegations [expressed concern] that a new legal regime regarding benefit-sharing would impede research and developments from which humanity at large benefited.

76. A number of delegations expressed support for the development of practical measures to enhance the conservation and sustainable use of marine genetic resources beyond areas of national jurisdiction. Several delegations stressed the need to address marine genetic resources beyond areas of national jurisdiction on the basis of integrated and ecosystem approaches. The view was expressed that activities related to marine genetic resources beyond areas of national jurisdiction should be carried out in accordance with principles of conservation and sustainable development and on the basis of a precautionary approach. Policies governing such activities should seek a balance between

environmental protection, freedom of scientific research and benefits to be derived by the international community.

77. Several delegations noted the need to take into account the work under other relevant forums, such as the Convention on Biological Diversity, FAO, the International Treaty on Plant Genetic Resources for Food and Agriculture and the World Intellectual Property Organization, when considering practical measures.

Notes

1. *Deep-sea Vent Resources and Marine Biotechnology*. Each year the pharmaceutical, enzyme, cosmetics, and nutritional supplement industries sell billions of dollars worth of marine biotechnology-related products. Biotechnology companies have obtained patents on genetic materials from living organisms located at deep-sea hydrothermal vents and have used those materials in products. These vents are home to abundant, unique, and diverse ecosystems. See Salvatore Arico & Charlotte Salpin, UNU-IAS Report: Bioprospecting the Genetic Resources in the Deep Seabed: Scientific, Legal and Policy Aspects (2005), available at http://www.iode.org/index.php?option=com_oe&task=viewDocumentRecord&docID=7517; David Leary et al., Marine Genetic Resources: A Review of Scientific and Commercial Interest, 33 Marine Policy 183 (2009).

2. *Marine Scientific Research*. The ISA may carry out marine scientific research in the Area, and it is obligated to encourage such research and coordinate and disseminate the results. LOS Convention, Article 143(2); 1994 Implementation Agreement, Annex, § 1(5)(h). All states and the Intergovernmental Oceanographic Commission also may conduct marine scientific research in the Area. LOS Convention, Articles 143(3), 256. Do the provisions on marine scientific research preclude companies from patenting and marketing the genetic resources they take from deep-sea vents? Must the results of companies' research into deep-sea vent resources at least be published and disseminated?

Is bioprospecting the same as marine scientific research? "Bioprospecting" is not defined in the LOS Convention, but the Conference of the Parties of the 1992 Convention on Biological Diversity has referred to bioprospecting as "the exploration of biodiversity for commercially valuable genetic and biochemical resources" and "the process of gathering information from the biosphere on the molecular composition of genetic resources for the development of new commercial product." Progress Report on the Implementation of the Programmes of Work on Biological Diversity of Inland Water Ecosystems,

Marine and Coastal Biological Diversity and Forest Biological Diversity ¶ 6, UNEP/CBD/COP/5/INF/7 (1999). See also UNEP/CBD/SBSTTA/8/INF/3/Rev.1 (2003), a study prepared by the Subsidiary Body on Scientific, Technical and Technological Advice concerning the relationship between the Convention on Biological Diversity and the LOS Convention with regard to the conservation and sustainable use of genetic resources on the deep seabed. Could states avoid their obligations with respect to marine scientific research—including the obligation in Article 143(1) of the LOS Convention to carry out such research in the Area "for the benefit of mankind as a whole"—by declaring that their activities with respect to genetic resources found at the deep seabed have a commercial purpose? If activities with respect to living deep-sea vent resources are deemed "bioprospecting," what law governs those activities?

3. *The International Seabed Authority and Regulation of Living Deep-sea Vent Resources.* Could the Authority's mandate to protect the marine environment be read broadly enough to allow it to regulate bioprospecting at deep-sea hydrothermal vents? See LOS Convention, Articles 145, 162(2)(x). See also id. Articles 162(2)(w) and 209(1) and Annex III, Article 17(1)(b)(ix), (xii); 1994 Implementation Agreement, Annex, § 1(5)(g), (7). Could the Authority rely on these Articles to ban bioprospecting at deep-sea vents? To what extent does the Article 145 phrase "in accordance with this Convention with respect to activities in the Area" restrict the ISA's regulatory authority? Recall the definition of "activities in the Area" in Article 1(1)(3) of the Convention.

4. *Legal Principles Applicable to Deep-sea Vent Resources.* Even if living resources of the deep seabed are not subject to direct regulation by the Authority, does the common heritage principle govern living organisms and genetic material at deep-sea hydrothermal vents? Article 136 of the LOS Convention provides that "[t]he Area and its resources are the common heritage of mankind." Recall that Article 133(a) defines "resources" for purposes of Part XI as "all solid, liquid or gaseous mineral resources *in situ* in the Area at or beneath the seabed, including polymetallic nodules." Does this definition limit the scope of Article 136? Of the meaning of "natural resources" in Article 145? Recall also that Article 1(1)(1) defines the "Area" as "the seabed and ocean floor and subsoil thereof, beyond the limits of national jurisdiction." Does the Area encompass various features that can be differentiated from the superjacent water column, such as hydrothermal vents, which emit heated water from under the seabed, and hypersaline brine pools, mud volcanoes, and cold seeps? Does the Area itself encompass organisms found in those features, or organisms that are sedentary on the seabed?

Instead of viewing deep-sea vent resources as subject to the common heritage principle, some states, along with Professor Allen, regard such resources as subject to the principle of high seas freedoms. Which freedoms may apply to bioprospecting? What limits apply to the exercise of high seas freedoms? See LOS Convention, Articles 87(2), 143, 192, 196(1).

Some have argued that existing law is insufficient to govern bioprospecting for deep-sea vent resources. Should states adopt an amendment to the LOS Convention or an implementing agreement? What should it provide?

Discussions continue. For reports of the U.N. Ad Hoc Open-ended Informal Working Group to study issues relating to the conservation and sustainable use of marine biological diversity beyond areas of national jurisdiction, see http://www.un.org/depts/los/biodiversityworkinggroup/biodiversityworkinggroup.htm.

CHAPTER 12

Protection and Preservation of the Marine Environment

The field of international environmental law has developed dramatically in the last few decades. It has become increasingly clear that pollution has had and is having a serious deleterious effect on the world environment in general, and on the oceans in particular, although it may be impossible to know all the precise effects of particular types of pollution. How the international legal system copes with scientific uncertainty, and how it accommodates the goals of protecting the environment and promoting economic activities (such as unhampered navigation of vessels), are among the most challenging problems facing international lawyers and policy makers. This chapter provides one example showing how difficult it can be to address these problems in a legal framework that is fragmented in terms of possible remedies at the global, regional, and national levels and that has difficulty protecting common goods such as the marine environment.

The example explored in this chapter deals with land-based pollution, the most important source of marine pollution. Despite its importance, land-based pollution is subject to less stringent international regulation than other sources. In the 1982 United Nations Convention on the Law of the Sea (LOS Convention), principles concerning regional and global cooperation with respect to land-based pollution are couched in much more cautious language than are the rules governing dumping, vessel-source pollution, and pollution of the Area. In fact, no global agreement deals specifically with land-based pollution. As of September 2013 only the nonbinding Global Program of Action for the Protection of the Marine Environment from Land-based Activities, UN Doc. UNEP(OCA)/LBA/IG.2/7 (1995), has been adopted, under the auspices of the United Nations Environment Programme. Where the exercise of legislative competence (jurisdiction) so clearly accommodates the territorial sovereignty of states, it is not surprising that international enforcement competence is not well developed. The MOX Plant cases, litigated in four different international forums over a span of seven years, illustrate just how complex proceedings concerning land-based pollution can be under international law.

 | DOI 10.1163/9789004203563_013

THE MOX PLANT CASE (ITLOS, PROVISIONAL MEASURES, 2001)

Dec. 3, 2001, Ireland v. United Kingdom (Provisional Measures), ITLOS Case No. 10 (2001), 2001 ITLOS Rep. 95, 41 Intl. Leg. Materials 405 (2002), available at http://www.itlos.org

[In 1993 local British authorities granted British Nuclear Fuels, a public limited company wholly owned by the United Kingdom, permission to build a mixed oxide (MOX) plant to process spent nuclear fuel so that it could be reused in nuclear reactors. This plant is located at Sellafield, in Cumbria, facing the Irish Sea. The Irish Sea is a semi-enclosed sea surrounded by Ireland and the United Kingdom, and Ireland feared that operation of the MOX plant would detrimentally affect the water quality of the Irish Sea and thus negatively influence the Irish fishing industry.

Ireland and the United Kingdom are both parties to the 1957 Treaty Establishing the European Atomic Energy Community. Its Article 37 obliges member states to provide the European Commission with information on any plan for the disposal of radioactive waste. The Commission would then determine whether implementing the plan would result in radioactive contamination of, inter alia, the waters of another member state. In 1997 the Commission, pointing out that Ireland lay at least 184 kilometers (approximately 100 nautical miles) away from the United Kingdom, found that the effects of the MOX plant on the marine environment of Ireland would be negligible. The Commission concluded that the planned operation of the plant would not result in impermissible radioactive contamination. 1997 O.J. C 68/03.

Ireland apparently did not agree with the Commission. On October 25, 2001, only weeks after the British Secretary of State for Environment, Food and Rural Affairs and the Secretary of State for Health approved the manufacture of MOX at Sellafield, Ireland instituted arbitration proceedings against the United Kingdom pursuant to Article 287 and Annex VII of the LOS Convention. On November 9, 2001, in accordance with Article 290(5) of the LOS Convention, Ireland also requested provisional measures from the International Tribunal for the Law of the Sea (ITLOS) pending the constitution of an Annex VII arbitral tribunal, in order to prevent serious harm to the marine environment. The 21 judges of the ITLOS, together with the ad hoc judge appointed by Ireland, unanimously issued the following order on December 3, 2001. (The ITLOS refers to the LOS Convention as "the Convention," while Ireland uses the acronym "UNCLOS.")]

THE TRIBUNAL . . .

Makes the following Order:

1. *Whereas* Ireland and the United Kingdom are States Parties to the Convention;

2. *Whereas*, on 9 November 2001, Ireland filed with the Registry of the Tribunal by facsimile a Request for the prescription of provisional measures under article 290, paragraph 5, of the Convention "in the dispute concerning the MOX plant, international movements of radioactive materials, and the protection of the marine environment of the Irish Sea" between Ireland and the United Kingdom;...

26. *Whereas*, in the Notification and Statement of Claim of 25 October 2001, Ireland requested the arbitral tribunal to be constituted under Annex VII (hereinafter "the Annex VII arbitral tribunal") to adjudge and declare:

> 1) That the United Kingdom has breached its obligations under Articles 192 and 193 and/or Article 194 and/or Article 207 and/or Articles 211 and 213 of UNCLOS in relation to the authorisation of the MOX plant, including by failing to take the necessary measures to prevent, reduce and control pollution of the marine environment of the Irish Sea from (1) intended discharges of radioactive materials and or wastes from the MOX plant, and/or (2) accidental releases of radioactive materials and/or wastes from the MOX plant and/or international movements associated the MOX plant, and/or (3) releases of radioactive materials and/or wastes from the MOX plant and/or international movements associated the MOX plant with the of resulting from terrorist act [sic];
>
> 2) That the United Kingdom has breached its obligations under Articles 192 and 193 and/or Article 194 and/or Article 207 and/or Articles 211 and 213 of UNCLOS in relation to the authorisation of the MOX plant by failing (1) properly or at all to assess the risk of terrorist attack on the MOX plant and international movements of radioactive material associated with the plant, and/or (2) properly or at all to prepare a comprehensive response strategy or plan to prevent, contain and respond to terrorist attack on the MOX plant and international movements of radioactive waste associated with the plant;
>
> 3) That the United Kingdom has breached its obligations under Articles 123 and 197 of UNCLOS in relation to the authorisation of the MOX plant, and has failed to cooperate with Ireland in the protection of the marine environment of the Irish Sea *inter alia* by refusing to share information with Ireland and/or refusing to carry out a proper environmental assessment of the impacts on the marine environment of the MOX plant and associated activities and/or proceeding to authorise the operation of the MOX plant whilst proceedings relating to the settlement of a dispute on access to information were still pending;

4) That the United Kingdom has breached its obligations under Article 206 of UNCLOS in relation to the authorisation of the MOX plant, including by

(a) failing, by its 1993 Environmental Statement, properly and fully to assess the potential effects of the operation of the MOX plant on the marine environment of the Irish Sea; and/or

(b) failing, since the publication of its 1993 Environmental Statement, to assess the potential effects of the operation of the MOX plant on the marine environment by reference to the factual and legal developments which have arisen since 1993, and in particular since 1998; and/or

(c) failing to assess the potential effects on the marine environment of the Irish Sea of international movements of radioactive materials to be transported to and from the MOX plant; and/or

(d) failing to assess the risk of potential effects on the marine environment of the Irish Sea arising from terrorist act or acts on the MOX plant and/or on international movements of radioactive material to and from the MOX plant.

5) That the United Kingdom shall refrain from authorizing or failing to prevent (a) the operation of the MOX plant and/or (b) international movements of radioactive materials into and out of the United Kingdom related to the operation of the MOX plant or any preparatory or other activities associated with the operation of the MOX [plant] until such time as (1) there has been carried out a proper assessment of the environmental impact of the operation of the MOX plant as well as related international movements of radioactive materials, and (2) it is demonstrated that the operation of the MOX plant and related international movements of radioactive materials will result in the deliberate discharge of no radioactive materials, including wastes, directly or indirectly into the marine environment of the Irish Sea, and (3) there has been agreed and adopted jointly with Ireland a comprehensive strategy or plan to prevent, contain and respond to terrorist attack on the MOX plant and international movements of radioactive waste associated with the plant; ...

29. *Whereas* Ireland, in its final submissions at the public sitting held on 20 November 2001, requested the prescription by the Tribunal of the following provisional measures:

(1) that the United Kingdom immediately suspend the authorisation of the MOX plant dated 3 October 2001, alternatively take such other

measures as are necessary to prevent with immediate effect the operation of the MOX plant;

(2) that the United Kingdom immediately ensure that there are no movements into or out of the waters over which it has sovereignty or exercises sovereign rights of any radioactive substances or materials or wastes which are associated with the operation of, or activities preparatory to the operation of, the MOX plant;

(3) that the United Kingdom ensure that no action of any kind is taken which might aggravate, extend or render more difficult of solution the dispute submitted to the Annex VII tribunal (Ireland hereby agreeing itself to act so as not to aggravate, extend or render more difficult of solution that dispute); and

(4) that the United Kingdom ensure that no action is taken which might prejudice the rights of Ireland in respect of the carrying out of any decision on the merits that the Annex VII tribunal may render (Ireland likewise will take no action of that kind in relation to the United Kingdom);

30. *Whereas*, at the public sitting held on 20 November 2001, the United Kingdom presented its final submissions as follows:

> The United Kingdom requests the International Tribunal for the Law of the Sea to:
>
> (1) reject Ireland's request for provisional measures; . . .

31. *Considering* that, in accordance with article 287 of the Convention, Ireland has, on 25 October 2001, instituted proceedings before the Annex VII arbitral tribunal against the United Kingdom "in the dispute concerning the MOX plant, international movements of radioactive materials, and the protection of the marine environment of the Irish Sea"; . . .

33. *Considering* that, on 9 November 2001, after the expiry of the time-limit of two weeks provided for in article 290, paragraph 5, of the Convention, and pending the constitution of the Annex VII arbitral tribunal, Ireland submitted to the Tribunal a Request for provisional measures;

34. *Considering* that article 290, paragraph 5, of the Convention provides in the relevant part that:

> Pending the constitution of an arbitral tribunal to which a dispute is being submitted under this section, any court or tribunal agreed upon by the parties or, failing such agreement within two weeks from the date of the request for provisional measures, the International Tribunal for the

> Law of the Sea ... may prescribe, modify or revoke provisional measures in accordance with this article if it considers that *prima facie* the tribunal which is to be constituted would have jurisdiction and that the urgency of the situation so requires;

35. *Considering* that, before prescribing provisional measures under article 290, paragraph 5, of the Convention, the Tribunal must satisfy itself that *prima facie* the Annex VII arbitral tribunal would have jurisdiction;

36. *Considering* that Ireland maintains that the dispute with the United Kingdom concerns the interpretation and application of certain provisions of the Convention, including, in particular, articles 123, 192 to 194, 197, 206, 207, 211, 212 and 213 thereof;

37. *Considering* that Ireland has invoked as the basis of jurisdiction of the Annex VII arbitral tribunal article 288, paragraph 1, of the Convention which reads as follows:

> A court or tribunal referred to in article 287 shall have jurisdiction over any dispute concerning the interpretation or application of this Convention which is submitted to it in accordance with this Part;

38. *Considering* that the United Kingdom maintains that Ireland is precluded from having recourse to the Annex VII arbitral tribunal in view of article 282 of the Convention which reads as follows:

> If the States Parties which are parties to a dispute concerning the interpretation or application of this Convention have agreed, through a general, regional or bilateral agreement or otherwise, that such dispute shall, at the request of any party to the dispute, be submitted to a procedure that entails a binding decision, that procedure shall apply in lieu of the procedures provided for in this Part, unless the parties to the dispute otherwise agree;

39. *Considering* that the United Kingdom maintains that the matters of which Ireland complains are governed by regional agreements providing for alternative and binding means of resolving disputes and have actually been submitted to such alternative tribunals, or are about to be submitted;

40. *Considering* that the United Kingdom referred to the fact that Ireland has under article 32 of the 1992 Convention for the Protection of the Marine Environment of the North-East Atlantic (hereinafter "the OSPAR Convention") submitted a dispute between Ireland and the United Kingdom "concerning access to information under article 9 of the OSPAR Convention in relation to

the economic 'justification' of the proposed MOX plant" to an arbitral tribunal (hereinafter "the OSPAR arbitral tribunal");

41. *Considering* that the United Kingdom has further stated that certain aspects of the complaints of Ireland are governed by the Treaty establishing the European Community (hereinafter "the EC Treaty") or the Treaty establishing the European Atomic Energy Community (hereinafter "the Euratom Treaty") and the Directives issued thereunder and that States Parties to those Treaties have agreed to invest the Court of Justice of the European Communities with exclusive jurisdiction to resolve disputes between them concerning alleged failures to comply with such Treaties and Directives; . . .

49. *Considering* that the dispute settlement procedures under the OSPAR Convention, the EC Treaty and the Euratom Treaty deal with disputes concerning the interpretation or application of those agreements, and not with disputes arising under the Convention;

50. *Considering* that, even if the OSPAR Convention, the EC Treaty and the Euratom Treaty contain rights or obligations similar to or identical with the rights or obligations set out in the Convention, the rights and obligations under those agreements have a separate existence from those under the Convention;

51. *Considering* also that the application of international law rules on interpretation of treaties to identical or similar provisions of different treaties may not yield the same results, having regard to, *inter alia*, differences in the respective contexts, objects and purposes, subsequent practice of parties and *travaux préparatoires*;

52. *Considering* that the Tribunal is of the opinion that, since the dispute before the Annex VII arbitral tribunal concerns the interpretation or application of the Convention and no other agreement, only the dispute settlement procedures under the Convention are relevant to that dispute;

53. *Considering* that, for the reasons given above, the Tribunal considers that, for the purpose of determining whether the Annex VII arbitral tribunal would have *prima facie* jurisdiction, article 282 of the Convention is not applicable to the dispute submitted to the Annex VII arbitral tribunal; . . .

62. *Considering* that, for the above reasons, the Tribunal finds that the Annex VII arbitral tribunal would *prima facie* have jurisdiction over the dispute;

63. *Considering* that, in accordance with article 290, paragraph 1, of the Convention, the Tribunal may prescribe provisional measures to preserve the respective rights of the parties to the dispute or to prevent serious harm to the marine environment;

64. *Considering* that, according to article 290, paragraph 5, of the Convention, provisional measures may be prescribed pending the constitution of the Annex VII arbitral tribunal if the Tribunal considers that the urgency

of the situation so requires in the sense that action prejudicial to the rights of either party or causing serious harm to the marine environment is likely to be taken before the constitution of the Annex VII arbitral tribunal;

65. *Considering* that the Tribunal must, therefore, decide whether provisional measures are required pending the constitution of the Annex VII arbitral tribunal. . . .

67. *Considering* that Ireland contends that its rights under certain provisions of the Convention, in particular articles 123, 192 to 194, 197, 206, 207, 211, 212 and 213 thereof, will be irrevocably violated if the MOX plant commences its operations before the United Kingdom fulfils its duties under the Convention;

68. *Considering* that Ireland contends further that once plutonium is introduced into the MOX plant and it commences operations some discharges into the marine environment will occur with irreversible consequences;

69. *Considering* that Ireland contends further that, if the plant becomes operational, the danger of radioactive leaks and emissions, whether arising from the operation of the plant, or resulting from industrial accidents, terrorist attacks, or other causes, would be greatly magnified;

70. *Considering* that Ireland argues that the commissioning of the plant is, in practical terms, itself a near-irreversible step and it is not possible to return to the position that existed before the commissioning of the MOX plant simply by ceasing to feed plutonium into the system;

71. *Considering* that Ireland argues that the precautionary principle places the burden on the United Kingdom to demonstrate that no harm would arise from discharges and other consequences of the operation of the MOX plant, should it proceed, and that this principle might usefully inform the assessment by the Tribunal of the urgency of the measures it is required to take in respect of the operation of the MOX plant;

72. *Considering* that the United Kingdom contends that it has adduced evidence to establish that the risk of pollution, if any, from the operation of the MOX plant would be infinitesimally small;

73. *Considering* that the United Kingdom maintains that the commissioning of the MOX plant on or around 20 December 2001 will not, even arguably, cause serious harm to the marine environment or irreparable prejudice to the rights of Ireland, in the period prior to the constitution of the Annex VII arbitral tribunal or at all;

74. *Considering* that the United Kingdom contends that neither the commissioning of the MOX plant nor the introduction of plutonium into the system is irreversible, although decommissioning would present the operator of the plant with technical and financial difficulties, if Ireland were to be successful in its claim before the Annex VII arbitral tribunal;

75. *Considering* that the United Kingdom argues that Ireland has failed to supply proof that there will be either irreparable damage to the rights of Ireland or serious harm to the marine environment resulting from the operation of the MOX plant and that, on the facts of this case, the precautionary principle has no application;

76. *Considering* that the United Kingdom states that the manufacture of MOX fuel presents negligible security risks and it has in place very extensive security precautions in terms of the protection of the Sellafield site;

77. *Considering* that the United Kingdom states that it hopes to reach agreement with Ireland on the constitution of the Annex VII arbitral tribunal within a short space of time;

78. *Considering* that, at the public sitting held on 20 November 2001, the United Kingdom has stated that "there will be no additional marine transports of radioactive material either to or from Sellafield as a result of the commissioning of the MOX plant";

79. *Considering* that at the same sitting the United Kingdom stated further that "there will be no export of MOX fuel from the plant until summer 2002" and that "there is to be no import to the THORP [Thermal Oxide Reprocessing Plant] plant of spent nuclear fuel pursuant to contracts for conversion to the MOX plant within that period either" and clarified that the word "summer" should be read as "October";

80. *Considering* that the Tribunal places on record the assurances given by the United Kingdom as specified in paragraphs 78 and 79;

81. *Considering* that, in the circumstances of this case, the Tribunal does not find that the urgency of the situation requires the prescription of the provisional measures requested by Ireland, in the short period before the constitution of the Annex VII arbitral tribunal;

82. *Considering*, however, that the duty to cooperate is a fundamental principle in the prevention of pollution of the marine environment under Part XII of the Convention and general international law and that rights arise therefrom which the Tribunal may consider appropriate to preserve under article 290 of the Convention;

83. *Considering* that, in accordance with article 89, paragraph 5, of the Rules, the Tribunal may prescribe measures different in whole or in part from those requested;

84. *Considering* that, in the view of the Tribunal, prudence and caution require that Ireland and the United Kingdom cooperate in exchanging information concerning risks or effects of the operation of the MOX plant and in devising ways to deal with them, as appropriate;

85. *Considering* that Ireland and the United Kingdom should each ensure that no action is taken which might aggravate or extend the dispute submitted to the Annex VII arbitral tribunal;…

89. For these reasons,

THE TRIBUNAL,

1. Unanimously,

Prescribes, pending a decision by the Annex VII arbitral tribunal, the following provisional measure under article 290, paragraph 5, of the Convention:

Ireland and the United Kingdom shall cooperate and shall, for this purpose, enter into consultations forthwith in order to:

(a) exchange further information with regard to possible consequences for the Irish Sea arising out of the commissioning of the MOX plant;

(b) monitor risks or the effects of the operation of the MOX plant for the Irish Sea;

(c) devise, as appropriate, measures to prevent pollution of the marine environment which might result from the operation of the MOX plant.

2. Unanimously,

Decides that Ireland and the United Kingdom shall each submit the initial report referred to in article 95, paragraph 1, of the Rules not later than 17 December 2001, and authorizes the President of the Tribunal to request such further reports and information as he may consider appropriate after that date.…

Joint Declaration of Judges Caminos, Yamamoto, Park, Akl, Marsit, Eiriksson, and Jesus

The dispute between Ireland and the United Kingdom as it appears before the Tribunal is characterized by an almost total lack of agreement on the scientific evidence with respect to the possible consequences of the operation of the MOX plant on the marine environment of the Irish Sea.

Under these circumstances of scientific uncertainty, the Tribunal might have been expected to have followed the path it took in the *Southern Bluefin Tuna Cases* to prescribe a measure preserving the existing situation. In its wisdom, it did not do so. It decided, in the circumstances of the case, that, in the short period before the constitution of an arbitral tribunal under Annex VII to the United Nations Convention on the Law of the Sea, the urgency of the situation did not require it to lay down, as binding legal obligations, the measures requested by Ireland.

We have supported this decision. The circumstances of the case which have influenced us in this regard include, first, as for Ireland's request that marine transport associated with the plant cease, that the United Kingdom has made assurances that there would be no such transport in the relevant period. Second, with respect to Ireland's request to prevent the commissioning of the plant, we are influenced by the United Kingdom statement that the commissioning of the plant and the introduction of plutonium into the system is not irreversible.

More importantly, our position is a response to another characteristic of the dispute as presented to the Tribunal, that is, the almost complete lack of cooperation between the Governments of Ireland and the United Kingdom with respect to the environmental impact of the planned operations. It is clear that this state of affairs has its origin in a long-standing dispute with respect to other activities at the Sellafield site, but those activities are not before the Tribunal.

The Tribunal has identified the duty to cooperate as a fundamental principle in the regime of the prevention of pollution of the marine environment under Part XII of the Convention and general international law. Against the background of that duty, we regard the most effective measure that the Tribunal could have adopted was to require the parties to cooperate forthwith. It is not, we trust, an idle hope that the results of the consultations prescribed will include a common understanding of the scientific evidence and a common appreciation of the measures which must be taken with respect to the plant to prevent harm to the marine environment.

DISPUTE CONCERNING ACCESS TO INFORMATION UNDER ARTICLE 9 OF THE OSPAR CONVENTION (OSPAR TRIBUNAL, FINAL AWARD, 2003)

July 2, 2003, Final Award, Ireland v. United Kingdom, Tribunal constituted pursuant to the 1992 Convention for the Protection of the Marine Environment of the North-East Atlantic (OSPAR Convention), 42 Intl. Leg. Materials 1118 (2003), 23 Rep. Intl. Arb. Awards 59 (2006), available at http://www.pca-cpa.org/showpage.asp?pag_id=1158

[As noted in the ITLOS case excerpted above (¶¶ 26(3) and 40), on June 25, 2001 Ireland requested that an arbitral tribunal be constituted under Article 32 of the 1992 OSPAR Convention before seeking provisional measures from the ITLOS on October 25, 2001. Both Ireland and the United Kingdom are parties to this regional Convention. It contains an access to information clause concerning activities or measures adversely affecting or likely to affect the maritime area. After five public consultations organized in the United Kingdom between 1997 and 2001, Ireland continued to argue that certain information, thought to be of a commercial nature by the United Kingdom, was being withheld from public scrutiny. The information in question concerned the reports of financial consultants, the PA Consulting Group of London, commissioned to prepare the second consultation, and of a consulting firm, Arthur D. Little, commissioned to prepare the fourth consultation. Both of these reports were presented in two versions: a full report for the commissioning agency and a second, redacted version for public consultation. In the following excerpt these reports are referred to as PA Report and ADL Report, respectively.

The arbitral tribunal focused on Article 9 of the OSPAR Convention, entitled "Access to Information," which reads as follows:

> 1. The Contracting Parties shall ensure that their competent authorities are required to make available the information described in paragraph 2 of this Article to any natural or legal person, in response to any reasonable request, without that person's having to prove an interest, without unreasonable charges, as soon as possible and at the latest within two months.
>
> 2. The information referred to in paragraph 1 of this Article is any available information in written, visual, aural or data-base form on the state of the maritime area, on activities or measures adversely affecting or likely to affect it and on activities or measures introduced in accordance with the Convention.
>
> 3. The provisions of this Article shall not affect the right of Contracting Parties, in accordance with their national legal systems and applicable international regulations, to provide for a request for such information to be refused where it affects:
>
> (a) the confidentiality of the proceedings of public authorities, international relations and national defence;
>
> (b) public security;
>
> (c) matters which are, or have been, sub judice, or under enquiry (including disciplinary enquiries), or which are the subject of preliminary investigation proceedings;
>
> (d) commercial and industrial confidentiality, including intellectual property;
>
> (e) the confidentiality of personal data and/or files;
>
> (f) material supplied by a third party without that party being under a legal obligation to do so;

(g) material, the disclosure of which would make it more likely that the environment to which such material related would be damaged.

4. The reasons for a refusal to provide the information requested must be given.

The arbitral tribunal constituted pursuant to the OSPAR Convention was composed of three arbiters, namely Professor Michael Reisman (Chairman), Dr. Gavan Griffith, and Lord Mustill. It rendered its award on July 2, 2003. On the issue of access to information it interpreted paragraphs 1 and 2 of Article 9 by a majority of two to one on the substantive issues. Griffith and Mustill formed the majority with respect to paragraph 1, Reisman and Mustill for paragraph 2. Before analyzing paragraphs 1 and 2, however, the tribunal clarifies the notion of "applicable international regulations" in paragraph 3.]

93. Article 9(3)(d) states that Parties have the right to refuse a request for information that qualifies under Article 9(2) "in accordance with their national legal systems and applicable international regulations" where the information affects "commercial and industrial confidentiality, including intellectual property. . . ."

94. Ireland acknowledged that the relevant national legal system applicable to Article 9(3) was English law.

95. Further, the Parties agreed that the 1992 Regulations [United Kingdom's Environmental Information Regulations 1992 of 18 December 1992, Statutory Instruments 1992 No. 3240], which give effect to Directive 90/313 [Council Directive 90/313/EEC of 7 June 1990 on the Freedom of Access to Information on the Environment, 1990 O.J. L 158/56], apply as the legislative component of the relevant national legal system. However, the Parties did not agree on their interpretation.

96. The Parties disagreed, in a number of ways, as to the reference of "applicable international regulations" in Article 9(3). Ireland contended that "applicable international regulations" means "international law and practice." The United Kingdom proposed a strict textual interpretation and submitted that there are no "applicable international regulations" for Article 9(3)(d) of the OSPAR Convention other than Directive 90/313, which was implemented in UK law.

97. On its broader submission, Ireland relied upon the Rio Declaration, in particular Principle 10, and the 1998 Aarhus Convention on Access to Information, Public Participation in Decision-making and Access to Justice in Environmental Matters (the "Aarhus Convention"), which entered into force

on 30 October 2001. The United Kingdom replied that the Rio Declaration was not a treaty and that the Aarhus Convention has been ratified by neither Ireland nor the United Kingdom.

98. In its Reply, Ireland submitted that "'regulations' include all the instruments relating to the environment and access to information referred to in detail in Ireland's Memorial...," and that such instruments are to be interpreted in light of "the evolving international law and practice on access to environmental information."

99. A jurisdictional clause may incorporate international law *in statu nascendi*. For example, the Special Agreement between Libya and Tunisia of 10 June 1977, submitting to the ICJ their continental shelf boundary dispute, incorporated as applicable law international maritime norms that had not yet become *lex lata*. Article 1 provided that:

> the Court shall take its decision according to equitable principles, and the relevant circumstances which characterize the area, as well as the new accepted trends in the Third Conference on the Law of the Sea.

When the Parties have so empowered an international arbitral tribunal, it may apply norms that are not *lex lata*, if, in the tribunal's judgment, the norms have been accepted and are soon likely to become part of the international *corpus juris*. But the arbitral tribunal then applies them because of the Parties' instructions, not because they are "almost" law.

100. As long as it is not inconsistent with *jus cogens*, Parties may also instruct a tribunal to apply a *lex specialis* that is not part of general international law at the time. But the OSPAR Convention does not incorporate such a reference. Without such an authorization, a tribunal established under the OSPAR Convention cannot go beyond existing law. This is not to say that a tribunal cannot apply customary international law of a recent vintage, but that it must in fact be customary international law.

101. Although the issue does not arise, the Tribunal agrees with Ireland's proposal to "draw on current international law and practice in considering whether a 'commercial confidentiality' exception to a request for information may be invoked," but only insofar as such law and practice are relevant and hence admissible under Article 31(3)(b) and (c) of the [1969] Vienna Convention [on the Law of Treaties [hereinafter Vienna Convention]]. However, the Tribunal has not been authorized to apply "evolving international law and practice" and cannot do so. In this regard, the Tribunal would note that the ICJ in its decision in the *Gabcikovo-Nagymaros* case, was not, as Ireland argued, proposing that

it—and arguably other international tribunals—had an inherent authority to apply law *in statu nascendi*. The ICJ said:

> new norms and standards have been developed, set forth in a great number of instruments during the last two decades. Such new norms have to be taken into consideration, and such new standards given proper weight, not only when States contemplate new activities but also when continuing with activities begun in the past.

102. The issue here is one of interpretation in good faith, as required by Article 31(1) of the Vienna Convention, if not by an essential ingredient of law itself. A treaty is a solemn undertaking and States Parties are entitled to have applied to them and to their peoples that to which they have agreed and not things to which they have not agreed.

103. Lest it produce anachronistic results that are inconsistent with current international law, a tribunal must certainly engage in *actualisation* or contemporization when construing an international instrument that was concluded in an earlier period. Oppenheim, after restating the so-called law of inter-temporality (i.e., that an instrument is to be interpreted in the light of the general rules of international law in force at the time of its conclusion), adds the qualification that "in some respects the interpretation of a treaty's provisions cannot be divorced from developments in the law subsequent to its adoption." But the reference in the Court's *dictum* and the doctrinal statement in Oppenheim based upon it is to developments in *law*. Wholly apart from the question of the need for actualization of a treaty made scarcely ten years earlier, the Court's reference in *Gabcikovo-Nagymaros* is to new *law* "in a great number of *instruments*" [italics supplied] and not material that has not yet become law. As stated, a tribunal must also adjust application of a treaty insofar as one of its provisions proves inconsistent with a *jus cogens* that subsequently emerged. The present case does not raise questions of *jus cogens*.

104. For these reasons, the Tribunal cannot accept Ireland's proposal that the Aarhus Convention or that "draft proposals for a new EC Directive" be applied.

105. Nonetheless, the Tribunal may apply, where appropriate, other extant international agreements insofar as they are admissible for purposes of interpretation under Article 31 of the Vienna Convention. . . .

[The Tribunal then interprets paragraph 1. According to Ireland, the requirement to make available the information described in paragraph 2 is an "obligation of result," providing it with a direct right. In contrast, the United Kingdom contends that this requirement is only an obligation to provide for a domestic regulatory framework, on the basis of which other states subsequently have a right to request information.]

118. The United Kingdom has characterized its objection to Ireland's claim under Article 9(1) as going to the lack of jurisdiction of the Tribunal and/or being inadmissible. However, in the unanimous view of the Tribunal the question posed by Ireland with respect to Article 9(1) is not one of jurisdiction or admissibility, but one of substance, namely what is the purport of Article 9(1) under the facts of this case. . . .

120. As noted above . . ., Regulation 3 of the 1992 Regulations giving effect to Directive 90/313 is relied upon by the United Kingdom as constituting its compliance under domestic law with the requirements of Article 9(1). The United Kingdom contends that the mandated regime under domestic law is not required to be expressed as being pursuant to the OSPAR Convention obligation. The Tribunal agrees that the standard may be satisfied in a form such as the 1992 Regulations, which are otherwise justified under Directive 90/313.

121. [I]t is no part of Ireland's claims in this dispute that there are defects within the domestic regime to the extent that the 1992 Regulations fall below the standards required by Article 9(1).

122. For the purpose of this issue of construction of Article 9(1), the Tribunal assumes that the redacted information sought by Ireland is of a sort required to be disclosed.

123. The issue remains one of interpretation of public international law, namely whether, as the United Kingdom contends, the obligation of a Contracting Party under Article 9(1) is completely discharged by putting in place an appropriate domestic regulatory framework so that disputes about specific applications of the obligations under Article 9 are to be exclusively determined within the municipal law of the Contracting Party. Should this be the case, the appropriate forum for Ireland with respect to its claims that information to which it was entitled under the OSPAR Convention was improperly withheld will be found in the United Kingdom municipal system.

124. If Article 9(1) is to be interpreted as maintained by Ireland, then this Tribunal may exercise its jurisdiction to consider the merits of the refusal of the United Kingdom's competent authorities to disclose information contained in the PA and ADL Reports, provided that such information falls within the definition of Article 9(2) of the OSPAR Convention.

125. Consistently with Article 31 of the Vienna Convention, the Parties have focused their arguments on the treaty text to determine the meaning of the Article 9(1) obligation. The Tribunal applies this approach to examine the terms of Article 9(1) in the context of the entire Article 9 and the OSPAR Convention.

126. The Tribunal first examines the meaning of the obligation in the context of the OSPAR Convention regime, taking into account its objects and purposes and also the fact that a dispute settlement clause is incorporated by Article 32. In confirmation of this analysis the Tribunal also is guided by Article 32(6)(a) to analyze the relevant rules of international law that inform the meaning of the obligation of Article 9(1), and in particular (the now superseded) Directive 90/313.

127. Article 9 is an access to information provision that must be taken to articulate the Contracting Parties' intentions as expressed within the framework of the general objectives and the particular other provisions of the OSPAR Convention. As much as do the other operative articles of the OSPAR Convention, the disputes clause, Article 32, applies Article 9 as an enforceable obligation in its particular subject matter. Its provisions for disclosure of defined information must be taken to have an intended bite beyond being an expression of aspirational objectives for the domestic laws of the Contracting Parties.

128. The main purpose of the OSPAR Convention is the protection of the marine environment and the elimination of the marine pollution in the North-East Atlantic. The objectives of the OSPAR Convention are set out in its Preamble and include, *inter alia*, obligations

- to protect the marine and other environments;
- to prevent and eliminate pollution;
- to prevent and punish infringements;
- to assist a Contracting Party;
- to conduct research; and
- to prevent dumping.

129. For the achievement of these aims the framers of the OSPAR Convention have carefully applied differential language to provide for stipulated levels of engagement of treaty obligation to achieve these objectives. There is a cascading standard of expression providing for the particular obligations imposed on a Contracting Party. For example, there are mandatory provisions that provide for Contracting Parties:

- to take some act ("shall apply," "shall include," "shall undertake," "shall co-operate" or "shall keep");
- actively to work towards an objective ("take all possible steps," "implement programs," "carry out programs");

- to deal with issues of planning for the objective ("establish programs," "adopt," "define," "draw up," "develop," "take account of"); and
- to take measures ("take," "adopt," "plan," "apply," "introduce," "prescribe," "take into account").

At a lesser level of engagement, other provisions provide for information to be dealt with ("collect," "access information") or that systems be set up ("provide for," "establish").

130. When read as a whole (including the Annexes), it is plain to the Tribunal that the entire text discloses a carefully crafted hierarchy of obligations or engagement to achieve the disparate objectives of the OSPAR Convention. Those who framed the OSPAR Convention expressed themselves in carefully chosen, rather than in loose and general, terms. They plainly identified matters for mandatory obligation for action by Contracting Parties, as in

- Article 5 ("The Contracting Party shall take");
- Article 6 ("The Contracting Party shall... undertake");
- Article 7 ("The Contracting Party shall co-operate..."); and
- Article 8 ("The Contracting Party shall establish...," "The Contracting Party shall have regard...").

131. Further, requirements for Contracting Parties to ensure a result are not confined to Article 9(1). Importantly, the general obligations expressed in Article 8(2) and embraced under Article 2(3)(b)(ii) are that the Contracting Parties shall "...ensure the application of best available techniques and best environmental practice..." Similarly, Article 4(1) of Annex II dealing with dumping requires that the Contracting Parties shall "ensure" the required result and, under Article 10(1), shall "ensure compliance" by vessels or aircraft. Likewise, Article 5(1) of Annex III demands that the Contracting Parties shall "ensure" that their competent authorities implement the relevant applicable decisions, recommendations, and all other agreements adopted under the OSPAR Convention.

132. The issue for determination is whether the requirement in Article 9(1) "to ensure" the obligated result, mandates a result rather than merely a municipal law system directed to obtain the result.

133. In the context of the language used within Article 9, it remains for the Tribunal to discern the extent of the comprised obligation. Whatever its particular replication of Directive 90/313, what does appear plain to the Tribunal is that the obligation expressed in Article 9(1) by the requirement that a

Contracting Party "shall ensure" the stipulated result is a reflection of a deliberate rather than a lax choice of vocabulary. It illustrates the application of a chosen (and strong) level of expression, deftly applied by the drafters to the particular and, to them, important subject matter of disclosure of information to any persons, whether nationals or not, who request it. It is expressed at the higher level of obligation, and when applying it in the complex of the provisions on disclosure of information embraced by the scheme of Article 9, the Tribunal sees no reason to read its particular language in a way that is discordant with the structure and use of language in the entire OSPAR Convention. The search is for conformity of meaning within the OSPAR Convention.

134. On that approach, the Tribunal finds that the obligation is to be construed as expressed at the mandatory end of the scale. The applied requirement of Article 9(1) is read by the Tribunal as imposing an obligation upon the United Kingdom, as a Contracting Party, to ensure something, namely that its competent authorities "are required to make available the information described in paragraph 2 . . . to any natural [or] legal person, in response to any reasonable request."

135. It appears to the Tribunal that to accept the expression of the requirement "to ensure" a result as expressed at the lesser level of setting up a regime or system directed to obtain the stipulated result under the domestic law of the Contracting Party, as is contended by the United Kingdom, would be to apply an impermissible gloss that does not appear as part of the unconditional primary obligation under Article 9(1). In contrast, a limitation of this sort is expressly embraced in the scheme of Article 9(3) providing for exceptions of disclosure expressed by reference to criteria to be imposed by the Contracting Parties "in accordance with their national legal systems." The fact that Article 9(3) engages such a limitation by reference to domestic law forecloses the possibility that Article 9(1) silently and similarly limits the obligation upon a Contracting Party to that of putting in place a domestic legal regime providing for disclosure in compliance with the Article 9 obligations.

136. A further matter that militates in favor of this interpretation is the fact that Article 9(1) identifies the objective criteria that should be met when a request to provide information is received by the competent authorities of a Contracting State. Hence, compliance by a Contracting State with these criteria may itself become a separate subject matter of arbitration under Article 32.

137. For these reasons in this aspect it appears to the Tribunal that Article 9(1) is advisedly pitched at a level that imposes an obligation of result rather than merely to provide access to a domestic regime which is directed at obtaining the required result.

138. In adopting this construction the Tribunal gives full effect to the terms of Article 9(1), including particularly the requirement that as a Contracting Party the United Kingdom "shall ensure that their competent authorities are required to make available the information." The Tribunal applies, rather than excises, this clause as the defining part of the obligation.

139. The Tribunal derives further support for its mere textual analysis of Article 9(1) from the relevant rules of international and European Union law.

140. The Parties are in agreement on the origins of Article 9(1) as derived from, and closely following, the language of Directive 90/313. As noted above, in support of its position the United Kingdom refers to the notion of a directive as defined in Article 249 of the EC Treaty as a measure which shall be "binding as to the result to be achieved, upon each Member State to which it is addressed, but shall leave to the national authorities the choice of form and methods." The United Kingdom submits that by adopting the language of the Directive, the Contracting Parties to the OSPAR Convention evinced their intention to adopt the same approach, namely that a State's only obligation is to take such legislative or administrative measures as may be appropriate to achieve the stated objective.

141. In considering these contentions the Tribunal first notes that the adoption of a similar or identical definition or term in international texts should be distinguished from the intention to bestow the same normative status upon both instruments. The complex of instruments whose wording was used by the drafters may include unilateral statements, position papers, declarations, recommendations, and the like. While the language of such sources might be instrumental to the extent that it allows one to trace and understand the origins of specific treaty terms, their normative value should not be attributed to similarly worded legal obligations imposed by that treaty. As the ITLOS has helpfully observed in its Order of 3 December 2001:

> [E]ven if the OSPAR Convention, the EC Treaty and the Euratom Treaty contain rights or obligations similar to or identical with the rights and obligations set out in [UNCLOS], the rights and obligations under those agreements have a separate existence from those under [UNCLOS].

Further,

> [T]he application of international law rules on interpretation of treaties to identical or similar provisions of different treaties may not yield the same results, having regard to, *inter alia*, differences in the respective contexts, objects and purposes, subsequent practice of parties and *travaux préparatoires*.

142. Each of the OSPAR Convention and Directive 90/313 is an independent legal source that establishes a distinct legal regime and provides for different legal remedies. The United Kingdom recognizes Ireland's right as an EU Member State to challenge the implementation of the Directive in the United Kingdom's domestic legal system before the ECJ. Similarly, a Contracting Party to the OSPAR Convention, with its elaborate dispute settlement mechanism, should be able to question the implementation of a distinct legal obligation imposed by the OSPAR Convention in the arbitral forum, namely this designated Tribunal.

143. Pursuant to Article 4 of Directive 90/313, legal action against a State in breach is to be pursued domestically. However, and in contrast, the OSPAR Convention contains a particular and self-contained dispute resolution mechanism in Article 32, in accordance with which this Tribunal acts. Article 9(1) does not provide for an exception to the OSPAR disputes clause by referring, for instance, to an exclusive municipal remedy, and is therefore as subject to review by an arbitral tribunal as any other provision of the OSPAR Convention. The similar language of the two legal instruments, as well as the fact that the 1992 Regulations are an implementing instrument for both Directive 90/313 and the OSPAR Convention, does not limit a Contracting Party's choice of a legal forum to only one of the two available, i.e. either the ECJ or an OSPAR tribunal. Nor, contrary to the United Kingdom's contention, does it suggest that the only cause of action available to Ireland is confined exclusively to those provided for by Directive 90/313 and implementing legislation. The primary purpose of employing the similar language is to create uniform and consistent legal standards in the field of the protection of the marine environment, and not to create precedence of one set of legal remedies over the other.

[The Tribunal also relies on contemporary principles of state responsibility to sustain its point of view, and concludes by summarizing its position with respect to Article 9(1):]

148. For these reasons the Tribunal rejects the contention of the United Kingdom based on Article 9(1), and determines that upon its proper construction Article 9(1) requires an outcome of result, namely that information falling within the meaning of Article 9(2) (and not excluded under Article 9(3)) is in fact disclosed in conformity with the Article 9 obligation imposed upon each Contracting Party.

[The Tribunal turns to paragraph 2. The parties contest its content. According to Ireland the information requested does not have to be directly related to activities that adversely affect the maritime area. This broad reading of paragraph 2 is disputed by the United Kingdom, which suggests a narrow reading that would require the information so requested to be directly and proximately related to the maritime area. In other words, not all information relating to the MOX plant needs to be disclosed, but only that part that relates to the maritime area.]

161. The Tribunal has not been requested to issue an advisory opinion as to the abstract meaning of Article 9(2) of the OSPAR Convention, but rather to apply the provision to a specific controversy about 14 categories of information redacted from the PA and ADL Reports. In its Memorial, Ireland identified those 14 categories as information relating to:

(A) Estimated annual production capacity of the MOX facility;
(B) Time taken to reach this capacity;
(C) Sales volumes;
(D) Probability of achieving higher sales volumes;
(E) Probability of being able to win contracts for recycling fuel in "significant quantities";
(F) Estimated sales demand;
(G) Percentage of plutonium already on site;
(H) Maximum throughput figures;
(I) Life span of the MOX facility;
(J) Number of employees;
(K) Price of MOX fuel;
(L) Whether, and to what extent, there are firm contracts to purchase MOX from Sellafield;
(M) Arrangements for transport of plutonium to, and MOX from Sellafield;
(N) Likely number of such transports.

It will be recalled that in its Amended Statement of Claim, the first relief which Ireland sought was an order and declaration that the United Kingdom had breached its obligations under Article 9 of the OSPAR Convention "by refusing to make available information deleted from the PA Report and the ADL Report." Ireland's second prayer for relief was, in effect, for an order for the provision by the United Kingdom of those parts of the PA and ADL Reports that had been redacted or, contingently, those parts that had been redacted but that did not affect commercial confidentiality within the meaning of Article 9(3)(d). The specific issue before the Tribunal is whether the redacted portions of the PA and ADL Reports, viewed as categories, constitute "information" within the meaning of Article 9(2)....

163. Article 9(2), whose chapeau is "Access to Information," establishes the scope of information to which, subject to specific enumerated rights of refusal

in Article 9(3), the obligation in Article 9(1) relates. The scope of the information in the provision is not environmental, in general, but, in keeping with the focus of the OSPAR Convention, "the state of the maritime area." It is manifest to the Tribunal that none of the above 14 categories in Ireland's list can plausibly be characterized as "information ... on the state of the maritime area." The Tribunal could, thus, rest its decision on the fact that none of the material in the 14 categories falls within the definition of "information" in Article 9(2).

164. In response to this, Ireland's submission of what might be called an interpretative theory of "inclusive causality" would overcome this difficulty. Ireland argued, it will be recalled,

> without the ADL report there would be no discharges from the MOX plant into the Irish Sea. It is hard to think how that report cannot even according to that test be direct and proximate.

Under an interpretative theory of inclusive causality, anything, no matter how remote, which facilitated the performance of an activity is to be deemed part of that activity. Legislators and drafters of treaties may adopt a theory of inclusive causality. The question is whether the drafters of the OSPAR Convention did. Some parts of Article 9(2) are, indeed, quite expansive, but other parts make abundantly clear that while the drafters sought inclusiveness with respect to some aspects of the information covered by Article 9(2), they had no intention of adopting a theory of inclusive causality. The Tribunal now turns its attention to these matters.

165. Article 9(2) identifies three categories, within each of which "any available information" falls within the obligations of Article 9, unless that category has a restriction. The drafters' selection of the adjectives "any" and "available" in Article 9(2) is significant.

166. The adjective "available" indicates that the drafters were not imposing an obligation on a Contracting Party to gather and process information of a certain sort upon the request of any natural or legal person, but rather were limiting the obligation of the Contracting Parties under Article 9 to information which had already been gathered and was already available to them. This provision is thus similar, in effect, to Article 14(1) of the Convention on Civil Liability for Damage Resulting from Activities Dangerous to the Environment of 1993, which establishes access to information simply if it is "held by public authorities." In this respect, the obligation of Article 9(2) differs from obligations in certain national instruments, under which a claimant with standing may require that a government or its agency or instrumentality gather, process, and make available certain types of information.

167. The adjective "any" indicates that, unless set out explicitly within the three categories enumerated in Article 9(2), no selections or restrictions are implied. One such explicit class of restrictions is to be found in the rights of refusal to a request for information under the grounds specified in Article 9(3). Apart from exceptions, the insertion by the drafters of the adjective "any" requires an applier to interpret extensively *within* each of the three categories. Once a matter is found to fall within one of the categories of Article 9(2), the presumption is that it is within the scope of the OSPAR Convention. This mandate for an extensive construction of the provision is reinforced by the drafters' selection of the term "information."

168. Article 1 does not define "information" but it is clear that it is a broad and inclusive reference with respect to the state of the maritime area. The point of emphasis, however, is that it is "information" about the state of the maritime area. The three categories of "information . . . on the state of the maritime area" in Article 9(2) are

(i) "any available information" on "the state of the maritime area,"
(ii) "any available information" on "activities or measures adversely affecting or likely to affect . . . the maritime area,"
(iii) "any available information" on "activities or measures introduced in accordance with the Convention."

169. In their submissions to the Tribunal, both Parties focused attention on the second category of Article 9(2). . . . . Accordingly, the Tribunal will direct its attention to this category. . . .

170. It is clear that Article 9(2) is not a general freedom of information statute. The information here is restricted in a number of ways. First, as noted, it is restricted by the term "maritime area," which appears in the first and second categories of Article 9(2), and is given a specific definition in Article 1(a) and 1(b), which provide

> (a) 'Maritime area' means the internal waters and the territorial seas of the Contracting Parties, the sea beyond and adjacent to the territorial sea under the jurisdiction of the coastal state to the extent recognised by international law, and the high seas, including the bed of all those waters and its sub-soil, situated within the following limits:
>
> (i) those parts of the Atlantic and Arctic Oceans and their dependent seas which lie north of 36° north latitude and between 42° west longitude and 51° east longitude, but excluding:

(1) the Baltic Sea and the Belts lying to the south and east of lines drawn from Hasenore Head to Gniben Point, from Korshage to Spodsbjerg and from Gilbjerg Head to Kullen,

(2) the Mediterranean Sea and its dependent seas as far as the point of intersection of the parallel of 36° north latitude and the meridian of 5° 36' west longitude;

(ii) that part of the Atlantic Ocean north of 59° north latitude and between 44° west longitude and 42° west longitude.

(b) 'Internal waters' means the waters on the landward side of the baselines from which the breadth of the territorial sea is measured, extending the case of watercourses up to the freshwater limit.

As so defined, the area covered by the OSPAR Convention includes the internal waters and territorial seas of Ireland and the United Kingdom as well as the Irish Sea between them, but Article 1 does not indicate whether particular information is relevant to that maritime area.

171. Each of the second and third categories of Article 9(2) relates to "activities or measures." Neither of these terms is defined in Article 1 of the Convention, but it is clear from other parts of the OSPAR Convention (e.g., Article 2(1)(a)) that the term "measures" refers generically to regulatory initiatives by any part of the governmental apparatus of the Contracting Parties with respect to matters covered by the OSPAR Convention, while "activities" refers to the actions, whether emanating from or effected by governmental or non-governmental entities, that would be the object of the "measures."

172. In commenting on identical language in Article 2(a) of Directive 90/313, the ECJ in *Mecklenburg* [Mecklenburg v. Kreis Pinneberg—Der Landrat, Case C-321/96, 1998 E.C.R. I-3809] remarked on "the term 'measures' as serving merely to make it clear that the acts governed by the directive included all forms of administrative activity." Plainly, the inclusion of both "activities" and "measures" indicates that the drafters intended a regime in the second category covering "any available information" about a wide, rather than narrow, range of matters relating to the specific subject matter of each of those categories, but the Tribunal notes, once again, that the information must relate to the state of the maritime area.

173. The second category of Article 9(2) relates to two types of activities or measures. First, activities or measures that are already adversely affecting the maritime area and, second, activities or measures that are likely to affect it. The second type of activity or measure may be underway and already be affecting or likely to affect adversely the maritime area or it may not be underway, but

if and when it is, it must be likely to affect adversely the maritime area if it is to fall within the second category. Thus the second category of Article 9(2) includes prospective activities and measures as well as activities and measures already underway.

174. Each of the three categories in Article 9(2) is cast in the broad terms that are consistent with the "any information" formula. As such, they might warrant an interpretation of inclusive causality. However, it is only the second category that contains an additional threshold of inclusion/exclusion that is manifestly designed by the drafters to be more restrictive than the first and third categories. While the scope of Article 9 covers *simpliciter* "any available information" "on the state of the maritime area" (first category) and "any available information" "on activities or measures introduced in accordance with the Convention" (third category), the second category of Article 9(2) qualifies the obligation to provide "any available information" on activities or measures "adversely affecting or likely to affect" the maritime area.

175. The adverb "adversely" qualifies both existing and prospective activities and measures and raises the threshold of inclusion, as does the adverb "likely." Even were the Tribunal to accept, *arguendo*, Ireland's submission of inclusive causality, the submission would founder on the adverb "adversely" and "likely." Had the adverbs "adversely" and "likely" not been inserted in the provision, the scope of that part of Article 9(2) would have included any present or prospective activity or measure having *any* effect on the maritime area and might, as a result, have indicated an intention of inclusive causality. By including those two adverbs, the drafters have excluded from the scope of the obligation of Article 9 current activities or measures that affected or were likely to affect the maritime area, but did not affect it *adversely* and prospective activities that were not likely to affect *adversely* the maritime area.

176. It may be that the object and purpose of this restrictive provision was based on a *de minimis* policy and was intended to preclude claims under Article 9 for available information about activities and measures that did not have adverse impacts on the maritime area. Alternatively, the restrictive character of the language may simply reflect a reluctance on the part of the Contracting Parties, at least at that stage, to undertake a broader obligation. In either case, the restrictive effect of the language in the second category is clear and is the standard which the Tribunal must apply.

177. The relevant parts of the *travaux préparatoires* show that Article 9(2) drew upon Directive 90/313. Article 2(a) of Directive 90/313, which speaks of "information relating to the environment," also establishes, as the criterion of inclusion, activities and measures "adversely affecting or likely so to affect..."

The decision of the ECJ in *Mecklenburg*..., relied upon in this regard by Ireland, is not helpful. The Court was not there concerned with how the word "adversely" should be interpreted, but with how inclusively the term "information relating to the environment" should be construed....

179. In the opinion of the Tribunal, Ireland has failed to demonstrate that the 14 categories of redacted items in the PA and ADL Reports, insofar as they may be taken to be activities or measures with respect to the commissioning and operation of a MOX Plant at Sellafield, are "information... on the state of the maritime area" or, even if they were, are likely adversely to affect the maritime area.

180. Rather than engage the requirement of establishing an adverse effect, Ireland has focused its arguments on the questions of directness of the effect and whether or not the information considered as a whole was "environmental." To buttress its arguments, Ireland has sought to rely upon treaties that are as yet unratified and not in force as between the Parties or regional legislative initiatives that have not been finalized nor entered into force for the Parties. Although, it is arguable—but in the view of the Tribunal not conclusive—that Ireland's claim might have succeeded under some of these drafts, the Tribunal is not empowered to apply legally unperfected instruments. The OSPAR Convention does not adopt a lower threshold requiring no more than an activity or measure that "affects" rather than one that "affects adversely" the maritime area.

181. Ireland has also argued that Article 9(2) relates to any environmental information as such. But, wholly aside from the difficult question of whether the PA and ADL Reports dealt with environmental information (as opposed to information about economic justification), the words "environmental information" do not appear in Article 9(2) nor, indeed, in any part of Article 9. Even if such words did, it is doubtful that the 14 categories listed in paragraph 161 above would come within that class.

182. Hence the Tribunal finds that Ireland has not established that the class of redacted information that it seeks from the PA and ADL Reports under the second category of Article 9(2) falls under Article 9(2)....

FINAL AWARD

The Claims by Ireland are dismissed.

DISPUTE CONCERNING THE MOX PLANT, INTERNATIONAL MOVEMENTS OF RADIOACTIVE MATERIALS, AND THE PROTECTION OF THE MARINE ENVIRONMENT OF THE IRISH SEA (ANNEX VII TRIBUNAL, JURISDICTIONAL MATTERS, 2003)

Ireland v. United Kingdom, Tribunal constituted pursuant to Article 287 and Article 1 of Annex VII of the LOS Convention

[As mentioned above, about two weeks before Ireland requested provisional measures from the ITLOS it had instituted arbitration proceedings against the United Kingdom pursuant to Article 287 of the LOS Convention. Unlike the United Kingdom, Ireland did not choose a particular means for the settlement of disputes from those listed in Article 287 of the LOS Convention, and thus arbitration in accordance with Annex VII became the default procedure pursuant to Article 287(3) and (5). This tribunal was constituted in February 2002 and consisted of Judge Thomas A. Mensah (President), Professor James Crawford, Maître L. Yves Fortier, Professor Gerhard Hafner, and Sir Arthur Watts. The oral hearings began on June 10, 2003, but only lasted for three days. This had much to do with the fact that only five days before the oral hearings began, the Tribunal was informed that the European Commission was considering whether to institute proceedings under Article 226 of the European Community Treaty, possibly leading to a seizure of the European Court of Justice. On June 13, 2003, therefore, the President made the following statement on behalf of the Tribunal, stressing that it was not an order. (The President usually refers to the LOS Convention as "the 1982 Convention.")]

STATEMENT BY THE PRESIDENT

June 13, 2003, available at http://www.pca-cpa.org/showpage.asp?pag_id=1148

2. The Tribunal considers that before proceeding to hear further evidence on the merits of the dispute, and in particular the witnesses presented by the parties on questions of fact and scientific opinion, it has first to determine that there is a reasonable likelihood that it has jurisdiction over the merits of the dispute, and to form a sufficiently clear view of the extent of that jurisdiction under the 1982 Convention on the Law of the Sea.

3. The jurisdictional objections presented by the United Kingdom fall into two groups. First, there are a number of questions of jurisdiction and admissibility raised in respect of the United Nations Convention on the Law of the Sea, itself, and other international commitments invoked or referred to by Ireland. I will refer to these, for present purposes, as the international

law points. Second, there are certain objections relating to the position of the parties under the law of the European Communities. I will refer to these as the EU law points.

4. The Tribunal would begin by observing that the parties are in agreement that there is a dispute concerning the MOX Plant, and that this dispute is a dispute concerning the interpretation and application of the 1982 Convention. The International Tribunal for the Law of the Sea held that it had *prima facie* jurisdiction over this dispute and so far the present Tribunal sees no reason to disagree.

5. As to the international law points raised by the United Kingdom, the Tribunal does not believe that these cast any doubt on its *prima facie* jurisdiction. There has already been (and the United Kingdom does not now contest this) an exchange of views between the parties as required by Article 283 of the 1982 Convention. It is true that the OSPAR Convention is relevant to some, at least, of the questions in issue between the parties, but the Tribunal does not regard that fact as calling into question the characterization of the present dispute as one essentially involving the interpretation and application of the 1982 Convention. Nor is it presently persuaded that the OSPAR Convention substantially covers the field of this dispute so as to trigger Articles 281 and 282 of the 1982 Convention on the Law of the Sea. The Tribunal agrees with the United Kingdom that there is a cardinal distinction to be drawn between the scope of its jurisdiction under Article 288 of the 1982 Convention and the applicable law under Article 293. It is also inclined to agree with the United Kingdom that aspects of the written pleadings of Ireland raised questions arising directly under other legal instruments, and it agrees that, to the extent this is so, any such claims would be inadmissible. It does not, however, agree that Ireland has failed to state and plead a case arising under the 1982 Convention. For these reasons, among others, the Tribunal maintains the view that it has *prima facie* jurisdiction under Article 288(1) of the Convention.

6. As to the EU law points, however, there is a serious difficulty. The Tribunal has been invited to consider the implications of the fact that the 1982 Convention is a mixed agreement to which the EC is a party along with its Member States. Moreover, the Tribunal is requested to consider the fact that, pursuant to Annex IX to the Law of the Sea Convention, it is for the EC, not its Member States, to exercise rights and obligations under the 1982 Convention in respect of matters in relation to which competence has been transferred to the EC by those of its Member States that are also parties to the Convention.

7. The Tribunal notes, in this regard, the statement in a Parliamentary Answer of 15 May 2003 by the European Commission to the effect that the provisions of the 1982 Convention on which Ireland relies in the present case must

be regarded as provisions of EC law, either generally or to the extent that they fall within EC competence. The Commission has added that it is examining the question whether to institute proceedings under article 226 of the EC Treaty.

8. There is, therefore, a real possibility that the European Court of Justice may be seised of the question whether the provisions of the 1982 Convention on which Ireland relies are matters relating to which competence has been transferred to the EC, and indeed that issues concerning the interpretation and application of the provisions of the Convention are as such matters of EC law. In these circumstances, whether, and if so to what extent, all or any of the provisions of the 1982 Convention fall within the competence of the EC or its Member States would fall to be decided by the European Court of Justice. Moreover, while neither the United Kingdom nor Ireland sought to sustain the view that the interpretation of the 1982 Convention in its entirety falls within the exclusive competence of the European Court of Justice as between Member States of the European Community, it cannot be said with certainty that this view would be rejected by the European Court of Justice. [T]he parties before us agreed in argument that, if this view were to be sustained, it would preclude the jurisdiction of the present Tribunal entirely, by virtue of Article 282 of the Convention. By contrast, the United Kingdom did not argue that its other EU law objections were such as wholly to preclude the jurisdiction of this Tribunal.

9. To decide on the jurisdictional issues raised by the United Kingdom in relation to European Community law, this Tribunal would need to determine, *inter alia*, whether the European Community or its Member States have competence in respect of all or some of the matters raised by the provisions invoked in this case. In other words the Tribunal must decide if, and to what extent, the rights and obligations arising under the provisions are exercisable by the European Community or by its Member States.

10. It is clear that any decision of the European Court of Justice on the issues identified above will be decisive and binding as to the question of European Union law. At the same time, by virtue of Article 11 of Annex VII to the 1982 Convention, the decision of the Tribunal will also be binding on Ireland and the United Kingdom as Parties to the dispute.

11. The Tribunal considers that a situation in which there might be two conflicting decisions on the same issues would not be helpful to the resolution of this international dispute. Nor would such a situation be in accord with the dictates of mutual respect and comity that should exist between judicial institutions deciding on rights and obligations as between States, and entrusted with the function of assisting States in the peaceful settlement of disputes that arise between them.

12. The Tribunal has, therefore, decided to suspend further proceedings in the case until not later than 1 December 2003. The Tribunal hopes that it will, at that time, have a clearer picture of the EC legal position. In this regard, the Tribunal urges the Parties to take the necessary steps to expedite the measures for the resolution of outstanding questions.

13. In the meantime, this Tribunal remains seised of the dispute. In the circumstances that now prevail, it is moreover willing to consider the possibility of prescribing provisional measures if either party considers that such measures are necessary in the circumstances to preserve the rights of the Parties or to prevent serious pollution of the marine environment. As Ireland has indicated that it will request the prescription of further provisional measures, the Parties will be given the opportunity during hearings next week to present their views on what, if any, provisional measures are appropriate and the conditions under which such measures may be prescribed. The hearings will commence on Tuesday 17 June and each party will be allocated one and a half days to make its submissions, with half a day for reply. Ireland will provide, as soon as possible and by no later than 5 pm on Monday 16 June, a written statement of the provisional measures it seeks.

14. An appropriate Order of the Tribunal will be issued subsequently, embodying the views as to *prima facie* jurisdiction which are set out above, and the eventual conclusions of the Tribunal on the Irish request for further provisional measures.

Order No. 3: Suspension of Proceedings on Jurisdiction and Merits, and Request for Further Provisional Measures

June 24, 2003, 42 Intl. Leg. Materials 1187 (2003), available at http://www.pca-cpa.org/showpage.asp?pag_id=1148

[As indicated in the Statement of the President excerpted above, Ireland did introduce a new request for further provisional measures on June 16, 2003. It asked the arbitral tribunal to decide that the United Kingdom should (a) stop any discharge of liquid waste from the MOX plant in the Irish Sea, (b) enhance its cooperation with respect to the exchange of information, and (c) be precluded from taking steps or making decisions that might make it impossible for the United Kingdom to give full effect to possible future orders of the tribunal. In its Order No. 3 issued on June 24, 2003, the tribunal rejects requests (a) and (c), and finds with respect to (b) that no further order is required. As indicated in the Statement of the President, it further elaborates the issue of the relevance of European Community law. (The arbitral tribunal constituted pursuant to Article 287 of the LOS Convention refers to that treaty as "the Convention.")]

20. With regard to the European Community law issues, however, certain problems have become apparent to the Tribunal in respect of some important and interrelated areas of European Community law as they appear to affect the dispute between the Parties before this Tribunal. These areas concern in particular:

(i) the standing of Ireland to institute proceedings before this Tribunal in reliance upon the Convention rights which it invokes;
(ii) the standing of the United Kingdom to respond to such proceedings;
(iii) the division of competences between the European Community (of which both Ireland and the United Kingdom are Member States) and its Member States in respect of the Convention, particularly in the light of the declarations made by the Parties and the European Community pursuant to article 5 of Annex IX to the Convention;
(iv) the extent to which provisions and instruments invoked by the Parties may properly be relied upon before this Tribunal; and
(v) the matters which, by agreement of the Parties, are subject to the exclusive jurisdiction of the European Court of Justice under European Community law.

21. These problems have become more acute following a Written Answer given by the Commission of the European Communities ("the European Commission") in the European Parliament on 15 May 2003, after the closure of the written pleadings in the present case. This Written Answer was brought to the Tribunal's attention on 5 June 2003, only five days before the commencement of the hearings. The Tribunal notes that the European Commission has indicated in its Written Answer that it is examining the question whether to institute proceedings under article 226 of the European Community Treaty. In these circumstances, there is a real possibility that the European Court of Justice may be seised of the question whether the provisions of the Convention on which Ireland relies are matters in relation to which competence has been transferred to the European Community and, indeed, whether the exclusive jurisdiction of the European Court of Justice, with regard to Ireland and the United Kingdom as Member States of the European Community, extends to the interpretation and application of the Convention as such and in its entirety.

22. While neither the United Kingdom nor Ireland sought to sustain the view that the interpretation of the Convention in its entirely fell within the exclusive competence of the European Court of Justice as between Member States of the European Union, it cannot be said with certainty that this view

would be rejected by the European Court of Justice. The Parties agreed in argument that, if this view were to be sustained, it would preclude the jurisdiction of the present Tribunal entirely, by virtue of article 282 of the Convention.

23. In these circumstances, the determination of the Tribunal's jurisdiction, particularly in the light of articles 281 and 282 of the Convention, and the identification of the treaty provisions and other rules of international law which the Tribunal could apply to the dispute brought before it by Ireland, are crucially dependent upon the resolution of the problems referred to above.

24. The Tribunal recognizes that the problems referred to above relate to matters which essentially concern the internal operation of a separate legal order (namely the legal order of the European Communities) to which both of the Parties to the present proceedings are subject and which, in the circumstances referred to in paragraph 21 above, are to be determined within the institutional framework of the European Communities. The European Community law issues are still to be resolved, and there is a risk of considerable further delay.

25. Despite this risk, the fact remains that, until these issues are definitively resolved, there remain substantial doubts whether the jurisdiction of the Tribunal can be firmly established in respect of all or any of the claims in the dispute.

26. Although it is possible that the Tribunal might conclude from the arguments of the Parties that at least certain provisions of the Convention do not fall within the exclusive jurisdiction and competence of the European Communities in the present case, it would still not be appropriate for the Tribunal to proceed with hearings on the merits in respect of any such provisions. For one thing, it is not at all clear at this stage that the Parties are able to identify with any certainty what such provisions might be; and the Tribunal is in no better position. For another, there is no certainty that any such provisions would in fact give rise to a self-contained and distinct dispute capable of being resolved by the Tribunal. Finally, the Tribunal notes that, whatever the Parties may agree in these proceedings as to the scope and effects of European Community law applicable in the present dispute, the question is ultimately not for them to decide but is rather to be decided within the institutions of the European Communities, and particularly by the European Court of Justice.

27. The Tribunal observes that the resolution of the essentially internal problems within the European Community legal order may involve decisions that are final and binding. The Tribunal further observes that its decision, including a decision on jurisdiction, will be final and binding on the Parties by virtue of article 296 of the Convention and article 11 of Annex VII to the Convention.

28. In the circumstances, and bearing in mind considerations of mutual respect and comity which should prevail between judicial institutions both of which may be called upon to determine rights and obligations as between two States, the Tribunal considers that it would be inappropriate for it to proceed further with hearing the Parties on the merits of the dispute in the absence of a resolution of the problems referred to. Moreover, a procedure that might result in two conflicting decisions on the same issue would not be helpful to the resolution of the dispute between the Parties.

Suspension of Further Proceedings on Jurisdiction and Merits

29. For these reasons, the Tribunal has decided, in exercise of its powers under article 8 of the Rules of Procedure, that further proceedings on jurisdiction and the merits in this arbitration will be suspended.

30. The Tribunal nevertheless remains seised of the dispute. Unless otherwise agreed or decided, the Tribunal will resume its proceedings not later than 1 December 2003. The Tribunal hopes that it will at that time have a clearer picture of the position regarding European Community law and possible proceedings thereunder insofar as they appertain to the present dispute.

COMMISSION OF THE EUROPEAN COMMUNITIES V. IRELAND (ECJ, JUDGMENT, 2006)

Case C-459/03 (ECJ Grand Chamber), 2006 E.C.R. I-463, 45 Intl. Leg. Materials 1051 (2006), available at http://eur-lex.europa.eu

[On October 15, 2003, the European Commission authorized the institution of proceedings against Ireland concerning Community law issues, based on of Article 226 of the Treaty on the European Union, which provides:

> If the Commission considers that a Member State has failed to fulfil an obligation under this Treaty, it shall deliver a reasoned opinion on the matter after giving the State concerned the opportunity to submit its observations. If the State concerned does not comply with the opinion within the period laid down by the Commission, the latter may bring the matter before the Court of Justice.

As the Annex VII tribunal had suspended its proceedings only until December 1, 2003 (see Order No. 3, ¶ 30, above), on November 14, 2003 it issued Order No. 4 extending the suspension period until the European Court of Justice (ECJ) rendered its judgment. It took the ECJ almost three years to reach the following decision on May 30, 2006. After describing the general legal context, the

Court addresses the background of the dispute. With respect to the proceedings under the 1992 OSPAR Convention, the Court is rather succinct.]

30. On 15 June 2001 Ireland forwarded to the United Kingdom a request for the constitution of an arbitral tribunal and a statement of claim pursuant to Article 32 of the Convention for the Protection of the Marine Environment of the North-East Atlantic, which was signed in Paris on 22 September 1992 and approved on behalf of the Community by Council Decision 98/249/EC of 7 October 1997 (OJ 1998 L 104, p. 1). That convention replaces, inter alia, the Paris conventions for the prevention of marine pollution from land-based sources to which the Community was already a party and which, as such, were mentioned in the annex to the Declaration of Community competence.

31. In that request, Ireland claimed that the United Kingdom had failed in its obligations under Article 9 of that convention by refusing to provide Ireland with a complete copy of the PA report.

32. On 2 July 2003 the arbitral tribunal constituted pursuant to that convention dismissed Ireland's claim.

33. The institution of those proceedings is not, however, covered by the present action for failure to fulfil obligations.

[The Court subsequently describes at some length the background of the proceedings before the Annex VII tribunal and the associated request for provisional measures from the ITLOS. It then turns to the three complaints of the European Commission. The first complaint is that Ireland failed to respect the exclusive jurisdiction of the Court to rule on issues concerning the interpretation and application of Community law. The ECJ concludes that the LOS Convention provisions relating to the prevention of marine pollution, on which Ireland relied, fell within the competence of the Community. (When the Court talks about "the Treaties," it is referring to the founding documents of the European Union, namely the Treaties of Paris (European Coal and Steel Community, April 18, 1951) and of Rome (European Economic Community and European Atomic Energy Community, both of March 25, 1957). To refer to an article of the Treaty on the European Union, the Court uses the abbreviation "EC." The relevant parts of these articles are added in brackets. When the Court mentions "the Convention," it is referring to the LOS Convention.)]

121. It follows that the provisions of the Convention relied on by Ireland in the dispute relating to the MOX plant and submitted to the Arbitral Tribunal are rules which form part of the Community legal order. The Court therefore has jurisdiction to deal with disputes relating to the interpretation and application of those provisions and to assess a Member State's compliance with them (see, in that connection, Case C-13/00 *Commission v Ireland*, paragraph 20, and Case C-239/03 *Commission v France*, paragraph 31).

122. It is, however, necessary to determine whether this jurisdiction of the Court is exclusive, such as to preclude a dispute like that relating to the MOX plant being brought by a Member State before an arbitral tribunal established pursuant to Annex VII to the Convention.

123. The Court has already pointed out that an international agreement cannot affect the allocation of responsibilities defined in the Treaties and, consequently, the autonomy of the Community legal system, compliance with which the Court ensures under Article 220 EC ["The Court of Justice and the Court of First Instance, each within its jurisdiction, shall ensure that in the interpretation and application of this Treaty the law is observed."]. That exclusive jurisdiction of the Court is confirmed by Article 292 EC ["Member States undertake not to submit a dispute concerning the interpretation or application of this Treaty to any method of settlement other than those provided for therein."], by which Member States undertake not to submit a dispute concerning the interpretation or application of the EC Treaty to any method of settlement other than those provided for therein (see, to that effect, Opinion 1/91 [1991] ECR I-6079, paragraph 35, and Opinion 1/00 [2002] ECR I-3493, paragraphs 11 and 12).

124. It should be stated at the outset that the Convention precisely makes it possible to avoid such a breach of the Court's exclusive jurisdiction in such a way as to preserve the autonomy of the Community legal system.

125. It follows from Article 282 of the Convention that, as it provides for procedures resulting in binding decisions in respect of the resolution of disputes between Member States, the system for the resolution of disputes set out in the EC Treaty must in principle take precedence over that contained in Part XV of the Convention.

126. It has been established that the provisions of the Convention in issue in the dispute concerning the MOX plant come within the scope of Community competence which the Community exercised by acceding to the Convention, with the result that those provisions form an integral part of the Community legal order.

127. Consequently, the dispute in this case is indeed a dispute concerning the interpretation or application of the EC Treaty, within the terms of Article 292 EC.

128. Furthermore, as it is between two Member States in regard to an alleged failure to comply with Community-law obligations resulting from those provisions of the Convention, this dispute is clearly covered by one of the methods of dispute settlement established by the EC Treaty within the terms of Article 292 EC, namely the procedure set out in Article 227 EC ["A Member State which considers that another Member State has failed to fulfil an obligation under this Treaty may bring the matter before the Court of Justice. Before

a Member State brings an action against another Member State for an alleged infringement of an obligation under this Treaty, it shall bring the matter before the Commission. The Commission shall deliver a reasoned opinion after each of the States concerned has been given the opportunity to submit its own case and its observations on the other party's case both orally and in writing. If the Commission has not delivered an opinion within three months of the date on which the matter was brought before it, the absence of such opinion shall not prevent the matter from being brought before the Court of Justice."].

129. In addition, it is not open to dispute that proceedings such as those brought by Ireland before the Arbitral Tribunal fall to be described as a method of settlement of a dispute within the terms of Article 292 EC inasmuch as, under Article 296 of the Convention, the decisions delivered by such a tribunal are final and binding on the parties to the dispute.

130. Ireland contends, however, by way of alternative submission, that, if the Court were to conclude that the provisions of the Convention invoked before the Arbitral Tribunal form an integral part of Community law, that conclusion would also be unavoidable with regard to the provisions of the Convention dealing with dispute settlement. Consequently, it submits, the initiation of proceedings before an arbitral tribunal referred to in Article 287(1)(c) of the Convention constitutes a method of dispute settlement provided for in the EC Treaty, within the terms of Article 292 EC.

131. That argument must be rejected.

132. As has been pointed out in paragraph 123 of the present judgment, an international agreement such as the Convention cannot affect the exclusive jurisdiction of the Court in regard to the resolution of disputes between Member States concerning the interpretation and application of Community law. Furthermore, as indicated in paragraphs 124 and 125 of the present judgment, Article 282 of the Convention precisely makes it possible to avoid such a breach occurring, in such a way as to preserve the autonomy of the Community legal system.

133. It follows from all of the foregoing that Articles 220 EC and 292 EC precluded Ireland from initiating proceedings before the Arbitral Tribunal with a view to resolving the dispute concerning the MOX plant.

[The second complaint of the European Commission asserts that Ireland breached Community law by referring to the Annex VII arbitral tribunal a dispute that requires for its resolution the interpretation and application of measures of Community law. Ireland, in its argument to the Annex VII tribunal, had urged the tribunal to apply several EU treaties and directives as international law. (When the Court talks about the "EAEC Treaty," it refers to the Treaty establishing the European Atomic Energy Community of March 25, 1957. To refer to an article of that treaty, the Court uses the abbreviation "EA.")]

146. It is common ground that, in its statement of claim and in its written submissions to the Arbitral Tribunal, Ireland invoked a number of Community measures.

147. In addition to the Convention for the Protection of the Marine Environment of the North-East Atlantic, the measures in question are essentially, in regard to the EC Treaty, Directives 85/337 and 90/313 and, in regard to the EAEC Treaty, Directives 80/836, 92/3 and 96/29.

148. It is also common ground that those Community measures were invoked by Ireland pursuant to Article 293(1) of the Convention, which provides that a tribunal such as the Arbitral Tribunal is to "apply this Convention and other rules of international law not incompatible with this Convention."

149. As the Advocate General has noted in points 49 and 50 of his Opinion, it follows from the different passages in the pleadings lodged by Ireland before the Arbitral Tribunal that that Member State presented those Community measures not only as relevant for the purpose of clarifying the meaning of the general provisions of the Convention in issue in the dispute but also as rules of international law to be applied by the Arbitral Tribunal pursuant to Article 293 of the Convention.

150. Thus, as the United Kingdom Government has submitted without being challenged on this point, Ireland argued inter alia before the Arbitral Tribunal that the 1993 environmental statement did not meet the requirements of Directive 85/337 and that the United Kingdom's refusal to disclose the operating plan for the MOX plant meant that it was not possible to evaluate the justification for that plant, as required under Directive 96/29, in addition to the contention that this refusal amounted to a breach of Article 6 of Directive 80/836 and of Article 6 of Directive 96/29.

151. It thus appears that Ireland submitted instruments of Community law to the Arbitral Tribunal for purposes of their interpretation and application in the context of proceedings seeking a declaration that the United Kingdom had breached the provisions of those instruments.

152. That is at variance with the obligation imposed on Member States by Articles 292 EC and 193 EA [identical to Article 292 EC] to respect the exclusive nature of the Court's jurisdiction to resolve disputes concerning the interpretation and application of provisions of Community law, in particular by having recourse to the procedures set out in Articles 227 EC and 142 EA [identical to Article 227 EC] for the purpose of obtaining a declaration that another Member State has breached those provisions.

153. Therefore, as some of the measures in question come within the scope of the EC Treaty and others within the scope of the EAEC Treaty, it must be held that there has been a breach of Articles 292 EC and 193 EA.

154. It must also be pointed out that the institution and pursuit of proceedings before the Arbitral Tribunal, in the circumstances indicated in paragraphs 146 to 150 of the present judgment, involve a manifest risk that the jurisdictional order laid down in the Treaties and, consequently, the autonomy of the Community legal system may be adversely affected.

155. That risk exists even though, as Ireland avers, it has given a formal assurance that it has not called on, and will not call on, the Arbitral Tribunal to examine or appraise, pursuant to Article 293 of the Convention or any other provision, whether the United Kingdom has breached any rule of Community law.

156. Furthermore, the existence of that risk renders entirely irrelevant the fact that Ireland may have called on the Arbitral Tribunal to apply Community law by way of *renvoi* or by recourse to any other technique.

157. The second head of complaint must accordingly be regarded as being well founded.

[The third complaint of the European Commission concerns Ireland's failure to comply with its duty of cooperation as provided under Community law by usurping a competence belonging to the Community and by failing to inform or consult with the competent Community institutions.]

168. The Commission first of all criticises Ireland for having failed in its duty of cooperation under Article 10 EC ["Member States shall take all appropriate measures, whether general or particular, to ensure fulfilment of the obligations arising out of this Treaty or resulting from action taken by the institutions of the Community. They shall facilitate the achievement of the Community's tasks. They shall abstain from any measure which could jeopardise the attainment of the objectives of this Treaty."] inasmuch as, by bringing arbitral proceedings under the Convention, Ireland exercised a competence which belongs to the Community.

169. The obligation devolving on Member States, set out in Article 292 EC, to have recourse to the Community judicial system and to respect the Court's exclusive jurisdiction, which is a fundamental feature of that system, must be understood as a specific expression of Member States' more general duty of loyalty resulting from Article 10 EC.

170. The unavoidable conclusion must also be drawn that this first part of the third head of complaint has the same subject-matter as the first head of complaint since it focuses on the same conduct on the part of Ireland, that is to say, the bringing by that Member State of the proceedings before the Arbitral Tribunal in contravention of Article 292 EC.

171. It is for that reason unnecessary to find that there has been a failure to comply with the general obligations contained in Article 10 EC that is distinct from the failure, already established, to comply with the more specific Community obligations devolving on Ireland pursuant to Article 292 EC.

172. Second, the Commission criticises Ireland for having breached Articles 10 EC and 192 EA [identical to Article 10 EC] by bringing the proceedings before the Arbitral Tribunal without having first informed and consulted the competent Community institutions....

174. The Court has pointed out that, in all the areas corresponding to the objectives of the EC Treaty, Article 10 EC requires Member States to facilitate the achievement of the Community's tasks and to abstain from any measure which could jeopardise the attainment of the objectives of the Treaty (see, inter alia, Opinion 1/03 [2006] E.C.R. I-1145, paragraph 119). The Member States assume similar obligations under the EAEC Treaty by virtue of Article 192 EA.

175. The Court has also emphasised that the Member States and the Community institutions have an obligation of close cooperation in fulfilling the commitments undertaken by them under joint competence when they conclude a mixed agreement (see [Dior and Others, Joined Cases C-300/98 and C-392/98, 2000 E.C.R. I-11307], paragraph 36).

176. That is in particular the position in the case of a dispute which, as in the present case, relates essentially to undertakings resulting from a mixed agreement which relates to an area, namely the protection and preservation of the marine environment, in which the respective areas of competence of the Community and the Member States are liable to be closely interrelated, as is, moreover, evidenced by the Declaration of Community competence and the appendix thereto.

177. The act of submitting a dispute of this nature to a judicial forum such as the Arbitral Tribunal involves the risk that a judicial forum other than the Court will rule on the scope of obligations imposed on the Member States pursuant to Community law.

178. Moreover, in their letter of 8 October 2001, the Commission's services had already contended that the dispute relating to the MOX plant, as referred by Ireland to the arbitral tribunal constituted pursuant to the Convention for the Protection of the Marine Environment of the North-East Atlantic, was a matter falling within the exclusive jurisdiction of the Court.

179. In those circumstances, the obligation of close cooperation within the framework of a mixed agreement involved, on the part of Ireland, a duty to inform and consult the competent Community institutions prior to instituting dispute-settlement proceedings concerning the MOX plant within the framework of the Convention.

180. The same duty of prior information and consultation was also imposed on Ireland by virtue of the EAEC Treaty in so far as that Member State contemplated invoking provisions of that Treaty and measures adopted pursuant to it within the framework of the proceedings which it was proposing to bring before the Arbitral Tribunal.

181. It is common ground that, at the date on which those proceedings were brought, Ireland had not complied with that duty of prior information and consultation.

182. Regard being had to the foregoing, the third head of complaint must be upheld in so far as it seeks a declaration by the Court that, by bringing proceedings under the dispute-settlement system set out in the Convention, without having first informed and consulted the competent Community institutions, Ireland has failed to comply with its duty of cooperation under Articles 10 EC and 192 EA.

183. The action must accordingly be upheld....

On those grounds, the Court (Grand Chamber) hereby:

1. Declares that, by instituting dispute-settlement proceedings against the United Kingdom of Great Britain and Northern Ireland under the United Nations Convention on the Law of the Sea concerning the MOX plant located at Sellafield (United Kingdom), Ireland has failed to fulfil its obligations under Articles 10 EC and 292 EC and under Articles 192 EA and 193 EA[.]

DISPUTE CONCERNING THE MOX PLANT, INTERNATIONAL MOVEMENTS OF RADIOACTIVE MATERIALS, AND THE PROTECTION OF THE MARINE ENVIRONMENT OF THE IRISH SEA (ANNEX VII TRIBUNAL, ORDER TERMINATING PROCEEDINGS, 2006)
Ireland v. United Kingdom, Tribunal constituted pursuant to Article 287 and Article 1 of Annex VII of the LOS Convention

[Although the European Court of Justice had clarified Community law competence, the legal proceedings between Ireland and the United Kingdom with respect to the MOX plant were not at an end. The arbitral tribunal constituted pursuant to Article 287 and Annex VII of the LOS Convention was still seized of the dispute and had only suspended its proceedings awaiting such a clarification. See the Dispute Concerning the MOX Plant, International Movements of Radioactive Materials, and the Protection of the Marine Environment of the Irish Sea (Part 1), Order No. 3, excerpted above. The Annex VII tribunal reacted within a week of the European Court of Justice's decision by issuing Order No. 6 on June 6, 2008.]

ORDER NO. 6: TERMINATION of PROCEEDINGS
June 6, 2008, available at http://www.pca-cpa.org/showpage.asp?pag_id=1148

The Arbitral Tribunal

Having regard to Articles 1 and 8 of the Rules of Procedure adopted by the Tribunal;

Having regard to the previous Orders of the Tribunal and in particular Order N° 3 of 24 June 2003 by which the Tribunal decided, *inter alia*, to suspend further proceedings in the case until the European Court of Justice had given judgment or the Tribunal otherwise determined;

Having regard to the Judgment of the European Court of Justice (ECJ) delivered on 30 May 2006 (Case C-459/03) and communicated to the Tribunal by the Agent for Ireland in his letter dated 31 May 2006;

Having regard to the letter dated 15 February 2007 by which the Agent for Ireland formally notified the Registry of the withdrawal by Ireland of the claim made by it against the United Kingdom regarding the MOX Plant in the proceedings before the Tribunal; . . .

Having regard to Article 16(1) of the Tribunal's Rules of Procedure which provides that, "Unless the Arbitral Tribunal determines otherwise because of the particular circumstances of the case, the costs of the Arbitral Tribunal, including the remuneration of its members, shall be borne by the Parties in equal shares";

Having regard to Article 17 of the Tribunal's Rules of Procedure which provides that, "The Arbitral Tribunal may make such award as appears appropriate in respect of the costs incurred by the Parties in presenting their respective cases";

Having regard to the sad passing away on 16 November 2007 of Sir Arthur Watts KCMG QC who served with distinction as a member of the Tribunal and made an important contribution to the development and practice of international law;

Having regard to the appointment on 31 January 2008 by the United Kingdom of The Rt. Hon. the Lord Mustill as replacement for Sir Arthur Watts KCMG QC in accordance with Article 7(1)(a) of the Tribunal's Rules of Procedure;

Whereas the Tribunal considers that there is no reason to depart from the practice of arbitral tribunals in inter-state litigation regarding apportionment of costs;

NOW THEREFORE the Arbitral Tribunal unanimously:

1. Decides to place on record the withdrawal by Ireland of the claim made by it against the United Kingdom in the MOX Plant case;
2. Decides, pursuant to Article 16(1) of the Tribunal's Rules of Procedure, that the expenses of the Tribunal shall be borne by the Parties in equal shares;
3. Decides, pursuant to Article 17 of the Tribunal's Rules of Procedure, that each Party shall bear the costs incurred by it in presenting its case;
4. Decides that these proceedings are terminated.

Notes

1. *Forum Shopping*. In Chapter 15 we will formally study the third-party dispute settlement system of the LOS Convention. Two of the four courts and tribunals involved in the MOX Plant cases—the ITLOS and the Annex VII arbitral tribunal—are part of that system. The other two—the OSPAR arbitral tribunal and the European Court of Justice (ECJ)—are each part of a different regional international treaty system. What are the implications of the proliferation of international courts and tribunals?

One logical result of this proliferation is forum shopping: states may bring a case before the courts or tribunals they believe will be most open to the kind of legal argument they intend to develop. For example, a country whose fishing vessels are denied access to a foreign port because those vessels do not respect a coastal state regulation applicable beyond 200 nautical miles from its baselines may well prefer to have the case heard by the Dispute Settlement Body of the World Trade Organization (WTO) rather than by the ITLOS. The WTO focuses on reducing or eliminating obstacles to trade, while the ITLOS is specifically created to interpret the LOS Convention with its strong Part XII on the protection and preservation of the marine environment. Vice versa, the coastal state involved in such a dispute may well prefer the ITLOS. This example is not hypothetical: compare the Case Concerning the Conservation and Sustainable Exploitation of Swordfish Stocks in the South-Eastern Pacific Ocean (Chile v. European Community), ITLOS Case No. 7 (2000), available at http://www.itlos.org, with the WTO Case on Measures Affecting the Transit and Importing of Swordfish (European Community v. Chile), WTO Doc. WT/DS193 (suspended Mar. 23, 2001). In the dispute over the MOX plant, why did Ireland take its claims to an OSPAR tribunal and a tribunal constituted pursuant to Article 287 of the LOS Convention instead of to the ECJ? How does the European Commission's 1997 opinion fit into your answer?

2. *Multiple Dispute Settlement Bodies Involved in the Same Dispute.* A related effect of the proliferation of international courts and tribunals is that the same dispute can be considered from different angles by more than one dispute settlement body. The MOX Plant cases are a good example. Indeed, there were litigation options even beyond the four bodies whose decisions are excerpted in this chapter—the OSPAR arbitral tribunal, the ITLOS, the arbitral tribunal created under Annex VII of the LOS Convention, and the ECJ. Besides those four global and regional courts and tribunals, municipal courts heard challenges involving the MOX plant. The non-governmental organization Greenpeace brought a case before local U.K. courts objecting to the October 3, 2001, decision approving the manufacture of MOX at Sellafield. See R (Friends of the Earth Ltd. and Greenpeace Ltd.) v. Secretary of State for the Environment, Food and Rural Affairs and Secretary of State for Health, 2001 EWHC Admin 914 (rejected), and R (Friends of the Earth Ltd. and Greenpeace Ltd.) v. Secretary of State for the Environment, Food and Rural Affairs, 2001 EWCA Civ 1847 (failed on appeal). Which level do you believe to be the most appropriate to solve the dispute over the MOX plant?

May the time taken by these bodies to render a decision affect the choice about which tribunal to use? For instance, it took the ITLOS less than one month to decide on provisional measures, while the ECJ needed three years to reach a decision. Is it simply a matter of comparing numbers here? What other factors affect the choice of forum?

With respect to the MOX Plant cases, one final question seems inescapable after reviewing the seven years of proceedings before four different international tribunals: What result did Ireland obtain at the end? Was it ever able to reach the substance of the case?

3. *The Proliferation of International Dispute Settlement Bodies and the Risk of Divergent Jurisprudence.* A negative side effect of the proliferation of international courts and tribunals is undoubtedly the risk that separate dispute settlement bodies, concerned with the same dispute, may interpret the law differently. Avoiding this danger does not seem an easy task.

When reading through the cases excerpted in this chapter, it might have struck you that more than 40 judges were involved. Only one judge, Thomas Mensah, served in two of the dispute settlement bodies, namely the ITLOS and the arbitral tribunal constituted on the basis of Annex VII of the LOS Convention; he served as President of the arbitral tribunal. Lord Mustill, who sat on the bench in the OSPAR arbitration, also filled a sudden vacancy on the Annex VII arbitral tribunal, but he only participated in the final decision made by that tribunal (Order No. 6). How is it possible that the unity of law has not yet seriously been threatened? Indeed, on more than one occasion decisions were taken unanimously, not only in a tribunal of five judges, but sometimes also in a judicial body of more than twenty.

Even within a particular dispute settlement body it might not be easy to come to an inherently logical and well-reasoned judgment. For example, in the OSPAR decision, the majorities formed among the three arbiters differed for the interpretation of Articles 9(1) and 9(2). The Chairman, Professor Michael Reisman, did not form part of the majority deciding on the interpretation of Article 9(1). In a declaration he appended to the judgment, he concluded that the OSPAR Convention only required parties to establish an internal regime making available certain information. According to him, implementation of that obligation could be secured on the national level. The United Kingdom thus only had an obligation to make adjustments in its domestic legal system. And because Ireland had never contested that the United Kingdom had made such appropriate adjustments, the United Kingdom had fulfilled its obligation under Article 9(1); no further procedures on the international level should have been allowed on this issue. Ireland v. United Kingdom, Tribunal constituted pursuant to the 1992 OSPAR Convention, Declaration of Professor W. Michael Reisman, 23 Rep. Intl. Arb. Awards 59, 113 (2006). How common is it for a majority to be formed without the Chairman being a part of it—especially if the tribunal is composed of three arbitrators, one of whom is appointed by the applicant, one by the respondent, and the third, i.e., the Chairman, by common agreement of the two party-appointed arbitrators? If in the OSPAR case the Chairman believed the dispute should have been settled on the national level, why did he join the majority concerning Article 9(2)?

If conflicts like this already burden decision making within one dispute settlement body, imagine how difficult it must be to safeguard the internal logic of international law when several such bodies are involved. What different techniques did the different dispute settlement bodies use to avoid undermining the unity of law? Compare the emphasis of the Annex VII arbitral tribunal on "mutual respect and comity" (Order No. 3, ¶ 28) with the heavy reliance of the ECJ on the importance of preserving the autonomy of the Community legal order. In discussing all three counts of the European Commission's complaint, the ECJ either directly or indirectly referred to this principle. Compare respectively paragraphs 124 and 132 (first complaint), 154 (second complaint), and 177 (third complaint). The ECJ also found support for this principle in Article 282 of the LOS Convention. Moreover, the ITLOS found no difficulty in different international legal instruments containing similar legal standards, but giving rise to different legal remedies (¶¶ 49–53), a point of view readily adopted by the OSPAR tribunal (see ¶¶ 141–43, literally reproducing paragraphs 50–51 of the ITLOS's opinion), while concluding that no single set of remedies takes precedence over the others (OSPAR Arbitration, ¶ 143).

That courts and arbitral tribunals have to tackle such problems is a rather new phenomenon. Consider in this respect the Statement of the President and Order No. 3 in the Annex VII arbitration. Why did the Statement precede the Order—with the President stressing the difference between the two—and what are the differences between the two? One difference was that the tribunal explicitly found in its Order No. 3 of June 24, 2003 that even if the parties agreed on the scope and effects of European Community law, the institutions of the European Communities must decide those effects. But see for instance the Iron Rhine Arbitration, Belgium/The Netherlands, May 24, 2005, ¶¶ 97–141, available at http://www.pca-cpa.org/showpage.asp?pag_id=1155, where the tribunal did not refer this issue back to the institutions of the European Communities but instead itself made the analysis. Note, however, that the European Commission did not stop the OSPAR proceedings. The ECJ simply found that the ECJ case did not concern the issue before the OSPAR tribunal (¶ 33). Nevertheless, the ECJ later mentioned the OSPAR issue as relevant (¶ 178).

4. *Prima Facie Competence of Court and Tribunals.* Every time provisional measures are requested, the court or tribunal must first make sure it has prima facie jurisdiction. How and why does the determination of prima facie jurisdiction differ from the determination of jurisdiction on the merits? In the MOX Plant case the issue of prima facie jurisdiction arose twice: once before the ITLOS and once before the Annex VII arbitral tribunal. Whose prima facie jurisdiction did each body have to assess? Why did Ireland have to address the issue twice in this case?

Two different dispute settlement bodies concluded that prima facie jurisdiction was present. See ¶ 34 of the ITLOS order and ¶¶ 4–5 of the President's Statement in the Annex VII arbitration. Nevertheless, the Annex VII tribunal, following its decision to suspend the proceedings awaiting a clarification from the ECJ, eventually terminated the arbitral proceedings. How does this ruling relate to the issue discussed in Note 3 above?

5. *The Duty to Cooperate, the LOS Convention, and the Protection and Preservation of the Marine Environment.* The duty to cooperate in international law might seem a good example of an oxymoron, i.e., a combination of contradictory or incongruous words, for it tries to combine a legal obligation (duty) with an action dependent on the good-will of those concerned (cooperation). International law does not contain a general customary obligation for states to cooperate. In some treaties, however, states have agreed on obligations to cooperate, especially in the field of environmental law. Early instances may

be found in bilateral agreements. International courts and tribunals have, for example, invoked duties to cooperate set out in bilateral treaties in the area of watercourses law. See, e.g., Case Concerning Pulp Mills on the River Uruguay (Argentina v. Uruguay), 2010 I.C.J. 14; Case Concerning the Gabčíkovo-Nagymaros Project (Hungary/Slovakia), 1997 I.C.J. 7; Lac Lanoux Arbitration (Spain v. France) (1957), 24 Intl. L. Rep. 101 (1957). The LOS Convention is an example of a multilateral agreement incorporating this duty, mainly by means of the phrase "shall cooperate" contained in several of its provisions, including Articles 199, 200, 201, 226(2), and 235(3) in Part XII (Protection and Preservation of the Marine Environment). See Seokwoo Lee, UNCLOS and the Obligation to Cooperate, in Maritime Energy Resources in Asia: Legal Regimes and Cooperation 23 (Clive Schofield ed., 2012).

In the MOX Plant cases, both the ITLOS (¶ 82; Joint Declaration of Judges Caminos, Yamamoto, Park, Akl, Marsit, Eiriksson, and Jesus, last paragraph) and the ECJ (¶¶ 168 and 182) relied on the duty to cooperate. What are the differences between these two instances of application? Do they relate to substance or procedure? In concrete terms, what action is required to fulfill a duty to cooperate? Do the treaty articles on which these judicial bodies relied explicitly mention a duty to cooperate? Do the articles relate to the protection and preservation of the environment? Can we speak today of a customary rule of international law, as opposed to a mere treaty rule, obliging states to cooperate in order to prevent pollution of the marine environment? Do you believe the ITLOS relied on Article 197 or on Article 123 to reach its conclusion concerning the duty to cooperate? Ireland and the United Kingdom were focusing on the Irish Sea, which can be characterized as a semi-enclosed sea according to Article 123 of the LOS Convention.

6. *Treaty Interpretation.* One difficult issue with respect to the interpretation of treaties relates to how courts and tribunals rely on new developments as a source of law. Consider the careful exposition of this issue in the OSPAR arbitration. May dispute settlement bodies rely on new developments? If so, under what circumstances? What did the OSPAR tribunal conclude about the applicability of new developments?

7. *Comparing International Legal Responses to Different Types of Marine Pollution.* The MOX Plant cases concerned land-based pollution. Other types of pollution of the marine environment have been the subject of detailed international regulation. For example, in Chapter 11, Section D we considered how pollution of the Area—the seabed and subsoil beyond the limits of national jurisdiction—is regulated. The International Maritime Organization, whose work we discussed in Chapter 4, Section A, has regulated vessel-source pollution in considerable detail in the 1973 Convention for the Prevention of

Pollution from Ships, as modified by the 1978 Protocol (MARPOL), and countries implement MARPOL requirements in their municipal law. See, e.g., 33 U.S.C. §§ 1901 et seq. Indeed, the LOS Convention itself regulates other types of pollution in much more detail than land-based pollution. See Chapter 7, Section C.

At a broad level, however, there are significant similarities among types of marine pollution. All marine pollution may affect non-polluting states and common spaces. Why, then, is there no detailed international regulation of land-based pollution? In the absence of an effective regulatory regime, or to supplement any such regime, is it appropriate to invoke principles of state responsibility to curb pollution? Should international courts and tribunals be bolder in fashioning or applying international legal principles to hold polluting states responsible? What techniques—both judicial and regulatory—can best cope with scientific uncertainty and the risks of various sources of marine pollution?

CHAPTER 13

Conservation and Management of High Seas Living Resources

Well over 90 percent of all commercially exploited fish species are found within 200 nautical miles from baselines. With the introduction of the exclusive economic zone (EEZ) concept in international law, the principle of freedom of fishing on the high seas correspondingly lost a lot of its luster. Indeed, the subject of conservation and management of high seas living resources did not attract much attention during the Third United Nations Conference on the Law of the Sea (1973–1982). Negotiators focused on the transfer of the bulk of marine fisheries resources from the global commons to the competence of coastal states, and they paid scant attention to the impact the new regime could have on the remaining commercially exploited high seas resources. High seas fisheries resources primarily fall into three categories: straddling stocks, highly migratory fish stocks, and discrete high seas stocks, i.e., stocks found only on the high seas. All of these fish stocks came under pressure soon after EEZs were established, because many owners of distant-water fishing fleets preferred to target these remaining stocks on the high seas rather than to assume the new regulatory and financial burdens normally associated with fishing inside the 200-nautical-mile limit.

Section A of this chapter digs back into history to consider whether Hugo Grotius, so often associated with the origins of high seas freedoms, was really as staunch a supporter of the freedom of fishing as he is generally depicted today. Section B addresses the period right after the entry into force of the 1982 United Nations Convention on the Law of the Sea (LOS Convention) when a dispute arose between Canada and the European Union (then still the European Communities) that spiraled out of control. It concerned the exploitation of a straddling fish stock on the high seas just beyond the Canadian EEZ, the management and conservation of which were entrusted to a regional fisheries management organization (RFMO), namely the Northwest Atlantic Fisheries Organization (NAFO). Finally, in Section C we analyze the contemporary period and the new legal framework that has been created to address the issue of overfishing on the high seas. We devote particular attention to RFMOs, as they are today the primary legal mechanism available to tackle this issue.

 | DOI 10.1163/9789004203563_014

A The Origins of the Modern Law of High Seas Fisheries

ERIK FRANCKX, FISHERIES IN THE SOUTH CHINA SEA: A CENTRIFUGAL OR CENTRIPETAL FORCE?

11 Chinese J. Intl. L. 727 (2012)

[In retrospect, it seems fair to conclude that Hugo de Groot (Grotius) won the so-called battle of the books that raged during the early 17th century against his major opponent, the Englishman John Selden. Selden defended the view of his government that the fish-rich waters around the British Isles could be closed off to foreign fishermen. Instead, the principle of the freedom of the high seas prevailed when the law of the sea was codified during the 20th century. The name of Hugo de Groot is consequently often associated not only with the freedom of navigation, a thesis he fiercely defended in support of the Netherlands' interest in free trade with its East Indian colonies, but also with the freedom of fisheries, another argument he developed. However, as this excerpt shows, he did not place both freedoms on an equal footing.]

[The fisheries] issue was introduced in general international law in the early 17th century by the Dutch jurist Hugo de Groot, or Hugo Grotius in Latin. His basic argument was that the oceans were so vast that anybody who would want to appropriate part of them and thus exclude others from fishing therein, would be regarded as a "seeker of immoderate power" and "he would not escape the stigma of monstrous cupidity."[1] This argument was later rephrased in his *opus magnus* written in 1625, where it was stated that the oceans were so vast that there was enough for all peoples to draw water, fish and navigate as they wished.[2] When the law of the sea was finally codified in 1958, and later in 1982, these ideas were reflected in the freedom of fisheries on the high seas. That freedom, as a principle, still applies today.

But much has changed in this area. After an unabated growth trend until the early 1990s of world capture fisheries production, that is excluding

1 Hugo Grotius, De Iure Praedae Commentarius [Commentary on the Law of Prize and Booty], trans. Gwladys L. Williams and Walter H. Zeydel (Geoffrey Cumberlege 1950), vol. 2, 239. This book, probably written in late 1604 to early 1605, was only found in 1864 and published four years later. The Latin text reads: "In tanto mari si quis usu promiscuo solum sibi imperium et dicionem exciperet, tamen immodicae dominationis affectator haberetur; si quis piscatu arceret alios, insanae cupiditatis notam non effugeret" (*id.*, 105).

2 Hugo Grotius, De Iure Belli Ac Pacis Libri Tres [On the Law of War and Peace: Three Books], trans. Francis W. Kelsey (Clarendon Press 1913), vol. 1, 190. The Latin text reads: "Est enim tanta maris magnitudo, ut ad quemvis usum omnibus populis sufficiat, ad aquam hauriendam, ad piscatum, ad navigationem" (*id.*, 114).

aquaculture, [world capture fisheries production] has stagnated and remained rather stable since then.[5] Moreover, if one further refines these statistics to cover only the fish species that Grotius had in mind, namely marine capture and thus excluding inland capture, this trend has been overall negative since the early 1990s,[6] clearly indicating that marine fisheries are not inexhaustible. Does this then mean that one of the fundamental premises on which Hugo Grotius based his argumentation turned out to be flawed since the end of the 20th century? This is an easy assumption to make today. However, it would not do full justice to the ingeniousness of this extremely talented Dutch lawyer, for one should not forget that Grotius only defended the position of his client. Indeed Part XII of *De Iure Praedae Commentarius*, which contained the first above-mentioned quote, was in fact identical, save some necessary adaptations to make it a free-standing publication, to his famous *Mare Liberum*, first published in 1609 as an anonymous pamphlet.[7] At that time Grotius worked for the Dutch government,[8] defending the interests of the Great United Company of the East Indies whose ships needed to be able to rely on the freedom of navigation in order to counter the monopoly claims by the Portuguese and the

5 Food and Agriculture Organization, The State of World Fisheries and Aquaculture 2010, Rome, FAO (2010), p. 5 and p. 6, Figure 3 (http://www.fao.org/docrep/013/i1820e/i1820e.pdf (accessed 8 November 2012)) (hereinafter SOFIA 2010).

6 SOFIA 2010, above n. 5, p. 5, Table 1 (covering the period 2004–2010), in combination with earlier FAO reports covering the period from 1990 until 2003 (http://www.fao.org/fishery/publications/sofia/en (accessed 8 November 2012)).

7 Hugo Grotius, Mare Liberum Sive De Iure Quod Batavis Competit Ad Indicana Commercia [The Freedom of the Seas or the Right Which Belongs to the Dutch to Take Part in the East Indian Trade] trans. Ralph van Deman Magoffin (Clarendon Press 1916) (hereinafter Mare Liberum). It was only after his work De Iure Praedae Commentarius was found (above n. 1), that this anonymous pamphlet could with certainty be attributed to Grotius because of the identical context. The above-cited statement on fisheries (above n. 1) is no exception, for it can be found at 38. See also an online copy of the original book, posted on the occasion of the 400th anniversary of its publication in 2009, p. 30 (http://www.kb.nl/bladerboek/mareliberum/browse/book.html (accessed 8 November 2012)).

8 Later in his lifetime, he had to flee The Netherlands, and finally even became an envoy of the Swedish government in France in 1634. In that capacity he had to adjust his position to take into account the four nautical mile zone claimed by that country to prohibit inter alia fisheries in front of its coast. It is only through a letter of Grotius dated 20 May 1637, in which he commented on John Selden's Mare Clausum, that it can be inferred that he had come to accept a zone along the coast of undetermined breadth in which the coastal State would have exclusive fishing rights. Frans Eric René De Pauw, Het Mare Liberum van Grotius en Pattijn (Die Keure 1960), 79–80.

Spanish at that time.[9] He consequently only used the freedom of fisheries as a secondary line of argumentation in order to prove with even more vigour his main point, namely the freedom of navigation.[10] Grotius indeed readily admitted in *Mare Liberum* that his argumentation based on living resources rested on weaker grounds than that concerning navigation, for he argued that even if it were possible to prohibit fishing because "in a way it can be maintained that fish are exhaustible," this still would not undermine his argumentation with respect to navigation because the sea is not "exhausted" by this use.[11]

Note

1. *The Exhaustibility of Marine Fisheries.* The exhaustible character of marine fisheries has only come to the fore rather recently. Early European settlers in North America were struck by "[t]he aboundance of sea fish . . . almost beyond believing." Rev. Francis Higgenson (1629), quoted in Mark Kurlansky, Cod: A Biography of the Fish That Changed the World 70 (1997). The view that fish resources were inexhaustible claimed adherents for centuries. In his 1883 inaugural address at the International Fisheries Exhibition in London, Thomas Henry Huxley, the acting Chairman of the British Royal Commission on Sea Fisheries instituted in 1863 to ascertain inter alia whether the supply of fish was diminishing, seized the occasion to expound on whether fisheries are exhaustible. P.R.S. Huxley, Inaugural Meeting of the Fishery Conferences, Delivered Monday, June 18, 1883, in IV The Fisheries Exhibition Literature 1 (1884). After having answered the question "yes" with respect to salmon fisheries—"it is possible to net the main stream, in such a manner, as to catch every salmon that tries to go up and every smolt that tries to go down," id. at 12—he turned to sea fisheries. Here his answer was primarily negative:

> I believe that it may be affirmed with confidence that, in relation to our present modes of fishing, a number of the most important sea fisheries,

9 When later in time he had to rely on these same works to defend the cause of the Dutch monopoly of the trade with the East Indies against the English, who specifically confronted him with his own earlier writings, this required some shrewd manipulation of his earlier arguments as demonstrated by De Pauw (*id.*, 49–65).

10 As emphasized by Tullio Scovazzi, "Dici quodammodo potest pisces exhauriri": Fishing in the Mare Liberum, in: R. Casado Raigon and G. Cataldi (eds.), L'évolution et l'état actuel du droit international de la mer. Mélanges de droit de la mer offerts à Daniel Vignes (Bruylant 2009), 861.

11 Mare Liberum, above n. 7, 35. The Latin text reads: "Et si quicquam eorum prohibere posset, puta piscaturam qua dici quodammodo potest pisces exhauriri, at navigationem non posset, per quam mari nihil perit."

> such as the cod fishery, the herring fishery, and the mackerel fishery, are inexhaustible. And I base this conviction on two grounds, first, that the multitude of these fishes is so inconceivably great that the number we catch is relatively insignificant; and, secondly, that the magnitude of the destructive agencies at work upon them is so prodigious, that the destruction effected by the fisherman cannot sensibly increase the death-rate.

Id. at 14. After having documented his argument with figures based on the Norwegian cod and herring fisheries, Huxley concluded:

> I believe, then, that the cod fishery, the herring fishery, the pilchard fishery, the mackerel fishery, and probably all the great sea fisheries, are inexhaustible; that is to say, that nothing we do seriously affects the number of the fish. And any attempt to regulate these fisheries seems consequently, from the nature of the case, to be useless.

Id. at 16. He finally added that oyster fisheries, and possibly other shell fisheries, might be rare examples that could well be exhaustible.

Was the argument of Hugo de Groot relating to the freedom of fisheries convincing in the early 17th century, when he first developed it? Even though de Groot was apparently aware of the fact that certain fish resources could be exhaustible, why did he not develop this point in his Mare Liberum? How was the issue of shell fisheries, raised by Huxley in the 19th century as an exception to what he believed to be the inexhaustibility of sea fisheries, tackled in the international law of the sea when it came to be codified?

Today, the exhaustibility of fish resources on the high seas is documented by the Food and Agriculture Organization (FAO). The biennial State of World Fisheries and Aquaculture (SOFIA) is the flagship publication of its Fisheries and Aquaculture Department. Since the late 1990s the Department has documented a steady decline in capture production in marine waters, i.e., excluding aquaculture and inland water fisheries. The 2012 report observed:

> The declining global marine catch over the last few years together with the increased percentage of overexploited fish stocks and the decreased proportion of non-fully exploited species around the world convey the strong message that the state of world marine fisheries is worsening and has had a negative impact on fishery production. Overexploitation not only causes negative ecological consequences, but it also reduces fish production, which further leads to negative social and economic consequences. To increase the contribution of marine fisheries to the food security, economies and well-being of the coastal communities, effective

> management plans must be put in place to rebuild overexploited stocks. The situation seems more critical for some highly migratory, straddling and other fishery resources that are exploited solely or partially in the high seas. The United Nations Fish Stocks Agreement that entered into force in 2001 should be used as a legal basis for management measures of the high seas fisheries.

FAO, State of World Fisheries and Aquaculture 2012, 12–13 (2012). Note the specific concern expressed by the FAO with respect to highly migratory, straddling, and discrete fish stocks of the high seas, namely those species still found today on the high seas.

B High Seas Fisheries after the Creation of the EEZ

FISHERIES JURISDICTION CASE
Spain v. Canada, 1998 I.C.J. 432

[This case before the International Court of Justice (ICJ) is excerpted not so much for the substance of its decision, which is touched on in one of the Notes following, but rather for the accurate overview of the facts in dispute.

Fish resources are not spread evenly over the world oceans. They tend to be more abundant in shallower areas. States with continental shelves extending beyond 200 nautical miles, like Canada on its Atlantic coast, consequently are highly likely to find fish resources straddling this man-made boundary. As indicated in Figure XIII.A, the Grand Banks, mostly located inside the Canadian 200-nautical-mile EEZ, is one such rich fishing ground, extending in two areas beyond that limit, called the Nose and the Tail. This case focuses on the Nose of the Grand Banks.]

14. On 10 May 1994 Canada deposited with the Secretary-General of the United Nations a declaration of acceptance of the compulsory jurisdiction of the Court which was worded as follows:

> On behalf of the Government of Canada,
>
> (1) I give notice that I hereby terminate the acceptance by Canada of the compulsory jurisdiction of the International Court of Justice hitherto effective by virtue of the declaration made on 10 September 1985 in conformity with paragraph 2 of Article 36 of the Statute of the Court.

> (2) I declare that the Government of Canada accepts as compulsory *ipso facto* and without special convention, on condition of reciprocity, the jurisdiction of the International Court of Justice, in conformity with paragraph 2 of Article 36 of the Statute of the Court, until such time as notice may be given to terminate the acceptance, over all disputes arising after the present declaration with regard to situations or facts subsequent to this declaration, other than:
>
> (*a*) disputes in regard to which the parties have agreed or shall agree to have recourse to some other method of peaceful settlement;
>
> (*b*) disputes with the Government of any other country which is a member of the Commonwealth, all of which disputes shall be settled in such manner as the parties have agreed or shall agree;
>
> (*c*) disputes with regard to questions which by international law fall exclusively within the jurisdiction of Canada; and
>
> (*d*) disputes arising out of or concerning conservation and management measures taken by Canada with respect to vessels fishing in the NAFO Regulatory Area, as defined in the Convention on Future Multilateral Co-operation in the Northwest Atlantic Fisheries, 1978, and the enforcement of such measures.
>
> (3) The Government of Canada also reserves the right at any time, by means of a notification addressed to the Secretary-General of the United Nations, and with effect as from the moment of such notification, either to add to, amend or withdraw any of the foregoing reservations, or any that may hereafter be added.
>
> It is requested that this notification be communicated to the Governments of all the States that have accepted the Optional Clause and to the Registrar of the International Court of Justice.

The three reservations set forth in subparagraphs (*a*), (*b*) and (*c*) of paragraph 2 of the above-mentioned declaration had already been included in Canada's prior declaration of 10 September 1985. Subparagraph (*d*) of the 1994 declaration, however, set out a new, fourth reservation[.]

15. On the same day that the Canadian Government deposited its new declaration, it submitted to Parliament Bill C-29 amending the Coastal Fisheries Protection Act by extending its area of application to include the Regulatory Area of the Northwest Atlantic Fisheries Organization (NAFO). Bill C-29 was adopted by Parliament, and received the Royal Assent on 12 May 1994. Section 2 of the Coastal Fisheries Protection Act as amended defined the

"NAFO Regulatory Area" as "that part of the Convention Area of the Northwest Atlantic Fisheries Organization that is on the high seas[.]"

The new Section 5.1 of the Act contained the following declaration:

> 5.1. Parliament, recognizing
>
> (*a*) that straddling stocks on the Grand Banks of Newfoundland are a major renewable world food source having provided a livelihood for centuries to fishers,
>
> (*b*) that those stocks are threatened with extinction,
>
> (*c*) that there is an urgent need for all fishing vessels to comply in both Canadian fisheries waters and the NAFO Regulatory Area with sound conservation and management measures for those stocks, notably those measures that are taken under the *Convention on Future Multilateral Co-operation in the Northwest Atlantic Fisheries*, done at Ottawa on October 24, 1978, Canada Treaty Series 1979 No. 11, and
>
> (*d*) that some foreign fishing vessels continue to fish for those stocks in the NAFO Regulatory Area in a manner that undermines the effectiveness of sound conservation and management measures,
>
> declares that the purpose of section 5.2. is to enable Canada to take urgent action necessary to prevent further destruction of those stocks and to permit their rebuilding, while continuing to seek effective international solutions to the situation referred to in paragraph (*d*).

The new Section 5.2 read as follows:

> 5.2. No person, being aboard a foreign fishing vessel of a prescribed class, shall, in the NAFO Regulatory Area, fish or prepare to fish for a straddling stock in contravention of any of the prescribed conservation and management measures.

Sections 7 ("Boarding by protection officer"), 7.1 ("Search") and 8.1 ("Use of force") of the Act as amended dealt with the activities of Canadian fisheries protection officers within the NAFO Regulatory Area. These sections read as follows:

> 7. A protection officer may
>
> (*a*) for the purpose of ensuring compliance with this Act and the regulations, board and inspect any fishing vessel found within Canadian fisheries waters or the NAFO Regulatory Area; and
>
> (*b*) with a warrant issued under section 7.1, search any fishing vessel found within Canadian fisheries waters or the NAFO Regulatory Area and its cargo.
>
> 7.1. (1) A justice of the peace who on *ex parte* application is satisfied by information on oath that there are reasonable grounds to believe that there is in any place, including any premises, vessel or vehicle, any fish or other thing that was obtained by or used in, or that will afford evidence in respect of, a contravention of this Act or the regulations, may issue a warrant authorizing the protection officer named in the warrant to enter and search the place for the fish or other thing subject to any conditions that may be specified in the warrant.
>
> (2) A protection officer may exercise the powers referred to in paragraph 7(*b*) without a warrant if the conditions for obtaining a warrant exist but, by reason of exigent circumstances, it would not be practical to obtain a warrant.
>
> 8.1. A protection officer may, in the manner and to the extent prescribed by the regulations, use force that is intended or is likely to disable a foreign fishing vessel, if the protection officer
>
> (*a*) is proceeding lawfully to arrest the master or other person in command of the vessel; and
>
> (*b*) believes on reasonable grounds that the force is necessary for the purpose of arresting that master or other person.

Finally, the new Section 18.1, which was concerned with the application of criminal law, stated:

> An act or omission that would be an offence under an Act of Parliament if it occurred in Canada is deemed to have been committed in Canada if it occurs, in the course of enforcing this Act,
>
> (*a*) in the NAFO Regulatory Area on board or by means of a foreign fishing vessel on board or by means of which a contravention of section 5.2 has been committed; or
>
> (*b*) in the course of continuing pursuit that commenced while a foreign fishing vessel was in Canadian fisheries waters or the NAFO Regulatory Area.

16. On 12 May 1994, following the adoption of Bill C-8, Canada also amended Section 25 of its Criminal Code relating to the use of force by police officers and other peace officers enforcing the law. This Section applied as well to fisheries protection officers, since their duties incidentally included those of peace officers.

17. On 25 May 1994 the Coastal Fisheries Protection Regulations were also amended.

The new Sections 19.3 to 19.5 regulated "the use of force" by Canadian fisheries protection officers pursuant to Section 8.1 of the amended Act.

The new subsection 2 of Section 21 of the Regulations provided as follows:

> (2) For the purposes of section 5.2 of the Act,
> (*a*) straddling stocks are,
> (i) in Division 3L, Division 3N and Division 30, the stocks of fish set out in Table 1 to this section, and
> (ii) in Division 3M, the stocks of fish set out in Table II to this section;
> (*b*) vessels without nationality and foreign fishing vessels that fly the flag of any state set out in Table III to this section are prescribed classes of vessels; and
> (*c*) a prohibition against fishing for straddling stocks, preparing to fish for straddling stocks or catching and retaining straddling stocks is a prescribed conservation and management measure.

The "straddling stocks" referred to in "Table 1" included the "Greenland halibut" (also called in French "flétan noir"). This was the only stock mentioned in "Table II." "Table III" specified Belize, the Cayman Islands, Honduras, Panama, Saint Vincent and the Grenadines and Sierra Leone.

18. These Regulations were further amended on 3 March 1995.

In their amended version, paragraphs (*b*) to (*d*) of Section 21(2) read as follows:

> (*b*) the following classes of foreign fishing vessels are prescribed classes namely
> (i) foreign fishing vessels without nationality,
> (ii) foreign fishing vessels that fly the flag of any state set out in Table III to this section, and
> (iii) foreign fishing vessels that fly the flag of any state set out in Table IV to this section;

(*c*) in respect of a foreign fishing vessel of a class prescribed by subparagraph (b)(i) or (ii), prohibitions against fishing for the straddling stocks set out in Table I or II to this section, preparing to fish for those straddling stocks and catching and retaining those straddling stocks are prescribed conservation and management measures; and

(*d*) in respect of a foreign fishing vessel of a class prescribed by subparagraph (b)(iii), the measures set out in Table V to this section are prescribed conservation and management measures.

"Table IV" referred to Spain and Portugal. "Table V," which was headed "Prescribed Conservation and Management Measures," began by laying down the following prohibitions:

1. Prohibitions against fishing for, or catching and retaining, Greenland halibut in Division 3L, Division 3M, Division 3N or Division 3O during the period commencing on March 3 and terminating on December 31 in any year.

19. On 9 March 1995, the *Estai*, a fishing vessel flying the Spanish flag and manned by a Spanish crew, was intercepted and boarded some 245 miles from the Canadian coast, in Division 3L of the NAFO Regulatory Area (Grand Banks area), by Canadian Government vessels. The vessel was seized and its master arrested on charges of violations of the Coastal Fisheries Protection Act and its implementing regulations. They were brought to the Canadian port of St. John's, Newfoundland, where they were charged with offences under the above legislation, and in particular illegal fishing for Greenland halibut; part of the ship's catch was confiscated. The members of the crew were released immediately. The master was released on 12 March 1995, following the payment of bail, and the vessel on 15 March 1995, following the posting of a bond.

20. The same day that the *Estai* was boarded, the Spanish Embassy in Canada sent two Notes Verbales to the Canadian Department of Foreign Affairs and International Trade. The second of these stated *inter alia* that: "the Spanish Government categorically condemn[ed] the pursuit and harassment of a Spanish vessel by vessels of the Canadian navy, in flagrant violation of the international law in force, since these acts [took] place outside the 200-mile zone." On 10 March 1995, the Spanish Ministry of Foreign Affairs sent a Note Verbale to the Canadian Embassy in Spain which contained the following passage:

> In carrying out the said boarding operation, the Canadian authorities breached the universally accepted norm of customary international law codified in Article 92 and articles to the same effect of the 1982 Convention on the Law of the Sea, according to which ships on the high seas shall be subject to the exclusive jurisdiction of the flag State ...
>
> The Spanish Government considers that the wrongful act committed by ships of the Canadian navy can in no way be justified by presumed concern to conserve fisheries in the area, since it violates the established provisions of the NAFO Convention to which Canada is a party.

In its turn, on 10 March 1995 the Canadian Department of Foreign Affairs and International Trade sent a Note Verbale to the Spanish Embassy in Canada, in which it was stated that "[t]he *Estai* resisted the efforts to board her made by Canadian inspectors in accordance with international practice" and that "the arrest of the *Estai* was necessary in order to put a stop to the overfishing of Greenland halibut by Spanish fishermen."

Also on 10 March 1995, the European Community and its member States sent a Note Verbale to the Canadian Department of Foreign Affairs and International Trade which included the following:

> The arrest of a vessel in international waters by a State other than the State of which the vessel is flying the flag and under whose jurisdiction it falls, is an illegal act under both the NAFO Convention and customary international law, and cannot be justified by any means. With this action Canada is not only flagrantly violating international law, but is failing to observe normal behaviour of responsible States.
>
> This act is particularly unacceptable since it undermines all the efforts of the international community, notably in the framework of the FAO and the United Nations Conference on Straddling Fish Stocks and Highly Migratory Fish Stocks, to achieve effective conservation through enhanced cooperation in the management of fisheries resources.
>
> This serious breach of international law goes far beyond the question of fisheries conservation. The arrest is a lawless act against the sovereignty of a Member State of the European Community. Furthermore, the behaviour of the Canadian vessels has clearly endangered the lives of the crew and the safety of the Spanish vessel concerned.
>
> The European Community and its Member States demand that Canada immediately release the vessel, repair any damages caused, cease and desist from its harassment of vessels flying the flag of Community Member States and immediately repeal the legislation under which it claims to take such unilateral action.

21. On 16 April 1995, an "Agreement constituted in the form of an Agreed Minute, an Exchange of Letters, an Exchange of Notes and the Annexes thereto between the European Community and Canada on fisheries in the context of the NAFO Convention" was initialled; this Agreement was signed in Brussels on 20 April 1995.

In Part A ("Control and Enforcement") of the Agreed Minute, the Community and Canada agreed on proposals which would "constitute the basis for a submission to be jointly prepared and made to the NAFO Fisheries Commission, for its consideration and approval, to establish a Protocol to strengthen the NAFO Conservation and Enforcement Measures"; at the same time the parties decided to implement immediately, on a provisional basis, certain control and enforcement measures. In Part B ("Total Allowable Catch and Catch Limits"), they agreed on the total allowable catch for 1995 for Greenland halibut within the area concerned, and to certain management arrangements for stocks of this fish. In Part C ("Other Related Issues") Canada undertook to

> repeal the provisions of the Regulation of 3 March 1995 pursuant to the Coastal Fisheries Protection Act which subjected vessels from Spain and Portugal to certain provisions of the Act and prohibited these vessels from fishing for Greenland halibut in the NAFO Regulatory Area;

it was further stated that, for the European Community, "any re-insertion by Canada of vessels from any European Community member State into legislation which subjects vessels on the high seas to Canadian jurisdiction" would be considered as a breach of the Agreed Minute. It was likewise stated in that Part that Canada would regard as a breach of the Agreed Minute

> any systematic and sustained failure of the European Community to control its fishing vessels in the NAFO Regulatory Area which clearly has resulted in violations of a serious nature of NAFO conservation and enforcement measures.

Point 1 of Part D ("General Provisions") of the Agreed Minutes provided as follows:

> The European Community and Canada maintain their respective positions on the conformity of the amendment of 25 May 1994 to Canada's Coastal Fisheries Protection Act, and subsequent regulations, with customary international law and the NAFO Convention. Nothing in this Agreed Minute shall prejudice any multilateral convention to which the European Community and Canada, or any Member State of the European

> Community and Canada, are parties, or their ability to preserve and defend their rights in conformity with international law, and the views of either Party with respect to any question relating to the Law of the Sea.

Finally, Part E ("Implementation") stated that the "Agreed Minute [would] cease to apply on 31 December 1995 or when the measures described in this Agreed Minute [were] adopted by NAFO, if this [should be] earlier."

The Exchange of Letters noted the agreement of the parties on two points. It was agreed, on the one hand, that the posting of a bond for the release of the vessel *Estai* and the payment of bail for the release of its master

> [could] not be interpreted as meaning that the European Community or its Member States recognize[d] the legality of the arrest or the jurisdiction of Canada beyond the Canadian 200-mile zone against fishing vessels flying the flag of another State

and, on the other hand, that

> the Attorney-General of Canada [would] consider the public interest in his decision on staying the prosecution against the vessel *Estai* and its master; in such case, the bond, bail and catch or its proceeds [would] be returned to the master.

The European Community emphasized that the stay of prosecution was essential for the application of the Agreed Minute.

22. On 18 April 1995 the proceedings against the *Estai* and its master were discontinued by order of the Attorney-General of Canada; on 19 April 1995 the bond was discharged and the bail was repaid with interest; and subsequently the confiscated portion of the catch was returned. On 1 May 1995 the Coastal Fisheries Protection Regulations were amended so as to remove Spain and Portugal from Table IV to Section 21. Finally, the Proposal for Improving Fisheries Control and Enforcement, contained in the Agreement of 20 April 1995, was adopted by NAFO at its annual meeting held in September 1995 and became measures binding on all contracting parties with effect from 29 November 1995.

Notes

1. *Flag State Jurisdiction*. Spain thought it had a strong case at international law on the merits, because Canada seized a Spanish vessel on the high seas

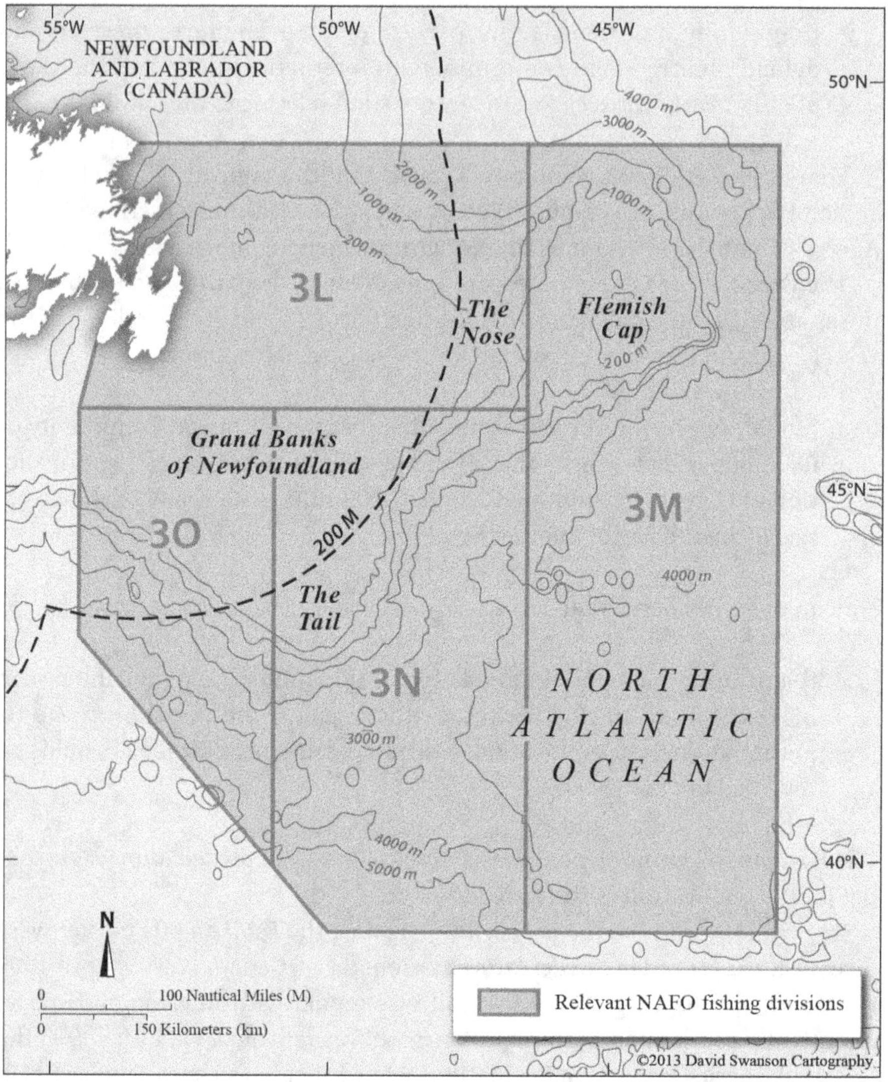

FIGURE XIII.A *Maritime Areas in 1995 Canada-European Union Fishing Dispute*

in the absence of any specific treaty in force between the parties authorizing such a seizure. See the discussion of flag state jurisdiction in Chapter 4, and the March 10, 1995 Note Verbale from the Spanish Ministry of Foreign Affairs to the Canadian Embassy, referred to in paragraph 20 of the ICJ decision and reproduced in full in Chapter 4, Section B. Spain argued before the ICJ that the dispute was about the seizure of ships on the high seas whereas Canada argued that it was instead a dispute over conservation and management measures. Why do you believe both parties took these positions? Are their positions explained solely by the parties' differing views on the merits of the dispute?

2. *Multiple Dispute Settlement Bodies Involved in the Same Dispute*. As in the MOX Plant case discussed in Chapter 12, legal battles stemming from the *Estai* incident were fought on several different levels. First, the company owning the vessel and the captain pursued a Canadian civil case to seek redress. Although the trial judge awarded damages of CAD 137,052.67 for out-of-pocket legal expenses, ship's agency fees during the sojourn, the lost fishing time because of the arrest and detention, and extra bunkers and lubrication, Jose Pereira E. Hijos S.A. v. Canada (Attorney General), 2005 FC 1011, 17 C.E.L.R. (3d) 1, this decision was reversed on appeal. 2007 FCA 20, 26 C.E.L.R. (3d) 169.

Second, Spain also sued on the regional European level. Spain contested the political compromise reached by Canada and the European Union on April 20, 1995, as mentioned in paragraph 21 of the ICJ's decision. The European Council later approved this compromise agreement. Council Decision of 22 December 1995 concerning the Conclusion of the Agreement Constituted in the Form of an Agreed Minute, an Exchange of Letters, an Exchange of Notes and the Annexes Thereto between the European Community and Canada on Fisheries in the Context of the NAFO Convention, (EC) No. 95/586, 1995 O.J. L. 327, 35. As a result of the E.U. Council decision, the E.U. Fisheries Council established a quota for E.U. fishermen of approximately nineteen percent of the total allowable catch (TAC) established by the NAFO. Regulation (EC) No. 1761/95, 1995 O.J.L. 171, 1. This quota represented a substantial reduction, for on the eve of the conflict in early 1995 the European Union, after having objected to a NAFO-adopted quota of 12.59 percent of the TAC, had unilaterally established for itself a quota of 69 percent. Spain strongly objected to the European Council's and the E.U. Fisheries Council's concessions and brought a claim before the European Court of First Instance (ECFI) seeking a declaration on the basis of the second paragraph of Article 288 of the EC Treaty ["In the case of non-contractual liability, the Union shall, in accordance with the general principles common to the laws of the Member States, make good any damage caused by its institutions or by its servants in the performance of their duties."] for the losses it had suffered following adoption of the lowered quota. Case T-196/99, Area Cova and Others v. Council of the European Union and Commission of the European Communities, Dec. 6, 2001, E.C.F.I. II, 3597 (2001). The ECFI dismissed all claims. According to that court, there was no misuse of E.U. powers either when making concessions in the bilateral agreement with Canada defusing the *Estai* dispute, or when adopting Regulation 1761, which substantially lowered the E.U.'s quota for Greenland halibut, because normalizing commercial relations forms an integral part of the Common Fisheries Policy. The conservation measure in question was thought not to damage Community vessel owners disproportionately, because European fishermen would benefit in the long run. Short-term benefits for some fishermen, in other words, did not outweigh the long-term development and availability of the resource for all.

Third, as indicated by the excerpt above, Spain also filed a claim before the ICJ. Spain challenged the amendment introduced by Canada on May 12, 1994 to its Coastal Fisheries Protection Act, the subsequent amendments to the regulations implementing that Act, and specific actions taken on the basis of the amended Act and its regulations, including the pursuit, boarding, and seizure of the *Estai* on March 9, 1995. The Court, however, did not have the chance to look into the merits of the case, for it decided, by a vote of twelve to five, that it lacked jurisdiction. Spain had argued that the Court had jurisdiction based on the Article 36(2) declarations made by both states. Article 36(2) of the ICJ Statute reads:

> The states parties to the present Statute may at any time declare that they recognize as compulsory ipso facto and without special agreement, in relation to any other state accepting the same obligation, the jurisdiction of the Court in all legal disputes concerning:
>
> a. the interpretation of a treaty;
> b. any question of international law;
> c. the existence of any fact which, if established, would constitute a breach of an international obligation;
> d. the nature or extent of the reparation to be made for the breach of an international obligation.

These so-called optional clauses may be made conditionally or unconditionally according to Article 36(3), and that is how one has to understand the Canadian declaration of May 10, 1994 mentioned in paragraph 14 of the ICJ judgment. Compared with its previous optional clause declaration, there was only one new condition, namely "disputes arising out of or concerning conservation and management measures taken by Canada with respect to vessels fishing in the NAFO Regulatory Area, as defined in the Convention on Future Multilateral Co-operation in the Northwest Atlantic Fisheries, 1978, and the enforcement of such measures." On the same day that Canada promulgated its new optional clause declaration, the government submitted a bill to Parliament that would make it possible to seize vessels like the *Estai* on the high seas. That bill was approved and received the required Royal Assent just two days later.

Are judicial procedures the best way to resolve the legal issues flowing from the *Estai* incident? Which level—national, regional, or global—was the most appropriate for addressing those issues?

3. *National Courts and the Exhaustion of Local Remedies.* When a foreign national challenges the legality under international law of a country's actions in that country's courts, the lawsuit often proves futile. Nevertheless, as stated by the ICJ in 1959, "[t]he rule that local remedies must be exhausted before international proceedings may be instituted is a well-established rule of customary international law." Interhandel (Switzerland v. United States), 1959 I.C.J. 6, 27. What is the rationale behind this rule? Typical cases involve individuals who have set up business entities abroad under the laws of the host country. Should the rule also apply in the absence of a voluntary link or territorial connection between the injured individual and the state committing an internationally wrongful act? In the *Estai* dispute Spain clearly had not subjected itself voluntarily to the jurisdiction of Canada. Consider Article 15(c) of the International Law Commission's Draft Articles on Diplomatic Protection, UN GAOR, 61st Sess., Supp. No. 10, UN Doc. A/61/10 (2006), which recognizes an exception to the exhaustion of local remedies rule where "[t]here was no relevant connection between the injured person and the State alleged to be responsible at the date of injury." Does this exception form part of the customary international law rule discerned by the ICJ in the Interhandel case? The ILC commented: "Neither judicial authority nor State practice provide clear guidance on the existence of such an exception to the exhaustion of local remedies rule." Id. at 81. If the ILC was not codifying existing international law, what exactly was it doing here?

4. *The European Legal System and the Allocation of National and Regional International Competence.* At the European regional level, division of competence with respect to fisheries is governed by the following rule of thumb: the European Union has exclusive competence with respect to establishing fisheries conservation and management rules, while enforcement of these rules remains a competence of the individual E.U. member states. One of Canada's concerns was that Spanish and Portuguese vessels misreported fish catches without there being any effective sanctioning of infractions committed by their vessels. Counter-Memorial of Canada, Fisheries Jurisdiction Case, Spain v. Canada, Feb. 1996, 18. How can the European Union make sure its Common Fisheries Policy, established in 1970 and giving it exclusive competence with respect to the conservation and management of fisheries, is implemented? Note that Spain was not a party to the political compromise finally reached with Canada that substantially lowered the European quota for Greenland

halibut. Nor is Spain a member of the NAFO, which later endorsed the political compromise reached between the European Union and Canada. How could Spain best protect its fishing interests after it became a member of the European Union in 1986? For discussion of how the principle of relative stability limited the possibilities for Spanish fishing vessels after Spain joined the European Union, see Erik Franckx, Sea Fisheries Cases before the European Court of Justice, in 9 Max Planck Encyclopedia of Public International Law 42 (Rüdiger Wolfrum ed., 2012); and see generally Robin Rolf Churchill & Daniel Owen, The EC Common Fisheries Policy (2010).

5. *The International Court of Justice and Limits on Access and Jurisdiction.* Was Spain prohibited from bringing the case before the ICJ because of the political compromise reached between Canada and the European Union, as set down in the agreement signed in Brussels on April 20, 1995? Because the dispute concerned an enforcement action with a non-E.U. member, Spain was not precluded from bringing this case to the ICJ. Compare the limitations placed on Ireland by the European Court of Justice in the MOX Plant case, discussed in Chapter 12.

Spain nevertheless was barred from obtaining a decision on the merits of the case because the ICJ decided it lacked jurisdiction. As suggested in Note 2, the basis for lack of jurisdiction was the change Canada made to its Article 36(2) optional clause declaration on the same day it submitted legislation to amend its national law to allow the arrest of vessels like the *Estai*. Does this Article 36(2) declaration change indicate that Canada doubted the international legal validity of its new legislation, since it was not willing to have the ICJ adjudge whether it was consistent with rules of contemporary international law?

Canada had already acted in a similar manner when it established its Arctic Waters Pollution Prevention Act in 1970, 9 Intl. Leg. Materials 543 (1970). The purpose of that Act was to prevent pollution in a 100-nautical-mile zone north of the 60th parallel. Although today a coastal state's pollution prevention measures in such a zone may well be in accordance with international law since the EEZ notion now forms part of international treaty law and customary international law (see Chapter 9), the Canadian Act was most certainly controversial in 1970. As admitted by E. Wang, Director of Legal Operations of the Canadian Department of External Affairs before the Standing Committee on External Affairs and National Defence of the House of Commons, this Act resulted in "a drawer full of protests." Quoted in Ted L. McDorman, The New Definition of "Canada Lands" and the Determination of the Outer Limit of the Continental Shelf, 14 J. Maritime L. & Commerce 195, 215 (1983).

On the same day that Canada adopted its 1970 Act, it added a new condition to its Article 36(2) ICJ optional clause acceptance, excluding all disputes arising "in respect of the prevention or control of pollution or contamination of the marine environment in marine areas adjacent to the coast of Canada." 9 Intl. Leg. Materials 589 (1970). This 1970 condition was never tested in practice before the ICJ. Canada withdrew the condition on September 10, 1985. Has the ICJ validated this kind of preventive action in the 1998 Fisheries Jurisdiction judgment by putting on record, in paragraph 54, that

> reservations from the Court's jurisdiction may be made by States for a variety of reasons; sometimes precisely because they feel vulnerable about the legality of their position or policy. Nowhere in the Court's case-law has it been suggested that interpretation in accordance with the legality under international law of the matters exempted from the jurisdiction of the Court is a rule that governs the interpretation of such reservations[.]

Why did the ICJ take this position? Does this statement imply that Canada bears no international responsibility for acts attributable to it that may have violated rights of Spain? How should these issues be resolved?

AGREEMENT FOR THE IMPLEMENTATION OF THE PROVISIONS OF THE [LOS CONVENTION] RELATING TO THE CONSERVATION AND MANAGEMENT OF STRADDLING FISH STOCKS AND HIGHLY MIGRATORY FISH STOCKS (1995 FISH STOCKS AGREEMENT)
Opened for signature Dec. 4, 1995, U.S. Sen. Treaty Doc. 104–24 (1996), 2167 U.N.T.S. 3, U.S. Sen. Treaty Doc. 104–24 (1996)

The States Parties to this Agreement,

Recalling the relevant provisions of the United Nations Convention on the Law of the Sea of 10 December 1982,

Determined to ensure the long-term conservation and sustainable use of straddling fish stocks and highly migratory fish stocks,

Resolved to improve cooperation between States to that end,

Calling for more effective enforcement by flag States, port States and coastal States of the conservation and management measures adopted for such stocks,

Seeking to address in particular the problems identified in chapter 17, programme area C, of Agenda 21 adopted by the United Nations Conference on Environment and Development, namely, that the management of high seas fisheries is inadequate in many areas and that some resources are overutilized; noting that there are problems of unregulated fishing, over-capitalization, excessive fleet size, vessel reflagging to escape controls, insufficiently selective gear, unreliable databases and lack of sufficient cooperation between States,

Committing themselves to responsible fisheries,

Conscious of the need to avoid adverse impacts on the marine environment, preserve biodiversity, maintain the integrity of marine ecosystems and minimize the risk of long-term or irreversible effects of fishing operations,

Recognizing the need for specific assistance, including financial, scientific and technological assistance, in order that developing States can participate effectively in the conservation, management and sustainable use of straddling fish stocks and highly migratory fish stocks,

Convinced that an agreement for the implementation of the relevant provisions of the [LOS] Convention would best serve these purposes and contribute to the maintenance of international peace and security,

Affirming that matters not regulated by the [LOS] Convention or by this Agreement continue to be governed by the rules and principles of general international law,

Have agreed as follows:

Part I: General Provisions . . .

Article 2: Objective

The objective of this Agreement is to ensure the long-term conservation and sustainable use of straddling fish stocks and highly migratory fish stocks through effective implementation of the relevant provisions of the [LOS] Convention.

Article 3: Application

1. Unless otherwise provided, this Agreement applies to the conservation and management of straddling fish stocks and highly migratory fish stocks beyond areas under national jurisdiction, except that articles 6 and 7 apply also to the conservation and management of such stocks within areas under national jurisdiction, subject to the different legal regimes that apply within areas under national jurisdiction and in areas beyond national jurisdiction as provided for in the [LOS] Convention. . . .

Article 4: Relationship between this Agreement and the [LOS] Convention

Nothing in this Agreement shall prejudice the rights, jurisdiction and duties of States under the [LOS] Convention. This Agreement shall be interpreted and applied in the context of and in a manner consistent with the [LOS] Convention.

Part II: Conservation and Management of Straddling Fish Stocks and Highly Migratory Fish Stocks . . .

Article 6: Application of the precautionary approach

1. States shall apply the precautionary approach widely to conservation, management and exploitation of straddling fish stocks and highly migratory fish stocks in order to protect the living marine resources and preserve the marine environment.

2. States shall be more cautious when information is uncertain, unreliable or inadequate. The absence of adequate scientific information shall not be used as a reason for postponing or failing to take conservation and management measures.

3. In implementing the precautionary approach, States shall:

(a) improve decision-making for fishery resource conservation and management by obtaining and sharing the best scientific information available and implementing improved techniques for dealing with risk and uncertainty;

(b) apply the guidelines set out in Annex II and determine, on the basis of the best scientific information available, stock-specific reference points and the action to be taken if they are exceeded;

(c) take into account, *inter alia*, uncertainties relating to the size and productivity of the stocks, reference points, stock condition in relation to such reference points, levels and distribution of fishing mortality and the impact of fishing activities on non-target and associated or dependent species, as well as existing and predicted oceanic, environmental and socio-economic conditions; and

(d) develop data collection and research programmes to assess the impact of fishing on non-target and associated or dependent species and their environment, and adopt plans which are necessary to ensure the conservation of such species and to protect habitats of special concern.

4. States shall take measures to ensure that, when reference points are approached, they will not be exceeded. In the event that they are exceeded, States shall, without delay, take the action determined under paragraph 3(b) to restore the stocks.

5. Where the status of target stocks or non-target or associated or dependent species is of concern, States shall subject such stocks and species to enhanced monitoring in order to review their status and the efficacy of conservation and

management measures. They shall revise those measures regularly in the light of new information.

6. For new or exploratory fisheries, States shall adopt as soon as possible cautious conservation and management measures, including, *inter alia*, catch limits and effort limits. Such measures shall remain in force until there are sufficient data to allow assessment of the impact of the fisheries on the long-term sustainability of the stocks, whereupon conservation and management measures based on that assessment shall be implemented. The latter measures shall, if appropriate, allow for the gradual development of the fisheries.

7. If a natural phenomenon has a significant adverse impact on the status of straddling fish stocks or highly migratory fish stocks, States shall adopt conservation and management measures on an emergency basis to ensure that fishing activity does not exacerbate such adverse impact. States shall also adopt such measures on an emergency basis where fishing activity presents a serious threat to the sustainability of such stocks. Measures taken on an emergency basis shall be temporary and shall be based on the best scientific evidence available.

Article 7: Compatibility of conservation and management measures

1. Without prejudice to the sovereign rights of coastal States for the purpose of exploring and exploiting, conserving and managing the living marine resources within areas under national jurisdiction as provided for in the [LOS] Convention, and the right of all States for their nationals to engage in fishing on the high seas in accordance with the [LOS] Convention:

(a) with respect to straddling fish stocks, the relevant coastal States and the States whose nationals fish for such stocks in the adjacent high seas area shall seek, either directly or through the appropriate mechanisms for cooperation provided for in Part III, to agree upon the measures necessary for the conservation of these stocks in the adjacent high seas area;

(b) with respect to highly migratory fish stocks, the relevant coastal States and other States whose nationals fish for such stocks in the region shall cooperate, either directly or through the appropriate mechanisms for cooperation provided for in Part III, with a view to ensuring conservation and promoting the objective of optimum utilization of such stocks throughout the region, both within and beyond the areas under national jurisdiction.

2. Conservation and management measures established for the high seas and those adopted for areas under national jurisdiction shall be compatible

in order to ensure conservation and management of the straddling fish stocks and highly migratory fish stocks in their entirety. In determining compatible conservation and management measures, States shall:

(a) take into account the conservation and management measures adopted and applied in accordance with article 61 of the [LOS] Convention in respect of the same stocks by coastal States within areas under national jurisdiction and ensure that measures established in respect of such stocks for the high seas do not undermine the effectiveness of such measures;

(b) take into account previously agreed measures established and applied for the high seas in accordance with the [LOS] Convention in respect of the same stocks by relevant coastal States and States fishing on the high seas;

(c) take into account previously agreed measures established and applied in accordance with the [LOS] Convention in respect of the same stocks by a subregional or regional fisheries management organization or arrangement;

(d) take into account the biological unity and other biological characteristics of the stocks and the relationships between the distribution of the stocks, the fisheries and the geographical particularities of the region concerned, including the extent to which the stocks occur and are fished in areas under national jurisdiction;

(e) take into account the respective dependence of the coastal States and the States fishing on the high seas on the stocks concerned; and

(f) ensure that such measures do not result in harmful impact on the living marine resources as a whole.

3. In giving effect to their duty to cooperate, States shall make every effort to agree on compatible conservation and management measures within a reasonable period of time.

4. If no agreement can be reached within a reasonable period of time, any of the States concerned may invoke the procedures for the settlement of disputes provided for in Part VIII. . . .

Part III: Mechanisms for International Cooperation Concerning Straddling Fish Stocks and Highly Migratory Fish Stocks

Article 8: Cooperation for conservation and management

1. Coastal States and States fishing on the high seas shall, in accordance with the [LOS] Convention, pursue cooperation in relation to straddling fish stocks and highly migratory fish stocks either directly or through appropriate

subregional or regional fisheries management organizations or arrangements, taking into account the specific characteristics of the subregion or region, to ensure effective conservation and management of such stocks.

2. States shall enter into consultations in good faith and without delay, particularly where there is evidence that the straddling fish stocks and highly migratory fish stocks concerned may be under threat of over-exploitation or where a new fishery is being developed for such stocks. To this end, consultations may be initiated at the request of any interested State with a view to establishing appropriate arrangements to ensure conservation and management of the stocks. Pending agreement on such arrangements, States shall observe the provisions of this Agreement and shall act in good faith and with due regard to the rights, interests and duties of other States.

3. Where a subregional or regional fisheries management organization or arrangement has the competence to establish conservation and management measures for particular straddling fish stocks or highly migratory fish stocks, States fishing for the stocks on the high seas and relevant coastal States shall give effect to their duty to cooperate by becoming members of such organization or participants in such arrangement, or by agreeing to apply the conservation and management measures established by such organization or arrangement. States having a real interest in the fisheries concerned may become members of such organization or participants in such arrangement. The terms of participation in such organization or arrangement shall not preclude such States from membership or participation; nor shall they be applied in a manner which discriminates against any State or group of States having a real interest in the fisheries concerned.

4. Only those States which are members of such an organization or participants in such an arrangement, or which agree to apply the conservation and management measures established by such organization or arrangement, shall have access to the fishery resources to which those measures apply.

5. Where there is no subregional or regional fisheries management organization or arrangement to establish conservation and management measures for a particular straddling fish stock or highly migratory fish stock, relevant coastal States and States fishing on the high seas for such stock in the subregion or region shall cooperate to establish such an organization or enter into other appropriate arrangements to ensure conservation and management of such stock and shall participate in the work of the organization or arrangement.

6. Any State intending to propose that action be taken by an intergovernmental organization having competence with respect to living resources should, where such action would have a significant effect on conservation and management measures already established by a competent subregional or

regional fisheries management organization or arrangement, consult through that organization or arrangement with its members or participants. To the extent practicable, such consultation should take place prior to the submission of the proposal to the intergovernmental organization....

Part VI: Compliance and Enforcement...

Article 21: Subregional and regional cooperation in enforcement

1. In any high seas area covered by a subregional or regional fisheries management organization or arrangement, a State Party which is a member of such organization or a participant in such arrangement may, through its duly authorized inspectors, board and inspect, in accordance with paragraph 2, fishing vessels flying the flag of another State Party to this Agreement, whether or not such State Party is also a member of the organization or a participant in the arrangement, for the purpose of ensuring compliance with conservation and management measures for straddling fish stocks and highly migratory fish stocks established by that organization or arrangement....

Article 23: Measures taken by a port State

1. A port State has the right and the duty to take measures, in accordance with international law, to promote the effectiveness of subregional, regional and global conservation and management measures. When taking such measures a port State shall not discriminate in form or in fact against the vessels of any State.

2. A port State may, *inter alia*, inspect documents, fishing gear and catch on board fishing vessels, when such vessels are voluntarily in its ports or at its offshore terminals.

3. States may adopt regulations empowering the relevant national authorities to prohibit landings and transshipments where it has been established that the catch has been taken in a manner which undermines the effectiveness of subregional, regional or global conservation and management measures on the high seas.

4. Nothing in this article affects the exercise by States of their sovereignty over ports in their territory in accordance with international law....

Part VIII: Peaceful Settlement of Disputes...

Article 30: Procedures for the settlement of disputes

1. The provisions relating to the settlement of disputes set out in Part XV of the [LOS] Convention apply *mutatis mutandis* to any dispute between States

Parties to this Agreement concerning the interpretation or application of this Agreement, whether or not they are also Parties to the [LOS] Convention.

2. The provisions relating to the settlement of disputes set out in Part XV of the [LOS] Convention apply *mutatis mutandis* to any dispute between States Parties to this Agreement concerning the interpretation or application of a subregional, regional or global fisheries agreement relating to straddling fish stocks or highly migratory fish stocks to which they are parties, including any dispute concerning the conservation and management of such stocks, whether or not they are also Parties to the [LOS] Convention.

Notes

1. *The 1995 Fish Stocks Agreement in Context.* The 1995 Fish Stocks Agreement was not the first legally binding post-LOS Convention document in which states sought to remedy overfishing on the high seas. Under the auspices of the FAO, the 1993 FAO Flag State Compliance Agreement had already been adopted. This document only focused on flag state competence. The 1995 Fish Stocks Agreement also contains a part on the duties of the flag state (Part V), but this part contains only one article; flag state control was certainly not the main focus of the 1995 Agreement. How did the 1995 Fish Stocks Agreement try to reconcile the interests of coastal states with those of the distant water fishing fleets? Is the language used in Articles 7(1)(a) and (b) much different from what the LOS Convention provides in Articles 63 and 64? Part III of the 1995 Fish Stocks Agreement is of course new, reflecting an emphasis different from that of the 1993 FAO Flag State Compliance Agreement.

The negotiations leading up to the 1993 FAO Flag State Compliance Agreement and the 1995 Fish Stocks Agreement both found their origin in Chapter 17, programme area C of Agenda 21 adopted by the United Nations Conference on Environment and Development (UNCED), held in Rio de Janeiro in 1992. UN Doc. A/CONF.151.26 (1992). See the fifth recital of the preamble of the 1995 Fish Stocks Agreement. Similarly, the fourth recital of the preamble of the 1993 FAO Flag State Compliance Agreement reads:

> *Recalling* that Agenda 21, adopted by the United Nations Conference on Environment and Development, calls upon States to take effective action, consistent with international law, to deter reflagging of vessels by their nationals as a means of avoiding compliance with applicable conservation and management rules for fishing activities on the high seas[.]

Why did the FAO initiative move faster than the one trying to implement the LOS Convention? The negotiations of the Fish Stocks Agreement lasted until August 1995. When Canada seized the *Estai* in March 1995, the negotiations of the 1995 Fish Stocks Agreement, adopted on August 4, 1995 and opened for signature on December 4, 1995, were in their final phase. The *Estai* incident certainly gave more content to the penultimate preambular paragraph of the 1995 Fish Stocks Agreement.

As mentioned in Chapter 7, port states today are also involved in the fight against what is commonly known as IUU (illegal, unreported, and unregulated) fishing on the high seas. Article 23 of the 1995 Fish Stocks Agreement shows this novel development, which later became the sole focus of a new treaty adopted under the auspices of the FAO, the 2009 Agreement on Port State Measures to Prevent, Deter and Eliminate Illegal, Unreported and Unregulated Fishing. This Agreement has not yet (as of September 2013) entered into force, and we do not further consider it here. By contrast, the 1995 Fish Stocks Agreement numbered 81 parties as of September 1, 2013. Over time, the international community has focused on different mediums or methods to curb IUU fishing on the high seas. Is there a logic to this shift in focus?

2. *Relationship between the 1995 Fish Stocks Agreement and the LOS Convention.* Consider the relationship between the 1995 Fish Stocks Agreement and the LOS Convention as specified in Article 4 of the 1995 Agreement. Part XIII of the 1995 Fish Stocks Agreement, entitled Final Provisions, makes clear that in order to become a party to that treaty, the state, entity, or international organization in question does not have to be a party to the LOS Convention. What is the advantage of not linking the two documents together as far as membership is concerned? Can you think of any disadvantages? Despite this general dissociation, why does the 1995 Agreement's rather elaborate formal title explicitly refer to the LOS Convention? As will be seen in Notes 3 and 4 below, many of the provisions contained in the 1995 Fish Stocks Agreement are rather new. Why does the title nevertheless contain the phrase "Agreement for the Implementation of the Provisions of the [LOS] Convention"? Compare in this respect the 1995 Fish Stocks Agreement with the 1994 Implementation Agreement analyzed in Chapter 11, Section C.

The European Union, which is a party to both the LOS Convention and the 1995 Fish Stocks Agreement, followed a different procedure to join each treaty, which happened on April 1, 1998 and December 19, 2003 respectively. In the case of the LOS Convention the majority of the member states needed to be parties before the European Union could join itself. Council Decision (E.C.) No. 98/392, 1998 O.J.L. 179, 1. The procedure adopted by the Council with respect to the 1995 Agreement was more restrictive:

> The President of the Council shall deposit, on behalf of the European Community, the instrument of ratification and the declaration of competence set out in Annex B to this Decision, together with the interpretative declarations set out in Annex C to this Decision, with the Secretary-General of the United Nations, in accordance with Articles 38, 47 and 49 of the Agreement.
>
> The instrument of ratification shall be deposited simultaneously with the instruments of ratification of all the Member States. At the same time the Member States shall confirm the declarations made by the Community on ratification of the Agreement.

Council Decision (E.C.) No. 98/414, art. 2, 1998 O.J.L. 189, 14. In view of the *Estai* case, how can one explain this difference?

3. *Duty to Cooperate.* In view of the discussion in Chapter 12, Note 5 on the duty to cooperate, why do you believe the negotiators of the 1995 Fish Stocks Agreement went on at such great length in Articles 7 and 8 to specify the framework for that obligation? Explain the relationship between these conventional provisions (also echoed in Articles 5 and 24(2), not excerpted here), and the much more general statement by the ITLOS when deciding on provisional measures in the MOX Plant case, excerpted in Chapter 12, that the duty to cooperate is a "fundamental principle in the prevention of pollution of the marine environment under Part XII of the LOS Convention and general international law." Ireland v. United Kingdom (Provisional Measures), ITLOS Case No. 10 (2001), ¶ 82, available at http://www.itlos.org.

4. *The Status of the Precautionary Approach under Contemporary International Law.* The precautionary approach is not mentioned in the LOS Convention. This should come as no surprise because the precautionary approach only began to be used in legally binding international instruments around the late 1980s and early 1990s. The 1995 Fish Stocks Agreement was one of the first multilateral international agreements to adopt the precautionary approach. As discussed in Note 1, that Agreement had its origins in the 1992 UNCED, and the final outcome of that Conference, namely the Rio Declaration on Environment and Development, contained Principle 15:

> In order to protect the environment, the precautionary approach shall be widely applied by States according to their capabilities. Where there are threats of serious or irreversible damage, lack of full scientific certainty shall not be used as a reason for postponing cost-effective measures to prevent environmental degradation.

UN Doc. A/CONF.151/26/Rev. 1 (Vol. I) (1992), 31 Intl. Leg. Materials 874, 879 (1992). Why does Article 6 of the Fish Stocks Agreement enter into so much detail about the precautionary approach? Annex II provides even more detail on how exactly to establish precautionary reference points.

The ITLOS has come close to embracing the notion of the precautionary approach. When having to decide on provisional measures in the MOX plant dispute, excerpted in Chapter 12, Ireland had raised the issue (¶ 71), while the United Kingdom had argued that it had no application in the case at hand (¶ 75). Because of the U.K.'s assurance that, at least until the arbitral tribunal dealing with the merits of the case was established, there would be no import or export of nuclear fuel to or from Sellafield, the ITLOS did not see the need to rely on this approach. However, the ITLOS had indirectly invoked the precautionary approach in the Southern Bluefin Tuna cases a few years earlier. In those cases the ITLOS found that "the parties should in the circumstances act with prudence and caution to ensure that effective conservation measures are taken to prevent serious harm to the stock of southern bluefin tuna." New Zealand v. Japan; Australia v. Japan, Requests for Provisional Measures, Order of Aug. 27, 1999, ITLOS Cases No. 3 and 4, 3 ITLOS Rep. 280, ¶ 77. The ITLOS, in view of the scientific uncertainty and the impossibility of conclusively assessing the scientific evidence presented by the parties, concluded that urgent measures should nevertheless be taken to avert further deterioration of the stock. (¶¶ 79–80) In these circumstances, did the ITLOS adopt the precautionary approach? In 2011 the Seabed Disputes Chamber of the ITLOS, in its advisory opinion in Responsibilities and Obligations of States Sponsoring Persons and Entities with Respect to Activities in the Area (excerpted in Chapter 11, Section D), noted that "the precautionary approach has been incorporated into a growing number of international treaties and other instruments, many of which reflect the formulation of Principle 15 of the Rio Declaration." The Chamber unanimously found that "this has initiated a trend towards making this approach part of customary international law." ITLOS Case No. 17 (2011), ¶ 135, available at http://www.itlos.org. Is it fair to conclude that the precautionary approach now forms part of customary international law? Legal scholars remain divided on the issue. For an overview, see, e.g., Jonathan B. Wiener, Precaution, in The Oxford Handbook of International Environmental Law 597 (Daniel Bodansky, Jutta Brunnée & Ellen Hey eds., 2007).

Compare the ITLOS's cautious reception of the precautionary approach with the situation in Europe, where the "precautionary principle"—terminology suggesting legal implication—has for some time formed part and parcel of the basic documents of the European Union:

> Union policy on the environment shall aim at a high level of protection taking into account the diversity of situations in the various regions of the Union. It shall be based on the precautionary principle and on the principles that preventive action should be taken, that environmental damage should as a priority be rectified at source and that the polluter should pay.

Treaty on the Functioning of the European Union, Article 191(2); ex Treaty establishing the European Community (as amended by the Treaty of Amsterdam [signed 1997; entered into force 1999] and the Treaty of Nice [signed 2001; entered into force 2003]), Article 174(2); ex Treaty establishing the European Community (as amended by the Treaty of Maastricht [signed 1992; entered into force 1993]), Article 130r(2). Why is the precautionary approach/principle so well established as a legal norm in the European Union, enshrined in its primary law, while still awaiting firm confirmation on the international level?

5. *Compulsory Third-party Dispute Settlement and the 1995 Fish Stocks Agreement.* The LOS Convention does not specify how to resolve conflicts between coastal states and distant water fishing states if they prove unable to "seek... to agree upon" or "cooperate... with a view to ensuring" the conservation of, respectively, the straddling or highly migratory resource in question. LOS Convention, Articles 63–64. Article 7(4) of the 1995 Fish Stocks Agreement, which refers to Part VIII on dispute settlement, tackles this problem. Article 30 of Part VIII contains an interesting technique to alleviate some of the negative consequences of the general dissociation of the Fish Stocks Agreement from the LOS Convention, a point discussed in Note 2. Article 30 of the Agreement incorporates by reference about ten percent of all the articles in the LOS Convention—those found in Part XV on dispute settlement—as well as the Convention's Annexes V–VIII. These LOS Convention provisions become automatically binding on each party to the 1995 Fish Stocks Agreement, even if it is not a party to the LOS Convention. The system of third-party dispute settlement under the LOS Convention is elaborated in Chapter 15.

Will a judge or arbitrator seized with a fishing dispute under the 1995 Fish Stocks Agreement be able to rule on the conservation measures applicable to straddling or highly migratory species in their entire range? Doing so could help ensure the compatibility of conservation and management measures applicable in the EEZ and on the high seas, as envisaged by Article 7 of the Fish Stocks Agreement. Are the automatic exceptions included in Article 297 of the LOS Convention also incorporated by reference in Article 30 of the 1995 Fish Stocks Agreement, or do states agree not to rely on LOS Convention

Article 297(3)(a) when they accept the Fish Stocks Agreement? When you answer this question, consider Article 3 of the Fish Stocks Agreement, which refers in turn to Article 7. What are the implications of your answer for the kind of management measures a judge or arbitrator will be able to prescribe?

C Regional Fishery Management Organizations under Contemporary International Law

The *Estai* dispute and especially the adoption and entry into force of the 1995 Fish Stocks Agreement have substantially altered the modern regime governing RFMOs. In the past these international organizations followed procedures typical of the time they were created. For example, the group of states creating an RFMO would determine its membership, and decisions were usually made behind closed doors based on unanimity. Since the 1990s, however, these organizations have adapted to new circumstances. If RFMOs are to play a central role in curbing IUU fishing on the high seas, they need more authority, as envisaged by the 1995 Fish Stocks Agreement. At the same time they need to become more transparent and to be held accountable for their actions.

Even though the 1995 Fish Stocks Agreement only applies to straddling and highly migratory fish stocks, new RFMOs concerned solely with discrete high seas stocks have used that Agreement as a blueprint for drafting their constitutive documents. Indeed, the Fisheries and Aquaculture Department of the FAO, in its 2012 biennial report on the state of world fisheries, excerpted in Section A, recommended that the best way to tackle the overfishing problem on the high seas is to follow the approach of the 1995 Fish Stocks Agreement for discrete high seas fish stocks, as well as for the straddling and highly migratory fish stocks that are currently covered by that Agreement.

This section takes a close look at the NAFO in order to see how this organization adapted to these new challenges, focusing on NAFO's decision-making procedures, which contributed essentially to the *Estai* dispute. The European Union and Canada, in the wake of the *Estai* incident, were instrumental in modernizing NAFO's founding document via a substantial amendment adopted on September 28, 2008. As of September 1, 2013, this amendment has not entered into force—three-fourths of NAFO member states must first accept it—but many members are considering ratification. We compare decision-making procedures in NAFO's 1978 founding document with the revised procedures called for in the 2008 amended version.

CONVENTION ON FUTURE COOPERATION IN THE NORTHWEST ATLANTIC FISHERIES

Oct. 24, 1978, 1135 U.N.T.S. 369

Article XII

1. If any Commission member presents to the Executive Secretary an objection to a proposal within sixty days of the date of transmittal specified in the notification of the proposal by the Executive Secretary, the proposal shall not become a binding measure until the expiration of forty days following the date of transmittal specified in the notification of that objection to the Contracting Parties. There upon any other Commission member may similarly object prior to the expiration of the additional forty-day period, or within thirty days after the date of transmittal specified in the notification to the Contracting Parties of any objection presented within that additional forty-day period, whichever shall be the later. The proposal shall then become a measure binding on all Contracting Parties, except those which have presented objections, at the end of the extended period or periods for objecting. If, however, at the end of such extended period or periods, objections have been presented and maintained by a majority of Commission members, the proposal shall not become a binding measure, unless any or all of the Commission members nevertheless agree as among themselves to be bound by it on an agreed date.

2. Any Commission member which has objected to a proposal may at any time withdraw that objection and the proposal immediately shall become a measure binding on such a member, subject to the objection procedure provided for in this Article.

3. At any time after the expiration of one year from the date on which a measure enters into force, any Commission member may give to the Executive Secretary notice of its intention not to be bound by the measure, and, if that notice is not withdrawn, the measure shall cease to be binding on that member at the end of one year from the date of receipt of the notice by the Executive Secretary. At any time after a measure has ceased to be binding on a Commission member under this paragraph, the measure shall cease to be binding on any other Commission member upon the date a notice of its intention not to be bound is received by the Executive Secretary.

4. The Executive Secretary shall immediately notify each Contracting Party of:

a) the receipt of each objection and withdrawal of objection under paragraphs 1 and 2;

b) the date on which any proposal becomes a binding measure under the provisions of paragraph 1; and

c) the receipt of each notice under paragraph 3.

Article XIII

1. The membership of the Commission shall be reviewed and determined by the General Council at its annual meeting and shall consist of:

a) each Contracting Party which participates in the fisheries of the Regulatory Area; and

b) any Contracting Party which has provided evidence satisfactory to the General Council that it expects to participate in the fisheries of the Regulatory Area during the year of that annual meeting or during the following calendar year.

2. Each Commission member shall appoint to the Commission not more than three representatives who may be accompanied at any of its meetings by alternates, experts and advisers.

3. Any Contracting Party that is not a Commission member may attend meetings of the Commission as an observer. . . .

Article XIV

1. Each Commission member shall have one vote in proceedings of the Commission.

2. Decisions of the Commission shall be taken by a majority of the votes of all Commission members present and casting affirmative or negative votes, provided that no vote shall be taken unless there is a quorum of at least two-thirds of the Commission members.

AMENDMENT TO THE CONVENTION ON FUTURE COOPERATION IN THE NORTHWEST ATLANTIC FISHERIES

Sept. 28, 2008, NAFO/GC Doc. 07/4, http://www.nafo.int/publications/amend-convention.html

Article XIII: Decision Making of the Commission

1. As a general rule, decision-making within the Commission shall be by consensus. For the purposes of this Article, "consensus" means the absence of any formal objection made at the time the decision was taken.

2. If the Chairperson considers that all efforts to reach consensus have been exhausted, decisions of the Commission shall, except where otherwise provided, be taken by two-thirds majority of the votes of all Contracting Parties present and casting affirmative or negative votes, provided that no vote shall be taken unless there is a quorum of at least two-thirds of the Contracting Parties. Each Contracting Party shall have one vote.

Article XIV: Implementation of Commission Decisions

1. Each measure adopted by the Commission pursuant to Article VI, paragraphs 8 [adoption by the Commission of conservation and management measures, TACs, and other measures in relation to the Regulatory Area] and 9 [adoption by the Commission of cooperative mechanisms for effective monitoring, control, surveillance, and enforcement of the conservation and management measures] shall become binding on each Contracting Party in the following manner:

(a) the Executive Secretary shall within five working days of adoption transmit the measure to each Contracting Party specifying the date of transmittal for the purposes of paragraph 2; and

(b) subject to paragraph 2, unless otherwise specified in the measure, it shall become binding on each Contracting Party sixty days following the date of transmittal.

2. Where any Contracting Party presents an objection to a measure by delivering it to the Executive Secretary within sixty days of the date of transmittal specified pursuant to subparagraph 1(a), any other Contracting Party may similarly present an objection prior to the expiration of an additional twenty day period, or within fifteen days after the date of transmittal specified in the notification to the Contracting Parties of any objection presented within that additional twenty day period, whichever shall be later. The measure shall then become binding on each Contracting Party, except any that has presented an objection. If, however, at the end of such extended period or periods, objections have been presented and maintained by a majority of Contracting Parties, the measure shall not become binding, unless any or all of the Contracting Parties nevertheless agree as among themselves to be bound by it on an agreed date.

3. Any Contracting Party that has presented an objection may withdraw it at any time and the measure shall then become binding on it.

4.

(a) Any time after the expiration of one year from the date on which a measure enters into force, any Contracting Party may notify the Executive Secretary of its intention not to be bound by the measure and, if that notification is not withdrawn, the measure shall cease to be binding on it at the end of one year from the date of receipt of such notification by the Executive Secretary.

(b) Any time after a measure has ceased to be binding on a Contracting Party pursuant to subparagraph (a), the measure shall cease to be binding on any other Contracting Party on the date the Executive Secretary receives notification of its intention not to be bound.

5. Any Contracting Party that has presented an objection to a measure pursuant to paragraph 2 or given notification of its intention not to be bound by a measure pursuant to paragraph 4 shall at the same time provide an explanation for its reasons for taking this action. This explanation shall specify whether it considers that the measure is inconsistent with the provisions of this Convention, or that the measure unjustifiably discriminates in form or fact against it. The explanation shall also include a declaration of the actions it intends to take following the objection or -notification, including a description of the alternative measures it intends to take or has taken for conservation and management of the relevant fishery resources consistent with the objective of this Convention.

6. The Executive Secretary shall immediately notify each Contracting Party of:

(a) the receipt or withdrawal of any objection pursuant to paragraph 2 or 3;

(b) the date on which any measure becomes binding pursuant to paragraph 1;

(c) the receipt of any notification pursuant to paragraph 4; and

(d) each explanation and description of alternative measures received pursuant to paragraph 5.

7. Any Contracting Party that invokes the procedure set out in paragraphs 2, 4 or 5, may at the same time submit the matter to *ad hoc* panel proceedings. Annex II shall apply *mutatis mutandis*.

8. Where a Contracting Party does not submit the matter to *ad hoc* panel proceedings pursuant to paragraph 7, the Commission shall decide by simple majority mail vote, whether to submit that Contracting Party's explanation made pursuant to paragraph 5 to such proceedings. Where the Commission decides to submit the matter to such proceedings, Annex II [entitled "Rules concerning the *ad hoc* panel procedure pursuant to Article XV"] shall apply *mutatis mutandis*.

9. Where, pursuant to paragraph 8, the Commission decides not to submit the matter to *ad hoc* panel proceedings, any Contracting Party may request a meeting of the Commission to review the measure adopted by the Commission and the explanation made pursuant to paragraph 5.

10. An *ad hoc* panel constituted pursuant to paragraph 7 or 8 shall review the explanation made pursuant to paragraph 5 and the measure to which it relates and make recommendations to the Commission on:

(a) whether the explanation provided by the Contracting Party pursuant to paragraph 5 is well founded, and if so, whether the measure should accordingly be modified or rescinded, or where it finds that the explanation is not well founded, whether the measure should be maintained; and

(b) whether the alternative measures set out in the explanation made by the Contracting Party pursuant to paragraph 5 are consistent with the objective of this Convention and preserve the respective rights of all Contracting Parties.

11. No later than thirty days following the termination of the *ad hoc* panel proceedings pursuant to this Article, the Commission shall meet to consider the recommendations of the *ad hoc* panel.

12. Where the procedures set out in paragraphs 7 to 11 have been concluded, any Contracting Party may invoke the dispute settlement procedures set out in Article XV.

Article XV: Settlement of Disputes

1. Contracting Parties shall co-operate in order to prevent disputes.

2. Where a dispute arises between two or more Contracting Parties concerning the interpretation or application of this Convention, including the explanation referred to in Article XIV, paragraph 5, any actions taken by a Contracting Party following an objection presented pursuant to Article XIV, paragraph 2, or any notification made pursuant of Article XIV, paragraph 4, those Contracting Parties, hereinafter referred to as "Contracting Parties to the dispute," shall seek to resolve their dispute by negotiation, inquiry, mediation, conciliation, arbitration, judicial settlement, *ad hoc* panel proceedings or other peaceful means of their choice.

3. Where a dispute concerns the interpretation or application of a measure adopted by the Commission pursuant to Article VI, paragraph 8 and 9, or matters related thereto, including the explanation referred to in Article XIV, paragraph 5, any actions taken by a Contracting Party to the dispute following an objection presented pursuant to Article XIV, paragraph 2, or notification made pursuant to Article XIV, paragraph 4, the Contracting Parties to the dispute may submit the dispute to non binding *ad hoc* panel proceedings pursuant to Annex II.

4. Where a dispute has been submitted to *ad hoc* panel proceedings, the *ad hoc* panel shall at the earliest opportunity confer with the Contracting Parties to the dispute with a view to resolving the dispute expeditiously. The *ad hoc* panel shall present a report to the Contracting Parties to the dispute and through the Executive Secretary to the other Contracting Parties. The report shall include any recommendations that the *ad hoc* panel considers appropriate to resolve the dispute.

5. Where the Contracting Parties to the dispute accept the recommendations of the *ad hoc* panel, they shall within fourteen days of receipt of the report of the *ad hoc* panel notify all other Contracting Parties, through the Executive Secretary, of the actions they intend to take with a view to implementing the recommendations. Thereupon, the recommendations of the *ad hoc* panel may be referred for consideration by the Commission in accordance with its appropriate procedures.

6. Where no settlement has been reached following the recommendations of the *ad hoc* panel, any of the Contracting Parties to the dispute may submit the dispute to compulsory proceedings entailing binding decisions pursuant to Section 2 of Part XV of the [LOS] Convention or Part VIII of the 1995 [Fish Stocks Agreement].

7. Where the Contracting Parties to a dispute have agreed to submit the dispute to *ad hoc* panel proceedings, they may at the same time agree to apply provisionally the relevant measure adopted by the Commission until the report of the *ad hoc* panel is presented unless they have settled the dispute by other means.

8. Where the Contracting Parties to a dispute are unable to agree on any peaceful means referred to in paragraph 2 to resolve their dispute or are unable to otherwise reach a settlement, the dispute shall at the request of one of them, be submitted to compulsory proceedings entailing a binding decision pursuant to Part XV, Section 2, of the [LOS] Convention or Part VIII of the 1995 [Fish Stocks Agreement].

9. Where recourse is made to compulsory proceedings entailing binding decisions, the Contracting Parties to the dispute shall, unless they agree otherwise, provisionally apply any recommendation made by the *ad hoc* panel pursuant to paragraph 4 or, where applicable, pursuant to Article XIV, paragraph 10. They shall continue to apply such provisional measures or any arrangements of equivalent effect agreed between them until a court or tribunal having jurisdiction over the dispute prescribes provisional measures or renders a decision, or, until the expiration of the measure in question.

10. The notification provisions of paragraph 5 shall apply *mutatis mutandis* with respect to provisional measures applied pursuant to paragraph 7 or prescribed pursuant to paragraph 9 or to any decision of a court or tribunal to which the dispute has been submitted.

11. A court, tribunal or *ad hoc* panel to which a dispute has been submitted pursuant to this Article shall apply the relevant provisions of this Convention, the [LOS] Convention, the 1995 [Fish Stocks Agreement], generally accepted standards for the conservation and management of living resources and other

rules of international law not incompatible with this Convention with a view to attaining the objective of this Convention.

12. Nothing in this Convention shall be argued or construed to prevent a Contracting Party to a dispute, as State Party to the [LOS] Convention, from submitting the dispute to compulsory procedures entailing binding decisions against another State Party pursuant to Section 2 of Part XV of the [LOS] Convention, or as State Party to the 1995 [Fish Stocks Agreement] from submitting the dispute to compulsory procedures entailing binding decisions against another State Party pursuant to Article 30 of the 1995 [Fish Stocks Agreement].

Notes

1. *Opting-out Procedures in Contemporary RFMOs*. Decision making of the NAFO Commission was a major point of contention between Canada and the European Union at the time of the *Estai* crisis. As Canada stressed in its pleadings before the ICJ in the Fisheries Jurisdiction case excerpted in Section B, the European Union had made use of the opting-out clause in Article XII of the 1978 Convention on almost 50 occasions between 1985 and 1991 in order to exceed NAFO-recommended quotas. Counter-Memorial of Canada, Fisheries Jurisdiction Case, Spain v. Canada, Feb. 1996, 13. In comparison to many other RFMOs, the NAFO is of rather recent origin. Its founding document did not contain the traditional unanimity voting clause. What exactly is the voting procedure in the Commission, and why was the opting-out clause necessary? Consider the sequence of articles in the 1978 Convention when assessing the importance of the opting-out clause.

Under the 2008 NAFO amendment, may states still opt out? What is new in that amendment? Is the ad hoc panel a dispute settlement body entitled to make binding decisions? Why does the 2008 version contain a complex and lengthy article on dispute settlement, whereas no such article appears in the original 1978 text? Had these amendments been in force in at the time of the *Estai* dispute, could the European Union have unilaterally defied the decisions taken by the NAFO Commission?

2. *NAFO's Contributions to RFMO Developments*. The goal of the ad hoc panel is to curb the discretionary power of a member state willing to opt out of a management or conservation measure adopted by the NAFO Commission. This ad hoc panel seems to have been a crucial factor in the envisaged 2008 modernization of the organization. Since the 2008 amendment has not, as of September 1, 2013, entered into force, the ad hoc panel process has not yet been tested in practice. It nevertheless has served as an example for certain other RFMOs established later. Compare for instance this 2008 NAFO amend-

ment, the negotiations for which began in 2005, with the 2009 Convention on South Pacific High Seas Fishery Resources. The articles in both documents on decision making and on implementing decisions exhibit common features, among them an intermediate body between the member states and a commission deciding on conservation and management measures, called the Review Panel in the case of the 2009 Convention on South Pacific High Seas Fishery Resources. A lengthy Annex II specifies the modus operandi of this Review Panel in great detail.

The first Review Panel constituted under the 2009 Convention on South Pacific High Seas Fishery Resources recently concluded that a Commission decision had discriminated against Russia, one of the Convention's member states. The Panel also found that the alternative measures proposed by Russia were not equivalent to the Commission's decision. The Panel instead recommended alternative measures, different from those Russia had proposed. Review Panel established under the Convention on the Conservation and Management of High Seas Fishery Resources in the South Pacific Ocean, Findings and Recommendations of July 5, 2013, http://www.pca-cpa.org/showpage.asp?pag_id=1520. What happens next? In such a case Annex II provides that

> the objecting member or members of the Commission shall, within 60 days, adopt measures recommended by the Review Panel as equivalent in effect to the decision to which objection has been presented or institute dispute settlement proceedings under this Convention. If the objecting member or members of the Commission adopt the measures recommended by the Review Panel these measures shall be deemed to be binding on the objecting member or members of the Commission in substitution for the decision. If the objecting member or members of the Commission choose to institute dispute settlement proceedings under this Convention then neither the decision nor any measures recommended by the Review Panel shall be binding on the objecting member or members of the Commission pending decisions made in those proceedings.

What are the advantages of such a strict regulation? In this instance, some of the facts of the case predate the Convention's entry into force on August 24, 2012, indicating the immediate interest generated by this new procedure. Why do member states apparently find this procedure more appealing than immediate recourse to third-party dispute settlement?

3. *Further Adaptation of the NAFO to Contemporary International Law Governing RFMOs*. The modified Commission decision-making procedures were not the only significant changes made in the 2008 NAFO amendment. The NAFO made additional changes in its founding document to accommodate new developments in international fisheries law. A good example is the acceptance of the precautionary approach, which had been included in the 1995 Fish Stocks Agreement, as discussed in Section B. Article III(c) of the 2008 NAFO amendment provides that one of the general principles that the contracting parties must apply when giving effect to the objective of the Convention is "the precautionary approach in accordance with Article 6 of the 1995 Agreement." Will this requirement also apply to a NAFO member that is not a party to the 1995 Fish Stocks Agreement, such as Cuba?

The NAFO has also agreed to a performance review conducted by four internal and three external experts. Their report was published on August 5, 2011. NAFO Performance Assessment Review 2011, http://www.nafo.int/publications/PAR-2011.pdf. Such periodic reviews are now envisaged by Article XVIII of the 2008 NAFO amendment. Why did the U.N. General Assembly in its 2006 resolution on sustainable fisheries encourage states to initiate performance review processes in RFMOs in which they were members? Sustainable Fisheries, Including through the [1995 Fish Stocks Agreement] and Related Instruments, UN Doc. A/RES/60/31, ¶ 60 (2006). What are the anticipated benefits of such reviews?

CHAPTER 14

Maritime Terrorism and Security

The dawn of modern-day maritime terrorism arose in October 1985, when members of the Palestine Liberation Front (PLF) boarded an Italian cruise ship as passengers and seized control of the vessel while it was sailing in the Mediterranean Sea. They threatened to destroy the ship, the *Achille Lauro*, its crew, and its passengers unless Israel released certain Palestinian prisoners. When Israel refused to accede to their demands, the terrorists killed an invalid Jewish-American passenger and threw his body and wheelchair overboard. Although the 1982 United Nations Convention on the Law of the Sea (LOS Convention) has provisions concerning several common crimes committed on the seas, including piracy, the slave trade, and illicit drug trafficking, the Convention did not sufficiently address acts of maritime terrorism that emerged after it had been signed.

This chapter discusses the measures states have developed over the past few decades to prevent maritime terrorism and to secure the safety of navigation. Section A reviews a call for action by the U.N. General Assembly, several conventions promulgated under the auspices of the International Maritime Organization (IMO), and the implementation of those conventions by states. The conventions respond to security risks facing vessels and other aspects of the complex maritime domain, including cargos, crews, and ports. Section B analyzes voluntary efforts undertaken by states, including the Proliferation Security Initiative, an informal cooperative framework initiated by the United States and widely (but not universally) endorsed by other countries.

A International Conventions Addressing Maritime Security

UNITED NATIONS GENERAL ASSEMBLY RESOLUTION 40/61
UN Doc. A/RES/40/61 (1985)

The General Assembly...

Deeply concerned about the world-wide escalation of acts of terrorism in all its forms, which endanger or take innocent human lives, jeopardize fundamental freedoms and seriously impair the dignity of human beings, ...

 | DOI 10.1163/9789004203563_015

Convinced of the importance of expanding and improving international co-operation among States, on a bilateral and multilateral basis, which will contribute to the elimination of acts of international terrorism and their underlying causes and to the prevention and elimination of this criminal scourge, . . .

1. *Unequivocally condemns*, as criminal, all acts, methods and practices of terrorism wherever and by whomever committed, including those which jeopardize friendly relations among States and their security;

2. *Deeply deplores* the loss of innocent human lives which results from such acts of terrorism;

3. *Also deplores* the pernicious impact of acts of international terrorism on relations of co-operation among States, including co-operation for development;

4. *Appeals* to all States that have not yet done so to consider becoming party to the existing international conventions relating to various aspects of international terrorism;

5. *Invites* all States to take all appropriate measures at the national level with a view to the speedy and final elimination of the problem of international terrorism, such as the harmonization of domestic legislation with existing international conventions, the fulfilment of assumed international obligations, and the prevention of the preparation and organization in their respective territories of acts directed against other States;

6. *Calls upon* all States to fulfil their obligations under international law to refrain from organizing, instigating, assisting or participating in terrorist acts in other States, or acquiescing in activities within their territory directed towards the commission of such acts;

7. *Urges* all States not to allow any circumstances to obstruct the application of appropriate law enforcement measures provided for in the relevant conventions to which they are party to persons who commit acts of international terrorism covered by those conventions;

8. *Also urges* all States to co-operate with one another more closely, especially through the exchange of relevant information concerning the prevention and combating of terrorism, the apprehension and prosecution or extradition of the perpetrators of such acts, the conclusion of special treaties and/or the incorporation into appropriate bilateral treaties of special clauses, in particular regarding the extradition or prosecution of terrorists;

9. *Further urges* all States, unilaterally and in co-operation with other States, as well as relevant United Nations organs, to contribute to the progressive elimination of the causes underlying international terrorism and to pay

special attention to all situations, including colonialism, racism and situations involving mass and flagrant violations of human rights and fundamental freedoms and those involving alien occupation, that may give rise to international terrorism and may endanger international peace and security;...

13. *Requests* the International Maritime Organization to study the problem of terrorism aboard or against ships with a view to making recommendations on appropriate measures[.]

Notes

1. *International Response to the* Achille Lauro *Incident.* U.N. General Assembly Resolution 40/61 was adopted by consensus in December 1985 in response to the *Achille Lauro* incident, and specifically condemns acts of terrorism as criminal. The IMO Assembly had previously adopted in November 1985 a resolution on "[m]easures to prevent unlawful acts [that] threaten the safety of ships and the security of their passengers and crews," which directed the IMO Maritime Safety Committee, in cooperation with other IMO committees, "to develop, on a priority basis, detailed and practical technical measures, including both shoreside and shipboard measures, which may be employed by Governments, port authorities and administrations, ship owners, ship operators, shipmasters and crews to ensure the security of passengers and crews on board ships." IMO Doc. A.584(14) (1985). In 1986, the IMO Maritime Safety Committee issued detailed, non-binding guidelines recommending that states implement a variety of preventive measures, including strengthened security in ports and on board ships, and control of access to vessels whether at sea or in port. IMO Doc. MSC/Circ.443 (1986). Additionally, the IMO Council established an Ad Hoc Preparatory Committee that began work on a comprehensive multilateral convention to address maritime security.

2. *Limitations of the LOS Convention's Definition of Piracy.* The United States charged the PLF members who hijacked the *Achille Lauro* with the crime of "piracy as defined by the law of nations." Criminal Complaint, United States v. Abu el-Abas (Misc. 85-0321, D.D.C.), 24 Intl. Leg. Materials 1553 (1985). Read again the definition of piracy found at LOS Convention, Article 101, and recall the materials on piracy in Chapter 4, Section D.1. If you were an attorney representing the hijackers, what arguments would you present to persuade a court that the activities of the hijackers did not constitute piracy? What other crimes might the PLF members have been charged with, and what countries would have had a jurisdictional basis to bring such charges?

CONVENTION FOR THE SUPPRESSION OF UNLAWFUL ACTS OF VIOLENCE AGAINST THE SAFETY OF MARITIME NAVIGATION (SUA CONVENTION)
1988 U.S.T. 198, 1678 U.N.T.S. 222, 27 Intl. Leg. Materials 668 (1988)

Article 3

1. Any person commits an offence if that person unlawfully and intentionally:

a. seizes or exercises control over a ship by force or threat thereof or any other form of intimidation; or

b. performs an act of violence against a person on board a ship if that act is likely to endanger the safe navigation of that ship; or

c. destroys a ship or causes damage to a ship or to its cargo which is likely to endanger the safe navigation of that ship; or

d. places or causes to be placed on a ship, by any means whatsoever, a device or substance which is likely to destroy that ship, or cause damage to that ship or its cargo which endangers or is likely to endanger the safe navigation of that ship; or

e. destroys or seriously damages maritime navigational facilities or seriously interferes with their operation, if any such act is likely to endanger the safe navigation of a ship; or

f. communicates information which he knows to be false, thereby endangering the safe navigation of a ship; or

g. injures or kills any person, in connection with the commission or the attempted commission of any of the offences set forth in subparagraphs (a) to (f).

2. Any person also commits an offence if that person:

a. attempts to commit any of the offences set forth in paragraph 1; or

b. abets the commission of any of the offences set forth in paragraph 1 perpetrated by any person or is otherwise an accomplice of a person who commits such an offence; or

c. threatens, with or without a condition, as is provided for under national law, aimed at compelling a physical or juridical person to do or refrain from doing any act, to commit any of the offences set forth in paragraph 1, subparagraphs (b), (c) and (e), if that threat is likely to endanger the safe navigation of the ship in question.

Article 4

1. This Convention applies if the ship is navigating or is scheduled to navigate into, through or from waters beyond the outer limit of the territorial sea of a single State, or the lateral limits of its territorial sea with adjacent States.

2. In cases where the Convention does not apply pursuant to paragraph 1, it nevertheless applies when the offender or the alleged offender is found in the territory of a State Party other than the State referred to in paragraph 1.

Article 5

Each State Party shall make the offences set forth in article 3 punishable by appropriate penalties which take into account the grave nature of those offences.

Article 6

1. Each State Party shall take such measures as may be necessary to establish its jurisdiction over the offences set forth in article 3 when the offence is committed:

a. against or on board a ship flying the flag of the State at the time the offence is committed; or

b. in the territory of that State, including its territorial sea; or

c. by a national of that State.

2. A State Party may also establish its jurisdiction over any such offence when:

a. it is committed by a stateless person whose habitual residence is in that State; or

b. during its commission a national of that State is seized, threatened, injured or killed; or

c. it is committed in an attempt to compel that State to do or abstain from doing any act.

3. Any State Party which has established jurisdiction mentioned in paragraph 2 shall notify the Secretary-General of the International Maritime Organization (hereinafter referred to as "the Secretary-General"). If such State Party subsequently rescinds that jurisdiction, it shall notify the Secretary-General.

4. Each State Party shall take such measures as may be necessary to establish its jurisdiction over the offences set forth in article 3 in cases where the

alleged offender is present in its territory and it does not extradite him to any of the States Parties which have established their jurisdiction in accordance with paragraphs 1 and 2 of this article.

5. This Convention does not exclude any criminal jurisdiction exercised in accordance with national law.

Article 7

1. Upon being satisfied that the circumstances so warrant, any State Party in the territory of which the offender or the alleged offender is present shall, in accordance with its law, take him into custody or take other measures to ensure his presence for such time as is necessary to enable any criminal or extradition proceedings to be instituted....

Article 10

1. The State Party in the territory of which the offender or the alleged offender is found shall, in cases to which article 6 applies, if it does not extradite him, be obliged, without exception whatsoever and whether or not the offence was committed in its territory, to submit the case without delay to its competent authorities for the purpose of prosecution, through proceedings in accordance with the laws of that State. Those authorities shall take their decision in the same manner as in the case of any other offence of a grave nature under the law of that State.

2. Any person regarding whom proceedings are being carried out in connection with any of the offences set forth in article 3 shall be guaranteed fair treatment at all stages of the proceedings, including enjoyment of all the rights and guarantees provided for such proceedings by the law of the State in the territory of which he is present.

Article 11

1. The offences set forth in article 3 shall be deemed to be included as extraditable offences in any extradition treaty existing between any of the States Parties. States Parties undertake to include such offences as extraditable offences in every extradition treaty to be concluded between them.

2. If a State Party which makes extradition conditional on the existence of a treaty receives a request for extradition from another State Party with which it has no extradition treaty, the requested State Party may, at its option, consider this Convention as a legal basis for extradition in respect of the offences set forth in article 3. Extradition shall be subject to the other conditions provided by the law of the requested State Party....

Article 13

1. States Parties shall co-operate in the prevention of the offences set forth in article 3, particularly by:

a. taking all practicable measures to prevent preparations in their respective territories for the commission of those offences within or outside their territories;

b. exchanging information in accordance with their national law, and coordinating administrative and other measures taken as appropriate to prevent the commission of offences set forth in article 3.

2. When, due to the commission of an offence set forth in article 3, the passage of a ship has been delayed or interrupted, any State Party in whose territory the ship or passengers or crew are present shall be bound to exercise all possible efforts to avoid a ship, its passengers, crew or cargo being unduly detained or delayed....

Notes

1. *Approval of the SUA Convention.* The Convention for the Suppression of Unlawful Acts against the Safety of Maritime Navigation (SUA Convention) and the related optional Protocol for the Suppression of Unlawful Acts against the Safety of Fixed Platforms were approved on March 10, 1988, at a diplomatic conference held at Rome. The 1988 SUA Convention parallels the 1970 Hague Convention for the Suppression of Unlawful Seizure of Aircraft and the 1971 Montreal Convention for the Suppression of Unlawful Acts Against the Safety of Civil Aviation. As of September 1, 2013, there were 161 parties to the 1988 SUA Convention, representing 94.51% of world tonnage, and 149 parties to the 1988 Fixed Platforms Protocol, representing 88.51% of world tonnage. Both treaties entered into force in 1992.

2. *What Constitutes Maritime Terrorism*? The SUA Convention does not define "maritime terrorism" nor even use the terms "terrorism" or "terrorist." Instead, it establishes several punishable offenses under Article 3. What difficulties might have been encountered if the IMO's Ad Hoc Preparatory Committee had attempted to define "maritime terrorism" in the SUA Convention? Is there an accepted definition of "terrorism" under customary international law? In 2011, the Special Tribunal for Lebanon, established by the U.N. Security Council in 2007 to prosecute persons responsible for the 2005 assassination of Lebanese Prime Minister Rafiq Hariri and others, issued a unanimous ruling addressing this question:

> 83. The Defence Office and the Prosecutor both forcefully assert that there is currently no settled definition of terrorism under customary international law. However, although it is held by many scholars and other legal experts that no widely accepted definition of terrorism has evolved in the world society because of the marked difference of views on some issues, closer scrutiny demonstrates that in fact such a definition has gradually emerged. . . .
>
> 85. As we shall see, a number of treaties, UN resolutions, and the legislative and judicial practice of States evince the formation of a general *opinio juris* in the international community, accompanied by a practice consistent with such *opinio*, to the effect that a customary rule of international law regarding the international crime of terrorism, at least *in time of peace*, has indeed emerged. This customary rule requires the following three key elements: (i) the perpetration of a criminal act (such as murder, kidnapping, hostage-taking, arson, and so on), or threatening such an act; (ii) the intent to spread fear among the population (which would generally entail the creation of public danger) or directly or indirectly coerce a national or international authority to take some action, or to refrain from taking it; (iii) when the act involves a transnational element.

Interlocutory Decision on the Applicable Law: Terrorism, Conspiracy, Homicide, Perpetration, Cumulative Charging, Case No. STL-11-01/I (Feb. 16, 2011), available at http://www.stl-tsl.org. Review the types of offenses that are punishable under Article 3 of the SUA Convention. Are there acts of violence that would fall under Article 3, but would not meet all of the elements of terrorism as defined by the Tribunal? Must there be an underlying political or ideological purpose to satisfy the Tribunal's element of "intent to spread fear among the population"? To constitute an offense under Article 3? In United States v. Shi, 525 F.3d 709 (9th Cir. 2008), a Chinese national who served as a cook on a Taiwanese-owned, Seychelles-flagged, Chinese-crewed fishing vessel was convicted in U.S. federal court under 18 U.S.C. § 2800 (implementing the SUA Convention) for killing two officers and ordering the remaining crew to sail back to their home port in China. Would this act constitute an act of terrorism as defined by the Tribunal?

3. *Acts Undertaken on behalf of Governments or against Governments*. Only offenses that are undertaken "unlawfully" and "intentionally" by persons are punishable under Article 3 of the SUA Convention. Would the "unlawful" requirement be met if a government employee were to commit one of the described acts while carrying out orders on behalf of the government?

Article 2 provides that the SUA Convention does not apply to warships and ships owned or operated by a state when being used as a naval auxiliary or for customs or police purposes. In October 2000, a U.S. naval vessel, the *U.S.S. Cole*, was attacked by a skiff manned by two militants linked to al-Qaida while it was refueling off of the coast of Yemen, resulting in the deaths of seventeen sailors. Would this attack against a government warship be punishable under the SUA Convention? If not, what reasons support excluding from the SUA Convention offenses directed toward a warship? What other criminal charges might be brought against the attackers?

Article 2 also specifies that the SUA Convention does not affect the immunities of warships and other government ships operated for non-commercial purposes.

4. *The Geographical Scope of the SUA Convention and Flag State Jurisdiction.* The SUA Convention has a broad geographical scope, applying to all ships (other than warships and certain other government ships as discussed in Note 3) that are navigating or scheduled to navigate beyond the territorial waters of a single state. Notably, however, Article 9 of the Convention preserves traditional rules concerning jurisdiction to enforce with respect to foreign flag vessels: "Nothing in this Convention shall affect in any way the rules of international law pertaining to the competence of States to exercise investigative or enforcement jurisdiction on board ships not flying their flag." Although Article 110 of the LOS Convention recognizes that the right of visit may be established by treaty, the SUA Convention does not create such a right.

5. *Appropriate Penalties and the Obligation to Extradite or Prosecute.* Parties are obligated under Article 5 to make the offenses described in Article 3 punishable by "appropriate penalties." Article 6 establishes two types of jurisdiction: mandatory and discretionary. In what instances must a state adopt measures that authorize it to exercise jurisdiction over an offender? When is the exercise of jurisdiction by a state party optional?

Article 10 of the SUA Convention incorporates an obligation to either extradite or prosecute an offender. Under Article 11, all offenses described in Article 3 are deemed to be extraditable offenses under extradition treaties in force between state parties. In the absence of an existing extradition treaty between a requesting and requested state party, the latter has the option to consider the SUA Convention as a legal basis for extradition.

Read Article 6(4) and Article 10(1). If an offender is present within the territory of a state party, is the state party obligated to prosecute the offender if no other state party has requested extradition, even though the jurisdictional connections specified in Articles 6(1) or (2) are not met? What if an offender is forcibly brought into the territory of a state party? These issues are discussed in the following case.

UNITED STATES V. SHIBIN
2012 U.S. Dist. LEXIS 97921 (E.D. Va. 2012), aff'd, 722 F.3d 233 (4th Cir. 2013)

[In May 2010, a group of Somali nationals seized a German vessel, the *Marida Marguerite*, on the high seas off of the coast of Somalia and held its crew members hostage. Defendant Shibin was not involved in the original attack, but was alleged to have boarded the *Marida Marguerite* following its seizure where he served for several months as a translator to facilitate negotiations for the crew members' ransom. The defendant allegedly received a share of ransom as compensation. In 2011, a U.S. federal grand jury returned an indictment against the defendant for violating, among other statutes, the U.S. statute implementing the SUA Convention (18 U.S.C. § 2280). While the defendant was in Somalia, and without a formal extradition request, the Somali police force delivered the defendant into the custody of agents of the U.S. Federal Bureau of Investigation (FBI), who subsequently transported him to the United States against his will. Prior to trial, the defendant sought to dismiss the criminal charges brought against him, alleging (among other reasons) that the United States lacked jurisdiction to prosecute him.]

Opinion by JUDGE DOUMAR

... Defendant's jurisdictional challenge can be summarized as follows: (i) the facts alleged in the Superseding Indictment do not satisfy the elements of piracy under 18 U.S.C. § 1651; (ii) therefore, universal jurisdiction does not exist to cover his alleged conduct; (iii) even if the Court finds that the facts alleged are sufficient to proceed on the piracy charges, the failure of the United States to formally extradite Defendant defeats jurisdiction; and (iv) even if the Court finds that universal jurisdiction applies to this case, certain charges against Defendant do not fall under the umbrella of universal jurisdiction, and are thus not properly before the Court....

Defendant[] challenges the Court's jurisdiction over the charges of Violence Against Maritime Navigation, in violation of 18 U.S.C. § 2280(a)(1)(A) and Hostage Taking, in violation of 18 U.S.C. § 1203(a). First, Defendant claims that these crimes do not fall under the umbrella of universal jurisdiction. Second, Defendant argues that that the failure of the United States to formally extradite Defendant to the United States defeats any claim to jurisdiction that this Court has over Defendant's prosecution. Specifically,

Defendant contends that the United States violated the Convention for the Suppression of Unlawful Acts of Violence Against the Safety of Maritime Navigation ("SUA Convention") and the International Convention Against the Taking of Hostages ("Convention Against Hostages"), because it did not request formal extradition from Somalia.

1. Violence Against Maritime Navigation

Defendant urges the Court to reject recent precedent from outside of this Circuit, see United States v. Shi, 525 F.3d 709 (9th Cir. 2008), and to hold that the doctrine of universal jurisdiction does not cover violations of 18 U.S.C. § 2280. To the Court's knowledge, the Fourth Circuit has not settled the question of whether the doctrine of universal jurisdiction covers conduct which extends beyond piracy, as proscribed by 18 U.S.C. § 1651. However, the Court need not reach this inquiry, because the statutory text of § 2280 itself supplies an adequate basis for jurisdiction over the charges now at issue. Because the statute provides an independent jurisdictional ground, Defendant's contention that customary international law does not extend universal jurisdiction over the charges at issue is inapposite. See United States v. Yousef, 327 F.3d 56, 91 (2d Cir. 2003) ("[I]rrespective of whether customary international law provides a basis for jurisdiction over [defendant]... United States law provides a separate and complete basis for jurisdiction over each of these counts and... United States law is not subordinate to customary international law...").

Domestic criminal laws may proscribe conduct which exceeds the scope of customary international law so long as such laws are clear in their extraterritorial scope and enacted pursuant to a constitutional exercise of Congressional power. United States v. Erdos, 474 F.2d 157, 159 (4th Cir. 1973). Courts should use caution in giving criminal laws extraterritorial effect absent a clear congressional directive. But "in fashioning the reach of [domestic] criminal law, 'Congress is not bound by international law'... 'If it choose to do so, it may legislate with respect to conduct outside the United States, in excess of the limits posed by international law.'" Yousef, 327 F.3d at 86 (internal citations omitted). Therefore, so long as § 2280 contains a clear manifestation of Congress' intent that the Act apply extraterritorially, and so long as Congress has the authority to apply the statute beyond United States borders, jurisdiction in this Court is proper. Id. ("As long as Congress has indicated its intent to reach [extraterritorial] conduct, a United States court is 'bound to follow the Congressional direction unless this would violate the due process clause of the Fifth Amendment'") (internal citations omitted).

To determine whether these criteria are satisfied here, we begin by looking to the text of the statute at issue. 18 U.S.C. § 2280(a) provides, in pertinent part, "A person who unlawfully and intentionally ... seizes or exercises control over a ship by force or threat thereof or any other form of intimidation ... [shall be liable under this title]." 18 U.S.C. § 2280(a)(1)(A). 18 U.S.C. § 2280(b), in turn, provides that there is jurisdiction over the conduct proscribed in § 2280(a) "in the case of a covered ship" if the ship flies the flag of the United States, the conduct is committed in the United States, a United States citizen is "seized, threatened, injured or killed" during the conduct, or the offender is "later found in the United States after such activity is committed." 18 U.S.C. §§ 2280(b)(1)(A)(i)–(ii), (b)(1)(B), (b)(1)(C). "A covered ship" is defined to include "a ship that is navigating or is scheduled to navigate into, through or from waters beyond the outer limit of the territorial sea of a single country." 18 U.S.C. § 2280(e). [T]he *Marida Marguerite* [is] alleged to have navigated in international waters beyond the outer limit of the territorial sea of a single country, and thus qualifies as a "covered ship" for the purposes of deciding the present motion.

That § 2280(b)(1)(A)(ii) grants jurisdiction over acts against maritime violence "if such activity is committed ... in the United States" but also provides four additional, independent conditions giving rise to jurisdiction clearly evinces congressional intent that the Act have extraterritorial reach. Congress' authority to give § 2280 extraterritorial reach is also manifest.... Congress enacted § 2280 in order to codify the United States' obligations under the SUA Convention. Such exercise of legislative authority is justified both by the Define and Punish Clause, which gives Congress the power to "define and punish Piracies and Felonies committed on the high Seas, and Offences against the Law of Nations" and the Necessary and Proper Clause, which vests Congress with the power to make "all Laws which shall be necessary and proper for carrying into Execution the foregoing Powers, and all other powers vested by this Constitution in the Government of the United States." U.S. Const. art. I, § 8, cl. 10, 18.

Having established that § 2280 can constitutionally be applied to proscribe conduct occurring outside of the United States, the sole question remaining is whether, as Defendant contends, the government's failure to extradite Defendant negates the Court's jurisdiction. Defendant argues that the requirement of § 1651 that a defendant be "brought into or found in the United States," is not met where, as here, a defendant is brought to the United States by "government action solely for the purpose of trial without a legal extradition process." However, Defendant cites no case, nor can the Court find any, in which jurisdiction was denied over charges pursuant to § 1651 on the grounds that the defendant was brought into the jurisdiction against his will and without legal extradition. On the contrary, under the "Ker-Frisbie Doctrine," the law has long been settled that "the power of a court to try a person for crime is not impaired by the fact that he had been brought within the court's jurisdiction by reason of a 'forcible abduction.'" Frisbie v. Collins, 342 U.S. 519, 522, 72 S. Ct. 509, 96 L.Ed. 541 (1952) (citing, inter alia, Ker v. Illinois, 119 U.S. 436, 7 S. Ct. 225, 30 L. Ed. 421 (1886))....

Finally, Defendant argues that because the SUA Convention contains an "extradite or prosecute" clause, the transfer of Defendant to the United States by an alternative procedure violated the Convention. This clause, found in Article 10.1 of the SUA Convention, provides,

> The State Party in the territory of which the offender or the alleged offender is found shall ... if it does not extradite him, be obliged, without exception whatsoever and whether or not the offence was committed in its territory, to submit the case without delay to its competent authorities for the purpose of prosecution, through proceedings in accordance with the laws of that State...

Convention on the Suppression of Unlawful Acts against the Safety of Maritime Navigation, art. 10, Mar. 10, 1988, 27 I.L.M. 668, 1678 U.N.T.S. 222. Nowhere does the Convention state that extradition is the exclusive means by which one state may lawfully turn over an offender to another state for prosecution. On the contrary, by establishing a protocol which must be followed "if [the state party] does not extradite [the defendant]," the Convention expressly acknowledges that extradition is not mandated. Moreover, as this Court has already explained, it is well-established that a court's jurisdiction over a defendant or the offenses he is alleged to have committed is not contingent on the means by which he was brought within such jurisdiction....

Therefore, extraterritorial application of § 2280 is proper, the government's failure to legally extradite Defendant does not defeat jurisdiction, and Defendant's Motion to Dismiss Counts Five and Thirteen is hereby denied.

Notes

1. *Basis of Jurisdiction.* As discussed in Chapter 4, unless the principle of universal jurisdiction applies, some connection must exist between a state, on the one hand, and the state's territory, citizens, vessels, government operations, or security, on the other, in order for the state validly to exercise jurisdiction under customary international law. The court did not address whether

maritime terrorism was a crime of universal jurisdiction, because it found that 18 U.S.C. § 1280 provided an independent basis for jurisdiction, namely, the defendant's involuntary presence in the United States. Although the Shibin court suggested that the U.S. Court of Appeals for the Ninth Circuit had previously ruled that maritime terrorism was a crime of universal jurisdiction, in that case the Ninth Circuit had determined that defendant Shi had engaged in piracy, a crime that does give rise to universal jurisdiction. United States v. Shi, 525 F.3d 709 (9th Cir. 2008).

Recall the Lotus case discussed in Chapter 4 involving a collision between a French and Turkish vessel; was the mere presence of the French officer in a Turkish port sufficient to provide Turkey with jurisdiction to prosecute him, or was another connection required? Under customary international law, is the presence of a foreign national who allegedly commits an act of terrorism in a distant foreign country against other foreign nationals a sufficient basis for a state to exercise jurisdiction? If not, do states have the ability to alter customary international law by entering into a treaty, such as the SUA Convention, that creates a right or obligation to prosecute based upon the mere presence of an alleged offender within the territory of a state party? In the absence of any requests for extradition, would the United States have been in breach of its obligations under the SUA Convention if it had not prosecuted Shibin for the alleged offense? Somalia was not a party to the SUA Convention (and remains a non-party as of September 1, 2013). Does international law allow a party to the SUA Convention to exercise jurisdiction over the national of a non-party state? In United States v. Ali, 885 F. Supp. 2d 17 (D.D.C. 2012), the court, in interpreting a similar U.S. statute implementing the 1979 Hostages Convention, stated that "given the contractual nature of treaty based jurisdiction, it remains an open question whether international law allows a state party to a treaty to assert 'found-in' or *aut dedere aut punire* [extradite or prosecute] jurisdiction over a non-state party's citizen in the absence of any other jurisdictional basis." How would you answer that "open question"?

2. *Elements of an Article 3 Offense*. Defendant Shibin was not involved in the actual seizure of the *Marida Marguerite* or the taking of the crew members as hostages. Does Shibin's on-board participation in negotiations for the crew members' ransom constitute an offense under Article 3(1) of the SUA Convention? Under Article 3(2)? At trial, the United States submitted evidence that Shibin, in his role as negotiator, psychologically and physically tortured the crew and stood guard over them with an AK-47 rifle. How do these additional facts impact your answers to the previous two questions? The jury's conviction of Shibin for violating the U.S. statute implementing the SUA Convention was upheld on appeal. United States v. Shibin, 722 F.3d 233 (4th Cir. 2013).

PROTOCOL OF 2005 TO THE CONVENTION FOR THE SUPPRESSION OF UNLAWFUL ACTS OF VIOLENCE AGAINST THE SAFETY OF MARITIME NAVIGATION

U.S. Sen. Treaty Doc. No. 110–8, IMO Doc. LEG/CONF.15/21 (2005)

[Under this 2005 Protocol, the following articles supplement the provisions of the 1988 SUA Convention.]

Article 3bis

1. Any person commits an offence within the meaning of this Convention if that person unlawfully and intentionally:

(a) when the purpose of the act, by its nature or context, is to intimidate a population, or to compel a government or an international organization to do or to abstain from doing any act:

(i) uses against or on a ship or discharges from a ship any explosive, radioactive material or BCN [biological, chemical, or nuclear] weapon in a manner that causes or is likely to cause death or serious injury or damage; or

(ii) discharges, from a ship, oil, liquefied natural gas, or other hazardous or noxious substance, which is not covered by subparagraph (a)(i), in such quantity or concentration that causes or is likely to cause death or serious injury or damage; or

(iii) uses a ship in a manner that causes death or serious injury or damage; or

(iv) threatens, with or without a condition, as is provided for under national law, to commit an offence set forth in subparagraph (a)(i), (ii) or (iii); or

(b) transports on board a ship:

(i) any explosive or radioactive material, knowing that it is intended to be used to cause, or in a threat to cause, with or without a condition, as is provided for under national law, death or serious injury or damage for the purpose of intimidating a population, or compelling a government or an international organization to do or to abstain from doing any act; or

(ii) any BCN weapon, knowing it to be a BCN weapon as defined in article 1; or

(iii) any source material, special fissionable material, or equipment or material especially designed or prepared for the processing, use or production of special fissionable material, knowing that it is intended to be used in a nuclear explosive activity or in any other nuclear activity not under safeguards pursuant to an IAEA [International Atomic Energy Agency] comprehensive safeguards agreement; or

(iv) any equipment, materials or software or related technology that significantly contributes to the design, manufacture or delivery of a BCN weapon, with the intention that it will be used for such purpose. . . .

Article 3ter

Any person commits an offence within the meaning of this Convention if that person unlawfully and intentionally transports another person on board a ship knowing that the person has committed an act that constitutes an offence set forth in article 3, 3*bis* or 3*quater* or an offence set forth in any treaty listed in the Annex, and intending to assist that person to evade criminal prosecution.

Article 3quater

Any person also commits an offence within the meaning of this Convention if that person:

(a) unlawfully and intentionally injures or kills any person in connection with the commission of any of the offences set forth in article 3, paragraph 1, article 3*bis*, or article 3*ter*; or

(b) attempts to commit an offence set forth in article 3, paragraph 1, article 3*bis*, paragraph 1(a)(i), (ii) or (iii), or subparagraph (a) of this article; or

(c) participates as an accomplice in an offence set forth in article 3, article 3*bis*, article 3*ter*, or subparagraph (a) or (b) of this article; or

(d) organizes or directs others to commit an offence set forth in article 3, article 3*bis*, article 3*ter*, or sub-paragraph (a) or (b) of this article; or

(e) contributes to the commission of one or more offences set forth in article 3, article 3*bis*, article 3*ter* or subparagraph (a) or (b) of this article, by a group of persons acting with a common purpose, intentionally and either:

(i) with the aim of furthering the criminal activity or criminal purpose of the group, where such activity or purpose involves the commission of an offence set forth in article 3, 3*bis* or 3*ter*; or

(ii) in the knowledge of the intention of the group to commit an offence set forth in article 3, 3*bis* or 3*ter*.

Notes

1. *2005 Protocols to the 1988 SUA Convention and 1988 Fixed Platforms Protocol.* Following the September 11, 2001 terrorist attacks on the United States, the IMO Assembly made it a "high priority" to review the 1988 SUA Convention, the 1988 Fixed Platforms Protocol, and other IMO instruments to determine whether more effective measures to improve maritime security and to suppress maritime terrorism should be adopted. IMO Doc. A 22/Res.924 (2002). The ensuing review, in which the United States played a leadership role, resulted in the approval in 2005 of amendments (in the form of protocols) to both the 1988 SUA Convention and the 1988 Fixed Platforms Protocol. Both 2005 Protocols entered into force in 2010. As of September 1, 2013, there were 27 parties to the 2005 Protocol to the SUA Convention, representing 36.04% of world tonnage, and 23 parties to the 2005 Fixed Platforms Protocol, representing 35.28% of world tonnage. A detailed analysis of these two Protocols may be found in U.S. Sen. Exec. Rpt. 110–25, Protocols of 2005 to the Convention concerning the Safety of Maritime Navigation and to the Protocol concerning the Safety of Fixed Platforms on the Continental Shelf (Sept. 16, 2008). See also Natalie Klein, Maritime Security and the Law of the Sea 170–92 (2011).

2. *Expansion of Punishable Offenses.* Compare the offenses described in Articles 3bis, 3ter, and 3quater of the 2005 SUA Convention Protocol to the offenses described in Article 3 of the 1988 SUA Convention. Under Article 3bis(1)(a), what new offenses have been added? What purpose must be present in connection with those offenses? How does the "purpose" element differ from the intent element under original Article 3 of the 1988 SUA Convention?

Article 3bis(1)(b) defines offenses concerning the transport of explosive and radioactive materials, biological, chemical, and nuclear (BCN) weapons, nuclear source materials, and related equipment. The 1968 Treaty on the Non-Proliferation of Nuclear Weapons prohibited contracting states that did not already have nuclear weapons from developing or acquiring them. The five "nuclear weapon" states were China, France, Russia, the United Kingdom, and the United States. In 2002, North Korea confirmed that it had been secretly developing nuclear weapons. Congressional Research Service, North Korea's Nuclear Weapons Program 4–5 (May 25, 2006). In 2004, Libya admitted to a "weapons of mass destruction" development program, but agreed to dismantle it. Congressional Research Service, Disarming Libya: Weapons of Mass Destruction (Apr. 22, 2004). Iran also developed uranium enrichment facilities, which it claimed were solely for peaceful purposes. Congressional Research Service, Iran's Nuclear Program: Status (Dec. 29, 2009). How does

Article 3bis(1)(b) address concerns about the escalating proliferation of BCN weapons? What facts must a state prove in order to successfully prosecute the member of a crew working on a ship that is transporting BCN weapons?

Article 3bis(2) creates exceptions from "offenses" for activities undertaken in compliance with the Non-Proliferation Treaty. As of September 1, 2013, there were 189 parties to the Non-Proliferation Treaty, excluding North Korea, which publicly announced its withdrawal from the treaty in January 2003. Other non-parties include India, Israel, and Pakistan.

Article 3ter makes it an offense for a person to unlawfully and intentionally transport another person on board a ship knowing that the person has committed an act that constitutes an offense under Article 3, 3bis or 3quater or an offense set forth in one of the treaties listed in the Annex to the Convention. What other element of intent must be satisfied?

3. *Right of Visit under the 2005 Protocol.* Article 8bis establishes a ship-boarding regime among contracting parties if there are "reasonable grounds to suspect" that a ship or a person on board the ship has been, is, or is about to be involved in the commission of an offense set forth in article 3, 3bis, 3ter, or 3quater. This regime is based on flag state consent, which corresponds to the concepts of vessel nationality and flag state jurisdiction introduced in Chapters 3 and 4. Flag state consent may be sought either on an ad hoc basis under Section 5(b) of Article 8bis or pursuant to a "prior consent" process that allows a party to file prior written notification of its consent to board vessels flying its flag with the IMO Secretary-General under Section 5(d) or (e). The flag state may withdraw this prior consent at any time.

If a flag state authorizes a requesting state to board a vessel, Sections 6 through 9 of Article 8bis impose conditions that protect the primacy of the flag state's jurisdiction over the boarded vessel. For example, the requesting state must inform the flag state of the results of a boarding and search, and may not detain the boarded vessel or take additional measures without prior flag state authorization. The flag state retains jurisdiction to prosecute if evidence of an offense is discovered. Section 10 sets out safeguards that the boarding state must respect, including, for example, the obligation to take into account the safety and security of the crew, ship, and cargo.

4. *Securing the Maritime Domain.* The SUA Conventions and Protocols focus on shipboard acts and threats to fixed platforms. However, the worldwide maritime network is extensive and consists of numerous components in addition to vessels and platforms, including ports, cargos, and crews. The stakeholders in this essential international transportation system are diverse, ranging from governments to ship owners to the manufacturers and consumers who rely on the maritime network to deliver goods. The following report analyzes the

challenges that the international community faces in securing this diverse and widespread "maritime domain." The following Notes highlight some of the international legal responses to those challenges.

SECURITY IN MARITIME TRANSPORT: THE RISK FACTORS AND ECONOMIC IMPACT

Organization for Economic Cooperation and Development [OECD], Maritime Transport Committee (July 2003), available at http://www.oecd.org

Executive Summary

1. Immediately after the devastating September 11th World Trade Center attacks in New York, governments around the world scrambled to assess their vulnerability to highly organised terrorist groups willing to sacrifice thousands of lives to achieve their aims. The risk of mega-terrorism, once the stuff of spy novels, suddenly became very real, and the maritime transport system loomed large in the eyes of security agencies worldwide as a prime target and/or vehicle for future attacks.

2. World trade is dependent on maritime transport and great strides have been made in recent years to render this system as open and frictionless as possible in order to spur even greater economic growth. However, the very things that have allowed maritime transport to contribute to economic prosperity also render it uniquely vulnerable to exploitation by terrorist groups. The risks are numerous and encompass both containerised and bulk shipping. The vulnerabilities are important, and range from the possibility for physical breaches in the integrity of shipments and vessels to documentary fraud and illicit money-raising for terrorist groups. Finally, the stakes are extremely high, as any important breakdown in the maritime transport system would fundamentally cripple the world economy[.]

2. Risk Factors: What are the Threats?

17. Perhaps foremost among the risk factors associated with maritime transport is the sheer volume and numbers of goods moving by sea. The United Nations Conference on Trade and Development (UNCTAD) estimates that 5.8 billion tons of goods were traded by sea at in 2001. This accounts for over 80% of world trade by volume. The bulk of this trade is carried by over 46 000 vessels servicing nearly 4 000 ports throughout the world. And there are no signs that world maritime trade will be decreasing any time soon, especially as international negotiations have expressly sought to facilitate and accelerate world trade rather than slow it down.

18. In addition to its size, the maritime sector, by its very nature as a complex, international open transportation network, poses several additional challenges from a security standpoint. One of these is the multiplicity of terrorist risk factors associated with shipping.

19. Sea-going vessels can be the vector for, or target of, attacks. They can also serve to facilitate other attacks and/or raise revenue for terrorist organisations. The principal risk factors related to shipping—cargo, vessels, people and financing—are also linked to the broader risk of major disruptions in world trade and increased economic costs linked to heightened security. It is important that governments address all of these risks with broad-based security policy responses, since simply responding to threats in isolation to one another can be both ineffective and costly.

Risk Factors: Cargo

Containers

20. Most of the world's non-bulk cargo travels in marine shipping containers. These standardised boxes have revolutionised the transport of goods by sea since their first appearance in the 1950's and have given rise to a multitude of specialised road and rail carriers, a fleet of over 2 700 modular container vessels and the emergence of a global network of over 430 highly automated port handling facilities. In 2002, the Bureau International des Containers (BIC) estimated that approximately 15 000 000 containers were in circulation—almost evenly shared between the self-owned and leased fleet. Data from Containerisation Online indicate that 232 million containers were moved through container ports in 2001. The staggering volume of container movements, their relatively high velocity in the international trading system and their uniformity all pose formidable challenges from a security perspective.

21. The first of these is that the system is porous enough that it can be relatively easily subverted from legitimate commercial purposes.... Suffice to say that the opportunities are numerous to misuse this mode of freight shipment.

22. Immediately following the World Trade Center attacks, attention quickly shifted to the possibility that containers could be used to conceal and deliver relatively crude weapons of mass destruction. In a worst case scenario, a terrorist organisation could pack a global positioning satellite-enabled weapon of mass destruction within a shipping container, introduce it into the international transport system using legitimate shippers, intermediaries and carriers,

and remotely detonate the weapon upon its arrival in the heart of a major population centre. All that would be required is a weapon, a few well-placed agents and a basic understanding of international trading practices. The likelihood of success of such an operation would be heightened by that fact that only a small number of containers are ever physically examined (e.g., approximately 2% in the United States prior to the World Trade Center attacks)[.]

Bulk shipments

31. The other principal maritime freight sector—bulk shipping—has generally received less scrutiny from security authorities. This sector is divided between bulk liquid shipments (ranging from crude oil, distilled oil derivatives, LPG [liquid propane gas] and LNG [liquid natural gas] to molasses and vegetable oils) and solid bulk cargoes. The risk posed by liquid bulk cargoes is commensurate with their volatility with some cargoes presenting extreme risks (gasoline, kerosene, LPG and LNG). Security efforts targeting bulk shipments have focused most on shipments of volatile liquid compounds—e.g., one of the first maritime related security actions taken following the World Trade Center attacks was to ban entry to a shipment of LNG to Baltimore harbour on 12 September 2001[.]

<u>Risk Factors: Vessels</u>

37. The previous section discusses the dangers posed by bulk vessel cargoes. These dangers highlight the potential for an entire vessel to be used as a weapon in a terrorist strike just as jet aircraft were used in the 2001 World Trade Center attacks. In such cases, a vessel can be used against a population centre adjacent to port facilities and/or shipping channels, to damage port facilities themselves or to sink the vessel(s) and block access to a port facility.

38. While the potential damage from such an attack is great, previous terrorist incidents involving ships have tended to target vessels rather than use them. The boarding of the cruise vessel Achille Lauro, the suicide attacks against the USS Cole and the oil tanker Limburg, and the discovery of an Al'Qaeda linked plot to attack vessels passing through the straits of Gibraltar, all point to the risk of attack faced by vessels. Given the relative difficulty in triggering a major explosion through an attack on a vessel, it is more likely that the principal motivation for terrorists to attack a vessel would be to hijack its cargo, hold its crew hostage for ransom or political purposes, sink the vessel and cause as much loss of life as possible, or cripple trade by threatening to close down access to ports and/or vulnerable trade routes.

Risk Factors: People

42. There are approximately 1 227 000 officers and ratings manning the merchant fleet. Not all of these seafarers operate on internationally trading commercial vessels but a significant portion do. The terrorism-related risk involving this vast labour force is two-fold. As seen in the previous section, seafarers are often directly targeted (in many cases of piracy) and/or indirectly suffer from terror attacks targeting vessels (as in the case of the Limburg). The second risk factor is that some seafarers, or individuals posing as seafarers, may actually be accomplices to and/or members of terrorist groups. The latter is especially worrisome given that seafarers have traditionally been granted relatively liberal travel rights by governments through non-immigrant crew list visas, or simply upon presentation of their seafarer identity documents[.]

4. International Cargo: Three Critical Flows

66. Previous attempts to address maritime security in international fora have focused on the vessel itself and, at most, the immediate area surrounding the vessel in port. This focus was an outgrowth of the ship-focused mandate given to the International Maritime Organization—the UN body responsible for developing the common regulatory framework for international maritime transport. Inspired by similar approaches in the passenger aviation sector, this vessel- and passenger-centric approach has obvious limitations when dealing with the international movement of cargo by sea.

67. The reality today is that while most of the world's trade travels by sea, the ocean voyage is only one element in a complex chain. A typical door-to-door journey using a shipping container will involve the interaction of approximately 25 different actors, generate 30–40 documents, use 2–3 different modes and be handled at as many as 12–15 physical locations. The complex web of people, interactions, movements, and information associated with the international movement of goods can be broken down into three principal flows:

- Movement of goods from place to place.
- Movement of custody from person to person.
- Movement of information regarding the cargo.

Places and Modes

68. The first chain involves the physical movement of cargo from place to place and from mode to mode. This is the most tangible chain from a secu-

rity perspective. Once suspected and/or confirmed, threats can be localised along this chain and actions can be taken to physically neutralise the threat. Knowing where a shipment originated, how it has travelled, where it can be localised and whether its integrity has been compromised are key questions for security agencies intent on intercepting threatening cargo. As such, it is important for policy-makers to also be aware of the physical reality of the cargo logistics chain.

69. Cargo originates from the manufacturer's premises. Here it is palletised and/or packed into a container and transported by road/rail either directly to a port, or to an intermediary's premises. In the latter case, the shipment will be consolidated with others and transported to a multi-modal staging area or to a port. While in transit, the container may be stationary for various periods of time as trucks are stopped on the roadside and/or container-carrying trains are being assembled in freight yards. Once in port, the container is sent to a staging area before it is placed immediately next to the vessel at quay. Even within the port area, a container may be moved several times as required by the port operator and/or customs. After being placed on board a ship, the container can be removed and trans-shipped in another port onto another vessel before arriving at its destination port. Here again, the container may be moved several times for customs clearance and into temporary storage areas while waiting to be picked up. Carried by road, rail or inland waterway to its final destination, the shipment may again transit through several intermediaries' facilities where the container is unpacked and the palletised shipments it contains are distributed.

70. The logistics chain described above is not uniformly secure and the level of protection offered containers and their contents can vary tremendously from node to node and among modes. The risk of security breaches at any one of its links compromises the security of the whole chain and imposes additional costs as additional security checks must be put in place to compensate. Also, the level of protection present at different nodes and in transit is often directly related to the value of the goods being shipped. A major electronics manufacturer will invest much more in securing his/her supply chain than will a small low-volume exporter of inexpensive porcelain objects. And even in cases where relatively high levels of protection are put in place, cargo theft remains a problem. There are literally tens of thousands "entry points" along modern logistics chains that could be exploited by terrorist groups.

Actors in the Logistics Chain

71. Every trade transaction involves dozens of primary agents. In addition, hundreds of people can potentially come into contact with containers and

their contents along the logistics chain described above. Understanding the flow of custody for the contents of a container and identifying and ensuring the security clearance of people who come into contact with containers are key challenges facing governments world-wide.

72. At the beginning of every container journey is a buyer and an originating shipper—most often a manufacturer. There are hundreds of thousands of manufacturers around the world and many of them are active in international trade. These manufacturers may produce high enough volumes or be located near enough to a port that they can ship full container loads directly. Most however, produce less than container load (LCL) shipments that must be consolidated before being shipped by sea.

73. Buying agents and/or freight forwarders serve as the most common intermediaries between originating shippers and ocean carriers. There are approximately 40 000 freight forwarders world-wide in an industry employing 8 to 10 million people. While many freight forwarders handle full container load shipments for their clients, their principal task revolves around the assembly and consolidation of LCL shipments into full containers. They also facilitate the entire international trade transaction by serving as agents for the cargo with other transport intermediaries, customs and other government agencies, banks and receiving parties. In some cases, the forwarder will negotiate each transaction on behalf of the shipper while in other cases, the forwarder will be the principal agent contracting with the shipper....

75. As with the security of nodes in the logistics chain, the level of scrutiny given every worker potentially coming into contact with containers and their contents varies considerably among companies and countries. While some companies may require extensive background checks for their workers, many do not. But even background checks do not represent a panacea as an entire company can be owned or operated by a terrorist group as has been seen in the past with the LTTE [Liberation Tigers of Emil Eelam].... The principal foil in such a case—where a terrorist group runs a "legitimate" operation for several years to build a reputation of trust—is better intelligence and transparency in company ownership disclosure requirements....

5. Maritime Security: Cost Considerations for Enacted and Proposed Security Measures

79. Very quickly after the World Trade Center attacks, attention shifted from aviation to maritime security as it became evident that the vulnerabilities detailed earlier in this report could potentially be targeted by organised terrorist groups such as Al'Qaeda. Following the unprecedented security measures

taken by the United States (e.g., the closing of its national airspace for 4 days), a concerted international effort was undertaken to rapidly develop a strategy to reduce the danger from terrorist acts on the maritime transport system. Four principal elements emerged as part of that strategy; the need to track vessels, the need to address the security of vessels and ports, the need to verify and authenticate the identity of seafarers and the need to ensure the integrity of containerised cargo. These four elements formed the basis of a draft proposal to the IMO that was reviewed at a special meeting of the Maritime Safety working group in February 2002. After some changes—notably the removal of IMO action on seafarer identity documents (transferred to the International Labour Organization)—the strategy was accepted at the September meeting of the working group and adopted at the IMO Maritime Safety Committee (MSC 76) meeting in December 2002.

Notes

1. *The ISPS Code and Related Measures.* The International Ship and Port Facility Security (ISPS) Code was adopted on December 17, 2002 at an IMO Diplomatic Conference on Maritime Security comprised of parties to the 1974 Safety of Life at Sea (SOLAS) Convention. IMO Doc. SOLAS/CONF.5/34, Annex 1. It entered into force in 2004 as an amendment (incorporated primarily into Chapter XI-2) of SOLAS. See the discussion of amendments to IMO conventions in Chapter 4, Section A.2. The ISPS Code contains mandatory measures to be implemented by governments, port authorities, and shipping companies for improved security of ships and port facilities (Part A), including the preparation, implementation, and regular assessment of security plans for ports and ships. The Code also contains a series of non-mandatory provisions (Part B) that provide guidance to states in implementing their obligations under Part A. Additional amendments to Chapter V of SOLAS provide for the installation of Long-Range Identification and Tracking (LRIT) systems for the global identification and tracking of ships and the use of ship-to-shore security alert systems. In 2006, the IMO established an arrangement for sharing LRIT information among SOLAS parties for security and search and rescue purposes. IMO Maritime Safety Comm. Res. 211(81), IMO Doc. MSC 81/25/Add.1, Annex 14 (2006). Ships must obtain an International Ship Security Certificate issued by the flag state or its designated agent as evidence of compliance with the ISPS Code.

State parties to SOLAS were required to implement the provisions of the ISPS Code and self-certify compliance by July 1, 2004. What if a state party fails to implement the risk assessment and other measures required under the ISPS Code? The IMO does not have the authority under SOLAS to impose penalties or otherwise enforce the ISPS Code. A port state is authorized to inspect and verify compliance of vessels within its ports. SOLAS, Chapter XI-2, reg. 9.1. Additionally, a port state may impose "control measures" on a vessel prior to its entrance into port if it has "clear grounds" to suspect that the arriving vessel or its port of origin are not compliant. These measures may include requesting security-related information, inspecting the ship in territorial waters, delaying or detaining the ship, restricting operations and movement within the port, or, if the vessel presents an immediate security threat, denying the ship entrance into port. Id., reg. 9.2. Port authorities must make every effort to avoid undue delay or detention of vessels; failure to do so may give rise to civil liability for any loss or damage suffered. Id., reg. 9.3. The United States and other countries have adopted legislation authorizing such enforcement actions. See, e.g., 46 U.S.C. § 70110; Regulation (EC) No 725/2004 of the European Parliament and of the Council of 31 March 2004 on enhancing ship and port facility security, 2004 O.J. L 129/6. Is it consistent with international law to apply these control measures to vessels of states that are not parties to the ISPS Code? For a discussion of these and other enforcement issues, see L. Stephen Cox, The Advent and Future of International Port Security Law, 1 Ntl. Security L.J. 77 (2013).

2. *Bilateral Port Inspection Arrangements.* Whereas the ISPS Code provides for port state enforcement authority regarding foreign vessels entering or within its ports, it contains no provisions allowing inspection by one state party of another state party's ports. Instead, the IMO anticipated that state parties would "cooperate" in ensuring compliance with the ISPS Code's port security provisions, and that the economic consequences of non-compliance would be a significant motivating factor. In 2002, the United States adopted legislation that required the U.S. Coast Guard to assess the effectiveness of the anti-terrorism measures maintained at foreign ports. 46 U.S.C. § 10108. If the assessment reveals that a foreign port does not maintain effective antiterrorism measures, the United States notifies the port in question of the findings and recommends steps to alleviate the situation. Id. at § 10109. If the foreign port fails to take remedial measures within 90 days, the U.S. government may impose conditions for access, or deny entry, into its ports for any vessel arriving from that foreign port or carrying cargo originating from or transshipped through that port. Id. at § 10110. Under international law, does the United States have the right to inspect the port of another state party for compliance with the ISPS Code without the port state's consent? Is a party to the SOLAS Convention required, as a component of its duty to cooperate in implementing the ISPS Code, to allow the United States to inspect its ports? What economic

or other incentives would prompt another state to allow inspection of its ports by the United States? Does the United States have the authority, on inspection of a foreign port, to unilaterally determine whether the foreign port is in compliance with the ISPS Code? The United States has inspected ports of more than 150 of its trading partners, and offers reciprocal rights to visit and inspect U.S. ports. Dan Orchard, International Port Security—A Global Challenge, 68 U.S. Coast Guard Proceedings 34, 35 (2011). The U.S. Coast Guard publishes a list of its port security advisory notices at http://homeport.uscg.mil.

3. *Seafarer Identification*. As noted in the OECD report, port states have historically granted seafarers relatively liberal visitation rights while in port, including temporary shore leave, transit in and out of a country to join or leave a crew, and the ability to change ships while in port. What potential security risks do these practices present? The 2003 Revised Seafarers' Identity Documents Convention (No. 185), drafted under the auspices of the International Labor Organization (ILO), a U.N. specialized agency, sets minimum standards for how parties produce and issue their seafarer identity documents, and requires the use of personally unique biometric information, such as fingerprints, retina, iris, or voice. A state party must, while a ship is in port, permit the entry into its territory of a seafarer holding a valid seafarer's identity document for purposes of temporary shore leave, transit, or transfer to another ship. Id., Article 6(4), (7). The Convention entered into force in 2005; as of September 1, 2013, there were 24 parties. For discussion, see Natalie Klein, Maritime Security and the Law of the Sea 235–39 (2011).

4. *U.N. Security Council Resolutions*. As discussed in Chapter 4, Section E, the U.N. Security Council has the authority, under Chapter VII of the U.N. Charter, to adopt legally binding decisions with respect to threats to the peace, breaches of the peace, and acts of aggression. In 2001, the Security Council declared that international terrorism constituted a threat to international peace and security and violated the principles of the U.N. Charter, and obligated states to implement measures to prevent the financing and commission of terrorist acts. UN Doc. S/RES/1373 (2001). In 2004, the Security Council determined that the proliferation of nuclear, chemical, and biological weapons, as well as their means of delivery, constituted a threat to international peace and security, and required states to adopt and enforce effective laws to "prohibit any non-State actor" from manufacturing, acquiring, possessing, developing, transporting, transferring, or using "nuclear, chemical or biological weapons and their means of delivery, in particular for terrorist purposes[.]" UN Doc. S/RES/1540 (2004). To what extent may states rely on these resolutions in support of the legality, under international law, of national legislation that enhances maritime security?

In 2006, the U.N. Security Council identified North Korea as a state of proliferation concern. UN Doc. S/RES/1718 (2006). In 2009, after escalation of North Korea's proliferation activities, the Security Council adopted Resolution 1874, in which the Council:

> 11. *Calls upon* all States to inspect, in accordance with their national authorities and legislation, and consistent with international law, all cargo to and from [North Korea], in their territory, including seaports and airports, if the State concerned has information that provides reasonable grounds to believe the cargo contains items the supply, sale, transfer, or export of which is prohibited . . . ;
>
> 12. *Calls upon* all Member States to inspect vessels, with the consent of the flag State, on the high seas, if they have information that provides reasonable grounds to believe that the cargo of such vessels contains items the supply, sale, transfer, or export of which is prohibited . . . ;
>
> 13. *Calls upon* all States to cooperate with inspections pursuant to paragraphs 11 and 12, and, if the flag State does not consent to inspection on the high seas, *decides* that the flag State shall direct the vessel to proceed to an appropriate and convenient port for the required inspection by the local authorities pursuant to paragraph 11[.]

UN Doc. S/RES/1874 (2009). What is the legal significance of the terminology "calls upon," as used in paragraphs 11–13, and "decides," as used in paragraph 13? Is the obligation imposed on flag states under paragraph 13 consistent with the principles of flag state jurisdiction discussed in Chapters 2 and 4?

After North Korea conducted a nuclear test in 2013, the Security Council adopted Resolution 2094 in which it "decided" that all states must inspect all cargo within or transiting through their territory that originated in or is destined for North Korea, if the state concerned has reasonable grounds to believe the cargo contains prohibited items. UN Doc. S/RES/2094, ¶ 16 (2013). Under this resolution, may a coastal state interdict a vessel engaged in innocent passage through its territorial waters (as discussed in Chapter 8, Section A.2) if it has reasonable grounds to believe that the vessel's cargo contains prohibited items? Does the Security Council have authority under Chapter VII to adopt a resolution that alters international law? Resolution 2094 also obligated all states to deny a vessel entry into its ports if the vessel refused to allow an inspection after the flag state had authorized the inspection pursuant to paragraph 12 of Resolution 1874. UN Doc. S/RES/2094, ¶ 16 (2013).

B Informal Measures Implemented by States

PROLIFERATION SECURITY INITIATIVE
White House Fact Sheet, Sept. 4, 2003

The Proliferation Security Initiative (PSI) is a response to the growing challenge posed by the proliferation of weapons of mass destruction (WMD), their delivery systems, and related materials worldwide. The PSI builds on efforts by the international community to prevent proliferation of such items, including existing treaties and regimes. It is consistent with and a step in the implementation of the UN Security Council Presidential Statement of January 1992, which states that the proliferation of all WMD constitutes a threat to international peace and security, and underlines the need for member states of the UN to prevent proliferation. The PSI is also consistent with recent statements of the G8 and the European Union, establishing that more coherent and concerted efforts are needed to prevent the proliferation of WMD, their delivery systems, and related materials. PSI participants are deeply concerned about this threat and of the danger that these items could fall into the hands of terrorists, and are committed to working together to stop the flow of these items to and from states and non-state actors of proliferation concern.

The PSI seeks to involve in some capacity all states that have a stake in nonproliferation and the ability and willingness to take steps to stop the flow of such items at sea, in the air, or on land. The PSI also seeks cooperation from any state whose vessels, flags, ports, territorial waters, airspace, or land might be used for proliferation purposes by states and non-state actors of proliferation concern. The increasingly aggressive efforts by proliferators to stand outside or to circumvent existing nonproliferation norms, and to profit from such trade, requires new and stronger actions by the international community. We look forward to working with all concerned states on measures they are able and willing to take in support of the PSI, as outlined in the following set of "Interdiction Principles."

Interdiction Principles for the Proliferation Security Initiative

PSI participants are committed to the following interdiction principles to establish a more coordinated and effective basis through which to impede and stop shipments of WMD, delivery systems, and related materials flowing to and from states and non-state actors of proliferation concern, consistent with national legal authorities and relevant international law and frameworks, including the UN Security Council. They call on all states concerned with this threat to international peace and security to join in similarly committing to:

1. Undertake effective measures, either alone or in concert with other states, for interdicting the transfer or transport of WMD, their delivery systems, and related materials to and from states and non-state actors of proliferation concern. "States or non-state actors of proliferation concern" generally refers to those countries or entities that the PSI participants involved establish should be subject to interdiction activities because they are engaged in proliferation through: (1) efforts to develop or acquire chemical, biological, or nuclear weapons and associated delivery systems; or (2) transfers (either selling, receiving, or facilitating) of WMD, their delivery systems, or related materials.

2. Adopt streamlined procedures for rapid exchange of relevant information concerning suspected proliferation activity, protecting the confidential character of classified information provided by other states as part of this initiative, dedicate appropriate resources and efforts to interdiction operations and capabilities, and maximize coordination among participants in interdiction efforts.

3. Review and work to strengthen their relevant national legal authorities where necessary to accomplish these objectives, and work to strengthen when necessary relevant international law and frameworks in appropriate ways to support these commitments.

4. Take specific actions in support of interdiction efforts regarding cargoes of WMD, their delivery systems, or related materials, to the extent their national legal authorities permit and consistent with their obligations under international law and frameworks, to include:

a. Not to transport or assist in the transport of any such cargoes to or from states or non-state actors of proliferation concern, and not to allow any persons subject to their jurisdiction to do so.

b. At their own initiative, or at the request and good cause shown by another state, to take action to board and search any vessel flying their flag in their internal waters or territorial seas, or areas beyond the territorial seas of any other state, that is reasonably suspected of transporting such cargoes to or from states or non-state actors of proliferation concern, and to seize such cargoes that are identified.

c. To seriously consider providing consent under the appropriate circumstances to the boarding and searching of its own flag vessels by other states, and to the seizure of such WMD-related cargoes in such vessels that may be identified by such states.

d. To take appropriate actions to (1) stop and/or search in their internal waters, territorial seas, or contiguous zones (when declared) vessels that are reasonably suspected of carrying such cargoes to or from states or non-state actors of proliferation concern and to seize such cargoes that are identified; and (2) to enforce conditions on vessels entering or leaving their ports, internal waters or territorial seas that are reasonably suspected of carrying such cargoes, such as requiring that such vessels be subject to boarding, search, and seizure of such cargoes prior to entry.

Notes

1. *Development of the Proliferation Security Initiative*. The *So San*, a vessel without a flag, left North Korea late in 2002. A Spanish frigate intercepted it on the high seas approximately 600 miles off the coast of Yemen. Spanish troops, with the assistance of U.S. personnel, boarded the vessel and discovered Scud missiles and tanks of rocket fuel on board. The cargo had been purchased by Yemen, and the United States believed that North Korea was using the currency from the sale of the cargo to fund its missile and nuclear weapons programs. The U.S. Navy took charge of the *So San*, but then released the vessel and allowed it and its cargo to proceed to Yemen. Although "there is authority to stop and search" the flagless vessel, said a White House spokesman, "in this instance there is no clear authority to seize the shipment of Scud missiles" and "there is no provision under international law prohibiting Yemen from accepting delivery of missiles from North Korea. And therefore, the merchant vessel is being released." Quoted in Robert M. Chesney, The Proliferation Security Initiative and WMD Interdiction on the High Seas, 25 Am. Bar Assoc. Ntl. Security L. Rep. No. 2 at 5 (Oct. 2003).

The *So San* incident spurred the development of the Proliferation Security Initiative (PSI), announced by President George W. Bush in May 2003. Australia, France, Germany, Italy, Japan, the Netherlands, Poland, Portugal, Spain, the United Kingdom, and the United States participated in meetings to formulate the initial PSI framework, resulting in the release of the PSI Statement of Interdiction Principles in September 2003. See http://www.psi-online.info/Vertretung/psi/en/Startseite.html. As of September 13, 2013, 102 countries voluntarily participated at some level in the PSI. The participating states are encouraged, among other measures, to conduct training exercises, exchange relevant information, and enter into agreements with other participating states to expedite requests to board and inspect suspicious vessels flying their flag.

See, for example, the 2005 United States-Belize Agreement on Cooperation to Suppress the Proliferation of Weapons of Mass Destruction, Their Delivery Systems, and Related Materials by Sea. The PSI does not have a secretariat or formal operating procedure. An Operational Expert Group comprised (as of September 1, 2013) of 21 participating states meets regularly to coordinate PSI activities, including training exercises. For a general discussion of the PSI, see Congressional Research Service, Proliferation Security Initiative, Rpt. No. RL34327 (June 15, 2012).

2. *Evaluating the PSI.* None of the major treaties addressing weapons of mass destruction—the 1968 Treaty on the Non-Proliferation of Nuclear Weapons, the 1972 Biological and Toxin Weapons Convention, and the 1993 Chemical Weapons Convention—authorizes the interdiction of vessels. Do the PSI Interdiction Principles purport to authorize any interdiction that would be illegal under international law?

Some concerns have been raised about the informal structure and procedures of the PSI, and the lack of publication and dissemination of uniform guidelines implementing its interdiction principles. Are the standards "of proliferation concern" and "good cause" in paragraph 4 too vague? As noted by one author:

> [T]he shipping commerce is a global industry, one that relies on a common framework of international conventions and treaties; the industry can operate efficiently only when regulations applicable to a particular ship are identical at the port of departure, on the high seas, and at the port of arrival. Since PSI focuses on enlarging national authorities rather than global rules, it is more likely to create inadvertently a web of inconsistent national laws than is the standardized international legal regime of SUA. The shipping industry is hopeful that the amended SUA 2005 will attract widespread support and enter into force quickly.

James Kraska, Grasping the Influence of Law on Sea Power, 62 Naval War College Rev. 113, 128 (2009). What are some of the advantages of the informal and non-binding nature of the PSI? What are the disadvantages? The PSI "has been criticized for lacking sufficient public accountability, stretching if not breaking the fundaments and limits of existing international law, undermining the UN system, adversely impacting legal trade, being politically divisive and having limited effectiveness." Mark J. Valencia, The Proliferation Security Initiative and Asia, in The Oceans in the Nuclear Age: Legacies and Risks 265, 265–66 (David D. Caron & Harry N. Scheiber eds., 2010). Are these fair criticisms? See also Donald R. Rothwell, The Proliferation Security Initiative: Amending the

Convention on the Law of the Sea by Stealth?, in id. at 285. Would ratification and implementation of the 2005 Protocol to the SUA Convention, discussed in Section A, provide a more effective international framework for combating the proliferation of WMD? Why have more than 100 states endorsed the PSI, while only 27 have ratified the 2005 Protocol to the SUA Convention as of September 1, 2013?

CSI [CONTAINER SECURITY INITIATIVE] IN BRIEF

U.S. Dept. of Homeland Security, Customs and Borders Protection (as of September 1, 2013), available at http://www.cbp.gov

As the single, unified border agency of the United States, U.S. Customs and Border Protection's (CBP) mission is extraordinarily important to the protection of America and the American people. In the aftermath of the terrorist attacks on September 11, 2001, U.S. Customs Service began developing antiterrorism programs to help secure the United States. Within months of these attacks, U.S. Customs Service had created the Container Security Initiative (CSI).

CSI addresses the threat to border security and global trade posed by the potential for terrorist use of a maritime container to deliver a weapon. CSI proposes a security regime to ensure all containers that pose a potential risk for terrorism are identified and inspected at foreign ports before they are placed on vessels destined for the United States. CBP has stationed multidisciplinary teams of U.S. officers from both CBP and Immigration and Customs Enforcement (ICE) to work together with our host foreign government counterparts. Their mission is to target and prescreen containers and to develop additional investigative leads related to the terrorist threat to cargo destined to the United States.

The three core elements of CSI are:

- Identify high-risk containers. CBP uses automated targeting tools to identify containers that pose a potential risk for terrorism, based on advance information and strategic intelligence.
- Prescreen and evaluate containers before they are shipped. Containers are screened as early in the supply chain as possible, generally at the port of departure.
- Use technology to prescreen high-risk containers to ensure that screening can be done rapidly without slowing down the movement of trade. This technology includes large-scale X-ray and gamma ray machines and radiation detection devices.

Through CSI, CBP officers work with host customs administrations to establish security criteria for identifying high-risk containers. Those administrations use non-intrusive inspection (NII) and radiation detection technology to screen high-risk containers before they are shipped to U.S. ports....

CSI is now operational at ports in North America, Europe, Asia, Africa, the Middle East, and Latin and Central America. CBP's 58 operational CSI ports now prescreen over 80 percent of all maritime containerized cargo imported into the United States.

Notes

1. *Voluntary Programs.* Approximately eleven million cargo containers arrive annually at U.S. ports. U.S. Dept. Transportation, Research and Innovative Technology Administration, Bureau of Transportation Statistics, America's Container Ports: Linking Markets at Home and Abroad (Jan. 2011). The goal of the Container Security Initiative, initiated in 2002, is to minimize the risks relating to containers by examining their contents and ensuring their integrity as far upstream in the shipping chain as possible. To that end, the United States has entered bilateral agreements with numerous trading partners to implement its CSI program. See, e.g., 2004 European Community-United States Container Security Cooperation Agreement. As of July 2013, the United States had established 58 CSI ports in 32 countries, representing over 80% of the container shipments into the United States. U.S. Government Accountability Office, Supply Chain Security: DHS [Department of Homeland Security] Could Improve Cargo Security by Periodically Assessing Risks from Foreign Ports, GAO Rpt. No. 13–764, 10 (2013).

In 2007, the U.S. Congress adopted legislation requiring 100% of U.S.-bound containers to be scanned with both radiation detection and non-intrusive imaging equipment by July 1, 2012. Pub. L. No. 110–53, § 1701. This requirement raised objections throughout the international community as being too extensive. The U.S. Customs and Border Protection agency failed to successfully implement this mandate by the prescribed deadline; the deadline for implementation of the 100% scanning requirement has been extended until July 2014. GAO Rpt. No. 13–764, supra, at 15; see also U.S. Government Accountability Office, Supply Chain Security: Container Security Programs Have Matured, but Uncertainty Persists over the Future of 100 Percent Scanning, GAO Rpt. No. 12–422T (Feb. 2012). Is the CSI program an appropriate national measure taken to comply with the obligations imposed by the Security Council Resolutions discussed in Note 4 at the end of Section A above? Does international law allow the United States to deny entrance into its ports of containers that have not been screened for radioactive materials? See the discussion of port state jurisdiction in Chapter 7. Why did the United States fail to implement the requirement of screening of 100% of U.S.-bound containers by its July 2012 deadline?

2. *Government-to-Business Partnerships*. While the CSI program involves bilateral agreements between the United States and other governments, the United States has also established a voluntary government-to-business partnership program that provides benefits to supply chain companies that comply with predetermined security measures. Why might such a voluntary program prove effective? Might some "non-binding" measures be as effective, or more effective, than legally binding ones? Under the Customs-Trade Partnership against Terrorism (C-TPAT) program, CBP officials work with private companies to review their supply chain security plans and improve members' security measures. In return, C-TPAT members may receive benefits, such as reduced scrutiny or expedited processing of their shipments. As of July 31, 2013, more than 10,000 companies have voluntarily participated in the program. GAO Rpt. No. 13–764, supra Note 1, at 30.

CHAPTER 15

Settlement of Disputes

The legal obligation to settle international disputes peacefully is set out in Articles 2(3) and 33 of the United Nations Charter and in Article 279 of the United Nations Convention on the Law of the Sea (LOS Convention). Most disputes are settled by negotiation, but many are the subject of more formal processes. Throughout this book, we have seen that international law of the sea cases may be heard in a variety of forums, including municipal courts, the International Court of Justice (ICJ), the International Tribunal for the Law of the Sea (ITLOS or Tribunal), the European Court of Justice, and international arbitral tribunals.

This chapter focuses on the dispute settlement system established in the LOS Convention. Under this system, many law of the sea disputes are subject to compulsory, binding, third-party dispute settlement. Section A of this chapter provides an overview of the dispute settlement provisions of the LOS Convention and how they were negotiated. Section B examines one of the components of the Convention's system of third-party dispute settlement, the International Tribunal for the Law of the Sea, which began operating after the Convention entered into force in 1994. The Tribunal has contributed to the law concerning a range of issues. In this chapter, we are particularly concerned with the Tribunal's structure, jurisdiction, and relationship to other dispute settlement bodies.

A The Dispute Settlement System of the 1982 LOS Convention

LOUIS B. SOHN, PEACEFUL SETTLEMENT OF DISPUTES IN OCEAN CONFLICTS: DOES UNCLOS III POINT THE WAY?
46 Law & Contemp. Probs. No. 2 at 195 (1983)

I. INTRODUCTION

One of the important accomplishments of the Third United Nations Law of the Sea Conference is the development of a veritable code for the settlement of the disputes which may arise with respect to the interpretation and application of the Law of the Sea Convention. It was recognized early in the negotiations that if the parties to the Convention had retained the right of

 | DOI 10.1163/9789004203563_016

unilateral interpretation, then the complex text drafted by the Conference would have lacked stability, certainty, and predictability. It is one of the prerogatives of sovereign equality that in the absence of an agreement on impartial third-party adjudication, the view of one state with respect to the interpretation of the Convention cannot prevail over the views of other member states. Each party can claim forever that its view alone is correct, but another party can make the same claim, resulting in an impasse.

The only effective remedy in such a situation is to provide in advance in the Convention itself for an effective method of settling future interpretation disputes. In the past, several groups of states have usually refused to accept such a solution, and at the 1958 Law of the Sea Conference, agreement was reached only on an optional protocol which very few states ratified. The general importance of the latest Law of the Sea Convention and the need to protect the agreed package of compromises against destruction through unchallengeable unilateral interpretations have led the reluctant states to abandon their opposition to binding provisions for the settlement of disputes.[5]

II. The General Framework for Dispute Settlement

The resulting system for the settlement of law of the sea disputes is at the same time simple and complex. Its simplicity is due to the fact that the Convention accepts as its guiding principle that in general the will of the parties to a dispute shall prevail and that the parties may by agreement select any dispute settlement method they wish. The more complex provisions apply only if the parties do not agree upon a dispute settlement method.

Even after a dispute has arisen, and even if one of the procedures provided for in the Convention has been started, the parties can agree "at any time" to adopt a special method for settling their dispute. Similarly, if the parties to a dispute have previously agreed, in a bilateral, regional, or general international agreement, to settle disputes (including those relating to the interpretation of international agreements between them) by a procedure entailing a binding decision, this procedure supersedes the procedure provided for in the Law of the Sea Convention.

For example, if the two parties to the dispute have agreed unconditionally to accept the jurisdiction of the International Court of Justice, either of them can refer the dispute to that forum. Some African countries have expressed

5 In particular, the Soviet Union and its allies, as well as the African states, have for the first time agreed to this method of settlement for an important general convention.

preference for submitting the disputes relating to the interpretation or application of the Law of the Sea Convention to the Commission of Mediation, Conciliation, and Arbitration of the Organization of African Unity; if they agree to accept as binding a decision of that Commission, such an agreement will prevail over the Law of the Sea Convention provisions for settlement of disputes. If, however, the procedure chosen by the parties does not lead to a binding decision, the jurisdiction of the institutions established by the Law of the Sea Convention revives, and a party to the dispute can resort to these institutions. Similarly, the provisions of the Convention come into play whenever the parties have not been able to settle the dispute by negotiations or conciliation and have not succeeded in agreeing on another method of settlement.

Flexibility does not stop at this stage. Unlike most other international instruments, the Law of the Sea Convention does not provide for a unitary system of dispute settlement. Various groups of states have expressed preferences for different methods of settling Convention disputes. Some states have argued for conferring the jurisdiction to interpret the Convention on the International Court of Justice;[13] others have expressed preferences for arbitration;[14] while some have supported special technical commissions;[15] a large group of states has opted for a permanent International Tribunal for the Law of the Sea.[16] After many other solutions were rejected, it was agreed that a state can choose any one of these four methods, but if the two states concerned have chosen different methods, the dispute may be submitted "only to arbitration." All states agreed that if they cannot have the tribunal of their choice they would be willing to go to arbitration. To ensure that this solution will work, an annex to the Convention provides an effective method for selecting the arbitral tribunal.

III. Settlement of Specific Categories of Disputes

Three categories of cases are subject, however, to different procedures: (a) Article 297 governs disputes relating to the exercise by a coastal state of its sovereign rights or jurisdiction in the Exclusive Economic Zone (EEZ); (b) Article 298 governs disputes relating to seaboundary delimitations, to military or law enforcement activities, or to disputes submitted to the Security Council of the United Nations; and (c) Articles 186–91 govern disputes relating

13 E.g., Japan and the Netherlands.

14 E.g., France, the United Kingdom, and the United States.

15 E.g., the Soviet Union and other Eastern European states.

16 Most African states and several Latin American states have supported this idea.

to seabed mining. The simplicity of the other provisions of the Convention is matched by the complexity of these three exceptions.

A. Exclusive Economic Zone

Disputes relating to the Exclusive Economic Zone are in turn subdivided into three categories:

(i) Disputes relating to violations by either the coastal state or any other state of the provisions of the Convention in regard to freedoms and rights of navigation, overflight, the laying of submarine cables and pipelines, or other internationally lawful uses of the sea, as well as those relating to violations by the coastal state of international rules and standards for the protection and preservation of the marine environment, are subject to the general system for the settlement of disputes.

(ii) Disputes relating to marine scientific research are further subdivided into three categories: Some are subject to the general system of dispute settlement; some are completely excluded from that system due to their discretionary character; and some are subject to compulsory conciliation (a procedure which can be resorted to by either party to the dispute but which leads only to a report, not to a binding decision).

(iii) Disputes relating to fisheries are similarly divided into three categories, paralleling those under (ii).

B. Sea Boundary Delimitations, Military or Law Enforcement Activities, and Disputes before the UN Security Council

While the exceptions relating to the EEZ are automatic, the exceptions enumerated in Article 298 are optional. In becoming party to the Convention, a state may make a declaration that it does not accept the dispute settlement procedures of the Convention with respect to one or more of the following three categories of disputes:

(i) Disputes concerning sea boundary delimitations or involving historic bays or titles are subdivided into four categories. Those which arose before the entry into force of the Convention are totally exempt from dispute settlement under the Convention; those which shall arise after the entry into force of the Convention will be subject to compulsory conciliation; mixed disputes which involve the concurrent consideration of sea boundaries and of any unsettled dispute concerning sovereignty or other rights over continental or insular land territory are totally excluded from dispute settlement under the Convention; and sea boundary disputes which have been finally settled by an arrangement between the parties or which are to be settled in accordance with an agreement between them are also totally excluded from dispute settlement under the Convention.

(ii) Disputes concerning military activities are completely exempt from dispute settlement under the Convention; disputes concerning law enforcement activities are exempt if they are connected with disputes involving fishing or marine scientific research since these latter disputes are themselves completely exempt from dispute settlement under [Article 297] of the Convention.

(iii) Disputes which are being dealt with by the UN Security Council are totally exempt from dispute settlement under the Convention as long as they are before the Council.

C. Seabed Mining

In earlier drafts of the Convention, disputes related to seabed mining were originally subject to a special Seabed Tribunal. However, once agreement was reached on an International Tribunal for the Law of the Sea, composed of twenty-one members elected at a meeting of all the parties to the Convention, many states became reluctant to maintain two separate tribunals. Further negotiations resulted in the unification of the two tribunals and the establishment within the International Tribunal for the Law of the Sea of a separate Seabed Disputes Chamber, composed of eleven members selected by a majority of the Tribunal from among its members. The jurisdiction of the Chamber embraces most disputes relating to seabed mining, except that some disputes are subject to other procedures and some disputes are completely exempt from any dispute settlement procedure.

While the general dispute settlement system applies only to disputes between states, the seabed dispute settlement system applies in addition to disputes between states and the International Seabed Authority and to contract disputes involving states, the Authority, the Enterprise (the mining arm of the Authority), state enterprises, and natural and juridical persons. The Seabed Disputes Chamber has exclusive jurisdiction over most of these disputes, but some disputes between states may be submitted instead to a smaller chamber, chosen either from the Tribunal as a whole or from the Seabed Disputes Chamber.

In view of the technical character of many contract disputes, it was agreed that at the request of any party to the dispute, such disputes shall be submitted to binding commercial arbitration, and that such arbitration shall be conducted in accordance with the generally accepted UNCITRAL Arbitration Rules, prepared by the UN Commission on International Trade Law and approved by the UN General Assembly in 1976. Similarly, commercial arbitration may be resorted to in disputes relating to transfer of seabed mining technology and to financial terms of mining contracts.

Some states strongly opposed the idea that should a dispute be a mixed one, involving the interpretation of both a contract and the Convention, the interpretation of the Convention would be referred to a commercial arbitral tribunal.[39] It was agreed, therefore, that in such a case the arbitral tribunal would refer the question of Convention interpretation to the Seabed Disputes Chamber for a ruling and that the tribunal's award should be rendered in accordance with such ruling.

Another difficulty arose concerning the power of the Seabed Disputes Chamber to declare that certain acts of the Authority were invalid. It was made clear that the Chamber would have no jurisdiction with respect to the exercise by the Authority of its discretionary powers, and that in no case should it substitute its discretion for that of the Authority. But if the Authority should act outside the limits of its discretion, lack competence, or misuse its powers, the Chamber would have jurisdiction to deal with such issues since such acts would not be considered discretionary. While the Chamber would have no power to declare any rules, regulations, or procedures invalid, it would be permitted to grant reparation or provide other remedies to the party which had suffered damage as a result of another party's failure to comply with its obligations under the Convention or a contract.

Despite the complexity of these provisions, in the last sessions of the Conference there was no disposition to challenge them, and it can be assumed that with respect to them a consensus has been reached. Of course, most of the substantive provisions of the Convention might come to reflect customary international law, so that nonparties to the Convention might be able to invoke them; yet the dispute settlement provisions will be available only to parties to the Convention.[43] Should a dispute arise between a state party to the Convention and a state not a party thereto, such a dispute would have to be resolved in accordance with procedures available to the parties to the dispute outside the Convention. At present, such procedures are seldom

39 E.g., the Soviet Union, India, and several Latin American States.

43 The provisions of part XV of the Convention relating to settlement of disputes apply only to "States Parties [to the Convention]." See id. art. 279. As the Permanent Court of International Justice has stated in the Eastern Carelia Case, "[i]t is well established in international law that no State can, without its consent, be compelled to submit its disputes with other States either to mediation or arbitration, or to any other kind of pacific settlement." P.C.I.J., Series B, No. 5, at 27 (1923).

available. As the United States has found out in its disputes with Canada and Latin American states in the last decades, without a satisfactory dispute settlement system even a powerful nation cannot adequately protect its citizens and ships against harmful acts of foreign governments who are not willing to submit to impartial adjudication. On the other hand, for disputes between parties to the Convention the system of dispute settlement provided by the Convention, though it appears extremely flexible and provides several options, in the great majority of cases can lead to a binding decision likely to be accepted and complied with by the parties to the dispute. This is the way to the rule of law and to ensuring that the peace of the world will not be jeopardized by a dangerous escalation of law of the sea controversies.

Notes

1. *The Third-party Dispute Settlement Provisions of the LOS Convention.* Prior to the LOS Convention, there had been no comprehensive law of the sea treaty and no experience with a widely accepted system for compulsory reference of law of the sea disputes to third parties for binding decisions. Relatively few states have accepted the 1958 Optional Protocol on Compulsory Dispute Settlement for law of the sea disputes. As of September 1, 2013, 38 states are bound by the Optional Protocol, with Montenegro being the most recent to adhere in 2000. In 1960 the U.S. Senate voted 49 to 30 in favor of the Optional Protocol, short of the two-thirds supermajority required under the U.S. Constitution for Senate advice and consent to U.S. acceptance of treaties.

Why, at the Third United Nations Conference on the Law of the Sea (UNCLOS III), did states reject the opt-in system of the Optional Protocol? Why did recourse to binding third-party dispute settlement seem particularly compelling, should informal means prove unsuccessful in resolving disputes? Why did developing states favor such a system? Why did the United States and other developed states also support a strong system of third-party dispute settlement? Why did states choose such a complex system?

Although states at UNCLOS III generally agreed on the desirability of provisions for compulsory third-party dispute settlement procedures entailing binding decisions, numerous details remained to be negotiated. How did the LOS Convention resolve the following questions:

- What should happen if the parties had previously agreed to accept a third-party dispute settlement mechanism that differed from the mechanism set forth in the LOS Convention?

- If parties were negotiating or addressing a dispute through informal means, at what point should one party be entitled to invoke a formal, binding third-party mechanism?
- What should happen if parties to a dispute each preferred different means of third-party dispute settlement?
- Should highly technical disputes, such as disputes over scientific research, be addressed in the same manner as less technical disputes?
- What provisions should be made for gathering facts?
- Should third-party procedures be available only to states, or also to other entities?
- Must states exhaust any remedies provided in municipal legal systems before proceeding to an international court or tribunal?
- Should provision be made for advisory opinions, and if so, who should be able to seek such opinions?
- What law should a court or tribunal apply under the Convention's dispute settlement system? Does the reference to "other rules of international law" in Article 287 allow tribunals operating under the LOS Convention to exercise jurisdiction over cases not related to the law of the sea?
- Should some sensitive matters be excluded from the third-party dispute settlement system altogether, and, if so, which ones?

See Part XV (Articles 279–299) of the LOS Convention, in the Appendix. The deep seabed mining dispute settlement provisions are found in Part XI of the Convention, at Articles 186–191.

2. *Negotiations at UNCLOS III.* It was difficult to reach consensus with respect to the questions highlighted in Note 1 at UNCLOS III, a huge diplomatic conference involving virtually every state in the world. The LOS Convention's dispute settlement provisions had to be negotiated along with provisions concerning a wide range of substantive law of the sea issues. How should negotiations be conducted in such a setting? Review the UNCLOS III negotiating process, summarized in Chapter 1, Section A. In line with that process, several states introduced proposals and informal working papers concerning dispute settlement.

The President of UNCLOS III and committee chairs played a significant role in developing texts that served as the basis of discussions at plenary sessions and in informal working groups. President Amerasinghe (Sri Lanka) revised informal working papers, preparing an "informal single negotiating text"—a code of 103 articles—on the settlement of disputes. UN Doc. A/CONF.62/WP.9 (1975), 5 UNCLOS III Official Records 111. A revised text, UN Doc. A/CONF.62/

WP.9/Rev.1 (1976), 5 id. 185, took into account the views that 72 delegates expressed at the April 1976 plenary debate in New York. Subsequent informal meetings of the plenary led to yet another revised text, UN Doc. A/CONF.62/WP.9/Rev.2 (1976), 6 id. 144, which provided a focal point for informal consultations in Geneva in March 1977. At the sixth session in New York in 1977 the dispute settlement code was incorporated, along with substantive texts, into the Informal Composite Negotiating Text. See UN Doc. A/CONF.62/WP.10/Add. 1 (1977), 8 id. 65, 70.

At this stage of the negotiations, negotiating groups were formed to deal with two "hard-core" dispute settlement issues, one relating to limitations on compulsory dispute settlement with respect to disputes about the living resources of the exclusive economic zone, and one relating to an optional exception for disputes concerning the delimitation of maritime boundaries between states. The next Note concerns the latter issue.

3. *The LOS Convention's Optional Exception for Maritime Boundary Disputes*. Negotiation of a provision concerning third-party settlement of maritime boundary disputes proved exceptionally difficult. Some states favored excluding such disputes from the possibility of third-party dispute settlement altogether, while other states argued for subjecting these disputes to the normal provisions on binding third-party dispute settlement. As Judge Manner (Finland), the head of UNCLOS III Negotiating Group 7, which dealt with this issue, put it in 1979, "the path leading to an acceptable compromise is very narrow." Informal Conference Doc. NG7/26 (Mar. 26, 1979), 9 Third United Nations Conference on the Law of the Sea: Documents 432, 434 (Renate Platzöder ed., 1986). Professor Louis B. Sohn of the United States chaired an expert group that surveyed possible compromises, helping to focus the discussion on a few alternatives, and an agreement was eventually reached. One particularly sensitive issue involved whether an exception should apply to all maritime delimitation disputes or only to future disputes. Another sensitive issue was whether non-binding compulsory conciliation should relate to the specific circumstances, principles, or methods to be considered in resolving a particular dispute, or should relate instead to the final delimitation itself.

How did Article 298(1)(a) resolve these issues? How is one to determine when "a dispute arises subsequent to the entry into force" of the Convention? Does Article 298(1)(a) embody other ambiguities that, perhaps, were the necessary price of compromise? Once a maritime boundary dispute has been finally settled by an arrangement between the parties, may it be reopened or interpreted pursuant to the Convention's dispute settlement provisions?

Would you expect most states to invoke the Article 298(1)(a) optional exception for maritime boundary delimitation disputes? What are the advantages and disadvantages of filing this and other optional exceptions? As of September 1, 2013, 21 of the 166 parties to the LOS Convention had claimed the Article 298(1)(a) optional exception. Those states are Argentina, Australia, Canada, Chile, China, Equatorial Guinea, France, Gabon, Ghana, Italy, Mexico, Montenegro, Palau, Portugal, the Republic of Korea, the Russian Federation, Spain, Thailand, Trinidad and Tobago, Tunisia, and the Ukraine. A few other states—Angola, Denmark, Iceland, Nicaragua, Norway, and Slovenia—had filed declarations that could significantly limit available forums in maritime boundary disputes, e.g., by excluding the settlement of such disputes by arbitration (the default third-party forum under Part XV of the LOS Convention). See http://www.un.org/Depts/los/convention_agreements/convention_declarations.htm. Arbitral tribunals constituted under Annex VII of the LOS Convention in accordance with the Convention's compulsory dispute settlement provisions have decided some maritime boundary disputes, with respect to which the parties had not filed Article 298 declarations. See In re Barbados/Trinidad & Tobago (Annex VII Arb., 2006), 45 Intl. Leg. Materials 798 (2006) (submitted before Trinidad and Tobago invoked the Article 298 exception); In re Guyana/Suriname (Annex VII Arb., 2007), 47 Intl. Leg. Materials 164 (2008).

All states, including those filing an Article 298(1)(a) exception, remain free to resolve maritime boundary delimitation disputes by formal or informal means of their choosing. Since the entry into force of the LOS Convention in November 1994, several states have specially agreed to submit particular maritime boundary delimitation disputes to the ICJ, the ITLOS, or arbitration tribunals for a binding decision. See Chapter 6.

4. *Jurisdiction Pursuant to Other Treaties*. According to Article 288(2) of the LOS Convention, an international agreement may provide for the jurisdiction of the ITLOS, the ICJ, or an arbitral or special arbitral tribunal, with respect to "any dispute concerning the interpretation or application of" that agreement. For example, Article 30 of the 1995 Fish Stocks Agreement provides in part:

> 1. The provisions relating to the settlement of disputes set out in Part XV of the [LOS] Convention apply *mutatis mutandis* to any dispute between States Parties to this Agreement concerning the interpretation or application of this Agreement, whether or not they are also Parties to the Convention.

> 2. The provisions relating to the settlement of disputes set out in Part XV of the Convention apply *mutatis mutandis* to any dispute between States Parties to this Agreement concerning the interpretation or application of a subregional, regional or global fisheries agreement relating to straddling fish stocks or highly migratory fish stocks to which they are parties, including any dispute concerning the conservation and management of such stocks, whether or not they are also Parties to the Convention.

See also Articles 7 and 31–32 of this Agreement. The United States is a party to the 1995 Fish Stocks Agreement and thus has accepted the LOS Convention's dispute settlement provisions with respect to disputes concerning the interpretation or application of the 1995 Agreement—even though the United States has not, as of September 1, 2013, accepted the LOS Convention. Does Article 30(2) of the 1995 Agreement effectively amend existing regional fisheries treaties, incorporating the Part XV dispute settlement provisions into them? Are disputes concerning straddling stocks fully subject to third-party process, in light of the limitation for EEZ fisheries disputes found in Article 297 of the LOS Convention? See the discussion of compulsory third-party dispute settlement and the 1995 Fish Stocks Agreement in Note 5 at the end of Chapter 13, Section B.

5. *Informal Means of Settling Disputes*. Despite the LOS Convention's provisions concerning third-party dispute settlement, informal means of settling disputes, such as negotiation, remain important. In what situations will they be used?

B The International Tribunal for the Law of the Sea

One of the institutions created by the LOS Convention is the International Tribunal for the Law of the Sea. The first reading in this section is the Tribunal's Statute (Annex VI of the Convention), which introduces its structure, jurisdiction, and operation. We next examine more closely the advisory jurisdiction of the ITLOS. The three cases excerpted at the end of this section relate to Article 292 applications for the prompt release of vessels and their crews and Article 290(5) provisional measures. These articles have provided the basis for most of the Tribunal's cases.

LAW OF THE SEA CONVENTION

Annex VI

See Appendix

Notes

1. *The International Tribunal for the Law of the Sea.* Recall from Section A of this chapter that the ITLOS is only one of several third-party forums that can render a legally binding decision should informal means of settling a dispute prove unsuccessful. How does the ITLOS differ from the Convention's other formal dispute settlement options?

Recall too that an arbitral tribunal will have jurisdiction over the merits of a dispute under Part XV of the Convention if the parties to a dispute have not both chosen another third-party mechanism. When and why, then, will the ITLOS be used? In what categories of cases will the ITLOS have jurisdiction?

2. *Jurisdiction Pursuant to Special Agreements.* One way the ITLOS may obtain jurisdiction in a contentious interstate case is by "special agreement," i.e., a treaty in which states agree, after a particular dispute has arisen, to bring that dispute to a specified forum. As noted in Chapter 6, states have submitted several maritime boundary disputes to the ICJ and to arbitral tribunals pursuant to special agreements. In March 2012 the ITLOS decided its first maritime boundary delimitation case—the Dispute concerning Delimitation of the Maritime Boundary between Bangladesh and Myanmar in the Bay of Bengal (Bangladesh/Myanmar), ITLOS Case No. 16, available at http://www.itlos.org. For a discussion of the peculiar way in which the ITLOS was seized, see Note 4 following the excerpt of the Bangladesh/Myanmar case in Chapter 6. Why would states choose the ITLOS to decide a maritime boundary delimitation dispute? Why an arbitral tribunal? Why the ICJ? Why perhaps a chamber of the ICJ or the ITLOS (which now has a Chamber for Maritime Delimitation Disputes)?

In most ITLOS cases, the Tribunal's jurisdiction has not been based on special agreements. See Declaration of Judge Treves in the Bangladesh/Myanmar case and the discussion of provisional measures and prompt release cases below. How could the ITLOS better attract special agreement cases?

DOO-YOUNG KIM, ADVISORY PROCEEDINGS BEFORE THE INTERNATIONAL TRIBUNAL FOR THE LAW OF THE SEA AS AN ALTERNATIVE PROCEDURE TO SUPPLEMENT THE DISPUTE-SETTLEMENT MECHANISM UNDER PART XV OF THE UNITED NATIONS CONVENTION ON THE LAW OF THE SEA

Issues in Legal Scholarship, Vol. 7, Issue 1: Frontier Issues in Ocean Law: Marine Resources, Maritime Boundaries, and the Law of the Sea, Article No. 6 (2008), available at http://www.degruyter.com/view/j/ils (published online 2010)

I. Introduction

Under Part XI (Area) of the United Nations Convention on the Law of the Sea (hereinafter "the Convention"), which confers exclusive jurisdiction on the Seabed Disputes Chamber in respect of disputes relating to activities in the international seabed, this Chamber is also empowered to give advisory opinions at the request of the Assembly or the Council of the International Seabed Authority (hereinafter "the Authority") on legal questions arising within the scope of their activities. Whereas the Convention expressly mandates the Seabed Disputes Chamber... to give advisory opinions to the Authority, it is not explicit with respect to the advisory role of the full Tribunal either under Part XV (Settlement of Disputes) or its Annex VI (Statute of the Tribunal).

...A proposal to give the Tribunal advisory power was first presented to the Tribunal at the first organizational session of the Tribunal in October 1996. [N]either the Convention nor the Statute expressly provided a basis for its advisory power. [However,] there was nothing in the Convention or the Statute itself to exclude or reject the advisory power of the Tribunal. The Rules of the Tribunal adopted on 28 October 1997 [included] a clause giving the advisory power to the Tribunal, which became article 138.

II. Legal Basis for the Advisory Power of the Tribunal

Article 21 (Jurisdiction) of the Statute of the Tribunal seems to confer a broad jurisdiction on it. It reads as follows:

> The jurisdiction of the Tribunal comprises all disputes and all applications submitted to it in accordance with this Convention and *all matters specifically provided for in any other agreement which confers jurisdiction on the Tribunal.* (emphasis added)

This article, with its broad wording, . . . provided the Tribunal with a legal basis for its advisory jurisdiction.

. . . The first part of [Article 21] deals with the Tribunal's jurisdiction to entertain all disputes and all applications submitted to it in accordance with the Convention. Given the ordinary meaning and usage of the words "disputes" and "applications" in this first part, it seems quite obvious that the first part covers only the contentious jurisdiction of the Tribunal. In the latter part of this article covering the compromissory jurisdiction of the Tribunal which is conferred upon it on the basis of an agreement, however, the Tribunal's jurisdiction is extended to "all matters specifically provided for in any other agreement [than the Convention] which confers jurisdiction on the Tribunal." Unlike the first part, here the Tribunal's jurisdiction is not restricted to "disputes" or "applications" and encompasses all matters specifically provided for in an agreement conferring jurisdiction upon the Tribunal. . . . If an agreement conferring jurisdiction upon the Tribunal contains a specific clause as regards the submission of the request for an advisory opinion to the Tribunal, such request could be characterized as being under "all matters." . . . This reading of the latter part of article 21 of the Statute seems to provide a legal basis for article 138 of the Rules granting the advisory capacity to the Tribunal. . . .

III. Requirements for the Exercise of the Advisory Jurisdiction of the Tribunal

[A]rticle 138 of the Rules of the Tribunal . . . reads [in part] as follows:

> 1. The Tribunal may give an advisory opinion on a legal question if an international agreement related to the purposes of the Convention specifically provides for the submission to the Tribunal of a request for such an opinion.
>
> 2. A request for an advisory opinion shall be transmitted to the Tribunal by whatever body is authorized by or in accordance with the agreement to make the request to the Tribunal. . . .

Legal question

An advisory opinion may be given by the Tribunal on a legal question and the question should be precisely formulated. [I]n its past several advisory opinions, the ICJ has declined to define the scope and meaning of a legal question narrowly when its advisory jurisdiction is being challenged on the grounds that the question on which an opinion was sought was political or deprived of a legal nature. [U]nlike the ICJ, which has competence in international law in general, the Tribunal is a specialized jurisdiction entrusted to deal with law of the sea matters under the Convention. The Tribunal may thus be required to read the term "legal" under article 138 of its Rules rather narrowly within the context of the law of the sea....

International agreement related to the purposes of the Convention

In order to request an advisory opinion from the Tribunal on the basis of an international agreement, such agreement should be related to the purposes of the Convention. Therefore, a request for an advisory opinion based upon an international agreement not related to the Convention cannot be dealt with by the Tribunal. A variety of international agreements—bilateral, regional or global—which are "related to the purposes of the Convention" can be concluded among States. For instance, an agreement establishing a regional fisheries organization may easily be characterized as an international agreement related to the purposes of the Convention. Other agreements concluded to implement provisions of the Convention relating to the protection of the marine environment could also be considered as being related to the purposes of the Convention.

Can an agreement related to the purposes of the Convention which is concluded between a State Party and a non-governmental entity be characterized as an international agreement within the context of paragraph 1 of article 138? [A]rticle 20, paragraph 2, of the Statute... states that "[t]he Tribunal shall be open to entities other than States Parties in any case expressly provided for in Part XI or in any case submitted pursuant to any other agreement conferring jurisdiction on the Tribunal which is accepted by all the parties to that case." This paragraph identifies two types of entities other than States Parties which can appear before the Seabed Disputes Chamber or the Tribunal. The first type is entities other than States Parties "in any case expressly provided for in Part XI." Those entities are entitled to appear before the Seabed Disputes Chamber but not before the Tribunal. In any event, under Part XI, only the Assembly and the Council of the Authority are permitted to request an advisory opinion from the Seabed Disputes Chamber. The second type of entities other than States Parties concerns those "in any case submitted pursuant to any other agreement conferring jurisdiction on the Tribunal which is accepted by all the parties to that case." It is envisaged that entities of this type may appear before the Tribunal. However, it does not seem to be entirely clear whether such other agreement concluded between a State Party and an entity such as a non-governmental organization and including a provision for the submission to the Tribunal of a request for an advisory opinion could be characterized as an international agreement related to the purposes of the Convention within the context of article 138, paragraph 1, of the Rules of the Tribunal.

Specificity of a provision in the agreement governing the submission to the Tribunal of a request for an advisory opinion

Pursuant to article 138, paragraph 1, of its Rules, the Tribunal may give an advisory opinion if the question asked of it is based upon a specific provision in an international agreement related to the purposes of the Convention. [A] request which does not clearly indicate a legal basis may be considered insufficient....

Authorization in the agreement for a body to request the Tribunal for an advisory opinion

[T]he advisory system of the ICJ ... restricts eligibility to request an advisory opinion from it to the General Assembly and the Security Council and other organs and specialized agencies so authorized by the General Assembly under article 96 of the Charter. Unlike the [U.N.] Charter, however, there is no such express provision in the Convention or the Statute of the Tribunal confining the bodies eligible to request an advisory opinion to the Tribunal.

[A]rticle 138, paragraph 2, is not explicit as to whether the body authorized to request an advisory opinion from the Tribunal should be a permanent one or whether it could also be an *ad hoc* body created by States Parties for the purpose of making such request to the Tribunal.... Judge Jesus [has expressed the view that:]

> ... any organ, entity, institution, organization or State that is indicated in such an international agreement as being empowered to request, on behalf of the parties concerned, an advisory opinion of the Tribunal, in accordance with the terms of the agreement, would be a "body" within the meaning of article 138, paragraph 2, of the Rules.... Its legitimacy to transmit the request is derived from the authority given to it by the agreement and not by its nature or any other structure or institutional considerations....

V. Advisory Proceedings under Article 138 of the Rules as an Alternative to Contentious Proceedings

. . . The non-binding character of advisory opinions may be more attractive and effective for certain States depending on the nature of the dispute or political and diplomatic considerations compared with final and binding decisions expected of contentious procedure.

[Most] of the advisory opinions given by the [Permanent Court of International Justice before World War II] related to existing disputes. . . .

Reading article 138 of the Rules of the Tribunal together with article 21 of its Statute, there does not seem to be any restriction preventing disputes formulated in legal questions from being referred to the Tribunal for the purpose of seeking advisory opinions. The parties to a dispute may agree to refer it to the Tribunal as a legal question for an opinion through a body authorized to do so as provided for in article 138, paragraph 2. . . .

VI. Conclusion . . .

As provided for in the Convention and the Statute, the Tribunal's jurisdiction in respect of law of the sea matters is broad[.] However, its use has been limited so far. [As of mid-2009] the Tribunal has dealt with 15 cases and out of those 15, 13 cases (nine prompt releases cases and four provisional measures cases requiring urgent handling) have been filed on the basis of the two special types of the Tribunal's compulsory jurisdiction provided for under articles 290, paragraph 5 (Provisional measures), and 292 (Prompt release of vessels and crews) of the Convention. The other two cases, . . . which concerned merits, were submitted to the Tribunal on the basis of a special agreement.

The limited use of the Tribunal by States Parties may be largely attributable to its narrow jurisdictional base. The number of treaties conferring jurisdiction upon it currently stands at only ten, five of which have not yet entered into force while, under article 287 of the Convention, out of 158 States Parties only 23 have so far chosen the Tribunal as their preferred forum. As a result most of the cases on merits arising under the Convention since 1997 were referred to Annex VII arbitral tribunals, which are default fora under article 287. It may also be noted that, since the Tribunal began its activities in October 1996, four cases concerning law of the sea matters have been submitted to the ICJ, whose jurisdiction is general and much broader than that of the Tribunal, which is a specialized jurisdiction in law of the sea matters.

...Part XV of the Convention is designed to deal with contentious cases, which would lead to binding decisions. The advisory procedure envisaged under article 138 of the Rules of the Tribunal, on the other hand, aims to give non-binding advisory opinions as is the case with the advisory opinions to be given by the Seabed Disputes Chamber or by the ICJ. As noted above, the eligibility requirement under article 138 seems to be much more flexible compared with that of the advisory system of the ICJ. For this reason, States Parties may be more interested and feel more comfortable by attempting to use the advisory procedure before the Tribunal instead of resorting to the contentious procedure resulting in a final and binding decision.

...Authoritative pronouncements of the Tribunal as to legal questions put to it through the advisory procedure could be a preliminary step before the parties to a dispute reach a definitive settlement and, in this respect, advisory proceedings could be a potential alternative to binding procedures under Part XV of the Convention.

Notes

1. *The Seabed Disputes Chamber and Advisory Opinions.* The LOS Convention provides explicitly that the Seabed Disputes Chamber of the ITLOS may issue advisory opinions when the International Seabed Authority's Assembly or Council requests them. LOS Convention, Articles 159(10), 191. What sorts of issues could be brought to and decided by the Chamber under these articles? We have seen one example, Responsibilities and Obligations of States Sponsoring Persons and Entities with Respect to Activities in the Area, ITLOS Case No. 17, 50 Intl. Leg. Materials 455 (2011), in Chapter 11.

2. *Advisory Opinions Pursuant to (International) Agreements.* It is not unusual for international courts and tribunals to have jurisdiction to give advisory opinions requested by an international organization. For example, in addition to Articles 159(10) and 191 of the LOS Convention, see Article 96 of the United Nations Charter and Article 65 of the ICJ Statute (providing for the advisory jurisdiction of the ICJ). ITLOS Rule 138, discussed in the reading above, is unusual in providing for advisory opinion requests pursuant to international agreements. In standard parlance, an "international agreement" is an interstate treaty or a treaty between a state and an international organization. Do you agree that it was appropriate for the Tribunal to adopt Rule 138? Should the Tribunal broaden the Rule to embrace requests for advisory opinions pursuant to "any other agreement," the language used in Article 21 of the Tribunal's Statute (Annex VI of the LOS Convention)? The phrase "any other agreement"

might encompass an agreement between a state and a private party, or even a purely private agreement. What sorts of issues could realistically be brought to the ITLOS under an expanded "any other agreement" basis for advisory jurisdiction? What might prompt parties to agree to seek advisory opinions if such a basis were available? What are the advantages and disadvantages of advisory opinions, compared to decisions rendered in contentious cases? Is it desirable to provide for referrals to the ITLOS from national courts, to enable them to seek advice on law of the sea matters? Could an ITLOS Rule 138 agreement permit such referrals?

In March 2013, the ITLOS received its first request for an advisory opinion not based on Part XI of the LOS Convention. See Request for an advisory opinion submitted by the Sub-Regional Fisheries Commission (SRFC), ITLOS Case No. 21, available at http://www.itlos.org; Michael A. Becker, Sustainable Fisheries and the Obligations of Coastal States: The Request by the Sub-Regional Fisheries Commission for an ITLOS Advisory Opinion, 17 ASIL Insights, Issue 19 (2013).

THE VOLGA CASE

Russian Federation v. Australia (Prompt Release), ITLOS Case No. 11, 126 Intl. L. Rep. 483 (2002), available at http://www.itlos.org

[The *Volga*, a long-line fishing vessel flying the Russian flag and owned by a Russian corporation, was boarded by Australian military personnel on February 7, 2002, arrested, and escorted to Freemantle, Australia. At the time of its arrest, the *Volga* was on the high seas just outside the EEZ of Australia's Heard Island. Heard Island and its surrounding waters are located in the Southern Ocean near Antarctica, within the region subject to the 1980 Convention on the Conservation of Antarctic Marine Living Resources.

According to Australia, an Australian fisheries protection vessel had warned the *Volga* on January 5, 2002, not to enter the EEZ around Heard Island. The *Volga*'s computer records indicated that it nonetheless proceeded to fish within the EEZ. Just before the *Volga*'s arrest, an Australian government aircraft observed the *Volga* within Australia's EEZ, heading for the high seas; the parties disagreed as to whether any Australian government aircraft or vessel gave the *Volga* an order to stop. The *Volga*'s cargo included 131 tons of Patagonian toothfish (Chilean sea bass), which Australia seized pursuant to its Fisheries Management Act.

Some of the *Volga*'s crew were detained in Australia, along with the vessel itself. Three crew members of Spanish nationality were finally permitted to leave Australia when the Supreme Court of Western Australia ruled, on

December 16, 2002, on their bail conditions. These conditions included the posting of a cash bail of AU$ 245,000 and the requirement that the crew members report periodically to the Australian Embassy in Madrid, Spain. The crew members accepted the bail conditions and left Australia.

The *Volga*'s owner pursued legal avenues in Australia, seeking to obtain the release of the vessel. During the course of the proceedings in Australia, the Australian government indicated that it would release the *Volga* on the posting of security amounting to AU$ 3,332,500. The owner, however, would agree only to a bond of AU$ 500,000.

The Russian Federation filed an application for the prompt release of the *Volga* and the three Spanish crew members with the ITLOS on December 2, 2002. The Tribunal rendered its judgment on December 23, 2002. In light of the crew's departure from Australia following the December 16th decision of the Supreme Court of Western Australia, the ITLOS found that "setting a bond in respect of the three members of the crew would serve no practical purpose." ¶ 74. The following excerpts from the Tribunal's judgment concern the bond conditions for the release of the *Volga* itself.]

55. The Tribunal will, at the outset, examine the question whether it has jurisdiction to entertain the Application and whether the Application is admissible. Article 292 of the Convention reads as follows:

Article 292
Prompt release of vessels and crews

> 1. Where the authorities of a State Party have detained a vessel flying the flag of another State Party and it is alleged that the detaining State has not complied with the provisions of this Convention for the prompt release of the vessel or its crew upon the posting of a reasonable bond or other financial security, the question of release from detention may be submitted to any court or tribunal agreed upon by the parties or, failing such agreement within 10 days from the time of detention, to a court or tribunal accepted by the detaining State under article 287 or to the International Tribunal for the Law of the Sea, unless the parties otherwise agree.
>
> 2. The application for release may be made only by or on behalf of the flag State of the vessel.
>
> 3. The court or tribunal shall deal without delay with the application for release and shall deal only with the question of release, without prejudice to the merits of any case before the appropriate domestic forum against the vessel, its owner or its crew. The authorities of the

> detaining State remain competent to release the vessel or its crew at any time.
>
> 4. Upon the posting of the bond or other financial security determined by the court or tribunal, the authorities of the detaining State shall comply promptly with the decision of the court or tribunal concerning the release of the vessel or its crew.

56. [T]he Respondent does not contest the jurisdiction of the Tribunal. The Russian Federation and Australia are both States Parties to the Convention.... The status of the Russian Federation as the flag State of the *Volga* is not disputed. The parties did not agree to submit the question of release from detention to any other court or tribunal within 10 days of the time of detention. The Application has been duly made by the Russian Federation in accordance with article 292, paragraph 2, of the Convention....

58. As regards admissibility, the Applicant alleges that the Respondent has not complied with the provisions of article 73, paragraph 2, of the Convention for the prompt release of a vessel and its crew because the bond set by the Respondent is in all circumstances unreasonable....

59. [A]rticle 73, paragraph 2, of the Convention is one of the provisions of the Convention "for the prompt release of the vessel or its crew upon the posting of a reasonable bond or other financial security" to which article 292, paragraph 1, refers. The Tribunal therefore finds that the Application is admissible.

60. The Applicant...submits that the Respondent has set conditions for the release of the vessel and three members of the crew which are not permissible under article 73, paragraph 2, or are unreasonable in terms of article 73, paragraph 2, of the Convention.

61. The Respondent maintains that the bond it has set for the release of the *Volga* is reasonable, having regard to the value of the *Volga*, its fuel, lubricants and the level of fishing equipment; the gravity of the offences and potential penalties; the level of international concern over illegal fishing; and the need to secure compliance with Australian laws and international obligations pending the completion of domestic proceedings....

62. When the Tribunal is called upon, under article 292 of the Convention, to assess whether the bond set by a party is reasonable, it must apply the Convention and other rules of international law not incompatible with the Convention.

63. In its previous judgments, the Tribunal indicated some of the factors that should be taken into account in assessing a reasonable bond for the release

of a vessel or its crew under article 292 of the Convention. In the *"Camouco" Case*, the Tribunal indicated factors relevant in an assessment of the reasonableness of bonds or other financial security, as follows:

> The Tribunal considers that a number of factors are relevant in an assessment of the reasonableness of bonds or other financial security. They include the gravity of the alleged offences, the penalties imposed or imposable under laws of the detaining State, the value of the detained vessel and of the cargo seized, the amount of bond imposed by the detaining State and its form. (Judgment of 7 February 2000, paragraph 67).

64. In the *"Monte Confurco" Case*, the Tribunal confirmed this statement and added that "[t]his is by no means a complete list of factors. Nor does the Tribunal intend to lay down rigid rules as to the exact weight to be attached to each of them" (Judgment of 18 December 2000, paragraph 76).

65. The Tribunal is required to determine whether or not the bond set by the Respondent is reasonable in terms of the Convention. As held in the *"Monte Confurco" Case*:

> [T]he object of article 292 of the Convention is to reconcile the interest of the flag State to have its vessel and its crew released promptly with the interest of the detaining State to secure appearance in its court of the Master and the payment of penalties.
>
> The balance of interests emerging from articles 73 and 292 of the Convention provides the guiding criterion for the Tribunal in its assessment of the reasonableness of the bond. [...] (Judgment of 18 December 2000, paragraphs 71 and 72).

In assessing the reasonableness of the bond or other security, due account must be taken of the terms of the bond or security set by the detaining State, having regard to all the circumstances of the particular case.

66. The Tribunal will now deal with the application of the various factors in the present case.

67. Turning first to the gravity of the offences alleged to have been committed in the present case, it is noted that the offences relate to the conservation of the fishery resources in the exclusive economic zone. The Respondent has submitted that the potential penalties under Australian law indicate the grave nature of the offence and support its contention that the bond set for the release of the vessel and members of its crew is reasonable. The

Respondent has pointed out that continuing illegal fishing in the area covered by the Convention for the Conservation of Antarctic Marine Living Resources ("CCAMLR") has resulted in a serious depletion of the stocks of Patagonian toothfish and is a matter of international concern. It has invited the Tribunal to take into account "the serious problem of continuing illegal fishing in the Southern Ocean" and the dangers this poses to the conservation of fisheries resources and the maintenance of the ecological balance of the environment. According to the Respondent, this problem and the international concern that it raises provide ample justification for the measures it has taken, including the penalties provided in its legislation and the high level of bond that it has set for the release of ships and their crews when charged with violation of its laws.

68. The Tribunal takes note of the submissions of the Respondent. The Tribunal understands the international concerns about illegal, unregulated and unreported fishing and appreciates the objectives behind the measures taken by States, including the States Parties to CCAMLR, to deal with the problem.

69. The Tribunal must, however, emphasize that, in the present proceedings, it is called upon to assess whether the bond set by the Respondent is reasonable in terms of article 292 of the Convention. The purpose of the procedure provided for in article 292 of the Convention is to secure the prompt release of the vessel and crew upon the posting of a reasonable bond, pending completion of the judicial procedures before the courts of the detaining State. Among the factors to be considered in making the assessment are the penalties that may be imposed for the alleged offences under the laws of the Respondent. It is by reference to these penalties that the Tribunal may evaluate the gravity of the alleged offences.... The Applicant does not deny that the alleged offences are considered to be grave under Australian law.

70. According to the laws of Australia, the maximum total of fines imposable on the three officers of the *Volga* is AU$ 1,100,000 and the vessel, its equipment and fish on board are liable to forfeiture.

71. There is no dispute between the parties as to the value of the vessel and its cargo. The vessel has been valued in the amount of US$ 1 million (approximately AU$ 1.8 million) and the value of fuel, lubricants and equipment amounts to AU$ 147,460. The catch and bait on board were sold by the Australian authorities for AU$ 1,932,579.28.

72. The bond sought by the Respondent is for AU$ 3,332,500. This consists of three components, namely:

- a security to cover the assessed value of the vessel, fuel, lubricants and fishing equipment (AU$ 1,920,000);

- an amount (AU$ 412,500) to secure payment of potential fines imposed in the criminal proceedings that are still pending against members of the crew;
- a security (AU$ 1,000,000) related to the carriage of a fully operational VMS [vehicle monitoring system] and observance of CCAMLR conservation measures.

73. In the view of the Tribunal, the amount of AU$ 1,920,00 sought by the Respondent for the release of the vessel, which represents the full value of the vessel, fuel, lubricants and fishing equipment and is not in dispute between the parties, is reasonable in terms of article 292 of the Convention. . . .

75. Besides requiring a bond, the Respondent has made the release of the vessel conditional upon the fulfillment of two conditions: that the vessel carry a VMS, and that information concerning particulars about the owner and ultimate beneficial owners of the ship be submitted to its authorities. The Respondent contends that the carrying of the VMS is necessary in order to prevent further illicit fishing once the ship is released. It further states that because the payment of a bond is a significant transaction it is entitled to know with whom the arrangements are to be made. The Applicant argues that such conditions find no basis in article 73, paragraph 2, and in the Convention in general, because only conditions that relate to the provision of a bond or security in the pecuniary sense can be imposed. . . .

77. In interpreting the expression "bond or other security" set out in article 73, paragraph 2, of the Convention, the Tribunal considers that this expression must be seen in its context and in light of its object and purpose. The relevant context includes the provisions of the Convention concerning the prompt release of vessels and crews upon the posting of a bond or security. These provisions are: article 292; article 220, paragraph 7; and article 226, paragraph 1(b). They use the expressions "bond or other financial security" and "bonding or other appropriate financial security." Seen in this context, the expression "bond or other security" in article 73, paragraph 2, should, in the view of the Tribunal, be interpreted as referring to a bond or security of a financial nature. The Tribunal also observes, in this context, that where the Convention envisages the imposition of conditions additional to a bond or other financial security, it expressly states so. Thus article 226, paragraph 1(c), of the Convention provides that "the release of a vessel may, whenever it would present an unreasonable threat of damage to the marine environment, be refused or made conditional upon proceeding to the nearest appropriate repair yard." It follows from the above that the non-financial conditions cannot be considered components of a bond or other financial security for the

purpose of applying article 292 of the Convention in respect of an alleged violation of article 73, paragraph 2, of the Convention....

78. The Respondent has required, as part of the security for obtaining the release of the *Volga* and its crew, payment by the owner of one million Australian dollars. According to the Respondent, the purpose of this amount is to guarantee the carriage of a fully operational monitoring system and observance of Commission for the Conservation of Marine Living Resources conservation measures until the conclusion of legal proceedings. The Respondent explained that this component of the bond was to ensure "that the *Volga* complies with Australian law and relevant treaties to which Australia is a party until the completion of the domestic legal proceedings"; that the ship does not "enter Australian territorial waters other than with permission or for the purpose of innocent passage prior to the conclusion of the forfeiture proceedings"; and further to ensure that the vessel "will not be used to commit further criminal offences."

79. The Tribunal cannot, in the framework of proceedings under article 292 of the Convention, take a position as to whether the imposition of a condition such as what the Respondent referred to as a "good behaviour bond" is a legitimate exercise of the coastal State's sovereign rights in its exclusive economic zone. The point to be determined is whether a "good behaviour bond" is a bond or security within the meaning of these terms in articles 73, paragraph 2, and 292 of the Convention.

80. [A]rticle 73... envisages enforcement measures in respect of violations of the coastal State's laws and regulations alleged to have been committed. In the view of the Tribunal, a "good behaviour bond" to prevent future violations of the laws of a coastal State cannot be considered as a bond or security within the meaning of article 73, paragraph 2, of the Convention read in conjunction with article 292 of the Convention....

83. In the view of the Tribunal, matters relating to the circumstances of the seizure of the *Volga*... are not relevant to the present proceedings for prompt release under article 292 of the Convention. The Tribunal therefore cannot take into account the circumstances of the seizure of the *Volga* in assessing the reasonableness of the bond.

84. The fish and bait that were on board the *Volga* at the time of its arrest have been sold by the Australian authorities. According to the Respondent, the proceeds are being held in trust, pending the final outcome of the proceedings against the members of the crew. The Applicant has invited the Tribunal to treat the proceeds of the sale of the catch as security given by the owner for the release of the vessel and its crew. The Respondent, however, contends that nei-

ther the fish nor the proceeds of their sale should be treated as security given by the owner, since the fish are subject to forfeiture under the laws of Australia.

85. Under the laws of Australia the fish on board the *Volga* are subject to confiscation, if the domestic courts find that they were illegally caught within the EEZ of the Respondent. However, the Respondent may be obliged to return the proceeds of the sale to the owner of the ship if the domestic courts conclude that the fish were not caught within the EEZ of Australia. In effect, the catch and the vessel, the fuel, lubricants and the equipment on board, all form part of the guarantee that the Respondent needs to ensure that the final decisions of the domestic courts can be fully enforced. However, a bond or other financial security for the purposes of article 292 of the Convention is needed only to ensure full protection of Australia's potential right in the vessel and possible fines against the members of the crew. No such bond is necessary in respect of the catch since Australia holds the proceeds of the sale....

88. On the basis of the above considerations, and keeping in view the overall circumstances of this case, the Tribunal considers that the bond as sought by Australia is not reasonable within the meaning of article 292 of the Convention.

89. For the above reasons, the Tribunal finds that the Application with respect to the allegation of non-compliance with article 73, paragraph 2, of the Convention is well-founded for the purposes of these proceedings and that, consequently, Australia must release promptly the *Volga* upon the posting of a bond or other financial security to be determined by the Tribunal.

90. On the basis of the foregoing considerations, the Tribunal is of the view that a bond for the release of the *Volga*, the fuel, lubricants and fishing equipment should be in the amount of AU$ 1,920,000.

[The Tribunal unanimously concludes that it has jurisdiction under Article 292 of the LOS Convention, that Russia's application is admissible, and that the form of the bond should be a bank guarantee. The findings and decisions on the matters discussed in paragraphs 89 and 90 above were by a vote of 19–2.]

THE TOMIMARU CASE

Japan v. Russian Federation (Prompt Release), ITLOS Case No. 15, 46 Intl. Leg. Materials 1185 (2007), available at http://www.itlos.org

[Russia licensed the *Tomimaru*, a Japanese-registered vessel owned by a Japanese company, to fish for walleye pollack and herring in the Russian exclusive economic zone. On October 31, 2006, Russian officials boarded the *Tomimaru* while it was fishing in Russia's EEZ. They discovered on board walleye pollack that the vessel had not entered in its logbook, as well as significant quantities of fish for which the vessel had no license. Russia seized and detained the *Tomimaru*, but released the crew (except for the master). On November 8, Russia instituted criminal proceedings against the master, alleging that he was engaged in illegal fishing and had caused environmental damage to living resources. On December 12, 2006, Russia set a bond of 8.8 million rubles (approximately US$ 345,000 at the time) for release of the vessel, which the owner did not pay. ¶ 36. On May 15, 2007, the master was fined 500,000 rubles (US$ 19,600) and ordered to pay nine million rubles (US$ 353,000) in damages; he paid the fine only but was allowed to leave Russia. ¶ 45.

Russia also pursued administrative proceedings with respect to the *Tomimaru*. The owner requested a bond for those proceedings, but was told that Russian law did not provide for one. The outcome of the Russian administrative proceedings is noted in the case excerpt below.

Japan filed a prompt release application with the ITLOS on July 6, 2007. The Tribunal found that it had jurisdiction under Article 292: Japan and the Russian Federation were both parties to the LOS Convention; Japan was the flag state of the *Tomimaru*; the *Tomimaru* was detained in Russia; Japan alleged noncompliance by Russia with Article 73(2) of the Convention; and the parties did not agree to submit the question of release of the vessel to another court or tribunal within ten days from the time of detention. The Tribunal then turned to the issue of the admissibility of Japan's prompt release application and the effect of Russia's confiscation of the *Tomimaru*, considered in the excerpt below. The ITLOS rendered its judgment on August 6, 2007.]

58. [T]he Application is based on article 292 read in conjunction with article 73, paragraph 2, of the Convention. The Applicant asks the Tribunal to exercise its power under article 292, paragraph 3, of the Convention, to order the release of the vessel and the crew upon the posting of a reasonable bond or other financial security.

59. The Respondent maintains that the judgment of the Kamchatka District Court confirming the confiscation of the *Tomimaru* renders the Application under article 292 of the Convention without object. The Respondent argues that, according to article 292, paragraph 3, of the Convention, when examining applications for release, the Tribunal should deal only with the question of release, without prejudice to the merits of any case before the appropriate domestic forum against the vessel, its owner or its crew. The Respondent states that the case has been considered before the appropriate domestic forum on the merits; that the decision rendered by that forum has already entered into

force and, moreover, has been executed. As a consequence, the Tribunal has no competence to examine an application for prompt release.

60. In support of this argument the Respondent states that on 28 December 2006 the Petropavlovsk-Kamchatskii City Court decided that the vessel should be confiscated and a fine of 2,865,149.5 roubles (approximately US$ 112,000) should be paid by the owner. This judgment was upheld on 24 January 2007 by the Kamchatka District Court, to which the owner had appealed....

64. The Applicant maintains that ... this case is still pending. The Applicant stresses ... that the Supreme Court of the Russian Federation may annul the decision of the Kamchatka District Court of 24 January 2007.

65. The Applicant further [argues] that [if] the confiscation of arrested vessels were allowed to prevent the Tribunal exercising its prompt release jurisdiction, the prompt release obligations and procedures under the Convention would lose all practical meaning....

66. [A]fter the closure of the [prompt release] hearing [before the ITLOS], on 26 July 2007, the Respondent informed the Tribunal that the Supreme Court of the Russian Federation had dismissed the complaint concerning the review of the decision on the confiscation of the *Tomimaru*....

71. The Tribunal now turns its attention to ... whether the confiscation of a vessel renders an application for its prompt release under article 292 of the Convention without object.

72. The Tribunal notes that article 73 of the Convention makes no reference to confiscation of vessels. The Tribunal is aware that many States have provided for measures of confiscation of fishing vessels in their legislation with respect to the management and conservation of marine living resources.

73. In considering whether confiscation renders an application for the prompt release of a vessel without object the Tribunal has to take into account the object and purpose of the prompt release procedure. Account has to be taken also of article 292, paragraph 3, of the Convention which reads:

> The court or tribunal shall deal without delay with the application for release and shall deal only with the question of release, without prejudice to the merits of any case before the appropriate domestic forum against the vessel, its owner or its crew.

74. As the Tribunal already stated in its judgment in the *"Monte Confurco" Case* (*ITLOS Reports 2000*, p. 86, at p. 108, para. 70), article 73 of the Convention establishes a balance between the interests of the coastal State in taking appropriate measures as may be necessary to ensure compliance with the laws and regulations adopted by it on the one hand and the interest of the flag State

in securing prompt release of its vessels and their crew upon the posting of a bond or other security on the other. The Tribunal wishes to emphasize that a judgment under article 292 of the Convention must be "without prejudice to the merits of any case" ("*sans préjudice de la suite qui sera donnée à toute action*") before the appropriate domestic forum against the vessel or its crew and that this, too, is a factor in maintaining the balance between the interests of the coastal State and of the flag State.

75. It is the view of the Tribunal that confiscation of a fishing vessel must not be used in such a manner as to upset the balance of the interests of the flag State and of the coastal State established in the Convention.

76. A decision to confiscate eliminates the provisional character of the detention of the vessel rendering the procedure for its prompt release without object. Such a decision should not be taken in such a way as to prevent the shipowner from having recourse to available domestic judicial remedies, or as to prevent the flag State from resorting to the prompt release procedure set forth in the Convention; nor should it be taken through proceedings inconsistent with international standards of due process of law. In particular, a confiscation decided in unjustified haste would jeopardize the operation of article 292 of the Convention.

77. In this context, the Tribunal emphasizes that, considering the objective of article 292 of the Convention, it is incumbent upon the flag State to act in a timely manner. This objective can only be achieved if the shipowner and the flag State take action within reasonable time either to have recourse to the national judicial system of the detaining State or to initiate the prompt release procedure under article 292 of the Convention.

78. The Tribunal emphasizes that, considering the object and purpose of the prompt release procedure, a decision to confiscate a vessel does not prevent the Tribunal from considering an application for prompt release of such vessel while proceedings are still before the domestic courts of the detaining State.

79. The Tribunal notes that the decision of the Supreme Court of the Russian Federation brings to an end the procedures before the domestic courts. This has not been contested by the Applicant. After being informed of that decision, the Applicant did not maintain its argument that the confiscation of the *Tomimaru* is not final. The Tribunal notes also that no inconsistency with international standards of due process of law has been argued and that no allegation has been raised that the proceedings which resulted in the confiscation were such as to frustrate the possibility of recourse to national or international remedies.

80. The Tribunal considers that a decision under article 292 of the Convention to release the vessel would contradict the decision which concluded the proceedings before the appropriate domestic fora and encroach upon national competences, thus contravening article 292, paragraph 3, of the Convention....

82. For these reasons,

THE TRIBUNAL,

Unanimously,

Finds that the Application of Japan no longer has any object and that the Tribunal is therefore not called upon to give a decision thereon.

Notes

1. *Residual Compulsory Jurisdiction.* The ITLOS has "residual compulsory jurisdiction" with respect to Article 292 prompt release applications and Article 290(5) provisional measures. As of September 2013 about half of the Tribunal's cases have been Article 292 prompt release applications, such as the Volga and Tomimaru cases. Many of the Tribunal's other cases have involved provisional measures, which we address in the next case and set of Notes. In Article 290(5) and Article 292 cases, in what sense is the Tribunal's jurisdiction "residual"? In what sense is it "compulsory"? Why did countries find it advisable to vest the Tribunal with residual compulsory jurisdiction in such cases?

2. *The Problem of Detained Vessels and Crews.* On the one hand, as the ITLOS recognized in paragraph 68 of its opinion in the Volga case, coastal state arrests and detentions of vessels and crews have been responses to the serious problem of illegal fishing and other violations of coastal state laws in EEZs. On the other hand, instances of prolonged coastal state detentions of foreign flag vessels and their crews may give rise to serious economic and human rights concerns. In light of Article 73 of the LOS Convention, did the Tribunal draw the appropriate balance in its order in the Volga case? Whose rights is the Tribunal balancing in its prompt release decisions?

3. *The Limited Scope of Prompt Release Proceedings.* Article 292 was narrowly tailored to address detentions only in particular situations. In a prompt release proceeding, according to Article 292(3), the court or tribunal (in practice, the ITLOS) "shall deal only with the question of release." That is, the legality of the coastal state's arrest of the vessel and questions concerning the

merits of the dispute between the flag state and coastal state are not at issue in a prompt release proceeding. The prompt release determination shall be "without prejudice to the merits of any case before the appropriate domestic forum against the vessel, its owner or its crew." Should the ITLOS be precluded from granting an order for prompt release if a detaining state, in an accelerated municipal proceeding, approves confiscation of the vessel in a "merits" ruling? Was the ITLOS's treatment of this issue in paragraph 76 of the Tomimaru case appropriate? Or does paragraph 76, as Judge Nelson argued in his separate declaration in that case, "run[] the risk of 'straying into territory which more properly belongs to the local court.'" Declaration of Judge Nelson, 2.

Article 292 does not apply to every foreign flag vessel or crew detained by coastal states. In order for Article 292 to come into play, it must be "alleged that the detaining State has not complied with the provisions of th[e] Convention for the prompt release of the vessel or its crew upon the posting of a reasonable bond or other financial security." Article 292(1). The Convention specifically refers to prompt release on the posting of a reasonable bond or financial security only in Article 73(2), at issue in the Volga case, and in a few of its marine pollution articles. See Articles 220 and 226. Article 73(2), for example, reads: "Arrested vessels and their crews shall be promptly released upon the posting of reasonable bond or other security."

Should the ITLOS judicially develop a "non-restrictive interpretation" of Article 292, under which the Tribunal could rule on detentions for other types of violations of coastal state laws? Or would such an interpretation upset the balance of coastal state vs. flag state rights contemplated in the Convention? The ITLOS has emphasized that "[t]he scope of the jurisdiction of the Tribunal in proceedings under article 292 of the Convention encompasses only cases in which 'it is alleged that the detaining State has not complied with the provisions of this Convention for the prompt release of the vessel or its crew upon the posting a reasonable bond or other financial security.'" Camouco Case (Panama v. France), ¶ 59, ITLOS Case No. 5 (2000), available at http://www.itlos.org (emphasis added). The text of Article 292(1) reinforces that view, as does Article 113(1) of the Rules of the Tribunal, ITLOS/8 (2009). In an application for prompt release based on Article 73(2), how close must be the relationship between the activity of a detained vessel and the subject matter of Article 73, in order for Article 292 to apply? For example, when a vessel supplies fuel oil to fishing vessels in a coastal state's EEZ and as a result is arrested and detained, is an allegation that the detention violates Article 73(2) sufficiently plausible to allow Article 292 to be invoked? See The M/V Saiga Case (St. Vincent and the Grenadines v. Guinea), ITLOS Case No. 1 (1997), available at http://www.itlos.org.

Despite the limited scope of Article 292, the ITLOS's decisions in its prompt release cases have addressed significant issues, such as prerequisites for vessel nationality. See, e.g., the excerpt from the Grand Prince case in Chapter 3, Section B.

4. *The Relationship between the ITLOS and Municipal Courts.* In some prompt release cases, the detaining state may simply have refused to set a bond. In other cases, however, national authorities have set a bond, and the flag state of the detained vessel challenges the bond's reasonableness. How is the ITLOS to determine the reasonableness of the bond? On this point, the LOS Convention provides no explicit guidance. Has the ITLOS determined the appropriate factors to consider, on this question of international law? How much deference should the ITLOS pay to a municipal court's determination as to what constitutes a reasonable bond? If a municipal court sets a bond, following its country's laws with respect to the proper amount, when, if ever, should the ITLOS find that bond to be unreasonable? Was the Tribunal correct to preclude a "good behavior bond" in the Volga case? In paragraph 7 of his dissent, Judge Anderson argued:

> My reading of the plain words of article 73 in their context and in the light of the object and purpose shows that the article contains no explicit restriction upon the imposition of non-financial conditions for release of arrested vessels. Where the Convention does limit the rights of coastal States in the matter of enforcement, it does so in express terms: article 73, paragraph 3, prohibits imprisonment and corporal punishment. In my view further limitations upon the rights of States Parties in what are important matters of domestic criminal procedure, are not to be easily implied.

Has the ITLOS taken insufficient account of the growing problem of illegal, unregulated, and unreported fishing in its prompt release decisions?

Does a flag state have to wait for a municipal court to rule on the conditions for release of a vessel or its crew before pursuing a prompt release application with the ITLOS? There was a delay between the detention and the Article 292 applications in both the Volga case and the Tomimaru case, but is "exhaustion of local remedies" required before the ITLOS may act on a prompt release application?

5. *"By or on behalf of the Flag State."* Article 292 proceedings are envisioned as flag state vs. coastal state proceedings, although Article 292(2) authorizes the flag state to designate another entity, such as the vessel owner, to act "on behalf of " the flag state as its agent in pursuing a prompt release application.

Two-thirds of the ITLOS's prompt release cases—though not the Volga case or the Tomimaru case—have been "on behalf of" cases. What difficulties could this system pose for the Tribunal? Recall the discussion in Note 1 following the Grand Prince case in Chapter 3, Section B. Should the LOS Convention have allowed private vessel owners to pursue prompt release applications directly, without the need to seek approval from the flag state? At the start of the negotiation of the LOS Convention, the United States proposed allowing direct private access to the Tribunal in such cases. See Article 8(2) of the 1973 U.S. Draft Articles on Dispute Settlement, UN Doc. A/AC.138/97, UNGAOR, 28th Sess., Supp. No. 21, vol. II at 22, UN Doc. A/9021 (1973).

SOUTHERN BLUEFIN TUNA CASE

Australia and New Zealand v. Japan, Arbitral Tribunal Constituted Under Annex VII of the United Nations Convention on the Law of the Sea (Award on Jurisdiction and Admissibility, Aug. 4, 2000), 39 Intl. Leg. Materials 1359 (2000)

[This case came to an Annex VII arbitral tribunal following proceedings before the ITLOS. In 1999, Australia and New Zealand, invoking Article 290(5) of the LOS Convention, sought and obtained provisional measures in the ITLOS with respect to Japanese experimental fishing for southern bluefin tuna (SBT) that allegedly contravened Articles 64 and 116–119 of the LOS Convention. Southern Bluefin Tuna Cases (New Zealand v. Japan; Australia v. Japan), ITLOS Cases Nos. 3 & 4 (1999), available at http://www.itlos.org. The application for provisional measures followed attempts at the Commission established under the 1993 Convention for the Conservation of Southern Bluefin Tuna (CCSBT) to resolve the dispute through informal means. In the course of its opinion, the ITLOS concluded that "the provisions of the Convention on the Law of the Sea invoked by Australia and New Zealand appear to afford a basis on which the jurisdiction of the arbitral tribunal might be founded" and that "the fact that the Convention of 1993 applies between the parties does not preclude recourse to the procedures in Part XV, section 2, of the Convention on the Law of the Sea." ¶¶ 52, 55. These conclusions respond to requirements found in Articles 281 and 290(5) of the LOS Convention.

An arbitral tribunal constituted under Articles 287–288 and Annex VII of the LOS Convention then heard the merits of the case. At issue before the arbitral tribunal was the significance of provisions in Article 16 of the 1993 CCSBT, concerning dispute settlement under that Convention:

> 1. If any dispute arises between two or more of the Parties concerning the interpretation or implementation of this Convention, those

> Parties shall consult among themselves with a view to having the dispute resolved by negotiation, inquiry, mediation, conciliation, arbitration, judicial settlement or other peaceful means of their own choice.
>
> 2. Any dispute of this character not so resolved shall, with the consent in each case of all parties to the dispute, be referred for settlement to the International Court of Justice or to arbitration; but failure to reach agreement on reference to the International Court of Justice or to arbitration shall not absolve parties to the dispute from the responsibility of continuing to seek to resolve it by any of the various peaceful means referred to in paragraph 1 above.
>
> 3. In cases where the dispute is referred to arbitration, the arbitral tribunal shall be constituted as provided in the Annex to this Convention.]

50. There is in fact no disagreement between the Parties over whether the dispute falls within the provisions of the 1993 Convention. The issue rather is, does it also fall within the provisions of UNCLOS? The Applicants maintain that Japan has failed to conserve and to cooperate in the conservation of the SBT stock, particularly by its unilateral experimental fishing for SBT in 1998 and 1999. They find a certain tension between cooperation and unilateralism. They contend that Japan's unilateral EFP [experimental fishing program] has placed it in breach of its obligations under Articles 64, 116, 117, 118 and 119 of UNCLOS. . . .

52. . . . There is no reason why a given act of a State may not violate its obligations under more than one treaty. There is frequently a parallelism of treaties, both in their substantive content and in their provisions for settlement of disputes arising thereunder. The current range of international legal obligations benefits from a process of accretion and cumulation; in the practice of States, the conclusion of an implementing convention does not necessarily vacate the obligations imposed by the framework convention upon the parties to the implementing convention. [T]he Tribunal concludes that the dispute between Australia and New Zealand, on the one hand, and Japan on the other, over Japan's role in the management of SBT stocks and particularly its unilateral experimental fishing program, while centered in the 1993 Convention, also arises under the United Nations Convention on the Law of the Sea. In its view, this conclusion is consistent with the terms of UNCLOS Article 311(2) and (5), and with the law of treaties, in particular Article 30(3) of the Vienna Convention on the Law of Treaties.

53. This holding, however, while critical to the case of the Applicants, is not dispositive of this case. It is necessary to examine a number of articles of Part XV of UNCLOS. Article 286 introduces section 2 of Part XV, a section entitled, "Compulsory Procedures Entailing Binding Decisions." Article 286

provides that, "Subject to section 3, any dispute concerning the interpretation or application of this Convention shall, where no settlement has been reached by recourse to section 1, be submitted at the request of any party to the dispute to the court or tribunal having jurisdiction under this section." Article 286 must be read in context, and that qualifying context includes Article 281(1)[.] Under Article 281(1), if the States which are parties to a dispute concerning the interpretation or application of UNCLOS (and the Tribunal has just held that this is such a dispute) have agreed to seek settlement of the dispute "by a peaceful means of their own choice," the procedures provided for in Part XV of UNCLOS apply only (a) where no settlement has been reached by recourse to such means and (b) the agreement between the parties "does not exclude any further procedure." ...

55. [T]he Tribunal is satisfied about fulfillment of condition (a) of Article 281(1). The Parties have had recourse to means set out in Article 16 of the CCSBT. Negotiations have been prolonged, intense and serious.... Manifestly, no settlement has been reached by recourse to such negotiations....

56. The Tribunal now turns to the second requirement of Article 281(1): that the agreement between the parties "does not exclude any further procedure." This is a requirement, it should be recalled, for applicability of "the procedures provided for in this Part," that is to say, the "compulsory procedures entailing binding decisions" dealt with in section 2 of UNCLOS Part XV. The terms of Article 16 of the 1993 Convention do not expressly and in so many words exclude the applicability of any procedure, including the procedures of section 2 of Part XV of UNCLOS.

57. Nevertheless, in the view of the Tribunal, the absence of an express exclusion of any procedure in Article 16 is not decisive. Article 16(1) requires the parties to "consult among themselves with a view to having the dispute resolved by negotiation, inquiry, mediation, conciliation, arbitration, judicial settlement or other peaceful means of their own choice." Article 16(2), in its first clause, directs the referral of a dispute not resolved by any of the above-listed means of the parties' "own choice" for settlement "to the International Court of Justice or to arbitration" but "with the consent in each case of all parties to the dispute." The ordinary meaning of these terms of Article 16 makes it clear that the dispute is not referable to adjudication by the International Court of Justice (or, for that matter, ITLOS), or to arbitration, "at the request of any party to the dispute" (in the words of UNCLOS Article 286). The consent in each case of all parties to the dispute is required. Moreover, the second clause of Article 16(2) provides that "failure to reach agreement on reference to the International Court of Justice or to arbitration shall not absolve the parties to the dispute from the responsibility of continuing to seek to resolve it by any of

the various peaceful means referred to in paragraph 1 above." The effect of this express obligation to continue to seek resolution of the dispute by the listed means of Article 16(1) is not only to stress the consensual nature of any reference of a dispute to either judicial settlement or arbitration. That express obligation equally imports, in the Tribunal's view, that the intent of Article 16 is to remove proceedings under that Article from the reach of the compulsory procedures of section 2 of Part XV of UNCLOS, that is, to exclude the application to a specific dispute of any procedure of dispute resolution that is not accepted by all parties to the dispute. Article 16(3) reinforces that intent by specifying that, in cases where the dispute is referred to arbitration, the arbitral tribunal shall be constituted as provided for in an annex to the 1993 Convention, which is to say that arbitration contemplated by Article 16 is not compulsory arbitration under section 2 of Part XV of UNCLOS but rather autonomous and consensual arbitration provided for in that CCSBT annex....

59. For all these reasons, the Tribunal concludes that Article 16 of the 1993 Convention "exclude[s] any further procedure" within the contemplation of Article 281(1) of UNCLOS.

60. There are two other considerations that, to the mind of the Tribunal, sustain this conclusion. The first consideration is the extent to which compulsory procedures entailing binding decisions have in fact been prescribed by Part XV of UNCLOS for all States Parties to UNCLOS. [The Tribunal reviews the limitations and optional exceptions to compulsory recourse to third-party dispute settlement contained in Articles 297 and 298 of the LOS Convention.]

62. It thus appears to the Tribunal that UNCLOS falls significantly short of establishing a truly comprehensive regime of compulsory jurisdiction entailing binding decisions....

63. The second consideration of a general character that the Tribunal has taken into account is the fact that a significant number of international agreements with maritime elements, entered into after the adoption of UNCLOS, exclude with varying degrees of explicitness unilateral reference of a dispute to compulsory adjudicative or arbitral procedures.... To hold that disputes implicating obligations under both UNCLOS and an implementing treaty such as the 1993 Convention—as such disputes typically may—must be brought within the reach of section 2 of Part XV of UNCLOS would be effectively to deprive of substantial effect the dispute settlement provisions of those implementing agreements which prescribe dispute resolution by means of the parties' choice....

65. It follows from the foregoing analysis that this Tribunal lacks jurisdiction to entertain the merits of the dispute brought by Australia and New Zealand against Japan....

66. In view of this Tribunal's conclusion that it lacks jurisdiction to deal with the merits of the dispute, and in view of the terms of Article 290(5) of UNCLOS providing that, "Once constituted, the tribunal to which the dispute has been submitted may modify, revoke or affirm those provisional measures...," the Order of the International Tribunal for the Law of the Sea of August 27, 1999, prescribing provisional measures, shall cease to have effect as of the date of the signing of this Award.

67. However, revocation of the Order prescribing provisional measures does not mean that the Parties may disregard the effects of that Order or their own decisions made in conformity with it. The Order and those decisions—and the recourse to ITLOS that gave rise to them—as well as the consequential proceedings before this Tribunal, have had an impact: not merely in the suspension of Japan's unilateral experimental fishing program during the period that the Order was in force, but on the perspectives and actions of the Parties....

70. The Tribunal recalls that Article 16(2) prescribes that failure to reach agreement on reference to arbitration shall not absolve the parties to the dispute from the responsibility of continuing to seek to resolve it by any of the various peaceful means referred to in paragraph 1; and among those means are negotiation, mediation and arbitration. The Tribunal further observes that, to the extent that the search for resolution of the dispute were to resort to third-party procedures, those listed in Article 16 are labels that conform to traditional diplomatic precedent. Their content and modus operandi can be refined and developed by the Parties to meet their specific needs. There are many ways in which an independent body can be configured to interact with the States party to a dispute. For example, there may be a combination or alternation of direct negotiations, advice from expert panels, benevolent supervision and good offices extended by a third-party body, and recourse to a third party for step-by-step aid in decision-making and for mediation, quite apart from third-party binding settlement rendered in the form of an arbitral award. Whatever the mode or modes of peaceful settlement chosen by the Parties, the Tribunal emphasizes that the prospects for a successful settlement of their dispute will be promoted by the Parties' abstaining from any unilateral act that may aggravate the dispute while its solution has not been achieved....

72. FOR THESE REASONS

The Arbitral Tribunal

By vote of 4 to 1,

1. Decides that it is without jurisdiction to rule on the merits of the dispute; and,

Unanimously,

2. Decides, in accordance with Article 290(5) of the United Nations Convention on the Law of the Sea, that provisional measures in force by Order of the International Tribunal for the Law of the Sea prescribed on August 27, 1999, are revoked from the day of the signature of this Award.

Separate Opinion of Justice Sir Kenneth Keith

1. . . . Each of the treaties in issue in this case sets up substantive obligations and obligations relating to peaceful settlement. The parallel and overlapping existence of the obligations arising under each treaty is fundamental in this case. I conclude that the one has not excluded or in any relevant way prejudiced the other.

2. This Tribunal has jurisdiction under section 2 of Part XV of UNCLOS "where no settlement has been reached by recourse to section 1" (article 286). Section 1 begins by imposing an obligation on States Parties [to settle disputes by peaceful means (article 279)]. Section 1 then saves the rights of States Parties to choose their own means of peaceful settlement and to settle the dispute by that means:

> *Article* 280
> *Settlement of disputes by any peaceful means chosen by the parties*
> Nothing in this Part impairs the right of any States Parties to agree at any time to settle a dispute between them concerning the interpretation or application of this Convention by any peaceful means of their own choice.

That provision, like article 281, depends on the Parties first agreeing to and then using a "peaceful means of their own choice." Article 281 however proceeds on the basis that the agreed procedure has failed:

> *Article* 281
> *Procedure where no settlement has been reached by the parties*
> 1. If the States Parties which are parties to a dispute concerning the interpretation or application of this Convention have agreed to seek

settlement of the dispute by a peaceful means of their own choice, the procedures provided for in this Part apply only where no settlement has been reached by recourse to such means and the agreement between the parties does not exclude any further procedure.

2. If the parties have also agreed on a time-limit, paragraph 1 applies only upon the expiration of that time-limit....

4. The two main issues which this provision raises in the circumstances of this case are:

(a) Have the Parties "agreed to seek settlement of the dispute by a peaceful means of their own choice"—that is by way of article 16 of the CCSBT or some other agreed means?

(b) Does article 16 "exclude any further procedure?"...

5. While my answer to question (a) is No so far as article 16 is concerned, I agree that there is a good argument that in their diplomatic exchanges the Parties did agree to attempt to settle the dispute by negotiation.

6. I do not however take that latter aspect of question (a) any further. Rather, I give my primary attention to question (b).... I answer question (b) No. The consequence is that, to my mind, that bar to the tribunal's jurisdiction is not established....

10. My reasons for concluding that article 16 does not exclude any further procedure and in particular the compulsory binding procedures under section 2 of Part XV are to be found in the ordinary meaning of the terms of the two treaties read in their context and in the light of their objects and purposes.

11. Part of the context is provided by the distinct and overlapping substantive obligations of UNCLOS and the CCSBT, a matter recognised by the Award.... The Award indeed recognises a longstanding and widespread parallelism of dispute settlement obligations as well as of substantive obligations. Three relevant categories of substantive obligations can be usefully distinguished:

(1) those which exist under both treaties;

(2) those which exist only under the CCSBT (such as the obligation to meet Secretariat budget obligations); and

(3) those which do or may exist only under UNCLOS; the Award mentions, for instance, the obligations of (a) each State, under article 117, to take such measures for their nationals as may be necessary for the conservation of the living resources of the high seas; and of (b) the three CCSBT Parties owed to third States.

Australia and New Zealand invoke UNCLOS procedures in respect of 1 and 3. Their contention is that the disputes between them and Japan concern "the interpretation or application of [the specified provisions of UNCLOS]."

12. That the disputes may or may not also concern the interpretation or implementation of the CCSBT is beside the point. Subject to the critical question stated in paragraph 4(b)—does article 16 "exclude" further procedures—the separate set of UNCLOS peaceful settlement obligations exists along with and distinct from the provisions of article 16.

13. But does article 16 "exclude" the UNCLOS set of obligations? It does not say that it does. It could have, given the timing of the drafting of the two treaties.... Next, it does not say that disputes concerning the CCSBT must be resolved *only* by procedures under it and *must not* be referred to any tribunal or other third party for settlement. Again it could have said that, as treaty parties have. But does it impliedly exclude the UNCLOS procedures?

14. To do that, article 16 would have to be capable of dealing with all the disputes relating to Southern Bluefin tuna arising between CCSBT parties and concerning the interpretation and application of the relevant provisions of UNCLOS. And, as well, it would have to *exclude* (impliedly) the UNCLOS procedures. I consider those two points in turn.

15. If it is the case, as the Award indicates, that Australia and New Zealand have appropriately invoked obligations which are not covered by the CCSBT it would be surprising were procedures for settlement of disputes *concerning that Convention* to be able to apply to disputes arising beyond it.... On their face, [article 16's] provisions ... do not exclude means to which the parties have separately agreed in respect of disputes concerning the interpretation or application of *other* treaties. What they do say is that the binding or indeed any non-binding procedures listed apply only if the parties agree. If any procedure is agreed to, that procedure applies to disputes concerning the interpretation or implementation (perhaps a wider word than "application") *of the CCSBT*.

16. ... The essential point is that the two treaty regimes (including their settlement procedures) remain distinct. The UNCLOS provisions are not to be seen in any sense as being part of, or being read into the other treaty system....

17. I return to the wording of article 281(1) of UNCLOS. The requirement is that the Parties have agreed to *exclude any* further procedure for the settlement of the dispute concerning UNCLOS. The French and Spanish texts have the same wording and structure. They require opting out. They do not require that the Parties positively agree to the binding procedure by opting in, by contrast to other provisions of Part XV: articles 282, 284(2) and (4) and 288(2)....

19. The need for clear wording to exclude the obligations to submit to the UNCLOS binding procedure, beyond the wording found in article 16, is further supported by other particular provisions of Part XV and by the pivotal role compulsory and binding peaceful settlement procedures played and play in the preparation and scheme of UNCLOS.

20. Article 282, the very next provision to that at centre stage, does indeed give preference to another agreed peaceful settlement procedure over Part XV, but it gives that preference only if that procedure "entails a binding decision"; and of course the terms of article 16 by themselves do not. . . .

21. The structure of Part XV and three elements of section 3 of that Part also contribute to an understanding of article 281(1) and the compulsory binding procedures of section 2 of Part XV. They too are part of the relevant context. Section 1, "General Provisions," begins with the obligation of the State Parties to settle UNCLOS disputes by peaceful means (article 279). Within that overall obligation, which is supported by obligations to exchange views about means of settlement (article 283) and the availability of a conciliation procedure (article 284 and Annex V), the emphasis of the section is on the Parties' freedom of choice of means (articles 280–282). If the Parties' chosen means does not lead to a settlement then one Party can submit the dispute to "Compulsory Procedures Entailing Binding Decisions," to quote the heading to section 2 (article 286). That power is however in turn subject to section 3 of the Part, "Limitations and Exceptions to Applicability of Section 2."

22. That structure itself supports the need for States to include clear wording in their agreements if they are to remove themselves from their otherwise applicable compulsory obligations arising under section 2 to submit to procedures entailing binding decisions. So, too, does the detail of section 3 which (1) enables States to opt out of certain otherwise compulsory, binding processes, (2) provides for non-binding processes in certain circumstances, and (3) limits the extent of the third party review of certain State actions. [S]ignificantly, the general run of fisheries disputes, such as the present, is not subject to those limitations and exceptions. Section 2, it is expressly said, continues to apply to them in full (article 297(3)).

23. Finally, in terms of the object and purpose of UNCLOS as a whole, I refer to the widely stated and shared understanding, expressed throughout all the stages of the Conference which prepared the Convention, about the critical central place of the provisions for the peaceful settlement of disputes. The States at that Conference moved decisively away from the freedom which they generally have in their international relations not to be subject in advance to dispute settlement processes, especially processes leading to binding outcomes. The processes in significant part were not to be optional and, in general,

third party binding decisions were to be available at the request of any party to the dispute. . . .

25. The President of the Conference, Ambassador H S Amerasinghe, in 1976 prepared an informal single negotiating text on the Settlement of Disputes. He explained his initiative in this way:

> Dispute settlement procedures will be the pivot upon which the delicate equilibrium of the compromise must be balanced. Otherwise the compromise [embodied in the whole UNCLOS text] will disintegrate rapidly and permanently. I should hope that it is the will of all concerned that the prospective convention should be fruitful and permanent. Effective dispute settlement would also be the guarantee that the substance and intention within the legislative language of a treaty will be interpreted both consistently and equitably. (A/CONF.62/WP.9/Add.1, 31 March 1976, para 6.) . . .

27. Ambassador T T B Koh, who succeeded to the Presidency of the Conference, in speaking at the final session in 1982 answered in the affirmative his question whether the Conference had produced a comprehensive constitution for the oceans which would stand the test of time. Among his reasons was the following:

> The world community's interest in the peaceful settlement of disputes and the prevention of use of force in the settlement of disputes between States has been advanced by the mandatory system of dispute settlement in the Convention.

He also stressed that the Convention forms an integral whole. States cannot pick what they like and disregard what they do not like.

28. The Japanese delegation had no doubt spoken for many when, early in the process, it similarly

> Emphasized the necessity of making the general obligation to settle disputes an integral part of the future convention. In his delegation's view, the solution adopted at the First United Nations Conference on the Law of the Sea in 1958, in the form of an Optional Protocol of Signature, was insufficient and unacceptable. (6 April 1976, 60th meeting, paragraph 56.) . . .

30. The objects and purposes of UNCLOS in general and its comprehensive, compulsory and where necessary, binding dispute settlement provisions

in particular, along with the plain wording of its article 281(1) and of article 16 of the CCSBT lead me to the conclusion that the latter does not "exclude" the jurisdiction of this tribunal in respect of disputes arising under UNCLOS....

32. I have accordingly voted in favour of holding that this Tribunal has jurisdiction and against the contrary decision of the Tribunal.

Notes

1. *The ITLOS, the ICJ, and Provisional Measures.* According to Article 41(1) of the ICJ Statute, "[t]he Court shall have the power to indicate, if it considers that circumstances so require, any provisional measures which ought to be taken to preserve the respective rights of either party." Note how that provision differs from Article 290 of the LOS Convention. First, Article 290 provisional measures may be prescribed not only to preserve the rights of the parties, but "to prevent serious harm to the marine environment." Does this language embody the precautionary principle, discussed in Chapter 11, Section D and Chapter 13, Section B? Second, the ICJ's provisional measures under Article 41 of its Statute would precede consideration of the merits of a case by the ICJ itself, while the ITLOS (or another tribunal agreed on by the parties) may, under Article 290(5), prescribe provisional measures in a case that may later be taken up by a different court or tribunal.

Are provisional measures under Article 290, such as those the ITLOS approved prior to the arbitral tribunal's decision in the Southern Bluefin Tuna case, legally binding? That is the apparent import of the use of the word "prescribe" in Article 290 and in Annex VI, Article 25(1), and of Article 290(6)'s reference to the obligation to "comply promptly" with provisional measures. The ICJ, according to Article 41 of its Statute, may only "indicate" provisional measures. Only in LaGrand (Germany v. United States), 2001 I.C.J. 466, did the ICJ specifically find, for the first time, that its orders indicating provisional measures were legally binding. According to ICJ Judge Bruno Simma, the ICJ felt "competitive pressure" from the ITLOS and wanted to "clarify" the status of its provisional measures in order not to "fall behind" the ITLOS. Bruno Simma & Carsten Hoppe, The LaGrand Case: A Story of Many Miscommunications, in International Law Stories 371, 383 (John E. Noyes et al. eds., 2007).

2. *The ITLOS's Prescription of Provisional Measures.* According to Article 89(5) of its Rules, the ITLOS may prescribe provisional measures other than those requested by the parties. Why does the ITLOS assume this authority, which it has exercised on several occasions? For example, in the Case Concerning Land Reclamation by Singapore In and Around the Straits of Johor (Malaysia v. Singapore), ITLOS Case No. 12 (2003), available at http://www.

itlos.org, the ITLOS ordered the parties to cooperate and to establish a Group of Experts that would file with the Tribunal reports on the status of the parties' negotiations. Neither party had requested those provisional measures. When the Annex VII arbitral tribunal handed down its award, it incorporated the agreed terms that were based on the report of this Group of Experts. Case Concerning Land Reclamation by Singapore In and Around the Straits of Johor (Malaysia v. Singapore) (Annex VII Arb., Award on Agreed Terms, 2005), available at http://www.pca-cpa.org. May the ITLOS's initiative in devising unrequested provisional measures in fact help the parties to resolve their disputes? See also paragraph 67 of the Southern Bluefin Tuna case, above.

3. *The Centrality of the LOS Convention's Provisions for Third-party Dispute Settlement.* Did the majority or dissent in the Southern Bluefin Tuna case have the better of the argument over how to interpret Article 16 of the CCSBT and Article 281 of the LOS Convention? Do the opinions reveal very different perspectives as to whether the LOS Convention is, on the one hand, deferential to states' abilities to fashion particular bilateral and regional relationships, or, on the other hand, akin to a constitution, creating a core set of rules, institutions, and dispute settlement mechanisms applicable to a broad range of issues? Are the different conclusions of the ITLOS and the arbitral tribunal with respect to jurisdiction fully explained by the fact that the ITLOS was making only a prima facie determination under Article 290(5)? What view should the ITLOS take in a similar case in the future, were the ITLOS asked to prescribe provisional measures? See Bernard H. Oxman, Complementary Agreements and Compulsory Jurisdiction, 95 Am. J. Intl. L. 277 (2001).

4. *The Proliferation of International Courts and Tribunals.* Today many dozens of international courts exist—some global, some regional, and some with limited and specialized jurisdiction. What are the advantages and disadvantages of having so many different international courts and tribunals? Does their proliferation create too many opportunities for forum shopping? What is the risk of divergent interpretations of international law? Those questions arose after Ireland claimed in 2001 that the commissioning of a British mixed oxide chemical plant posed an immediate threat to the marine environment. Four different international tribunals—the ITLOS, an Annex VII arbitral tribunal, an arbitral tribunal constituted pursuant to the 1992 Convention for the Protection of the Marine Environment of the North-East Atlantic (OSPAR Convention), and the European Court of Justice—addressed at least aspects of the MOX plant dispute, which is featured in Chapter 12 on the marine environment.

APPENDIX

United Nations Convention on the Law of the Sea

U.S. Sen. Treaty Doc. 103–39 (1994), 1833 U.N.T.S. 397

Preamble

The States Parties to this Convention,

Prompted by the desire to settle, in a spirit of mutual understanding and cooperation, all issues relating to the law of the sea and aware of the historic significance of this Convention as an important contribution to the maintenance of peace, justice and progress for all peoples of the world,

Noting that developments since the United Nations Conferences on the Law of the Sea held at Geneva in 1958 and 1960 have accentuated the need for a new and generally acceptable Convention on the law of the sea,

Conscious that the problems of ocean space are closely interrelated and need to be considered as a whole,

Recognizing the desirability of establishing through this Convention, with due regard for the sovereignty of all States, a legal order for the seas and oceans which will facilitate international communication, and will promote the peaceful uses of the seas and oceans, the equitable and efficient utilization of their resources, the conservation of their living resources, and the study, protection and preservation of the marine environment,

Bearing in mind that the achievement of these goals will contribute to the realization of a just and equitable international economic order which takes into account the interests and needs of mankind as a whole and, in particular, the special interests and needs of developing countries, whether coastal or land-locked,

Desiring by this Convention to develop the principles embodied in resolution 2749 (XXV) of 17 December 1970 in which the General Assembly of the United Nations solemnly declared *inter alia* that the area of the seabed and ocean floor and the subsoil thereof, beyond the limits of national jurisdiction, as well as its resources, are the common heritage of mankind, the exploration and exploitation of which shall be carried out for the benefit of mankind as a whole, irrespective of the geographical location of States,

Believing that the codification and progressive development of the law of the sea achieved in this Convention will contribute to the strengthening of peace, security, cooperation and friendly relations among all nations in conformity with the principles

 | DOI 10.1163/9789004203563_017

of justice and equal rights and will promote the economic and social advancement of all peoples of the world, in accordance with the Purposes and Principles of the United Nations as set forth in the Charter,

Affirming that matters not regulated by this Convention continue to be governed by the rules and principles of general international law,

Have agreed as follows:

Part I Introduction

Article 1
Use of terms and scope

1. For the purposes of this Convention:

(1) "Area" means the seabed and ocean floor and subsoil thereof, beyond the limits of national jurisdiction;

(2) "Authority" means the International Seabed Authority;

(3) "activities in the Area" means all activities of exploration for, and exploitation of, the resources of the Area;

(4) "pollution of the marine environment" means the introduction by man, directly or indirectly, of substances or energy into the marine environment, including estuaries, which results or is likely to result in such deleterious effects as harm to living resources and marine life, hazards to human health, hindrance to marine activities, including fishing and other legitimate uses of the sea, impairment of quality for use of sea water and reduction of amenities;

(5)(a) "dumping" means:

(i) any deliberate disposal of wastes or other matter from vessels, aircraft, platforms or other man-made structures at sea;

(ii) any deliberate disposal of vessels, aircraft, platforms or other man-made structures at sea;

(b) "dumping" does not include:

(i) the disposal of wastes or other matter incidental to, or derived from the normal operations of vessels, aircraft, platforms or other man-made structures at sea and their equipment, other than wastes or other matter transported by or to vessels, aircraft, platforms or other man-made structures at sea, operating for the purpose of disposal of such matter or derived from the treatment of such wastes or other matter on such vessels, aircraft, platforms or structures;

(ii) placement of matter for a purpose other than the mere disposal thereof, provided that such placement is not contrary to the aims of this Convention.

2. (1) "States Parties" means States which have consented to be bound by this Convention and for which this Convention is in force.

(2) This Convention applies *mutatis mutandis* to the entities referred to in article 305, paragraph l(b), (c), (d), (e) and (f), which become Parties to this Convention in accordance with the conditions relevant to each, and to that extent "States Parties" refers to those entities.

Part II Territorial Sea and Contiguous Zone

Section 1 General Provisions

Article 2

Legal status of the territorial sea, of the air space over the territorial sea and of its bed and subsoil

1. The sovereignty of a coastal State extends, beyond its land territory and internal waters and, in the case of an archipelagic State, its archipelagic waters, to an adjacent belt of sea, described as the territorial sea.

2. This sovereignty extends to the air space over the territorial sea as well as to its bed and subsoil.

3. The sovereignty over the territorial sea is exercised subject to this Convention and to other rules of international law.

Section 2 Limits of the Territorial Sea

Article 3

Breadth of the territorial sea

Every State has the right to establish the breadth of its territorial sea up to a limit not exceeding 12 nautical miles, measured from baselines determined in accordance with this Convention.

Article 4

Outer limit of the territorial sea

The outer limit of the territorial sea is the line every point of which is at a distance from the nearest point of the baseline equal to the breadth of the territorial sea.

Article 5

Normal baseline

Except where otherwise provided in this Convention, the normal baseline for measuring the breadth of the territorial sea is the low-water line along the coast as marked on large-scale charts officially recognized by the coastal State.

Article 6

Reefs

In the case of islands situated on atolls or of islands having fringing reefs, the baseline for measuring the breadth of the territorial sea is the seaward low-water line of the reef, as shown by the appropriate symbol on charts officially recognized by the coastal State.

Article 7

Straight baselines

1. In localities where the coastline is deeply indented and cut into, or if there is a fringe of islands along the coast in its immediate vicinity, the method of straight baselines joining appropriate points may be employed in drawing the baseline from which the breadth of the territorial sea is measured.

2. Where because of the presence of a delta and other natural conditions the coastline is highly unstable, the appropriate points may be selected along the furthest seaward extent of the low-water line and, notwithstanding subsequent regression of the low-water line, the straight baselines shall remain effective until changed by the coastal State in accordance with this Convention.

3. The drawing of straight baselines must not depart to any appreciable extent from the general direction of the coast, and the sea areas lying within the lines must be sufficiently closely linked to the land domain to be subject to the regime of internal waters.

4. Straight baselines shall not be drawn to and from low-tide elevations, unless lighthouses or similar installations which are permanently above sea level have been built on them or except in instances where the drawing of baselines to and from such elevations has received general international recognition.

5. Where the method of straight baselines is applicable under paragraph 1, account may be taken, in determining particular baselines, of economic interests peculiar to the region concerned, the reality and the importance of which are clearly evidenced by long usage.

6. The system of straight baselines may not be applied by a State in such a manner as to cut off the territorial sea of another State from the high seas or an exclusive economic zone.

Article 8

Internal waters

1. Except as provided in Part IV, waters on the landward side of the baseline of the territorial sea form part of the internal waters of the State.

2. Where the establishment of a straight baseline in accordance with the method set forth in article 7 has the effect of enclosing as internal waters areas which had not

previously been considered as such, a right of innocent passage as provided in this Convention shall exist in those waters.

Article 9

Mouths of rivers

If a river flows directly into the sea, the baseline shall be a straight line across the mouth of the river between points on the low-water line of its banks.

Article 10

Bays

1. This article relates only to bays the coasts of which belong to a single State.

2. For the purposes of this Convention, a bay is a well-marked indentation whose penetration is in such proportion to the width of its mouth as to contain land-locked waters and constitute more than a mere curvature of the coast. An indentation shall not, however, be regarded as a bay unless its area is as large as, or larger than, that of the semi-circle whose diameter is a line drawn across the mouth of that indentation.

3. For the purpose of measurement, the area of an indentation is that lying between the low-water mark around the shore of the indentation and a line joining the low-water mark of its natural entrance points. Where, because of the presence of islands, an indentation has more than one mouth, the semi-circle shall be drawn on a line as long as the sum total of the lengths of the lines across the different mouths. Islands within an indentation shall be included as if they were part of the water area of the indentation.

4. If the distance between the low-water marks of the natural entrance points of a bay does not exceed 24 nautical miles, a closing line may be drawn between these two low-water marks, and the waters enclosed thereby shall be considered as internal waters.

5. Where the distance between the low-water marks of the natural entrance points of a bay exceeds 24 nautical miles, a straight baseline of 24 nautical miles shall be drawn within the bay in such a manner as to enclose the maximum area of water that is possible with a line of that length.

6. The foregoing provisions do not apply to so-called "historic" bays, or in any case where the system of straight baselines provided for in article 7 is applied.

Article 11

Ports

For the purpose of delimiting the territorial sea, the outermost permanent harbour works which form an integral part of the harbour system are regarded as forming part of the coast. Off-shore installations and artificial islands shall not be considered as permanent harbour works.

Article 12

Roadsteads

Roadsteads which are normally used for the loading, unloading and anchoring of ships, and which would otherwise be situated wholly or partly outside the outer limit of the territorial sea, are included in the territorial sea.

Article 13

Low-tide elevations

1. A low-tide elevation is a naturally formed area of land which is surrounded by and above water at low tide but submerged at high tide. Where a low-tide elevation is situated wholly or partly at a distance not exceeding the breadth of the territorial sea from the mainland or an island, the low-water line on that elevation may be used as the baseline for measuring the breadth of the territorial sea.

2. Where a low-tide elevation is wholly situated at a distance exceeding the breadth of the territorial sea from the mainland or an island, it has no territorial sea of its own.

Article 14

Combination of methods for determining baselines

The coastal State may determine baselines in turn by any of the methods provided for in the foregoing articles to suit different conditions.

Article 15

Delimitation of the territorial sea between States with opposite or adjacent coasts

Where the coasts of two States are opposite or adjacent to each other, neither of the two States is entitled, failing agreement between them to the contrary, to extend its territorial sea beyond the median line every point of which is equidistant from the nearest points on the baselines from which the breadth of the territorial seas of each of the two States is measured. The above provision does not apply, however, where it is necessary by reason of historic title or other special circumstances to delimit the territorial seas of the two States in a way which is at variance therewith.

Article 16

Charts and lists of geographical coordinates

1. The baselines for measuring the breadth of the territorial sea determined in accordance with articles 7, 9 and 10, or the limits derived therefrom, and the lines of

delimitation drawn in accordance with articles 12 and 15 shall be shown on charts of a scale or scales adequate for ascertaining their position. Alternatively, a list of geographical coordinates of points, specifying the geodetic datum, may be substituted.

2. The coastal State shall give due publicity to such charts or lists of geographical coordinates and shall deposit a copy of each such chart or list with the Secretary-General of the United Nations.

Section 3 Innocent Passage in the Territorial Sea

SUBSECTION A. RULES APPLICABLE TO ALL SHIPS

Article 17

Right of innocent passage

Subject to this Convention, ships of all States, whether coastal or land-locked, enjoy the right of innocent passage through the territorial sea.

Article 18

Meaning of passage

1. Passage means navigation through the territorial sea for the purpose of:

(a) traversing that sea without entering internal waters or calling at a roadstead or port facility outside internal waters; or

(b) proceeding to or from internal waters or a call at such roadstead or port facility.

2. Passage shall be continuous and expeditious. However, passage includes stopping and anchoring, but only in so far as the same are incidental to ordinary navigation or are rendered necessary by *force majeure* or distress or for the purpose of rendering assistance to persons, ships or aircraft in danger or distress.

Article 19

Meaning of innocent passage

1. Passage is innocent so long as it is not prejudicial to the peace, good order or security of the coastal State. Such passage shall take place in conformity with this Convention and with other rules of international law.

2. Passage of a foreign ship shall be considered to be prejudicial to the peace, good order or security of the coastal State if in the territorial sea it engages in any of the following activities:

(a) any threat or use of force against the sovereignty, territorial integrity or political independence of the coastal State, or in any other manner in violation of the principles of international law embodied in the Charter of the United Nations;

(b) any exercise or practice with weapons of any kind;

(c) any act aimed at collecting information to the prejudice of the defense or security of the coastal State;

(d) any act of propaganda aimed at affecting the defence or security of the coastal State;

(e) the launching, landing or taking on board of any aircraft;

(f) the launching, landing or taking on board of any military device;

(g) the loading or unloading of any commodity, currency or person contrary to the customs, fiscal, immigration or sanitary laws and regulations of the coastal State;

(h) any act of wilful and serious pollution contrary to this Convention;

(i) any fishing activities;

(j) the carrying out of research or survey activities;

(k) any act aimed at interfering with any systems of communication or any other facilities or installations of the coastal State;

(l) any other activity not having a direct bearing on passage.

Article 20

Submarines and other underwater vehicles

In the territorial sea, submarines and other underwater vehicles are required to navigate on the surface and to show their flag.

Article 21

Laws and regulations of the coastal State relating to innocent passage

1. The coastal State may adopt laws and regulations, in conformity with the provisions of this Convention and other rules of international law, relating to innocent passage through the territorial sea, in respect of all or any of the following:

(a) the safety of navigation and the regulation of maritime traffic;

(b) the protection of navigational aids and facilities and other facilities or installations;

(c) the protection of cables and pipelines;

(d) the conservation of the living resources of the sea;

(e) the prevention of infringement of the fisheries laws and regulations of the coastal State;

(f) the preservation of the environment of the coastal State and the prevention, reduction and control of pollution thereof;

(g) marine scientific research and hydrographic surveys;

(h) the prevention of infringement of the customs, fiscal, immigration or sanitary laws and regulations of the coastal State.

2. Such laws and regulations shall not apply to the design, construction, manning or equipment of foreign ships unless they are giving effect to generally accepted international rules or standards.

3. The coastal State shall give due publicity to all such laws and regulations.

4. Foreign ships exercising the right of innocent passage through the territorial sea shall comply with all such laws and regulations and all generally accepted international regulations relating to the prevention of collisions at sea.

Article 22

Sea lanes and traffic separation schemes in the territorial sea

1. The coastal State may, where necessary having regard to the safety of navigation, require foreign ships exercising the right of innocent passage through its territorial sea to use such sea lanes and traffic separation schemes as it may designate or prescribe for the regulation of the passage of ships.

2. In particular, tankers, nuclear-powered ships and ships carrying nuclear or other inherently dangerous or noxious substances or materials may be required to confine their passage to such sea lanes.

3. In the designation of sea lanes and the prescription of traffic separation schemes under this article, the coastal State shall take into account:

(a) the recommendations of the competent international organization;
(b) any channels customarily used for international navigation;
(c) the special characteristics of particular ships and channels; and
(d) the density of traffic.

4. The coastal State shall clearly indicate such sea lanes and traffic separation schemes on charts to which due publicity shall be given.

Article 23

Foreign nuclear-powered ships and ships carrying nuclear or other inherently dangerous or noxious substances

Foreign nuclear-powered ships and ships carrying nuclear or other inherently dangerous or noxious substances shall, when exercising the right of innocent passage through the territorial sea, carry documents and observe special precautionary measures established for such ships by international agreements.

Article 24

Duties of the coastal State

1. The coastal State shall not hamper the innocent passage of foreign ships through the territorial sea except in accordance with this Convention. In particular, in the application of this Convention or of any laws or regulations adopted in conformity with this Convention, the coastal State shall not:

(a) impose requirements on foreign ships which have the practical effect of denying or impairing the right of innocent passage; or

(b) discriminate in form or in fact against the ships of any State or against ships carrying cargoes to, from or on behalf of any State.

2. The coastal State shall give appropriate publicity to any danger to navigation, of which it has knowledge, within its territorial sea.

Article 25

Rights of protection of the coastal State

1. The coastal State may take the necessary steps in its territorial sea to prevent passage which is not innocent.

2. In the case of ships proceeding to internal waters or a call at a port facility outside internal waters, the coastal State also has the right to take the necessary steps to prevent any breach of the conditions to which admission of those ships to internal waters or such a call is subject.

3. The coastal State may, without discrimination in form or in fact among foreign ships, suspend temporarily in specified areas of its territorial sea the innocent passage of foreign ships if such suspension is essential for the protection of its security, including weapons exercises. Such suspension shall take effect only after having been duly published.

Article 26

Charges which may be levied upon foreign ships

1. No charge may be levied upon foreign ships by reason only of their passage through the territorial sea.

2. Charges may be levied upon a foreign ship passing through the territorial sea as payment only for specific services rendered to the ship. These charges shall be levied without discrimination.

SUBSECTION B. RULES APPLICABLE TO MERCHANT SHIPS AND GOVERNMENT SHIPS OPERATED FOR COMMERCIAL PURPOSES

Article 27

Criminal jurisdiction on board a foreign ship

1. The criminal jurisdiction of the coastal State should not be exercised on board a foreign ship passing through the territorial sea to arrest any person or to conduct any investigation in connection with any crime committed on board the ship during its passage, save only in the following cases:

(a) if the consequences of the crime extend to the coastal State;

(b) if the crime is of a kind to disturb the peace of the country or the good order of the territorial sea;

(c) if the assistance of the local authorities has been requested by the master of the ship or by a diplomatic agent or consular officer of the flag State; or

(d) if such measures are necessary for the suppression of illicit traffic in narcotic drugs or psychotropic substances.

2. The above provisions do not affect the right of the coastal State to take any steps authorized by its laws for the purpose of an arrest or investigation on board a foreign ship passing through the territorial sea after leaving internal waters.

3. In the cases provided for in paragraphs 1 and 2, the coastal State shall, if the master so requests, notify a diplomatic agent or consular officer of the flag State before taking any steps, and shall facilitate contact between such agent or officer and the ship's crew. In cases of emergency this notification may be communicated while the measures are being taken.

4. In considering whether or in what manner an arrest should be made, the local authorities shall have due regard to the interests of navigation.

5. Except as provided in Part XII or with respect to violations of laws and regulations adopted in accordance with Part V, the coastal State may not take any steps on board a foreign ship passing through the territorial sea to arrest any person or to conduct any investigation in connection with any crime committed before the ship entered the territorial sea, if the ship, proceeding from a foreign port, is only passing through the territorial sea without entering internal waters.

Article 28

Civil jurisdiction in relation to foreign ships

1. The coastal State should not stop or divert a foreign ship passing through the territorial sea for the purpose of exercising civil jurisdiction in relation to a person on board the ship.

2. The coastal State may not levy execution against or arrest the ship for the purpose of any civil proceedings, save only in respect of obligations or liabilities assumed or incurred by the ship itself in the course or for the purpose of its voyage through the waters of the coastal State.

3. Paragraph 2 is without prejudice to the right of the coastal State, in accordance with its laws, to levy execution against or to arrest, for the purpose of any civil proceedings, a foreign ship lying in the territorial sea, or passing through the territorial sea after leaving internal waters.

Subsection C. Rules Applicable to Warships and Other Government Ships Operated for Non-Commercial Purposes

Article 29

Definition of warships

For the purposes of this Convention, "warship" means a ship belonging to the armed forces of a State bearing the external marks distinguishing such ships of its nationality, under the command of an officer duly commissioned by the government of the State and whose name appears in the appropriate service list or its equivalent, and manned by a crew which is under regular armed forces discipline.

Article 30

Non-compliance by warships with the laws and regulations of the coastal State

If any warship does not comply with the laws and regulations of the coastal State concerning passage through the territorial sea and disregards any request for compliance therewith which is made to it, the coastal State may require it to leave the territorial sea immediately.

Article 31

Responsibility of the flag State for damage caused by a warship or other government ship operated for non-commercial purposes

The flag State shall bear international responsibility for any loss or damage to the coastal State resulting from the non-compliance by a warship or other government ship operated for non-commercial purposes with the laws and regulations of the coastal State concerning passage through the territorial sea or with the provisions of this Convention or other rules of international law.

Article 32

Immunities of warships and other government ships operated for non-commercial purposes

With such exceptions as are contained in subsection A and in articles 30 and 31, nothing in this Convention affects the immunities of warships and other government ships operated for non-commercial purposes.

Section 4 Contiguous Zone

Article 33

Contiguous zone

1. In a zone contiguous to its territorial sea, described as the contiguous zone, the coastal State may exercise the control necessary to:

(a) prevent infringement of its customs, fiscal, immigration or sanitary laws and regulations within its territory or territorial sea;

(b) punish infringement of the above laws and regulations committed within its territory or territorial sea.

2. The contiguous zone may not extend beyond 24 nautical miles from the baselines from which the breadth of the territorial sea is measured.

Part III Straits Used for International Navigation

Section 1 General Provisions

Article 34

Legal status of waters forming straits used for international navigation

1. The regime of passage through straits used for international navigation established in this Part shall not in other respects affect the legal status of the waters forming such straits or the exercise by the States bordering the straits of their sovereignty or jurisdiction over such waters and their air space, bed and subsoil.

2. The sovereignty or jurisdiction of the States bordering the straits is exercised subject to this Part and to other rules of international law.

Article 35

Scope of this Part

Nothing in this Part affects:

(a) any areas of internal waters within a strait, except where the establishment of a straight baseline in accordance with the method set forth in article 7 has the effect of enclosing as internal waters areas which had not previously been considered as such;

(b) the legal status of the waters beyond the territorial seas of States bordering straits as exclusive economic zones or high seas; or

(c) the legal regime in straits in which passage is regulated in whole or in part by long-standing international conventions in force specifically relating to such straits.

Article 36

High seas routes or routes through exclusive economic zones through straits used for international navigation

This Part does not apply to a strait used for international navigation if there exists through the strait a route through the high seas or through an exclusive economic zone of similar convenience with respect to navigational and hydrographical characteristics; in such routes, the other relevant Parts of this Convention, including the provisions regarding the freedoms of navigation and overflight, apply.

Section 2 Transit Passage

Article 37

Scope of this section

This section applies to straits which are used for international navigation between one part of the high seas or an exclusive economic zone and another part of the high seas or an exclusive economic zone.

Article 38

Right of transit passage

1. In straits referred to in article 37, all ships and aircraft enjoy the right of transit passage, which shall not be impeded; except that, if the strait is formed by an island of a State bordering the strait and its mainland, transit passage shall not apply if there exists seaward of the island a route through the high seas or through an exclusive economic zone of similar convenience with respect to navigational and hydrographical characteristics.

2. Transit passage means the exercise in accordance with this Part of the freedom of navigation and overflight solely for the purpose of continuous and expeditious transit of the strait between one part of the high seas or an exclusive economic zone and another part of the high seas or an exclusive economic zone. However, the requirement of continuous and expeditious transit does not preclude passage through the strait for the purpose of entering, leaving or returning from a State bordering the strait, subject to the conditions of entry to that State.

3. Any activity which is not an exercise of the right of transit passage through a strait remains subject to the other applicable provisions of this Convention.

Article 39

Duties of ships and aircraft during transit passage

1. Ships and aircraft, while exercising the right of transit passage, shall:

(a) proceed without delay through or over the strait;

(b) refrain from any threat or use of force against the sovereignty, territorial integrity or political independence of States bordering the strait, or in any other manner in violation of the principles of international law embodied in the Charter of the United Nations;

(c) refrain from any activities other than those incident to their normal modes of continuous and expeditious transit unless rendered necessary by *force majeure* or by distress;

(d) comply with other relevant provisions of this Part.

2. Ships in transit passage shall:

(a) comply with generally accepted international regulations, procedures and practices for safety at sea, including the International Regulations for Preventing Collisions at Sea;

(b) comply with generally accepted international regulations, procedures and practices for the prevention, reduction and control of pollution from ships.

3. Aircraft in transit passage shall:

(a) observe the Rules of the Air established by the International Civil Aviation Organization as they apply to civil aircraft; state aircraft will normally comply with such safety measures and will at all times operate with due regard for the safety of navigation;

(b) at all times monitor the radio frequency assigned by the competent internationally designated air traffic control authority or the appropriate international distress radio frequency.

Article 40

Research and survey activities

During transit passage, foreign ships, including marine scientific research and hydrographic survey ships, may not carry out any research or survey activities without the prior authorization of the States bordering straits.

Article 41

Sea lanes and traffic separation schemes in straits used for international navigation

1. In conformity with this Part, States bordering straits may designate sea lanes and prescribe traffic separation schemes for navigation in straits where necessary to promote the safe passage of ships.

2. Such States may, when circumstances require, and after giving due publicity thereto, substitute other sea lanes or traffic separation schemes for any sea lanes or traffic separation schemes previously designated or prescribed by them.

3. Such sea lanes and traffic separation schemes shall conform to generally accepted international regulations.

4. Before designating or substituting sea lanes or prescribing or substituting traffic separation schemes, States bordering straits shall refer proposals to the competent international organization with a view to their adoption. The organization may adopt only such sea lanes and traffic separation schemes as may be agreed with the States bordering the straits, after which the States may designate, prescribe or substitute them.

5. In respect of a strait where sea lanes or traffic separation schemes through the waters of two or more States bordering the strait are being proposed, the States concerned shall cooperate in formulating proposals in consultation with the competent international organization.

6. States bordering straits shall clearly indicate all sea lanes and traffic separation schemes designated or prescribed by them on charts to which due publicity shall be given.

7. Ships in transit passage shall respect applicable sea lanes and traffic separation schemes established in accordance with this article.

Article 42

Laws and regulations of States bordering straits relating to transit passage

1. Subject to the provisions of this section, States bordering straits may adopt laws and regulations relating to transit passage through straits, in respect of all or any of the following:

(a) the safety of navigation and the regulation of maritime traffic, as provided in article 41;

(b) the prevention, reduction and control of pollution, by giving effect to applicable international regulations regarding the discharge of oil, oily wastes and other noxious substances in the strait;

(c) with respect to fishing vessels, the prevention of fishing, including the stowage of fishing gear;

(d) the loading or unloading of any commodity, currency or person in contravention of the customs, fiscal, immigration or sanitary laws and regulations of States bordering straits.

2. Such laws and regulations shall not discriminate in form or in fact among foreign ships or in their application have the practical effect of denying, hampering or impairing the right of transit passage as defined in this section.

3. States bordering straits shall give due publicity to all such laws and regulations.

4. Foreign ships exercising the right of transit passage shall comply with such laws and regulations.

5. The flag State of a ship or the State of registry of an aircraft entitled to sovereign immunity which acts in a manner contrary to such laws and regulations or other provisions of this Part shall bear international responsibility for any loss or damage which results to States bordering straits.

Article 43

Navigational and safety aids and other improvements and the prevention, reduction and control of pollution

User States and States bordering a strait should by agreement cooperate:

(a) in the establishment and maintenance in a strait of necessary navigational and safety aids or other improvements in aid of international navigation; and

(b) for the prevention, reduction and control of pollution from ships.

Article 44

Duties of States bordering straits

States bordering straits shall not hamper transit passage and shall give appropriate publicity to any danger to navigation or overflight within or over the strait of which they have knowledge. There shall be no suspension of transit passage.

Section 3 Innocent Passage

Article 45

Innocent passage

1. The regime of innocent passage, in accordance with Part II, section 3, shall apply in straits used for international navigation:

(a) excluded from the application of the regime of transit passage under article 38, paragraph 1; or

(b) between a part of the high seas or an exclusive economic zone and the territorial sea of a foreign State.

2. There shall be no suspension of innocent passage through such straits.

Part IV Archipelagic States

Article 46

Use of terms

For the purposes of this Convention:

(a) "archipelagic State" means a State constituted wholly by one or more

(b) archipelagos and may include other islands; "archipelago" means a group of islands, including parts of islands, interconnecting waters and other natural features which are so closely interrelated that such islands, waters and other natural features form an intrinsic geographical, economic and political entity, or which historically have been regarded as such.

Article 47

Archipelagic baselines

1. An archipelagic State may draw straight archipelagic baselines joining the outermost points of the outermost islands and drying reefs of the archipelago provided that within such baselines are included the main islands and an area in which the ratio of the area of the water to the area of the land, including atolls, is between 1 to 1 and 9 to 1.

2. The length of such baselines shall not exceed 100 nautical miles, except that up to 3 per cent of the total number of baselines enclosing any archipelago may exceed that length, up to a maximum length of 125 nautical miles.

3. The drawing of such baselines shall not depart to any appreciable extent from the general configuration of the archipelago.

4. Such baselines shall not be drawn to and from low-tide elevations, unless lighthouses or similar installations which are permanently above sea level have been built on them or where a low-tide elevation is situated wholly or partly at a distance not exceeding the breadth of the territorial sea from the nearest island.

5. The system of such baselines shall not be applied by an archipelagic State in such a manner as to cut off from the high seas or the exclusive economic zone the territorial sea of another State.

6. If a part of the archipelagic waters of an archipelagic State lies between two parts of an immediately adjacent neighbouring State, existing rights and all other legitimate interests which the latter State has traditionally exercised in such waters and all rights stipulated by agreement between those States shall continue and be respected.

7. For the purpose of computing the ratio of water to land under paragraph l, land areas may include waters lying within the fringing reefs of islands and atolls, including that part of a steep-sided oceanic plateau which is enclosed or nearly enclosed by a chain of limestone islands and drying reefs lying on the perimeter of the plateau.

8. The baselines drawn in accordance with this article shall be shown on charts of a scale or scales adequate for ascertaining their position. Alternatively, lists of geographical coordinates of points, specifying the geodetic datum, may be substituted.

9. The archipelagic State shall give due publicity to such charts or lists of geographical coordinates and shall deposit a copy of each such chart or list with the Secretary-General of the United Nations.

Article 48

Measurement of the breadth of the territorial sea, the contiguous zone, the exclusive economic zone and the continental shelf

The breadth of the territorial sea, the contiguous zone, the exclusive economic zone and the continental shelf shall be measured from archipelagic baselines drawn in accordance with article 47.

Article 49

Legal status of archipelagic waters, of the air space over archipelagic waters and of their bed and subsoil

1. The sovereignty of an archipelagic State extends to the waters enclosed by the archipelagic baselines drawn in accordance with article 47, described as archipelagic waters, regardless of their depth or distance from the coast.

2. This sovereignty extends to the air space over the archipelagic waters, as well as to their bed and subsoil, and the resources contained therein.

3. This sovereignty is exercised subject to this Part.

4. The regime of archipelagic sea lanes passage established in this Part shall not in other respects affect the status of the archipelagic waters, including the sea lanes, or the exercise by the archipelagic State of its sovereignty over such waters and their air space, bed and subsoil, and the resources contained therein.

Article 50

Delimitation of internal waters

Within its archipelagic waters, the archipelagic State may draw closing lines for the delimitation of internal waters, in accordance with articles 9, 10 and 11.

Article 51

Existing agreements, traditional fishing rights and existing submarine cables

1. Without prejudice to article 49, an archipelagic State shall respect existing agreements with other States and shall recognize traditional fishing rights and other legitimate activities of the immediately adjacent neighbouring States in certain areas falling within archipelagic waters. The terms and conditions for the exercise of such rights and activities, including the nature, the extent and the areas to which they apply, shall, at the request of any of the States concerned, be regulated by bilateral agreements between them. Such rights shall not be transferred to or shared with third States or their nationals.

2. An archipelagic State shall respect existing submarine cables laid by other States and passing through its waters without making a landfall. An archipelagic State shall permit the maintenance and replacement of such cables upon receiving due notice of their location and the intention to repair or replace them.

Article 52

Right of innocent passage

1. Subject to article 53 and without prejudice to article 50, ships of all States enjoy the right of innocent passage through archipelagic waters, in accordance with Part II, section 3.

2. The archipelagic State may, without discrimination in form or in fact among foreign ships, suspend temporarily in specified areas of its archipelagic waters the innocent passage of foreign ships if such suspension is essential for the protection of its security. Such suspension shall take effect only after having been duly published.

Article 53

Right of archipelagic sea lanes passage

1. An archipelagic State may designate sea lanes and air routes thereabove, suitable for the continuous and expeditious passage of foreign ships and aircraft through or over its archipelagic waters and the adjacent territorial sea.

2. All ships and aircraft enjoy the right of archipelagic sea lanes passage in such sea lanes and air routes.

3. Archipelagic sea lanes passage means the exercise in accordance with this Convention of the rights of navigation and overflight in the normal mode solely for the purpose of continuous, expeditious and unobstructed transit between one part of the high seas or an exclusive economic zone and another part of the high seas or an exclusive economic zone.

4. Such sea lanes and air routes shall traverse the archipelagic waters and the adjacent territorial sea and shall include all normal passage routes used as routes for international navigation or overflight through or over archipelagic waters and, within such routes, so far as ships are concerned, all normal navigational channels, provided that duplication of routes of similar convenience between the same entry and exit points shall not be necessary.

5. Such sea lanes and air routes shall be defined by a series of continuous axis lines from the entry points of passage routes to the exit points. Ships and aircraft in archipelagic sea lanes passage shall not deviate more than 25 nautical miles to either side of such axis lines during passage, provided that such ships and aircraft shall not navigate closer to the coasts than 10 per cent of the distance between the nearest points on islands bordering the sea lane.

6. An archipelagic State which designates sea lanes under this article may also prescribe traffic separation schemes for the safe passage of ships through narrow channels in such sea lanes.

7. An archipelagic State may, when circumstances require, after giving due publicity thereto, substitute other sea lanes or traffic separation schemes for any sea lanes or traffic separation schemes previously designated or prescribed by it.

8. Such sea lanes and traffic separation schemes shall conform to generally accepted international regulations.

9. In designating or substituting sea lanes or prescribing or substituting traffic separation schemes, an archipelagic State shall refer proposals to the competent international organization with a view to their adoption. The organization may adopt only such sea lanes and traffic separation schemes as may be agreed with the archipelagic State, after which the archipelagic State may designate, prescribe or substitute them.

10. The archipelagic State shall clearly indicate the axis of the sea lanes and the traffic separation schemes designated or prescribed by it on charts to which due publicity shall be given.

11. Ships in archipelagic sea lanes passage shall respect applicable sea lanes and traffic separation schemes established in accordance with this article.

12. If an archipelagic State does not designate sea lanes or air routes, the right of archipelagic sea lanes passage may be exercised through the routes normally used for international navigation.

Article 54

Duties of ships and aircraft during their passage, research and survey activities, duties of the archipelagic State and laws and regulations of the archipelagic State relating to archipelagic sea lanes passage

Articles 39, 40, 42 and 44 apply *mutatis mutandis* to archipelagic sea lanes passage.

Part V Exclusive Economic Zone

Article 55

Specific legal regime of the exclusive economic zone

The exclusive economic zone is an area beyond and adjacent to the territorial sea, subject to the specific legal regime established in this Part, under which the rights and jurisdiction of the coastal State and the rights and freedoms of other States are governed by the relevant provisions of this Convention.

Article 56

Rights, jurisdiction and duties of the coastal State in the exclusive economic zone

1. In the exclusive economic zone, the coastal State has:

(a) sovereign rights for the purpose of exploring and exploiting, conserving and managing the natural resources, whether living or non-living, of the waters superjacent to the seabed and of the seabed and its subsoil, and with regard to other activities for the economic exploitation and exploration of the zone, such as the production of energy from the water, currents and winds;

(b) jurisdiction as provided for in the relevant provisions of this Convention with regard to:

(i) the establishment and use of artificial islands, installations and structures;

(ii) marine scientific research;

(iii) the protection and preservation of the marine environment;

(c) other rights and duties provided for in this Convention.

2. In exercising its rights and performing its duties under this Convention in the exclusive economic zone, the coastal State shall have due regard to the rights and duties of other States and shall act in a manner compatible with the provisions of this Convention.

3. The rights set out in this article with respect to the seabed and subsoil shall be exercised in accordance with Part VI.

Article 57

Breadth of the exclusive economic zone

The exclusive economic zone shall not extend beyond 200 nautical miles from the baselines from which the breadth of the territorial sea is measured.

Article 58

Rights and duties of other States in the exclusive economic zone

1. In the exclusive economic zone, all States, whether coastal or land-locked, enjoy, subject to the relevant provisions of this Convention, the freedoms referred to in article 87 of navigation and overflight and of the laying of submarine cables and pipelines, and other internationally lawful uses of the sea related to these freedoms, such as those associated with the operation of ships, aircraft and submarine cables and pipelines, and compatible with the other provisions of this Convention.

2. Articles 88 to 115 and other pertinent rules of international law apply to the exclusive economic zone in so far as they are not incompatible with this Part.

3. In exercising their rights and performing their duties under this Convention in the exclusive economic zone, States shall have due regard to the rights and duties of the coastal State and shall comply with the laws and regulations adopted by the coastal State in accordance with the provisions of this Convention and other rules of international law in so far as they are not incompatible with this Part.

Article 59

Basis for the resolution of conflicts regarding the attribution of rights and jurisdiction in the exclusive economic zone

In cases where this Convention does not attribute rights or jurisdiction to the coastal State or to other States within the exclusive economic zone, and a conflict arises between the interests of the coastal State and any other State or States, the conflict should be resolved on the basis of equity and in the light of all the relevant circumstances, taking into account the respective importance of the interests involved to the parties as well as to the international community as a whole.

Article 60

Artificial islands, installations and structures in the exclusive economic zone

1. In the exclusive economic zone, the coastal State shall have the exclusive right to construct and to authorize and regulate the construction, operation and use of:

(a) artificial islands;

(b) installations and structures for the purposes provided for in article 56 and other economic purposes;

(c) installations and structures which may interfere with the exercise of the rights of the coastal State in the zone.

2. The coastal State shall have exclusive jurisdiction over such artificial islands, installations and structures, including jurisdiction with regard to customs, fiscal, health, safety and immigration laws and regulations.

3. Due notice must be given of the construction of such artificial islands, installations or structures, and permanent means for giving warning of their presence must be maintained. Any installations or structures which are abandoned or disused shall be removed to ensure safety of navigation, taking into account any generally accepted international standards established in this regard by the competent international organization. Such removal shall also have due regard to fishing, the protection of the marine environment and the rights and duties of other States. Appropriate publicity shall be given to the depth, position and dimensions of any installations or structures not entirely removed.

4. The coastal State may, where necessary, establish reasonable safety zones around such artificial islands, installations and structures in which it may take appropriate measures to ensure the safety both of navigation and of the artificial islands, installations and structures.

5. The breadth of the safety zones shall be determined by the coastal State, taking into account applicable international standards. Such zones shall be designed to ensure that they are reasonably related to the nature and function of the artificial islands, installations or structures, and shall not exceed a distance of 500 metres around them, measured from each point of their outer edge, except as authorized by generally accepted international standards or as recommended by the competent international organization. Due notice shall be given of the extent of safety zones.

6. All ships must respect these safety zones and shall comply with generally accepted international standards regarding navigation in the vicinity of artificial islands, installations, structures and safety zones.

7. Artificial islands, installations and structures and the safety zones around them may not be established where interference may be caused to the use of recognized sea lanes essential to international navigation.

8. Artificial islands, installations and structures do not possess the status of islands. They have no territorial sea of their own, and their presence does not affect the delimitation of the territorial sea, the exclusive economic zone or the continental shelf.

Article 61

Conservation of the living resources

1. The coastal State shall determine the allowable catch of the living resources in its exclusive economic zone.

2. The coastal State, taking into account the best scientific evidence available to it, shall ensure through proper conservation and management measures that the maintenance of the living resources in the exclusive economic zone is not endangered by over-exploitation. As appropriate, the coastal State and competent international organizations, whether subregional, regional or global, shall cooperate to this end.

3. Such measures shall also be designed to maintain or restore populations of harvested species at levels which can produce the maximum sustainable yield, as qualified by relevant environmental and economic factors, including the economic needs of coastal fishing communities and the special requirements of developing States, and taking into account fishing patterns, the interdependence of stocks and any generally recommended international minimum standards, whether subregional, regional or global.

4. In taking such measures the coastal State shall take into consideration the effects on species associated with or dependent upon harvested species with a view to maintaining or restoring populations of such associated or dependent species above levels at which their reproduction may become seriously threatened.

5. Available scientific information, catch and fishing effort statistics, and other data relevant to the conservation of fish stocks shall be contributed and exchanged on a regular basis through competent international organizations, whether subregional, regional or global, where appropriate and with participation by all States concerned, including States whose nationals are allowed to fish in the exclusive economic zone.

Article 62
Utilization of the living resources

1. The coastal State shall promote the objective of optimum utilization of the living resources in the exclusive economic zone without prejudice to article 61.

2. The coastal State shall determine its capacity to harvest the living resources of the exclusive economic zone. Where the coastal State does not have the capacity to harvest the entire allowable catch, it shall, through agreements or other arrangements and pursuant to the terms, conditions, laws and regulations referred to in paragraph 4, give other States access to the surplus of the allowable catch, having particular regard to the provisions of articles 69 and 70, especially in relation to the developing States mentioned therein.

3. In giving access to other States to its exclusive economic zone under this article, the coastal State shall take into account all relevant factors, including, *inter alia*, the significance of the living resources of the area to the economy of the coastal State concerned and its other national interests, the provisions of articles 69 and 70, the requirements of developing States in the subregion or region in harvesting part of the surplus and the need to minimize economic dislocation in States whose nationals

have habitually fished in the zone or which have made substantial efforts in research and identification of stocks.

4. Nationals of other States fishing in the exclusive economic zone shall comply with the conservation measures and with the other terms and conditions established in the laws and regulations of the coastal State. These laws and regulations shall be consistent with this Convention and may relate, *inter alia*, to the following:

(a) licensing of fishermen, fishing vessels and equipment, including payment of fees and other forms of remuneration, which, in the case of developing coastal States, may consist of adequate compensation in the field of financing, equipment and technology relating to the fishing industry;

(b) determining the species which may be caught, and fixing quotas of catch, whether in relation to particular stocks or groups of stocks or catch per vessel over a period of time or to the catch by nationals of any State during a specified period;

(c) regulating seasons and areas of fishing, the types, sizes and amount of gear, and the types, sizes and number of fishing vessels that may be used;

(d) fixing the age and size of fish and other species that may be caught;

(e) specifying information required of fishing vessels, including catch and effort statistics and vessel position reports;

(f) requiring, under the authorization and control of the coastal State, the conduct of specified fisheries research programmes and regulating the conduct of such research, including the sampling of catches, disposition of samples and reporting of associated scientific data;

(g) the placing of observers or trainees on board such vessels by the coastal State;

(h) the landing of all or any part of the catch by such vessels in the ports of the coastal State;

(i) terms and conditions relating to joint ventures or other cooperative arrangements;

(j) requirements for the training of personnel and the transfer of fisheries technology, including enhancement of the coastal State's capability of undertaking fisheries research;

(k) enforcement procedures.

5. Coastal States shall give due notice of conservation and management laws and regulations.

Article 63

Stocks occurring within the exclusive economic zones of two or more coastal States or both within the exclusive economic zone and in an area beyond and adjacent to it

1. Where the same stock or stocks of associated species occur within the exclusive economic zones of two or more coastal States, these States shall seek, either directly

or through appropriate subregional or regional organizations, to agree upon the measures necessary to coordinate and ensure the conservation and development of such stocks without prejudice to the other provisions of this Part.

2. Where the same stock or stocks of associated species occur both within the exclusive economic zone and in an area beyond and adjacent to the zone, the coastal State and the States fishing for such stocks in the adjacent area shall seek, either directly or through appropriate subregional or regional organizations, to agree upon the measures necessary for the conservation of these stocks in the adjacent area.

Article 64
Highly migratory species

1. The coastal State and other States whose nationals fish in the region for the highly migratory species listed in Annex I shall cooperate directly or through appropriate international organizations with a view to ensuring conservation and promoting the objective of optimum utilization of such species throughout the region, both within and beyond the exclusive economic zone. In regions for which no appropriate international organization exists, the coastal State and other States whose nationals harvest these species in the region shall cooperate to establish such an organization and participate in its work.

2. The provisions of paragraph 1 apply in addition to the other provisions of this Part.

Article 65
Marine mammals

Nothing in this Part restricts the right of a coastal State or the competence of an international organization, as appropriate, to prohibit, limit or regulate the exploitation of marine mammals more strictly than provided for in this Part. States shall cooperate with a view to the conservation of marine mammals and in the case of cetaceans shall in particular work through the appropriate international organizations for their conservation, management and study.

Article 66
Anadromous stocks

1. States in whose rivers anadromous stocks originate shall have the primary interest in and responsibility for such stocks.

2. The State of origin of anadromous stocks shall ensure their conservation by the establishment of appropriate regulatory measures for fishing in all waters landward of the outer limits of its exclusive economic zone and for fishing provided for in paragraph 3(b). The State of origin may, after consultations with the other States

referred to in paragraphs 3 and 4 fishing these stocks, establish total allowable catches for stocks originating in its rivers.

3. (a) Fisheries for anadromous stocks shall be conducted only in waters landward of the outer limits of exclusive economic zones, except in cases where this provision would result in economic dislocation for a State other than the State of origin. With respect to such fishing beyond the outer limits of the exclusive economic zone, States concerned shall maintain consultations with a view to achieving agreement on terms and conditions of such fishing giving due regard to the conservation requirements and the needs of the State of origin in respect of these stocks.

(b) The State of origin shall cooperate in minimizing economic dislocation in such other States fishing these stocks, taking into account the normal catch and the mode of operations of such States, and all the areas in which such fishing has occurred.

(c) States referred to in subparagraph (b), participating by agreement with the State of origin in measures to renew anadromous stocks, particularly by expenditures for that purpose, shall be given special consideration by the State of origin in the harvesting of stocks originating in its rivers.

(d) Enforcement of regulations regarding anadromous stocks beyond the exclusive economic zone shall be by agreement between the State of origin and the other States concerned.

4. In cases where anadromous stocks migrate into or through the waters landward of the outer limits of the exclusive economic zone of a State other than the State of origin, such State shall cooperate with the State of origin with regard to the conservation and management of such stocks.

5. The State of origin of anadromous stocks and other States fishing these stocks shall make arrangements for the implementation of the provisions of this article, where appropriate, through regional organizations.

Article 67

Catadromous species

1. A coastal State in whose waters catadromous species spend the greater part of their life cycle shall have responsibility for the management of these species and shall ensure the ingress and egress of migrating fish.

2. Harvesting of catadromous species shall be conducted only in waters landward of the outer limits of exclusive economic zones. When conducted in exclusive economic zones, harvesting shall be subject to this article and the other provisions of this Convention concerning fishing in these zones.

3. In cases where catadromous fish migrate through the exclusive economic zone of another State, whether as juvenile or maturing fish, the management, including harvesting, of such fish shall be regulated by agreement between the State mentioned in

paragraph 1 and the other State concerned. Such agreement shall ensure the rational management of the species and take into account the responsibilities of the State mentioned in paragraph 1 for the maintenance of these species.

Article 68
Sedentary species

This Part does not apply to sedentary species as defined in article 77, paragraph 4.

Article 69
Right of land-locked States

1. Land-locked States shall have the right to participate, on an equitable basis, in the exploitation of an appropriate part of the surplus of the living resources of the exclusive economic zones of coastal States of the same subregion or region, taking into account the relevant economic and geographical circumstances of all the States concerned and in conformity with the provisions of this article and of articles 61 and 62.

2. The terms and modalities of such participation shall be established by the States concerned through bilateral, subregional or regional agreements taking into account, *inter alia*:

(a) the need to avoid effects detrimental to fishing communities or fishing industries of the coastal State;

(b) the extent to which the land-locked State, in accordance with the provisions of this article, is participating or is entitled to participate under existing bilateral, subregional or regional agreements in the exploitation of living resources of the exclusive economic zones of other coastal States;

(c) the extent to which other land-locked States and geographically disadvantaged States are participating in the exploitation of the living resources of the exclusive economic zone of the coastal State and the consequent need to avoid a particular burden for any single coastal State or a part of it;

(d) the nutritional needs of the populations of the respective States.

3. When the harvesting capacity of a coastal State approaches a point which would enable it to harvest the entire allowable catch of the living resources in its exclusive economic zone, the coastal State and other States concerned shall cooperate in the establishment of equitable arrangements on a bilateral, subregional or regional basis to allow for participation of developing land-locked States of the same subregion or region in the exploitation of the living resources of the exclusive economic zones of coastal States of the subregion or region, as may be appropriate in the circumstances and on terms satisfactory to all parties. In the implementation of this provision the factors mentioned in paragraph 2 shall also be taken into account.

4. Developed land-locked States shall, under the provisions of this article, be entitled to participate in the exploitation of living resources only in the exclusive economic zones of developed coastal States of the same subregion or region having regard to the extent to which the coastal State, in giving access to other States to the living resources of its exclusive economic zone, has taken into account the need to minimize detrimental effects on fishing communities and economic dislocation in States whose nationals have habitually fished in the zone.

5. The above provisions are without prejudice to arrangements agreed upon in subregions or regions where the coastal States may grant to land-locked States of the same subregion or region equal or preferential rights for the exploitation of the living resources in the exclusive economic zones.

Article 70

Right of geographically disadvantaged States

1. Geographically disadvantaged States shall have the right to participate, on an equitable basis, in the exploitation of an appropriate part of the surplus of the living resources of the exclusive economic zones of coastal States of the same subregion or region, taking into account the relevant economic and geographical circumstances of all the States concerned and in conformity with the provisions of this article and of articles 61 and 62.

2. For the purposes of this Part, "geographically disadvantaged States" means coastal States, including States bordering enclosed or semi-enclosed seas, whose geographical situation makes them dependent upon the exploitation of the living resources of the exclusive economic zones of other States in the subregion or region for adequate supplies of fish for the nutritional purposes of their populations or parts thereof, and coastal States which can claim no exclusive economic zones of their own.

3. The terms and modalities of such participation shall be established by the States concerned through bilateral, subregional or regional agreements taking into account, *inter alia*:

(a) the need to avoid effects detrimental to fishing communities or fishing industries of the coastal State;

(b) the extent to which the geographically disadvantaged State, in accordance with the provisions of this article, is participating or is entitled to participate under existing bilateral, subregional or regional agreements in the exploitation of living resources of the exclusive economic zones of other coastal States;

(c) the extent to which other geographically disadvantaged States and land-locked States are participating in the exploitation of the living resources of the exclusive economic zone of the coastal State and the consequent need to avoid a particular burden for any single coastal State or a part of it;

(d) the nutritional needs of the populations of the respective States.

4. When the harvesting capacity of a coastal State approaches a point which would enable it to harvest the entire allowable catch of the living resources in its exclusive economic zone, the coastal State and other States concerned shall cooperate in the establishment of equitable arrangements on a bilateral, subregional or regional basis to allow for participation of developing geographically disadvantaged States of the same subregion or region in the exploitation of the living resources of the exclusive economic zones of coastal States of the subregion or region, as may be appropriate in the circumstances and on terms satisfactory to all parties. In the implementation of this provision the factors mentioned in paragraph 3 shall also be taken into account.

5. Developed geographically disadvantaged States shall, under the provisions of this article, be entitled to participate in the exploitation of living resources only in the exclusive economic zones of developed coastal States of the same subregion or region having regard to the extent to which the coastal State, in giving access to other States to the living resources of its exclusive economic zone, has taken into account the need to minimize detrimental effects on fishing communities and economic dislocation in States whose nationals have habitually fished in the zone.

6. The above provisions are without prejudice to arrangements agreed upon in subregions or regions where the coastal States may grant to geographically disadvantaged States of the same subregion or region equal or preferential rights for the exploitation of the living resources in the exclusive economic zones.

Article 71
Non-applicability of articles 69 and 70

The provisions of articles 69 and 70 do not apply in the case of a coastal State whose economy is overwhelmingly dependent on the exploitation of the living resources of its exclusive economic zone.

Article 72
Restrictions on transfer of rights

1. Rights provided under articles 69 and 70 to exploit living resources shall not be directly or indirectly transferred to third States or their nationals by lease or licence, by establishing joint ventures or in any other manner which has the effect of such transfer unless otherwise agreed by the States concerned.

2. The foregoing provision does not preclude the States concerned from obtaining technical or financial assistance from third States or international organizations in order to facilitate the exercise of the rights pursuant to articles 69 and 70, provided that it does not have the effect referred to in paragraph 1.

Article 73

Enforcement of laws and regulations of the coastal State

1. The coastal State may, in the exercise of its sovereign rights to explore, exploit, conserve and manage the living resources in the exclusive economic zone, take such measures, including boarding, inspection, arrest and judicial proceedings, as may be necessary to ensure compliance with the laws and regulations adopted by it in conformity with this Convention.

2. Arrested vessels and their crews shall be promptly released upon the posting of reasonable bond or other security.

3. Coastal State penalties for violations of fisheries laws and regulations in the exclusive economic zone may not include imprisonment, in the absence of agreements to the contrary by the States concerned, or any other form of corporal punishment.

4. In cases of arrest or detention of foreign vessels the coastal State shall promptly notify the flag State, through appropriate channels, of the action taken and of any penalties subsequently imposed.

Article 74

Delimitation of the exclusive economic zone between States with opposite or adjacent coasts

1. The delimitation of the exclusive economic zone between States with opposite or adjacent coasts shall be effected by agreement on the basis of international law, as referred to in Article 38 of the Statute of the International Court of Justice, in order to achieve an equitable solution.

2. If no agreement can be reached within a reasonable period of time, the States concerned shall resort to the procedures provided for in Part XV.

3. Pending agreement as provided for in paragraph 1, the States concerned, in a spirit of understanding and cooperation, shall make every effort to enter into provisional arrangements of a practical nature and, during this transitional period, not to jeopardize or hamper the reaching of the final agreement. Such arrangements shall be without prejudice to the final delimitation.

4. Where there is an agreement in force between the States concerned, questions relating to the delimitation of the exclusive economic zone shall be determined in accordance with the provisions of that agreement.

Article 75

Charts and lists of geographical coordinates

1. Subject to this Part, the outer limit lines of the exclusive economic zone and the lines of delimitation drawn in accordance with article 74 shall be shown on charts of a scale or scales adequate for ascertaining their position. Where appropriate, lists of

geographical coordinates of points, specifying the geodetic datum, may be substituted for such outer limit lines or lines of delimitation.

2. The coastal State shall give due publicity to such charts or lists of geographical coordinates and shall deposit a copy of each such chart or list with the Secretary-General of the United Nations.

Part VI Continental Shelf

Article 76
Definition of the continental shelf

1. The continental shelf of a coastal State comprises the seabed and subsoil of the submarine areas that extend beyond its territorial sea throughout the natural prolongation of its land territory to the outer edge of the continental margin, or to a distance of 200 nautical miles from the baselines from which the breadth of the territorial sea is measured where the outer edge of the continental margin does not extend up to that distance.

2. The continental shelf of a coastal State shall not extend beyond the limits provided for in paragraphs 4 to 6.

3. The continental margin comprises the submerged prolongation of the land mass of the coastal State, and consists of the seabed and subsoil of the shelf, the slope and the rise. It does not include the deep ocean floor with its oceanic ridges or the subsoil thereof.

4. (a) For the purposes of this Convention, the coastal State shall establish the outer edge of the continental margin wherever the margin extends beyond 200 nautical miles from the baselines from which the breadth of the territorial sea is measured, by either:

(i) a line delineated in accordance with paragraph 7 by reference to the outermost fixed points at each of which the thickness of sedimentary rocks is at least 1 per cent of the shortest distance from such point to the foot of the continental slope; or

(ii) a line delineated in accordance with paragraph 7 by reference to fixed points not more than 60 nautical miles from the foot of the continental slope.

(b) In the absence of evidence to the contrary, the foot of the continental slope shall be determined as the point of maximum change in the gradient at its base.

5. The fixed points comprising the line of the outer limits of the continental shelf on the seabed, drawn in accordance with paragraph 4 (a)(i) and (ii), either shall not exceed 350 nautical miles from the baselines from which the breadth of the territorial sea is measured or shall not exceed 100 nautical miles from the 2,500 metre isobath, which is a line connecting the depth of 2,500 metres.

6. Notwithstanding the provisions of paragraph 5, on submarine ridges, the outer limit of the continental shelf shall not exceed 350 nautical miles from the baselines from which the breadth of the territorial sea is measured. This paragraph does not apply to submarine elevations that are natural components of the continental margin, such as its plateaux, rises, caps, banks and spurs.

7. The coastal State shall delineate the outer limits of its continental shelf, where that shelf extends beyond 200 nautical miles from the baselines from which the breadth of the territorial sea is measured, by straight lines not exceeding 60 nautical miles in length, connecting fixed points, defined by coordinates of latitude and longitude.

8. Information on the limits of the continental shelf beyond 200 nautical miles from the baselines from which the breadth of the territorial sea is measured shall be submitted by the coastal State to the Commission on the Limits of the Continental Shelf set up under Annex II on the basis of equitable geographical representation. The Commission shall make recommendations to coastal States on matters related to the establishment of the outer limits of their continental shelf. The limits of the shelf established by a coastal State on the basis of these recommendations shall be final and binding.

9. The coastal State shall deposit with the Secretary-General of the United Nations charts and relevant information, including geodetic data, permanently describing the outer limits of its continental shelf. The Secretary-General shall give due publicity thereto.

10. The provisions of this article are without prejudice to the question of delimitation of the continental shelf between States with opposite or adjacent coasts.

Article 77

Rights of the coastal State over the continental shelf

1. The coastal State exercises over the continental shelf sovereign rights for the purpose of exploring it and exploiting its natural resources.

2. The rights referred to in paragraph 1 are exclusive in the sense that if the coastal State does not explore the continental shelf or exploit its natural resources, no one may undertake these activities without the express consent of the coastal State.

3. The rights of the coastal State over the continental shelf do not depend on occupation, effective or notional, or on any express proclamation.

4. The natural resources referred to in this Part consist of the mineral and other non-living resources of the seabed and subsoil together with living organisms belonging to sedentary species, that is to say, organisms which, at the harvestable stage, either are immobile on or under the seabed or are unable to move except in constant physical contact with the seabed or the subsoil.

Article 78

Legal status of the superjacent waters and air space and the rights and freedoms of other States

1. The rights of the coastal State over the continental shelf do not affect the legal status of the superjacent waters or of the air space above those waters.

2. The exercise of the rights of the coastal State over the continental shelf must not infringe or result in any unjustifiable interference with navigation and other rights and freedoms of other States as provided for in this Convention.

Article 79

Submarine cables and pipelines on the continental shelf

1. All States are entitled to lay submarine cables and pipelines on the continental shelf, in accordance with the provisions of this article.

2. Subject to its right to take reasonable measures for the exploration of the continental shelf, the exploitation of its natural resources and the prevention, reduction and control of pollution from pipelines, the coastal State may not impede the laying or maintenance of such cables or pipelines.

3. The delineation of the course for the laying of such pipelines on the continental shelf is subject to the consent of the coastal State.

4. Nothing in this Part affects the right of the coastal State to establish conditions for cables or pipelines entering its territory or territorial sea, or its jurisdiction over cables and pipelines constructed or used in connection with the exploration of its continental shelf or exploitation of its resources or the operations of artificial islands, installations and structures under its jurisdiction.

5. When laying submarine cables or pipelines, States shall have due regard to cables or pipelines already in position. In particular, possibilities of repairing existing cables or pipelines shall not be prejudiced.

Article 80

Artificial islands, installations and structures on the continental shelf

Article 60 applies *mutatis mutandis* to artificial islands, installations and structures on the continental shelf.

Article 81

Drilling on the continental shelf

The coastal State shall have the exclusive right to authorize and regulate drilling on the continental shelf for all purposes.

Article 82
Payments and contributions with respect to the exploitation of the continental shelf beyond 200 nautical miles

1. The coastal State shall make payments or contributions in kind in respect of the exploitation of the non-living resources of the continental shelf beyond 200 nautical miles from the baselines from which the breadth of the territorial sea is measured.

2. The payments and contributions shall be made annually with respect to all production at a site after the first five years of production at that site. For the sixth year, the rate of payment or contribution shall be 1 per cent of the value or volume of production at the site. The rate shall increase by 1 per cent for each subsequent year until the twelfth year and shall remain at 7 per cent thereafter. Production does not include resources used in connection with exploitation.

3. A developing State which is a net importer of a mineral resource produced from its continental shelf is exempt from making such payments or contributions in respect of that mineral resource.

4. The payments or contributions shall be made through the Authority, which shall distribute them to States Parties to this Convention, on the basis of equitable sharing criteria, taking into account the interests and needs of developing States, particularly the least developed and the land-locked among them.

Article 83
Delimitation of the continental shelf between States with opposite or adjacent coasts

1. The delimitation of the continental shelf between States with opposite or adjacent coasts shall be effected by agreement on the basis of international law, as referred to in Article 38 of the Statute of the International Court of Justice, in order to achieve an equitable solution.

2. If no agreement can be reached within a reasonable period of time, the States concerned shall resort to the procedures provided for in Part XV.

3. Pending agreement as provided for in paragraph 1, the States concerned, in a spirit of understanding and cooperation, shall make every effort to enter into provisional arrangements of a practical nature and, during this transitional period, not to jeopardize or hamper the reaching of the final agreement. Such arrangements shall be without prejudice to the final delimitation.

4. Where there is an agreement in force between the States concerned, questions relating to the delimitation of the continental shelf shall be determined in accordance with the provisions of that agreement.

Article 84

Charts and lists of geographical coordinates

1. Subject to this Part, the outer limit lines of the continental shelf and the lines of delimitation drawn in accordance with article 83 shall be shown on charts of a scale or scales adequate for ascertaining their position. Where appropriate, lists of geographical coordinates of points, specifying the geodetic datum, may be substituted for such outer limit lines or lines of delimitation.

2. The coastal State shall give due publicity to such charts or lists of geographical coordinates and shall deposit a copy of each such chart or list with the Secretary-General of the United Nations and, in the case of those showing the outer limit lines of the continental shelf, with the Secretary-General of the Authority.

Article 85

Tunnelling

This Part does not prejudice the right of the coastal State to exploit the subsoil by means of tunnelling, irrespective of the depth of water above the subsoil.

Part VII High Seas

Section 1 General Provisions

Article 86

Application of the provisions of this Part

The provisions of this Part apply to all parts of the sea that are not included in the exclusive economic zone, in the territorial sea or in the internal waters of a State, or in the archipelagic waters of an archipelagic State. This article does not entail any abridgement of the freedoms enjoyed by all States in the exclusive economic zone in accordance with article 58.

Article 87

Freedom of the high seas

1. The high seas are open to all States, whether coastal or land-locked. Freedom of the high seas is exercised under the conditions laid down by this Convention and by other rules of international law. It comprises, *inter alia*, both for coastal and land-locked States:

(a) freedom of navigation;

(b) freedom of overflight;

(c) freedom to lay submarine cables and pipelines, subject to Part VI;

(d) freedom to construct artificial islands and other installations permitted under international law, subject to Part VI;

(e) freedom of fishing, subject to the conditions laid down in section 2;

(f) freedom of scientific research, subject to Parts VI and XIII.

2. These freedoms shall be exercised by all States with due regard for the interests of other States in their exercise of the freedom of the high seas, and also with due regard for the rights under this Convention with respect to activities in the Area.

Article 88

Reservation of the high seas for peaceful purposes

The high seas shall be reserved for peaceful purposes.

Article 89

Invalidity of claims of sovereignty over the high seas

No State may validly purport to subject any part of the high seas to its sovereignty.

Article 90

Right of navigation

Every State, whether coastal or land-locked, has the right to sail ships flying its flag on the high seas.

Article 91

Nationality of ships

1. Every State shall fix the conditions for the grant of its nationality to ships, for the registration of ships in its territory, and for the right to fly its flag. Ships have the nationality of the State whose flag they are entitled to fly. There must exist a genuine link between the State and the ship.

2. Every State shall issue to ships to which it has granted the right to fly its flag documents to that effect.

Article 92

Status of ships

1. Ships shall sail under the flag of one State only and, save in exceptional cases expressly provided for in international treaties or in this Convention, shall be subject to its exclusive jurisdiction on the high seas. A ship may not change its flag during a voyage or while in a port of call, save in the case of a real transfer of ownership or change of registry.

2. A ship which sails under the flags of two or more States, using them according to convenience, may not claim any of the nationalities in question with respect to any other State, and may be assimilated to a ship without nationality.

Article 93

Ships flying the flag of the United Nations, its specialized agencies and the International Atomic Energy Agency

The preceding articles do not prejudice the question of ships employed on the official service of the United Nations, its specialized agencies or the International Atomic Energy Agency, flying the flag of the organization.

Article 94

Duties of the flag State

1. Every State shall effectively exercise its jurisdiction and control in administrative, technical and social matters over ships flying its flag.

2. In particular every State shall:

(a) maintain a register of ships containing the names and particulars of ships flying its flag, except those which are excluded from generally accepted international regulations on account of their small size; and

(b) assume jurisdiction under its internal law over each ship flying its flag and its master, officers and crew in respect of administrative, technical and social matters concerning the ship.

3. Every State shall take such measures for ships flying its flag as are necessary to ensure safety at sea with regard, *inter alia*, to:

(a) the construction, equipment and seaworthiness of ships;

(b) the manning of ships, labour conditions and the training of crews, taking into account the applicable international instruments;

(c) the use of signals, the maintenance of communications and the prevention of collisions.

4. Such measures shall include those necessary to ensure:

(a) that each ship, before registration and thereafter at appropriate intervals, is surveyed by a qualified surveyor of ships, and has on board such charts, nautical publications and navigational equipment and instruments as are appropriate for the safe navigation of the ship;

(b) that each ship is in the charge of a master and officers who possess appropriate qualifications, in particular in seamanship, navigation, communications and marine engineering, and that the crew is appropriate in qualification and numbers for the type, size, machinery and equipment of the ship;

(c) that the master, officers and, to the extent appropriate, the crew are fully conversant with and required to observe the applicable international regulations concerning the safety of life at sea, the prevention of collisions, the prevention, reduction and control of marine pollution, and the maintenance of communications by radio.

5. In taking the measures called for in paragraphs 3 and 4 each State is required to conform to generally accepted international regulations, procedures and practices and to take any steps which may be necessary to secure their observance.

6. A State which has clear grounds to believe that proper jurisdiction and control with respect to a ship have not been exercised may report the facts to the flag State. Upon receiving such a report, the flag State shall investigate the matter and, if appropriate, take any action necessary to remedy the situation.

7. Each State shall cause an inquiry to be held by or before a suitably qualified person or persons into every marine casualty or incident of navigation on the high seas involving a ship flying its flag and causing loss of life or serious injury to nationals of another State or serious damage to ships or installations of another State or to the marine environment. The flag State and the other State shall cooperate in the conduct of any inquiry held by that other State into any such marine casualty or incident of navigation.

Article 95

Immunity of warships on the high seas

Warships on the high seas have complete immunity from the jurisdiction of any State other than the flag State.

Article 96

Immunity of ships used only on government non-commercial service

Ships owned or operated by a State and used only on government non-commercial service shall, on the high seas, have complete immunity from the jurisdiction of any State other than the flag State.

Article 97

Penal jurisdiction in matters of collision or any other incident of navigation

1. In the event of a collision or any other incident of navigation concerning a ship on the high seas, involving the penal or disciplinary responsibility of the master or of any other person in the service of the ship, no penal or disciplinary proceedings may be instituted against such person except before the judicial or administrative authorities either of the flag State or of the State of which such person is a national.

2. In disciplinary matters, the State which has issued a master's certificate or a certificate of competence or licence shall alone be competent, after due legal process, to pronounce the withdrawal of such certificates, even if the holder is not a national of the State which issued them.

3. No arrest or detention of the ship, even as a measure of investigation, shall be ordered by any authorities other than those of the flag State.

Article 98
Duty to render assistance

1. Every State shall require the master of a ship flying its flag, in so far as he can do so without serious danger to the ship, the crew or the passengers:

(a) to render assistance to any person found at sea in danger of being lost;

(b) to proceed with all possible speed to the rescue of persons in distress, if informed of their need of assistance, in so far as such action may reasonably be expected of him;

(c) after a collision, to render assistance to the other ship, its crew and its passengers and, where possible, to inform the other ship of the name of his own ship, its port of registry and the nearest port at which it will call.

2. Every coastal State shall promote the establishment, operation and maintenance of an adequate and effective search and rescue service regarding safety on and over the sea and, where circumstances so require, by way of mutual regional arrangements cooperate with neighbouring States for this purpose.

Article 99
Prohibition of the transport of slaves

Every State shall take effective measures to prevent and punish the transport of slaves in ships authorized to fly its flag and to prevent the unlawful use of its flag for that purpose. Any slave taking refuge on board any ship, whatever its flag, shall *ipso facto* be free.

Article 100
Duty to cooperate in the repression of piracy

All States shall cooperate to the fullest possible extent in the repression of piracy on the high seas or in any other place outside the jurisdiction of any State.

Article 101
Definition of piracy

Piracy consists of any of the following acts:

(a) any illegal acts of violence or detention, or any act of depredation, committed for private ends by the crew or the passengers of a private ship or a private aircraft, and directed:

(i) on the high seas, against another ship or aircraft, or against persons or property on board such ship or aircraft;

(ii) against a ship, aircraft, persons or property in a place outside the jurisdiction of any State;

(b) any act of voluntary participation in the operation of a ship or of an aircraft with knowledge of facts making it a pirate ship or aircraft;

(c) any act of inciting or of intentionally facilitating an act described in subparagraph (a) or (b).

Article 102

Piracy by a warship, government ship or government aircraft whose crew has mutinied

The acts of piracy, as defined in article 101, committed by a warship, government ship or government aircraft whose crew has mutinied and taken control of the ship or aircraft are assimilated to acts committed by a private ship or aircraft.

Article 103

Definition of a pirate ship or aircraft

A ship or aircraft is considered a pirate ship or aircraft if it is intended by the persons in dominant control to be used for the purpose of committing one of the acts referred to in article 101. The same applies if the ship or aircraft has been used to commit any such act, so long as it remains under the control of the persons guilty of that act.

Article 104

Retention or loss of the nationality of a pirate ship or aircraft

A ship or aircraft may retain its nationality although it has become a pirate ship or aircraft. The retention or loss of nationality is determined by the law of the State from which such nationality was derived.

Article 105

Seizure of a pirate ship or aircraft

On the high seas, or in any other place outside the jurisdiction of any State, every State may seize a pirate ship or aircraft, or a ship or aircraft taken by piracy and under the control of pirates, and arrest the persons and seize the property on board. The courts of the State which carried out the seizure may decide upon the penalties to be imposed, and may also determine the action to be taken with regard to the ships, aircraft or property, subject to the rights of third parties acting in good faith.

Article 106

Liability for seizure without adequate grounds

Where the seizure of a ship or aircraft on suspicion of piracy has been effected without adequate grounds, the State making the seizure shall be liable to the State the nationality of which is possessed by the ship or aircraft for any loss or damage caused by the seizure.

Article 107

Ships and aircraft which are entitled to seize on account of piracy

A seizure on account of piracy may be carried out only by warships or military aircraft, or other ships or aircraft clearly marked and identifiable as being on government service and authorized to that effect.

Article 108

Illicit traffic in narcotic drugs or psychotropic substances

1. All States shall cooperate in the suppression of illicit traffic in narcotic drugs and psychotropic substances engaged in by ships on the high seas contrary to international conventions.

2. Any State which has reasonable grounds for believing that a ship flying its flag is engaged in illicit traffic in narcotic drugs or psychotropic substances may request the cooperation of other States to suppress such traffic.

Article 109

Unauthorized broadcasting from the high seas

1. All States shall cooperate in the suppression of unauthorized broadcasting from the high seas.

2. For the purposes of this Convention, "unauthorized broadcasting" means the transmission of sound radio or television broadcasts from a ship or installation on the high seas intended for reception by the general public contrary to international regulations, but excluding the transmission of distress calls.

3. Any person engaged in unauthorized broadcasting may be prosecuted before the court of:

(a) the flag State of the ship;
(b) the State of registry of the installation;
(c) the State of which the person is a national;
(d) any State where the transmissions can be received; or
(e) any State where authorized radio communication is suffering interference.

4. On the high seas, a State having jurisdiction in accordance with paragraph 3 may, in conformity with article 110, arrest any person or ship engaged in unauthorized broadcasting and seize the broadcasting apparatus.

Article 110

Right of visit

1. Except where acts of interference derive from powers conferred by treaty, a warship which encounters on the high seas a foreign ship, other than a ship entitled to complete immunity in accordance with articles 95 and 96, is not justified in boarding it unless there is reasonable ground for suspecting that:

(a) the ship is engaged in piracy;

(b) the ship is engaged in the slave trade;

(c) the ship is engaged in unauthorized broadcasting and the flag State of the warship has jurisdiction under article 109;

(d) the ship is without nationality; or

(e) though flying a foreign flag or refusing to show its flag, the ship is, in reality, of the same nationality as the warship.

2. In the cases provided for in paragraph 1, the warship may proceed to verify the ship's right to fly its flag. To this end, it may send a boat under the command of an officer to the suspected ship. If suspicion remains after the documents have been checked, it may proceed to a further examination on board the ship, which must be carried out with all possible consideration.

3. If the suspicions prove to be unfounded, and provided that the ship boarded has not committed any act justifying them, it shall be compensated for any loss or damage that may have been sustained.

4. These provisions apply *mutatis mutandis* to military aircraft.

5. These provisions also apply to any other duly authorized ships or aircraft clearly marked and identifiable as being on government service.

Article 111

Right of hot pursuit

1. The hot pursuit of a foreign ship may be undertaken when the competent authorities of the coastal State have good reason to believe that the ship has violated the laws and regulations of that State. Such pursuit must be commenced when the foreign ship or one of its boats is within the internal waters, the archipelagic waters, the territorial sea or the contiguous zone of the pursuing State, and may only be continued outside the territorial sea or the contiguous zone if the pursuit has not been interrupted. It is not necessary that, at the time when the foreign ship within the territorial sea or the contiguous zone receives the order to stop, the ship giving the order should likewise be within the territorial sea or the contiguous zone. If the foreign ship is within a contiguous zone, as defined in article 33, the pursuit may only be undertaken if there has been a violation of the rights for the protection of which the zone was established.

2. The right of hot pursuit shall apply *mutatis mutandis* to violations in the exclusive economic zone or on the continental shelf, including safety zones around continental shelf installations, of the laws and regulations of the coastal State applicable in accordance with this Convention to the exclusive economic zone or the continental shelf, including such safety zones.

3. The right of hot pursuit ceases as soon as the ship pursued enters the territorial sea of its own State or of a third State.

4. Hot pursuit is not deemed to have begun unless the pursuing ship has satisfied itself by such practicable means as may be available that the ship pursued or one of its boats or other craft working as a team and using the ship pursued as a mother ship is within the limits of the territorial sea, or, as the case may be, within the contiguous zone or the exclusive economic zone or above the continental shelf. The pursuit may only be commenced after a visual or auditory signal to stop has been given at a distance which enables it to be seen or heard by the foreign ship.

5. The right of hot pursuit may be exercised only by warships or military aircraft, or other ships or aircraft clearly marked and identifiable as being on government service and authorized to that effect.

6. Where hot pursuit is effected by an aircraft:

(a) the provisions of paragraphs 1 to 4 shall apply *mutatis mutandis*;

(b) the aircraft giving the order to stop must itself actively pursue the ship until a ship or another aircraft of the coastal State, summoned by the aircraft, arrives to take over the pursuit, unless the aircraft is itself able to arrest the ship. It does not suffice to justify an arrest outside the territorial sea that the ship was merely sighted by the aircraft as an offender or suspected offender, if it was not both ordered to stop and pursued by the aircraft itself or other aircraft or ships which continue the pursuit without interruption.

7. The release of a ship arrested within the jurisdiction of a State and escorted to a port of that State for the purposes of an inquiry before the competent authorities may not be claimed solely on the ground that the ship, in the course of its voyage, was escorted across a portion of the exclusive economic zone or the high seas, if the circumstances rendered this necessary.

8. Where a ship has been stopped or arrested outside the territorial sea in circumstances which do not justify the exercise of the right of hot pursuit, it shall be compensated for any loss or damage that may have been thereby sustained.

Article 112

Right to lay submarine cables and pipelines

1. All States are entitled to lay submarine cables and pipelines on the bed of the high seas beyond the continental shelf.

2. Article 79, paragraph 5, applies to such cables and pipelines.

Article 113

Breaking or injury of a submarine cable or pipeline

Every State shall adopt the laws and regulations necessary to provide that the breaking or injury by a ship flying its flag or by a person subject to its jurisdiction of a submarine cable beneath the high seas done wilfully or through culpable negligence, in such a manner as to be liable to interrupt or obstruct telegraphic or telephonic communications, and similarly the breaking or injury of a submarine pipeline or high-voltage power cable, shall be a punishable offence. This provision shall apply also to conduct calculated or likely to result in such breaking or injury. However, it shall not apply to any break or injury caused by persons who acted merely with the legitimate object of saving their lives or their ships, after having taken all necessary precautions to avoid such break or injury.

Article 114

Breaking or injury by owners of a submarine cable or pipeline of another submarine cable or pipeline

Every State shall adopt the laws and regulations necessary to provide that, if persons subject to its jurisdiction who are the owners of a submarine cable or pipeline beneath the high seas, in laying or repairing that cable or pipeline, cause a break in or injury to another cable or pipeline, they shall bear the cost of the repairs.

Article 115

Indemnity for loss incurred in avoiding injury to a submarine cable or pipeline

Every State shall adopt the laws and regulations necessary to ensure that the owners of ships who can prove that they have sacrificed an anchor, a net or any other fishing gear, in order to avoid injuring a submarine cable or pipeline, shall be indemnified by the owner of the cable or pipeline, provided that the owner of the ship has taken all reasonable precautionary measures beforehand.

Section 2 Conservation and Management of the Living Resources of the High Seas

Article 116

Right to fish on the high seas

All States have the right for their nationals to engage in fishing on the high seas subject to:

(a) their treaty obligations;

(b) the rights and duties as well as the interests of coastal States provided for, *inter alia*, in article 63, paragraph 2, and articles 64 to 67; and

(c) the provisions of this section.

Article 117

Duty of States to adopt with respect to their nationals measures for the conservation of the living resources of the high seas

All States have the duty to take, or to cooperate with other States in taking, such measures for their respective nationals as may be necessary for the conservation of the living resources of the high seas.

Article 118

Cooperation of States in the conservation and management of living resources

States shall cooperate with each other in the conservation and management of living resources in the areas of the high seas. States whose nationals exploit identical living resources, or different living resources in the same area, shall enter into negotiations with a view to taking the measures necessary for the conservation of the living resources concerned. They shall, as appropriate, cooperate to establish subregional or regional fisheries organizations to this end.

Article 119

Conservation of the living resources of the high seas

1. In determining the allowable catch and establishing other conservation measures for the living resources in the high seas, States shall:

(a) take measures which are designed, on the best scientific evidence available to the States concerned, to maintain or restore populations of harvested species at levels which can produce the maximum sustainable yield, as qualified by relevant environmental and economic factors, including the special requirements of developing States, and taking into account fishing patterns, the interdependence of stocks and any generally recommended international minimum standards, whether subregional, regional or global;

(b) take into consideration the effects on species associated with or dependent upon harvested species with a view to maintaining or restoring populations of such associated or dependent species above levels at which their reproduction may become seriously threatened.

2. Available scientific information, catch and fishing effort statistics, and other data relevant to the conservation of fish stocks shall be contributed and exchanged on a regular basis through competent international organizations, whether subregional, regional or global, where appropriate and with participation by all States concerned.

3. States concerned shall ensure that conservation measures and their implementation do not discriminate in form or in fact against the fishermen of any State.

Article 120

Marine mammals

Article 65 also applies to the conservation and management of marine mammals in the high seas.

Part VIII Regime of Islands

Article 121
Regime of islands

1. An island is a naturally formed area of land, surrounded by water, which is above water at high tide.

2. Except as provided for in paragraph 3, the territorial sea, the contiguous zone, the exclusive economic zone and the continental shelf of an island are determined in accordance with the provisions of this Convention applicable to other land territory.

3. Rocks which cannot sustain human habitation or economic life of their own shall have no exclusive economic zone or continental shelf.

Part IX Enclosed or Semi-Enclosed Seas

Article 122
Definition

For the purposes of this Convention, "enclosed or semi-enclosed sea" means a gulf, basin or sea surrounded by two or more States and connected to another sea or the ocean by a narrow outlet or consisting entirely or primarily of the territorial seas and exclusive economic zones of two or more coastal States.

Article 123
Cooperation of States bordering enclosed or semi-enclosed seas

States bordering an enclosed or semi-enclosed sea should cooperate with each other in the exercise of their rights and in the performance of their duties under this Convention. To this end they shall endeavour, directly or through an appropriate regional organization:

(a) to coordinate the management, conservation, exploration and exploitation of the living resources of the sea;

(b) to coordinate the implementation of their rights and duties with respect to the protection and preservation of the marine environment;

(c) to coordinate their scientific research policies and undertake where appropriate joint programmes of scientific research in the area;

(d) to invite, as appropriate, other interested States or international organizations to cooperate with them in furtherance of the provisions of this article.

Part X Right of Access of Land-Locked States to and from the Sea and Freedom of Transit

Article 124

Use of terms

1. For the purposes of this Convention:

(a) "land-locked State" means a State which has no sea-coast;

(b) "transit State" means a State, with or without a sea-coast, situated between a land-locked State and the sea, through whose territory traffic in transit passes;

(c) "traffic in transit" means transit of persons, baggage, goods and means of transport across the territory of one or more transit States, when the passage across such territory, with or without trans-shipment, warehousing, breaking bulk or change in the mode of transport, is only a portion of a complete journey which begins or terminates within the territory of the land-locked State;

(d) "means of transport" means:

(i) railway rolling stock, sea, lake and river craft and road vehicles;

(ii) where local conditions so require, porters and pack animals.

2. Land-locked States and transit States may, by agreement between them, include as means of transport pipelines and gas lines and means of transport other than those included in paragraph 1.

Article 125

Right of access to and from the sea and freedom of transit

1. Land-locked States shall have the right of access to and from the sea for the purpose of exercising the rights provided for in this Convention including those relating to the freedom of the high seas and the common heritage of mankind. To this end, land-locked States shall enjoy freedom of transit through the territory of transit States by all means of transport.

2. The terms and modalities for exercising freedom of transit shall be agreed between the land-locked States and transit States concerned through bilateral, subregional or regional agreements.

3. Transit States, in the exercise of their full sovereignty over their territory, shall have the right to take all measures necessary to ensure that the rights and facilities provided for in this Part for land-locked States shall in no way infringe their legitimate interests.

Article 126

Exclusion of application of the most-favoured-nation clause

The provisions of this Convention, as well as special agreements relating to the exercise of the right of access to and from the sea, establishing rights and facilities on account of the special geographical position of land-locked States, are excluded from the application of the most-favoured-nation clause.

Article 127

Customs duties, taxes and other charges

1. Traffic in transit shall not be subject to any customs duties, taxes or other charges except charges levied for specific services rendered in connection with such traffic.

2. Means of transport in transit and other facilities provided for and used by land-locked States shall not be subject to taxes or charges higher than those levied for the use of means of transport of the transit State.

Article 128

Free zones and other customs facilities

For the convenience of traffic in transit, free zones or other customs facilities may be provided at the ports of entry and exit in the transit States, by agreement between those States and the land-locked States.

Article 129

Cooperation in the construction and improvement of means of transport

Where there are no means of transport in transit States to give effect to the freedom of transit or where the existing means, including the port installations and equipment, are inadequate in any respect, the transit States and land-locked States concerned may cooperate in constructing or improving them.

Article 130

Measures to avoid or eliminate delays or other difficulties of a technical nature in traffic in transit

1. Transit States shall take all appropriate measures to avoid delays or other difficulties of a technical nature in traffic in transit.

2. Should such delays or difficulties occur, the competent authorities of the transit States and land-locked States concerned shall cooperate towards their expeditious elimination.

Article 131

Equal treatment in maritime ports

Ships flying the flag of land-locked States shall enjoy treatment equal to that accorded to other foreign ships in maritime ports.

Article 132

Grant of greater transit facilities

This Convention does not entail in any way the withdrawal of transit facilities which are greater than those provided for in this Convention and which are agreed between States Parties to this Convention or granted by a State Party. This Convention also does not preclude such grant of greater facilities in the future.

Part XI The Area

Section 1 General Provisions

Article 133

Use of terms

For the purposes of this Part:

(a) "resources" means all solid, liquid or gaseous mineral resources *in situ* in the Area at or beneath the seabed, including polymetallic nodules;

(b) resources, when recovered from the Area, are referred to as "minerals".

Article 134

Scope of this Part

1. This Part applies to the Area.
2. Activities in the Area shall be governed by the provisions of this Part.
3. The requirements concerning deposit of, and publicity to be given to, the charts or lists of geographical coordinates showing the limits referred to in article 1, paragraph 1(1), are set forth in Part VI.
4. Nothing in this article affects the establishment of the outer limits of the continental shelf in accordance with Part VI or the validity of agreements relating to delimitation between States with opposite or adjacent coasts.

Article 135

Legal status of the superjacent waters and air space

Neither this Part nor any rights granted or exercised pursuant thereto shall affect the legal status of the waters superjacent to the Area or that of the air space above those waters.

Section 2 Principles Governing the Area

Article 136

Common heritage of mankind

The Area and its resources are the common heritage of mankind.

Article 137

Legal status of the Area and its resources

1. No State shall claim or exercise sovereignty or sovereign rights over any part of the Area or its resources, nor shall any State or natural or juridical person appropriate any part thereof. No such claim or exercise of sovereignty or sovereign rights nor such appropriation shall be recognized.

2. All rights in the resources of the Area are vested in mankind as a whole, on whose behalf the Authority shall act. These resources are not subject to alienation. The minerals recovered from the Area, however, may only be alienated in accordance with this Part and the rules, regulations and procedures of the Authority.

3. No State or natural or juridical person shall claim, acquire or exercise rights with respect to the minerals recovered from the Area except in accordance with this Part. Otherwise, no such claim, acquisition or exercise of such rights shall be recognized.

Article 138

General conduct of States in relation to the Area

The general conduct of States in relation to the Area shall be in accordance with the provisions of this Part, the principles embodied in the Charter of the United Nations and other rules of international law in the interests of maintaining peace and security and promoting international cooperation and mutual understanding.

Article 139

Responsibility to ensure compliance and liability for damage

1. States Parties shall have the responsibility to ensure that activities in the Area, whether carried out by States Parties, or state enterprises or natural or juridical persons which possess the nationality of States Parties or are effectively controlled by them or their nationals, shall be carried out in conformity with this Part. The same responsibility applies to international organizations for activities in the Area carried out by such organizations.

2. Without prejudice to the rules of international law and Annex III, article 22, damage caused by the failure of a State Party or international organization to carry out its responsibilities under this Part shall entail liability; States Parties or international organizations acting together shall bear joint and several liability. A State Party shall not however be liable for damage caused by any failure to comply with this Part by a person whom it has sponsored under article 153, paragraph 2(b), if the State Party has taken all necessary and appropriate measures to secure effective compliance under article 153, paragraph 4, and Annex III, article 4, paragraph 4.

3. States Parties that are members of international organizations shall take appropriate measures to ensure the implementation of this article with respect to such organizations.

Article 140

Benefit of mankind

1. Activities in the Area shall, as specifically provided for in this Part, be carried out for the benefit of mankind as a whole, irrespective of the geographical location of States, whether coastal or land-locked, and taking into particular consideration the interests and needs of developing States and of peoples who have not attained full independence or other self-governing status recognized by the United Nations in accordance with General Assembly resolution 1514 (XV) and other relevant General Assembly resolutions.

2. The Authority shall provide for the equitable sharing of financial and other economic benefits derived from activities in the Area through any appropriate mechanism, on a non-discriminatory basis, in accordance with article 160, paragraph 2(f)(i).

Article 141

Use of the Area exclusively for peaceful purposes

The Area shall be open to use exclusively for peaceful purposes by all States, whether coastal or land-locked, without discrimination and without prejudice to the other provisions of this Part.

Article 142

Rights and legitimate interests of coastal States

1. Activities in the Area, with respect to resource deposits in the Area which lie across limits of national jurisdiction, shall be conducted with due regard to the rights and legitimate interests of any coastal State across whose jurisdiction such deposits lie.

2. Consultations, including a system of prior notification, shall be maintained with the State concerned, with a view to avoiding infringement of such rights and interests. In cases where activities in the Area may result in the exploitation of resources lying within national jurisdiction, the prior consent of the coastal State concerned shall be required.

3. Neither this Part nor any rights granted or exercised pursuant thereto shall affect the rights of coastal States to take such measures consistent with the relevant provisions of Part XII as may be necessary to prevent, mitigate or eliminate grave and imminent danger to their coastline, or related interests from pollution or threat thereof or from other hazardous occurrences resulting from or caused by any activities in the Area.

Article 143

Marine scientific research

1. Marine scientific research in the Area shall be carried out exclusively for peaceful purposes and for the benefit of mankind as a whole, in accordance with Part XIII.

2. The Authority may carry out marine scientific research concerning the Area and its resources, and may enter into contracts for that purpose. The Authority shall promote and encourage the conduct of marine scientific research in the Area, and shall coordinate and disseminate the results of such research and analysis when available.

3. States Parties may carry out marine scientific research in the Area. States Parties shall promote international cooperation in marine scientific research in the Area by:

(a) participating in international programmes and encouraging cooperation in marine scientific research by personnel of different countries and of the Authority;

(b) ensuring that programmes are developed through the Authority or other international organizations as appropriate for the benefit of developing States and technologically less developed States with a view to:

(i) strengthening their research capabilities;

(ii) training their personnel and the personnel of the Authority in the techniques and applications of research;

(iii) fostering the employment of their qualified personnel in research in the Area;

(c) effectively disseminating the results of research and analysis when available, through the Authority or other international channels when appropriate.

Article 144
Transfer of technology

1. The Authority shall take measures in accordance with this Convention:

(a) to acquire technology and scientific knowledge relating to activities in the Area; and

(b) to promote and encourage the transfer to developing States of such technology and scientific knowledge so that all States Parties benefit therefrom.

2. To this end the Authority and States Parties shall cooperate in promoting the transfer of technology and scientific knowledge relating to activities in the Area so that the Enterprise and all States Parties may benefit therefrom. In particular they shall initiate and promote:

(a) programmes for the transfer of technology to the Enterprise and to developing States with regard to activities in the Area, including, *inter alia*, facilitating the access of the Enterprise and of developing States to the relevant technology, under fair and reasonable terms and conditions;

(b) measures directed towards the advancement of the technology of the Enterprise and the domestic technology of developing States, particularly by providing opportunities to personnel from the Enterprise and from developing States for training in marine science and technology and for their full participation in activities in the Area.

Article 145
Protection of the marine environment

Necessary measures shall be taken in accordance with this Convention with respect to activities in the Area to ensure effective protection for the marine environment from harmful effects which may arise from such activities. To this end the Authority shall adopt appropriate rules, regulations and procedures for *inter alia*:

(a) the prevention, reduction and control of pollution and other hazards to the marine environment, including the coastline, and of interference with the ecological balance of the marine environment, particular attention being paid to the need for protection from harmful effects of such activities as drilling, dredging, excavation, disposal of waste, construction and operation or maintenance of installations, pipelines and other devices related to such activities;

(b) the protection and conservation of the natural resources of the Area and the prevention of damage to the flora and fauna of the marine environment.

Article 146
Protection of human life

With respect to activities in the Area, necessary measures shall be taken to ensure effective protection of human life. To this end the Authority shall adopt appropriate rules, regulations and procedures to supplement existing international law as embodied in relevant treaties.

Article 147
Accommodation of activities in the Area and in the marine environment

1. Activities in the Area shall be carried out with reasonable regard for other activities in the marine environment.

2. Installations used for carrying out activities in the Area shall be subject to the following conditions:

(a) such installations shall be erected, emplaced and removed solely in accordance with this Part and subject to the rules, regulations and procedures of the Authority. Due notice must be given of the erection, emplacement and removal of such installations, and permanent means for giving warning of their presence must be maintained;

(b) such installations may not be established where interference may be caused to the use of recognized sea lanes essential to international navigation or in areas of intense fishing activity;

(c) safety zones shall be established around such installations with appropriate markings to ensure the safety of both navigation and the installations. The configuration and location of such safety zones shall not be such as to form a belt impeding the lawful access of shipping to particular maritime zones or navigation along international sea lanes;

(d) such installations shall be used exclusively for peaceful purposes;

(e) such installations do not possess the status of islands. They have no territorial sea of their own, and their presence does not affect the delimitation of the territorial sea, the exclusive economic zone or the continental shelf.

3. Other activities in the marine environment shall be conducted with reasonable regard for activities in the Area.

Article 148

Participation of developing States in activities in the Area

The effective participation of developing States in activities in the Area shall be promoted as specifically provided for in this Part, having due regard to their special interests and needs, and in particular to the special need of the land-locked and geographically disadvantaged among them to overcome obstacles arising from their disadvantaged location, including remoteness from the Area and difficulty of access to and from it.

Article 149

Archaeological and historical objects

All objects of an archaeological and historical nature found in the Area shall be preserved or disposed of for the benefit of mankind as a whole, particular regard being paid to the preferential rights of the State or country of origin, or the State of cultural origin, or the State of historical and archaeological origin.

Section 3 Development of Resources of the Area

Article 150

Policies relating to activities in the Area

Activities in the Area shall, as specifically provided for in this Part, be carried out in such a manner as to foster healthy development of the world economy and balanced growth of international trade, and to promote international cooperation for the over-all development of all countries, especially developing States, and with a view to ensuring:

(a) the development of the resources of the Area;

(b) orderly, safe and rational management of the resources of the Area, including the efficient conduct of activities in the Area and, in accordance with sound principles of conservation, the avoidance of unnecessary waste;

(c) the expansion of opportunities for participation in such activities consistent in particular with articles 144 and 148;

(d) participation in revenues by the Authority and the transfer of technology to the Enterprise and developing States as provided for in this Convention;

(e) increased availability of the minerals derived from the Area as needed in conjunction with minerals derived from other sources, to ensure supplies to consumers of such minerals;

(f) the promotion of just and stable prices remunerative to producers and fair to consumers for minerals derived both from the Area and from other sources, and the promotion of long-term equilibrium between supply and demand;

(g) the enhancement of opportunities for all States Parties, irrespective of their social and economic systems or geographical location, to participate in the development of the resources of the Area and the prevention of monopolization of activities in the Area;

(h) the protection of developing countries from adverse effects on their economies or on their export earnings resulting from a reduction in the price of an affected mineral, or in the volume of exports of that mineral, to the extent that such reduction is caused by activities in the Area, as provided in article 151;

(i) the development of the common heritage for the benefit of mankind as a whole; and

(j) conditions of access to markets for the imports of minerals produced from the resources of the Area and for imports of commodities produced from such minerals shall not be more favourable than the most favourable applied to imports from other sources.

Article 151

Production policies

1. (a) Without prejudice to the objectives set forth in article 150 and for the purpose of implementing subparagraph (h) of that article, the Authority, acting through existing forums or such new arrangements or agreements as may be appropriate, in which all interested parties, including both producers and consumers, participate, shall take measures necessary to promote the growth, efficiency and stability of markets for those commodities produced from the minerals derived from the Area, at prices remunerative to producers and fair to consumers. All States Parties shall cooperate to this end.

(b) The Authority shall have the right to participate in any commodity conference dealing with those commodities and in which all interested parties including both producers and consumers participate. The Authority shall have the right to become a party to any arrangement or agreement resulting from such conferences. Participation of the Authority in any organs established under those arrangements or agreements shall be in respect of production in the Area and in accordance with the relevant rules of those organs.

(c) The Authority shall carry out its obligations under the arrangements or agreements referred to in this paragraph in a manner which assures a uniform and non-discriminatory implementation in respect of all production in the Area of the minerals concerned. In doing so, the Authority shall act in a manner consistent with the terms of existing contracts and approved plans of work of the Enterprise.

2. (a) During the interim period specified in paragraph 3, commercial production shall not be undertaken pursuant to an approved plan of work until the operator has applied for and has been issued a production authorization by the Authority. Such production authorizations may not be applied for or issued more than five years prior to the planned commencement of commercial production under the plan of work unless, having regard to the nature and timing of project development, the rules, regulations and procedures of the Authority prescribe another period.

(b) In the application for the production authorization, the operator shall specify the annual quantity of nickel expected to be recovered under the approved plan of work. The application shall include a schedule of expenditures to be made by the operator after he has received the authorization which are reasonably calculated to allow him to begin commercial production on the date planned.

(c) For the purposes of subparagraphs (a) and (b), the Authority shall establish appropriate performance requirements in accordance with Annex III, article 17.

(d) The Authority shall issue a production authorization for the level of production applied for unless the sum of that level and the levels already authorized exceeds the nickel production ceiling, as calculated pursuant to paragraph 4 in the year of issuance of the authorization, during any year of planned production falling within the interim period.

(e) When issued, the production authorization and approved application shall become a part of the approved plan of work.

(f) If the operator's application for a production authorization is denied pursuant to subparagraph (d), the operator may apply again to the Authority at any time.

3. The interim period shall begin five years prior to 1 January of the year in which the earliest commercial production is planned to commence under an approved plan of work. If the earliest commercial production is delayed beyond the year originally planned, the beginning of the interim period and the production ceiling originally calculated shall be adjusted accordingly. The interim period shall last 25 years or until the end of the Review Conference referred to in article 155 or until the day when such new arrangements or agreements as are referred to in paragraph 1 enter into force, whichever is earliest. The Authority shall resume the power provided in this article for the remainder of the interim period if the said arrangements or agreements should lapse or become ineffective for any reason whatsoever.

4. (a) The production ceiling for any year of the interim period shall be the sum of:

(i) the difference between the trend line values for nickel consumption, as calculated pursuant to subparagraph (b), for the year immediately prior to the year of the earliest commercial production and the year immediately prior to the commencement of the interim period; and

(ii) sixty per cent of the difference between the trend line values for nickel consumption, as calculated pursuant to subparagraph (b), for the year for which the production authorization is being applied for and the year immediately prior to the year of the earliest commercial production.

(b) For the purposes of subparagraph (a):

(i) trend line values used for computing the nickel production ceiling shall be those annual nickel consumption values on a trend line computed during the year in which a production authorization is issued. The trend line shall be derived from a linear regression of the logarithms of actual nickel consumption for the most recent 15-year period for which such data are available, time being the independent variable. This trend line shall be referred to as the original trend line;

(ii) if the annual rate of increase of the original trend line is less than 3 per cent, then the trend line used to determine the quantities referred to in subparagraph (a) shall instead be one passing through the original trend line at the value for the first year of the relevant 15-year period, and increasing at 3 per cent annually; provided however that the production ceiling established for any year of the interim period may not in any case exceed the difference between the original trend line value for that year and the original trend line value for the year immediately prior to the commencement of the interim period.

5. The Authority shall reserve to the Enterprise for its initial production a quantity of 38,000 metric tonnes of nickel from the available production ceiling calculated pursuant to paragraph 4.

6. (a) An operator may in any year produce less than or up to 8 per cent more than the level of annual production of minerals from polymetallic nodules specified in his production authorization, provided that the over-all amount of production shall not exceed that specified in the authorization. Any excess over 8 per cent and up to 20 per cent in any year, or any excess in the first and subsequent years following two consecutive years in which excesses occur, shall be negotiated with the Authority, which may require the operator to obtain a supplementary production authorization to cover additional production.

(b) Applications for such supplementary production authorizations shall be considered by the Authority only after all pending applications by operators who have not yet received production authorizations have been acted upon and due account has been taken of other likely applicants. The Authority shall be guided by the principle of not exceeding the total production allowed under the production ceiling in any year of the interim period. It shall not authorize the production under any plan of work of a quantity in excess of 46,500 metric tonnes of nickel per year.

7. The levels of production of other metals such as copper, cobalt and manganese extracted from the polymetallic nodules that are recovered pursuant to a production authorization should not be higher than those which would have been produced had the operator produced the maximum level of nickel from those nodules pursuant to this article. The Authority shall establish rules, regulations and procedures pursuant to Annex III, article 17, to implement this paragraph.

8. Rights and obligations relating to unfair economic practices under relevant multilateral trade agreements shall apply to the exploration for and exploitation of minerals from the Area. In the settlement of disputes arising under this provision, States Parties which are Parties to such multilateral trade agreements shall have recourse to the dispute settlement procedures of such agreements.

9. The Authority shall have the power to limit the level of production of minerals from the Area, other than minerals from polymetallic nodules, under such conditions and applying such methods as may be appropriate by adopting regulations in accordance with article 161, paragraph 8.

10. Upon the recommendation of the Council on the basis of advice from the Economic Planning Commission, the Assembly shall establish a system of compensation or take other measures of economic adjustment assistance including cooperation with specialized agencies and other international organizations to assist developing countries which suffer serious adverse effects on their export earnings or economies resulting from a reduction in the price of an affected mineral or in the volume of exports of that mineral, to the extent that such reduction is caused by activities in the Area. The Authority on request shall initiate studies on the problems of those States which are likely to be most seriously affected with a view to minimizing their difficulties and assisting them in their economic adjustment.

Article 152

Exercise of powers and functions by the Authority

1. The Authority shall avoid discrimination in the exercise of its powers and functions, including the granting of opportunities for activities in the Area.

2. Nevertheless, special consideration for developing States, including particular consideration for the land-locked and geographically disadvantaged among them, specifically provided for in this Part shall be permitted.

Article 153

System of exploration and exploitation

1. Activities in the Area shall be organized, carried out and controlled by the Authority on behalf of mankind as a whole in accordance with this article as well as other relevant provisions of this Part and the relevant Annexes, and the rules, regulations and procedures of the Authority.

2. Activities in the Area shall be carried out as prescribed in paragraph 3:

(a) by the Enterprise, and

(b) in association with the Authority by States Parties, or state enterprises or natural or juridical persons which possess the nationality of States Parties or are effectively controlled by them or their nationals, when sponsored by such States, or any group of the foregoing which meets the requirements provided in this Part and in Annex III.

3. Activities in the Area shall be carried out in accordance with a formal written plan of work drawn up in accordance with Annex III and approved by the Council after review by the Legal and Technical Commission. In the case of activities in the Area carried out as authorized by the Authority by the entities specified in paragraph 2(b), the plan of work shall, in accordance with Annex III, article 3, be in the form of a contract. Such contracts may provide for joint arrangements in accordance with Annex III, article 11.

4. The Authority shall exercise such control over activities in the Area as is necessary for the purpose of securing compliance with the relevant provisions of this Part and the Annexes relating thereto, and the rules, regulations and procedures of the Authority, and the plans of work approved in accordance with paragraph 3. States Parties shall assist the Authority by taking all measures necessary to ensure such compliance in accordance with article 139.

5. The Authority shall have the right to take at any time any measures provided for under this Part to ensure compliance with its provisions and the exercise of the functions of control and regulation assigned to it thereunder or under any contract. The Authority shall have the right to inspect all installations in the Area used in connection with activities in the Area.

6. A contract under paragraph 3 shall provide for security of tenure. Accordingly, the contract shall not be revised, suspended or terminated except in accordance with Annex III, articles 18 and 19.

Article 154

Periodic review

Every five years from the entry into force of this Convention, the Assembly shall undertake a general and systematic review of the manner in which the international regime of the Area established in this Convention has operated in practice. In the light of this review the Assembly may take, or recommend that other organs take, measures in accordance with the provisions and procedures of this Part and the Annexes relating thereto which will lead to the improvement of the operation of the regime.

Article 155
The Review Conference

1. Fifteen years from 1 January of the year in which the earliest commercial production commences under an approved plan of work, the Assembly shall convene a conference for the review of those provisions of this Part and the relevant Annexes which govern the system of exploration and exploitation of the resources of the Area. The Review Conference shall consider in detail, in the light of the experience acquired during that period:

(a) whether the provisions of this Part which govern the system of exploration and exploitation of the resources of the Area have achieved their aims in all respects, including whether they have benefited mankind as a whole;

(b) whether, during the 15-year period, reserved areas have been exploited in an effective and balanced manner in comparison with non-reserved areas;

(c) whether the development and use of the Area and its resources have been undertaken in such a manner as to foster healthy development of the world economy and balanced growth of international trade;

(d) whether monopolization of activities in the Area has been prevented;

(e) whether the policies set forth in articles 150 and 151 have been fulfilled; and

(f) whether the system has resulted in the equitable sharing of benefits derived from activities in the Area, taking into particular consideration the interests and needs of the developing States.

2. The Review Conference shall ensure the maintenance of the principle of the common heritage of mankind, the international regime designed to ensure equitable exploitation of the resources of the Area for the benefit of all countries, especially the developing States, and an Authority to organize, conduct and control activities in the Area. It shall also ensure the maintenance of the principles laid down in this Part with regard to the exclusion of claims or exercise of sovereignty over any part of the Area, the rights of States and their general conduct in relation to the Area, and their participation in activities in the Area in conformity with this Convention, the prevention of monopolization of activities in the Area, the use of the Area exclusively for peaceful purposes, economic aspects of activities in the Area, marine scientific research, transfer of technology, protection of the marine environment, protection of human life, rights of coastal States, the legal status of the waters superjacent to the

Area and that of the air space above those waters and accommodation between activities in the Area and other activities in the marine environment.

3. The decision-making procedure applicable at the Review Conference shall be the same as that applicable at the Third United Nations Conference on the Law of the Sea. The Conference shall make every effort to reach agreement on any amendments by way of consensus and there should be no voting on such matters until all efforts at achieving consensus have been exhausted.

4. If, five years after its commencement, the Review Conference has not reached agreement on the system of exploration and exploitation of the resources of the Area, it may decide during the ensuing 12 months, by a three-fourths majority of the States Parties, to adopt and submit to the States Parties for ratification or accession such amendments changing or modifying the system as it determines necessary and appropriate. Such amendments shall enter into force for all States Parties 12 months after the deposit of instruments of ratification or accession by three fourths of the States Parties.

5. Amendments adopted by the Review Conference pursuant to this article shall not affect rights acquired under existing contracts.

Section 4 The Authority

Subsection A. General Provisions

Article 156

Establishment of the Authority

1. There is hereby established the International Seabed Authority, which shall function in accordance with this Part.

2. All States Parties are *ipso facto* members of the Authority.

3. Observers at the Third United Nations Conference on the Law of the Sea who have signed the Final Act and who are not referred to in article 305, paragraph 1(c), (d), (e) or (f), shall have the right to participate in the Authority as observers, in accordance with its rules, regulations and procedures.

4. The seat of the Authority shall be in Jamaica.

5. The Authority may establish such regional centres or offices as it deems necessary for the exercise of its functions.

Article 157

Nature and fundamental principles of the Authority

1. The Authority is the organization through which States Parties shall, in accordance with this Part, organize and control activities in the Area, particularly with a view to administering the resources of the Area.

2. The powers and functions of the Authority shall be those expressly conferred upon it by this Convention. The Authority shall have such incidental powers, consistent with this Convention, as are implicit in and necessary for the exercise of those powers and functions with respect to activities in the Area.

3. The Authority is based on the principle of the sovereign equality of all its members.

4. All members of the Authority shall fulfil in good faith the obligations assumed by them in accordance with this Part in order to ensure to all of them the rights and benefits resulting from membership.

Article 158

Organs of the Authority

1. There are hereby established, as the principal organs of the Authority, an Assembly, a Council and a Secretariat.

2. There is hereby established the Enterprise, the organ through which the Authority shall carry out the functions referred to in article 170, paragraph 1.

3. Such subsidiary organs as may be found necessary may be established in accordance with this Part.

4. Each principal organ of the Authority and the Enterprise shall be responsible for exercising those powers and functions which are conferred upon it. In exercising such powers and functions each organ shall avoid taking any action which may derogate from or impede the exercise of specific powers and functions conferred upon another organ.

Subsection B. The Assembly

Article 159

Composition, procedure and voting

1. The Assembly shall consist of all the members of the Authority. Each member shall have one representative in the Assembly, who may be accompanied by alternates and advisers.

2. The Assembly shall meet in regular annual sessions and in such special sessions as may be decided by the Assembly, or convened by the Secretary-General at the request of the Council or of a majority of the members of the Authority.

3. Sessions shall take place at the seat of the Authority unless otherwise decided by the Assembly.

4. The Assembly shall adopt its rules of procedure. At the beginning of each regular session, it shall elect its President and such other officers as may be required. They shall hold office until a new President and other officers are elected at the next regular session.

5. A majority of the members of the Assembly shall constitute a quorum.

6. Each member of the Assembly shall have one vote.

7. Decisions on questions of procedure, including decisions to convene special sessions of the Assembly, shall be taken by a majority of the members present and voting.

8. Decisions on questions of substance shall be taken by a two-thirds majority of the members present and voting, provided that such majority includes a majority of the members participating in the session. When the issue arises as to whether a question is one of substance or not, that question shall be treated as one of substance unless otherwise decided by the Assembly by the majority required for decisions on questions of substance.

9. When a question of substance comes up for voting for the first time, the President may, and shall, if requested by at least one fifth of the members of the Assembly, defer the issue of taking a vote on that question for a period not exceeding five calendar days. This rule may be applied only once to any question, and shall not be applied so as to defer the question beyond the end of the session.

10. Upon a written request addressed to the President and sponsored by at least one fourth of the members of the Authority for an advisory opinion on the conformity with this Convention of a proposal before the Assembly on any matter, the Assembly shall request the Seabed Disputes Chamber of the International Tribunal for the Law of the Sea to give an advisory opinion thereon and shall defer voting on that proposal pending receipt of the advisory opinion by the Chamber. If the advisory opinion is not received before the final week of the session in which it is requested, the Assembly shall decide when it will meet to vote upon the deferred proposal.

Article 160
Powers and functions

1. The Assembly, as the sole organ of the Authority consisting of all the members, shall be considered the supreme organ of the Authority to which the other principal organs shall be accountable as specifically provided for in this Convention. The Assembly shall have the power to establish general policies in conformity with the relevant provisions of this Convention on any question or matter within the competence of the Authority.

2. In addition, the powers and functions of the Assembly shall be:

(a) to elect the members of the Council in accordance with article 161;

(b) to elect the Secretary-General from among the candidates proposed by the Council;

(c) to elect, upon the recommendation of the Council, the members of the Governing Board of the Enterprise and the Director-General of the Enterprise;

(d) to establish such subsidiary organs as it finds necessary for the exercise of its functions in accordance with this Part. In the composition of these subsidiary organs due account shall be taken of the principle of equitable geographical distribution and of special interests and the need for members qualified and competent in the relevant technical questions dealt with by such organs;

(e) to assess the contributions of members to the administrative budget of the Authority in accordance with an agreed scale of assessment based upon the scale used for the regular budget of the United Nations until the Authority shall have sufficient income from other sources to meet its administrative expenses;

(f) (i) to consider and approve, upon the recommendation of the Council, the rules, regulations and procedures on the equitable sharing of financial and other economic benefits derived from activities in the Area and the payments and contributions made pursuant to article 82, taking into particular consideration the interests and needs of developing States and peoples who have not attained full independence or other self-governing status. If the Assembly does not approve the recommendations of the Council, the Assembly shall return them to the Council for reconsideration in the light of the views expressed by the Assembly;

(ii) to consider and approve the rules, regulations and procedures of the Authority, and any amendments thereto, provisionally adopted by the Council pursuant to article 162, paragraph 2 (o)(ii). These rules, regulations and procedures shall relate to prospecting, exploration and exploitation in the Area, the financial management and internal administration of the Authority, and, upon the recommendation of the Governing Board of the Enterprise, to the transfer of funds from the Enterprise to the Authority;

(g) to decide upon the equitable sharing of financial and other economic benefits derived from activities in the Area, consistent with this Convention and the rules, regulations and procedures of the Authority;

(h) to consider and approve the proposed annual budget of the Authority submitted by the Council;

(i) to examine periodic reports from the Council and from the Enterprise and special reports requested from the Council or any other organ of the Authority;

(j) to initiate studies and make recommendations for the purpose of promoting international cooperation concerning activities in the Area and encouraging the progressive development of international law relating thereto and its codification;

(k) to consider problems of a general nature in connection with activities in the Area arising in particular for developing States, as well as those problems for States in connection with activities in the Area that are due to their geographical location, particularly for land-locked and geographically disadvantaged States;

(l) to establish, upon the recommendation of the Council, on the basis of advice from the Economic Planning Commission, a system of compensation or other measures of economic adjustment assistance as provided in article 151, paragraph 10;

(m) to suspend the exercise of rights and privileges of membership pursuant to article 185;

(n) to discuss any question or matter within the competence of the Authority and to decide as to which organ of the Authority shall deal with any such question or matter not specifically entrusted to a particular organ, consistent with the distribution of powers and functions among the organs of the Authority.

Subsection C. The Council

Article 161

Composition, procedure and voting

1. The Council shall consist of 36 members of the Authority elected by the Assembly in the following order:

(a) four members from among those States Parties which, during the last five years for which statistics are available, have either consumed more than 2 per cent of total world consumption or have had net imports of more than 2 per cent of total world imports of the commodities produced from the categories of minerals to be derived from the Area, and in any case one State from the Eastern European (Socialist) region, as well as the largest consumer;

(b) four members from among the eight States Parties which have the largest investments in preparation for and in the conduct of activities in the Area, either directly or through their nationals, including at least one State from the Eastern European (Socialist) region;

(c) four members from among States Parties which on the basis of production in areas under their jurisdiction are major net exporters of the categories of minerals to be derived from the Area, including at least two developing States whose exports of such minerals have a substantial bearing upon their economies;

(d) six members from among developing States Parties, representing special interests. The special interests to be represented shall include those of States with large populations, States which are land-locked or geographically disadvantaged, States which are major importers of the categories of minerals to be derived from the Area, States which are potential producers of such minerals, and least developed States;

(e) eighteen members elected according to the principle of ensuring an equitable geographical distribution of seats in the Council as a whole, provided that each geographical region shall have at least one member elected under this subparagraph. For this purpose, the geographical regions shall be Africa, Asia, Eastern European (Socialist), Latin America and Western European and Others.

2. In electing the members of the Council in accordance with paragraph 1, the Assembly shall ensure that:

(a) land-locked and geographically disadvantaged States are represented to a degree which is reasonably proportionate to their representation in the Assembly;

(b) coastal States, especially developing States, which do not qualify under paragraph 1(a), (b), (c) or (d) are represented to a degree which is reasonably proportionate to their representation in the Assembly;

(c) each group of States Parties to be represented on the Council is represented by those members, if any, which are nominated by that group.

3. Elections shall take place at regular sessions of the Assembly. Each member of the Council shall be elected for four years. At the first election, however, the term of one half of the members of each group referred to in paragraph 1 shall be two years.

4. Members of the Council shall be eligible for re-election, but due regard should be paid to the desirability of rotation of membership.

5. The Council shall function at the seat of the Authority, and shall meet as often as the business of the Authority may require, but not less than three times a year.

6. A majority of the members of the Council shall constitute a quorum.

7. Each member of the Council shall have one vote.

8. (a) Decisions on questions of procedure shall be taken by a majority of the members present and voting.

(b) Decisions on questions of substance arising under the following provisions shall be taken by a two-thirds majority of the members present and voting, provided that such majority includes a majority of the members of the Council: article 162, paragraph 2, subparagraphs (f); (g); (h); (i); (n); (p); (v); article 191.

(c) Decisions on questions of substance arising under the following provisions shall be taken by a three-fourths majority of the members present and voting, provided that such majority includes a majority of the members of the Council: article 162, paragraph 1; article 162, paragraph 2, subparagraphs (a); (b); (c); (d); (e); (l); (q); (r); (s); (t); (u) in cases of non-compliance by a contractor or a sponsor; (w) provided that orders issued thereunder may be binding for not more than 30 days unless confirmed by a decision taken in accordance with subparagraph (d); article 162, paragraph 2, subparagraphs (x); (y); (z); article 163, paragraph 2; article 174, paragraph 3; Annex IV, article 11.

(d) Decisions on questions of substance arising under the following provisions shall be taken by consensus: article 162, paragraph 2(m) and (o); adoption of amendments to Part XI.

(e) For the purposes of subparagraphs (d), (f) and (g), "consensus" means the absence of any formal objection. Within 14 days of the submission of a proposal to the Council, the President of the Council shall determine whether there would be a formal objection to the adoption of the proposal. If the President determines that there would be such an objection, the President shall establish and convene, within three days following such determination, a conciliation committee consisting of not more than nine members of the Council, with the President as chairman, for the purpose of reconciling the differences and producing a proposal which can be adopted by consensus. The committee shall work expeditiously and report to the Council within 14 days following its establishment. If the committee is unable to recommend a proposal which can be adopted by consensus, it shall set out in its report the grounds on which the proposal is being opposed.

(f) Decisions on questions not listed above which the Council is authorized to take by the rules, regulations and procedures of the Authority or otherwise shall be taken pursuant to the subparagraphs of this paragraph specified in the rules, regulations and procedures or, if not specified therein, then pursuant to the subparagraph determined by the Council if possible in advance, by consensus.

(g) When the issue arises as to whether a question is within subparagraph (a), (b), (c) or (d), the question shall be treated as being within the subparagraph requiring the higher or highest majority or consensus as the case may be, unless otherwise decided by the Council by the said majority or by consensus.

9. The Council shall establish a procedure whereby a member of the Authority not represented on the Council may send a representative to attend a meeting of the Council when a request is made by such member, or a matter particularly affecting it is under consideration. Such a representative shall be entitled to participate in the deliberations but not to vote.

Article 162

Powers and functions

1. The Council is the executive organ of the Authority. The Council shall have the power to establish, in conformity with this Convention and the general policies established by the Assembly, the specific policies to be pursued by the Authority on any question or matter within the competence of the Authority.

2. In addition, the Council shall:

(a) supervise and coordinate the implementation of the provisions of this Part on all questions and matters within the competence of the Authority and invite the attention of the Assembly to cases of non-compliance;

(b) propose to the Assembly a list of candidates for the election of the Secretary-General;

(c) recommend to the Assembly candidates for the election of the members of the Governing Board of the Enterprise and the Director-General of the Enterprise;

(d) establish, as appropriate, and with due regard to economy and efficiency, such subsidiary organs as it finds necessary for the exercise of its functions in accordance with this Part. In the composition of subsidiary organs, emphasis shall be placed on the need for members qualified and competent in relevant technical matters dealt with by those organs provided that due account shall be taken of the principle of equitable geographical distribution and of special interests;

(e) adopt its rules of procedure including the method of selecting its president;

(f) enter into agreements with the United Nations or other international organizations on behalf of the Authority and within its competence, subject to approval by the Assembly;

(g) consider the reports of the Enterprise and transmit them to the Assembly with its recommendations;

(h) present to the Assembly annual reports and such special reports as the Assembly may request;

(i) issue directives to the Enterprise in accordance with article 170;

(j) approve plans of work in accordance with Annex III, article 6. The Council shall act upon each plan of work within 60 days of its submission by the Legal and Technical Commission at a session of the Council in accordance with the following procedures:

(i) if the Commission recommends the approval of a plan of work, it shall be deemed to have been approved by the Council if no member of the Council submits in writing to the President within 14 days a specific objection alleging noncompliance with the requirements of Annex III, article 6. If there is an objection, the conciliation procedure set forth in article 161, paragraph 8(e), shall apply. If, at the end of the conciliation procedure, the objection is still maintained, the plan of work shall be deemed to have been approved by the Council unless the Council disapproves it by consensus among its members excluding any State or States making the application or sponsoring the applicant;

(ii) if the Commission recommends the disapproval of a plan of work or does not make a recommendation, the Council may approve the plan of work by a three-fourths majority of the members present and voting, provided that such majority includes a majority of the members participating in the session;

(k) approve plans of work submitted by the Enterprise in accordance with Annex IV, article 12, applying, *mutatis mutandis*, the procedures set forth in subparagraph (j);

(l) exercise control over activities in the Area in accordance with article 153, paragraph 4, and the rules, regulations and procedures of the Authority;

(m) take, upon the recommendation of the Economic Planning Commission, necessary and appropriate measures in accordance with article 150, subparagraph (h), to provide protection from the adverse economic effects specified therein;

(n) make recommendations to the Assembly, on the basis of advice from the Economic Planning Commission, for a system of compensation or other measures of economic adjustment assistance as provided in article 151, paragraph 10;

(o) (i) recommend to the Assembly rules, regulations and procedures on the equitable sharing of financial and other economic benefits derived from activities in the Area and the payments and contributions made pursuant to article 82, taking into particular consideration the interests and needs of the developing States and peoples who have not attained full independence or other self-governing status;

(ii) adopt and apply provisionally, pending approval by the Assembly, the rules, regulations and procedures of the Authority, and any amendments thereto, taking into account the recommendations of the Legal and Technical Commission or other subordinate organ concerned. These rules, regulations and procedures shall relate to prospecting, exploration and exploitation in the Area and the financial management and internal administration of the Authority. Priority shall be given to the adoption of rules, regulations and procedures for the exploration for and exploitation of polymetallic nodules. Rules, regulations and procedures for the exploration for and exploitation of any resource other than polymetallic nodules shall be adopted within three years from the date of a request to the Authority by any of its members to adopt such rules, regulations and procedures in respect of such resource. All rules, regulations and procedures shall remain in effect on a provisional basis until approved by the Assembly or until amended by the Council in the light of any views expressed by the Assembly;

(p) review the collection of all payments to be made by or to the Authority in connection with operations pursuant to this Part;

(q) make the selection from among applicants for production authorizations pursuant to Annex III, article 7, where such selection is required by that provision;

(r) submit the proposed annual budget of the Authority to the Assembly for its approval;

(s) make recommendations to the Assembly concerning policies on any question or matter within the competence of the Authority;

(t) make recommendations to the Assembly concerning suspension of the exercise of the rights and privileges of membership pursuant to article 185;

(u) institute proceedings on behalf of the Authority before the Seabed Disputes Chamber in cases of non-compliance;

(v) notify the Assembly upon a decision by the Seabed Disputes Chamber in proceedings instituted under subparagraph (u), and make any recommendations which it may find appropriate with respect to measures to be taken;

(w) issue emergency orders, which may include orders for the suspension or adjustment of operations, to prevent serious harm to the marine environment arising out of activities in the Area;

(x) disapprove areas for exploitation by contractors or the Enterprise in cases where substantial evidence indicates the risk of serious harm to the marine environment;

(y) establish a subsidiary organ for the elaboration of draft financial rules, regulations and procedures relating to:

(i) financial management in accordance with articles 171 to 175; and

(ii) financial arrangements in accordance with Annex III, article 13 and article 17, paragraph 1(c);

(z) establish appropriate mechanisms for directing and supervising a staff of inspectors who shall inspect activities in the Area to determine whether this Part, the rules, regulations and procedures of the Authority, and the terms and conditions of any contract with the Authority are being complied with.

Article 163

Organs of the Council

1. There are hereby established the following organs of the Council:

(a) an Economic Planning Commission;

(b) a Legal and Technical Commission.

2. Each Commission shall be composed of 15 members, elected by the Council from among the candidates nominated by the States Parties. However, if necessary, the Council may decide to increase the size of either Commission having due regard to economy and efficiency.

3. Members of a Commission shall have appropriate qualifications in the area of competence of that Commission. States Parties shall nominate candidates of the highest standards of competence and integrity with qualifications in relevant fields so as to ensure the effective exercise of the functions of the Commissions.

4. In the election of members of the Commissions, due account shall be taken of the need for equitable geographical distribution and the representation of special interests.

5. No State Party may nominate more than one candidate for the same Commission. No person shall be elected to serve on more than one Commission.

6. Members of the Commissions shall hold office for a term of five years. They shall be eligible for re-election for a further term.

7. In the event of the death, incapacity or resignation of a member of a Commission prior to the expiration of the term of office, the Council shall elect for the remainder of the term, a member from the same geographical region or area of interest.

8. Members of Commissions shall have no financial interest in any activity relating to exploration and exploitation in the Area. Subject to their responsibilities to the Commissions upon which they serve, they shall not disclose, even after the termination of their functions, any industrial secret, proprietary data which are transferred to

the Authority in accordance with Annex III, article 14, or any other confidential information coming to their knowledge by reason of their duties for the Authority.

9. Each Commission shall exercise its functions in accordance with such guidelines and directives as the Council may adopt.

10. Each Commission shall formulate and submit to the Council for approval such rules and regulations as may be necessary for the efficient conduct of the Commission's functions.

11. The decision-making procedures of the Commissions shall be established by the rules, regulations and procedures of the Authority. Recommendations to the Council shall, where necessary, be accompanied by a summary on the divergencies of opinion in the Commission.

12. Each Commission shall normally function at the seat of the Authority and shall meet as often as is required for the efficient exercise of its functions.

13. In the exercise of its functions, each Commission may, where appropriate, consult another commission, any competent organ of the United Nations or of its specialized agencies or any international organizations with competence in the subject-matter of such consultation.

Article 164

The Economic Planning Commission

1. Members of the Economic Planning Commission shall have appropriate qualifications such as those relevant to mining, management of mineral resource activities, international trade or international economics. The Council shall endeavour to ensure that the membership of the Commission reflects all appropriate qualifications. The Commission shall include at least two members from developing States whose exports of the categories of minerals to be derived from the Area have a substantial bearing upon their economies.

2. The Commission shall:

(a) propose, upon the request of the Council, measures to implement decisions relating to activities in the Area taken in accordance with this Convention;

(b) review the trends of and the factors affecting supply, demand and prices of minerals which may be derived from the Area, bearing in mind the interests of both importing and exporting countries, and in particular of the developing States among them;

(c) examine any situation likely to lead to the adverse effects referred to in article 150, subparagraph (h), brought to its attention by the State Party or States Parties concerned, and make appropriate recommendations to the Council;

(d) propose to the Council for submission to the Assembly, as provided in article 151, paragraph 10, a system of compensation or other measures of economic adjustment assistance for developing States which suffer adverse effects caused by activities in the Area. The Commission shall make the recommendations to the Council that are necessary for the application of the system or other measures adopted by the Assembly in specific cases.

Article 165

The Legal and Technical Commission

1. Members of the Legal and Technical Commission shall have appropriate qualifications such as those relevant to exploration for and exploitation and processing of mineral resources, oceanology, protection of the marine environment, or economic or legal matters relating to ocean mining and related fields of expertise. The Council shall endeavour to ensure that the membership of the Commission reflects all appropriate qualifications.

2. The Commission shall:

(a) make recommendations with regard to the exercise of the Authority's functions upon the request of the Council;

(b) review formal written plans of work for activities in the Area in accordance with article 153, paragraph 3, and submit appropriate recommendations to the Council. The Commission shall base its recommendations solely on the grounds stated in Annex III and shall report fully thereon to the Council;

(c) supervise, upon the request of the Council, activities in the Area, where appropriate, in consultation and collaboration with any entity carrying out such activities or State or States concerned and report to the Council;

(d) prepare assessments of the environmental implications of activities in the Area;

(e) make recommendations to the Council on the protection of the marine environment, taking into account the views of recognized experts in that field;

(f) formulate and submit to the Council the rules, regulations and procedures referred to in article 162, paragraph 2(o), taking into account all relevant factors including assessments of the environmental implications of activities in the Area;

(g) keep such rules, regulations and procedures under review and recommend to the Council from time to time such amendments thereto as it may deem necessary or desirable;

(h) make recommendations to the Council regarding the establishment of a monitoring programme to observe, measure, evaluate and analyse, by recognized scientific methods, on a regular basis, the risks or effects of pollution of the marine environment resulting from activities in the Area, ensure that existing regulations are adequate and are complied with and coordinate the implementation of the monitoring programme approved by the Council;

(i) recommend to the Council that proceedings be instituted on behalf of the Authority before the Seabed Disputes Chamber, in accordance with this Part and the relevant Annexes taking into account particularly article 187;

(j) make recommendations to the Council with respect to measures to be taken, upon a decision by the Seabed Disputes Chamber in proceedings instituted in accordance with subparagraph (i);

(k) make recommendations to the Council to issue emergency orders, which may include orders for the suspension or adjustment of operations, to prevent serious harm to the marine environment arising out of activities in the Area. Such recommendations shall be taken up by the Council on a priority basis;

(l) make recommendations to the Council to disapprove areas for exploitation by contractors or the Enterprise in cases where substantial evidence indicates the risk of serious harm to the marine environment;

(m) make recommendations to the Council regarding the direction and supervision of a staff of inspectors who shall inspect activities in the Area to determine whether the provisions of this Part, the rules, regulations and procedures of the Authority, and the terms and conditions of any contract with the Authority are being complied with;

(n) calculate the production ceiling and issue production authorizations on behalf of the Authority pursuant to article 151, paragraphs 2 to 7, following any necessary selection among applicants for production authorizations by the Council in accordance with Annex III, article 7.

3. The members of the Commission shall, upon request by any State Party or other party concerned, be accompanied by a representative of such State or other party concerned when carrying out their function of supervision and inspection.

SUBSECTION D. THE SECRETARIAT

Article 166

The Secretariat

1. The Secretariat of the Authority shall comprise a Secretary-General and such staff as the Authority may require.

2. The Secretary-General shall be elected for four years by the Assembly from among the candidates proposed by the Council and may be re-elected.

3. The Secretary-General shall be the chief administrative officer of the Authority, and shall act in that capacity in all meetings of the Assembly, of the Council and of any subsidiary organ, and shall perform such other administrative functions as are entrusted to the Secretary-General by these organs.

4. The Secretary-General shall make an annual report to the Assembly on the work of the Authority.

Article 167

The staff of the Authority

1. The staff of the Authority shall consist of such qualified scientific and technical and other personnel as may be required to fulfil the administrative functions of the Authority.

2. The paramount consideration in the recruitment and employment of the staff and in the determination of their conditions of service shall be the necessity of securing the highest standards of efficiency, competence and integrity. Subject to this consideration, due regard shall be paid to the importance of recruiting the staff on as wide a geographical basis as possible.

3. The staff shall be appointed by the Secretary-General. The terms and conditions on which they shall be appointed, remunerated and dismissed shall be in accordance with the rules, regulations and procedures of the Authority.

Article 168

International character of the Secretariat

1. In the performance of their duties the Secretary-General and the staff shall not seek or receive instructions from any government or from any other source external to the Authority. They shall refrain from any action which might reflect on their position as international officials responsible only to the Authority. Each State Party undertakes to respect the exclusively international character of the responsibilities of the Secretary-General and the staff and not to seek to influence them in the discharge of their responsibilities. Any violation of responsibilities by a staff member shall be submitted to the appropriate administrative tribunal as provided in the rules, regulations and procedures of the Authority.

2. The Secretary-General and the staff shall have no financial interest in any activity relating to exploration and exploitation in the Area. Subject to their responsibilities to the Authority, they shall not disclose, even after the termination of their functions, any industrial secret, proprietary data which are transferred to the Authority in accordance with Annex III, article 14, or any other confidential information coming to their knowledge by reason of their employment with the Authority.

3. Violations of the obligations of a staff member of the Authority set forth in paragraph 2 shall, on the request of a State Party affected by such violation, or a natural or juridical person, sponsored by a State Party as provided in article 153, paragraph 2(b), and affected by such violation, be submitted by the Authority against the staff member concerned to a tribunal designated by the rules, regulations and procedures of the Authority. The Party affected shall have the right to take part in the

proceedings. If the tribunal so recommends, the Secretary-General shall dismiss the staff member concerned.

4. The rules, regulations and procedures of the Authority shall contain such provisions as are necessary to implement this article.

Article 169

Consultation and cooperation with international and non-governmental organizations

1. The Secretary-General shall, on matters within the competence of the Authority, make suitable arrangements, with the approval of the Council, for consultation and cooperation with international and non-governmental organizations recognized by the Economic and Social Council of the United Nations.

2. Any organization with which the Secretary-General has entered into an arrangement under paragraph 1 may designate representatives to attend meetings of the organs of the Authority as observers in accordance with the rules of procedure of these organs. Procedures shall be established for obtaining the views of such organizations in appropriate cases.

3. The Secretary-General may distribute to States Parties written reports submitted by the non-governmental organizations referred to in paragraph 1 on subjects in which they have special competence and which are related to the work of the Authority.

SUBSECTION E. THE ENTERPRISE

Article 170

The Enterprise

1. The Enterprise shall be the organ of the Authority which shall carry out activities in the Area directly, pursuant to article 153, paragraph 2(a), as well as the transporting, processing and marketing of minerals recovered from the Area.

2. The Enterprise shall, within the framework of the international legal personality of the Authority, have such legal capacity as is provided for in the Statute set forth in Annex IV. The Enterprise shall act in accordance with this Convention and the rules, regulations and procedures of the Authority, as well as the general policies established by the Assembly, and shall be subject to the directives and control of the Council.

3. The Enterprise shall have its principal place of business at the seat of the Authority.

4. The Enterprise shall, in accordance with article 173, paragraph 2, and Annex IV, article 11, be provided with such funds as it may require to carry out its functions, and shall receive technology as provided in article 144 and other relevant provisions of this Convention.

Subsection F. Financial Arrangements of the Authority

Article 171

Funds of the Authority

The funds of the Authority shall include:

(a) assessed contributions made by members of the Authority in accordance with article 160, paragraph 2(e);

(b) funds received by the Authority pursuant to Annex III, article 13, in connection with activities in the Area;

(c) funds transferred from the Enterprise in accordance with Annex IV, article 10;

(d) funds borrowed pursuant to article 174;

(e) voluntary contributions made by members or other entities; and

(f) payments to a compensation fund, in accordance with article 151, paragraph 10, whose sources are to be recommended by the Economic Planning Commission.

Article 172

Annual budget of the Authority

The Secretary-General shall draft the proposed annual budget of the Authority and submit it to the Council. The Council shall consider the proposed annual budget and submit it to the Assembly, together with any recommendations thereon. The Assembly shall consider and approve the proposed annual budget in accordance with article 160, paragraph 2(h).

Article 173

Expenses of the Authority

1. The contributions referred to in article 171, subparagraph (a), shall be paid into a special account to meet the administrative expenses of the Authority until the Authority has sufficient funds from other sources to meet those expenses.

2. The administrative expenses of the Authority shall be a first call upon the funds of the Authority. Except for the assessed contributions referred to in article 171, subparagraph (a), the funds which remain after payment of administrative expenses may, *inter alia*:

(a) be shared in accordance with article 140 and article 160, paragraph 2(g);

(b) be used to provide the Enterprise with funds in accordance with article 170, paragraph 4;

(c) be used to compensate developing States in accordance with article 151, paragraph 10, and article 160, paragraph 2(l).

Article 174

Borrowing power of the Authority

1. The Authority shall have the power to borrow funds.

2. The Assembly shall prescribe the limits on the borrowing power of the Authority in the financial regulations adopted pursuant to article 160, paragraph 2(f).

3. The Council shall exercise the borrowing power of the Authority.

4. States Parties shall not be liable for the debts of the Authority.

Article 175

Annual audit

The records, books and accounts of the Authority, including its annual financial statements, shall be audited annually by an independent auditor appointed by the Assembly.

SUBSECTION G. LEGAL STATUS, PRIVILEGES AND IMMUNITIES

Article 176

Legal status

The Authority shall have international legal personality and such legal capacity as may be necessary for the exercise of its functions and the fulfillment of its purposes.

Article 177

Privileges and immunities

To enable the Authority to exercise its functions, it shall enjoy in the territory of each State Party the privileges and immunities set forth in this subsection. The privileges and immunities relating to the Enterprise shall be those set forth in Annex IV, article 13.

Article 178

Immunity from legal process

The Authority, its property and assets, shall enjoy immunity from legal process except to the extent that the Authority expressly waives this immunity in a particular case.

Article 179

Immunity from search and any form of seizure

The property and assets of the Authority, wherever located and by whomsoever held, shall be immune from search, requisition, confiscation, expropriation or any other form of seizure by executive or legislative action.

Article 180

Exemption from restrictions, regulations, controls and moratoria

The property and assets of the Authority shall be exempt from restrictions, regulations, controls and moratoria of any nature.

Article 181

Archives and official communications of the Authority

1. The archives of the Authority, wherever located, shall be inviolable.

2. Proprietary data, industrial secrets or similar information and personnel records shall not be placed in archives which are open to public inspection.

3. With regard to its official communications, the Authority shall be accorded by each State Party treatment no less favourable than that accorded by that State to other international organizations.

Article 182

Privileges and immunities of certain persons connected with the Authority

Representatives of States Parties attending meetings of the Assembly, the Council or organs of the Assembly or the Council, and the Secretary-General and staff of the Authority, shall enjoy in the territory of each State Party:

(a) immunity from legal process with respect to acts performed by them in the exercise of their functions, except to the extent that the State which they represent or the Authority, as appropriate, expressly waives this immunity in a particular case;

(b) if they are not nationals of that State Party, the same exemptions from immigration restrictions, alien registration requirements and national service obligations, the same facilities as regards exchange restrictions and the same treatment in respect of travelling facilities as are accorded by that State to the representatives, officials and employees of comparable rank of other States Parties.

Article 183

Exemption from taxes and customs duties

1. Within the scope of its official activities, the Authority, its assets and property, its income, and its operations and transactions, authorized by this Convention, shall be exempt from all direct taxation and goods imported or exported for its official use shall be exempt from all customs duties. The Authority shall not claim exemption from taxes which are no more than charges for services rendered.

2. When purchases of goods or services of substantial value necessary for the official activities of the Authority are made by or on behalf of the Authority, and when the price of such goods or services includes taxes or duties, appropriate measures shall, to the extent practicable, be taken by States Parties to grant exemption from such taxes or duties or provide for their reimbursement. Goods imported or purchased under an

exemption provided for in this article shall not be sold or otherwise disposed of in the territory of the State Party which granted the exemption, except under conditions agreed with that State Party.

3. No tax shall be levied by States Parties on or in respect of salaries and emoluments paid or any other form of payment made by the Authority to the Secretary-General and staff of the Authority, as well as experts performing missions for the Authority, who are not their nationals.

Subsection H. Suspension of the Exercise of Rights and Privileges of Members

Article 184

Suspension of the exercise of voting rights

A State Party which is in arrears in the payment of its financial contributions to the Authority shall have no vote if the amount of its arrears equals or exceeds the amount of the contributions due from it for the preceding two full years. The Assembly may, nevertheless, permit such a member to vote if it is satisfied that the failure to pay is due to conditions beyond the control of the member.

Article 185

Suspension of exercise of rights and privileges of membership

1. A State Party which has grossly and persistently violated the provisions of this Part may be suspended from the exercise of the rights and privileges of membership by the Assembly upon the recommendation of the Council.

2. No action may be taken under paragraph 1 until the Seabed Disputes Chamber has found that a State Party has grossly and persistently violated the provisions of this Part.

Section 5 Settlement of Disputes and Advisory Opinions

Article 186

Seabed Disputes Chamber of the International Tribunal for the Law of the Sea

The establishment of the Seabed Disputes Chamber and the manner in which it shall exercise its jurisdiction shall be governed by the provisions of this section, of Part XV and of Annex VI.

Article 187

Jurisdiction of the Seabed Disputes Chamber

The Seabed Disputes Chamber shall have jurisdiction under this Part and the Annexes relating thereto in disputes with respect to activities in the Area falling within the following categories:

(a) disputes between States Parties concerning the interpretation or application of this Part and the Annexes relating thereto;

(b) disputes between a State Party and the Authority concerning:

(i) acts or omissions of the Authority or of a State Party alleged to be in violation of this Part or the Annexes relating thereto or of rules, regulations and procedures of the Authority adopted in accordance therewith; or

(ii) acts of the Authority alleged to be in excess of jurisdiction or a misuse of power;

(c) disputes between parties to a contract, being States Parties, the Authority or the Enterprise, state enterprises and natural or juridical persons referred to in article 153, paragraph 2(b), concerning:

(i) the interpretation or application of a relevant contract or a plan of work; or

(ii) acts or omissions of a party to the contract relating to activities in the Area and directed to the other party or directly affecting its legitimate interests;

(d) disputes between the Authority and a prospective contractor who has been sponsored by a State as provided in article 153, paragraph 2(b), and has duly fulfilled the conditions referred to in Annex III, article 4, paragraph 6, and article 13, paragraph 2, concerning the refusal of a contract or a legal issue arising in the negotiation of the contract;

(e) disputes between the Authority and a State Party, a state enterprise or a natural or juridical person sponsored by a State Party as provided for in article 153, paragraph 2(b), where it is alleged that the Authority has incurred liability as provided in Annex III, article 22;

(f) any other disputes for which the jurisdiction of the Chamber is specifically provided in this Convention.

Article 188

Submission of disputes to a special chamber of the International Tribunal for the Law of the Sea or an ad hoc chamber of the Seabed Disputes Chamber or to binding commercial arbitration

1. Disputes between States Parties referred to in article 187, subparagraph (a), may be submitted:

(a) at the request of the parties to the dispute, to a special chamber of the International Tribunal for the Law of the Sea to be formed in accordance with Annex VI, articles 15 and 17; or

(b) at the request of any party to the dispute, to an ad hoc chamber of the Seabed Disputes Chamber to be formed in accordance with Annex VI, article 36.

2. (a) Disputes concerning the interpretation or application of a contract referred to in article 187, subparagraph (c)(i), shall be submitted, at the request of any party to the dispute, to binding commercial arbitration, unless the parties otherwise

agree. A commercial arbitral tribunal to which the dispute is submitted shall have no jurisdiction to decide any question of interpretation of this Convention. When the dispute also involves a question of the interpretation of Part XI and the Annexes relating thereto, with respect to activities in the Area, that question shall be referred to the Seabed Disputes Chamber for a ruling.

(b) If, at the commencement of or in the course of such arbitration, the arbitral tribunal determines, either at the request of any party to the dispute or *proprio motu*, that its decision depends upon a ruling of the Seabed Disputes Chamber, the arbitral tribunal shall refer such question to the Seabed Disputes Chamber for such ruling. The arbitral tribunal shall then proceed to render its award in conformity with the ruling of the Seabed Disputes Chamber.

(c) In the absence of a provision in the contract on the arbitration procedure to be applied in the dispute, the arbitration shall be conducted in accordance with the UNCITRAL Arbitration Rules or such other arbitration rules as may be prescribed in the rules, regulations and procedures of the Authority, unless the parties to the dispute otherwise agree.

Article 189

Limitation on jurisdiction with regard to decisions of the Authority

The Seabed Disputes Chamber shall have no jurisdiction with regard to the exercise by the Authority of its discretionary powers in accordance with this Part; in no case shall it substitute its discretion for that of the Authority. Without prejudice to article 191, in exercising its jurisdiction pursuant to article 187, the Seabed Disputes Chamber shall not pronounce itself on the question of whether any rules, regulations and procedures of the Authority are in conformity with this Convention, nor declare invalid any such rules, regulations and procedures. Its jurisdiction in this regard shall be confined to deciding claims that the application of any rules, regulations and procedures of the Authority in individual cases would be in conflict with the contractual obligations of the parties to the dispute or their obligations under this Convention, claims concerning excess of jurisdiction or misuse of power, and to claims for damages to be paid or other remedy to be given to the party concerned for the failure of the other party to comply with its contractual obligations or its obligations under this Convention.

Article 190

Participation and appearance of sponsoring States Parties in proceedings

1. If a natural or juridical person is a party to a dispute referred to in article 187, the sponsoring State shall be given notice thereof and shall have the right to participate in the proceedings by submitting written or oral statements.

2. If an action is brought against a State Party by a natural or juridical person sponsored by another State Party in a dispute referred to in article 187, subparagraph (c),

the respondent State may request the State sponsoring that person to appear in the proceedings on behalf of that person. Failing such appearance, the respondent State may arrange to be represented by a juridical person of its nationality.

Article 191

Advisory opinions

The Seabed Disputes Chamber shall give advisory opinions at the request of the Assembly or the Council on legal questions arising within the scope of their activities. Such opinions shall be given as a matter of urgency.

Part XII Protection and Preservation of the Marine Environment

Section 1 General Provisions

Article 192

General obligation

States have the obligation to protect and preserve the marine environment.

Article 193

Sovereign right of States to exploit their natural resources

States have the sovereign right to exploit their natural resources pursuant to their environmental policies and in accordance with their duty to protect and preserve the marine environment.

Article 194

Measures to prevent, reduce and control pollution of the marine environment

1. States shall take, individually or jointly as appropriate, all measures consistent with this Convention that are necessary to prevent, reduce and control pollution of the marine environment from any source, using for this purpose the best practicable means at their disposal and in accordance with their capabilities, and they shall endeavour to harmonize their policies in this connection.

2. States shall take all measures necessary to ensure that activities under their jurisdiction or control are so conducted as not to cause damage by pollution to other States and their environment, and that pollution arising from incidents or activities under their jurisdiction or control does not spread beyond the areas where they exercise sovereign rights in accordance with this Convention.

3. The measures taken pursuant to this Part shall deal with all sources of pollution of the marine environment. These measures shall include, *inter alia*, those designed to minimize to the fullest possible extent:

(a) the release of toxic, harmful or noxious substances, especially those which are persistent, from land-based sources, from or through the atmosphere or by dumping;

(b) pollution from vessels, in particular measures for preventing accidents and dealing with emergencies, ensuring the safety of operations at sea, preventing intentional and unintentional discharges, and regulating the design, construction, equipment, operation and manning of vessels;

(c) pollution from installations and devices used in exploration or exploitation of the natural resources of the seabed and subsoil, in particular measures for preventing accidents and dealing with emergencies, ensuring the safety of operations at sea, and regulating the design, construction, equipment, operation and manning of such installations or devices;

(d) pollution from other installations and devices operating in the marine environment, in particular measures for preventing accidents and dealing with emergencies, ensuring the safety of operations at sea, and regulating the design, construction, equipment, operation and manning of such installations or devices.

4. In taking measures to prevent, reduce or control pollution of the marine environment, States shall refrain from unjustifiable interference with activities carried out by other States in the exercise of their rights and in pursuance of their duties in conformity with this Convention.

5. The measures taken in accordance with this Part shall include those necessary to protect and preserve rare or fragile ecosystems as well as the habitat of depleted, threatened or endangered species and other forms of marine life.

Article 195

Duty not to transfer damage or hazards or transform one type of pollution into another

In taking measures to prevent, reduce and control pollution of the marine environment, States shall act so as not to transfer, directly or indirectly, damage or hazards from one area to another or transform one type of pollution into another.

Article 196

Use of technologies or introduction of alien or new species

1. States shall take all measures necessary to prevent, reduce and control pollution of the marine environment resulting from the use of technologies under their jurisdiction or control, or the intentional or accidental introduction of species, alien or new, to a particular part of the marine environment, which may cause significant and harmful changes thereto.

2. This article does not affect the application of this Convention regarding the prevention, reduction and control of pollution of the marine environment.

Section 2 Global and Regional Cooperation

Article 197

Cooperation on a global or regional basis

States shall cooperate on a global basis and, as appropriate, on a regional basis, directly or through competent international organizations, in formulating and elaborating international rules, standards and recommended practices and procedures consistent with this Convention, for the protection and preservation of the marine environment, taking into account characteristic regional features.

Article 198

Notification of imminent or actual damage

When a State becomes aware of cases in which the marine environment is in imminent danger of being damaged or has been damaged by pollution, it shall immediately notify other States it deems likely to be affected by such damage, as well as the competent international organizations.

Article 199

Contingency plans against pollution

In the cases referred to in article 198, States in the area affected, in accordance with their capabilities, and the competent international organizations shall cooperate, to the extent possible, in eliminating the effects of pollution and preventing or minimizing the damage. To this end, States shall jointly develop and promote contingency plans for responding to pollution incidents in the marine environment.

Article 200

Studies, research programmes and exchange of information and data

States shall cooperate, directly or through competent international organizations, for the purpose of promoting studies, undertaking programmes of scientific research and encouraging the exchange of information and data acquired about pollution of the marine environment. They shall endeavour to participate actively in regional and global programmes to acquire knowledge for the assessment of the nature and extent of pollution, exposure to it, and its pathways, risks and remedies.

Article 201

Scientific criteria for regulations

In the light of the information and data acquired pursuant to article 200, States shall cooperate, directly or through competent international organizations, in establishing appropriate scientific criteria for the formulation and elaboration of rules, standards and recommended practices and procedures for the prevention, reduction and control of pollution of the marine environment.

Section 3 Technical Assistance

Article 202

Scientific and technical assistance to developing States

States shall, directly or through competent international organizations:

(a) promote programmes of scientific, educational, technical and other assistance to developing States for the protection and preservation of the marine environment and the prevention, reduction and control of marine pollution. Such assistance shall include, *inter alia*:

(i) training of their scientific and technical personnel;

(ii) facilitating their participation in relevant international programmes;

(iii) supplying them with necessary equipment and facilities;

(iv) enhancing their capacity to manufacture such equipment;

(v) advice on and developing facilities for research, monitoring, educational and other programmes;

(b) provide appropriate assistance, especially to developing States, for the minimization of the effects of major incidents which may cause serious pollution of the marine environment;

(c) provide appropriate assistance, especially to developing States, concerning the preparation of environmental assessments.

Article 203

Preferential treatment for developing States

Developing States shall, for the purposes of prevention, reduction and control of pollution of the marine environment or minimization of its effects, be granted preference by international organizations in:

(a) the allocation of appropriate funds and technical assistance; and

(b) the utilization of their specialized services.

Section 4 Monitoring and Environmental Assessment

Article 204

Monitoring of the risks or effects of pollution

1. States shall, consistent with the rights of other States, endeavour, as far as practicable, directly or through the competent international organizations, to observe, measure, evaluate and analyse, by recognized scientific methods, the risks or effects of pollution of the marine environment.

2. In particular, States shall keep under surveillance the effects of any activities which they permit or in which they engage in order to determine whether these activities are likely to pollute the marine environment.

Article 205

Publication of reports

States shall publish reports of the results obtained pursuant to article 204 or provide such reports at appropriate intervals to the competent international organizations, which should make them available to all States.

Article 206

Assessment of potential effects of activities

When States have reasonable grounds for believing that planned activities under their jurisdiction or control may cause substantial pollution of or significant and harmful changes to the marine environment, they shall, as far as practicable, assess the potential effects of such activities on the marine environment and shall communicate reports of the results of such assessments in the manner provided in article 205.

Section 5 International Rules and National Legislation to Prevent, Reduce, and Control Pollution of the Marine Environment

Article 207

Pollution from land-based sources

1. States shall adopt laws and regulations to prevent, reduce and control pollution of the marine environment from land-based sources, including rivers, estuaries, pipelines and outfall structures, taking into account internationally agreed rules, standards and recommended practices and procedures.

2. States shall take other measures as may be necessary to prevent, reduce and control such pollution.

3. States shall endeavour to harmonize their policies in this connection at the appropriate regional level.

4. States, acting especially through competent international organizations or diplomatic conference, shall endeavour to establish global and regional rules, standards and recommended practices and procedures to prevent, reduce and control pollution of the marine environment from land-based sources, taking into account characteristic regional features, the economic capacity of developing States and their need for economic development. Such rules, standards and recommended practices and procedures shall be re-examined from time to time as necessary.

5. Laws, regulations, measures, rules, standards and recommended practices and procedures referred to in paragraphs 1, 2 and 4 shall include those designed to minimize, to the fullest extent possible, the release of toxic, harmful or noxious substances, especially those which are persistent, into the marine environment.

Article 208

Pollution from seabed activities subject to national jurisdiction

1. Coastal States shall adopt laws and regulations to prevent, reduce and control pollution of the marine environment arising from or in connection with seabed activities subject to their jurisdiction and from artificial islands, installations and structures under their jurisdiction, pursuant to articles 60 and 80.

2. States shall take other measures as may be necessary to prevent, reduce and control such pollution.

3. Such laws, regulations and measures shall be no less effective than international rules, standards and recommended practices and procedures.

4. States shall endeavour to harmonize their policies in this connection at the appropriate regional level.

5. States, acting especially through competent international organizations or diplomatic conference, shall establish global and regional rules, standards and recommended practices and procedures to prevent, reduce and control pollution of the marine environment referred to in paragraph 1. Such rules, standards and recommended practices and procedures shall be re-examined from time to time as necessary.

Article 209

Pollution from activities in the Area

1. International rules, regulations and procedures shall be established in accordance with Part XI to prevent, reduce and control pollution of the marine environment from activities in the Area. Such rules, regulations and procedures shall be re-examined from time to time as necessary.

2. Subject to the relevant provisions of this section, States shall adopt laws and regulations to prevent, reduce and control pollution of the marine environment from activities in the Area undertaken by vessels, installations, structures and other devices flying their flag or of their registry or operating under their authority, as the case may be. The requirements of such laws and regulations shall be no less effective than the international rules, regulations and procedures referred to in paragraph 1.

Article 210

Pollution by dumping

1. States shall adopt laws and regulations to prevent, reduce and control pollution of the marine environment by dumping.

2. States shall take other measures as may be necessary to prevent, reduce and control such pollution.

3. Such laws, regulations and measures shall ensure that dumping is not carried out without the permission of the competent authorities of States.

4. States, acting especially through competent international organizations or diplomatic conference, shall endeavour to establish global and regional rules, standards and recommended practices and procedures to prevent, reduce and control such pollution. Such rules, standards and recommended practices and procedures shall be re-examined from time to time as necessary.

5. Dumping within the territorial sea and the exclusive economic zone or onto the continental shelf shall not be carried out without the express prior approval of the coastal State, which has the right to permit, regulate and control such dumping after due consideration of the matter with other States which by reason of their geographical situation may be adversely affected thereby.

6. National laws, regulations and measures shall be no less effective in preventing, reducing and controlling such pollution than the global rules and standards.

Article 211
Pollution from vessels

1. States, acting through the competent international organization or general diplomatic conference, shall establish international rules and standards to prevent, reduce and control pollution of the marine environment from vessels and promote the adoption, in the same manner, wherever appropriate, of routeing systems designed to minimize the threat of accidents which might cause pollution of the marine environment, including the coastline, and pollution damage to the related interests of coastal States. Such rules and standards shall, in the same manner, be re-examined from time to time as necessary.

2. States shall adopt laws and regulations for the prevention, reduction and control of pollution of the marine environment from vessels flying their flag or of their registry. Such laws and regulations shall at least have the same effect as that of generally accepted international rules and standards established through the competent international organization or general diplomatic conference.

3. States which establish particular requirements for the prevention, reduction and control of pollution of the marine environment as a condition for the entry of foreign vessels into their ports or internal waters or for a call at their off-shore terminals shall give due publicity to such requirements and shall communicate them to the competent international organization. Whenever such requirements are established in identical form by two or more coastal States in an endeavour to harmonize policy, the communication shall indicate which States are participating in such cooperative arrangements. Every State shall require the master of a vessel flying its flag or of its registry,

when navigating within the territorial sea of a State participating in such cooperative arrangements, to furnish, upon the request of that State, information as to whether it is proceeding to a State of the same region participating in such cooperative arrangements and, if so, to indicate whether it complies with the port entry requirements of that State. This article is without prejudice to the continued exercise by a vessel of its right of innocent passage or to the application of article 25, paragraph 2.

4. Coastal States may, in the exercise of their sovereignty within their territorial sea, adopt laws and regulations for the prevention, reduction and control of marine pollution from foreign vessels, including vessels exercising the right of innocent passage. Such laws and regulations shall, in accordance with Part II, section 3, not hamper innocent passage of foreign vessels.

5. Coastal States, for the purpose of enforcement as provided for in section 6, may in respect of their exclusive economic zones adopt laws and regulations for the prevention, reduction and control of pollution from vessels conforming to and giving effect to generally accepted international rules and standards established through the competent international organization or general diplomatic conference.

6. (a) Where the international rules and standards referred to in paragraph 1 are inadequate to meet special circumstances and coastal States have reasonable grounds for believing that a particular, clearly defined area of their respective exclusive economic zones is an area where the adoption of special mandatory measures for the prevention of pollution from vessels is required for recognized technical reasons in relation to its oceanographical and ecological conditions, as well as its utilization or the protection of its resources and the particular character of its traffic, the coastal States, after appropriate consultations through the competent international organization with any other States concerned, may, for that area, direct a communication to that organization, submitting scientific and technical evidence in support and information on necessary reception facilities. Within 12 months after receiving such a communication, the organization shall determine whether the conditions in that area correspond to the requirements set out above. If the organization so determines, the coastal States may, for that area, adopt laws and regulations for the prevention, reduction and control of pollution from vessels implementing such international rules and standards or navigational practices as are made applicable, through the organization, for special areas. These laws and regulations shall not become applicable to foreign vessels until 15 months after the submission of the communication to the organization.

(b) The coastal States shall publish the limits of any such particular, clearly defined area.

(c) If the coastal States intend to adopt additional laws and regulations for the same area for the prevention, reduction and control of pollution from vessels, they shall, when submitting the aforesaid communication, at the same time notify the organization thereof. Such additional laws and regulations may relate to discharges or navigational practices but shall not require foreign vessels to observe design, construction, manning or equipment standards other than generally accepted international rules and standards; they shall become applicable to foreign vessels 15 months after the submission of the communication to the organization, provided that the organization agrees within 12 months after the submission of the communication.

7. The international rules and standards referred to in this article should include *inter alia* those relating to prompt notification to coastal States, whose coastline or related interests may be affected by incidents, including maritime casualties, which involve discharges or probability of discharges.

Article 212

Pollution from or through the atmosphere

1. States shall adopt laws and regulations to prevent, reduce and control pollution of the marine environment from or through the atmosphere, applicable to the air space under their sovereignty and to vessels flying their flag or vessels or aircraft of their registry, taking into account internationally agreed rules, standards and recommended practices and procedures and the safety of air navigation.

2. States shall take other measures as may be necessary to prevent, reduce and control such pollution.

3. States, acting especially through competent international organizations or diplomatic conference, shall endeavour to establish global and regional rules, standards and recommended practices and procedures to prevent, reduce and control such pollution.

Section 6 Enforcement

Article 213

Enforcement with respect to pollution from land-based sources

States shall enforce their laws and regulations adopted in accordance with article 207 and shall adopt laws and regulations and take other measures necessary to implement applicable international rules and standards established through competent international organizations or diplomatic conference to prevent, reduce and control pollution of the marine environment from land-based sources.

Article 214

Enforcement with respect to pollution from seabed activities

States shall enforce their laws and regulations adopted in accordance with article 208 and shall adopt laws and regulations and take other measures necessary to implement applicable international rules and standards established through competent international organizations or diplomatic conference to prevent, reduce and control pollution of the marine environment arising from or in connection with seabed activities subject to their jurisdiction and from artificial islands, installations and structures under their jurisdiction, pursuant to articles 60 and 80.

Article 215

Enforcement with respect to pollution from activities in the Area

Enforcement of international rules, regulations and procedures established in accordance with Part XI to prevent, reduce and control pollution of the marine environment from activities in the Area shall be governed by that Part.

Article 216

Enforcement with respect to pollution by dumping

1. Laws and regulations adopted in accordance with this Convention and applicable international rules and standards established through competent international organizations or diplomatic conference for the prevention, reduction and control of pollution of the marine environment by dumping shall be enforced:

(a) by the coastal State with regard to dumping within its territorial sea or its exclusive economic zone or onto its continental shelf;

(b) by the flag State with regard to vessels flying its flag or vessels or aircraft of its registry;

(c) by any State with regard to acts of loading of wastes or other matter occurring within its territory or at its off-shore terminals.

2. No State shall be obliged by virtue of this article to institute proceedings when another State has already instituted proceedings in accordance with this article.

Article 217

Enforcement by flag States

1. States shall ensure compliance by vessels flying their flag or of their registry with applicable international rules and standards, established through the competent international organization or general diplomatic conference, and with their laws and regulations adopted in accordance with this Convention for the prevention, reduction and control of pollution of the marine environment from vessels and shall accordingly adopt laws and regulations and take other measures necessary for their implementation. Flag States shall provide for the effective enforcement of such rules, standards, laws and regulations, irrespective of where a violation occurs.

2. States shall, in particular, take appropriate measures in order to ensure that vessels flying their flag or of their registry are prohibited from sailing, until they can

proceed to sea in compliance with the requirements of the international rules and standards referred to in paragraph 1, including requirements in respect of design, construction, equipment and manning of vessels.

3. States shall ensure that vessels flying their flag or of their registry carry on board certificates required by and issued pursuant to international rules and standards referred to in paragraph 1. States shall ensure that vessels flying their flag are periodically inspected in order to verify that such certificates are in conformity with the actual condition of the vessels. These certificates shall be accepted by other States as evidence of the condition of the vessels and shall be regarded as having the same force as certificates issued by them, unless there are clear grounds for believing that the condition of the vessel does not correspond substantially with the particulars of the certificates.

4. If a vessel commits a violation of rules and standards established through the competent international organization or general diplomatic conference, the flag State, without prejudice to articles 218, 220 and 228, shall provide for immediate investigation and where appropriate institute proceedings in respect of the alleged violation irrespective of where the violation occurred or where the pollution caused by such violation has occurred or has been spotted.

5. Flag States conducting an investigation of the violation may request the assistance of any other State whose cooperation could be useful in clarifying the circumstances of the case. States shall endeavour to meet appropriate requests of flag States.

6. States shall, at the written request of any State, investigate any violation alleged to have been committed by vessels flying their flag. If satisfied that sufficient evidence is available to enable proceedings to be brought in respect of the alleged violation, flag States shall without delay institute such proceedings in accordance with their laws.

7. Flag States shall promptly inform the requesting State and the competent international organization of the action taken and its outcome. Such information shall be available to all States.

8. Penalties provided for by the laws and regulations of States for vessels flying their flag shall be adequate in severity to discourage violations wherever they occur.

Article 218
Enforcement by port States

1. When a vessel is voluntarily within a port or at an off-shore terminal of a State, that State may undertake investigations and, where the evidence so warrants, institute proceedings in respect of any discharge from that vessel outside the internal waters, territorial sea or exclusive economic zone of that State in violation of applicable international rules and standards established through the competent international organization or general diplomatic conference.

2. No proceedings pursuant to paragraph 1 shall be instituted in respect of a discharge violation in the internal waters, territorial sea or exclusive economic zone of another State unless requested by that State, the flag State, or a State damaged or threatened by the discharge violation, or unless the violation has caused or is likely to cause pollution in the internal waters, territorial sea or exclusive economic zone of the State instituting the proceedings.

3. When a vessel is voluntarily within a port or at an off-shore terminal of a State, that State shall, as far as practicable, comply with requests from any State for investigation of a discharge violation referred to in paragraph 1, believed to have occurred in, caused, or threatened damage to the internal waters, territorial sea or exclusive economic zone of the requesting State. It shall likewise, as far as practicable, comply with requests from the flag State for investigation of such a violation, irrespective of where the violation occurred.

4. The records of the investigation carried out by a port State pursuant to this article shall be transmitted upon request to the flag State or to the coastal State. Any proceedings instituted by the port State on the basis of such an investigation may, subject to section 7, be suspended at the request of the coastal State when the violation has occurred within its internal waters, territorial sea or exclusive economic zone. The evidence and records of the case, together with any bond or other financial security posted with the authorities of the port State, shall in that event be transmitted to the coastal State. Such transmittal shall preclude the continuation of proceedings in the port State.

Article 219
Measures relating to seaworthiness of vessels to avoid pollution

Subject to section 7, States which, upon request or on their own initiative, have ascertained that a vessel within one of their ports or at one of their off-shore terminals is in violation of applicable international rules and standards relating to seaworthiness of vessels and thereby threatens damage to the marine environment shall, as far as practicable, take administrative measures to prevent the vessel from sailing. Such States may permit the vessel to proceed only to the nearest appropriate repair yard and, upon removal of the causes of the violation, shall permit the vessel to continue immediately.

Article 220
Enforcement by coastal States

1. When a vessel is voluntarily within a port or at an off-shore terminal of a State, that State may, subject to section 7, institute proceedings in respect of any violation of its laws and regulations adopted in accordance with this Convention or applicable international rules and standards for the prevention, reduction and control of pol-

lution from vessels when the violation has occurred within the territorial sea or the exclusive economic zone of that State.

2. Where there are clear grounds for believing that a vessel navigating in the territorial sea of a State has, during its passage therein, violated laws and regulations of that State adopted in accordance with this Convention or applicable international rules and standards for the prevention, reduction and control of pollution from vessels, that State, without prejudice to the application of the relevant provisions of Part II, section 3, may undertake physical inspection of the vessel relating to the violation and may, where the evidence so warrants, institute proceedings, including detention of the vessel, in accordance with its laws, subject to the provisions of section 7.

3. Where there are clear grounds for believing that a vessel navigating in the exclusive economic zone or the territorial sea of a State has, in the exclusive economic zone, committed a violation of applicable international rules and standards for the prevention, reduction and control of pollution from vessels or laws and regulations of that State conforming and giving effect to such rules and standards, that State may require the vessel to give information regarding its identity and port of registry, its last and its next port of call and other relevant information required to establish whether a violation has occurred.

4. States shall adopt laws and regulations and take other measures so that vessels flying their flag comply with requests for information pursuant to paragraph 3.

5. Where there are clear grounds for believing that a vessel navigating in the exclusive economic zone or the territorial sea of a State has, in the exclusive economic zone, committed a violation referred to in paragraph 3 resulting in a substantial discharge causing or threatening significant pollution of the marine environment, that State may undertake physical inspection of the vessel for matters relating to the violation if the vessel has refused to give information or if the information supplied by the vessel is manifestly at variance with the evident factual situation and if the circumstances of the case justify such inspection.

6. Where there is clear objective evidence that a vessel navigating in the exclusive economic zone or the territorial sea of a State has, in the exclusive economic zone, committed a violation referred to in paragraph 3 resulting in a discharge causing major damage or threat of major damage to the coastline or related interests of the coastal State, or to any resources of its territorial sea or exclusive economic zone, that State may, subject to section 7, provided that the evidence so warrants, institute proceedings, including detention of the vessel, in accordance with its laws.

7. Notwithstanding the provisions of paragraph 6, whenever appropriate procedures have been established, either through the competent international organization

or as otherwise agreed, whereby compliance with requirements for bonding or other appropriate financial security has been assured, the coastal State if bound by such procedures shall allow the vessel to proceed.

8. The provisions of paragraphs 3, 4, 5, 6 and 7 also apply in respect of national laws and regulations adopted pursuant to article 211, paragraph 6.

Article 221

Measures to avoid pollution arising from maritime casualties

1. Nothing in this Part shall prejudice the right of States, pursuant to international law, both customary and conventional, to take and enforce measures beyond the territorial sea proportionate to the actual or threatened damage to protect their coastline or related interests, including fishing, from pollution or threat of pollution following upon a maritime casualty or acts relating to such a casualty, which may reasonably be expected to result in major harmful consequences.

2. For the purposes of this article, "maritime casualty" means a collision of vessels, stranding or other incident of navigation, or other occurrence on board a vessel or external to it resulting in material damage or imminent threat of material damage to a vessel or cargo.

Article 222

Enforcement with respect to pollution from or through the atmosphere

States shall enforce, within the air space under their sovereignty or with regard to vessels flying their flag or vessels or aircraft of their registry, their laws and regulations adopted in accordance with article 212, paragraph 1, and with other provisions of this Convention and shall adopt laws and regulations and take other measures necessary to implement applicable international rules and standards established through competent international organizations or diplomatic conference to prevent, reduce and control pollution of the marine environment from or through the atmosphere, in conformity with all relevant international rules and standards concerning the safety of air navigation.

Section 7 Safeguards

Article 223

Measures to facilitate proceedings

In proceedings instituted pursuant to this Part, States shall take measures to facilitate the hearing of witnesses and the admission of evidence submitted by authorities of another State, or by the competent international organization, and shall facilitate the attendance at such proceedings of official representatives of the competent international organization, the flag State and any State affected by pollution arising out of any violation. The official representatives attending such proceedings shall have such rights and duties as may be provided under national laws and regulations or international law.

Article 224

Exercise of powers of enforcement

The powers of enforcement against foreign vessels under this Part may only be exercised by officials or by warships, military aircraft, or other ships or aircraft clearly marked and identifiable as being on government service and authorized to that effect.

Article 225

Duty to avoid adverse consequences in the exercise of the powers of enforcement

In the exercise under this Convention of their powers of enforcement against foreign vessels, States shall not endanger the safety of navigation or otherwise create any hazard to a vessel, or bring it to an unsafe port or anchorage, or expose the marine environment to an unreasonable risk.

Article 226

Investigation of foreign vessels

1. (a) States shall not delay a foreign vessel longer than is essential for purposes of the investigations provided for in articles 216, 218 and 220. Any physical inspection of a foreign vessel shall be limited to an examination of such certificates, records or other documents as the vessel is required to carry by generally accepted international rules and standards or of any similar documents which it is carrying; further physical inspection of the vessel may be undertaken only after such an examination and only when:

(i) there are clear grounds for believing that the condition of the vessel or its equipment does not correspond substantially with the particulars of those documents;

(ii) the contents of such documents are not sufficient to confirm or verify a suspected violation; or

(iii) the vessel is not carrying valid certificates and records.

(b) If the investigation indicates a violation of applicable laws and regulations or international rules and standards for the protection and preservation of the marine environment, release shall be made promptly subject to reasonable procedures such as bonding or other appropriate financial security.

(c) Without prejudice to applicable international rules and standards relating to the seaworthiness of vessels, the release of a vessel may, whenever it would present an unreasonable threat of damage to the marine environment, be refused or made conditional upon proceeding to the nearest appropriate repair yard. Where release has been refused or made conditional, the flag State of the vessel must be promptly notified, and may seek release of the vessel in accordance with Part XV.

2. States shall cooperate to develop procedures for the avoidance of unnecessary physical inspection of vessels at sea.

Article 227

Non-discrimination with respect to foreign vessels

In exercising their rights and performing their duties under this Part, States shall not discriminate in form or in fact against vessels of any other State.

Article 228

Suspension and restrictions on institution of proceedings

1. Proceedings to impose penalties in respect of any violation of applicable laws and regulations or international rules and standards relating to the prevention, reduction and control of pollution from vessels committed by a foreign vessel beyond the territorial sea of the State instituting proceedings shall be suspended upon the taking of proceedings to impose penalties in respect of corresponding charges by the flag State within six months of the date on which proceedings were first instituted, unless those proceedings relate to a case of major damage to the coastal State or the flag State in question has repeatedly disregarded its obligation to enforce effectively the applicable international rules and standards in respect of violations committed by its vessels. The flag State shall in due course make available to the State previously instituting proceedings a full dossier of the case and the records of the proceedings, whenever the flag State has requested the suspension of proceedings in accordance with this article. When proceedings instituted by the flag State have been brought to a conclusion, the suspended proceedings shall be terminated. Upon payment of costs incurred in respect of such proceedings, any bond posted or other financial security provided in connection with the suspended proceedings shall be released by the coastal State.

2. Proceedings to impose penalties on foreign vessels shall not be instituted after the expiry of three years from the date on which the violation was committed, and shall not be taken by any State in the event of proceedings having been instituted by another State subject to the provisions set out in paragraph 1.

3. The provisions of this article are without prejudice to the right of the flag State to take any measures, including proceedings to impose penalties, according to its laws irrespective of prior proceedings by another State.

Article 229

Institution of civil proceedings

Nothing in this Convention affects the institution of civil proceedings in respect of any claim for loss or damage resulting from pollution of the marine environment.

Article 230

Monetary penalties and the observance of recognized rights of the accused

1. Monetary penalties only may be imposed with respect to violations of national laws and regulations or applicable international rules and standards for the prevention, reduction and control of pollution of the marine environment, committed by foreign vessels beyond the territorial sea.

2. Monetary penalties only may be imposed with respect to violations of national laws and regulations or applicable international rules and standards for the prevention, reduction and control of pollution of the marine environment, committed by foreign vessels in the territorial sea, except in the case of a wilful and serious act of pollution in the territorial sea.

3. In the conduct of proceedings in respect of such violations committed by a foreign vessel which may result in the imposition of penalties, recognized rights of the accused shall be observed.

Article 231

Notification to the flag State and other States concerned

States shall promptly notify the flag State and any other State concerned of any measures taken pursuant to section 6 against foreign vessels, and shall submit to the flag State all official reports concerning such measures. However, with respect to violations committed in the territorial sea, the foregoing obligations of the coastal State apply only to such measures as are taken in proceedings. The diplomatic agents or consular officers and where possible the maritime authority of the flag State, shall be immediately informed of any such measures taken pursuant to section 6 against foreign vessels.

Article 232

Liability of States arising from enforcement measures

States shall be liable for damage or loss attributable to them arising from measures taken pursuant to section 6 when such measures are unlawful or exceed those reasonably required in the light of available information. States shall provide for recourse in their courts for actions in respect of such damage or loss.

Article 233

Safeguards with respect to straits used for international navigation

Nothing in sections 5, 6 and 7 affects the legal regime of straits used for international navigation. However, if a foreign ship other than those referred to in section 10 has committed a violation of the laws and regulations referred to in article 42, paragraph 1(a) and (b), causing or threatening major damage to the marine environment of the straits, the States bordering the straits may take appropriate enforcement measures and if so shall respect *mutatis mutandis* the provisions of this section.

Section 8 Ice-Covered Areas

Article 234

Ice-covered areas

Coastal States have the right to adopt and enforce non-discriminatory laws and regulations for the prevention, reduction and control of marine pollution from vessels in ice-covered areas within the limits of the exclusive economic zone, where particularly severe climatic conditions and the presence of ice covering such areas for most of the year create obstructions or exceptional hazards to navigation, and pollution of the marine environment could cause major harm to or irreversible disturbance of the ecological balance. Such laws and regulations shall have due regard to navigation and the protection and preservation of the marine environment based on the best available scientific evidence.

Section 9 Responsibility and Liability

Article 235

Responsibility and liability

1. States are responsible for the fulfillment of their international obligations concerning the protection and preservation of the marine environment. They shall be liable in accordance with international law.

2. States shall ensure that recourse is available in accordance with their legal systems for prompt and adequate compensation or other relief in respect of damage caused by pollution of the marine environment by natural or juridical persons under their jurisdiction.

3. With the objective of assuring prompt and adequate compensation in respect of all damage caused by pollution of the marine environment, States shall cooperate in the implementation of existing international law and the further development of international law relating to responsibility and liability for the assessment of and compensation for damage and the settlement of related disputes, as well as, where appropriate, development of criteria and procedures for payment of adequate compensation, such as compulsory insurance or compensation funds.

Section 10 Sovereign Immunity

Article 236

Sovereign immunity

The provisions of this Convention regarding the protection and preservation of the marine environment do not apply to any warship, naval auxiliary, other vessels or aircraft owned or operated by a State and used, for the time being, only on government non-commercial service. However, each State shall ensure, by the adoption of appropriate measures not impairing operations or operational capabilities of such vessels or aircraft owned or operated by it, that such vessels or aircraft act in a manner consistent, so far as is reasonable and practicable, with this Convention.

Section 11 Obligations Under Other Conventions on the Protection and Preservation of the Marine Environment

Article 237

Obligations under other conventions on the protection and preservation of the marine environment

1. The provisions of this Part are without prejudice to the specific obligations assumed by States under special conventions and agreements concluded previously which relate to the protection and preservation of the marine environment and to agreements which may be concluded in furtherance of the general principles set forth in this Convention.

2. Specific obligations assumed by States under special conventions, with respect to the protection and preservation of the marine environment, should be carried out in a manner consistent with the general principles and objectives of this Convention.

Part XIII Marine Scientific Research

Section 1 General Provisions

Article 238

Right to conduct marine scientific research

All States, irrespective of their geographical location, and competent international organizations have the right to conduct marine scientific research subject to the rights and duties of other States as provided for in this Convention.

Article 239

Promotion of marine scientific research

States and competent international organizations shall promote and facilitate the development and conduct of marine scientific research in accordance with this Convention.

Article 240

General principles for the conduct of marine scientific research

In the conduct of marine scientific research the following principles shall apply:

(a) marine scientific research shall be conducted exclusively for peaceful purposes;

(b) marine scientific research shall be conducted with appropriate scientific methods and means compatible with this Convention;

(c) marine scientific research shall not unjustifiably interfere with other legitimate uses of the sea compatible with this Convention and shall be duly respected in the course of such uses;

(d) marine scientific research shall be conducted in compliance with all relevant regulations adopted in conformity with this Convention including those for the protection and preservation of the marine environment.

Article 241

Non-recognition of marine scientific research activities as the legal basis for claims

Marine scientific research activities shall not constitute the legal basis for any claim to any part of the marine environment or its resources.

Section 2 International Cooperation

Article 242

Promotion of international cooperation

1. States and competent international organizations shall, in accordance with the principle of respect for sovereignty and jurisdiction and on the basis of mutual benefit, promote international cooperation in marine scientific research for peaceful purposes.

2. In this context, without prejudice to the rights and duties of States under this Convention, a State, in the application of this Part, shall provide, as appropriate, other States with a reasonable opportunity to obtain from it, or with its cooperation, information necessary to prevent and control damage to the health and safety of persons and to the marine environment.

Article 243

Creation of favourable conditions

States and competent international organizations shall cooperate, through the conclusion of bilateral and multilateral agreements, to create favourable conditions for the conduct of marine scientific research in the marine environment and to integrate the efforts of scientists in studying the essence of phenomena and processes occurring in the marine environment and the interrelations between them.

Article 244

Publication and dissemination of information and knowledge

1. States and competent international organizations shall, in accordance with this Convention, make available by publication and dissemination through appropriate channels information on proposed major programmes and their objectives as well as knowledge resulting from marine scientific research.

2. For this purpose, States, both individually and in cooperation with other States and with competent international organizations, shall actively promote the flow of scientific data and information and the transfer of knowledge resulting from marine scientific research, especially to developing States, as well as the strengthening of the autonomous marine scientific research capabilities of developing States through, *inter alia*, programmes to provide adequate education and training of their technical and scientific personnel.

Section 3 Conduct and Promotion of Marine Scientific Research

Article 245

Marine scientific research in the territorial sea

Coastal States, in the exercise of their sovereignty, have the exclusive right to regulate, authorize and conduct marine scientific research in their territorial sea. Marine scientific research therein shall be conducted only with the express consent of and under the conditions set forth by the coastal State.

Article 246

Marine scientific research in the exclusive economic zone and on the continental shelf

1. Coastal States, in the exercise of their jurisdiction, have the right to regulate, authorize and conduct marine scientific research in their exclusive economic zone and on their continental shelf in accordance with the relevant provisions of this Convention.

2. Marine scientific research in the exclusive economic zone and on the continental shelf shall be conducted with the consent of the coastal State.

3. Coastal States shall, in normal circumstances, grant their consent for marine scientific research projects by other States or competent international organizations in their exclusive economic zone or on their continental shelf to be carried out in accordance with this Convention exclusively for peaceful purposes and in order to increase scientific knowledge of the marine environment for the benefit of all mankind. To this end, coastal States shall establish rules and procedures ensuring that such consent will not be delayed or denied unreasonably.

4. For the purposes of applying paragraph 3, normal circumstances may exist in spite of the absence of diplomatic relations between the coastal State and the researching State.

5. Coastal States may however in their discretion withhold their consent to the conduct of a marine scientific research project of another State or competent international organization in the exclusive economic zone or on the continental shelf of the coastal State if that project:

(a) is of direct significance for the exploration and exploitation of natural resources, whether living or non-living;

(b) involves drilling into the continental shelf, the use of explosives or the introduction of harmful substances into the marine environment;

(c) involves the construction, operation or use of artificial islands, installations and structures referred to in articles 60 and 80;

(d) contains information communicated pursuant to article 248 regarding the nature and objectives of the project which is inaccurate or if the researching State or competent international organization has outstanding obligations to the coastal State from a prior research project.

6. Notwithstanding the provisions of paragraph 5, coastal States may not exercise their discretion to withhold consent under subparagraph (a) of that paragraph in respect of marine scientific research projects to be undertaken in accordance with the provisions of this Part on the continental shelf, beyond 200 nautical miles from the baselines from which the breadth of the territorial sea is measured, outside those specific areas which coastal States may at any time publicly designate as areas in which exploitation or detailed exploratory operations focused on those areas are occurring or will occur within a reasonable period of time. Coastal States shall give reasonable notice of the designation of such areas, as well as any modifications thereto, but shall not be obliged to give details of the operations therein.

7. The provisions of paragraph 6 are without prejudice to the rights of coastal States over the continental shelf as established in article 77.

8. Marine scientific research activities referred to in this article shall not unjustifiably interfere with activities undertaken by coastal States in the exercise of their sovereign rights and jurisdiction provided for in this Convention.

Article 247

Marine scientific research projects undertaken by or under the auspices of international organizations

A coastal State which is a member of or has a bilateral agreement with an international organization, and in whose exclusive economic zone or on whose continental shelf that organization wants to carry out a marine scientific research project, directly or under its auspices, shall be deemed to have authorized the project to be carried out in conformity with the agreed specifications if that State approved the detailed project when the decision was made by the organization for the undertaking of the project, or is willing to participate in it, and has not expressed any objection within four months of notification of the project by the organization to the coastal State.

Article 248

Duty to provide information to the coastal State

States and competent international organizations which intend to undertake marine scientific research in the exclusive economic zone or on the continental shelf of a coastal State shall, not less than six months in advance of the expected starting date of the marine scientific research project, provide that State with a full description of:

(a) the nature and objectives of the project;

(b) the method and means to be used, including name, tonnage, type and class of vessels and a description of scientific equipment;

(c) the precise geographical areas in which the project is to be conducted;

(d) the expected date of first appearance and final departure of the research vessels, or deployment of the equipment and its removal, as appropriate;

(e) the name of the sponsoring institution, its director, and the person in charge of the project; and

(f) the extent to which it is considered that the coastal State should be able to participate or to be represented in the project.

Article 249

Duty to comply with certain conditions

1. States and competent international organizations when undertaking marine scientific research in the exclusive economic zone or on the continental shelf of a coastal State shall comply with the following conditions:

(a) ensure the right of the coastal State, if it so desires, to participate or be represented in the marine scientific research project, especially on board research vessels and other craft or scientific research installations, when practicable, without payment of any remuneration to the scientists of the coastal State and without obligation to contribute towards the costs of the project;

(b) provide the coastal State, at its request, with preliminary reports, as soon as practicable, and with the final results and conclusions after the completion of the research;

(c) undertake to provide access for the coastal State, at its request, to all data and samples derived from the marine scientific research project and likewise to furnish it with data which may be copied and samples which may be divided without detriment to their scientific value;

(d) if requested, provide the coastal State with an assessment of such data, samples and research results or provide assistance in their assessment or interpretation;

(e) ensure, subject to paragraph 2, that the research results are made internationally available through appropriate national or international channels, as soon as practicable;

(f) inform the coastal State immediately of any major change in the research programme;

(g) unless otherwise agreed, remove the scientific research installations or equipment once the research is completed.

2. This article is without prejudice to the conditions established by the laws and regulations of the coastal State for the exercise of its discretion to grant or withhold consent pursuant to article 246, paragraph 5, including requiring prior agreement for making internationally available the research results of a project of direct significance for the exploration and exploitation of natural resources.

Article 250

Communications concerning marine scientific research projects

Communications concerning the marine scientific research projects shall be made through appropriate official channels, unless otherwise agreed.

Article 251

General criteria and guidelines

States shall seek to promote through competent international organizations the establishment of general criteria and guidelines to assist States in ascertaining the nature and implications of marine scientific research.

Article 252

Implied consent

States or competent international organizations may proceed with a marine scientific research project six months after the date upon which the information required pursuant to article 248 was provided to the coastal State unless within four months of the receipt of the communication containing such information the coastal State has informed the State or organization conducting the research that:

(a) it has withheld its consent under the provisions of article 246; or

(b) the information given by that State or competent international organization regarding the nature or objectives of the project does not conform to the manifestly evident facts; or

(c) it requires supplementary information relevant to conditions and the information provided for under articles 248 and 249; or

(d) outstanding obligations exist with respect to a previous marine scientific research project carried out by that State or organization, with regard to conditions established in article 249.

Article 253

Suspension or cessation of marine scientific research activities

1. A coastal State shall have the right to require the suspension of any marine scientific research activities in progress within its exclusive economic zone or on its continental shelf if:

(a) the research activities are not being conducted in accordance with the information communicated as provided under article 248 upon which the consent of the coastal State was based; or

(b) the State or competent international organization conducting the research activities fails to comply with the provisions of article 249 concerning the rights of the coastal State with respect to the marine scientific research project.

2. A coastal State shall have the right to require the cessation of any marine scientific research activities in case of any non-compliance with the provisions of article 248 which amounts to a major change in the research project or the research activities.

3. A coastal State may also require cessation of marine scientific research activities if any of the situations contemplated in paragraph 1 are not rectified within a reasonable period of time.

4. Following notification by the coastal State of its decision to order suspension or cessation, States or competent international organizations authorized to conduct marine scientific research activities shall terminate the research activities that are the subject of such a notification.

5. An order of suspension under paragraph 1 shall be lifted by the coastal State and the marine scientific research activities allowed to continue once the researching State or competent international organization has complied with the conditions required under articles 248 and 249.

Article 254

Rights of neighbouring land-locked and geographically disadvantaged States

1. States and competent international organizations which have submitted to a coastal State a project to undertake marine scientific research referred to in article 246, paragraph 3, shall give notice to the neighbouring land-locked and geographically disadvantaged States of the proposed research project, and shall notify the coastal State thereof.

2. After the consent has been given for the proposed marine scientific research project by the coastal State concerned, in accordance with article 246 and other relevant provisions of this Convention, States and competent international organizations undertaking such a project shall provide to the neighbouring land-locked and

geographically disadvantaged States, at their request and when appropriate, relevant information as specified in article 248 and article 249, paragraph 1(f).

3. The neighbouring land-locked and geographically disadvantaged States referred to above shall, at their request, be given the opportunity to participate, whenever feasible, in the proposed marine scientific research project through qualified experts appointed by them and not objected to by the coastal State, in accordance with the conditions agreed for the project, in conformity with the provisions of this Convention, between the coastal State concerned and the State or competent international organizations conducting the marine scientific research.

4. States and competent international organizations referred to in paragraph 1 shall provide to the above-mentioned land-locked and geographically disadvantaged States, at their request, the information and assistance specified in article 249, paragraph 1(d), subject to the provisions of article 249, paragraph 2.

Article 255
Measures to facilitate marine scientific researchand assist research vessels

States shall endeavour to adopt reasonable rules, regulations and procedures to promote and facilitate marine scientific research conducted in accordance with this Convention beyond their territorial sea and, as appropriate, to facilitate, subject to the provisions of their laws and regulations, access to their harbours and promote assistance for marine scientific research vessels which comply with the relevant provisions of this Part.

Article 256
Marine scientific research in the Area

All States, irrespective of their geographical location, and competent international organizations have the right, in conformity with the provisions of Part XI, to conduct marine scientific research in the Area.

Article 257
Marine scientific research in the water column beyond the exclusive economic zone

All States, irrespective of their geographical location, and competent international organizations have the right, in conformity with this Convention, to conduct marine scientific research in the water column beyond the limits of the exclusive economic zone.

Section 4 Scientific Research Installations or Equipment in the Marine Environment

Article 258

Deployment and use

The deployment and use of any type of scientific research installations or equipment in any area of the marine environment shall be subject to the same conditions as are prescribed in this Convention for the conduct of marine scientific research in any such area.

Article 259

Legal status

The installations or equipment referred to in this section do not possess the status of islands. They have no territorial sea of their own, and their presence does not affect the delimitation of the territorial sea, the exclusive economic zone or the continental shelf.

Article 260

Safety zones

Safety zones of a reasonable breadth not exceeding a distance of 500 metres may be created around scientific research installations in accordance with the relevant provisions of this Convention. All States shall ensure that such safety zones are respected by their vessels.

Article 261

Non-interference with shipping routes

The deployment and use of any type of scientific research installations or equipment shall not constitute an obstacle to established international shipping routes.

Article 262

Identification markings and warning signals

Installations or equipment referred to in this section shall bear identification markings indicating the State of registry or the international organization to which they belong and shall have adequate internationally agreed warning signals to ensure safety at sea and the safety of air navigation, taking into account rules and standards established by competent international organizations.

Section 5 Responsibility and Liability

Article 263

Responsibility and liability

1. States and competent international organizations shall be responsible for ensuring that marine scientific research, whether undertaken by them or on their behalf, is conducted in accordance with this Convention.

2. States and competent international organizations shall be responsible and liable for the measures they take in contravention of this Convention in respect of marine scientific research conducted by other States, their natural or juridical persons or by competent international organizations, and shall provide compensation for damage resulting from such measures.

3. States and competent international organizations shall be responsible and liable pursuant to article 235 for damage caused by pollution of the marine environment arising out of marine scientific research undertaken by them or on their behalf.

Section 6 Settlement of Disputes and Interim Measures

Article 264

Settlement of disputes

Disputes concerning the interpretation or application of the provisions of this Convention with regard to marine scientific research shall be settled in accordance with Part XV, sections 2 and 3.

Article 265

Interim measures

Pending settlement of a dispute in accordance with Part XV, sections 2 and 3, the State or competent international organization authorized to conduct a marine scientific research project shall not allow research activities to commence or continue without the express consent of the coastal State concerned.

Part XIV Development and Transfer of Marine Technology

Section 1 General Provisions

Article 266

Promotion of the development and transfer of marine technology

1. States, directly or through competent international organizations, shall cooperate in accordance with their capabilities to promote actively the development and transfer of marine science and marine technology on fair and reasonable terms and conditions.

2. States shall promote the development of the marine scientific and technological capacity of States which may need and request technical assistance in this field, particularly developing States, including land-locked and geographically disadvantaged States, with regard to the exploration, exploitation, conservation and management of marine resources, the protection and preservation of the marine environment, marine scientific research and other activities in the marine environment compatible with this Convention, with a view to accelerating the social and economic development of the developing States.

3. States shall endeavour to foster favourable economic and legal conditions for the transfer of marine technology for the benefit of all parties concerned on an equitable basis.

Article 267

Protection of legitimate interests

States, in promoting cooperation pursuant to article 266, shall have due regard for all legitimate interests including, *inter alia*, the rights and duties of holders, suppliers and recipients of marine technology.

Article 268

Basic objectives

States, directly or through competent international organizations, shall promote:

(a) the acquisition, evaluation and dissemination of marine technological knowledge and facilitate access to such information and data;

(b) the development of appropriate marine technology;

(c) the development of the necessary technological infrastructure to facilitate the transfer of marine technology;

(d) the development of human resources through training and education of nationals of developing States and countries and especially the nationals of the least developed among them;

(e) international cooperation at all levels, particularly at the regional, subregional and bilateral levels.

Article 269

Measures to achieve the basic objectives

In order to achieve the objectives referred to in article 268, States, directly or through competent international organizations, shall endeavour, *inter alia*, to:

(a) establish programmes of technical cooperation for the effective transfer of all kinds of marine technology to States which may need and request technical assistance in this field, particularly the developing land-locked and geographically disadvantaged States, as well as other developing States which have not been able either to establish or develop their own technological capacity in marine science and in the exploration and exploitation of marine resources or to develop the infrastructure of such technology;

(b) promote favourable conditions for the conclusion of agreements, contracts and other similar arrangements, under equitable and reasonable conditions;

(c) hold conferences, seminars and symposia on scientific and technological subjects, in particular on policies and methods for the transfer of marine technology;

(d) promote the exchange of scientists and of technological and other experts;

(e) undertake projects and promote joint ventures and other forms of bilateral and multilateral cooperation.

Section 2 International Cooperation

Article 270

Ways and means of international cooperation

International cooperation for the development and transfer of marine technology shall be carried out, where feasible and appropriate, through existing bilateral, regional or multilateral programmes, and also through expanded and new programmes in order to facilitate marine scientific research, the transfer of marine technology, particularly in new fields, and appropriate international funding for ocean research and development.

Article 271

Guidelines, criteria and standards

States, directly or through competent international organizations, shall promote the establishment of generally accepted guidelines, criteria and standards for the transfer of marine technology on a bilateral basis or within the framework of international organizations and other fora, taking into account, in particular, the interests and needs of developing States.

Article 272

Coordination of international programmes

In the field of transfer of marine technology, States shall endeavour to ensure that competent international organizations coordinate their activities, including any regional or global programmes, taking into account the interests and needs of developing States, particularly land-locked and geographically disadvantaged States.

Article 273

Cooperation with international organizations and the Authority

States shall cooperate actively with competent international organizations and the Authority to encourage and facilitate the transfer to developing States, their nationals and the Enterprise of skills and marine technology with regard to activities in the Area.

Article 274

Objectives of the Authority

Subject to all legitimate interests including, *inter alia*, the rights and duties of holders, suppliers and recipients of technology, the Authority, with regard to activities in the Area, shall ensure that:

(a) on the basis of the principle of equitable geographical distribution, nationals of developing States, whether coastal, land-locked or geographically disadvantaged, shall be taken on for the purposes of training as members of the managerial, research and technical staff constituted for its undertakings;

(b) the technical documentation on the relevant equipment, machinery, devices and processes is made available to all States, in particular developing States which may need and request technical assistance in this field;

(c) adequate provision is made by the Authority to facilitate the acquisition of technical assistance in the field of marine technology by States which may need and request it, in particular developing States, and the acquisition by their nationals of the necessary skills and know-how, including professional training;

(d) States which may need and request technical assistance in this field, in particular developing States, are assisted in the acquisition of necessary equipment, processes, plant and other technical know-how through any financial arrangements provided for in this Convention.

Section 3 National and Regional Marine Scientific and Technological Centres

Article 275

Establishment of national centres

1. States, directly or through competent international organizations and the Authority, shall promote the establishment, particularly in developing coastal States, of national marine scientific and technological research centres and the strengthening of existing national centres, in order to stimulate and advance the conduct of marine scientific research by developing coastal States and to enhance their national capabilities to utilize and preserve their marine resources for their economic benefit.

2. States, through competent international organizations and the Authority, shall give adequate support to facilitate the establishment and strengthening of such national centres so as to provide for advanced training facilities and necessary equipment, skills and know-how as well as technical experts to such States which may need and request such assistance.

Article 276

Establishment of regional centres

1. States, in coordination with the competent international organizations, the Authority and national marine scientific and technological research institutions, shall promote the establishment of regional marine scientific and technological research centres, particularly in developing States, in order to stimulate and advance the

conduct of marine scientific research by developing States and foster the transfer of marine technology.

2. All States of a region shall cooperate with the regional centres therein to ensure the more effective achievement of their objectives.

Article 277

Functions of regional centres

The functions of such regional centres shall include, *inter alia*:

(a) training and educational programmes at all levels on various aspects of marine scientific and technological research, particularly marine biology, including conservation and management of living resources, oceanography, hydrography, engineering, geological exploration of the seabed, mining and desalination technologies;

(b) management studies;

(c) study programmes related to the protection and preservation of the marine environment and the prevention, reduction and control of pollution;

(d) organization of regional conferences, seminars and symposia;

(e) acquisition and processing of marine scientific and technological data and information;

(f) prompt dissemination of results of marine scientific and technological research in readily available publications;

(g) publicizing national policies with regard to the transfer of marine technology and systematic comparative study of those policies;

(h) compilation and systematization of information on the marketing of technology and on contracts and other arrangements concerning patents;

(i) technical cooperation with other States of the region.

Section 4 Cooperation among International Organizations

Article 278

Cooperation among international organizations

The competent international organizations referred to in this Part and in Part XIII shall take all appropriate measures to ensure, either directly or in close cooperation among themselves, the effective discharge of their functions and responsibilities under this Part.

Part XV Settlement of Disputes

Section 1 General Provisions

Article 279

Obligation to settle disputes by peaceful means

States Parties shall settle any dispute between them concerning the interpretation or application of this Convention by peaceful means in accordance with Article 2, paragraph 3, of the Charter of the United Nations and, to this end, shall seek a solution by the means indicated in Article 33, paragraph 1, of the Charter.

Article 280

Settlement of disputes by any peaceful means chosen by the parties

Nothing in this Part impairs the right of any States Parties to agree at any time to settle a dispute between them concerning the interpretation or application of this Convention by any peaceful means of their own choice.

Article 281

Procedure where no settlement has been reached by the parties

1. If the States Parties which are parties to a dispute concerning the interpretation or application of this Convention have agreed to seek settlement of the dispute by a peaceful means of their own choice, the procedures provided for in this Part apply only where no settlement has been reached by recourse to such means and the agreement between the parties does not exclude any further procedure.
2. If the parties have also agreed on a time-limit, paragraph 1 applies only upon the expiration of that time-limit.

Article 282

Obligations under general, regional or bilateral agreements

If the States Parties which are parties to a dispute concerning the interpretation or application of this Convention have agreed, through a general, regional or bilateral agreement or otherwise, that such dispute shall, at the request of any party to the dispute, be submitted to a procedure that entails a binding decision, that procedure shall apply in lieu of the procedures provided for in this Part, unless the parties to the dispute otherwise agree.

Article 283

Obligation to exchange views

1. When a dispute arises between States Parties concerning the interpretation or application of this Convention, the parties to the dispute shall proceed expeditiously

to an exchange of views regarding its settlement by negotiation or other peaceful means.

2. The parties shall also proceed expeditiously to an exchange of views where a procedure for the settlement of such a dispute has been terminated without a settlement or where a settlement has been reached and the circumstances require consultation regarding the manner of implementing the settlement.

Article 284

Conciliation

1. A State Party which is a party to a dispute concerning the interpretation or application of this Convention may invite the other party or parties to submit the dispute to conciliation in accordance with the procedure under Annex V, section 1, or another conciliation procedure.

2. If the invitation is accepted and if the parties agree upon the conciliation procedure to be applied, any party may submit the dispute to that procedure.

3. If the invitation is not accepted or the parties do not agree upon the procedure, the conciliation proceedings shall be deemed to be terminated.

4. Unless the parties otherwise agree, when a dispute has been submitted to conciliation, the proceedings may be terminated only in accordance with the agreed conciliation procedure.

Article 285

Application of this section to disputes submitted pursuant to Part XI

This section applies to any dispute which pursuant to Part XI, section 5, is to be settled in accordance with procedures provided for in this Part. If an entity other than a State Party is a party to such a dispute, this section applies *mutatis mutandis*.

Section 2 Compulsory Procedures Entailing Binding Decisions

Article 286

Application of procedures under this section

Subject to section 3, any dispute concerning the interpretation or application of this Convention shall, where no settlement has been reached by recourse to section 1, be submitted at the request of any party to the dispute to the court or tribunal having jurisdiction under this section.

Article 287

Choice of procedure

1. When signing, ratifying or acceding to this Convention or at any time thereafter, a State shall be free to choose, by means of a written declaration, one or more of the

following means for the settlement of disputes concerning the interpretation or application of this Convention:

(a) the International Tribunal for the Law of the Sea established in accordance with Annex VI;

(b) the International Court of Justice;

(c) an arbitral tribunal constituted in accordance with Annex VII;

(d) a special arbitral tribunal constituted in accordance with Annex VIII for one or more of the categories of disputes specified therein.

2. A declaration made under paragraph 1 shall not affect or be affected by the obligation of a State Party to accept the jurisdiction of the Seabed Disputes Chamber of the International Tribunal for the Law of the Sea to the extent and in the manner provided for in Part XI, section 5.

3. A State Party, which is a party to a dispute not covered by a declaration in force, shall be deemed to have accepted arbitration in accordance with Annex VII.

4. If the parties to a dispute have accepted the same procedure for the settlement of the dispute, it may be submitted only to that procedure, unless the parties otherwise agree.

5. If the parties to a dispute have not accepted the same procedure for the settlement of the dispute, it may be submitted only to arbitration in accordance with Annex VII, unless the parties otherwise agree.

6. A declaration made under paragraph 1 shall remain in force until three months after notice of revocation has been deposited with the Secretary-General of the United Nations.

7. A new declaration, a notice of revocation or the expiry of a declaration does not in any way affect proceedings pending before a court or tribunal having jurisdiction under this article, unless the parties otherwise agree.

8. Declarations and notices referred to in this article shall be deposited with the Secretary-General of the United Nations, who shall transmit copies thereof to the States Parties.

Article 288
Jurisdiction

1. A court or tribunal referred to in article 287 shall have jurisdiction over any dispute concerning the interpretation or application of this Convention which is submitted to it in accordance with this Part.

2. A court or tribunal referred to in article 287 shall also have jurisdiction over any dispute concerning the interpretation or application of an international agreement related to the purposes of this Convention, which is submitted to it in accordance with the agreement.

3. The Seabed Disputes Chamber of the International Tribunal for the Law of the Sea established in accordance with Annex VI, and any other chamber or arbitral

tribunal referred to in Part XI, section 5, shall have jurisdiction in any matter which is submitted to it in accordance therewith.

4. In the event of a dispute as to whether a court or tribunal has jurisdiction, the matter shall be settled by decision of that court or tribunal.

Article 289

Experts

In any dispute involving scientific or technical matters, a court or tribunal exercising jurisdiction under this section may, at the request of a party or *proprio motu*, select in consultation with the parties no fewer than two scientific or technical experts chosen preferably from the relevant list prepared in accordance with Annex VIII, article 2, to sit with the court or tribunal but without the right to vote.

Article 290

Provisional measures

1. If a dispute has been duly submitted to a court or tribunal which considers that *prima facie* it has jurisdiction under this Part or Part XI, section 5, the court or tribunal may prescribe any provisional measures which it considers appropriate under the circumstances to preserve the respective rights of the parties to the dispute or to prevent serious harm to the marine environment, pending the final decision.

2. Provisional measures may be modified or revoked as soon as the circumstances justifying them have changed or ceased to exist.

3. Provisional measures may be prescribed, modified or revoked under this article only at the request of a party to the dispute and after the parties have been given an opportunity to be heard.

4. The court or tribunal shall forthwith give notice to the parties to the dispute, and to such other States Parties as it considers appropriate, of the prescription, modification or revocation of provisional measures.

5. Pending the constitution of an arbitral tribunal to which a dispute is being submitted under this section, any court or tribunal agreed upon by the parties or, failing such agreement within two weeks from the date of the request for provisional measures, the International Tribunal for the Law of the Sea or, with respect to activities in the Area, the Seabed Disputes Chamber, may prescribe, modify or revoke provisional measures in accordance with this article if it considers that *prima facie* the tribunal which is to be constituted would have jurisdiction and that the urgency of the situation so requires. Once constituted, the tribunal to which the dispute has been submitted may modify, revoke or affirm those provisional measures, acting in conformity with paragraphs 1 to 4.

6. The parties to the dispute shall comply promptly with any provisional measures prescribed under this article.

Article 291

Access

1. All the dispute settlement procedures specified in this Part shall be open to States Parties.

2. The dispute settlement procedures specified in this Part shall be open to entities other than States Parties only as specifically provided for in this Convention.

Article 292

Prompt release of vessels and crews

1. Where the authorities of a State Party have detained a vessel flying the flag of another State Party and it is alleged that the detaining State has not complied with the provisions of this Convention for the prompt release of the vessel or its crew upon the posting of a reasonable bond or other financial security, the question of release from detention may be submitted to any court or tribunal agreed upon by the parties or, failing such agreement within 10 days from the time of detention, to a court or tribunal accepted by the detaining State under article 287 or to the International Tribunal for the Law of the Sea, unless the parties otherwise agree.

2. The application for release may be made only by or on behalf of the flag State of the vessel.

3. The court or tribunal shall deal without delay with the application for release and shall deal only with the question of release, without prejudice to the merits of any case before the appropriate domestic forum against the vessel, its owner or its crew. The authorities of the detaining State remain competent to release the vessel or its crew at any time.

4. Upon the posting of the bond or other financial security determined by the court or tribunal, the authorities of the detaining State shall comply promptly with the decision of the court or tribunal concerning the release of the vessel or its crew.

Article 293

Applicable law

1. A court or tribunal having jurisdiction under this section shall apply this Convention and other rules of international law not incompatible with this Convention.

2. Paragraph 1 does not prejudice the power of the court or tribunal having jurisdiction under this section to decide a case *ex aequo et bono*, if the parties so agree.

Article 294

Preliminary proceedings

1. A court or tribunal provided for in article 287 to which an application is made in respect of a dispute referred to in article 297 shall determine at the request of a party,

or may determine *proprio motu*, whether the claim constitutes an abuse of legal process or whether *prima facie* it is well founded. If the court or tribunal determines that the claim constitutes an abuse of legal process or is *prima facie* unfounded, it shall take no further action in the case.

2. Upon receipt of the application, the court or tribunal shall immediately notify the other party or parties of the application, and shall fix a reasonable time-limit within which they may request it to make a determination in accordance with paragraph 1.

3. Nothing in this article affects the right of any party to a dispute to make preliminary objections in accordance with the applicable rules of procedure.

Article 295

Exhaustion of local remedies

Any dispute between States Parties concerning the interpretation or application of this Convention may be submitted to the procedures provided for in this section only after local remedies have been exhausted where this is required by international law.

Article 296

Finality and binding force of decisions

1. Any decision rendered by a court or tribunal having jurisdiction under this section shall be final and shall be complied with by all the parties to the dispute.

2. Any such decision shall have no binding force except between the parties and in respect of that particular dispute.

Section 3 Limitations and Exceptions to Applicability of Section 2

Article 297

Limitations on applicability of section 2

1. Disputes concerning the interpretation or application of this Convention with regard to the exercise by a coastal State of its sovereign rights or jurisdiction provided for in this Convention shall be subject to the procedures provided for in section 2 in the following cases:

(a) when it is alleged that a coastal State has acted in contravention of the provisions of this Convention in regard to the freedoms and rights of navigation, overflight or the laying of submarine cables and pipelines, or in regard to other internationally lawful uses of the sea specified in article 58;

(b) when it is alleged that a State in exercising the aforementioned freedoms, rights or uses has acted in contravention of this Convention or of laws or regulations adopted by the coastal State in conformity with this Convention and other rules of international law not incompatible with this Convention; or

(c) when it is alleged that a coastal State has acted in contravention of specified international rules and standards for the protection and preservation of the marine environment which are applicable to the coastal State and which have been established by this Convention or through a competent international organization or diplomatic conference in accordance with this Convention.

2. (a) Disputes concerning the interpretation or application of the provisions of this Convention with regard to marine scientific research shall be settled in accordance with section 2, except that the coastal State shall not be obliged to accept the submission to such settlement of any dispute arising out of:

(i) the exercise by the coastal State of a right or discretion in accordance with article 246; or

(ii) a decision by the coastal State to order suspension or cessation of a research project in accordance with article 253.

(b) A dispute arising from an allegation by the researching State that with respect to a specific project the coastal State is not exercising its rights under articles 246 and 253 in a manner compatible with this Convention shall be submitted, at the request of either party, to conciliation under Annex V, section 2, provided that the conciliation commission shall not call in question the exercise by the coastal State of its discretion to designate specific areas as referred to in article 246, paragraph 6, or of its discretion to withhold consent in accordance with article 246, paragraph 5.

3. (a) Disputes concerning the interpretation or application of the provisions of this Convention with regard to fisheries shall be settled in accordance with section 2, except that the coastal State shall not be obliged to accept the submission to such settlement of any dispute relating to its sovereign rights with respect to the living resources in the exclusive economic zone or their exercise, including its discretionary powers for determining the allowable catch, its harvesting capacity, the allocation of surpluses to other States and the terms and conditions established in its conservation and management laws and regulations.

(b) Where no settlement has been reached by recourse to section 1 of this Part, a dispute shall be submitted to conciliation under Annex V, section 2, at the request of any party to the dispute, when it is alleged that:

(i) a coastal State has manifestly failed to comply with its obligations to ensure through proper conservation and management measures that the maintenance of the living resources in the exclusive economic zone is not seriously endangered;

(ii) a coastal State has arbitrarily refused to determine, at the request of another State, the allowable catch and its capacity to harvest living resources with respect to stocks which that other State is interested in fishing; or

(iii) a coastal State has arbitrarily refused to allocate to any State, under articles 62, 69 and 70 and under the terms and conditions established by the coastal State consistent with this Convention, the whole or part of the surplus it has declared to exist.

(c) In no case shall the conciliation commission substitute its discretion for that of the coastal State.

(d) The report of the conciliation commission shall be communicated to the appropriate international organizations.

(e) In negotiating agreements pursuant to articles 69 and 70, States Parties, unless they otherwise agree, shall include a clause on measures which they shall take in order to minimize the possibility of a disagreement concerning the interpretation or application of the agreement, and on how they should proceed if a disagreement nevertheless arises.

Article 298

Optional exceptions to applicability of section 2

1. When signing, ratifying or acceding to this Convention or at any time thereafter, a State may, without prejudice to the obligations arising under section 1, declare in writing that it does not accept any one or more of the procedures provided for in section 2 with respect to one or more of the following categories of disputes:

(a) (i) disputes concerning the interpretation or application of articles 15, 74 and 83 relating to sea boundary delimitations, or those involving historic bays or titles, provided that a State having made such a declaration shall, when such a dispute arises subsequent to the entry into force of this Convention and where no agreement within a reasonable period of time is reached in negotiations between the parties, at the request of any party to the dispute, accept submission of the matter to conciliation under Annex V, section 2; and provided further that any dispute that necessarily involves the concurrent consideration of any unsettled dispute concerning sovereignty or other rights over continental or insular land territory shall be excluded from such submission;

(ii) after the conciliation commission has presented its report, which shall state the reasons on which it is based, the parties shall negotiate an agreement on the basis of that report; if these negotiations do not result in an agreement, the parties shall, by mutual consent, submit the question to one of the procedures provided for in section 2, unless the parties otherwise agree;

(iii) this subparagraph does not apply to any sea boundary dispute finally settled by an arrangement between the parties, or to any such dispute which is to be settled in accordance with a bilateral or multilateral agreement binding upon those parties;

(b) disputes concerning military activities, including military activities by government vessels and aircraft engaged in non-commercial service, and disputes concerning law enforcement activities in regard to the exercise of sovereign rights or jurisdiction excluded from the jurisdiction of a court or tribunal under article 297, paragraph 2 or 3;

(c) disputes in respect of which the Security Council of the United Nations is exercising the functions assigned to it by the Charter of the United Nations, unless the Security Council decides to remove the matter from its agenda or calls upon the parties to settle it by the means provided for in this Convention.

2. A State Party which has made a declaration under paragraph 1 may at any time withdraw it, or agree to submit a dispute excluded by such declaration to any procedure specified in this Convention.

3. A State Party which has made a declaration under paragraph 1 shall not be entitled to submit any dispute falling within the excepted category of disputes to any procedure in this Convention as against another State Party, without the consent of that party.

4. If one of the States Parties has made a declaration under paragraph 1(a), any other State Party may submit any dispute falling within an excepted category against the declarant party to the procedure specified in such declaration.

5. A new declaration, or the withdrawal of a declaration, does not in any way affect proceedings pending before a court or tribunal in accordance with this article, unless the parties otherwise agree.

6. Declarations and notices of withdrawal of declarations under this article shall be deposited with the Secretary-General of the United Nations, who shall transmit copies thereof to the States Parties.

Article 299

Right of the parties to agree upon a procedure

1. A dispute excluded under article 297 or excepted by a declaration made under article 298 from the dispute settlement procedures provided for in section 2 may be submitted to such procedures only by agreement of the parties to the dispute.

2. Nothing in this section impairs the right of the parties to the dispute to agree to some other procedure for the settlement of such dispute or to reach an amicable settlement.

Part XVI General Provisions

Article 300
Good faith and abuse of rights

States Parties shall fulfill in good faith the obligations assumed under this Convention and shall exercise the rights, jurisdiction and freedoms recognized in this Convention in a manner which would not constitute an abuse of right.

Article 301
Peaceful uses of the seas

In exercising their rights and performing their duties under this Convention, States Parties shall refrain from any threat or use of force against the territorial integrity or political independence of any State, or in any other manner inconsistent with the principles of international law embodied in the Charter of the United Nations.

Article 302
Disclosure of information

Without prejudice to the right of a State Party to resort to the procedures for the settlement of disputes provided for in this Convention, nothing in this Convention shall be deemed to require a State Party, in the fulfillment of its obligations under this Convention, to supply information the disclosure of which is contrary to the essential interests of its security.

Article 303
Archaeological and historical objects found at sea

1. States have the duty to protect objects of an archaeological and historical nature found at sea and shall cooperate for this purpose.
2. In order to control traffic in such objects, the coastal State may, in applying article 33, presume that their removal from the seabed in the zone referred to in that article without its approval would result in an infringement within its territory or territorial sea of the laws and regulations referred to in that article.
3. Nothing in this article affects the rights of identifiable owners, the law of salvage or other rules of admiralty, or laws and practices with respect to cultural exchanges.
4. This article is without prejudice to other international agreements and rules of international law regarding the protection of objects of an archaeological and historical nature.

Article 304
Responsibility and liability for damage

The provisions of this Convention regarding responsibility and liability for damage are without prejudice to the application of existing rules and the development of further rules regarding responsibility and liability under international law.

Part XVII Final Provisions

Article 305
Signature

1. This Convention shall be open for signature by:

(a) all States;

(b) Namibia, represented by the United Nations Council for Namibia;

(c) all self-governing associated States which have chosen that status in an act of self-determination supervised and approved by the United Nations in accordance with General Assembly resolution 1514 (XV) and which have competence over the matters governed by this Convention, including the competence to enter into treaties in respect of those matters;

(d) all self-governing associated States which, in accordance with their respective instruments of association, have competence over the matters governed by this Convention, including the competence to enter into treaties in respect of those matters;

(e) all territories which enjoy full internal self-government, recognized as such by the United Nations, but have not attained full independence in accordance with General Assembly resolution 1514 (XV) and which have competence over the matters governed by this Convention, including the competence to enter into treaties in respect of those matters;

(f) international organizations, in accordance with Annex IX.

2. This Convention shall remain open for signature until 9 December 1984 at the Ministry of Foreign Affairs of Jamaica and also, from 1 July 1983 until 9 December 1984, at United Nations Headquarters in New York.

Article 306
Ratification and formal confirmation

This Convention is subject to ratification by States and the other entities referred to in article 305, paragraph 1(b), (c), (d) and (e), and to formal confirmation, in accordance with Annex IX, by the entities referred to in article 305, paragraph 1(f). The instruments of ratification and of formal confirmation shall be deposited with the Secretary-General of the United Nations.

Article 307

Accession

This Convention shall remain open for accession by States and the other entities referred to in article 305. Accession by the entities referred to in article 305, paragraph l(f), shall be in accordance with Annex IX. The instruments of accession shall be deposited with the Secretary-General of the United Nations.

Article 308

Entry into force

1. This Convention shall enter into force 12 months after the date of deposit of the sixtieth instrument of ratification or accession.

2. For each State ratifying or acceding to this Convention after the deposit of the sixtieth instrument of ratification or accession, the Convention shall enter into force on the thirtieth day following the deposit of its instrument of ratification or accession, subject to paragraph 1.

3. The Assembly of the Authority shall meet on the date of entry into force of this Convention and shall elect the Council of the Authority. The first Council shall be constituted in a manner consistent with the purpose of article 161 if the provisions of that article cannot be strictly applied.

4. The rules, regulations and procedures drafted by the Preparatory Commission shall apply provisionally pending their formal adoption by the Authority in accordance with Part XI.

5. The Authority and its organs shall act in accordance with resolution II of the Third United Nations Conference on the Law of the Sea relating to preparatory investment and with decisions of the Preparatory Commission taken pursuant to that resolution.

Article 309

Reservations and exceptions

No reservations or exceptions may be made to this Convention unless expressly permitted by other articles of this Convention.

Article 310

Declarations and statements

Article 309 does not preclude a State, when signing, ratifying or acceding to this Convention, from making declarations or statements, however phrased or named, with a view, *inter alia,* to the harmonization of its laws and regulations with the provisions of this Convention, provided that such declarations or statements do not purport to exclude or to modify the legal effect of the provisions of this Convention in their application to that State.

Article 311

Relation to other conventions and international agreements

1. This Convention shall prevail, as between States Parties, over the Geneva Conventions on the Law of the Sea of 29 April 1958.

2. This Convention shall not alter the rights and obligations of States Parties which arise from other agreements compatible with this Convention and which do not affect the enjoyment by other States Parties of their rights or the performance of their obligations under this Convention.

3. Two or more States Parties may conclude agreements modifying or suspending the operation of provisions of this Convention, applicable solely to the relations between them, provided that such agreements do not relate to a provision derogation from which is incompatible with the effective execution of the object and purpose of this Convention, and provided further that such agreements shall not affect the application of the basic principles embodied herein, and that the provisions of such agreements do not affect the enjoyment by other States Parties of their rights or the performance of their obligations under this Convention.

4. States Parties intending to conclude an agreement referred to in paragraph 3 shall notify the other States Parties through the depositary of this Convention of their intention to conclude the agreement and of the modification or suspension for which it provides.

5. This article does not affect international agreements expressly permitted or preserved by other articles of this Convention.

6. States Parties agree that there shall be no amendments to the basic principle relating to the common heritage of mankind set forth in article 136 and that they shall not be party to any agreement in derogation thereof.

Article 312

Amendment

1. After the expiry of a period of 10 years from the date of entry into force of this Convention, a State Party may, by written communication addressed to the Secretary-General of the United Nations, propose specific amendments to this Convention, other than those relating to activities in the Area, and request the convening of a conference to consider such proposed amendments. The Secretary-General shall circulate such communication to all States Parties. If, within 12 months from the date of the circulation of the communication, not less than one half of the States Parties reply favourably to the request, the Secretary-General shall convene the conference.

2. The decision-making procedure applicable at the amendment conference shall be the same as that applicable at the Third United Nations Conference on the

Law of the Sea unless otherwise decided by the conference. The conference should make every effort to reach agreement on any amendments by way of consensus and there should be no voting on them until all efforts at consensus have been exhausted.

Article 313

Amendment by simplified procedure

1. A State Party may, by written communication addressed to the Secretary-General of the United Nations, propose an amendment to this Convention, other than an amendment relating to activities in the Area, to be adopted by the simplified procedure set forth in this article without convening a conference. The Secretary-General shall circulate the communication to all States Parties.

2. If, within a period of 12 months from the date of the circulation of the communication, a State Party objects to the proposed amendment or to the proposal for its adoption by the simplified procedure, the amendment shall be considered rejected. The Secretary-General shall immediately notify all States Parties accordingly.

3. If, 12 months from the date of the circulation of the communication, no State Party has objected to the proposed amendment or to the proposal for its adoption by the simplified procedure, the proposed amendment shall be considered adopted. The Secretary-General shall notify all States Parties that the proposed amendment has been adopted.

Article 314

Amendments to the provisions of this Convention relating exclusively to activities in the Area

1. A State Party may, by written communication addressed to the Secretary-General of the Authority, propose an amendment to the provisions of this Convention relating exclusively to activities in the Area, including Annex VI, section 4. The Secretary-General shall circulate such communication to all States Parties. The proposed amendment shall be subject to approval by the Assembly following its approval by the Council. Representatives of States Parties in those organs shall have full powers to consider and approve the proposed amendment. The proposed amendment as approved by the Council and the Assembly shall be considered adopted.

2. Before approving any amendment under paragraph 1, the Council and the Assembly shall ensure that it does not prejudice the system of exploration for and exploitation of the resources of the Area, pending the Review Conference in accordance with article 155.

Article 315

Signature, ratification of, accession to and authentic texts of amendments

1. Once adopted, amendments to this Convention shall be open for signature by States Parties for 12 months from the date of adoption, at United Nations Headquarters in New York, unless otherwise provided in the amendment itself.

2. Articles 306, 307 and 320 apply to all amendments to this Convention.

Article 316

Entry into force of amendments

1. Amendments to this Convention, other than those referred to in paragraph 5, shall enter into force for the States Parties ratifying or acceding to them on the thirtieth day following the deposit of instruments of ratification or accession by two thirds of the States Parties or by 60 States Parties, whichever is greater. Such amendments shall not affect the enjoyment by other States Parties of their rights or the performance of their obligations under this Convention.

2. An amendment may provide that a larger number of ratifications or accessions shall be required for its entry into force than are required by this article.

3. For each State Party ratifying or acceding to an amendment referred to in paragraph 1 after the deposit of the required number of instruments of ratification or accession, the amendment shall enter into force on the thirtieth day following the deposit of its instrument of ratification or accession.

4. A State which becomes a Party to this Convention after the entry into force of an amendment in accordance with paragraph 1 shall, failing an expression of a different intention by that State:

(a) be considered as a Party to this Convention as so amended; and

(b) be considered as a Party to the unamended Convention in relation to any State Party not bound by the amendment.

5. Any amendment relating exclusively to activities in the Area and any amendment to Annex VI shall enter into force for all States Parties one year following the deposit of instruments of ratification or accession by three fourths of the States Parties.

6. A State which becomes a Party to this Convention after the entry into force of amendments in accordance with paragraph 5 shall be considered as a Party to this Convention as so amended.

Article 317

Denunciation

1. A State Party may, by written notification addressed to the Secretary-General of the United Nations, denounce this Convention and may indicate its reasons. Failure to indicate reasons shall not affect the validity of the denunciation. The denunciation

shall take effect one year after the date of receipt of the notification, unless the notification specifies a later date.

2. A State shall not be discharged by reason of the denunciation from the financial and contractual obligations which accrued while it was a Party to this Convention, nor shall the denunciation affect any right, obligation or legal situation of that State created through the execution of this Convention prior to its termination for that State.

3. The denunciation shall not in any way affect the duty of any State Party to fulfil any obligation embodied in this Convention to which it would be subject under international law independently of this Convention.

Article 318

Status of Annexes

The Annexes form an integral part of this Convention and, unless expressly provided otherwise, a reference to this Convention or to one of its Parts includes a reference to the Annexes relating thereto.

Article 319

Depositary

1. The Secretary-General of the United Nations shall be the depositary of this Convention and amendments thereto.

2. In addition to his functions as depositary, the Secretary-General shall:

(a) report to all States Parties, the Authority and competent international organizations on issues of a general nature that have arisen with respect to this Convention;

(b) notify the Authority of ratifications and formal confirmations of and accessions to this Convention and amendments thereto, as well as of denunciations of this Convention;

(c) notify States Parties of agreements in accordance with article 311, paragraph 4;

(d) circulate amendments adopted in accordance with this Convention to States Parties for ratification or accession;

(e) convene necessary meetings of States Parties in accordance with this Convention.

3. (a) The Secretary-General shall also transmit to the observers referred to in article 156:

(i) reports referred to in paragraph 2(a);

(ii) notifications referred to in paragraph 2(b) and (c); and

(iii) texts of amendments referred to in paragraph 2(d), for their information.

(b) The Secretary-General shall also invite those observers to participate as observers at meetings of States Parties referred to in paragraph 2(e).

Article 320

Authentic texts

The original of this Convention, of which the Arabic, Chinese, English, French, Russian and Spanish texts are equally authentic, shall, subject to article 305, paragraph 2, be deposited with the Secretary-General of the United Nations.

IN WITNESS WHEREOF, the undersigned Plenipotentiaries, being duly authorized thereto, have signed this Convention.

DONE AT MONTEGO BAY, this tenth day of December, one thousand nine hundred and eighty-two.

Annex I Highly Migratory Species

1. Albacore tuna: *Thunnus alalunga.*
2. Bluefin tuna: *Thunnus thynnus.*
3. Bigeye tuna: *Thunnus obesus.*
4. Skipjack tuna: *Katsuwonus pelamis.*
5. Yellowfin tuna: *Thunnus albacares.*
6. Blackfin tuna: *Thunnus atlanticus.*
7. Little tuna: *Euthynnus alletteratus; Euthynnus affinis.*
8. Southern bluefin tuna: *Thunnus maccoyii.*
9. Frigate mackerel: *Auxis thazard; Auxis rochei.*
10. Pomfrets: Family *Bramidae.*
11. Marlins: *Tetrapturus angustirostris; Tetrapturus belone; Tetrapturus pfluegeri; Tetrapturus albidus; Tetrapturus audax; Tetrapturus georgei; Makaira mazara; Makaira indica; Makaira nigricans.*
12. Sail-fishes: *Istiophorus platypterus; Istiophorus albicans.*
13. Swordfish: *Xiphias gladius.*
14. Sauries: *Scomberesox saurus; Cololabis saira; Cololabis adocetus; Scomberesox saurus scombroides.*
15. Dolphin: *Coryphaena hippurus*; *Coryphaena equiselis.*
16. Oceanic sharks: *Hexanchus griseus*; *Cetorhinus maximus*; Family *Alopiidae*; *Rhincodon typus*; Family *Carcharhinidae*; Family *Sphyrnidae*; Family *Isurida.*
17. Cetaceans: Family *Physeteridae*; Family *Balaenopteridae*; Family *Balaenidae*; Family *Eschrichtiidae*; Family *Monodontidae*; Family *Ziphiidae*; Family *Delphinidae.*

Annex II Commission on the Limits of the Continental Shelf

Article 1

In accordance with the provisions of article 76, a Commission on the Limits of the Continental Shelf beyond 200 nautical miles shall be established in conformity with the following articles.

Article 2

1. The Commission shall consist of 21 members who shall be experts in the field of geology, geophysics or hydrography, elected by States Parties to this Convention from among their nationals, having due regard to the need to ensure equitable geographical representation, who shall serve in their personal capacities.

2. The initial election shall be held as soon as possible but in any case within 18 months after the date of entry into force of this Convention. At least three months before the date of each election, the Secretary-General of the United Nations shall address a letter to the States Parties, inviting the submission of nominations, after appropriate regional consultations, within three months. The Secretary-General shall prepare a list in alphabetical order of all persons thus nominated and shall submit it to all the States Parties.

3. Elections of the members of the Commission shall be held at a meeting of States Parties convened by the Secretary-General at United Nations Headquarters. At that meeting, for which two thirds of the States Parties shall constitute a quorum, the persons elected to the Commission shall be those nominees who obtain a two-thirds majority of the votes of the representatives of States Parties present and voting. Not less than three members shall be elected from each geographical region.

4. The members of the Commission shall be elected for a term of five years. They shall be eligible for re-election.

5. The State Party which submitted the nomination of a member of the Commission shall defray the expenses of that member while in performance of Commission duties. The coastal State concerned shall defray the expenses incurred in respect of the advice referred to in article 3, paragraph 1(b), of this Annex. The secretariat of the Commission shall be provided by the Secretary-General of the United Nations.

Article 3

1. The functions of the Commission shall be:

(a) to consider the data and other material submitted by coastal States concerning the outer limits of the continental shelf in areas where those limits extend beyond 200 nautical miles, and to make recommendations in accordance with article 76 and the Statement of Understanding adopted on 29 August 1980 by the Third United Nations Conference on the Law of the Sea;

(b) to provide scientific and technical advice, if requested by the coastal State concerned during the preparation of the data referred to in subparagraph (a).

2. The Commission may cooperate, to the extent considered necessary and useful, with the Intergovernmental Oceanographic Commission of UNESCO, the International Hydrographic Organization and other competent international organizations with a view to exchanging scientific and technical information which might be of assistance in discharging the Commission's responsibilities.

Article 4

Where a coastal State intends to establish, in accordance with article 76, the outer limits of its continental shelf beyond 200 nautical miles, it shall submit particulars of such limits to the Commission along with supporting scientific and technical data as soon as possible but in any case within 10 years of the entry into force of this Convention for that State. The coastal State shall at the same time give the names of any Commission members who have provided it with scientific and technical advice.

Article 5

Unless the Commission decides otherwise, the Commission shall function by way of sub-commissions composed of seven members, appointed in a balanced manner taking into account the specific elements of each submission by a coastal State. Nationals of the coastal State making the submission who are members of the Commission and any Commission member who has assisted a coastal State by providing scientific and technical advice with respect to the delineation shall not be a member of the sub-commission dealing with that submission but has the right to participate as a member in the proceedings of the Commission concerning the said submission. The coastal State which has made a submission to the Commission may send its representatives to participate in the relevant proceedings without the right to vote.

Article 6

1. The sub-commission shall submit its recommendations to the Commission.

2. Approval by the Commission of the recommendations of the sub-commission shall be by a majority of two thirds of Commission members present and voting.

3. The recommendations of the Commission shall be submitted in writing to the coastal State which made the submission and to the Secretary-General of the United Nations.

Article 7

Coastal States shall establish the outer limits of the continental shelf in conformity with the provisions of article 76, paragraph 8, and in accordance with the appropriate national procedures.

Article 8

In the case of disagreement by the coastal State with the recommendations of the Commission, the coastal State shall, within a reasonable time, make a revised or new submission to the Commission.

Article 9

The actions of the Commission shall not prejudice matters relating to delimitation of boundaries between States with opposite or adjacent coasts.

Annex III Basic Conditions of Prospecting, Exploration and Exploitation

Article 1

Title to minerals

Title to minerals shall pass upon recovery in accordance with this Convention.

Article 2

Prospecting

1. (a) The Authority shall encourage prospecting in the Area.

(b) Prospecting shall be conducted only after the Authority has received a satisfactory written undertaking that the proposed prospector will comply with this Convention and the relevant rules, regulations and procedures of the Authority concerning cooperation in the training programs referred to in articles 143 and 144 and the protection of the marine environment, and will accept verification by the Authority of compliance therewith. The proposed prospector shall, at the same time, notify the Authority of the approximate area or areas in which prospecting is to be conducted.

(c) Prospecting may be conducted simultaneously by more than one prospector in the same area or areas.

2. Prospecting shall not confer on the prospector any rights with respect to resources. A prospector may, however, recover a reasonable quantity of minerals to be used for testing.

Article 3

Exploration and exploitation

1. The Enterprise, States Parties, and the other entities referred to in article 153, paragraph 2(b), may apply to the Authority for approval of plans of work for activities in the Area.

2. The Enterprise may apply with respect to any part of the Area, but applications by others with respect to reserved areas are subject to the additional requirements of article 9 of this Annex.

3. Exploration and exploitation shall be carried out only in areas specified in plans of work referred to in article 153, paragraph 3, and approved by the Authority in accordance with this Convention and the relevant rules, regulations and procedures of the Authority.

4. Every approved plan of work shall:

(a) be in conformity with this Convention and the rules, regulations and procedures of the Authority;

(b) provide for control by the Authority of activities in the Area in accordance with article 153, paragraph 4;

(c) confer on the operator, in accordance with the rules, regulations and procedures of the Authority, the exclusive right to explore for and exploit the specified categories of resources in the area covered by the plan of work. If, however, the applicant presents for approval a plan of work covering only the stage of exploration or the stage of exploitation, the approved plan of work shall confer such exclusive right with respect to that stage only.

5. Upon its approval by the Authority, every plan of work, except those presented by the Enterprise, shall be in the form of a contract concluded between the Authority and the applicant or applicants.

Article 4

Qualifications of applicants

1. Applicants, other than the Enterprise, shall be qualified if they have the nationality or control and sponsorship required by article 153, paragraph 2(b), and if they follow the procedures and meet the qualification standards set forth in the rules, regulations and procedures of the Authority.

2. Except as provided in paragraph 6, such qualification standards shall relate to the financial and technical capabilities of the applicant and his performance under any previous contracts with the Authority.

3. Each applicant shall be sponsored by the State Party of which it is a national unless the applicant has more than one nationality, as in the case of a partnership or consortium of entities from several States, in which event all States Parties involved shall sponsor the application, or unless the applicant is effectively controlled by another State Party or its nationals, in which event both States Parties shall sponsor the application. The criteria and procedures for implementation of the sponsorship requirements shall be set forth in the rules, regulations and procedures of the Authority.

4. The sponsoring State or States shall, pursuant to article 139, have the responsibility to ensure, within their legal systems, that a contractor so sponsored shall carry out activities in the Area in conformity with the terms of its contract and its obligations under this Convention. A sponsoring State shall not, however, be liable for damage caused by any failure of a contractor sponsored by it to comply with its obligations if that State Party has adopted laws and regulations and taken administrative measures which are, within the framework of its legal system, reasonably appropriate for securing compliance by persons under its jurisdiction.

5. The procedures for assessing the qualifications of States Parties which are applicants shall take into account their character as States.

6. The qualification standards shall require that every applicant, without exception, shall as part of his application undertake:

(a) to accept as enforceable and comply with the applicable obligations created by the provisions of Part XI, the rules, regulations and procedures of the Authority, the decisions of the organs of the Authority and terms of his contracts with the Authority;

(b) to accept control by the Authority of activities in the Area, as authorized by this Convention;

(c) to provide the Authority with a written assurance that his obligations under the contract will be fulfilled in good faith;

(d) to comply with the provisions on the transfer of technology set forth in article 5 of this Annex.

Article 5

Transfer of technology

1. When submitting a plan of work, every applicant shall make available to the Authority a general description of the equipment and methods to be used in carrying out activities in the Area, and other relevant non-proprietary information about the characteristics of such technology and information as to where such technology is available.

2. Every operator shall inform the Authority of revisions in the description and information made available pursuant to paragraph 1 whenever a substantial technological change or innovation is introduced.

3. Every contract for carrying out activities in the Area shall contain the following undertakings by the contractor:

(a) to make available to the Enterprise on fair and reasonable commercial terms and conditions, whenever the Authority so requests, the technology which he uses in carrying out activities in the Area under the contract, which the contractor is legally entitled to transfer. This shall be done by means of licences or other appropriate arrangements which the contractor shall negotiate with the Enterprise and which shall be set forth in a specific agreement supplementary to the contract. This undertaking may be invoked only if the Enterprise finds that it is unable to obtain the same or equally efficient and useful technology on the open market on fair and reasonable commercial terms and conditions;

(b) to obtain a written assurance from the owner of any technology used in carrying out activities in the Area under the contract, which is not generally available on the open market and which is not covered by subparagraph (a), that the owner will, whenever the Authority so requests, make that technology available to the Enterprise under licence or other appropriate arrangements and on fair and reasonable commercial terms and conditions, to the same extent as made available to the contractor. If this assurance is not obtained, the technology in question shall not be used by the contractor in carrying out activities in the Area;

(c) to acquire from the owner by means of an enforceable contract, upon the request of the Enterprise and if it is possible to do so without substantial cost to the contractor, the legal right to transfer to the Enterprise any technology used by the contractor, in carrying out activities in the Area under the contract, which the contractor is otherwise not legally entitled to transfer and which is not generally available on the open market. In cases where there is a substantial corporate relationship between the contractor and the owner of the technology, the closeness of this relationship and the degree of control or influence shall be relevant to the determination whether all feasible measures have been taken to acquire such a right. In cases where the contractor exercises effective control over the owner, failure to acquire from the owner the legal right shall be considered relevant to the contractor's qualification for any subsequent application for approval of a plan of work;

(d) to facilitate, upon the request of the Enterprise, the acquisition by the Enterprise of any technology covered by subparagraph (b), under licence or other appropriate arrangements and on fair and reasonable commercial terms and conditions, if the Enterprise decides to negotiate directly with the owner of the technology;

(e) to take the same measures as are prescribed in subparagraphs (a), (b), (c) and (d) for the benefit of a developing State or group of developing States which has applied for a contract under article 9 of this Annex, provided that these measures shall be limited to the exploitation of the part of the area proposed by the contractor which has been reserved pursuant to article 8 of this Annex and provided that activities under the contract sought by the developing State or group of developing States would not involve transfer of technology to a third State or the nationals of a third State. The obligation under this provision shall only apply with respect to any given contractor where technology has not been requested by the Enterprise or transferred by that contractor to the Enterprise.

4. Disputes concerning undertakings required by paragraph 3, like other provisions of the contracts, shall be subject to compulsory settlement in accordance with Part XI and, in cases of violation of these undertakings, suspension or termination of the contract or monetary penalties may be ordered in accordance with article 18 of this Annex. Disputes as to whether offers made by the contractor are within the range of fair and reasonable commercial terms and conditions may be submitted by either party to binding commercial arbitration in accordance with the UNCITRAL Arbitration Rules or such other arbitration rules as may be prescribed in the rules, regulations and procedures of the Authority. If the finding is that the offer made by the contractor is not within the range of fair and reasonable commercial terms and conditions, the contractor shall be given 45 days to revise his offer to bring it within that range before the Authority takes any action in accordance with article 18 of this Annex.

5. If the Enterprise is unable to obtain on fair and reasonable commercial terms and conditions appropriate technology to enable it to commence in a timely manner

the recovery and processing of minerals from the Area, either the Council or the Assembly may convene a group of States Parties composed of those which are engaged in activities in the Area, those which have sponsored entities which are engaged in activities in the Area and other States Parties having access to such technology. This group shall consult together and shall take effective measures to ensure that such technology is made available to the Enterprise on fair and reasonable commercial terms and conditions. Each such State Party shall take all feasible measures to this end within its own legal system.

6. In the case of joint ventures with the Enterprise, transfer of technology will be in accordance with the terms of the joint venture agreement.

7. The undertakings required by paragraph 3 shall be included in each contract for the carrying out of activities in the Area until 10 years after the commencement of commercial production by the Enterprise, and may be invoked during that period.

8. For the purposes of this article, "technology" means the specialized equipment and technical know-how, including manuals, designs, operating instructions, training and technical advice and assistance, necessary to assemble, maintain and operate a viable system and the legal right to use these items for that purpose on a non-exclusive basis.

Article 6

Approval of plans of work

1. Six months after the entry into force of this Convention, and thereafter each fourth month, the Authority shall take up for consideration proposed plans of work.

2. When considering an application for approval of a plan of work in the form of a contract, the Authority shall first ascertain whether:

(a) the applicant has complied with the procedures established for applications in accordance with article 4 of this Annex and has given the Authority the undertakings and assurances required by that article. In cases of non-compliance with these procedures or in the absence of any of these undertakings and assurances, the applicant shall be given 45 days to remedy these defects;

(b) the applicant possesses the requisite qualifications provided for in article 4 of this Annex.

3. All proposed plans of work shall be taken up in the order in which they are received. The proposed plans of work shall comply with and be governed by the relevant provisions of this Convention and the rules, regulations and procedures of the Authority, including those on operational requirements, financial contributions and the undertakings concerning the transfer of technology. If the proposed plans of work conform to these requirements, the Authority shall approve them provided that they are in accordance with the uniform and non-discriminatory requirements set forth in the rules, regulations and procedures of the Authority, unless:

(a) part or all of the area covered by the proposed plan of work is included in an approved plan of work or a previously submitted proposed plan of work which has not yet been finally acted on by the Authority;

(b) part or all of the area covered by the proposed plan of work is disapproved by the Authority pursuant to article 162, paragraph 2(x); or

(c) the proposed plan of work has been submitted or sponsored by a State Party which already holds:

(i) plans of work for exploration and exploitation of polymetallic nodules in non-reserved areas that, together with either part of the area covered by the application for a plan of work, exceed in size 30 per cent of a circular area of 400,000 square kilometres surrounding the centre of either part of the area covered by the proposed plan of work;

(ii) plans of work for the exploration and exploitation of polymetallic nodules in non-reserved areas which, taken together, constitute 2 per cent of the total seabed area which is not reserved or disapproved for exploitation pursuant to article 162, paragraph (2)(x).

4. For the purpose of the standard set forth in paragraph 3(c), a plan of work submitted by a partnership or consortium shall be counted on a *pro rata* basis among the sponsoring States Parties involved in accordance with article 4, paragraph 3, of this Annex. The Authority may approve plans of work covered by paragraph 3(c) if it determines that such approval would not permit a State Party or entities sponsored by it to monopolize the conduct of activities in the Area or to preclude other States Parties from activities in the Area.

5. Notwithstanding paragraph 3(a), after the end of the interim period specified in article 151, paragraph 3, the Authority may adopt by means of rules, regulations and procedures other procedures and criteria consistent with this Convention for deciding which applicants shall have plans of work approved in cases of selection among applicants for a proposed area. These procedures and criteria shall ensure approval of plans of work on an equitable and non-discriminatory basis.

Article 7

Selection among applicants for production authorizations

1. Six months after the entry into force of this Convention, and thereafter each fourth month, the Authority shall take up for consideration applications for production authorizations submitted during the immediately preceding period. The Authority shall issue the authorizations applied for if all such applications can be approved without exceeding the production limitation or contravening the obligations of the Authority under a commodity agreement or arrangement to which it has become a party, as provided in article 151.

2. When a selection must be made among applicants for production authorizations because of the production limitation set forth in article 151, paragraphs 2 to 7, or because of the obligations of the Authority under a commodity agreement or arrangement to which it has become a party, as provided for in article 151, paragraph 1, the Authority shall make the selection on the basis of objective and non-discriminatory standards set forth in its rules, regulations and procedures.

3. In the application of paragraph 2, the Authority shall give priority to those applicants which:

(a) give better assurance of performance, taking into account their financial and technical qualifications and their performance, if any, under previously approved plans of work;

(b) provide earlier prospective financial benefits to the Authority, taking into account when commercial production is scheduled to begin;

(c) have already invested the most resources and effort in prospecting or exploration.

4. Applicants which are not selected in any period shall have priority in subsequent periods until they receive a production authorization.

5. Selection shall be made taking into account the need to enhance opportunities for all States Parties, irrespective of their social and economic systems or geographical locations so as to avoid discrimination against any State or system, to participate in activities in the Area and to prevent monopolization of those activities.

6. Whenever fewer reserved areas than non-reserved areas are under exploitation, applications for production authorizations with respect to reserved areas shall have priority.

7. The decisions referred to in this article shall be taken as soon as possible after the close of each period.

Article 8
Reservation of areas

Each application, other than those submitted by the Enterprise or by any other entities for reserved areas, shall cover a total area, which need not be a single continuous area, sufficiently large and of sufficient estimated commercial value to allow two mining operations. The applicant shall indicate the coordinates dividing the area into two parts of equal estimated commercial value and submit all the data obtained by him with respect to both parts. Without prejudice to the powers of the Authority pursuant to article 17 of this Annex, the data to be submitted concerning polymetallic nodules shall relate to mapping, sampling, the abundance of nodules, and their metal content. Within 45 days of receiving such data, the Authority shall designate which part is to be reserved solely for the conduct of activities by the Authority through the Enterprise or in association with developing States. This designation may be deferred for a further period of 45 days if the Authority requests an independent expert to assess whether all data required by this article has been submitted. The area designated shall become a reserved area as soon as the plan of work for the non-reserved area is approved and the contract is signed.

Article 9

Activities in reserved areas

1. The Enterprise shall be given an opportunity to decide whether it intends to carry out activities in each reserved area. This decision may be taken at any time, unless a notification pursuant to paragraph 4 is received by the Authority, in which event the Enterprise shall take its decision within a reasonable time. The Enterprise may decide to exploit such areas in joint ventures with the interested State or entity.

2. The Enterprise may conclude contracts for the execution of part of its activities in accordance with Annex IV, article 12. It may also enter into joint ventures for the conduct of such activities with any entities which are eligible to carry out activities in the Area pursuant to article 153, paragraph 2(b). When considering such joint ventures, the Enterprise shall offer to States Parties which are developing States and their nationals the opportunity of effective participation.

3. The Authority may prescribe, in its rules, regulations and procedures, substantive and procedural requirements and conditions with respect to such contracts and joint ventures.

4. Any State Party which is a developing State or any natural or juridical person sponsored by it and effectively controlled by it or by other developing State which is a qualified applicant, or any group of the foregoing, may notify the Authority that it wishes to submit a plan of work pursuant to article 6 of this Annex with respect to a reserved area. The plan of work shall be considered if the Enterprise decides, pursuant to paragraph 1, that it does not intend to carry out activities in that area.

Article 10

Preference and priority among applicants

An operator who has an approved plan of work for exploration only, as provided in article 3, paragraph 4(c), of this Annex shall have a preference and a priority among applicants for a plan of work covering exploitation of the same area and resources. However, such preference or priority may be withdrawn if the operator's performance has not been satisfactory.

Article 11

Joint arrangements

1. Contracts may provide for joint arrangements between the contractor and the Authority through the Enterprise, in the form of joint ventures or production sharing,

as well as any other form of joint arrangement, which shall have the same protection against revision, suspension or termination as contracts with the Authority.

2. Contractors entering into such joint arrangements with the Enterprise may receive financial incentives as provided for in article 13 of this Annex.

3. Partners in joint ventures with the Enterprise shall be liable for the payments required by article 13 of this Annex to the extent of their share in the joint ventures, subject to financial incentives as provided for in that article.

Article 12

Activities carried out by the Enterprise

1. Activities in the Area carried out by the Enterprise pursuant to article 153, paragraph 2(a), shall be governed by Part XI, the rules, regulations and procedures of the Authority and its relevant decisions.

2. Any plan of work submitted by the Enterprise shall be accompanied by evidence supporting its financial and technical capabilities.

Article 13

Financial terms of contracts

1. In adopting rules, regulations and procedures concerning the financial terms of a contract between the Authority and the entities referred to in article 153, paragraph 2(b), and in negotiating those financial terms in accordance with Part XI and those rules, regulations and procedures, the Authority shall be guided by the following objectives:

(a) to ensure optimum revenues for the Authority from the proceeds of commercial production;

(b) to attract investments and technology to the exploration and exploitation of the Area;

(c) to ensure equality of financial treatment and comparable financial obligations for contractors;

(d) to provide incentives on a uniform and non-discriminatory basis for contractors to undertake joint arrangements with the Enterprise and developing States or their nationals, to stimulate the transfer of technology thereto, and to train the personnel of the Authority and of developing States;

(e) to enable the Enterprise to engage in seabed mining effectively at the same time as the entities referred to in article 153, paragraph 2(b); and

(f) to ensure that, as a result of the financial incentives provided to contractors under paragraph 14, under the terms of contracts reviewed in accordance with article 19 of this Annex or under the provisions of article 11 of this Annex with respect to joint ventures, contractors are not subsidized so as to be given an artificial competitive advantage with respect to land-based miners.

2. A fee shall be levied for the administrative cost of processing an application for approval of a plan of work in the form of a contract and shall be fixed at an amount of $US 500,000 per application. The amount of the fee shall be reviewed from time to time by the Council in order to ensure that it covers the administrative cost incurred. If such administrative cost incurred by the Authority in processing an application is less than the fixed amount, the Authority shall refund the difference to the applicant.

3. A contractor shall pay an annual fixed fee of $US 1 million from the date of entry into force of the contract. If the approved date of commencement of commercial production is postponed because of a delay in issuing the production authorization, in accordance with article 151, the annual fixed fee shall be waived for the period of postponement. From the date of commencement of commercial production, the contractor shall pay either the production charge or the annual fixed fee, whichever is greater.

4. Within a year of the date of commencement of commercial production, in conformity with paragraph 3, a contractor shall choose to make his financial contribution to the Authority by either:

(a) paying a production charge only; or

(b) paying a combination of a production charge and a share of net proceeds.

5. (a) If a contractor chooses to make his financial contribution to the Authority by paying a production charge only, it shall be fixed at a percentage of the market value of the processed metals produced from the polymetallic nodules recovered from the area covered by the contract. This percentage shall be fixed as follows:

(i) years 1–10 of commercial production 5 per cent

(ii) years 11 to the end of commercial production 12 per cent

(b) The said market value shall be the product of the quantity of the processed metals produced from the polymetallic nodules extracted from the area covered by the contract and the average price for those metals during the relevant accounting year, as defined in paragraphs 7 and 8.

6. If a contractor chooses to make his financial contribution to the Authority by paying a combination of a production charge and a share of net proceeds, such payments shall be determined as follows:

(a) The production charge shall be fixed at a percentage of the market value, determined in accordance with subpara-graph (b), of the processed metals produced from the polymetallic nodules recovered from the area covered by the contract. This percentage shall be fixed as follows:

(i) first period of commercial production 2 per cent

(ii) second period of commercial production 4 per cent

If, in the second period of commercial production, as defined in subparagraph (d), the return on investment in any accounting year as defined in subparagraph (m) falls below 15 per cent as a result of the payment of the production charge at 4 per cent, the production charge shall be 2 per cent instead of 4 per cent in that accounting year.

(b) The said market value shall be the product of the quantity of the processed metals produced from the polymetallic nodules recovered from the area covered by the contract and the average price for those metals during the relevant accounting year as defined in paragraphs 7 and 8.

(c) (i) The Authority's share of net proceeds shall be taken out of that portion of the contractor's net proceeds which is attributable to the mining of the resources of the area covered by the contract, referred to hereinafter as attributable net proceeds.

(ii) The Authority's share of attributable net proceeds shall be determined in accordance with the following incremental schedule:

Portion of attributable net proceeds	*Share of the Authority*	
	First period of commercial production	*Second period of commercial production*
That portion representing a return on investment which is greater than 0 per cent, but less than 10 per cent	35 per cent	40 per cent
That portion representing a return on investment which is 10 per cent or greater, but less than 20 per cent	42.5 per cent	50 per cent
That portion representing a return on investment which is 20 per cent or greater	50 per cent	70 per cent

(d) (i) The first period of commercial production referred to in subparagraphs (a) and (c) shall commence in the first accounting year of commercial production and terminate in the accounting year in which the contractor's development costs with interest on the unrecovered portion thereof are fully recovered by his cash surplus, as follows:

In the first accounting year during which development costs are incurred, unrecovered development costs shall equal the development costs less cash surplus in that year. In each subsequent accounting year, unrecovered development costs shall equal the unrecovered development costs at the end of the preceding accounting year, plus interest thereon at the rate of

10 per cent per annum, plus development costs incurred in the current accounting year and less contractor's cash surplus in the current accounting year. The accounting year in which unrecovered development costs become zero for the first time shall be the accounting year in which the contractor's development costs with interest on the unrecovered portion thereof are fully recovered by his cash surplus. The contractor's cash surplus in any accounting year shall be his gross proceeds less his operating costs and less his payments to the Authority under subparagraph (c).

(ii) The second period of commercial production shall commence in the accounting year following the termination of the first period of commercial production and shall continue until the end of the contract.

(e) "Attributable net proceeds" means the product of the contractor's net proceeds and the ratio of the development costs in the mining sector to the contractor's development costs. If the contractor engages in mining, transporting polymetallic nodules and production primarily of three processed metals, namely, cobalt, copper and nickel, the amount of attributable net proceeds shall not be less than 25 per cent of the contractor's net proceeds. Subject to subparagraph (n), in all other cases, including those where the contractor engages in mining, transporting polymetallic nodules, and production primarily of four processed metals, namely, cobalt, copper, manganese and nickel, the Authority may, in its rules, regulations and procedures, prescribe appropriate floors which shall bear the same relationship to each case as the 25 per cent floor does to the three-metal case.

(f) "Contractor's net proceeds" means the contractor's gross proceeds less his operating costs and less the recovery of his development costs as set out in subparagraph (j).

(g) (i) If the contractor engages in mining, transporting polymetallic nodules and production of processed metals, "contractor's gross proceeds" means the gross revenues from the sale of the processed metals and any other monies deemed reasonably attributable to operations under the contract in accordance with the financial rules, regulations and procedures of the Authority.

(ii) In all cases other than those specified in subparagraphs (g)(i) and (n)(iii), "contractor's gross proceeds" means the gross revenues from the sale of the semi-processed metals from the polymetallic nodules recovered from the area covered by the contract, and any other monies deemed reasonably attributable to operations under the contract in accordance with the financial rules, regulations and procedures of the Authority.

(h) "Contractor's development costs" means:

(i) all expenditures incurred prior to the commencement of commercial production which are directly related to the development of the productive capacity of the area covered by the contract and the activities related thereto for operations under the contract in all cases other than that specified in subparagraph (n), in conformity with generally recognized accounting principles, including, *inter alia*, costs of machinery, equipment, ships, processing plant, construction, buildings, land, roads, prospecting and exploration of the area covered by the contract, research and development, interest, required leases, licences and fees; and

(ii) expenditures similar to those set forth in (i) above incurred subsequent to the commencement of commercial production and necessary to carry out the plan of work, except those chargeable to operating costs.

(i) The proceeds from the disposal of capital assets and the market value of those capital assets which are no longer required for operations under the contract and which are not sold shall be deducted from the contractor's development costs during the relevant accounting year. When these deductions exceed the contractor's development costs the excess shall be added to the contractor's gross proceeds.

(j) The contractor's development costs incurred prior to the commencement of commercial production referred to in subparagraphs (h)(i) and (n)(iv) shall be recovered in 10 equal annual instalments from the date of commencement of commercial production. The contractor's development costs incurred subsequent to the commencement of commercial production referred to in subparagraphs (h)(ii) and (n)(iv) shall be recovered in 10 or fewer equal annual instalments so as to ensure their complete recovery by the end of the contract.

(k) "Contractor's operating costs" means all expenditures incurred after the commencement of commercial production in the operation of the productive capacity of the area covered by the contract and the activities related thereto for operations under the contract, in conformity with generally recognized accounting principles, including, *inter alia*, the annual fixed fee or the production charge, whichever is greater, expenditures for wages, salaries, employee benefits, materials, services, transporting, processing and marketing costs, interest, utilities, preservation of the marine environment, overhead and administrative costs specifically related to operations under the contract, and any net operating losses carried forward or backward as specified herein. Net operating losses may be carried forward for two consecutive years except in the last two years of the contract in which case they may be carried backward to the two preceding years.

(l) If the contractor engages in mining, transporting of polymetallic nodules, and production of processed and semi-processed metals, "development costs of the mining sector" means the portion of the contractor's development costs which is directly related to the mining of the resources of the area covered by the contract, in conformity with generally recognized accounting principles, and the financial rules, regulations and procedures of the Authority, including, *inter alia*, application fee, annual fixed fee and, where applicable, costs of prospecting and exploration of the area covered by the contract, and a portion of research and development costs.

(m) "Return on investment" in any accounting year means the ratio of attributable net proceeds in that year to the development costs of the mining sector. For the purpose of computing this ratio the development costs of the mining sector shall include expenditures on new or replacement equipment in the mining sector less the original cost of the equipment replaced.

(n) If the contractor engages in mining only:

(i) "attributable net proceeds" means the whole of the contractor's net proceeds;

(ii) "contractor's net proceeds" shall be as defined in subparagraph (f);

(iii) "contractor's gross proceeds" means the gross revenues from the sale of the polymetallic nodules, and any other monies deemed reasonably attributable to operations under the contract in accordance with the financial rules, regulations and procedures of the Authority;

(iv) "contractor's development costs" means all expenditures incurred prior to the commencement of commercial production as set forth in subparagraph (h)(i), and all expenditures incurred subsequent to the commencement of commercial production as set forth in subparagraph (h)(ii), which are directly related to the mining of the resources of the area covered by the contract, in conformity with generally recognized accounting principles;

(v) "contractor's operating costs" means the contractor's operating costs as in subparagraph (k) which are directly related to the mining of the resources of the area covered by the contract in conformity with generally recognized accounting principles;

(vi) "return on investment" in any accounting year means the ratio of the contractor's net proceeds in that year to the contractor's development costs. For the purpose of computing this ratio, the contractor's development costs shall include expenditures on new or replacement equipment less the original cost of the equipment replaced.

(o) The costs referred to in subparagraphs (h), (k), (l) and (n) in respect of interest paid by the contractor shall be allowed to the extent that, in all the circumstances, the Authority approves, pursuant to article 4, paragraph 1, of this Annex, the debt-equity ratio and the rates of interest as reasonable, having regard to existing commercial practice.

(p) The costs referred to in this paragraph shall not be interpreted as including payments of corporate income taxes or similar charges levied by States in respect of the operations of the contractor.

7. (a) "Processed metals", referred to in paragraphs 5 and 6, means the metals in the most basic form in which they are customarily traded on international terminal markets. For this purpose, the Authority shall specify, in its financial rules, regulations and procedures, the relevant international terminal market. For the metals which are not traded on such markets, "processed metals" means the metals in the most basic form in which they are customarily traded in representative arm's length transactions.

(b) If the Authority cannot otherwise determine the quantity of the processed metals produced from the polymetallic nodules recovered from the area covered by the contract referred to in paragraphs 5(b) and 6(b), the quantity shall be determined on the basis of the metal content of the nodules, processing recovery efficiency and other relevant factors, in accordance with the rules, regulations and procedures of the Authority and in conformity with generally recognized accounting principles.

8. If an international terminal market provides a representative pricing mechanism for processed metals, polymetallic nodules and semi-processed metals from the nodules, the average price on that market shall be used. In all other cases, the Authority shall, after consulting the contractor, determine a fair price for the said products in accordance with paragraph 9.

9. (a) All costs, expenditures, proceeds and revenues and all determinations of price and value referred to in this article shall be the result of free market or arm's length transactions. In the absence thereof, they shall be determined by the Authority, after consulting the contractor, as though they were the result of free market or arm's length transactions, taking into account relevant transactions in other markets.

(b) In order to ensure compliance with and enforcement of the provisions of this paragraph, the Authority shall be guided by the principles adopted for, and the interpretation given to, arm's length transactions by the Commission on Transnational Corporations of the United Nations, the Group of Experts on Tax Treaties between Developing and Developed Countries and other international organizations, and shall, in its rules, regulations and procedures, specify uniform and internationally acceptable accounting rules and procedures, and the means of selection by the contractor of certified independent accountants acceptable to the Authority for the purpose of carrying out auditing in compliance with those rules, regulations and procedures.

10. The contractor shall make available to the accountants, in accordance with the financial rules, regulations and procedures of the Authority, such financial data as are required to determine compliance with this article.

11. All costs, expenditures, proceeds and revenues, and all prices and values referred to in this article, shall be determined in accordance with generally recognized accounting principles and the financial rules, regulations and procedures of the Authority.

12. Payments to the Authority under paragraphs 5 and 6 shall be made in freely usable currencies or currencies which are freely available and effectively usable on the major foreign exchange markets or, at the contractor's option, in the equivalents of processed metals at market value. The market value shall be determined in accordance with paragraph 5(b). The freely usable currencies and currencies which are freely available and effectively usable on the major foreign exchange markets shall be defined in the rules, regulations and procedures of the Authority in accordance with prevailing international monetary practice.

13. All financial obligations of the contractor to the Authority, as well as all his fees, costs, expenditures, proceeds and revenues referred to in this article, shall be adjusted by expressing them in constant terms relative to a base year.

14. The Authority may, taking into account any recommendations of the Economic Planning Commission and the Legal and Technical Commission, adopt rules, regulations and procedures that provide for incentives, on a uniform and non-discriminatory basis, to contractors to further the objectives set out in paragraph 1.

15. In the event of a dispute between the Authority and a contractor over the interpretation or application of the financial terms of a contract, either party may submit the dispute to binding commercial arbitration, unless both parties agree to settle the dispute by other means, in accordance with article 188, paragraph 2.

Article 14
Transfer of data

1. The operator shall transfer to the Authority, in accordance with its rules, regulations and procedures and the terms and conditions of the plan of work, at time intervals determined by the Authority all data which are both necessary for and relevant to the effective exercise of the powers and functions of the principal organs of the Authority in respect of the area covered by the plan of work.

2. Transferred data in respect of the area covered by the plan of work, deemed proprietary, may only be used for the purposes set forth in this article. Data necessary for the formulation by the Authority of rules, regulations and procedures concerning protection of the marine environment and safety, other than equipment design data, shall not be deemed proprietary.

3. Data transferred to the Authority by prospectors, applicants for contracts or contractors, deemed proprietary, shall not be disclosed by the Authority to the Enterprise or to anyone external to the Authority, but data on the reserved areas may be disclosed to the Enterprise. Such data transferred by such persons to the Enterprise shall not be disclosed by the Enterprise to the Authority or to anyone external to the Authority.

Article 15

Training programmes

The contractor shall draw up practical programmes for the training of personnel of the Authority and developing States, including the participation of such personnel in all activities in the Area which are covered by the contract, in accordance with article 144, paragraph 2.

Article 16

Exclusive right to explore and exploit

The Authority shall, pursuant to Part XI and its rules, regulations and procedures, accord the operator the exclusive right to explore and exploit the area covered by the plan of work in respect of a specified category of resources and shall ensure that no other entity operates in the same area for a different category of resources in a manner which might interfere with the operations of the operator. The operator shall have security of tenure in accordance with article 153, paragraph 6.

Article 17

Rules, regulations and procedures of the Authority

1. The Authority shall adopt and uniformly apply rules, regulations and procedures in accordance with article 160, paragraph 2(f)(ii), and article 162, paragraph 2(o)(ii), for the exercise of its functions as set forth in Part XI on, *inter alia*, the following matters:

(a) administrative procedures relating to prospecting, exploration and exploitation in the Area;

(b) operations:

(i) size of area;

(ii) duration of operations;

(iii) performance requirements including assurances pursuant to article 4, paragraph 6(c), of this Annex;

(iv) categories of resources;

(v) renunciation of areas;

(vi) progress reports;

(vii) submission of data;

(viii) inspection and supervision of operations;

(ix) prevention of interference with other activities in the marine environment;

(x) transfer of rights and obligations by a contractor;

(xi) procedures for transfer of technology to developing States in accordance with article 144 and for their direct participation;

(xii) mining standards and practices, including those relating to operational safety, conservation of the resources and the protection of the marine environment;

(xiii) definition of commercial production;

(xiv) qualification standards for applicants;

(c) financial matters:

(i) establishment of uniform and non-discriminatory costing and accounting rules and the method of selection of auditors;

(ii) apportionment of proceeds of operations;

(iii) the incentives referred to in article 13 of this Annex;

(d) implementation of decisions taken pursuant to article 151, paragraph 10, and article 164, paragraph 2(d).

2. Rules, regulations and procedures on the following items shall fully reflect the objective criteria set out below:

(a) Size of areas:

The Authority shall determine the appropriate size of areas for exploration which may be up to twice as large as those for exploitation in order to permit intensive exploration operations. The size of area shall be calculated to satisfy the requirements of article 8 of this Annex on reservation of areas as well as stated production requirements consistent with article 151 in accordance with the terms of the contract taking into account the state of the art of technology then available for seabed mining and the relevant physical characteristics of the areas. Areas shall be neither smaller nor larger than are necessary to satisfy this objective.

(b) Duration of operations:

(i) Prospecting shall be without time-limit;

(ii) Exploration should be of sufficient duration to permit a thorough survey of the specific area, the design and construction of mining equipment for the area and the design and construction of small and medium-size processing plants for the purpose of testing mining and processing systems;

(iii) The duration of exploitation should be related to the economic life of the mining project, taking into consideration such factors as the depletion of the ore, the useful life of mining equipment and processing facilities and commercial viability. Exploitation should be of sufficient duration to permit commercial extraction of minerals of the area and should include a reasonable time period for construction of commercial-scale mining and processing systems, during which period commercial production should not be required. The total duration of exploitation, however, should also be short enough to give the Authority an opportunity to amend the terms and conditions of the plan of work at the time it considers renewal in accordance with rules, regulations and procedures which it has adopted subsequent to approving the plan of work.

(c) Performance requirements:

The Authority shall require that during the exploration stage periodic expenditures be made by the operator which are reasonably related to the size of the area covered by the plan of work and the expenditures which would be expected of a *bona fide* operator who intended to bring the area into commercial production within the time-limits established by the Authority. The required expenditures should not be established at a level which would discourage prospective operators with less costly technology than is prevalently in use. The Authority shall establish a maximum time interval, after the exploration stage is completed and the exploitation stage begins, to achieve commercial production. To determine this interval, the Authority should take into consideration that construction of large-scale mining and processing systems cannot be initiated until after the termination of the exploration stage and the commencement of the exploitation stage. Accordingly, the interval to bring an area into commercial production should take into account the time necessary for this construction after the completion of the exploration stage and reasonable allowance should be made for unavoidable delays in the construction schedule. Once commercial production is achieved, the Authority shall within reasonable limits and taking into consideration all relevant factors require the operator to maintain commercial production throughout the period of the plan of work.

(d) Categories of resources:

In determining the category of resources in respect of which a plan of work may be approved, the Authority shall give emphasis *inter alia* to the following characteristics:

(i) that certain resources require the use of similar mining methods; and

(ii) that some resources can be developed simultaneously without undue interference between operators developing different resources in the same area.

Nothing in this subparagraph shall preclude the Authority from approving a plan of work with respect to more than one category of resources in the same area to the same applicant.

(e) Renunciation of areas:

The operator shall have the right at any time to renounce without penalty the whole or part of his rights in the area covered by a plan of work.

(f) Protection of the marine environment:

Rules, regulations and procedures shall be drawn up in order to secure effective protection of the marine environment from harmful effects directly resulting from activities in the Area or from shipboard processing immediately above a mine site of minerals derived from that mine site, taking into account the extent to which such harmful effects may directly result from drilling, dredging, coring and excavation and from disposal, dumping and discharge into the marine environment of sediment, wastes or other effluents.

(g) Commercial production:

Commercial production shall be deemed to have begun if an operator engages in sustained large-scale recovery operations which yield a quantity of materials sufficient to indicate clearly that the principal purpose is large-scale production rather than production intended for information gathering, analysis or the testing of equipment or plant.

Article 18

Penalties

1. A contractor's rights under the contract may be suspended or terminated only in the following cases:

(a) if, in spite of warnings by the Authority, the contractor has conducted his activities in such a way as to result in serious, persistent and wilful violations of the fundamental terms of the contract, Part XI and the rules, regulations and procedures of the Authority; or

(b) if the contractor has failed to comply with a final binding decision of the dispute settlement body applicable to him.

2. In the case of any violation of the contract not covered by paragraph 1(a), or in lieu of suspension or termination under paragraph 1(a), the Authority may impose upon the contractor monetary penalties proportionate to the seriousness of the violation.

3. Except for emergency orders under article 162, paragraph 2(w), the Authority may not execute a decision involving monetary penalties, suspension or termination until the contractor has been accorded a reasonable opportunity to exhaust the judicial remedies available to him pursuant to Part XI, section 5.

Article 19

Revision of contract

1. When circumstances have arisen or are likely to arise which, in the opinion of either party, would render the contract inequitable or make it impracticable or impossible to achieve the objectives set out in the contract or in Part XI, the parties shall enter into negotiations to revise it accordingly.

2. Any contract entered into in accordance with article 153, paragraph 3, may be revised only with the consent of the parties.

Article 20

Transfer of rights and obligations

The rights and obligations arising under a contract may be transferred only with the consent of the Authority, and in accordance with its rules, regulations and procedures. The Authority shall not unreasonably withhold consent to the transfer if the proposed transferee is in all respects a qualified applicant and assumes all of the obligations of the transferor and if the transfer does not confer to the transferee a plan of work, the approval of which would be forbidden by article 6, paragraph 3(c), of this Annex.

Article 21

Applicable law

1. The contract shall be governed by the terms of the contract, the rules, regulations and procedures of the Authority, Part XI and other rules of international law not incompatible with this Convention.

2. Any final decision rendered by a court or tribunal having jurisdiction under this Convention relating to the rights and obligations of the Authority and of the contractor shall be enforceable in the territory of each State Party.

3. No State Party may impose conditions on a contractor that are inconsistent with Part XI. However, the application by a State Party to contractors sponsored by it, or to ships flying its flag, of environmental or other laws and regulations more stringent than those in the rules, regulations and procedures of the Authority adopted pursuant to article 17, paragraph 2(f), of this Annex shall not be deemed inconsistent with Part XI.

Article 22

Responsibility

The contractor shall have responsibility or liability for any damage arising out of wrongful acts in the conduct of its operations, account being taken of contributory acts or omissions by the Authority. Similarly, the Authority shall have responsibility or liability for any damage arising out of wrongful acts in the exercise of its powers and functions, including violations under article 168, paragraph 2, account being taken of contributory acts or omissions by the contractor. Liability in every case shall be for the actual amount of damage.

Annex IV Statute of the Enterprise

Article 1
Purposes

1. The Enterprise is the organ of the Authority which shall carry out activities in the Area directly, pursuant to article 153, paragraph 2(a), as well as the transporting, processing and marketing of minerals recovered from the Area.

2. In carrying out its purposes and in the exercise of its functions, the Enterprise shall act in accordance with this Convention and the rules, regulations and procedures of the Authority.

3. In developing the resources of the Area pursuant to paragraph 1, the Enterprise shall, subject to this Convention, operate in accordance with sound commercial principles.

Article 2
Relationship to the Authority

1. Pursuant to article 170, the Enterprise shall act in accordance with the general policies of the Assembly and the directives of the Council.

2. Subject to paragraph l, the Enterprise shall enjoy autonomy in the conduct of its operations.

3. Nothing in this Convention shall make the Enterprise liable for the acts or obligations of the Authority, or make the Authority liable for the acts or obligations of the Enterprise.

Article 3
Limitation of liability

Without prejudice to article 11, paragraph 3, of this Annex, no member of the Authority shall be liable by reason only of its membership for the acts or obligations of the Enterprise.

Article 4
Structure

The Enterprise shall have a Governing Board, a Director-General and the staff necessary for the exercise of its functions.

Article 5
Governing Board

1. The Governing Board shall be composed of 15 members elected by the Assembly in accordance with article 160, paragraph 2(c). In the election of the members of the Board, due regard shall be paid to the principle of equitable geographical distribution. In submitting nominations of candidates for election to the Board, members of the

Authority shall bear in mind the need to nominate candidates of the highest standard of competence, with qualifications in relevant fields, so as to ensure the viability and success of the Enterprise.

2. Members of the Board shall be elected for four years and may be re-elected; and due regard shall be paid to the principle of rotation of membership.

3. Members of the Board shall continue in office until their successors are elected. If the office of a member of the Board becomes vacant, the Assembly shall, in accordance with article 160, paragraph 2(c), elect a new member for the remainder of his predecessor's term.

4. Members of the Board shall act in their personal capacity. In the performance of their duties they shall not seek or receive instructions from any government or from any other source. Each member of the Authority shall respect the independent character of the members of the Board and shall refrain from all attempts to influence any of them in the discharge of their duties.

5. Each member of the Board shall receive remuneration to be paid out of the funds of the Enterprise. The amount of remuneration shall be fixed by the Assembly, upon the recommendation of the Council.

6. The Board shall normally function at the principal office of the Enterprise and shall meet as often as the business of the Enterprise may require.

7. Two thirds of the members of the Board shall constitute a quorum.

8. Each member of the Board shall have one vote. All matters before the Board shall be decided by a majority of its members. If a member has a conflict of interest on a matter before the Board he shall refrain from voting on that matter.

9. Any member of the Authority may ask the Board for information in respect of its operations which particularly affect that member. The Board shall endeavour to provide such information.

Article 6

Powers and functions of the Governing Board

The Governing Board shall direct the operations of the Enterprise. Subject to this Convention, the Governing Board shall exercise the powers necessary to fulfil the purposes of the Enterprise, including powers:

(a) to elect a Chairman from among its members;

(b) to adopt its rules of procedure;

(c) to draw up and submit formal written plans of work to the Council in accordance with article 153, paragraph 3, and article 162, paragraph 2(j);

(d) to develop plans of work and programmes for carrying out the activities specified in article 170;

(e) to prepare and submit to the Council applications for production authorizations in accordance with article 151, paragraphs 2 to 7;

(f) to authorize negotiations concerning the acquisition of technology, including those provided for in Annex III, article 5, paragraph 3(a), (c) and (d), and to approve the results of those negotiations;

(g) to establish terms and conditions, and to authorize negotiations, concerning joint ventures and other forms of joint arrangements referred to in Annex III, articles 9 and 11, and to approve the results of such negotiations;

(h) to recommend to the Assembly what portion of the net income of the Enterprise should be retained as its reserves in accordance with article 160, paragraph 2(f), and article 10 of this Annex;

(i) to approve the annual budget of the Enterprise;

(j) to authorize the procurement of goods and services in accordance with article 12, paragraph 3, of this Annex;

(k) to submit an annual report to the Council in accordance with article 9 of this Annex;

(l) to submit to the Council for the approval of the Assembly draft rules in respect of the organization, management, appointment and dismissal of the staff of the Enterprise and to adopt regulations to give effect to such rules;

(m) to borrow funds and to furnish such collateral or other security as it may determine in accordance with article 11, paragraph 2, of this Annex;

(n) to enter into any legal proceedings, agreements and transactions and to take any other actions in accordance with article 13 of this Annex;

(o) to delegate, subject to the approval of the Council, any non-discretionary powers to the Director-General and to its committees.

Article 7

Director-General and staff of the Enterprise

1. The Assembly shall, upon the recommendation of the Council and the nomination of the Governing Board, elect the Director-General of the Enterprise who shall not be a member of the Board. The Director-General shall hold office for a fixed term, not exceeding five years, and may be re-elected for further terms.

2. The Director-General shall be the legal representative and chief executive of the Enterprise and shall be directly responsible to the Board for the conduct of the operations of the Enterprise. He shall be responsible for the organization, management, appointment and dismissal of the staff of the Enterprise in accordance with the rules and regulations referred to in article 6, subparagraph (l), of this Annex. He shall participate, without the right to vote, in the meetings of the Board and may participate, without the right to vote, in the meetings of the Assembly and the Council when these organs are dealing with matters concerning the Enterprise.

3. The paramount consideration in the recruitment and employment of the staff and in the determination of their conditions of service shall be the necessity of securing the highest standards of efficiency and of technical competence. Subject to this consideration, due regard shall be paid to the importance of recruiting the staff on an equitable geographical basis.

4. In the performance of their duties the Director-General and the staff shall not seek or receive instructions from any government or from any other source external to the Enterprise. They shall refrain from any action which might reflect on their position as international officials of the Enterprise responsible only to the Enterprise. Each State Party undertakes to respect the exclusively international character of the responsibilities of the Director-General and the staff and not to seek to influence them in the discharge of their responsibilities.

5. The responsibilities set forth in article 168, paragraph 2, are equally applicable to the staff of the Enterprise.

Article 8

Location

The Enterprise shall have its principal office at the seat of the Authority. The Enterprise may establish other offices and facilities in the territory of any State Party with the consent of that State Party.

Article 9

Reports and financial statements

1. The Enterprise shall, not later than three months after the end of each financial year, submit to the Council for its consideration an annual report containing an audited statement of its accounts and shall transmit to the Council at appropriate intervals a summary statement of its financial position and a profit and loss statement showing the results of its operations.

2. The Enterprise shall publish its annual report and such other reports as it finds appropriate.

3. All reports and financial statements referred to in this article shall be distributed to the members of the Authority.

Article 10

Allocation of net income

1. Subject to paragraph 3, the Enterprise shall make payments to the Authority under Annex III, article 13, or their equivalent.

2. The Assembly shall, upon the recommendation of the Governing Board, determine what portion of the net income of the Enterprise shall be retained as reserves of the Enterprise. The remainder shall be transferred to the Authority.

3. During an initial period required for the Enterprise to become self-supporting, which shall not exceed 10 years from the commencement of commercial production by it, the Assembly shall exempt the Enterprise from the payments referred to in paragraph 1, and shall leave all of the net income of the Enterprise in its reserves.

Article 11

Finances

1. The funds of the Enterprise shall include:

(a) amounts received from the Authority in accordance with article 173, paragraph 2(b);

(b) voluntary contributions made by States Parties for the purpose of financing activities of the Enterprise;

(c) amounts borrowed by the Enterprise in accordance with paragraphs 2 and 3;

(d) income of the Enterprise from its operations;

(e) other funds made available to the Enterprise to enable it to commence operations as soon as possible and to carry out its functions.

2. (a) The Enterprise shall have the power to borrow funds and to furnish such collateral or other security as it may determine. Before making a public sale of its obligations in the financial markets or currency of a State Party, the Enterprise shall obtain the approval of that State Party. The total amount of borrowings shall be approved by the Council upon the recommendation of the Governing Board.

(b) States Parties shall make every reasonable effort to support applications by the Enterprise for loans on capital markets and from international financial institutions.

3. (a) The Enterprise shall be provided with the funds necessary to explore and exploit one mine site, and to transport, process and market the minerals recovered therefrom and the nickel, copper, cobalt and manganese obtained, and to meet its initial administrative expenses. The amount of the said funds, and the criteria and factors for its adjustment, shall be included by the Preparatory Commission in the draft rules, regulations and procedures of the Authority.

(b) All States Parties shall make available to the Enterprise an amount equivalent to one half of the funds referred to in subparagraph (a) by way of long-term interest-free loans in accordance with the scale of assessments for the United Nations regular budget in force at the time when the assessments are made, adjusted to take into account the States which are not members of the United Nations. Debts incurred by the Enterprise in raising the other half of the funds shall be guaranteed by all States Parties in accordance with the same scale.

(c) If the sum of the financial contributions of States Parties is less than the funds to be provided to the Enterprise under subparagraph (a), the Assembly shall, at its first session, consider the extent of the shortfall and adopt by consensus measures for dealing with this shortfall, taking into account the obligation of States Parties under subparagraphs (a) and (b) and any recommendations of the Preparatory Commission.

(d) (i) Each State Party shall, within 60 days after the entry into force of this Convention, or within 30 days after the deposit of its instrument of ratification or accession, whichever is later, deposit with the Enterprise irrevocable, non-negotiable, non-interest-bearing promissory notes in the amount of the share of such State Party of interest-free loans pursuant to subparagraph (b).

(ii) The Board shall prepare, at the earliest practicable date after this Convention enters into force, and thereafter at annual or other appropriate intervals, a schedule of the magnitude and timing of its requirements for the funding of its administrative expenses and for activities carried out by the Enterprise in accordance with article 170 and article 12 of this Annex.

(iii) The States Parties shall, thereupon, be notified by the Enterprise, through the Authority, of their respective shares of the funds in accordance with subparagraph (b), required for such expenses. The Enterprise shall encash such amounts of the promissory notes as may be required to meet the expenditure referred to in the schedule with respect to interest-free loans.

(iv) States Parties shall, upon receipt of the notification, make available their respective shares of debt guarantees for the Enterprise in accordance with subparagraph (b).

(e) (i) If the Enterprise so requests, State Parties may provide debt guarantees in addition to those provided in accordance with the scale referred to in subparagraph (b).

(ii) In lieu of debt guarantees, a State Party may make a voluntary contribution to the Enterprise in an amount equivalent to that portion of the debts which it would otherwise be liable to guarantee.

(f) Repayment of the interest-bearing loans shall have priority over the repayment of the interest-free loans. Repayment of interest-free loans shall be in accordance with a schedule adopted by the Assembly, upon the recommendation of the Council and the advice of the Board. In the exercise of this function the Board shall be guided by the relevant provisions of the rules, regulations and procedures of the Authority, which shall take into account the paramount importance of ensuring the effective functioning of the Enterprise and, in particular, ensuring its financial independence.

(g) Funds made available to the Enterprise shall be in freely usable currencies or currencies which are freely available and effectively usable in the major foreign exchange markets. These currencies shall be defined in the rules, regulations and procedures of the Authority in accordance with prevailing international monetary practice. Except as provided in paragraph 2, no State Party shall maintain or impose restrictions on the holding, use or exchange by the Enterprise of these funds.

(h) "Debt guarantee" means a promise of a State Party to creditors of the Enterprise to pay, *pro rata* in accordance with the appropriate scale, the financial obligations of the Enterprise covered by the guarantee following notice by the creditors to the State Party of a default by the Enterprise. Procedures for the payment of those obligations shall be in conformity with the rules, regulations and procedures of the Authority.

4. The funds, assets and expenses of the Enterprise shall be kept separate from those of the Authority. This article shall not prevent the Enterprise from making arrangements with the Authority regarding facilities, personnel and services and arrangements for reimbursement of administrative expenses paid by either on behalf of the other.

5. The records, books and accounts of the Enterprise, including its annual financial statements, shall be audited annually by an independent auditor appointed by the Council.

Article 12

Operations

1. The Enterprise shall propose to the Council projects for carrying out activities in accordance with article 170.

possess the goods and services required for its operations it may procure Such proposals shall include a formal written plan of work for activities in the Area in accordance with article 153, paragraph 3, and all such other information and data as may be required from time to time for its appraisal by the Legal and Technical Commission and approval by the Council.

2. Upon approval by the Council, the Enterprise shall execute the project on the basis of the formal written plan of work referred to in paragraph 1.

3. (a) If the Enterprise does not them. For that purpose, it shall issue invitations to tender and award contracts to bidders offering the best combination of quality, price and delivery time.

(b) If there is more than one bid offering such a combination, the contract shall be awarded in accordance with:

(i) the principle of non-discrimination on the basis of political or other considerations not relevant to the carrying out of operations with due diligence and efficiency; and

(ii) guidelines approved by the Council with regard to the preferences to be accorded to goods and services originating in developing States, including the land-locked and geographically disadvantaged among them.

(c) The Governing Board may adopt rules determining the special circumstances in which the requirement of invitations to bid may, in the best interests of the Enterprise, be dispensed with.

4. The Enterprise shall have title to all minerals and processed substances produced by it.

5. The Enterprise shall sell its products on a non-discriminatory basis. It shall not give non-commercial discounts.

6. Without prejudice to any general or special power conferred on the Enterprise under any other provision of this Convention, the Enterprise shall exercise such powers incidental to its business as shall be necessary.

7. The Enterprise shall not interfere in the political affairs of any State Party; nor shall it be influenced in its decisions by the political character of the State Party concerned. Only commercial considerations shall be relevant to its decisions, and these considerations shall be weighed impartially in order to carry out the purposes specified in article 1 of this Annex.

Article 13

Legal status, privileges and immunities

1. To enable the Enterprise to exercise its functions, the status, privileges and immunities set forth in this article shall be accorded to the Enterprise in the territories of States Parties. To give effect to this principle the Enterprise and States Parties may, where necessary, enter into special agreements.

2. The Enterprise shall have such legal capacity as is necessary for the exercise of its functions and the fulfillment of its purposes and, in particular, the capacity:

(a) to enter into contracts, joint arrangements or other arrangements, including agreements with States and international organizations;

(b) to acquire, lease, hold and dispose of immovable and movable property;

(c) to be a party to legal proceedings.

3. (a) Actions may be brought against the Enterprise only in a court of competent jurisdiction in the territory of a State Party in which the Enterprise:

(i) has an office or facility;

(ii) has appointed an agent for the purpose of accepting service or notice of process;

(iii) has entered into a contract for goods or services;

(iv) has issued securities; or

(v) is otherwise engaged in commercial activity.

(b) The property and assets of the Enterprise, wherever located and by whomsoever held, shall be immune from all forms of seizure, attachment or execution before the delivery of final judgment against the Enterprise.

4. (a) The property and assets of the Enterprise, wherever located and by whomsoever held, shall be immune from requisition, confiscation, expropriation or any other form of seizure by executive or legislative action.

(b) The property and assets of the Enterprise, wherever located and by whomsoever held, shall be free from discriminatory restrictions, regulations, controls and moratoria of any nature.

(c) The Enterprise and its employees shall respect local laws and regulations in any State or territory in which the Enterprise or its employees may do business or otherwise act.

(d) States Parties shall ensure that the Enterprise enjoys all rights, privileges and immunities accorded by them to entities conducting commercial activities in their territories. These rights, privileges and immunities shall be accorded to the Enterprise on no less favourable a basis than that on which they are accorded to entities engaged in similar commercial activities. If special privileges are provided by States Parties for developing States or their commercial entities, the Enterprise shall enjoy those privileges on a similarly preferential basis.

(e) States Parties may provide special incentives, rights, privileges and immunities to the Enterprise without the obligation to provide such incentives, rights, privileges and immunities to other commercial entities.

5. The Enterprise shall negotiate with the host countries in which its offices and facilities are located for exemption from direct and indirect taxation.

6. Each State Party shall take such action as is necessary for giving effect in terms of its own law to the principles set forth in this Annex and shall inform the Enterprise of the specific action which it has taken.

7. The Enterprise may waive any of the privileges and immunities conferred under this article or in the special agreements referred to in paragraph 1 to such extent and upon such conditions as it may determine.

Annex V Conciliation

Section 1 Conciliation Procedure Pursuant to Section 1 of Part XV

Article 1

Institution of proceedings

If the parties to a dispute have agreed, in accordance with article 284, to submit it to conciliation under this section, any such party may institute the proceedings by written notification addressed to the other party or parties to the dispute.

Article 2

List of conciliators

A list of conciliators shall be drawn up and maintained by the Secretary-General of the United Nations. Every State Party shall be entitled to nominate four conciliators, each of whom shall be a person enjoying the highest reputation for fairness, competence and integrity. The names of the persons so nominated shall constitute the list. If at any time the conciliators nominated by a State Party in the list so constituted shall be fewer than four, that State Party shall be entitled to make further nominations as necessary. The name of a conciliator shall remain on the list until withdrawn by the State Party which made the nomination, provided that such conciliator shall continue to serve on any conciliation commission to which that conciliator has been appointed until the completion of the proceedings before that commission.

Article 3

Constitution of conciliation commission

The conciliation commission shall, unless the parties otherwise agree, be constituted as follows:

(a) Subject to subparagraph (g), the conciliation commission shall consist of five members.

(b) The party instituting the proceedings shall appoint two conciliators to be chosen preferably from the list referred to in article 2 of this Annex, one of whom may be its national, unless the parties otherwise agree. Such appointments shall be included in the notification referred to in article 1 of this Annex.

(c) The other party to the dispute shall appoint two conciliators in the manner set forth in subparagraph (b) within 21 days of receipt of the notification referred to in article 1 of this Annex. If the appointments are not made within that period, the party instituting the proceedings may, within one week of the expiration of that period, either terminate the proceedings by notification addressed to the other party or request the Secretary-General of the United Nations to make the appointments in accordance with subparagraph (e).

(d) Within 30 days after all four conciliators have been appointed, they shall appoint a fifth conciliator chosen from the list referred to in article 2 of this Annex, who shall be chairman. If the appointment is not made within that period, either party may, within one week of the expiration of that period, request the Secretary-General of the United Nations to make the appointment in accordance with subparagraph (e).

(e) Within 30 days of the receipt of a request under subparagraph (c) or (d), the Secretary-General of the United Nations shall make the necessary appointments from the list referred to in article 2 of this Annex in consultation with the parties to the dispute.

(f) Any vacancy shall be filled in the manner prescribed for the initial appointment.

(g) Two or more parties which determine by agreement that they are in the same interest shall appoint two conciliators jointly. Where two or more parties have separate interests or there is a disagreement as to whether they are of the same interest, they shall appoint conciliators separately.

(h) In disputes involving more than two parties having separate interests, or where there is disagreement as to whether they are of the same interest, the parties shall apply subparagraphs (a) to (f) in so far as possible.

Article 4

Procedure

The conciliation commission shall, unless the parties otherwise agree, determine its own procedure. The commission may, with the consent of the parties to the dispute, invite any State Party to submit to it its views orally or in writing. Decisions of the commission regarding procedural matters, the report and recommendations shall be made by a majority vote of its members.

Article 5

Amicable settlement

The commission may draw the attention of the parties to any measures which might facilitate an amicable settlement of the dispute.

Article 6

Functions of the commission

The commission shall hear the parties, examine their claims and objections, and make proposals to the parties with a view to reaching an amicable settlement.

Article 7

Report

1. The commission shall report within 12 months of its constitution. Its report shall record any agreements reached and, failing agreement, its conclusions on all questions of fact or law relevant to the matter in dispute and such recommendations as the commission may deem appropriate for an amicable settlement. The report shall be deposited with the Secretary-General of the United Nations and shall immediately be transmitted by him to the parties to the dispute.

2. The report of the commission, including its conclusions or recommendations, shall not be binding upon the parties.

Article 8

Termination

The conciliation proceedings are terminated when a settlement has been reached, when the parties have accepted or one party has rejected the recommendations of the report by written notification addressed to the Secretary-General of the United Nations, or when a period of three months has expired from the date of transmission of the report to the parties.

Article 9

Fees and expenses

The fees and expenses of the commission shall be borne by the parties to the dispute.

Article 10

Right of parties to modify procedure

The parties to the dispute may by agreement applicable solely to that dispute modify any provision of this Annex.

Section 2 Compulsory Submission to Conciliation Procedure Pursuant to Section 3 of Part XV

Article 11

Institution of proceedings

1. Any party to a dispute which, in accordance with Part XV, section 3, may be submitted to conciliation under this section, may institute the proceedings by written notification addressed to the other party or parties to the dispute.

2. Any party to the dispute, notified under paragraph 1, shall be obliged to submit to such proceedings.

Article 12

Failure to reply or to submit to conciliation

The failure of a party or parties to the dispute to reply to notification of institution of proceedings or to submit to such proceedings shall not constitute a bar to the proceedings.

Article 13

Competence

A disagreement as to whether a conciliation commission acting under this section has competence shall be decided by the commission.

Article 14

Application of section 1

Articles 2 to 10 of section l of this Annex apply subject to this section.

Annex VI Statute of the International Tribunal for the Law of the Sea

Article 1

General provisions

1. The International Tribunal for the Law of the Sea is constituted and shall function in accordance with the provisions of this Convention and this Statute.

2. The seat of the Tribunal shall be in the Free and Hanseatic City of Hamburg in the Federal Republic of Germany.

3. The Tribunal may sit and exercise its functions elsewhere whenever it considers this desirable.

4. A reference of a dispute to the Tribunal shall be governed by the provisions of Parts XI and XV.

Section 1 Organization of the Tribunal

Article 2

Composition

1. The Tribunal shall be composed of a body of 21 independent members, elected from among persons enjoying the highest reputation for fairness and integrity and of recognized competence in the field of the law of the sea.

2. In the Tribunal as a whole the representation of the principal legal systems of the world and equitable geographical distribution shall be assured.

Article 3

Membership

1. No two members of the Tribunal may be nationals of the same State. A person who for the purposes of membership in the Tribunal could be regarded as a national of more than one State shall be deemed to be a national of the one in which he ordinarily exercises civil and political rights.

2. There shall be no fewer than three members from each geographical group as established by the General Assembly of the United Nations.

Article 4

Nominations and elections

1. Each State Party may nominate not more than two persons having the qualifications prescribed in article 2 of this Annex. The members of the Tribunal shall be elected from the list of persons thus nominated.

2. At least three months before the date of the election, the Secretary-General of the United Nations in the case of the first election and the Registrar of the Tribunal in

the case of subsequent elections shall address a written invitation to the States Parties to submit their nominations for members of the Tribunal within two months. He shall prepare a list in alphabetical order of all the persons thus nominated, with an indication of the States Parties which have nominated them, and shall submit it to the States Parties before the seventh day of the last month before the date of each election.

3. The first election shall be held within six months of the date of entry into force of this Convention.

4. The members of the Tribunal shall be elected by secret ballot. Elections shall be held at a meeting of the States Parties convened by the Secretary-General of the United Nations in the case of the first election and by a procedure agreed to by the States Parties in the case of subsequent elections. Two thirds of the States Parties shall constitute a quorum at that meeting. The persons elected to the Tribunal shall be those nominees who obtain the largest number of votes and a two-thirds majority of the States Parties present and voting, provided that such majority includes a majority of the States Parties.

Article 5

Term of office

1. The members of the Tribunal shall be elected for nine years and may be re-elected; provided, however, that of the members elected at the first election, the terms of seven members shall expire at the end of three years and the terms of seven more members shall expire at the end of six years.

2. The members of the Tribunal whose terms are to expire at the end of the above-mentioned initial periods of three and six years shall be chosen by lot to be drawn by the Secretary-General of the United Nations immediately after the first election.

3. The members of the Tribunal shall continue to discharge their duties until their places have been filled. Though replaced, they shall finish any proceedings which they may have begun before the date of their replacement.

4. In the case of the resignation of a member of the Tribunal, the letter of resignation shall be addressed to the President of the Tribunal. The place becomes vacant on the receipt of that letter.

Article 6

Vacancies

1. Vacancies shall be filled by the same method as that laid down for the first election, subject to the following provision: the Registrar shall, within one month of the occurrence of the vacancy, proceed to issue the invitations provided for in article 4 of this Annex, and the date of the election shall be fixed by the President of the Tribunal after consultation with the States Parties.

2. A member of the Tribunal elected to replace a member whose term of office has not expired shall hold office for the remainder of his predecessor's term.

Article 7

Incompatible activities

1. No member of the Tribunal may exercise any political or administrative function, or associate actively with or be financially interested in any of the operations of any enterprise concerned with the exploration for or exploitation of the resources of the sea or the seabed or other commercial use of the sea or the seabed.

2. No member of the Tribunal may act as agent, counsel or advocate in any case.

3. Any doubt on these points shall be resolved by decision of the majority of the other members of the Tribunal present.

Article 8

Conditions relating to participation of members in a particular case

1. No member of the Tribunal may participate in the decision of any case in which he has previously taken part as agent, counsel or advocate for one of the parties, or as a member of a national or international court or tribunal, or in any other capacity.

2. If, for some special reason, a member of the Tribunal considers that he should not take part in the decision of a particular case, he shall so inform the President of the Tribunal.

3. If the President considers that for some special reason one of the members of the Tribunal should not sit in a particular case, he shall give him notice accordingly.

4. Any doubt on these points shall be resolved by decision of the majority of the other members of the Tribunal present.

Article 9

Consequence of ceasing to fulfill required conditions

If, in the unanimous opinion of the other members of the Tribunal, a member has ceased to fulfill the required conditions, the President of the Tribunal shall declare the seat vacant.

Article 10

Privileges and immunities

The members of the Tribunal, when engaged on the business of the Tribunal, shall enjoy diplomatic privileges and immunities.

Article 11

Solemn declaration by members

Every member of the Tribunal shall, before taking up his duties, make a solemn declaration in open session that he will exercise his powers impartially and conscientiously.

Article 12

President, Vice-President and Registrar

1. The Tribunal shall elect its President and Vice-President for three years; they may be re-elected.
2. The Tribunal shall appoint its Registrar and may provide for the appointment of such other officers as may be necessary.
3. The President and the Registrar shall reside at the seat of the Tribunal.

Article 13

Quorum

1. All available members of the Tribunal shall sit; a quorum of 11 elected members shall be required to constitute the Tribunal.
2. Subject to article 17 of this Annex, the Tribunal shall determine which members are available to constitute the Tribunal for the consideration of a particular dispute, having regard to the effective functioning of the chambers as provided for in articles 14 and 15 of this Annex.
3. All disputes and applications submitted to the Tribunal shall be heard and determined by the Tribunal, unless article 14 of this Annex applies, or the parties request that it shall be dealt with in accordance with article 15 of this Annex.

Article 14

Seabed Disputes Chamber

A Seabed Disputes Chamber shall be established in accordance with the provisions of section 4 of this Annex. Its jurisdiction, powers and functions shall be as provided for in Part XI, section 5.

Article 15

Special chambers

1. The Tribunal may form such chambers, composed of three or more of its elected members, as it considers necessary for dealing with particular categories of disputes.
2. The Tribunal shall form a chamber for dealing with a particular dispute submitted to it if the parties so request. The composition of such a chamber shall be determined by the Tribunal with the approval of the parties.

3. With a view to the speedy dispatch of business, the Tribunal shall form annually a chamber composed of five of its elected members which may hear and determine disputes by summary procedure. Two alternative members shall be selected for the purpose of replacing members who are unable to participate in a particular proceeding.

4. Disputes shall be heard and determined by the chambers provided for in this article if the parties so request.

5. A judgment given by any of the chambers provided for in this article and in article 14 of this Annex shall be considered as rendered by the Tribunal.

Article 16

Rules of the Tribunal

The Tribunal shall frame rules for carrying out its functions. In particular it shall lay down rules of procedure.

Article 17

Nationality of members

1. Members of the Tribunal of the nationality of any of the parties to a dispute shall retain their right to participate as members of the Tribunal.

2. If the Tribunal, when hearing a dispute, includes upon the bench a member of the nationality of one of the parties, any other party may choose a person to participate as a member of the Tribunal.

3. If the Tribunal, when hearing a dispute, does not include upon the bench a member of the nationality of the parties, each of those parties may choose a person to participate as a member of the Tribunal.

4. This article applies to the chambers referred to in articles 14 and 15 of this Annex. In such cases, the President, in consultation with the parties, shall request specified members of the Tribunal forming the chamber, as many as necessary, to give place to the members of the Tribunal of the nationality of the parties concerned, and, failing such, or if they are unable to be present, to the members specially chosen by the parties.

5. Should there be several parties in the same interest, they shall, for the purpose of the preceding provisions, be considered as one party only. Any doubt on this point shall be settled by the decision of the Tribunal.

6. Members chosen in accordance with paragraphs 2, 3 and 4 shall fulfil the conditions required by articles 2, 8 and 11 of this Annex. They shall participate in the decision on terms of complete equality with their colleagues.

Article 18

Remuneration of members

1. Each elected member of the Tribunal shall receive an annual allowance and, for each day on which he exercises his functions, a special allowance, provided that in any year the total sum payable to any member as special allowance shall not exceed the amount of the annual allowance.

2. The President shall receive a special annual allowance.

3. The Vice-President shall receive a special allowance for each day on which he acts as President.

4. The members chosen under article 17 of this Annex, other than elected members of the Tribunal, shall receive compensation for each day on which they exercise their functions.

5. The salaries, allowances and compensation shall be determined from time to time at meetings of the States Parties, taking into account the workload of the Tribunal. They may not be decreased during the term of office.

6. The salary of the Registrar shall be determined at meetings of the States Parties, on the proposal of the Tribunal.

7. Regulations adopted at meetings of the States Parties shall determine the conditions under which retirement pensions may be given to members of the Tribunal and to the Registrar, and the conditions under which members of the Tribunal and Registrar shall have their travelling expenses refunded.

8. The salaries, allowances, and compensation shall be free of all taxation.

Article 19

Expenses of the Tribunal

1. The expenses of the Tribunal shall be borne by the States Parties and by the Authority on such terms and in such a manner as shall be decided at meetings of the States Parties.

2. When an entity other than a State Party or the Authority is a party to a case submitted to it, the Tribunal shall fix the amount which that party is to contribute towards the expenses of the Tribunal.

Section 2 Competence

Article 20

Access to the Tribunal

1. The Tribunal shall be open to States Parties.

2. The Tribunal shall be open to entities other than States Parties in any case expressly provided for in Part XI or in any case submitted pursuant to any other agreement conferring jurisdiction on the Tribunal which is accepted by all the parties to that case.

Article 21

Jurisdiction

The jurisdiction of the Tribunal comprises all disputes and all applications submitted to it in accordance with this Convention and all matters specifically provided for in any other agreement which confers jurisdiction on the Tribunal.

Article 22

Reference of disputes subject to other agreements

If all the parties to a treaty or convention already in force and concerning the subject-matter covered by this Convention so agree, any disputes concerning the interpretation or application of such treaty or convention may, in accordance with such agreement, be submitted to the Tribunal.

Article 23

Applicable law

The Tribunal shall decide all disputes and applications in accordance with article 293.

Section 3 Procedure

Article 24

Institution of proceedings

1. Disputes are submitted to the Tribunal, as the case may be, either by notification of a special agreement or by written application, addressed to the Registrar. In either case, the subject of the dispute and the parties shall be indicated.
2. The Registrar shall forthwith notify the special agreement or the application to all concerned.
3. The Registrar shall also notify all States Parties.

Article 25

Provisional measures

1. In accordance with article 290, the Tribunal and its Seabed Disputes Chamber shall have the power to prescribe provisional measures.
2. If the Tribunal is not in session or a sufficient number of members is not available to constitute a quorum, the provisional measures shall be prescribed by the chamber of summary procedure formed under article 15, paragraph 3, of this Annex. Notwithstanding article 15, paragraph 4, of this Annex, such provisional measures may be adopted at the request of any party to the dispute. They shall be subject to review and revision by the Tribunal.

Article 26
Hearing

1. The hearing shall be under the control of the President or, if he is unable to preside, of the Vice-President. If neither is able to preside, the senior judge present of the Tribunal shall preside.

2. The hearing shall be public, unless the Tribunal decides otherwise or unless the parties demand that the public be not admitted.

Article 27
Conduct of case

The Tribunal shall make orders for the conduct of the case, decide the form and time in which each party must conclude its arguments, and make all arrangements connected with the taking of evidence.

Article 28
Default

When one of the parties does not appear before the Tribunal or fails to defend its case, the other party may request the Tribunal to continue the proceedings and make its decision. Absence of a party or failure of a party to defend its case shall not constitute a bar to the proceedings. Before making its decision, the Tribunal must satisfy itself not only that it has jurisdiction over the dispute, but also that the claim is well founded in fact and law.

Article 29
Majority for decision

1. All questions shall be decided by a majority of the members of the Tribunal who are present.

2. In the event of an equality of votes, the President or the member of the Tribunal who acts in his place shall have a casting vote.

Article 30
Judgment

1. The judgment shall state the reasons on which it is based.

2. It shall contain the names of the members of the Tribunal who have taken part in the decision.

3. If the judgment does not represent in whole or in part the unanimous opinion of the members of the Tribunal, any member shall be entitled to deliver a separate opinion.

4. The judgment shall be signed by the President and by the Registrar. It shall be read in open court, due notice having been given to the parties to the dispute.

Article 31

Request to intervene

1. Should a State Party consider that it has an interest of a legal nature which may be affected by the decision in any dispute, it may submit a request to the Tribunal to be permitted to intervene.

2. It shall be for the Tribunal to decide upon this request.

3. If a request to intervene is granted, the decision of the Tribunal in respect of the dispute shall be binding upon the intervening State Party in so far as it relates to matters in respect of which that State Party intervened.

Article 32

Right to intervene in cases of interpretation or application

1. Whenever the interpretation or application of this Convention is in question, the Registrar shall notify all States Parties forthwith.

2. Whenever pursuant to article 21 or 22 of this Annex the interpretation or application of an international agreement is in question, the Registrar shall notify all the parties to the agreement.

3. Every party referred to in paragraphs 1 and 2 has the right to intervene in the proceedings; if it uses this right, the interpretation given by the judgment will be equally binding upon it.

Article 33

Finality and binding force of decisions

1. The decision of the Tribunal is final and shall be complied with by all the parties to the dispute.

2. The decision shall have no binding force except between the parties in respect of that particular dispute.

3. In the event of dispute as to the meaning or scope of the decision, the Tribunal shall construe it upon the request of any party.

Article 34

Costs

Unless otherwise decided by the Tribunal, each party shall bear its own costs.

Section 4 Seabed Disputes Chamber

Article 35

Composition

1. The Seabed Disputes Chamber referred to in article 14 of this Annex shall be composed of 11 members, selected by a majority of the elected members of the Tribunal from among them.

2. In the selection of the members of the Chamber, the representation of the principal legal systems of the world and equitable geographical distribution shall be assured. The Assembly of the Authority may adopt recommendations of a general nature relating to such representation and distribution.

3. The members of the Chamber shall be selected every three years and may be selected for a second term.

4. The Chamber shall elect its President from among its members, who shall serve for the term for which the Chamber has been selected.

5. If any proceedings are still pending at the end of any three-year period for which the Chamber has been selected, the Chamber shall complete the proceedings in its original composition.

6. If a vacancy occurs in the Chamber, the Tribunal shall select a successor from among its elected members, who shall hold office for the remainder of his predecessor's term.

7. A quorum of seven of the members selected by the Tribunal shall be required to constitute the Chamber.

Article 36

Ad hoc chambers

1. The Seabed Disputes Chamber shall form an ad hoc chamber, composed of three of its members, for dealing with a particular dispute submitted to it in accordance with article 188, paragraph 1(b). The composition of such a chamber shall be determined by the Seabed Disputes Chamber with the approval of the parties.

2. If the parties do not agree on the composition of an ad hoc chamber, each party to the dispute shall appoint one member, and the third member shall be appointed by them in agreement. If they disagree, or if any party fails to make an appointment, the President of the Seabed Disputes Chamber shall promptly make the appointment or appointments from among its members, after consultation with the parties.

3. Members of the ad hoc chamber must not be in the service of, or nationals of, any of the parties to the dispute.

Article 37

Access

The Chamber shall be open to the States Parties, the Authority and the other entities referred to in Part XI, section 5.

Article 38

Applicable law

In addition to the provisions of article 293, the Chamber shall apply:

(a) the rules, regulations and procedures of the Authority adopted in accordance with this Convention; and

(b) the terms of contracts concerning activities in the Area in matters relating to those contracts.

Article 39

Enforcement of decisions of the Chamber

The decisions of the Chamber shall be enforceable in the territories of the States Parties in the same manner as judgments or orders of the highest court of the State Party in whose territory the enforcement is sought.

Article 40

Applicability of other sections of this Annex

1. The other sections of this Annex which are not incompatible with this section apply to the Chamber.

2. In the exercise of its functions relating to advisory opinions, the Chamber shall be guided by the provisions of this Annex relating to procedure before the Tribunal to the extent to which it recognizes them to be applicable.

Section 5 Amendments

Article 41

Amendments

1. Amendments to this Annex, other than amendments to section 4, may be adopted only in accordance with article 313 or by consensus at a conference convened in accordance with this Convention.

2. Amendments to section 4 may be adopted only in accordance with article 314.

3. The Tribunal may propose such amendments to this Statute as it may consider necessary, by written communications to the States Parties for their consideration in conformity with paragraphs 1 and 2.

Annex VII Arbitration

Article 1

Institution of proceedings

Subject to the provisions of Part XV, any party to a dispute may submit the dispute to the arbitral procedure provided for in this Annex by written notification addressed to the other party or parties to the dispute. The notification shall be accompanied by a statement of the claim and the grounds on which it is based.

Article 2

List of arbitrators

1. A list of arbitrators shall be drawn up and maintained by the Secretary-General of the United Nations. Every State Party shall be entitled to nominate four arbitrators, each of whom shall be a person experienced in maritime affairs and enjoying the highest reputation for fairness, competence and integrity. The names of the persons so nominated shall constitute the list.

2. If at any time the arbitrators nominated by a State Party in the list so constituted shall be fewer than four, that State Party shall be entitled to make further nominations as necessary.

3. The name of an arbitrator shall remain on the list until withdrawn by the State Party which made the nomination, provided that such arbitrator shall continue to serve on any arbitral tribunal to which that arbitrator has been appointed until the completion of the proceedings before that arbitral tribunal.

Article 3

Constitution of arbitral tribunal

For the purpose of proceedings under this Annex, the arbitral tribunal shall, unless the parties otherwise agree, be constituted as follows:

(a) Subject to subparagraph (g), the arbitral tribunal shall consist of five members.

(b) The party instituting the proceedings shall appoint one member to be chosen preferably from the list referred to in article 2 of this Annex, who may be its national. The appointment shall be included in the notification referred to in article 1 of this Annex.

(c) The other party to the dispute shall, within 30 days of receipt of the notification referred to in article 1 of this Annex, appoint one member to be chosen preferably from the list, who may be its national. If the appointment is not made within that period, the party instituting the proceedings may, within two weeks of the expiration of that period, request that the appointment be made in accordance with subparagraph (e).

(d) The other three members shall be appointed by agreement between the parties. They shall be chosen preferably from the list and shall be nationals of third States unless the parties otherwise agree. The parties to the dispute shall appoint the President of the arbitral tribunal from among those three members. If, within 60 days of receipt of the notification referred to in article 1 of this Annex, the parties are unable to reach agreement on the appointment of one or more of the members of the tribunal to be appointed by agreement, or on the appointment of the President, the remaining appointment or appointments shall be made in accordance with subparagraph (e), at the request of a party to the dispute. Such request shall be made within two weeks of the expiration of the aforementioned 60-day period.

(e) Unless the parties agree that any appointment under subparagraphs (c) and (d) be made by a person or a third State chosen by the parties, the President of the International Tribunal for the Law of the Sea shall make the necessary appointments. If the President is unable to act under this subparagraph or is a national of one of the parties to the dispute, the appointment shall be made by the next senior member of the International Tribunal for the Law of the Sea who is available and is not a national of one of the parties. The appointments referred to in this subparagraph shall be made from the list referred to in article 2 of this Annex within a period of 30 days of the receipt of the request and in consultation with the parties. The members so appointed shall be of different nationalities and may not be in the service of, ordinarily resident in the territory of, or nationals of, any of the parties to the dispute.

(f) Any vacancy shall be filled in the manner prescribed for the initial appointment.

(g) Parties in the same interest shall appoint one member of the tribunal jointly by agreement. Where there are several parties having separate interests or where there is disagreement as to whether they are of the same interest, each of them shall appoint one member of the tribunal. The number of members of the tribunal appointed separately by the parties shall always be smaller by one than the number of members of the tribunal to be appointed jointly by the parties.

(h) In disputes involving more than two parties, the provisions of subparagraphs (a) to (f) shall apply to the maximum extent possible.

Article 4

Functions of arbitral tribunal

An arbitral tribunal constituted under article 3 of this Annex shall function in accordance with this Annex and the other provisions of this Convention.

Article 5

Procedure

Unless the parties to the dispute otherwise agree, the arbitral tribunal shall determine its own procedure, assuring to each party a full opportunity to be heard and to present its case.

Article 6

Duties of parties to a dispute

The parties to the dispute shall facilitate the work of the arbitral tribunal and, in particular, in accordance with their law and using all means at their disposal, shall:

(a) provide it with all relevant documents, facilities and information; and

(b) enable it when necessary to call witnesses or experts and receive their evidence and to visit the localities to which the case relates.

Article 7

Expenses

Unless the arbitral tribunal decides otherwise because of the particular circumstances of the case, the expenses of the tribunal, including the remuneration of its members, shall be borne by the parties to the dispute in equal shares.

Article 8

Required majority for decisions

Decisions of the arbitral tribunal shall be taken by a majority vote of its members. The absence or abstention of less than half of the members shall not constitute a bar to the tribunal reaching a decision. In the event of an equality of votes, the President shall have a casting vote.

Article 9

Default of appearance

If one of the parties to the dispute does not appear before the arbitral tribunal or fails to defend its case, the other party may request the tribunal to continue the proceedings and to make its award. Absence of a party or failure of a party to defend its case shall not constitute a bar to the proceedings. Before making its award, the arbitral tribunal must satisfy itself not only that it has jurisdiction over the dispute but also that the claim is well founded in fact and law.

Article 10

Award

The award of the arbitral tribunal shall be confined to the subject-matter of the dispute and state the reasons on which it is based. It shall contain the names of the members who have participated and the date of the award. Any member of the tribunal may attach a separate or dissenting opinion to the award.

Article 11

Finality of award

The award shall be final and without appeal, unless the parties to the dispute have agreed in advance to an appellate procedure. It shall be complied with by the parties to the dispute.

Article 12

Interpretation or implementation of award

1. Any controversy which may arise between the parties to the dispute as regards the interpretation or manner of implementation of the award may be submitted by either party for decision to the arbitral tribunal which made the award. For this purpose, any vacancy in the tribunal shall be filled in the manner provided for in the original appointments of the members of the tribunal.

2. Any such controversy may be submitted to another court or tribunal under article 287 by agreement of all the parties to the dispute.

Article 13

Application to entities other than States Parties

The provisions of this Annex shall apply *mutatis mutandis* to any dispute involving entities other than States Parties.

Annex VIII Special Arbitration

Article 1
Institution of proceedings

Subject to Part XV, any party to a dispute concerning the interpretation or application of the articles of this Convention relating to (1) fisheries, (2) protection and preservation of the marine environment, (3) marine scientific research, or (4) navigation, including pollution from vessels and by dumping, may submit the dispute to the special arbitral procedure provided for in this Annex by written notification addressed to the other party or parties to the dispute. The notification shall be accompanied by a statement of the claim and the grounds on which it is based.

Article 2
Lists of experts

1. A list of experts shall be established and maintained in respect of each of the fields of (1) fisheries, (2) protection and preservation of the marine environment, (3) marine scientific research, and (4) navigation, including pollution from vessels and by dumping.

2. The lists of experts shall be drawn up and maintained, in the field of fisheries by the Food and Agriculture Organization of the United Nations, in the field of protection and preservation of the marine environment by the United Nations Environment Programme, in the field of marine scientific research by the Intergovernmental Oceanographic Commission, in the field of navigation, including pollution from vessels and by dumping, by the International Maritime Organization, or in each case by the appropriate subsidiary body concerned to which such organization, programme or commission has delegated this function.

3. Every State Party shall be entitled to nominate two experts in each field whose competence in the legal, scientific or technical aspects of such field is established and generally recognized and who enjoy the highest reputation for fairness and integrity. The names of the persons so nominated in each field shall constitute the appropriate list.

4. If at any time the experts nominated by a State Party in the list so constituted shall be fewer than two, that State Party shall be entitled to make further nominations as necessary.

5. The name of an expert shall remain on the list until withdrawn by the State Party which made the nomination, provided that such expert shall continue to serve on any

special arbitral tribunal to which that expert has been appointed until the completion of the proceedings before that special arbitral tribunal.

Article 3

Constitution of special arbitral tribunal

For the purpose of proceedings under this Annex, the special arbitral tribunal shall, unless the parties otherwise agree, be constituted as follows:

(a) Subject to subparagraph (g), the special arbitral tribunal shall consist of five members.

(b) The party instituting the proceedings shall appoint two members to be chosen preferably from the appropriate list or lists referred to in article 2 of this Annex relating to the matters in dispute, one of whom may be its national. The appointments shall be included in the notification referred to in article 1 of this Annex.

(c) The other party to the dispute shall, within 30 days of receipt of the notification referred to in article 1 of this Annex, appoint two members to be chosen preferably from the appropriate list or lists relating to the matters in dispute, one of whom may be its national. If the appointments are not made within that period, the party instituting the proceedings may, within two weeks of the expiration of that period, request that the appointments be made in accordance with subparagraph (e).

(d) The parties to the dispute shall by agreement appoint the President of the special arbitral tribunal, chosen preferably from the appropriate list, who shall be a national of a third State, unless the parties otherwise agree. If, within 30 days of receipt of the notification referred to in article 1 of this Annex, the parties are unable to reach agreement on the appointment of the President, the appointment shall be made in accordance with subparagraph (e), at the request of a party to the dispute. Such request shall be made within two weeks of the expiration of the aforementioned 30-day period.

(e) Unless the parties agree that the appointment be made by a person or a third State chosen by the parties, the Secretary-General of the United Nations shall make the necessary appointments within 30 days of receipt of a request under subparagraphs (c) and (d). The appointments referred to in this subparagraph shall be made from the appropriate list or lists of experts referred to in article 2 of this Annex and in consultation with the parties to the dispute and the appropriate international organization. The members so appointed shall be of different nationalities and may not be in the service of, ordinarily resident in the territory of, or nationals of, any of the parties to the dispute.

(f) Any vacancy shall be filled in the manner prescribed for the initial appointment.

(g) Parties in the same interest shall appoint two members of the tribunal jointly by agreement. Where there are several parties having separate interests or where there is disagreement as to whether they are of the same interest, each of them shall appoint one member of the tribunal.

(h) In disputes involving more than two parties, the provisions of subparagraphs (a) to (f) shall apply to the maximum extent possible.

Article 4

General provisions

Annex VII, articles 4 to 13, apply *mutatis mutandis* to the special arbitration proceedings in accordance with this Annex.

Article 5

Fact finding

1. The parties to a dispute concerning the interpretation or application of the provisions of this Convention relating to (1) fisheries, (2) protection and preservation of the marine environment, (3) marine scientific research, or (4) navigation, including pollution from vessels and by dumping, may at any time agree to request a special arbitral tribunal constituted in accordance with article 3 of this Annex to carry out an inquiry and establish the facts giving rise to the dispute.

2. Unless the parties otherwise agree, the findings of fact of the special arbitral tribunal acting in accordance with paragraph 1, shall be considered as conclusive as between the parties.

3. If all the parties to the dispute so request, the special arbitral tribunal may formulate recommendations which, without having the force of a decision, shall only constitute the basis for a review by the parties of the questions giving rise to the dispute.

4. Subject to paragraph 2, the special arbitral tribunal shall act in accordance with the provisions of this Annex, unless the parties otherwise agree.

Annex IX Participation by International Organizations

Article 1

Use of terms

For the purposes of article 305 and of this Annex, "international organization" means an intergovernmental organization constituted by States to which its member States have transferred competence over matters governed by this Convention, including the competence to enter into treaties in respect of those matters.

Article 2

Signature

An international organization may sign this Convention if a majority of its member States are signatories of this Convention. At the time of signature an international organization shall make a declaration specifying the matters governed by this Convention in respect of which competence has been transferred to that organization by its member States which are signatories, and the nature and extent of that competence.

Article 3

Formal confirmation and accession

1. An international organization may deposit its instrument of formal confirmation or of accession if a majority of its member States deposit or have deposited their instruments of ratification or accession.

2. The instruments deposited by the international organization shall contain the undertakings and declarations required by articles 4 and 5 of this Annex.

Article 4

Extent of participation and rights and obligations

1. The instrument of formal confirmation or of accession of an international organization shall contain an undertaking to accept the rights and obligations of States under this Convention in respect of matters relating to which competence has been transferred to it by its member States which are Parties to this Convention.

2. An international organization shall be a Party to this Convention to the extent that it has competence in accordance with the declarations, communications of information or notifications referred to in article 5 of this Annex.

3. Such an international organization shall exercise the rights and perform the obligations which its member States which are Parties would otherwise have under this Convention, on matters relating to which competence has been transferred to it by those member States. The member States of that international organization shall not exercise competence which they have transferred to it.

4. Participation of such an international organization shall in no case entail an increase of the representation to which its member States which are States Parties would otherwise be entitled, including rights in decision-making.

5. Participation of such an international organization shall in no case confer any rights under this Convention on member States of the organization which are not States Parties to this Convention.

6. In the event of a conflict between the obligations of an international organization under this Convention and its obligations under the agreement establishing the organization or any acts relating to it, the obligations under this Convention shall prevail.

Article 5

Declarations, notifications and communications

1. The instrument of formal confirmation or of accession of an international organization shall contain a declaration specifying the matters governed by this Convention in respect of which competence has been transferred to the organization by its member States which are Parties to this Convention.

2. A member State of an international organization shall, at the time it ratifies or accedes to this Convention or at the time when the organization deposits its instrument of formal confirmation or of accession, whichever is later, make a declaration specifying the matters governed by this Convention in respect of which it has transferred competence to the organization.

3. States Parties which are member States of an international organization which is a Party to this Convention shall be presumed to have competence over all matters governed by this Convention in respect of which transfers of competence to the organization have not been specifically declared, notified or communicated by those States under this article.

4. The international organization and its member States which are States Parties shall promptly notify the depositary of this Convention of any changes to the distribution of competence, including new transfers of competence, specified in the declarations under paragraphs 1 and 2.

5. Any State Party may request an international organization and its member States which are States Parties to provide information as to which, as between the organization and its member States, has competence in respect of any specific question which has arisen. The organization and the member States concerned shall provide this information within a reasonable time. The international organization and the member States may also, on their own initiative, provide this information.

6. Declarations, notifications and communications of information under this article shall specify the nature and extent of the competence transferred.

Article 6

Responsibility and liability

1. Parties which have competence under article 5 of this Annex shall have responsibility for failure to comply with obligations or for any other violation of this Convention.

2. Any State Party may request an international organization or its member States which are States Parties for information as to who has responsibility in respect of any specific matter. The organization and the member States concerned shall provide this information. Failure to provide this information within a reasonable time or the provision of contradictory information shall result in joint and several liability.

Article 7

Settlement of disputes

1. At the time of deposit of its instrument of formal confirmation or of accession, or at any time thereafter, an international organization shall be free to choose, by means of a written declaration, one or more of the means for the settlement of disputes concerning the interpretation or application of this Convention, referred to in article 287, paragraph 1(a), (c) or (d).

2. Part XV applies *mutatis mutandis* to any dispute between Parties to this Convention, one or more of which are international organizations.

3. When an international organization and one or more of its member States are joint parties to a dispute, or parties in the same interest, the organization shall be deemed to have accepted the same procedures for the settlement of disputes as the member States; when, however, a member State has chosen only the International Court of Justice under article 287, the organization and the member State concerned shall be deemed to have accepted arbitration in accordance with Annex VII, unless the parties to the dispute otherwise agree.

Article 8

Applicability of Part XVII

Part XVII applies *mutatis mutandis* to an international organization, except in respect of the following:

(a) the instrument of formal confirmation or of accession of an international organization shall not be taken into account in the application of article 308, paragraph 1;

(b) (i) an international organization shall have exclusive capacity with respect to the application of articles 312 to 315, to the extent that it has competence under article 5 of this Annex over the entire subject-matter of the amendment;

(ii) the instrument of formal confirmation or of accession of an international organization to an amendment, the entire subject-matter over which the international organization has competence under article 5 of this Annex, shall be considered to be the instrument of ratification or accession of each of the member States which are States Parties, for the purposes of applying article 316, paragraphs 1, 2 and 3;

(iii) the instrument of formal confirmation or of accession of the international organization shall not be taken into account in the application of article 316, paragraphs 1 and 2, with regard to all other amendments;

(c) (i) an international organization may not denounce this Convention in accordance with article 317 if any of its member States is a State Party and if it continues to fulfill the qualifications specified in article 1 of this Annex;

(ii) an international organization shall denounce this Convention when none of its member States is a State Party or if the international organization no longer fulfils the qualifications specified in article 1 of this Annex. Such denunciation shall take effect immediately.

Agreement Relating to the Implementation of Part XI of the United Nations Convention on the Law of the Sea of 10 December 1982

U.S. Sen. Treaty Doc. No. 103-39 (1994); 1836 U.N.T.S. 3

The States Parties to this Agreement,

Recognizing the important contribution of the United Nations Convention on the Law of the Sea of 10 December 1982 (hereinafter referred to as "the Convention") to the maintenance of peace, justice and progress for all peoples of the world,

Reaffirming that the seabed and ocean floor and subsoil thereof, beyond the limits of national jurisdiction (hereinafter referred to as "the Area"), as well as the resources of the Area, are the common heritage of mankind,

Mindful of the importance of the Convention for the protection and preservation of the marine environment and of the growing concern for the global environment,

Having considered the report of the Secretary-General of the United Nations on the results of the informal consultations among States held from 1990 to 1994 on outstanding issues relating to Part XI and related provisions of the Convention (hereinafter referred to as "Part XI"),

Noting the political and economic changes, including market-oriented approaches, affecting the implementation of Part XI,

Wishing to facilitate universal participation in the Convention,

Considering that an agreement relating to the implementation of Part XI would best meet that objective,

Have agreed as follows:

Article 1

Implementation of Part XI

1. The States Parties to this Agreement undertake to implement Part XI in accordance with this Agreement.
2. The Annex forms an integral part of this Agreement.

Article 2

Relationship between this Agreement and Part XI

1. The provisions of this Agreement and Part XI shall be interpreted and applied together as a single instrument. In the event of any inconsistency between this Agreement and Part XI, the provisions of this Agreement shall prevail.
2. Articles 309 to 319 of the Convention shall apply to this Agreement as they apply to the Convention.

Article 3

Signature

This Agreement shall remain open for signature at United Nations Headquarters by the States and entities referred to in article 305, paragraph 1(a), (c), (d), (e) and (f), of the Convention for 12 months from the date of its adoption.

Article 4

Consent to be bound

1. After the adoption of this Agreement, any instrument of ratification or formal confirmation of or accession to the Convention shall also represent consent to be bound by this Agreement.

2. No State or entity may establish its consent to be bound by this Agreement unless it has previously established or establishes at the same time its consent to be bound by the Convention.

3. A State or entity referred to in article 3 may express its consent to be bound by this Agreement by:

(a) Signature not subject to ratification, formal confirmation or the procedure set out in article 5;

(b) Signature subject to ratification or formal confirmation, followed by ratification or formal confirmation;

(c) Signature subject to the procedure set out in article 5; or

(d) Accession.

4. Formal confirmation by the entities referred to in article 305, paragraph 1(f), of the Convention shall be in accordance with Annex IX of the Convention.

5. The instruments of ratification, formal confirmation or accession shall be deposited with the Secretary-General of the United Nations.

Article 5

Simplified procedure

1. A State or entity which has deposited before the date of the adoption of this Agreement an instrument of ratification or formal confirmation of or accession to the Convention and which has signed this Agreement in accordance with article 4, paragraph 3(c), shall be considered to have established its consent to be bound by this Agreement 12 months after the date of its adoption, unless that State or entity notifies the depositary in writing before that date that it is not availing itself of the simplified procedure set out in this article.

2. In the event of such notification, consent to be bound by this Agreement shall be established in accordance with article 4, paragraph 3(b).

Article 6

Entry into force

1. This Agreement shall enter into force 30 days after the date on which 40 States have established their consent to be bound in accordance with articles 4 and 5, provided that such States include at least seven of the States referred to in paragraph l(a) of resolution II of the Third United Nations Conference on the Law of the Sea (hereinafter referred to as "resolution II") and that at least five of those States are developed States. If these conditions for entry into force are fulfilled before 16 November 1994, this Agreement shall enter into force on 16 November 1994.

2. For each State or entity establishing its consent to be bound by this Agreement after the requirements set out in paragraph 1 have been fulfilled, this Agreement shall enter into force on the thirtieth day following the date of establishment of its consent to be bound.

Article 7

Provisional application

1. If on 16 November 1994 this Agreement has not entered into force, it shall be applied provisionally pending its entry into force by:

(a) States which have consented to its adoption in the General Assembly of the United Nations, except any such State which before 16 November 1994 notifies the depositary in writing either that it will not so apply this Agreement or that it will consent to such application only upon subsequent signature or notification in writing;

(b) States and entities which sign this Agreement, except any such State or entity which notifies the depositary in writing at the time of signature that it will not so apply this Agreement;

(c) States and entities which consent to its provisional application by so notifying the depositary in writing;

(d) States which accede to this Agreement.

2. All such States and entities shall apply this Agreement provisionally in accordance with their national or internal laws and regulations, with effect from 16 November 1994 or the date of signature, notification of consent or accession, if later.

3. Provisional application shall terminate upon the date of entry into force of this Agreement. In any event, provisional application shall terminate on 16 November 1998 if at that date the requirement in article 6, paragraph 1, of consent to be bound by this Agreement by at least seven of the States (of which at least five must be developed States) referred to in paragraph 1(a) of resolution II has not been fulfilled.

Article 8

States Parties

1. For the purposes of this Agreement, "States Parties" means States which have consented to be bound by this Agreement and for which this Agreement is in force.

2. This Agreement applies *mutatis mutandis* to the entities referred to in article 305, paragraph 1(c), (d), (e) and (f), of the Convention which become Parties to this Agreement in accordance with the conditions relevant to each, and to that extent "States Parties" refers to those entities.

Article 9

Depositary

The Secretary-General of the United Nations shall be the depositary of this Agreement.

Article 10

Authentic texts

The original of this Agreement, of which the Arabic, Chinese, English, French, Russian and Spanish texts are equally authentic, shall be deposited with the Secretary-General of the United Nations.

IN WITNESS WHEREOF, the undersigned Plenipotentiaries, being duly authorized thereto, have signed this Agreement.

DONE AT NEW YORK, this twenty-eighth day of July, one thousand nine hundred and ninety-four.

Annex

Section 1 Costs to States Parties and Institutional Arrangements

1. The International Seabed Authority (hereinafter referred to as "the Authority") is the organization through which States Parties to the Convention shall, in accordance with the regime for the Area established in Part XI and this Agreement, organize and control activities in the Area, particularly with a view to administering the resources of the Area. The powers and functions of the Authority shall be those expressly conferred upon it by the Convention. The Authority shall have such incidental powers, consistent with the Convention, as are implicit in, and necessary for, the exercise of those powers and functions with respect to activities in the Area.

2. In order to minimize costs to States Parties, all organs and subsidiary bodies to be established under the Convention and this Agreement shall be cost-effective. This principle shall also apply to the frequency, duration and scheduling of meetings.

3. The setting up and the functioning of the organs and subsidiary bodies of the Authority shall be based on an evolutionary approach, taking into account the functional needs of the organs and subsidiary bodies concerned in order that they may discharge effectively their respective responsibilities at various stages of the development of activities in the Area.

4. The early functions of the Authority upon entry into force of the Convention shall be carried out by the Assembly, the Council, the Secretariat, the Legal and Technical Commission and the Finance Committee. The functions of the Economic Planning Commission shall be performed by the Legal and Technical Commission until such time as the Council decides otherwise or until the approval of the first plan of work for exploitation.

5. Between the entry into force of the Convention and the approval of the first plan of work for exploitation, the Authority shall concentrate on:

(a) Processing of applications for approval of plans of work for exploration in accordance with Part XI and this Agreement;

(b) Implementation of decisions of the Preparatory Commission for the International Seabed Authority and for the International Tribunal for the Law of the Sea (hereinafter referred to as "the Preparatory Commission") relating to the registered pioneer investors and their certifying States, including their rights and obligations, in accordance with article 308, paragraph 5, of the Convention and resolution II, paragraph 13;

(c) Monitoring of compliance with plans of work for exploration approved in the form of contracts;

(d) Monitoring and review of trends and developments relating to deep seabed mining activities, including regular analysis of world metal market conditions and metal prices, trends and prospects;

(e) Study of the potential impact of mineral production from the Area on the economies of developing land-based producers of those minerals which are likely to be most seriously affected, with a view to minimizing their difficulties and assisting them in their economic adjustment, taking into account the work done in this regard by the Preparatory Commission;

(f) Adoption of rules, regulations and procedures necessary for the conduct of activities in the Area as they progress. Notwithstanding the provisions of Annex III, article 17, paragraph 2(b) and (c), of the Convention, such rules, regulations and procedures shall take into account the terms of this Agreement, the prolonged delay in commercial deep seabed mining and the likely pace of activities in the Area;

(g) Adoption of rules, regulations and procedures incorporating applicable standards for the protection and preservation of the marine environment;

(h) Promotion and encouragement of the conduct of marine scientific research with respect to activities in the Area and the collection and dissemination of the results of such research and analysis, when available, with particular emphasis on research related to the environmental impact of activities in the Area;

(i) Acquisition of scientific knowledge and monitoring of the development of marine technology relevant to activities in the Area, in particular technology relating to the protection and preservation of the marine environment;

(j) Assessment of available data relating to prospecting and exploration;

(k) Timely elaboration of rules, regulations and procedures for exploitation, including those relating to the protection and preservation of the marine environment.

6. (a) An application for approval of a plan of work for exploration shall be considered by the Council following the receipt of a recommendation on the application from the Legal and Technical Commission. The processing of an application for approval of a plan of work for exploration shall be in accordance with the provisions of the Convention, including Annex III thereof, and this Agreement, and subject to the following:

(i) A plan of work for exploration submitted on behalf of a State or entity, or any component of such entity, referred to in resolution II, paragraph 1(a)(ii) or (iii), other than a registered pioneer investor, which had already undertaken substantial activities in the Area prior to the entry into force of the Convention, or its successor in interest, shall be considered to have met the financial and technical qualifications necessary for approval of a plan of work if the sponsoring State or States certify that the applicant has expended an amount equivalent to at least US$ 30 million in research and exploration activities and has expended no less than 10 per cent of that amount in the location, survey and evaluation of the area referred to in the plan of work. If the plan of work otherwise satisfies the requirements of the Convention and any rules, regulations and procedures adopted pursuant thereto, it shall be approved by the Council in the form of a contract. The provisions of section 3, paragraph 11, of this Annex shall be interpreted and applied accordingly;

(ii) Notwithstanding the provisions of resolution II, paragraph 8(a), a registered pioneer investor may request approval of a plan of work for exploration within 36 months of the entry into force of the Convention. The plan of work for exploration shall consist of documents, reports and other data submitted to the Preparatory Commission both before and after registration and shall be accompanied by a certificate of compliance, consisting of a factual report describing the status of fulfilment of obligations under the pioneer investor regime, issued by the Preparatory Commission in accordance with resolution II, paragraph 11(a). Such a plan of work shall be considered to be approved. Such an approved plan of work shall be in the form of a contract concluded between the Authority and the registered pioneer investor in accordance with Part XI and this Agreement. The fee of US$ 250,000 paid pursuant to resolution II, paragraph 7(a), shall be deemed to be the fee relating to the exploration phase pursuant to section 8, paragraph 3, of this Annex. Section 3, paragraph 11, of this Annex shall be interpreted and applied accordingly;

(iii) In accordance with the principle of non-discrimination, a contract with a State or entity or any component of such entity referred to in subparagraph (a)(i) shall include arrangements which shall be similar to and no less favourable than those agreed with any registered pioneer investor referred to in subparagraph (a)(ii). If any of the States or entities or any components of such entities referred to in subparagraph (a)(i) are granted more favourable arrangements, the Council shall make similar and no less favourable arrangements with regard to the rights and obligations assumed by the registered pioneer investors referred to in subparagraph (a)(ii), provided that such arrangements do not affect or prejudice the interests of the Authority;

(iv) A State sponsoring an application for a plan of work pursuant to the provisions of subparagraph (a)(i) or (ii) may be a State Party or a State which is applying this Agreement provisionally in accordance with article 7, or a State which is a member of the Authority on a provisional basis in accordance with paragraph 12;

(v) Resolution II, paragraph 8(c), shall be interpreted and applied in accordance with subparagraph (a)(iv).

(b) The approval of a plan of work for exploration shall be in accordance with article 153, paragraph 3, of the Convention.

7. An application for approval of a plan of work shall be accompanied by an assessment of the potential environmental impacts of the proposed activities and by a description of a programme for oceanographic and baseline environmental studies in accordance with the rules, regulations and procedures adopted by the Authority.

8. An application for approval of a plan of work for exploration, subject to paragraph 6(a)(i) or (ii), shall be processed in accordance with the procedures set out in section 3, paragraph 11, of this Annex.

9. A plan of work for exploration shall be approved for a period of 15 years. Upon the expiration of a plan of work for exploration, the contractor shall apply for a plan of work for exploitation unless the contractor has already done so or has obtained an extension for the plan of work for exploration. Contractors may apply for such extensions for periods of not more than five years each. Such extensions shall be approved if the contractor has made efforts in good faith to comply with the requirements of the plan of work but for reasons beyond the contractor's control has been unable to complete the necessary preparatory work for proceeding to the exploitation stage or if the prevailing economic circumstances do not justify proceeding to the exploitation stage.

10. Designation of a reserved area for the Authority in accordance with Annex III, article 8, of the Convention shall take place in connection with approval of an application for a plan of work for exploration or approval of an application for a plan of work for exploration and exploitation.

11. Notwithstanding the provisions of paragraph 9, an approved plan of work for exploration which is sponsored by at least one State provisionally applying this Agreement shall terminate if such a State ceases to apply this Agreement provisionally and has not become a member on a provisional basis in accordance with paragraph 12 or has not become a State Party.

12. Upon the entry into force of this Agreement, States and entities referred to in article 3 of this Agreement which have been applying it provisionally in accordance with article 7 and for which it is not in force may continue to be members of the Authority on a provisional basis pending its entry into force for such States and entities, in accordance with the following subparagraphs:

(a) If this Agreement enters into force before 16 November 1996, such States and entities shall be entitled to continue to participate as members of the Authority on a provisional basis upon notification to the depositary of the Agreement by such a State or entity of its intention to participate as a member on a provisional basis. Such membership shall terminate either on 16 November 1996 or upon the entry into force of this Agreement and the Convention for such member, whichever is earlier. The Council may, upon the request of the State or entity concerned, extend such membership beyond 16 November 1996 for a further period or periods not exceeding a total of two years provided that the Council is satisfied that the State or entity concerned has been making efforts in good faith to become a party to the Agreement and the Convention;

(b) If this Agreement enters into force after 15 November 1996, such States and entities may request the Council to grant continued membership in the Authority on a provisional basis for a period or periods not extending beyond 16 November 1998. The Council shall grant such membership with effect from the date of the request if it is satisfied that the State or entity has been making efforts in good faith to become a party to the Agreement and the Convention;

(c) States and entities which are members of the Authority on a provisional basis in accordance with subparagraph (a) or (b) shall apply the terms of Part XI and this Agreement in accordance with their national or internal laws, regulations and annual budgetary appropriations and shall have the same rights and obligations as other members, including:

(i) The obligation to contribute to the administrative budget of the Authority in accordance with the scale of assessed contributions;

(ii) The right to sponsor an application for approval of a plan of work for exploration. In the case of entities whose components are natural or juridical persons possessing the nationality of more than one State, a plan of work for exploration shall not be approved unless all the States whose natural or juridical persons comprise those entities are States Parties or members on a provisional basis;

(d) Notwithstanding the provisions of paragraph 9, an approved plan of work in the form of a contract for exploration which was sponsored pursuant to subparagraph (c)(ii) by a State which was a member on a provisional basis shall terminate if such membership ceases and the State or entity has not become a State Party;

(e) If such a member has failed to make its assessed contributions or otherwise failed to comply with its obligations in accordance with this paragraph, its membership on a provisional basis shall be terminated.

13. The reference in Annex III, article 10, of the Convention to performance which has not been satisfactory shall be interpreted to mean that the contractor has failed to comply with the requirements of an approved plan of work in spite of a written warning or warnings from the Authority to the contractor to comply therewith.

14. The Authority shall have its own budget. Until the end of the year following the year during which this Agreement enters into force, the administrative expenses of the Authority shall be met through the budget of the United Nations. Thereafter, the administrative expenses of the Authority shall be met by assessed contributions of its members, including any members on a provisional basis, in accordance with articles 171, subparagraph (a), and 173 of the Convention and this Agreement, until the Authority has sufficient funds from other sources to meet those expenses. The

Authority shall not exercise the power referred to in article 174, paragraph 1, of the Convention to borrow funds to finance its administrative budget.

15. The Authority shall elaborate and adopt, in accordance with article 162, paragraph 2(o)(ii), of the Convention, rules, regulations and procedures based on the principles contained in sections 2, 5, 6, 7 and 8 of this Annex, as well as any additional rules, regulations and procedures necessary to facilitate the approval of plans of work for exploration or exploitation, in accordance with the following subparagraphs:

(a) The Council may undertake such elaboration any time it deems that all or any of such rules, regulations or procedures are required for the conduct of activities in the Area, or when it determines that commercial exploitation is imminent, or at the request of a State whose national intends to apply for approval of a plan of work for exploitation;

(b) If a request is made by a State referred to in subparagraph (a) the Council shall, in accordance with article 162, paragraph 2(o), of the Convention, complete the adoption of such rules, regulations and procedures within two years of the request;

(c) If the Council has not completed the elaboration of the rules, regulations and procedures relating to exploitation within the prescribed time and an application for approval of a plan of work for exploitation is pending, it shall none the less consider and provisionally approve such plan of work based on the provisions of the Convention and any rules, regulations and procedures that the Council may have adopted provisionally, or on the basis of the norms contained in the Convention and the terms and principles contained in this Annex as well as the principle of non-discrimination among contractors.

16. The draft rules, regulations and procedures and any recommendations relating to the provisions of Part XI, as contained in the reports and recommendations of the Preparatory Commission, shall be taken into account by the Authority in the adoption of rules, regulations and procedures in accordance with Part XI and this Agreement.

17. The relevant provisions of Part XI, section 4, of the Convention shall be interpreted and applied in accordance with this Agreement.

Section 2 Costs to States Parties and Institutional Arrangements

1. The Secretariat of the Authority shall perform the functions of the Enterprise until it begins to operate independently of the Secretariat. The Secretary-General of the Authority shall appoint from within the staff of the Authority an interim Director-General to oversee the performance of these functions by the Secretariat. These functions shall be:

(a) Monitoring and review of trends and developments relating to deep seabed mining activities, including regular analysis of world metal market conditions and metal prices, trends and prospects;

(b) Assessment of the results of the conduct of marine scientific research with respect to activities in the Area, with particular emphasis on research related to the environmental impact of activities in the Area;

(c) Assessment of available data relating to prospecting and exploration, including the criteria for such activities;

(d) Assessment of technological developments relevant to activities in the Area, in particular technology relating to the protection and preservation of the marine environment;

(e) Evaluation of information and data relating to areas reserved for the Authority;

(f) Assessment of approaches to joint-venture operations;

(g) Collection of information on the availability of trained manpower;

(h) Study of managerial policy options for the administration of the Enterprise at different stages of its operations.

2. The Enterprise shall conduct its initial deep seabed mining operations through joint ventures. Upon the approval of a plan of work for exploitation for an entity other than the Enterprise, or upon receipt by the Council of an application for a joint-venture operation with the Enterprise, the Council shall take up the issue of the functioning of the Enterprise independently of the Secretariat of the Authority. If joint-venture operations with the Enterprise accord with sound commercial principles, the Council shall issue a directive pursuant to article 170, paragraph 2, of the Convention providing for such independent functioning.

3. The obligation of States Parties to fund one mine site of the Enterprise as provided for in Annex IV, article 11, paragraph 3, of the Convention shall not apply and States Parties shall be under no obligation to finance any of the operations in any mine site of the Enterprise or under its joint-venture arrangements.

4. The obligations applicable to contractors shall apply to the Enterprise. Notwithstanding the provisions of article 153, paragraph 3, and Annex III, article 3, paragraph 5, of the Convention, a plan of work for the Enterprise upon its approval shall be in the form of a contract concluded between the Authority and the Enterprise.

5. A contractor which has contributed a particular area to the Authority as a reserved area has the right of first refusal to enter into a joint-venture arrangement with the Enterprise for exploration and exploitation of that area. If the Enterprise does not submit an application for a plan of work for activities in respect of such a reserved area within 15 years of the commencement of its functions independent of

the Secretariat of the Authority or within 15 years of the date on which that area is reserved for the Authority, whichever is the later, the contractor which contributed the area shall be entitled to apply for a plan of work for that area provided it offers in good faith to include the Enterprise as a joint-venture partner.

6. Article 170, paragraph 4, Annex IV and other provisions of the Convention relating to the Enterprise shall be interpreted and applied in accordance with this section.

Section 3 Decision-Making

1. The general policies of the Authority shall be established by the Assembly in collaboration with the Council.

2. As a general rule, decision-making in the organs of the Authority should be by consensus.

3. If all efforts to reach a decision by consensus have been exhausted, decisions by voting in the Assembly on questions of procedure shall be taken by a majority of members present and voting, and decisions on questions of substance shall be taken by a two-thirds majority of members present and voting, as provided for in article 159, paragraph 8, of the Convention.

4. Decisions of the Assembly on any matter for which the Council also has competence or on any administrative, budgetary or financial matter shall be based on the recommendations of the Council. If the Assembly does not accept the recommendation of the Council on any matter, it shall return the matter to the Council for further consideration. The Council shall reconsider the matter in the light of the views expressed by the Assembly.

5. If all efforts to reach a decision by consensus have been exhausted, decisions by voting in the Council on questions of procedure shall be taken by a majority of members present and voting, and decisions on questions of substance, except where the Convention provides for decisions by consensus in the Council, shall be taken by a two-thirds majority of members present and voting, provided that such decisions are not opposed by a majority in any one of the chambers referred to in paragraph 9. In taking decisions the Council shall seek to promote the interests of all the members of the Authority.

6. The Council may defer the taking of a decision in order to facilitate further negotiation whenever it appears that all efforts at achieving consensus on a question have not been exhausted.

7. Decisions by the Assembly or the Council having financial or budgetary implications shall be based on the recommendations of the Finance Committee.

8. The provisions of article 161, paragraph 8(b) and (c), of the Convention shall not apply.

9. (a) Each group of States elected under paragraph 15(a) to (c) shall be treated as a chamber for the purposes of voting in the Council. The developing States elected under paragraph 15(d) and (e) shall be treated as a single chamber for the purposes of voting in the Council.

(b) Before electing the members of the Council, the Assembly shall establish lists of countries fulfilling the criteria for membership in the groups of States in paragraph 15(a) to (d). If a State fulfils the criteria for membership in more than one group, it may only be proposed by one group for election to the Council and it shall represent only that group in voting in the Council.

10. Each group of States in paragraph 15(a) to (d) shall be represented in the Council by those members nominated by that group. Each group shall nominate only as many candidates as the number of seats required to be filled by that group. When the number of potential candidates in each of the groups referred to in paragraph 15(a) to (e) exceeds the number of seats available in each of those respective groups, as a general rule, the principle of rotation shall apply. States members of each of those groups shall determine how this principle shall apply in those groups.

11. (a) The Council shall approve a recommendation by the Legal and Technical Commission for approval of a plan of work unless by a two-thirds majority of its members present and voting, including a majority of members present and voting in each of the chambers of the Council, the Council decides to disapprove a plan of work. If the Council does not take a decision on a recommendation for approval of a plan of work within a prescribed period, the recommendation shall be deemed to have been approved by the Council at the end of that period. The prescribed period shall normally be 60 days unless the Council decides to provide for a longer period. If the Commission recommends the disapproval of a plan of work or does not make a recommendation, the Council may nevertheless approve the plan of work in accordance with its rules of procedure for decision-making on questions of substance.

(b) The provisions of article 162, paragraph 2(j), of the Convention shall not apply.

12. Where a dispute arises relating to the disapproval of a plan of work, such dispute shall be submitted to the dispute settlement procedures set out in the Convention.

13. Decisions by voting in the Legal and Technical Commission shall be by a majority of members present and voting.

14. Part XI, section 4, subsections B and C, of the Convention shall be interpreted and applied in accordance with this section.

15. The Council shall consist of 36 members of the Authority elected by the Assembly in the following order:

(a) Four members from among those States Parties which, during the last five years for which statistics are available, have either consumed more than 2 per cent in value terms of total world consumption or have had net imports of more than 2 per cent in value terms of total world imports of the commodities produced from the categories of minerals to be derived from the Area, provided that the four members shall include one State from the Eastern European region having the largest economy in that region in terms of gross domestic product and the State, on the date of entry into force of the Convention, having the largest economy in terms of gross domestic product, if such States wish to be represented in this group;

(b) Four members from among the eight States Parties which have made the largest investments in preparation for and in the conduct of activities in the Area, either directly or through their nationals;

(c) Four members from among States Parties which, on the basis of production in areas under their jurisdiction, are major net exporters of the categories of minerals to be derived from the Area, including at least two developing States whose exports of such minerals have a substantial bearing upon their economies;

(d) Six members from among developing States Parties, representing special interests. The special interests to be represented shall include those of States with large populations, States which are land-locked or geographically disadvantaged, island States, States which are major importers of the categories of minerals to be derived from the Area, States which are potential producers of such minerals and least developed States;

(e) Eighteen members elected according to the principle of ensuring an equitable geographical distribution of seats in the Council as a whole, provided that each geographical region shall have at least one member elected under this subparagraph. For this purpose, the geographical regions shall be Africa, Asia, Eastern Europe, Latin America and the Caribbean and Western Europe and Others.

16. The provisions of article 161, paragraph 1, of the Convention shall not apply.

Section 4 Review Conference

The provisions relating to the Review Conference in article 155, paragraphs 1, 3 and 4, of the Convention shall not apply. Notwithstanding the provisions of article 314, paragraph 2, of the Convention, the Assembly, on the recommendation of the Council, may undertake at any time a review of the matters referred to in article 155, paragraph 1, of the Convention. Amendments relating to this Agreement and Part XI shall be subject to the procedures contained in articles 314, 315 and 316 of the Convention, provided that the principles, regime and other terms referred to in article 155, paragraph 2, of the Convention shall be maintained and the rights referred to in paragraph 5 of that article shall not be affected.

Section 5 Transfer of Technology

1. In addition to the provisions of article 144 of the Convention, transfer of technology for the purposes of Part XI shall be governed by the following principles:

(a) The Enterprise, and developing States wishing to obtain deep seabed mining technology, shall seek to obtain such technology on fair and reasonable commercial terms and conditions on the open market, or through joint-venture arrangements;

(b) If the Enterprise or developing States are unable to obtain deep seabed mining technology, the Authority may request all or any of the contractors and their respective sponsoring State or States to cooperate with it in facilitating the acquisition of deep seabed mining technology by the Enterprise or its joint venture, or by a developing State or States seeking to acquire such technology on fair and reasonable commercial terms and conditions, consistent with the effective protection of intellectual property rights. States Parties undertake to cooperate fully and effectively with the Authority for this purpose and to ensure that contractors sponsored by them also cooperate fully with the Authority;

(c) As a general rule, States Parties shall promote international technical and scientific cooperation with regard to activities in the Area either between the parties concerned or by developing training, technical assistance and scientific cooperation programmes in marine science and technology and the protection and preservation of the marine environment.

2. The provisions of Annex III, article 5, of the Convention shall not apply.

Section 6 Production Policy

1. The production policy of the Authority shall be based on the following principles:

(a) Development of the resources of the Area shall take place in accordance with sound commercial principles;

(b) The provisions of the General Agreement on Tariffs and Trade, its relevant codes and successor or superseding agreements shall apply with respect to activities in the Area;

(c) In particular, there shall be no subsidization of activities in the Area except as may be permitted under the agreements referred to in subparagraph (b). Subsidization for the purpose of these principles shall be defined in terms of the agreements referred to in subparagraph (b);

(d) There shall be no discrimination between minerals derived from the Area and from other sources. There shall be no preferential access to markets for such minerals or for imports of commodities produced from such minerals, in particular:

(i) By the use of tariff or non-tariff barriers; and

(ii) Given by States Parties to such minerals or commodities produced by their state enterprises or by natural or juridical persons which possess their nationality or are controlled by them or their nationals;

(e) The plan of work for exploitation approved by the Authority in respect of each mining area shall indicate an anticipated production schedule which shall include the estimated maximum amounts of minerals that would be produced per year under the plan of work;

(f) The following shall apply to the settlement of disputes concerning the provisions of the agreements referred to in subparagraph (b):

(i) Where the States Parties concerned are parties to such agreements, they shall have recourse to the dispute settlement procedures of those agreements;

(ii) Where one or more of the States Parties concerned are not parties to such agreements, they shall have recourse to the dispute settlement procedures set out in the Convention;

(g) In circumstances where a determination is made under the agreements referred to in subparagraph (b) that a State Party has engaged in subsidization which is prohibited or has resulted in adverse effects on the interests of another State Party and appropriate steps have not been taken by the relevant State Party or States Parties, a State Party may request the Council to take appropriate measures.

2. The principles contained in paragraph 1 shall not affect the rights and obligations under any provision of the agreements referred to in paragraph 1(b), as well as the relevant free trade and customs union agreements, in relations between States Parties which are parties to such agreements.

3. The acceptance by a contractor of subsidies other than those which may be permitted under the agreements referred to in paragraph 1(b) shall constitute a violation of the fundamental terms of the contract forming a plan of work for the carrying out of activities in the Area.

4. Any State Party which has reason to believe that there has been a breach of the requirements of paragraphs 1(b) to (d) or 3 may initiate dispute settlement procedures in conformity with paragraph 1(f) or (g).

5. A State Party may at any time bring to the attention of the Council activities which in its view are inconsistent with the requirements of paragraph 1(b) to (d).

6. The Authority shall develop rules, regulations and procedures which ensure the implementation of the provisions of this section, including relevant rules, regulations and procedures governing the approval of plans of work.

7. The provisions of article 151, paragraphs 1 to 7 and 9, article 162, paragraph 2(q), article 165, paragraph 2(n), and Annex III, article 6, paragraph 5, and article 7, of the Convention shall not apply.

Section 7 Economic Assistance

1. The policy of the Authority of assisting developing countries which suffer serious adverse effects on their export earnings or economies resulting from a reduction in the price of an affected mineral or in the volume of exports of that mineral, to the extent that such reduction is caused by activities in the Area, shall be based on the following principles:

(a) The Authority shall establish an economic assistance fund from a portion of the funds of the Authority which exceeds those necessary to cover the administrative expenses of the Authority. The amount set aside for this purpose shall be determined by the Council from time to time, upon the recommendation of the Finance Committee. Only funds from payments received from contractors, including the Enterprise, and voluntary contributions shall be used for the establishment of the economic assistance fund;

(b) Developing land-based producer States whose economies have been determined to be seriously affected by the production of minerals from the deep seabed shall be assisted from the economic assistance fund of the Authority;

(c) The Authority shall provide assistance from the fund to affected developing land-based producer States, where appropriate, in cooperation with existing global or regional development institutions which have the infrastructure and expertise to carry out such assistance programmes;

(d) The extent and period of such assistance shall be determined on a case-by-case basis. In doing so, due consideration shall be given to the nature and magnitude of the problems encountered by affected developing land-based producer States.

2. Article 151, paragraph 10, of the Convention shall be implemented by means of measures of economic assistance referred to in paragraph 1. Article 160, paragraph 2(l), article 162, paragraph 2(n), article 164, paragraph 2(d), article 171, subparagraph (f), and article 173, paragraph 2(c), of the Convention shall be interpreted accordingly.

Section 8 Financial Terms of Contracts

1. The following principles shall provide the basis for establishing rules, regulations and procedures for financial terms of contracts:

(a) The system of payments to the Authority shall be fair both to the contractor and to the Authority and shall provide adequate means of determining compliance by the contractor with such system;

(b) The rates of payments under the system shall be within the range of those prevailing in respect of land-based mining of the same or similar minerals in order to avoid giving deep seabed miners an artificial competitive advantage or imposing on them a competitive disadvantage;

(c) The system should not be complicated and should not impose major administrative costs on the Authority or on a contractor. Consideration should be given to the adoption of a royalty system or a combination of a royalty and profit-sharing system. If alternative systems are decided upon, the contractor has the right to choose the system applicable to its contract. Any subsequent change in choice between alternative systems, however, shall be made by agreement between the Authority and the contractor;

(d) An annual fixed fee shall be payable from the date of commencement of commercial production. This fee may be credited against other payments due under the system adopted in accordance with subparagraph (c). The amount of the fee shall be established by the Council;

(e) The system of payments may be revised periodically in the light of changing circumstances. Any changes shall be applied in a non-discriminatory manner. Such changes may apply to existing contracts only at the election of the contractor. Any subsequent change in choice between alternative systems shall be made by agreement between the Authority and the contractor;

(f) Disputes concerning the interpretation or application of the rules and regulations based on these principles shall be subject to the dispute settlement procedures set out in the Convention.

2. The provisions of Annex III, article 13, paragraphs 3 to 10, of the Convention shall not apply.

3. With regard to the implementation of Annex III, article 13, paragraph 2, of the Convention, the fee for processing applications for approval of a plan of work limited to one phase, either the exploration phase or the exploitation phase, shall be US$ 250,000.

Section 9 The Finance Committee

1. There is hereby established a Finance Committee. The Committee shall be composed of 15 members with appropriate qualifications relevant to financial matters. States Parties shall nominate candidates of the highest standards of competence and integrity.

2. No two members of the Finance Committee shall be nationals of the same State Party.

3. Members of the Finance Committee shall be elected by the Assembly and due account shall be taken of the need for equitable geographical distribution and the representation of special interests. Each group of States referred to in section 3, paragraph 15(a), (b), (c) and (d), of this Annex shall be represented on the Committee by at least one member. Until the Authority has sufficient funds other than assessed contributions to meet its administrative expenses, the membership of the Committee shall include representatives of the five largest financial contributors to the administrative budget of the Authority. Thereafter, the election of one member from each group shall be on the basis of nomination by the members of the respective group, without prejudice to the possibility of further members being elected from each group.

4. Members of the Finance Committee shall hold office for a term of five years. They shall be eligible for re-election for a further term.

5. In the event of the death, incapacity or resignation of a member of the Finance Committee prior to the expiration of the term of office, the Assembly shall elect for the remainder of the term a member from the same geographical region or group of States.

6. Members of the Finance Committee shall have no financial interest in any activity relating to matters upon which the Committee has the responsibility to make recommendations. They shall not disclose, even after the termination of their functions, any confidential information coming to their knowledge by reason of their duties for the Authority.

7. Decisions by the Assembly and the Council on the following issues shall take into account recommendations of the Finance Committee:

(a) Draft financial rules, regulations and procedures of the organs of the Authority and the financial management and internal financial administration of the Authority;

(b) Assessment of contributions of members to the administrative budget of the Authority in accordance with article 160, paragraph 2(e), of the Convention;

(c) All relevant financial matters, including the proposed annual budget prepared by the Secretary-General of the Authority in accordance with article 172 of the Convention and the financial aspects of the implementation of the programmes of work of the Secretariat;

(d) The administrative budget;

(e) Financial obligations of States Parties arising from the implementation of this Agreement and Part XI as well as the administrative and budgetary implications of proposals and recommendations involving expenditure from the funds of the Authority;

(f) Rules, regulations and procedures on the equitable sharing of financial and other economic benefits derived from activities in the Area and the decisions to be made thereon.

8. Decisions in the Finance Committee on questions of procedure shall be taken by a majority of members present and voting. Decisions on questions of substance shall be taken by consensus.

9. The requirement of article 162, paragraph 2(y), of the Convention to establish a subsidiary organ to deal with financial matters shall be deemed to have been fulfilled by the establishment of the Finance Committee in accordance with this section.

Index

www.ingramcontent.com/pod-product-compliance
Lightning Source LLC
LaVergne TN
LVHW010555300926
849162LV00002B/333